Fodor's
ESSENTIAL
NEW ZEALAND

WELCOME TO NEW ZEALAND

From the Bay of Islands' pristine beaches in the north to the soaring pinnacles of Milford Sound in the south, New Zealand is a stunner. Glaciated mountains, steaming volcanoes, and lush forests give adventurers a vast array of ecological playgrounds to explore. While hikers retreat to 14 national parks, bird-watchers find their bliss on peaceful Stewart Island. But it's not all parks and rec. Māori enclaves display deep native heritage, idyllic vineyards produce world-class wines, and vibrant dining and arts scenes thrive in cities like Auckland and Wellington.

TOP REASONS TO GO

★ **Landscapes:** Deep blue lakes, alpine peaks, green valleys—the scenery is breathtaking.

★ **Superb Wine:** Hawkes Bay's Bordeaux blends, Marlborough's Sauvignon Blancs, and more.

★ **Hobbits:** *Lord of the Rings* tours in Glenorchy and Matamata take fans to Middle Earth.

★ **Water Sports:** Incredible sailing, surfing, rafting, kayaking, and diving.

★ **Māori Culture:** Native traditions are shared in craft workshops and ceremonial feasts.

★ **The Great Walks:** Nine famous trails, including the Milford Track, entice hikers.

Fodor's ESSENTIAL NEW ZEALAND

Publisher: Amanda D'Acierno, *Senior Vice President*

Design: Tina Malaney, *Associate Art Director*; Erica Cuoco, *Production Designer*

Photography: Jennifer Arnow, *Senior Photo Editor*; Mary Robnett, *Photo Researcher*

Maps: Rebecca Baer, *Senior Map Editor*; Ed Jacobus, David Lindroth, Mark Stroud (Moon Street Cartography), *Cartographers*

Production: Angela L. McLean, *Senior Production Manager*

Sales: Jacqueline Lebow, *Sales Director*

Marketing & Publicity: Heather Dalton, *Marketing Director*; Katherine Punia, *Publicity Director*

Business & Operations: Susan Livingston, *Senior Vice President, Strategic Business Planning*; Sue Daulton, *Vice President, Operations*

Fodors.com: Megan Bell, *Executive Director, Revenue & Business Development*; Yasmin Marinaro, *Senior Director, Marketing & Partnerships*

Copyright © 2017 by Fodor's Travel, a division of Penguin Random House LLC

Writers: Anabel Darby, Gerard Hindmarsh, Claire Kenny, Bob Marriott, Kathy Ombler, Richard Pamatatau, Mike Stearne

Editors: Róisín Cameron, Salwa Jabado, Teddy Minford

Production Editor: Elyse Rozelle

1st Edition

ISBN 978–1–101–87988–7

ISSN 2470–9441

All details in this book are based on information supplied to us at press time. Always confirm information when it matters, especially if you're making a detour to visit a specific place. Fodor's expressly disclaims any liability, loss, or risk, personal or otherwise, that is incurred as a consequence of the use of any of the contents of this book.

SPECIAL SALES

This book is available at special discounts for bulk purchases for sales promotions or premiums. For more information, e-mail specialmarkets@penguinrandomhouse.com.

PRINTED IN THE UNITED STATES OF AMERICA

10 9 8 7 6 5 4 3 2 1

CONTENTS

MAPS

ABOUT THIS GUIDE

Fodor's Recommendations

Everything in this guide is worth doing— we don't cover what isn't—but exceptional sights, hotels, and restaurants are recognized with additional accolades. **Fodor's**Choice★ indicates our top recommendations. Care to nominate a new place? Visit Fodors.com/contact-us.

Trip Costs

We list prices wherever possible to help you budget well. Hotel and restaurant price categories from **$** to **$$$$** are noted alongside each recommendation. For hotels, we include the lowest cost of a standard double room in high season. For restaurants, we cite the average price of a main course at dinner or, if dinner isn't served, at lunch. For attractions, we always list adult admission fees; discounts are usually available for children, students, and senior citizens.

Hotels

Our local writers vet every hotel to recommend the best overnights in each price category, from budget to expensive. Unless otherwise specified, you can expect private bath, phone, and TV in your room. For expanded hotel reviews visit Fodors.com.

Top Picks		Hotels & Restaurants	
★ **Fodor's**Choice		🏨	Hotel
		🛏	Number of rooms
Listings			
⊠	Address	🍽	Meal plans
⊠	Branch address	✕	Restaurant
☎	Telephone	🕮	Reservations
🖷	Fax	🏛	Dress code
⊕	Website	▭	No credit cards
🖃	E-mail	$	Price
▱	Admission fee		
☉	Open/closed times	**Other**	
Ⓜ	Subway	⇨	See also
✛	Directions or Map coordinates	☞	Take note
		🏌	Golf facilities

Restaurants

Unless we state otherwise, restaurants are open for lunch and dinner daily. We mention dress code only when there's a specific requirement and reservations only when they're essential or not accepted.

Credit Cards

The hotels and restaurants in this guide typically accept credit cards. If not, we'll say so.

EUGENE FODOR

Hungarian-born Eugene Fodor (1905–91) began his travel career as an interpreter on a French cruise ship. The experience inspired him to write *On the Continent* (1936), the first guidebook to receive annual updates and discuss a country's way of life as well as its sights. Fodor later joined the U.S. Army and worked for the OSS in World War II. After the war, he kept up his intelligence work while expanding his guidebook series. During the Cold War, many guides were written by fellow agents who understood the value of insider information. Today's guides continue Fodor's legacy by providing travelers with timely coverage, insider tips, and cultural context.

EXPERIENCE
NEW ZEALAND

NEW ZEALAND TODAY

Kia ora, or welcome, to the "Youngest Country on Earth." New Zealand's moniker may specifically reference its place as the last landmass to be discovered, but it speaks to the constant geological, social, and political shifts the country has undergone as it has tried to find its national identity. Tectonic hotbeds include three active volcanoes—Tongariro, Ngauruhoe, and Ruapehu—on the Central Plateau of the North Island and the still-growing Southern Alps on the South Island. In a nation of farmers with frontier ancestors, Georgina Beyer, a transsexual former prostitute, won a rural seat against a conservative opponent in 1999. New Zealand's Ernest Rutherford was the first person to split the atom, but the country remains passionately anti–nuclear technology. The national rugby team, the All Blacks continue to dominate the field as one of the best rugby teams in the world, though many Kiwis still consider themselves to be underdogs in sport.

A Tale of Two Islands

Together, the North and South Islands make up the majority of *Aotearoa*—Land of the Long White Cloud. New Zealand is roughly the size of Colorado (with a slightly smaller population), but you are never more than 150 miles from the sea. New Zealand's two main islands are more than 1,000 miles long and together encompass nearly every environment on the planet: glaciers, white-sand beaches, fjords, rain forests, alpine forest and lakes, agricultural plains, and volcanic craters and cones.

The South Island is the stunner: the colorful beaches, inlets, and sunny vineyards of the north give way to the Southern Alps, a mountain range that can only be crossed in three places (Arthur's Pass,

Lewis Pass, and Haast Pass). Aoraki/ Mount Cook National Park contains New Zealand's tallest mountain (Aoraki/ Mt. Cook, 12,316 feet) and another 19 peaks that are more than 10,000 feet. Forty percent of the park is covered by glaciers. On the West Coast, dense native forest, wild weather, and a sparse population provide a frontier feel. At the southern end of the West Coast is primeval Fiordland National Park, more than 3 million acres of raw wilderness. Together, Fiordland, Aoraki/Mount Cook, Westland Tai Poutini, and Mount Aspiring national parks form Te Wāhiponamu, a UNESCO World Heritage site encompassing 6.4 million acres, nearly 10% of New Zealand's total landmass.

On the East Coast of the South Island, sea life ranges from the giant 65-foot male sperm whale to the 5-foot Hector's Dolphin. On land, ideas of preserving the wildlife are different from what you'd expect. Saving birds and trees entails ridding the area of possums and cats—mammals that are not native to New Zealand.

Fourteen miles separate the North and South Islands over the rough Cook Strait, but the two islands are worlds apart. Due to its volcanic origins, the North Island has fertile farmlands and rejuvenated native forest. More than three-quarters of New Zealand's 4.2 million people live on the North Island, which tends to have milder weather and a more forgiving landscape. Long beaches sweep up both coasts past small communities (many still predominantly Māori). Te Urewera National Park and two out of three of New Zealand's longest rivers (Waikato and Wanganui) are found near the Central Plateau. Here you'll also discover New Zealand's largest lake (Taupo).

A Tale of Two Cultures

New Zealand is 900 miles from the nearest landmass. Its relative isolation and geographical diversity has affected its population. On a whole, New Zealanders are genial, reserved, and friendly, but they don't suffer fools or braggarts lightly. An isolated past, when things were either unavailable or expensive, led to a nation of inventors: Kiwis invented the jet-boat, bungy jumping, and the electric fence, to name a few. They were the first to climb Mt. Everest, and the first to give women the vote.

New Zealand is a bicultural nation. New Zealanders of European descent (*Pakeha*) make up 80% of the population, while Māori make up 15% (the rest is largely Pacific Islanders and Asian), and the future is still unclear. There are two camps: most New Zealanders want to move forward as "one New Zealand," but a significant portion still sees Māoridom as a culture set apart. Although many New Zealanders consider the reconciliation process to be labored and an impediment to forward progress, Māori is an oral culture, and many feel that continuing to discuss the past is a way of making certain it isn't lost in the present.

Kiwi Quality of Life

New Zealand is consistently rated as one of the best places to live and is one of the most active nations: Kiwis seem to be born with a love of the outdoors, and families tramp, caravan, sail, and play rugby, cricket, and netball together. Most New Zealanders are well educated. They value travel highly, with one-quarter of the population traveling overseas every year, often for their post-school O.E. (overseas experience). Kiwis don't tend to be religious, with two-thirds lightly following one of the four main Christian religions (Catholic, Methodist, Presbyterian, and Anglican). New Zealand isn't a wealthy nation, either: most Kiwis prefer a good work–life balance to an overflowing bank account.

100% Pure

Despite their quality of life, many New Zealanders express concern for the country's future. The Department of Conservation now focuses on environmental issues, reflecting the national love of the outdoors and the importance of the landscape to the country's burgeoning tourism industry. Although New Zealand is making great strides in sustainability, the country aims for a "100% Pure" lifestyle. New Zealand is also facing a challenge in rising obesity in 25% of adults, a binge-drinking problem, youth gang culture and violent crime, and an increase in poverty. Basically, New Zealand is facing many of the same problems as the Western world—just on a smaller scale.

WHAT'S WHERE

1 Auckland. Auckland, the City of Sails, is New Zealand's biggest city, its economic capital, and its most multicultural city, home to Polynesians, Asians, and other immigrants. Dynamic, driven, and gorgeous, Auckland is the city the rest of New Zealand loves to hate.

2 Northland and the Bay of Islands. Northland has a large population of Māori, ancient kauri forests, salty harbors, and ocean inlets. The Bay of Islands is known for diving, sailing, and sunning on and around the isolated beaches on its 100-plus islands.

3 The Coromandel and the Bay of Plenty. Close to Auckland, the Coromandel and the Bay of Plenty have white-sand beaches, blue seas, native birds, and steep hills carpeted with forest. The Coromandel has a café-and-board-shorts culture, while the Bay of Plenty is a Māori cultural hub.

4 East Coast and the Volcanic Zone. Taupo, a vibrant city next to New Zealand's largest lake, is bordered by volcanoes in Tongariro National Park; nearby Turangi claims to be the trout-fishing capital of the world. Te Urewera's wilderness contrasts with the mix of arty café towns like Napier, wineries, and beach towns like Ruatoria and Tolaga Bay, where Māori community life is still present.

5 North Island's West Coast. Mt. Taranaki broods over Egmont National Park and the rural industrial area affectionately known as the 'Naki. A thin highway loops through surf towns, tropical coastline, black-sand beaches, and the lower West Coast farmland. Outside of Wellington, SH1 is bordered by Kapiti Coast beach towns, farmland, and the Tararua Ranges. Kapiti Island is a protected reserve where endangered birdlife thrives.

6 Wellington and the Wairarapa. Cafés, art galleries, and cinemas overflow in the capital city, giving it a vibrant quality. It's bordered by steep hillsides studded with Victorian homes and an expansive harbor and crowned by Te Papa, New Zealand's largest museum. Lyall and Houghton bays attract surfers, while the Miramar Peninsula is home to Peter Jackson's film empire. The Wairarapa, northeast of Wellington, features some of New Zealand's best wine country and windswept coasts.

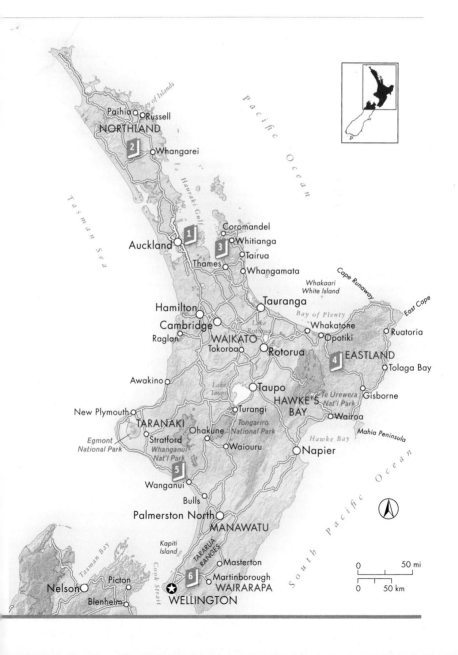

Pacific Ocean

Bay of Islands
Paihia○ ○Russell
NORTHLAND
2 ○Whangarei

Tasman Sea

Hauraki Gulf

Coromandel
○
Auckland○ 1 ○Whitianga
3 ○Tairua
○Thames ○Whangamata

Whakaari
White Island

Cape Runaway

Tauranga
Bay of Plenty
Hamilton ○Whakatane East Cape
○ ○Opotiki
Cambridge ○ Lake
Raglan○ Rotorua ○Ruatoria
WAIKATO
Tokoroa○ ○**Rotorua** **EASTLAND**
4 ○Tolaga Bay

Awakino○ Lake
Taupo ○**Taupo** Te Urewera ○Gisborne
Nat'l Park
New Plymouth○ ○Turangi **HAWKE'S**
TARANAKI Tongariro **BAY** ○Wairoa
○Ohakune National Park Mahia Peninsula
Egmont ○ Hawke Bay
National Park ○Stratford
Whanganui ○Waiouru ○**Napier**
Nat'l Park
5
Wanganui○

Bulls○
Palmerston North○
MANAWATU
Kapiti
Island TARARUA ○Masterton
RANGES
○Martinborough
6 **WAIRARAPA**
Picton○ Cook
Nelson○ Strait ★
Blenheim○ **WELLINGTON**

Tasman Bay

South Pacific Ocean

0   50 mi
0   50 km

WHAT'S WHERE

7 Upper South Island and the West Coast. Across the Cook Strait is the Marlborough Sounds, known for seafood, sunshine, Sauvignon Blanc, sailing, and the Queen Charlotte Track. To the southeast, the wineries of Blenheim rise up into snowcapped mountains plunging to the Kaikoura coastline. To the west, the artistic town of Nelson gives way to Abel Tasman National Park. The West Coast is rugged with sights like the Punakaiki Pancake Rocks and the twin glaciers, Franz Josef and Fox.

8 Christchurch and Canterbury. Easygoing Christchurch, with its British-style gardens and meandering Avon River, is bordered in the north by the thermal resort town, Hanmer Springs. To the east is the Banks Peninsula, another volcanic remnant of green hills and hidden ocean inlets, as well as the French-flavored town of Akaroa. To the west, the flat, vast Canterbury Plains extends to remote Arthur's Pass and the Southern Alps and Aoraki (Mt. Cook), New Zealand's tallest peak.

9 The Southern Alps and Fiordland. The Southern Alps is populated by alpine towns. Queenstown is known as the Adventure Capital of the World and offers up any extreme sport you can think of. Wanaka is quieter, though no less scenic, while artsy Arrowtown displays the area's gold-rush history. Remote Glenorchy is the gateway to spectacular hiking tracks. Best known for the Milford Sound and track, Fiordland is a raw, brooding forest.

10 Otago, Invercargill, and Stewart Island. The southern part of the South Island has two main towns: Invercargill and Dunedin. Dunedin is the livelier of the two, due in part to its university. The towns are bordered by the Otago Peninsula, rich in albatrosses, seals, and penguin colonies, and the Catlins, known for its bird-rich forests. To the very south lies Stewart Island, with its colonies of kiwi birds and Rakiura National Park.

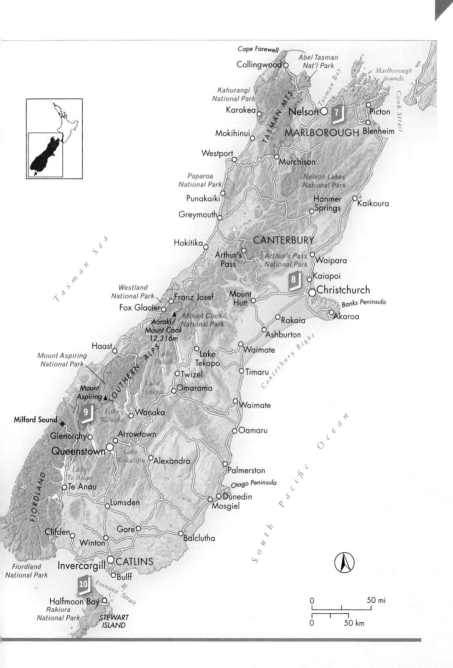

Cape Farewell
Collingwood
Abel Tasman Nat'l Park
Marlborough Sounds
Kahurangi National Park
Karakea
TASMAN MTS
Nelson
Tasman Bay
7
Picton
Cook Strait
MARLBOROUGH
Blenheim
Mokihinui
Westport
Murchison
Paparoa National Park
Nelson Lakes National Park
Punakaiki
Hanmer Springs
Kaikoura
Greymouth
Hokitika
CANTERBURY
Arthur's Pass
Arthur's Pass National Park
Waipara
Kaiapoi
8
Christchurch
Tasman Sea
Westland National Park
Franz Josef
Mount Hutt
Fox Glacier
Aoraki/ Mount Cook National Park
Banks Peninsula
Akaroa
Mount Cook 12,316m
Rakaia
Haast
Ashburton
SOUTHERN ALPS
Lake Pukaki
Lake Tekapo
Waimate
Mount Aspiring National Park
Twizel
Timaru
Lake Hawea
Omarama
Canterbury Bight
Mount Aspiring
Lake Wanaka
Waimate
9
Wanaka
Oamaru
Milford Sound
Glenorchy
Arrowtown
South Pacific Ocean
Queenstown
Lake Wakatipu
Alexandra
Palmerston
FIORDLAND
Lake Te Anau
Otago Peninsula
Te Anau
Dunedin
Lumsden
Mosgiel
Clifden
Gore
Winton
Balclutha
Fiordland National Park
Invercargill
CATLINS
10
Bluff
Foveaux Strait
Halfmoon Bay
Rakiura National Park
STEWART ISLAND

0   50 mi

0   50 km

NEED TO KNOW

NEW ZEALAND

Wellington

AT A GLANCE

Capital: Wellington

Population: 4,538,358

Currency: New Zealand dollar

Money: ATMs common; credit cards accepted

Language: English

Country Code: 64

Emergencies: 111

Driving: Left

Electricity: 230-40V/50Hz; electrical plugs have two flat prongs in a V

Time: 16 hours ahead of New York

Documents: Up to 90 days with valid passport

Mobile Phones: GSM (900 and 1800 bands)

Major Mobile Companies: Vodafone, Telecom, 2degrees

WEBSITES

NZ Tourism:
⊕ www.newzealand.com

NZ Tourism Guide:
⊕ www.tourism.net.nz

The New Zealand Herald:
⊕ www.nzherald.co.nz

GETTING AROUND

✈ **Air Travel:** Air New Zealand and Qantas are the two main carriers, with most international flights arriving to Auckland Airport.

🚌 **Bus Travel:** There is well-organized bus transport throughout both islands. The main companies are Inter-City and Newlands.

🚗 **Car Travel:** Rent a car or camper but know that gas can be expensive and purchase insurance; you can use your country's driver's license.

🚆 **Train Travel:** Tranz Scenic offers rail journeys between Auckland and Wellington, Christchurch and Picton, and Christchurch and Greymouth, as well as shorter trips.

PLAN YOUR BUDGET

	HOTEL ROOM	MEAL	ATTRACTIONS
Low Budget	NZ$35	NZ$7	Mount Cook National Park visitor center, free
Mid Budget	NZ$120	NZ$35	Camping at Abel Tasman National Park, NZ$14
High Budget	NZ$240	NZ$90	Auckland Bridge bungy jump, NZ$120

WAYS TO SAVE

Rent an apartment. Particularly in big cities, hotel costs are high. In a flat, you'll have more space and a kitchen.

Pack a picnic. Gorgeous parks abound, so eat outdoors with picnic provisions.

Go by bus. If you're traveling solo, car costs can be prohibitively expensive; buses offer a cheaper alternative.

Go hiking. Sweeping vistas are what you've come for and access to parks is generally free.

PLAN YOUR TIME

Hassle Factor	Medium. There are no direct flights from the U.S. east coast. Most flights have anywhere from 4- to 24-hour layovers.
3 days	Explore Auckland and see why it's one of the world's most livable cities. Adrenaline junkies can go bungy jumping off the Auckland Harbour Bridge. Take a ferry to Waiheke Island.
1 week	From Auckland, take the ferry to Waiheke for beach and wine. The next day, fly to Wellington and take the cable car to the Botanic Gardens, then fly on to Christchurch; drive to Akaroa to watch dolphins and stroll the town's quaint streets.
2 weeks	Get your bearings in Auckland with swim and sun on Waiheke Island. Your next stop is Rotorua, for hot springs and Māori culture, then to Wellington and Queenstown with wine tasting stops.

WHEN TO GO

High Season: It's best to visit from October to April, especially in alpine areas. The summer holidays (mid-December to February) can be crowded, with scarce car rentals and accommodations and expensive flights.

Low Season: June through September (winter) is the least expensive time to visit New Zealand, although flights from the United States may not be at their lowest. Prices in ski areas do remain high June through August but accommodations on weekdays will not be hard to come by.

Value Season: March to May and September to November, fall and spring respectively, offer the best combination of temperature, weather, and moderate prices. One exception is Easter weekend, when many families take vacations.

BIG EVENTS

February: Kwhia Kai Festival celebrates traditional and contemporary Māori food and culture. ⊕ www.kawhiakaifestival.co.nz

February and March: New Zealand Festival is three-plus weeks of dance, film, theater, music, visual arts, and writing events. ⊕ www.festival.co.nz

June: Run, bike, ski, take a hot tub dip, and watch performances and sports matches at the Queenstown Winter Festival. ⊕ www.winterfestival.co.nz

July: A week of family-friendly activities make up the annual Cadbury Chocolate Carnival. ⊕ www.chocolatecarnival.co.nz

READ THIS

■ *The Luminaries,* Eleanor Catton. Walter Moody is pulled into strange and secretive events.

■ *The Bone People,* Keri Hulme. A Māori-European artist meets a feral boy and his foster father.

■ *Long Cloud Ride,* Josie Dew. Dew bikes across New Zealand over nine months.

WATCH THIS

■ *My Wedding and Other Secrets.* A Chinese-Kiwi's struggle to get her family to accept her boyfriend.

■ *Lord of the Rings; The Hobbit.* Peter Jackson's epic adventure trilogies were filmed here.

■ *Whale Rider.* A Māori girl dreams of becoming her tribe's chief.

EAT THIS

■ *Pavlova*: A meringue dessert with a crispy outer shell and a soft interior

■ *Wine*: Excellent Sauvignon Blanc and Chardonnay

■ *Lamingtons*: Sponge cake coated in chocolate and rolled in shredded coconut

■ *Vegemite*: A salty, bitter, malty spread

■ *Fish-and-chips*: Cod or haddock battered and fried with thick-cut fries

■ *Roast lamb*: Leg or shoulder with potatoes

ESSENTIAL NEW ZEALAND TOP ATTRACTIONS

Abel Tasman National Park

(A) Abel Tasman National Park is New Zealand's smallest and most visited park. At the north end of the South Island, this park is an explosion of color: green waves lap orange-tinted sand fringed by green forest. Made up of limestone and marble, Abel Tasman is studded with caves and rock formations that make it an excellent hiking or kayaking destination.

Aoraki/Mt. Cook

(B) Rising 12,316 feet out of the Mackenzie Plains, the South Island's Aoraki (cloud piercer) is aptly named. Aoraki (also known as Mt. Cook) is the largest mountain in New Zealand, the crown jewel of the sparkling Southern Alps. Nearby are two glacier lakes (Lake Tekapo and Lake Pukaki) of such startling turquoise they hurt the eyes. This is where Sir Edmund Hillary cut his climbing teeth.

Bay of Islands

(C) On the north finger of the North Island is the Bay of Islands, a 100-island maze that is a stronghold of New Zealand history. Captain Cook first sailed here in 1769. In 1840, the Treaty of Waitangi was signed here. Today, New Zealanders flock to the area for the warm temperatures and pristine beaches, making it a haven for sailing, boating, and big-game fishing.

The Coromandel

(D) The Coromandel Peninsula is that local spot Kiwis don't want you to know about. Only two hours from Auckland, the Coromandel is a remote getaway of white-sand beaches, native forest, quirky cafés, and bustling marinas. Highlights include bountiful fishing, kayaking to Cathedral Cove (a huge limestone arch), and digging your own hot-tub on Hot Water Beach.

Hawke's Bay

(**E**) Napier, Hawke's Bay, and East Cape area on the East Coast of the North Island comprise three distinct areas hemmed in by Te Urewera National Park on one side, and the curving coastline of the Pacific Ocean on the other. Napier is a quirky coastal city, an art deco phoenix risen from the ashes of a 7.9 earthquake in 1931. Hawke's Bay is known for its wine. Farther north, from Gisborne up to the East Cape, is a string of quiet coastal towns.

Otago Peninsula

(**F**) Tiny, rugged Otago Peninsula, only 18 miles long, is jam-packed with wildlife, including a yellow-eyed penguin reserve and the world's only mainland royal albatross colony. Little Blue penguins, sea lions, and New Zealand fur seals are abundant, and Larnach Castle towers over it all at the peninsula's highest point.

Queenstown

(**G**) Queenstown has long been known as the Adventure Capital of the World. The city is a small and lively maze of restaurants and shops, but the surrounding landscape is the real playground. The Queenstown area, including mild Wanaka and isolated Glenorchy, is a jumble of ski slopes, rivers, and alpine areas that make it a haven for hiking, skiing, paragliding, white-water rafting, kayaking, and—after the adrenaline wears off—wine tasting.

Waitomo Caves

(**H**) Between Auckland and Taupo are the Waitomo Caves, a massive system of underground limestone caves. Three main caves—Glowworm Cave (named for its electric blue inhabitants), Ruakuri Cave (a *wahi tapu,* or sacred site), and Aranui Cave (known for its fantastic limestone formations)—can be rafted, hiked, or rappelled.

IF YOU LIKE

Beaches

New Zealand has more than 15,000 km (9,300 miles) of coastline, which ripples and zigzags to create bays, coves, fjords, and countless beaches. These run the gamut from surfing hot spots to quiet sheltered lagoons to rugged, boulder-studded strands. Most are open to the public, and few are crowded. The greatest hazards are sunburn—the lack of smog and a subequatorial location mean the sun is strong—and strong currents.

On the North Island, Coromandel's eastern shore and the Bay of Plenty—especially busy **Mount Maunganui**—are favorites during summer "time off." The black "iron sand" on the West Coast of the North Island is a result of volcanic activity. **Karekare Beach,** west of Auckland, is the striking, cliff-backed beach that was made famous in Jane Campion's film *The Piano*. The dunes at **90 Mile Beach** in Northland are spectacular, and nearby **Doubtless Bay** has some of the country's loveliest caramel-color beaches. New Zealand's most famous surf breaks are near the laid-back west-coast towns of **Raglan** and **Oakura**; you can "hang-10" here or at **Piha** near Auckland or at the Bay of Plenty beaches.

South Island beaches are captivating, particularly in **Abel Tasman National Park** and neighboring **Golden Bay.** The sands are golden, and the water is jade green. Westerly winds carry driftwood, buoys, entire trees, and a fascinating variety of flotsam from as far away as South America to Stewart Island's **Mason Bay,** making this dramatic sweep of sand a beachcomber's paradise. The sand is crisscrossed with the tracks of kiwis (the birds) that reside in the area by the thousands.

Birds

It is one thing to read "9.6-foot wingspan," but it is quite another to watch the magnificent northern royal albatross spread its wings and soar through your field of vision. You don't have to be a twitcher (bird-watching nut) to appreciate New Zealand's feathered population—this country will turn you into a bird nerd. The birds of New Zealand are extraordinary to behold: a raft of thousands of sooty shearwaters (aka muttonbirds or *titi*) move like smoke over the water; a yellow-eyed penguin pops like a cork from the bright green surf and waddles up the beach; fantails squeak and follow you through the forest; the soft cry of the *morepork* (owl) is interrupted by the otherworldly call of the kiwi. Pelagic birds such as the royal albatross will take your breath away; the Otago Peninsula colony (off Dunedin) is the only mainland breeding colony for these perfect flying machines. It may be ornithologically incorrect to say so, but many of the native birds are simply hilarious. Penguins always make people smile, and New Zealand is home to the Little Blue (or fairy), the extremely rare *hoiho* (or yellow-eyed), and the Fiordland crested penguin. The kea and its cousin the kaka are wild and clever parrots whose antics crack people up—these birds like to hang upside down from gutters, drink from water fountains, and remove windshield wipers from cars. And, of course, there is the star of the bird show: the kiwi. You won't ever see another bird like this staunch flightless brown bird, and to glimpse a kiwi is an unforgettable and joyful experience. Hot bird spots include Kapiti Island off the North Island and Stewart Island way down south.

Boating

There are boating and fishing options to match any mood.

If you're feeling cruisy, rent a kayak and paddle around the golden beaches and inlets of Abel Tasman National Park, or the penguin-filled waters of Paterson Inlet. Take a canoe on the Whanganui River, or sail the Bay of Islands. Feeling really lazy? Just charter a boat and captain and take in the scenery of the Marlborough Sounds or busy Auckland Hauraki Gulf. Fly-fish a trout from a caldera in Lake Taupo, or from one of the many pristine rivers and lakes throughout the country.

If you want some fun and a bit of a rush, much of the fishing in the South is simple rod or hand-lining for groper (grouper), trumpeter, and greenbone. Northerners argue their snapper is superior to the succulent Stewart Island blue cod; sample both to weigh in on this tasty debate. Go on a creaky wooden boat for the local old-school experience (some skippers will fry your catch), or opt for a sleeker vessel and a bird tour and let your heart soar with the mollymawks.

Up north ups the excitement, with big-game fishing out of Russell and Paihia for big fish such as striped marlin. Tuna is always a challenging catch, and the **Hokitika Trench** off Greymouth is one of the few places in the world where the three species of bluefin tuna gather.

If you want a major adrenaline buzz, go jet-boating on the **Shotover River** near Queenstown, or raft the North Island's **Kaituna River**, near Rotorua, which has the highest commercially rafted waterfall (22 feet) in the Southern Hemisphere. Or get off the boat and go spearfishing for *moki* in the kelp forests beneath the waves.

Bushwalking

The traditional way to hike in New Zealand is freedom walking. Freedom walkers carry their sleeping bags, food, and cooking gear and sleep in basic huts. A more refined alternative—usually on more popular trails—is the guided walk, on which you trek with a light day pack, guides do the cooking, and you sleep in heated lodges.

The most popular walks are in the Southern Alps. The **Milford Track,** one of New Zealand's nine Great Walks, is a four-day walk through breathtaking scenery to the edge of Milford Sound (Great Walks need to booked in advance, ⊕ *www.doc. govt.nz*). The **Queen Charlotte Track** (71 km [45 miles]) winds along the jagged coast of the Marlborough Sounds region; you can often see seals and dolphins from the waterside cliffs.

Rakiura National Park's **North West Circuit** is a challenging hike. The 10- to 12-day trek will sometimes feel more like mud wrestling than walking, but the scenic rewards are immeasurable, as is the pint of beer waiting at the South Sea Hotel when it's over. To experience Rakiura, do the three-day **Rakiura Track**, or have a water taxi drop you along one of the many coastal trails and walk back.

On the North Island the Coromandel has forests of regenerating kauri trees, more than 100 years old; 80-foot-tall tree ferns; a gorgeous coastline; and well-marked trails. You can hike among active volcanic peaks in **Tongariro National Park.** On a nub of the West Coast sits the majestic **Mt. Taranaki.** If time is short, set aside a few hours for trekking in the **Waitakere Ranges,** a short drive from Auckland city.

Luxe Lodging

If you think New Zealand is provincial in its accommodations, think again—Kiwis know how to live in their landscape, and that knowledge is reflected in lodging options on offer.

Check out stunning **Blanket Bay** (⊕ *www. blanketbay.com*) on the end of Lake Wakatipu near Glenorchy, with its schist-stone chalets under the shadow of the Remarkables mountain range, if you can spend more than NZ$1,000 per night. Or try **Wharekauhau Lodge** (⊕ *www. wharekauhau.co.nz*), 5,500 acres of quiet luxury surrounded by native forest and overlooking Palliser Bay, 90 minutes from Wellington.

Blend into the native forest at one of the environmentally friendly eco-villas at **Punakaiki Resort** (⊕ *www.punakaiki-resort. co.nz*) on the wild West Coast of the South Island with views of the ocean or the rain forest in Paparoa National Park. Stay in the treetops at Kaikoura's **Hapuku Lodge & Tree Houses** (⊕ *www.hapukulodge.com*).

Kick it old-style at the granddaddy of all New Zealand lodges, **Chateau Tongariro** (⊕ *www.chateau.co.nz*), an iconic heritage building at the base of active volcano Mt. Ruapehu in Tongariro National Park.

Dream of grapes growing on the vine? Stay at one of the two cottages in Hawke's Bay's **Craggy Range Winery** (⊕ *www. craggyrange.com*) near Napier, or at **Owhanake Bay Estate** (⊕ *www.owhanake. co.nz*), a boutique accommodation and vineyard on Waiheke Island near Auckland.

Wild and rugged station life and genuine Kiwi company come with a taste of the good life at **Mt. Nicholas Lodge** (⊕ *www. mtnicholaslodge.co.nz*), a 100,000-acre working station near Queenstown.

Skiing

With all of its mountains, New Zealand is a skier's paradise, from the volcanic cones in the North Island to the massive Southern Alps on the South Island.

North Island skiing centers on **Mt. Ruapehu,** an active volcano with two skiing areas: Whakapapa (the larger of the two, with 30 groomed trails) and Turoa (20 groomed trails, including the country's longest vertical drop of 2,369 feet). Mt. Ruapehu is New Zealand's largest ski area, and no wonder: who would pass up the opportunity to ski down Mt. Doom from *Lord of the Rings*? The nearby town of Ohakune is also the Queenstown of the north in the wintertime, famous for its lively hospitality.

The South Island provides a few more major fields to choose from. Near Queenstown, the **Remarkables** is a popular area with three basins and one heckuva view. **Coronet Peak** is known for its excellent facilities, treeless slopes, and night skiing, with a wide range of terrain for all levels.

Wanaka's **Treble Cone** is the most challenging field in New Zealand, with intermediate and advanced downhill powder runs on a vertical drop of 2,313 feet. Nearby **Cardrona** is more suited to families, with more rolling slopes for beginners.

Mt. Hutt near **Methven** (Canterbury) is New Zealand's best and highest ski slope with first-rate powder skiing; it also has the longest season.

Heli-skiing, snowboarding terrain parks, and cross-country skiing are also popular, so check out the local regions to see what's available.

Surfing

New Zealand's 15,000 km (9,300-plus) miles of coastline provides excellent surfing beaches for experts and beginners alike. The water is cold, so bring a wet suit. Since many beaches have a notorious rips, be sure to talk to the locals and check the weather before heading out.

The North Island has the highest concentration of surf beaches, with **Northland** providing ample opportunities. In **Auckland, Te Arai Point, Mangawhai, Piha,** and **Muriwai** are popular hot spots, and **Coromandel's Whangamata** is a favorite.

Find white-sand, cliff-side beaches in the **East Cape** area, including **Ruatoria, Tokomaru Bay, Tolaga Bay,** and **Gisborne.** *Whale Rider* was filmed in this area. The locals are fiercely protective of their land, so tread gently. Farther south are the beaches of the **Napier** and **Wairarapa** area: **Mahia, Ocean Beach, Castlepoint,** and **Cape Palliser.**

Raglan, New Zealand's most famous surf beach, is on the West Coast of the North Island. Its breaks were featured in the 1964 cult-classic *The Endless Summer.* Farther south, **Taranaki's Surf Highway,** a 43-mile stretch from New Plymouth to Hawera on State Highway 45, provides inlets and remote beaches.

The South Island's coast is more difficult to get to and colder, so there are fewer surfing opportunities. **Kaikoura, Christchurch, Hokitika, Greymouth,** and **Dunedin** all have good breaks.

For a list of surf schools, events, and news, check out Surfing NZ (⊕ *www.surfingnz. co.nz*). Surf.co.nz (⊕ *surf.co.nz*) has surf reports.

Wine

With its cool winters and mild summers, New Zealand is fast becoming famous for fine white wines and rich reds.

The largest, most well-known region is **Marlborough,** on the top of the South Island, which produces 70% of the national crop. Marlborough produces fine Sauvignon Blancs, as well as unique Rieslings and Pinot Noirs.

Hawke's Bay is the second-largest region, located on the East Coast of the North Island. New Zealand's premiere food and wine destination is known for Chardonnays, Cabernet Sauvignons, Syrahs, and Merlots.

Auckland has about 100 vineyards and wineries. It is known for rich, Bordeaux-style reds, as well as the boutique vineyards on Waiheke Island.

Gisborne, also on the East Coast of the North Island, is the fourth-largest grape-growing region, and produces buttery-rich tones in its tasty Chardonnays.

The **Wairarapa** features small wineries, most of which are within walking distance of the town square. This is Pinot Noir country, and it produces some of New Zealand's best.

Nelson, another small, idyllic wine region in the north of South Island, is known for light reds as well as its artistic flair.

Canterbury, in the east of the South Island, is the country's newest wine region, but its Rieslings and Pinot Noirs stand out.

Central Otago, near Queenstown in the South Island, wins the most handsome wine region award: vineyards are hemmed in by staggering white-capped mountain ranges, producing earthy rich reds.

SPEAK LIKE A LOCAL

From the moment you begin your New Zealand (or *Aotearoa,* as you'll learn in the airport) adventure, you'll confront the mélange of Māori words, Briticisms, and uniquely Kiwi phrases that make the language vibrant . . . but perhaps a bit hard for American ears to navigate.

New Zealand is a bilingual nation, as reflected in its national anthem. Although Māori isn't conversational language, a basic knowledge of Māori is essential for understanding phrases, the meaning of place-names, as well as the pronunciation of certain words or place-names. ■ TIP➔ **For a crash course in the best way to pronounce New Zealand place-names, the best thing to do is watch the weather report on the news.**

Talking Kiwi is not as daunting as Māori pronunciations for those with the English language under their belt. New Zealanders tend to use the Queen's English, colored up with their unique brand of abbreviated slang. Most Kiwi turns-of-phrase are easy to unravel—a *car park* is a parking lot, for example. Others, like *dairy* (a convenience or corner store), can be confused with American terminology. Only occasionally will you find yourself at a complete loss (with words like *jandal,* for example—Kiwi for flip-flop), and even then New Zealanders will be happy to set you right. Below are common Māori and Kiwi phrases that you'll likely hear throughout the country.

Māori Pronunciation

Knowing how to pronounce Māori words can be important while traveling around New Zealand. Even if you have a natural facility for picking up languages, you'll find many Māori words to be quite baffling. The West Coast town of Punakaiki (pronounced poon-ah- *kye*-kee) is relatively straightforward, but when you get to places such as Whakatane, the going gets tricky—the opening *wh* is pronounced like an *f,* and the accent is placed on the last syllable: "fa-ca-tawn- *e.*" Sometimes it is the mere length of words that makes them difficult, as in the case of Waitakaruru (why- *ta*-ka-ru-ru) or Whakarewarewa (fa-ca- *re*-wa- *re*-wa). You'll notice that the ends of both of these have repeats—of "ru" and "rewa," which is something to look out for to make longer words more manageable. In other instances, a relatively straightforward name like Taupo can sound completely different than you expected (Toe-paw). Town names like Waikanea (*why*-can-eye) you'll just have to repeat to yourself a few times before saying them without pause.

The Māori *r* is rolled so that it sounds a little like a *d.* Thus the Northland town of Whangarei is pronounced "fang-ah-day," and the word *Māori* is pronounced "mah- *aw*-dee," or sometimes "mo-dee," with the *o* sounding like it does in the word *mold,* and a rolled *r.* A macron indicates a lengthened vowel. In general, *a* is pronounced *ah* as in "car"; *e* is said as the *ea* in "weather." *O* is pronounced like "awe," rather than *oh,* and *u* sounds like the *u* of "June." *Ng,* meanwhile, has a soft, blunted sound, as the *ng* in "singing." All of this is a little too complicated for those who still choose not to bother with Māori pronunciations. So in some places, if you say you've just driven over from "fahng-ah-ma- *ta,*" the reply might be: "You mean 'wang-ah- *ma*-tuh'." You can pronounce these words either way, but more and more people these days are pronouncing Māori words correctly.

MĀORI GLOSSARY

Common Māori Words

Aotearoa: Land of the long white cloud (New Zealand's Māori name)

Haere mai: Welcome, come here

Haere rā: Farewell, good-bye

Haka: "Dance," implies history, life-force, rhythm, words and meaning of the haka, made internationally famous by the All Blacks, who perform it before each match

Hāngi: Earth oven, food from an earth oven, also used to describe a feast

Hongi: Press noses in greeting

Hui: Gathering

Iwi: People, tribe

Ka pai: Good, excellent

Kai: Food, eat, dine

Karakia: Ritual chant, prayer, religious service

Kaumātua: Elder

Kia ora: Hello, thank you

Koha: Customary gift, donation

Kūmara: Sweet potato

Mana: Influence, prestige, power

Marae: Traditional gathering place, sacred ground

Moko: Tattoo

Pā: Fortified village

Pākehā: Non-Māori, European, Caucasian

Pounamu: Greenstone

Rangatira: Chief, person of rank

Reo: Language

Tāne: Man

Tangata whenua: People of the land, local people

Taonga: Treasure

Tapu: Sacred, under religious restriction, taboo

Wahine: Woman

Waiata: Sing, song

Waka: Canoe

Whakapapa: Genealogy, cultural identity

Whānau: Family

KIWI GLOSSARY

Common Kiwi Words

Across the ditch: Over the Tasman Sea in Australia (Australians are called Aussies)

Bach: Vacation house (pronounced *batch*)

Cabbage: Stupid

Crook: Sick

Fanny: Woman's privates (considered obscene)

Footie: Rugby football

Gutted: Very upset

Kiwi: A native, brown flightless bird, the people of New Zealand, or the furry fruit

Knackered: Tired

Nappie: Diaper

Pissed: Drunk

Sealed road: Paved road

Shout: Buy a round of drinks

Sticking plaster or plaster: Adhesive bandage

Stuffed up: Made a mistake

Sweet as: All good

Ta: Thanks

Torch: Flashlight

Tramping: Hiking

Whinge: To whine

NEW ZEALAND HISTORY

Aotearoa

According to Māori legend, the demigod Maui sailed from Hawaiki (believed to be one of the French Polynesian islands) in his canoe, and he caught a huge fish, which he dragged to the surface. The fish is the North Island; Maui's canoe is the South Island.

This legend describes New Zealand's history, which is one of hardship, fortitude, and discovery. This brave, isolated, and young country is still creating its history, day by day.

Māori oral traditions say it began with the moa hunters, believed to have arrived in the 9th century, possibly from east Polynesia, which could make them related to present-day Māori. In AD 925, Kupe sailed from Hawaiki and discovered New Zealand. He returned to Hawaiki, named it Aotearoa (Land of the Long White Cloud), and passed on the sailing coordinates. In AD 1350, eight war canoes landed in New Zealand, marking the beginning of Māori culture on the landmass. Their existence was a battle of brutality and beauty. Warriors were trained at a young age, and tribal warfare and sheer survival led to a low life expectancy. At the same time, Māori became accomplished tattoo, carving, and weaving artists.

Europeans Arrive

In 1642, the Dutch captain Abel Tasman sighted the South Island, near Punakaiki, and officially put New Zealand on the map. Captain Tasman never actually set foot in New Zealand, though—he left after his boat was attacked by Māori in Golden Bay.

In 1767, Captain James Cook visited "Nieuw Zeeland" (as it had been named) in the *Endeavour,* and he is responsible for accurately charting the coastline. The whalers and sealers arrived in the 1790s, nearly obliterating sea-life populations in a matter of decades. Māori also suffered from the introduction of European diseases and firearms, which they used on each other in their brutal land wars.

The Treaty of Waitangi

The date February 6, 1840, is one of the most important dates in New Zealand history. Māori signed the Treaty of Waitangi with the British. The Treaty guaranteed Māori rights to their land, but it gave the British sovereignty. The hope of this treaty was that it would end land wars, tame lawlessness, and put New Zealand beyond the reach of French settlement. The New Zealand capital was moved from Russell in the Bay of Islands to Auckland, where it remained for 25 years.

It wasn't long, however, before Māori continued to lose their land to both the government and local settlers. When Pakeha outnumbered Māori for the first time in 1858, Māori tribes banded together, declaring Waikato's Te Wherowhero the first Māori king. This only galvanized the British further, and violent land wars continued well into the 1860s.

Boom Years and Social Changes

Meanwhile, on the South Island, gold was discovered, leading to a booming period of growth in the areas around Queenstown, Arrowtown, and Otago, including the establishment of New Zealand's first university in 1869 in Dunedin. The nation's capital was also moved to Wellington (1865), and Māori were given representation in parliament two years later. By 1880, the government had established free public schooling, and railroads and roads were beginning to crisscross the country. New Zealand also became the first country to legalize unions in 1878, and it was the first country to give women the vote in 1893.

Although well versed in land wars, New Zealand got its first taste of international war in 1899, when it backed the British in the Boer War. New Zealand's allegiance to the Crown made for a bloody 50 years. In World War I, New Zealanders were part of the epic battle at Gallipoli in Turkey; 10% of the population joined the Australian and New Zealand Army Corps (ANZAC), which helped to form the strange and unique bond with Australia, but nearly 17,000 New Zealanders died in the conflict. New Zealand also entered the fray in World War II, once again sustaining heavy casualties that rocked the tiny country's population.

The Post-WWII Years

The 1950s through the 1980s were a time of huge economic growth, then bust, populated with local tragedies. In 1952 the country's population soared to more than 2 million, and in 1953 local boy Edmund Hillary with Sherpa Tenzing Norgay became the first to summit Mt. Everest. Postwar, the economy was at an all-time high. Within the next few decades, however, disaster struck again and again, including the 1953 Mt. Ruapehu eruption that killed 151 people when a lahar derailed a train, the sinking of the ferry *Wahine* off Wellington's coast in 1968, and the plane crash in Antarctica in 1979 that killed all 257 passengers. The economy went into a slump, and mad-dash government efforts only seemed to make things worse.

The 1980s were defined by stands that started to give New Zealand her own identity. In 1981 much of the population was in an uproar about the South African rugby team touring New Zealand. Apartheid protesters flocked to the streets and clashed with Kiwis who felt that politics had no place in rugby. In 1984, the Labour government put a ban on nuclear-powered or -armed ships, despite pressure from the United States because of its anti-nuke stand. In 1985, the Greenpeace ship *Rainbow Warrior* was blown up in Auckland by the French. In 1987, New Zealand won the inaugural Rugby World Cup—a feat it repeated in 2011.

In the New Millennium

Māori culture has experienced a resurgence and greater integration, but in 2003 a new debate flared as Māori requested a legal inquiry into their precolonial customary ownership of the seabed and shore. Thousands of protesters marched on Parliament in support of Māori claims. New Zealand ratified the Kyoto Treaty in late 2002; it bound itself to new environmental regulations. By 2007, the former Prime Minister, Helen Clarke, announced the country's goals for eventual carbon neutrality. In February 2008, the National Party defeated her Labour Party and John Key became Prime Minister. On February 22, 2011, a magnitude 6.3 earthquake caused massive destruction in Christchurch and killed 181 people. Shortly after these trying times, the Rugby World Cup 2011 was a much needed tonic. The country burst with pride as the All Blacks defeated France in the final tournament in October 2011. A contest in 2015 allowed designers to come up with ideas for a new flag, and the people a chance to vote on which image best represents the country. The finalist went up against the current flag in a 2016 referendum, but voters chose to retain the current flag.

GREAT ITINERARIES

BEST OF THE NORTH ISLAND, 8 TO 10 DAYS

It can be difficult to decide which island to focus on, but this much is true: each of the islands is uniquely memorable, so no matter where you go, you will bring home a story. You will find volcanic springs, worm caves, and subterranean excitement in the North Island. Most of your time can be spent exploring the busy cities and close-to-ground activities. It's generally quicker and easier to get from place to place by car. If you travel by bus, consider adding a few hours to the itinerary, since buses make frequent stops and weave in and out of towns.

Fly in: Auckland Airport (AKL)

Fly out: Auckland Airport (AKL)

DAYS 1 AND 2: AUCKLAND

After a long international flight, stretch your legs and invigorate your circulation with a walk around the city center, with perhaps stops at **Auckland Museum** and **Auckland Domain** or **Albert Park.** Head to the harbor (or "harbour") and take a ferry ride round-trip between Auckland and Devonport for a great view of the city from the water. Have an early dinner and turn in to get over the worst of the jet lag.

On your second day, you'll have more wind in your sails to explore the City of Sails. Depending on your interests, head to **Kelly Tarlton's Antarctic Encounter and Underwater World,** the **New Zealand National Maritime Museum,** the **Auckland Art Gallery,** or the **Parnell** neighborhood for window-shopping. If you're feeling energetic, you can even do a bit of kayaking (or just sunbathing) at **Mission Bay** or **Karekare Beach.**

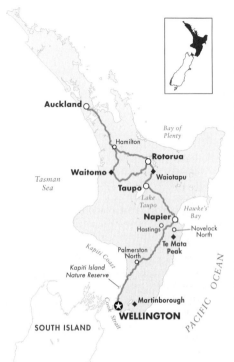

DAYS 3 AND 4: WAITOMO AND ROTORUA

Waitomo is known for what's beneath the surface—intricate limestone caves filled with stalactites, stalagmites, and galaxies of glowworms. If this is up your alley, get an early start from **Auckland** to arrive here before 11 am and sign up for a cave tour. Afterward, continue on to **Rotorua,** which seethes with geothermal activity. In the late afternoon you should have time for a walk around the town center, strolling through the **Government Gardens,** and perhaps also **Kuirau Park.** If you decide to skip the **Waitomo** worms, you can zip straight down from Auckland to Rotorua. In addition to the town proper, visit some of the eye-popping thermal areas nearby, such as **Waikite Valley Thermal Pools.** At night, be a guest at a *hāngi,* a Māori feast accompanied by a cultural performance. On the next day, you can either see some of the outlying thermal areas or continue south to **Taupo. Logistics:** 3–3.5 hours by car.

DAY 5: TAUPO

Midway between Auckland and Wellington, the resort town of **Taupo**, on its giant namesake lake, is the perfect base for a day full of aquatic activities. If you're at all interested in trout fishing, this is the place to do it. You can also bathe in the volcanic springs in the park that is open to the public night and day. **Logistics:** 1–1.5 hours by car.

DAY 6: NAPIER

The small town of **Napier** is an art deco period piece; after a devastating Richter 7.9 earthquake in 1931, the center of town was rebuilt in the distinctive style, and it's been carefully preserved ever since. Take a guided or self-guided walk around the heritage (historically significant) neighborhood. If you have a car, drive out of town and visit one of the 30-odd wineries around **Hawke's Bay**. In the afternoon, take a drive to the top of **Te Mata Peak**, or visit nearby towns **Hastings** or **Havelock North**. Otherwise, hang out at the waterfront or visit the aquarium. **Logistics:** 1.5–2 hours by car.

DAYS 7 AND 8: WELLINGTON

New Zealand's capital, **Wellington**, is a terrific walking city, and there's even a cable car to help you with the hills. The big cultural draw is **Te Papa Tongarewa**—the Museum of New Zealand, which, with five floors and great interactive activities for kids, can take a full day to explore. You may wish to spend the rest of your first day here along the waterfront, winding up with dinner in the area. Be sure to check out the entertainment listings, too; you could be in town during one of the many festivals or catch a cool local band. On your second day, explore more of the urban highlights, like the **City Gallery** and the **Museum of Wellington City &**

Sea, followed by a bit of browsing on the main shopping drags or a trip up into the hills to the **Botanic Garden.** If you'd prefer more time out in the country and have a car, drive up the **Kapiti Coast** and book to visit **Kapiti Island Nature Reserve**, or sip acclaimed Pinot Noir in the wine center of **Martinborough. Logistics:** 4–5 hours by car.

OTHER TOP OPTIONS

With at least one more day at your disposal, you could squeeze in one of the following destinations. **The Tongariro Crossing,** a challenging but spectacular daylong hike, could be added to your Taupo stay. You'll "tramp" up close to three volcanoes: **Tongariro, Ngauruhoe,** and **Ruapehu.** If you have two days and are keen on swimming with dolphins or doing some diving, loop up to **Paihia**, a small seaside town and gateway to the **Bay of Islands,** after your initial two days in Auckland. You can dip into the mellow, rural **Coromandel Peninsula,** perhaps the gateway town of **Thames**, before going south to Rotorua. Most places on the Coromandel are within 1 to 1½ hours' drive from the Thames township.

BEST OF THE SOUTH ISLAND, 10 TO 13 DAYS

The South Island is where you'll find yourself recharging that camera battery. For breathtaking scenery and daredevil activities like skydiving, skiing, exotic wildlife viewing, and trekking, this island has the most to offer. Spend a few days on a biking or hiking trip, and a few days on a wine tour, and you've got yourself quite a suitable itinerary. Driving on this island can take longer between towns since the roads weave in and out of mountains.

Fly in: Wellington International Airport (WLG)

Fly out: Wellington International Airport (WLG)

DAYS 1-2: PICTON AND BLENHEIM

Hop or drive onto the ferry from Wellington to Picton. This small seaside township is the Marlborough region's main commercial port, and the gateway to the gorgeously scalloped coastline of **Marlborough Sounds.** Hop on a mail boat, which makes stops at coves and islands along the Sounds; take a day walk along the famous **Queen Charlotte Track** for spectacular water views; or join a kayak tour (you might just see some seals and dolphins as you paddle around). Have dinner along the foreshore and turn in early.

The next morning, head out of town to the **Blenheim** region, where the rolling hills are covered with grapevines and filled with scores of wineries. Stop in for tastings at esteemed spots like the **Seresin Estate, Cloudy Bay,** and **Allan Scott Wines**; if you've made reservations, you might also be able to dine at **Herzog** or **Hunter's Garden Cafe.** Be sure to pick up a few bottles of wine and olive oil to take with you.

DAY 3: KAIKOURA

Get an early start and continue down the South Island's eastern coast to the seaside settlement of **Kaikoura,** where you can go whale-watching, reef diving, swimming with dolphins or seals, or stay on land and indulge in a big crayfish lunch ("Kaikoura" actually means "meal of crayfish" in the Māori language). **Logistics:** 1–3 hours by car.

DAYS 4 AND 5: CHRISTCHURCH

2010 and 2011 brought three significant earthquakes that rocked **Christchurch,** the South Island's largest city. The city center and some outlying suburbs were significantly damaged and are in the process of being rebuilt. Although this will take some time, "The Garden City" still lives up to its name: after you arrive from Kaikoura, spend the afternoon strolling around 395-acre **Hagley Park** and the neighboring **Christchurch Botanic Gardens,** a sprawling wonderland with more than 10,000 exotic and indigenous plants. Or take a punt on the meandering **Avon River,** followed by a coffee at a local café. For a two-day stay, fit in a couple of hours at the **International Antarctic Centre,** or spend the day in **Akaroa,** swimming with the endangered Hector's dolphins or enjoying the French-influenced atmosphere. The next morning, get an early start to make the push to Queenstown. **Logistics:** 2 hours from Kaikoura.

DAYS 6 THROUGH 8: QUEENSTOWN

Depending on your appetite for adventure, **Queenstown** may be the focus of your South Island trip. Take the plunge with **AJ Hackett Bungy,** free-fall on the **Shotover Canyon Swing,** try a jet-boat ride, or go rafting. As the town is set on **Lake Wakatipu** with the jagged peaks of the **Remarkables** mountains around it, you won't lack for scenic distractions. If you're interested in the area's gold-mining history, detour to nearby **Arrowtown** and see the **Lake District Museum & Gallery**. If the area looks familiar, you're not dreaming: many scenes from the *Lord of the Rings* film trilogy were shot here. **Logistics:** 5–6 hours by car.

DAYS 9 AND 10: FIORDLAND NATIONAL PARK

Follow your extreme sports adventure with some extremely splendid landscapes. At **Milford and Doubtful sounds** in **Fiordland National Park,** deep green slopes fall steeply down to crystalline waters. Rare species live in the unique underwater environment here, so try to visit the **Milford Deep Underwater Observatory.** Drink in the views by catamaran, by kayak, or by flightseeing. Whatever you do, don't forget your rain gear and bug repellent! If pressed, you could make a trip to Milford Sound a long day's trip from Queenstown.

■ **TIP→ The road to Milford Sound can be a bit precarious. You can get more out of taking a bus through Fiordland National Park as the bus driver also serves as a tour guide, and stops at various attractions. The bus trip is 4–5 hours, and you can ogle the mountains from the windows.**

OTHER TOP OPTIONS

With more time in your schedule, build in a couple of low-key days to offset the thrills-and-chills outdoor activities. After you arrive at Picton, you can drive or take a bus to Nelson, a relaxed waterfront town that's a good base for arts-and-crafts shopping and wine tasting. One fun stop is the **World of Wearable Art & Classic Cars Museum**. If ice is on your mind and you're willing to brave rainy conditions, push on down the rugged West Coast, stopping at the **Pancake Rocks**—columns of limestone resembling stacks of pancakes—on your way to the **Fox** or **Franz Josef Glacier** in **Westland Tai Poutini National Park.** Their flow rates are up to 10 times the speed of most valley glaciers. (To do this, plan on three days, as it's a long drive and you'll want at least one full day at the glaciers.)

NEW ZEALAND TRIP OF A LIFETIME, 16 DAYS

New Zealand may be small, but it is one of the most geographically diverse places on the planet. This ever-changing landscape is ideal to experience from the road. Although we suggest taking your time to see both islands, if you've only got two or three weeks to do it all, here's a quick-hit itinerary for both islands. Start your way at the bottom and work your way up or do it the other way around, although if you plan on leaving after seeing Queenstown, you might want to extend your flight. The whole span of the country is roughly the length of the East Coast of the United States, so if you were to drive from top to bottom, you'd cover it in a day. This tight but action-packed itinerary gives you suitable amount of time in each of New Zealand's top sites, and will give you a sense of accomplishment at the end of the trip. Consider renting a car, as public transportation every day could rack up the bills and become more of a hassle. Most people only fly if they have to get to the major cities in less than two hours. For a leisurely vacation, getting around by car would be the best.

NORTH ISLAND

Day 1: Auckland. Stop at the city's museums and galleries, but save some time to shop in the Parnell neighborhood.

Day 2: Taupo. Try trout fishing, or tramp the best one-day walk in the world: the Tongariro Crossing.

Day 3: Wellington. Take in Te Papa Tongarewa—the Museum of New Zealand, and then have dinner along the waterfront.

SOUTH ISLAND

Days 4 and 5: Christchurch. Visit the Botanic Gardens, Hagley Park, or the International Antarctic Centre with a side trip to Hanmer Springs, Kaikoura, or the Banks Peninsula.

Day 6: Aoraki/Mt. Cook. Experience the nearby glacier lakes. En route from Christchurch, stop for a picnic by Caribbean-color Lake Tekapo or Lake Pukaki.

Days 7 and 8: Queenstown. Bungy jump, take a jet-boat ride, or go rafting. Or, just take in stunning Lake Wakatipu and the Remarkables.

Day 9: Milford Sound. Spend the morning driving through Fiordland, and then take an overnight cruise.

Days 10 and 11: Wanaka. Go fishing, canyoning, kayaking, mountain biking, hiking, museum-visiting, or shopping.

Day 12: Franz Josef or Fox Glacier. See cascading waterfalls, forests, and icy blue rivers and pools before taking a glacier tour (book in advance).

Day 13: Hokitika. Stroll the town shops, carve your own piece of greenstone, and have coffee on the beach. At dusk, walk to the glowworm grotto.

Day 14: Arthur's Pass. Take in remote terrain before heading back to Christchurch.

Days 15 and 16: Christchurch. Return to Christchurch and then homeward from Auckland the next day.

FLAVORS OF NEW ZEALAND

The New Zealand food and wine scene had an earthy beginning. Traditional Māori staples included fish, birds, and root vegetables like *kūmara* (sweet potato) cooked slowly in an underground oven known as a *hāngi*. With the Europeans came livestock (sheep, cattle, and pigs) and a meat-and-potato diet. However, the past 30 years have seen a growth spurt in the New Zealand food and wine industries. Farmers and consumers are quickly developing a taste and reputation for sustainable, seasonable fare, and more and more chefs have incorporated foreign influences into local cuisine.

New Zealand food has been described as "Pacific Rim" or "Pacific Rim fusion," which is an expansive term that incorporates Asian and Pacific Island influences with traditional European-style mainstays. Breakfast includes eggs, muesli, and fruit. Sandwiches and sushi are common lunches, and Indian food, seafood, fish-and-chips, and game meats (steak, boar, and venison) are common for dinner. Although vegetarian restaurants are rare, most restaurants serve vegetarian options.

Not much cuisine is unique to New Zealand, although it's well known for pavlova (meringue topped with cream and fruit), hokey pokey ice cream (vanilla with golden toffee), hāngi, and Manuka honey.

Seafood
New Zealand has some of the largest fishing grounds in the world, so seafood is a must-have. Greenshell mussels, often cooked with lemongrass and coconut, are large and succulent. Bluff Oysters are pulled from the deep waters off the South Island late March to late August. *Paua* (abalone mother of pearl) are also abundant along the coast, as are crayfish (rock lobster) and hundreds of fish

varieties, including Marlborough-farmed salmon, trout, and *terakihi*. A local favorite is whitebait, a small fish caught in rivers and marine estuaries from August to November.

Fruits and Vegetables
Kiwis are also known for their kiwifruits and other fresh produce, such as olives, citrus fruit, and green vegetables. The best produce is found at roadside stalls or farmers' markets, which have become hugely popular weekend morning haunts. Favorite markets include the Hawke's Bay Farmers' Market, the Wellington Harbourside Market, and the Nelson Farmers' Market @ Founders.

Wine, Beverages, and Festivals
New Zealand's wine industry has flourished along with its cuisine. Marlborough produces award-winning Sauvignon Blancs, and Pinots and Chardonnays are also making names for themselves. Wines are reasonably priced and boutique vineyards are inviting.

There's also a variety of quality beers, microbrews, and liquor: check out 42 Below vodka in flavors like feijoa and Manuka honey. Coffee is serious business, alongside the burgeoning café culture. Flat whites (steamed milk over a shot of espresso) are the favorite. Kiwis take their tea British-style, with milk, so order it black if that's your preference.

Kiwis love to combine quality cuisine with a good party. Hokitika Wildfoods Festival, Toast Martinborough, the Bluff Oyster & Southland Seafood Festival, Auckland's Devonport Food, Wine and Music Festival, the Gisborne Wine & Food Festival, and Harvest Hawke's Bay Wine and Food Festival are just a few local celebrations.

TOUR OPERATORS

You can always travel without a guide, but in unfamiliar territory you'll learn more with a knowledgeable local by your side. If you're interested in a multiday excursion book it at least several weeks in advance. The companies listed here cover large regions of one or both islands.

With most adventure-tour companies, the guides' knowledge of the environment is matched by a level of competence that ensures your safety even in dangerous situations. The safety record of adventure operators is extremely good. Be aware, however, that most adventure-tour operators require you to sign waivers absolving the company of responsibility in the event of an accident. Courts normally uphold such waivers except in cases of significant negligence.

For additional regional tour operator recommendations and contact information see the Tours and Sports and the Outdoors sections in individual chapters.

BICYCLING

Season: October–March.

Best Locations: Countrywide.

Cost: Multiday tours start around NZ$1,700 per person, including food, lodging, and guide services. Supplemental fees are commonly charged for single riders.

New Zealand Pedaltours. New Zealand Pedaltours operates on both islands, with tours of 2 to 37 days. Tour options include the Coromandel Peninsula, the Southern Alps, and the Central Otago Rail Trail. Both islands. ⊠ *45 Tarawera Terr., Kohimarama, Auckland* ☎ *09/585–1338, 09/585–1339* ⊕ *www.pedaltours.co.nz.*

South Island Contacts Adventure South. ⊠ *29 Iversen Terr., Christchurch* ☎ *0800/00–1166* ⊕ *www.advsouth.co.nz.* **Pacific Cycle Tours.** ⊠ *Unit 3, 14 Kennaway Rd., Christchurch* ☎ *03/982–9933* ⊕ *www. bike-nz.com.*

CANOEING

Season: Year-round, best October–April.

Best Locations: Whanganui River, North Island.

Cost: From NZ$80 per person for single-day tours to NZ$225 per person for five-day trips. Tents, sleeping bags, and bedrolls can be rented for an additional fee.

Blazing Paddles Canoe Adventures. Blazing Paddles Canoe Adventures runs one- to five-day trips on the Whanganui River, during which you can ride mild rapids, and see waterfalls, pristine forests, and birdlife. Overnight stays are spent camping or in huts, depending on the trip. Blazing Paddles has a provisional OutdoorMark safety rating and now holds a DOC concession for self-catered guiding trips on the Whanganui River. ⊠ *1033 State Hwy. 4, Taumarunui* ☎ *07/895–5261, 0800/252–9464* ⊕ *www. blazingpaddles.co.nz* ☞ *From NZ$80 for a day trip to NZ$225 for a 5-day trip.*

CROSS-COUNTRY SKIING

Season: July–September.

Best Location: Aoraki (Mount Cook) and Wanaka, South Island.

Cost: Around NZ$850 for two to five days, NZ$1,170–NZ$1,700 for five days high on Mt. Cook alpine skiing, which includes equipment, meals, hut accommodation, a guide, and transport.

Alpine Recreation Canterbury. In winter (July–September), Alpine Recreation Canterbury runs multiday backcountry skiing trips on the glaciers of Aoraki/ Mount Cook and Westland National Parks and in the Two Thumb Range above Lake Tekapo, with terrains to suit all reasonably fit skiers. In the National Parks, Alpine and Telemark Tours typically start with a flight to the alpine hut that becomes your base; from there the group sets out each day. In the Lake Tekapo High Country you hike three hours to a private hut, from which you do day tours. Snowshoeing tours are also possible from here.

In summer (November–April), Alpine Recreation Canterbury runs guided treks, mountaineering courses, and guided ascents in Aoraki/Mount Cook and Westland National Parks. They have their own private hut straight opposite the mighty Caroline Face of Mt. Cook, which is used for the Aoraki Mt. Cook Trek, the Ball Pass Crossing, and climbing courses. ✉ *30 Murray Pl., Lake Tekapo, Christchurch* ☎ *03/680–6736, 0800/006–096* ⊕ *www. alpinerecreation.com.*

DIVING

Season: Year-round.

Best Locations: Bay of Islands, Poor Knights Islands, Great Barrier Island, Goat Island Marine Reserve, and the Coromandel Peninsula, North Island. Also, Milford Sound, South Island.

Cost: A two-dive day trip without rental gear runs about NZ$150, with gear around NZ$240.

Yukon Dive. Pacific Hideaway Charters runs dives at the Poor Knights Islands, Mokohinau Islands, and the coastal regions around Tutukaka—all of which are home to manta rays, large kingfish, and lots of other sea life. Day trips include tea, coffee, and snacks, as well as kayaks to borrow if you want to stay on the surface. ✉ *Marina A8, Tutukaka* ☎ *09/ 434–4506, 0800/693–483* ⊕ *yukon.co.nz/ pacifichideaway.*

North Island Contacts Paihia Dive Hire and Charter. ☎ *0800/107–551, 09/402–7551* ⊕ *www.divenz.com.*

FISHING

Licenses and Limits: Different regions require different licenses when fishing for trout, so check at the local tackle store or visit ⊕ *www.fishandgame.org.nz.* Fees are approximately NZ$124 per year, but at most tackle shops, you can purchase a daily or weekly license. No license is needed for saltwater fishing.

Season: Varies by region.

Best Locations: Countrywide.

Cost: Big-game fishing: NZ$300 per person, per day. Heli-fishing: from NZ$560 per person, per day. Trolling and fly-fishing for lake trout: from NZ$90 per hour (one to four people). Charter costs vary widely.

North Island Contacts Blue Ocean Charters. ✉ *Tauranga* ☎ *0800/224–278* ⊕ *www. blueocean.co.nz.* **Brett Cameron Central Plateau Fishing.** ☎ *07/378–8192* ⊕ *www.cpf. net.nz.* **Te Ra Charters.** ✉ *Whangamata* ☎ *07/865–8681* ⊕ *tera.whangamata.co.nz.*

South Island Contacts New Zealand Fly Fishing Guide. ✉ *Queenstown* ☎ *03/442– 7061* ⊕ *www.flyfishing.net.nz.* **Toa Tai Charters.** ☎ *021/169–2257* ⊕ *www. soundsfishing.co.nz.*

HIKING

Season: October–March for high-altitude walks, year-round for others.

Best Locations: Any of the national parks or New Zealand's nine Great Walks.

Cost: One- to three-day guided hikes are NZ$170 to NZ$1,070. Prices for longer hikes vary widely.

Hiking New Zealand. Hiking New Zealand has hiking tours to suit everyone on both islands, from 5 to 20 days. ☎ *0800/697–232, 03/310–8188* ⊕ *www. HikingNewZealand.com.*

North Island Contacts Bush and Beach. ☎ *09/837–4130, 0800/423–224* ⊕ *www. bushandbeach.co.nz.* **Kiwi Dundee Adventures, Ltd.** ☎ *07/865–8809* ⊕ *www. kiwidundee.co.nz.*

South Island Contacts Alpine Guides Ltd. ☎ *03/435–1834* ⊕ *www.alpineguides. co.nz.* **Alpine Recreation.** ☎ *03/680–6736* ⊕ *www.alpinerecreation.com.* **Guided Walks New Zealand Ltd.** ☎ *03/442–3000, 0800/832–226* ⊕ *www.nzwalks.com.* **Marlborough Sounds Adventure Company.** ⊠ *London Quay, Picton* ☎ *03/573–6078* ⊕ *www.marlboroughsounds.co.nz.* **Ultimate Hikes.** ⊠ *The Station Bldg., Duke St. Entrance, Queenstown* ☎ *03/450–1940* ⊕ *www.ultimatehikes.co.nz.* **Wild West Adventure Co.** ⊠ *8 Whall St., Greymouth* ☎ *03/768–6649, 0800/946–543* ⊕ *www. fun-nz.com.*

HORSE TREKKING

Season: All year-round on the North Island; may be weather dependent on the South Island.

Best Locations: Northland and the Coromandel Peninsula in the North Island, Nelson and Canterbury high country in the South Island.

Cost: Prices range from about NZ$125 for two hours to NZ$240 for a day trip, or NZ$500 for overnight; contact outfitters for specifics on shorter or multiday trips.

South Island Contacts

Cape Farewell Horse Treks. ⊠ *23 McGowan St., Puponga* ☎ *03/524–8031* ⊕ *www. horsetreksnz.com* ▣ *From NZ$80.*

Dart Stables Glenorchy. ⊠ *58 Coll St., Glenorchy* ☎ *03/442–5688, 0800/474–3464* ⊕ *www.dartstables.com.*

North Island Contacts

Pakiri Beach Horse Rides. ⊠ *317 Rahuikiri Rd., Pakiri Beach, R.D. 2, Wellsford* ☎ *09/422–6275* ⊕ *www.horseride-nz. co.nz* ▣ *NZ$175 ½-day, NZ$299 full-day, including packed lunch.*

Rangihau Ranch. ⊠ *Rangihau Rd., Coroglen* ☎ *07/866–3875* ⊕ *www. rangihauranch.co.nz.*

SAILING

Season: Year-round.

Best Locations: Bay of Islands, Auckland and Wellington in the North Island, upper and lower South Island, including the Marlborough Sounds.

Cost: Bay of Islands from NZ$90 for a day trip to NZ$700 to NZ$850; Doubtful Sound from NZ$1,750 for five days; Fiordland National Park from NZ$3,700 for eight days.

South Island Contacts Catamaran Sailing Charters. ⊠ *46 Martin St., Nelson* ☎ *03/547–6666, 0800/467–245* ⊕ *www. sailingcharters.co.nz.* **Heritage Expeditions.** ☎ *03/365–3500* ⊕ *www.heritage-expeditions.com.*

TRAMPING NEW ZEALAND
by Oliver Wigmore

Tramping (hiking) in the backcountry is a sacred kiwi pastime. Pristine coastal beaches, meandering rivers, glaciated peaks, steaming volcanoes, isolated lakes, cascading waterfalls, and lush native forest are often just an hour's drive from the major cities. You can "get amongst it" all with short walks, one-day tramps, or multiday hikes.

Many of New Zealand's best tramps are within the 14 national parks. The Department of Conservation (DOC) manages these parks and additional lands totalling over 5 million hectares, almost 30 percent of New Zealand. DOC maintains a range of tracks, walkways, huts, and campgrounds throughout these areas.

The Great Walks are the nine most renowned hiking (though one is technically a canoeing route) tracks, which traverse the country's volcanic plateau beaches, temperate rainforest, fjords, and mountain ranges. The most famous, Milford Track, is commonly called "the finest walk in the world." Collectively the Great Walks see over 86,000 trampers annually.

However hundreds of other tracks and routes crisscross the country, ranging from gruelling week-long, self-guided adventures to mellow, half-hour strolls through native bush. Often on these tracks you'll have the scenery to yourself. The range of difficulty and variety of terrain means almost anyone can experience tramping in New Zealand.

Milford Track.

PLANNING TIPS

■ During summer book accommodations well in advance, especially for the **Milford Track**.

■ DOC lowers fees from May to September. However alpine tracks may be impassable or closed.

■ Skip popular day walks such as the **Tongariro Alpine Crossing** over long weekends to avoid crowds.

■ Many tracks require transport. Book in advance through local tour operators.

BEST ONE-DAY HIKES

You don't need to commit to a three-day trek in order to see New Zealand by foot. These one-day hikes will give you a sense of New Zealand's landscapes sans huts and tents.

Tongariro Alpine Crossing: Explore the central North Island's alpine scenery, steaming fumaroles, volcanic craters, and brilliant emerald lakes on the country's most popular day walk. In summer the hike is somewhat strenuous, though not technically difficult. In winter it requires high-alpine experience. Hikers generally walk from Mangatepopo to Ketetahi, with side trips to the summits of Ngauruhoe and Tongariro.

Abel Tasman National Park: The park's easily-accessible, golden-sand coastlines require limited fitness. Perhaps the best of the many day walks on the Abel Tasman Coast Track is from Totaranui to Separation Point, where seals are visible in winter and autumn. Water taxi from Marahau transport visitors to a number of different points along the track.

Fiordland National Park: There are a number of short walks from the roadside on the drive to Milford Sound. These range from easy to difficult and from 30 minutes to a day. Key Summit (medium) and Gertrude Saddle (difficult) take in some of New Zealand's most amazing mountain scenery. Don't miss Bowen Falls, an easy 30 minute walk along Milford Sound's foreshore.

Queenstown: A number of day walks start at Glenorchy at Lake Wakatipu's north end. You can access short sections of the Routeburn, Caples, and Greenstone tracks, where alpine scenery is the star. The walk to Routeburn Falls is particularly spectacular, well graded, and of medium difficulty.

(top left) Hollyford Track, Fiordland National Park. (right) Routeburn Falls, Mt. Aspiring National Park. (bottom left) Anchorage Hut, Abel Tasman National Park. (opposite page) Routeburn Track.

GREAT WALKS

NORTH ISLAND TRACK	DIFFICULTY	ACTIVITIES / ATTRACTIONS
❶ LAKE WAIKAREMOANA TRACK, Te Urewera National Park (Ch. 5) 46 km (28.5mi), 3-4 days	**Moderate.** The tougest part is the climb from lake edge to Panekiri Bluffs. Heavy rain, mosquitoes and sand-flies are common.	Much of the track runs through podocarp forest. Track condition is generally good. The best views are from Panekiri Bluffs. See a variety of birds: kaka, parakeets, paradise ducks, whiteheads, fantails, silvereyes, morepork (native owl) kiwi. Don't miss the short uphill side trip to Korokoro waterfall. Advance booking advised.
❷ TONGARIRO NORTHERN CIRCUIT, Tongariro National Park (Ch. 5) 41 km (25 mi), 3-4 days	**Moderate.** Take good gear especially for the toughest section, the "Staircase." Do not attempt the track in rain or snow. Volcano erruptions are possible; stay back from steam vents.	This is one of New Zealand's best walks, with wonderful alpine and volcanic vistas, warm blue-green lakes, and steam vents, but mountains are often in heavy clouds. You'll see Mt. Ngauruhoe—a.k.a Mt. Doom in *The Lord of the Rings*.
❸ WHANGANUI JOURNEY, Whanganui National Park, near Taumarunui (Ch. 8) Full Trip: 145 km (90 mi,) 5 days Short Trip: 88 km (54.5 mi,) 3 days	**Moderate.** Those with experience can swim, canoe, and kayak. Be prepared for rain and floods.	Although a river journey, Whanganui is a Great Walk, and there is a 3-day version from Whaka-horo to Pipiriki. The Whanganui river takes a twisting path to sea; en route, expect narrow gorges, high cliffs, waterfalls, glowworm grottos. Tieke Marae has good huts and facilities, but you'll follow Maori protocol; koha (a gift of money) will be expected. Book trip and hire kayaks in advance from operators in Turangi, Taumaruni, or Ohakune.

For mountain landscapes and alpine scenery, the South Island and stunning **Fiordland National Park** are the clear winners.

Auckland

NORTH ISLAND — Rotorua ❶

❸ ❷

Napier

WELLINGTON

❹ Nelson

❺

Christchurch

SOUTH ISLAND

❻

❼ Te Anau

❽

❾ Stewart Is.

NORTH ISLAND
Tramping on the North Island is hard to beat: rivers, beaches, and otherworldly volcanic cones are all on offer here.

SOUTH ISLAND
Abel Tasman National Park provides beauti-ful beaches and lazy days. Warm, more stable weather generally occurs between January and April, but they're also the busiest.

SOUTH ISLAND TRACK	DIFFICULTY	ACTIVITIES/ATTRACTIONS
❹ ABEL TASMAN COAST TRACK, Abel Tasman National Park, near Nelson (Ch. 8) 54 km (34 mi), 3–5 days	**Moderate.** In autumn and winter, walking and weather conditions are good and the track is less crowded.	Follow the coast across beautiful golden sand beaches, rocks, and regenerating rain forests (with nikau palms, ferns, and forest gians). The two estuaries are only passable around low tide. You may spot seals and penguins.
❺ HEAPHY TRACK, Kahurangie National Park, near Nelson (Ch. 8) 78 km (48 mi), 4–6 days	**Moderate.** The most difficult section is between Brown and Perry Saddle huts. While normally a drier area, it does rain on the western slopes.	The track begins in dense beech and podocarp forest in north; continues up to snow tussock plateaus; and descends into palm-studded forests, rugged West Coast beaches. See bird, including kiwis and pipits, along one of the country's finest routes. This is primarily a summer route; snow can block the track in winter.
❻ ROUTEBURN TRACK, Mount Aspiring and Fiordland national parks (Ch. 10) 32 km (20 mi), 2–3 days	**Moderate.** Heavy rain, clouds, snow, and ice can be factors. On mountaintops, winter avalanches are possible.	Travel in either direction through beech forest and onto exposed mountaintops for spectacular scenery. In summer flowers, many unique to New Zealand, cover the alpine slopes. You'll need good equipment to travel this route.
❼ MILFORD TRACK, Fiordland National Park, near Te Anau (Ch. 10) 54 km (33.5 mi), 4–5 days.	**Moderate.** There are two strenuous climbs, one with a very steep descent. It frequently rains. Beware of avalanche conditions at Mackinnon Pass in winter.	You can only hike in on direction (south to north) along New Zealand's most popular track. Clinton River (often muddy) crosses Mackinnon Pass, goes through alpine meadows, and passes waterfalls, including NZ's highest, Sutherland Falls. Thick forests bookend the track, and lots of kea (mountain parrots) greet trampers. Book at least four months ahead; sandfly repellent is a must.
❽ KEPLER TRACK, Fiordland National Park, near Te Anau (Ch. 10) 60 km (37 mi), 3–4 days	**Moderate.** Day one includes a steep climb from lake to tops.	The hike goes through beech forests to sometimes snow-covered tussock tops with wonderful views in clear weather. Geology buffs will appreciate this trek, especially Mt. Luxmore. Detour to Iris Burn waterfall, 20-minute walk from Iris Burn hut.
❾ RAKIURA TRACK, Rakiura National Park, Steward Island (Ch. 11) 36 km (22 mi, including road walk), 3 days.	**Moderate.** There are two short uphill climbs. Be prepared to get muddy in the wet changeable weather. Expect mosquitoes and sandflies.	Follows the coastline through beech forest, subalpine scrub, and remote beaches. Mt. Anglem, a 3–4 hour side trip (one-way), provides wonderful views. Birdlife includes kiwi, bellbirds, tui, fantails, and parakeets. You may see seals and penguins. Hut tickets are required; there's some camping. Pack extra food and insect repellent.

WHAT TO BRING

Weather in New Zealand is unpredictable to say the least, so it is extremely important to be prepared and to carry the right equipment. In the mountains you should prepare for cold, wet weather year-round; in the north you can generally travel a little lighter, but there is nothing worse than walking for five hours shivering and wet because you forgot a decent jacket.

Tramping gear is widely available throughout New Zealand for rental or purchase, but is usually more expensive than in the United States. You must declare all used camping and hiking equipment on arrival. The Ministry of Agriculture and Fisheries (MAF) will inspect and sterilize your equipment, which is usually available for immediate collection. By not declaring your gear you risk not only a hefty fine but also the fragile New Zealand ecosystem, which is extremely susceptible to invasive foreign species.

The equipment you carry and the fitness required depends hugely on where you are heading and how long and at what time of year you're going. In general you should carry:

A good-quality three-season hiking tent (for overnighters).

Tramping clothes, i.e., polypropylene underwear, fleece, etc.

Warm sleeping bag in the winter (year-round in the South Island).

Personal first-aid kit and insect repellent.

Topographic maps (widely available throughout the country). Though not required for the majority of marked tracks, they should be carried when venturing into the back country.

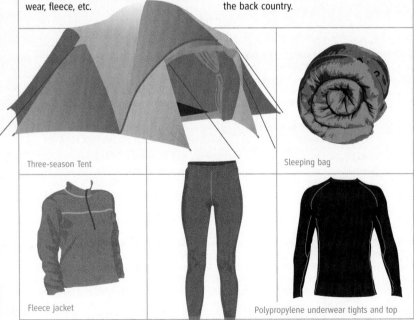

Three-season Tent

Sleeping bag

Fleece jacket

Polypropylene underwear tights and top

WHAT TO WEAR

BASE LAYER: Wear lightweight thermal underwear, preferably polypropylene or other moisture wicking synthetic fabric.

MID LAYER: Fleece, wool, or synthetic jersey (preferable for their lighter weight and rapid drying time) go over the base layer. This layer should keep you warm when wet (no cotton sweatshirts).

BACKPACK: Take a sturdy, comfortable pack that fits you well. Take a larger pack for longer tracks. Strong canvas fabric is best.

GAITERS: If walking through thick mud, water, or snow, tramping gaiters (covers for your shoes and pants) are a must.

The key thing to remember is layering. Wearing multiple layers of clothing allows you to rapidly adjust to changing temperatures and different exertion levels. Modern synthetic fabrics are preferable for their lightweight, quick drying times, and ability to keep you warm when wet.

HAT AND GLOVES: Bring a warm hat and gloves made from wool or synthetic.

SUN PROTECTION: Bring a sunhat and sunglasses.

OUTER LAYER: A water- and windproof outer layer, is necessary. In addition to a jacket bring overtrousers for many tracks, especially in the winter.

TROUSERS/SHORTS: Strong synthetic fabrics are best because they dry quickly when wet. No jeans!

SOCKS: Wool or synthetic hiking socks to keep your feet warm.

FOOTWEAR: The most important part, boots should be strong, sturdy, and waterproof. For longer, more rugged tramps full leather boots are best, but on shorter tramps and day walks lightweight fabric boots are often sufficient.

CHOOSING YOUR TRACK

Pick your hike based on the type of experience you're looking for and the time of year you plan on visiting. The DOC has five classifications for walks to help you decide which tracks are best suited for your experience and fitness level.

Short Walks: These easy walks last up to an hour along an even, graded surface and are suitable for all fitness levels.

Walking Tracks: These easy to moderate walks take from a few minutes to a day on reasonably well-formed but occasionally steep tracks. They are clearly signposted and suitable for people with low to moderate fitness. You may need light hiking boots in winter.

Easy Tramping Tracks: These single or multiday, signposted tracks for people of moderate fitness are well formed but may be steep and muddy. Wear light hiking boots. This category includes all the Great Walks.

Tramping Tracks: Trampers need good fitness and moderate back country experience, including navigation and survival skills, to walk these challenging single or multiday unformed trails. Generally marked with poles or rock cairns, trails may include unbridged river crossings; appropriate equipment, sturdy hiking boots, and preparation are required.

Route: You need a lot of backcountry survival and navigational experience, a high level of fitness, sturdy hiking boots and equipment, and preparation for these treks through natural terrain. Tracks may have basic markings, but trampers should be self-sufficient.

Visit DOC's information offices, in all major towns and the national parks, for information and lists of experienced guides, and to register your intentions. Inexperienced trampers should consider guided trips, which remove some of the organizational hassle and provide additional safety. Guides are generally friendly and extremely knowledgeable, and group trips are a great way to meet other travelers.

HUTS

DOC maintains a network of over 950 backcountry huts throughout New Zealand's conservation areas that are available for a small fee. Accommodations range from basic 4-person shelters offering a roof and a mattress to 20-person buildings complete with cooking facilities, toilets, lights, and heating. It's best to book huts well in advance. Book huts on the DOC Web site or by contacting the local DOC office. During the busy months custodians check for payment; however in the off season, respect the honesty system. Fees keep these places pristine and accessible to the public.

AUCKLAND

WELCOME TO AUCKLAND

TOP REASONS TO GO

★ **Boating and Sailing:** Aucklanders love boating. You can join them on a commuter ferry, a sailboat, or a racing yacht.

★ **Cuisine and Café Culture:** You'll find some of the country's finest restaurants, plus bistro bars, noodle houses, and vibrant neighborhood eateries.

★ **Year-Round Golf:** Lydia Ko started playing in a town with 20-plus golf courses, from informal to challenging championship level. The Muriwai Golf Club fronts a great surf beach.

★ **Art and Culture:** The revamped Auckland Art Gallery, Auckland Museum, theater companies, and live music scene draw crowds.

★ **Gorgeous Beaches:** The West Coast's black-sand beaches attract surfers from around the world; the safest swimming is on the East Coast. Takapuna Beach and Mission Bay are good places to swim but are very crowded on a sunny day. Remember to swim between the flags and slather on the sunscreen.

1 City Center and Parnell. Aucklanders see the central business district as the waterfront and Queen Street. Major international designers are opening stores in this part of town. To the east of the city center, Parnell has historic buildings, good restaurants, and water views, and is frequented by the upmarket "coffee set." This neighborhood also includes the Domain—home to Auckland Museum and a park with good walking and running trails, stunning harbor views, gardens and sculptures.

2 Ponsonby. Explore narrow streets lined with wooden Victorian villas and stroll the main strip lined with cafés, bars, restaurants, and local designer clothing stores.

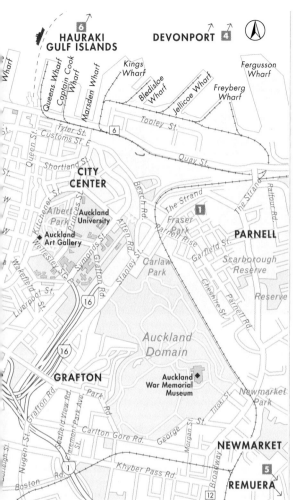

HAURAKI GULF ISLANDS

DEVONPORT

GETTING ORIENTED

The drive from the airport (often slow since Auckland's road network has not kept apace with the city's growth) will take you past some dramatic sculpture and industrial parks and into the standard image of New Zealand—cleanish and greenish with the landscape dominated by the city's 50 or so volcanic hills. Many of these hills have been set aside as parks, some with livestock. The Auckland region is geographically diverse, and Auckland city sits on an isthmus between the Waitemata (to the east) and Manukau Harbour (to the southwest). At its narrowest point the isthmus is only 1 km (½ mile) wide. The Orakei and Panmure basins, which are east of the city, are actually large craters that have been invaded by the sea. There's plenty of outdoor activity on the easy rolling terrain outside the central suburban areas and in some of the city's big parks. The many islands of the Hauraki Gulf, off Auckland's East Coast, are a must; ferries go to most at least once a day.

3 Western Springs. A park and suburb west of Auckland, and named after the springs that bubble into the lake, this makes a nice retreat from the city with little ones in tow.

4 Devonport. Across Waitemata Harbour, this moneyed suburb has great views of the harbour and a grand dame hotel.

5 Remuera. "Old money" families like to live in this tony suburb close to the Domain.

6 Hauraki Gulf Islands. Rangitoto, Waiheke, Rakino, and Motutapu islands have great walking and nature sites while Waiheke draws visitors to its wineries, restaurants, and Easter Jazz Festival.

SNACKING IN AUCKLAND

There is a raft of eating places in Auckland: eateries of all kinds use the freshest ingredients and simple preparation. Although you won't always get high-end cuisine most good places use unprocessed, pure, often locally sourced foods to turn out good honest fare that can surprise and delight.

Many of Auckland's best dining options are in its residential neighborhoods that you can get to by bus or taxi. Break away from the tourist-filled cafés on Viaduct Harbour and pull up a chair in a hidden Parnell garden, or a bustling Ponsonby sidewalk café, catch the ferry to Devonport or cab it to Takapuna for an alfresco meal enjoyed the way Kiwis do it, with good wine and friends.

English influences are everywhere but with a modern sensibility. Your afternoon tea just might be a slice of passion fruit cake and a flat white. Nearly every street with shops has a few eateries, a fish-and-chips shop, and several places for a great coffee.

PERFECT PICNICS

Auckland's many parks, with impressive native and introduced trees, beckon the outdoor diner. Supermarkets, gourmet shops, and most small cafés will make you a picnic. You can get a luxury hamper at one of many delicatessens, or select fresh fruit from numerous vendors.

Faster food is already wrapped and waiting at Wishbone, a unique elegant take-out chain found around the city. On tap are creative daily soups and special salads, and light sandwiches, like chicken, Brie, and cranberries.

SNACKING THE KIWI WAY

Hokey-Pokey Ice Cream. Chances are you've never had dairy as fresh as New Zealand butter or cream. Go for the full-fat version of this vanilla ice cream dotted with toffee bits.

Kūmara Fries. Packed with potassium and fiber, *kūmara* fries are guilt-free delicious snacks. The kūmara, or sweet potato, has a rich heritage as a Māori food staple. Red, gold, and orange varieties are plentiful in New Zealand today. Orange is the sweetest, especially fried and served with sweet chili sauce and sour cream. These fries are soft rather than crunchy.

Pavlova. Like the ballerina for whom it was named, this national dessert is feather light—a meringue topped with fruit, sauce, and fresh cream. The confection is essentially hollow, but it forms the tough core of one of the many Kiwi and Aussie rivalries: who invented it first and named it after Anna Pavlova? So far, Kiwis have the edge: a recipe predating the Australian one by six years. Look for the treat on the menu around Christmastime.

Whitebait Fritters. The Kiwi passion for this seafood, a smeltlike fish caught as juveniles as they head upriver to spawn, is so intense that the media reports the start of whitebait season. Find the pancake-size fritters at markets or as a daily special in cafés. Strict controls

and popularity make it a delicious and pricey delicacy.

THE CAFFERATTI

Auckland is home to the self-described cafferatti—those who live for coffee. Aucklanders happily tick off lists of go-to coffee shops and joints to avoid. A top-notch barista is key. In fact, some follow baristas from café to café. Locals prefer small independent shops that often operate in tiny spots with room for little more than a coffee machine, a small food cabinet, and a few stools. Aucklanders drink on the run, so you may see people present their own cups (some use brightly colored "keepcups") to be filled. To blend in with the cafferatti, order a **double shot flat white**—thicker and less milky than a latte, with a smoother, richer flavor than cappuccino—or a **short black** (espresso). And true members of the cafferatti never order flavoring, so save your caramel craving for when you return home.

(top left) Diners enjoy outdoor seating at an Auckland café; *(top)* Homemade pavlova with pomegranate and cream; *(bottom)* Latte art adds whimsy to a caffeine fix.

CITY OF SAILS

In Auckland you're never far from the water; on the East Coast it's the Waitemata Harbour and Hauraki Gulf and on the West Coast dramatic surf beaches. Residents make the most of it and the number of watercraft make it clear why they call Auckland the City of Sails. There are lots of opportunities for you to take part in the fun.

There are more yachts here per capita than in any other city in the world, and some of the world's fastest vessels are built and crewed by Kiwis. New Zealand has won two America's Cup competitions and hosts regattas of all sizes. In summer, Viaduct Harbour dazzles with some of the sleekest racing boats and splashiest yachts and superyachts in the hemisphere. Aquatic innovation isn't just about racing, though. A New Zealand farmer invented the jet-boat, a high-octane contraption that thrills adrenaline junkies on shallow inland rivers.

There are plenty of charter companies ready to take you out for a day on the water around Auckland, and they offer a wide array of experiences, from gentle, 1½-hour trips for the sea-wary to multi-day treks along the coast.

TOP OPERATORS

Fullers Ferries. See the Auckland skyline on Fullers's 1½-hour **Auckland Harbour cruise.** Commentary runs while taking passengers past the Harbour Bridge, Devonport's naval base, and Bean Rock Lighthouse. There's a brief stopover at Rangitoto Island in the Hauraki Gulf. Various day tours of Waiheke Island are also available. **Departure:** 10:30 am and

2

1:30 pm from the Downtown Ferry Terminal. Pier 1, Ferry Terminal, 99 Quay St. ☎ *09/367–9111* ⊕ *www.fullers.co.nz* *NZ$40.*

Pride of Auckland. Pride of Auckland trips keep customers well fed and active as they take in the sights of Waitemata Harbour. Affiliated with Sail NZ, this fleet of purpose-built sailboats plus serious racing yachts is based in Viaduct Harbour in downtown Auckland. Don't get too relaxed, since helping the crew is part of the experience. For those wanting a classic, more sedate day out, the company also offers a classic wooden launch. You'll eat well on trips timed for lunch, dinner, and coffee breaks. The fee includes entrance to the New Zealand National Maritime Museum, where you can explore the country's seafaring past. **Departure:** 1 pm, 2:45 pm, 3:45 pm, and 5:30 pm from Viaduct Harbour. Auckland NZ Maritime Museum, corner Quay and Hobson Sts. ☎ *09/373–4557* ⊕ *www.exploregroup. net NZ$75–NZ$160.*

Ross Adventures. Ross Adventures proves there's more to Waiheke Island than relaxed beaches and wineries. Half-day (appropriate for beginners), full-day, and multiday kayaking trips take paddlers past coastal cliffs and inlets. Explore caves, beaches, and Māori pā sites (depending on the day's route). Full-day trips include swimming and snorkeling,

and you may spot blue penguins or dolphins as you kayak. **Departure:** 9 am from the kayak shed at Matiatia. Waiheke Island ☎ *09/372–5550* ⊕ *www. kayakwaiheke.co.nz NZ$125–NZ$195.*

Sail NZ. Sail on America's Cup racing yachts in Viaduct or Waitemata harbors (depending on the trip). With Sail NZ's **America's Cup Sailing Experience** you can sail with a racing crew (or relax while they do the work). For more thrills participate in the **America's Cup Match Racing** trip. This three-hour experience includes practice drills followed by a race against other yachts with a race crew. **Departure:** Daily from Viaduct Harbour. Booking Kiosk, Viaduct Harbour ☎ *09/359–5987* ⊕ *www. exploregroup.net NZ$160.*

(top left) Yacht passing Auckland, the City of Sails; *(top)* Charter a yacht in Auckland and find yourself in an immense cruising ground of islands; *(bottom)* Sailing on Hauraki Bay, Auckland

Updated
by Richard
Pamatatau

Auckland is called the City of Sails, and visitors flying in will see why. On the East Coast is the Waitemata Harbour—a Māori word meaning sparkling waters—which is bordered by the Hauraki Gulf, an aquatic playground peppered with small islands where many Aucklanders can be found "mucking around in boats."

Not surprisingly, Auckland has some 70,000-plus boats. About one in four households in Auckland has a seacraft of some kind, and there are 102 beaches within an hour's drive depending on the traffic; during the week many are quite empty except for the two weeks that include Christmas and New Year. Even the airport is by the water; it borders the Manukau Harbour, which also takes its name from the Māori language and means solitary bird.

According to Māori tradition, the Auckland isthmus was originally peopled by a race of giants and fairy folk. When Europeans arrived in the early 19th century, however, the Ngāti-Whātua tribe was firmly in control of the region. The British began "negotiations" with the Ngāti Whātua in 1840 to purchase the isthmus and establish the colony's first capital. (The Government is still dealing with the fallout from the British negotiations and redress for land theft continues between Ngāti-Whātua and the Crown.) In September of that year the British flag was hoisted to mark the township's foundation, and Auckland remained the capital until 1865, when the seat of government was moved to Wellington. Aucklanders expected to suffer from the shift; it hurt their pride but not their pockets. As the terminal for the South Sea shipping routes, Auckland was already an established commercial center. Since then the urban sprawl has made this city of approximately 1.4 million people one of the world's largest geographically.

A couple of days in the city will reveal just how developed and sophisticated Auckland is—the Mercer City Survey 2014 saw it ranked as the third-highest city for quality of life—though those seeking a New York in the South Pacific will be disappointed. Auckland is more get-up and go-outside than get-dressed-up and go-out. That said, most shops are open daily, central bars and a few nightclubs buzz well into the wee hours, especially Thursday through Saturday, and a mix of Māori, Pacific people, Asians, and Europeans contributes to the cultural milieu. Auckland has the world's largest single population of Pacific Islanders living outside their home countries, though many of them live outside the central parts of the city and in Manukau to the south. The Samoan language is the second most spoken in New Zealand. Most Pacific people came to New Zealand seeking a better life. When the plentiful, low-skilled work that attracted them dried up, the dream soured, and the population has suffered with poor health and education. Luckily, policies are now addressing that, and change is slowly coming. The Pacifica Festival in March is the region's biggest cultural event, attracting thousands to Western Springs with fantastic food, stunning performances and art and craft from the region. The annual Pacific Island Secondary Schools' Competition, also in March, sees young Pacific Islander and Asian students compete in traditional dance, drumming, and singing. This event is open to the public.

At the geographical center of Auckland city is the 1,082-foot Sky Tower, a convenient landmark for those exploring on foot and some say a visible sign of the city's naked aspiration. It has earned nicknames like the Needle and the Big Penis—a counterpoint to a poem by acclaimed New Zealand poet James K. Baxter, which refers to Rangitoto Island as a clitoris in the harbor.

The Waitemata Harbour has become better known since New Zealand staged its first defense of the America's Cup in 2000 and the successful Louis Vuitton Pacific Series in early 2009. The first regatta saw major redevelopment of the waterfront. The area, where many of the city's most popular bars, cafés, and restaurants are located, is now known as Viaduct Basin or, more commonly, the Viaduct. A recent expansion has created another area, Wynyard Quarter, which is slowly adding restaurants.

AUCKLAND PLANNER

WHEN TO GO
Auckland's weather can be unpredictable, but don't let that put you off. There is always something to do whatever the weather. The warmest months are December through April and a sun hat is a good idea. Winter is between July and October. It can be humid in summer and quite chilly in winter. It often rains, so be prepared.

PLANNING YOUR TIME
Auckland is big, so plan ahead. Allow yourself three days to navigate the city.

Day 1: Go outdoors out west. The Waitakere Ranges' native forests provide easy walks. Bring walking shoes, a day pack, water, a raincoat, and a sweater. Stop at a West Coast beach, too.

Day 2: Go shopping in Newmarket or Ponsonby in the morning before ferrying to Waiheke Island to tour wineries and have dinner.

Day 3: Take in some adventure or culture. Sky Tower has high-flying city views. See Māori artifacts at Auckland War Memorial Museum, the latest exhibitions at the Auckland City Gallery, or get out of town for a game of golf.

GETTING HERE AND AROUND

AIR TRAVEL

Auckland International Airport (AKL) lies 21 km (13 miles) southwest of the city center, about a 30-minute drive away. It has adopted a "quiet airport" policy, so it doesn't use loudspeakers to announce boarding times. Look for flight info on screens, which abound.

A free inter-terminal bus links the international and domestic terminals from 6 am to 10 pm. Otherwise, the walk between the two terminals takes about 10 minutes. Luggage for flights aboard the two major domestic airlines, Air New Zealand and Qantas Airways, can be checked at the international terminal.

Air New Zealand and Jetstar, Qantas's budget airline, are the main domestic carriers serving Auckland. Air New Zealand connects with 25 domestic cities a day, and makes about 10 flights a day to Australia. Jetstar also connects Auckland with many cities and complements Qantas's cross-Tasman service; Jetstar is now competing with Air New Zealand on some regional flights. It can have unpredictable service and requires check-in one hour before departure. Air Tahiti Nui stops off in Auckland on its LA and New York runs.

Airport Auckland International Airport. ⊠ *Ray Emery Dr.* ☎ *09/275–0789* ⊕ *www.aucklandairport.co.nz.*

BUS TRAVEL

BUS TRAVEL WITHIN AUCKLAND The easily recognizable red, green, and orange Link Buses, run by Maxx, circle the inner city and close suburbs every 10 minutes between 6 am and 7 pm weekdays, and then every 15 minutes until about 11:30 pm. Weekend service runs from 7 am to 6 pm. The route includes the Britomart Centre between Customs and Quay streets, Queen Street, Parnell, Newmarket (near the Auckland War Memorial Museum), Ponsonby, and Karangahape Road. The fares range from NZ$1 for the inner city NZ$4.50 to the close suburbs. You can pay in cash using change or else buy a Hop prepay card available widely.

Auckland's bus and train network is slowly being united with new electronic ticketing, but it is in a state of flux. If you're not feeling intrepid, it's best to hire a car or take a taxi. For travel farther afield, Auckland Transport offers services as far north as Orewa on the Hibiscus Coast and south to Pukekohe. A Discovery Pass (NZ$16 a day for unlimited travel) is the best deal for extensive bus and ferry travel; it covers all travel on Auckland Transport. You can buy passes from the ferry office. The information office at Britomart provides maps and timetables.

Information Office. The information center provides timetable information and tickets for all services. ⊠ *Britomart Transport Centre, Queen Elizabeth Sq., Queen and Quay Sts., City Center* ☎ *09/366–6400 public service number* ⊕ *https://at.govt.nz/bus-train-ferry/.*

BUS TOURS **Explorer Bus.** This yellow double-decker stops at nine city attractions; you can hop on and off anywhere along the way. Buses begin at the Ferry Building between 9 and 4 daily. Buy tickets from the driver or at the Fullers office in the Ferry Building. ⊠ *Ferry Bldg., Queen's Wharf, 30 Custom St.* ☎ *0800/439–756* ⊕ *www.explorerbus.co.nz* ⊂ *From NZ$45 a day.*

InterCity's TravelPass (☎ *0800/222–146* ⊕ *flexipass.intercity.co.nz*) provides set itineraries on comfortable buses and commentary on the passing scenery. For the independent traveler, the **InterCity Flexipass** lets you travel where and when it suits you. Based on hours of travel, it lets you hop on and off and stay as long as you like. Passes are valid for 12 months from activation.

Grayline Tours. A variety of guided bus tours leave from Quay Street, just across from the Ferry Building at 9:15. Itineraries might take in city highlights or West Coast beaches. ⊠ *172 Quay St.* ⊹ *Opposite Ferry Bldg.* ☎ *09/307–7880* ⊕ *www.graylinetours.co.nz* ⊂ *From NZ$59.*

CAR AND TAXI TRAVEL

Auckland traffic is unpredictable due to a road network groaning under the pressure of a rapidly growing population. An incident on any part of the road network lead to gridlock across the whole city. Local rush hours last from 6 to 9:30 am and 3.30 to 6:30 pm, but if it's wet add an hour at least. Massive road upgrades are under way across the motorway system, so traffic can be disrupted at any time. The main motorways all have convenient city turnoffs, but watch the signs carefully. The main road into and out of Auckland is State Highway 1. Off-ramps are clearly marked. Most areas have meter parking, and you can pay by coin or credit card. Fines are hefty if you overstay your time.

Auckland taxi rates vary with the company. Most are around NZ$2 per km (½ mile), but some charge as much as NZ$4. Flag-fall, when the meters start, is usually NZ$2. The rates are listed on the driver's door. Most taxis accept major credit cards.

Alert Taxis. This efficient taxi company has clean cars. ⊠ *918b Great South Rd.* ☎ *09/309–2000* ⊕ *www.alerttaxis.co.nz.*

Auckland Cooperative Taxi Service. This is Auckland's largest fleet of well-maintained cars. ⊠ *10 Macaulay St.* ☎ *09/300–3000* ⊕ *www.cooptaxi.co.nz.*

Corporate Cabs. This upmarket cab company has branches in New Zealand's major tourist cities. ⊠ *161 Manukau Rd.* ☎ *09/377–0773* ⊕ *www.corporatecabs.co.nz.*

Eastern Taxis. Affiliated with Alert Taxis, this small company services East and South Auckland. ⊠ *918B Great South Rd.* ☎ *09/534–4644* ⊕ *www.easterntaxis.nz.*

TRAIN TRAVEL

KiwiRail, New Zealand's train operator, has a terminal and booking office at the **Britomart Transportation Centre**, on the harbor end of Queen Street. Service leaves Auckland for Wellington Monday, Thursday, and Saturday and returns Tuesday, Friday, and Sunday.

Britomart Transport Centre. The hub of Auckland's growing rail network system is built in the city's historic central post office with a modern annex that houses the train hub. There is a currency exchange in the renovated old building that is adjacent to the fast-growing Britomart Precinct, with its trendy eateries and fashion stores. ⊠ *Queen Elizabeth Sq., Queen and Quay Sts.* ☎ *0800/467–536* ⊕ *www.britomart.co.nz.*

TOURS

Several companies run city orientation tours or special-interest excursions outside town.

HORSE TREKKING

FAMILY **Pakiri Beach Horse Rides.** Pakiri Beach Horse Rides, north of Auckland, runs trips from several hours to several days, all incorporating a ride on the namesake white-sand beach. You might ride through groves of *pohutukawa,* which are ablaze with red flowers in the summer, or across the sand dunes with inspiring views of islands on the horizon or even go from the East to the West Coast. The proprietors are very conscious of horse welfare and don't take riders who weigh more than 210 lbs without prior arrangement. ⊠ *317 Rahuikiri Rd., Pakiri Beach, R.D. 2, Wellsford* ☎ *09/422–6275* ⊕ *www.horseride-nz.co.nz* ⊠ *NZ$175 half-day, NZ$299 full-day, including packed lunch.*

MĀORI-THEME TOURS

FAMILY
Fodor'sChoice
★
Potiki Adventures. Potiki Adventures cultivates an air of intimacy with its small groups and friendly, open tour guides. You'll travel to Waiheke Island by ferry for an experience that includes a trip around the island, visit to an ancient fortified village, a weaving demonstration, and the chance to hear and play Māori musical instruments. Lunch is at one of the many cafés on the island. Potiki also offers customized private tours that include meeting Māori artists and gallery visits. ⊠ *68 Ocean Rd., Waiheke Island, Hauraki Gulf Islands* ☎ *09/372–3477* ⊕ *www. potikiadventures.co.nz* ⊠ *From NZ$150 excluding ferry fares.*

FAMILY
Fodor'sChoice
★
TIME Unlimited. You'll have the time of your life on any of the tours offered by TIME Unlimited. The company integrates Māori culture with activities like kayak-fishing and trail walking and can arrange an overnight stay at a *marae* (meetinghouse). TIME, through its concessions with the Department of Conservation and Māori tribes, can take visitors to places often out of reach of other tours, and they will customize a tour to meet your specific needs and time frame. Transport is in late-model Mercedes vehicles. ⊠ *Suite 276, 92 Franklin Rd., Freemans Bay* ✛ *In heart of Ponsonby* ☎ *09/446–6677* ⊕ *www.newzealandtours. travel* ⊠ *From NZ$265.*

WILDERNESS TOURS

FAMILY **Auckland Adventures.** This long-established company offers half- and full-day trips featuring tours ranging from visits to the West's vineyards and a beach or two, to mountain biking, to a compressed overview of Auckland. Personalized tours can be arranged. ⊠ *Auckland* ☎ *09/379–4545* ⊕ *www.aucklandadventures.co.nz* ⊠ *From NZ$145.*

Bush and Beach Ltd. Whether you are a *Lord of the Rings* fan, an outdoor adventurer, or a wine buff you'll find something from Bush and Beach to meet your needs and time frame. Tours range from a quick-ish tour of *Lord of the Rings* set Hobbiton to a full-day excursion that includes rain forest plus black-sand West Coast beaches, wineries, and a visit to where Jane Campion's *The Piano* was filmed. There are also tours of Great Barrier Island in the Hauraki Gulf. Custom tours are also available. ✉ *Auckland* ☎ *09/837–4130* ⊕ *www.bushandbeach.co.nz* 🖾 *From NZ$78 for 3-hr city tour.*

WINE TOURS

Fine Wine Tours. The four-hour West Auckland tour takes in several wineries and includes a picnic lunch and, weather permitting, a visit to a black-sand beach. The full-day Waiheke Island tour covers a number of wineries and lunch. Tour host Phil Parker is an authority on New Zealand wines (you may meet his pooch Merlot who sometimes goes on the tour) and he has published a guide to the country's wine regions. Custom tours can be arranged. ☎ *09/845–6971* ⊕ *www.insidertouring. co.nz* 🖾 *From NZ$269.*

NZWinePro Auckland Wine Tours. If you are pushed for time, but still want to fit in a vineyard, these four-hour tours may be the ticket. They are based around wine-growing areas to Auckland's north and west, plus Waiheke Island. The company also tailors tours to your grape or wine choice. ✉ *417a Tamaki Dr.* ☎ *09/575–1958* ⊕ *www.nzwinepro.co.nz* 🖾 *From NZ$185.*

VISITOR INFORMATION

Need some travel advice? Drop in at one of Auckland's many i-SITEs and other visitor centers. Employees will help plan trips, provide sightseeing information, and point you toward a well-priced lunch.

Contacts Auckland International Airport Visitor Centre. ✉ *Ray Emery Dr., next to arrivals exit, ground floor, International terminal* ☎ *09/275–0789.* **Auckland i-SITE Visitor Centre.** ✉ *Atrium, Sky City, Victoria and Federal Sts.* ☎ *09/367–6009* ⊕ *www.aucklandnz.com.*

EXPLORING

You can get around city center and the suburbs close to the harbor like Ponsonby, Devonport, and Parnell, on foot, by bus, and by ferry. Elsewhere, Auckland is not as easy to explore. The neighborhoods and suburbs sprawl from the Waitemata and Manukau harbors to rural areas, and complicated roads, frequent construction, and heavy traffic can make road travel a challenge. Still it's best to have a car for getting between neighborhoods and some city center sights. What might look like an easy walking distance on a map can turn out to be a 20- to 30-minute hilly trek, and stringing a few of those together can get frustrating.

If you're nervous about driving on the left, especially when you first arrive, purchase a one-day Link Bus Pass that covers the inner-city neighborhoods and central business district (CBD) or, for a circuit of the main sights, a Discovery Pass. Take a bus to get acquainted with the city layout. Getting around Auckland by bus is easy and inexpensive. The region's bus services are coordinated through the Auckland Transport. You can buy electronic Hop cards which can be used on buses, trains and ferries and its website can provide door-to-door information, including bus route numbers, to most places in the greater Auckland area. Timetables are available at most information centers.

CITY CENTER AND PARNELL

Auckland's city center includes the working port area, much of it reclaimed from the sea in the latter half of the 19th century. While it's easy to walk around this area, some of the best views can be marred by the container and car import terminal which is behind a large red iron fence. Successive city administrators neglected Auckland's older buildings, too, so Queen Street and its surroundings are a mix of glass-tower office buildings and a dwindling number of older, some say more gracious, buildings. Tucked away in Lorne and High streets, running parallel with Queen Street, are good examples of the city's early architecture, now home to the shops of some of New Zealand's leading fashion designers. The central business district (CBD) has been energized by a residential surge since the late 1990s and a move to create pedestrian friendly strips, which is boosted by apartment development and an influx of Asian students. The Auckland Domain and Parnell areas have the city's preeminent museums and art gallery as well as historic homes and shops. Parnell was Auckland's first suburb, established in 1841, and is a good place to look for arts and crafts or to sample some of Auckland's most popular cafés, bars, and restaurants.

A dozen "city ambassadors" patrol the city center on weekdays between 8:30 and 5, providing directions and answering questions. They're identified by their yellow-and-gray uniforms with "ambassador" written on their tops in red.

TOP ATTRACTIONS

FAMILY **Albert Park.** These 15 acres of formal gardens, fountains, and statue- and sculpture-studded lawns are a favorite for Aucklanders, who pour out of nearby office buildings, and two adjacent universities to eat lunch and lounge under trees on sunny days. Good cafés at the universities serve well-priced take-out food and coffee. The park is built on the site of an 1840s–50s garrison, which protected settlers from neighboring Māori tribes. On the park's east side, behind Auckland University's general library are remnants of stone walls with rifle slits. In late February the park is home to the Auckland Lantern Festival, organized by the Asian community, which celebrates Chinese New Year with lantern lightings and stalls selling authentic Asian food from 5 to 10:30 pm daily. ⊠ *Bounded by Wellesley St. W, Kitchener St., Waterloo Quad, City Center.*

Fodor's Choice **Auckland Art Gallery Toi o Tāmaki.** The modernist addition to the Auck-
★ land Art Gallery has breathed life and light into a structure built in the 1880s. The soaring glass, wood, and stone addition, which some say looks like stylized trees, both complements and contrasts with the formal château-like main gallery. A courtyard and fountain space at the front is home to ever-changing works. The gallery, adjacent to Albert Park has some 15,000 items dating from the 12th century but also shows innovative and challenging contemporary art that draws big

crowds. Historic portraits of Māori chiefs by well-known New Zealand painters C.F. Goldie and Gottfried Lindauer offer an ethnocentric view of people once seen as fiercely martial. Goldie often used the same subject repeatedly—odd, considering his desire to document what he considered a dying race. New Zealand artists Frances Hodgkins, Doris Lusk, and Colin McCahon are also here, as are shows and performances. Free collection tours are given at 11:30 and 1:30. The café is hip and busy and the gift shop offers a range of books, original artworks, and keepsakes. ⊠ *5 Kitchener St., at Wellesley St. E, City Center* ☎ *09/379–1349* ⊕ *www.aucklandartgallery.com* ⊠ *Free, except for special exhibits* ⊙ *Daily 10–5.*

FAMILY   **Auckland Domain.** Saturday cricketers, Sunday picnickers, and morning runners are some of the Aucklanders who enjoy this rolling, 340-acre park—not to mention loads of walkers, particularly the "Remuera Bobs," women with rich husbands who like their wives trim and young looking. Running trails range from easy to challenging, and organized 10-km (6-mile) runs occur throughout the year. The Domain contains some magnificent sculpture as well as the domed **Wintergardens** (open daily 10–4), which houses tropical and seasonally displayed hothouse plants. In summer watch the local paper for free weekend-evening concerts, which usually include opera and fireworks. Take a bottle of wine and a basket of goodies and join the locals—up to 300,000 per show. ⚠ **While the Domain is safe during the day it is not a place to be at night unless you're there for a concert with a big crowd.** ⊠ *Entrances at Stanley St., Park Rd., Carlton Gore Rd., and Maunsell Rd., Parnell.*

FAMILY   **Auckland War Memorial Museum.** The Māori artifact collection here is
Fodor's Choice   one of the largest in the world, housed in a Greek Revival building in
★   one of the city's finest parks, with views to match. Must-sees include a fine example of a *pātaka* (storehouse), a fixture in Māori villages, and Te Toki a Tapiri, the last great Māori *waka* (canoe). Made of a single log and measuring 85 feet long, it could carry 100 warriors, and its figurehead shows tremendous carving. To learn more about Māori culture, attend one of the performances, held at least three times daily, that demonstrate Māori song, dance, weaponry, and the *haka* (a ceremonial dance the All Blacks rugby team has adopted as an intimidating pregame warm-up). The museum also holds an exceptional collection of Pacific artifacts and hosts high-quality visiting or issue-specific exhibitions. If you want a bit of talk and music in the evening check out the once-a-month panel discussion followed by live music known as Late at the Museum. On Anzac Day (April 25), thousands gather in front of the museum in a dawn service to recognize the gallantry of the country's servicemen and women. ⊠ *Auckland Domain, Park Rd., Parnell* ☎ *09/309–0443* ⊕ *www.aucklandmuseum.com* ⊠ *NZ$25, NZ$45 with Māori performance* ⊙ *Daily 10–5.*

FAMILY   **Civic Theatre.** This extravagant art nouveau movie theater was the talk of the town when it opened in 1929, but nine months later the owner, Thomas O'Brien, went bust and fled, taking the week's revenues and an usherette with him. During World War II a cabaret show in the basement was popular with Allied servicemen. One of the entertainers, Freda Stark, is said to have appeared regularly wearing nothing more

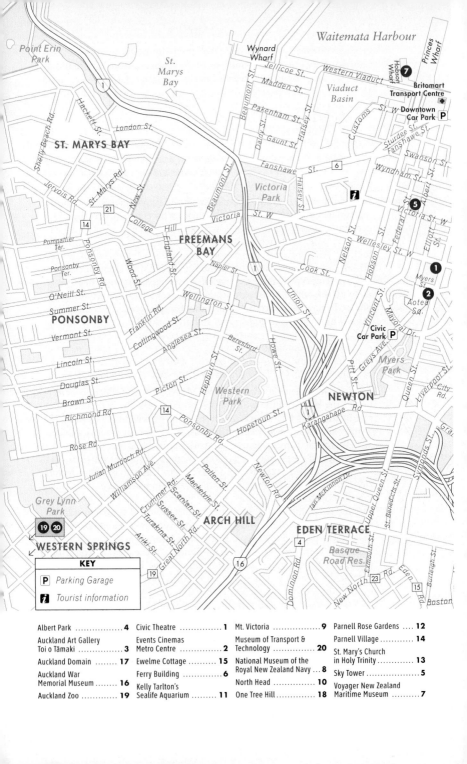

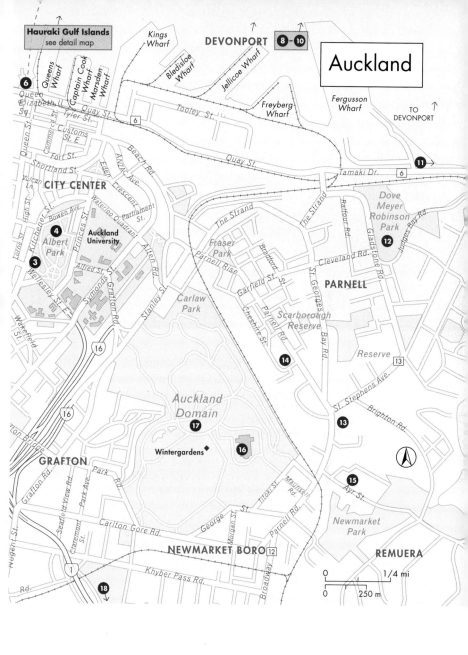

Visitors go under the sea at Kelly Tarlton's Sealife Aquarium.

than a coat of gold paint. Now the café at the front of the Civic bears her name. When you sit down to a show or movie you'll see a simulated night sky on the ceiling and giant lions with lights for eyes on stage. The theater is host to an ever-changing raft of movie premieres, intimate rock concerts, live theater, and dance parties. ⊠ *Queen and Wellesley Sts., City Center* ☎ *09/309–2677.*

FAMILY

Fodor's Choice
★

Kelly Tarlton's Sealife Aquarium. This harborside marine park—the creation of New Zealand's most celebrated undersea explorer and treasure hunter—offers a fish's-eye view of the sea. A transparent tunnel, 120 yards long, makes a bewitching circuit past moray eels, lobsters, sharks, and stingrays. You can also have an encounter with King and Gentoo penguins and their keepers in their icy home, and take home photos to prove it. This attraction is popular and limited to four people a day so it pays to book ahead. ⊠ *Orakei Wharf, 23 Tamaki Dr., 5 km (3 miles) east of downtown Auckland* ☎ *09/531–5065* ⊕ *www.kellytarltons.co.nz* ⊠ *NZ$39; online discounts* ☉ *Daily 9:30–5:30, last admission at 4.*

FAMILY

One Tree Hill. The largest of Auckland's extinct volcanoes and one of the best lookout points, One Tree Hill, or Maungakiekie, was the site of three Māori *pā* (fortifications). It used to have a single pine tree on its summit, but that was attacked several times by activists who saw it as a symbol of colonialism, and in 2000 it was taken down. Sir John Logan Campbell, the European founding father of the city, is buried on the summit. There is fantastic walking and running in the surrounding acreage known as Cornwall Park, with avenues of oaks, a kauri plantation, and an old olive grove. Or just take a mat and read under an old tree. Free

CLOSE UP

Kelly Tarlton

"Diver, dreamer, explorer, inventor, instigator, worker, storyteller, father, a man who linked us all with his love of the sea." This inscription on the bust of the celebrated figure that stands in the eponymous Kelly Tarlton's Sea Life Aquarium reveals something of the man whose charisma and vision brought together a team of fellow adventurers.

In 1956 Kelly Tarlton was set to join a climbing expedition to the Andes. When political unrest in Peru canceled the trip, he was left at loose ends. Bored, he went to see the Jacques Cousteau film *Silent World* and thought diving looked like more fun than climbing, with no politics to worry about.

With typical Kiwi No. 8 fencing wire ingenuity (aka a do-it-yourself mentality), he built much of his own diving gear, got an underwater camera, and devised housings for the camera and flash.

In the 1960s, Tarlton focused on photographing marine life. In 1967 a trip to the Three Kings Islands to photograph and collect marine specimens whetted his appetite for treasure hunting. He and companion Wade Doak found the wreck of the *Elingamite*, which had foundered on the islands in 1902 with thousands of pounds in gold bullion on board, much of which they recovered.

One of Tarlton's most celebrated finds was the jewels of Isodore Rothschild on the *Tasmania*, which had sunk in 1897. Through his characteristic detailed research, Tarlton pinpointed the whereabouts of the wreck and succeeded in salvaging most of the jewelry in the late 1970s. The treasure was put on display in his now defunct Museum of Shipwrecks in Paihia but was then stolen by a staff member. Though the thief was imprisoned, he has never revealed the jewelry's fate.

Tarlton's interest broadened to marine archaeology. His first major success was finding the first de Surville anchor. Jean François Marie de Surville sailed the *St. Jean Baptiste* into Doubtless Bay in Northland in 1769, where three of his anchors were lost in a storm. Tarlton plotted their whereabouts from crew accounts of the ship's dangerous proximity to a "big rock" and its position "a pistol shot" from shore, and by calculating the magnetic variations and wind directions from the original maps. The anchor is now in Wellington's Te Papa Museum.

But Tarlton is perhaps best known for the aquarium he built on Auckland's waterfront. Not having the funds to buy ready-molded acrylic to build his planned transparent viewing tunnels, Tarlton said that if he could mold his own camera housings, he could create his own tunnels, too. And do it he did, with a team of skilled and loyal friends, building an "oven" for the molding and inventing a gluing technique to form the curving tunnels.

Opened in January 1985, the aquarium was a huge success. After only seven weeks Tarlton shook the hand of the 100,000th visitor, an image captured in the last photo of him. Tragically, he died that very night, at the age of 47, of a heart complication.

—Toni Mason

electric barbecue sites are also available. Because the park is a working farm of sheep and cattle, you'll need to be wary of cows with their calves along the paths. There's also a cricket club with old-style seating, where you can watch a game in summer, and a pavilion where you can buy refreshments. ⊠ *Greenlane Rd. W, Parnell* ⊕ *www.cornwallpark.co.nz.*

FAMILY **Sky Tower.** This 1,082-foot beacon is the first place many Aucklanders take visiting friends to give them a view of the city. Up at the main observation level, glass floor panels let you look past your feet to the street hundreds of yards below. Adults step gingerly onto the glass, while kids delight in jumping up and down on it. Through glass panels in the floor of the elevator you can see the counterweight of the **Sky Jump,** a controlled leap off the 630-foot observation deck that provides an adrenaline rush. ⊠ *Victoria and Federal Sts., City Center* ☎ *09/912–6000* ⊕ *www.skycity. co.nz* ⊠ *NZ\$28; NZ\$65 for family pass; jump NZ\$225* ⊗ *Sun.–Thurs. 8:30 am–11 pm, last elevator 10:30 pm; Fri. and Sat. 8:30 am–midnight, last elevator 11:30 pm; Sky Jump daily 10–5:15, weather permitting.*

FAMILY **Voyager New Zealand Maritime Museum.** New Zealand's rich seafaring history is on display at this marina complex on Auckland Harbour. The collection includes Pacific and Māori seagoing canoes as well as a range of European sailing boats. There are detailed exhibits on early whaling and a superb collection of yachts and ship models, including *KZ1,* the 133-foot racing sloop built for the America's Cup challenge in 1988. A scow conducts short harbor trips twice a day on Tuesday, Thursday, and weekends, and there's a wharf-side eatery. Seriously rich people's yachts are moored in the adjacent Viaduct Basin. ⊠ *Eastern Viaduct, Quay St., City Center* ☎ *09/373–0800* ⊕ *www.maritimemuseum.co.nz* ⊠ *NZ\$17; NZ\$29 with harbor sail* ⊗ *Daily 9–5.*

WORTH NOTING

FAMILY **Event Cinemas Metro Centre.** If you are struck with inclement weather and need to take in a movie the Metro Centre is worth a look. The architecture references science-fiction movies with spiral staircases, bridges designed to look like film, and elevators in the shape of rockets. The Metro Centre incorporates a 13-screen cineplex, an international food court with good inexpensive food, especially Asian, and several bars. ⊠ *291–297 Queen St., City Center* ☎ *09/309–9137* ⊕ *www. eventcinemas.co.nz* ⊗ *Daily 9 am–midnight.*

Ewelme Cottage. Built between 1863 and 1864 by the curiously named Reverend Vicesimus Lush (*vicesimus* is Latin for "20th," his birth order) and inhabited by his descendants for more than a century, this historic cottage stands behind a picket fence. The house was constructed of kauri, a resilient timber highly prized by the Māori for their war canoes and later by Europeans for ship masts and floors. The home contains much of the original furniture and personal effects of the Lush family. You have to duck as you climb the steep, narrow stairs to the small pitched-roof bedrooms, made up as the Lushes might have left them. The drawing room, veranda, and garden appeared in Jane Campion's film *The Piano.* ⊠ *14 Ayr St., Parnell* ☎ *09/379–0202* ⊠ *NZ\$8.50* ⊗ *Fri.–Sun. 10:30–noon and 1–4:30.*

Ferry Building. This magnificent 1912 Edwardian building continues to stand out on Auckland's waterfront. It's still used for its original purpose, launching ferries to Devonport as well as to Waiheke and other Hauraki Gulf islands. The building also houses bars and restaurants. Nearby, and easily seen from here, is Marsden Wharf, where French frogmen bombed and sank the Greenpeace vessel *Rainbow Warrior* in 1985. ⊠ *Quay St., City Center.*

FAMILY **Parnell Rose Gardens.** When you tire of boutiques and cafés, take 10 minutes (or more) to gaze upon and sniff this collection of some 5,000 rosebushes. The main beds contain mostly modern hybrids, with new introductions planted regularly. The adjacent **Nancy Steen Garden** has antique varieties. And don't miss the incredible trees. There is a 200-year-old *pohutukawa* (puh-hoo-too- *ka*-wa), whose weighty branches touch the ground and rise up again, and a *kanuka* that is one of Auckland's oldest trees. In summer it's a popular site for wedding photographs. ⊠ *85 Gladstone Rd., Parnell* 🖃 *Free* ☉ *Daily dawn–dusk.*

Parnell Village. The lovely Victorian timber villas along the upper slope of Parnell Road have been transformed into antique shops, designer boutiques, cafés, and restaurants. Parnell Village is the creation of Les Harvey, who saw the potential of the old, run-down shops and houses and almost single-handedly snatched them from the jaws of the developers' bulldozers in the early 1960s by buying them, renovating them, and leasing them out. Today this village of trim pink-and-white timber facades is one of the most delightful parts of the city. At night, the area's restaurants and bars attract Auckland's well-heeled set. There are some good jewelry stores, including Hartfields and Sutcliffe, as well as a couple of upmarket art galleries. ⊠ *Parnell Rd. between St. Stephen's Ave. and Augustus Rd., Parnell* ⊕ *www.parnell.net.nz.*

St. Mary's Church in Holy Trinity. This Gothic Revival wooden church was built in 1886, by the early Anglican missionary Bishop Selwyn. The craftsmanship inside the kauri church is remarkable, down to the hand-finished columns. One of the carpenters left his trademark, an owl, sitting in the beams to the right of the pulpit. If you stand in the pulpit and clasp the lectern, you'll feel something lumpy under your left hand—a mouse, the trademark of another of the craftsmen who made the lectern, the so-called Mouse Man of Kilburn. The story of the church's relocation is also remarkable. St. Mary's originally stood on the other side of Parnell Road, and in 1982 the entire structure was moved across the street to be next to the new church, the Cathedral of the Holy Trinity. ⊠ *Parnell Rd. and St. Stephen's Ave., Parnell* ⊕ *www. holy-trinity.org.nz* ☉ *Daily 8–6.*

PONSONBY

Some of the city's best cafés are on Ponsonby Road. Breakfast is a specialty because of the high demand from locals looking to grab a coffee and something to eat before heading to a glass tower, media company, or studio downtown. It's difficult to single out any café as all are pretty good because the competition and expectations are high. If you are an architecture buff wander the streets and look at how smart renovation brings modern living and life to former working-class homes.

WESTERN SPRINGS

Western Springs Park is both a suburb and a park in the inner west part of Auckland. It takes its name from the lake there, fed by a natural spring. Today the park, which houses the zoo and the Museum of Transport and Technology, is home to Pacifica, the giant culture, food, and art festival that takes place in summer, generally in March. The speedway sometimes hosts rock concerts.

The lake, which is full of eels, swans, and ducks, has many surrounding paths popular with dog walkers and joggers alike. See native plants and wild fowl, including native pūkeko, teal, Australian coot, and shovelers, around the shores and wetlands.

Across the road from Western Springs is the Chamberlain Park Golf Course, which is open to the public. Western Springs is a good place to read a book or have a picnic.

FAMILY **Auckland Zoo.** Since the 1990s, this zoo, 6 km (4 miles) west of Auckland, has focused on providing its animals with the most natural habitats possible, as well as on breeding and conservation. To catch a glimpse of New Zealand flora and fauna, spend time in the New Zealand Native Aviary, where you walk among the birds, and the Kiwi and Tuatara Nocturnal House. A number of music events are held in summer in the zoo grounds. ⊠ *Motions Rd., Western Springs* ⚓ *By car, take Karangahape Rd. (which turns into Great North Rd.) west out of city, past Western Springs. Take right onto Motions Rd. Buses from city stop opposite Motions Rd.* ☎ *09/360–3805* ⊕ *www.aucklandzoo.co.nz* 💰 *NZ$28* ⊗ *June–Aug., daily 9:30–5; Sept.–May, daily 9:30–5:30.*

FAMILY **Museum of Transport & Technology.** Six km (4 miles) west of Auckland, this is a fantastic place for anyone with a technical bent. A fascinating collection of vehicles, telephones, cameras, locomotives, steam engines, and farm equipment is a tribute to Kiwi ingenuity. The aviation collection includes the only surviving Solent flying boat. One of the most intriguing exhibits is the remains of an aircraft built by New Zealand aviation pioneer Robert Pearse. There is a reproduction of another he built in which he made a successful powered flight around the time the Wright brothers first took to the skies. The flight ended inauspiciously when his plane crashed into a hedge. But Pearse, considered a wild eccentric by his farming neighbors, is recognized today as a mechanical genius. MOTAT, as the museum is called, also has the scooter that former Prime Minister Helen Clark rode to the university. ⊠ *825 Great North Rd., off Northwestern Motorway (Rte. 16), Western Springs* ☎ *09/846–0199* ⊕ *www.motat.org.nz* 💰 *NZ$16* ⊗ *Daily 10–5.*

DEVONPORT

The 20-minute ferry to Devonport across Waitemata Harbour provides a fine view of Auckland's busy harbor. Originally known as Flagstaff, after the signal station on the summit of Mt. Victoria, Devonport was the first settlement on the north side of the harbor. Later the area drew some of the city's wealthiest traders, who built their homes where they

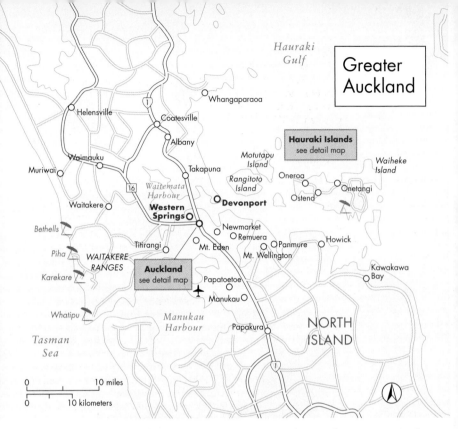

Haraki Gulf

Whangaparaoa

Helensville

Coatesville

Albany

Waimauku

Takapuna

Muriwai

Motutapu Island

Waiheke Island

Oneroa

Rangitoto Island

Onetangi

Waitemata Harbour

Ostend

Waitakere

Western Springs

Devonport

Bethells

Newmarket

Remuera

Titirangi

Piha

WAITAKERE RANGES

Mt. Eden

Panmure

Howick

Mt. Wellington

Karekare

Kawakawa Bay

Auckland
see detail map

Papatoetoe

Manukau

Whatipu

Manukau Harbour

Papakura

NORTH ISLAND

Tasman Sea

Hauraki Islands
see detail map

0   10 miles

0   10 kilometers

could watch their sailing ships arriving with cargo from Europe. Auck-landers have fixed up and repopulated its great old houses, laying claim to the suburb's relaxed and moneyed seaside aura.

The Esplanade Hotel is one of the first things you'll see as you leave the ferry terminal. It stands at the harbor end of Victoria Road, a pleasant street for stopping at a shop, a bookstore, or a café; we recommend picking up some fish-and-chips to eat under the giant Moreton Bay fig tree on the green across the street.

GETTING HERE AND AROUND

Various companies serve Waitemata Harbour; one of the best and least expensive is Fullers. The ferry terminal is on the harbor side of the Ferry Building on Quay Street, near the corner of Albert Street. Boats leave here for Devonport Monday through Thursday 6:15 am–11 pm, Friday and Saturday 6:15 am–1 am, and Sunday 7:15 am–10 pm at half-hour intervals, except for one 45-minute interval between the 9:15 am and 10 am sailings. From 8 pm Monday through Thursday and from 7 pm on Sunday they sail on the hour. The cost is NZ$11 round-trip.

Ferry Information Fullers Booking Office. ⊠ *Ferry Bldg., Quay St., Devonport* ☎ *09/367–9111* ⊕ *www.fullers.co.nz.*

WORTH NOTING

FAMILY **Mt. Victoria.** Long before European settlement, this ancient volcano was the site of a Māori *pā* (fortified village) of the local Kawerau tribe. On the northern and eastern flanks of the hill you can still see traces of the terraces once protected by palisades of sharpened stakes. Don't be put off by its name—this is more molehill than mountain. The climb is easy, but the views are outstanding. Mt. Victoria is signposted on Victoria Road, a few minutes' walk from the Esplanade Hotel. ⊠ *Kerr St., off Victoria Rd., Devonport.*

National Museum of the Royal New Zealand Navy. New Zealand's navy is recognized in this small museum. Also known as Te Waka Huia O Te Taua Moana O Aoteoroa, or Torpedo Bay Navy Museum, it holds a trove of material that reflects the country from a naval perspective. You'll see not only predictable naval material like firearms, swords, and militaria but also memorabilia from those connected to the Navy. Entry is free. ⊠ *64 King Edward Parade, Torpedo Bay, Devonport* ☏ *09/445–5186* ⊕ *www.navymuseum.co.nz* 🖾 *Donations welcome* ⊙ *Daily 10–4:30.*

North Head. Jutting out from Devonport into Auckland's harbor, the position of an ancient Māori defense site was enough to convince European settlers that they, too, should use North Head for strategic purposes. Rumor has it that veteran aircraft are still stored in the dark, twisting tunnels under the head, but plenty of curious explorers have not found any. You can still get into most tunnels (they're safe), climb all over the abandoned antiaircraft guns, and get great views of Auckland and the islands to the east. It's one of the best places to watch yacht racing on the harbor. North Head is a 20-minute walk east of the ferry terminal on King Edward Parade, left onto Cheltenham Street, and then out Takarunga Road. The visitor information center can say when the local folk-music club will have events in one of the old bunkers. ⊠ *Takarunga Rd., Devonport.*

REMUERA

Remuera was established by Auckland's merchant families and it's full of big houses, big trees, and bigger gardens. They built to make the most of the sweeping north-facing harbor views, hence an affectionate nickname for the suburb is "the Northern slopes." Many of the big houses survive but a stroll along Remuera streets reveals just how big the properties originally were when you see how many new homes fit behind them. Auckland's well-heeled populate this tony suburb, which they like to say is "close to everything." Remuera abounds with good walking and parks for pooches, and the shopping precinct has good shops selling high-quality products. There is also a great bookshop tucked in behind the main strip next to the supermarket.

HAURAKI GULF ISLANDS

More than 50 islands lie in the Hauraki Gulf, forming the Hauraki Gulf Marine Park, managed by the Department of Conservation (DOC). Many of the islands are nature reserves, home to endangered plants and birds, and public access to these is restricted. Others are public reserves that can be reached by ferry, and a few are privately owned.

GETTING HERE AND AROUND

Fullers operates ferries year-round to Rangitoto daily at 9:15 and 12:15, departing the island at 12:45 and 3:30. The fare is NZ$29 round-trip; boats leave from the Ferry Building. Fullers also arranges Volcanic Explorer tours, which include a guided ride to the summit in a covered carriage. It's NZ$60 for the tour and ferry ride, and you must book in advance.

Fullers ferries make the 35-minute run from the Ferry Building to Waiheke Island from 5:30 am to 11:45 pm at a cost of NZ$36 round-trip. Return ferries leave every hour on the hour, and every half hour at peak commuter times. Buses meet ferries at the Waiheke terminal and loop the island. If you're planning on going farther afield on the island, you can purchase an all-day bus pass from Fullers Booking Office (NZ$9 to Oneroa, Palm Beach, Onetangi, and Rocky Bay), but you need to take the 10 am ferry (return time optional). Fullers also provides tours, after which passengers may use their ticket to travel free on regular island buses that day. Note that crossings can be canceled if seas are rough and that ferries are very crowded on busy holiday weekends.

SeaLink runs car and passenger ferries to Waiheke, leaving from Half-moon Bay in the east of the city. The round-trip fare is NZ$152 per car, plus NZ$36.50 for each adult. On Waiheke you can also take a shuttle to beaches or vineyards; Waiheke Shuttles has reliable service, but it pays to book well ahead in summer.

Ferry and Bus Information Fullers Booking Office. ⊠ *Ferry Bldg., Quay St.* ☎ *09/367–9111* ⊕ *www.fullers.co.nz.* **SeaLink.** ⊠ *Ara-Tai Dr., Halfmoon Bay* ☎ *09/300–5900* ⊕ *www.sealink.co.nz.* **Waiheke Shuttles.** ☎ *09/280–3993* ⊕ *www.gotowaiheke.co.nz/taxi.htm.*

TOP ATTRACTIONS

Fodor's Choice ★ **Goldie Vineyard.** First to plant grapes on Waiheke were Kim and Jeanette Goldwater, whose eponymous wines have earned a reputation for excellence. They donated the vineyard to the University of Auckland, and it's now home to the Wine Research Institute for postgraduate research into wine as well the Goldie Room, a fantastic eatery that offers superb food and of course wine. Personalized tours can be arranged. The estate is known for the Long Lunch which is a nine-course degustation menu that is held about four times a year and sells out very quickly. ⊠ *18 Causeway Rd., Waiheke Island, Surfdale* ☎ *09/372–7493* ⊕ *www.thegoldieroom. co.nz* ☺ *Mar.–Nov., Wed.–Sun. noon–4; Dec.–Feb., daily noon–4.*

Fodor's Choice ★ **Rangitoto Island.** When Rangitoto Island emerged from the sea in a series of fiery eruptions 600 years ago, it had an audience. Footprints in the ash on its close neighbor Motutapu Island prove that Māori people watched Rangitoto's birth. It is the largest and youngest of about 50

Rangitoto Island emerged from the sea in a dramatic volcanic eruption 600 years ago.

volcanic cones and craters in the Auckland volcanic field, and scientists are confident that it will not blow again. During the 1920s and '30s hundreds of prisoners built roads and trails on the island, some of which are still used as walkways. Small beach houses were erected by families in the early 20th century. Many were pulled down in the 1970s before their historical significance was recognized. Thirty-two remain, and a few are still used by leaseholders, who are allowed to use them during their lifetimes. (Afterward, they'll be relinquished to the DOC.)

The island's most popular activity is the one-hour summit walk, beginning at Rangitoto Wharf and climbing through lava fields and forest to the peak. At the top, walkers are rewarded with panoramic views of Auckland and the Hauraki Gulf. Short detours lead to lava caves and to the remnants of a botanical park planned in 1915. Wear sturdy shoes and carry water because parts of the walk are on exposed lava flows, which are hot in the sun. You can swim at Islington Bay and at the Rangitoto wharf in a specially made pool. ⊕ *www.rangitoto.org.*

Fodor's Choice
★ **Stonyridge Vineyard.** This vineyard has followers all over the world. The Stonyridge Larose, made from the classic Bordeaux varieties, is excellent and the vintage often sells out. Reservations for lunch at the Veranda Café, which uses local produce including olive oil and wine, are essential. This place is popular with the helicopter-in crowd. ⊠ *80 Onetangi Rd., Waiheke Island, Ostend* ☎ *09/372–8822* ⊕ *www.stonyridge.co.nz* ⊘ *Daily 11:30–5.*

Fodor's Choice
★ **Te Motu Vineyard.** The friendly Dunleavy family started planting vines in 1989. Now its Te Motu Bordeaux blend, which is made only when conditions are right, is on the wine list at many Michelin-starred restaurants

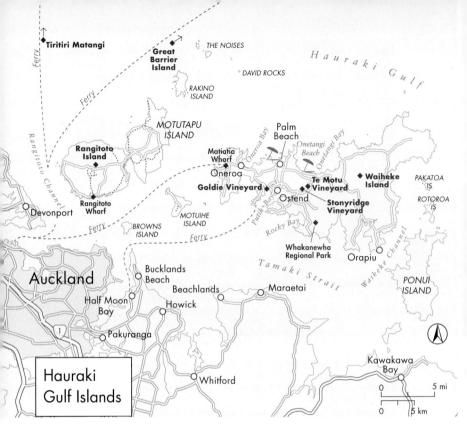

Tiritiri Matangi

THE NOISES

Great
Barrier
Island

DAVID ROCKS

Hauraki Gulf

RAKINO
ISLAND

MOTUTAPU
ISLAND

Palm
Beach

Onetangi
Beach

Matiatia
Wharf

Rangitoto
Island

Oneroa

Te Motu
Vineyard

Waiheke
Island

PAKATOA
IS

Goldie Vineyard

Ostend

Stonyridge
Vineyard

ROTOROA
IS

Devonport

Rangitoto
Wharf

MOTUIHE
ISLAND

BROWNS
ISLAND

Ferry

Rocky Bay

Whakanewha
Regional Park

Orapiu

PONUI
ISLAND

Auckland

Bucklands
Beach

Tamaki Strait

Beachlands

Maraetai

Waiheke Channel

Half Moon
Bay

Howick

Pakuranga

Whitford

Kawakawa
Bay

Hauraki
Gulf Islands

0   5 mi
0   5 km

in France. The winery gives tastings, but it's best to call first to check
for times. Don't be fooled by the restaurant's name, the Shed; it caters
to a fussy clientele for its grown-on-site garden-to-plate cooking. The
wine list, which always feature Te Motu wines from the heritage cellar,
changes monthly. Reservations are essential. ⊠ *76 Onetangi Rd., Waiheke Island, Onetangi* ☎ *09/372–6884* ⊕ *www.temotu.co.nz* ☉ *Wed.–
Sun., times vary.*

Fodor'sChoice
★

Tiritiri Matangi. You can see rare native birds up close at Tiritiri Matangi,
a bird sanctuary open to the public and accessible by ferry from Auckland or Gulf Harbour on the Whangaparoa Peninsula. Gentle, well-
maintained, signposted trails lead to the top of the island and the oldest
lighthouse in the gulf, still in operation. The island is free from predators, and the birds are unafraid. Tiritiri is home to at least 18 *takahe*,
large blue-and-green flightless birds with red beaks. You can usually
spot them eating grass near the lighthouse. The grave of Mr. Blue, the
hand-reared male of the first pair on the island, is marked by a plaque
at his favorite spot near the lighthouse. ⊕ *www.tiritirimatangi.org.nz.*

FAMILY
Fodor'sChoice
★

Waiheke Island. Once Waiheke was a sleepy summer vacation retreat,
and hippie haven, with beach houses dotting its edges. Now you'll
find some 35 vineyards, many the passion projects of their owners,
architectural holiday homes owned by the well heeled, and old-school

CLOSE UP

Volcano Views

Auckland is built on and around 48 volcanoes, and the tops provide sweeping views of the city.

Mt. Eden. This is the highest volcano on the Auckland isthmus. Several bus tours include this central site. It's a popular spot at night when the city's lights below make a spectacular show, and many go there to canoodle or even propose! At the base of the mountain is Mount Eden village, known for its good places to eat and boutique stores. ⊕ www.mounteden.co.nz

One Tree Hill. One Tree Hill, the largest of Auckland's extinct volcanoes, was the site of an early Māori settlement. The surrounding park is great for picnics and running or walking. ⊕ www.cornwallpark.co.nz

Rangitoto Island. Rangitoto Island has an even better vista than One Tree Hill. This volcano emerged from the sea 600 years ago, no doubt much to the wonder of the Māori people living next door on Motutapu Island. Take a ferry to the island; then take a short ride on a covered carriage towed by a jeep or walk to the top to get a 360-degree view of the city and the Hauraki Gulf islands. There are paths round the island where you can take a peek at some holiday homes. ⊕ www.rangitoto.org

It's thought that Māori settled on the volcanoes beginning in the 14th century, taking advantage of the fertile soils. There's evidence that in the 16th century the Māori used the cones as defensive pā (fortified villages). Remains of complex earthworks can be seen on Mt. Eden and One Tree Hill, where Māori cleared volcanic stone to develop garden plots and formed the terraces that are features of pā.

2

tiny weekend escapes side by side. The island is earning a reputation for its vineyards, and many local cafés stock wines unavailable elsewhere. The annual Waiheke Jazz Festival at Easter attracts renowned overseas performers.

From the ferry landing at Matiatia Wharf you can walk five minutes to the small town of **Oneroa,** the island's hub, with its shops, cafés, bars, and real estate agents. Another minute's walk gets you to **Oneroa Beach,** one of the most accessible beaches. The north-facing beaches—sheltered bays with little surf—are the best for swimming. The most popular is **Palm Beach,** 10 minutes by bus from Oneroa. Around the rocks to the left is **Little Palm Beach,** one of Auckland's three nudist beaches. Another great beach, **Onetangi,** is on the north side of the island, 20 minutes from Matiatia by bus. **Whakanewha Regional Park,** on the south side, is a lovely bush reserve leading down to a half-moon bay. You can hike and picnic here, and the wetlands is home to rare birds such as the New Zealand dotterel. You can get to the park from Oneroa by shuttle bus. If you go in summer or on weekends, it pays to get ferry tickets early as the island draws big crowds on fine days.

WORTH NOTING

FAMILY **Great Barrier Island.** Great Barrier Island known, also as Aotea, is the largest in the gulf with a population of around 1,100, and is mostly agricultural. It's popular with surfers—particularly Awana Beach and the population swells in summer as the boating crowd moves in mooring in its many sheltered bays. Motuihe Island, a popular swimming and picnic spot, was a prisoner-of-war camp during World War I and the scene of a daring escape: Count Felix Von Luckner, known as the Sea Devil, commandeered the camp commander's boat and got as far as the Kermadec Islands before being recaptured. Access is by ferry, air, or yacht.

GREATER AUCKLAND

West Auckland has black-sand KareKare and Muriwai beaches, the former with a famous gannett bird colony, as well as vineyards. North Auckland includes Takapuna Beach, a ritzy seaside suburb.

Artisan Wines. This producer of high-quality wine uses grapes sourced from around New Zealand. Though it's open daily, coming Saturday is best because there is a busy farmers' market, and you can try a wide range of Artisan wines alongside local produce, much of it organic. There's a busy restaurant on-site as well as tasting and sales. From time to time the vineyard, which has organic status, also provides courses in things like cheese making. Allow at least 60 to 80 minutes from central Auckland because the Northwestern Motorway can be like a parking lot even at weekends. ⊠ *99 Parrs Cross Rd., Oratia, Waitakere City* ☏ *09/838–7979* ⊕ *www.artisanwines.co.nz* ⊗ *Daily 11–5.*

Babich Wines. The Babich family has been making wine in New Zealand since 1916, beginning first in the far north, where Josip Babich joined his brothers from Croatia and planted grapes near the gum fields. The 72-acre Henderson cellar site has a range of tastings and snacks; years ago it was amid farmland but now is almost surrounded by houses as the population in west Auckland has grown. ⊠ *15 Babich Rd., Henderson, Waitakere City* ☏ *09/833–7859* ⊕ *www.babichwines.co.nz* ⊗ *Weekdays 9–5, Sat. 10–5.*

Villa Maria Winery. This winery has grown from a small company founded by the Fistonich family to one of the country's biggest producers, with a wide range of wines using different grapes. It is recognized for its consistency, and Sir George Fistonich, the founder, has done much for the grape industry in New Zealand. The tasting room offers selections from most of the company's vineyards (shipping can be arranged if you decide to buy). Villa Maria also hosts outdoor summer concerts from jazz to classical. ⊠ *118 Montgomerie Rd., Mangere, Manukau City* ☏ *09/255–0660* ⊕ *www.villamaria.co.nz* ⊗ *Weekdays 9–6, weekends 9–4.*

BEACHES

GREATER AUCKLAND

FAMILY **KareKare.** Film buffs will recognize KareKare and its black sand from the dramatic opening scenes of *The Piano*. Its size means you will never feel hemmed in, even in the peak summer months when it attracts big visitor numbers despite the steep road access and you'll need to pack a lunch as there are no shops.

The pounding waves make for great swimming and surfing, but again, go in only when the surf patrol is operating as there are strong rips and undertows. Fit walkers should explore the southern end of the beach. You can venture past the point but only go at low tide because getting back is difficult when the tide comes in. The sunsets are spectacular anytime of year. **Amenities:** lifeguards in summer; free parking and toilets; picnic areas. **Best for:** surfing; swimming; sunset; walking. ⊠ *KareKare Rd.*

FAMILY **Mission Bay.** Mission Bay off Tamaki Drive—about 10 minutes drive from the central city—draws the crowds year-round and summertime can see families and community groups from all of Auckland picnicking side by side. It's also a popular place for triathlons and related water and running activities in summer. Dining options run the gamut from fast food to formal-ish restaurants. Three extremely good ice-cream parlors and an abundance of good coffee round out the culinary options, and it's not uncommon to see long lines at each joint and then people eating sitting on the seawall. Be aware though it can get very busy in summer and finding a park can be a nightmare. **Amenities:** food and drink; showers; toilets; parking. **Best for:** sunrise; swimming. ⊠ *Tamaki Dr.*

FAMILY **Muriwai Beach.** The black sand of Muriwai Beach is a must for those exploring the West Coast. Combine a trip here with a visit to any of the many wineries in the area. The beach is great for surfing, kitesurfing, walking, and swimming. It is a dangerous beach so don't venture into the water if the surf patrol is not operating, and always swim between the red and yellow flags. It is a great spot for a long, long walk and in summer it draws huge crowds. In winter you may be accompanied by wild winds, but it's still enjoyable if you're warmly dressed. Alternatively, get up-close-and-personal with the local gannet colony from the DOC viewing platforms; see the chicks in December and January. **Amenities:** food and drink; lifeguards in summer; parking; showers; toilets. **Best for:** sunset; walking; swimming. ⊠ *Motutara Rd.*

FAMILY **Takapuna Beach.** You'll see some of New Zealand's most expensive houses along Takapuna Beach on Auckland's North Shore. If architecture (or being nosey) isn't your thing, it's a safe swimming beach in summer and there are many picnic areas. It's good for walking and in the mornings and evenings it's where the well-sneakered walk their pooches. Sailors, kayakers, and triathletes all use this beach for training. Stand-up paddle boarding is also very popular here. The many cafés in Takapuna township are two minutes away from the sand. **Amenities:** food and drink; parking; showers; toilets; water sports. **Best for:** sunrise; swimming; walking. ⊠ *The Promenade.*

WHERE TO EAT

Princes Wharf and adjoining Viaduct Quay, an easy stroll from the city's major thoroughfare, Queen Street, offer dozens of eateries in every style from cheap-and-cheerful to superposh. High Street, running parallel to Queen Street on the Albert Park side of town, is a busy café and restaurant strip. Vulcan Lane, between Queen and High streets, has some pleasant bars. Asian immigrants have created a market for a slew of cheap noodle and sushi bars throughout the inner city; the more crowded, the better.

Outside the city center, the top restaurant areas are a 10-minute bus or cab ride away on Ponsonby and Parnell roads. Dominion and Mt. Eden roads in the city, as well as Hurstmere Road in the seaside suburb of Takapuna (just over the Harbour Bridge) are also worth exploring with the creation of a dining precinct called The Commons. The mix is eclectic—Indian, Chinese, Japanese, Italian, and Thai eateries sit alongside casual taverns, pizzerias, and high-end restaurants.

DINING PLANNER

Hours. Peak dinnertime in Auckland is between 8 and 9, with some kitchens staying open until at least 10 pm. Many restaurants, particularly in Ponsonby and Parnell, serve food all day; some have a limited menu between 3 and 6 pm or close between services. On Sunday and Monday, check whether a place is open.

What to Wear. Only in the most formal restaurants (and there are not many of those) do men need to wear a jacket. Some restaurants have started charging a 15% surcharge on public holidays.

Use the coordinate (⊕ B2) at the end of each listing to locate a site on the corresponding map.

WHAT IT COSTS IN NEW ZEALAND DOLLARS

	$	$$	$$$	$$$$
Restaurants	under NZ$15	NZ$15–NZ$20	NZ$21–NZ$30	over NZ$30

Prices are per person for a main course at dinner, or the equivalent.

CITY CENTER AND PARNELL

CITY CENTER

$$$$ NEW ZEALAND Fodor's Choice ★

🍴 **Fish.** Stylish and smart, this light-filled restaurant with floor-to-ceiling glass looks across the harbor to trendy Devonport and the Bayswater boat marina. The ambience is bright and buzzy and the food superb. The menu changes frequently and is based on high-quality fresh local produce, particularly fish. Meat is cooked to perfection, and salads are made the minute before they are served. As the windows are so big you might need your sunglasses on a bright day, and reservations are advised. Special dinners around Christmas and New Year's satisfy festive spirits. [$] *Average main: NZ$38* ✉ *Hilton Auckland, Princes Wharf, 147 Quay St., City Center* ☎ *09/978–2000* 🌐 *www.fishrestaurant.co.nz* ⊕ *D1.*

$$$$ ✕ **The French Café.** It's not really a café, and it's not strictly French—
EUROPEAN that aside, it is one of Auckland's best and most consistent restaurants.
Fodor'sChoice Simon Wright is an informed chef who creates inspired dishes that
★ revolve around what is in season. At TFC (as some call it), one table
will be chatty young entrepreneurs while the next is old-money dowa-
gers having a "girls' night out." Service is understand and smart—efficient, friendly without attitude. The wine list is comprehensive and
includes hard-to-find vintages. There is also an excellent *degustation*
menu. $ *Average main: NZ$38* ✉ *210B Symonds St., near Kyber Pass
Rd., Eden Terr., City Center* ☎ *09/377–1911* ⊕ *www.thefrenchcafe.
co.nz* ☉ *Closed Sun. and Mon. Closed the first 2 wks in July* ⚐ *Reservations essential* ✛ *D6.*

$$ ✕ **Galbraith's Ale House.** Brew lovers and Brits craving a taste of home
BRITISH head straight for Keith Galbraith's alehouse, which occupies the former
Grafton Library, with its neo-Palladian facade. It hosts a big crowd
that comes before and after rugby matches at nearby Eden Park, and
it's also popular with academics who come to discuss the New Zealand
political scene on Friday night. The English-style ales are made on the
premises and served at proper cellar temperature. Keith learned the art
of brewing in the United Kingdom and sticks religiously to the style.
Order a pint and dig into bangers and mash (seriously good sausages
made by a local butcher with meat marinated in the Grafton Porter ale
atop creamy mashed potatoes). The food is well priced and tasty. People
also come for the smoked fish platter—a selection of fish and seafood
smoked at the Coromandel smokehouse. There's also a reasonable selec-
tion of whiskey. $ *Average main: NZ$20* ✉ *2 Mt. Eden Rd., Eden Terr.*
☎ *09/379–3557* ⊕ *www.alehouse.co.nz* ✛ *D6.*

$$$$ ✕ **Harbourside Ocean Bar Grill.** Overlooking the water from the upper
SEAFOOD level of the restored Ferry Building, this seafood restaurant is an Auck-
land institution. It serves New Zealand seafood, which, depending on
the season and availability, is likely to include tuna, salmon, snapper,
pipi (a type of shellfish), and *tuatua* (a type of clam), on a menu that
references a number of cuisine styles but steers clear of fads. You can
also select crayfish direct from the tank. Meat-eaters can choose lamb,
eye fillet (beef tenderloin), and perhaps *cervena* (farmed venison). On
warm nights, reserve a table outside on the balcony, where you can
watch the ferries come and go. $ *Average main: NZ$50* ✉ *Ferry Bldg.,
Quay St., City Center* ☎ *09/307–0486* ⊕ *www.harbourside.co* ✛ *E2.*

$$$ ✕ **La Zeppa Kitchen and Bar.** *Zeppa* is Italian for "wedge," but you won't
ECLECTIC get the thin end here. Tapas-style dishes are served in this generous
warehouselike space that, despite its size, is always lively. It's popular
with the after-work set and on a Friday and Saturday can be packed
with people either on the way home from work, or on the way to
something. The dishes are inspired by Mediterranean and Asian flavors
and many of the dishes are designed for sharing. Often on weekends
there is a DJ spinning and the place can get very animated. $ *Aver-
age main: NZ$25* ✉ *33 Drake St., Victoria Park Market, City Center*
☎ *09/379–8167* ⊕ *www.lazeppa.co.nz* ☉ *No lunch Mon.–Thurs.* ✛ *C3.*

$$$$
NEW ZEALAND
FAMILY
Fodor'sChoice
★

✕ **Mecca on the Viaduct.** It's buzzy and busy and in the heart of the Viaduct, downtown on the water. Mecca serves New Zealand cuisine with a Middle Eastern twist. Open all day, it's designed to cope with anything—from tables for two to larger groups without fuss. The menu changes at least four times a year. The two signature dishes are lamb shanks slow-cooked in a fragrant tomato gravy and in-season fish baked with fresh vegetables, garlic, and chilies. People have been trying to get the shank recipe out of the owner for years. Like many of the Viaduct places, it can get busy, and only a limited number of reservations are taken. The wine list has a great selection of the bigger (and a few smaller) New Zealand producers. $ *Average main: NZ$34* ✉ *Viaduct Harbour, City Center* ☎ *09/358–1093* ⊕ *www.meccacafe.com* ✛ *D2.*

$$$$
MODERN NEW
ZEALAND
Fodor'sChoice
★

✕ **Merediths.** A fixture in Auckland's dining landscape, this degustation-menu-only restaurant serves sublime food. Six-course, eight-course, nine-course, and plant-only menus can be matched with wines if you choose. The wine list is outstanding. Start with an amuse-bouche of king salmon, chorizo, and ricotta; follow it with *chook* (chicken) and egg, pea, mustard, and cheddar; and finish with chocolate and beet. On Tuesday there is a four-course dine-by-donation menu with all proceeds going to a different charity each month. Merediths is intimate, fabulous, and always busy. It can be hard to get a table, with people booking months ahead. $ *Average main: NZ$90* ✉ *365 Dominion Rd., Mt. Eden* ☎ *09/623–3140* ⊕ *www.merediths.co.nz* ☾ *Closed Sun. and Mon. No lunch Tues.–Thurs. and Sat.* ☙ *Reservations essential* ✛ *C6.*

$$$
MEXICAN
FAMILY

✕ **Mexican Café.** The worn red paint on the steps leading to this lively favorite is a testament to its longevity. It's been serving up great Mexican style food since 1983. Get here at least a half hour before you want to dine, since it's a busy place. People go as much for the noisy, friendly vibe as they do for the food. The menu is packed with traditional choices such as nachos, tacos, and enchiladas. $ *Average main: NZ$25* ✉ *67 Victoria St. W, City Center* ☎ *09/373–2311* ⊕ *www. mexicancafe.co.nz* ✛ *D3.*

$$$$
NEW ZEALAND

✕ **Number 5 Restaurant.** The sign outside declares, "Life is too short to drink bad wine." Accordingly, the wine list here is designed to prevent such a mishap, with a vast selection by the glass and the bottle. Unlike many high-end restaurants, Number 5 is happy to serve just a small dish with a glass of wine. The menu is imaginative and accessible, not too eclectic, and the food, whether meat, fish, or vegetables, is cooked with flair and finesse. Regulars here are foodies who are prepared to pay for it, but aren't interested in the latest fad in dining. $ *Average main: NZ$38* ✉ *5 City Rd., City Center* ☎ *09/309–9273* ⊕ *www.number5. co.nz* ☾ *Closed Sun. No lunch* ✛ *E4.*

$$$$
NEW ZEALAND
Fodor'sChoice
★

✕ **O'Connell Street Bistro.** This former bank vault, on one of the city's fashionable backstreets, has a cozy bar from which you can watch passersby through thin venetian blinds. It has garnered a loyal clientele who keep returning for the food and service. The wine list is big and imaginative, showcasing varieties rarely seen elsewhere. Great for lunch, the bistro is popular with the business crowd. $ *Average main: NZ$42* ✉ *3 O'Connell St., City Center* ☎ *09/377–1884* ⊕ *www.oconnellstbistro. com* ☾ *Closed Sun. No lunch Sat.* ✛ *E3.*

2

$$$$ ✕ **Ostro Brasserie and Bar.** Housed in the artfully renovated Seafarers
MODERN NEW   Building overlooking the harbor, Ostro has a buzzy bar, superb food,
ZEALAND   and some of the best people-watching in Auckland. Enjoy lunch, dinner, or something in-between in a relaxed brasserie style. Reservations
are only accepted for large groups, so walk in, wait and enjoy. $ *Aver-
age main: NZ$40* ✉ *Seafarers Bldg., Tyler St.* ☎ *09/3029888* ⊕ *www.
seafarers.co.nz* ✛ *E2.*

$$$$ ✕ **Soul Bar and Bistro.** There's always something to see at the Soul Bar
NEW ZEALAND   and Bistro which fronts the Viaduct Basin on the harbor. On the terrace you're close enough to the moorings to study the paintwork on
the yachts and, when it gets crowded, to see which of the patrons (both
men and women) have been to see Dr. Botox. The menu is modern with
a traditional twist (pork belly with pork-and-apple strudel, parsnip
purée, and parsley slaw, for example) and always good whether your
want fresh fish, meat, or something from the plant family. At night,
the bar and outside tables are packed with a polished and often noisy
crowd, and the wine list is sensational. $ *Average main: NZ$39* ✉ *Viaduct Harbour, City Center* ☎ *09/356–7249* ⊕ *www.soulbar.co.nz* ✛ *D2.*

$$$$ ✕ **The Sugar Club.** For a high-end dining experience, this is the place to
MODERN NEW   go—53 floors up in the Sky Tower. The decor is reminiscent of 1930s
ZEALAND   Italy, while the food and views attract a range of diners. Dishes are
served in starter-size portions and you order in sets of three through
to six. It's not cheap, but the span of the cuisine speaks to innovation and fun, with options from a spicy, smoked duck *laksa* to grilled
scallops to slow-roasted pork belly. $ *Average main: NZ$90* ✉ *Level
53, Sky Tower, Federal and Victoria Sts., City Center* ☎ *09/363–6365*
⊕ *www.skycityauckland.co.nz/restaurants/the-sugar-club* ⟁ *Reservations essential* ✛ *D3.*

$$$ ✕ **Tanuki's Cave.** A flight of dimly lighted stairs leads down to a buzzing
JAPANESE   Japanese yakitori and sake bar. The oblong bar is usually jammed with
film-festival types, the young art and fashion crowd or classical music
lovers eating before a concert in the nearby Town Hall. Order small
plates of skewers like grilled chicken, with or without cheese. Deep-fried
fish balls are also popular, served with Japanese mayonnaise. In addition
to more than 20 types of sake by the glass, you'll see large bottles of
sake on the "bottle-keep" shelves—these are for people who keep their
own bottle to have when they come to eat. While the price of individual
items is relatively small, the bill can mount up quickly, and watch the
stairs on the way out. $ *Average main: NZ$28* ✉ *319B Queen St., City
Center* ☎ *09/379–5151* ⊕ *www.sakebars.co.nz/cave* ☾ *No lunch* ✛ *D4.*

PARNELL

$$ ✕ **Alphabet Bistro.** Take a table on the sidewalk for a breakfast or brunch
NEW ZEALAND   that will set you up for the day. Classics such as eggs Benedict and boiled
FAMILY   eggs with "toast soldiers" (strips of toasted bread for dipping) are done
just right, and the coffee is great. Alphabet has a strong support from
locals and while not hip you may have to wait for a table. It's also good
for a well-priced lunch. $ *Average main: NZ$18* ✉ *193 Parnell Rd.,
Parnell* ☎ *09/307–2223* ☾ *Closed Sun. No dinner* ⟁ *Reservations not
accepted* ✛ *G4.*

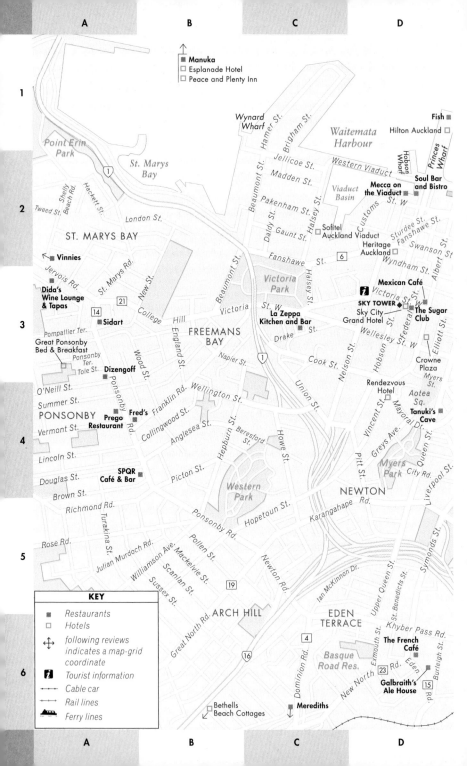

A

B

C

D

1

↑ ■ Manuka
□ Esplanade Hotel
□ Peace and Plenty Inn

Point Erin Park

St. Marys Bay

Wynard Wharf

Hamer St.

Brigham St.

Waitemata Harbour

Hilton Auckland □

Fish ■

Jellicoe St.

Western Viaduct

Hobson Wharf

Princes Wharf

Madden St.

Beaumont St.

Viaduct Basin

Soul Bar and Bistro ■

Mecca on the Viaduct ■

Customs St. W

2

Tweed St.

Shelly Beach Rd.

Hackett St.

London St.

Pakenham St.

Daldy St.

Gaunt St.

Halsey St.

Sofitel Auckland Viaduct □

Sturdee St.

Fanshawe St.

Swanson St.

Albert St.

Heritage Auckland □

Wyndham St.

ST. MARYS BAY

Fanshawe St.

6

← ■ Vinnies

Jervois Rd.

St. Marys Rd.

New St.

Beaumont St.

Victoria Park

Halsey St.

Mexican Café ■

Victoria St.

SKY TOWER ◆

■ The Sugar Club

Dida's Wine Lounge & Tapas

21

College Hill

Victoria

St. W

La Zeppa Kitchen and Bar ■

Sky City Grand Hotel □

Federal St.

Customs St. W

Elliott St.

3

14

■ Sidart

Pompallier Ter.

England St.

FREEMANS BAY

Drake St.

Wellesley St.

Hobson St.

Crowne Plaza □

Pompallier Ter.

Great Ponsonby Bed & Breakfast □

Ponsonby Ter.

Napier St.

Cook St.

Nelson St.

Myers St.

Tole St.

■ Dizengoff

Wood St.

1

Rendezvous Hotel □

Aotea Sq.

O'Neill St.

Ponsonby Rd.

Franklin Rd.

Wellington St.

Union St.

Vincent St.

Tanuki's Cave ■

Summer St.

PONSONBY

■ Fred's

Collingwood St.

Anglesea St.

Hepburn St.

Beresford St.

Howe St.

Greys Ave.

Mayoral Dr.

Queen St.

4

Vermont St.

Prego Restaurant ■

Picton St.

Pitt St.

Myers Park

City Rd.

Liverpool St.

Lincoln St.

Douglas St.

SPQR Café & Bar ■

Brown St.

Richmond Rd.

Turakina St.

Western Park

Ponsonby Rd.

Hopetoun St.

NEWTON

Karangahape Rd.

5

Rose Rd.

Julian Murdoch Rd.

Williamson Ave.

Mackelvie St.

Scanlan St.

Pollen St.

Sussex St.

19

Newton Rd.

Ian McKinnon Dr.

Upper Queen St.

St. Benedicts St.

Symonds St.

ARCH HILL

Great North Rd.

4

Dominion Rd.

EDEN TERRACE

Basque Road Res.

New North Rd.

Exmouth St.

Khyber Pass Rd.

The French Café ■

23

Eden Rd.

Burleigh St.

6

16

Bethells Beach Cottages □

■ Merediths

Galbraith's Ale House ■

15

KEY

■ *Restaurants*
□ *Hotels*
⬌ *following reviews indicates a map-grid coordinate*
🛈 *Tourist information*
━━ *Cable car*
┼┼┼ *Rail lines*
⛴ *Ferry lines*

A

B

C

D

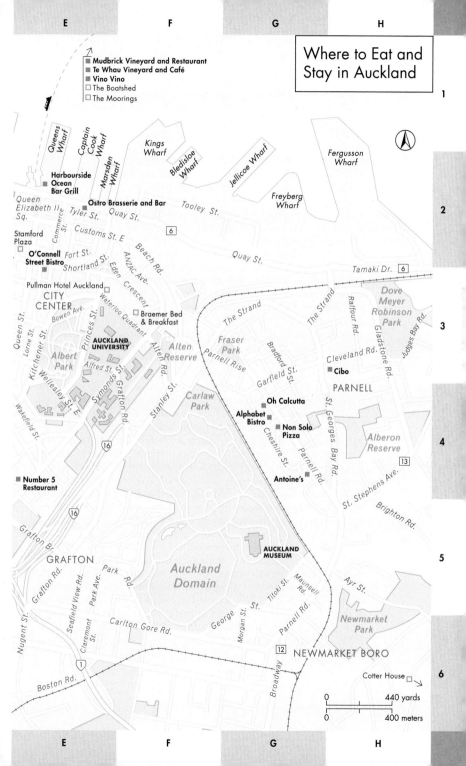

$$$$ NEW ZEALAND Fodor's Choice ★ 🍴 **Antoine's.** Owners Tony and Beth Astle have run this renowned restaurant for more than a quarter century, and it retains a reputation as a place for special occasions and business dining. The decor is conservative and low-key, the service immaculate, and the food delicious—and expensive. Tony is still at the stove, and his "table menu" reads as if it were designed by a chef half his age and is based on seasonal produce. His "nostalgic menu" has such classics as raw spinach salad with chicken livers, and oxtail with baby mushrooms. The wine list is extensive. [$] *Average main: NZ$48* ✉ *333 Parnell Rd., Parnell* ☎ *09/379–8756* 🌐 *www.antoinesrestaurant.co.nz* 🕒 *Closed Sun. No lunch Mon., Tues., and Sat.* ✍ *Reservations essential* ✥ *G4.*

$$$$ MODERN NEW ZEALAND Fodor's Choice ★ 🍴 **Cibo.** When you are in the mood for really good food without any drama head to Cibo. It's Italian for "good food," and it is apt for this restaurant, which has been around for more than 20 years. Chef Kate Fay is known for smart innovative food and the service is led by co-owner Jeremy Turner, who is possibly Auckland's best maître d' and an avid cyclist. In an old chocolate factory, the restaurant opens onto a quiet courtyard, where you can dine by a fishpond lined with rushes and lotus plants. Or take a table inside, where palms grow toward the high skylights. Everything is cooked with aplomb, and the menu reflects the best available produce. This is a popular venue for weddings, so don't be surprised if you can't get a table on a summer Saturday. The wine list at this grown-up place is remarkably good. [$] *Average main: NZ$45* ✉ *91 St. Georges Bay Rd., Parnell* ☎ *09/303–9660* 🌐 *www.cibo.co.nz* 🕒 *Closed Sun. No lunch Sat.* ✥ *H3.*

$$$$ ITALIAN 🍴 **Non Solo Pizza.** If you've had a busy day and want to roll on and be surrounded by animated diners this place is for you. The food is good and you can order pasta individually or with bowls to be shared by the table. Lunchtimes are busy when people head for a table in the Italian-style courtyard. There's always pizza with traditional toppings, and the green salad is excellent. [$] *Average main: NZ$35* ✉ *259 Parnell Rd., Parnell* ☎ *09/379–5358* 🌐 *www.nonsolopizza.co.nz* ✍ *Reservations essential* ✥ *G4.*

$$$ INDIAN 🍴 **Oh Calcutta.** Executive chef Meena Anand applies traditional cooking skills while focusing on fresh seafood and vegetables. The results are consistent and efficient, which is why the place is always busy with people eating in, or locals taking out. There are plenty of traditional dishes—the butter chicken and lamb dishes are excellent—but her lighter interpretations of traditional dishes, such as prawn *malabari* (fat shelled prawns sautéed with onions, peppers, coriander, and fresh coconut cream) are a hallmark. The wine list is average, and though the restaurant does have a bring-your-own license (there are a number of excellent wineshops in Parnell), each person is charged a corkage fee. [$] *Average main: NZ$25* ✉ *149–155 Parnell Rd., Parnell* ☎ *09/377–9090* 🌐 *www.ohcalcutta.co.nz* 🕒 *No lunch* ✍ *Reservations essential* ✥ *G4.*

PONSONBY

$$$ ✕ **Dida's Wine Lounge & Tapas.** In 1941 a grocer's shop stood on this site,
SPANISH   run by a Croatian, Joseph Jakicevich, who also made his own wine.
Today, three generations on, his descendants run this lively wine-and-
tapas bar in the same building, alongside one of the wineshops in their
Glengarry chain. A photo of *Dida*, Croatian for "grandfather," hangs
on the wall in the company of many family photos, and it is likely you'll
be served by one of his great grandchildren. More than 100 wines are
offered by the glass to accompany a menu of around 18 tapas—Span-
ish with a Kiwi twist—which vary depending on the season. There
might be risotto balls with a kiwifruit relish or chicken wings with
smoked spiced almonds. Breakfast is served, too. Locals love this place,
so you may need to arrive early to get a table inside or out especially
on a Thursday or Friday night. $ *Average main: NZ$22* ✉ *54 Jervois
Rd., Ponsonby* ☎ *09/376–2813* ⊕ *www.didas.co.nz* ⌧ *Reservations not
accepted* ✛ *A3.*

$$ ✕ **Dizengoff.** The food is Jewish, though not kosher. The most popular
ISRAELI   breakfast dish is scrambled eggs and veal sausages with homemade pesto
Fodor's Choice   and French bread followed by toast and an unbelievably creamy lemon-
★   curd spread. At lunch try the beet salad (baby beets with fava beans in a
balsamic dressing, topped with pesto and shaved Parmesan) or the salad
made with shredded poached chicken, parsley, and lemon. The coffee is
among the best around and there is an ever-changing selection of New
Zealand art. This place is always busy; avoid weekends unless you get
here early for breakfast (no later than 8). The lemon poppy-seed muffins
and coffee make an excellent take-out option along with the bagel filled
with chicken and red cabbage. $ *Average main: NZ$15* ✉ *256 Ponsonby
Rd., Ponsonby* ☎ *09/360–0108* ☽ *No dinner* ✛ *A3.*

$$ ✕ **Fred's.** Fred's is a very hip and small joint at the top of one of Auck-
MODERN NEW   land's hippest and expensive streets. It serves soda with its own flavor-
ZEALAND   ings while remaining "in" with the coffee crowd. It attracts a wide age
range and locals don't mind the random seating and big table in the
sunny window. The breakfast offerings range of eggs and sausages to
vegetarian options plus delicious small cakes, and soups in winter. While
the address is on Ponsonby Road, the entrance is on Franklin Road. It's
easy to find. Just follow the trendily dressed patrons. $ *Average main:
NZ$15* ✉ *181 Ponsonby Rd., Ponsonby* ☎ *09/360–1551* ☽ *No dinner*
⌧ *Reservations not accepted* ✛ *A4.*

$$$ ✕ **Prego Restaurant.** It's no mean feat being the longest-running restau-
ITALIAN   rant in Ponsonby, where the locals and their guests are fussy. The broad
Fodor's Choice   Italian menu includes wood-fired pizzas and good pasta. Also worth
★   trying, the fish of the day is served in many ways. Prego is extremely
noisy, so don't go there for an intimate chat, though you may find the
courtyard quieter. It is always full; a wait is likely, but the expert staff
will usher you to the bar. The wine list is comprehensive. $ *Average
main: NZ$30* ✉ *226 Ponsonby Rd., Ponsonby* ☎ *09/376–3095* ⊕ *www.
prego.co.nz* ⌧ *Reservations not accepted* ✛ *A4.*

$$$$ ✕ **Sidart.** Sidart takes modern cooking to a whole new level. The chefs
MODERN NEW   take a slew of the finest ingredients and combine them in ways that
ZEALAND   will delight and astound the taste buds. The sweet and the savory are

combined on beautiful plates with foam, or the finest au jus. There is no à la carte and Tuesday is Test Kitchen night where the diners get to try new ideas. The dining room has a stunning evening view of Auckland's CBD. [$] *Average main: NZ$150* ✉ *Three Lamps Plaza, 283 Ponsonby Rd.* ☎ *09/360–2122* 🌐 *www.sidart.co.nz* 💳 *No credit cards* ✥ *A3.*

$$$$ ITALIAN 🍴 **SPQR Cafe & Bar.** This former motorcycle shop is one of the best places on Ponsonby Road for people-watching. If you want to fit in, wear black and big sunglasses. Should an outside table not be an option, you can sit in the minimalist concrete interior. You can keep your shades on there, too. With the eclectic clientele, the people-watching is just as good inside. The excellent food is largely Italian, and it's known for its thin-crust pizzas. It's also known for the attitude of the staff, who sometimes neglect customers, but the food mostly makes up for service. The bar cranks up as the sun goes down. On weekend mornings, aspiring celebrities and the "love your work set" can be seen having a late breakfast in public. A lot of air-kissing goes on at SPQR, and it is decidedly popular with the gay community. [$] *Average main: NZ$35* ✉ *150 Ponsonby Rd., Ponsonby* ☎ *09/360–1710* 🌐 *www.spqrnz.co.nz* ✍ *Reservations not accepted* ✥ *B4.*

$$$$ NEW ZEALAND 🍴 **Vinnies.** This shop-front restaurant has a warm, intimate quality. Specialty local produce is prepared with elegant flair by Chef Geoff Scott. The menu changes to suit the season, but you can be assured everything is prepared to make the most of the produce and served to satisfy the customer. The wine list is excellent. Given this spot's lovely character and reputation, it's often busy, so it pays to book ahead. [$] *Average main: NZ$42* ✉ *166 Jervois Rd., Herne Bay, St Mary's Bay* ☎ *09/376–5597* 🌐 *www.vinnies.co.nz* 🕒 *Closed Sun. and Mon. No lunch* ✥ *A2.*

DEVONPORT

$$$ NEW ZEALAND 🍴 **Manuka.** A corner on Devonport's main street is a good place to people-watch and rest after exploring, and Manuka is a relaxed spot with wooden tables and stacks of newspapers and magazines. Weekend brunch is hectic when the locals turn out, but tables turn over quickly. Wood-fired pizzas are available all day, with toppings ranging from classic pepperoni to smoked chicken, Brie, and roasted cashews. There are also vegetarian options. [$] *Average main: NZ$28* ✉ *49 Victoria Rd., Devonport* ☎ *09/445–7732* 🌐 *http://manukarestaurant.co.nz/* ✥ *B1.*

HAURAKI GULF ISLANDS

WAIHEKE ISLAND

$$$$ EUROPEAN 🍴 **Mudbrick Vineyard and Restaurant.** This is a good place to try wines that never make it to the mainland. The vineyard produces a small portfolio of whites and reds and serves them along with those of other tiny producers. Because Bordeaux varieties predominate on the island, the food emphasis is on red meat; particular favorites are the rack of lamb and Black Angus eye fillet. The front terrace is the best spot to take in the harbor views. Mudbrick is open for lunch and dinner daily, year-round, and many people like to arrive by helicopter. It's a popular spot for weddings so it pays to ring before heading there. [$] *Average*

main: NZ$50 ✉ Church Bay Rd., Hauraki Gulf Islands ☎ 09/372–9050 🌐 www.mudbrick.co.nz ✣ E1.

$$$$ MODERN NEW ZEALAND Fodor's Choice ★ 🍴 **Te Whau Vineyard and Café.** With a big wine list of the finest New Zealand and international wines, this award-winning restaurant has been described as one of the best in the world for wine lovers. Many of the vintages are only available here. Spectacularly perched atop a finger of land, the restaurant commands a nearly 360-degree view. Te Whau's own Bordeaux blend is much praised, and the Chardonnay can only be had here. The menu changes according to the season and what produce is available. Some examples: a grilled beef eye fillet with smoked potato crème, beet chips, and mushroom ketchup and a market fish with clams, vegetable ragout, and gluten-free tomato jus. [$] *Average main: NZ$40 ✉ 218 Te Whau Dr., Te Whau Point, Hauraki Gulf Islands ☎ 09/372–7191 🌐 www.tewhau.com ⏲ Easter–Oct., closed Mon.–Thurs., no dinner Fri. and Sun.; Nov.–Easter, no dinner Sun.–Wed. ✣ E1.*

$$$ MEDITERRANEAN 🍴 **Vino Vino.** Waiheke's longest-running restaurant perches on Oneroa's main street, with a large all-weather deck overlooking the bay. The platters—Mediterranean, grilled (with Italian sausages and calamari), or seafood—are perennial favorites. It's popular in the busy summer months. [$] *Average main: NZ$30 ✉ 3/153 Ocean View Rd., Oneroa, Hauraki Gulf Islands ☎ 09/372–9888 🌐 www.vinovino.co.nz ✍ Reservations essential ✣ E1.*

WHERE TO STAY

As New Zealand's gateway city, Auckland has most of the large international chain hotels, as well as plenty of comfortable bed-and-breakfasts, mom-and-pop motels, and other individually owned places. Many of the large brand-name hotels cluster around the central business district (CBD), whereas B&Bs tend to congregate in trendier neighborhoods. Many of the best are in suburbs close to the city center like Devonport and Ponsonby. You'll find your hosts quite chatty and keen to recommend local sights but equally happy to offer you privacy.

November to March are the busiest months for Auckland hotels, so it pays to book by August to ensure you get your first choice. All the major hotels have parking at a price. A number of the B&Bs offer parking, an especially useful perk since they're usually in narrow city center streets. Better yet, B&Bs generally don't charge for parking. Wi-Fi access is standard in hotels and B&Bs, and a computer is almost always available if you didn't bring your own device. B&B owners offer insider knowledge on what's best close by, and many will make reservations or other arrangements for you. Only the hotels tend to have air-conditioning, but this isn't a problem when you can fling open the windows and let in the fresh air.

Hotel reviews have been shortened. For full information, visit Fodors.com. Use the coordinate (✣ B2) at the end of each listing to locate a site on the corresponding map.

WHAT IT COSTS IN NEW ZEALAND DOLLARS				
	$	$$	$$$	$$$$
Hotels	under NZ$125	NZ$125–NZ$200	NZ$201–NZ$300	over NZ$300

Prices are for a standard double room in high season, including 12.5% tax.

CITY CENTER AND PARNELL

$$$ ⛉ **Braemar Bed & Breakfast.** This gorgeous Edwardian town house in
B&B/INN the heart of the city is close to all of Auckland's enchantments, such
Fodor's Choice as the art gallery, food places, parks, museums, and designer shops.
★ **Pros:** lovely historic building; endearing hosts. **Cons:** no outdoor space.
⑤ *Rooms from: NZ$250* ✉ *7 Parliament St., City Center* ☎ *09/377–
5463* ⊕ *www.parliamentstreet.co.nz* ⫽ *4 rooms* ⑩ *Breakfast* ✛ *F3.*

$$$$ ⛉ **Crowne Plaza.** An escalator connects the atrium of this hotel to the
HOTEL Atrium on Elliot, an average shopping complex with a remarkably
good food court that is a short walk from Queen Street via one of
Auckland's new shared pedestrian and car spaces. **Pros:** close to town;
well priced; good café. **Cons:** often frequented by conference goers;
shopping center is drab. ⑤ *Rooms from: NZ$550* ✉ *128 Albert St.,
City Center* ☎ *09/302–1111* ⊕ *www.crowneplazaauckland.co.nz*
⫽ *352 rooms* ⑩ *No meals* ✛ *D3.*

$$$$ ⛉ **Heritage Auckland.** This hotel mixes the historical and the contempo-
HOTEL rary; it's housed in one of Auckland's landmark buildings, the Farmers
Department Store, but has an additional tower wing. **Pros:** close to city
center; clean; good views from some rooms. **Cons:** interior is a little tired.
⑤ *Rooms from: NZ$450* ✉ *35 Hobson St., City Center* ☎ *09/379–8553*
⊕ *www.heritagehotels.co.nz* ⫽ *224 rooms, 243 suites* ✛ *D2.*

$$$$ ⛉ **Hilton Auckland.** Perched on the end of Princes Wharf, the Hilton
HOTEL resembles the cruise ships that dock alongside it, with white walls and
Fodor's Choice neutral furnishings in chic, clean-lined rooms that allow your eyes
★ to drift to the views, which are best in the bow and starboard. **Pros:**
lovely views; good rooms; close to central city and ferry terminal. **Cons:**
ships mooring nearby can be noisy. ⑤ *Rooms from: NZ$369* ✉ *Princes
Wharf, 147 Quay St., City Center* ☎ *09/978–2000* ⊕ *www.hilton.com*
⫽ *160 room, 6 suites, 35 apartments* ⑩ *No meals* ✛ *D1.*

$$$ ⛉ **Pullman Hotel Auckland.** This hotel offers a mix of hotel rooms and
HOTEL apartments: the Residences wing with beautiful balconied rooms and
at least partial harbor views, and the Tower with more conventional
rooms and suites. **Pros:** close to city center; reliable service; nice spa.
Cons: can be busy. ⑤ *Rooms from: NZ$280* ✉ *Princes St. and Water-
loo Quadrant, City Center* ☎ *09/353–1000* ⊕ *www.pullmanhotels.com*
⫽ *254 rooms, 140 suites* ✛ *E3.*

$$ ⛉ **Rendezvous Hotel.** This hotel is close to the Aotea Centre performance
HOTEL venue—an underground tunnel runs from the hotel to Aotea Square—
and its central locale close to many well-priced restaurants appeals to
business travelers. **Pros:** central to the city; bath pillows. **Cons:** decor
needs a refresh. ⑤ *Rooms from: NZ$200* ✉ *Mayoral Dr. at Vincent
St., City Center* ☎ *09/366–3000* ⊕ *www.rendezvoushotels.com* ⫽ *440
rooms, 15 suites* ⑩ *No meals* ✛ *D4.*

$$$ 🏨 **Sky City Grand Hotel.** The specially commissioned works of top New
HOTEL   Zealand artists hanging in the soaring lobby are testimony to the atten-
FAMILY tion to design throughout—even the staff uniforms were designed by
local fashion leaders. **Pros:** close to the city center and casino; good res-
taurants. **Cons:** can be busy with conferences. 💲 *Rooms from: NZ$250*
✉ *90 Federal St., City Center* ☎ *09/363–7000* ⊕ *www.skycitygrand.
co.nz* 🛏 *296 rooms, 20 suites* ✛ *D3.*

$$$ 🏨 **Sofitel Auckland Viaduct.** This waterfront hotel presents the customer
HOTEL   with both luxury and a friendly environment, as well as views of the
ever-changing Viaduct Basin from some rooms. **Pros:** well situated, with
waterside dining; excellent rooms; close to Victoria Park. **Cons:** Viaduct
area can be noisy. 💲 *Rooms from: NZ$300* ✉ *21 Viaduct Harbour Ave.,
City Center* ☎ *09/909–9000* ⊕ *www.sofitel.com* 🛏 *172 suites* ✛ *C2.*

$$$ 🏨 **Stamford Plaza.** Constant upgrades, noteworthy service, and attention
HOTEL   to detail keep this mid-city hotel at the top of its game. **Pros:** close to
town; good service and lovely staff. **Cons:** tends to get busy with group
tours. 💲 *Rooms from: NZ$225* ✉ *Albert St. and Swanson St., City Cen-
ter* ☎ *09/309–8888* ⊕ *www.stamford.com.au/spak* 🛏 *329 rooms* ✛ *E2.*

PONSONBY

$$$$ 🏨 **Great Ponsonby Bed & Breakfast.** Convivial hosts Gerry and Sally wel-
B&B/INN come all to their Pacific-theme villa on a quiet street off Ponsonby Road.
Pros: friendly; relaxed; low-key. **Cons:** sophisticates may find it a bit
too homey. 💲 *Rooms from: NZ$355* ✉ *30 Ponsonby Terr., Ponsonby*
☎ *09/376–5989* ⊕ *www.greatpons.co.nz* 🛏 *12 rooms, 1 penthouse
suite* 🍽 *Breakfast* ✛ *A3.*

DEVONPORT

$$$ 🏨 **Esplanade Hotel.** Commanding the corner opposite the pier, this turn-
HOTEL   of-the-20th-century Edwardian baroque-revival hotel is the first thing
FAMILY you see when approaching Devonport by ferry. **Pros:** stunning views;
lovely character. **Cons:** poor parking lot. 💲 *Rooms from: NZ$300* ✉ *1
Victoria Rd., Devonport* ☎ *09/445–1291* ⊕ *www.esplanadehotel.co.nz*
🛏 *15 rooms, 2 suites* 🍽 *Breakfast* ✛ *B1.*

$$$ 🏨 **Peace and Plenty Inn.** Antiques brought over from England fill this
B&B/INN lovely B&B, which is a mix of luxury and simplicity and is close to
two lovely beaches and the trendy Devonport precinct. **Pros:** lovely
environment; good food; close to Devonport. **Cons:** some may find
the antiques too fussy. 💲 *Rooms from: NZ$265* ✉ *6 Flagstaff Terr.,
Devonport* ☎ *09/445–2925* ⊕ *www.peaceandplenty.co.nz* 🛏 *7 rooms*
🍽 *Breakfast* ✛ *B1.*

REMUERA

$$$$ 🏨 **Cotter House.** This 1847 Regency mansion, the fifth-oldest house in
B&B/INN   Auckland, has been refurbished in original style, with classic features
FAMILY   such as egg-and-dart molding, recessed arches, and narrow shutters on
Fodor'sChoice   the high windows, and it's private with security gates. **Pros:** like staying
★   in a magical, private country house; close to upmarket Remuera and

Newmarket for shopping. **Cons:** grounds are a little small. $ *Rooms from: NZ$650* ✉ *4 St. Vincent Ave., Remuera* ☎ *09/529–5156* ⊕ *www.cotterhouse.com* ⇨ *2 rooms, 1 suite* ⦿ *Breakfast* ✦ *H6*.

HAURAKI GULF ISLANDS

WAIHEKE ISLAND

$$$$
B&B/INN
The Boatshed. If you feel like staying in a "lighthouse" without the responsibility for ships, this two-story turret suite at The Boatshed maybe the place for you. **Pros:** gorgeous location with bay views; lovely rooms and decks. **Cons:** pricey. $ *Rooms from: NZ$800* ✉ *Tawa and Huia Sts., Little Oneroa, Waiheke Island, Hauraki Gulf Islands* ☎ *09/372–3242* ⊕ *www.boatshed.co.nz* ⇨ *4 rooms, 1 suite* ⦿ *Breakfast* ✦ *E1*.

$$$
RENTAL
The Moorings. From the bright guest rooms of this L-shape Mediterranean farmhouse-style home, you can look outward or inward: out onto Matiatia Bay or into a sheltered courtyard with lavender hedges and lemon trees. **Pros:** clean; informal; lovely location. **Cons:** no room service. $ *Rooms from: NZ$250* ✉ *9 Oceanview Rd., Oneroa, Waiheke Island, Hauraki Gulf Islands* ☎ *09/372–8283* ⊕ *www.themoorings.gen.nz* ⇨ *2 rooms* ⦿ *Breakfast* ✦ *E1*.

GREATER AUCKLAND

$$$$
B&B/INN
FAMILY
Bethells Beach Cottages. Surrounded by pohutukawa trees and overlooking one of West Auckland's beautiful rugged beaches, these two cottages plus an apartment offer a true Kiwi *bach* (rustic beach house) experience. **Pros:** relaxed environment; cozy; close to magnificent beach. **Cons:** some may find it too rustic. $ *Rooms from: NZ$330* ✉ *267 Bethells Rd., Te Henga (Bethells Beach)* ☎ *09/810–9581* ⊕ *www.bethellsbeach.com* ⇨ *2 cottages, 1 apartment* ✦ *B6*.

NIGHTLIFE AND PERFORMING ARTS

For the latest information on nightclubs get your hands on *What's On Auckland,* a pocket-size booklet available at all visitor information bureaus. The monthly *Metro* magazine, available at newsstands, has a guide to theater, arts, and music, and can also give you a helpful nightlife scoop. *City Mix* magazine, also published monthly and stocked at newsstands, has a complete guide to what's happening in the city, and the Friday and Saturday editions of the *New Zealand Herald* run a gig guide and full cinema and theater listings.

NIGHTLIFE

After sunset the bar action is split across four distinct areas, with the waterfront and central city a common ground between the largely loyal Parnell and Ponsonby crowds. Be warned that Auckland can be quite unpleasant in the small hours of the morning when young people from the far suburbs spill out of bars drunk and rowdy. To avoid this, head to Parnell where the restaurants and bars are frequented by a polished, free-spending crowd, or for a more relaxed scene, head to Ponsonby Road, west of the city center, where you'll find street-side dining and packed bars. If you prefer to stay in the city center, the place to be for bars is the Viaduct, particularly in summer, or High Street and nearby O'Connell Street, with a sprinkling of bars in between. At the Queen Street end of Karangahape Road (just north of Highway 1) you'll find shops, lively bars, cafés, and nightspots including gay clubs. Not many venues are aimed at the gay and lesbian market in Auckland—that's probably because in Auckland the car you drive or your home renovations are more important than your sexual preference. The best place to scout for bars is the gay news site *GayNZ.com*. It is the best guide to bars and events; some bars have women-only evenings, but this changes often. Nightclubs, meanwhile, are transient animals with names and addresses changing monthly if not weekly.

There is also a growing nightlife scene on the North Shore—particularly in the upmarket seaside suburb of Takapuna. If you make the trip over the bridge, you'll be rewarded by bars and restaurants with a particularly relaxed vibe. From Sunday to Tuesday many bars close around midnight, and nightclubs, if open, close about midnight or 1 am. From Thursday to Saturday, most bars stay open until 2 or 3 am. Nightclubs keep rocking until at least 4 am and some for a couple of hours after that.

CITY CENTER AND PARNELL
BARS
Wine Loft. Quotes from the famous are scrawled on the walls, and wines seldom available by the glass can be had here. Jocular lawyers, other suits, and trendy academics make up most of the after-work crowd, who share the small and tasty tasting dishes while imbibing. This is not a place for a quiet drink. ⊠ *67 Shortland St., City Center* ☎ *09/379–5070* ⊕ *www.wineloft.co.nz.*

COMEDY
Classic Comedy & Bar. At Auckland's main venue for live comedy, acts of varying caliber are a mix of well-known Kiwi comedians, fresh faces, and the occasional international act. The Classic hosts the International Laugh Festival every April, which draws international comics and very big crowds. ⊠ *321 Queen St., City Center* ☎ *09/373–4321* ⊕ *www.comedy.co.nz.*

LIVE MUSIC AND NIGHTCLUBS
The live music scene in Auckland is growing—bands often perform in unexpected and sometimes out-of-the-way locations (a bowling alley isn't unheard of), so keep an eye on the entertainment guides. Live bands tend to start late so make sure you eat first because at most venues food is not a priority.

Fodor's Choice ★ **Kings Arms Tavern.** One of Auckland's longest-running music institutions, this is often a launch pad for bands that cross the indie and rock boundary. Very good local and established bands also play here, as do small international acts before they hit the big time. Gigs sell out fast at the small venue. This place may not be everyone's cup of tea, especially for those after a sophisticated nightclub atmosphere. If it all gets a bit too much or too noisy, head to the outdoor beer garden. It's in an out-of-the-way area so best to take a taxi. ✉ *59 France St., South Newton, City Center* ☎ *09/373–3240* ⊕ *www.kingsarms.co.nz.*

PONSONBY

BARS

Lime. You might as well leave your inhibitions at the door when you enter, because everybody else does. People pack this friendly and often noisy, narrow bar on the weekend. ✉ *167 Ponsonby Rd., Ponsonby* ☎ *09/360–7167.*

PERFORMING ARTS

The Auckland arts scene is busy, particularly in the area of visual arts, with some 60 dealer galleries operating. Theater is on the rise and more touring exhibitions and performing companies are coming through the city than ever before. The Auckland Philharmonia Orchestra performs regularly, including at the summer series of free concerts in the park at the Domain, when thousands of music lovers sit with picnics under the stars. The Vector Arena by the harbor attracts plenty of rock acts, too.

Ticketek. This is the central ticket agency for all theater, music, and dance performances, as well as for major sporting events and it advertises its content months ahead of time. It offers a smart phone app and tickets are delivered by app, email, or collection at the venue. ☎ *09/307–5000* ⊕ *www.ticketek.co.nz.*

ART GALLERIES AND STUDIOS

Artspace. This independent contemporary gallery shows both international artists and the best of local artists. There are also talks and seminars from time to time. ✉ *300 Karangahape Rd.* ☎ *09/303–4965* ⊕ *www.artspace.org.nz.*

Fodor's Choice ★   **Fresh Gallery Otara.** This gallery, funded by Auckland Council, is a little off the beaten art track in the Otara Town Centre (in one of Auckland's poor and ethnically diverse areas), but it's worth visiting for the extraordinary work it shows. Emerging artists, many from the Pacific, test boundaries not only in materials used, but also with content and techniques. The space is also used by the South Auckland Poets' Collective for performance poetry that plays to packed houses. ✉ *5/46 Fairmall, Otara Town Centre, Otara* ☎ *09/271–6019* ⊙ *Closed Sun.*

Masterworks. This gallery exhibits and sells contemporary New Zealand art, glass, ceramics, and jewelry and is the place to go if you are looking for something different. Its location on Upper Queen Street is an easy walk from the center of town. Masterworks holds some 15 group and individual exhibitions a year including student work and will pack and ship any item purchased. ✉ *71 Upper Queen St., City Center* ☎ *09/373–5446* ⊕ *www.masterworksgallery.co.nz* ⊙ *Closed Sun. and Mon.*

West Coast Gallery Piha. It's well worth driving the winding road to this West Coast beach to see work by some 200 artists living in the region: paintings, ceramics, sculpture, jewelry, photography, glasswork, books, and CDs. Prices range from NZ$20 or NZ$30 to thousands.

The gallery hosts regular events and occasional themed art projects that get locals involved. ⊠ *Seaview Rd., Piha* ⊕ *www.westcoastgallery. co.nz* ⊙ *Closed Mon. and Tues.*

MUSIC AND OPERA

Aotea Centre. This is Auckland's main venue for the performing arts and medium-size conferences, and it often mounts free art exhibitions in its public spaces. There is a good café on the steps leading into the main foyer. The **New Zealand Opera** performs three annual main-stage seasons here, accompanied by either the **Auckland Philharmonia Orchestra** or the **New Zealand Symphony Orchestra.** ⊠ *Aotea Sq., 50 Mayoral Dr., City Center* ⊹ *Best accessed from Queen St.* ☎ *09/309–2677* ⊕ *www.the-edge.co.nz/aoteacentre.*

Auckland Town Hall. Though they play at the Aotea Centre on occasion, both the New Zealand Symphony and Auckland Philharmonia Orchestra perform here more regularly. The centerpiece is the Great Hall, seating up to 1,529 people in theater style on three levels. Some say it has some of the finest acoustics in the world. It also features the recently restored Auckland Town Hall Organ, which dates from 1911 and is the largest musical instrument in the country. More intimate concerts take place in the Concert Chamber. ⊠ *303 Queen St., City Center* ☎ *09/309–2677* ⊕ *www.the-edge.co.nz/aucklandtownhall.*

Civic Theatre. This theater hosts many performances by international touring companies and artists. For general inquiries about all three venues, check with the information desk on Level Three of the Aotea Centre. ⊠ *Queen and Wellesley Sts., City Center* ☎ *09/309–2677* ⊕ *www. the-edge.co.nz/thecivic.*

THEATER

Auckland Theatre Company (ATC). While Aucklanders endure accusations of philistinism, mostly from Wellingtonians, over the lack of theater in the city, there is one shining light: the Auckland Theatre Company (ATC). The ATC has a mixed repertory that includes New Zealand and international contemporary drama and the classics. The company performs at the Herald Theatre at the Aotea Centre, Sky City Theatre, and the Maidment Theatre at Auckland University. ☎ *09/309–0390* ⊕ *www.atc.co.nz.*

SHOPPING

Auckland's main shopping precincts for clothes and shoes are Queen Street, the Britomart precinct behind the train station and Newmarket; Queen Street is particularly good for outdoor gear, duty-free goods, greenstone jewelry, and souvenirs and big-name international brands. O'Connell and High streets also have a good smattering of designer boutiques, bookstores, and other specialty shops. Ponsonby is known for its design stores and fashion boutiques.

CITY CENTER AND PARNELL

BOOKS

Unity Books. If you are after New Zealand–related books, travel, and fiction this is the place for you. Smart staff will help you find that special text. ⊠ *19 High St., City Center* ☎ *09/307–0731* ⊕ *www.unitybooks. co.nz.*

CLOTHING AND ACCESSORIES

Fodor's Choice
★

Fingers. Six jewelers started Fingers in the 1970s as a place to display and sell their work. Now it showcases unique contemporary work by about 45 New Zealand artists, working with fine metals and stones. It's jewelry as art. Many of the artists have work in the New Zealand national collection, and customers who purchased items at an early stage of a maker's career are being rewarded with significant increases in value. Look out for works that combine precious metal with more mundane materials like rocks or seashells or even plastic. ⊠ *2 Kitchener St., City Center* ☎ *09/373–3974* ⊕ *www.fingers.co.nz.*

Karen Walker. You'll find tailored or easy-to-wear women's clothing lat Karen Walker, one of New Zealand's most recognized fashion designers. She also has a line of jewelry and eyewear. ⊠ *128A Ponsonby Rd., City Center* ☎ *09/309–6299* ⊕ *www.karenwalker.com.*

Trelise Cooper. Bohemian glamour with a deconstructed and sometimes raggedy edge, flamboyantly feminine designs popular with older curvy women, plush fabrics, extravagant use of colors that make the wearers look like tropical birds, and intricate detailing are the hallmarks of this New Zealand frock designer. Dame Trelise Cooper also makes jewelry and clothes for children. ⊠ *536 Parnell Rd., Parnell* ☎ *09/379–5005* ⊕ *www.trelisecooper.com.*

WORLD. Quirky WORLD is one of New Zealand's groundbreaking fashion labels, making contemporary clothing with its version of attitude. The flagship store is in trendy Tyler Street, near the Britomart train station in downtown Auckland. ⊠ *60 Tyler St., City Center* ☎ *09/373–3034* ⊕ *www.worldbrand.co.nz.*

Fodor's Choice
★

Zambesi. Always among the top New Zealand designers, this fashion label run by an informed family team has always charted its own course. ⊠ *56 Tyler St., near Britomart, City Center* ☎ *09/303–1701* ⊕ *www. zambesistore.co.nz.*

DEPARTMENT STORES

Smith and Caughey's Ltd. This is a good place to see plenty of local and international brands under one roof, coupled with extremely good service. The clothing runs the gamut from homegrown favorites such as Trelise Cooper to international megabrands such as Armani. The lingerie department is known for its large, plush dressing rooms. Also here are the largest cosmetics hall in the city, a good selection of conservative but well-made menswear, and good-quality china and crystal. ⊠ *253–261 Queen St., City Center* ☎ *09/377–4770* ⊕ *www. smithandcaugheys.co.nz.*

2

SOUVENIRS AND GIFTS

Elephant House. Follow elephant footprints down an alley in Parnell Village to the more than 30-year-old Elephant House. Its extensive collection of souvenirs and crafts, many unavailable elsewhere, include one-off hand-turned bowls, pottery, glass, and New Zealand jade, known as greenstone or *pounamu*. ⊠ *237 Parnell Rd., Parnell* ☎ *09/309–8740* ⊕ *www.nzcrafts.co.nz.*

Pauanesia. The sign hanging above this gift shop sets the tone—the letters are shaped from *paua* shell, which resembles abalone. You'll find one-off bags, place mats, picture frames, cushions, jewelry, and many other handmade items. ⊠ *35 High St., City Center* ☎ *09/366–7282* ⊕ *www.pauanesia.co.nz.*

SPORTS GEAR

Kathmandu. New Zealand–made outdoor clothing and equipment runs from fleece jackets to sleeping bags to haul-everything packs. ⊠ *200 Victoria St. W, City Center* ☎ *09/377–7560* ⊕ *www.kathmandu.co.nz.*

SPAS

Spa culture has developed slowly and against the grain of New Zealand's Calvinist roots and view that spas are an extravagance. But over the last few years a number of spas have firmly established themselves, with organic products and a strong Eastern influence. The range of spas, some in hotels, provide everything from steam treatment to pore cleanse to deep laser therapy and heated, smooth basalt pebbles and scented oils.

Fodor's Choice
★

East Day Spa. You may bump into visiting stars at this spa where treatments blend Eastern, particularly Indian, culture with a more Western approach to beauty. Treatments include shiatsu, Swedish, and Balinese massage, total body exfoliation, manicures, pedicures, facials, and waxing. Packages include a massage and pedicure from NZ$150 or a massage and organic facial for NZ$250. ⊠ *Ground level, 123 Albert St., City Center* ☎ *09/363–7050* ⊕ *www.eastdayspa.com* ☾ *Weekdays 9–9, weekends 9–8.*

Erban Spa. This spa offers a range of treatments for men and women and treats couples together. You'll enjoy a range of body treatments such as massage (Eastern, Swedish, herbal, and couples), body scrubs, and wraps. Beauty treatments such as facials, skin polishing, and waxing begin at NZ$45. Basic massage starts at NZ$110. ⊠ *86 Symonds St., City Center* ☎ *09/377–5955* ⊕ *www.erbanspa.co.nz* ☾ *Tues.–Sun. 9:30–6.*

PONSONBY

SPAS

White Beauty Spa. This spa and salon, known as White Beauty Spa, is loved by the trendy set who live in the comfortable suburbs of Ponsonby and Grey Lynn. It offers a wide range of therapies, including full-body massages, some using heated stones, as well as nail care and facials, many of which are tailor-made after a skin-type assessment. It also offers a flotation lounge where you are encased in a pod filled with warm water. There is a range of treatments including the 4½-hour White Cocoon package at NZ$480, which includes facials, brow work, massage, and a flotation session. There are also packages for men. ✉ *182 Jervois Rd., Ponsonby* ☎ *09/376–9969* ⊕ *www.whitespa.co.nz* ⊗ *Tues. and Thurs. 10–8, Wed. and Fri. 9–6, Sat. 9–4.*

GREATER AUCKLAND

MALLS

Dress-Smart. With more than 70 factory outlets, this is the place to go for high-quality, low-priced goods. You'll find books, music, children's toys, bags, jewelry, and housewares. Expect to pay 30%–70% less than regular retail. Take the inexpensive **shuttle service** (☎ *0800/748–885*), or, if you're driving, take the Penrose turnoff from the Southern Motorway and follow the signs to Onehunga. This is the heart of Auckland suburbia, so a detailed road map helps. Dress-Smart is close to Onehunga Mall, which has interesting antiques shops. ✉ *151 Arthur St., Onehunga* ☎ *09/622–2400* ⊕ *www.dress-smart.co.nz.*

STREET MARKETS

Otara Market. For many years people from all over Auckland have headed south on a Saturday morning looking for bargains to the sounds of hip-hop beats and island music. Vegetable stalls groan with produce such as taro, yams, and coconuts. More Asian food stalls are joining the traditional Polynesian tapa cloths, paua-shell jewelry, greenstone, and bone carvings, reflecting the city's increasingly multicultural profile, but sadly some junky stuff is creeping in. Nonetheless, watch for T-shirts bearing puns on famous brands, such as "Mikey" or "Cocolicious." The T-shirts designed by the Niuean poet Vela Manusaute are particularly sought by collectors. The market opens around 6, and stalls come down around midday. Exit the Southern Motorway at the East Tamaki off-ramp, turn left, and take the second left. ✉ *Newbury St., Otara.*

FAMILY **Takapuna Market.** The Takapuna parking lot comes alive on Sunday mornings, with organic cheese, meat, vegetables, homemade jams, small goods, and a slew of sweet and savory items from boutique bakers on sale. There's also clothing from designers starting out, interesting imports, as well as crafts and bric-a-brac. That saucer to complete the family dinner set might be lurking in a pile on a trestle table. ✉ *Corner Lake Rd. and Anzac St.* ☎ *021/127–2529* ⊕ *www.aucklandmarkets. co.nz/north-shore.html.*

SPORTS AND THE OUTDOORS

Aucklanders love sport, whether as spectators or participants. The nation's psyche is embedded in rugby—where men (most of the time) chase an elliptical ball around hoping to land it under goalposts to score what is known as a "try." The city is home to two rugby teams—the Auckland Blues and the North Harbour team known as Harbour.

For those not in love with rugby there is soccer and, in summer, cricket. Increasingly, more people are taking up cycling and mountain biking, and it's easy to rent a bike. For many women the big sport is netball, which is akin to basketball. There are a number of venues around the city.

For those who prefer water sports, Auckland has plenty of sailing, surfing, and kite-surfing. Beaches—commonly categorized as east, west, or north—generally have great views and are good for walking. The eastern beaches, such as those along Tamaki Drive on the south side of the harbor, are closer to the city and don't have heavy surf. West-coast black-sand beaches are popular (and hot) in summer, and can have rough seas with sudden rips and holes. (Surfboards can be rented at Muriwai and Piha.) And across Waitemata Harbour from the city, a chain of magnificent beaches stretches north as far as the Whangaparoa Peninsula.

BIKING

Auckland can be good for cycling if you stick to certain areas, such as around the waterfront. With a road bike, you can join a "bunch ride." Cyclists leave designated points most mornings and welcome guests; cycle shops can point you in the right direction. On weekends bunch rides can cover up to 150 km (93 miles) and will show you parts of the countryside that most won't get to see, plus stop off for a mandatory coffee.

Adventure Cycles. This outfit can provide maps of biking routes that avoid pitfalls such as traffic and roadwork (and there's always roadwork in Auckland). Bikes run from NZ$25 for a full day to NZ$230 for a month. You can even bring your own saddle and pedals. A full range of related gear, like panniers, helmets, and lights, can also be rented. Here for a while? The friendly crew will sell you a bike and then buy it back for half price. Though the company does not organize bike tours, it provides as much information as needed. It's closed Tuesday and Wednesday. ⊠ *9 Premier Ave., Western Springs* ☎ *09/940–2453* ⊕ *www.adventure-auckland.co.nz/adventurecycles.*

BOATING AND SAILING

If you're in Auckland in February, be sure to check out the Auckland Anniversary Regatta (⊕ *www.regatta.org.nz*). The Yachting New Zealand website has a calendar of events throughout the year (⊕ *www. yachtingnz.org.nz*). *(See also "City of Sails" at the beginning of this chapter for more on sailing.)*

INDEPENDENT MULTIDAY TRIPS

If you'd like an independent trip, but you'd rather someone else take the actual helm, New Zealand ports offer scores of options for skippered personalized itineraries. Choices include high-speed catamarans, luxury yachts, and restored tall ships, and these vessels run the gamut from basic to swank (which, unsurprisingly, directly corresponds to cost). Skippered boats during peak season cost anywhere from NZ$1,000 to NZ$3,000 a day. While most have habitual cruising grounds near their home ports, many skippers are happy to discuss an itinerary that includes destinations far and wide.

America's Cup

The uninitiated will be hard-pressed to avoid talk of Auckland's regattas and races, and inevitably, of the America's Cup. The history of this prestigious sailing race includes the longest winning streak in sports history: the United States held the prize from the race's 1851 inception until Australia successfully challenged for it in 1983. Perhaps due to the healthy rivalry New Zealand has long had with its trans-Tasman neighbor, the Kiwis developed a keen interest in the "Auld Mug" (as the silver trophy has affectionately been dubbed).

In 1995 Team New Zealand, aka Black Magic (its yacht was black), challenged for the cup and won, becoming the second non-U.S. nation to ever do so. And people are still talking about it. This was an enormous coup for a nation relatively small of stature and piggy bank, and New Zealanders rode an ecstatic wave of national pride. Team leaders Sir Peter Blake and Russell Coutts gained hero status, and Blake's lucky red socks were elevated to icons of the Kiwi effort.

The glory continued into 2000, when New Zealand was again the victor, becoming the first non-U.S. team to successfully defend the cup. But then tragedy, infighting, equipment failure, and disappointment took the wind out of New Zealand's sails. In 2001 Sir Peter Blake was murdered by Amazonian pirates; in 2003 skipper Coutts controversially "defected" to the challenging Swiss team, which won the cup away from New Zealand. Kiwi musician Dave Dobbyn's yachting anthem "Loyal" played endlessly and bitterly amid cries of *Traitor*. Another devastating loss came in 2013, when the Kiwis failed to capitalize on a seemingly insurmountable lead.

The race has long been plagued by legal wrangling, and as bigger dollars and egos scrap for the mug the battleground is often more courtroom than high seas. Despite all of this unfortunate nonsense, there is still a great sailing race to behold: land-based bipeds scamper frantically over multimillion-dollar super-engineered vessels, which skim over waves in an often-vain but always magnificent bid to harness the forces of nature. It makes for a powerful, heart-in-the-mouth display, and it's understandable that since the Kiwis have had a sip from the sailing grail, they are thirsty for more. So if you mention Black Magic, the Auld Mug, or cheap red socks to a Kiwi, you'll elicit a somewhat rueful smile: the America's Cup has been heartwarming and heartbreaking for this nation and there are high hopes for a win in the future. ⊕ *www.americascup.com.*

—Jessica Kany

You can spend a couple of days tooling around the Hauraki Gulf, three days visiting the beaches of Abel Tasman, or three weeks exploring the sub-Antarctic Islands. Many vessels provide equipment for fishing and diving and other toys suited to the cruising area. The Bay of Islands, Hauraki Gulf, and Marlborough sounds are maritime reserves and popular for sailing in season.

TOURS

Fodor's Choice ★ **Explore America's Cup Sail Auckland.** No experience is necessary to sail on America's Cup yachts *NZL 40* and *NZL 41* with Sail NZ. With the America's Cup Sailing Experience can help sail with a racing crew or relax while they do the work. For more thrills, participate in the America's Cup Match Racing trip, a three-hour experience that includes practice drills followed by a race against other yachts with a race crew. ⊠ *Viaduct Harbour* ☎ *09/359–5987* ⊕ *www.exploregroup.co.nz/en/unique-experiences/americas-cup-sail-auckland/* 🖃 *From NZ$160.*

FAMILY **Explore Auckland Harbor Sailing.** Customers are kept well fed and active while taking in the sights of Waitemata Harbour on trips timed for lunch, dinner, and snack time. Don't get too relaxed; working alongside the crew on the purpose-built yachts is encouraged. This outfit also offers sails on a fast racing yacht used by New Zealand to contest the America's Cup. ⊠ *Viaduct Harbour* ✛ *Near Maritime Museum* ☎ *09/359–5987* ⊕ *www.exploregroup.co.nz/en/new-zealand/* 🖃 *From NZ$120.*

Fullers. To get a sense of Auckland, the Auckland skyline, and the size of Sky Tower, take a 1½-hour Auckland Harbour cruise that leaves from the Ferry Building. Commentary runs while the boat passes the Harbour Bridge, Devonport's naval base, and Bean Rock Lighthouse. There's a brief stopover on Rangitoto Island in the Harauki Gulf. Various day tours of Waiheke Island are also available. ⊠ *Ferry Bldg., 99 Quay St.* ☎ *09/367–9111* ⊕ *www.fullers.co.nz* 🖃 *From NZ$40.*

BRIDGE ADVENTURES

AJ Hackett Bungy—Auckland Harbour Bridge. The only bungy (New Zealand spelling for bungee) jumping in Auckland, this company operates off the Harbour Bridge year-round. The Harbour Bridge Experience is a 1½-hour bridge climb with commentary on the history of the bridge and the region. Needless to say, views from the bridge walk are outstanding. There are three trips a day, and reservations are essential. ⊠ *Westhaven Reserve, Curran St., Herne Bay* ☎ *09/360–7748* ⊕ *www.bungy.co.nz* 🖃 *From NZ$125 for the walk and NZ$160 for the bungy.*

GOLF

Chamberlain Park Golf Course. This 18-hole public course in a parkland is a five-minute drive off Northwestern Motorway (Route 16) from the city. It's a popular course with open fairways, controlled rough, and big old specimen trees. The course is popular with the first tee at 6 am. Because it is publicly owned you don't need membership anywhere else to play, but call ahead to book because Chamberlain Park is busy. The club shop rents clubs, shoes, and carts. It's one of the cheapest golf courses in Auckland, and because it's on volcanic rock, the course holds up in wet weather. ⊠ *46 Linwood Ave., Western Springs* ☎ *09/815–4999* ⊕ *www.chamberlainpark.co.nz* 🖃 *NZ$30* 🏌 *18 holes, 5553 yards, par 69.*

Rugby Madness

Rugby evolved out of soccer in 19th-century Britain. It was born at the elitist English school of Rugby, where in 1823 a schoolboy by the name of William Webb Ellis became bored with kicking a soccer ball and picked it up and ran with it. Rugby is similar to American football, except players are not allowed to pass the ball forward and they wear no protective gear. There's a World Cup for the sport, every four years since 1987.

Rugby developed among the upper classes of Britain, whereas soccer remained a predominantly working-class game. However, in colonial New Zealand, a country largely free from the rigid class structure of Britain, the game developed as the nation's number-one winter sport. One reason was the success of New Zealand teams in the late 19th and early 20th centuries. This remote outpost of the then British empire, with a population of only 750,000 in 1900, was an impressive rugby force, and it became a source of great national pride. Today, in a country of 4-plus million, the national sport is played by 250,000 New Zealanders at the club level.

The top-class rugby season in the Southern Hemisphere kicks off in February with the Super15, which pits professional teams from provincial franchises in New Zealand, South Africa, and Australia against one another. New Zealand's matches are generally held in main cities, and you should be able to get tickets without too much trouble. The international season runs from June to late August. This is your best chance to see the national team, the All Blacks, and the major cities are again the place to be. National provincial championship games hit towns all over the country from late August to mid-October. A winner-takes-all game decides who attains the domestic rugby Holy Grail, the Ranfurly Shield. If you can't catch a live game, you can always join a crowd watching a televised match at a local pub or sports bar.

Gulf Harbour Country Club. Designed by Robert Trent Jones Jr. (some say the world's finest designer of classic golf courses), this course is about 40 minutes north of Auckland (if the traffic is flowing) on the East Coast's Whangaparaoa Peninisula. Some have called it the Pebble Beach of New Zealand and there's a dress code here: collared shirts, golf slacks or shorts, and no metal spike shoes with socks. The first nine holes are hilly while the last nine offer amazing views of the Hauraki Gulf. Winter specials are posted on the website. After a round, take a stroll around the Gulf Harbour Marina to look at the range of yachts and launches. ⊠ *Gulf Harbour Dr., Rodney District* ☎ *09/424–0971* ⊕ *www.gulfharbourcountryclub.co.nz* ▭ *NZ$180* ⚐ *18 holes, 7000 yards, par 72.*

Muriwai Golf Club. A 40-minute drive (depending on traffic) northwest of the city brings you to this links course near a bird sanctuary, with outstanding views of the coast, even from the "19th hole." Because the links are on sandy soil, they can be played even if the rest of Auckland is sodden and the course is often home to tournaments and training. If your partner is not a golfer there are some great beach and forest walks close by. ⊠ *Coast Rd., Muriwai Beach* ☎ *09/411–8454* ⊕ *www. muriwaigolfclub.co.nz* ✉ *NZ$70* ⚐ *18 holes, 6800 yards, par 72.*

Titirangi Golf Club. Designed by renowned golf architect Alister MacKenzie, this is one of the country's finest (and oldest) 18-hole courses. The club was established in 1909 and takes pride in its rolling fairways, and challenging bunkers and greens. Golfers might be distracted by the magnificent setting and specimen trees. Nonmembers are welcome to play provided they contact the course in advance (and get through the painful automated phone system). Once booked, you must show evidence of membership at an overseas club and the dress code must be adhered to. Tailored shirts and pants are a must and no beachwear of any kind is allowed. Massive road works that are due for completion in 2017 mean Titirangi can be a 50-minute drive from the city. ⊠ *Links Rd., Waitakere City* ☎ *09/827–5749* ⊕ *www.titirangigolf.co.nz* ✉ *NZ$150* ⚐ *18 holes, 6600 yards, par 70.*

HIKING

Tāmaki Hīkoi. For a Māori perspective on Auckland, take this walking tour with guides from the local Ngāti Whatua tribe, who tell ancient stories and recount their history on a trek from Mt. Eden through sacred landmarks to the harbor. The three-hour tour departs at 9 am and 1:30 pm from the visitor centers at Princes Wharf and Sky City. ⊠ *Auckland i-SITE Visitor Centre, Princes Wharf, 137 Quay St., Viaduct* ☎ *021/146–9593* ⊕ *www.tamakihikoi.co.nz* ✉ *From NZ$95.*

Waitakere Ranges. These scenic hills west of Auckland are a favorite walking and picnic spot for locals. The bush-clad ranges, rising sharply from West Coast beaches, are threaded by streams and waterfalls. The highlight of a great, easy hour-long trail, **Auckland City Walk**, is Cascade Falls, just off the main track. The 20-minute **Arataki Nature Trail** is a great introduction to kauri and other native trees. Providing information on the Waitakeres and other Auckland parks, the **Arataki Visitor Centre** displays modern Māori carvings. Some tracks may be closed as a fungus is infecting some trees and you may be required to use the disinfectant provided to clean your shoes before and after your walk.

To get to the Waitakeres, head along the Northwestern Motorway (Route 16) from central Auckland, take the Waterview turnoff, and keep heading west to the gateway village of Titirangi. A sculpture depicting fungal growths tells you you're heading in the right direction. From here the best route to follow is Scenic Drive, with spectacular views of Auckland and its two harbors. The visitor center is 5 km (3 miles) along the drive. ⊠ *300 Scenic Dr.* ☎ *09/817–0077* ⊕ *regionalparks.aucklandcouncil.govt.nz/aratakivisitorcentre.*

KAYAKING

Ferg's Kayaks. Instead of taking the ferry to Rangitoto, why not paddle? Ferg's Kayaks, run by four-time Olympic gold medal winner Ian Ferguson, takes guided trips to the island twice daily, leaving at 9:30 am and 5:30 pm. The round-trip takes about seven hours, including two to paddle each way and one to climb the volcano. On the later trip you paddle back in the dark toward the city lights. Booking is essential, and trips are dependent on weather and numbers. ✉ *12 Tamaki Dr.* ☎ *09/529–2230* ⊕ *www.fergskayaks.co.nz* 🎬 *From NZ$140.*

Ross Adventures. There's more to Waiheke Island than relaxed beaches and wineries. Half, full-day, and overnight kayaking trips take paddlers past coastal cliffs and inlets. Explore caves, beaches, and Māori pā sites, and have coffee and snacks or lunch at a private beach depending on the day's route. Full-day trips include swimming and snorkeling, and you may spot blue penguins or dolphins as you kayak. ✉ *Matiatia Wharf, Ocean View Rd.* ☎ *09/372–5550* ⊕ *www.kayakwaiheke.co.nz* 🎬 *From NZ$125.*

SPORTS VENUE

Eden Park. The city's major stadium is the best place (in winter) to see New Zealand's sporting icon: the All Blacks, one of the best rugby teams in the world. More frequently, it sees the Auckland Blues, a Super 15 rugby team that plays professional franchise opponents from Australia, South Africa, and other parts of New Zealand. Cricket teams arrive in summer. For information on sporting events, check out *What's On Auckland,* a monthly guide available from the Auckland i-SITE Visitor Centre. ✉ *Reimers Ave.* ⊕ *www.edenpark.co.nz.*

Ticketek. The big games sell fast through this ticket agency. ☎ *09/307–5000* ⊕ *www.ticketek.co.nz.*

NORTHLAND AND THE BAY OF ISLANDS

WELCOME TO NORTHLAND AND THE BAY OF ISLANDS

TOP REASONS TO GO

★ **Boating and Fishing:** Take a cruise to an island, whale-watch, swim with dolphins, or fish with the Bay of Islands as the hub.

★ **Bountiful Beaches:** Most Northland beaches are safe for swimming. On the 90 Mile Beach you can swim in both the Tasman Sea and the Pacific Ocean. Experienced surfers head to Shipwreck Bay for great waves.

★ **Coastal Views:** Take the Old Coast Road to Russell for superb views of islands and (almost) hidden bays and places to picnic.

★ **Superb Diving:** Dive at the Poor Knights Islands, known for their huge variety of subtropical fish, or the wreck of the Greenpeace vessel *Rainbow Warrior*, sunk by French agents in 1985.

★ **Walking and Hiking:** Superb bushwalking (hiking) provides a close look at ancient kauri trees (a local species of pine) and interesting birds, such as *tūī* (too-ee), fantails, wood pigeons.

1 **Northland.** *Te Tai Tokerau*, or Northland, with its no-frills, tiny, friendly towns and high rates of unemployment, is extremely different from the affluent Bay of Islands. However, the scenery is just as stunning. But without the infrastructure that goes along with organized tourism you will feel a little off the beaten path. The best approach is to travel in a relaxed fashion: explore Cape Reinga, the tip of the country; take the car ferry out past the mangroves and cruise across Hokianga Harbour. The ferry is busy over summer but half the fun is people-watching— this quiet route gets its fair share of movie and music stars looking to get away from it all. Some visitors will stand in awe at the base of a giant kauri tree; others eat fish-and-chips on Opononi Beach and enjoy the views of the enormous golden sand dunes across the water.

2 **The Bay of Islands.** This sweep of coastline is home to 144 islands amid a mild, subtropical climate and excellent game-fishing waters. That combination makes the Bay of Islands ideal—with a slew of things to do while visiting. You'll feel well catered to, whether your interests lie in the history of Waitangi (and New Zealand) or the sunken *Rainbow Warrior*, staying somewhere with your own private beach, or trying to catch the biggest marlin on record.

GETTING ORIENTED

3

As the map indicates, Northland includes the Bay of Islands, but we've divided this chapter into two sections—Northland and the Bay of Islands. The West Coast, from Dargaville to Cape Reinga seems empty. The unassuming little towns along the way and the lumbering Kohu Ra Tuama Hokianga Harbour ferry contrast the luxurious lodges and fancy yachts around the Bay of Islands. No matter where you are in the North, you're never far from the water and the combination of coast, rolling pastures, and ancient native forest is unlike any other part of the country.

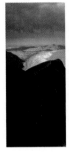

Updated
by Richard
Pamatatau

Northland is the place to go when you seek more than great restaurants and shopping. You'll be best served on a trip here by taking in inspiring views from winding coastal roads or reading on a quiet beach with some fruit from owner-operated shops. While there are pockets of relative sophistication that offer good coffee and fancy food, much of this part of the country is about the views.

There's a rawness to the North. Social tensions are exacerbated by high unemployment, particularly among the area's Māori population, and political neglect, but the scenery is truly majestic, going from rugged to pastoral in a matter of kilometers.

You will notice the change about an hour after leaving the sometimes-confusing jumble that makes up Auckland. With the city behind you the air starts to clear and you can see what some call the Northland light. The lack of industry in Northland alongside a declining population means less pollution, and may account for the fact that it seems brighter the farther north you go, even on overcast days.

The Tasman Sea to the west and the Pacific Ocean to the east meet at the top of North Island at Cape Reinga. No matter what route you take, you'll pass farms and forests, marvelous beaches, and great open spaces. Even though the East Coast, up to the Bay of Islands, is Northland's most densely populated, often with cashed-up migrants from bigger cities—looking for a more relaxed life—it still feels uncrowded.

The first decision on the drive north comes at the foot of the Brynderwyn Hills. Turning left will take you up the West Coast through areas once covered with forests and now used for either agricultural or horticulture.

Driving over "the Brynderwyns," as they are known, takes you to Whangarei, the only city in Northland. If you're in the mood for a diversion, you can slip to the beautiful coastline and take in Waipu Cove, an area settled by Scots, and Laings Beach, where million-dollar homes sit next to small Kiwi beach houses.

An hour's drive farther north is the Bay of Islands, known all over the world for its beauty. Here you will find lush forests, splendid beaches, and shimmering harbors. The Treaty of Waitangi was signed here in 1840 between Māori and the British Crown, establishing the basis for the modern New Zealand state. Every year on February 6, the extremely beautiful Waitangi Treaty Ground (the name means weeping waters) is the site of a celebration of the treaty, and of protests by Māori unhappy with it.

Continuing north on the East Coast, the agricultural backbone of the region is even more evident and a series of winding loop roads off the main highway leads to beaches that are both beautiful and isolated where you can swim, dive, picnic, or just laze.

The West Coast is even less populated, and the coastline is rugged and windswept. In the Waipoua Forest, you will find some of New Zealand's oldest and largest kauri trees; the winding road will also take you past mangrove swamps.

Crowning the region is the spiritually significant Cape Reinga, the headland at the top of the vast stretch of 90 Mile Beach, where it's believed Māori souls depart after death. Today Māori make up roughly a quarter of the area's population (compared with the national average of about 15%). The legendary Māori navigator Kupe was said to have landed on the shores of Hokianga Harbour, where the first arrivals made their home. Many different *iwi* (tribes) lived throughout Northland, including Ngapuhi (the largest), Te Roroa, Ngāti Wai, Ngāti Kuri, Te Aupouri, Ngaitakoto, Ngāti Kahu, and Te Rarawa. Many Māori here can trace their ancestry to the earliest inhabitants.

PLANNING

Plan to spend three days in Northland. On Day 1 take in the main town of Paihia, and then catch the ferry to Russell for lunch and sightseeing. Drive north on the second day, stopping at beaches and Cape Reinga. Meander home via the Hokianga on Day 3 by winding south through the forests along the West Coast to Kohukohu. Ferry south across serene Hokianga Harbour to Rawene. From Opononi, closer to the harbor's mouth, continue down the Kauri Coast to the Waipoua Forest. From there, Highway 12 runs to the arty town of Dargaville, and on to Matakohe, site of the renowned Kauri Museum. It's another half-hour to Brynderwyn, where you rejoin State Highway 1 about an hour north of Auckland.

WHEN TO GO

Snow doesn't fall in the "winterless north," but it can get cool. The best time to go is between mid-November and mid-April; peak season is December through March. During the quiet months of July and August it can be wet. For game fishing, arrive from February to June.

GETTING HERE AND AROUND

BOAT AND FERRY TRAVEL

Three passenger boats cross between Paihia and Russell, with departures at least once every 20 minutes in each direction from 7:20 am to 10:30 pm from Paihia, and 7 am to 10 pm from Russell. The one-way fare is NZ$6. Or, join the car ferry at nearby Opua, about 5 km (3 miles) south of Paihia. It operates from 6:50 am to 9:50 pm, with departures at approximately 10-minute intervals from either shore. The last boat leaves from Okiato on the Russell side at 9:50 pm. The one-way fare is NZ$11 for car and driver plus NZ$1 for each adult passenger. Buy your tickets on board (cash only). Save time by crossing the Hokianga Harbour between Rawene and Kohukohu (with or without a car) by ferry.

BUS TRAVEL

Taking a bus is a cheap and also easy alternative to driving. Several companies serve all but the most out-of-the-way spots. InterCity (contact the Paihia branch), runs several times daily between Auckland and the Bay of Islands and connect to the other Northland centers at least once a day. Auckland to Paihia takes about 4½ hours and to Kerikeri about 5½ hours.

Contacts InterCity. 📞 09/583–5780 ⊕ www.intercity.co.nz.

CAR TRAVEL

It's best to see Northland's many lovely bays, sandy beaches, and worthwhile sights by car. Northland roads are generally just two lanes wide with many one-lane bridges in remote areas. Take care on the narrow—and often unsealed—roads that thread through the region. Don't risk a drive along 90 Mile Beach; the quicksand and tides can leave you stuck, and your rental car insurance won't cover any accidents here. You can easily find a tour company to take you along 90 Mile Beach.

From Auckland, drive up the East Coast on State Highway 1 and return down the West Coast on Highway 12 (or vice versa), but make sure to check out smaller, winding coastal roads with their stunning coastlines and dramatic island views.

RESTAURANTS

Seafood abounds in the north with scallops and oysters farmed throughout the region, though occasional sewerage scares and algae blooms put them off-limits. Snapper and kingfish are available year-round, and marlin and broad-bill swordfish are abundant between January and June.

The region prides itself on its local produce, and with more skillful chefs arriving in the region, the restaurant food has improved.

People eat earlier in Northland than in the cities, with restaurants filling around 7. Dress is casual—jeans are acceptable in all but the most upscale lodges. From May through September, many restaurants close or reduce their opening hours, some to four nights a week. October sees regular hours resume.

HOTELS

Northland accommodations vary from basic motels to luxury lodges. Your hosts, particularly in the bed-and-breakfasts, share their local knowledge and are a great resource on less-obvious attractions.

Paihia is a hub for Northland and has plenty of vacation apartments and standard motels. You'll also find in places like Russell, a range of high-end B&Bs, and luxury lodges sometimes with private bays.

High season runs from December through March. Some lodges have shoulder seasons in April and May, and September and October. Overall, room rates drop between May and October though many places also close for a break.

Hotel reviews have been shortened. For full information, visit Fodors.com.

WHAT IT COSTS IN NEW ZEALAND DOLLARS			
	$	$$	$$$	$$$$
Restaurants	under NZ$15	NZ$15–NZ$20	NZ$21–NZ$30	over NZ$30
Hotels	under NZ$125	NZ$125–NZ$200	NZ$201–NZ$300	over NZ$300

Restaurant prices are the average cost of a main course at dinner or, if dinner is not served, at lunch. Hotel prices are the lowest cost of a standard double room in high season.

VISITOR INFORMATION

Local visitor bureaus, many known as i-SITEs, have information on the whole region, with more extensive information on their particular environs. In addition, some helpful community Web resources include ⊕ *www.kerikeri.co.nz,* ⊕ *www.dargaville.co.nz,* and ⊕ *www.paihia. co.nz.* Destination Northland, a regional tourism organization, maintains ⊕ *www.northland.org.nz.*

NORTHLAND

The Bay of Islands is the destination for most tourists while the rest of Northland has large stretches of green farmland separating the mostly tiny towns. Some areas, particularly in the Far North and Hokianga, have higher-than-average unemployment, and many New Zealanders joke that cannabis cultivation fuels a giant hidden economy.

Northland today is also home to many wealthy people retreating from the city who may live close to people who have never left the area.

Whatever their occupation, Northland residents are generally good-humored and hospitable, and proud of their varied lifestyles and exceptional scenery.

European settlement began in Northland in the 18th century, starting with whalers around the Bay of Islands, Scots who settled at Waipu on the East Coast, and Dalmatians who worked the West Coast's kauri-gum fields. Anglican missionaries started arriving in Northland in the early 19th century. The first mission was established at Kerikeri by the Reverend Samuel Marsden of the Church Missionary Society, who went about trying to "civilize" the Māori before conversion to Christianity. He also planted the first grapevines in New Zealand.

If you're driving up the East Coast toward the Bay of Islands in December, you'll see scarlet blossoms blazing along the roadside. These are *pohutukawa* trees in flower, turning crimson in time for the Kiwi Christmas, hence their *Pākehā* (non-Māori) name: "the New Zealand Christmas tree." To the Māori, the flowers had another meaning: the beginning of shellfish season. Along Northland roads you might also see clumps of spiky-leaf New Zealand flax (the Māori used the fibers of this plant, the raw material for linen, to weave into clothing), huge tree ferns known as *punga,* and giant mangrove swamps.

WARKWORTH

59 km (36 miles) north of Auckland.

A sleepy town on the banks of the Mahurangi River, Warkworth was established in 1853. With lime mined from the local river, it became the first cement-manufacturing site in the southern hemisphere. Today, race boatbuilding and refitting are the main industries though slowly boutique food producers are opening shop. Warkworth also serves as a service town for the surrounding farms and market gardens. It's a convenient stopping point en route to nearby marine reserve Goat Island or the superb vineyards at Matakana.

GETTING HERE AND AROUND

There are two ways to get to Warkworth—bus or car. It's on the major bus routes north, and all you need do is let the driver know where you want to get off. InterCity has ticketing options that lets you explore, and regular service. However, bus travel can be limiting because attractions are spread out. For more flexibility rent a car and rove the countryside more freely, especially if you are heading to Matakana to explore the wineries. There are about 100 white-sand beaches in the area, which are easy to get to and often deserted.

VISITOR INFORMATION

Contacts Warkworth Visitor Information Centre. ⊠ *1 Baxter St.* ☎ *09/425–9081* ⊕ *www.matakanacoast.co.nz.*

EXPLORING
TOP ATTRACTIONS

McKinney Kauri. Two giants stand in Warkworth, near the Warkworth Museum—two giant kauri trees, that is. The larger one, the McKinney Kauri, measures almost 25 feet around its base, yet this 800-year-old colossus is a mere adolescent by kauri standards. Look a few yards to the west and you'll see the Simpson Kauri. Kauri trees were highly prized by Māori canoe builders because a canoe capable of carrying 100 warriors could be made from a single trunk. These same characteristics—strength, size, and durability—made kauri timber ideal for ships, furniture, and housing, and the kauri forests were rapidly depleted by early European settlers. Today the trees are protected by law; infant kauri are appearing in the forests of the North Island, although their growth rate is painfully slow. ⊠ *Parry Kauri Park* ⊕ *www.waymarking. com/waymarks/WMJR9.*

WORTH NOTING

FAMILY **SheepWorld.** Head for SheepWorld about an hour North of Auckland for a taste of life on a typical New Zealand sheep farm. Twice a day demonstrations show working farm dogs rounding up sheep, before shearers take over. An ecotrail meanders through the bush, providing information on native trees, birds (and their calls), and boxes of *weta*, large, ugly—yet impressive—native insects. On the weekends, the farm dogs even herd ducks. Children can take pony rides, and, in August, bottle-feed lambs. Depending on the weather there is also eel feeding. ⊠ *324 State Hwy. 1* ☎ *09/425–7444* ⊕ *www.sheepworld.co.nz* ☜ *NZ$10, NZ$27 including sheep and dog shows* ⊙ *Daily 9–5; sheep-and-dog show at 11 and 2.*

FAMILY **Warkworth Museum.** For a glimpse of Northland's pioneering past pay a visit to the Warkworth District Museum. It's a must if you are interested in learning about how smaller settlements in New Zealand developed. This eclectic collection includes Māori artifacts plus farming and domestic implements from the early days of European settlement including implements used to dig for kauri gum. Rotating textile displays cover clothing and lace dating to the late 1700s. There is also a display of a school dental clinic—what Kiwi children called the "murder house." Outside is a collection of old buildings, including a bushman's hut and an army hut used by Americans stationed at Warkworth in World War II. ⊠ *Tudor Collins Dr.* ☎ *09/425–7093* ⊕ *warkworthmuseum.co.nz* ☜ *NZ$7* ⊙ *Daily 10–3. Closed Christmas Day, Good Friday.*

EN ROUTE **Goat Island.** Take a trip to the Goat Island or Te Hawere-a-Maki marine reserve where fishing is prohibited and marine life has returned in abundance. Prominent species include blue *maomao* fish, snapper, and cod. It does get crowded here, and midweek is best. You can put on a snorkel and get up-close-and-personal with a school of maomao. The beach area is good for a picnic, as well.

To get to Goat Island head toward Leigh, 21 km (13 miles) northeast of Warkworth. From Leigh, take a left turn and follow the signs for a couple of miles. If you arrive by 10, you should avoid the masses especially midweek and in winter. If you want to stay there are camping grounds near by and the Warkworth Visitor Centre will direct you. ⊠ *Goat Island Rd.* ⊕ *www.discovergoatisland.co.nz/reserve.html.*

Glass Bottom Boat. Just as the name promises, Glass Bottom Boat takes a glass-bottom boat around the island and gives you an aquarium eye view of waters teaming with fish. If the weather isn't ideal, there is an inner reef trip. Call ahead, because trips don't run if there is too much of a swell. You can also rent flippers, masks, and snorkels if you want to get up really close. ⊠ *Goat Island Rd.* ☎ *09/422–6334* ⊕ *www. glassbottomboat.co.nz* ☜ *From NZ$28* ⊙ *Fri. and weekends.*

Octopus Hideaway. You can rent a mask, snorkel, and flippers (NZ$15)—and a wet suit if it's too cold for you (NZ$15)—from Octopus Hideaway; their sign is about 1 km (½ mile) before the beach on the main drag, Goat Island Road. The operators of this business are knowledgeable and very helpful. ⊠ *7 Goat Island Rd.* ☎ *09/422–6212* ⊕ *www.theoctopushideaway.nz.*

WHANGAREI

127 km (79 miles) north of Warkworth, 196 km (123 miles) north of Auckland.

The main center in Northland is the Whangarei (*fahng*-ar-ay) District; Whangarei Harbour was traditionally a meeting place for Māori tribes traveling south by *waka* (canoe). The full Māori name of the harbor, Whangarei Terenga Paraoa, means "swimming place of whales" but is also interpreted as "the meeting place of chiefs." Europeans started to settle in the area from the mid-1800s; now it's a town of roughly 45,000 people, rooted in the agriculture, forestry, and fishing industries. Boatbuilding is a traditional business, manufacturing everything from superyachts to charter boats. There is also a growing community of artists who have retreated to the North where housing is cheaper. The mouth of the harbor is dominated by the volcanic peaks of Whangarei Heads, atop Bream Bay. The drive from town to the Whangarei Heads takes about 20 minutes heading out on Riverside Drive, past mangrove-lined bays. At the Heads are stunning white-sand beaches and coves with safe swimming, and several hikes, including up the peaks of Mt. Manaia.

GETTING HERE AND AROUND

Whangarei is about two hours by car from Auckland on State Highway One. Bus services also travel this route but take longer as they stop at many small towns along the way.

You can fly from Auckland to Whangarei, but factoring arriving at the airport and checking in, it's often quicker to drive to Whangarei. There is no train service.

VISITOR INFORMATION

Contacts Northland Coach and Travel Centre. ✉ *Northland Coach and Travel Bldg., 3C Bank St.* ☎ *09/438–2653.* **Whangarei Visitor Information Centre.** ✉ *92 Otaika Rd.* ☎ *09/438–1079* ⊕ *whangareinz.com/i-site.*

EXPLORING

TOP ATTRACTIONS

FAMILY **Claphams Clocks—The National Clock Museum.** If you want to while away some time this clock museum is the place for you. About every conceivable method of telling time is represented. The collection of more than 1,500 clocks includes primitive water clocks, ships' chronometers, and ornate masterworks from Paris and Vienna. Some of the most intriguing examples were made by the late Mr. Clapham himself, such as his World War II air-force clock. Ironically, the one thing you won't find here is the correct time. If all the bells, chimes, gongs, and cuckoos went off together, the noise would be deafening, so the clocks are set to different times. ✉ *Town Basin, Dent St.* ☎ *09/438–3993* ⊕ *www.claphamsclocks. com* 🖅 *NZ$10* ☉ *Daily 9–5.*

Historical Reyburn House. This is the oldest kauri villa in Whangarei. It is home to the Northland Society of Arts plus hosts exhibitions from New Zealand artists. Original works from well-known artists are available for purchase. The permanent collection focuses on the 1880s

The Treaty of Waitangi

The controversial cornerstone of New Zealand's Māori and Pākehā relations is the 1840 Treaty of Waitangi, the first formal document that bound the Māori to the British crown. This contract became the basis for Britain's claim to the entire country as its colony.

In the mid-1830s, Britain became increasingly concerned about advances by French settlers and the inroads made by the New Zealand Company, a private emigration organization. The British government had an official Resident at Waitangi, James Busby, but no actual means to protect its interests. In 1835, Busby helped orchestrate an alliance among more than 30 North Island Māori chiefs.

In 1840, Captain William Hobson arrived in Waitangi to negotiate a transfer of sovereignty. Hobson and Busby hurriedly drew up a treaty in both English and Māori, and presented it to the Māori confederation on February 5, 1840. On the following day, about 40 chiefs signed the treaty.

But there were significant differences between the Māori and English versions. In the first article, the English version said the Māori would cede sovereignty to the Queen of England. But the Māori translation used the word *kāwanatanga* (governorship), which did not mean that the Māori were ceding the right to *mana* (self-determination).

The second article guaranteed the chiefs the "full, exclusive and undisturbed possession of their lands, estates, forests, fisheries, and other properties," but granted the right of preemption to the crown. The Māori translation did not convey the crown's exclusive right to buy Māori land, which caused friction over the decades. The third article granted the Māori protection as British citizens—and thus held them accountable to British law.

After the initial wave of signatures at Waitangi, signatures were gathered elsewhere in the North Island and on the South Island. In spring 1840 Hobson claimed all of New Zealand as a British colony. He had not, however, gotten signatures from some of the most powerful Māori chiefs, and this came back to haunt the crown during the Land Wars of 1860.

What wasn't confiscated after the Land Wars was taken by legislation. In 1877 Chief Justice Prendergast ruled that the treaty was "a simple nullity" that lacked legal validity because one could not make a treaty with "barbarians." At first European contact, 66.5 million acres of land was under Māori control, but by 1979 only 3 million remained—of mostly marginal lands.

The battle to have the treaty honored and reinterpreted is ongoing. In 1973, February 6 was proclaimed the official Waitangi Day holiday. From the get-go, the holiday sparked debate, as Māori activists protest the celebration of such a divisive document. The Waitangi Tribunal was established in 1975 to allow Māori to rule on alleged breaches of the treaty, and in 1985 the tribunal's powers were made retrospective to 1840. It has its hands full, as the claims continue to be one of New Zealand's largest sociopolitical issues. The treaty is now in the National Archives in Wellington.

Scuba divers examine the notoriously friendly subtropical fish in the Poor Knights Islands Marine Reserve.

to the present and some well-known New Zealand artists are represented. ✉ *Town Basin, Reyburn House La.* ☎ *09/438–3074* ⊕ *www.reyburnhouse.co.nz* ✉ *Donation* ☉ *Tues.–Fri. 10–4, weekends 1–4.*

FAMILY **Kiwi North.** Minutes out of town, this 61-acre park is home to a nocturnal kiwi house, several Heritage buildings, and the Whangarei Museum. The museum has some 40,000 items in its collection including fine examples of pre-European Māori cloaks, waka (canoes), and tools. Photographers will love the early pictures of the area. You can also check out Glorat, an original 1886 kauri homestead, and the world's smallest consecrated chapel, built in 1859 from a single kauri tree. On the third Sunday of every month and on selected "Live Days" (call for dates), you can cruise around the park on model reproductions of steam and electric trains, as well as on a full-size diesel train. ✉ *500 State Hwy. 14, Maunu* ☎ *09/438–9630* ⊕ *kiwinorth.co.nz/* ✉ *Park free, kiwi house and Whangarei Museum NZ$15–NZ$35 family ticket* ☉ *Daily 10–4.*

WORTH NOTING

FAMILY **Whangarei Falls.** The falls are a lovely picnic spot, located on Ngunguru Road, 5 km (3 miles) northeast of town. Viewing platforms are atop the falls, and a short trail runs through the local bush. ✉ *12 Ngunguru Rd., Glenbervie* ⊕ *www.whangareifalls.co.nz.*

Whangarei Town Basin. People often bypass Whangarei on their way to the Bay of Islands. It's easy to see why, as the town has a confusing traffic system, but if you can brave it the area known as the Whangarei Town Basin is worth a look. The marina is now a haven for visiting yachts and has cafés, restaurants, galleries, and crafts shops. There's parking behind the basin off Dent Street. ✉ *Dent St.* ⊕ *www.wdc.govt.nz.*

The Poor Knights Islands

Jacques Cousteau once placed the Poor Knights Islands among the world's top 10 dive locations. Underwater archways, tunnels, caves, and rocky cliffs provide endless opportunities for viewing many species of subtropical fish. On a good day you'll see soft coral, sponge gardens, gorgonian fields, and forests of kelp.

Two large islands and many islets make up the Poor Knights, remnants of an ancient volcanic eruption 12 nautical miles off the stunning Tutukaka coast, a half-hour drive east of Whangarei. The ocean around them is a marine reserve, extending 800 meters (½ mile) from the islands. Indeed the islands themselves are a nature reserve; landing on them is prohibited.

At 7.9 million cubic feet, Rikoriko Cave, on the southern island's northwest side, is one of the world's largest sea caves. It's known for its acoustics. Ferns hang from its roof, and underwater cup coral grows toward the rear of it. (Normally found at depths of 200 meters, the cave light has tricked the coral into thinking it is deeper.) Visibility at the Poor Knights is between 20 and 30 meters, but in Rikoriko Cave it goes up to 35 to 45 meters.

A dense canopy of regenerated *pohutukawa* covers the islands, flowering brilliant scarlet around Christmas time. Native Poor Knights lilies cling to cliff faces, producing bright red flowers in October. Rare bellbirds (*koromikos*) and red-crowned parakeets (*kakarikis*) thrive in the predator-free environment. Between October and May, millions of seabirds come to breed, including the Buller's shearwaters that arrive from the Arctic Circle. But possibly the most distinguished resident is the New Zealand native *tuatara*, a reptile species from the dinosaur age that survives only on offshore islands.

New Zealand fur seals bask on the rocks and feed on the abundant fish life, mostly from July to October, and year-round dolphins, whales, and bronze whaler sharks can be seen in the surrounding waters. In summer you can see minke and rare Bryde's whales, too. In March stingrays stack in the hundreds in the archways for their mating season.

Conditions rarely prevent diving, which is good year-round. That said, don't expect the same experience you'll get diving off Australia's Great Barrier Reef. There aren't as many colorful fish, and the water is cooler. In October, the visibility drops to about 18 to 20 meters because of a spring plankton bloom, though this attracts hungry marine life. The best places for novices are Nursery Cove and shallower parts of the South Harbour.

—Richard Pamatatau and Toni Mason

WHERE TO EAT

$$$$
MODERN NEW
ZEALAND

✗ **à Deco.** In a faithfully restored art deco house, this restaurant maintains a high standard, its reputation built on straightforward flavors and inventive twists using fresh, often organic, Northland ingredients. The ever-changing tasting menu includes either five or seven courses, each matched with local wine. The restaurant is closed for about two weeks over the Christmas break. $ *Average main: NZ$40* ⊠ *70 Kamo Rd.* ☎ *09/459–4957* ☉ *Closed Mon.*

$$$$ ✕ **Tonic.** Owner-chef Brad O'Connell's seasonal menu may be French-
FRENCH inspired, but it's flavored with New Zealand. You could say it is a form
Fodor's Choice of fusion cooking. Whenever possible Brad tries to buy local—anything
★ from lamb to pork—and his wine list includes a big selection from the
region. Whatever seafood the market has in the morning will be on
the menu in the evening. The local love for Tonic is intense, so be prepared to wait for a table. $ *Average main: NZ$32* ⊠ *239a Kamo Rd.*
☎ *09/437–5558* ⊕ *www.tonicrestaurant.co.nz/* ⊗ *No lunch.*

WHERE TO STAY

$$ ☉ **Chelsea House.** This beautiful renovated villa is a welcoming and
B&B/INN warm bed-and-breakfast establishment, and from the moment you step
onto the return veranda you might not want to leave. **Pros:** low key;
lovely environment. **Cons:** some may find it a bit basic. $ *Rooms from:*
NZ$135 ⊠ *83 Hatea Dr. 0112* ☎ *09/437–7115* ⊕ *www.chelsea-house.*
co.nz ⥅ *3 rooms.*

$$$ ☉ **Lodge Bordeaux.** With obvious references to France (but in a very Kiwi
B&B/INN way) Lodge Bordeaux offers comfortable and stylish accommodation.
FAMILY **Pros:** big; airy; smart. **Cons:** slightly clinical; is on a busy state highway. $ *Rooms from: NZ$270* ⊠ *361 Western Hills Dr.* ☎ *09/438–0404*
⊕ *www.lodgebordeaux.co.nz* ⥅ *15 rooms.*

$$$ ☉ **Lupton Lodge.** The country setting of Lupton Lodge makes it a per-
B&B/INN fect place to retreat to after a day's traveling in the North, with five
rooms, two apartments, a lovely big swimming pool, and gorgeous
gardens. **Pros:** knowledgeable, friendly hosts; pleasant locale; safe bike
storage. **Cons:** distance from town might be problematic for some
guests. $ *Rooms from: NZ$235* ⊠ *555 Ngunguru Rd.* ☎ *09/437–2989*
⊕ *www.luptonlodge.co.nz/* ⥅ *7 rooms.*

NIGHTLIFE

Killer Prawn Restaurant and Bar. This eatery doubles as Whangarei's night-
life hub and is part of the town's scenery. The food is good (but not
terribly chic). That said, they do know how to cook prawns. It's a great
place if you want a noisy, buzzy evening. ⊠ *28 Bank St.* ☎ *09/430–3333*
⊕ *www.killerprawn.co.nz.*

SHOPPING

Fodor's Choice **Burning Issues Gallery.** Specializing in contemporary fine glass, ceramics,
★ and jewelry, Burning Issues Gallery is one of the best places in North-
land to buy locally made arts and crafts and work from some of the
country's best artisans. Look for beautifully carved *pounamu* (New
Zealand greenstone) and bone pendants. The silver and gold jewelry
and small ceramic items are perfect for tiny take-home gifts. ⊠ *8 Quay-*
side, Town Basin ☎ *64 9/438–3108* ⊕ *www.burningissuesgallery.co.nz.*

Quarry Craft Co-op Shop. A cooperative of local craftspeople, including
jewelers, potters, wood turners, and weavers, runs the Quarry Craft
Co-op Shop. You will find unique crafts, including jewelry made from
kauri gum. The cooperative also runs courses—some only a day long—
so check the website. You may end up making your own souvenir.
The co-op is also home to residential craftspeople dedicated to pre-
serving the art of wood turning and hand-printing. ⊠ *21 Selwyn Ave.*
☎ *09/438–9884* ⊕ *www.quarryarts.org.*

SPORTS AND THE OUTDOORS
DIVING
Dive Tutukaka. Dive trips with Dive Tutukaka to the spectacular Poor Knights Islands include rented gear. Lunch is extra but inexpensive. You can also sail on *The Perfect Day*, a 70-foot luxury multilevel boat between November and April. This trip includes a half day of sightseeing, with the option to go kayaking, snorkeling, and diving. Free transfers to and from Whangarei are provided. ⊠ *Poor Knights Dive Centre, Marina Rd., Tutukaka* ☎ *09/434–3867* ⊕ *www.diving.co.nz* ✉ *From NZ$269.*

3

HOKIANGA AND THE KAURI COAST

85 km (53 miles) west of Paihia.

A peaceful harbor moves inland into the Hokianga region. It's a quiet area with small towns, unspoiled scenery, and proximity to the giant kauri trees on the Kauri Coast, a 20-minute drive south on Highway 12. Here the highway winds through Waipoua State Forest, then stretches south to Kaipara Harbour. Giant golden sand dunes tower over the mouth of Hokianga Harbour, across the water from the twin settlements of Omapere and Opononi. Opononi is the place where Opo, a tame dolphin, came to play with swimmers in the mid-1950s, putting the town on the national map for the first and only time in its history. A statue in front of the pub commemorates the much-loved creature.

GETTING HERE AND AROUND
The best way to get to the Hokianga is to drive; from Auckland turn left at the bottom of the Bryderwyn Hills and follow the road. There is generally one bus service a day from Auckland, but there is no airport or train service.

TOURS
Footprints–Waipoua. The night tours to see Tane Mahuta and Te Matua Ngahere are led by local Māori guides, experienced bushmen who enrich your experience with their knowledge of the forest and wildlife, *waiata* (traditional Māori song), and tales from Māori legend. Spend four hours on the Twilight Encounter; a shortened version, Meet Tane at Night, takes 1½ hours. If you're really pressed for time, but want more than your own self-guided 10-minute jaunt, there is also a 40-minute tour. ⊠ *334 State Hwy. 12, Omapere* ☎ *09/405–8207* ⊕ *www.footprintswaipoua.co.nz* ✉ *From NZ$25.*

VISITOR INFORMATION
Contacts Hokianga Visitor Information Centre. ⊠ 29 State Hwy. 12, Omapere ☎ 09/405–8869 ⊕ www.northlandnz.com. **Kauri Coast i-SITE Visitor Centre.** ⊠ 4 Murdoch St., Dargaville ☎ 09/439–4975 ⊕ www.kauriinfocentre.co.nz.

EXPLORING
TOP ATTRACTIONS
Matakohe Kauri Museum. South of Dargaville is Matakohe, a pocket-size town with an outstanding attraction: the Matakohe Kauri Museum. The museum's intriguing collection of artifacts, tools, photographs, documents, and memorabilia traces the story of the pioneers who settled

this area in the second half of the 19th century—a story interwoven with the kauri forests. The furniture and a complete kauri house are among the superb examples of craftsmanship. One of the most fascinating displays is of kauri gum, the transparent lumps of resin that form when the sticky sap of the kauri tree hardens. This gum, which was used to make varnish, can be polished to a warm, lustrous finish that looks remarkably like amber—right down to the occasional insects trapped and preserved inside—and this collection is the biggest in the world. **Volunteers Hall** contains a huge kauri slab running from one end of the hall to the other, and there is also a reproduction of a cabinet-maker's shop, and a chain-saw exhibit. The Steam Saw Mill illustrates how the huge kauri logs were cut into timber. Perhaps the best display is the two-story replica of a late 1800s to early 1900s boardinghouse. Rooms are set up as they were more than 100 years ago; you can walk down the hallways and peer in at the goings-on of the era. If you like the whirring of engines, the best day to visit is Wednesday, when much of the museum's machinery is started up. ⊠ *5 Church Rd., Matakohe* ☎ *09/431–7417* ⊕ *www.kaurimuseum.com* ⌦ *NZ$25* ☉ *Daily 9–5.*

Fodor's Choice   **Waipoua State Forest.** Kauri forests once covered this region. Waipoua
★   State Forest contains the largest collection of the remaining trees. A short path leads from the parking area on the main road through the forest to **Tane Mahuta,** "Lord of the Forest," and the largest tree in New Zealand. It stands nearly 173 feet high, measures 45 feet around its base, and is 1,200 to 2,500 years old. The second-largest tree, older by some 800 years, is **Te Matua Ngahere,** about a 20-minute walk from the road. If you have a few hours to spare you can visit Te Matua Ngahere and other trees of note. Head to the Kauri Walks parking lot about a mile south of the main Tane Mahuta parking lot. From there you trek past the **Four Sisters,** four kauri trees that have grown together in a circular formation, then the **Yakas Tree** (named after an old kauri-gum digger), and Te Matua Ngahere. The forest has a campground—check at the visitor center before you pitch a tent. Facilities include toilets, hot showers, and a communal cookhouse. When it's wet, you may spot large kauri snails in the forest. Also, the successful eradication of predators such as weasels and stoats has led to a rise in the number of kiwis in the forest. You'll need a flashlight to spot one because the birds only come out at night. The Waipoua campground and Waipoua Visitor Centre is managed by Te Iwi O Te Roroa, the local Māori tribe. ⊠ *Waipoua Visitor Centre, 1 Waipoua River Rd., Waipoua* ☎ *09/439–6445* ⊕ *www. kauricoast.com/waipoua-forest-visitors-centre/.*

WORTH NOTING

Dargaville. Sixty-four kilometers (40 miles) south of the Waipoua Forest along the Kaihu River, you'll come to sleepy Dargaville, once a thriving river port and now a good place to stock up if you're planning to camp in any of the nearby forests. It has some good craft stores, too. The surrounding region is best known for its main cash crop, the purple-skinned sweet potato known as *kūmara.* You'll see field after field dedicated to this root vegetable. ⊠ *Dargaville* ☎ *09/439–4975* ⊕ *www.dargaville.co.nz/.*

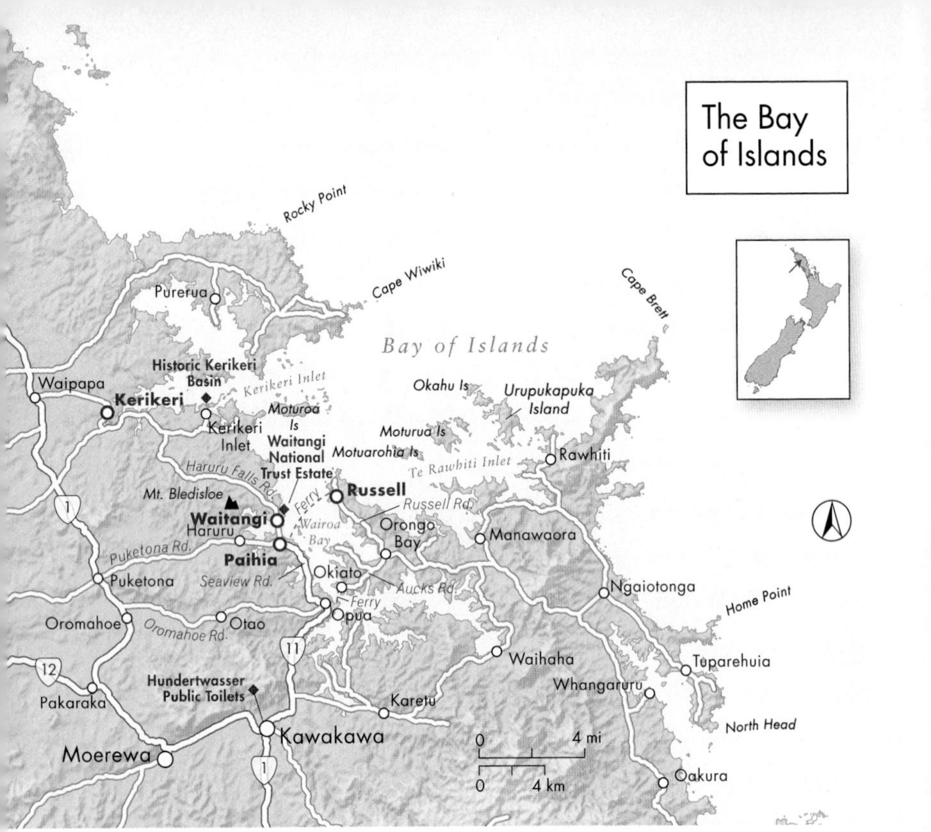
The Bay of Islands
Rocky Point
Cape Wiwiki
Cape Brett
Purerua
Bay of Islands
Historic Kerikeri Basin
Kerikeri Inlet
Waipapa
Kerikeri
Okahu Is
Urupukapuka Island
Moturoa Is
Kerikeri Inlet
Moturua Is
Waitangi National Trust Estate
Motuarohia Is
Te Rawhiti Inlet
Rawhiti
Haruru Falls Rd.
Mt. Bledisloe
Russell
Ferry
Russell Rd.
Waitangi
Haruru
Wairoa Bay
Orongo Bay
Manawaora
Puketona Rd.
Paihia
Puketona
Seaview Rd.
Okiato
Aucks Rd.
Ngaiotonga
Home Point
Ferry
Opua
Oromahoe
Otao
Oromahoe Rd.
Waihaha
Tuparehuia
Hundertwasser Public Toilets
Whangaruru
Pakaraka
Karetu
North Head
Kawakawa
Moerewa
0
4 mi
0
4 km
Oakura

Mangungu Mission House. The 1838 Mangungu Mission House is an overlooked stop on the tourist trail. Although Waitangi is the most famous site of New Zealand's founding document, this unassuming spot, which looks out over Hokianga Harbour, was the scene of the second signing of the Treaty. Here, on February 12, 1840, the largest gathering of Māori chiefs signed the Treaty of Waitangi (73 chiefs, compared with about 40 in Waitangi's signing). The house is now a museum, furnished with pre-Treaty missionary items, including portraits, photographs, and furniture. ✉ *Motukiore Rd., Hokianga Harbour, Horeke* ☎ *09/407–0470* 🌐 *www.heritage.org.nz/places/places-to-visit/northland-region/mangungu-mission* 🎟 *NZ$10* 🕓 *Nov.–Apr., weekends noon–4; May–Oct., Sun. noon–4; summer and Easter school holidays, Thurs.–Mon. noon–4.*

WHERE TO EAT AND STAY

$ 🍴 **Boatshed Café and Crafts.** This café is on the waterfront adjacent to the
NEW ZEALAND Rawene supermarket, craft shop, and ferry ramp. It's got a lovely outdoor deck and is a good place to take a coffee and slice of pizza while waiting for the ferry. [$] *Average main: NZ$13* ✉ *8 Clendon Esplanade, Rawene* ☎ *09/405–7728* 🕓 *No dinner.*

$$ 🏨 **Copthorne Hotel and Resort Hokianga.** From the deck of this charming
HOTEL seaside hotel you look straight out to the mouth of Hokianga Har-
FAMILY bour, where the view hasn't changed since, according to legend, the

Polynesian navigator Kupe first arrived in New Zealand 1,000 years ago. **Pros:** low key; on the beach; great views. **Cons:** rooms without a view aren't as special; service can be patchy. $ *Rooms from: NZ$139* ⊠ *State Hwy. 12, Omapere* ☎ *09/405–8737* ⊕ *www.millenniumhotels. co.nz/copthornehokianga/* ⤶ *37 rooms, 9 suites.*

$$ **RENTAL** 🖫 **Kauri Coast Top 10 Holiday Park.** Come for the spotless and varied lodging configurations—cabins with or without kitchens, and with or without bathrooms, as well as self-contained apartments; stay for the spectacular nighttime exploration of Trounson Kauri Park that promises looming kauri trees and maybe even a kiwi bird or two. **Pros:** good for families; inexpensive. **Cons:** gets crowded; not private. $ *Rooms from: NZ$135* ⊠ *Trounson Park Rd., 70 km (43 miles) south of Opononi, Kaihu* ☎ *09/439–0621* ⊕ *www.kauricoasttop10.co.nz* ⤶ *2 motel units, 3 apartments, 8 cabins, 60 campsites.*

$$$$ **B&B/INN** **Fodor's Choice** ★ 🖫 **Waipoua Lodge.** Renovations of this 100-year-old kauri farmhouse and its buildings have created a sophisticated and relaxing place to stay in the northern end of the North Island. **Pros:** friendly and warm; peaceful, gorgeous location; beautiful gardens. **Cons:** for some, the isolation may be too much. $ *Rooms from: NZ$583* ⊠ *State Hwy. 12, Waipoua* ☎ *09/439–0422* ⊕ *www.waipoualodge.co.nz* ⤶ *4 suites* ⊙| *Breakfast.*

THE BAY OF ISLANDS

The Bay of Islands was a large Māori settlement when Captain James Cook first anchored off Roberton Island in 1769. He noted "the inhabitants in this bay are far more numerous than in any other part of the country that we had visited." When the English started a convict settlement in Australia a couple of decades later, many boats stayed in the South Pacific to go whaling and sealing, and the Bay of Islands became a port of call. Consequently, many of the early European arrivals were sailors and whalers, stopping to blow off steam, have a few drinks, and trade with the local Māori. A missionary, Henry Williams, wrote in 1828 that a whaling captain had told him, "all the Europeans were in a state of intoxication, except himself and two others."

It took nearly a century for the Bay of Islands to get some positive reviews. American author Zane Grey visited in the 1920s to fish for marlin and was so impressed that he wrote a book about the bay called *Tales of the Angler's Eldorado.* Game fishing remains one of the bay's many draws, with record catches of marlin and mako shark, along with diving, boating, and swimming with dolphins. Many of the 144 islands were farms, but now only one, Motoroa, is still farmed; most others are now used for vacation homes.

TOURS

Great Sights. Book a one-, two-, or three-day trips to the Bay of Islands with this Auckland-based company. The one-day tour stops at Kaiwaka for morning tea and goes on to visit the Waitangi Treaty House and to cruise out to the Hole in the Rock. You can opt for a tour of historic Russell instead of the cruise. Taking the two-day tour allows you both to cruise and visit Russell, and the three-day itinerary adds a trip along 90 Mile Beach to Cape Reinga, where the Tasman Sea and

Pacific Ocean meet. ✉ *Discover New Zealand Centre, 102 Hobson St., Auckland* ☎ *09/583–5790* ⊕ *www.greatsights.co.nz* ✉ *From NZ$240.*

PAIHIA AND WAITANGI

69 km (43 miles) north of Whangarei.

As the main vacation base for the Bay of Islands, Paihia is an unremarkable stretch of motels at odds with the quiet beauty of the island-studded seascape. With its handful of hostels, plus the long and safe swimming beach, it's popular with a young backpacker crowd. Most of the boat and fishing tours leave from the central wharf, as do the passenger ferries to the historic village of Russell. The nearby suburb of Waitangi, however, is one of the country's most important historic sites. The Treaty Grounds, a lovely nearby park, was where the Treaty of Waitangi, the founding document for modern New Zealand, was signed.

The main Bay of Islands visitor bureau, in Paihia, is open daily. There is a really good toilet facility at the southern end of the strip.

GETTING HERE AND AROUND

Bus Depot Paihia. ✉ *InterCity Travel Centre, Maritime Bldg., Marsden Rd., Paihia* ☎ *09/402–7857.*

VISITOR INFORMATION

Contacts Bay of Islands Visitor Information Centre Paihia. ✉ *Marsden Rd., Paihia* ☎ *09/402–7345* ⊕ *www.bayofislands.co.nz.*

EXPLORING

TOP ATTRACTIONS

Fodor'sChoice
★
Waitangi National Trust Estate. Take in a major site in New Zealand's history at the northern end of Paihia. You'll gain a better understanding of the at-times tangled relationship between Māori and the British colonizers. The visitor center presents the events that led to the Treaty of Waitangi. You'll also be able to experience *kapa haka,* a live Māori cultural performance. The center also displays Māori artifacts and weapons, including a musket that belonged to Hone Heke Pokai, the first Māori chief to sign the treaty. After his initial enthusiasm for British rule, Hone Heke was quickly disillusioned, and less than five years later he attacked the British in their stronghold at Russell. From the visitor center, follow a short track (trail) through the forest to **Ngatoki Matawhaorua** (ng-ga-to-ki ma-ta- *fa*-oh- *roo*-ah), a Māori war canoe. This huge kauri canoe, capable of carrying 80 paddlers and 55 passengers, named after the vessel in which Kupe, the Polynesian navigator, is said to have discovered New Zealand. It was built in 1940 to mark the centennial of the signing of the Treaty of Waitangi.

The **Treaty House** in Waitangi Treaty Grounds is a simple white-timber cottage. The interior is fascinating, especially the back, where exposed walls demonstrate the difficulties that early administrators faced—such as an acute shortage of bricks (since an insufficient number had been shipped from New South Wales, as Australia was known at the time) with which to finish the walls.

3

The Treaty House was prefabricated in New South Wales for British Resident James Busby, who arrived in New Zealand in 1832. Busby had been appointed to protect British commerce and put an end to the brutalities of the whaling captains against the Māori, but he lacked the judicial authority and the force of arms necessary to impose peace. On one occasion, unable to resolve a dispute between Māori tribes, Busby was forced to shelter the wounded of one side in his house. While tattooed warriors screamed war chants outside the windows, one of the Māori sheltered Busby's infant daughter, Sarah, in his cloak.

The real significance of the Treaty House lies in the events that took place here on February 6, 1840, the day the Treaty of Waitangi was signed by Māori chiefs and Captain William Hobson, representing the British crown. The Treaty House has not always received the care its significance merits. When Lord Bledisloe, New Zealand's governor-general between 1930 and 1935, bought the house and presented it to the nation in 1932, it was being used as a shelter for sheep.

Whare Runanga (fah-ray roo-nang-ah) is a traditional meetinghouse with elaborate Māori carvings inside. The house is on the northern boundary of Waitangi Treaty Grounds. ⊠ *Waitangi Rd., Waitangi* ☎ *09/402–7437* ⊕ *www.waitangi.org.nz* ✏ *Adult NZ$25, under 18 free, guided tour add NZ$10, cultural performance add NZ$10, package NZ$40* ☉ *Daily 9–5.*

WORTH NOTING

FAMILY **Mt. Bledisloe.** On the National Trust Estate beyond the Treaty Grounds, Mt. Bledisloe showcases the splendid view across Paihia and the Bay of Islands. The handsome ceramic marker at the top showing the distances to major world cities was made by Doulton in London and presented by Lord Bledisloe in 1934 during his term as governor-general of New Zealand. The mount is 3 km (2 miles) from the Treaty House, on the other side of the Waitangi Golf Course. From a small parking area on the right of Waitangi Road, a short track rises above a pine forest to the summit. ⊠ *Mt Bledisloe, Waitangi.*

EN ROUTE **The Hundertwasser Public Toilets.** On the main street of Kawakawa, a nondescript town just off State Highway 1 south of Paihia, stand surely the most outlandish public toilets in the country—a must-go even if you don't need to. Built by Austrian artist and architect Friedensreich Hundertwasser in 1997, the toilets are fronted by brightly colored ceramic columns supporting an arched portico, which in turn supports a garden of grasses. There are no straight lines in the building, which is furnished inside with mostly white tiles, punctuated with primary colors, and set in black grout (something like a Mondrian after a few drinks). Plants sprout from the roof. If you sit in one of the cafés across the road you can watch the tourist buses stop so the visitors can take pictures of the facilities. ⊠ *Gillies St.* ⊕ *www.bay-of-islands-nz.com/hundertwasser.shtml.*

WHERE TO STAY

$$$ ⊞ **Abri.** These freestanding studio apartments resemble tree houses and HOTEL provide lovely sea views from the bush behind the Paihia beachfront. **Pros:** close to town; friendly hosts; whirlpool baths. **Cons:** entrance

The Māori National Festival in Waitangi commemorates the signing of the Waitangi treaty.

up a staircase. $ *Rooms from: NZ$235* ✉ *10–12 Bayview Rd., Paihia* ☎ *09/402–8003* ⊕ *www.abriapartments.co.nz/* ➥ *2 studios, 1 suite* ⦿ *No meals.*

$
HOTEL

🛏 **Austria Motel.** The large, double-bed rooms are typical of motel accommodations in the area—clean and moderately comfortable but devoid of character. **Pros:** friendly; covered off-street parking; close to town. **Cons:** basic. $ *Rooms from: NZ$95* ✉ *36 Selwyn Rd., Paihia* ☎ *09/402–7480* ⊕ *www.austria.motel.net.nz* ➥ *8 rooms* ⦿ *No meals.*

$$$
HOTEL

🛏 **Bay Adventurer.** If you are traveling on a budget with the family this place is perfect, with dorm rooms, studios, and one-bedroom apartments, which have kitchens, bathrooms, and TVs, and two-bedroom apartments. **Pros:** some women-only dorms; fun environment; pool and hot tub. **Cons:** noisy; eclectic clientele. $ *Rooms from: NZ$225* ✉ *28 Kings Rd., Paihia* ☎ *09/402–5162* ⊕ *www.bayadventurer.co.nz* ➥ *14 dorm rooms, 7 doubles, 9 apartments* ⦿ *Breakfast.*

$$
HOTEL

🛏 **Copthorne Hotel and Resort Bay of Islands.** The biggest hotel north of Auckland and a favorite with tour groups, this complex sprawls along a peninsula within walking distance of the Treaty House. **Pros:** most rooms have a terrace or patio; French provincial style; lovely location. **Cons:** some rooms need refreshing. $ *Rooms from: NZ$200* ✉ *Tau Henare Dr., Waitangi* ☎ *09/402–7411* ⊕ *www.copthornebayofislands.co.nz* ➥ *138 rooms, 7 suites* ⦿ *Breakfast.*

$$$$
RESORT
FAMILY

🛏 **Paihia Beach Resort and Spa.** A large *pohutukawa* tree stands next to the heated saltwater pool in front, and all of the rooms have bay views, a deck or patio, and a large whirlpool tub in the bathroom. **Pros:** close to town; stunning views; family packages available. **Cons:** road noise.

$ *Rooms from: NZ$555* ✉ *116 Marsden Rd., Paihia* ☎ *09/402–0111* ⊕ *www.paihiabeach.co.nz* ⤳ *19 rooms, 2 suites* ☯ *Breakfast.*

SPORTS AND THE OUTDOORS

Getting out on the water is a highlight of the Bay of Islands whether on the ferry crossing from Paihia to Russell or on a trip. The coastal areas are also lovely places to stroll, especially in summer. Those who love to fish will find the charter providers all have their secret spots to snag the big one.

BOATING

Carino NZ Sailing and Dolphin Adventures. Get close to dolphins (primarily bottlenose) and penguins. Passengers on the 50-foot red catamaran can just relax or pitch in with sailing. This full-day trip (NZ$120) includes a barbecue lunch at one of the islands, weather permitting, and a full bar is on board. This company has a permit that allows guests to swim with dolphins. The tours do not run in the winter months. ✉ *Paihia Wharf Marsden Rd.* ☎ *09/402–8040* ⊕ *www.sailingdolphins.co.nz.*

Fodor's Choice ★

Dolphin Eco Experience. Trips come with an option to "Swim with the Dolphins." You might also spot Bryde's whales, migrating humpback and orca whales, or groups of tiny blue penguins. Prices begin at NZ$102. ✉ *Marsden and Williams Rds., Paihia* ☎ *09/402–7421* ⊕ *www.dolphincruises.co.nz.*

Fodor's Choice ★

Fullers. Cruises and sea-based adventure trips depart daily from both Paihia and Russell. The most comprehensive sightseeing trip is the six-hour, summer-only Best of the Bay Supercruise (NZ$127) aboard a high-speed catamaran. You'll follow about half of what was once called the "Cream Trip" route, but nowadays, instead of picking up cream from farms, the boat delivers mail and supplies to vacation homes. Fullers also visits Urupukapuka Island, once home to a *hapu* (subtribe) of the Ngare Raumati Māori. Little is known about their life, but there are numerous archaeological sites. It's also the only one to go to Otehei Bay, one of the island's most spectacular bays. On this particular trip, the boat stops for 1½ hours on the island, where you can go kayaking, take a short hike, or have lunch at the Zane Grey Café. The trip also takes in the Hole in the Rock, a natural hole at sea level in Piercy Island that boats pass through if the tide is right. During winter there is a shorter NZ$105 trip that is mostly focused on finding dolphins. ✉ *Maritime Bldg., Marsden Rd., Paihia* ☎ *09/402–7421* ⊕ *www.dolphincruises.co.nz.*

DIVING

The Bay of Islands has some of the finest scuba diving in the country, particularly around Cape Brett, where the marine life includes moray eels, stingrays, and grouper. The wreck of the Greenpeace vessel *Rainbow Warrior,* bombed and sunk by French agents in 1985, is another underwater highlight. The wreck was transported to the Cavalli Islands in 1987 and is now covered in soft corals and jewel anemones; it's full of fish life. Water temperature at the surface varies from 16°C (62°F) in July to 22°C (71°F) in January. From September through November, underwater visibility can be affected by a plankton bloom.

Continued on page 132

CARVING

Although pre-European Māori did not have a written language, their traditional carvings served as a historical record. Every piece has a *kaupapa* (story), which can be read by those who know how. The shape of the heads, position of the body, and surface patterns work together to commemorate important events.

MĀORI ART

By
Debra A. Klein

Kiwi culture weaves together Māori and *Pakeha* (European) traditions. Māori symbols crop up in everything from the popular whale's tail pendants to a major airline's modernized koru logo. Today Māori art, likewise, melds traditional storytelling with modern concerns.

It wasn't always this way, but since the 1970s there has been a resurgence of, and interest in, Māori culture throughout New Zealand. Days begin with the Māori greeting, "kia ora," literally "be well," offered by Māoris and pakeha alike. Kiwis cheer the world-famous All Blacks rugby squad when they perform the *haka*—that fierce warrior dance that intimidates opposing teams.

There has even been a renaissance in Māori arts, crafts, and body art. Weavers gather by the hundreds to participate in the *hui* workshop. Reviving an ancient tradition they work their *harakeke* (flax) materials into baskets and skirts.

Tens of thousands of spectators attend the biannual Māori performance competition at the Te Matatini arts festival. In Rotorua, center of modern Māori life in New Zealand, there are nightly traditional chants and *hangi* feasts. Galleries all over New Zealand celebrate works of contemporary artists who express strong or glancing Māori influences in their pieces, and visitors and locals alike mimic traditional Māori *moku*, or tattoos.

Many Māori artisans see this integration as essential to preserving their culture.

Above: Whare runanga (meeting house), Waitangi

TRADITIONAL ART

Traditional Māori art is symbolic, not literal, and recurring motifs appear on meeting houses, in jewelry, and on objects. Some shapes and symbols come from nature, others represent ancestors or the geographical region of an *iwi*, or tribe.

Koru—The curled fern frond symbolizes beginnings or life, as well as peace and strength.

Hei Matau—The fish hook is a popular talisman for safe journeys over water. It also represents prosperity.

Hei Tiki—The small human figure with a tilted head depicts a fetus in the womb and symbolizes fertility.

Hiku—New Zealanders frequently wear the whale's tail, which is a sign of strength and speed.

MASKS

North Island styles of face mask include Tai Tokerau, Tai Rawhiti, and Rongo-whakaata, and are distinguished by the parallel, angular lines framing the eyes. Koruru, found in the mid-North Island area, are masks characterized by rounded, bulging eyes. The point at the top of the Taranaki mask symbolizes Mount Taranaki. In the Coromandel area, look for tell-tale paua shell eyes in the Pare Hauraki and hollow eye sockets in the Te Whanau a Apanui. The Te Arawa Māori, who live between Rotorua and Lake Taupo, make Ruru masks with pointed ears representing a small owl.

WOOD CARVING

Whakairo (carving) holds an important place in Māori culture; it functions as both an art form and a historical record. Each line and shape has meaning, and each design connects the physical object with *mana*, or spiritual power. Intricately carved Māori meeting houses and raised storehouses, seen on both islands, demonstrate the Māori practice of designing and patterning objects to imbue them with the spirits of ancestors. For an excellent example, visit the meeting house and war canoe on the Treaty of Waitangi grounds on the North Island.

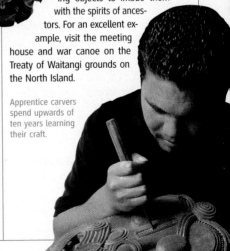

Apprentice carvers spend upwards of ten years learning their craft.

TEKOTEKO AND OTHER OBJECTS

This ancestral face on an archway greets visitors to a marae.

Tekoteko, carved human figures, adorn Māori meeting houses, homes, and, traditionally, canoe prows. These symbolic ancestors' defiant stances, protruding tongues, and weapons ward off intruders. Other carved items include ceremonial war paddles (*wahaika*), spears (*taiaha*), treasure boxes, and sticks. Look for these carvings at a marae or in museums and galleries.

PAINTINGS (KOWHAIWHAI)

Decorative patterns, called *kowhaiwhai*, are considered less sacred than wood carvings or tattoo-making and can be done by anyone. Find these temporary designs on meeting-house ridgepoles and rafters, canoe bottoms, and paddles. The standard black, white, and red paints mimic the colors produced by red ochre, white clay, and charcoal, the materials used by Māori ancestors. Designs can represent speed and swiftness or hospitality and strength.

Above: The koru symbol is common in Māori style painting.

MĀORI TA MOKO

Unlike contemporary ink tattoos, traditional Māori *moku* (tattoos) were literally carved into the body with a tool called an *uhi*, filled with soot from burnt plants or caterpillars, and covered with leaves to heal.

Only those of high rank wore facial tattoos, and they were recognized by these patterns rather than by the natural features we use to describe people today. Segments of the face were reserved for identifying features related to the social rank of the wearer's family; for example, sections on each side of the face depicted the ancestry from the mother's and father's sides.

Markings also commemorated important events in a person's life and, except for some tribes that had tattoos on their legs and buttocks, were confined to the face. Women's tattoos were, and still are, limited to an outline around the lips and thin lines from the lips down the chin. This pattern is still worn in ink tattoos today.

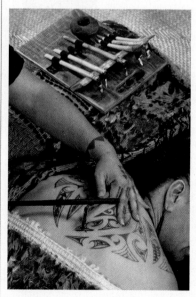

Today, talented Ta Moko artists continue the deeply spiritual traditions of ancient Māori tattooing.

MODERN MĀORI ART

Contemporary Māori artists work in every medium, including music, weaving, crafts, film, and visual entertainment and often contain subtle cultural references or overt interpretations of historic symbols.

Museums, such as the comprehensive **Te Papa** (in Wellington), the **Auckland Art Gallery**, and tiny **Suter Art Gallery** (in Nelson), exhibit a range of art that may include portraits of Māori and their Ta Moku from the last century or modern, mixed-media art by pan-Pacific artists commenting on current events.

Contemporary artwork with traditional Māori influences

MĀORI JEWELRY AND SOUVENIRS

Māori symbols are common in contemporary pendants that are crafted of plastic and wood and hung on a braided cord. More expensive versions are made of greenstone (jade), once used for chisels and weaponry, or bone. These necklaces are popular souvenirs.

Traditional Māori pendant carved from greenstone (jade)

Many contemporary artists take the idea of these traditional pendants and reinterpret motifs in fresh ways. A modern necklace may reference a pattern from a chief's cloak or hint at the fish hook without mimicking the the pattern. While such jewelry may come in greenstone, some artists work with metals like silver or gold instead.

Modern angular and traditional rounded wooden treasure boxes, called *wakahuia*, incorporate Māori symbols.

Contemporary textile artists blend traditional materials such as flax, tree bark pigments, and feathers with nontraditional colors to craft modern purses and wall hangings.

Popular souvenirs include greenstone, ceramics, synthetic feathers, decorative flax designs, replicas of paddles and war clubs, clothing, and jewelry. The Toi Iho certifies that items were produced by Māori artists (⊕ *www.toiiho. co.nz*). Not all Māori artists participate in the program; check carefully for authenticity.

This girl wears a greenstone pendant

BUYING MĀORI ART

Woven Kete pikau (back pack)

Māori ceramics with traditional motifs

WHERE TO BUY

Those seriously interested in Māori art and culture should visit Rotorua. Creative Rotorua (⊕ *www.creativerotorua.org.nz*) is an umbrella organization that links to arts organizations, performances, various area artists, and the local Māori Arts Trail, which maps out studios you can visit. If your trip coincides with Te Matatini, a dance showcase as well as the largest Māori arts festival in the world, scour the booths for authentic crafts (⊕ *www.tematatini.org.nz*).

If Rotorua isn't on your itinerary, seek out Māori galleries in Christchurch, Queenstown, Auckland, Wellington, and Whangarei. The Te Papa Museum in Wellington has a range of Māori-influenced New Zealand artworks, jewelry and prints. Most museum shops have reproductions of pieces in the collection and rare art books.

HOW TO CHOOSE

Buy what you like or choose a depiction of a place you visited. The connection you feel should motivate you more than the piece's resale value. If quality is important, seek authentication from a dealer.

CUSTOM MADE FOR YOU

New Zealand's small population and informal atmosphere allow for direct contact with artists. Visit their studios, attend a workshop, or chat with them about their pieces. Most artisans and craftspeople will happily custom-make a piece to forward to you at home. There are also dozens of online shops offering various Māori-themed wares if you regret not making a purchase after you return. By purchasing directly from the artist you'll get a one-of-a-kind piece, but don't expect a discount.

USEFUL WEB SITES

⊕ *www.maoriart.org.nz*
⊕ *www.maori.com*

The Moko, or facial tattoo, on this carved figure displays ancestral and tribal messages that apply to the wearer. These messages represent the wearer's family, sub-tribal and tribal affiliations, and his place within these social structures. This carving commemorates an ancestor.

Paihia Dive Compass Ltd. This company will take you around two significant sunken ships: the Greenpeace vessel *Rainbow Warrior* plus the former Royal New Zealand Navy vessel *Canterbury*. Accredited divers can rent equipment and the unaccredited can sign up for dive courses. Prices including equipment begin at NZ$229. ⊠ *7 Williams Rd., Paihia* ☎ *09/402–7551, 0800/107–551* ⊕ *www.divenz.com.*

FISHING

Spot-X. Charter a boat for the whole day for up to six people (about NZ$1,200) and leave as early as you like. If you don't have a whole day, a four-hour trip is on offer, too. You'll need to bring your lunch and cold drinks but the team that takes you out will supply tea and coffee and snacks. Word is these people know some good fishing spots and are skilled at filleting your catch, so you can take it back to where you're staying and cook it. They leave from Paihia but if you are staying in Russell or Waitangi they'll pick you up there. ☎ *09/402–7123* ⊕ *www.fish-spot-x.co.nz.*

RUSSELL

4 km (2½ miles) east of Paihia by ferry, 13 km (8 miles) by road and car ferry.

Russell is regarded as the "second" town in the Bay of Islands, but it's far more interesting, and pleasant, than Paihia. Hard as it is to believe, sleepy little Russell was once dubbed the "Hellhole of the Pacific." In the mid- to late 19th century (when it was still known by its Māori name, Kororareka) it was a swashbuckling frontier town, a haven for sealers and whalers who found the East Coast of New Zealand to be one of the richest whaling grounds on Earth.

Tales of debauchery abound. British administrators in New South Wales were sufficiently concerned to dispatch a British resident agent in 1832 to impose law and order. After the Treaty of Waitangi, Russell was the capital until 1844, when the Māori chief Hone Heke, disgruntled with newly imposed harbor dues and his loss of authority, cut down the flagstaff flying the Union Jack above the town three times before attacking the British garrison. Most of the town burned to the ground in what is known as the Sacking of Kororareka. Hone Heke was finally defeated in 1846, but Russell never recovered its former prominence, and the seat of government was shifted first to Auckland, then to Wellington.

Today Russell is a delightful town of timber houses and big trees that hang low over the seafront, framing the yachts and game-fishing boats in the harbor. The relaxed vibe can best be absorbed in a stroll along the Strand, the path along the waterfront. There are several safe swimming beaches, some in secluded bays, as well as the aptly named Long Beach, over the hill from the township.

GETTING HERE AND AROUND

The road between Russell and Paihia is long and tortuous. The best way to travel between the two is by passenger ferry, which leaves from the Russell Wharf, or by car ferry, which departs from Okiato, about 9 km (5½ miles) southwest of town.

VISITOR INFORMATION

Contacts Russell Information Centre. ✉ *Russell Wharf* ☎ *09/403–8020* ⊕ *www.russellinfo.co.nz.*

EXPLORING

TOP ATTRACTIONS

Christ Church. One of the donors to the construction of New Zealand's oldest church was Charles Darwin, who at that time in 1835 was making his way around the globe on board the HMS *Beagle*. Behind the white picket fence that borders the churchyard, gravestones tell a fascinating and brutal story of life in the colony's early days. Several graves belong to sailors from the HMS *Hazard* who were killed in this churchyard by Hone Heke's warriors in 1845. Another headstone marks the grave of a Nantucket sailor from the whaler *Mohawk*. As you walk around the church, look for the musket holes made when Hone Heke besieged the church. The interior is simple and charming—embroidered cushions on the pews are examples of a still-vibrant folk-art tradition ✉ *Church and Robertson Sts.* ⊙ *Daily 8–5.*

WORTH NOTING

FAMILY **Pompallier Mission.** New Zealand's oldest industrial building, the Pompallier Mission, at the southern end of the Strand, was named after the first Catholic bishop of the South Pacific. Marist missionaries built the original structure out of rammed earth, because they lacked the funds to buy timber. For several years the priests and brothers operated a press here, printing Bibles in the Māori language. From December through April you can visit independently, but from May to November the mission organizes tours at set times. ✉ *The Strand* ☎ *09/403–9025* ⊕ *www.pompallier.co.nz* 💲 *NZ$10* ⊙ *Daily 10–5.*

WHERE TO EAT

$$$$
MODERN NEW
ZEALAND
Fodor's Choice
★

✗ **The Gables Restaurant.** One of Russell's oldest buildings (built in 1847) is home to an up-to-the-minute kitchen, serving the finest cuts of meat, fresh fish, and imaginative vegetarian options. In for lunch? Try the chowder or the open steak sandwich. In the evening, slow-cooked oxtail or baked snapper are excellent options. The atmosphere is calm, the wine list decent, and the service is on point. 💲 *Average main: NZ$32* ✉ *19 The Strand* ☎ *09/403–7670* ⊕ *www.thegablesrestaurant.co.nz.*

$$$
SEAFOOD
FAMILY

✗ **Sally's.** At this restaurant overlooking Kororareka Bay from the Bay of Islands Swordfish Club building, Sally's seafood chowder, packed with fresh mussels, shrimp, and fish, is the most popular dish—despite numerous requests, the chef refuses to divulge the recipe. The Orongo Bay oysters (if available) are served three ways, and there's always the fish of the day and related seasonal produce. It gets very busy during the summer break. 💲 *Average main: NZ$30* ✉ *The Strand* ☎ *09/403–7652* ⊕ *sallysrestaurant.co.nz.*

$$$
NEW ZEALAND
Fodor's Choice
★

✗ **The Wharf.** The prime dining spot in Russell, this waterfront restaurant combines subtly prepared yet flavorsome cuisine with arguably the best restaurant view in town—especially if you nab a table up front. It specializes in cooking on very hot stones—everything from fish and steak to chicken and vegetables. There are tables across the road from the kitchen on the waterfront. It gets very busy in the holiday periods so book ahead. $ *Average main: NZ$30* ✉ *29 The Strand* ☎ *09/403–7771* ⊕ *thewharfrussell.co.nz/* ⊘ *Closed Mon.*

WHERE TO STAY

$$$
B&B/INN
Fodor's Choice
★

🏨 **Arcadia Lodge.** Rumor had it that this B&B, perched over Matauwhi Bay, a few minutes' walk from town, had been supported for more than 100 years by whale vertebrae. **Pros:** fantastic hosts; lovely rooms; spectacular views; decadent breakfast. **Cons:** finding the car park is tricky so follow the directions on the website. $ *Rooms from: NZ$295* ✉ *10 Florance Ave.* ☎ *09/403–7756* ⊕ *www.arcadialodge.co.nz/* ⇄ *5 rooms* ⦿ *Breakfast.*

$$$$
HOTEL

🏨 **Duke of Marlborough Hotel.** This waterfront hotel is a favorite with the yachting fraternity, for whom ready access to the harbor and the bar downstairs are the most important considerations. **Pros:** prime waterfront position; busy, lively crowd. **Cons:** can be too close to the action; quite noisy; no privacy. $ *Rooms from: NZ$360* ✉ *The Strand* ☎ *09/403–7829* ⊕ *www.theduke.co.nz* ⇄ *19 rooms, 6 suites, 1 cottage* ⦿ *Breakfast.*

$$$$
B&B/INN

🏨 **Flagstaff Lodge and Day Spa.** Though little about the exterior of this 1912 villa has changed, the inside has been restored with all modern conveniences and the addition of New Zealand art. **Pros:** good facilities; spa; hill-free stroll to the village; local wine and canapes in the evening. **Cons:** some might see its setting as a bit suburban. $ *Rooms from: NZ$425* ✉ *17 Wellington St.* ☎ *09/403–7117, 0800/403–711* ⊕ *www.flagstafflodge.co.nz* ⇄ *4 rooms* ⦿ *Breakfast.*

$$$$
B&B/INN

🏨 **The Homestead at Orongo Bay.** Tucked away in gardens off the road between the car-ferry landing and Russell, this historic lodge, built in 1865, soothes with peace and quiet—which is why it has hosted people like Jane Fonda and Joanna Lumley. **Pros:** convivial host; really good food; lovely garden. **Cons:** slightly out of town. $ *Rooms from: NZ$350* ✉ *45 Aucks Rd.* ☎ *09/403–7527* ⊕ *www.thehomestead.co.nz* ⇄ *3 rooms* ⦿ *Breakfast.*

SPORTS AND THE OUTDOORS

FISHING

Major Tom Charters. Chase game fish such as marlin, kingfish, *hapuka* (grouper), snapper, broadbill, and tuna. A full day, with a maximum of four anglers, is NZ$1,600 including lunch (hopefully you catch dinner). ☎ *09/403–8553* ⊕ *www.majortom.co.nz.*

HIKING

There are several pleasant walks around the Russell area; the most challenging—and spectacular—is the **Cape Brett Tramping Track** out to the lighthouse. It takes about eight hours round-trip. It costs NZ$30 to walk the track and you can stay in a hut for NZ$15 a night. You must book and pay in advance, as this is a popular walk. It is not for the unfit, and good shoes are a must. Check with the Russell Information Center on the wharf. For a shorter jaunt on your own (an hour each way), follow the **Whangamumu Walking Track** to the remnants of a whaling station. Many relics such as an old boiler and vats are still left at the station.

KERIKERI

20 km (12 miles) north of Paihia.

Kerikeri is often referred to as the cradle of the nation because so much of New Zealand's earliest history, especially interactions between Māori and Europeans, took place here. A major citrus and kiwifruit growing area, it was once principally a service town for the whole mid-north region. Though newcomers have flocked to Kerikeri for its low-key lifestyle, it still feels like a small town. The Sunday farmers' market is a treat.

The **Kerikeri Proctor Library,** open weekdays 8 to 5, and Saturday from 9:30 to 2, is the only place in Kerikeri that provides visitor information, and it's far less extensive than other bureaus.

GETTING HERE AND AROUND

Kerikeri is about four hours' drive from Auckland following State Highway 1. Buses connect from Auckland directly and from the other centers. There is also a good airport with regular flights, but it is expensive to fly, particularly from Auckland. There is no train service.

VISITOR INFORMATION

Contacts Kerikeri Proctor Library. ✉ *6 Cobham Rd.* ☎ *09/407–9297* ⊕ *www.kerikeri.co.nz.*

EXPLORING

TOP ATTRACTIONS

FAMILY **Historic Kerikeri Basin.** Most of the interest in Kerikeri lies just northeast of the modern town on the Kerikeri Inlet where you'll see the Stone Store, the country's oldest stone building. It was designed by the Wesleyan missionary John Hobbs, and built by Australian convict William Parrott. Behind it is Kemp House, known also as the Kerikeri Mission House, built about the same time as the store between 1832 and 1836 by the London-based Church Missionary Society.

It was built for the Reverend John Butler by missionary carpenters (though Māori sawed the timber) and the two-story structure is of simple Georgian design, with a hipped roof and symmetrical facade.

Viewers should be able to take from these buildings an idea of how Anglican missionaries attempted to re-create some of what they had left behind. They were invited to Kerikeri by its most famous historical figure, the great Māori chief Hongi Hika. The chief visited England in 1820, where he was showered with gifts. On his way back to New Zealand, during a stop in Sydney, he traded many of these presents for muskets. Having the advantage of these prized weapons, he set in motion plans to conquer other Māori tribes, enemies of his own Ngapuhi people. The return of his raiding parties over five years, with many slaves and gruesome trophies of conquest, put considerable strain between Hongi Hika and the missionaries. Eventually his warring ways were Hongi's undoing. He was shot in 1827 and died from complications from the wound a year later. ✉ *Kerikeri Basin, 246 Kerikeri Rd.*

Fodor's Choice ★   **Kerikeri Farmers' market.** If you're in Kerikeri on a Sunday, head to the market to sample and buy the best the region has to offer, from music to fresh produce, local wines, cheeses, preserves, oils, and handmade soaps. Grab a locally roasted coffee and wander among the stalls. ⊠ *Parking lot, off Hobson Ave.* ⊕ *www.kerikeri.co/bay-of-islands-farmers-market-kerikeri* ☉ *Sun. 9–noon.*

FAMILY   **Kerikeri Mission Station.** The station, which includes the 1821 **Mission House** and the **Stone Store**, provides a fascinating and rare look at pre-treaty New Zealand. **Kemp House,** otherwise known as Mission House, has gone through many changes since 1821, but ironically, a major flood in 1981 inspired its "authentic" restoration. The flood washed away the garden and damaged the lower floor, and during repair much information about the original structure of the house was revealed. Its ground floor and garden have been restored to the style of missionary days, and the upper floor retains its Victorian decoration.

Stone Store, New Zealand's oldest stone building, is a striking example of early colonial architecture. Designed by Wesleyan missionary John Hobbs and built by an Australian convict stonemason between 1832 and 1836, the Store was meant to house New Zealand mission supplies and large quantities of wheat from the mission farm at Te Waimate. When the wheat failed, the building was mainly leased as a kauri gum-trading store. The ground floor is still a shop. The upper stories display the goods of a culture trying to establish itself in a new country, such as red Hudson Bay blankets, which were sought after by Māori from the *pā* (hilltop fortification), forged goods, steel tools, an old steel flour mill, and tools and flintlock muskets—also prized by local Māori. Guided tours are available; bookings are essential. ⊠ *Kerikeri Historic Basin, Kerikeri Rd.* ☎ *09/407–9236* 🖾 *NZ$10* ☉ *Daily 10–4.*

WORTH NOTING

Kororipo Pā. Across the road from the Kerikeri Basin's Stone Store is a path leading to the historic site of Kororipo Pā, the fortified headquarters of chief Hongi Hika. Untrained eyes may have difficulty figuring out exactly where the pā (Māori fortification) was, as no structures are left. The pā was built on a steep-sided promontory between the Kerikeri River and the Wairoa Stream. ⊠ *Kororipo Pā.*

FAMILY   **Rewa's Village.** This museum re-creates a *kāinga* (unfortified fishing village) where local Māori lived in peaceful times. In times of war they took refuge in nearby Kororipo Pā. In the village are good reproductions of the chief Hongi Hika's house, the weapons store, and the family enclosure, as well as two original canoes dug up from local swamps and original *hāngi* stones which were heated by fire and used to cook traditional Māori feasts, found on-site. A "discoverers garden" takes you on a winding path past indigenous herbs and other plants; information is posted describing the uses of each plant. ⊠ *Kerikeri Historic Basin, Kerikeri Rd.* ☎ *09/407–6454* ⊕ *www.kerikeri.co.nz/Rewas_Village.cfm* 🖾 *NZ$5* ☉ *Nov.–Apr., daily 9:30–5:30; May–Oct., daily 10–4; Jan. and Feb., daily 9–5.*

CLOSE UP

Northern Northland

Above the Bay of Islands Northland are many small communities. For many the big attraction is **90 Mile Beach,** a 100-km (60-mile) or so long clear stretch of golden sand running up North Island's tip. You access it from **Kaitaia,** a vibrant town with an extremely good café—Birdies—where the omelets are not only delicious, they will set you up for the day. If you want to travel the beach, take a tour. Don't roll your eyes—a tour is the safest bet. The beach is virtually off-limits to independent travelers, as, thanks to quicksand and incoming tides, rental-car insurance won't cover you here.

Just out of Kaitaia are the beaches at Ahipara and Shipwrecks. Surfers love the long lines and almost perfect waves here. Many surfers head south around the point for even better waves and fewer people.

Cape Reinga, at the peninsula's end, is a sacred Māori area. They believe that spirits depart for the underworld by sliding down the roots of the headland's gnarled *pohutukawa* tree (reputed to be 800 years old) and into the sea. A much-photographed solitary lighthouse stands here.

You can easily drive into the Far North, barring 90 Mile Beach. From the Bay of Islands on State Highway 10 you'll reach Mangonui, a former whaling port on the southeast side of **Doubtless Bay.** Beach lovers should head for the Karikari Peninsula, on Doubtless Bay's northwestern side. From Doubtless Bay it's less than a half-hour drive west to Awanui, near the service town of Kaitaia. Fill your gas tank in one of these two towns, then head north on Highway 1. The last few miles to Cape Reinga aren't paved.

3

WHERE TO EAT

$$ CAFÉ 🍴 **Fishbone Café.** The coffee is good as is the big range of egg dishes, salads, and sandwiches. The menu for meals changes frequently and is built around seasonal produce, much of it from local suppliers. The wine list mixes local and international. [$] *Average main: NZ$20* ✉ *88 Kerikeri Rd.* ☎ *09/407–6065* 🌐 *www.fishbonecafe.co.nz* 🕒 *No dinner.*

$$$ ECLECTIC 🍴 **Marsden Estate Winery and Restaurant.** Named after the missionary Samuel Marsden, who planted New Zealand's first grapevines in Kerikeri in 1819, this winery is a popular lunch spot and for good reason. On a fine day ask for a table on the terrace. The seasonal menu is eclectic and is built around fresh seasonal produce. It is a great place for breakfast with vegan and gluten-free options available. Of the winery's small but notable output, the full-bodied Black Rocks Chardonnay has won national and international awards. All grapes are handpicked and grown on-site with the exception of the Viognier, which comes from a vineyard 90 minutes south, and the Sauvignon Blanc, which is from Marlborough in the South Island. [$] *Average main: NZ$30* ✉ *Wiroa Rd.* ☎ *09/407–9398* 🌐 *www.marsdenestate.co.nz* 🕒 *No dinner Sun.–Thurs.*

WHERE TO STAY

$$$$ B&B/INN 🏨 **Cavalli Beach House Retreat.** Curving down a cliff face like a spinnaker in full sail, this retreat overlooks a private horseshoe-shape bay. **Pros:** gorgeous architecture; superb location; intimate. **Cons:** not cheap. [$] *Rooms from: NZ$450* ✉ *Mahinepua Rd., Kaeo* ☎ *09/405–1049* 🌐 *www.cavallibeachhouse.com* 🛏 *1 suite, 2 rooms* 🍴 *Breakfast.*

$$$$ RESORT FAMILY Fodor's Choice ★ 🏨 **Kauri Cliffs Lodge.** Several holes of a par-72 championship golf course sweep past this cliff-top lodge, which is truly outstanding. **Pros:** absolute luxury; superb environment; sophisticated. **Cons:** possibly overwhelming for first-timers. [$] *Rooms from: NZ$725* ✉ *139 Tepene Tablelands Rd., Matauri Bay* ☎ *09/407–0010* 🌐 *www.kauricliffs.com* 🛏 *22 suites* 🍴 *Some meals.*

$ HOTEL 🏨 **Kauri Park.** This small cluster of chalets is a notch above the usual, with contemporary style and a magnificent setting among fruit trees adjacent to farmland. **Pros:** clean; relaxed; friendly. **Cons:** not within walking distance of town. [$] *Rooms from: NZ$110* ✉ *512 Kerikeri Rd.* ☎ *09/407–7629* 🌐 *www.kauripark.co.nz* 🛏 *9 units* 🍴 *No meals.*

$ HOTEL 🏨 **Mangonui Hotel.** This classic wooden two-story pub sits just a few feet from Mangonui's harbor and has a New Zealand Historic Places Trust classification. **Pros:** old-fashioned; in town; a place to meet locals. **Cons:** really basic; can be noisy. [$] *Rooms from: NZ$100* ✉ *Beach Rd., Mangonui* ☎ *09/406–0003* 🌐 *www.mangonuihotel.co.nz* 🛏 *13 rooms.*

$$ B&B/INN 🏨 **Paheke.** An enormous cedar of Lebanon stands in front of this gracious 1864 kauri homestead; both the tree and the house are listed with the Historic Places Trust. **Pros:** well priced; relaxing; stunning grounds. **Cons:** not close to town. [$] *Rooms from: NZ$195* ✉ *State Hwy. 1, Ohaeawai* ☎ *09/405–9623* 🌐 *www.paheke.co.nz* 🛏 *4 rooms, 2 with bath* 🍴 *Breakfast.*

SHOPPING

FAMILY **Makana Confections.** Favorites include the macadamia butter toffee crunch; chocolate-coated, locally grown macadamias; and liqueur truffles. The products at this boutique place are fabulous. ✉ *504 Kerikeri Rd.* ☎ *09/407–6800* 🌐 *www.makana.co.nz.*

SPORTS AND THE OUTDOORS

GOLF

Fodor's Choice ★ **Kauri Cliffs.** The spectacular par-72 championship course at Kauri Cliffs has four sets of tees to challenge every skill level. Fifteen holes have views of the Pacific, and six are played alongside the cliffs. Kauri Cliffs is approximately 45 minutes' drive from Kerikeri. ✉ *139 Tepene Tablelands Rd., Matauri Bay* ☎ *09/407–0010* 🌐 *www.kauricliffs.com* 🎟 *NZ$475 per person, Oct.–Apr.; NZ$313, May–Sept.*

THE COROMANDEL
AND THE BAY
OF PLENTY

WELCOME TO THE COROMANDEL AND THE BAY OF PLENTY

TOP REASONS TO GO

★ **Beach Bounty:** The seemingly endless coastline here is replete with forest-fringed inlets, sprawling sand dunes, and many of the country's most popular beaches.

★ **Vistas:** From the Coromandel's coastal cliffs to Bay of Plenty's volcanic peak, Mauao, great views abound.

★ **Walking and Hiking:** Climb Mauao (The Mount) for stunning coastal views, or take a forest walk to swim in a lagoon formed by Kaiate Falls. Coromandel Forest Park has a network of trails.

★ **Cycling and Gold:** Explore gold-mining history as you ride the gentle Hauraki Cycle Trail, through forested Karangahake and Waikino gorges.

★ **Watery Wonders:** Dive or snorkel in the region's marine reserves, or swim with dolphins. Charter a deep-sea fishing trip, or kayak beneath glowworms by moonlight.

1 **The Coromandel.** The Coromandel Peninsula beckons from the Hauraki Plains like a big lizard lying in the sun—the dark forest on the central mountainous spine promising more than just pretty pictures. When you arrive at the peninsula you'll be surprised how lush the forest growth is, wonder at how the road hugs the coast literally feet above the water, and understand why people like living here.

2 **The Bay of Plenty.** People refer to the Bay of Plenty as New Zealand's food bowl—as in plenty of food. Some of the most fertile land for fruit and vegetables is found in the region, and seafood is abundant.

GETTING ORIENTED

The Coromandel and Bay of Plenty regions are about two to three hours southeast of Auckland and west of the Waikato farming district and are a mix of rugged and forested hill country and rich plains used for horticulture. They are about a seven- to nine-hour drive from Wellington and one to two hours from Hamilton and Rotorua. Many of the Coromandel's small settlements are based on former ports, established to transport logs in earlier days, when the forests were milled. Bay of Plenty, with its strong horticultural focus, is dotted with small rural towns fanning out from Tauranga's large port. You can fly over or take a boat to see an active marine volcano on White Island off the coast of Whakatane. The steaming fissures are dramatic whether viewed by sea, air, or standing on the marine volcano itself.

4

Updated by
Kathy Ombler

Beautiful sandy beaches, lush native forests, and some steamy geothermal activity make the Coromandel and Bay of Plenty quite a departure from urban Auckland. Many residents live in fishing villages or small rural towns, with the occasional artsy or alternative-lifestyle community thrown in, particularly in the Coromandel.

Both areas bask in more than their fair share of sun for much of the year, so avocado, citrus, kiwifruit, nuts, and even subtropical fruits flourish here, and many growers adopt organic practices. Keep an eye out for the ubiquitous unmanned fruit stands accompanied by "honesty boxes."

Both regions are hugely popular holiday spots for New Zealanders, the beaches and bays, the fishing, surfing, and kayaking on the water and the land-based bush and coastal walks and cycle trails draw people, especially in the summer holidays in January. Join them, or perhaps more wisely, time your trip to avoid the crowds—the weather will still be good.

Follow State Highway 25—the Pacific Coast Highway—as it meanders up the west coast and down the east coast of the peninsula. Traffic can build up on this road, particularly in the busy summer months or weekends. As you drive south down the peninsula's east coast, the Pacific Highway stretches out to the coastal plains and forests of the Bay of Plenty.

From the Bay of Plenty's northern gateway of Katikati as far as Whakatane and Ohope Beach, the coastline consists of huge stretches of sand, interrupted by rivers, estuaries, and sandbars. Inland, the soil is rich and fertile; this is horticulture territory with sprawling canopies of kiwifruit vines, fields of corn and other produce, and pockets of dense native forest. You'll see people fishing in some of the bays, but others have strict conservation rules; signs in the shape of a fish outline whether you can fish.

Bay of Plenty was one of the country's first areas settled by Māori. In Whakatane look for the landing site of the *Mataatua*, one of the great migratory *waka* (canoes), and visit the beautiful Mataatua meetinghouse.

PLANNING

WHEN TO GO

These regions are well loved for their beaches, and they are crowded between December and February when the hot summer weather draws thousands of holiday makers; sleepy seaside towns become filled with city folk with a tourist surge during the weeks around Christmas and the New Year. Don't overlook the off-season (March through September). The weather's usually sunny, climate is temperate, prices are lower, and locals have more time to chat. Some of the more hardy locals swim whatever the weather.

MAKING THE MOST OF YOUR TIME

Set aside four to five days and get a rental car. Bay of Plenty and the Coromandel need to be approached with flexibility. These regions have much to provide in a relatively small area. Allow for five-minute stops at the beach to become long coastal walks. Likewise, the many forest walks can be as challenging as you choose—from an hour to a whole day or overnight. You can approach the journey many ways, perhaps as a coastal exploration from Auckland along the "Seabird Coast," home to Miranda, an internationally recognized wetland on the Firth of Thames—then cross the fertile farmland of the Hauraki Plains to the base of Coromandel Peninsula. From here try a loop of the Coromandel that begins in Thames and ends in Whangamata, then continue along the coast to Bay of Plenty, Tauranga, and Whakatane. And be patient—the curvy roads challenge many drivers, especially tourists in campervans.

GETTING HERE AND AROUND

AIR TRAVEL

There are some tiny airstrips along the Coromandel Peninsula and a commercial airport at Tauranga and Whakatane. A number of scenic-flight operators offer trips over the region.

BUS TRAVEL

Contacts **Go Kiwi Shuttles.** ☎ *0800/446–549* ⊕ *www.go-kiwi.co.nz.* **Inter-City Coachlines.** ☎ *0800/222–146* ⊕ *www.intercity.co.nz.* **nakedbus.com.** ☎ *0900/62533* ⊕ *nakedbus.com.*

CAR TRAVEL

The best way to explore is by car. Most roads are well maintained and clearly signposted, and a car gives you the freedom to explore attractions such as short walks and waterfalls along side roads.

There are two main ways to drive to the Coromandel from Auckland. First take the Southern Motorway, following signs to Hamilton. Just as you get over the "Bombay Hills," turn left onto State Highway 2 (it's clearly signposted to Coromandel); then take the turnoff to State Highway 25, signposted between the small towns of Maramarua and Mangatarata. Follow the signs to Thames. Allow 1½ to 2½ hours for the 118-km (73-mile) journey. An arguably more scenic—though longer—way is to detour off the Southern Motorway at Manurewa, travel through Clevedon and follow the Seabird Coast, past tiny Kaiaua village, Miranda thermal springs, and alongside the Firth of Thames, home to thousands of seabirds attracted here to the internationally recognized Ramsar wetland of Miranda. From Thames, State Highway 25 is the main loop that travels around the peninsula, and though winding, the road is in good condition.

To reach the Bay of Plenty from Auckland, take the Southern Motorway, following signs to Hamilton. Just past the "Bombay Hills," turn left onto State Highway 2, and stay on Highway 2 all the way to Tauranga, driving through Paeroa, the scenic Karangahake Gorge (stop for walks and photos), Waihi, and Katikati on the way. The driving time between Auckland and Katikati is around 2 hours, 40 minutes. Between Auckland and Tauranga, it's at least 3 hours, 15 minutes.

FERRY TRAVEL

360 Discovery. Auckland ferry company 360 Discovery operates a ferry service from downtown Auckland to Coromandel, daily during peak summer holiday season, five days per week during the rest of summer and three days a week during winter. The sailing takes just under two hours and travels via Waiheke Island to Hannafords Wharf, 7 km (4 miles) from Coromandel township. A free shuttle service operates into town. One-way fare is NZ$55. ☎ 0800/360–3472.

RESTAURANTS

There are many dining options across the Coromandel and Bay of Plenty. You can buy everything from fruit from roadside orchard stalls and take-out fish-and-chips joints to cafés serving sandwiches and espresso coffee, right through to fine-dining affairs. Even when restaurants are formal in appearance, diners and hosts tend toward a relaxed country-casualness. Restaurant owners make a point of using the region's abundant resources: the fish is likely to have been caught that morning from a nearby bay, and shellfish are from local mussel and scallop farms. A huge community of artists lives in the region and their work is likely to be for sale even though it adorns restaurant walls.

Dinner service begins about 6 pm in the winter and around 7 pm during the summer months, though many places have "all-day menus." In peak season most places keep serving until at least 9 pm. For many restaurants reservations are a good idea, especially in the summer around the Coromandel. In winter, phone ahead to check if the restaurant will stay open.

HOTELS

Like mellow places around the world, you'll find plenty of comfortable bed-and-breakfasts and stylish motels, but both Coromandel and Bay of Plenty also have a sprinkling of luxe boutique lodges tucked away in the forest or along coastal coves. In peak season, from October through March, advance booking is essential across the board and many of the better places have long-term customers who book as much as a year in advance.

Hotel reviews have been shortened. For full information, visit Fodors.com.

Use the coordinate (✛ B2) at the end of each listing to locate a site on the corresponding map.

WHAT IT COSTS IN NEW ZEALAND DOLLARS				
	$	$$	$$$	$$$$
Restaurants	under NZ$15	NZ$15–NZ$20	NZ$21–NZ$30	over NZ$30
Hotels	under NZ$125	NZ$125–NZ$200	NZ$201–NZ$300	over NZ$300

Restaurant prices are the average cost of a main course at dinner or, if dinner is not served, at lunch. Hotel prices are the lowest cost of a standard double room in high season.

TOURS

Coromandel Adventures. If you don't have your own transport, that's not a problem. Coromandel Adventures will happily drive you to any or all of the sights listed here, and beyond. The small tour company has a range of tailor-made tours that will show you the best and some secret spots of the Coromandel, including the northern peninsula tip and beautiful Hot Water Beach and Cathedral Cove on the eastern side. Check their website for online specials. ☎ *0800/462–676* ⊕ *www. coromandeladventures.co.nz* ✉ *From NZ$25.*

VISITOR INFORMATION

The Coromandel, Katikati, Tauranga, Thames, Pauanui, Tairua, Waihi, Whakatane, Whangamata, and Whitianga visitor centers are open daily between at least 10 and 4. For tidal information, check the back page of the *New Zealand Herald* newspaper. *Tait's Fun Maps* of Coromandel, Thames, and Whitianga are not drawn to scale, but they clearly mark roads and main attractions. Pick up a copy at almost any hotel, tour-operator office, or visitor center, or check ⊕ *www.coromandelfun.co.nz.*

THE COROMANDEL

New Zealand has countless pockets of beauty that escape standard itineraries. As with so many other lands "discovered" by Europeans, the Coromandel was looted for its valuable resources: kauri trees, then kauri gum from the peninsula's forests, and finally gold from the southern hills and around Waihi and Coromandel towns in the 1870s. Relative quiet since the 1930s has allowed the region to recover its natural beauty and attract many life-styler types.

In the 1960s and 1970s, dairy farms and orchards sprang up, as did communes, spiritual retreats, and artists' communities. The population is now a mix of artists, those who appreciate the country lifestyle (and the easy access to organic food), and a growing number of Aucklanders looking for a weekend or retirement home.

A craggy range of peaks rises sharply to almost 3,000 feet and dominates the center of the peninsula. The west coast cradles the tidal Firth of Thames, and along the east coast the Pacific has carved out a succession of beaches and inlets separated by rearing headlands. Because of its rich soil, the peninsula has many spectacular gardens; some are open to the public. From the town of Thames, the gateway to the region, State Highway 25 and the 309 Road circle the lower two-thirds of the

ON THE ROAD

Slow down! Some of the Coromandel's best bits aren't points A or B but what's stumbled on in between. Lopsided signs advertising local artists beckon from gateposts; green-and-yellow DOC (Department of Conservation) signs point out short walks off the road; and those bags of feijoas, avocados, and oranges at that roadside stand will beat their grocery store counterparts in a taste test every time.

Coromandel's meandering, winding roads mean that locals tend to measure driving distance by time, not kilometers. Listen to them when they tell you it will take an hour to get from Coromandel to Whitianga, even though it's only 60 km (37 miles)—you'll drop down to 25 km per hour (16 mph) for every other dip and curve. Watch for the one-way bridges and give way if the red arrow is on your side. Keep left.

peninsula—an exhilarating drive starting with the sea on one side and a jumble of forested ranges on the other.

THAMES

120 km (75 miles) southeast of Auckland.

The peninsula's oldest town, Thames has evolved from a gold-mining hotbed in the late 1800s to an agricultural center. Locals have a saying that when the gold ran out, "Thames went to sleep awaiting the kiss of a golden prince—and instead it awoke to the warm breath of a cow." The main street was once lined with nearly 100 hotels (read: bars—gold mining and logging was thirsty work). Only a handful of these hotels still operate, but the town and environs provide glimpses of the mining era. In 1872 two towns, Grahamstown in the north and Shortland in the south, merged to form Thames, and many locals still refer to upper Thames as Grahamstown. Thames today is also the gateway to Kauaeranga Valley, part of Coromandel Forest Park, home to waterfalls, kauri groves, and the dramatic Pinnacles formations. Pinnacles Hut is a popular overnight hiking destination. Thames is also the northern entry point for the two- to three-day Hauraki Rail Trail. This is part of Nga Haerenga, the New Zealand Cycle Trail. The 82-km (51-mile) trail travels in part on former railway lines, including tunnels (the grade is easy), and explores farmland, the coast around Thames, gold-mining history, and the scenic Karangahake Gorge.

GETTING HERE AND AROUND

If you're not driving, you can take a public bus to Thames from Auckland, Hamilton, Tauranga, or any of the smaller towns on the main road en route from these cities. If you're coming from the nearest big city, *such as the ones mentioned above,* a bus ticket shouldn't cost you more than about NZ$15–NZ$25.

You can pick up a rental car at the Auckland airport and drive on down to Coromandel, or you can take a bus and rent a car when you arrive in Thames. At the Thames i-SITE Information Centre, located right where the bus deposits you, ask for rental car advice.

Bus Depot Bus Depot. ⊠ *Thames i-SITE Visitor Infomation Centre, 200 Mary St.* ☎ *07/868–7284.*

Car Rentals Saunders Rental Cars. ⊠ *201 Pollen St.* ☎ *07/868–8398* ⊕ *www.saundersmotorgroup.co.nz.*

VISITOR INFORMATION

Contacts Thames i-SITE Visitor Centre. ⊠ *200 Mary St.* ☎ *07/868–7284* ⊕ *www.thamesinfo.co.nz.*

EXPLORING
TOP ATTRACTIONS

FAMILY **Butterfly and Orchid Garden.** A few minutes' (3 km, 1.8 mile) drive north on the way out of Thames, it's easy to miss this garden unless you're specifically looking for the signs. Roger and Sabine Gass have brought some color to the Coromandel with a flock of butterflies from Australia. Now, up to 20 species and hundreds of butterflies from all over the world may be on view at any time, including large Birdwing butterflies. Birds such as finches, doves, and quails join the butterflies along with about 100 different plant species. The heliconia (or false bird-of-paradise) and orchids are particularly stunning. ⊠ *Dickson Holiday Park, Victoria St.* ☎ *07/868–8080* ⊕ *www.butterfly.co.nz* 🖾 *NZ$12* ⊙ *Sept.–May, daily 9:30–4:30.*

Goldmine Experience. To learn about early gold-mining efforts in the Coromandel, stop in at the Goldmine Experience, a few minute's drive north of town. Take a 40-minute underground tour of the old Golden Crown Claim, which was first worked in 1868. From early 2014 the mine has reopened after a major upgrade and installation of new stampers. You'll need sturdy, closed-toe footwear because it can be muddy underground. You can also pan for gold on the surface. Five hundred feet below, the Caledonia strike was one of the richest in the world. Be sure to call or email first to book a tour; attendance here is a bit haphazard. ⊠ *Corner of State Hwy. 25 and Moanawataiari Creek Rd.* ☎ *07/868–8154* ⊕ *www.goldmine-experience.co.nz* 🖾 *NZ$15.*

Grahamstown Saturday Market. On Saturday morning, the northern end of Thames's main street is transformed into a bustling market. Stalls

---

ONE-LANE BRIDGES

During your travels throughout the Coromandel, you'll become familiar with a sign showing two arrows: one big (white or black), one small and red. This means you're about to approach a really narrow section of road—often a bridge—that only allows room for cars traveling in one direction at a time. If you're heading in the direction of the smaller, red arrow, you must yield to oncoming traffic and wait until the road is clear. Even if you're heading in the direction of the bigger arrow, take it easy. These narrow stretches often include a blind corner or two.

4

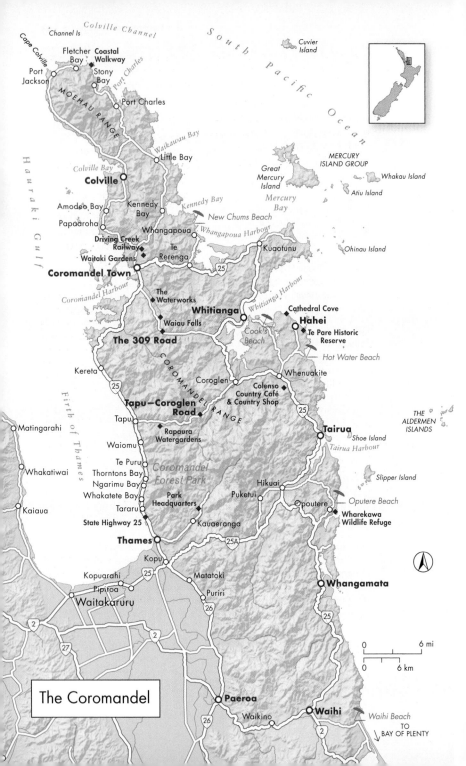

The Coromandel

Channel Is
Colville Channel
South Pacific Ocean
Cuvier Island

Cape Colville
Fletcher Bay
Coastal Walkway
Stony Bay
Port Charles
Port Jackson
Port Charles

MOEHAU RANGE

Waikawau Bay

Little Bay

Hauraki Gulf

Colville Bay
Colville

MERCURY ISLAND GROUP

Great Mercury Island

Whakau Island

Atiu Island

Mercury Bay

Amodeo Bay
Kennedy Bay
Papaaroha
Kennedy Bay
New Chums Beach
Whangapoua
Whangapoua Harbour

Ohinau Island

Driving Creek Railway
Te Rerenga
Waitaki Gardens
Kuaotunu

Coromandel Town

25

Coromandel Harbour

The Waterworks
Whitianga
Whitianga Harbour
Cathedral Cove
Hahei
Te Pare Historic Reserve

Waiau Falls

The 309 Road

Cook's Beach

Hot Water Beach

Coroglen
Whenuakite

Kereta

25

Colenso Country Café & Country Shop

25

THE ALDERMEN ISLANDS

Tapu–Coroglen Road

COROMANDEL RANGE

Tapu
Tairua
Shoe Island
Tairua Harbour

Matingarahi

Rapaura Watergardens

Waiomu

Firth of Thames

Whakatiwai

Te Puru
Thorntons Bay
Ngarimu Bay
Whakatete Bay
Tararu

Coromandel Forest Park

Park Headquarters

Hikuai
Puketui
Opoutere
Oputere Beach

Slipper Island

Kaiaua

Wharekawa Wildlife Refuge

State Highway 25
Kauaeranga

Thames

25A

Kopu

Whangamata

Kopuarahi
Matatoki
25
Puriri
Pipiroa
26
Waitakaruru
25

2

27

26

Paeroa

Waikino

Waihi

Waihi Beach
TO
BAY OF PLENTY

2

0   6 mi
0   6 km

line the street, with vendors selling local organic produce and cheeses, antiques, jewelry, and arts and crafts. Most, if not all, of the shops get in on the act as well. ⊠ *Upper Pollen St.* ⊘ *Sat. 8–1.*

NEED A BREAK?

Waiomu Beach Cafe. Waiomu Beach Cafe sits across from Waiomu Beach, and if you've had enough of the twists and turns of the coastal road, this is the spot to stop. The café serves everything from ice cream (the best on the coast, some say) to pizza. Burgers and fries aren't the focus here. Local favorites like Coromandel mussel sausages, the "half kilo" shellfish dish of *pipi*, cockles, and mussels, and the Coromandel's ubiquitous mussel chowder deserve your attention. Coffee is great, too. Sit at the picnic tables to the side, or cross over to Waiomu Beach Park and have a picnic. You'll know you've hit Waiomu Bay when you see the perennial striped umbrellas in front of the café. ⊠ *622 Thames Coast Rd., Tapu* ☎ *07/868–2554* ⊘ *Closed evenings, from 4 pm weekdays, from 6 pm weekends.*

4

WORTH NOTING

Thames Historical Museum. At this tiny museum you can look into earlier ways of life in the town. The museum contains photographic displays of the gold-rush and logging industries, good re-creations of period rooms from the 1800s, and info on the original Māori inhabitants and early European settlers. A nice feature here are the grounds, the memorial garden, with period roses and other flora that settlers commonly planted, is a nice place to rest and reflect. Run by volunteers. ⊠ *Pollen and Cochrane Sts.* ☎ *07/868–8509* ⊕ *www.thamesinfo.co.nz/Museum* ⌨ *NZ$5* ⊘ *Daily 1–4, Sat. 10–4.*

Thames School of Mines Mineralogical Museum. From the mid-1800s, the School of Mines was an internationally recognized institution, teaching all aspects of mining. A diploma from here guaranteed a job anywhere in the world. The museum was established in 1900 to exhibit geological samples. The school closed decades ago, but the museum's still kicking, displaying those turn-of-the-20th-century rock specimens along with scales, models of stamper batteries, and other gold-mining paraphernalia. ⊠ *Brown and Cochrane Sts.* ☎ *07/868–6227* ⊕ *www.nzmuseums. co.nz/account/3309* ⌨ *NZ$10* ⊘ *Wed.–Sun. 11–3.*

WHERE TO EAT

$$$

NEW ZEALAND
FAMILY

✕ **The Junction Hotel.** Named for its location between the old towns of Grahamstown and Shortland (they merged into Thames in 1872), this is one of the few hotels remaining from the gold rush days, when more than 100 bars lined the streets. The character of that era remains but the decor is considerably smartened. If you're in the mood for casual but classy pub grub in a convivial atmosphere with the locals, this is your place. The GBD is the main restaurant bar, serving everything from breakfast to lunch to bar snacks, pizzas, and tapas to evening main courses (herb-crusted baked fish with pea risotto) to desserts. Weekends will get busy after dinner with music gigs, and comedy shows are a regular feature. Down the back is a more casual bar with pool tables; upstairs, some basic but clean budget and excellent value accommodation. Open daily 11 to 9, and weekends for breakfast

from 8:30. [$] *Average main: NZ$25* ✉ *700 Pollen St.* ☎ *07/868–6008* 🌐 *www.thejunction.net.nz.*

$ VEGETARIAN 🍴 **Sola Café.** This little community café is consistently good. Don't be fooled by the vegetarian menu; this is no health bar. The counter displays risotto cakes, Florentines, and apple, pear, apricot, and fig shortbread; the berry friend (a small, sweet cake made from ground almonds and egg whites, often topped or filled with fruit) is as good as any you will find. Try a breakfast of potato-and-fresh-herb frittata, or panfried polenta with smoked field mushroom, spinach, and feta for lunch. Wheat and gluten-free diets are well catered to. The wraps are irresistible, and the local cheeses and chutneys from the deli counter make great picnic fixings. The store sells local cheeses outside the door during the Grahamstown Saturday Market. [$] *Average main: NZ$11* ✉ *720b Pollen St.* ☎ *07/868–8781* 🌐 *www.solacafe.co.nz* ⏲ *Closed Sun.*

WHERE TO STAY

$$ HOTEL 🏨 **Coastal Motor Lodge.** Set in 3 acres of gardens, with native bushwalks to the rear of the property and the Thames coast just across the road, this is a spacious, scenic spot to bed down and get your bearings as you enter the Coromandel. **Pros:** close to Thames; lovely views; obliging hosts. **Cons:** basic furnishings. [$] *Rooms from: NZ$165* ✉ *608 Tararu Rd.* ☎ *07/868–6843* 🌐 *www.stayatcoastal.co.nz* 🔑 *4 cottages, 10 studios, 2-bedroom unit in lodge* 🍽 *No meals.*

$$ B&B/INN FAMILY 🏨 **Grafton Cottage & Chalets.** These six independent units set among a hillside garden overlooking the sea offer a relaxing ambience and great sunsets. **Pros:** views; peaceful garden setting; friendly hosts. **Cons:** steep driveway; some steps and stairs to access units. [$] *Rooms from: NZ$140* ✉ *304 Grafton Rd.* ☎ *07/868–9971* 🌐 *www.graftoncottage.co.nz* 🔑 *6 units* 🍽 *Breakfast* 💳 *No credit cards.*

EN ROUTE The Coromandel Ranges drop right down to the seafront **State Highway 25** as it winds up the west coast of the peninsula. When you top the hills north of Kereta on the way to Coromandel town, mountains, pastures, and islands in the Firth of Thames open before you. It's quite wonderful to watch the sunset from this part of the coastal highway. Some of the vantage points along the way offer opportunities for stunning photographs. The area is popular with landscape painters.

SPORTS AND THE OUTDOORS

Short walks and longer day and overnight forest walks are a big attraction, especially in Kauaeranga Valley. Camping is also popular in the valley or at coastal camping grounds. On the water, try fishing around the mussel and scallop farms, or bird-watching.

HIKING

Fodor's Choice ★ **Coromandel Forest Park—Kauaeranga Valley.** This area of the forest park has more than 20 walking trails that offer everything from a 15-minute stroll to an overnight trek. The hike to the interesting Pinnacles formations is a steep climb yet probably the most popular walk in the park; the trek from the trailhead to the Pinnacles hut takes three hours one-way. From the hut you can continue (about one hour one-way) to the Pinnacles and a viewpoint that spans both coasts, the Firth of Thames and Pacific Ocean. An overnight in Pinnacles hut costs NZ$15;

you need to reserve it either through a DOC visitor center or online (⊕ *booking.doc.govt.nz*). You can hike back via the three-hour-long Webb Creek trail or come down the longer (four-hour) alternative route, the Billy Goat track.

Always read the signs at the start of the track to check their state. Summer holiday season is busy, so book well ahead. Generally, midweek is less crowded than weekends throughout summer. There are also delightful camping areas along the valley floor (from NZ$10; powered sites should be booked in advance). To reach Kauaeranga Valley, head south from Thames and on the outskirts of the town turn left on Banks Street, then right on Parawai Road, which becomes Kauaeranga Valley Road. Thirteen kilometers (8½ miles) from Thames you'll come to the DOC Visitor Centre, which opens from 8:30 to 4 (possibly later in summer, give them a call first).

The visitor center offers up-to-date information on track conditions and camping facilities, educational displays, plus information on many other Coromandel walks or hikes, to places such as Fantail Bay, Cathedral Cove, or Opera Point. ☎ *07/867–9080* ⊕ *www.doc.govt.nz.*

Department of Conservation Visitors Center. The most accessible starting point is the delightful Kauaeranga Valley Road, where the Department of Conservation Visitors Center provides maps and information. Open hours are generally from 8:30 to 4 daily, with extended hours in peak summer holidays. Phone first to be sure. ✉ *995 Kauaeranga Valley Rd.* ☎ *07/867–9080* ⊕ *www.doc.govt.nz.*

Fodor's Choice ★ **Sleeping God Canyon.** This is one of New Zealand's most epic outdoor and cultural adventures, set in Coromandel Forest Park, a spectacularly steep, forested canyon in Kauearanga Valley. Not for the fainthearted, here you'll rappel, zipline, jump, water slide, and swim down and through a series of waterfalls and pools, a total 300-meter (984-foot) descent. The big jumps are optional, the rappels are not. You're in safe hands, as the guides have practiced for years in the underground canyons of the Waitomo Caves and are fully accredited, DOC-approved operators. You'll also hike 45 minutes through the forest to reach your jump-off point, during which your guides will share their Māori history and culture about this special place they know as Atuatumoa. It's a full day trip, 8:30 to 6:30, and canyoning equipment, lunch, and barbecue finale are supplied. Transport is offered from Thames and Hamilton. A good level of fitness and an adventurous spirit are essential for this excursion. ✉ *1160 Kauaeranga Valley Rd.* ☎ *0800/422–696* ⊕ *www.canyonz.co.nz* ✉ *NZ$360 per person.*

TAPU–COROGLEN ROAD

25 km (16 miles) north of Thames.

The 28-km-long (17-mile-long), intermittently paved **Tapu–Coroglen Road** turns off State Highway 25 in the hamlet of Tapu to wind into the mountains. It's a breathtaking route where massive tree ferns blanket the roadside hills. Take it slowly: stretches of the road are quite narrow with access for only one vehicle. Signs indicate these places.

GETTING HERE AND AROUND

About 6½ km (4 miles) from Tapu you come to the magical Rapaura Watergardens. Travel another 3½ km (2 miles) along the road and pull over to climb the 187 steps up to the huge, 1,200-year-old **Square Kauri**, so named for its unusual square shape. At 133 feet tall and 30 feet around, this is the 15th-largest kauri in New Zealand. From a tree-side platform there is a splendid view across the valley to Mau Mau Paki, one of the peaks along the Coromandel Range. Continuing east across the peninsula, the road passes through forests and sheep paddocks—a shimmeringly gorgeous drive in sun or mist.

EXPLORING

Rapaura Watergardens. Rapaura Watergardens is in a 64-acre private estate nestled beside Coromandel Forest Park. This property, which has been nurtured more than 40 years, features ponds and streams, fountains, and water features set in lush green lawns and native forest, and adorned with garden art. A 45-minute walk leads you through seasonal displays of exotic flora, primulas and spring bulbs, azaleas, rhododendrons, camellias, lilies, and hydrangeas, interspersed with native grasses and bushes. There's also the Big Pond, where water lilies flower through summer, and a forest walk to cascading waterfalls. The on-site vegetable and herb gardens supply Koru at Rapaura, the highly recommended café at the garden that serves wholesome home baking, local fare, and daily-baked beer bread. Rapaura also offers self-catering accommodation in either a Boutique Lodge or Garden Cottage. After 5, the garden becomes your private playground. You can swim beneath the falls, cook up a barbecue dinner, and enjoy nature at its best. Rates for two range from NZ$165 to NZ$285, including continental breakfast provisions. ⊠ *586 Tapu–Coroglen Rd., 6 km (4 miles) east of Tapu, Tapu* ☎ *07/868–4821* ⊕ *www.rapaurawatergardens.co.nz* ⊠ *NZ$12* ☾ *Daily 9–5 summer, winter hrs vary; café open summer (Oct.–Apr.) 9–4.*

COROMANDEL TOWN

60 km (38 miles) north of Thames, 29 km (18 miles) northwest of Whitianga.

Coromandel town became the site of New Zealand's first gold strike in 1852 when sawmill worker Charles Ring found gold-bearing quartz at Driving Creek, just north of the town. The find was important for New Zealand, because the country's workforce had been severely depleted by the gold rushes in California and Australia. Ring hurried to Auckland to claim the reward that had been offered to anyone finding "payable" gold. The town's population soared, but the reef gold could be mined only by heavy and expensive machinery. Within a few months Coromandel resumed its former sleepy existence as a timber town—and Charles Ring was refused the reward.

Nowadays, Coromandel is a popular holiday town but manages to retain a low-key charm even when SUVs and campervans fill the streets. With 19th-century buildings lining both sides of its single main street, an active artists' collective, and the requisite fish-and-chips shops at either end, you could not find a truer example of a relaxed and slightly hippie Kiwi town. The local mussel farms mean that mussels are served every which way, from smoked-mussel pies to chowder.

GETTING HERE AND AROUND

As with every town in the Coromandel, you can arrange to be dropped off or collected by any of the three main bus companies—Nakedbus. com, Go Kiwi, or InterCity. There is no rental car company in Coromandel town, so if you decide you want to get around by yourself, you'll need to rent a car in neighboring towns of Thames or Whitianga. Alternatively, Coromandel Adventures offer daily, customized tours.

If locals walks are your thing, upon arriving, head over to the Coromandel Town Information Centre and ask for a photocopy of "Coromandel's Walking Tracks," a small booklet they'll copy for you for the princely sum of 50 cents.

Bus Depot Bus Depot. ⊠ *Coromandel Town Information Centre, 85 Kapanga Rd., Coromandel* ☎ *07/866–8598.*

Ferry Information Coromandel-Auckland Ferry. ⊠ *Hannaford's Wharf, Te Kouma Rd., Coromandel* ☎ *0800/360–3472* ⊕ *www.360discovery.co.nz.*

VISITOR INFORMATION

Coromandel Adventures. Whether it's a shuttle ride to town from the Coromandel ferry, a packaged multiday tour of all Coromandel's highlights, or transport to one of the region's walkways, this company will put it all together for you. Transport to the Coromandel Coastal Walkway, which follows the very northern tip of the peninsula, is particularly useful given the two ends of the walkway are several kilometers apart. ☎ *0800/462–676 NZ only, 07/866–7014* ⊕ *www. coromandeladventures.co.nz.*

Coromandel Town Information Centre. ⊠ *85 Kapanga Rd., Coromandel* ☎ *07/866–8598* ⊕ *www.coromandeltown.co.nz.*

EXPLORING

Coromandel Gold Stamper Battery. Nothing quirky or gimmicky here. This is the real thing, with a Category One Historic Places Trust rating. Started up around 1900, this was the first diesel-powered gold processing plant in New Zealand and its last original stamper battery, the only six-head stamper battery in the world. Geologist Ash Franklin offers an enthusiastic tour of the plant and brings alive the region's fascinating mining and geology history. Tours last one hour, and entry to the battery is by guided tour only. Ash also runs, on demand, an evening "Lamplight Tour," which he describes as spooky. Check the website or give him a call. Located 2 km (1 mile) north of Coromandel township and clearly signposted at the start of Buffalo Road. ⊠ *410 Buffalo Rd., Coromandel* ☎ *021/0232–8262* ⊕ *www.coromandelstamperbattery.weebly.com* ▣ *NZ$15 (cash only)* ⊗ *Daily 10, 11, noon, 1, 2, 3.*

FAMILY **Driving Creek Railway.** Barry Brickell's fascinating project has become a major tourist attraction. Mr. Brickell is a potter who discovered that the clay on his land was perfect for his work. The problem was the deposit lay at the top of a very steep slope, so he hacked a path through the forest and built a narrow gauge railway to bring the clay down to his studio. Visitors began asking if they could go along for a ride and specially designed passenger trains now run daily tours.

The diesel-powered locomotive route incorporates a double-deck viaduct, three tunnels, a spiral, and switchback through native forest, lined with terra-cotta sculptures all the way to the "Eyefull Tower," modeled on a hexagonal lighthouse tower, and viewing platform. On a clear day you can see across the Hauraki Gulf. The railway also funds a reforestation program; to date more than 25,000 native trees have been planted and a 1.6-acre fenced wildlife sanctuary has been established. The railway round-trip takes about 60 minutes. There is also a pottery shop at the "station" and an art gallery with changing exhibitions. You'll find it all just 3 km (2 miles) north of Coromandel township. ■ TIP→ Bookings are advised, and essential during the peak summer months. ✉ *380 Driving Creek Rd., Coromandel* ☎ *07/866–8703* ⊕ *www.drivingcreekrailway.co.nz* ☜*NZ$30* ⊙ *9–5, trains run 6 times a day in summer, twice in winter (10:15 am and 2 pm). Extra trains run for 5 or more adults.*

The Source. This local arts collective gallery sells many mediums of art–jewelry, pottery, clothing, sculpture, and more. There's an outdoor courtyard where you'll find huge ceramic works inspired by native plants and recycled metal items. Everything, including the largest sculptures, can be broken down for shipping overseas. Call in, you're likely to meet one of the artists on roster behind the counter. ✉ *31 Kapanga Rd., Coromandel* ☎ *07/866–7345* ⊙ *Daily 10–4, in peak summer 10–5.*

Weta Design. The Weta Design gallery is named after the country's largest native insect, which looks like a grasshopper with armor. This gallery has a wide range of items, from large and really lovely glass totems to small, finely made tiles, not to mention fabric art, carving, and ceramics. The gallery also has New Zealand jewelry. Keep an eye out for the silver work by Anna Hallissey. Her delicate brooches are based on the tiny branches of the manuka tree, while a wittier piece is a silver version of the plastic clip used to close bread bags. For a truly unique gift they sell a surprisingly packaged weta. ✉ *46 Kapanga Rd., Coromandel* ☎ *07/866–8823* ⊕ *www.wetadesign.co.nz* ⊙ *Daily 10–4.*

EN ROUTE **Waitati Gardens.** Waitati Gardens is recognized as a Garden of Significance by the New Zealand Gardens Trust. Walkways meander through trees and shrubs, perennial flower borders, a rhododendron glade, and native plantings. Water pools and native birdsong provide a peaceful backdrop. ✉ *485 Buffalo Rd., Coromandel* ☎ *07/866–8659* ☜*NZ$7* ⊙ *Daily Sept.–May, dawn–dusk; winter by appointment.*

WHERE TO EAT

$$$
SEAFOOD
FAMILY

✕ **Coromandel Mussel Kitchen.** Think of any conceivable way to serve fresh, fat mussels and you'll find it here, in the café established by the original mussel-farming family in the district. Big bold pictures of the aquaculture farms grace the walls. Start with a simple hot-steamed mussel pot, maybe with garlic and wine, or coconut cream and green curry. Or sample grilled mussels in half shells, or fill up on a classic mussel kitchen chowder or fritters. Branch out and simply ask for fish-and-chips, or a generous salad, or burger, or massage the sweet tooth with ice cream. Wash it all down with a natural craft beer brewed on-site by the MK Brewing Company, and after you've mussel-ed up, there's a big tempting cabinet crammed with goodies such as vacuum-packed mussel chowder or smoked mussels that you can purchase for later. Located 4 km (2½ miles) south of Coromandel township. [$] *Average main: NZ$21* ✉ *At State Hwy. 25 and 309 Rd., Coromandel* ☎ *07/866–7245* 🌐 *www.musselkitchen.co.nz* 🕒 *No dinner Mar. 1–Dec. 26.*

$$ VEGETARIAN FAMILY 🍴 **Driving Creek Cafe.** Fresh food, generous portions, and reasonable prices in a rural setting are the draw here. The café captures the essence of the communes that used to thrive on the peninsula, while providing food that appeals to the masses. It is surrounded by fruit trees with outdoor seating in a sculpture garden and on the porch. The vegetarian menu includes breakfasts (omelets, scrambled tofu, bagels, pancakes, mushrooms, and muesli). For lunch there's the Indian-style dhal; tofu burger; or 6-inch sandwich with sprouts and gherkins, cheese, tomato, and lettuce; plus piles of baked goods, locally roasted coffee, and fresh juices (e.g., liver booster) and smoothies. They also sell a small range of organic goods, local art, and pottery. There's space for the kids to play and free, fast Internet available. [$] *Average main: NZ$15* ✉ *180 Driving Creek Rd., Coromandel* ☎ *07/866–7066* 🌐 *www.drivingcreekcafe.com* 🕒 *Closed Wed. May–July.*

$$$ NEW ZEALAND 🍴 **Pepper Tree Restaurant and Bar.** The standout restaurant in town is also a regular award winner—Silver Fern Farmslamb awards and Monteiths Wild Food Challenge finalist for five years running, for example. Coromandel seafood is showcased (think Mussel Pot, sautéed scallops or oysters, or macadamia dukkah crusted rack of lamb). All-day brunches and light lunches are also served. Lunch easily segues into dinner in the sheltered courtyard or in front of the fire, depending on the season. Open daily 10 am to 9 pm. [$] *Average main: NZ$30* ✉ *31 Kapanga Rd., Coromandel* ☎ *07/866–8211.*

$$ CAFÉ 🍴 **UMU Café.** Like many places to eat on the peninsula, this café does a roaring trade with mussels—chowders, and a platter with mussels served every which way you could imagine. There's also salmon bagels for breakfast, and fresh line-caught fish. Pizzas are popular, or you could try beef-cheek pie. The dinner menu serves all the classics, including lamb, beef fillet, chicken, and vegetarian specials as well as seafood. Quiches, cakes, and sandwiches are handmade every day, and the coffee is Fair Trade. [$] *Average main: NZ$17* ✉ *22 Wharf Rd., Coromandel* ☎ *07/866–8618.*

WHERE TO STAY

$$ HOTEL 🏨 **Anchor Lodge.** Spa apartments, motel units, and backpacker accommodations are cozy and clean, with views from that encompass the Coromandel Harbour and a bank of native forest. **Pros:** wide choice of accommodations to suit range of travelers; heated swimming pool and whirlpool; bikes available. **Cons:** outward appearance is underwhelming, 200-meter (656-foot) walk to town. [$] *Rooms from: NZ$175* ✉ *448 Wharf Rd., Coromandel* ☎ *07/866–7992* 🌐 *www.anchorlodgecoromandel.co.nz* 🛏 *25 rooms* 🍽 *No meals.*

$$$ B&B/INN 🏨 **Buffalo Lodge.** Perched on a hillside and surrounded by bush just out of Coromandel town, this lodge looks across the Hauraki Gulf toward

Auckland. **Pros:** splendid breakfasts; private; multilingual host. **Cons:** town is a short drive away; not suitable for children under 14. $ *Rooms from: NZ$225* ✉ *860 Buffalo Rd., Coromandel* ☎ *07/866–8960* ⊕ *www. buffalolodge.co.nz* ⊘ *Closed May–Sept.* ⇆ *3 rooms* ⚭ *Breakfast.*

$$ ⛱ **Coromandel Court Motel.** Tucked away in a hidden spot just behind
HOTEL Coromandel township, these down-to-earth units are fresh, clean, and well set out. **Pros:** in town; friendly; free Wi-Fi throughout. **Cons:** generic; uninspiring. $ *Rooms from: NZ$180* ✉ *365 Kapanga Rd., Coromandel* ☎ *07/866–8402* ⊕ *www.coromandelcourtmotel.co.nz* ⇆ *10 units* ⚭ *No meals.*

$$$ ⛱ **Coromandel Top 10 Holiday Park.** Whether you choose a luxury villa,
HOTEL rustic Fisherman's Nest cottage, self-catering motel, cabin, backpacker,
FAMILY or powered campervan site, you can enjoy the plentiful facilities at this park: a big swimming pool (heated, with a jumping pillow for the kids), BBQ areas with indoor/outdoor dining options, laundry, playground, and fish- and boat-cleaning facilities for the successful fishers. **Pros:** there's so much to do; Wi-Fi throughout; three-minute walk to excellent restaurants. **Cons:** crowded with families in summer. $ *Rooms from: NZ$250* ✉ *636–732 Rings Rd.* ☎ *0800/267–646, 07/866–8830* ⊕ *www.coromandeltop10.co.nz* ⇆ *24 rooms* ⚭ *No meals.*

$$$$ ⛱ **Driving Creek Villas.** This delightfully private, restful retreat within
HOTEL the trees of Fraser Reserve is a great place to spread out and use as a
FAMILY base for a few days. **Pros:** close to town; secluded; lots of space; good for families. **Cons:** can feel a little isolated after dark. $ *Rooms from: NZ$325* ✉ *21a Colville Rd., Coromandel* ☎ *07/866–7755* ⊕ *www. drivingcreekvillas.com* ⇆ *3 villas.*

$$ ⛱ **Hush Boutique Accommodation.** Built around one of the main gold-
HOTEL mining spots in Coromandel, and part of the growing Driving Creek community, these small cabins are set up to resemble a more comfortable version of an old mining village. **Pros:** affordable; unique; nature is the feature here. **Cons:** small cabins; shared facilities may get on your nerves depending on your fellow guests. $ *Rooms from: NZ$195* ✉ *425 Driving Creek Rd., Coromandel* ☎ *07/866–7771* ⊕ *www. hushaccommodation.co.nz* ⇆ *4 studios, one 3-bedroom house and one self-contained 1-bedroom unit* ⚭ *Breakfast.*

$$$ ⛱ **Indigo Bush Studios.** From burnished clay floors, copper pipes, and old
B&B/INN beams of timber arise two creatively designed studios where Balinese doors, Egyptian louvres, and Afghani furniture add to the eclectic ambience. **Pros:** secluded; visually lovely. **Cons:** not suitable for children. $ *Rooms from: NZ$225* ✉ *19 Flays Rd., Coromandel* ☎ *07/866–7388* ⊕ *www.indigo-bush-studios.co.nz* ⇆ *2 studios* ⚭ *No meals.*

$$ ⛱ **Te Kouma Harbour Cottages.** A little off-the-beaten-track, on a 680-acre
HOTEL deer and cattle farm, these single-story wooden chalets are excellent
FAMILY for families or groups who want plenty of activities: kayaking, soccer, pétanque (the French game similar to boccie), and swimming in the pool. **Pros:** fantastic views; spacious; self-contained. **Cons:** a little out of town; basic furnishings; can be busy at times. $ *Rooms from: NZ$180* ✉ *1159 State Hwy. 25, Te Kouma Harbour, Coromandel* ☎ *07/866– 8747* ⊕ *www.tekoumacottages.co.nz* ⇆ *6 cabins, 6 cottages, 1 lodge, 1 log home* ⚭ *No meals.*

SPORTS AND THE OUTDOORS

Fishing and forest walks are what most outdoorsy people do around here. Or, if fishing isn't your thing—simply cruising through the little islands to see the mussel farms is a great scenic, and social, thing to do.

FISHING

Mussel Barge Snapper Safaris. If you've been in Coromandel for more than five minutes, you'll know mussel farming is big business. Here's your chance to take a closer look, on board the mussel barge that heads through sheltered waters past offshore islands to these marine farms in the Hauraki Gulf. The large concentration of so much *kaimoana* (seafood) means the farms are also a hit with the local fish population looking for lunch, mostly snapper and very tasty in their own right. Thus fishing for snapper around the farms can be rewarding—not to mention exciting! There's shelter and a barbecue on board, cruises last about four to five hours and depart daily at 7 am and 1 pm from Sugar Loaf Wharf, Te Kouma, 7 km (4½ miles) south of Coromandel township. (Be there 15 minutes before sailings.) Fishing lines are available for hire and bait is available for sale (must be preordered), if you don't have your own. ✉ *Hannafords Wharf, Te Kouma Rd., Coromandel* ☎ *07/866–7667* ⊕ *www.musselbargesafaris.co.nz* 🖃 *NZ$55 per person (minimum of 8 bookings required).*

Top Catch: Bait, Tackle, Advice. The name says it all. If you're new in town and are hankering for a spot of fishing, start here. These guys can arrange fishing trips with local fishing boats to suit all levels. They also sell all the fishing gear you could need, although they don't hire out equipment—generally, that is arranged through the fishing boats. Advice is given freely, although it may be—by proprietor Wayne's own admission—dodgy. And although this might be one of a national chain of fishing shops, the knowledge is definitely local. ✉ *2 Kapanga Rd., Coromandel* ☎ *07/866–7397* ☉ *Daily in summer (end of Oct.–end of Apr.), in winter Wed.–Sun.*

HIKING

Kauri Block Pā Track. On a clear day, head up to the Kauri Block Pā Track (1½ hours return), which provides panoramic views over the town, harbor, and coast. Follow the main road to Coromandel town's western outskirts, where a signpost points out the start of the trail at 356 Wharf Road. The trail goes through native and regenerating bush to the summit, a Māori *pā* site, before winding down through the bush and emerging onto Harbour View Road, which you follow back to town. ✉ *356 Wharf Rd., Coromandel* ⊕ *www.doc.govt.nz* 🖃 *Free.*

Long Bay Scenic Reserve and Kauri Grove. A gentle 40-minute walk (one-way) will take you to one of the lovelier beaches in the immediate area. Pack a picnic and enjoy a relaxing afternoon. The track starts at the end of Long Bay Road, at the Long Bay Motor Camp (about 3 km [1.8 miles] from Coromandel town), and slopes up through a grove of young kauri trees (and one much bigger, older kauri that happily evaded the early loggers) and down to the secluded Tucks Bay, a prime spot to unpack a picnic lunch. Either turn back here, or head across Tucks Bay and follow the coastal track back to the motor camp. Be sure to wash your footwear where indicated, to help thwart the spread of kauri die-back disease. ⊠ *3200 Long Bay Rd., Coromandel.*

THE 309 ROAD

Although named for a journey that used to (apparently) take 309 minutes, the 309 Road cuts right across the peninsula and is now the shortest route between Coromandel and Whitianga. The mostly unpaved road is winding and narrow and takes 35–40 minutes to cross, not counting the stops you'll want to make along the way.

GETTING HERE AND AROUND

If you are traveling in a campervan, it's best to leave early in the morning to avoid traffic. Pull over where you can to let traffic behind you pass. If you end up behind a campervan, be patient. The surrounding landscape alternates between farmland, pine trees, and native forest, with numerous reasons to stop along the way. Look for the 309 Road brochure at visitor information centers.

EXPLORING

TOP ATTRACTIONS

FAMILY **The Waterworks.** Five kilometers (3 miles) from Coromandel, The Waterworks is a quirky playground designed with recycled materials in a series of grassy clearings surrounded by bush, ponds, streams, and a river with a swimming hole. The roadside sign "For kids up to the age of 84," and the water that trickles on your car as you drive in the gateway, are a hint of the fun to come. There are sculpture gardens, a number of water-powered artworks, and some unusual takes on playground equipment that invite children and inner children to come out and play. ⊠ *471, 309 Rd., Coromandel* ☎ *07/866–7191* ⊕ *www.thewaterworks. co.nz* ⊠ *NZ$24* ☉ *Daily 10–4 (winter, Apr., Nov.), 10–6 (summer, Dec.–Mar.).*

WORTH NOTING

Waiau Falls. About 7½ km (4½ miles) from Coromandel, stop for a swim at Waiau Falls, a forest-fringed waterfall lagoon that's just a three-minute walk down a few steps from the road. The track starts close to the Waiau Falls Scenic Reserve sign. Additional walking tracks lead farther into the woods. Less than 2 km (1 mile) east of Waiau Falls, a series of easy, clearly marked gravel paths and wooden walkways takes you through lush forest to a protected giant kauri grove. ■ TIP ➡ **The full walk takes about 15 minutes, but the trees are so majestic that you may want to allow a half hour to stroll through this ancient forest.** ⊠ *Free*

COLVILLE AND BEYOND

30 km (19 miles) north of Coromandel.

To reach land's end in the very north of the Coromandel Peninsula—with rugged coastline, delightful coves, and pastures—take the 30-minute drive from Coromandel up to **Colville**. The town has a grocery store–gas station, post office, community hall, and café. There is also an interesting Buddha shrine, or stupa, by the Mahamudra Buddhist Centre on the drive in and public toilets with a mosaic worthy of a

Farmland outside of Coromandel town

picture. Colville is the gateway to some of the peninsula's most untamed landscape. Maps of the area are available in Coromandel at the Town Information Centre and in Colville at the General Store.

GETTING HERE AND AROUND

Other than driving to Colville, you can get here by bus or small touring company. If you're staying in Coromandel town and you don't have a car but want to explore some of the more remote bays, such as Fletcher Bay, you could call Coromandel Adventures, which offers excursions and shuttle transport around the area.

EXPLORING

Fletcher Bay. Beyond Colville, a twisty, gravel (but well-maintained) road will take you to Fletcher Bay, the northernmost end of the peninsula. (It's impossible to fully circumnavigate the peninsula by road.) The road to Fletcher Bay goes north from Colville, coming to a T-junction about 5 km (3 miles) out of the settlement. The road to your left follows the west coast to a stunning sandy beach at Port Jackson, then continues along the cliff top and down to Fletcher Bay, a smaller, sandy cove banked by green pasture rolling down to the beach. It's 60 km (38 miles) from Coromandel—a 1¼-hour drive. There's a small camping ground here, tracks and beaches to explore, and the bay is considered one of the top spots to kayak in New Zealand. From Fletcher Bay, hikers can follow the signposted **Coromandel Coastal Walkway** to Stony Bay. The Coromandel Coastal Walkway follows an old bridle trail along the very northeastern tip of Coromandel Peninsula. It's a charming three- to four-hour walk, partly along cliff tops with grand views across to the Mercury Islands, and at times dipping down to secluded, forest-fringed beaches.

General Store. Colville's classic counterculture General Store is run by a local co-operative. It sells foodstuffs (there's a well-stocked organic section), wine, beer, and gasoline. It's kind of like the general store that used to be in all country areas. It's also the northernmost supplier on the peninsula, so don't forget to fill your tank. ✉ *2314, Colville Rd., Coromandel* ☎ *07/866–6805.*

WHERE TO EAT

$$ MODERN NEW ZEALAND

🍴 **Hereford 'n' a Pickle.** Homegrown fare is at its best here; the meat and produce in this café and store all come from the owner's local farm, Kairaumati Hereford Stud. The meat is processed on-site, the sausages made from an old family recipe, and the free-range eggs, honey, vegetables, jams, and pickles are all homegrown. Enjoy a barbecue breakfast, or for lunch there's a range of homemade, sandwiches, muffins, and cakes, plus freshly brewed coffee and real fruit ice cream. You can dine alfresco, relaxing in the garden or tree-shaded picnic area. On your way out, pick up a pack of farm-fresh meat and some condiments for later enjoyment. Open daily 8 to 5 (winter months call or text first). [$] *Average main: NZ$15* ✉ *2318 Colville Rd.* ☎ *21/136–8952* 🌐 *www.kairaumatipolledherefords.com.*

WHERE TO STAY

$$ HOTEL

🏨 **Anglers Lodge Motel and Holiday Park.** In a valley off the main road between Coromandel and Colville, these wooden accommodation units face the Motukawa Islands of Amodeo Bay. The beach is just over the road; it's a fisherman's paradise. **Pros:** friendly operators; stunning location. **Cons:** far from town. [$] *Rooms from: NZ$140* ✉ *Amodeo Bay, 1446 Colville Rd., Colville* ☎ *07/866–8584* 🌐 *www.anglers.co.nz* 🛏 *10 units, 1- and 2-bedroom cabins and flats, a 1-bedroom penthouse* 🍽 *No meals.*

$$$ HOTEL Fodor's Choice ★

🏨 **Tangiaro Kiwi Retreat.** This place is like the pot of gold at the end of the rainbow—it's quite a drive to get there but, hey, there are not many places in New Zealand where you can stay in simple, understated luxury, hear kiwi call at night, have a massage from a professional therapist, and soak in a private hot tub in the native bush. **Pros:** prolific birdlife—nearly 50 kiwi live in the local reserve; close to great beaches and forest walks; Wi-Fi throughout the property; quality touches throughout. **Cons:** if you like crowds, you might feel lonely here. [$] *Rooms from: NZ$260* ✉ *1299 Port Charles Rd., Coromandel* ☎ *07/866–6614, 0800/826–4276* 🌐 *www.kiwiretreat.co.nz* 🛏 *14 rooms* 🍽 *No meals.*

WHITIANGA

46 km (29 miles) southeast of Coromandel.

As you descend from the hills on the Coromandel's east coast, you'll enter Whitianga township. Here you'll find Buffalo Beach, named for the British ship that used to ferry convicts from the United Kingdom to Australia. The ship ran ashore and sank in 1840, and still lies buried in the sandy bottom of the bay.

The beachfront is lined with motels and hostels, all within walking distance of the shops of Whitianga, the main township on this side of the peninsula, and the ferry across Whitianga Harbour to Flaxmill Bay and Cooks Beach. Many people use the town as a base for fishing or boating trips, and others stock up for camping at nearby beaches. Over summer it hosts some great rock music and jazz shows, and people use it as a base for enjoying the region's gorgeous beaches.

The Whitianga i-SITE Visitor Centre can help you choose an excursion and has a full list of the many B&Bs in the area.

EN ROUTE

If you're driving between Whitianga and Coromandel and the sun is shining, make some time to head north toward Whangapoua. Park your car and grab your bathing suit and a surfboard if you're keen, and make the 30-minute trek over to New Chums beach, a native forest-fringed bay of golden sand. It's accessible only by foot, and you have to wade through an estuary to get there, but the secluded beach—once rated by the U.K. *Observer* as one of the world's top 20 deserted beaches—is well worth the walk.

4

GETTING HERE AND AROUND

Unless you're driving or on a charter flight from Auckland, bus is the only way to get to Whitianga (with the exception of those stalwart few who are conquering the Coromandel by bicycle). Bus companies stop at the Whitianga i-SITE Visitor Centre.

A nice way to explore Flaxmill Bay or Whitianga (if you're based at either of these points) is to leave your car on the dock and take the NZ$4 (NZ$6 return) ferry across and explore the beaches and cafés on foot.

Bus Depot Whitianga. ⊠ *Whitianga i-SITE Visitor Information Centre, 66 Albert St.* ☎ *07/866–5555* ⊕ *www.thecoromandel.com.*

TOURS

Fodor's Choice
★

Ocean Leopard Tours. Explore the drama of the volcanic coastline from the comfort of this sleek craft purpose-built for the task at hand. As a boy, skipper Jason came to Coromandel every year for family holidays. Now, after sailing international superyachts, he's returned to settle in the area and just loves to share his old holiday haunts with visitors. Justin's boat is also covered—great to keep the rain and sun at bay without spoiling the amazing views. The sturdy little craft can get right up close against towering sea cliffs, blowholes, and even into sea caves. Trips leave from both Whitianga Wharf and Ferry Landing (on the Cooks Beach side of the estuary). Excursions include "The Full Monty" (two hours), with options to add a snorkeling component or, by request only, "The Whirlwind Tour" (one hour). Bookings, available online, are essential in summer. ☎ *0800/843–8687* ⊕ *www.oceanleopardtours. co.nz* ⊠ *From NZ$60.*

Sea Cave Adventures. This company uses a smaller boat that can get you into the sea caves and blowholes (weather and tide dependent) as well as showcase all the sheer volcanic coastal cliffs and white-sand beaches. The skipper knows the best spots and you can shelter from the sun under the boat's awning. Two-hour trips leave from Whitianga Wharf at 8, 11, 2, and 4:30 (other times by request). Reservations recommended. ⊠ *Whitianga Wharf* ☎ *0800/80–6060* ⊕ *www.whitianga-adventures. co.nz* ⊠ *From NZ$75.*

VISITOR INFORMATION

Contacts Whitianga i-SITE Visitor Centre. ✉ *66 Albert St.* ☎ *07/866–5555* 🌐 *www.thecoromandel.com.*

EXPLORING

The Lost Spring. There are spas, and then there is The Lost Spring; thermal pools, day spa, and licensed restaurant set in the middle of town yet landscaped as if they're hidden in the forest. After 20 years of listening to local lore, planning, and digging, owner Alan Hopping finally struck gold, in this case tapping into hot,16,000-year-old mineral water that comes from 2,113 feet, underground and now fills a man-made haven of steaming lagoons, waterfalls, and quartz-studded caves. Lie back in the water and watch native birds eating berries from the trees and ferns, and butterflies darting among the hibiscus. Waiters deliver snacks, fresh juices, beer, wine, or cocktails right to the water's edge. Wander along the paths and over the swing bridge to the restaurant or upstairs to the Day Spa for a massage or any other therapeutic treatment (book ahead). The only thing stopping The Lost Spring from being a truly therapeutic health spa is your thermal:cocktail ratio. ✉ *121 A Cook Dr.* ☎ *07/866–0456* 🌐 *www.thelostspring.co.nz* 🎟 *NZ$38 (90-min pass); NZ$68 (all-day pass)* 🕒 *Daily 10:30–6 (8 Sat.)* ☞ *Restricted to 14 yrs and over.*

WHERE TO EAT

$ CAFÉ 🍴 **Cafe Nina.** Folks come here for breakfast and lunch every day of the week and you might have to wait a bit during holiday time, but locals think it's worth it. For breakfast, "The Classic" (bacon, sausages, eggs, fried potatoes, tomato, and toast) will set most people up for the day. At lunch you'll find hearty salads and seafood chowder, a staple for regulars. Cakes are seriously good, as is the coffee. Dine inside or out. Jasmine vines cloak the front porch of this adorable 1890 miner's cottage. [$] *Average main: NZ$14* ✉ *20 Victoria St.* ☎ *07/866–5440* 🕒 *Closed evenings (from 3 pm).*

$$$$ FRENCH FUSION 🍴 **Poivre & Sel.** French chef Samuel Goslin understands the Kiwi taste is for less salt, and less fat, so his French-fusion menu caters to suit. You can depend on locally famed Ora King salmon and Coromandel scallops, and perhaps garlic butter snails, roast quail, or wild goat. You must spare room for dessert; the chef's specialty is playing with flavors from flowers, and creating his own, exquisitely decorated chocolate. Wife Severine guides front of house, a sophisticated yet relaxed ambience, inside or in the cottage garden. Dining is not rushed. Reservations recommended. [$] *Average main: NZ$36* ✉ *2 Mill Rd.* ☎ *07/866–0053* 🌐 *www.poivresel.co.nz* 🕒 *Closed Sun. and Mon.*

$$$ NEW ZEALAND 🍴 **Salt Restaurant and Bar.** Put a slightly upmarket yet still casual restaurant in a popular local hotel, with a waterside location in a holiday town, and you've got Salt, a can't-miss dining spot. There is more casual restaurant dining in the hotel's bars, but Salt is the star. The table-studded, tiered deck reaches all the way down to the palm-edged marina. The menu changes with the seasons, sometimes offering free-range pork belly with prawn dumplings, lamb backstrap, or grass-fed eye fillet with béarnaise sauce. Bar snacks include lots of fresh seafood such as Coromandel mussels. During the summer make reservations. [$] *Average main: NZ$30*

✉ *1 Blacksmith La.* ☎ *07/866–5818* ⊕ *www.whitiangahotel.co.nz* ⊙ *Closed Mon. and Tues. May–Oct.*

WHERE TO STAY

$$$$ 🏨 **Admiralty Lodge.** A mile from the town center, but only across the road from Buffalo Beach, this is a good spot if you're planning on a few days beachside. **Pros:** views; big swimming pool; beach location. **Cons:** right beside the road. $ *Rooms from: NZ$325* ✉ *69–71 Buffalo Beach Rd.* ☎ *07/866–0181, 0508/236–472* ⊕ *www.admiraltylodge.co.nz* ⇆ *18 rooms* ⫶◉⫶ *Breakfast.*
HOTEL

$$$ 🏨 **Beachfront Resort.** You can step out of this tiny, family-run property's garden onto a breathtaking beach. **Pros:** stunning location; friendly hosts; good self-contained accommodations. **Cons:** a bit too far to walk to town. $ *Rooms from: NZ$300* ✉ *111–113 Buffalo Beach Rd.* ☎ *07/866–5637* ⊕ *www.beachfrontresort.co.nz* ⇆ *8 rooms* ⫶◉⫶ *Breakfast.*
B&B/INN

$$$ 🏨 **Oceanside Motel.** The views are great from any of the stylish studio suites or one-bedroom units. **Pros:** Wi-Fi throughout; friendly hosts; kayaks and guest barbecue available. **Cons:** small rooms. $ *Rooms from: NZ$235* ✉ *32 Buffalo Beach Rd.* ☎ *07/866–5766* ⊕ *www.oceansidemotel.co.nz* ⇆ *9 rooms* ⫶◉⫶ *Breakfast.*
B&B/INN

SPORTS AND THE OUTDOORS

Fishing, swimming, and diving are popular activities around this seaside town. There's kayaking along the dramatic coastline, with its rock arches and caves, or cruising the clear waters in a glass-bottom boat. Inland, old miner's trails now make interesting forest walks.

BOATING, FISHING, AND DIVING

Cathedral Cove Scenic Cruises. After coming to Coromandel for 20 years for holidays, owner/operator Ken Hindmarsh decided it was time to move here. Ken has a wealth of knowledge about the local history, geology, and marine life and he'll share it all with you as he shows you the special spots of this spectacular coastline. He even has an underwater camera installed on his boat, so you can check out the fish without getting wet, or you can jump right in and snorkel. Several tours leave daily from Whitianga Wharf (with Ferry Landing pickups an option). Reservations recommended. ✉ *Whitianga Wharf* ☎ *0800/888–688* ⊕ *www.cathedralcovecruises.co.nz* ⌦ *From NZ$60.*

Cave Cruzer. The Cave Cruzer gives you an unusual spin on an ex-Navy rescue boat, exploring Cathedral Cove, blowholes, and sea caves, with time for snorkeling if you wish. At one point, you'll head into a cave and your guides will provide a surprising acoustical demonstration. Two trip options are the standard 2- to 2½-hour Scenic and Sound, and 1-hour Express. There's no shade on this boat, but lots of

---

SCALLOPS GALORE

Whitianga Scallop Festival.
The Whitianga Scallop Festival, held during September, is one of the region's main events. Stalls serve scallops prepared every which way, and there are music performances, kids' activities, and cook-offs. No worries that it's only early spring, the vibes are warm enough. Keep an eye on the website, tickets sell quickly. ⊕ *www.scallopfestival.co.nz.*

personality. ☎ 07/866–0611, 0800/427–893 ⊕ *www.cavecruzer.co.nz* ✉ *From NZ$50.*

Dive Zone Whitianga. The place in Whitianga to go for scuba diving gear, training, and dive boat trips, this company runs PADI courses right up to five-star instructor development level. ✉ *7 Blacksmith La.* ☎ *07/867–1580* ⊕ *www.divezonewhitianga.co.nz.*

Glass Bottom Boat. Glass Bottom Boat cruises take you to Te Whanganui-A-Hei Marine Reserve, where you can see multitudes of marine life through the bottom of their boat. Informed guides discuss the formation and history of the land, Captain Cook's explorations along this coast during the 1700s, the Ngāti Hei, the Māori tribe who were the earliest settlers of the region, and more recent history of Narnia film locations. Daily trips year-round (10:30 am and 1:30 pm) plus 8 am and 4 pm, December to February (weather permitting), all leave from Whitianga Wharf. The trips take two hours. When the water's warm, they'll also stop for a snorkel. Bookings are essential. ☎ *07/867–1962* ⊕ *www. glassbottomboatwhitianga.co.nz* ✉ *From NZ$95.*

Water's Edge Charters. This highly experienced operator charters fishing and diving trips, specializing in half and full day outings, from Whitianga Marina. Skipper Craig will also share local stories and show you the great scenery and abundant birdlife. ☎ *07/866–5760.*

Whitianga Sports Centre. You can rent both diving and fishing gear from the Whitianga Sports Centre. ✉ *32 Albert St.* ☎ *07/866–5295.*

GUIDED HORSE TREKS

FAMILY   **Rangihau Ranch.** Rangihau Ranch offers guided horse rides into the rugged Coromandel ranges. Treks from 30 minutes to two hours will take you through native bush and across open pasture into the hills and valleys surrounded by spectacular views across the peninsula. All abilities are well catered to and preschoolers are welcome. Accommodation available. ✉ *111 Rangihau Rd., Coroglen* ☎ *07/866–3875* ⊕ *www. rangihauranch.co.nz* ✉ *From NZ$25.*

AROUND HAHEI

57 km (35 miles) southeast of Coromandel, 64 km (40 miles) northeast of Thames.

The beaches, coves, and seaside villages around Hahei make for a great day of exploring—or lounging. If you're craving a true beach vacation, consider basing yourself in Hahei rather than in Whitianga. From Hahei, you can easily reach Cathedral Cove, the Purangi Estuary, Cooks Beach, Flaxmill Bay (where the little passenger ferry crosses to Whitianga township); the famous Hot Water Beach is only minutes away.

GETTING HERE AND AROUND

If you're day-tripping from Whitianga, take the five-minute ferry ride (which leaves every hour, NZ$6 round-trip) across to Flaxmill Bay and explore by foot. Alternatively, follow State Highway 25 south from Whitianga. The road takes you past the Wilderland Community's roadside stand (selling organic produce and delicious honey

Swimmers enjoy the blue waters in Te-Whanganui-a-Hei (Cathedral Cove) Marine Reserve, Coromandel Peninsula.

from a community-run organic farm) and on a loop around to Hahei, Cooks Beach, and Flaxmill Bay. If you want to explore Cathedral Cove you can walk the steepish track, or simply catch a water taxi off the beach at Hahei.

Contacts Cathedral Cove Water Taxi. ☎ *027/919–0563*
⊕ *www.cathedralcovewatertaxi.co.nz.*

EXPLORING
TOP ATTRACTIONS
Cathedral Cove. The spectacular Cathedral Cove rock arch and white-sand crescent-shape beach is possibly the most visited feature in Coromandel. The two-hour return walk is steep but incredibly popular. The water at the cove is usually calm and clear, good for swimming and snorkeling, plus along the way there is a sidetrack (albeit steep) to Gemstone Bay, a rocky beach with an underground snorkel trail. To get there, travel along Hahei Beach Road, turn right toward town and the sea, and then, just past the shops, turn left onto Grange Road and follow the signs. In the height of summer the parking lot is likely to be full and you can start your walk down at the northern end of Hahei Beach, though it takes an extra 25 minutes and involves a bit of a climb. Another option is to jump on the Cathedral Cove Water Taxi that operates off Hahei Beach and can buzz you around to Cathedral Cove in a few minutes. Or you could paddle there with Cathedral Cove Kayaks. A good plan is to visit outside peak summer holiday season, January in particular. ⊠ *Trail head car park, end of Grange Rd., Hahei.*

WORTH NOTING

EN
ROUTE

Colenso Country Café and Shop. On State Highway 25 just south of the Hahei turnoff on the way to Tairua, this is a relaxed cottage café named after William Colenso, an early explorer of New Zealand. Set in a garden full of citrus and olive trees, lavender, and kitchen herbs, the café serves soups, moreish country-style pies, salads, an ever-changing variety of cakes, addictive chocolate fudge biscuits (also called slices), and Devonshire teas. In the shop you can procure tasty chutneys, jams, organic honey, and giftware. The open grassy space, play area, and tame donkeys make this an especially good place to stop with kids. ⊠ *State Hwy. 25, Whenuakite* ☎ *07/866–3725* ⊘ *Closed evenings (from 4 pm in winter, 5 pm in summer).*

Te Pare Historic Reserve. Overlooking Hahei Beach, and accessed via Pa Road, is Te Pare Historic Reserve, the site of a Māori *pā* (fortified village). Although no trace remains of the defensive terraces and wooden spikes that once ringed the hill, the stunning outlook, which made it an ideal defensive sight in years past, remains. At high tide, the blowhole at the foot of the cliffs adds a booming bass note to the sound of waves and the sighing of the wind in the grass. To reach the actual pā site, follow the red arrow down the hill from the parking area. After some 50 meters (164 feet), take the right fork through a grove of giant *pohutukawa* trees, then go through a gate and across an open, grassy hillside. You can also pick up the trail onto the headland from the southern end of Hahei Beach, at mid- to low tide. There's no entry fee. ⊠ *End of Pa Rd., Hahei.*

BEACHES

Cook's Beach. Cook's Beach lies along Mercury Bay, so named for Captain James Cook's observation of the transit of the planet Mercury in November 1769. The beach is notable because of the captain's landfall—it was the first by a European. It's a beautiful expanse of white sandy beach, albeit backed by growing sprawl of holiday homes. Forest-covered headlands overlook each end (take the walking track to Shakespeare Cliff Scenic and Historic Reserve, on the northern headland for the view), plus a pleasant inlet and river mouth at the south end. The beach is a good safe family swimming spot, likely to be crowded in peak summer (January) and delightfully quiet at other times of the year. As well as private holiday homes, B&Bs and a holiday park with campsites, backpacker huts, and studio units are located at the beach. **Amenities:** boat launching ramps; cafés (a few blocks back from the actual beach); parking (free); toilets. **Best for:** swimming; sunrise; walking. ⊠ *Marine Parade, Cooks Beach, Coromandel.*

Hot Water Beach. The popular Hot Water Beach is a wild beach to wander and a delightful thermal oddity. A warm spring seeps beneath the beach, and by scooping a shallow hole in the sand, you can create a pool of warm water; the deeper you dig, the hotter the water becomes. The phenomenon occurs only at low to mid-tide, so time your trip accordingly. In summer you'll be joined by hundreds of other spade-toting, wannabe bathers—plan your visit outside of busy January, if you can. If you are an adventurous sort, it can be fun in winter to sit in warm water while it rains. Hot Water Beach is well signposted off Hahei Beach

Road from Whenuakite (fen-oo-ah- *kye*-tee). ⚠ **Do not swim in the surf at Hot Water Beach; the spot is notorious for drownings.** However, nearby, at the end of Hahei Beach Road, you'll find one of the finest protected coves on the coast, with sands tinted pink from crushed shells; it's safe to swim here. If you need to while away some time before the tide goes out, there is a beachside café plus the Moko Artspace gallery across the road. **Amenities:** cafés and art gallery; changing rooms and showers; toilets; parking (small fee). **Best for:** natural hot water tubs in the sand; surfing (for experienced surfers only); walking. ✉ *Hot Water Beach Rd., Hot Water Beach, Coromandel.*

4

WHERE TO EAT

$$$ ECLECTIC Fodor's Choice ★

🍴 **Eggsentric Café.** Energetic owner Dave Fowell (hence the "egg" references) has created a community hub in his restaurant. More than great food—there are live music and jam sessions, poetry readings, film nights, and a sculpture symposium in summer. The menu reaches beyond standard café fare; try duck three ways, or fresh kingfish on lemon risotto with the famous local scallops. There's also a great range of classic breakfasts and fresh baking, and be sure to check the on-site shop, ''Eggstras" for quality deli goods to take on your journey. To get here, drive just beyond Cook's Beach on Purangi Road or take the ferry from Whitianga to Flaxmill Bay. The café is about 1 km (.6 mile) from the ferry landing. There's a free pick-up service if you don't fancy the 10-minute walk. [$] *Average main: NZ$29* ✉ *1049 Purangi Rd., Flaxmill Bay* ☎ *07/866–0307* 🌐 *www.eggsentriccafe.co.nz* 🕒 *Closed May 1–Oct. 1.*

$$ MODERN NEW ZEALAND

🍴 **Go Vino.** Small plates to share are the standout here, all featuring an eclectic fusion of Asian and classic European flavors with a strong Kiwi touch. Try the Tea Leaf Salad, Burmese style, with roasted soy beans, peanuts, *kawakawa* (a pepper-flavored native plant), cabbage, and tomato; ostrich and beef cheek; or the braised octopus with nectarines. You can share the smaller plates (NZ$13 to NZ$22) or let the chef treat you with a NZ$45 degustation menu. Sit inside in candlelight or under the trees in the buzzy garden with the locals. Open 9 am to late. [$] *Average main: NZ$18* ✉ *19 Captain Cook Rd., Cook's Beach* ☎ *07/867–1215* 🌐 *www.govino.co.nz* 🕒 *Closed Tues. (except in peak summer), Tues. and Wed. in mid-winter.*

WHERE TO STAY

$$$ HOTEL

🏨 **The Church Accommodation.** Originally a 1916 Methodist church from another town, dismantled, shifted, and rebuilt, the Church is worth a visit even if you're not staying the night. **Pros:** range of accommodations; lovely garden; free Wi-Fi throughout. **Cons:** at least 10-minute walk to the beach. [$] *Rooms from: NZ$205* ✉ *87 Hahei Beach Rd., Hahei* ☎ *07/866–3533* 🌐 *www.thechurchhahei.co.nz* 🕒 *Closed a few wks mid-winter. Dates vary, so check first* 🛏 *11 wooden cottages, 1 3-bedroom house* 🍽 *No meals.*

$$$ B&B/INN Fodor's Choice ★

🏨 **Mussel Bed.** Every detail of guest comfort and privacy is considered at this delightful, friendly B&B. **Pros:** down-to-earth, friendly, Kiwi hosts; excellent breakfasts and fresh baking; you can paddle or walk to the beach. **Cons:** away from town a bit; can't see the beach; you can't stay forever. $ *Rooms from: NZ$285* ⊠ *892 Purangi Rd., Cooks Beach* ☎ *07/866–5786* ⊕ *www.musselbed.co.nz* ⇨ *3 suites, 1 2-bedroom cottage* ¶○¶ *Breakfast.*

$$$
HOTEL

▢ **Tatahi Lodge.** In the center of Hahei and 100 meters (328 feet) down the street from the beach, this lodge comprises a number of low-lying wooden buildings in hidden, parklike surroundings. **Pros:** range of accommodation; good for budget travelers; close to everything. **Cons:** a bit crammed and can get crowded with younger travelers. $ *Rooms from: NZ$215* ⊠ *9 Grange Rd., Hahei* ☎ *07/866–3992* ⊕ *www.tatahilodge.co.nz* ⇨ *10 units, backpacker lodge* ¶○¶ *No meals.*

$$
B&B/INN

▢ **Wairua Lodge.** Amid 15 acres of native forest flanked by creeks and swimming holes sit four studios—known to the hosts as "snugs" because they're so cozy—and the two-bedroom River Deck suite. **Pros:** divine location; fantastic river swimming. **Cons:** unsealed road access—albeit a short distance—can make driving challenging, particularly if traveling at night. $ *Rooms from: NZ$195* ⊠ *251 Old Coach Rd., Hahei* ☎ *07/866–0304* ⊕ *www.wairualodge.co.nz* ⇨ *4 rooms, 1 2-bedroom suite* ¶○¶ *Breakfast.*

SPORTS AND THE OUTDOORS

Cathedral Cove Dive and Snorkel Hahei. Cathedral Cove Dive and Snorkel Hahei gives beginner, advanced, and dive-master courses, as well as daily dive trips in the Te Whanganui-A-Hei Marine Reserve, Cathedral Cove, and around the outer islands and pinnacles. Most dive sites are a 10-minute boat ride away. ⊠ *48 Hahei Beach Rd., Hahei* ☎ *07/866–3955* ⊕ *www.hahei.co.nz/diving.*

Fodor'sChoice
★

Cathedral Cove Kayak Tours. A great way to see this spectacular volcanic coastline is on a sea-kayaking tour with Cathedral Cove Sea Kayaking; and they're happy to work with beginners. You can paddle off the beach at Hahei and along the coast to the famous Cathedral Cove (the only kayak company licensed to land here), be served a cappuccino on the beach—and that's just the standard trip. They take groups of eight in double kayaks and pride themselves on taking visitors to places they are unlikely to see on foot. Other options, weather permitting, include full-day paddles (think caves, blowholes, and beaches all to yourselves), a sunrise or a sunset paddle, a family classic, and a remote coast tour. ⊠ *88 Hahei Beach Rd., Hahei* ☎ *07/866–3877, 0800/529–258* ⊕ *www.seakayaktours.co.nz* ▱ *From NZ$105 for standard ½ day.*

Hahei Explorer. *Hahei Explorer*, a sturdy, eight-seater rigid inflatable boat, explores this volcanic coastline's sea caves, blowhole, beaches, headlands, and spectacular Cathedral Cove. One-hour trips depart directly off Hahei Beach (the southeastern end) at 10 and 2 daily, also 9 and 3 in summer. Bookings essential; arrive 15 minutes before departure. ⊠ *Hahei* ✛ *South end of beach* ☎ *07/866–3910* ⊕ *www.haheiexplorer.co.nz* ▱ *NZ$85.*

TAIRUA

28 km (18 miles) south of Hahei, 37 km (23 miles) north of Whangamata.

Tairua is one of the larger communities along the coast, and one of the prettiest, nestled beside an estuary, harbor, and hills, with an ocean beach close by. Because State Highway 25 is the town's main road, it's also convenient for a bite en route to other seaside spots around Whitianga and Hahei. In Tairua, the twin volcanic peaks of Paku rise up beside the harbor. The five-minute ferry ride from Tairua across the harbor to the holiday homes of Pauanui takes you to the immediate area's best beach. The ferry runs hourly through summer school holidays, weekends and long weekends: NZ$5 round-trip. If you're here at the end of March you can get fully immersed, literally, in the Tairu Wet & Wild weekend—involving lots of water-sports fun. For year-round activities and maps check out the Pauanui and Tairua information centers.

GETTING HERE AND AROUND

If you're based in Thames, Tairua is an easy drive across the base of the Coromandel Peninsula along State Highway 25A. Otherwise, whether you're heading up or down the eastern side of the Coromandel, you can't miss it. The information center on the main road is a good place to stop in and get your bearings.

VISITOR INFORMATION

Contacts Pauanui Information Centre. ✉ *Vista Paku and Shepherd Ave.* ☎ *07/864–7101.* **Tairua Information Centre.** ✉ *223 Main Rd., Tairua* ☎ *07/864–7575* ⊕ *www.tairua.info/index.html.*

WHERE TO EAT

$$$ ✕ **Manaia Café and Bar.** This spacious, centrally located restaurant is
ECLECTIC welcoming and it shows—it can get busy. You can sit inside or out, depending on your mood and the weather. Try the slow-cooked lamb, or there's a generous selection of vegetarian dishes and hearty salads if meat isn't your thing. Gluten-free meals are also available. The café is also open for breakfast—the smoked-salmon eggs Benedict and blueberry muffins are popular. Open daily through the height of summer. If you arrive during the day, pop into the adjacent Manaia Gallery, which sells jewelry, art, and crafts. $ *Average main: NZ$26* ✉ *228 Main Rd.* ☎ *07/864–9050* ⊙ *Closed Tues. and Wed. in winter.*

$ ✕ **Surf and Sand.** Enjoy a New Zealand takeaway experience. This is the
SEAFOOD spot to get a quintessential Kiwi-style beachside lunch of *kūmara* chips, Coromandel mussels, fresh fish, or burgers of many kinds, including gluten free and vegetarian. You could even wash it down with a bottle of Lemon & Paeroa (L&P—the iconic Kiwiana soda made not too far from the Coromandel). The chips are crisp (they're fried in rice bran oil). $ *Average main: NZ$12* ✉ *Shop 7, Main Rd.* ☎ *07/864–8617.*

WHERE TO STAY

$$$ ⌂ **Blue Water Motel.** These bright and cheery colorful units are at the
HOTEL southern end of Tairua, across the street from a small sandy beach. **Pros:** simple and basic; close to the beach; outstandingly helpful hosts; free Wi-Fi. **Cons:** a bit crammed; beside the main road. $ *Rooms from:*

NZ$220 ✉ *213 Main Rd.* ☎ *07/864–8537* 🌐 *www.bluewatermotel.co.nz* 🛏 *5 studios, 1 1-bedroom unit, 2 2-bedroom units, 2 chalets (bigger studios)* 🍴 *No meals.*

$$$ HOTEL 🏨 **Pacific Harbour Lodge.** With a grand Pacific-styled portico, this resort property on the main street in Tairua looks like a tropical island getaway. **Pros:** tropical island ambience; good location; well priced. **Cons:** front units right beside main road. [$] *Rooms from: NZ$249* ✉ *223 Main Rd.* ☎ *07/864–8581* 🌐 *www.pacificharbour.co.nz* 🛏 *31 rooms* 🍴 *No meals.*

$$$ HOTEL 🏨 **Puka Park Resort Grand Mecure.** This hillside hideaway, managed by the international Accor hotel chain, nestles in native bushland on Pauanui Beach, at the seaward end of Tairua Harbor. **Pros:** upmarket and well appointed; close to the beach; pool, tennis court, and bikes are among amenities. **Cons:** somewhat formal for the region; access to rooms not easy. [$] *Rooms from: NZ$279* ✉ *Mount Ave., Pauanui* ☎ *07/864–8088* 🌐 *www.pukapark.co.nz* 🛏 *48 rooms* 🍴 *No meals.*

EN ROUTE

Wharekawa Wildlife Refuge. Stop at the dazzling, white-sand Opoutere Beach and Wharekawa (fah-ray- *ka*-wa) Wildlife Refuge, reached by a five-minute drive off SH25, turning left 8½ km (5 miles) south of Tairua. The road travels along the edge of Wharekawa Estuary to a car park. From here cross a wooden footbridge and follow the trail for 10 minutes through the forest to the beach. The long beach is bounded at either end by headlands, and there are outlooks to Slipper Island. Much of the estuary and headland area is part of the wildlife refuge, a breeding ground for shorebirds, including the endangered New Zealand dotterel. For information and maps about the Wharekawa Wildlife Refuge, ask at the Tairua or Whangamata information centers.

WHANGAMATA

37 km (23 miles) south of Tairua, 60 km (38 miles) east of Thames.

The Coromandel Ranges back Whangamata (fahng-a-ma- *ta*), another harborside town, with a population of around 3,500. Once a town of modest houses, it's been discovered by city people wanting to work remotely from the beach, and some mighty big homes have now been constructed here. The harbor, surf beaches, mangroves, and coastal islands are glorious. In summer, the population more than triples. It's a great spot for deep-sea fishing, and its bar break creates some of the best waves in New Zealand. For classic- and muscle-car enthusiasts, the Whangamata Beach Hop held each year at the end of April is a must-go. You'll see amazing classic cars and listen to some of the best rock-and-roll bands around. In October, British cars and bikes are a feature during the "Brits at the Beach" festival.

GETTING HERE AND AROUND

Whangamata is the Coromandel's last coastal port of call, as you travel southward into the Bay of Plenty. If you're only passing through but you've got a couple of hours to spare, check out some of the short bush walks in the area, or, of course, head down to the beach.

VISITOR INFORMATION

Contacts Whangamata Information Centre. ✉ *616 Port Rd.* ☎ *07/865–8340* ⊕ *www.whangamatanz.com.*

WHERE TO EAT

$$$$
MODERN NEW ZEALAND
✕ **Argo Restaurant.** Sophisticated, seasonal cuisine as created here by German chef Francisco Kurnak may not be what you'd expect in this small seaside town. The menu favors simple, and classic dishes such as rustic beef of the day with herb crème fraîche, jüs, and fries. Reservations preferred, especially on weekends. $ *Average main: NZ$31* ✉ *328 Ocean Rd.* ☎ *07/865–7157* ⊕ *www.argorestaurant.co.nz* ⊘ *Closed July and Aug. No lunch weekdays Apr.–July and Sept.–Nov.*

$$
CAFÉ
✕ **El Barrio Cafe & Bar.** Once a truck repair yard, now a quaint café. El Barrio opens early, at 7:30 am, so breakfasts are popular, as is the Atomic coffee. For lunch and later, however, it's the tapas that are the point of difference here, as well as lots of local seafood options (scallops, salmon fillet, and mussel fritters), plus falafel, house-made tortillas, hearty salads, steak sandwiches, and other, seriously good café food. $ *Average main: NZ$16* ✉ *101 Winifred Ave.* ☎ *07/865–6400* ⊘ *Closed Mon. and Tues. No dinner Wed., Thurs., and weekends.*

$$
CAFÉ
✕ **SixfortySix.** This café boasts of being the friendliest place in town, and the daylong crowds support the claim. Good coffee, fresh pastries, plus a paper roll menu (as they call it) listing breakfasts (pancakes, eggs, bagels) and lunch/dinners of beer-battered fish, chicken, papaya salads, and classic (huge) burgers. There's a generous selection of gluten- and dairy-free options, too. It's the sort of place where surfers might be seated alfresco next to older folks out for a balmy afternoon coffee. $ *Average main: NZ$20* ✉ *646 Port Rd.* ☎ *07/865–6117* ⊕ *www. sixfortysix.co.nz* ⊘ *No dinner Wed.–Fri.*

WHERE TO STAY

$$$$
B&B/INN
🏨 **Brenton Lodge.** Looking out over Whangamata and the islands in its harbor from your hillside suite, you'll feel rested and pampered, especially after being greeted with fresh flowers, fruit, and handmade chocolates. **Pros:** peaceful setting; pool and hot tub; breathtaking views. **Cons:** a little too far from town to walk home in the evening. $ *Rooms from: NZ$435* ✉ *2 Brenton Pl.* ☎ *07/865–8400* ⊕ *www.brentonlodge. co.nz* ⊘ *Closed June and July* ⤳ *3 suites* ⫶⊙⫶ *Breakfast.*

$$
HOTEL
🏨 **Pipinui Motel.** Tucked away down a quiet street, yet just a two-minute walk to Whangamata marina and a 10-minute walk to the beach, this motel has two studios and two one-bedroom units, all self-contained with modern kitchens, big bathrooms, peaceful pastel colors, and small private decks. **Pros:** modern and spacious; well serviced; good location. **Cons:** if you want to stay around Christmas you'll need to book months ahead. $ *Rooms from: NZ$190* ✉ *805 Martyn Rd.* ☎ *07/865–6796* ⊕ *www.pipinuimotel.co.nz* ⤳ *2 studios, 2 1-bedroom units, and 1 3-bedroom apartment* ⫶⊙⫶ *No meals.*

SPORTS AND THE OUTDOORS

The beach is where it's at here. Surfers and swimmers share the waves; farther offshore big-game fishing is popular.

SPORTS TOURS

Kiwi Dundee Adventures. Doug Johansen (Kiwi Dundee) and Jan Poole offer personalized, guided tours throughout New Zealand but they have a special focus on their home region, Coromandel. Their total enthusiasm for the region rubs off on anyone who takes a Kiwi Dundee tour. There are 1-day or 3-day walks and tours, plus 14- to 20-day tours all over New Zealand if you'd like more. ☏ *07/865–8809* ⊕ *www. kiwidundee.co.nz.*

Te Ra Charters. Te Ra (The Sun) skipper Chris Jones has been doing this job for more than 20 years, so he knows what he's doing. Half-day fishing trips are available during the day on Wednesday and Friday evenings throughout the year, and two trips daily during January. Or you can charter the boat for the day. Te Ra is also licensed for marine-mammal watching, so keep an eye out for the big guys while you're on board. Divers are welcome but must bring their own gear. ⊠ *120 Moana Anu Anu Ave.* ☏ *07/865–8681* ⊕ *tera.whangamata.co.nz* 🗌*NZ$ 55 per person for ½-day trips; NZ$650 full-day charter.*

SURFING

Whangamata Surf Shop. They know all about surfing in this town. If you're looking for a quick introduction to surfing, check out the Whangamata Surf Shop, owned by local surfing legend, Dean Williams (whose daughter Ella is World Junior Champ). The shop, in the center of town and recognized by its bright orange exterior, has surfboards, boogie boards, and wet suits for rent, plus they also offer one-on-one surfing lessons. You can book at the shop, or, during summer, they're also set up down on the beach. ⊠ *634 Port Rd.* ☏ *07/865–8252* 🗌*$80 (1 hr, including instructor and surfboard).*

WALKING

Wentworth Valley. Regenerating forest, gold mine history, and the 150-foot-high Wentworth Falls are all features on this quality walk in the hills of southern Coromandel Forest park, behind Whangamata. There's also a Department of Conservation campsite in the valley, and lots of swimming holes for cooling off on hot summer days. From Whangamata township drive south on SH25 for 2.5 km (1½ miles). Turn right off the highway into Wentworth Valley Road. The track starts at the road end. ⊠ *Wentworth Valley Rd.* ☏ *07/865–7032* ⊕ *www.wentworthvalleycamp.co.nz.*

WAIHI TO PAEROA

Waihi is 30 km (18.6 miles) south of Whangamata, 20 km (12.4 miles) from Paeroa.

The southern Coromandel is bounded by the historic and scenic Karangahake Gorge and smaller, adjoining Waikino Gorge. State Highway 2 wends its way through the forest-covered, gorged terrain from small farming town Paeroa, to the gold-mining center of Waihi. While the towns are just 20 km (12.4 miles) apart, there is much to see and do along the way. Try to give yourself some time to explore the forest walks to old mining sites, batteries, and tunnels. Better still, take a bike ride on the Hauraki Rail Trail (including through the tunnels). Check out the gold-mining history in Waihi. If you're not beached-out after the Coromandel, head to beautiful Waihi Beach, 11½ km (7 miles) from Waihi.

Gold mining has helped shaped the history of this region. From the late 1800s to early 1900s, hundreds of miners toiled in both underground and open pit mines. You can reflect on their efforts at heritage sites and in museums, and even visit a working mine, as mining still continues in Waihi.

Today a new rush of people come here to explore the walking trails and heritage mining sites and tunnels, to cycle the Hauraki Rail Trail and the Goldfields Heritage Railway, and to visit the cafés and wineries.

GETTING HERE AND AROUND

If you've headed south down the east coast of the Coromandel, Waihi is your last port of call before you arrive into the Bay of Plenty. Consider a break here, or at least a detour to the west on State Highway 2. This will lead you into the Waikino, then Karangahake Gorge in Coromandel Forest Park, then you'll emerge into open farmland country and Paeroa township. InterCity run daily bus services to the region.

Bus Travel InterCity. ☏ *07/868–7251, 0800/446–549 NZ only* ⊕ *www.intercity.co.nz.*

VISITOR INFORMATION

Contacts Paeroa Information Centre. ⊠ *101 Normanby Rd., Paeroa* ☏ *07/862–8636.* **Waihi i-SITE Visitor Centre.** ⊠ *126 Seddon St., Waihi* ☏ *07/863–9015* ⊕ *golddiscoverycentre.co.nz.*

EXPLORING

FAMILY **Gold Discovery Centre and Gold Mine Tour.** Head underground to this interactive museum explaining the region's gold-mining history. The roof is lined with timbers as if you are in a real mine shaft. You can operate a compressor drill, fire the explosives, learn of the local geology and the role of stamper batteries in extracting gold from rock, and understand the social upheavals of striking miners, unions, and bosses. Each visit is personally introduced. If you want to see the real thing, you can also take a tour (1½ hours) to Waihi's still-working mine. Tours leave from the center, bookings recommended. ⊠ *126 Seddon St., Waihi* ☏ *07/863–9015* ⊕ *www.golddiscoverycentre.co.nz* ☏ *NZ$25 (Gold Discovery Centre), NZ$29 (gold mine tour), NZ$46 (combo ticket)* ⊙ *Daliy: 9–5 (Gold Discovery Centre), 10:30 and 12:30 (gold-mine tours; extra times may be offered in summer, check website).*

FAMILY **Goldfields Railway.** This half-hour, 7-km (4.3-mile) heritage-train journey into the Karangahake Gorge follows part of the former Waihi to Paeroa line, built in 1905 after five years of challenging construction in the steep gorge country. The train travels from historic Waihi Railway Station to the Waikino Station Café, which, luckily, has great homemade food. Travel one way or return, or bring your bike—from Waikino to Paeroa the former railway line now forms part of the Hauraki Rail Trail for bikers and walkers. Reservations for the train are recommended. ⊠ *30 Wrigley St., Waihi* ☏ *07/863–9020* ⊕ *www.waihirail.co.nz* ☏ *NZ$12 (one-way), NZ$18 (return)* ⊙ *Departs Waihi 11:45* *daily, plus 10 and 1:45 weekends and public holidays. Departures can be variable so check website for up-to-date times.*

Martha Mine. Gaze in awe into the huge open pit of the Martha Mine, right in the center of Waihi, and one of the world's most significant gold and silver mines of its time. Between the late 1800s and 1952, thousands of miners worked here, extracting 174,000 kilograms of gold and more than a million kilos of silver. Cross the road from the Waihi i-SITE Visitor Information Centre to the towering Cornish Pumphouse (relocated here) for a glimpse into the pit, and perhaps walk around the Pit Rim Walkway (5 km/3 miles). It's an easy, obvious trail with historic information to read along the way. ✉ *Seddon St., Waihi.*

BEACHES

Waihi Beach. Waihi Beach, 19 km (12 miles) north of Katikati, is ideal for swimming and surfing and has access to numerous walkways. With 9 km (5½ miles) of sweeping white sand, the beach is one of the region's safest for swimming, surfing, and kayaking, and is particularly popular in peak summer (January). A surf club offers beach patrols at the beach's northern end and, in summer, at the far Bowentown end in the south, though you'll find people splashing about all along the long white stretch. At low tide, people dig in the sand looking for *tuatua* and *pipi*—delicious shellfish that you boil until they open. Don't miss the drive to the top of the Bowentown heads at the southern end of Waihi Beach. This is an old Māori pā (fortified village) with stunning views. A short but steep walk from here leads to Cave Bay directly below the viewing point. ⚠ **Don't swim at Cave Bay; there are dangerous currents.** The Waihi Beach township encompasses restaurants and shops and there is a full range of accommodations, from holiday parks to boutique lodges. **Amenities:** food and drink; lifeguard; toilets; parking; surf school. **Best for:** kayaking; swimming; sunrise; surfing; walking; windsurfing. ✉ *The Esplanade, Waihi Beach* 🌐 *www.waihibeachinfo.co.nz.*

WHERE TO EAT

$$$$ MODERN NEW ZEALAND

🍴 **Bistro at the Falls Retreat.** It might be way out in the bush but this restaurant could stand proud in any big city. Dine inside or out, beneath the trees, and watch the chefs in the open kitchen firing up the wood-fired oven for pizzas or creating contemporary cuisine with organic-farmed beef and lamb and vegetables straight from the garden. For flavor and innovation, try the chef's choice of three seasonal tasters. This is a great option for family dining—there's so much space and a little playground—and it's actually only about 10 minutes away from town, Waihi or Paeroa. Open 11 am to late. [$] *Average main: NZ$33* ✉ *25 Waitawheta Rd., Karangahake Gorge* ☎ *07/863–8770* 🌐 *www.fallsretreat.co.nz* 🕓 *Closed Mon. and Tues. Apr.–Oct. (approximately).*

$$$ MODERN NEW ZEALAND

🍴 **Ohinemuri Estate.** Hidden away in the forest of Karangahake Gorge, the café is here to attract people to the winery and does a great job of doing so. The comprehensive à la carte menu changes with the seasons but always offers a mix of chowders and soups, pastas and salads, lamb, pork, and seafood, desserts, and a Vintner's Platter, for sharing. Dishes are designed to complement the wines, which are made with grapes sourced from sustainable vineyards throughout all New Zealand's major wine regions. The café is set in an old stable building that opens to a delightful cottage garden, and it's right on the Hauraki Rail Trail. Park your bike and imbibe. Open 10–5 daily December to February, Thursday through Monday 10–4 March to November. $ *Average main: NZ$28* ✉ *Moresby St., Karangahake Gorge* ☎ *07/862–8874* ⊕ *www. ohinemuri.co.nz* ⊗ *Closed Mon. and Tues. in winter.*

$ ✕ **The Refinery.** Hidden down a side street (look for the sign on the main

CAFÉ street), is this gourmet home-cooking surprise. This excellent coffee shop and café serves breakfasts, home-baked muffins, scones, cakes and shortcakes, build-your-own bagels, and counter "sammies" crammed with choices of grilled meats, *haloumi* (salty cheese of goat and sheep's milk), and vegetables (the corned beef on rye Reuben is a signature). Most ingredients are free range, organically grown. The setting is a heritage building originally a bank gold refinery, built during the height of this district's gold-mining days. Open 9:30 to 3:30, Wednesday to Sunday. The Refinery also encompasses a boutique one-bedroom accommodation, the Refinery Guard's Cottage, NZ$140/night. $ *Average main: NZ$13* ✉ *5 Willoughby St., Paeroa* ☎ *07/862–7678* ⊕ *the-refinery.co. nz* ⊗ *Closed Mon. and Tues.*

$$$ ✕ **Waitete Restaurant, Cafe & Ice Creamery.** Enjoy the finest local produce,

MODERN NEW and, of course, the house-made ice cream at this peaceful country setting

ZEALAND on the edge of town. The German-born chef makes his own stocks and sauces and cooks everything to order. Seafood risotto or grilled duck and lentil stew, or wild hare marinated in red wine are tempting main courses, all matched with wine recommendations by the master sommelier. There is also a degustation menu. $ *Average main: NZ$29* ✉ *31 Orchard Rd., Waihi* ☎ *07/863–8980* ⊕ *www.waitete.co.nz* ⊗ *Closed Mon. and 4–6 Tues.–Sun.*

WHERE TO STAY

$$$$ ⬚ **Manawa Ridge.** Everything about this luxury eco-retreat, with its three

B&B/INN guest suites, is outstanding. **Pros:** 360-degree farm, forest, and coastal

Fodor's Choice views; hospitable hosts; gourmet breakfasts. **Cons:** 9 km (5.6 miles)

★ out of town. $ *Rooms from: NZ$950* ✉ *267 Ngatitangata Rd., Waihi* ☎ *07/863–9400* ⊕ *manawaridge.co.nz* ⤳ *3 suites* ⦿ *Breakfast* ⊟ *No credit cards.*

SPORTS AND THE OUTDOORS
BICYCLING

FAMILY **Hauraki Rail Trail.** Join the many Kiwi families discovering this new, gen-

Fodor's Choice tly graded 82-km (51-mile) bike trail. It starts from Thames, crosses

★ Hauraki Plains farmland to Paeroa, then follows the old railway line through scenic Karangahake Gorge to Waihi. Heritage gold-mine sites, bridges, and tunnels are part of the drama, so bring a torch. Take a break at a country café, camp, or stopover at a B&B en route. You can even ride the Goldfields Railway train along with your bike for the final stretch. This trail is one of the New Zealand Cycle Trails' "Great Rides." ✉ *Karangahake Gorge* ☎ *07/868–5140* ⊕ *www.haurakiRailTrail.co.nz.*

HIKING

FAMILY **Karangahake Gorge Walks.** Rivers, waterfalls, and steep, forested-sided ravines, plus old railway tunnels and gold-mining sites can all be explored on the walkways in Karangahake Gorge. The trails are well maintained by the Department of Conservation (DOC) and designed to showcase the best natural and heritage features. Recommended are Windows Walk (one hour), Rail Tunnel Loop (one hour), and Karangahake Historic Walkway (three hours). Some tracks are shared with bikers on the Hauraki Rail Trail, but there's plenty of room. Look for the large riverside car park and DOC signs part way through the gorge, opposite Moresby Road (to tiny Karangahake village). Most tracks begin across a footbridge from here. DOC camping spots, and several good cafés, are also in the area. Pick up a DOC brochure at local i-SITE Visitor Information Centres. ⊠ *Karangahake* ⊕ *www.doc.govt.nz.*

THE BAY OF PLENTY

Explorer Captain James Cook gave the Bay of Plenty its name for the abundant sources of food he found here; these days it's also known for its plentiful supply of beaches. Places like Mount Maunganui and Whakatane overflow with sunseekers during peak summer-vacation periods, but even at the busiest times you need to travel only a few miles to find a largely secluded stretch of beach.

The Bay of Plenty has a significant Māori history; this is the first landing place of *Takitimu, Tainui, Arawa,* and *Mataatua,* four of the seven Māori migration *waka* (canoes) that arrived in New Zealand from the Polynesian Pacific Islands, and from what they call their traditional homeland, Hawaiki. These first arrivals formed the ancestral base for the Māori tribes of the Tauranga region: Ngāti Ranginui, Ngāti Te Rangi, and Ngāti Pûkenga.

The central city base of "The Bay" is Tauranga and associated port, Mount Maunganui. Both have retained a relaxed vacation-town vibe despite ongoing expansion. From here and from the next major town, Whakatane, you can take day trips to beaches, the bush, and offshore attractions such as volcanic White Island. "Laid-back sophistication," is an apt description of what this region can offer its visitors.

KATIKATI

62 km (39 miles) southeast of Thames, 35 km (22 miles) northwest of Tauranga.

The small town of Katikati was built on land confiscated from local Māori after the 1863 land wars and given to Irish Protestant settlers by the Central Government, the only planned Irish settlement anywhere. Long before the Irish arrived, Māori had recognized the area's potential for growing food crops. These days, fruit growing—particularly kiwifruit and avocado—keeps the Katikati economy afloat, perhaps providing one of (many) explanations for Katikati's name, "to nibble" in Māori. Katikati's most noticeable features are more than 50 murals around town, depicting its history. Another interesting attraction is the

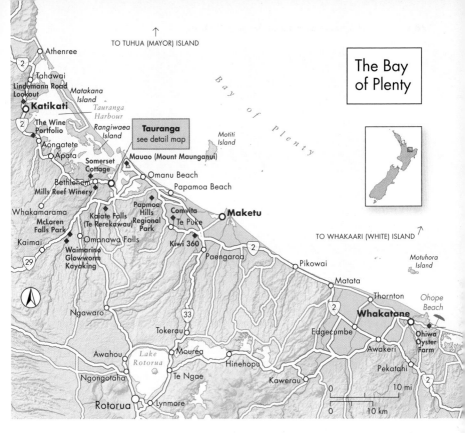

The Bay
of Plenty

TO TUHUA (MAYOR) ISLAND

TO WHAKAARI (WHITE) ISLAND

Haiku Pathway, a walking trail studded with haiku-etched boulders. The path starts on Katikati's Main Street and leads down to the river. Pick up a map of the route at Katikati Visitor Information.

GETTING HERE AND AROUND

While remaining on the Pacific Coast Highway, head south from the Coromandel toward the Bay of Plenty. At Waihi, State Highway 25 switches and becomes State Highway 2. The next town you'll meet along State Highway 2 is Katikati, better known for its agricultural bounty than as a beach or fishing town (though the sea is very close by).

VISITOR INFORMATION

Contacts Katikati Visitor Information. ⊠ *36 Main Rd.* ☎ *07/549–1658* ⊕ *www.katikati.org.nz.*

EXPLORING

Lindemann Road Lookout. For great views over the Bay of Plenty, go a couple of minutes north of Katikati on State Highway 2 to the Lindemann Road Lookout. It's signposted where Lindemann Road turns off the main road. Drive 3.5 km (2 miles) to the road end and the lookout. The road is good but narrow in parts. At the lookout you'll find a map embedded in rock to help orient you. Look for Tuhua (Mayor Island) just to the north and Mauao (Mt. Maunganui) to the south. If the weather is clear you might even see volcanic White Island, farther to the south.

The Wine Portfolio. Just south of Katikati on Highway 2, you'll spot the Cape Dutch design of the winery's cellar door. Originally the home of Morton Estate Wines, this boutique, specialist winery now produces vintages from grapes grown in leading New Zealand wine regions Hawke's Bay and Marlborough. Here's your chance to sample the country's best, all in one place. The Cellar Door is open for tastings daily from 9:30 to 5. ✉ *2389 Main Rd.* ☎ *07/552–0795* 🌐 *www.wineportfolio.co.nz* 🕐 *Daily 9:30–5.*

WHERE TO EAT

$$$ NEW ZEALAND 🍴 **The Landing.** The Landing restaurant in the 1876-built Talisman Hotel offers a range pub fare including wood-fired pizzas and seafood chowder. For something more substantial, try the pork belly or the fillet steak served with scallops and prawns in a white-wine-and-cream sauce. Open daily from 11:30 am to late. [$] *Average main: NZ$28* ✉ *7–9 Main Rd., State Hwy. 2* ☎ *07/549–3218* 🌐 *www.talismanhotel.co.nz.*

WHERE TO STAY

$$ B&B/INN 🏨 **Crindau Lodge.** Gardens, grassy paths, ferns, and a feijoa orchard surround this stylish accommodation, actually a barn renovated with two custom-designed, fully self-contained guest suites, and the views stretch all the way to Mauao (Mt. Maunganui). **Pros:** appealing environment; thoughtfully appointed furnishings and art. **Cons:** out of the way; units are self-catering, so you'll need to bring your own provisions. [$] *Rooms from: NZ$185* ✉ *530A Lund Rd.* ☎ *07/549–4750* 🌐 *www.crindaulodge.co.nz* 🛏 *2 rooms* 🍽 *No meals.*

$$ HOTEL 🏨 **Kaimai View Motel.** Right on Katikati's main strip, with panoramic views of the Kaimai Range, this motel is close to area activities, making it a low-key and handy base. **Pros:** disabled access in one unit; warmly decorated. **Cons:** traffic noise. [$] *Rooms from: NZ$165* ✉ *84 Main Rd., State Hwy. 2* ☎ *07/549–0398* 🌐 *www.kaimaiview.co.nz* 🛏 *7 rooms, 7 suites* 🍽 *No meals.*

$$$$ HOTEL Fodor'sChoice ★ 🏨 **Matahui Lodge.** This lodge on 6 acres of manicured gardens and vineyards is an outstanding example of the boutique home-hosted properties popping up in this region. **Pros:** substantial breakfasts; lovely gardens; good wine list. **Cons:** a little far from town for some. [$] *Rooms from: NZ$475* ✉ *187 Matahui Rd., 9 km (5½ miles) south of Katikati* ☎ *07/571–8121* 🌐 *www.matahui-lodge.co.nz* 🛏 *3 suites* 🍽 *Breakfast.*

TAURANGA

216 km (134 miles) southeast of Auckland.

The population center of the Bay of Plenty, Tauranga is one of New Zealand's fastest-growing cities. Along with neighboring town, Whakatane, this seaside city also rates as one of the country's sunniest spots. Unlike most local towns, Tauranga doesn't grind to a halt in the off-season, because it has one of the busiest ports in the country, and the excellent waves at the neighboring beach resort of Mount Maunganui—just across Tauranga's harbor bridge—always draw surfers and holiday folk.

GETTING HERE AND AROUND

Whether you self-drive, catch a bus, or fly, getting to Tauranga is simple. Air New Zealand flies daily from major cities throughout New Zealand to Tauranga Airport. By road, Tauranga is about a 50-minute drive northeast of Rotorua. From Auckland, allow 2½ hours for the drive south. You can travel either on State Highway 2 through the southern Coromandel and northern Bay of Plenty regions (arguably more scenic) or on State Highway 1 to Waikato then State Highway 29, which crosses over the Kaimai Ranges—a steep-ish but scenic drive through farmland and native forest. InterCity buses travel daily to Tauranga from Auckland, Hamilton, and Rotorua. The Tauranga bus depot is in the city center, handy to shops and accommodations.

Once you are here, major and clearly signposted roads lead from Tauranga to coastal resorts, Mount Maunganui and Papamoa, and south through kiwifruit orchard country to Whakatane. A toll expressway bypasses some of these places, for example, Te Puke, should you be in such a hurry on your vacation. Local bus company the Bay Bus (sometimes called the Bay Hopper) travels regularly between Tauranga and regional towns including Mount Maunganui, Te Puke, Katikati, and Whakatane. Activity operators, for example, swim with dolphins, kayaking, fishing, and walking tours, are mostly based in or close to the city or will collect you from your accommodations.

Bus Contacts Bay Bus. ✉ *Tauranga* ☎ *0800/422–928* ⊕ *www.baybus.co.nz.* **InterCity Tauranga Depot.** ✉ *95 Willow St.* ☎ *07/578–8103.*

VISITOR INFORMATION

Contacts Tauranga i-SITE Visitor Information Centre. ✉ *95 Willow St.* ☎ *07/578–8103* ⊕ *www.bayofplentynz.com.*

EXPLORING

To explore the town center, start at the **Strand,** where palm trees separate the shops from the sea. Bars, restaurants, and cafés line the Strand and nearby side streets. If you're interested in the beachier side of Tauranga, head 8 km (5 miles) east out of the city center and over the Harbor Bridge to Mount Maunganui. Here, you'll find one of the best surf spots in the country along the 20-km (12½-mile) shoreline, a sheltered, harborside swimming spot, as well as shopping, restaurants, and walking tracks up and around the prominent, small, and dormant volcano Mauao (Mt. Maunganui or, as locals say, The Mount).

TOP ATTRACTIONS

Kaiate Falls (Te Rerekawau). The falls are a little off-the-beaten-track but worth the trip, driving past kiwifruit orchards, farms, and forest. About 15 minutes southeast of Tauranga, just off Welcome Bay Road, the Kaiate Stream drops over bluffs in a series of waterfalls and rocky lagoons, culminating in a deep green lagoon flanked by moss- and fern-fringed cliffs. A 20- to 30-minute loop trail takes you down to the main lagoon and through lush greenery. The falls' summit (and the parking lot) affords views over Tauranga and the coast. To get there, turn off Welcome Bay Road onto Waitao Road, after a few kilometers turn onto Kaiate Falls Road, after 1 km (½ mile) turn into the Kaiate

Falls Scenic Reserve parking lot. The track is clearly signposted from here. ⊠ *Kaiate Falls Rd.* ☎ *07/578–7677.*

FAMILY **Mauao (Mt. Maunganui).** This dormant volcanic mountain is the region's geological icon, with its conical rocky outline rising 761 feet above sea level. White-sand beaches with clear water stretch for miles from Mauao—this is one of New Zealand's best swimming and surfing areas. One of the early Māori canoes, *Takitimu*, landed at the base of the mountain. A system of trails around Mauao includes an easy walk around its base and the more strenuous climb to the summit from the campground at the base of the mountain. The trails are clearly signposted and heavily used, so no bushwhacking is necessary. All roads lead to "The Mount," as they say; follow any road running parallel to the beach. The Mount Maunganui area gets crowded around Christmas and New Year's Eve; to see it at its best, come in November, early December, or between mid-January and late March. Walks along the beach and up Mauao are a delight. In January, you can watch the fit folk competing in the three-day Festival of Multisport while drinking coffee at a sidewalk café (or you can join them).

WORTH NOTING

Comvita. This company has developed a worldwide following for its honey-based health products. Put yourself in the place of real honeybee in their interactive 3-D experience during a guided tour of the forest, where you will learn about the healing nature of native New Zealand plants, in particular the manuka tree. Tours (40 minutes) start at 11, 1, and 3, bookings recommended. You can also treat yourself to a therapy treatment using Comvita health products (bookings and prices through website), relax in the café, and explore the retail store, where fully trained staff will help you understand the range of health, wellness, and beauty products. ⊠ *23 Wilson Rd., Paengaroa, Te Puke* ☎ *07/533–1987, 0800/493–782* ⊕ *www.experiencecomvita.com* ☎ *NZ$18 (for guided tour, entry free to shop and café)* ⊙ *Daily 8:30–5.*

Elms Mission House. Built in 1847, this was the first Christian missionary station in the Bay of Plenty. The lovely late-Georgian house, named for the 50 elms that grew on the property, was home to descendants of pioneer missionaries until the mid-1990s. You can explore the lush grounds, but the real appeal lies in the main house, the small wooden chapel, and the collection of furniture, crockery, and other period items. ⊠ *15 Mission St.* ☎ *07/577–9772* ⊕ *www.theelms.org.nz* ☎ *NZ$5 (tour of library and house), free (gardens)* ⊙ *Daily 10–4.*

Kiwi 360. Te Puke rightfully claims the title of kiwifruit capital of the world, as the major kiwifruit growing and exporting region of New Zealand. Kiwi 360 is devoted to this furry little vitamin C–loaded fruit. You can tour an actual kiwifruit orchard on a cute little KiwiKart train and learn all about the complexities of raising an export-ready crop, learn why it grows so well in this fertile region—and sample the harvest. Tours depart every hour, from 9 to 4 (summer) and 10 to 3 (winter). Then you can enjoy the wholesome food in the Kiwi 360 café, and browse the huge range of quality designer products and mementos in the Kiwi 360 store. To find it, look for the giant kiwifruit, just beside SH2 five minutes' drive south of Te Puke (take the free SH2 road, not the toll expressway). ✉ *24 Young Rd., Paengaroa* ☎ *07/573–6340* 🌐 *kiwi360.com* 🎟 *NZ$20 for 1-hr KiwiKart tour* 🕑 *Daily 9–5.*

McLaren Falls Park. A 15-minute drive south of Tauranga off State Highway 29, this extensive, open park offers a 10-minute easy bushwalk to the falls and more strenuous walks to Pine Tree Knoll or the Ridge for great vistas across the park. The park is also a great spot for a picnic with picnic tables and coin-operated barbecues. Watch out for big and hungry geese. ✉ *State Hwy. 29* ☎ *07/578–8103.*

Mills Reef Winery. Established by the Preston family, enhanced by winemaker Paul Dawick, and using quality grapes from renowned Hawke's Bay vineyards, Mills Reef Winery has built a fine reputation for its award-winning wines. The winery itself is a treat to visit; the spacious, landscaped, 20-acre complex includes an art deco–style tasting room and restaurant. You can dine alfresco on baked salmon, slow-braised beef, organic lamb rump, and a scrumptious range of salads, matched with classy Mills Reef wines, including the highly regarded Elsbeth range. Mains range from NZ$27 to NZ$38.The restaurant is open daily for brunch and lunch, and from Thursday to Saturday for dinner during the peak of summer. Dinner reservations are essential because the venue is often booked for weddings. The cellar door/tasting room is open daily 10 to 5 (except public holidays). ✉ *143 Moffat Rd., Bethlehem* ✥ *About 5 km (3 miles) north of Tauranga* ☎ *07/576–8800* 🌐 *www.millsreef.co.nz* 🕑 *Closed evenings Sun.–Wed.*

4

FAMILY **Papamoa Hills Regional Park.** Twenty kilometers (12½ miles) from Tauranga, the 45-minute summit walk through the 108-acre park on the Papamoa Hills (Te Rae o Papamoa) will take you past Māori pā (fortified village) sites dating back to 1460, considered some of the most important and earliest archaeological sites in the region. You climb through pine forest, then open farmland. As you emerge from the trees, views take in everything between Mauao and White Island. Follow the clearly marked track from the car park, which is at the end of Poplar Lane, which turns off old SH2. (You'll need to get off the tolled Expressway for access. If traveling from Tauranga, take the Papamoa exit then follow the signs indicating free road to Te Puke. Go past Welcome Bay Road then look for Poplar Lane, on the right.) ✉ *Poplar La., Papamoa Hills.*

WHERE TO EAT

$$ ITALIAN 🍴 **Bella Mia.** Pizza- and pasta-maker Guisseppe Scorce re-created a little piece of Italia here in central Tauranga in 1978 and has been going strong ever since. The decor is classic Italian, with red-and-white checked tablecloths and grapes hanging from the ceiling, and the pasta is homemade—the tortellini is prepared every afternoon—and the flavorful pizzas are thin-crusted. Be sure to leave room for dessert—Bella Mia makes its own gelato, sorbets, and tiramisu. They only open for dinner during winter but if you're keen for lunch (and it's not Sunday, and there's more than two of you), just give them a call the night before and they'll open up. [$] *Average main: NZ$20* ✉ *73A Devonport Rd.* ☎ *07/578–4996* ✥ *B3.*

$$$

NEW ZEALAND

✗ **Bravo Restaurant Café.** With jazz music and tables spilling out onto the sidewalk patio, this restaurant is popular right from the start of the day with brunch, when you can sip a strong latte and enjoy a dish of smoked salmon with scallion, fried potatoes, poached eggs, and hollandaise sauce. Actually there's a huge range on the daylong menu. Produce is handpicked from local suppliers and the restaurant is a regular winner of the NZ Beef and Lamb Excellence Awards. Focaccias, hot sandwiches, shared platters, salads, satays, and pizzas are delivered by young, energetic, efficient staff. In the evening the casual café turns into a dinner restaurant. $ *Average main: NZ$22* ✉ *Red Sq.* ☎ *07/578–4700* ⊕ *www.cafebravo.co.nz* ⊗ *No dinner Sun.–Tues.* ✛ *B3.*

$$$$

MODERN NEW

ZEALAND

✗ **Harbourside.** The food and the view will vie for your attention here, as you dine on contemporary New Zealand cuisine, created largely from local artisan and organic products, and admire Tauranga Harbour from the stunning waterfront location. The menu mixes starters (smoked salmon rillette) or starters to share; light meals (chicken thigh stack) and main courses which come with matches of vegetables and eight different sauces. Dessert classics include panna cotta, pavlova, sticky date pudding, and more. Reservations are recommended, particularly if you want a spot on the over-water balcony. $ *Average main: NZ$37* ✉ *Old Yacht Club Bldg., 150 The Strand* ☎ ⊕ *www. harboursidetauranga.co.nz* ✛ *B3.*

$$$$

NEW ZEALAND

Fodor's Choice

★

✗ **Mount Bistro.** The prices set this restaurant apart from other Mount Maunganui options, but then so does the chef and his menu. The streetside restaurant looks out onto Mauao (Mt. Maunganui). In the open-plan kitchen, nationally renowned chef Stephen Barry fuses indigenous ingredients with Pacific Rim flavors. From the à la carte menu, the appetizer of "Sword n Sauce-ry" (skewer of scallops, prawn tail, crayfish, salmon, fresh fish flambéed with horopito and lime vodka served with dipping sauces) is just one of Barry's standout, signature dishes. Menu choices range from small tapas to share, to medium appetizers to main courses and, for those who inevitably want a taste of all the desserts, there's a tasting platter. Reservations recommended. $ *Average main: NZ$32* ✉ *6 Adams Ave., Mount Maunganui* ☎ *07/575–3872* ⊕ *www. mountbistro.nz* ⊗ *Closed Mon. No lunch* ✛ *B1.*

$

CAFÉ

✗ **Sidetrack Cafe.** At the base of Mauao and across the street from the beach, this bustling café is a great place for breakfast or lunch after a climb or swim. Grab a table (there are more outside than in) for a blueberry muffin, blue cheese scone, a falafel, a salad, or a dense chocolate brownie. Or get a huge sandwich and a smoothie to go, and head off to a quiet spot on the trail that rings The Mount. $ *Average main: NZ$12* ✉ *Shop 3, Marine Parade, Mount Maunganui* ☎ *07/575–2145* ⊗ *No dinner* ✛ *B1.*

$$$$

MODERN NEW

ZEALAND

✗ **Somerset Cottage.** The name says it all—Somerset is a genuine country cottage, and many locals consider it one of the region's best restaurants. A smaller lunch menu (Wednesday to Friday) serves the same menu as in the evening, just with smaller portions. For dinner the menu is split in two—one includes signature dishes such as braised lamb shank with roasted garlic, olive and potato pie, oven-roasted duck, and vanilla-and-coconut-scented mash with orange sauce. The other menu changes weekly,

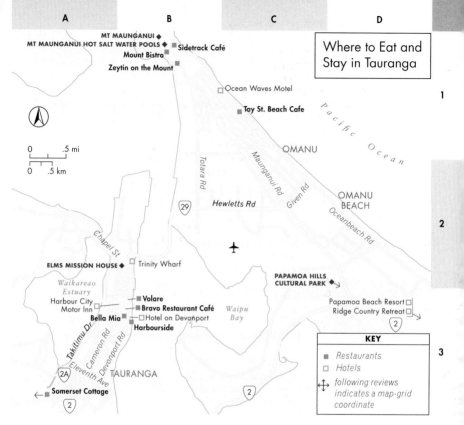

MT MAUNGANUI ◆
MT MAUNGANUI HOT SALT WATER POOLS ◆ ■ Sidetrack Café
Mount Bistro ■
Zeytin on the Mount ■

□ Ocean Waves Motel

■ **Tay St. Beach Cafe**

Pacific Ocean

OMANU

Maunganui Rd

Totara Rd

Given Rd

29

Hewletts Rd

OMANU BEACH

Oceanbeach Rd

0 ___ .5 mi
0 ___ .5 km

ELMS MISSION HOUSE ◆   □ Trinity Wharf

Waikareao Estuary

Harbour City Motor Inn □

■ **Volare**
■ **Bravo Restaurant Café**
Bella Mia ■   □ Hotel on Devonport
■ **Harbourside**

Waipu Bay

PAPAMOA HILLS CULTURAL PARK ◆ ↘

Papamoa Beach Resort □
Ridge Country Retreat □ ↘

2

Takitimu Dr
Cameron Rd
Devonport Rd
Eleventh Ave

2A

TAURANGA

← ■ **Somerset Cottage**

2

2

KEY

■ *Restaurants*
□ *Hotels*
⊹ *following reviews indicates a map-grid coordinate*

1

2

3

incorporating fresh and seasonal produce. Somerset also sells some of the products they cook and hosts a regular cooking school. $ *Average main: NZ$39* ⊠ *30 Bethlehem Rd., 5 km (3 miles) north of Tauranga center on State Hwy. 2* ☎ *07/576–6889* ⊕ *www.somersetcottage.co.nz* ⊙ *No lunch Sat.–Tues. No dinner Sun.* ⌕ *Reservations essential* ⊹ *A3.*

$$$ ✕ **Tay Street Beach Cafe.** The tables out on the patio across the road from
CAFÉ   the dunes of Maunganui Beach are the place to be when the weather's nice; otherwise, head inside to the cool, grey, vinyl bench seats. Tay Street's menu serves a range of dishes, from all-day brunch favorites like eggs Benedict or creamy mushrooms and bacon, to seared tuna, energy salad, or confit duck with edamame and wasabi puree. $ *Average main: NZ$26* ⊠ *At Tay St. and Marine Parade, Mount Maunganui* ☎ *07/572–0691* ⊕ *www.taystreetbeachcafe.co.nz* ⊙ *Winter has variable hrs, check first* ⊹ *C1.*

$$$ ✕ **Volare.** Although this restaurant is crammed in between half a dozen
ITALIAN   other restaurants overlooking the marina, the Italian opera music, bare wood floors, exposed beams, and brick walls create an environment that is miles away from Tauranga. The lounge bar is at street level; head up the wrought-iron staircase to the restaurant, where a comprehensive menu is divided helpfully into chicken, meat, and seafood; pasta and risotto; and pizza. All the classics, and more, are there for you to choose from. $ *Average main: NZ$30* ⊠ *85 The Strand* ☎ *07/578–6030* ⊕ *www.volaretga.com* ⊙ *Closed Mon.* ⊹ *B3.*

$$ ✕ **Zeytín at The Mount.** This café (not to be confused with the separately
TURKISH   owned Zeytin on the Strand, in Tauranga) is a good bet when in Mount
Maunganui. Their Moroccan tagines (lamb and apricot or chicken,
date, and almond) are great, as is the haloumi (salty cheese of goat
and sheep's milk), roasted beet salad with toasted walnuts and minted
yogurt, and any breads or pizzas smoky-fresh from the wood-fired oven.
The Kurdish baklava with vanilla ice cream will keep you coming back.
$ *Average main: NZ$20* ⊠ *118 Maunganui Rd., Mount Maunganui*
☎ *07/574–3040* ☾ *Closed Mon.* ✛ *B1.*

WHERE TO STAY

$$$ ◫ **Harbour City Motor Inn.** A Qualmark four-star-plus and environment
HOTEL   bronze-rated property, this bright yellow inn features smart, comfort-
able, and spacious self-contained studio and one-bedroom units. **Pros:**
central location; units have cooking facilities; bathrooms have spa
baths. **Cons:** built around a car park; no outdoor spaces; not particularly kid-friendly. $ *Rooms from: NZ$220* ⊠ *50 Wharf St.* ☎ *07/571–
1435* ⊕ *www.taurangaharbourcity.co.nz* ⤺ *20 rooms* ✛ *B3.*

$$$ ◫ **Hotel on Devonport.** At the most central hotel in Tauranga, each earth-
HOTEL   toned room has a balcony looking over the city, the harbor, or the port.
Pros: smart; modern; access to the adjacent private members' club.
Cons: slightly impersonal vibe. $ *Rooms from: NZ$210* ⊠ *72 Devon-
port Rd.* ☎ *07/578–2668* ⊕ *www.hotelondevonport.net.nz* ⤺ *38 rooms*
⦿ *Breakfast* ✛ *B3.*

$$ ◫ **Ocean Waves Motel.** These stylish, fully self-contained motel units are
HOTEL   directly across the road from Mt. Maunganui's stunning beachfront.
FAMILY   **Pros:** proximity to beach and Maunganui attractions. **Cons:** on the main
waterfront road; can be noisy. $ *Rooms from: NZ$170* ⊠ *74 Marine
Parade., Mount Maunganui* ☎ *07/575–4594, 0800/303–160* ⊕ *www.
oceanwaves.co.nz* ⤺ *9 rooms* ⦿ *No meals* ✛ *C1.*

$$ ◫ **Papamoa Beach Resort.** This resort complex has the widest range of
RESORT   accommodations in the area, and they're all on the beach, about a
FAMILY   10-minute drive down the road from the madding Mount Maunganui
crowd. **Pros:** wide range of accommodations; cheap; on the beach.
Cons: gets busy over summer; can be noisy. $ *Rooms from: NZ$135*
⊠ *535 Papamoa Beach Rd.* ☎ *07/572–0816* ⊕ *www.papamoabeach.
co.nz* ⤺ *250 campsites, 9 cabins, 7 holiday units, 2 baches, 19 beach-
front and garden-view villas* ⦿ *No meals* ✛ *D3.*

$$$$ ◫ **Ridge Country Retreat.** Set on 35 acres—a 30-minute drive from
HOTEL   town—the lodge overlooks a brilliant green valley, all the way to
Fodor'sChoice   Mauao and the ocean. **Pros:** handsome lodge without being overdone;
★   superb location. **Cons:** out in the country. $ *Rooms from: NZ$310*
⊠ *300 Rocky Cutting Rd.* ☎ *07/542–1301* ⊕ *www.rcr.co.nz* ⤺ *11 suites*
⦿ *All-inclusive* ✛ *D3.*

$$$$ ◫ **Trinity Wharf.** Perched over the edge of Tauranga Harbor, this is one of
HOTEL   the top-end hotels in the Bay of Plenty. **Pros:** fantastic views; comfort-
able, spacious rooms; warm staff. **Cons:** 10-minute walk into the city
center; some rooms have parking-lot views. $ *Rooms from: NZ$450*
⊠ *51 Dive Crescent* ☎ *07/577–8700* ⊕ *www.trinitywharf.co.nz* ⤺ *120
rooms* ⦿ *No meals* ✛ *B2.*

SPORTS AND THE OUTDOORS

Surfing, swimming, kayaking, dolphin watching, fishing, big-game fishing—yes, it's mostly on the water that visitors (and locals) enjoy the outdoors around here. There are great short walks around estuaries to forested waterfalls and on historic Māori sites.

BOATING AND FISHING

Blue Ocean Charters. Blue Ocean Charters operates three vessels and has full-day and evening reef fishing trips and overnight excursions, including special trips to chase the prized hapuka. Fishing equipment is available for hire. These guys can also take you saltwater fly-fishing, freshwater fishing for trout, and hunting for wild deer and pig. Phone ahead; they get busy. ✉ *Tauranga Bridge Marina, Te Awanui Dr.* ☎ *07/544–3072* ⊕ *www.blueocean.co.nz* ⌨ *NZ$100 (day and evening reef fishing), NZ$165 (overnight), NZ$185 (overnight hapuka fishing).*

HELICOPTER TOURS

Aerius Helicopters. If you think this is a scenic place on the ground, take in the view from a helicopter. Aerius are the local scenic flight specialists, they'll buzz you up and around Mauo (Mt. Maunganui), over the Papamoa Hills (historic Māori sites and kiwifruit country), above the beaches and, the most dramatic, to the steamingly active volcanic White Island. Flights leave from either Tauranga Airport or Kiwi 360 (just south of Te Puke on SH2). ✉ *Jean Batten Dr., Tauranga Airport* ☎ *0800/864–354* ⊕ *aerius.co.nz* ⌨ *NZ$115 (Mauo and Tauranga, 12 mins), NZ$210 (Papamoa Hills, 20 mins), NZ$680 (White Island, 70 mins); all prices quoted from Tauranga.*

KAYAKING

Fodor'sChoice
★

Waimarino Glowworm Kayaking. After you've had your fill of local award-winning Mills Reef wines, cheeses, and fresh fruit on the banks of Lake McLaren at dusk, plus a careful safety talk, the guides of Waimarino Glowworm Kayaking will help you into your kayak and take you on a gentle, two-hour, nighttime trip across the lake and into a narrow canyon, where the walls are lined with thousands of glowworms. Floating in the dark and the silence (everyone has to be quiet or the glowworms "turn off") is an amazing sensation. You don't need kayaking expertise; you will be well cared for. The whole tour takes about 3½ hours. Transport to the lake (about a 15-minute drive) is included, from Waimarino Adventure Park. Departure times change as the evenings draw out, check the website for exact times. These guys can also take you for genteel daytime paddles on Lake McLaren, or even at sea. ✉ *36 Taniwha Pl., Wairoa River, Bethlehem* ☎ *07/576–4233* ⊕ *www. waimarino.com* ⌨ *NZ$130.*

SURFING

Hibiscus Surf School. Mt. Maunganui is one of New Zealand's premier surfing beaches, so where better to learn to surf? These surfing dudes reckon that by the end of your first two-hour lesson, you'll be riding waves and feeling the good vibes. They take care of everyone, from beginner to advanced, from daily lessons to multiday packages; they also rent surfboards, full body wet suits, body boards, and stand-up paddleboards. You'll find them on Main Beach in Mount Maunganui—look

For a relaxing swim, take a dip in Mt. Maunganui Hot Salt Water Pools.

for the Hibiscus surf van or red Hibiscus gazebo across from Leisure (Moturiki) Island. Open daily from 9 to 5:30 in summer. ⊠ *Main Beach, Mt. Maunganui* ☎ *07/575–3792* ⊕ *surfschool.co.nz* ✉ *From NZ$85.*

SWIMMING

Mt. Maunganui Hot Salt Water Pools. Heated saltwater bathing is reputed to be a great healing process, and these pools offer just that, nestled beneath Mauao, Mt. Maunganui. The complex includes a cool pool with marked lanes for anyone who wants some serious exercise, but most visitors prefer to soak in the hotter saltwater pools. If that's not enough, book a session with one of the in-house massage therapists. ⊠ *Adams Ave.* ☎ *07/575–0868* ⊕ *www.bayvenues.co.nz* ✉ *NZ$10.80* ⊙ *Mon.–Sat. 6 am–10 pm, Sun. 8 am–10 pm.*

SWIMMING WITH DOLPHINS

Swimming with dolphins is a big summer activity in the Bay of Plenty. Most cruises leave from the Tauranga Bridge Marina. Bookings are essential and should be arranged at least one day prior. The Department of Conservation licenses and regularly inspects operators and sets limits on the number of boats allowed around any pod of dolphins.

Dolphin Blue. Aside from the dolphins, a highlight of this trip is the classic, 54-foot wooden launch you sail in. It makes a comfortable trip out to dolphin world (keeping in mind the cruise travels into open waters). Small groups, no more than 15, provide an intimate, boutique experience on the water. Trips leave Tauranga at 8:30 am and return at about 4 pm. Skipper Paul will give a talk first setting out clearly what you can expect during this long day on the water. The vessel is fitted with a "swim rope" for you to hold while the dolphins dart around you. They also have a couple of kayaks on board, and might pull into an island for guests to have a paddle, while waiting for dolphins to show. As with other such tours, if no dolphins or whales are spotted you can return for a free trip, with no time restriction on when you do. ✉ *Sulphur Point Marina, Keith Allen Dr.* ☎ *027/666–8047* 🌐 *www.dolphinblue.co.nz* 🎟 *NZ$150.*

Dolphin Seafaris. Dolphin Seafaris will really look after you on your dolphin encounter. Wet suits, dive gear, and towels, plus warm muffins, juices, and hot drinks, are included for a trip leaving at 8 am (from Tauranga, a bit later from Mt. Maunganui) and back around 1 pm. All guides are qualified marine biologists. Donations from every booking goes toward prevention of the slaughter of dolphins and whales. Bookings are essential. Phone ahead for daily departure times from the Tauranga Bridge Marina. **■ TIP→ September to November is whale migration season. You'll likely see as many whales as dolphins.** ✉ *Berth D1, Tauranga Bridge Marina* ☎ *07/577–0105, 0800/326–8747* 🌐 *www.nzdolphin.com* 🎟 *NZ$150.*

4

MAKETU

39 km (25 miles) southeast of Tauranga.

About halfway between Tauranga and Whakatane is the small seaside village of Maketu, one of the area's least-developed places and one of the first points of Māori landfall. Maketu is an important area for seabirds, and is host to a small colony of endangered New Zealand dotterel.

WHERE TO EAT

$$$ CAFÉ 🍴 **Maketu Beachside Cafe.** With a wraparound enclosed porch overlooking the beach, and a menu focused on fresh local seafood, this is as good a place to take time out and enjoy the superslow pace of Maketu. It's not high end—what's different here is the local quirkiness and historic location. The café sits on the shore where one of the migratory canoes, *Te Arawa*, landed several hundred years ago, and there are monuments here to remember this and other early history. The café also serves takeout, if you want a casual picnic on the beach. Open 10 to 7 weekdays, 9 to 8 weekends. [$] *Average main: NZ$29* ✉ *Townpoint Rd.* ☎ *07/533–2381* 💳 *No credit cards.*

SHOPPING

Maketu Pies. You'll find Maketu Pies in almost every supermarket and dairy throughout the country, but this little pie shop is where it all began. Hardly haute cuisine or healthy, the humble pie is one of New Zealand's icons—you have to at least try one. Choose from more than 20 flavors, everything from traditional mince, steak, and chicken to fancy seafood mornay or Moroccan lamb. There's even a veggie choice. Come to the original shop, or check the website for other locations. ✉ *6 Little Waihi Rd.* ☎ *0800/367–7437* 🌐 *www.maketupies.co.nz* 🕒 *Weekdays 7:30–3:30.*

WHAKATANE

100 km (62 miles) southeast of Tauranga.

For yet another chance to laze on the beach, Whakatane (fah-kah-*tah*-ne) is indisputably the North Island's sunniest town. The harbor here was a landfall site of *Mataatua*, one of the first migratory Māori canoes, and the fertile hinterland was among the first areas of the country to be farmed.

GETTING HERE AND AROUND

Whakatane is an easy one-hour drive down the Tauranga Eastern Link Expressway from Tauranga (NZ$2 toll) or, if you want to see more attractions, about 1½ hours on the old SH2. Whichever you choose you'll travel along a spectacular stretch of coast. Keep your eyes on the road—it's easy to lapse when you've got such spectacular ocean scenery.

Bus Depot InterCity Whakatane Depot. ⊠ *Quay and Kakahoroa Sts.* ☎ *0800/942–528.*

VISITOR INFORMATION

Contacts Whakatane i-SITE Visitor Information Centre. ⊠ *Quay and Kakahoroa Sts., on the Strand* ☎ *07/306–2030, 0800/942–528* ⊕ *www.whakatane.com.*

EXPLORING

Mataatua Maori Marae. Mataatua, one of the most beautiful carved *wharenui* (meetinghouses) in Maoridom, endured a 130-year-long indignity, traveling to museums around New Zealand, Australia, and England, and being rebuilt in various forms. In 2011 the house was returned home to the Ngāti Awa people of this area and restored. For a truly enriching cultural experience, take a tour with these people as they explain tribal protocols, share the history of their wharenui (including song and chants and an outstanding light show), and host you with refreshments. The adjacent retail store showcases contemporary designer clothing and jewelry. ⊠ *105 Muriwai Dr.* ☎ *07/308–4271* ⊕ *www.mataatua.com* 🖃 *NZ$49* ⊙ *Mid-Nov.–end Mar., daily 9–4 (tours at 10, noon, 2, 4); Apr.–mid-Nov., daily 9:30–3 (tours 10, noon, 2).*

Ohiwa Oyster Farm. Just beyond Ohope, following Wainui Road around the huge Ohiwa Harbour, it's not uncommon to see locals (plus the prolific number of resident wading birds) out on the mudflats harvesting dinner. However, the oyster beds here are currently recovering from a debilitating viral attack that occurred in 2010. Nevertheless, the Ohiwa Oyster Farm continues to serve up takeaway food like fish-and-chips, and burgers and mussel fritters, and the harborside is a lovely setting for eating them. ⊠ *Wainui Rd., Ohope.*

Whakatane Observatory. If you've a hankering to see the stars from an antipodean perspective, check out the Whakatane Observatory, up on a hill above the town. With no city lights to obscure the view, the skies here rate among the clearest in the country. Showings are obviously weather dependent, however on a good night you will see in stark clarity sights such as the "jewel box," a cluster of multicolor

Continued on page 197

STAYING ON A FARM

By Alia Bloom

Farmstays are an increasingly popular choice with travelers to New Zealand, whether you're the type to roll up your sleeves and "muck in" (i.e., help out) or recline on a porch with a glass of wine and watch the sunset. Here's how to plan an unforgettable farm visit.

New Zealand's farm experiences are ideal for active vacationers and visitors interested in local Kiwi culture. On some farmstays, guests can arrange to participate in farm activities—from simply touring the farm's facilities to milking cows, harvesting produce, rounding up livestock, and even shearing sheep. And itineraries can easily be customized to fit a visitor's interests.

With more than half of the country's land dedicated to farming, there are numerous options available for overnight or weeklong stays. More than 1,000 farmers around the country welcome travelers to their farms, ranging from a 14-acre country manor with apple orchard near Hawke's Bay to a 4,000-acre, high-country cattle farm (with fly-fishing) in Canterbury. The accommodations range from bunk beds with shared baths to luxurious private cottages on the property and are affordable when compared to hotels with similar amenities.

Leading farmstay providers such as **Rural Tours** and **Rural Holidays NZ** emphasize that farmstays are as much about tasting a slice of rural life, meeting locals, and experiencing a down-to-earth brand of Kiwi hospitality as they are about helping out with whatever needs to be done on the property. In their words: you can bet the farm on it.

(Above) Sheep herder at Grassmere Lodge, Arthur's Pass National Park, Southern Alps

WHICH FARM SHOULD I CHOOSE?

Four Peaks Lodge, Geraldine

Farms are as diverse as the New Zealand countryside. Some are smack in the middle of the grasslands; others stretch for miles along the coast. Note that most farms raise and harvest several types of plants and animals, even if they specialize in a single species. Here are the main types of farms you're likely to encounter, and a few property recommendations (find more suggestions on the Rural Tourism and Rural Holidays NZ sites).

BEEF/DAIRY FARMS

These farms often stretch over several hundred acres. Other than checking for broken fences, or offloading feed in the fields, there may not be much hands-on farm work to be done. But there are ample opportunities for hiking, fishing, and riding horses on most properties. **Hiwinui Country Estate** (see review in Palmerston North section of Ch. 6) is a rare combination of a luxury lodge and a 1,100-acre working dairy and sheep farm, with an award-winning focus on environmental sustainability. Guests are as likely to enjoy a spa treatment as they are to climb aboard a four-wheeler and help round up the cows for milking.

SHEEP STATIONS

As a guest, you might find yourself rounding up livestock, watching the shearing gang at work, or taking a turn bottle-feeding an orphaned baby lamb. You'll have plenty of photo ops with New Zealand's woolly icon, and the possibility of enjoying slow-cooked, honey-braised lamb shanks for your dinner. **Linburn Farmstay** (see review in Gisborne section of Ch. 5) is home to cattle and sheep. Depending on the season, you might be around for lambing, rounding up stock, or shearing. Bush walking trails provide entertainment for those less keen on the grittier side of farming.

ORCHARD & GARDEN PROPERTIES

New Zealand has some special plant life resulting from the country's geographic isolation. Whether your interest is in wild flora or cultivated fruit species, numerous properties around the country welcome guests. If you arrive on the orchard at harvest time, your help as an extra hand picking fruit could be welcome.

WINERIES

The environment and activities here are more refined than those at most farmstays, but you could still find yourself helping with the grape harvest, and, of course, helping with the terribly arduous task of sampling the wines. Wineries are often similar to upscale B&Bs.

LODGING TYPES

Accommodations listed as a "farmstay" run an enormous gamut, from cottages to backpacker-type dorms. Some farms offer upscale accommodations (hot tubs and pools, gourmet meals, and designer furnishings), while others provide simple lodgings and a hearty meal.

WHAT CAN I EXPECT?

Hay bales in a field near Queenstown

Grape harvest in Martinborough

If you work with a farmstay provider such as **Rural Tours** or **Rural Holidays NZ,** you can ask them for recommendations based on your interests and budget. A typical reservation includes overnight lodging, breakfast, and dinner. Check to see whether lunch is also included with your booking. Rural Tours offers the choice of standard or deluxe options; "deluxe" ensures your own ensuite, private bathroom, whereas "standard" usually includes a shared bathroom.

Some farmstays offer accommodations without meals included. These "self-catered" accommodations may be a shared dorm, a cottage, or a suite

attached to the main house. The self-catering option works best if you're staying in less remote areas, where you're close to restaurants or grocery stores.

COSTS

Farmstays cost less than most hotels. Guests can expect to pay between NZ$100-NZ$300 per person, per night. Unlike New Zealand's burgeoning industry of luxury lodges (and upmarket winery stays), which can charge upwards of NZ$300 per night, farmstays tend to have more of a "down home" feel, and this is reflected in the price.

WHAT CAN I DO ON THE FARM?

A sheep-shearer at work

Just-picked Cabernet Sauvignon grapes

Farmstay hosts are keen to share their lifestyle with international visitors. Here are a few activities you might observe or participate in:

Guided tour of the farm: Don a spare pair of gumboots before getting into a four-wheel drive or climbing on the back of a tractor to explore the terrain. You'll have the opportunity to interact with farm animals while farming activities are viewed and explained.

Milking cows: Depending on the farm, this could be a vast, machinery-operated process in a milking shed, where you might watch hundreds of cows being milked in tandem, or perhaps you'll join your host with their resident cow and nothing more than a tin pail.

Harvesting produce: Depending on the season and the farm's particular produce, you could find yourself armed with a basket as you pick a bushel of blueberries, apricots, or cherries. But you won't be put to work if you don't

want to be, and some farms may not consider it safe for visitors to take part in the harvest, depending on the types of machinery used.

Sheep shearing: A day's shearing has been compared by more than one shearer to running a marathon, and seeing a team shear 300 sheep in a day will make you tired just watching. Shearing occurs

DINING ON THE FARM

Some farmstays offer gourmet meals with wine pairings, while others offer more humbler farm fare. Most farms provide home-grown vegetables and meat from the farm, or at least offer meals made from locally sourced ingredients.

Traditional dishes likely to make it on the menu include a classic roast dinner—lamb, chicken, or beef, depending on the farm—with home-harvested vegetables and gravy, followed by a fruit crumble or another New Zealand staple: Pavlova (an airy meringue) with fresh whipped cream and fruit. If you visit during the summer months, you're likely to eat barbecue and overdo it on smoky, grilled lamb chops and potato salad. Discuss any special dietary needs when you make your reservation.

Tending to dairy calves in Westland

FAMILIES & FARMSTAYS

Most farmstays are family friendly, offering activities designed to appeal to a range of ages, including horseback riding, feeding farm animals, sheep shearing demonstrations, forest walks, and river swims.

Farmstays offering self-contained accommodations, such as cottages, are a fantastic option if you're traveling with your children. You get the perks of being off the hotel circuit, but can still spread out and make the place your own.

Inquire ahead to make sure the farm you're staying at has animals that are friendly and comfortable being touched and hand-fed. Many smaller farms are better able to provide these experiences. The larger working farms do not always have animals that closely interact with children or adults, and you may miss out on a hands-on experience.

about four times per year, so there's a good chance you'll get to see shearers in action. Otherwise, some farms will shear a sheep at the time of your visit, so you can see how it's done.

Feeding and interacting with farm animals: Almost every farm will provide the opportunity to feed the animals, whether throwing grain to the chickens, feeding lambs, kids, and calves, or tossing hay to sheep and cattle.

Riding tractors, trail bikes, and horses: During feeding seasons, you may be able to hitch a tractor ride with a farmer as they disperse hay among the stock. Or you could find yourself on the back of a trail bike rounding up sheep.

Lambing: The months of August to October are lambing time. Lambing tends to be a hands-off experience from a farmer's perspective, as sheep often give birth in pastures unassisted. If you time your visit with the beginning of lambing season, you'll be able to see sheep giving birth, help tag newborns (putting a plastic tag on their ears to help keep track of them), and bottle-feed lambs.

Many kids enjoy hand-feeding lambs

WHEN SHOULD I GO?

The season of your trip will help shape your farmstay experience. Farming life goes on, no matter the season or the weather. In winter, some South Island farms set high in the foothills of the Alps will have snow to contend with, while mud could be in abundance in the North Island. This is also the time when farmers "feed out" hay and crops to their stock, which is great to be a part of. Rural Tours has a chart on their website that describes the activities on cattle, sheep, dairy, and deer farms on a monthly basis to help you time your visit.

Lunch in the garden at Four Peaks Lodge

How far in advance should you plan your farmstay? Last-minute reservations don't allow host farmers much time out of their schedule to prepare for your stay. For best results, reserve at least a few days in advance (a few weeks is better).

A tip from Rural Tours: Remember that the farm is a working establishment. Please be guided by your hosts with regards to safety on the property. Don't forget to shut farm gates, and keep away from any paddock or areas that the farmer asks you to avoid.

Note that farmstays booked through **Rural Tours** and **Rural Holidays NZ** must comply with the New Zealand Government's health and safety regulations; you may not be able to take the tractor for a spin or go horseback riding. Let Rural Tours and Rural Holidays know in advance what you're interested in, and they can advise accordingly.

USEFUL WEB SITES & RESOURCES

Rural Tours (⊕ www.ruraltourism.co.nz) is New Zealand's largest database of farmstays. You can choose from a range of rural B&Bs and farms (cattle, beef, dairy, sheep, etc.), selecting by region and type of farm. The detailed descriptions make it easy to compile a shortlist. Upon choosing a farm that captures your interest, Rural Tours staff then work with you to arrange your stay and make sure your requirements are met.

Rural Holidays NZ (⊕ www.ruralholidays. co.nz) is also a national database of more than 500 farmstays, country home stays, and city home stays, divided by region. Descriptions of each property are brief and frustratingly coded; however, staff are helpful and come from both a farming and tourism background. They avoid listing properties with self-contained accommodation, preferring for guests to fully immerse themselves in rural New Zealand life.

Tourism New Zealand (⊕ www.newzealand.com) provides a massive database of accommodations, sights, and activities listings, along with general information about New Zealand. The farmstay section of the database has about 100 listings, and you can contact each property directly and make your own booking.

New Zealand Tourism Guide (⊕ www.tourism.net.nz) includes a national database of accommodations that are thematically grouped (farmstays, winery stays, eco-lodges, etc.). Similar to the New Zealand Tourism Board site, you can make your own inquiries and bookings.

stars near the Southern Cross. Nighttime presentations are informal and informative, led by local astrologer Norm Izett. ✉ *Hurinui Ave.* ☎ *07/308–6495* 🎟 *NZ$15* 🕒 *Tues. and Fri., opens between 7:30 pm and 8:30 pm (depending on how late the sun sets).*

BEACHES

FAMILY **Ohope Beach.** The most popular and safest swimming beach in the area (and, according to several traveler polls, in New Zealand) is the 11-km-long (7-mile-long) Ohope Beach, in Ohope, a 10-minute drive east of Whakatane. Take the well-signposted Ohope Road out of Whakatane's town center and over the hills to the beach. Pohutukawa Avenue, Ohope's main road, runs parallel to the beach, flanked by native *pohutukawa* forest, citrus trees, and grazing cows, as well as private residences. The beach is far less developed than others along the bay, nevertheless you can camp or park your campervan in the Top 10 Holiday Park or choose from a range of holiday homes or friendly B&Bs. There's lots to do: try fishing off the beach, riding the waves with the local surf school, walking the rocky coastline at Kohi Point Walk, or just getting up early to catch the sunrise. The beach will buzz with families over summer school holidays (Christmas through January), but after that you'll pretty much have it to yourself. **Amenities:** food and drink (a block back from the beach); toilets; lifeguards; parking (free); surf school. **Best for:** surfing; swimming; walking. ✉ *Pohutukawa Ave., Ohope Beach* 🌐 *www.ohopebeach.info.*

WHERE TO EAT

$$$ SRI LANKAN 🍴 **Babinka Restaurant and Bar.** Authentic curries from the Sri Lankan chefs are a specialty here, but modern New Zealand classics are also on the menu in this delightful spot. Both the Asian and Kiwi dishes might feature salmon, prawns, calamari, spice lamb rump, or pork medallions. There's also a breakfast menu (for later risers, from 10).There's a buzzy atmosphere whether you're eating inside or out. Local and imported beers and wines feature from the bar. [$] *Average main: NZ$26* ✉ *62 The Strand* ☎ *07/307–0009* 🌐 *www.babinka.co.nz* 🕒 *Closed 2–5* 💳 *No credit cards.*

$ CAFÉ 🍴 **The Bean Cafe and Roastery.** Mellow jazz might be playing in the background, local art graces the walls, and the retro couches and armchairs are a great spot to chill out and enjoy a coffee, which is freshly roasted every day in the café. When you walk in you'll see—and smell—the roasting machine. Snack options include bagels with any filling you desire, egg and bacon rolls, sandwiches, cakes, and slices. [$] *Average main: NZ$14* ✉ *72 The Strand* ☎ *07/307–0494* 🌐 *www.thebeancafe.co.nz* 🕒 *No dinner.*

$ NEW ZEALAND 🍴 **Peejays Coffee House.** Peejays, based at White Island Tours, specializes in breakfast and lunch. It opens up early (6:30 am) so if you're preparing for a trip out to White Island, nab a table on the deck to get a glimpse of your destination (weather permitting), and then fuel up with a big Kiwi breakfast (sausages, bacon, and eggs), three-egg omelet, or salmon kedgeree. The coffee's great, too. [$] *Average main: NZ$14* ✉ *15 The Strand E* ☎ *07/308–9588, 0800/242–299* 🕒 *Closed from 4 pm daily.*

4

WHERE TO STAY

$$ B&B/INN **Moanarua Beach Cottage.** Hosts Miria and Taroi Black provide their own variety of Māori *manaakitanga* (hospitality) for a truly cultural homestay experience. **Pros:** welcoming, relaxed environment; close to beach; kayaks available to rent. **Cons:** not luxurious; may be too far off-the-beaten-track for some. [$] *Rooms from: NZ$160* ✉ *2 Hoterini St., Ohope Beach* ☎ *07/312–5924* 🌐 *www.moanarua.co.nz* 💳 *No credit cards* 🛏 *2 rooms* 🍴 *Breakfast.*

$$ HOTEL **White Island Rendezvous.** Convenient if you're heading out to White Island this motel, run by the owners of White Island Tours, is across the road from the marina and within walking distance of town. **Pros:** friendly hosts; clean and relaxed; café on-site. **Cons:** seagulls can be noisy. [$] *Rooms from: NZ$160* ✉ *15 The Strand E* ☎ *07/308–9500, 0800/242–299* 🌐 *www.whiteislandrendezvous.co.nz* 🛏 *27 rooms.*

SPORTS AND THE OUTDOORS

Fishing, diving, and swimming with dolphins are popular activities in the Whakatane area. The water surrounding White Island and Whale Island has some great dive sites, with volcanic formations and abundant marine life. Moutohora (Whale Island) sanctuary is home to many endangered native species.

DOLPHIN- AND SEAL-WATCHING

FAMILY **Dolphin and Seal Encounters.** For closer aqueous encounters of the mammalian kind, local boating/diving/fishing experts, Diveworks, will take you on a four-hour cruise from Whakatane Wharf. First you'll check out the dolphins (there's a 97% success rate of finding them), then you'll head to Whale Island where the seals will be waiting. They will often jump off the rocks and swim out to meet the boat. Wet suits and snorkels for swimming with the dolphins and seals are provided, or you can just watch. From November though March, cruises leave daily at 8 am; other times of the year times depend on weather and demand. ✉ *96 The Strand* ☎ *0800/354–7737, 07/308–2001* 🌐 *www.diveworks-charters.com* 🎫 *NZ$160 (swimmer), NZ$130 (watching only).*

FISHING AND DIVING

FAMILY **Diveworks.** Diveworks provide a range of specialist diving and fishing trips. Their afternoon fishing venture, chasing snapper and gurnard, is especially suited to families. Rods, bait, and filleting all the fish you might catch are all included. Beginners are welcome. There's also a full-day option plus a White Island expedition, where game fish bluenose, hapuka, and kingfish could be the quarry. Dive trips include a full day exploring the unique volcanic features and teeming marine life around White Island, and a half day closer to shore, around Whale Island. Minimum numbers apply for longer trips and bookings are essential. ✉ *The Strand* ☎ *07/308–2001, 0800/354–7737* 🌐 *www.diveworks-charters.com* 🎫 *Fishing trips NZ$90 (1–5 daily in summer), NZ$160 (full day), NZ$335 (White Island 8–4 year-round, minimum of 6); dive trips NZ$120 (Whale Island, afternoons, minimum 6, 2 dives) NZ$300 (White Island, 8–4, minimum 6, 2 dives).*

HIKING

Hiking trails. The native forest reserves around Whakatane provide a range of bushwalks and hiking trails. The 6-km (4-mile) walkway called *Nga Tapuwae o Toi* ("the footprints of Toi") is named for a descendant of Tiwakawaka, one of the first Māori to settle in New Zealand. In total it takes about four hours, it's also divided into eight shorter walks that take you past historic pā (fortified village) sites, along the coastline and the Whakatane River, around Kohi Point (which separates Whakatane from Ohope), and through the Ohope and Makaroa Bush Scenic Reserves. These shorter sections range from one to three hours. No guide is necessary, and most tourist operators and the i-SITE visitor information center in Whakatane stocks free trail maps. The main trailhead starts from Canning Place, behind the Whakatane Hotel on the corner of George Street and the Strand. Follow the steps up the cliff and you'll be at the beginning of the trail. For an easier wander (30 minutes round-trip), start at the west end of Ohope Beach and head over to Otarawairere, a delightful secluded cove. ■TIP➔ Some trail crossings depend on the tidal schedule, so be sure to check low-tide times or you might end up swimming across! ⊠ *Canning Pl., Whakatane.*

FAMILY **Whale Island Tours.** Cruise to and walk on this special island wildlife reserve, home of endangered species such as kiwi, saddleback, parakeet, and *tuatara*. Your skipper, Phil van Dusschoten, has been a stalwart of the restoration program on Moutohora (Whale Island), just off shore of Whakatane, for 25 years. Let him share his knowledge as he guides you over the gentle island trails. You'll need to check your bags first, to ensure you're not carrying any sneaky, egg-eating pests, such as rats or mice. Tours usually leave at 1 pm and return at 5 pm, check when booking (which is essential). ⊠ *96 The Strand* ☎ *0800/354–7737* ⊕ *www.whaleislandtours.com* ✉ *NZ$120.*

WHAKAARI (WHITE) ISLAND

49 km (29 miles) off the coast of Whakatane.

With its billowing plumes of steam, the active volcano of Whakaari (White) Island makes for an awesome geothermal experience. The island is New Zealand's only active marine volcano—and New Zealand's most active volcano overall. The last major eruption was in 2012, and steam issues continuously from the many *fumeroles* (vents) and from the central crater, and the area reeks of sulfur. The island itself is eerie but exquisite, with fluorescent sulfuric crystal formations and boiling mud pools.

TOURS

From Whakatane or Tauranga, you can fly over the island on a fixed-wing plane or land there by helicopter; however, the least expensive way to get there is by boat. As a bonus, you might see dolphins, seals, and even a whale en route.

Frontier Helicopters. Frontier is licensed to fly from both Whakatane and Tauranga and to land on this very active marine volcano. From Whakatane, the flight each way is 30 minutes and you get a one-hour guided tour on the island. Bookings essential. ☎ *0800/804–354* ⊕ *www. frontierhelicopters.co.nz* ⌨ *NZ$650 per person (minimum of 2).*

White Island Flights. Take a close look at this steaming island volcano from a safe distance. This company flies fixed-wing aircraft to and over the island and its crater (they can't land). The trips last one hour. ☎ *0800/944–834* ⊕ *www.whiteislandflights.co.nz* ⌨ *NZ$249.*

White Island Tours. Peter and Jenny Tait, "official guardians" for the private owners of White Island, operate White Island Tours, which takes people out to the island by boat. En route to the island you will be issued with a hard hat and gas mask (yes, these can be necessary because of the sulfur fumes), and after landing you'll be guided on a walk around the volcano and through the remains of a sulfur mine. The island is 49 km (30 miles) off the coast of Whakatane, the boat trip is about 80 minutes each way (look for dolphins), and you spend two hours on the island. Trips run daily, weather permitting, and you'll leave Whakatane about 9:15 am (give or take a bit, depending on the tides). Check-in is at White Island Rendezvous, the tour office on The Strand. The main trip is not suitable for small children (it's recommended for ages eight and over—check with the tour operators for their family-friendly shorter tours). The island remains in a fluctuating state of volcanic alert. Peter and Jenny have been running tours for more than two decades and are experienced in dealing with varying activity levels. Bookings essential, by email or phone. ✉ *15 The Strand E, Whakatane* ☎ *09/308–9588, 0800/733–529 Freephone in New Zealand* ⊕ *www.whiteisland.co.nz* ⌨ *NZ$199 per person.*

EAST COAST AND THE VOLCANIC ZONE

WELCOME TO EAST COAST AND THE VOLCANIC ZONE

TOP REASONS TO GO

★ **Hiking and Walking:** Central North Island has great trails, including the famed Tongariro Alpine Crossing in Tongariro National Park. Some of the country's most rugged bush is in Te Urewera National Park.

★ **Māori Ceremonial Feast:** Rotorua may be the best place in New Zealand to indulge in the traditional Māori feast known as a *hāngi*.

★ **Soaking:** In Rotorua and Taupo, thermal springs are on tap. Soak in your own thermal bath in some Rotorua lodgings or take advantage of public facilities like the Polynesian Spa.

★ **Surfing:** Gisborne is blessed with fine (and often underused) surfing beaches; there are options for both beginners and seasoned surfers.

★ **Fishing:** Central North Island is trout country. You can fish any designated lake or waterway if you have your own gear and a license—but local guides know the right spots.

1 The Rotorua Area. Home of geothermal unrest and oddities, Rotorua today is almost entirely a product of the late-19th-century fad for spa towns; its elaborate bathhouses and formal gardens date to this era. You'll find surreal wonders that include limestone caverns, volcanic waste-lands, steaming geysers, and bubbling ponds.

2 Lake Taupo and Tongariro National Park. Fishing and water sports are popular activities in Lake Taupo, New Zealand's largest lake, and on the rivers running into it. The area also has its share of geothermal features. Tongariro National Park, dominated by three volcanic peaks, has some great otherworldly hiking trails.

White Island
Cape Runaway
Midway Point
Hicks Bay
Bay *of* *Plenty*
Te Araroa
Te Kaha
35
Omaio
Tikitiki
Ruatoria
Torere
Aorangi
Whareponga
Opotiki
Kutarere
Waioeka
Waipiro
Te Puia
RAUKUMARA RANGE
Toatoa
Tokomaru Bay
Matahi
Oponae
Motu
EASTLAND
35
Matawai
Mangatuna
Rakauroa
Tolaga Bay
2
Te Karaka
Te Urewera National Park
Hexton
Whangara
Manutuke
4
Tiniroto
Gisborne
Tuai
Te Reinga
38
Omahanui
Marumaru
Rangiahua
Frasertown
2
Ohinepaka
Wairoa
Nuhaka
Waihua
Oraka Beach
Table Cape
Long Point
MAHIA PENINSULA
H a w k e
B a y
Portland Island
South Pacific Ocean

0 — 20 mi
0 — 20 km

GETTING ORIENTED

Covering some of the most splendid natural areas in the country, this region lies to the northeast of the North Island. The main towns are busy despite being connected by isolated roads that wind across mountain ranges through vast areas of bush. Expect steaming thermal regions, rolling farmland, or peaceful sun-drenched vineyards.

5

3 **Napier and Hawke's Bay.** On the shores of Hawke's Bay, you'll find a fabulous architectural anomaly: the town of Napier, a time capsule of colorful art deco architecture. The countryside here is thick with vineyards, as this is one of the country's major wine-producing areas.

4 **Gisborne and Eastland.** Gisborne is the area's largest town. Above it juts the largely agricultural East Cape, a sparsely populated area ringed with stunning beaches; inland lies the haunting beauty of Te Urewera National Park.

TONGARIRO NATIONAL PARK

Tongariro National Park is the oldest national park in New Zealand and the largest on the North Island. Gifted to the nation by the Ngāti Tuwharetoa people in 1887, this stunning mountainous region provided much of the dramatic scenery for the *Lord of the Rings* films.

The park has a spectacular combination of dense forest, wild open countryside, crater lakes, barren lava fields, and rock-strewn mountain slopes. Its rugged beauty and convenient location, almost in the center of the North Island, make it the most popular and accessible of New Zealand's parks. Three volcanoes, Tongariro, Ngauruhoe, and Ruapehu, tower above its Central Plateau overlooking miles of untamed country that stretch to the West Coast on one side and the aptly named Desert Road on the other. The volcanoes are no sleeping giants; Tongariro is the least active, but Ngauruhoe and Ruapehu have both erupted in recent years. In 1995, 1996, and again in 2007, Ruapehu spewed ash, created showers of rock, and released lahars (landslides of volcanic debris) that burst through the walls of the crater lake.

BEST TIME TO GO

Your best window for decent weather is November through March, and the busiest time is between Christmas and New Year. Keep in mind, however, that even during summer you may feel like you're experiencing all four seasons in a single day, with weather ranging from hot and sunny to cool and rainy, and even snowy at higher elevations. In winter, cold alpine conditions are not uncommon. Suitable clothing should always be carried and sensible footwear worn.

BEST ACTIVITIES

Hiking and Tramping. The **Tongariro Alpine Crossing** has been described as the best one-day walk in the world. Approach it with the expectation that sudden changes of weather, even during summer, are always possible. There are numerous other trails covering the area and various types of accommodations, from cheap backpacker campgrounds to lodges and at least one first-class hotel. Most of these will organize transport to get the keen walkers to places where hikes can vary from an hour to several days. The longer trails will have huts to provide basic overnight stopovers.

Skiing. June through October (give or take a week or two, depending on conditions), the slopes of Mt. Ruapehu come to life with hundreds of skiing and snowboarding enthusiasts. On occasion the runs have to be cleared when the mountain's crater lake threatens to overflow, but this hasn't decreased the area's popularity. The combined fields of Turoa and Whakapapa form the largest ski slope in New Zealand and have brought a measure of prosperity to the once sleepy villages of National Park and Ohakune.

Viewing Volcanoes. Massive and downright awesome, Tongariro, Ngauruhoe, and Ruapehu dominate from whichever direction one approaches, and the views from Desert Road are a photographer's dream. If you travel from the south on State Highway 1 on a clear day, the first

glimpse of Ruapehu as the road crests will take your breath away. Farther north on the same road, the enormous, almost perfectly truncated, cone-shaped bulk of Ngauruhoe looms alongside a series of hairpin bends.

ONE-DAY ITINERARY

The best one-day itinerary is indisputably the **Tongariro Alpine Crossing.** The 19.4-km (12½-mile) walk starts and finishes in different places, so make arrangements for drop-off and pickup points. Several firms and most lodgings will organize this at a reasonable charge *(see the Tongariro section later in the chapter).* Check on the condition of the trail before you depart—there have been geological disturbances and, as a result, some parts of the track may not be accessible. Good footwear is essential and you should carry warm clothing, even in summer. Bring food and drink because there's none to be found along the route.

The trail makes its way up the Mangate-popo Valley, a reasonable incline running by a stream and old lava flows. It's a harsh environment for vegetation, but you'll spot moss and lichens and occasional wetland plants. It's a steep climb to the Mangetepopo Saddle, which lies between Tongariro and Ngauruhoe, but the views on a clear day can seem endless. For the adventurous, an unmarked

(above left) Emerald Lakes; *(bottom)* The crater lake of Mt. Ruahepu; *(above)* Lake Taupo

5

South Crater at Mt. Tongariro with Mt. Ngauruhoe beyond

track leads to the top of Mt. Ngauruhoe (Mount Doom if you're a *Lord of the Rings* fan). It's very steep and estimated to be a three-hour trip; adding this excursion requires a high level of fitness. The main trail proceeds to the south crater of Tongariro to a ridge leading up Red Crater. Here you can often smell sulfur. Rising 6,120 feet, the Red Crater's summit is the highest point of the Tongariro Alpine Crossing. From here the trail has a lot of loose stones and gravel and is extremely rough underfoot as it descends down to three smaller water-filled craters known as the Emerald Lakes (so named for their brilliant greenish color). The trail then continues across Central Crater to the Blue Lake to lead across the North Crater and downhill all the way to the Ketetahi Hut, where you'll be glad to sit and take a breather. Afterward, hike on to the springs of the same name; these are on private land, which the trail artfully skirts, but their steam cloud is impossible to miss. From here it's pretty much all downhill through tussock slopes to the start of the bush line and a long descent through forest to your pickup at the end. As you fall asleep in the transport (and no doubt you will), you'll delight in the knowledge that you have accomplished something to boast about for years to come.

THREE-DAY ITINERARY

Serious walkers with time to spare might wish to tackle the **Tongariro Northern Circuit.** This well-marked 43-km (26½-mile) route, which encompasses parts of the shorter Tongariro Alpine Crossing, offers up volcanic terrain and outstanding mountain vistas. Hikers following it can take advantage of several comfortable, well-maintained huts. These must be booked in advance at the Tongariro National Park Visitor Centre for the "Great Walks Season" (the third week in October to the last week in April); at other times, hut availability is on a first come–first served basis. Note that the circuit is best tackled in the warmer months (November through March), and a good degree of fitness is required.

Updated by
Bob Marriott

When you get to Rotorua, after a trip through the rolling, sheep-speckled fields of the Waikato and the wild Mamaku Ranges, the aptly named "Sulfur City"—with its mud pots, geysers, and stinky air—comes as a complete surprise. Rotorua, the mid-island's major city and Māori hub, has been a tourist magnet since the 19th century, when Europeans first heard of the healing powers of local hot springs.

South of Rotorua is the small town of Taupo; it stands alongside the lake of the same name (Australasia's largest) and is the geographical bull's-eye of the North Island. From the lake, you'll have a clear shot at Ruapehu, the island's tallest peak and a top ski area, and its symmetrically cone-shape neighbor, Ngauruhoe. Ruapehu dominates Tongariro National Park, a haunting landscape of craters, volcanoes, and lava flows that ran with molten rock as recently as 1988. As part of the Pacific Ring of Fire (a zone that's earthquake- and volcanic-eruption prone), the area's thermal features remain an ever-present hazard—and a thrilling attraction.

Southeast of Lake Taupo lies Hawke's Bay and the laid-back art deco town of Napier. Laze the days away drinking at the local vineyards or, to truly get off the beaten path, head north to Gisborne; it's the easy-going center of isolated Eastland, the thick thumb of land that's east of Rotorua.

PLANNING

WHEN TO GO

November through mid-April is the best time in Central and Eastern North Island. The weather is generally balmy and everything is open. This is also the season for vineyard festivals, so keep an eye on the local calendars. Try to avoid the school holidays (from mid-December to late January), when the roads and hotels get clogged with Kiwi vacationers.

To see the gannet colony at Cape Kidnappers, you need to go between October and April, when the birds are nesting and raising their young.

Hawke's Bay and Gisborne can be remarkably mild in winter; Rotorua and Taupo, however, can get quite cold and wet. If you want to do some skiing, you can hit the slopes of Tongariro National Park from June through October, but you will be competing with families if you are there during the school break.

GETTING HERE AND AROUND

AIR TRAVEL

Air New Zealand offers daily direct flights from Wellington, Auckland, and Christchurch to Napier and Rotorua; direct flights from Wellington and Auckland also land in Gisborne. Budget carrier **Jetstar** serves Napier with direct flights from Auckland.

Contacts Air New Zealand. ⊠ *Rotorua* ☎ *0800/737–000* ⊕ *www.airnewzealand.co.nz.* **Jetstar.** ☎ *0800/800–995* ⊕ *www.jetstar.com.*

BUS TRAVEL

InterCity provides regular bus service for the entire region. Comfortable, reasonably priced, and efficient, it's particularly useful to backpackers and people who are in no particular hurry. The Napier-to-Auckland trip takes 8 hours, Napier–Rotorua is 3½ hours, Napier–Taupo is 2¼ hours, and Napier–Wellington is 6 hours. Frequent local services go between Napier and Hastings. There's also a daily bus to Gisborne from either Auckland, via Rotorua, or from Wellington, via Napier.

Nakedbus runs an alternative, low-cost operation that serves some 300 cities and towns around New Zealand.

Contacts Inter-City. ⊠ *Rotorua* ☎ *09/913–6100* ⊕ *www.intercitycoach.co.nz.* **Nakedbus.** ☎ *09/979–1616* ⊕ *nakedbus.com.*

CAR TRAVEL

The best way to travel in this region is by car. Rotorua is about three hours from Auckland, four if you leave Auckland during the rush hour or if there is a motorway holdup. Take Highway 1 south past Hamilton and Cambridge to Tirau, where Highway 5 breaks off to Rotorua. Roads in this region are generally in good condition.

The main route between Napier and the north is Highway 5. Driving time from Taupo is two hours, five if you're coming straight from Auckland. Highway 2 is the main route heading south; it connects Hastings and Napier; from Wellington, driving time is 4½ hours to the former, 5 hours to the latter.

The most direct route from the north to Gisborne is to follow State Highway 2 around the Bay of Plenty to Opotiki, Eastland's northern gateway, then continue to Gisborne through the Waioeka Gorge Scenic Reserve. The drive from Auckland to Gisborne takes seven hours. South from Gisborne, continuing on Highway 2, you pass through Wairoa, about 90 minutes away, before passing Napier, Hawke's Bay, and Wairarapa on the way to Wellington.

TRAIN TRAVEL

Northern Explorer, a scenic 10-hour train connecting Auckland and Wellington, stops at National Park village and Ohakune. The journey from Wellington passes over five high viaducts. The train from Auckland goes around the remarkable Raurimu Spiral, where the track rises 660 feet in a stretch only 6 km (3½ miles) long.

Contacts **Northern Explorer.** ☎ *0800/872–467* ⊕ *www.kiwirailscenic.co.nz.*

PLANNING YOUR TIME

Start in Rotorua and then head down to Taupo and the National Park region. If fishing is your game, stop at Turangi. Napier and Hastings, with Hawke's Bay, is an area not to be missed. Prepare for a lengthy drive to Gisborne and the East Cape, and if you have the time (allow for 2½ hours each way and don't forget to fill the tank in Wairoa), take the rugged side road to Lake Waikaremoana. It's a little piece of heaven.

North Island's East Coast and volcanic zone include some of the country's most popular attractions. Plenty of excellent tours and bus routes hit most highlights, but having your own vehicle gives you the flexibility to seek out an untrammeled scenic spot or that lesser-known-but-outstanding winery.

Information centers known as i-SITEs are found throughout the region. They supply free information and brochures on where to go and how to get there, available accommodations, car rentals, bus services, restaurants, and tourist venues. The centers often serve as bus and tour stops, too.

RESTAURANTS

Rotorua has the area's most diverse dining scene. You can order anything from Indian to Japanese fare, or, for true local flavor, try a Māori *hāngi* (a traditional meal cooked in an earth oven or over a steam vent). Hawke's Bay is another hot spot; its winery restaurants emphasize sophisticated preparations and food-and-wine pairings. Around Eastland, which is so laid-back it's nearly horizontal, the choices are simpler, and you'll be treated with the area's characteristic friendliness. One thing you won't find on any menu is fresh trout. Laws prohibit selling this fish, but if you catch a trout, chefs at most lodging establishments will cook it for you.

Dressing up for dinner, or any other meal, is a rarity, expected at only the most high-end lodges and restaurants.

HOTELS

Accommodations range from super-expensive lodges to multistory hotels and budget motels. Bed-and-breakfast establishments—whether in town centers or in the depths of the countryside where you can succumb to the silence, curl up and read a book, or cast a fly in a quiet stream—are another excellent option.

Rotorua has lodgings in all price ranges. If you're willing to stay out of the town center, you can find bargain rates virtually year-round. In both Rotorua and Taupo, many hotels and motels give significant discounts on their standard rates off-season, from June through September. For stays during the school holidays in December and January, book well in advance. Also note that peak season in Tongariro National Park and other ski areas is winter (June–September); summer visitors can usually find empty beds and good deals. Many places, even the fanciest lodges, don't have air-conditioning, as the weather doesn't call for it.

Hotel reviews have been shortened. For full information, visit Fodors. com.

WHAT IT COSTS IN NEW ZEALAND DOLLARS				
	$	$$	$$$	$$$$
Restaurants	under NZ$15	NZ$15–NZ$20	NZ$21–NZ$30	over NZ$30
Hotels	under NZ$125	NZ$125–NZ$200	NZ$201–NZ$300	over NZ$300

Restaurant prices are the average cost of a main course at dinner or, if dinner is not served, at lunch. Hotel prices are the lowest cost of a standard double room in high season.

THE ROTORUA AREA

Rotorua sits on top of the most active segment of the Taupo Volcanic Zone, which runs in a broad belt from White Island in the Bay of Plenty to Tongariro National Park south of Lake Taupo. In many parts of this extraordinary area, the earth bubbles, boils, spits, and oozes; and recently, due to a ban on hydro bores, some dormant geysers are coming back to life. Drainpipes steam, flower beds hiss, jewelry tarnishes, and cars corrode. In Rotorua the rotten-egg smell of hydrogen sulfide hangs in the air, and even the local golf course has its own thermal hot spots where a lost ball stays lost forever.

ROTORUA

Visitors tend to have a love-hate relationship with Rotorua (ro-to-roo-ah). Millions of them—both from New Zealand and abroad—flock in each year, sometimes embracing and sometimes ignoring the unashamedly touristy vibe that has earned it the nickname Rotovegas. In either case, there's no denying that Rotorua has long capitalized on nature's gifts. After all, the influx is nothing new. The "Great South Seas Spa," as the city was once known, ranks among the country's oldest tourism ventures and has been luring vacationers since the late 19th century.

Rotorua's Māori community traces its ancestry to the great Polynesian migration of the 14th century through the Arawa tribe, whose ancestral home is Mokoia Island in Lake Rotorua. The whole area is steeped in Māori history and legend—for hundreds of years, they have settled by the lake and harnessed the geological phenomena, cooking and bathing in the hotpools. Today there are still many places where you can soak in the naturally heated water—and soak up the traditional Māori atmosphere.

Whakarewarewa, at the southern end of Tryon Street, is the most accessible of these and also the most varied. Whaka, as the locals call it, has two parts (the Living Thermal Village and Te Puia), both of which give firsthand exposure to the hotpools and Māori culture. The community was founded by people who moved here from Te Wairoa after the eruption in 1886.

GETTING HERE AND AROUND
Air New Zealand runs daily direct flights from Wellington, Auckland, and Christchurch to the Rotorua Regional Airport (ROT). It's located 10 km (6 miles) from the city center on Highway 33. Taxi fare into the city is NZ$25 to NZ$30. You could also arrange for a ride (NZ$26) with Super Shuttle; call ahead for a reservation.

In regular traffic, you can drive here from Auckland in about 3 hours; it will take about 5½ to come from Wellington. If you don't have your own vehicle, InterCity and Nakedbus both provide long-distance bus service.

The city itself is easy to navigate as streets follow a neat grid pattern. Entering Rotorua from Taupo, Fenton Street (the wide main drag) starts around Whakarewarewa. For about 3 km (2 miles), it's lined with lodgings until just before it reaches the lakefront, where shops and restaurants dominate. The Rotorua i-SITE Visitor Information Centre at 1167 Fenton is a good first stop: facilities include a tour-reservation desk and a map shop operated by the Department of Conservation.

Airport Rotorua Regional Airport. ✉ *Te Ngae Rd.* ☎ *07/345–8800* ⊕ *www.rotorua-airport.co.nz.*

Airport Transfers Rotorua Taxis. ✉ *Rotorua* ☎ *07/348–1111.* **Super Shuttle.** ✉ *Rotorua* ☎ *07/345–7790* ⊕ *www.supershuttle.co.nz.*

Bus Depot Rotorua Bus Depot. ✉ *Rotorua i-SITE Visitor Information Centre, 1167 Fenton St.*

TOURS
HELICOPTER TOURS **Volcanic Air.** Helicopters and floatplanes fly from the Volcanic Air office on the Rotorua Lakefront. Trips include over-city flights, crater-lake flights, and excursions to Orakei Korako and White Island. The floatplane trip over the Mount Tarawera volcano is extremely popular. ✉ *Memorial Dr.* ☎ *07/348–9984* ⊕ *www.volcanicair.co.nz* ✈ *From NZ$95.*

VISITOR INFORMATION
Rotorua i-SITE Visitor Information Centre. ✉ *1167 Fenton St.* ☎ *07/348–5179* ⊕ *www.rotoruanz.com.*

EXPLORING
TOP ATTRACTIONS
The Living Thermal Village. For an introduction to Māori life, visit this authentic village. On a guided tour you'll see thermal pools where villagers bathe, boiling mineral pools, and natural steam vents where residents cook. You can add on a cultural performance and *hāngi* meal to complete the experience. Arts and crafts are available at local shops in case you want to take home a memento. ✉ *17 Tryon St.* ☎ *07/349–3463* ⊕ *www.whakarewarewa.com* ✈ *NZ$35, NZ$66 with cultural show and hāngi* ⊙ *Daily 8:30–5.*

The Hinemoa Legend

One of the great Māori love stories has a special local connection, because it takes place on Mokoia Island in Lake Rotorua—and it's a true tale at that. Hinemoa, the daughter of an influential chief, lived on the lakeshore. Because of her father's status she was declared *puhi* (singled out to marry into another chief's family), and the tribal elders planned to choose a husband for her when she reached maturity. Although she had many suitors, none gained the approval of her tribe.

Tutanekai was the youngest son of a family who lived on Mokoia Island. Each of his older brothers had sought the hand of Hinemoa, but none had been accepted. Tutanekai knew that because of his lowly rank he would never win approval from her family. But he was handsome and

an excellent athlete—and eventually Hinemoa noticed him and fell in love.

From the lakeshore, Hinemoa would hear Tutanekai play his flute, his longing music drifting across the water. Hinemoa's family, suspicious that their daughter would try to reach the island, beached their canoes so that she could not paddle across to Mokoia. The sound of Tutanekai's flute lured Hinemoa to try to swim to the island. After lashing gourds together to help her float, she slipped into the lake; guided by the music, she reached Mokoia. Cold and naked, she submerged herself in a hotpool, where she was discovered by Tutanekai. Enchanted, he slipped her into his home for the rest of the night. When they were discovered, Tutanekai's family feared an outbreak of war with Hinemoa's tribe, but instead the two tribes were peacefully united.

Te Puia. The grounds here are home to silica terraces, mud pools, and the Pohutu Geyser (the largest active one in the southern hemisphere). Te Puia also contains the New Zealand Māori Arts & Crafts Institute, where you can watch skilled carvers and weavers at work. Don't miss the Nocturnal Kiwi House, where you might spot one of New Zealand's beloved national birds. Day passes include a guided tour; packages with extras like a cultural performance or *hāngi* feast are also available. ⊠ *Hemo Rd.* ☎ *07/348–9047* ⊕ *www.tepuia.com* 🖃 *NZ$51, packages from NZ$64* ⊙ *Daily Oct.–Mar., 8–6; Apr.– Sept., 8–5.*

WORTH NOTING

Blue Baths. At the southern end of the Government Gardens you can soak in this thermally heated swimming pool, which was built in the 1930s. ⊠ *Queens Dr.* ☎ *07/350–2119* ⊕ *www.bluebaths.co.nz* 🖃 *NZ$11* ⊙ *Daily 10–6.*

Government Gardens. Heading south from Lake Rotorua takes you to the Government Gardens, which occupy a small peninsula. The Māori call this area Whangapiro (fang-ah- *pee*-ro, "evil-smelling place"), an appropriate name for these gardens, where sulfur pits bubble and fume behind manicured rose beds and bowling lawns. The high point is the extraordinary neo-Tudor Bath House. Built as a spa at the turn of the 20th century, it is now the **Rotorua Museum.** One wing on the ground floor is devoted to the eruption of Mt. Tarawera in 1886. On display are a number of artifacts unearthed from the debris plus remarkable photographs of the silica terraces of Rotomahana before the eruption. Be sure to check out the old bathrooms, where some equipment would be right at home in a torture chamber—one soaking tub even administered electric current to the body. ✉ *Government Gardens, Oruawhata Dr.* ☎ *07/350–1814* 🌐 *www.rotoruamuseum.co.nz* 🎟 *NZ$20* 🕓 *Dec.–Feb., daily 9–6; Mar.–Nov., daily 9–5.*

Kuirau Park. This public park is a local hot spot—literally. Mud pools and hot springs sit alongside the flower beds, which at times are almost hidden by floating clouds of steam. You can wander around or join the locals soaking their weary feet in shallow warm pools. Because this thermally active place can change overnight, you should stay well outside the fences as you stroll through. ✉ *Kuirau St., south from Lake Rd.* 🎟 *Free.*

5

Fodor's Choice ★

Polynesian Spa. Follow pumice paths from the Government Gardens to naturally heated relaxation. Considered one of the best spas of its kind, it has a wide choice of mineral baths available, from large communal pools to family pools to small, private baths for two. You can also treat yourself to a massage or spa treatments; for a scenic soak, the Lake Spa has exclusive bathing in shallow rock pools overlooking Lake Rotorua. ✉ *Hinemoa St.* ☎ *07/348–1328* 🌐 *www.polynesianspa.co.nz* 🎟 *Family pool NZ$39, private pool NZ$27 per ½ hr, lake spa NZ$45* 🕓 *Daily 8 am–11 pm.*

St. Faith's. A short walk north from the Rotorua lakefront brings you to the Māori *pā* (fortress) of Ohinemutu, the region's original Māori settlement. It's a still-thriving community, centered around its *marae* (meetinghouse) and St. Faith's, the lakefront Anglican church. The interior of the church is richly decorated with carvings inset with mother-of-pearl. Sunday services feature the sonorous, melodic voices of the Māori choir. The service at 9 am is in Māori and English. ✉ *Tunohopu St.*

WHERE TO EAT

$$$ NEW ZEALAND FAMILY Fodor's Choice ★

🍴 **Capers Epicurean.** The pleasing scent of spices may entice you into this large, open restaurant, which serves meals from 7 am to 9 pm daily. If you're in the mood for something sustaining, try the chicken shiitake linguine (a grilled chicken breast set on pasta tossed in a creamy mushroom sauce, then topped with crispy prosciutto). Afterward, wander to the dessert cabinet and choose from goodies like the chocolate-cherry frangipani tart. Half of the space is a delicatessen that sells preserves and specialty foods, such as chutney made from kūmara (a local sweet potato) and a rub made from *kawa kawa* (a native herb). [$] *Average main: NZ$25* ✉ *1181 Eruera St.* ☎ *07/348–8818* 🌐 *www.capers.co.nz.*

$$$ ECLECTIC

🍴 **Eat Streat.** If you are not good at making decisions, Eat Streat could drive you crazy. This area at the northern end of Tutanekai Street is covered with a retractable roof and has 15-odd restaurants and bars. Standing cheek by jowl, they tempt tourists and locals with a variety of cuisines. The place is certainly buzzing at night. [$] *Average main: NZ$25* ✉ *Tutanekai St.*

CLOSE UP

Dinner on the Rocks

Rotorua is the best place to experience a *hāngi*, a traditional Māori feast featuring food cooked over steaming vents. Several local venues offer the opportunity for you to try this slow-cooked treat, paired with a concert—an evening that may remind you of a Hawaiian luau.

As a *manuhiri* (guest), you'll typically get the full treatment, beginning with a *powhiri*, the awe-inspiring Māori welcome that generally includes the *wero* (challenge), the *karanga* (cries of welcome), and the *hongi*, or pressing together of noses, an age-old Māori gesture that shows friendship.

While the meal cooks, a show begins with haunting harmonious singing, foot stamping, and *poi* twirling (rhythmic swinging of balls on strings). The performance might raise the hair on the back of your neck—but this will be assuaged with food, glorious food. The lifting of the *hāngi* will produce pork, sometimes lamb and chicken, *kūmara* (sweet potato), vegetables, and maybe fish and other seafood, followed by dessert.

Cultural enclaves like the **Living Thermal Village** (✉ 17 Tryon St. ☎ *07/349–3463* 🌐 *www.whakarewarewa.com* NZ$66) and **Te Puia** (✉ Hemo Rd. ☎ *07/348–9047* 🌐 *www.tepuia.com* NZ$116) are only two of the places where you can get a true taste of local flavor.

The **Holiday Inn Rotorua** also has an excellent cultural performance and *hāngi* (✉ 10 Tryon St. ☎ *07/348–1189* 🌐 *www.holidayinnrotorua.co.nz* NZ$69); and the **Matariki Hāngi and Concert** combines an informative, enthusiastic show with ample, delicious food (✉ Tutanekai St. ☎ *07/346–3888* 🌐 *www.accorhotels.com* NZ$69, NZ$39 concert only).

$$$ ECLECTIC FAMILY 🍴 **The Fat Dog Café and Bar.** The eclectic style and fine food here attract young, old, and everyone in between. A line of paw prints trails along the maroon ceiling. Poetry of somewhat dubious merit also winds along the walls, is painted on the chair backs, and even circles the extremities of plates. On the psychedelic blackboard menu look for beef fillet served on a warm, roasted vegetable salad with red onion marmalade. For dessert, try the caramelized banana waffle with vanilla ice cream. If you are traveling with children, there is a kid's menu, too. [$] *Average main: NZ$28* ✉ *69 Arawa St.* ☎ *07/347–7586* 🌐 *www.fatdogcafe.co.nz.*

$$$ NEW ZEALAND 🍴 **Pig & Whistle.** The name of this 1940s landmark winks at its previous incarnation—a police station. Expect pub fare at its absolute best, with seafood chowder, Kentucky bourbon pork belly, New Zealand lamb salad, and their famous pigtail fries. In summer, finish off your meal with a snooze under the enormous elm tree outside. Large, high-definition TVs in the garden bar make this the perfect place to watch the big game. On Thursday, Friday, and Saturday nights, you can catch live music, too. [$] *Average main: NZ$27* ✉ *1182 Tutanekai St.* ☎ *07/347–3025* 🌐 *www.pigandwhistle.co.nz.*

$$$ ITALIAN FAMILY 🍴 **Zanelli's.** The green casements on a terra-cotta wall perfectly highlight the homey interior of this classic Italian restaurant. Study the shots of the Italian countryside after ordering *Filetto di Agnello*, a grilled lamb

fillet with rosemary potatoes in a red wine-and-mint sauce; then savor some vino while waiting for *Torta di Cioccloato,* a moist dark chocolate cake drizzled with chocolate sauce and garnished with whipped cream and fruit. It's all delightful. $ *Average main: NZ$28* ✉ *1243 Amohia St.* ☎ *07/348–4908* ⊕ *www.zanellis.net.nz* ☾ *Closed Sun. and Mon. No lunch.*

WHERE TO STAY

$$ 🏨 **Arista of Rotorua.** These spacious two-story units, about 1 km (½ mile)
HOTEL   from the city center, are a good value—especially for families. **Pros:**
FAMILY   within walking distance of town; a parking space for each unit; fenced playground for children. **Cons:** Fenton is a busy road and can be noisy. $ *Rooms from: NZ$135* ✉ *296 Fenton St.* ☎ *07/349–0300* ⊕ *www. aristaofrotorua.co.nz* ↝ *16 rooms* ⦿ *No meals.*

$ 🏨 **Ashleigh Court Motel.** Each bright, well-maintained unit here has an
HOTEL   individual whirlpool tub, which helps distinguish Ashleigh Court from
FAMILY   the many motels on Fenton Street. **Pros:** clean and tidy; reasonably priced; close to Whakarewarewa and the golf course. **Cons:** Fenton Street is busy and can be noisy; no swimming pool. $ *Rooms from: NZ$119* ✉ *337 Fenton St.* ☎ *07/348–7456* ⊕ *www.ashleighcourtrotorua.co.nz* ↝ *13 rooms* ⦿ *No meals.*

$ 🏨 **The Backyard Inn.** This complex overlooking the thermal Kuirau Park
HOTEL   has basic lodge rooms with shared facilities starting at NZ$29 per person, plus 29 en suite chalets priced from NZ$87 per room. **Pros:** nice quiet location; you could snag an en suite chalet. **Cons:** it's a 10-minute walk to town; can get busy in summer. $ *Rooms from: NZ$87* ✉ *60 Tarewa Rd.* ☎ *07/347–0931* ⊕ *www.thebackyardinn.co.nz* ↝ *64 lodge rooms, 29 chalets* ⦿ *No meals.*

$ 🏨 **Base-Rotorua.** At Base-Rotorua, you can choose between dorm rooms
HOTEL   that sleep anywhere from 4 to 12 people and private rooms, including doubles that comes with en suite baths and balconies. **Pros:** heated swimming pool; convenient to Kuirau Park. **Cons:** the disco could keep you awake; limited parking. $ *Rooms from: NZ$80* ✉ *1286 Arawa St.* ☎ *07/348–8636* ⊕ *www.stayatbase.com* ↝ *13 rooms, 18 dorm rooms* ⦿ *No meals.*

$$ 🏨 **Holiday Inn Rotorua.** From the massive but welcoming entrance foyer
HOTEL   with its huge stone fireplace to the lake views from the tower wing, this hotel spells class. **Pros:** top-class accommodations at all levels; a Māori concert and hāngi on the premise; complimentary shuttle service to town. **Cons:** it's close enough to Whakarewarewa to get more than a whiff of the local vapor. $ *Rooms from: NZ$129* ✉ *10 Tryon St.* ☎ *07/348–1189* ⊕ *www.holidayinnrotorua.co.nz* ↝ *203 rooms, 3 suites* ⦿ *No meals.*

$$$ 🏨 **Princes Gate Hotel.** This ornate timber hotel was built in 1897 on the
HOTEL   Coromandel Peninsula; its large, wonderfully appointed guest rooms were transported here in 1920. **Pros:** elegant and sophisticated; has an air of old-fashioned charm. **Cons:** you'll feel you have to whisper in the lounge; if you want clinical and modern it's not for you. $ *Rooms from: NZ$220* ✉ *1057 Arawa St.* ☎ *07/348–1179* ⊕ *www.princesgate. co.nz* ↝ *34 rooms, 16 suites* ⦿ *No meals.*

$$$
RESORT
FAMILY

🏨 **Regal Palms 5 Star City Resort.** The well-appointed studio, one-bedroom, and two-bedroom suites at this resort, located 2 km (1 mile) from downtown Rotorua, have a contemporary look plus mod cons like air-conditioning and Wi-Fi. **Pros:** good recreational facilities; roomy accommodations are good for families. **Cons:** you'll want to take the car to town; there may be some traffic noise. $ *Rooms from: NZ$280* ✉ *350 Fenton St.* ☎ *07/350–3232* ⊕ *www.regalpalms.co.nz* 🛏 *44 suites* ⦿| *No meals.*

$$
HOTEL

🏨 **Rotorua Lakeside.** This snazzy spot has the handiest position of any of the large downtown hotels—it overlooks the lake and is a two-minute walk from restaurants and shops. **Pros:** you might get a room with a lake view; the Matariki Concert Hall is right alongside. **Cons:** corporate feel; disappointing view if not lakefront. $ *Rooms from: NZ$195* ✉ *Tutanekai St.* ☎ *07/346–3888* ⊕ *www.accorhotels.com* 🛏 *199 rooms* ⦿| *No meals.*

SHOPPING

Te Puia. Te Puia was established in 1963 to preserve Māori heritage and crafts. At the institute you can watch wood-carvers and flax weavers at work and see New Zealand greenstone (jade) sculpted into jewelry. The gift shop sells fine examples of this work as well as other items, from small wood-carved kiwis to decorative flax skirts worn in the Māori cultural shows. ✉ *Hemo Rd.* ☎ *07/348–9047* ⊕ *www.tepuia.com.*

SPORTS AND THE OUTDOORS
BOATING

Kawarau Jet. This company, which is best known for jet-boat trips on Lake Rotorua, has extended its offerings to include parasailing adventures and hot springs excursions. Packages begin at NZ$85 and the team goes out of its way to make sure you have a safe, memorable experience. ✉ *Memorial Dr.* ☎ *07/343–7600* ⊕ *www.nzjetboat.co.nz.*

Lakeland Queen. Licensed for 300 passengers, the *Lakeland Queen*, a genuine stern-wheel paddle ship, has breakfast, lunch, and dinner cruises. One popular trip includes an onboard barbecue (NZ$59). ✉ *Memorial Dr.* ☎ *07/348–0265* ⊕ *www.lakelandqueen.com.*

NEARBY ROTORUA

The countryside near Rotorua includes magnificent untamed territory with lakes and rivers full of some of the largest rainbow and brown trout on Earth. From here down through Taupo and on into Tongariro National Park, fishing is a booming business. So if you're dreaming of landing the "big one," this is the place to do it.

GETTING HERE AND AROUND

Most of the sights outside the Rotorua city area can be reached from State Highway 30, which branches right off Fenton Street at the southern corner of town. Lake Tarawera, the Blue and Green lakes, and the Buried Village are all accessed from Highway 30; farther east, you reach the airport, Lakes Rotoiti and Rotoma, and Hells Gate. Keeping on Fenton Street will lead to Lake Road and back onto Highway 5, which goes to Paradise Valley, Fairy Springs Road, and farther out of town to Ngongotaha and the Agrodome. If you don't have a car, sightseeing buses operated by Geyser Link Shuttles will transport you to a number of thermal sites in the area, Waimangu and Waiotapu among them; buses leave from Rotorua's i-SITE center on Fenton Street.

Bus Contacts Geyser Link Shuttles. ☎ 0800/304–333 ⊕ travelheadfirst.com/ local-legends/geyser-link-shuttle.

EXPLORING
TOP ATTRACTIONS

FAMILY **Agrodome.** At this working sheep-and-cattle farm, 6 km (4 miles) north of Rotorua, you can get up close and personal with the animals on a guided tour and pay a visit to the kiwifruit orchard. The main attraction, though, is the farm show. Well-trained dogs run across the backs of sheep, and there's a sheep-shearing demonstration. Heads-up to the uninitiated: what the shearer is wearing is *not* an undershirt but a shearing vest, a classic Kiwi item. Expect plenty of wisecracks about pulling the wool over your eyes and about Whoopi Goldberg (here, a Lincoln sheep with dreadlock-style wool). Sure, it's corny, but it's fun. Shows are at 9:30, 11, and 2:30 daily. ⊠ 141 Western Rd., Ngongotaha, Rotorua ☎ 07/357–1050 ⊕ www.agrodome.co.nz ✉ Farm show NZ$32.50, farm show and tour NZ$62 ☉ Daily 8:30–5.

Buried Village Te Wairoa. At the end of the 19th century, Te Wairoa (tay why- *ro*-ah, "the buried village") was the starting point for expeditions to the pink-and-white terraces of Rotomahana, on the slopes of Mt. Tarawera. As mineral-rich geyser water cascaded down the mountainside, it formed a series of baths, which became progressively cooler as they neared the lake. In the latter half of the 19th century these fabulous terraces were the country's major attraction, but they were destroyed when Mt. Tarawera erupted in 1886. The explosion, heard as far away as Auckland, killed 153 people and buried the village of Te Wairoa under a sea of mud and hot ash. The village has been excavated, and of special interest is the *whare* (*fah*-ray, "hut") of the *tohunga* (priest) Tuhoto Ariki, who predicted the destruction. Eleven days before the eruption, two separate tourist parties saw a Māori war canoe emerge from the mists of Lake Tarawera and disappear again—a vision the 100-year-old tohunga interpreted as a sign of impending disaster. Four days after the eruption, he was dug out of his buried hut still alive, only to die a few days later. An interesting museum contains artifacts, photographs, and models re-creating the day of the disaster, and a number of small dwellings remain basically undisturbed beneath mud and ash. A path circles the excavated village, then continues on as a delightful trail to the waterfall, the lower section of which is steep and slippery in places. Te Wairoa is 14 km (9 miles) southeast of Rotorua. ⊠ 1180 Tarawera Rd., Rotorua ☎ 07/362–8287 ⊕ www.buriedvillage. co.nz ✉ NZ$32.50 ☉ Oct.–Apr., daily 9–5; May–Sept., daily 9–4:30.

Hells Gate. Located 15 km (9 miles) east of Rotorua, Hells Gate is arguably the most active thermal reserve in the area. Its 50 acres hiss and bubble with steaming fumaroles and boiling mud pools. Among the attractions here is the Kakahi Falls, reputedly the largest hot waterfall in the southern hemisphere, where, according to legend, Māori warriors

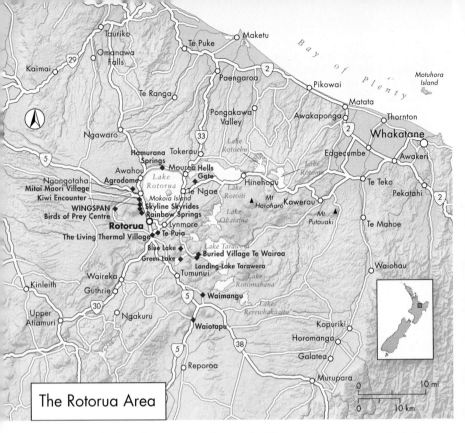

The Rotorua Area

bathed their wounds after battle. Warm mud pools are available for public bathing; at the Hellsgate Mud Spa, you can soak in a mud bath or try a *mirimiri* (a traditional Māori massage). ✉ *State Hwy. 30, Tikitere, Rotorua* ☎ *07/345–3151* ⊕ *www.hellsgate.co.nz* 🖃 *NZ$35, spa and mud treatments NZ$75–NZ$240* ⊗ *Daily 8:30 am–10 pm.*

FAMILY **Kiwi Encounter.** This conservation center next to Rainbow Springs receives kiwi eggs, then hatches and rears the endangered birds before returning them to the wild. From September to April you'll see eggs or baby chicks, which have an extremely high cute factor. ✉ *Fairy Springs Rd., Rotorua* ☎ *07/350–0440* ⊕ *www.rainbowsprings.co.nz* 🖃 *NZ$50 includes admission to Rainbow Springs* ⊗ *Daily 10–5.*

Fodor's Choice **Mitai Māori Village.** Rewind time by spending an evening at Mitai Māori ★ Village, where you can listen to the harmonious chant of traditionally clad warriors as they paddle a *waka* (war canoe) along the Wai-o-whiro stream, then watch a top-notch cultural show, and enjoy a delicious *hāngi* feast. Getting the chance to see glowworms on a short, guided bush walk is an added bonus. ✉ *196 Fairy Springs Rd., Rotorua* ☎ *07/343–9132* ⊕ *www.mitai.co.nz* 🖃 *NZ$116* ⊗ *Daily 5:30 pm–8:30 pm.*

FAMILY **Rainbow Springs.** Stroll through the bush and take a close-up look at native birds such as *tūī, kea, kereru,* and *kakariki.* You can also eyeball a *tuatara* (an endangered lizard) and see skinks, geckos, plus some mighty trout. Children will love the Big Splash boat ride and daily bird show. ⊠ *192 Fairy Springs Rd., Rotorua* ☎ *07/350–0440* ⊕ *www. rainbowsprings.co.nz* ⌑ *NZ$40* ⊙ *Daily 8:30 am–10 pm.*

FAMILY **Skyline Skyrides.** A 2,900-foot cable-car system carries you up Mt. Ngongotaha for spectacular views over Lake Rotorua. At the summit, 1,600-feet above sea level, there's a café, a restaurant, a souvenir shop, and several Kiwi ways to trigger a heart attack—including the Sky Swing, a giant three-person swing that hits speeds up to 150 kph (93 mph). As an alternative, try the luge track, where you can take hair-raisingly fast rides on wheeled bobsled-like contraptions (you can also go slowly; a braking system gives you full control of your speed). The track runs partway down the mountain, winding through the redwood trees; from the bottom, you can return to the summit on a separate chairlift. For further thrills, consider ziplining or mountain biking. ⊠ *Fairy Springs Rd., Rotorua* ☎ *07/347–0027* ⊕ *www.skyline.co.nz* ⌑ *Cable car NZ$28, swing NZ$40, luge NZ$22, zipline NZ$45, bike-lift pass from NZ$55* ⊙ *Daliy 9 am–late (last gondola descends when restaurant closes).*

Fodor's Choice **Waimangu.** When Mt. Tarawera erupted in 1886, destroying Rotoma-
★ hana's terraces, not all was lost. A volcanic valley emerged from the ashes, extending southwest from Lake Rotomahana. It's consequently one of the world's newest thermal-activity areas, encompassing the boiling water of the massive Inferno Crater, plus steaming cliffs, bubbling springs, and bush-fringed terraces. A path (one–two hours) runs through the valley down to the lake, where a shuttle bus can get you back to the entrance. You can also cap your trip by taking a cruise on the lake itself. Waimangu is 26 km (16 miles) southeast of Rotorua; to reach it, take Highway 5 south (Taupo direction) and look for the turn after 19 km (12 miles). ⊠ *587 Waimangu Rd., Rotorua* ☎ *07/366–6137* ⊕ *www.waimangu.co.nz* ⌑ *NZ$37, NZ$79.50 with cruise* ⊙ *Daily 8:30–5; last entry at least 1 hr prior to closing.*

Waiotapu. This is a freakish landscape of deep, sulfur-crusted pits, jade-color ponds, silica terraces, and a steaming lake edged with red algae and bubbling with tiny beads of carbon dioxide. The **Lady Knox Geyser** erupts precisely at 10:15 daily; other points of interest include the Devil's Ink Pots, a series of evil-looking, bubbling, plopping mud pools, and the spectacular, gold-edged Champagne Pool, which is 195 feet wide and equally deep. Birds nest in holes around the aptly named Birds' Nest Crater—the heat presumably allows the adult birds more time away from the eggs. Waiotapu is 30 km (19 miles) southeast of Rotorua; follow Highway 5 south (Taupo direction) and look for the signs. ⊠ *State Hwy. 5, Rotorua* ☎ *07/366–6333* ⊕ *www.waiotapu.co.nz* ⌑ *NZ$32.50* ⊙ *Daily 8:30–5; last entry at 3:45.*

WORTH NOTING

Blue and Green Lakes. You'll find these vibrant lakes on the road to Te Wairoa and Lake Tarawera. The Green Lake is off-limits except for its viewing area, but the Blue Lake is popular for picnics and swimming. The best place to see their rich color is from the isthmus between the two. Take Highway 30 east (Te Ngae Road) and turn right onto

Tarawera Road at the signpost for the lakes and Buried Village. The road loops through forests and skirts the edge of the lakes. ✉ *Tarawera Rd., Rotorua.*

Hamurana Springs. For stunning scenery and idyllic picnic spots, drive around Lake Rotorua. Look for Hamurana Springs, a large area of land with free public access where crystal-clear water bubbles from springs forming a river that flows into the lake. Walking through this area you will see birdlife and pass through several groves of magnificent redwood trees. It's about 15 km (9 miles) northeast of Rotorua. ✉ *Hamurana Rd., Rotorua.*

Landing-Lake Tarawera. On Tarawera Road, 2 km (1 mile) beyond the Buried Village, this clear, blue lake offers a number of water activities. Boats and kayaks can be hired and there are water taxis and trout fishing available. The Landing Café has a small but varied menu and a decent wine list. Clearwater Cruises will design a custom trip for you on its 50-foot launch. ✉ *Clearwater Cruises, 1064B Tarawera Rd., Rotorua* ☎ *07/345–6688* 🌐 *www.clearwater.co.nz.*

FAMILY **Paradise Valley Springs Wildlife Sanctuary.** Popular with families, this wildlife park is a great place for kids to meet all kinds of critters in a native bush setting. You can hand-feed trout and maybe even handle cubs up to six-months old in the lion enclosure. ✉ *467 Paradise Valley Rd., Rotorua* ☎ *07/348–9667* 🌐 *www.paradisevalleysprings.co.nz* 🎟 *NZ$30* 🕒 *Daily 8–5.*

FAMILY
Fodor's Choice ★
WINGSPAN Birds of Prey Centre. A must-see for ornithology fans, WINGSPAN has 10 light and roomy aviaries where you can see native birds of prey. In Māori mythology, falcons, harriers, and *moreporks* (little owls) all acted as messengers to the gods. The aviaries, which are connected by an undercover walkway, echo with the cries of these fierce raptors, and they can be seen flying, feeding, and nesting. Open-air flying and obedience displays take place daily at 2. Some of the birds are brought in to recuperate from injury before being released back into the wild. ✉ *1164 Paradise Valley Rd., Rotorua* ☎ *07/357–4469* 🌐 *www.wingspan.co.nz* 🎟 *NZ$25* 🕒 *Daily 9–3.*

WHERE TO STAY

$$ B&B/INN FAMILY
🏨 **Arias Farm.** This modern home is set on peaceful farmland overlooking Rotorua, but it's only a few minutes from the city center. **Pros:** quiet and peaceful; lovely welcoming hosts; on the hill away from sulfur smells. **Cons:** 10-minute drive to town. [$] *Rooms from: NZ$130* ✉ *396 Clayton Rd., Rotorua* ☎ *07/348–0790, 021/753–691 cell* 🌐 *www.ariasfarm.com* 🛏 *2 rooms, 3 cottages* 🍴 *Breakfast.*

$$$$ B&B/INN
🏨 **City Lights Boutique Lodge.** On the hills overlooking the lights of Rotorua, this stylish modern home has an inviting lounge where you can relax in front of the large-screen television, plus a spacious outside area where you can soak in the hot tub, savor the silence, and watch alpacas roam the fields. **Pros:** modern, comfortable accommodation; very peaceful location. **Cons:** about a 10-minute drive to nearest restaurant; need transport to town. [$] *Rooms from: NZ$325* ✉ *56c Mountain Rd., Pleasant Heights, Rotorua* ☎ *07/349–1413* 🌐 *www.citylights.net.nz* 🛏 *3 rooms* 🍴 *Breakfast.*

$$$ B&B/INN **Cottage at Paradise.** A 20-minute drive from the city center, this two-bedroom cottage stands back from the road on a 12-acre block of rural land (called a "lifestyle block"). **Pros:** quiet and remote; great trout fishing at the doorstep. **Cons:** it's a fair drive to town and a decent restaurant. [$] *Rooms from: NZ$220* ✉ *801 Paradise Valley Rd., Rotorua* ☎ *07/357–5006* 🌐 *www.cottagesatparadise.co.nz* 🛏 *1 cottage* 🍴 *Breakfast.*

$$$ B&B/INN **Country Villa.** Morning sunshine floods through the stained-glass windows of this lovely country home, which has scenic views of the lake and Mt. Tarawera. **Pros:** great country location; beautiful gardens. **Cons:** it's a bit of a drive to town; not close to restaurants. [$] *Rooms from: NZ$280* ✉ *351 Dalbeth Rd., Rotorua* ☎ *07/357–5893* 🌐 *www.countryvilla.biz* 🛏 *5 rooms* 🍴 *Breakfast.*

$$$$ HOTEL Fodor's Choice ★ **Solitaire Lodge.** Nestled in native bush on a private peninsula, the luxurious Solitaire Lodge commands extensive views over Lake Tarawera and the legendary mountain. **Pros:** quiet, secluded class in superb surroundings; good fishing. **Cons:** remote location comes at a high price; no golf course. [$] *Rooms from: NZ$1690* ✉ *16 Ronald Rd., Rotorua* ☎ *07/362–8208* 🌐 *www.solitairelodge.co.nz* 🛏 *8 suites, 2 villas* 🍴 *All-inclusive.*

SHOPPING

Mountain Jade. Look for beautifully made, high-quality jade items in this bright, spacious shop. ✉ *1288 Fenton St., Rotorua* ☎ *07/349–1828* 🌐 *www.mountainjade.co.nz.*

Simply New Zealand. This spot stocks an excellent range of New Zealand gifts and souvenirs. ✉ *1105 Pukuatua St., Rotorua* ☎ *07/348–8273* 🌐 *www.simplynewzealand.co.nz.*

SPORTS AND THE OUTDOORS

The trout fishing on area lakes, streams, and rivers is some of the finest in the world. For outdoor enthusiasts there is also no shortage of activities such as trail biking, white-water rafting, and bungy jumping.

BIKING

Planet Bike. First-timers and experts alike will find the perfect mountain-bike adventures with Planet Bike. You can ride for a couple of hours or several days, and some tours combine biking with rafting, kayaking, indoor climbing, or horseback riding. A full day rental (helmet included) starts at NZ$60. ✉ *8 Waipa Bypass Rd., off Waipa State Mill Rd., Rotorua* ☎ *027/280–2817* 🌐 *www.planetbike.co.nz.*

EXTREME ADVENTURE

Agroventures Adventure Park. Part of the Agrodome complex, this is the place to get your adrenaline pumping. Bungy jump from a 140-foot-high crane or the opt for the **Swoop**, where one, two, or three people are put into a hang-gliding harness and raised 120 feet off the ground before a rip cord is released. The **Agrojet** boat ride and **Freefall Extreme** (picture yourself being blown into the air by a giant fan) are high-octane alternatives. On-site you can also try the **Shweeb**, a five-car monorail racetrack that operates on pedal power. The cost to get you screaming is NZ$49 each for the Swoop, Agrojet, Freefall Extreme, and

The geothermal activity at Waimangu keeps the water of Inferno Crater Lake at a boil.

Shweeb; NZ$109 for the bungy jump. ✉ *1335 Paradise Rd., Ngongotaha, Rotorua* ☎ *07/357–4747* ⊕ *www.agroventures.co.nz* ☺ *Daily 9–5.*

FISHING

If you want to keep the trout of a lifetime from becoming just another fish story, go with a registered guide. Prices vary, but expect to pay about NZ$100–NZ$120 per hour for a fishing guide and a 20-foot cruiser that takes up to six passengers. The minimum charter period is two hours; gear and tackle are included in the price. A one-day fishing license costs NZ$25 per person and is available on the boat. (You'll need a special license to fish in the Rotorua area and in Taupo.) For general information about local lake and river conditions, check with the Rotorua i-SITE Visitor Information Centre.

Bryan Colman. Troll Lake Rotorua or try fly-fishing on the region's many streams, including a private-land source. Bryan takes up to four anglers at a time, and a daylong trip is NZ$860. ✉ *32 Kiwi St., Rotorua* ☎ *07/348–7766* ⊕ *www.TroutFishingRotorua.com.*

Gordon Randle. A trip with Gordon Randle will set you back about NZ$110 per hour; you can also charter the boat (and Gordon) for the day at a cost of NZ$680. ✉ *11 Te Ana Pl., Rotorua* ☎ *07/349–2555, 0274/938–733 boat* ⊕ *www.rotoruatrout.co.nz.*

Silver Hilton Trout Fishing. Fly-fish all year with this outfit, which takes out one or two people at a time. The price (NZ$650 per day, plus license) includes all equipment and lunch. ✉ *4A Ward Rd., Hamurana, Rotorua* ☎ *07/332–3488* ⊕ *www.troutfly.co.nz.*

RAFTING AND KAYAKING

The Rotorua region has rivers with Grade III to Grade V rapids that make excellent white-water rafting. For scenic beauty—and best for first-timers—the Rangitaiki River (Grades III–IV) is recommended. For experienced rafters, the Wairoa River has exhilarating Grade V rapids. The climax of a rafting trip on the Kaituna River is the drop over the 21-foot Okere Falls, among the highest to be rafted by a commercial operator anywhere. The various operators run similar trips on a daily schedule, though different rivers are open at different times of year, depending on water levels. All equipment and instruction are provided, plus transportation to and from the departure points—which can be up to 80 km (50 miles) from Rotorua. Prices start around NZ$90 for the short (one-hour) Kaituna run; a half day on the Rangitaiki costs from NZ$120. Many operators sell combination trips.

Kaitiaki Adventures. The well-qualified team at Kaitiaki Adventures leads daily rafting trips on the Kaituna River (NZ$95). For a variation on the theme, try white-water sledging—you'll shoot the rapids on a specially designed plastic raft the size of a boogie board, and then soak in a natural hotpool; the cost is NZ$109 to NZ$299, gear included. ✉ *1135 Te Ngae Rd., Rotorua* ☎ *0800/338-736* ⊕ *www.kaitiaki.co.nz.*

Kaituna Cascades. This company knows the river it takes its name from like the back of its hand. It organizes one-day or multiday expeditions using rafts or kayaks with a focus on fun and safety. A rafting trip will cost NZ$89; a double kayak ride is NZ$140 (note that there is a 185-pounds weight limit). ✉ *Trout Pool Rd., Rotorua* ☎ *07/345-4199, 0800/524-8862* ⊕ *www.kaitunacascades.co.nz.*

Raftabout. This outfit focuses on day trips, some pairing rafting with jet-boating. ✉ *State Hwy. 33, Okere Falls* ☎ *07/343-9500, 0800/723-822* ⊕ *www.raftabout.co.nz.*

River Rats. Day trips to the main rivers are organized by River Rats; adventure packages are available, too. ✉ *391 State Hwy. 33, Mourea* ☎ *07/345-6543, 0800/333-900* ⊕ *www.riverrats.co.nz.*

Wet 'n' Wild Rafting. One-day itineraries cover the Rangitaiki, Wairoa, and Kaituna rivers. Wet 'n' Wild Rafting also has multi-adventure and double-trip options. ✉ *2 White St., Rotorua* ☎ *07/348-3191, 0800/462-7238* ⊕ *www.wetnwildrafting.co.nz.*

LAKE TAUPO AND TONGARIRO NATIONAL PARK

The town of Taupo on Lake Taupo's northeastern shore has blossomed into a major outdoor activities center, providing everything from rafting to skydiving. Taupo is also home to geothermal wonders.

Fishing is a major lure, both on the lake itself and on the rivers to the south. These are some of the few places where tales of the "big one" can actually be believed. The Tongariro River is particularly well known as an angler's paradise.

Southwest of Lake Taupo rise the three volcanic peaks that dominate Tongariro National Park. Even if you don't have much time, skirting the peaks provides a rewarding route on your way south to Wanganui or Wellington.

TAUPO

82 km (51 miles) south of Rotorua, 150 km (94 miles) northwest of Napier.

The tidy town of Taupo is the base for exploring Lake Taupo, the country's largest lake. Its placid shores are backed by volcanic mountains, and in the vicinity you'll see more of the geothermal activity that characterizes this zone. Water sports are popular here—notably sailing, cruising, and waterskiing—but Taupo is most known for fishing. The town is the rainbow-trout capital of the universe: the average Taupo trout weighs in around 4 pounds, and the lake is open year-round. Meanwhile, the backpacker crowd converges on Taupo for its adventure activities. The town has skydiving and bungy-jumping opportunities, and white-water rafting and jet-boating are available on the local rivers.

GETTING HERE AND AROUND

Taupo is four hours from Auckland, taking Highway 1 the whole way. It's 70 minutes from Rotorua, also via Highway 1. If you are coming by bus, InterCity Buses has daily service to Taupo from Auckland (approximately 5 hours) and from Rotorua (1 hour and 20 minutes).

Within the town, streets are laid out in a grid pattern. Lake Terrace runs along the waterfront; it turns into Tongariro Street as it heads north, crossing the Waikato River and the gates that control the flow of water from the lake. Heu Heu, the main shopping street, runs from the traffic lights on Tongariro Street.

Bus Depot Taupo Bus Depot. ⊠ *Taupo i-SITE Visitor Information Centre, 30 Tongariro St.*

TOURS

BOAT TOURS **Barbary.** This 1920s yacht, believed to have once been the property of golden-age film star Errol Flynn, has short cruises departing at 10:30, 2, and 5. They take in giant carvings on a lakefront cliff face and, depending on the weather, let you swim off the boat when it's smooth. On board, you can help hoist the sails or just sit back and dream in one of the big beanbags. ⊠ *10 Ferry Rd.* ☎ *07/378–5879* ⊕ *www.sailbarbary. com* 🖃 *From NZ$44.*

Maid of the Falls. Board the *Maid of the Falls* for a Huka Falls cruise. She leaves from Aratiatia Dam, 10 km (6 miles) north of Taupo, at 10:30, 12:30, and 2:30; a 4:30 trip is added in summer. The vessel has a viewing platform on the front and takes you up close to the falls, which push a huge amount of water through a narrow gap in the rocks. ⊠ *630 Aratiatia Rd.* ☎ *0800/278–336* ⊕ *www.hukafallscruise.co.nz* 🖃 *NZ$37.*

BUS TOURS **Paradise Tours.** Bus tours operated by this outfit visit attractions in and around Taupo, including Huka Falls and Craters of the Moon. ⊠ *Taupo* ☎ *07/378–9955* ⊕ *www.paradisetours.co.nz* 🖃 *From NZ$99.*

VISITOR INFORMATION

Contacts **Taupo i-SITE Visitor Information Centre.** ✉ *30 Tongiriro St.* ☎ *07/376–0027* ⊕ *www.greatlaketaupo.com.*

EXPLORING
TOP ATTRACTIONS

Huka Falls. The Waikato River thunders through a narrow chasm and over a 35-foot rock ledge at Huka Falls. The fast-flowing river produces almost 50% of the North Island's required power, and its force is extraordinary, with the falls dropping into a seething, milky-white pool 200 feet across. The view from the footbridge is superb; for an even more impressive look, both the *Maid of the Falls* and vessels operated by Hukafalls Jet get close to the maelstrom. The falls are 3 km (2 miles) north of town; to reach them, turn right off Highway 1 onto Huka Falls Road. ✉ *Huka Falls Rd.*

Orakei Korako. Even if you've seen enough bubbling pools and fuming craters to last a lifetime, the thermal valley of Orakei Korako is still likely to captivate you. Geyser-fed streams hiss and steam as they flow into the waters of the lake, and a cream-and-pink silica terrace is believed to be the largest in the world since the volcanic destruction of the terraces of Rotomahana. At the bottom of Aladdin's Cave, the vent of an ancient volcano, a jade-green pool was once used by Māori women as a beauty parlor, which is where the name *Orakei Korako* (a place of adorning) originated. The valley is 37 km (23 miles) north of Taupo, via Highway 1, and takes about 25 minutes to reach by car; you could always see it en route to or from Rotorua, which lies another 68 km (43 miles) northeast of the valley. ✉ *494 Orakeikorako Rd., Reporoa* ☎ *07/378–3131* ⊕ *www.orakeikorako.co.nz* 🎫 *NZ$36* ⊙ *Oct.–May, daily 8–4:30; June–Sept., daily 8–4.*

WORTH NOTING

Aratiatia Dam. The Waikato River is dammed along its length; the first construction is the Aratiatia Dam, 10 km (6 miles) northeast of Taupo. The river below it is virtually dry most of the time, but three times a day (at 10, noon, and 2), and four times a day in summer (October–March, also at 4), the dam gates are opened and the gorge is dramatically transformed into a raging torrent. Watch the spectacle from the road bridge over the river or from one of two lookout points a 15-minute walk downriver through the bush. To access the dam from Taupo, turn right off Highway 5. ✉ *Aratiatia Rd.*

Craters of the Moon. The construction of the local geothermal project had an impressive—and unforeseen—effect. Boiling mud pools, steaming vents, and large craters appeared in an area now known as Craters of the Moon. A marked walkway snakes for 3 km (2 miles) through the belching, sulfurous landscape, past boiling pits and hissing crevices. The craters are up Karapiti Road, across from the Huka Falls turnoffs on Highway 1, 3 km (2 miles) north of Taupo. ✉ *171 Karapiti Rd.* ☎ *0276/564–684* ⊕ *www.cratersofthemoon.co.nz* 🎫 *NZ$8* ⊙ *Dec.– Apr., daily 8:30–6; others months based on daylight.*

FAMILY **Huka Prawn Park.** This is the only prawn farm in New Zealand where you can take a tour. It's a curious mix of cheesy and really interesting.

Check out the holding tanks where prawns are bred in specially heated river water (in some, baby prawns eat out of your hand). You can also catch your own prawns using a small rod and fishing line, or just buy some on-site; either way you can have them cooked and served as you like in the adjoining café. If you are feeling young at heart try some of the fun, self-activated water features. ⊠ *Huka Falls Rd., Wairakei Park* ☎ *07/374–8474* ⊕ *www.prawnpark.co.nz* ⊠ *NZ$28* ☉ *Weekdays 9–3:30, weekends 9–4.*

Taupo Museum. You'll find Māori treasures and contemporary art on display at this museum; the volcanic eruptions that have shaped the area are also chronicled. The star attraction, however, is the glorious Ora Garden, which was granted Garden of National Significance status in 2011. ⊠ *Story Pl. Taupo* ☎ *07/376–0414* ⊕ *www.taupomuseum.co.nz* ⊠ *NZ$5* ☉ *Daily 10–4:30.*

WHERE TO EAT

$$$$
EUROPEAN
Fodor'sChoice
★

✕ **The Bistro.** Jude Messenger, an award-winning young chef, aims for "simple but nice" at his unpretentious, family-owned eatery. Large cylindrical lamp shades brighten the modern interior, creating a contemporary bistro vibe. The food follows suit, focusing on what's fresh and seasonal. Try the crackled pork belly with kūmara (sweet potato) and pickled red cabbage or the sweet corn cakes with roasted red-pepper sauce, either of which can be topped off with a selection of house-made sweets. $ *Average main: NZ$32* ⊠ *17 Tamamutu St.* ☎ *07/377–3111* ⊕ *www.thebistro.co.nz* ☉ *No lunch.*

$$$
CONTEMPORARY

✕ **Brantry Restaurant.** The menu is updated seasonally at this converted 1950s town house on a suburban street not far from the shores of Lake Taupo. Owners Prue and Felicity Campbell know what they're doing and use the best local ingredients to make delicious things to satisfy all palates. One good choice is eye fillet of beef with roasted beetroot, baby spinach, and red onion-walnut salsa. Wines include those from emerging and boutique vineyards. $ *Average main: NZ$29* ⊠ *45 Rifle Range Rd.* ☎ *07/378–0484* ⊕ *www.thebrantry.co.nz* ☉ *Closed Sun. and Mon.* ⟁ *Reservations essential.*

$$
CAFÉ
FAMILY
Fodor'sChoice
★

✕ **The Replete Food Company.** There's no wine license here, but the food brings in crowds for breakfast and lunch. In the morning, try the Complete Replete Breakfast: honey-cured bacon, tomato relish, poached eggs, roasted field mushrooms, and grilled focaccia. (It is a big hit with the many multisport athletes who frequent this sports-mad town.) The Vietnamese pork clay pot and prawn linguine are especially popular at midday. Tasty salads, including Thai beef with coconut-lime dressing or Asian chicken with crispy noodles, are top picks, too. $ *Average main: NZ$16* ⊠ *45 Heu Heu St.* ☎ *07/377–3011* ⊕ *www.replete.co.nz* ☉ *No dinner.*

WHERE TO STAY

$$
B&B/INN

🛏 **b&b @ number ten.** The sunny en suite guest rooms at this newly built B&B have panoramic views of Lake Taupo and French doors that let you take full advantage of the vistas. **Pros:** good location; not far to town; free Wi-Fi. **Cons:** you might not want to leave. $ *Rooms from: NZ$195* ⊠ *10 Coprosma Crescent, Botanical Heights* ☎ *07/378–6823, 021/237–2405* ⊕ *www.bnbnumberten.co.nz* ⤸ *2 rooms* ⊺⊙⊺ *Breakfast.*

Kayakers paddle the Waikato River, New Zealand's longest waterway.

$$ **HOTEL**  **Comfort Inn Cascades.** The pleasing brick-and-timber rooms in this lakeside motel (formerly called the Cascades Motor Lodge) are large, comfortable, and smartly decorated. **Pros:** on the lakeside with a safe beach; heated pool. **Cons:** 3 km (2 miles) from town center; units near road may get some traffic noise. [$] *Rooms from: NZ$145* ⊠ *303 Lake Terr., just south of State Hwy. 5 (Napier) turnoff* ☎ *07/378–3774* ⊕ *www.cascades.co.nz* ⇥ *24 units* ⦿ *No meals.*

$$$$ **HOTEL** **FAMILY** **Fodor's Choice** ★ **Huka Lodge.** Set on 17 blissful acres, this riverfront lodge is one of the country's finest and has seen its fair share of prominent guests over the years. **Pros:** one of the world's best lodges with a knowing and established clientele. **Cons:** perfection does not come cheap. [$] *Rooms from: NZ$1650* ⊠ *77–105 Huka Falls Rd.* ☎ *647/378–5791* ⊕ *www. hukalodge.co.nz* ⇥ *25 suites* ⦿ *Some meals* ☞ *Average room price is per person per night.*

$$$ **B&B/INN**  **The Pillars.** This modern, Mediterranean-style country manor features four large en suite rooms, a spacious guest lounge, a conservatory, and patio areas where a complimentary evening drink can be enjoyed. **Pros:** has a pool and tennis court; free Wi-Fi; delightful, friendly hosts. **Cons:** you need transport to see the sights; with such a warm welcome you won't want to leave. [$] *Rooms from: NZ$275* ⊠ *7 Deborah Rise, Bonshaw Park* ☎ *07/378–1512* ⊕ *www.pillarstaupo.co.nz* ⇥ *4 suites* ⦿ *Breakfast.*

$$$ **B&B/INN**  **Richlyn Homestay.** Located 8 km (5 miles) southeast of Taupo, the home of eponymous owners Richard and Lyn is surrounded by well-tended gardens, and the patio is a peaceful haven where the silence is broken only by birdsong. **Pros:** spacious and tasteful; a great cooked breakfast. **Cons:** you might prefer to be nearer the bright lights and the lake. Ⓢ *Rooms from: NZ$250* ✉ *1 Mark Wynd, Bonshaw Park* ☎ *07/378–8023* ⊕ *www.richlyn.co.nz* ⤴ *4 rooms* ⓧ *Breakfast.*

SPORTS AND THE OUTDOORS

The Central North Island region is an absolute must for anyone keen on hunting, fishing, canoeing, hiking, or just about any other outdoor activity. Travel with an expert to get the most out of classic New Zealand wilderness.

BUNGY JUMPING

Taupo Bungy. Plunge from a cantilevered platform that projects out from a cliff 150 feet above the Waikato River. You can go for the "water touch" or dry versions. Even if you have no intention of "walking the plank," go and watch the jumpers from the nearby lookout point, 1 km (½ mile) north of town. Jumps cost from NZ$169 a shot and are available daily from 9 to 5. ✉ *202 Spa Rd., off Tongariro St.* ☎ *07/377–1135, 0800/888–408* ⊕ *www.taupobungy.com.*

FISHING

There is some great fishing in the Taupo area and an attendant number of guides with local expertise who work the Tongariro River and the lake. High season runs from October to April. Costs are usually around NZ$250 for a half day and include all equipment plus a fishing license (note that you need a special license to fish here and in Rotorua). Book at least a day in advance.

Chris Jolly Outdoors. Staffed by people with a love of the outdoors, this company can take you mountain biking, hiking, hunting, cruising, and, of course, fishing. Try fly-fishing or cast for trout on a chartered boat trip. A half-day fly-fishing expedition costs NZ$484 for two people, all equipment included. ✉ *Berth 4, Taupo Boat Harbour, Ferry Rd.* ☎ *07/378–0623, 0800/252–628* ⊕ *chrisjolly.co.nz.*

Fishy Steve. Steve Sprague leads a number of trips, among them a half-day fly-fishing excursion for beginners (NZ$300); 4X4 bush outings and helicopter trips into the wilderness are available, too. ✉ *Taupo* ☎ *07/378–2192, 027/293–5335* ⊕ *www.fishysteve.com.*

Mark Aspinall. Fly-fish for rainbow and brown trout with Mark Aspinall. He will organize a custom trip to meet your needs and collect you from wherever you are staying. A half-day trip, all gear included, will set you back NZ$300; a full-day with lunch costs NZ$500. ✉ *Taupo* ☎ *07/378–4453, 021/500–384* ⊕ *www.markaspinall.com.*

JET-BOATING

Hukafalls Jet. For high-speed thrills on the Waikato River, take a ride with Hukafalls Jet; its jet-boats spin and skip between the Aratiatia Dam and Huka Falls multiple times per day. The 30-minute trip costs NZ$115 (NZ$69 for children who are under 15 years old and at least 3.3-feet tall). ✉ *200 Karetoto Rd.* ☎ *07/374–8572* ⊕ *www.hukafallsjet.com.*

RAFTING

Rafting New Zealand. The Wairoa and Mohaka rivers are accessible from Taupo, as are the Rangitaiki and the more family-friendly Tongariro. Rafting New Zealand provides transportation, wet suits, equipment, and much-needed hot showers at the end. Prices start at NZ$90. ⊠ *41 Ngawaka Pl.* ☎ *07/386–0352, 0800/865–226* ⊕ *www. raftingnewzealand.com.*

SKYDIVING

Call at least one day in advance to arrange your jump—weather permitting—and expect to pay NZ$249–NZ$339 per, more if you want to add on a video or other mementos to commemorate your experience.

Skydive Taupo. On a tandem jump you're attached to a professional skydiver for a breathtaking descent. Depending on altitude, free fall can last from a few seconds to close to a minute. Prices start at NZ$249. ⊠ *Anzac Memorial Dr.* ☎ *0800/586–766* ⊕ *www.skydivetaupo.co.nz.*

Taupo Tandem Skydiving. For a thrill—along with a bird's eye view of Taupo—try Taupo Tandem Skydiving. Prices start at NZ$249 for a 12,000-foot jump. ⊠ *Anzac Memorial Dr.* ☎ *07/377–0428, 0800/826– 336* ⊕ *taupotandemskydiving.com.*

TONGARIRO NATIONAL PARK

110 km (69 miles) southwest of Taupo.

Tongariro has a spectacular combination of dense forest, wild open countryside, crater lakes, barren lava fields, and rock-strewn mountain slopes. Its rugged beauty and convenient location, almost in the center of the North Island, make it the most popular and accessible of New Zealand's parks.

GETTING HERE AND AROUND

The park is best reached by car. The approach from the north is along Highway 4 on the park's western side; turn off at the village of National Park for Whakapapa. Coming from the south, turn off State Highway 1 at Waiouru for Ohakune. From Taupo to the park, follow State Highway 1 south and turn off at Turangi onto State Highway 47. The roads are generally good; however, snow and ice can be a problem around the park in winter.

It's difficult to reach Tongariro National Park by public transportation, though InterCity does run a daily bus in summer (mid-October–April) between Taupo, Whakapapa, and National Park village; the trip takes around 1½ hours. Numerous local shuttle operators also provide transportation for hikers to and from the park.

Northern Explorer, a scenic train that links Auckland and Wellington, stops at National Park village and Ohakune; it travels southbound on Monday, Thursday, and Saturday and northbound on Tuesday, Friday, and Sunday.

Whakapapa, on the north side of Ruapehu, is the only settlement within the park with services, and it is the jump-off point for the Whakapapa ski slopes. The second ski area is Turoa, and its closest town is Ohakune, which is just beyond the southern boundary of the park. Both towns keep their doors open for hikers and other travelers when the snow melts.

The Tongariro National Park Visitor Centre is the best place to get maps, guides, and, if needed, hut passes. If you want to do some online research, the Department of Conservation's website (🌐 *www.doc.govt.nz*) is another helpful resource.

TOURS

Tongariro Expeditions. This outfit runs a shuttle to Tongariro National Park from the Taupo, Turangi, and Tongariro Base Camp and Ketetahi car park in summer. Only guided trips, which include gear and return transportation, are available in winter. Shuttle prices start at NZ$30. ✉ *Taupo* ☎ *07/377–0435, 0800/828–763* 🌐 *www.tongariroexpeditions.com.*

VISITOR INFORMATION

Contacts Tongariro National Park Visitor Centre. ✉ *Whakapapa Village, State Hwy. 48, Mt. Ruapehu* ☎ *07/892–3729* 🌐 *www.doc.govt.nz.*

WHERE TO EAT

$$$ NEW ZEALAND 🍴 **Eivins Bar & Bistro.** Popular with the ski set in winter and other outdoorsy types in summer, this modern eatery offers panoramic mountain views from its front veranda. The Scotch fillet cooked to your liking with a stuffed baked potato might take your fancy. Just don't let it go cold while you're gazing at the mountains. [$] *Average main: NZ$24* ✉ *State Hwy. 4, National Park Village* ☎ *07/892–2844* 🌐 *eivins.co.nz* ⏲ *No lunch.*

$$$ NEW ZEALAND FAMILY 🍴 **The Station Cafe, Bar, & Restaurant.** Paintings by local artists adorn the dusky pink and wood-paneled walls of this café-cum-bar, which has the tracks of the north–south railway right outside its door. Look for standard café fare during the day (think breakfast classics, plus soups, sandwiches, and salads). In the evening, order the beef eye fillet with French mustard jus and rösti or, perhaps, the grilled pork tenderloin with a creamy blue-cheese sauce. Finish off with the chef's homemade cheesecake; it goes down well with Baileys coffee. This is a great place if you need to refuel while exploring the Central Plateau. [$] *Average main: NZ$29* ✉ *Findlay St., National Park Village* ☎ *07/892–2881* 🌐 *www.stationcafe.co.nz.*

WHERE TO STAY

$$ HOTEL 🏨 **Chateau Tongariro.** Built in 1929, this French neo-Georgian-style property in Whakapapa hosts everyone from well-heeled movie types to people who tramp and ski by day, then switch their clothing to dress in heels or jacket and tie for the evening. **Pros:** classy, restful place; enormous lounge area has a welcoming open fire and billiard table. **Cons:** when the mist comes down you won't get a view from even the most expensive suite; a long way from the nearest town. [$] *Rooms from: NZ$195* ✉ *99 State Hwy. 48, Mt. Ruapehu* ☎ *07/892–3809, 0800/242–832* 🌐 *www.chateau.co.nz* 🛏 *101 rooms, 5 suites, 9 villas* 🍽 *No meals.*

$$ HOTEL FAMILY 🏨 **Discovery Lodge.** The only tourist lodging in the park to give a panoramic view of three active volcanoes is this friendly complex, only minutes from the ski slopes. **Pros:** handy to the village; close to the start of the Tongariro Alpine Crossing and their shuttle gets you there quite early. **Cons:** a long way from shops. [$] *Rooms from: NZ$145* ✉ *State Hwy. 47, Whakapapa Village* ☎ *07/892–2744, 0800/122–122* 🌐 *www.discovery.net.nz* 🛏 *2 rooms, 6 chalets, 14 apartments* 🍽 *No meals.*

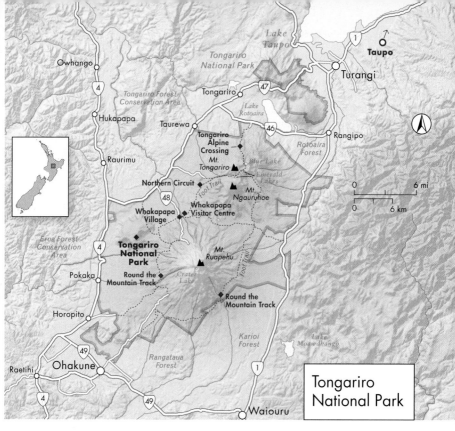

Tongariro
National Park

EN
ROUTE

Straddling State Highway 1 between National Park village and Taupo sits the small town of **Turangi**. A regular stopover for motorists on the main north–south route, its number-one attraction is trout fishing on some of the world's most productive rivers, but there is also great local walking, kayaking, and white-water rafting. Hotpools are also close by. The Turangi i-SITE Visitor Information Centre (☎ *07/386–8999,* ⊕ *www.greatlaketaupo.com*) is on Ngawhaka Place, Turangi.

SPORTS AND THE OUTDOORS
HIKING

Fodor'sChoice
★

The **Tongariro Alpine Crossing** grabs the hiking limelight. Starting at Mangatepopo, the one-way crossing is a spectacular seven- to nine-hour hike that follows a 19.4-km (12½-mile) trail up and over the namesake mountain, passing craters, the evocatively named Emerald Lakes, old lava flows, and hot springs. Although children and school groups commonly do the hike, it is not to be taken lightly. Prepare yourself for rapidly changing weather conditions by bringing warm and waterproof clothing. Wear sturdy footwear, and carry food, plenty of water, sunblock, and sunglasses—and don't forget a hat. Also, be careful not to get too close to steam vents; the area around them can be dangerously hot. From late November to May, you'll be sharing the trail with many other hikers. In the colder months, it's really only for experienced winter hikers who can deal with snow and ice; some transport companies will take you only if you have an ice axe and crampons. It is recommended that you get up-to-date trail and weather conditions from the Department of Conservation's Tongariro National Park Visitor Centre before starting out. A number of trail transport operators provide shuttles to and from the Tongariro Alpine Crossing. Many of the motels and lodges in National Park village can also arrange transport for about NZ$15.

The longest hikes in the park are the three-day **Northern Circuit,** which goes over Tongariro and around Ngauruhoe, and the four-day **Round-the-Mountain Track,** which circles Ruapehu. There are trailside huts throughout the park to use on overnight trips. You'll need to buy a hut pass at the visitor center; it costs NZ$32 from October 1 to the first weekend in June and NZ$10 the rest of the year. During the "Great Walks Season"(the third week in October to last week in April), huts musts be booked ahead; otherwise it's first come–first served. Gas cookers are available in the huts. You can also tackle short half-hour to two-hour walks if all you want is a flavor of the region. A 90-minute round-trip trek to the Tawhai Falls via the **Whakapapanui Track** takes you through the forest, and a two-hour round-trip to Taranaki Falls showcases subalpine scenery.

Mountain Shuttle. Transport to the trailhead from Turangi costs NZ$45. For an extra charge boots, clothing, day packs, and more can be supplied. ⊠ *Taupo* ☎ *0800/117–686* ⊕ *www.tongarirocrossing.com.*

SKIING

Mt. Ruapehu ski slopes. Combined, the Mt. Ruapehu ski slopes add up to New Zealand's most extensive skiing and snowboarding area. **Whakapapa,** on the mountain's north side, has more than 30 groomed trails, including beginners' slopes. **Turoa,** on the south side, has a half-pipe. Ski season generally runs from June through October, depending on snow conditions. Expect to pay about NZ$95 for a full day, all-mountain lift pass; lessons and rental equipment are also available. In summer, lifts operate for those wanting to enjoy a little alpine sightseeing. ⊠ *Taupo* ⊕ *www.mtruapehu.com.*

NAPIER AND HAWKE'S BAY

New Zealand prides itself on natural wonders, but Napier (population 50,000) is best known for its architecture. After an earthquake devastated this coastal city in 1931, residents rebuilt it in the art deco style of the day. Its well-kept uniformity of style makes it an exceptional period piece. There's a similar aspect to Napier's less-visited twin city, Hastings, just to the south, which was also remodeled following the earthquake. Once you've ogled the architecture, be sure to go on a brief wine-tasting tour—the region produces some of the country's best wines. The mild climate and beaches of Hawke Bay make this a popular vacation area. (Hawke Bay is the body of water; Hawke's Bay is the region.) Make a point of visiting the gannet colony at Cape Kidnappers, which is best seen between October and April.

NAPIER

150 km (94 miles) southeast of Taupo, 345 km (215 miles) northeast of Wellington.

The earthquake that struck Napier at 10:46 am on February 3, 1931, was—at 7.8 on the Richter scale—the largest quake ever recorded in New Zealand. The coastline was wrenched upward several feet. Almost all of the town's brick buildings collapsed, and many people were killed on the footpaths as they rushed outside. The quake triggered fires throughout town, and with water mains shattered, little could be done to stop the blazes that devoured the remaining wooden structures. Only a few buildings survived (the Public Service Building with its neoclassical pillars is one), and the death toll was well over 100.

The surviving townspeople set up tents and cookhouses in Nelson Park, and then tackled the city's reconstruction at a remarkable pace. In the rush to rebuild, Napier went mad for art deco, the bold, geometric style that had burst on the global design scene in 1925. Now a walk through the art deco district, concentrated between Emerson, Herschell, Dalton, and Browning streets, is a stylistic immersion. The decorative elements are often above the ground floors, so keep your eyes up.

GETTING HERE AND AROUND

Driving is more relaxed around this region, and you won't experience the traffic problems often found in the larger cities. If you'd rather not take the wheel yourself, InterCity and Nakedbus have daily service to Napier from Auckland, Hamilton, Rotorua, Wellington, and other destinations. GoBay also runs a limited public bus service covering Hawke's Bay and Napier.

Air travelers can catch direct Air New Zealand flights from Wellington, Auckland, and Christchurch; these arrive daily at the small Hawke's Bay Airport (NPE). Direct Jetstar flights from Auckland land here as well. The airport is 5 km (3 miles) north of Napier. Rental cars are available at the airport. Taxis and shuttles also provide transportation into the city: the former will take you to the center of Napier for about NZ$28.

Airport Hawke's Bay Airport. ✉ *111 Main North Rd.* ☏ *06/834–0742* ⊕ *www.hawkesbay-airport.co.nz.*

Bus Depot GoBay. ✉ *Napier* ☏ *06/878–9250* ⊕ *www.gobus.co.nz/urban/ hawkes-bay.* **Napier Bus Depot.** ✉ *Carlyle St.*

TOURS

Absolute de Tours. This company organizes a series of tours, among them art deco–themed outings in Napier, longer excursions to scenic points of interest in the area, and half- or full-day vineyard visits. Custom tours are also available from Napier, Hastings, and Havelock North. ✉ *112 Avenue Rd., Greenmeadows* ☏ *06/844–8699* ⊕ *www.absolutedetours. co.nz* 🚐 *From NZ$40.*

Art Deco Trust. The Trust leads excellent themed tours that highlight Napier's architectural heritage. A one-hour walk starts daily at 10 from the Napier i-SITE Visitor Information Centre (NZ$18); a two-hour version, which includes an audiovisual introduction, starts at 2 from the Art Deco Centre (NZ$20). If you'd rather not hoof it, sign on for the Deco Bus Tour (NZ$40) or, to really immerse yourself in the 1930s aesthetic, see the sights from a vintage car (NZ$160 for up to four people). DIY types can pick up the Trust's Art Deco Tour Map, which plots a self-drive route through Napier and Hastings. ⊠ *Art Deco Centre, 7 Tennyson St.* ☎ *06/835–0022* ⊕ *www.artdeconapier.com* ✉ *From NZ$18.*

VISITOR INFORMATION

Contacts Napier i-SITE Visitor Information Centre. ⊠ *100 Marine Parade* ☎ *06/834–1911* ⊕ *www.napiernz.com.*

EXPLORING
TOP ATTRACTIONS

Brookfields Vineyard. One of this region's most attractive wineries features rose gardens and a tasting room that overlooks the vines. The Chardonnay and Pinot Gris are usually outstanding, but the showpiece is the reserve Cabernet Sauvignon–Merlot, a powerful red that ages well. Syrah grapes are proving spectacular as is the Brookfields Hillside Syrah. From Napier take Marine Parade toward Hastings and turn right on Awatoto Road. Follow it to Brookfields Road and turn left. Signs will point to the winery. ⊠ *376 Brookfields Rd.* ☎ *06/834–4615* ⊕ *www. brookfieldsvineyards.co.nz* ✉ *Tastings free* ☉ *Daily 10:30–4:30.*

Fodor's Choice
★

MTG Hawke's Bay. Thanks to a multimillion-dollar renovation, the Hawke's Bay Museum has morphed into the MTG Hawke's Bay—a space that is home to a museum, a theater, and a gallery. The museum component's curatorial team is engaged, and the exhibitions ponder a range of local and international issues, so you might see a temporary display devoted to an exploration of memory alongside a cutting-edge digital presentation. There's also a significant collection of newspaper reports, photographs, and audiovisuals that re-create the suffering caused by the 1931 earthquake, plus a unique collection of artifacts—including vessels, decorative work, and statues—relating to the Ngāti Kahungunu Māori people of the East Coast. ⊠ *1 Tennyson St.* ☎ *06/835–7781* ⊕ *www.mtghawkesbay.com* ✉ *NZ$10* ☉ *Daily 10–5.*

FAMILY
Fodor's Choice
★

National Aquarium. Stand on a moving conveyor that takes you through the world of sharks, rays, and fish. Environmental and ecological displays showcase tropical fish, sea horses, tuatara, and other creatures. For NZ$82—all gear provided—you can even swim with the sharks. There is also a kiwi enclosure where these birds can be seen in ideal viewing conditions. ⊠ *Marine Parade* ☎ *06/834–1404* ⊕ *www. nationalaquarium.co.nz* ✉ *NZ$20* ☉ *Daily 9–5.*

Ocean Spa. In a place where the beaches are not really suitable for swimming, this complex is a delight for the sun- and water-seeking tourist, its open-air pools being right alongside the beach. Sun beds and spa treatments are available at extra charge. ⊠ *42 Marine Parade* ☎ *06/835–8553* ⊕ *www.oceanspapier.co.nz* ✉ *NZ$10.70* ☉ *Mon.– Sat. 6–10, Sun. 8–10.*

Silky Oak Chocolate Company. This enticing spot—which includes a factory, museum, shop, and café—is a chocoholic's dream come true. The museum details the story of chocolate through the ages, while the café

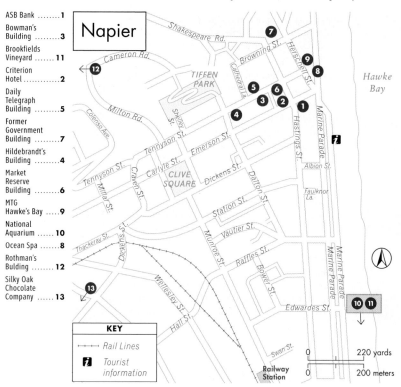

Napier

Hawke Bay

KEY

├───┤ *Rail Lines*

🛈 *Tourist information*

Railway Station

0 — 220 yards
0 — 200 meters

5

serves a nice selection of goodies. ✉ *1131 Links Rd.* ☎ *06/845–0908* ⊕ *www.silkyoakchocs.co.nz* 🖃 *Museum-tasting tours NZ$8–$79* ⊙ *Mon.–Thurs. 9–5, Fri. 9–4, weekends 10–4.*

WORTH NOTING

ASB Bank. One of Napier's more notable buildings is at the corner of Hastings and Emerson streets. The Māori theme on the lintels is probably the country's finest example of *kowhaiwhai* (rafter) patterns decorating a European building. The traditional red, white, and black pattern is also continued inside around a coffered ceiling. ✉ *100 Hastings St.*

Bowman's Building. Erected in 1932, the Bowman's Building is a Louis Hay design in brick veneer with the characteristic eyebrow (brick or tiles, often curved, set over a window). Some of Hay's work was influenced by Chicago's Louis Sullivan. ✉ *36 Tennyson St.*

Criterion Hotel. This is typical of the Spanish Mission style, which Napier took on because of its success in Santa Barbara, California, where an earthquake had similarly wreaked havoc just a few years before the New Zealand catastrophe. It has smooth plastered concrete walls (in imitation of adobe construction) and tiled parapets. The small square windows and larger round-arched glass doors also reflect features of mud-brick construction. ✉ *48 Emerson St.*

Daily Telegraph Building. Now a real-estate office, the Daily Telegraph Building is another Napier classic. It has almost all the deco style, incorporating zigzags, fountain shapes, ziggurats, and a sunburst. ✉ *49 Tennyson St.*

Former Government Building. A decorative lighthouse pillar at the front takes on the almost-Gothic menace that art deco architecture sometimes has (picture New York's Chrysler Building). ✉ *Browning St.*

Hildebrandt's Building. Hildebrandt's has an excellent frieze, which is best viewed from across Dalton Street. The original owner was a German who migrated to New Zealand—hence the German flag at one end, the New Zealand at the other; the wavy lines in the middle symbolize the sea passage between the two countries. ✉ *90 Tennyson St.*

Market Reserve Building. On Tennyson and Hastings, this was the first building to rise after the earthquake. Its steel metal frame was riveted, not welded, so that the construction noise would give residents the message that the city was being rebuilt. The bronze storefronts with their "crown of thorns" patterned leaded glass are still original. ✉ *28 Tennyson St.*

Rothman's Building. A little over a kilometer (½ mile) north of the central core stands one of the area's finest deco edifices. The 1932 structure has been totally renovated and its original name reinstated: the National Tobacco Company Building. It has a rose theme on the stained-glass windows and on a magnificent glass dome over the entrance hall. ✉ *1 Ossian St.*

WHERE TO EAT

$$$ NEW ZEALAND 🍴 **Caution Dining Lounge.** Massive wood-frame mirrors reflect the candles behind the bar in this northern Napier spot overlooking the boat masts in the basin. Try the pork ribs in homemade barbecue sauce or opt for the lamb ragout. You can cap your meal with crème caramel or a trio of local cheeses, and then savor the view outside on the deck. The menu and ownership is shared with the attached Shed 2, a casual eatery that's open for lunch and dinner. [$] *Average main: NZ$23* ✉ *At Lever St., West Quay, Ahuhiri* ☎ *06/835–2202* 🌐 *www.shed2.com* 🕒 *No lunch.*

$$$ MEXICAN 🍴 **Mexi Mama.** With its huge wrought-iron chandelier and candle-lit shrine to St. Theresa, this cheery Mexican restaurant is a feast for the eyes as well as the stomach. The menu includes many shared plates—the spicy pork tostaditas and *tortitas de pollo* are both recommended. You'll need a cold *cerveza* (beer) to cool you down. [$] *Average main: NZ$25* ✉ *58 West Quay* ☎ *027/804–5812* 🌐 *www.meximama.co.nz* 🕒 *No lunch.*

$$$$ NEW ZEALAND 🍴 **The Old Church Restaurant & Bar.** From the high-vaulted ceiling to the overly ornate fittings, this restaurant (a converted church) is a stunner. Sit on red velvet upholstered chairs by an open fire while waiting for your meal to arrive. Tempting main courses include miso-rubbed South Island salmon, wild hare gnocchi, and a surf-and-turf combo with pork belly and black tiger prawns. For a sweet finish, try the apple brûlée topped with Hawke's Bay apple chips and edible flowers. [$] *Average main: NZ$33* ✉ *199 Meanee Rd.* ☎ *06/844–8866* 🌐 *www.theoldchurch.co.nz* 🕒 *No lunch Tues.*

$$$$ NEW ZEALAND Fodor's Choice ★ 🍴 **Pacifica Restaurant.** Enter this weathered blue bungalow and watch classically trained chef Jeremy Remeka produce delicious dishes. These are worked into a pair of five-course degustation menus, one devoted exclusively to seafood and one mixed. Each reflects his creativity and his commitment to using the finest local products. [$] *Average main: NZ$50* ✉ *209 Marine Parade* ☎ *06/833–6335* 🌐 *www.pacificarestaurant.co.nz* ⏰ *Closed Sun. and Mon. No lunch.*

WHERE TO STAY

$$$$ HOTEL 🏨 **The County Hotel.** Built in 1909 as the Hawke's Bay County Council headquarters, this is one of the few Napier buildings that survived the 1931 earthquake; wood paneling, chandeliers, and claw-foot bathtubs conjure up that more gracious era. **Pros:** you'll sleep in a room with a bit of history; dine well without leaving the building. **Cons:** wood paneling is not everyone's choice of decor. [$] *Rooms from: NZ$375* ✉ *12 Browning St.* ☎ *06/835–7800* 🌐 *www.countyhotel.co.nz* 🛏 *18 rooms* 🍽 *No meals.*

$$ B&B/INN 🏨 **Esk Valley Lodge.** Eileen and Jes Roddy are the warm owners of this lovely homestead, set in peaceful surroundings with expansive views over acres of vines. **Pros:** quiet rural setting handy to Napier/Taupo highway; congenial hosts. **Cons:** 15-minute drive to town center; not near restaurants. [$] *Rooms from: NZ$185* ✉ *342 Hill Rd., RD2* ☎ *06/836–7904* 🌐 *www.eskvalleylodge.co.nz* 🛏 *2 rooms, 1 suite* 🍽 *Breakfast.*

$$ B&B/INN 🏨 **Homestay 157.** You'll be made to feel very welcome at this luxurious yet comfortable home, which features a lovely en suite bedroom, a private guest lounge, and a covered veranda that provides spectacular views over the ocean to the Mahia Peninsula. **Pros:** genuine welcoming hosts; free Wi-Fi. **Cons:** it's downstairs to the guest suite; a fair distance from town. [$] *Rooms from: NZ$145* ✉ *157 Thompson Rd.* ☎ *06/835–0117* 🛏 *1 suite* 🍽 *Breakfast* 💳 *No credit cards.*

$$$$ B&B/INN 🏨 **McHardy Lodge.** The gardens at this historic mansion, high on Napier Hill, have panoramic views of the Pacific Ocean and the splendid Kaweka Ranges. **Pros:** has that grand mansion feel; fabulous views; heated pool and full-size billiard table. **Cons:** it could be hard to find on a dark night; hard uphill walk from town center. [$] *Rooms from: NZ$495* ✉ *11 Bracken St.* ☎ *06/835–0605* 🌐 *www.mchardylodge.co.nz* 🛏 *2 rooms, 4 suites* 🍽 *Some meals.*

$$$ B&B/INN 🏨 **Mon Logis.** Built in the 1860s and one of the few houses that escaped destruction in 1931, this splendid mansion–cum–boutique hotel feels like a little piece of France. **Pros:** a superb breakfast with Gerard, a genial Gallic host; sea views; great location. **Cons:** Gerard actually supports the French rugby team. [$] *Rooms from: NZ$220* ✉ *415 Marine Parade* ☎ *06/835–2125* 🌐 *www.monlogis.co.nz* 🛏 *4 rooms* 🍽 *Breakfast.*

$$$ B&B/INN 🏨 **Napier Bed and Breakfast—Tequila Sunrise.** This modern hilltop residence with sweeping views over countryside and ocean was purpose-built as a B&B; its spacious, airy rooms are comfortably furnished, and one is wheelchair friendly. **Pros:** quality accommodation; plenty of parking space. **Cons:** 20-minute drive to town; long way from restaurants.

$ *Rooms from: NZ$210* ⊠ *123 Eskridge Dr.* ☎ *06/836–7373* ⊕ *www. napierbandb.co.nz* ⬏ *4 suites* ⦵ *Breakfast.*

$$
HOTEL
📶 **Shoreline Motel.** The rooms at this Marine Parade place are well appointed and well equipped; each comes with its own spa pool, a flat-screen TV, and free Wi-Fi. **Pros:** comfortable accommodation close to town; 28 rooms have a sea view; free off-street parking. **Cons:** could be full in the holiday season; two flights of outside stairs to top units. $ *Rooms from: NZ$180* ⊠ *377 Marine Parade* ☎ *06/835–5222* ⊕ *www.shorelinenapier.co.nz* ⬏ *38 rooms* ⦵ *No meals.*

SHOPPING

Art Deco Centre. Napier's Art Deco Trust maintains a perfectly laid-out shop that sells everything from table lamps to ceramics, as well as an amazing selection of hats, toys, jewelry, rugs, and wineglasses. You can also purchase booklets outlining self-guided walks through town. ⊠ *7 Tennyson St.* ☎ *06/835–0022* ⊕ *www.artdeconapier.com.*

Opossum World. This fascinating spot sells opossum products and houses a mini-museum about the opossum's effects on New Zealand's environment. Fur items include hats, gloves, and rugs; a soft blend of merino wool and opossum fur is also made into sweaters, scarves, and socks. ⊠ *157 Marine Parade* ☎ *06/835–7697* ⊕ *www.opossumworld.co.nz.*

HAWKE'S BAY

320 km (205 miles) northeast of Wellington, 165 km (100 miles) southeast of Taupo.

Bounded by the Kaweka and Ruahine ranges, Hawke's Bay is known as the fruit basket of New Zealand. You can't travel far without seeing a vineyard or an orchard, and the region produces some of the country's finest wines. Roughly 25 years ago, a dry, barren area known as the **Gimblett Gravels** was about to be mined for gravel. Then an enterprising vine grower took a gamble and purchased the land. The stony soil turned out to be a boon for grapevines because it retains heat, and now several wineries benefit from its toasty conditions. Chardonnay is the most important white variety here; you'll also find Sauvignon Blanc, Bordeaux varieties, and Syrah.

On the coast east of Hawke's Bay is Cape Kidnappers, a fascinating spot that is home to as many as 20,000 gannets. To the south, you'll find Hastings, which is blessed with art deco buildings, and adorable Havelock North (known locally as "the Village"), with the Te Mata Peak rising dramatically beyond.

Farther south, a hill near Porangahau is the place with **the longest name in the world.** Take a deep breath and say, "Taumatawhakatangihangakoau-auotamateaturipukakapikimaungahoronukupokaiwhenuakitanatahu." Now, that wasn't too hard, was it? Just remember it as "the place where Tamatea, the man with the big knees who slid, climbed, and swallowed mountains, known as land-eater, played his flute to his loved one," and it should be no problem at all.

A gannet comes in for a landing on the rocks of Cape Kidnappers in Hawke's Bay.

GETTING HERE AND AROUND

Distances here are comparatively short: Hastings, for instance, is only 18 km (11 miles) south of Napier, so driving is the optimal way to get around. If you don't have a car, check out GoBay, the regional public transit system.

Bus Contacts GoBay. ✉ *Napier* ☎ *06/878–9250* ⊕ *www.gobus.co.nz/urban/hawkes-bay.*

TOURS

FAMILY

Fodor's Choice

★

Gannet Beach Adventures. Make the most of your trip to the Cape Kidnappers gannet colony by boarding a trailer towed by a 1949 Minneapolis-Moline tractor. Along the way, you'll hear commentary about the geological features of this amazing coastline. Tours lasting about four hours run daily, October through late April. They depart approximately two hours before low tide from Clifton Reserve; transport from the Napier or Hastings i-SITEs is available. ✉ *475 Clifton Rd., Clifton, Napier* ☎ *06/875–0898* ⊕ *www.gannets.com* 🖅 *NZ$44.*

Gannet Safaris Overland. Accessing the gannet colony across private farmland, this outfit runs a four-wheel-drive bus to Cape Kidnappers from its base, just past Te Awanga. The three-hour tour includes commentary and stops within a few feet of the gannets—no walking required. Buses leave daily at 9:30 and 1:30, September through April. Advance booking is essential; and transportation from Napier or Hastings can be arranged at extra cost. ✉ *396 Clifton Rd., Clifton, Napier* ☎ *06/875–0888* ⊕ *www.gannetsafaris.co.nz* 🖅 *NZ$75 (4-person minimum).*

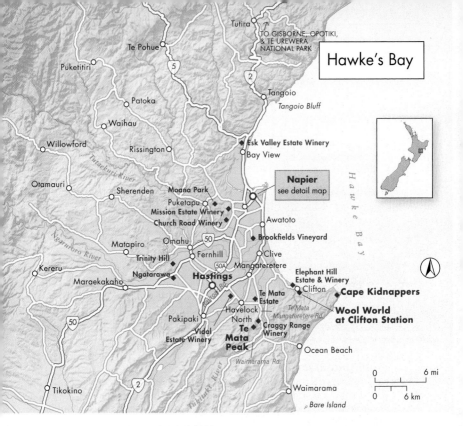

Hawke's Bay

Tutira
TO GISBORNE, OPOTIKI, & TE UREWERA NATIONAL PARK

Te Pohue
Puketitiri
Patoka
Waihau
Willowford
Rissington
Otamauri
Sherenden
Moana Park
Puketapu
Mission Estate Winery
Church Road Winery
Matapiro
Omahu
Trinity Hill
Fernhill
Kereru
Ngatarawa
Maraekakaho
Hastings
Matua
Te Mata Estate
Havelock North
Pakipaki
Vidal Estate Winery
Te Mata Peak
Craggy Range Winery
Tikokino
Waimarama
Bare Island

Tangoio
Tangoio Bluff
Esk Valley Estate Winery
Bay View
Napier
see detail map
Awatoto
Brookfields Vineyard
Clive
Mangateretere
Elephant Hill Estate & Winery
Clifton
Cape Kidnappers
Wool World at Clifton Station
Ocean Beach

Te Mata Mangateretere Rd.
Waimarama Rd.

Hawke Bay

Tutaekuri River
Ngaruroro River
Tukituki River

0   6 mi
0   6 km

VISITOR INFORMATION

Contacts Hastings i-SITE Visitor Information Centre. ✉ Westerman's Bldg., at Russell St. N and Heretaunga St., Hastings ☎ 0800/429–537 ⊕ www.visithastings.co.nz. **Havelock North i-SITE Visitor Information Centre.** ✉ At Te Aute and Middle Rds., Havelock North ☎ 06/877–9600 ⊕ www.havelocknorthnz.com.

EXPLORING
TOP ATTRACTIONS

Cape Kidnappers. This outstanding spot was named by Captain James Cook after local Māori tried to kidnap the servant of his Tahitian interpreter. It's believed to be the only mainland **gannet sanctuary** in existence. Gannets—large white seabirds with black-tipped flight feathers, a golden crown, and a wingspan that can reach 6 feet—generally nest only on remote islands. But between October and April, thousands of them build their nests here, hatch their young, and prepare them for their long migratory flight. Watching them dive for their dinner is particularly impressive; when the birds find a shoal of fish, they fold their wings and plunge straight into the sea at tremendous speed.

You can walk to the sanctuary along the beach from Clifton, a community located about 24 km (15 miles) south of Napier—but not at high tide. The 8-km (5-mile) walk must begin no earlier than three hours after the high-tide mark, and the return journey must begin no later than four hours before the next high tide. Tidal information is available at area i-SITE Visitor Information Centres. A rest hut with refreshments is near the colony. ⊠ *Cape Kidnappers, Clifton, Napier.*

WORTH NOTING

Hastings. Napier's twin city doesn't have the same concentrated architectural interest. But the 1931 earthquake also did a great deal of damage here, and buildings in its center exhibit similar art deco flourishes. The Westerman's Building, on the corner of Russell and Heretaunga, is one prime example; it now houses the town's i-SITE center. Hastings is 18 km (11 miles) south of Napier, down Highway 2. ⊠ *Hastings.*

Hawke's Bay Farmers' Market. For picnic supplies, visit the Hawke's Bay Farmers' Market. It's held at the A&P Showgrounds on Sunday from 8:30 to 12:30. Local products include handmade cheese, breads, ice cream, and fruit. This is also a good place to people-watch. ⊠ *Kenilworth Rd., Hastings* ⊕ *hawkesbayfarmersmarket.co.nz.*

Te Mata Peak. It's possible to gaze across the plains to Napier and the rumpled hills beyond from this famed local viewpoint. The summit is a 15-minute (signposted) drive along Te Mata Peak Road from the village of Havelock North. ⊠ *Te Mata Peak Rd., Havelock North.*

Wool World at Clifton Station. Capture the rustic aura of life on the farm in an original 1890s woolshed. View century-old equipment, learn the history of wool in Hawke's Bay, and watch sheep being shorn daily at 2 pm by hand and machine. The small shop has a nice range of mainly New Zealand–made articles. ⊠ *459 Clifton Rd., Clifton, Napier* ☎ *06/875–0611, 027/451–2512* ⌨ *NZ$5 museum; NZ$20 show* ☺ *Daily 10–4.*

WINERIES

Church Road Winery. Although owned by Pernod-Ricard, this winery operates pretty much as a separate entity, and its wines bear a Church Road label. The Chardonnay is a nationwide restaurant staple, and the many variations on the Cabernet Sauvignon and Merlot themes are all worth sampling. A McDonald series features limited-release wines with styles and varieties unique to Church Road. Tours of the wine museum and expertly restored cellars are given daily (NZ$17.50, tasting included); a behind-the-scenes version is also available (NZ$35, with wine-and-food pairings). Bookings are essential. The winery's on-site restaurant is open for lunch daily. ⊠ *150 Church Rd., Taradale, Napier* ☎ *06/833–8234* ⊕ *www.churchroad.co.nz* ⌨ *Tours from NZ$17.50* ☺ *Daily 10:30–4:30.*

Fodor's Choice ★ **Craggy Range Winery.** Situated by a small lake with the towering Te Mata Peak beyond, this vineyard has a stellar backdrop. The wines include single-varietal Chardonnay, Merlot, and Syrah; a predominantly Merlot blend called Sophia; and a Pinot Noir dubbed Aroha. You can take an in-depth tour of the facility that follows the path of the grape from vine to glass, or simply sample wines at the cellar door; leave time to linger over a meal at Terroir, a French-inspired restaurant overlooking the lake. ⊠ *253 Waimarama Rd., Havelock North* ☎ *06/873-7126* ⊕ *www.craggyrange.com* ⌨ *Tastings NZ$7.50 (refundable with purchase); tours by appointment NZ$35 (NZ$15 refundable with purchase)* ☺ *Winery Apr.–Oct., daily 10–5; Nov.–Mar., daily 10–6. Restaurant*

Apr.–Oct., lunch Wed.–Sun. and dinner Wed.–Sat.; Nov.–Mar., lunch daily and dinner Mon.–Sat.

Elephant Hill Estate & Winery. Blending contemporary architecture with the traditional aspect of wine making, this stunning estate overlooks jagged rows of vines with expansive views from the terrace taking in the ocean and Cape Kidnappers. Sip a glass of wine in the sunken lounge or enjoy a meal in the ultramodern dining room—it's an unforgettable experience. ✉ *86 Clifton Rd., Te Awanga* ☎ *06/872–6073 winery, 06/872–6060 restaurant* ⊕ *www.elephanthill.co.nz* 🍷 *Tastings NZ$5 (refundable with purchase)* ⊗ *Winery Apr.–Nov., daily 11–4; Dec.–Mar., daily 11–5. Restaurant lunch daily; dinner daily Dec.–Mar. and Thurs.– Sat. Apr.–Nov.*

Esk Valley Estate Winery. Winemaker Gordon Russell produces Merlot, Syrah, and blends with Cabernet Sauvignon, Merlot, Cabernet Franc, and Malbec in various combinations, including a rare and expensive red simply called The Terraces. White varieties include Chardonnay, Sauvignon Blanc, Riesling, Verdelho, Chenin Blanc, and Pinot Gris. Look for the Wine-Makers reserve versions of Chardonnay, Syrah, and Merlot-Malbec blend to find out what he has done with the best grapes from given years. The vineyard's position, in a sheltered valley overlooking the Pacific, ensures it captures full sun; it's located 12 km (8 miles) north of Napier, just north of the town of Bay View before Highways 2 and 5 split. ✉ *745 Main Rd., Bay View* ☎ *06/872–7430* ⊕ *www.eskvalley.co.nz* 🍷 *Tastings NZ$5 (refundable with purchase)* ⊗ *June–Aug., Mon.–Sat. 10–4:30; other months, daily 9–5.*

Fodor's Choice
★

Mission Estate Winery. Surrounded by gardens, this classic winery—the country's oldest—stands in the Taradale hills overlooking Napier. Dating back to 1851, it deserves to be added to your "must-see" list. Award-winning wines, including the Mission Jewelstone range, can be bought or tasted at the cellar door. Learn more about the mission's history by joining one of the twice-daily tours; or order a meal in the on-site restaurant, which serves lunch and dinner daily (take a seat on the terrace for a terrific view of the vineyard and Napier). Also check out the website—the winery occasionally hosts concerts by big-name performers. To get here, leave Napier by Kennedy Road, heading southwest from the city center toward Taradale. Just past Anderson Park, turn right into Avenue Road and continue to its end at Church Road. ✉ *198 Church Rd., Taradale* ☎ *06/845–9350* ⊕ *www.missionestate. co.nz* 🍷 *Tastings free* ⊗ *Mon.–Sat. 9–5, Sun. 10–4:30.*

Moana Park. Specific wine styles are selected and handcrafted from each vintage at this small boutique producer, based on its Gimblett Gravels and Dartmoor Valley vineyards. All grapes are grown on either organic or sustainable sites and are vegetarian approved. There's no café here, but platters of local produce are available; you're also welcome to bring along a picnic as there are plenty of tables on the lovely grounds. ✉ *530 Puketapu Rd., Taradale* ☎ *06/844–8269* ⊕ *www.moanapark.co.nz* 🍷 *Tastings free* ⊗ *Nov.–Apr., daily 10–5; May–Oct., daily noon–4.*

Ngatarawa. Set among superb countryside, this former racing stable has become a medium-size boutique winery. Producing premium wines in the Alwyn Proprietors Reserve, Glazebrook, and Stables ranges and drawing grapes from around the region, the wines are often referred to as being in the classic style. ✉ *305 Ngatarawa Rd., Bridge Pā* ☎ *06/879–7603* ⊕ *www.ngatarawa.co.nz* 🍷 *Tastings free* ☉ *Nov.–Apr., daily 11–5; May–Oct., daily 10–4.*

Te Mata Estate. This is one of New Zealand's oldest and best wineries. Coleraine, a rich but elegant Cabernet–Merlot blend named after the much-photographed home of the owner, John Buck, is considered the archetypal Hawke's Bay red. Bullnose Syrah, Elston Chardonnay, and Cape Crest Sauvignon Blanc show similar restraint and balance. If there's any Zara Viognier open (it's made only in tiny quantities), try it—it's excellent. From Napier head south on Marine Parade through Clive and turn left at the Mangateretere School. Signs will then lead you to Te Mata Road and the estate. ✉ *349 Te Mata Rd., Havelock North* ☎ *06/877–4399* ⊕ *www.temata.co.nz* 🍷 *Tastings NZ$5 (refundable with purchase)* ☉ *Weekdays 9–5, Sat. 10–5, Sun. 11–4.*

Trinity Hill. Situated in the Gimblett Gravels region, this winery produces distinctive wines reflecting the character of the vineyard sites. Its diverse range includes classic varieties as well as lesser known ones, such as Tempranillo, Montepulciano, and Marsame-Viognier. At the cellar door, visitors can sample a generous selection of Trinity Hill's best products. ✉ *2.396 State Hwy. 50, Hastings* ☎ *06/879–7778* ⊕ *www.trinityhill.com* 🍷 *Tastings NZ$5 (refundable with purchase)* ☉ *Oct.–Easter, daily 10–5; Easter–Oct., daily 11–4.*

Vidal Estate Winery. Founded in 1905, this is one of Hawke's Bay's oldest boutique wineries and a producer of premium quality wines. The popular Vidal Estate Winery Restaurant is a wonderful place to laze away the afternoon with a glass of Sauvignon Blanc, Chardonnay, or Syrah. ✉ *913 St. Aubyn St. E, Hastings* ☎ *06/872–7440* ⊕ *www.vidal.co.nz* 🍷 *Tastings NZ$5 (refundable with purchase)* ☉ *Winery Mon.–Sat. 10–5, Sun. 11–4. Restaurant Mon.–Sat. lunch and dinner, Sun. lunch only.*

WHERE TO EAT

$$$
CONTEMPORARY
✕ **Jarks Cityside.** On sunny days, you can sit outside on the patio here. In winter, a large fireplace warms the rustic interior, and candles on the tables enhance the scene. Either way, the service is efficient and friendly. One good choice from the varied menu is lamb shank on saffron mash with seasonal vegetables and red wine jus; you can cap your meal by ordering the cheesecake of the day. $ *Average main: NZ$26* ✉ *118 Maraekakoho Rd., Hastings* ☎ *06/870–8333* ⊕ *www.jarks.co.nz* ☉ *Closed Sun.*

$$$
IRISH
✕ **Rose & Shamrock.** This lovely old-world pub in the heart of Havelock North has the largest selection of tap beer in Hawke's Bay. The pints mix with reasonably priced pub fare, including Scotch fillet, Irish sausages, and hearty beef-and-Guinness pie. If you like a good pub quiz, then the brain-testing competition it hosts the first Tuesday of each month may be just the ticket. $ *Average main: NZ$22* ✉ *At Napier Rd. and Porter Dr., Havelock North* ☎ *06/877–2999* ⊕ *www.roseandshamrock.co.nz.*

$$$$ FRENCH Fodor's Choice ★ 🍴 **Terroir Restaurant.** The massive cedar doors, high circular roof, and open wood fire give this well-regarded restaurant at Craggy Range Winery a rustic character. Although the menu is loosely country French, "rustic" here is far from unsophisticated. Start with venison tartare or the twice-baked goat cheese soufflé; then move on to mouthwatering main courses like wood-fired whole fish with fried potatoes and aioli. For a sweet finish, the eclectic dessert menu features a classic vanilla crème brûlée. On warm evenings, you can dine on the terrace with views of Te Mata Peak. [$] *Average main: NZ$39* ✉ *253 Waimarama Rd., Havelock North* ☎ *06/873–0143* 🌐 *www.craggyrange.com* 🕒 *No dinner Sun.; Apr.–Oct., closed Mon. and Tues.*

$$$$ CONTEMPORARY 🍴 **Vidal Estate Winery Restaurant.** Vidal's is acknowledged as one of Hawke's Bay's finest eateries. Appetizers like the gin-infused crab cakes will whet your appetite for the main event (picture an eye fillet with potato gnocchi or Cajun chicken with chorizo-and-chickpea stew). Add a fudge brownie with salted caramel sauce, and you have all the makings of a memorable meal. [$] *Average main: NZ$34* ✉ *913 St. Aubyn St. E, Hastings* ☎ *06/872–7440* 🌐 *www.vidal.co.nz* 🕒 *No dinner Sun.* ✍ *Reservations essential.*

WHERE TO STAY

$$ HOTEL FAMILY 🏨 **Harvest Lodge.** Close to the center of Havelock North, this up-to-the-minute motel has spacious units with original artwork and comfortable king-size beds. **Pros:** close to the Rose & Shamrock pub; handy to restaurants. **Cons:** near busy road; there may be some traffic noise. [$] *Rooms from: NZ$165* ✉ *23 Havelock Rd., Havelock North* ☎ *06/877–9500* 🌐 *www.harvestlodge.co.nz* 🛏 *19 units* 🍽 *No meals.*

$$$$ HOTEL 🏨 **Mangapapa Hotel.** Built in 1885, the restored residence of Sir James Wattie stands in 20 acres of working orchards. **Pros:** a private, quiet place; luxury to lighten your heart. **Cons:** you won't want to leave. [$] *Rooms from: NZ$320* ✉ *466 Napier Rd., Havelock North* ☎ *06/878–3234* 🌐 *www.mangapapa.co.nz* 🛏 *12 suites* 🍽 *No meals.*

$$ HOTEL 🏨 **Portmans Motor Lodge.** Conveniently located near the center of Hastings, this motel has 20 modern units surrounding a spacious courtyard; 10 have whirlpool baths, and all are comfortably equipped. **Pros:** reasonably priced accommodations; really handy to town. **Cons:** some parking is a little cramped; pool isn't heated. [$] *Rooms from: NZ$130* ✉ *401 Railway Rd., Hastings* ☎ *06/878–8332* 🌐 *www.portmans.co.nz* 🛏 *20 rooms* 🍽 *No meals.*

GISBORNE AND EASTLAND

Traveling to Eastland takes you well away from the tourist track in the North Island. Once here, you will find rugged coastline, beaches, dense forests, gentle nature trails, and small, predominantly Māori communities. Eastland provides one of the closest links with the nation's earliest past. Kaiti Beach, near the city of Gisborne, is where the *Horouta* landed, and nearby Titirangi was named by the first Māori settlers in remembrance of a mountain in Hawaiki, their Polynesian island of origin. Kaiti Beach is also where Captain Cook—the first European to set foot on New Zealand soil—landed in 1769. His initial foray

Bikers tour Gimblett Gravels Vineyard in Hawke's Bay.

was unsuccessful, for even though the natives were friendly, several were killed because of misunderstandings. When Cook left, he named the place Poverty Bay "as it afforded us not one thing we wanted." Although Cook's name stuck to the body of water that hugs the eastern shore, the region is now generally known as Eastland.

Gisborne's warm climate and fertile soil produce some of New Zealand's top wines. Often overshadowed by Hawke's Bay (and its PR machine), Gisborne has about 7,000 acres under vine, and it is the country's largest supplier of Chardonnay grapes.

The region also has some of the finest and often almost deserted surfing beaches in the country; it's ideal for walking, fishing, horse trekking, and camping as well. The international spotlight focused briefly on Eastland when scenes for the film *Whale Rider* were shot at Whangara, north of Gisborne, but there have been few changes to what is mainly a quiet, rural place.

GISBORNE

210 km (130 miles) northeast of Napier, 500 km (310 miles) southeast of Auckland.

The Māori name for the Gisborne district is Tairawhiti (tye-ra-*fee*-tee), "the coast upon which the sun shines across the water," and Gisborne is indeed the first city in New Zealand to see sunrise. With a population of just 30,000, it's hardly large; however, you'll need a day or so to get around properly. The landmark Town Clock stands in the middle of Gladstone Road; nearby, in a house on Grey Street, Kiri Te Kanawa,

New Zealand's world-famous opera diva, was born in 1944 (the house is no longer there).

Europeans settled the Gisborne area early in the 19th century. A plaque on the waterfront commemorates the first official sale—of an acre of land—on June 30, 1831. On that site, the first European house and store was reportedly erected (it's long gone, too).

GETTING HERE AND AROUND

Air New Zealand flies daily to Gisborne from Auckland and Wellington. The small Gisborne Airport (GIS) is about 5 km (3 miles) from the city center; you can catch a taxi in for NZ$20. InterCity buses also link Gisborne to Auckland and Wellington once per day.

Motorists should note that Gisborne is a long way from almost anywhere, but the coastal and bush scenery makes the drive wholly worthwhile. Most of the town's historical sights and other attractions are too spread out to explore by foot, and a car is needed for the spectacular countryside. The main driving approach is by State Highway 2, which becomes Gladstone Street as it enters the town.

Airport Gisborne Airport. ⊠ *Aerodrome Rd.* ☎ *06/867–1608* ⊕ *www.eastland. co.nz/gisborne-airport.*

Bus Depot Gisborne Bus Depot. ⊠ *Gisborne i-SITE Visitor Information Centre, 209 Grey St.*

VISITOR INFORMATION

Contacts Gisborne i-SITE Visitor Information Centre. ⊠ *209 Grey St.* ☎ *06/868–6139* ⊕ *www.gisbornenz.com.*

EXPLORING

Cook Landing Site National Historic Reserve. This place has deep historical significance for New Zealanders. A statue of Captain James Cook, who first landed here on October 9, 1769, stands on Kaiti Beach, across the river southeast of the city center. The beach itself attracts interesting birdlife at low tide. ⊠ *Esplanade on south end of Turanganui River.*

Tairawhiti Museum. With its Māori and *Pākehā* (non-native) artifacts and an extensive photographic collection, this small but interesting museum provides a good introduction to the region's history. A maritime gallery covers seafaring matters, and there are changing exhibits of local and national artists' work. The pottery displays are particularly outstanding. An on-site shop sells locally made items. Check out Wyllie Cottage before leaving the grounds (although it stands outside, it's part of the museum). Built in 1872, this colonial-style house is the oldest in town. ⊠ *Kelvin Park, 10 Stout St.* ☎ *06/867–3832* ⊕ *www.tairawhitimuseum. org.nz* ⊠ *NZ$5 Tues.–Sun.; free Mon.* ☉ *Mon.–Sat. 10–4, Sun. 1:30–4.*

Te Poho o Rawiri Meeting House. One of the largest Māori marae (meetinghouses) in New Zealand has an intriguing interior with complex traditional carvings. One example is the *tekoteko*, a kneeling human figure with the right hand raised to challenge those who enter. There are also unusual alcoves and a stage framed by carvings; it's essentially a meetinghouse within a meetinghouse. Photography is not allowed inside. On the side of the hill stands the 1930s Toko Toro Tapu Church. You'll need permission to explore either site; contact the Gisborne i-SITE Visitor Information Centre. ✉ *At Ranfurly St. and Queens Dr., Kaiti Hill* 🖃 *Donations requested.*

Titirangi Domain. This was the site of an extensive *pā* (fortified village), which can be traced back at least 24 Māori generations. It has excellent views of Gisborne, Poverty Bay, and the surrounding rural areas. **Titirangi Recreational Reserve** is a part of the Domain, and it makes a great place for a picnic or a walk. The Domain is south of Turanganui River. Pass the harbor and turn right onto Esplanade, left onto Crawford Road, then right onto Queens Drive, and follow it to several lookout points in the Domain where the views are extraordinary. ✉ *Gisborne.*

WINERIES

Bushmere Estate. In the Central Valley region of Gisborne, only a few minutes' drive from the city center, this small estate grows mainly Chardonnay grapes along with some Gewürztraminer, Viognier, Pinot Gris, and Merlot. Its restaurant, The Vines, serves lunches that highlight fresh, seasonal ingredients. ✉ *166 Main Rd.* 📞 *06/868–9317* ⊕ *www.bushmerevines.co.nz* 🖃 *Tastings NZ$5 (refundable with purchase)* ⊗ *Sept.–May, Wed.–Sun. 11–3.*

Kirkpatrick Estate Winery. This unique boutique winery is located on the Patutahi Plateau in a lovely environment with fabulous views out to the hills. Its range includes Chardonnay, Merlot, Malbec, Gewürztraminer, and Viognier. Antipasto plates are available during the summer. ✉ *569 Wharekopae Rd., RD2* 📞 *06/862–7722* ⊕ *www.kew.co.nz* 🖃 *Tastings NZ$10 for 7 wines; free if you buy 2 bottles* ⊗ *Daily noon–4.*

Millton Vineyard. The first New Zealand facility to attain organic certification specializes in making fine wine from estate-grown grapes sourced from single vineyards and grown in the traditional manner using biodynamic techniques. It's a great place to sample, sit, and relax. There are no restaurant facilities here, but you're welcome to bring a picnic. The vineyard is signposted off State Highway 2, about 11 km (7 miles) south of Gisborne. ✉ *119 Papatu Rd., Manutuke* 📞 *06/862–8680* ⊕ *www.millton.co.nz* 🖃 *Tastings free* ⊗ *Nov.–Mar., Mon.–Sat. 10–5; Apr.–Oct., by appointment.*

OFF THE BEATEN PATH

Eastwoodhill Arboretum. Inspired by the gardens seen on a trip to England in 1910, William Douglas Cook returned home and began planting 160 acres. His brainchild became a stunning collection of more than 600 genera of trees from around the world. In spring and summer daffodils mass yellow, magnolias bloom in clouds of pink and white, and cherries, crab apples, wisteria, and azalea add to the spectacle. The main trails in the park can be walked in about 45 minutes. Maps and self-guided tour booklets are available. Drive west from Gisborne center on State Highway 2 toward Napier, cross the bridge, and turn at the rotary onto the Ngatapa–Rere Road. Follow it 35 km (22 miles) to the arboretum. ✉ *2392 Wharekopae Rd., Ngatapa* 📞 *06/863–9003* ⊕ *www.eastwoodhill.org.nz* 🖃 *NZ$15* ⊗ *Daily 9–5.*

OFF THE BEATEN PATH

Morere Hot Springs. Set in 1,000 acres of native bush, this place provides modern bathing facilities in an unusual natural environment. A cold outdoor pool is alongside a warm indoor pool, and in the forest a few minutes' walk away are smaller hot or warm pools with a cold plunge pool. Two private hotpools are also available. Following the walking trails through the forest can take 20 minutes or stretch to two to three hours. Morere is roughly halfway between Wairoa and Gisborne, north of the Mahia turnoff. ✉ *State Hwy. 2, Morere* ☎ *06/837–8856* 🌐 *www.morerehotsprings.co.nz* 🎟 *NZ$12, private pools NZ$15 per ½ hr* 🕒 *June–Oct., daily 10–6; Nov.–May, daily 10–9.*

WHERE TO EAT

$ CAFÉ

🍴 **Exhibit Café.** The Tairawhiti Museum's bright, friendly café has a sunny veranda overlooking the river and wharf. Expect light, lunchworthy fare plus a delicious assortment of sweet offerings for your morning or afternoon tea break. [$] *Average main: NZ$14* ✉ *Kelvin Park, 10 Stout St.* ☎ *06/867–3832* 🌐 *www.tairawhitimuseum.org.nz* 🕒 *Closed weekends. No dinner.*

$$$$ FRENCH

🍴 **The Marina Restaurant & Bar.** Originally the ballroom of a stately home, this high-ceilinged restaurant lives up to its pedigree. Light filters through stained glass, and floor-length cappuccino-color silk drapes grace windows that frame the river; crisp white table linens and sparkling glassware further enhance the interior. On the menu, look for the steamed fresh fish fillet with crushed new potatoes and bell-pepper confit. The dark chocolate mousse cake with praline crunch and cocoa sorbet is a divine dessert choice. [$] *Average main: NZ$36* ✉ *Marina Park, Vogel St.* ☎ *06/868–5919* 🌐 *www.marinarestaurant.co.nz* 🕒 *Closed Sun. and Mon. No lunch Tues.–Wed.*

$$$ IRISH

🍴 **The Rivers.** A casual place to hoist a few pints while dining on hearty pub fare, The Rivers is popular with Gisborne's locals. Stained-glass partitions separate the dining alcoves, which have brass chandeliers, dark woodwork, and green leather upholstery. Guinness pie with creamy mashed potatoes and chicken calypso topped with a tangy mango sauce are two favorite dishes; washed down with a glass of ale, could you say no to that? [$] *Average main: NZ$25* ✉ *At Reads Quay and Gladstone Rd.* ☎ *06/863–3733* 🌐 *www.therivers.co.nz.*

$$$$ NEW ZEALAND

🍴 **The Wharf Café Bar Restaurant.** Overlooking the Gisborne Wharf, this erstwhile storage shed with seating indoors and out is a scenic spot. Come for a big breakfast, or arrive later in the day when choices include herb-roasted chicken with apricot rice, steamed greens, and chorizo stuffing (it pairs well with a glass of Matawhero Chardonnay). [$] *Average main: NZ$31* ✉ *60 The Esplanade* ☎ *06/868–4876* 🌐 *www.wharfbar.co.nz* 🕒 *Closed Mon. No dinner Sun.*

$$$$ NEW ZEALAND

🍴 **The Works Café & Winery.** This eatery in the former Gisborne Freezing Works embraces its industrial roots (note the large drive shaft and pulleys on the brick walls). The menu builds on local products, from cheeses to fruit, scallops to calamari. The sticky pork ribs served with a rich barbecue sauce, potato wedges, and coleslaw is one popular choice; the panfried fish of the day in white wine sauce is another. [$] *Average main: NZ$32* ✉ *41 The Esplanade* ☎ *06/868–9699.*

WHERE TO STAY

$$
B&B/INN
Linburn Farm Stay. The 1920s home of Karyn and Mark Watson is situated on a working farm that breeds sheep and cattle. **Pros:** great getaway for peace and quiet; set in picturesque countryside. **Cons:** 20-minute drive to the city; location might seem a little isolated. $ *Rooms from: NZ$140* ✉ *1279 Waimata Valley Rd.* ☎ *06/867–0375* ⊕ *www.geocities. ws/linburnfarmstay/* ▬ *No credit cards* ⌁ *2 rooms* ⦿*Breakfast.*

$$
HOTEL
FAMILY
Ocean Beach. A surfer's paradise, this Mediterranean-look motel complex is a five-minute drive north of Gisborne, close to Wainui Beach. **Pros:** ideal situation for beach-type holiday; spacious accommodation. **Cons:** there may be traffic noise in the season; need transport into town. $ *Rooms from: NZ$170* ✉ *7 Oneroa Rd., Wainui Beach* ☎ *06/868–6186* ⊕ *www.oceanbeach.co.nz* ⌁ *15 rooms* ⦿*No meals.*

$$
HOTEL
Senator Motor Inn. Offering comfortable, modern accommodations with lovely views over the marina and inner harbor on one side and main-street shopping on the doorstep, this motel has an ideal location that ticks all the boxes. **Pros:** great views; close to all amenities; free Wi-Fi and off-street parking. **Cons:** may be full in high season. $ *Rooms from: NZ$155* ✉ *2 Childers Rd.* ☎ *06/868–8877* ⊕ *www. senatormotorinn.co.nz* ⌁ *4 studios, 12 suites* ⦿*No meals.*

SPORTS AND THE OUTDOORS

DIVING AND SNORKELING

Fodor's Choice
★
Dive Tatapouri. Dean and Chrissie lead an extremely popular snorkeling excursion that lets you swim freely with stingrays, eagle rays, kingfish, crayfish, octopuses, and other ocean creatures. You'll get to observe, touch, and feed them in their natural habitat (NZ$70, wet suits, snorkels, and masks provided). If you'd rather not dive right in, try the Reef Tour. On this one you wade out to spy all manner of marine life. Huge rays slide up the rocks and put their head clear of the water; when you pop a morsel into their mouth, they take it gently, and then glide silently away (NZ$45, waders included). Tours are available year-round but are dependent on tides. Dive Tatapouri is (9 miles) north of the city, off State Highway 35. ✉ *Whangara Rd.* ☎ *06/868–5153* ⊕ *www. divetatapouri.com* ⌁ *From NZ$45.*

FISHING

Touchwood Fishing Charter. Albacore, yellowfin tuna, mako shark, and marlin along with the yellow-tail kingfish are prized catches from January to April (no license required). There are various operators who will help you land one—including Touchwood. Its boat has a full range of safety equipment, plus fish-finding electronics that help it target a number of species from the lesser-known hot spots around Gisborne. Prepare to pay NZ$1,765 per day for a private charter or NZ$150 per person for a party of 10, tackle and bait included. ✉ *37a Massey Rd.* ☎ *06/867–1066* ⊕ *touchwoodfishingchartersgisborne.co.nz.*

GOLF

Poverty Bay Golf Course. This 18-hole championship course ranks among the top five in the country. Established in 1893, the links-style, par 72 course is open for play daily. The green fee is NZ$45 for nonaffiliated players; otherwise it's NZ$40. ✉ *Lytton and Awapuni Rds., Elgin* ☎ *06/867–4402* ⊕ *www.gisbornegolf.co.nz.*

CLOSE UP

Te Urewera National Park

Remote Te Urewera National Park is rugged and mountainous. Lake Waikaremoana formed more than 2,000 years ago when a massive landslide blocked the Waikaretaheke River. It's not easily accessible—the road from the north is narrow, winding, and mostly unpaved, and the road from Wairoa is still gravel in parts. However, both pass through spectacular countryside of high, misty ridges covered with silver and mountain beech. Waterfalls and streams abound, and on the lower levels the forest giants, *rimu, rata, kamahi, totara,* and *tawa* attract native birds like the New Zealand falcon, North Island brown kiwi, *kaka,* and *kokako.* The Lake Waikaremoana Track, one of New Zealand's great walks, is here.

The Best Time to Go. The summer months (October to March) are prime time, but even then there are many misty, rainy days. Summer is also when local tourists flock to the park, so accommodations may be limited.

Hiking and Walking. For the nature lover who likes solitude, Te Urewera is paradise. Trails by the lake reveal great fishing and swimming spots, and many follow old Māori tracks. Bird-watchers can catch glimpses of native species that are rare in other parts of the country, including the largest surviving population of kokako. You might even spot native bats, green gecko, and skinks. The most popular walk is the Lake Waikaremoana Track, or Great Lake Walk, a three- to four-day tramp that mostly follows the Western Lake shore. The three- to four-day Manuoha–Sandy Track takes you to the highest part of the park, where on a clear day you can see the volcanoes of Tongariro National Park. Hikes are generally moderate to difficult.

Water Sports. Take a canoe trip along the lakeshore for a picnic or a spot of fishing. In this secluded realm, birdsong and the insect chirps are often the only sounds. The adventurous can kayak to remote spots around the lake. Kayaks and canoes can be hired at the Aniwaniwa Visitor Centre. The walk to Lake Waikareti, a much smaller lake that stands a thousand feet higher and is 2½ miles to the northeast, is one of the forest's finest.

SURFING

FAMILY   **Surfing with Frank.** Gisborne has three good surfing beaches close to town. Waikanae Beach, a short walk from the i-SITE Visitor Information Centre on Grey Street, usually has good learners' surf; the Pipe and the Island are for the more experienced. The former is just south of Waikanae; the latter fronts the Titarangi Domain. You can arrange for lessons at Surfing with Frank. Private lessons are NZ$90 for two hours; group rates start at NZ$60; surfboard and wet suit hire is NZ$30. ✉ *Gisborne* ☎ *06/867–0823* ⊕ *www.surfingwithfrank.com.*

Gisborne–Opotiki Loop. Soak in the beauty of Eastland by driving the Provincial Highway 35 loop between Gisborne and Opotiki—it's one of the country's ultimate roads-less-traveled. The 330-km (205-mile) trip takes about five hours without stops. En route, rolling green hills drop into wide crescent beaches or rock-strewn coves; and small towns appear, only to fade into the surrounding landscape. Some scenic highlights are **Anaura Bay,** with rocky headlands, a long beach favored by surfers, and nearby islands; it is between **Tolaga Bay** and **Tokomaru Bay,** two former shipping towns. Tolaga Bay has an incredibly long wharf stretching over a white-sand beach into the sea, and Cooks Cove Walkway is a pleasant amble through the countryside past a rock arch. Farther up the coast in **Tikitiki,** you'll find both a gas station and an Anglican church full of carved Māori panels and beams.

East of the small town of **Te Araroa,** which has the oldest *pohutukawa* (po-hoo-too- *ka*-wa) tree in the country, the coast is about as remote as you could imagine. At the tip of the cape, 21 km (13 miles) from Te Araroa, the East Cape Lighthouse promises fantastic views after a long, steep climb from the beach. **Hicks Bay** has another long beach. Back toward Opotiki, **Whanarua** (fahn-ah- *roo*-ah) **Bay** is one of the most gorgeous on the East Cape, with isolated beaches ideal for a picnic and a swim. Farther on, there is an intricately carved Māori marae (meetinghouse) called Tukaki in **Te Kaha.**

If you choose to spend a night along the loop, there are motels at various points on the cape and some superbly sited motor camps and backpackers' lodges, though you'll need to be well stocked with foodstuffs before you set off. Gisborne's i-SITE Centre can provide information about lodging.

TE UREWERA NATIONAL PARK

163 km (101 miles) west of Gisborne.

New Zealand's fourth-largest national park protects the biggest area of native forest remaining on the North Island. The ancestral home of the Tuhoe people, its main attraction is Lake Waikaremoana, which draws hikers, canoeists, and fishing enthusiasts from around the world.

GETTING HERE AND AROUND

Local bus service is extremely limited, so the best way to get around is by car. Campervans are also popular, as there is plenty of space for the outdoor style of living. Access to the park is from Wairoa, 100 km (62 miles) southwest of Gisborne down Highway 2. It's then another 63 km (39 miles) northwest from Wairoa along Highway 38 to Lake Waikaremoana.

VISITOR INFORMATION

Contacts Department of Conservation Visitor Centre. ✉ *State Hwy. 38, Aniwaniwa* ☎ *06/837–3803* ⊕ *www.doc.govt.nz.*

EXPLORING

Fodor's Choice ★ **Te Urewera National Park.** This park's outstanding feature is glorious Lake Waikaremoana ("sea of rippling waters"), a forest-girded lake with good swimming, boating, and fishing. The lake is encircled by a 50-km (31-mile) walking trail, which takes three or four days to complete; it's a popular trek, and the lakeside hiking huts are heavily used in the summer months. The Department of Conservation Visitor Centre at Aniwaniwa is stocked with maps and informative leaflets; staff will also give advice about other park walks, like the one to the **Aniwaniwa Falls** (30 minutes round-trip) or to **Lake Waikareiti** (five to six hours round-trip). A motor camp on the lakeshore, not far from the visitor center, has cabins, chalets, and motel units; in summer, a launch operates sightseeing and fishing trips from it. Note that there are areas of private Māori land within the park, so be sure to stay on marked paths. ⊠ *Te Urewera National Park, Gisborne.*

NORTH ISLAND'S WEST COAST

WELCOME TO
NORTH ISLAND'S WEST COAST

TOP REASONS TO GO

★ **Caving:** Beneath Waitomo, underground passageways, fossils, limestone formations, and glowworms await. Explore by walking, boating, "black-water" rafting, or rappelling.

★ **Kayaking and Canoeing:** Ideal for beginners, the Whanganui is New Zealand's longest navigable river. Paddling trips promise amazing scenery and historic Māori settlements.

★ **Walking and Hiking:** Take a short walk or multiday trek through the wetlands, alpine fields, and lowland rain forest of Egmont National Park.

★ **Surfing:** The black-sand surfing beaches here are among the world's best. Near Raglan try Whale Bay and Manu Bay; in Taranaki "Surf Highway 45" accesses premier breaks.

★ **Scenic Drives:** Rolling green farmlands, dense forests, mountain ranges, river gorges, and dramatic coastlines—you can see them all from the comfort of your car.

1 **Waikato and Waitomo.** Waikato's landscape is a mosaic of dairy farms, stud-horse farms, and rural service towns. In the west, forest-covered ranges form a buffer between the farms and famed West Coast surfing beaches of Raglan. To the south, the Waitomo Caves region is nestled in steep country, a mix of forest reserve and sheep-and-cattle farms.

2 **New Plymouth and Taranaki.** Taranaki juts away west from the North Island landmass. Dominating the landscape is Mt. Taranaki (Egmont is its English name), the nearly perfectly symmetrical volcano that forms the basis of Egmont National Park. The mountain's lower, forested slopes give way to farmland, interspersed with outstanding public gardens. Along the coastline are popular surf beaches. Anchored by New Plymouth, it's a place known for climbing, hiking, surfing, fishing, and cultural museums.

3 **Wanganui, the Whanganui River, and Palmerston North.** The Whanganui River, flowing through a vast, forest-covered wilderness from the central North Island mountains, is the focus here. At its mouth, Wanganui city was established when river travel was the main form of transport. Today, kayakers and jet-boaters enjoy the scenic, historic, and wilderness experiences of Whanganui National Park. Close by is Palmerston North, a university city and farming center.

GETTING ORIENTED

The region's landscape includes the majestic volcano, Mt. Taranaki; the gorges and wilderness of the Whanganui River; the underground wonders of the Waitomo Caves; world-renowned surfing beaches; two national parks; and a host of forest-covered conservation areas, along with highly productive farmland. In the north, Cambridge is close to Hamilton and about a two-hour drive from Auckland, on the main State Highway 1. Surfing town Raglan is in a sparsely populated area of the West Coast, yet an easy hour's drive from Hamilton. Continuing south, Waitomo sits on a popular North Island tourist trail linking Rotorua and Tongariro National Park. It's also on the westward route to New Plymouth and the Taranaki region. While State Highway 1 traverses the center of the North Island, State Highway 3 travels the West Coast through the Taranaki bight to Wanganui, then meets again with State Highway 1 close to Palmerston North.

6

EGMONT NATIONAL PARK

On the western tip of the North Island, Mt. Taranaki (or Mt. Egmont, as Captain Cook called it) is a steeply sloped, symmetrically shaped volcanic peak that dominates the region's landscape, weather, and history.

New Zealand's second-oldest national park, Egmont, was created in 1900 to protect the 8,261-foot-high mountain and its surrounding forests. From a distance the landscape of this national park looks simple; a cone-shape mountain draped white with snow in winter and flanked by a near-perfect circle of forest. Look closer, or try walking on the park trails, and a different picture emerges. Thousands of years of volcanic buildup and erosion have crafted steep gullies and rivers, immense lava bluffs, unstable slips, and forests of everything from moss-covered "goblin" trees to tall, ancient forest giants. It makes a fascinating place to explore, and thankfully there are many ways of doing this no matter what your level of fitness.

BEST TIME TO GO

December through March is the best time for walking, hiking, viewing alpine flowers, and making summit ascents. Experienced or guided mountaineers can snow- and ice-climb in July and August. Skiing is available July through September (depending on snow levels).

BEST WAYS TO EXPLORE

Take a Short Walk. Several gentle, well-signposted walking trails leave from the three main park entrances. Some top examples are Wilkies Pools, which takes in mountain streams, sculpted rocks, and goblin forest (1½-hour round-trip); Patea Loop, encompassing mountain cedar forest and stony riverbeds (two hours); and Potaema, with giant *rimu* and *rata* forest plus a vast wetland (20 minutes).

Take a Scenic Drive. Three main access roads lead into the park, climbing steeply (allow 10 to 20 minutes) up the mountain's forest-lined lower slopes and, in some areas, opening up stunning views. Short strolls along these roads enable you to appreciate the plants, trees, waterfalls, and streams. The interesting displays and photos at the main North Egmont Visitor Centre enhance the experience—as will the taste temptations in the café.

Take a Long Hike. The two- to three-day Pouakai Circuit explores all the park's landscapes: subalpine terrain, lava cliffs and gorges, the vast Ahukawakawa wetland, the tussock tops of the Pouakai Range, and lichen-covered goblin forest. The one-day Pouakai Crossing takes in much of the Pouakai Circuit and descends through forest to the western park boundary (transport shuttles required). Hiking around the mountain (four to five days) is another option, if you're keen to climb in and out of steep gullies and through mud. A second mountain loop above the tree line (three to four days) can be stunning in summer, icy in winter, and exposed to extreme weather at any time.

Climb the Mountain. The steep climb is a serious undertaking, especially with frequent bad weather. The mountain is sacred to the local Māori people, so they ask that climbers respect its spirituality and not clamber over the summit rocks. The main summer route (seven to eight hours round-trip) follows the northeast ridge. When there's no snow, it's all rock underfoot—slippery shingle or big tangled boulders. In winter, climbing is technical, requiring snow- and ice-climbing gear and expertise. Mountain guides can be hired in both winter and summer.

EGMONT ECO-STAYS

If you stay in the park rather than driving in and out from city accommodations, you'll have a better chance of becoming one with this magnificent natural realm. Experience sunset or sunrise, watch the light change across the summit snows, and hear the birds waking in the forest. **The Camphouse** (⊕ *www.doc. govt.nz/parks-and-recreation/national-parks/egmont/places-to-stay*), in North Egmont, provides self-catering, backpacker-style accommodations in a grand setting, just above the tree line. Set 2,625 feet up the mountain, **Ngati Ruanui Stratford Mountain House**, in East Egmont, promises forest freshness, cool air, and camera-ready views *(see review in this chapter)*.

(top left) View from the summit of Mt. Egmont/Mt. Taranaki; *(bottom)* Trampers taking in the mountain views; *(top)* Dawson Falls

6

WHANGANUI NATIONAL PARK

New Zealand's longest navigable river cuts through the single largest tract of lowland forest remaining in the North Island. For centuries, Māori people have lived beside the river, its gentle rapids and long gorges providing transportation routes long before roads and railways were built.

The Whanganui's special characteristics—its often muddy appearance, fearsome floods, deep-cut gorges, bluffs, and waterfalls—are all outcomes of the easily eroded sandstones and volcanic soils in which the lowland forest thrives. Māori still live along the lower reaches, some farming, others welcoming visitors into their villages on tours. In the early 1900s, riverboats carried thousands of admiring passengers along the waterway. Now protected as national park, the wild landscape remains intact, and you can see it from a canoe, kayak, or speedy jet-boat; alternately, you can drive the Whanganui River Road through a most scenic slice of backcountry New Zealand.

BEST TIME TO GO

Anytime. Guided river trips generally operate in summer; however, the climate is mild and a winter journey, while a little cooler and possibly wetter, is equally rewarding—and less crowded. The historic Whanganui River Road is open year-round.

BEST WAYS TO EXPLORE

Paddle the River. The Whanganui, New Zealand's most canoed river, is popular both for the terrain it transects and its suitability for beginners. Although the water flows through gorges and forested wilderness, its gradient is gentle and most of its 239 named rapids have little more than a 3-foot fall. The river is suitable for all kinds of craft, from kayaks to open-style Canadian canoes. Department of Conservation huts and campsites provide basic (but very scenic) riverside accommodations. Most people take a three- or five-day trip through the heart of the wilderness to Pipiriki, though paddling the lower reaches past historic Māori settlements is also appealing.

Take a Hike. Two three-day hiking trails (one is also a mountain-bike trail) traverse the park, and each has a distinctive character. Regenerating forests along Mangapurua–Kaiwhakauka Track tell the story of failed farming attempts in these remote valleys. The old farming road was upgraded in 2010 and is now popular with mountain-bikers. In contrast, the Matemateaonga Track passes through the park's most pristine forested areas. Jet-boats can be chartered for access to the river end of each walk.

Take a Drive. The narrow Whanganui River Road follows the water's lower reaches, climbing around bluffs and steep gullies and passing through historic Māori settlements. Heritage stops include an old flour mill, mission settlement, village churches, and traditional Māori *marae* (villages)—check with a local before venturing into these. You can drive yourself, or take the daily mail delivery tour from Wanganui.

Ride a Bike. Much of the Mountains to Sea—Nga Ara Tuhono Cycle Trail passes through Whanganui National Park. Remote, at times challenging, mountain-bike sections traverse the bluff-lined Kaiwhakauka and Mangapurua valleys. The last section follows the narrow, twisting, and very scenic Whanganui River Road before linking with off-road trails through Wanganui city to the sea. Jet-boat shuttles can be booked for the 32-km (20-mile) section of river gorge that links two trail sections. Several companies offer packages including jet-boat shuttles, accommodation, bike rentals, and a guide.

6

(top left) Canoers on the Whanganui River; *(bottom)* Tramp to waterfalls within the park; *(top)* A peaceful stretch of the river

Updated by
Kathy Ombler

The North Island's West Coast encompasses a diversity of landscapes: top surfing beaches; world-renowned limestone caves; and two national parks, one centered on a volcanic mountain, the other on a wilderness river.

The land is generally rural, ranging from tidy thoroughbred horse stud farms to sheep-and-cattle farms located in remote, rolling hill country and a jumble of forest-covered mountain ranges. The long coastline is captivating; world-class surfing breaks meet sandy swimming beaches and craggy cliffs. Small cities and rural towns throughout the region provide a high level of sophistication for their size; they may have started as service communities, but delve closer and you'll find galleries, art studios, farmers' markets, designer stores, museums, and funky cafés.

Waikato and Waitomo is a region of surprises. Gently rolling dairy farms and thoroughbred horse studs emanate from Cambridge, a genteel, English-style town with tree-lined streets. Then things get wilder. To the west are the famed surfing beaches of Raglan, guarded by ancient forest-covered volcanoes. In the south, 30 million years of Mother Nature's handiwork have created the Waitomo Caves, an underground spectacle that thousands of visitors now explore each year, be it by foot, boat, or rappelling rope.

The Taranaki region sprang from the ocean floor in a series of volcanic blasts, creating that distinctive curve along the West Coast of the North Island. The cone of Mt. Taranaki is the province's dramatic symbol and the backdrop for climbing routes and hiking tracks (trails). Agriculture thrives in the area's fertile volcanic soil, and the gardens around Taranaki and New Plymouth are some of the country's most spectacular. The mythology and historic sites relating to the local people are an integral part of Taranaki, too.

Farther south, the Whanganui River wends its scenic way through the forest-covered ridges and valleys that encompass Whanganui National Park. The river is steeped in history, for centuries forming the "road" for the Māori who lived on its banks, then a major route for tourists traveling by steamer. Today it draws canoeists, hikers, and other outdoor enthusiasts. As you veer inland, from river city Wanganui through to the Manawatu region and Palmerston North, the land gives way to prosperous sheep and cattle farms.

PLANNING

Whether surfing or just enjoying the harbor, spare at least a couple of days for Raglan, another day or two for exploring the Waitomo Caves. Cambridge also warrants a day, perhaps en route to Rotorua. From Waitomo travel southwest to Taranaki, where two to three days would allow exploration of the gardens and museums, plus a beach trip and a short walk in Egmont National Park—allow longer for more serious hiking, climbing, or surfing adventures. Wanganui city is worth a day or two. A river jet-boat or road trip provides a quick glimpse of the area; for an in-depth tour try a five-day kayak journey, then take a good day or two to absorb the university town of Palmerston North before heading on south to Wellington.

WHEN TO GO

Although the most popular period is from November through mid-April, most attractions can be enjoyed year-round. Spring is garden festival time in Taranaki. Summer is obviously warmer and great for swimming or surfing. However, the weather is often more settled during winter—unlike some South Island regions, it generally has no harsh snow or ice conditions to thwart travel—and there are fewer people.

GETTING HERE AND AROUND

AIR TRAVEL

Airports serve the main centers but driving or taking a bus is best for other areas. **Air New Zealand** operates flights daily from Auckland and Wellington to Hamilton, New Plymouth, Wanganui, and Palmerston North; and from Christchurch to New Plymouth and Palmerston North. Budget carrier Jetstar also serves New Plymouth and Palmerston North, while Originair connects Palmerston North and Nelson.

Contacts Air New Zealand. ☎ 0800/737–000 ⊕ www.airnewzealand.co.nz. **Jetstar.** ☎ 0800/800–995 ⊕ www.jetstar.com. **Originair.** ☎ 0800/380–380 ⊕ originair.co.nz.

BUS TRAVEL

InterCity links all cities and towns throughout the region with regular daily service. Flexible travel passes let passengers stop off as they please along the way. **Nakedbus** provides an alternative, low-cost service throughout the region. The **Waitomo Wanderer** links Rotorua and Taupo with Waitomo, once daily each way. From Otorohanga, the **Waitomo Shuttle** (book in advance) connects with major bus and train arrivals.

Contacts InterCity. ☎ 09/913–6100 ⊕ www.intercity.co.nz. **Nakedbus.** ☎ 09/979–1616 ⊕ nakedbus.com. **Waitomo Shuttle.** ☎ 0800/808–279 ✍ waikiwi@ihug.co.nz. **Waitomo Wanderer.** ☎ 0800/304–333 ⊕ www.travelheadfirst.com.

CAR TRAVEL

Driving is the most flexible way to travel through this region. Roads are nearly all clearly signposted, and drivers pass through diverse and scenic landscapes of farmland, forest-covered ranges, and rugged coastline.

TRAIN TRAVEL

Northern Explorer, the scenic 10-hour Auckland–Wellington train, stops at Hamilton, Otorohanga (near Waitomo), and Palmerston North; it travels southbound on Monday, Thursday, and Saturday and northbound on Tuesday, Friday, and Sunday.

Contacts Northern Explorer. ☎ 0800/872–467 ⊕ *www.kiwirailscenic.co.nz.*

RESTAURANTS

Throughout western North Island, provincial city restaurants and small, tourist-town cafés feature an overall sophistication you might not expect away from major urban centers: think wholesome and hearty fare, local organic produce, good espresso and loose-leaf teas, high-quality New Zealand wines, plus local craft beers. Counter food is generally fresh salads, paninis, filled rolls, sweet or savory pies, and homemade soups.

Dinner menus in the higher-end restaurants include the chef's latest creations using high-quality New Zealand eye fillet of beef (beef tenderloin), fish, lamb racks, pork fillets, and chicken. The best chefs change menus regularly to focus on fresh regional and seasonal ingredients. You will also find Indian, Thai, Malaysian, Japanese, Mexican, Turkish, and Italian restaurants, even in smaller centers. "Smart-casual" is about as formal as attire gets.

HOTELS

Bed-and-breakfasts are often stylishly converted country homesteads; sometimes they're custom built. There are also luxury lodges and a wonderful range of self-catering villas and cottages (some on working farms, others with spectacular coastal locations, and a few deep in the forest-covered hinterland). National parks have mountain lodges, river lodges, basic backcountry huts, and camping spots managed by the Department of Conservation.

In tourist towns and larger cities, there's the full range of options: boutique hotels, standard hotels with basic rooms, motels with full kitchens, holiday parks with RV sites and sometimes apartment units, as well as backpacker hostels. Although hostels are generally budget options with shared facilities, an increasing number are modern and feature private en suite rooms.

Hotel reviews have been shortened. For full information, visit Fodors.com.

WHAT IT COSTS IN NEW ZEALAND DOLLARS				
	$	$$	$$$	$$$$
Restaurants	under NZ$15	NZ$15–NZ$20	NZ$21–NZ$30	over NZ$30
Hotels	under NZ$125	NZ$125–NZ$200	NZ$201–NZ$300	over NZ$300

Restaurant prices are the average cost of a main course at dinner or, if dinner is not served, at lunch. Hotel prices are the lowest cost of a standard double room in high season.

PLANNING YOUR TIME

If you are making just one trip to New Zealand, you're probably starting from Auckland and working your way south; in doing so, you should also consider making some "dog-leg" detours across the North Island.

For example, between Cambridge and the Waitomo Caves head east to catch the geothermal action of Rotorua. Or, from the Waitomo Caves, before turning west to Taranaki head south an hour or so to Whaka-papa, the northern gateway to Tongariro National Park. From the south, turn inland from Wanganui to reach the park before heading to Palmerston North.

For a backcountry adventure go south from surfing spot Raglan, keeping close to the coast, then inland to the Waitomo Caves before heading back to the coast to follow the Marakopa Road to Taranaki.

VISITOR INFORMATION

Hamilton and Waikato Regional Tourism (⊕ *www.hamiltonwaikato.com*) is a helpful regional resource. The regional tourism organization in Taranaki also maintains a website (⊕ *www.taranaki.info/visit*) with local listings and event information.

WAIKATO AND WAITOMO

Some think of the Waikato region—a fertile, temperate, agricultural district south of Auckland—as the heartland of the North Island. It's home to New Zealand's largest inland city (Hamilton) and some of the most important pre-European sites. Polynesian sailors first landed on the region's West Coast as early as the mid-14th century; by way of contrast, Europeans (mainly British) didn't settle here until the 1830s. In the 1860s, the Waikato's many tribes united to elect a king in an attempt to resist British encroachment. This King Movement, as it is known, is still a significant cultural and political force within Waikato Māoridom.

Hamilton is essentially a service city, but well worth a pause for the city center's good restaurants and sprawling Hamilton Gardens, with areas dedicated to garden cultures worldwide. Other regional attractions are the surfing hot spots and magnificent harbor of Raglan, on the West Coast; delightful tree-lined Cambridge, an agricultural town renowned as a horse-breeding center; and the extraordinary cave formations at Waitomo.

RAGLAN

176 km (110 miles) south of Auckland, 44 km (27 miles) west of Hamilton.

It's hard to think of a more laid-back, welcoming spot than Raglan. ■ **TIP→ On the drive out, tune in to radio station Raglan FM 98.1 to catch the local news and grooves.** On sheltered Raglan Harbour, and in the lee of Mt. Karioi, the tiny town owes its easygoing ways to the legions of young surfers drawn to the legendary breaks at Manu Bay, 8 km (5 miles) southwest of town, and Whale Bay, just beyond. The Raglan surf is featured in movies and regularly plays host to international competitions. When the surf's up, you can drive out to the parking areas above the sweeping bays to see scores of enthusiasts tackling what's reputed to be the world's longest, most consistent left-hand break.

Surfers have made this seaside village cool, and along the main drag, Bow Street, barefoot dudes in designer shades pad in and out of the hip café-bars or hang in the smattering of craft and surf-wear shops; there is, however, much more to Raglan. The huge harbor, with its long Māori history, sandy beaches, and opportunities for kayaking, fishing, and relaxation, draws vacationers throughout the year.

GETTING HERE AND AROUND

The main road route to Raglan is from Hamilton, a pleasant hour's drive away. Travelers from Auckland can turn off State Highway 1 at Ngaruawahia (10 minutes north of Hamilton) and follow State Highway 39 to Whatawhata to join the road from Hamilton. Turn right to Raglan. Buses to Raglan (NZ$9) run from Hamilton several times daily.

Bus Depot Raglan Bus Depot. ✉ *Waikato District Library Raglan, 7 Bow St.*

VISITOR INFORMATION

Contacts Raglan i-SITE Visitor Information Centre. ✉ *13 Wainui Rd.* ☎ *07/825–0556* 🌐 *www.raglan.org.nz.*

WHERE TO EAT

$$$ NEW ZEALAND

🍴 **Orca Restaurant and Bar.** This waterside restaurant has big windows and the best views in Raglan—when orca swim into the harbor, you can see them from your table. Brunch is served all day (picture free-range eggs with Kranksy sausage, or eggs Benedict with house-smoked salmon). At lunch, look for platters, flatbreads, burgers, and more. Dinner brings out the chef's creativity; his signature dish is braised beef cheek with balsamic pickled onions and garlic mash. The food-and-wine matches are recommended, with selections from international and Kiwi wineries. Orca also has a casual bar, where you can watch the sunset over the harbor, play a game of pool, or listen to live music on weekends. [$] *Average main: NZ$22* ✉ *2 Wallis St.* ☎ *07/825–6543* 🌐 *www.orcarestaurant.co.nz.*

$$ MODERN NEW ZEALAND

🍴 **Rock-It Kitchen.** Occupying a 100-year old shearing shed, the funky, rustic Rock-it serves wholesome Kiwi fare and local Raglan Roast coffee. Try the beef sliders, cauliflower soup, all-day brunch, or a casual dinner, either inside or out on the huge deck. This place is also home to a surf shop, art studio, and live-music venue. It's 3 km (2 miles) from town on the way to Ocean Beach—so you can paddle a kayak up the

Wainui estuary instead of coming by car if you want. $ *Average main: NZ$19* ⊠ *248 Wainui Rd.* ☎ *07/825–8233* ⊕ *www.rockitraglan.co.nz* ⊟ *No credit cards.*

$$	✕ **The Shack.** Provenance is important at The Shack, a buzzing corner
CAFÉ	café that is truly local and consistently good. Surfers—who come for
Fodor's Choice	great local espresso and organic, free-range food—cram the couches
★	and Formica tables beneath walls decorated with surfboards and Rag-

lan Beach scenes. The menu is huge and the meals hearty, starting with breakfast at 8. All-day dishes hail from around the globe: Mexican-style fish tortillas or Thai salad, for example. The dinner menu (Thursday through Saturday only) changes with the seasons, and plates are designed for sharing. There's also a great selection of beers, wines, loose-leaf teas, smoothies, and juices (local and organic, of course). $ *Average main: NZ$16* ⊠ *19 Bow St.* ☎ *07/825–0027* ⊕ *www.theshackraglan. com* ⊙ *No dinner Apr.–late Oct. and Sun.–Wed.*

WHERE TO STAY

$$$	⌂ **Raglan Sunset Motel.** Accommodations at the modern, family-friendly
HOTEL	Raglan Sunset Motel range from studio units to a self-contained,
FAMILY	two-bedroom/two-bathroom apartment with a kitchen, lounge/din-

ing area, and private courtyard. **Pros:** lovely barbecue area; quiet yet close to shops and restaurants; free Wi-Fi throughout. **Cons:** grounds not hugely spacious. $ *Rooms from: NZ$220* ⊠ *7 Bankart St.* ☎ *07/825–0050* ⊕ *www.raglansunsetmotel.co.nz* ⇆ *23 studios, 1 apartment* ⊠ *No meals.*

$$	⌂ **Waters Edge.** Checking out will be the hardest part when you stay in
B&B/INN	either the 100-year old cottage or modern apartment on this waterfront
Fodor's Choice	garden property. **Pros:** welcoming hosts; lovely over-water outlook;
★	quiet, relaxing environment. **Cons:** three-minute drive from town; your

visit might not coincide with the orcas. $ *Rooms from: NZ$195* ⊠ *100 E. Greenslade Rd.* ☎ *07/825–0567* ⊕ *www.watersedge.co.nz* ⇆ *1 cottage, 1 apartment* ⊠ *No meals.*

SPORTS AND THE OUTDOORS

Surfing (with waves to attract both beginners and the world's top surfers), kite surfing, fishing, kayaking, and just cruising in the vast harbor are the big water-sport attractions. Coastal walks and forest walks, from one hour to one day, are also popular.

BOATING AND KAYAKING

Fodor's Choice **Raglan Boat Charters.** If it's a social harbor cruise you're after, try a two-★ hour sunset sail aboard the *Wahinemoe*, a 70-person purpose-built catamaran. It runs daily November to April and includes a barbecue dinner (NZ$49). For a quieter, more low-key one-hour cruise, opt for Harmony Scenic Cruises, whose skipper, Ian Hardie, knows his way around the harbor's tidal inlets and bays (NZ$30). From *Harmony III,* you can see forest reserves, historic habitation sites, isolated beaches, the "pancakes" (limestone outcrops), seabirds, and perhaps the pod of orca that occasionally visits the harbor. This tour runs all year, with times based on the tides. Reservations are essential for both cruises. The *Wahinemoe* operates from Raglan Wharf, in Wallis Street, while *Harmony III* sets off from the Raglan jetty, in the township at the end of Bow Street. ⊠ *Raglan* ☏ *07/825–7873* ⊕ *www.raglanboatcharters.co.nz.*

Fodor'sChoice
★
Raglan Kayak. There's no better way to explore huge Raglan Harbour than on nature's terms with Steve and Candide Reid and their enthusiastic guides. Local boy Steve searched the world for the perfect place to work on water, then realized it was back home. People of any age and ability are welcome on his daily trip, where the focus is on paddling with the tide and wind, swimming on secluded beaches, great scenery, espresso, and home-baked goodies. Trips run for three hours (NZ$75). Kayaks are also available for rent (NZ$20 single, NZ$30 tandem per hour; NZ$40–NZ$60 per half day; NZ $50–NZ$80 per day), as are paddleboards (NZ$20 per hour; NZ$40 per half day). ☏ *07/825–8862* ⊕ *raglaneco.co.nz* ⊗ *Closed Easter–Oct.*

**OFF THE
BEATEN
PATH**
Kawhia. With time on your hands, explore the road from Raglan to this isolated coastal settlement 55 km (34 miles) to the south. It's a remote country route through forest and farmland, skirting the eastern flank of Mt. Karioi and passing the turnoff for Waireinga/Bridal Veil Falls, but much of the road is gravel. The little-developed region is steeped in the past: this was where the Tainui people, the region's earliest Polynesian settlers, first landed after their arduous sea voyage. Beside Kawhia Wharf, the Kawhia Regional Museum Gallery and Information Centre interprets this long history (open 11 to 4 daily). What those in the know come for, however, are the Te Puia hot springs at Ocean Beach, east of town. There's road access to the beach (or it's a two-hour walk from Kawhia). Ask a friendly local for directions. You can find the springs only by digging into the sand a couple of hours either side of low tide, so check the tide tables in Raglan before you set off.

SURFING

Raglan Surf Co. If you're itching to hit the waves, stop by this top surfing store. Starting out as a factory and producing high-performance boards for years, it now stocks homegrown boards as well as the leading brands. The shop also rents surfboards, wet suits, and boogie boards, and staffers pass along helpful tips. ⊠ *3 Wainui Rd.* ☏ *07/825–8988* ⊕ *www.raglansurf.com.*

Raglan Surfing School. Past and even present national surfing champions often work as instructors at the RSS. Three-hour group and private lessons are available for beginners (NZ$89 and NZ$149 respectively, board and wet suit included). Two- to five-day Surf Adventure Packages include transport, daily lessons, and lodgings, plus other adventures, such as rappelling, paragliding, and jet-boating. "Surf dame" programs (luxury surfing retreats for women) are also offered throughout the year. You can rent gear at the RSS-operated trailer on Ocean (Ngarunui) Beach in summer or at the school itself year-round. Note that its location is a little out of town, but transportation from Raglan is provided. ⊠ *5b Whaanga Rd., Whale Bay* ☏ *07/825–7873* ⊕ *www.raglansurfingschool.co.nz.*

Raglan surfers head along the beach to catch some waves.

SWIMMING

Although the surf looks inviting at most of the West Coast beaches, there can be dangerous rips and undertows, so be careful where you take a dip. The safest spots around Raglan are Te Aro Bay (Wallis and Puriri streets), Te Kopua, and at Cox and Lorenzen bays during high tide. Call the Raglan i-SITE Visitor Information Centre (☎ 07/825–0556) for tide times. In summer, lifeguards patrol the beach at Ocean (Ngarunui); to avoid the strong rips, swim between the flags.

WALKING AND HIKING

From Raglan, a number of walks and hikes give you wonderful views of the coastline and take you through splendid native bush. The closest and easiest is from the township itself through Wainui Reserve to gorgeous Ocean (Ngarunui) Beach. You can climb above coastal bluffs to a lookout point and enjoy the drama of the kite surfers at play, or follow the beach for 6 km (4 miles), except during high spring tides. Ask for a brochure at the Raglan i-SITE Visitor Information Centre. ■ TIP➔ Don't leave valuables in your vehicle while you're away walking.

Mt. Karioi. The trek up Mt. Karioi is significantly more difficult than the Waireinga/Bridal Veil Falls trail. Some sections are quite steep, so good walking gear and a positive attitude are required; fantastic views of the coast, however, make the challenge worthwhile. The Mt. Karioi Track, from Te Toto Gorge at Whaanga Road, climbs to a lookout and then the summit (3–3½ hours one-way). Wairake Track, from Karioi Road, is a shorter, steeper summit option (2–3 hours one-way).

Waireinga/Bridal Veil Falls. A 15-minute shaded hike from the parking lot leads through native forest to the spectacle of the falls. Two viewing platforms are poised near the top of the 150-foot drop. This section of trail is wheelchair accessible. Another much steeper track continues to a midway-viewing platform; from there a 10-minute trail descends to a bridge and viewing platform at the base of the falls. The tall trees and the sight of the water cascading over the hard basalt cliff justify the effort required for the return climb. The falls are 20 km (12 miles) south of Raglan via the Kawhia road. ⊕ *www.doc.govt.nz.*

CAMBRIDGE

53 km (33 miles) east of Raglan.

For many travelers, Cambridge provides a good lunch break on their way elsewhere. But this cute town, with its historic buildings and rural English character, merits a closer look. The tree-lined Village Square provides plenty of entertainment, including summer cricket matches, the Farmers' Market (Saturday 8–noon), and the Lions Trash and Treasure Market (the second Sunday of each month). Cambridge is known for its English trees, which provide an elegant canopy over the town's designer shops, art galleries, and cafés. It's also home to the country's thoroughbred industry.

GETTING HERE AND AROUND

The Waikato Expressway, now the main State Highway 1 route south from Auckland, opened in late 2015 and bypasses Cambridge. But the beautiful town is well worth a stopover, so exit the Expressway at the Cambridge signs, or travel on State Highway 1B (which avoids Hamilton city and is clearly signposted from Taupiri); Cambridge is an easy two-hour drive from Auckland and 20 minutes from Hamilton. Continuing south, Rotorua is a one-hour drive, while Taupo is 90 minutes away. InterCity coach services connect daily from these cities and towns.

If you're arriving by air, Hamilton Airport (HLZ) is 14 km (9 miles) northwest of Cambridge. Air New Zealand offers daily direct flights from Wellington, Palmerston North, and Christchurch, with connecting flights to most domestic destinations. You can rent a car at the airport; a shuttle will also take you into Cambridge for about NZ$48. The best way to explore the town itself is to visit the Village Square, i-SITE Visitor Information Centre, and historic Town Hall, before strolling down to Victoria, Empire, and Commerce streets.

Airport Hamilton Airport. ✉ *Airport Rd.* ☎ *07/848–9027* ⊕ *www.hamiltonairport.co.nz.*

Bus Depot Cambridge Bus Depot. ✉ *Lake St.*

TOURS

Waikato Thoroughbred Stud Tours. Pete Evans provides an up-close look at the renowned Waikato horse industry, offering professional insight along with access to famous studs farms (Cambridge, Trelawney, and Windsor Park) not normally on view. Tours are personalized for small groups of up to four and include options to visit training facilities. The cost varies depending on your choices but generally works out to NZ$100 per group for about 90 minutes. Evans can pick you up from your accommodation. He also leads hunting and trout-fishing trips. ☎ *022/600–5783 cell* 🌐 *www.troutstalker.co.nz* 🎫 *NZ$100 per group.*

VISITOR INFORMATION

Contacts Cambridge i-SITE Visitor Information Centre. ✉ *Queen and Victoria Sts.* ☎ *07/823–3456* 🌐 *www.cambridge.co.nz.*

WHERE TO EAT

$ CAFÉ 🍴 **Fran's Café.** Snag a table in the main room, the comfy lounge, or the sunny courtyard garden, and enjoy your choice of amazing homemade sandwiches, pasta, frittatas, and salads. Fran's menu changes regularly and reflects the owners' interest in a variety of foods and styles. Note that this is the only place in New Zealand that sells the famous Granny Dunn's Preserves; it also sells a selection of local art. If all that's not enough to interest you, take a look at the incredible teapot collection. [$] *Average main: NZ$10* ✉ *62 Victoria St.* ☎ *07/827–3946* 🌐 *www.franscafe.co.nz* 🕒 *No dinner.*

$$$$ MODERN NEW ZEALAND Fodor's Choice ★ 🍴 **Onyx.** A consistent draw for a sleepy Sunday brunch, ladies who lunch, and that special-occasion dinner, Onyx starts with coffee and cakes at 9. At brunch and lunch, a wood-fired oven adds pizza to the menu, which also includes lighter fusion and contemporary fare. At dinner, signature items—such as slow-cooked duck with hoisin Chinese plum jus and Asian vegetables, or Hereford prime sirloin steak with prawn and garlic butter—are complemented by dishes that highlight the finest seasonal ingredients. Good George craft beer, brewed in nearby Hamilton, appears on the full beverage menu. Onyx offers seating both indoors and out; minimalist decor with hard surfaces can make the former noisy, but the great food and service are ample compensation. [$] *Average main: NZ$32* ✉ *70 Alpha St.* ☎ *07/827–7740* 🌐 *www.onyxcambridge.co.nz.*

$$ CAFÉ 🍴 **Rouge Cafe.** Hidden away but always busy with in-the-know locals, this family-run café emphasizes local organic produce. Come for a full breakfast (options include eggs Benedict with salmon, house-made gluten-free muesli, and more), or at lunch, when you can choose between open sandwiches made to order and an incredible cabinet selection (think cheese-and-bacon scones, risotto cakes, tasty salads, plus gourmet pies). Good coffee and a range of wines, beers, and juices can also be savored either indoors or at a courtyard table. [$] *Average main: NZ$15* ✉ *11 Empire St.* ☎ *07/823–9178* 🌐 *www.rougeempire.co.nz.*

$$$ NEW ZEALAND 🍴 **Stables Bar and Grill.** With a cozy stone fireplace, three inside bars, a garden bar, and a gaming room, this casual spot aims to please everyone. Its gastropub fare is good quality and good value; steak-house standards are prominently featured, but the menu also lists salads, seafood, and pastas, with lighter options available for lunch. Stables also has a strong community vibe; it sponsors local teams, DJs and bands perform regularly, and the sporting event of the moment will be playing on at least one of the big screens. [$] *Average main: NZ$22* ✉ *72 Alpha St.* ☎ *07/827–6699* 🌐 *www.stablesbar.co.nz.*

WHERE TO STAY

$$ **Cambridge Mews.** All of these self-contained units, ranging from
HOTEL studios to two-bedroom apartments, have cooking facilities and modern amenities—including whirlpool baths and flat-screen TVs; however, each is configured differently, so you can pick the arrangement that best suits your party. **Pros:** modern; caring hosts; well equipped. **Cons:** some traffic noise. $ *Rooms from: NZ$180* ⊠ *20 Hamilton Rd.* ☎ *07/827–7166* ⊕ *www.cambridgemews.co.nz* ⇨ *6 studios, 4 apartments* ⦿| *No meals.*

$$$$ **Karapiro Lodge.** In 2004, Ed and Ann Rompelberg constructed a modern Edwardian mansion 20 km (12 miles) from Cambridge, where luxury
B&B/INN only begins with the grand views across Lake Karapiro and Maungatautiri Mountain. **Pros:** luxurious facilities, ambience, and service; great views. **Cons:** out of town. $ *Rooms from: NZ$450* ⊠ *1829F State Hwy. 1, Lake Karapiro* ☎ *07/823–7414* ⊕ *www.lakekarapirolodge.co.nz* ⇨ *5 rooms* ⦿| *Breakfast.*

$$ **Out in the Styx Cafe and Guesthouse.** As the name suggests, this place
B&B/INN is in the country, a 25-minute drive from Cambridge, and the delightful
Fodor's Choice rural environment includes a view of Maungatautari. **Pros:** four-course
★ dinner and breakfast included in price; environmental focus; hot tubs. **Cons:** country isolation. $ *Rooms from: NZ$$130* ⊠ *2117 Arapuni Rd., Pukeatua* ☎ *0800/461–559* ⊕ *www.styx.co.nz* ⇨ *9 rooms, 3 bunkrooms* ⦿| *Some meals.*

Sanctuary Mountain Maungatautari. Walk among some of the most ancient
OFF THE forests in the region at the small "mountain" called Maungatautari,
BEATEN where the Maungatautari Ecological Island Trust, in conjunction with
PATH the Department of Conservation, is carrying out one of New Zealand's many successful conservation stories. The trust has built a NZ$14-million, 50-km (31-mile) pest-proof fence around 8,400 acres of native forest, creating a refuge for some of New Zealand's rarest native species. Several endangered birds, including the kaka bush parrot, kiwi, takahe, and saddleback have been reintroduced here. The best place to start is at the Manu Tioriori Visitor Centre, which has information and refreshments; it's on the southern side of the mountain at the end of Tari Road in Pukeatua, 32 km (20 miles) outside of Cambridge. From here you can explore on your own or take a short guided walk through the Southern Enclosure (1½-hours, NZ$30). Five kilometers (3 miles) of high-quality trails lead through forest to a 52-foot viewing tower in the treetops, where you can be one with the birds. Other guided walks include Tautari Wetland (1½ hours, NZ$30) and Sanctuary by Night (summer Saturdays or by arrangement, two hours, NZ$50). Keen walkers can tackle the Over the Mountain trail, a full-day walk from one side to the other. ⊠ *Tari Rd., Pukeatua* ☎ *07/870–5180* ⊕ *www. sanctuarymountain.co.nz* ⬚ *NZ$16* ⊗ *Daily 8:30–4.*

WAITOMO

80 km (50 miles) southwest of Hamilton, 65 km (41 miles) southwest of Cambridge, 150 km (95 miles) west of Rotorua.

Fodor's Choice ★ Waitomo is a busy little village located a short drive from the main highway. Above ground, the surrounding hills are a mix of native bush and verdant farmland. Below ground you'll find the region's famous cave systems, and Waitomo caters to the tourists who come to ogle them. Despite its small size—everything here is within walking distance—the village promises a good selection of cafés, a tavern, plus some 20 different cave tour options ranging from gentle walking on well-lighted pathways to rappelling, tubing, and climbing underground waterfalls.

The Waitomo Caves are part of an ancient seabed that was lifted and then spectacularly eroded into a surreal subterranean landscape of limestone formations, gushing rivers, and contorted caverns. The name, a combination of *wai* (water) and *tomo* (cave), refers to the Waitomo River that vanishes into the hillside here. Many of the amazing underground passages are still unexplored, but four major cave systems are open for guided tours: Ruakuri, Spellbound, Aranui, and Waitomo Glowworm Cave. Each has its own special characteristics, and you won't be disappointed by any.

After all, notable features include not only stalactites and stalagmites but also glowworms—the 1- to 2-inch larvae of *Arachnocampa luminosa*, which live on cave ceilings. They snare prey by dangling sticky filaments, trapping insects attracted to the light they emit. A single worm produces far less than any firefly, but when massed in great numbers in the dark, it's like looking at the night sky in miniature. The guides who introduce you to all of this below-ground beauty may be descendants of local chief Tane Tinorau (who discovered Waitomo Glowworm Cave); they will certainly be local caving experts who have spent years exploring the amazing network of shafts and passageways around Waitomo.

GETTING HERE AND AROUND

Although it's in the countryside, Waitomo is close to State Highway 3, one of the major highways linking Waikato and Rotorua with Taranaki and Tongariro. The Waitomo Wanderer offers daily round-trip bus service from both Rotorua and Taupo, arriving mid-morning and departing late afternoon. Day-trippers wishing to see the caves can also take advantage of bus-tour packages offered by InterCity and Nakedbus; these originate in Auckland or Rotorua.

If you'd rather ride the rails, the Auckland–Wellington *Northern Explorer* train stops in Otorohanga, 16 km (10 miles) from Waitomo. The Waitomo Shuttle (NZ$12 per person) can be booked to meet the train and bring you into town; contact the Waitomo i-SITE Discovery Centre or email waikiwi@ihug.co.nz for bookings.

Bus Depot Waitomo Bus Depot. ⊠ *Waitomo i-SITE Discovery Centre, Waitomo Village Rd., Waitomo Caves Village.*

Train Station Otorohanga Train Station. ⊠ *7 Wahanui Cres., Otorohanga.*

VISITOR INFORMATION

There are two visitor centers in Waitomo village. Waitomo Glowworm Caves Visitor Centre is managed by the company that owns access to the Waitomo Glowworm, Ruakuri, and Aranai caves. The independent Waitomo i-SITE Discovery Centre offers impartial advice to help you decide which tour is most suitable as well as bookings for all cave tours and other regional attractions. Bookings may also be made with the individual tour operators.

Contacts Waitomo Glowworm Caves Visitor Centre. ⊠ *39 Waitomo Village Rd.* ☎ *0800/456–922* ⊕ *www.waitomo.com.* **Waitomo i-SITE Discovery Centre.** ⊠ *Waitomo Village Rd., Waitomo Caves Village* ☎ *07/878–7640* ⊕ *www.waitomocaves.com.*

EXPLORING

TOP ATTRACTIONS

Ruakuri Cave. Discovered several hundred years ago by a Māori hunting party, Ruakuri takes its name from the pack of wild dogs that used to inhabit the cave entrance—*rua* means "den" or "pit," and *kuri* means "dog." Its original entrance, an *urupa* (burial site) for Māori, has been closed. Visitors now enter through a dramatic, man-made spiral "drum passage," then proceed through narrow passages. Surrounded by magical limestone formations, you hear the roar of hidden waterfalls, pass beneath ancient rock falls, and follow a dark underground river that twinkles with glowworm reflections. The two-hour tours (reservations suggested) are limited to 15 people. This is the longest cave-walking tour in Waitomo, but it's easily managed by people of reasonable fitness. All pathways are wheelchair accessible. Tours meet at the Waitomo Glowworm Caves Visitor Centre or the Long Black Café (585 Waitomo Village Road). ⊠ *39 Waitomo Village Rd.* ☎ *0800/228–464* ⊕ *www. waitomo.com* 🎫 *Tours NZ$69; multicave tickets available* ⊘ *Tours daily at 9, 10, 11, 12:30, 1:30, 2:30, and 3:30.*

Spellbound and Te Ana o te Atua Caves. This tour offers two different underground experiences as well as an opportunity to see glowworms close up and learn about their amazing life cycle. The short but scenic above-ground walk is an added bonus. At Spellbound, a raft gently floats through a glowworm chamber that was filmed by Sir David Attenborough for the BBC. At Te Ana o te Atua (Cave of the Spirit), which has been known to the Ngati Kinohaku people for centuries, you proceed on foot through a chamber that features limestone formations, fossils, and bones. The combo includes tea or coffee and is limited to 12 people. Tours (3½-hours, advance booking advised) leave from the general store in the middle of Waitomo Village. ⊠ *Waitomo Village Rd., Waitomo Village* ☎ *0800/773–552* ⊕ *www.glowworm.co.nz* 🎫 *Tours NZ$75* ⊘ *Tours daily at 10, 11, 2, and 3.*

Fodor's Choice ★ **Waitomo Glowworm Cave.** The most "genteel" of all the cave tours leads through the Waitomo Glowworm Cave, which was first officially explored in 1887 by local Chief Tane Tinorau and English surveyor Fred Mace. They built a raft of flax stems and, with candles for light, floated into the cave where the stream goes underground. Now visitors enter via high-quality pathways. You explore the limestone cathedral

Novice spelunkers learn about the natural wonders of the Waitomo Caves.

(and, like opera diva Kiri Te Kanawa, are invited to sing to make best use of the amazing acoustics here), then board a boat for a magical cruise beneath the "starry" glowworm-lit ceiling, floating out of the cave on the Waitomo River. Tours last 45 minutes and start at the magnificent Waitomo Glowworm Cave Visitor Centre, about 330 feet beyond the Waitomo i-SITE Discovery Centre. ✉ *39 Waitomo Village Rd.* ☎ *0800/456–922* ⊕ *www.waitomo.com* 🎫 *Tours NZ$49; multi-cave tickets available* 🕙 *Tours every ½ hr: Apr. 1–Oct. 31, daily 9–5; Nov. 1–Mar. 31, daily 9–5:30.*

Waitomo Glowworm Caves Visitor Centre. Unveiled in 2010, this striking and sustainable structure has an open design that reflects the drama of the limestone landscape surrounding it. Artwork honors Māori culture. Inside, you can buy tickets to visit the caves, find information about the region, relax in the café and restaurant, or browse the gift shop. ✉ *39 Waitomo Village Rd.* ☎ *0800/456–922* ⊕ *www.waitomo.com* 🕙 *Apr. 1–Oct. 31, daily 9–5; Nov. 1–Mar. 31, daily 9–5:30.*

WORTH NOTING

Aranui Cave. Eons of dripping water have sculpted a delicate garden of pink-and-white limestone here. Keep an eye out for the resident cave wetas; these native insects stretch up to 4 inches in length and have long antennae, but don't worry—though scary looking, they're very passive and will most likely hide if they sense you coming. Aranui is named after Te Rutuku Aranui, who discovered the cave in 1910 when his dog disappeared inside in pursuit of a wild pig. Today, hour-long tours lead along boardwalks into tall, narrow chambers. Reservations are essential; tours meet in the Ruakuri Reserve car park on Tumutumu

Road, 3 km (2 miles) beyond Waitomo Caves Village. ⊠ *Cave entrance at Ruakuri Reserve, Tumutumu Rd.* ☎ *0800/456–922* ⊕ *www.waitomo. com* ⊠ *Tours NZ$49; multicave tickets available* ☉ *Tours daily 9–4.*

Waitomo Walkway. Passing through forests and impressive limestone outcrops, the 5-km (3-mile) Waitomo Walkway—which begins across the road from the i-SITE Discovery Centre and follows the Waitomo River—is one of the country's most interesting short treks. You can walk back to Waitomo Caves Village on the same path or follow the road, a distance of just over 2 km (1 mile). For a shorter alternative that still includes the most spectacular section, take Te Anga Road from the village, turn left onto Tumutumu Road, and park at Ruakuri Reserve. Walk the 30-minute loop through natural rock tunnels and across cantilevered bridges beneath limestone bluffs. Note that the trail can be slippery following wet weather, and there are steep sections, so wear good walking shoes. ■TIP➔ Many people come after dusk for a free view of the local glowworms; bring a flashlight to find your way. ⊕ *www.doc.govt.nz.*

WHERE TO EAT

$$$

MODERN NEW ZEALAND

✕ **HUHU Cafe.** Locals smile quietly when visitors inevitably express surprise that such an urban-chic café exists "way out here in the country." (The moniker "café" doesn't do HUHU justice.) Chef-owner Andy showcases local food, and his Te Kuiti slow-cooked lamb shoulder has won national acclaim. The same contemporary New Zealand–style menu runs from lunch through dinner, with a mix of smaller and larger plates that (mostly) stay under NZ$30. Traditional *rewana* (Māori bread) is usually featured, and top New Zealand wines plus craft beers from throughout the North Island are available. Big windows with great views encourage diners to linger, but leave time to check out the classy New Zealand giftware, ceramics, and jewelry downstairs in the HUHU Gallery. $ *Average main: NZ$28* ⊠ *10 Waitomo Village Rd., Waitomo Village* ☎ *07/878–6674* ⊕ *www.huhucafe.co.nz.*

WHERE TO STAY

$$

B&B/INN

Fodor'sChoice

★

🛏 **Abseil Breakfast Inn.** The sign at the bottom of this B&B's steep driveway—"Approach with Enthusiasm"—sets a convivial tone. **Pros:** quirky, helpful hosts; John's big breakfasts; comfy rooms. **Cons:** steep driveway; not for those who like big, impersonal hotels. $ *Rooms from: NZ$160* ⊠ *709 Waitomo Village Rd.* ☎ *07/878–7815* ⊕ *www. abseilinn.co.nz* ⮑ *4 rooms* ⦿ *Breakfast.*

$$

HOTEL

FAMILY

🛏 **Waitomo Top 10 Holiday Park.** Modern, clean, and rated Qualmark four-star-plus, this delightful holiday park in the heart of Waitomo Village offers tents, powered campervan sites, cabins, and a self-contained motel. **Pros:** central location; spacious rural environment with great views of the surrounding forest; friendly hosts. **Cons:** likely to be busy in summer; kid-friendly environment may not suit some. $ *Rooms from: NZ$135* ⊠ *12 Waitomo Village Rd., Waitomo Caves Village* ☎ *07/878–7639* ⊕ *www.waitomopark.co.nz* ⮑ *8 motel units, 10 cabins, 50 tent sites, 26 powered sites* ⦿ *No meals.*

SPORTS AND THE OUTDOORS
CAVE ADVENTURES

Many of Waitomo's subterranean adventure tours involve black-water rafting—that is, floating through the underground caverns on inflated inner tubes, dressed in wet suits and equipped with cavers' helmets. Be prepared for pitch darkness and freezing cold water. Your reward is an exhilarating trip gliding through vast glowworm-lighted caverns, clambering across rocks, and jumping over waterfalls. There are also dry options. Some tours involve steep rappelling and tight underground squeezes. Each company runs several trips daily.

Kiwi Cave Rafting. Thrill-seekers can venture down below on a five-hour combo adventure that includes rappelling, black-water rafting, rock climbing, caving, and checking out the glowworms—a pretty good value at NZ$225. Alternatively, you can keep dry on a three-hour tour (NZ$125) that still includes the thrilling rappel. ✉ 95 *Waitomo Village Rd.* ☎ *07/873–9149* ⊕ *www.caveraft.com.*

The Legendary Black Water Rafting Company. Most adventurous types can handle the basic, three-hour Black Labyrinth trip (NZ$128), which finishes with a welcome hot shower and mug of soup back at base. Then there's the more intense Black Odyssey (NZ$179), with four hours of twisting and turning "dry caving," and the five-hour Black Abyss (NZ$231). Though the guides and the underground scenery are great (you'll learn caving techniques from experts), these are staunch physical and emotional challenges and can be scary. Departure times depend on demand. ✉ *585 Waitomo Caves Rd.* ☎ *07/878–6219, 0800/228–464* ⊕ *www.waitomo.com.*

Fodor'sChoice ★ **Waitomo Adventures.** Five different trips with these caving enthusiasts release serious adrenaline. A 328-foot rappel into the famous Lost World cave system is spectacular—not just for a thumping heart, but also for the underground landscape, illuminated by daylight sneaking in through a couple of surface openings. Other tours include TumuTumu Toobing (climbing, swimming, tubing, and rafting), Haggas Honking Holes (rappelling, rock climbing, and crawling), and the seven-hour Lost World Epic (rappelling, wading, swimming, and climbing). These caves are a little way out of the main Waitomo tourist center, beneath picturesque farmland. Prices start at NZ$190; book ahead for discounted rates. ✉ *Waitomo Adventure Centre, Waitomo Village Rd.* ☎ *07/878-7788, 0800/924–866* ⊕ *www.waitomo.co.nz.*

NEW PLYMOUTH AND TARANAKI

On a clear day, sometimes with a cover of snow, Mt. Taranaki (also known as Mt. Egmont) towers above green flanks of forest and farmland. The solitary volcano peak, symmetrical in shape like Japan's Mt. Fuji, sits at the heart of the Taranaki region, and the province has shaped itself around it. Northeast of Taranaki, the provincial city of New Plymouth hugs the coast, and smaller rural towns dot the roads that circle the mountain's base.

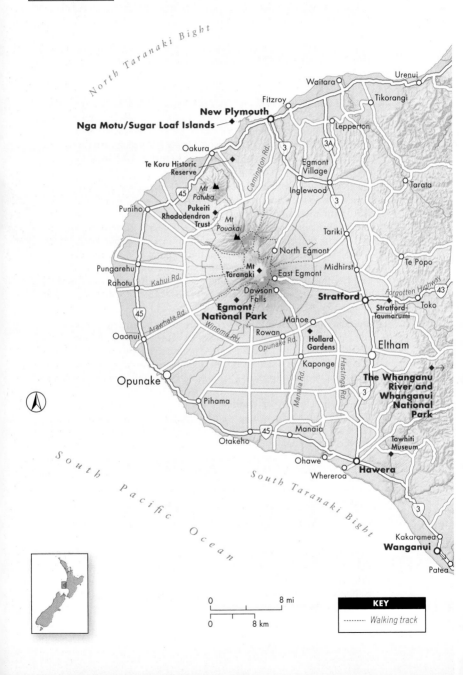

Taranaki

North Taranaki Bight

Urenui

Waitara

Tikorangi

Fitzroy

New Plymouth

Nga Motu/Sugar Loaf Islands

Lepperton

Oakura

Camington Rd.

3

3A

Te Koru Historic Reserve

Egmont Village

45

Mt Patuha

Inglewood

Tarata

Puniho

Pukeiti Rhododendron Trust

Mt Pouakai

3

Tariki

Pungarehu

North Egmont

Te Popo

Mt Taranaki

East Egmont

Midhirst

Rahotu

Kahui Rd.

Forgotten Highway

43

Dawson Falls

Stratford

Egmont National Park

45

Stratford-Taumarunu

Toko

Arawhata Rd.

Mahoe

Oaonui

Winemd Rd.

Rowan

Opunake Rd.

Hollard Gardens

Eltham

Kaponge

Mania Rd.

Hastings Rd.

Opunake

3

The Whanganu River and Whanganui National Park

Pihama

45

Manaia

Tawhiti Museum

Otakeho

Ohawe

Hawera

Whereroa

South Pacific Ocean

South Taranaki Bight

3

Kakaramea

Wanganui

Patea

0 — 8 mi

0 — 8 km

KEY
.... *Walking track*

Mt. Taranaki and Egmont National Park are tucked away on the western tip of the North Island, but visitors who make the journey are rewarded with mountain climbing (a serious challenge requiring expertise), hiking, and short forest walks to streams and waterfalls. Heading seaward, there's some 200 km (124 miles) of shoreline—complete with top surf breaks, beach walks, shipwrecks, seal colonies, small estuaries, and fishing spots—to discover along the Taranaki coast.

THE FICKLE SKIES

The weather here is constantly in flux—dictated by the peak of Mt. Taranaki, which is said to be brooding over lost love when hidden by cloud. Day in and day out, this meteorological mix makes for stunning contrasts of sun and clouds on and around the mountain.

Taranaki is a productive agricultural region; layers of volcanic ash have created free-draining topsoil and the western, coastal location ensures abundant rainfall. What serves farmers also serves gardeners. Some of the country's most magnificent gardens grow in the rich soil, including many "significant" and "nationally significant" gardens, as rated by the New Zealand Gardens Trust. New Plymouth's Te Kainga Marire is one of only four New Zealand gardens of international significance. Some, such as Pukekura Park, Pukeiti, and Hollard, are public, but many are private, open only by appointment and during the annual Taranaki Garden Spectacular and Taranaki Fringe Garden Festival. During these spring events, more than 100 splendid gardens celebrate the area's green-fingered excellence, particularly its rhododendrons.

These and other festivals, such as the biannual Taranaki International Arts Festival and annual World of Music, Art, and Dance (WOMAD), the Parihaka Peace Festival (a cultural celebration with great Kiwi music), and the World Cup Triathlon, as well as regular appearances by top international performers at the Bowl of Brooklands in Pukekura Park, add immensely to the area's attractions.

Taranaki has other delights as well. The striking Len Lye Centre, in New Plymouth, celebrates the eponymous kinetic artist. Out of town and by the water's edge—along "Surf Highway" (Highway 45), which traverses coastal farmland around the Taranaki bight—you can surf, swim, and fish. Several museums also delve into Taranaki history, which is particularly rich on the subject of the Māori.

NEW PLYMOUTH

375 km (235 miles) south of Auckland, 190 km (120 miles) southwest of Waitomo, 163 km (102 miles) northwest of Wanganui.

New Plymouth serves one of New Zealand's most productive dairy regions as well as the gas and oil industries. This natural wealth translates into an optimistic outlook that is reflected in New Plymouth's healthy arts scene, the abundance of cafés and restaurants, and a lifestyle that maximizes the great outdoors.

Taranaki has a strong Māori history and a strong history of Māori–European interaction, not all of it friendly. Before the arrival of Europeans in 1841, *kainga* (villages) and *pā* (fortified villages) spread along the coast. In the mid-1800s, European land disputes racked Taranaki. An uneasy formal peace was made between the government and local Māori tribes in 1881, and New Plymouth began to play its current role as a trading port. On the edge of the Tasman Sea, today's city is second to its surroundings, but its few surviving colonial buildings, cafés, stores, galleries, museums, and extensive parklands merit a half-day's exploration.

GETTING HERE AND AROUND

Air New Zealand flies daily to New Plymouth from Auckland, Wellington, and Christchurch, while Jetstar flies direct from Auckland. New Plymouth Airport (NPL) is about 12 km (7½ miles) from the city center; expect to pay about NZ$42 for a taxi to town. Scott's Airport Shuttle runs a door-to-door service from the airport for NZ$22 (first person, plus NZ$4 each additional passenger); book ahead online or by phone.

Coach companies (InterCity and Nakedbus) provide daily service linking New Plymouth, Stratford, and Hawera. Local service provider CityLink runs from New Plymouth to nearby Waitara and the surfing village of Oakura.

Travel by private car, however, is the best option for getting around New Plymouth and Taranaki. The roads are generally paved and in good condition. From the north, State Highway 3 passes through Te Kuiti, near Waitomo, and then heads west to New Plymouth. The highway continues south through Taranaki to Wanganui and onto Bulls, where it connects with State Highway 1. New Plymouth is a six- to seven-hour drive from Auckland and a five-hour drive from Wellington. If you're traveling west on a sunny afternoon, watch out for strong glare from the setting sun.

You can take in most of Taranaki in a couple of days, using New Plymouth as a base, but that would keep you on the run. Ideally, treat yourself to a leisurely week, choosing accommodations from fine lodges, B&Bs, motels, backpacker hostels, and holiday parks spread throughout the region.

Airport New Plymouth Airport. ⊠ *192 Airport Dr.* ☎ *06/755–2250.*

Airport Transfers Scott's Airport Shuttle. ☎ *06/769–5974, 0800/373–001* ⊕ *www.npairportshuttle.co.nz.*

Bus Depot Ariki Street Bus Station. ⊠ *19 Ariki St., City Center.*

Bus Information CityLink. ⊕ *www.trc.govt.nz/taranaki-bus-information.*

VISITOR INFORMATION

Contacts New Plymouth i-SITE Visitor Information Centre. ⊠ *Puke Ariki, 65 St. Aubyn St.* ☎ *06/759–0897* ⊕ *www.newplymouthnz.com.*

EXPLORING

TOP ATTRACTIONS

Govett-Brewster Art Gallery. Regarded as one of the country's leading modern art museums, this gallery boasts a strong collection of New Zealand conceptual, abstract, and contemporary pieces from the 1970s to today. It hosts regular visiting exhibitions from abroad and has a prolific publishing and events program revolving around works from New Zealand and the Pacific. It's also the home of the internationally acclaimed Len Lye collection. ⊠ *42 Queen St.* ☎ *06/759–6060* ⊕ *www. govettbrewster.com* 🖅 *Free (some charges for special events)* ☉ *Wed. and Fri.–Mon. 10–6, Thurs. 10–9.*

Fodor's Choice
★
Len Lye Centre. Len Lye—a native-born artist famous for his experimental films and kinetic sculpture—believed "great architecture goes 50/50 with great art," and the twisted towers of glass and steel housing his work bear that out. Inside the drama continues with changing exhibitions of Lye's thought-provoking pieces. Designed by New Zealand architect Andrew Patterson, who used traditional Māori aesthetics to convey the essence of the artist, the stunning venue opened in 2015. It adjoins the Govett-Brewster Art Gallery and is the only museum in the country devoted to a single artist. ⊠ *42 Queen St* ☎ *06/759–6060* ⊕ *www.govettbrewster.com/len-lye/centre* 🖅 *Free* ☉ *Wed. and Fri.– Mon. 10–6, Thurs. 10–9.*

New Plymouth Coastal Walkway. To get a feel for the landscape, take a stroll or ride a rented bike along this gentle path, which extends for 7 km (4 miles) from Port Taranaki to Lake Rotomanu—winding by beaches, over rivers, through playgrounds, and past a golf course. It runs under the *Wind Wand,* a sculpture almost as iconic to New Plymouth residents as the *Statue of Liberty* is to New Yorkers. Created by the late New Zealand artist Len Lye, the red carbon-fiber tube stands 148 feet high and, like a conductor's baton, dances in the wind as Lye's tribute to what he called "tangible motion." Near the path's northeastern end, the bold, white Te Rewa Rewa Bridge crosses Waiwhakaiho River in grand style. The framed view of Mt. Taranaki through the bridge's struts makes a great photo.

Fodor's Choice
★
Puke Ariki. Across the road from the *Wind Wand* is the region's heritage, research, and information center. Though not as large as Wellington's Museum of New Zealand Te Papa Tongarewa, Puke Ariki tells compelling stories of the region, from its volcanic inception to the Land Wars to the discovery of natural oil and gas in 1959 to today's surfing culture. Interactive science exhibits for children are on the lower level. The in-house Arborio Café is worth a stop, too, as demonstrated by the presence of locals. ⊠ *Puke Ariki Landing, 1 Ariki St.* ☎ *06/759–6060* ⊕ *www.pukeariki.com* 🖅 *Free* ☉ *Mon., Tues., Thurs., and Fri. 9–6; Wed. 9–9; weekends 9–5.*

Pukeiti Gardens. Established by the Pukeiti Rhododendron Trust, these 900 acres of lush, native rain forest are surrounded by farmland. The Pukeiti (poo-ke- *ee*-tee) collection of 2,500 varieties of rhododendrons is the largest in New Zealand. Many were first grown here, such as the giant winter-blooming *R. protistum var. giganteum*, collected from seed in 1953 and now standing 15 feet tall, and the delightful Lemon

Lodge and Spring Honey hybrids, which bloom in spring. *Kyawi*, a large red "rhodo," is the last to bloom, in April (autumn). Rhododendrons aside, there are many other rare and special plants here. All winter long the Himalayan daphnes fragrance the pathways. Spring-to-summer-growing candelabra primroses reach up to 4 feet; and, for a month around Christmas, spectacular 8-foot Himalayan *cardiocrinum* lilies bear heavenly scented, 12-inch, white trumpet flowers. Located 20 km (12½ miles) southwest of New Plymouth's center, Pukeiti is also a wonderful bird habitat. ✉ *2290 Carrington Rd.* ☎ *06/752–4141* ⊕ *www.trc.govt.nz/pukeiti-home* 🎫 *Free* ⊘ *Daily 9–5.*

FAMILY **Pukekura Park and Brooklands Park.** Together the expansive lawns, lakes, groves, and woodlands of these connected parks make up a tranquil, 128-acre urban oasis. From mid-December through January during the Festival of Lights, and again in March during the WOMAD Festival, **Pukekura Park** is beautifully illuminated at night. Special lighting effects transform the gardens and giant trees into a visual delight. At any time of year, visitors can hire a rowboat (from near the lakeside café) and explore the small islands and nooks and crannies of the main lake. The park also has a fernery—caverns carved out of the hillside that connect through fern-cloaked tunnels—and botanical display houses.

On Brooklands Road, **Brooklands Park** was once a great estate, laid out in 1843 around the house of Captain Henry King, New Plymouth's first magistrate. Today, Brooklands is best known for its amazing variety of trees. Mostly planted in the second half of the 19th century, they include giant copper beeches, pines, walnuts, and oaks. The Monterey pine, magnolia *soulangeana*, ginkgo, and native karaka and kohekohe are all the largest of their kind in New Zealand. Take a walk along the outskirts of the park on trails leading through subtropical bush. This area has been relatively untouched for the last few thousand years, and 1,500-year-old trees are not uncommon. A puriri tree near the Somerset Street entrance—one of 20 in the park—is believed to be more than 2,000 years old. Brooklands also has a rhododendron dell and the extremely popular Bowl of Brooklands, a stage and natural amphitheater used for a variety of concerts and events. Brooklands Zoo has frogs, fish, meerkats, monkeys, and a bird aviary. For a reminder of colonial days, visit the Gables, a former hospital built in 1847 that is now an art gallery. ✉ *Park entrances on Brooklands Park Dr. and Liardet, Somerset and Rogan Sts.* ☎ *06/758–6060 for zoo only* 🎫 *Free* ⊘ *Daily dawn–dusk; restaurant Wed.–Mon. dawn–dusk; display houses daily 8:30–4; zoo daily 9–5.*

Te Kainga Marire. In 1972, Valda Poletti and Dave Clarkson began transforming what was then a clay wasteland into one of New Zealand's few "gardens of international significance." Featured in the BBC documentary *Around the World in 80 Gardens*, Te Kainga Marire resembles a piece of native New Zealand bush and features everything from alpine to forest plants. There's even a hunter's camp and bushman's hut, legacies of Dave's earlier days as a professional deer hunter. Though within the city limits, this gorgeous green refuge certainly lives up to its name—which means "peaceful encampment" in Māori. ✉ *15 Spencer Pl.* ☎ *06/758–8693* ⊕ *www.tekaingamarire.co.nz* 🎫 *NZ$10* ⊘ *Sept.–Apr., daily 9–5; May–Aug. by appointment.*

DID YOU KNOW?

Underground streams slowly dissolved limestone to form the Waitomo Caves over thousands of years. The water picked up lime and, as it moved, left deposits that eventually formed intricate, beautiful stalactites and stalagmites.

WORTH NOTING

Te Koru Historic Reserve. To get a sense of the Taranaki's turbulent history, drive inland through the countryside from Oakura to this reserve. A Department of Conservation trail leads ½ km (about ¼ mile) from the parking lot to the site of a pā (fortified village), a former stronghold of the Nga Mahanga a Tairi *hapū* (subtribe). Regenerating native forest has covered part of the site, but still visible are the main defensive ditch and stonewall terraces that drop a considerable way from the highest part of the village to the Oakura River. There are no facilities. Take Highway 45 southwest out of New Plymouth to the beach suburb of Oakura, 17 km (10 miles) away. On the far side of the township, turn left onto Wairau Road and follow the signs, veering left onto Surrey Hill Road and left again onto Koru Hill Pa Road for 4 km (2½ miles). ✉ *Koru Hill Pa Rd., Oakura* ☎ *06/759–0350 Department of Conservation* 🖃 *Free* ☉ *Daily dawn–dusk.*

**OFF THE
BEATEN
PATH**

Taranaki–Waitomo. Mt. Taranaki is an ever-receding presence in your rearview mirror as you head northeast up the Taranaki coast from New Plymouth on Highway 3. The highway provides the most direct route to Waitomo Caves and Hamilton, turning inland at Awakino, 90 km (56 miles) from New Plymouth. The Awakino Gorge, between Mahoenui and the coast, is particularly appealing. Forest-filled scenic reserves are interspersed with stark, limestone outcrops and verdant farmland, where sheep have worn trails that hang on the sides of steep green hills. At the mouth of the Awakino River, little whitebaiting shacks dot the water's edge. **Awakino** is worth a stop; pull into the family-oriented Awakino Hotel (☎ *06/752–9815,* ⊕ *www.awakinohotel.co.nz*) or turn off the main road by the hotel for a lovely, sheltered picnic spot beneath the summer-flowering pohutukawa trees. A little farther along is **Mokau,** with a couple of little cafés where, if the whitebait are running, delicious whitebait fritters might be on the menu from September to November.

From Awakino, you could be in Waitomo within the hour if you stick to the main highway, but if time is not your master, a far more adventurous route is to follow the minor road north, at the turnoff just beyond Awakino. This runs for 58 km (36 miles) to Marokopa. It's a gravel road for the most part, but a reasonable trip, provided you take care and remember to keep left—especially on blind corners. The drive is through superb sheep country, passing through the Manganui Gorge, and with a possible 4-km (2½-mile) detour down the Waikawau Road to the stunningly isolated Waikawau Beach. The sweep of black sand here, backed by high cliffs, is reached through a hand-dug drover's tunnel. Total driving time from Awakino to Marokopa, including a picnic stop, is about three hours, plus another hour from Marokopa to Waitomo.

BEACHES

Fitzroy Beach. Just 1½ km (¾ mile) from the center of New Plymouth, this reasonably exposed beach is easily accessible. You can even come on foot or by bike via the New Plymouth Coastal Walkway. Changeable surf makes it a bit wild, so be sure to swim between the patrol flags. There's interesting rock-pool exploring to be had here and at other beaches along this coast, courtesy of the black sand and rocky outcrops. Expect crowds on hot summer days, when pohutukawa trees provide shade in some spots. Nearby accommodations include the Fitzroy Beach Motel and the popular Fitzroy Beach Holiday Park (camp and campervan sites and cabins, some with kitchenettes). **Amenities:** lifeguards (summer); parking (free); toilets. **Best for:** surfing; swimming; walking. ✉ *Beach St., Fitzroy.*

FAMILY **Ngamotu Beach.** This black-sand strand beside the busy container wharves and sheds of Port Taranaki is not the most picturesque of beaches; nevertheless, it's good for families, as the swimming is safe and there's a playground. There's also lots of history here involving early Māori and European altercations. Belt Road Seaside Holiday Park (tent and campervan sites, cabins, and motel studios) is close by, as are the cafés of Port Taranaki. Regular beach events include kids' triathlons, open-water swims, and Sunday markets. **Amenities:** parking (free); toilets. **Best for:** surfing; swimming; walking. ✉ *Ocean View Parade.*

WHERE TO EAT

$$$ NEW ZEALAND 🍴 **Caffe Windsor.** Energizing the café scene in little Inglewood, midway between New Plymouth and Stratford, this eatery occupies a charming building that was originally the Inglewood Butchery, built in 1878. Indoor-outdoor dining and wholesome homemade food draw both locals and travelers. Breakfast includes omelets and corn fritters; lunch features salads, pastas, soups, and curries; and dinner (Thursday to Saturday only) focuses on seasonal, contemporary New Zealand–style fare. [$] *Average main: NZ$25* ✉ *1 Kelly St., Inglewood* ☎ *06/756–6665* 🌐 *www.caffewindsor.co.nz* 🕒 *No dinner Sun.–Wed.*

$ CAFÉ 🍴 **Empire Tea & Coffee.** This charming spot serves excellent espressos but is best known for its huge range of loose-leaf teas, including jasmine, rose, sunflower, and calendula. There are mixes such as Cooletta, a refreshing and fruity blend of rose hip, hibiscus, papaya, blackberry leaves, and mango. Food includes a full breakfast menu, filled rolls, crepes, salads, and hearty soups. Vegetarian and gluten-free options are available. [$] *Average main: NZ$10* ✉ *112 Devon St. W* ☎ *06/758–1148* 🕒 *Closed Sun. No dinner.*

$$$ ECLECTIC 🍴 **Our Place.** Featuring big couches, booths, and a cool outdoor area, this restaurant–cum–cocktail lounge morphs into a club later at night, with DJ music, especially on weekends. Pizzas, mixed platters, and appealing à la carte dishes like eye fillet or confit duck will give you the stamina to stay up. [$] *Average main: NZ$25* ✉ *75 Devon St.* ☎ *06/758–8444* 🕒 *Closed Mon. and Tues. No lunch.*

$$ JAPANESE FUSION 🍴 **Snug Lounge.** The casual yet stylish setup at this Japanese yakitori grill and cocktail bar is designed to bring people together, and it works. The menu focuses on small plates to share. Opt for savory steamed buns and dumplings with assorted fillings, spicy meat skewers (the teriyaki-marinated chicken is to die for), tempura vegetables, or any of the many deep-fried *kusiage* delights. Fancy a dessert? They're part cocktail here—for example, lemon meringue or cookies and cream, alcohol infused. Good-quality wines, craft beers, and sake are also available. Located in the heritage-listed White Heart Hotel, the Snug has cozy nooks and crannies plus a sheltered courtyard with massive gas fire and barbecue. Lunch is served on Friday, but otherwise it's dinner only, from 4 until late. [$] *Average main: NZ$18* ✉ *124 Devon St. W* ☎ *06/757–9130* 🌐 *www.snuglounge.co.nz* 🕒 *Closed Sun. and Mon. No lunch Sat.–Thurs.*

WHERE TO STAY

$$$ HOTEL Fodor's Choice ★ **Ahu Ahu Beach Villas.** Set on a coastal clifftop about 15 minutes south of New Plymouth, these rustic-chic villas promise stunning sea views. **Pros:** dramatic coastal views; handsome design; Wi-Fi available. **Cons:** a drive to town. [$] *Rooms from: NZ$210* ✉ *321 Ahu Ahu Rd., RD4, Oakura* ☎ *06/752–7370* 🌐 *www.ahu.co.nz* 🛏 *5 villas* 🍴 *No meals.*

$ HOTEL **Ducks and Drakes Hotel.** A place for travelers rather than party animals, Ducks and Drakes offers character, color, and modern accommodations within walking distance of shops, cafés, and Pukekura Park. **Pros:** comfortable lounge; lots of books to read; friendly hosts. **Cons:** old, steep staircase in main building. [$] *Rooms from: NZ$90* ✉ *48 Lemon St.* ☎ *06/758–0404* 🌐 *www.ducksanddrakes.co.nz* 🛏 *13 rooms, 5 cottages* 🍴 *No meals.*

$$$ HOTEL **Nice Hotel.** Personable owner Terry Parkes has transformed this 19th-century hospital into an opulent city retreat decorated with contemporary art by leading Taranaki artists Don Driver, Tom Kriesler, and Michael Smither. **Pros:** boutique character; original artwork; fine in-house restaurant; complimentary port in the library. **Cons:** reservations a must for hotel and restaurant; parking is difficult to find. [$] *Rooms from: NZ$250* ✉ *71 Brougham St.* ☎ *06/758–6423* 🌐 *www.nicehotel.co.nz* 🛏 *8 rooms, 4 suites* 🍴 *No meals.*

$$ B&B/INN **Villa Heights B&B.** Retired farmers John and Rosemary will pour you a cup of tea and make you feel welcome when you arrive at their restored Victorian villa just 15 minutes from the city. **Pros:** welcoming hosts; great views; spacious en suite rooms. **Cons:** might be too far out of town for some. [$] *Rooms from: NZ$185* ✉ *333 Upland Rd.* ☎ *06/755–2273* 🌐 *www.villaheights.co.nz* 🛏 *3 rooms* 🍴 *Breakfast.*

$$$ HOTEL **The Waterfront Hotel.** Stylish and modern, New Plymouth's only waterfront lodging is handily placed next to the Puke Ariki Museum. **Pros:** proximity to the beach and Puke Ariki Museum; city right next door; good restaurant. **Cons:** port traffic rumbles past. [$] *Rooms from: NZ$250* ✉ *1 Egmont St.* ☎ *06/769–5301* 🌐 *www.waterfront.co.nz* 🛏 *42 rooms, 2 suites* 🍴 *No meals.*

SHOPPING

Devon Street, which runs from Fitzroy in the east to Blagdon in the west, is New Plymouth's main shopping thoroughfare.

Et Vous. Thanks to leading New Zealand, Australian, French, and Danish labels, this boutique has the best selection of designer clothing in town. It also stocks items for the larger form, as well as European shoes. If you work up an appetite browsing, just wander through to the adjoining bakery and café. ✉ *118 Devon St. W.* ☎ *06/759–1360* 🌐 *www.etvous.co.nz.*

Kina NZ Design + Art Space. For magnificent locally made arts and crafts with an edge, visit Kina, which exhibits the works of Taranaki artists and carries contemporary design pieces, from jewelry to sculpture. ✉ *101 Devon St. W* ☎ *06/759–1201* 🌐 *www.kina.co.nz.*

Taranaki Hardcore. Designer surf- and snow-wear and gear are sold at Taranaki Hardcore. ✉ *454 Devon St. E* ☎ *06/758–1757* 🌐 *www.taranakihardcore.co.nz.*

SPORTS AND THE OUTDOORS

Surfing is the big thing along the Taranaki coast, but the beaches and coastal walkways also draw swimmers and beachcombers. Fishing, be it surfcasting from the shore, trailing a line from a boat, or netting the delicacy whitebait at stream mouths during the season, is also popular.

BICYCLING

Cycle Inn. To ride the New Plymouth Coastal Walkway, rent a touring (aka road, not mountain) bike and a helmet at Cycle Inn. Expect to pay NZ$10 for two hours, NZ$20 for a full day. Lockers are provided if needed. ✉ *133 Devon St.* ☎ *06/758–7418.*

BOATING AND KAYAKING

Canoe & Kayak Taranaki. Guided trips taking in the best of the region's ocean and river paddling include the Nga Motu–Sugar Loaf Islands Marine Park (three hours; NZ$95 per person, minimum two people); the scenic Mokau River (one day; NZ$110 per person, minimum five people); and the more challenging Waitara River with its Class II rapids (four hours; NZ$85 per person, minimum three people). ✉ *468 St. Aubyn St.* ☎ *06/769–5506* ⊕ *www.canoeandkayak.co.nz/Taranaki.*

Happy Chaddy's Charters. A launch with this outfit inevitably starts with the guide announcing, "Hold on to your knickers, because we're about to take off." Then the old English lifeboat rocks back and forth in its shed (with you on board), slides down its rails, and hits the sea with a spray of water. Even if your time is limited, spare an hour for this trip, during which you'll see seals, get a close-up view of the Nga Motu–Sugar Loaf Islands, and be thoroughly entertained by skipper and former fisherman Happy Chaddy (NZ$40). Rental kayaks (singles NZ$15 per hour, doubles NZ$30 per hour) and paddleboards (NZ$30 per hour) are also available here. Note that Chaddy usually takes a break in midwinter. ✉ *Ocean View Parade* ☎ *06/758–9133* ⊕ *www.chaddyscharters.co.nz.*

SURFING

The coastal road between New Plymouth and Hawera is known as the **Surf Highway,** though, to be realistic, it mostly passes through green Taranaki farmland. To see the actual surf generally involves short detours, albeit attractive ones, a kilometer or so down side roads. Nevertheless, it is a pleasant rural journey. Note the little grassy mounds scattered across the farmland, the result of volcanic debris avalanches pouring from Mt. Taranaki. **Oakura,** a village 17 km (10 miles) southwest of New Plymouth, has good surf as well as cafés and crafts shops. Its environmental efforts have been recognized by the international Blue Flag program, dedicated to developing sustainable beaches and marinas. Closer to New Plymouth, Fitzroy, East End, Back, and Bell Block beaches are all popular with surfers. **Opunake,** in South Taranaki, has an artificial surf reef.

Beach Street Surf Shop. Local legend Wayne Arthur has all the equipment surfers need and will give you the lowdown on the hot spots in Taranaki. ✉ *39 Beach St., Fitzroy Beach* ☎ *06/758–0400* ⊕ *lostinthe60s.com.*

Vertigo Surf. In Oakura, this is the place to get the latest in surfing gear and advice on local conditions. A webcam shows what the Oakura Beach surf is doing at that moment. ✉ *605 Surf Hwy. 45, Oakura* ☎ *06/752–7363* ⊕ *www.vertigosurf.com.*

NGA MOTU–SUGAR LOAF ISLANDS

About 17,000 seabirds nest in the Nga Motu–Sugar Loaf Islands Marine Protected Area, located just off shore from the Taranaki Port, near New Plymouth. Shearwaters, petrels, terns, penguins, shags, and herons, some of them threatened species, nest and feed on and around these little islands. They are also a breeding colony and hauling grounds for New Zealand fur seals; in winter more than 400 seals congregate here. Dolphins, orca, and pilot whales frequent the waters around the islands, and humpback whales migrate past in August and September.

Beneath the water's surface, caves, crevices, boulder fields, and sand flats, together with the merging of warm and cool sea currents, support a wealth of marine life. More than 80 species of fish have been recorded here, along with jewel and striped anemones, sponges, and rock lobsters.

On land, more than 80 different native plant species grow. Cook's scurvy grass, almost extinct on the mainland, grows on two of them. The palatable species is rich in vitamin C and was sought by early sailors to treat scurvy.

GETTING HERE AND AROUND

Nga Motu–Sugar Loaf Islands are managed by the Department of Conservation, and landing on them is not permitted. You can, however, reach the area and view the marine life by boat. Kayaking tours and chartered launch trips leave regularly from New Plymouth. Contact the New Plymouth i-SITE Visitors Information Centre for details (☎ *06/759–0897* ⊕ *visitnewplymouth.nz*).

SPORTS AND THE OUTDOORS

Oceans Alive NZ. The diving here is fabulous; the best times to explore the marine reserve are summer and autumn, when visibility extends up to 65 feet. ✉ *35A Ocean View Parade, New Plymouth* ☎ *06/758–3348* ⊕ *www.oceansalive.co.nz.*

EGMONT NATIONAL PARK

North Egmont Visitor Centre is 26 km (16 miles) south of New Plymouth, Dawson Falls Visitor Centre is 68 km (42 miles) southwest of New Plymouth.

Fodor's Choice ★

Rising 8,261 feet above sea level, Mt. Taranaki dominates the landscape of this national park. It's difficult not to be drawn toward it. The lower reaches are cloaked in dense and mossy rain forests; above the tree line, lower-growing tussocks and subalpine shrubs cling to spectacularly steep slopes. Taranaki is the mountain's Māori name. James Cook gave it its English name, Egmont, in 1770, to honor the Earl of Egmont, who supported his exploration. Both are officially acceptable today.

Mt. Taranaki is notorious for its changing weather conditions, and many climbers and hikers are caught with insufficient gear. On a clear day, from even the mountain's lower slopes you can see the three mountains of Tongariro National Park in the central North Island—and sometimes even as far as the South Island.

GETTING HERE AND AROUND

Three well-marked main roads provide access up the mountain and to walking trails, lodgings, and visitor centers. Egmont Road, the first mountain turnoff as you drive south from New Plymouth on State Highway 3, leads to the start of many walking trails and the **North Egmont Visitor Centre.** Drop in to peruse the excellent displays and grab a bite at the café. Pembroke Road, the second road up the mountain from State Highway 3, goes to the Ngati Ruanui Stratford Mountain House hotel, a few walking trails, and, a little farther on, **Stratford Plateau,** where there are stunning views and access to the mountain's small ski slope. A third turnoff (Manaia Road) turns right off Opunake Road coming from Stratford, and leads up the south side of the mountain to the **Dawson Falls Visitor Centre.**

You can book a local transport operator from New Plymouth through the New Plymouth i-SITE Visitor Information Centre.

TOURS

Helicopter flights are a quick but spectacular way to enjoy views of Taranaki. Not surprisingly, the most popular flight is around the Mt. Taranaki summit.

Beck Helicopters. This outfit flies out of Eltham in south Taranaki, lifting quickly above the farmland and heading over the steep forests, deep ravines, and spectacular volcanic peak of Egmont National Park. Coastal views are an added bonus. Flights last 25 to 30 minutes. ✉ *4512 Mountain Rd., Eltham* ☎ *06/764–7073* 🌐 *www.heli.co.nz* 🎟 *NZ$995 for 4 passengers.*

Precision Helicopters. Based in the eastern Taranaki town of Urenui, Precision Helicopters offers anything from a scenic 12-minute hop to extended flightseeing tours that deliver views of the summit, plus beaches, waterfalls, and river valleys. ✉ *450 Kaipikari Rd. Upper, Urenui* ☎ *0800/246–359* 🌐 *www.precisionhelicopters.com* 🎟 *From NZ$480 for 4 passengers.*

VISITOR INFORMATION

Contacts Dawson Falls Visitor Centre. ✉ *Upper Manaia Rd., RD29, Kaponga* ☎ *027/443–0248* 🌐 *www.doc.govt.nz.* **North Egmont Visitor Centre.** ✉ *Egmont Rd.* ☎ *06/756–0990* 🌐 *www.doc.govt.nz.*

WHERE TO STAY

$$$ HOTEL 🏨 **Dawson Falls Mountain Lodge.** Markus, a highly qualified Swiss hotelier, first met Sera on this mountain; now they've returned with their family to run a charming alpine-style lodge on the southern slopes of Mt. Taranaki. **Pros:** bush backdrop, waterfalls, birdsong; superb hosts; quality cuisine. **Cons:** way out in the country. [$] *Rooms from: NZ$210* ✉ *Manaia Rd., off Opunake Rd., Dawson Falls* ☎ *06/765–5457* 🌐 *dawsonfallsmountainlodge.kiwi.nz* 🛏 *12 rooms* 🍴 *Breakfast.*

$$ HOTEL **Ngati Ruanui Stratford Mountain House.** High on Mt. Taranaki, this hotel and restaurant has a long-standing reputation for its dramatic setting and fine food. **Pros:** dramatic mountain views; fine food. **Cons:** it can rain often on the mountain. [$] *Rooms from: NZ$155* ✉ *Pembroke Rd., E. Egmont* ☎ *06/765–6100* 🌐 *www.stratfordmountainhouse.co.nz* 🛏 *10 rooms* 🍴 *No meals.*

SPORTS AND THE OUTDOORS

Whether your thing is climbing sheer rocky crags or taking a 10-minute stroll to a forest waterfall, you'll find something to wow you in this national park. Short walks to natural features, multiday hikes using park huts for accommodation, and day climbs of the mountain (rocky in summer, icy and snowy in winter) are all popular. There's also a very basic slope for skiers.

MOUNTAINEERING

Mt. Taranaki Guided Tours. Mt. Taranaki is a potentially perilous mountain to climb; unpredictable weather and steep upper slopes with sheer bluffs and ice are an extremely dangerous combination. For summit climbs in winter, use a local guide like Ian McAlpine of Mt. Taranaki Guided Tours. McAlpine—who has made more than 1,800 ascents of Mt. Taranaki and climbed in Nepal, India, and Antarctica—leads individuals and groups. He also organizes other one-day and multiday walks that explore the park's forests, waterfalls, gorges, old lava flows, and alpine plants. A particular favorite is the Pouakai Crossing, which encompasses volcanic, wetland, and forest landscapes. Summit-climb rates depend on the season and group size. ☎ *0274/417–042 cell* 🌐 *www.mttaranakiguidedtours.co.nz.*

SKIING

Manganui. Owned by a small club, the sole ski slope on Mt. Taranaki only operates for 10 to 30 days each winter (June–October), based on snow conditions. The terrain is for intermediate and advanced skiers; nonmembers can buy daily tow passes for NZ$45. Note that facilities are limited, and it's a 20-minute walk from the parking lot to the ski area. ✉ *Egmont National Park* 🌐 *www.skitaranaki.co.nz.*

WALKING AND HIKING

Hiking. Egmont National Park has more than 188 km (116 miles) of walking trails that lead around the mountain and across to the adjoining Pouakai Range, through dense forests, across the higher subalpine slopes, past waterfalls, across mountain streams, and beneath massive lava bluffs. There are signposted short walks, suitable for all ages, from each of the three main park access roads. The best trails for sampling the park's forested scenery start from the Dawson Falls Visitor Centre. Most popular are the Wilkies Pools Loop Track and Kapuni Loop Track to Dawson Falls; each takes 60 to 90 minutes.

For a multiday hiking trip, consider the well-signed Pouakai Circuit, which has accommodation huts (NZ$15 a night) at one-day intervals. The Pouakai Crossing, an increasingly popular one-day walk, takes in the diverse landscape features of the Pouakai Circuit, but because the start and finish are several kilometers apart, transportation must be arranged. (Check with the visitor center.) For those who want to stay on the mountain, the Camphouse has budget bunkhouses at North Egmont (NZ$25 per person, including bed linen). Reservations are required. ⊕ *www.doc.govt.nz.*

STRATFORD

41 km (27 miles) southeast of New Plymouth.

Sitting under the eastern side of Mt. Taranaki, Stratford is a service town for surrounding farms. Its streets are named after characters from Shakespeare's works, and it has the first glockenspiel in New Zealand, which chimes four times a day. A number of the country's most interesting private gardens, including Hollard, are also found in the rich volcanic soil here. Because the town is at the junction of two highways, you'll likely pass through at some stage if you're exploring Taranaki.

GETTING HERE AND AROUND

Stratford is in central Taranaki, at the junction of State Highway 3, which passes through the region along the eastern side of Mt. Taranaki, and State Highway 43, aka the Forgotten World Highway. The town is just more than a 30-minute drive from New Plymouth. Daily bus service through Stratford, linking New Plymouth and Wanganui, is provided by InterCity and Nakedbus; bookings can be made via i-SITE Visitor Information Centres in the area.

Bus Depot Stratford Bus Depot. ⊠ *By Stratford i-SITE Visitor Information Centre, 56 Miranda St.*

VISITOR INFORMATION

Contacts Stratford i-SITE Visitor Information Centre. ⊠ *Prospero Pl.* ☎ *06/765–6708, 0800/765–6708* ⊕ *stratfordnz.co.nz.*

EXPLORING

Fodor's Choice **Hollard Gardens.** A detour into dairy country, 16 km (10 miles) south-
★ west of Stratford, brings you to this well-regarded horticultural haven. In 1927, dairy farmers Bernie and Rose Hollard fenced a 14-acre patch of native bush and started what is now a garden of "national significance." There are two distinct sections. One is an old woodland garden of mature native and exotic trees, with closely underplanted rhododendrons, azaleas, camellias, and perennials. The other, established in 1982, has broad lawns, paths with mixed borders, hidden paths, a children's play area, and vistas of Mt. Taranaki. Managed by the Taranaki Regional Council for all to enjoy, the gardens are particularly colorful during the rhododendron flowering season from September to late November. Self-contained campervans can stay overnight. ⊠ *1686 Upper Manaia Rd., off Opunake Rd., Kaponga* ☎ *0800/736–222* ⊕ *www.hollardgardens.info* ⊡ *Free* ⊙ *Daily 9–5.*

**OFF THE
BEATEN
PATH**
Stratford–Taumarunui. Known as the Forgotten World Highway, Highway 43, heading northeast from Stratford, takes you on an intriguing, heritage-rich journey back in time as it winds through rolling farmland and dense rain forests to Taumarunui, the northern access point for the Whanganui River. You'll see few cars here, but there's no shortage of scenic sights. Highlights include Mt. Damper Falls (a side trip); spectacular views from three saddles and a lookout point; the steep,

forest-filled Tangarakau Gorge; a road tunnel and historic railway; plus Whanganui River views. The 155-km (96-mile) highway is sealed for all but 11 km (7 miles). Allow three hours, and be sure to fill your tank before leaving Stratford. If you need a break, drop into the vintage **Whangamomona Hotel** (⊠ *6018 Ohura Rd.,* ☎ *06/762–5823,* ⊕ *www. whangamomonahotel.co.nz*). More than a century old, it's the only place to stop for refreshments along the Forgotten World Highway.

Travelers who don't feel like driving a car can sign on with **Forgotten World Adventures** (⊕ *www.forgottenworldadventures.co.nz*), an outfit that lets you "ride the rails"—golf carts mounted on a decommissioned railway line. The self-drive carts reach a top speed of 20 kph (12 mph) as you're led along 140 km (87 miles) of stunning track; one- and two-day guided trips are available.

SHOPPING

Envirofur. This small but thriving business near Stratford is turning possum, a local environmental pest, into high-end items using all-natural tanning processes. Designer fur and leather products such as hats, rugs, coats, and scarves are sold. It's open weekdays 9–5 and weekends 10–4. ⊠ *1103 Opunake Rd., Mahoe* ☎ *06/764–6133* ⊕ *www.envirofur.co.nz.*

HAWERA

29 km (18 miles) south of Stratford.

This quiet country town, a hub for the farming community, provides a close look at the local history and way of life. Brush up on its backstory at the Tawhiti Museum—it's a national gem.

GETTING HERE AND AROUND

Hawera is in southern Taranaki on State Highway 3, which passes through the region along the eastern side of Mt. Taranaki. Traveling by car, it's one hour south of New Plymouth and just more than an hour north of Wanganui. InterCity and Nakedbus coaches serving the New Plymouth-to-Wanganui route drive into Hawera daily; bookings can be made through area i-SITE Visitor Information Centres.

Bus Depot Hawera Bus Depot. ⊠ *South Taranaki i-SITE Visitor Information Centre, 55 High St.*

VISITOR INFORMATION

Contacts South Taranaki i-SITE Visitor Information Centre. ⊠ *55 High St.* ☎ *06/278–8599* ⊕ *www.southtaranaki.com.*

EXPLORING

KD's Elvis Presley Museum. An unlikely find in Hawera, this private museum is devoted to "The King." The collection includes more than 10,000 records, books, and impressive memorabilia. The museum doesn't keep regular hours, so phone ahead for an appointment with KD (try his cell number first); he's more likely to be able to accommodate evenings. ⊠ *51 Argyle St.* ☎ *06/278–7624, 0274/982–942 cell* ⊕ *www.elvismuseum.co.nz* ✉ *Donations welcome.*

FAMILY **Tawhiti Museum.** No boring old museum this. Nigel Ogle's labor of love is an outstanding presentation of regional history. The former school-teacher-cum-historian bought an old cheese factory in 1975 and proceeded to fill it with life-size figures from Taranaki's past. He creates the fiberglass figures from molds of local people and sets them in scenes depicting the pioneering days. Nigel is continually adding "stories"; dioramas depict the huge intertribal wars of the 1830s and European–Māori land wars of the 1860s. More than 800 model warriors, none of them the same, have been created. Separate from the main museum is the amazing "Traders and Whalers," where you glide by lantern light on a boat through an eerie world of traders and whalers and witness their first encounters with Māori tribes. On the first Sunday of every month and Sundays during school holidays the Tawhiti Bush Railway springs to life, rattling through a variety of outdoor displays that highlight historical logging operations in Taranaki. Also in the museum is Mr. Badger's Café, with its *Wind in the Willows* theme, and a quaint gift shop. To reach the museum, take Tawhiti Road northeast out of Hawera and continue 4 km (2½ miles). ✉ *401 Ohangai Rd.* ☎ *06/278-6837* ⊕ *www.tawhitimuseum.co.nz* ✉ *Museum NZ$12, Traders and Whalers NZ$12, Bush Railway NZ$6* ☉ *June–Aug., Sun. 10–4; Sept.–late Dec. and Feb.–May, Fri.–Mon. 10–4; Dec. 26–Jan., daily 10–4.*

WHERE TO STAY

$$ 🏨 **Tairoa Lodge.** *Tairoa*, meaning "linger, stay longer," is a fitting name
B&B/INN   for this relaxing B&B. **Pros:** spacious accommodations; inviting swimming pool; quiet, rural location. **Cons:** not for those who prefer larger hotels; by main road (but not a busy one). $ *Rooms from: NZ$195* ✉ *3 Puawai St.* ☎ *06/278-8603* ⊕ *www.tairoa-lodge.co.nz* ↪ *3 rooms, 2 cottages* 🍴 *Breakfast.*

WANGANUI, THE WHANGANUI RIVER, AND PALMERSTON NORTH

163 km (102 miles) southeast of New Plymouth, 193 km (121 miles) north of Wellington, 225 km (141 miles) southwest of Taupo.

Wanganui is a river city and the Whanganui River its raison d'être. It began as a small port settlement and a transportation junction between the sea and the river, which is navigable for miles into the forested interior.

For hundreds of years, the Māori people have lived along the banks of this waterway. In the 1840s, European settlers started moving to the area; the subsequent appropriation of land caused conflict, and a British garrison was temporarily established in the town. Beginning in the 1880s, the port and riverboat transport that provided a link to the North Island interior led to a prosperous time for trade and tourism. That changed in 1908, when the completion of the main railway line meant Wanganui was essentially bypassed. With trains, roads, and later planes stealing the transportation limelight, Wanganui sat quietly for some years while other North Island towns flourished. Today, though, there has been a considerable resurgence of the small-but-appealing provincial city.

6

Palmerston North sits in the heart of farming country, an easy one-hour drive southeast of Wanganui. With a population of about 80,000, it ranks as New Zealand's seventh largest city. "Palmy," as it's affectionately known, is home to Massey University, and a youthful demographic helps keep it young at heart.

WANGANUI

A major gateway to Whanganui National Park, Wanganui is worthy in its own right. Its compact center has lively streets with shops and galleries, plus restored heritage buildings that hark back to colonial times and the busy trading days. The city is home to a vibrant arts community, and locals gather at the River Traders riverside market on Saturday morning for fresh produce and crafts. Restored riverboats cruise the river's lower reaches; gardens, parks, an interesting regional museum, and fine cafés and restaurants complete the picture.

GETTING HERE AND AROUND

Air New Zealand flies here from Auckland three times a day, landing at Wanganui Airport (WAG). It's located south of the river, approximately 4 km (2½ miles) from the center of Wanganui; you can catch a taxi in for about NZ$25.

If you're driving, Wanganui is three hours from Wellington; take State Highway 1 north to Sanson and Highway 3 west from there. From New Plymouth drive south on State Highway 3, allowing about 90 minutes for the journey. Access to the lower and middle reaches of the Whanganui River from the city is via the scenic Whanganui River Road—expect it to take two hours to drive from Wanganui to Pipiriki. Remember to keep left on the narrow corners. For a scenic backcountry day trip, drive north up the Whanganui River Road, cut east along the minor road connecting Pipiriki to Raetihi, and then return down Highway 4, a paved though winding route through steep farmland and forest, to Wanganui. To reach the kayak starting points, take Highway 4 north from Wanganui; it's a three-hour drive to Taumarunui, via Raetihi.

Note that the river is named Whanganui, the traditional spelling. The city can officially be spelled Wanganui or Whanganui.

Airport Wanganui Airport. ✉ *Airport Rd.* ☎ *06/348–0536*
🌐 *www.wanganuiairport.co.nz.*

Bus Depot Wanganui Travel Centre. ✉ *156 Ridgeway St.*

VISITOR INFORMATION

Contacts Wanganui i-SITE Visitor Information Centre. ✉ *31 Taupo Quay*
☎ *06/349–0508* 🌐 *whanganuinz.com.*

EXPLORING
TOP ATTRACTIONS

Durie Hill Lookout. This lookout provides spectacular views, but reaching it—via an elevator that runs through the hill—is something else. On the opposite side of the river from the city center, directly across the bridge from the bottom of Victoria Avenue, you first walk through a

700-foot tunnel to the elevator shaft. The elevator concierge, who waits at the top, will see you on camera and lower the elevator for you. Alternatively, you can climb several hundred steps up to the lookout, plus another 176 steps up the nearby Durie Hill Memorial Tower. ⊠ *Durie Hill* 🖃 *NZ$2 each way (cash only)* ☉ *Weekdays 7:30–6, weekends and public holidays 10–5.*

Sarjeant Gallery. One of New Zealand's finest art galleries and most handsome heritage buildings sits on a small hill overlooking the city. Renowned for its domed neoclassical architecture, natural lighting, and magnificent display spaces, The Sarjeant also wins praise for the quality of its 6,000-piece collection and regularly changing exhibits spotlighting local, national, and international artists. Works in its care include 19th- and 20th-century paintings from home and abroad, photography, and a dynamic assortment of contemporary New Zealand pieces. The shop stocks fine glasswork and jewelry, much of it crafted by locals. ⊠ *Queens Park* 🕾 *06/349–0506* ⊕ *www.sarjeant.org.nz* 🖃 *Donations welcome* ☉ *Daily 10:30–4:30.*

Fodor's Choice ★ **Whanganui Regional Museum.** For an overview of the region's history and one of the country's best collections of Māori artifacts, drop into this museum by Queens Park. It contains *taonga* (Māori ancestral treasures) of the river people and some wonderful *waka* (canoes), as well as carvings, jewelry, ornaments, kiwi-feather cloaks, greenstone clubs, tools, bone flutes, and ceremonial portraits. The museum also re-creates 19th-century pioneer-town Wanganui in a series of traditional shop windows filled with relics and curios. Another highlight is Te Pataka Whakaahua (the Lindauer Gallery), which displays 19th-century paintings of Māori leaders by respected artist Gottfried Lindauer. ⊠ *Watt St.* 🕾 *06/349–1110* ⊕ *www.wrm.org.nz* 🖃 *Free* ☉ *Daily 10–4:30.*

WORTH NOTING

Chronicle Glass Studio. Wanganui is home to more than 30 glass artisans who exhibit internationally. This studio, owned and operated by Lyndsay Patterson and Katie Brown, is open to the public, and you're welcome to watch them at work (generally on weekdays). The master glassblowers also offer one-hour classes (NZ$100), during which participants are guided through the hot-glass process to craft their own paperweight. A mezzanine retail gallery sells stunning glass pieces. ⊠ *2 Rutland St.* 🕾 *06/347–1921* ⊕ *www.chronicleglass.co.nz* 🖃 *Free* ☉ *Tues. 10–1, Wed.–Fri. 9:30–5, Sat. 10–4.*

Virginia Lake. Winter or summer, the formal gardens of Virginia Lake are a delight by day, and, at night, the trees and fountain are softly illuminated. A gentle 25-minute stroll leads around the lake through woodlands and gardens and past rose-and-wisteria pergolas. There's a pleasant café here, too, with indoor and outdoor dining. The lake is just north of Wanganui, off State Highway 3. 🖃 *Free*

Waimarie *and Whanganui Riverboat Centre.* For a taste of the old days on the river, catch a ride on the *Waimarie,* a vintage coal-fired paddle steamer. A two-hour cruise takes you up the Whanganui to the village of Upokongaro. You might even be invited into the engine room to help stoke the boiler. Built in 1899, the *Waimarie* sank in 1952. Critics said she couldn't be salvaged, let alone restored to working order, but a dedicated volunteer team proved them wrong. Cruises run on weekends in summer, and daily during the December–January holiday season (call ahead to ask about other dates). If you don't have time to take one, check out the museum at the Riverboat Centre, which displays photographs and related artifacts from the era when riverboats were commonplace here. Note that opening hours are variable at this volunteer operation: summer weekends are your best bet. ✉ *Whanganui Riverboat Centre, 1A Taupo Quay* ☎ *06/347–1863* 🌐 *www.riverboats.co.nz* 🎟 *Cruise NZ$45, museum by donation* 🕒 *Variable hrs, check with Wanganui i-SITE Visitor Information Centre.*

Wairua. Rescued from the muddy riverbed and restored to first-class order, the *Wairua* plied the river's remote middle reaches in the early 1900s, moving not only people but also cattle, sheep, and horses. Now based in Wanganui, this classic riverboat makes regular two- and three-hour trips upriver. They're run by Skipper Dave McDermid, one of the team who rescued the vessel. Operating times vary; however, scheduled cruises depart Tuesday, Wednesday, and Thursday at 11, from approximately November to April. Other sailings are by arrangement. ✉ *Taupo Quay, 1 Halswell St.* ☎ *027/555–4201 cell* 🌐 *www.whanganuiriverboat.co.nz* 🎟 *NZ$36.*

6

WHERE TO EAT

$$$ MODERN NEW ZEALAND FAMILY

🍴 **Angora Cafe and Restaurant.** Turkish classics, like köfte and kebobs, share the menu here with fillet steak, fresh-caught fish, and other Kiwi favorites. Flatbreads and pizzas also emerge from the constantly glowing wood-fired oven at this cozy, family-friendly spot. Open daily from 5:30 until late, it's popular with locals and features live piano music most nights. [$] *Average main: NZ$25* ✉ *199 Victoria Ave.* ☎ *06/348–8334* 🌐 *angora.co.nz* 🕒 *No lunch.*

$$$ MODERN NEW ZEALAND

🍴 **The Big Orange and Ceramic Lounge.** Mingle with the many locals who gather here, be it for their first coffee of the day, a social weekend brunch, lunch or dinner, late-night wine, or a music gig in the laid-back lounge. The multi-format café–restaurant–wine bar caters to every meal or mood. By day there are homemade cakes, to-die-for caramelized onion muffins, and a full breakfast menu. In the evening, main courses encompass contemporary Kiwi flavors with an international twist. Local lamb is always on the menu, as are tapas. Dine alfresco on the Victoria Avenue pavement, or snuggle into a leather banquette in the lounge. [$] *Average main: NZ$28* ✉ *51 Victoria Ave.* ☎ *06/348–4449* 🌐 *www.bigorange.co.nz.*

$$$ PIZZA

🍴 **Stellar.** This relaxed restaurant specializes in giant gourmet pizzas with ominous names, like "Ren and Stinky" (lots of mozzarella) and "Foul Play" (yes, chicken), but it also serves a variety of light meals, salads, and meaty main courses. The space, which includes a bar and music venue, retains the brick-and-stone interior of an erstwhile 1850s hotel. There's a strong Kiwi vibe throughout, with stained-and-polished wool presses for bar stands and giant plasma TVs for engaging in that favorite Kiwi pastime: watching sports. A spacious veranda, free Wi-Fi for diners, and stylish bathrooms are also notable. Happy hour, 4:30–6:30 on weeknights, is a bargain, and there's live music some nights after 10. $ *Average main: NZ$26* ✉ *2 Victoria Ave.* ☎ *06/345–7278* ⊕ *www.stellarwanganui.co.nz.*

$$

CAFÉ

✕ **Yellow House Café.** Spread throughout the veranda, garden, and several intimate rooms of this old multicolor villa (it used to be yellow—hence the name) is a cozy café that also displays local art. It serves excellent buttermilk pancakes and eggs Benedict for breakfast or brunch, as well as soups, salads, and other wholesome food for lunch. The Yellow House Café is across the road from the river and a two-minute drive from the city center. $ *Average main: NZ$19* ✉ *17 Pitt St., at Dublin St.* ☎ *06/345–0083* ⊘ *No dinner.*

WHERE TO STAY

$$

HOTEL

FAMILY

Fodor'sChoice

★

Anndion Lodge. With its blend of upmarket "flashpacker" lodge rooms and stylish self-contained suites and apartments, Anndion is a market leader. **Pros:** free extras; thoughtful hosts; personal attention. **Cons:** a few minutes' drive from downtown. $ *Rooms from: NZ$140* ✉ *143 Anzac Parade* ☎ *06/343–3593, 0800/343–056* ⊕ *www.anndionlodge. co.nz* ⬑ *11 rooms, 8 suites, 2 apartments* ⫿⊙⫾ *No meals.*

$$

HOTEL

Aotea Motor Lodge. The stylish modern apartments here include studio, one-bedroom, and two-bedroom units. **Pros:** amenities include double whirlpool baths and free Wi-Fi; close to supermarkets and fast-food restaurants. **Cons:** beside busy road. $ *Rooms from: NZ$190* ✉ *390 Victoria Ave.* ☎ *06/345–0303* ⊕ *www.aoteamotorlodge.co.nz* ⬑ *28 apartments* ⫿⊙⫾ *No meals.*

$$

HOTEL

Bushy Park Homestead. This grand old Edwardian B&B is surrounded by the Bushy Park Trust native bird sanctuary. **Pros:** outstanding forest reserve location; varied accommodation options. **Cons:** the birds' dawn chorus may wake you; 24 km (15 miles) northwest of Wanganui. $ *Rooms from: NZ$145* ✉ *Rangitautau East Rd.* ☎ *06/342–9879* ⊕ *www.bushyparksanctuary.org.nz* ⬑ *6 rooms, 1 bunkhouse* ⫿⊙⫾ *Breakfast.*

$$

HOTEL

FAMILY

151 on London. In a quiet location close to the city center, this upmarket motel-style complex incorporates rustic barnlike iron cladding and farming memorabilia into amenity-packed units. **Pros:** modern; high-quality amenities; handy location. **Cons:** close to busy roads; industrial location lacks charm. $ *Rooms from: NZ$185* ✉ *151 London St.* ☎ *06/345–8668* ⊕ *www.151onlondon.co.nz* ⬑ *26 units* ⫿⊙⫾ *No meals.*

$$

B&B/INN

Rutland Arms. Reproduction Victorian furniture and lots of mahogany make this renovated Edwardian inn in the center of Wanganui a top choice if you're looking for elegance and character. **Pros:** central location; old-world elegance; rooms refurbished in 2015. **Cons:** no elevator; on busy main street, so some noise. $ *Rooms from: NZ$160* ✉ *Victoria Ave. and Ridgeway St.* ☎ *06/347–7677* ⊕ *www.rutlandarms.co.nz* ⬑ *8 suites* ⫿⊙⫾ *Breakfast.*

THE WHANGANUI RIVER AND WHANGANUI NATIONAL PARK

The Whanganui, the longest continually navigable river in New Zealand, flows through one of the country's largest remaining areas of native lowland forest, much of which is protected in Whanganui

The *Waimarie* paddle steamer plies the Whanganui River.

National Park. Canoeing, jet-boating, hiking, and mountain biking are the main recreational activities here.

GETTING HERE AND AROUND

Whanganui National Park, through which the eponymous river flows, is in the hinterland of the central North Island. The closest access points are Wanganui in the south and the township of Taumarunui to the north. The latter sits on State Highway 4 and is served by daily InterCity buses from Auckland and Wellington.

Traditional entry points for a Whanganui River journey are Taumarunui and the small settlements of Whakahoro and Pipiriki. To reach Whakahoro, turn off State Highway 4 at Owhango, just south of Taumarunui. Pipiriki is 27 km (17 miles) from Raetihi (also on State Highway 4) and 79 km (49 miles) from Wanganui, via the Whanganui River Road. Shuttle services for kayakers, hikers, and jet-boat travelers are run by tourism operators based in the Whanganui/Ruapehu region, including the towns of Ohakune, National Park, Taumarunui, and Pipiriki.

Bus Depot Taumarunui Bus Depot. ⊠ *Taumarunui i-SITE Visitor Information Centre, 116 Hakiaha St., Taumarunui.*

TOURS

Fodor's Choice ★ **Whanganui River Adventures.** Ken and Josephine Haworth, who grew up on the river, now run a Pipiriki-based company that leads tours to the Bridge to Nowhere plus shorter trips to such scenic delights as the Drop Scene and Manganui o te Ao River. Shuttles for mountain bikers, canoeists, and hikers are available as well. They also operate a café and nicely landscaped campground for tents and campervans on the grounds of the former Pipiriki School. ⊠ *RD 6, Pipirki, Wanganui* ☎ *06/385–3246, 0800/862–743* ⊕ *www.whanganuiriveradventures. co.nz* ✉ *Tours from NZ$80.*

Whanganui River Road Mail Tour. Run by Whanganui Tours, this early-morning trip goes to Pipiriki and back by midafternoon; precise times vary depending on how much mail the postman has to deliver and whether he waits while you enjoy an optional jet-boat ride. Pickups are from city accommodations, and reservations are essential.

Sights en route include the remains of giant, fossilized oyster shells at **Oyster Cliffs** (28 km [17 miles] from Wanganui) and the village of **Koriniti** (47 km [29 miles]), which contains historic but still much-used Māori ceremonial buildings and a small Anglican church. If there's anything happening, just ask whether it's appropriate to visit—unless it's a private funeral, you're likely to be made completely welcome. The restored **Kawana Flour Mill** and colonial miller's cottage (56 km [35 miles]) provide a glimpse of bygone pioneer life. In the farming settlement of **Ranana** (60 km [37 miles]), a Roman Catholic church from the 1890s remains a place of worship; the larger St. Joseph's Church and Catholic Mission, established by Home of Compassion founder Mother Aubert, is in picturesque **Hiruharama** (66 km [41 miles]), better known locally as Jerusalem. In **Pipiriki** (79 km [49 miles]), the turnaround point, it's possible to arrange a jet-boat tour up to the magnificent river gorges or farther still to Mangapurua Landing. From the landing, an easy 40-minute walk through forested terrain leads to the remote Bridge to Nowhere; this huge concrete span is a remnant of the Mangapurua farming settlement, abandoned in 1942. ☎ *06/345–3475* ⊕ *www. whanganuitours.co.nz* ✉ *NZ$63* ⊙ *Weekdays at 7 am, weekends by arrangement (3-person minimum).*

Whanganui Scenic Experience Jet. Mark and Claire Wickham, a pair of knowledgeable locals, offer two- to eight-hour tours that can include morning or afternoon tea stops at scenic and historic spots along the river. Trips start from the Wickham family farm, a 30-minute drive from Wanganui. Other options include self-guided kayak tours (lasting from a few hours to a few days) and jet-boat/canoe combos. Overnight parking for campervans is available at the farm, and cottage accommodations can be arranged at the neighbour's River Time Lodge. ⊠ *1195 Whanganui River Rd., Wanganui* ☎ *06/342–5599, 0800/945–335* ⊕ *www.whanganuiscenicjet.com* ✉ *Tours from NZ$80.*

VISITOR INFORMATION

Contacts Taumarunui i-SITE Visitor Information Centre. ⊠ *116 Hakiaha St., Taumarunui* ☎ *07/895–7494* ⊕ *www.visitruapehu.com.* **Wanganui i-SITE Visitor Information Centre.** ⊠ *31 Taupo Quay, Wanganui* ☎ *06/349–0508* ⊕ *whanganuinz.com.*

EXPLORING

Whanganui National Park. Flowing through the heart of this national park, the Whanganui River begins its journey high on the mountains of Tongariro National Park and travels 329 km (204 miles) through steep gorges, forested wilderness, and isolated pockets of farmland. For several hundred years the *Te Atihau nui a paparangi* tribe of Māori has lived along the riverbanks, and they still regard the waterway as their spiritual ancestor.

The river's wilderness, its rich culture and history, and its relatively easy navigability are the main draws. Scenic jet-boat trips operate throughout the year from several points along the river. Single and multiday kayak trips, both guided and independent, are extremely popular. Most visitors kayak in summer, but a river trip is feasible at any time. Two major two- to three-day walks and many shorter ones explore the lowland forest. Totaling 317 km (197 miles), the Mountains to Sea—Nga Ara Tuhono Cycle Trail traverses remote forest tracks (challenging for mountain bikes) and roads through Tongariro and Whanganui national parks from Mt. Ruapehu to the river's mouth. It can be ridden in stages. 🌐 *www.doc.govt.nz/parks-and-recreation/national-parks/whanganui.*

Whanganui River Road. Visitors without the time or inclination to travel by kayak or jet-boat can explore the river's lower reaches by following the Whanganui River Road from the city of Wanganui. Built in the 1930s to provide access to communities otherwise reliant on the less-frequent riverboat service, the narrow backcountry road runs for 79 km (49 miles) north, as far as Pipiriki. It passes several small villages and historic sites along the way. Be sure to keep left, take it slowly, and keep an eye out for wandering livestock. ✉ *Whanganui River Rd., Wanganui.*

6

WHERE TO STAY

$$ B&B/INN 🏨 **Bridge to Nowhere Lodge.** Deep inside Whanganui National Park, roughly 30 miles upriver from Pipiriki, this private enclave can only be reached by jet-boat; however, the remote location rewards you with magnificent forest vistas, birdsong at dawn, and the chance to bathe under the stars in an outdoor tub. **Pros:** memorable wilderness experience; range of lodging styles; packages including meals and jet-boat transport available. **Cons:** river access only. [$] *Rooms from: NZ$145* ✉ *Whanganui River, Box 4203* ☎ *06/385–4622, 0800/480–308* 🌐 *www.bridgetonowhere.co.nz* 🛏 *6 rooms, 2 bunkrooms, 4 cabins* 🍴 *Some meals.*

$$ B&B/INN Fodor's Choice ★ 🏨 **The Flying Fox.** The arrival is exceptional—whether by boat or the namesake Flying Fox, a cable car that carries you across to the remote, west bank of the Whanganui River. **Pros:** river wilderness; eco-friendly and organic; getting there. **Cons:** no cell phone reception. [$] *Rooms from: NZ$200* ✉ *Whanganui River Rd., Koriniti* ☎ *06/342–8160* 🌐 *www.theflyingfox.co.nz* 🛏 *2 cottages, 1 cabin* 🍴 *Some meals.*

SPORTS AND THE OUTDOORS

CANOEING AND KAYAKING

The main season for Whanganui River trips is between October and Easter; the busiest period is during the summer holidays (Christmas–January). Winter trips are also doable; the weather will be slightly colder, but you'll probably have the river to yourself. In summer, although there can be several hundred folks on the water at any one time, they are all moving in one direction, so a group can travel long periods without seeing another soul. The time they do come together is in the evenings, at park huts and campsites.

Travel on the river is generally in open, two-seater canoes or in kayaks. Tour options range from one-day picnic trips to five-day camping expeditions. What's known as the **Whanganui Journey** is regarded as one of nine "Great Walks" in New Zealand's national parks. Most tours go from Taumarunui to Pipiriki (a four- to five-day trip) or from Whakahoro to Pipiriki (three to four days). The latter is a true wilderness experience; there is no road access. A lower-river trip, from Pipiriki to Wanganui, passes through a mix of native forest, farmland, and several small communities.

To arrange a trip, contact a licensed commercial operator or the **Department of Conservation** (☎ 06/349–2100 ⊕ www.doc.govt.nz). No experience is necessary as the Whanganui is considered a beginner's river; however, while it's definitely not a white-water adventure, the river should be respected, and one or two rapids can play nasty tricks on paddlers. Operators can supply all equipment, transfers, and the necessary hut and campsite passes, whether the trip is independently undertaken or guided and catered. Prices vary considerably according to the length and style of the journey, but you can expect to pay from about NZ$55 for a simple one-day outing and in the NZ$600 to NZ$800 range for an all-inclusive three-day excursion.

Canoe Safaris. This operator's "big boats," six-person open canoes, are built along the lines of those once used by Canadian fur-trappers. Whanganui trips start at NZ$795 for a three-day safari with all equipment, including a waterproof gear bag and a Department of Conservation User Pass. These guides have been working the river for more than a quarter of a century, and they whip up mean three-course meals at campsites. Kayak and canoe rentals and combo jet-boat trips are also offered. ☎ 06/385–9237, 0800/272–3353 ⊕ www.canoesafaris.co.nz.

Yeti Tours. This outfit has been paddling the river for 25-plus years and knows how the water flows. Fully catered choices range from 2-day trips (NZ$420) to the only comprehensive 10-day guided tour from Taumarunui to Wanganui (most trips stop at Pipiriki). They include meals, kayaks, and a Department of Conservation pass. You provide (or rent) your own camping gear. ✉ 61 Clyde St., Ohakune ☎ 06/385–8197, 0800/322–388 ⊕ www.yetitours.co.nz.

WHANGANUI ECO-STAYS

The Flying Fox Lodge has cute, comfortable cottages built from recycled timbers; and the property, which is certified organic, is dotted with vegetable gardens and heritage fruit trees.

Accessible only by water, the **Bridge to Nowhere Lodge** is nestled on a small riverside patch of farmland. There's no electric power, but diesel generators, wood-fueled stoves, and helpful hosts provide all the comforts of home. Basic campsites are also available.

Both lodges are surrounded by Whanganui National Park and offer water activities.

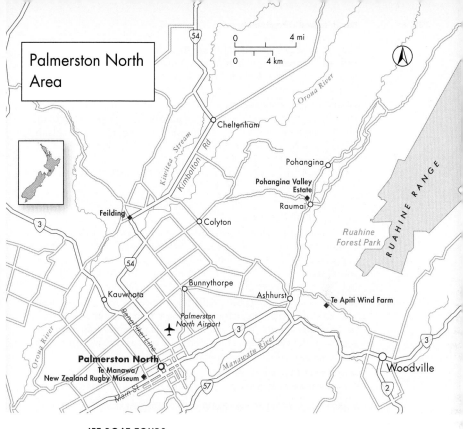

Palmerston North Area

JET-BOAT TOURS

Bridge to Nowhere. Jet-boats make the trip from Pipiriki to the Bridge to Nowhere (NZ$130) as well as to other natural and historic sights. The company also offers a host of additional activities, including canoeing, canoe/jet-boat combos, accommodations at the Bridge to Nowhere Lodge, and transport for mountain bikers tackling the Bridge to Nowhere section of the Mountains to Sea—Nga Ara Tuhono Cycle Trail. ☎ 0800/480–308 ⊕ www.bridgetonowhere.co.nz.

PALMERSTON NORTH

145 km (87 miles) northeast of Wellington, 72 km (45 miles) southeast of Wanganui.

Palmerston North—or "Palmy" as the locals call it—is home to several major educational and research institutes. Thanks to these, students make up one-third of the population. The biggest influence on the city is Massey University, one of the country's leading postsecondary institutions. It is set among huge trees and lovely gardens just across the Manawatu River on Palmerston North's southern edge. The campus includes the Sport and Rugby Institute, which serves as a training facility for players on the All Blacks (New Zealand's revered national rugby team) and other elite athletes.

The city provides services for the surrounding agricultural industry as well. Rolling sheep and cattle farms, stunning gardens, and country homestay retreats are all in close proximity, nestling at the foot of the steep Ruahine Ranges.

GETTING HERE AND AROUND

The Palmerston North Airport (PMR) is 5 km (3 miles) northeast of the city. Air New Zealand serves it with daily direct flights from Auckland, Hamilton, Wellington, and Christchurch; Jetstar flies direct from Auckland; and Originair flies direct from Nelson. Ground transportation options to the city center include Super Shuttle (NZ$18) and Palmerston North Taxis (NZ$25–NZ$30).

The scenic *Northern Explorer* train also stops here as it travels between Auckland and Wellington.

If you're driving, Palmerston North is about two hours north of Wellington (allow more time during busy holiday weekends), and six to seven hours south of Auckland, following State Highway 1 through the central North Island. Wanganui is a one-hour drive to the northwest, and Napier is just over a two-hour drive to the northeast.

InterCity and Nakedbus offer daily bus services from all major North Island communities. They arrive and depart from the Palmerston North i-SITE Visitor Information Centre. Activity in the city is centered on the streets around the Square. From there, you can easily explore the cafés, boutiques, art galleries, and museums on foot.

Airport Palmerston North Airport. ⊠ *Airport Dr.* ☎ *06/351–4415* ⊕ *www.pnairport.co.nz.*

Airport Transfers Palmerston North Taxis. ⊠ *Palmerston North* ☎ *06/355–5333.* **Super Shuttle.** ⊠ *Palmerston North* ☎ *0800/748–885* ⊕ *www.supershuttle.co.nz.*

Bus Depot Palmerston North Bus Depot. ⊠ *Palmerston North i-SITE Visitor Information Centre, The Square.*

Train Station Palmerston North Train Station. ⊠ *Matthew Ave.*

TOURS

Manawatu Gorge Experience Jet. Few rivers cut right through a mountain range, as does the Manawatu. It scythes a deep, forest-lined gorge through the North Island divide, separating the Ruahine and Tararua ranges. This company runs trips into the gorge on jet-boats, which climb narrow chutes, skim past huge boulders, and reveal scenery that road travelers can't see. The 25-minute rides depart from the eastern side of the gorge, a 25-minute drive from Palmerston North. Reservations are essential, and a minimum of six passengers is required. ⊠ *Napier Rd. (State Hwy. 3), Woodville* ☎ *0800/945–335* ✍ *tours@ manawatugorgejet.com* 🖱 *NZ$75.*

VISITOR INFORMATION

Contacts Palmerston North i-SITE Visitor Information Centre. ⊠ *The Square* ☎ *06/350–1922, 0800/626–292* ⊕ *www.manawatunz.co.nz.*

EXPLORING

New Zealand Rugby Museum. The only one of its kind in the country, this museum—located upstairs in the Te Manawa complex—is worth a visit whether or not you're a rugby fan because it offers insight into a sport that many New Zealanders treat like a religion. The growing collection of rugby memorabilia dates back to the start of this national game in 1870. Interactive components even let visitors "have a go"; you can kick, tackle, and jump in the lineout, testing your playing skills quite safely. ⊠ *326 Main St.* ☏ *06/358–6947* ⊕ *www.rugbymuseum.co.nz* 🎫 *NZ$12.50* ⊘ *Daily 10–5.*

Pohangina Valley Estate. Sheltered beneath the Ruahine Ranges, 30 minutes from Palmerston North, this young winery is the only vineyard in the delightful Pohangina Valley. It is unpretentious, even though its products have collected coveted Bragato awards, among others. You can mingle with the chooks and dogs as you chat with the owners, sisters Fiona and Bronwyn, about the hands-on work of running a wine business. Pick up a bottle or two before you leave (tastings are available); oil from the estate's olive grove can be purchased, too. ⊠ *1034 Valley Rd., Pohangina* ☏ *06/354–7948* ⊕ *www.pohanginavalleyestate. co.nz* 🎫 *Free* ⊘ *Jan.–Apr., weekdays 11–4:30; Oct.–Dec., Sun. 11–4:30, other times by appointment.*

Te Apiti Wind Farm. The original New Zealand wind farm makes a dramatic sight on the ranges that overlook Palmerston North. A drive up steep Saddle Road to the largest windmills (there is a parking lot beneath a huge one) yields fantastic views. Look south and you'll also see the Tararua Wind Farm, currently the country's biggest. Returning to the city via Woodville and the Manawatu Gorge makes an enjoyable, scenic road trip. Maps are available from Palmerston North's i-SITE Centre. ⊠ *Saddle Rd., Ashhurst.*

FAMILY **Te Manawa.** This distinctive complex is divided into three sections that weave together the region's art, science, and history, including natural history and the history of Rangitane, the local Māori people. For young ones, the Mind Science Centre, with its quirky interactive exhibits, is entertaining and educational. Te Manawa also houses the New Zealand Rugby Museum. ⊠ *326 Main St.* ☏ *06/355–5000* ⊕ *www. temanawa.co.nz* 🎫 *Life and Art galleries free; charges for some exhibitions* ⊘ *Daily 10–5.*

OFF THE BEATEN PATH

Feilding. For a look at an authentic New Zealand farming town, take a side trip to Feilding, 20 km (12 miles) northwest of Palmerston North.

The Feilding Saleyards, which rank among the largest livestock sale yards in the southern hemisphere, are close to the Edwardian-style town square. At least twice weekly, farmers buy and sell more than 15,000 sheep and 1,400 head of cattle here. Every Friday at 11, the Feilding Saleyards Guided Tour (NZ$10, bookings essential) takes you through the sheep pens and state-of-the-art computerized cattle auction pavilion, providing a fascinating glimpse at one of New Zealand's oldest farming traditions. After the tour, visit the rustic Saleyards Café, where farmers meet for pie and chips or a toasted steak sandwich. Other local attractions include the Friday morning farmers' market, the

Coachhouse Museum (displaying restored vehicles from the pioneering era; NZ$10), and Manfeild Park (which hosts events from motor sports to equestrian). You could putter about for half a day in the town itself, browsing through bookshops, art galleries, the community Arts Centre, and Focal Point (a boutique movie theater and café). From Feilding, Kimbolton Road passes through prime sheep-farming country to Kimbolton Village, 28 km (17 miles) away. Within a few minutes' drive of it are two outstanding gardens with rhododendrons and myriad other plants: Cross Hills (NZ$10; daily September–May) and Heritage Park Garden (NZ$7; daily year-round). ✉ *Feilding* ☎ *06/323–3318 Feilding & District Information Centre* 🌐 *www.feilding.co.nz.*

WHERE TO EAT

$$$$ INTERNATIONAL Fodor'sChoice ★ 🍴 **Bella's Café.** Serving a mix of Mediterranean and Pacific Rim dishes, with a touch of Thai flavor, Bella's has been a city favorite for more than a decade. Smart and cheerful, it's right on the Square. Start the day right by ordering breakfast here (anyone for toasted brioche with Bella's own preserves?) or end in it style by choosing from the tempting dinner menu. Try a cashew-and-coconut prawn appetizer, followed by a classic char-grilled beef fillet with truffle-mushroom bread-and-butter pudding or perhaps panfried venison with a caramelized onion and blue cheese tart. The dark chocolate mousse with Chantilly cream is a perfect finishing touch. [$] *Average main: NZ$36* ✉ *2 The Square* ☎ *06/357–8616* 🌐 *www.bellas.co.nz.*

$$$ NEW ZEALAND FAMILY 🍴 **Brewer's Apprentice.** Plenty of brick, stone, and timber lend character to this restaurant near the Square, while open fires, a pair of bars, plus a quiet dining alcove add ambience. In addition to the entire range of New Zealand–crafted Monteith's beer, the menu lists lunchtime favorites like big burgers and Monteith's-battered fish-and-chips. Dinner goes upscale, with choices including pulled pork ragout with pappardelle and top-quality beef dishes (picture Angus fillets or beef bourguignonne). Look for specials, such as NZ$15 steak nights. Events and live music provide entertainment through the week. [$] *Average main: NZ$29* ✉ *334 Church St.* ☎ *06/358–8888* 🌐 *www.brewersapprentice.co.nz.*

$$ NEW ZEALAND FAMILY 🍴 **Café Cuba.** Just off the Square, funky Café Cuba is a popular local haunt for breakfast, brunch, lunch, dinner, and after shows. Laid-back music plays in the background, and there are plenty of magazines to peruse over breakfast options like bubble-and-squeak with bacon or the ubiquitous eggs Benedict. Later in the day, classic fish-and-chips, *kūmara* (sweet potato) cakes, and herbed mussels satisfy. Pastas, salads, and sweet things fill the lunch cabinet, and the counter staff tempts with interesting smoothies and milk shakes. If you're traveling with children, this place has a great kids' menu, too. [$] *Average main: NZ$17* ✉ *Cuba and George Sts.* ☎ *06/356–5750* 🌐 *www.cafecuba.co.nz.*

$$ CAFÉ FAMILY 🍴 **The Herb Farm and Cafe.** About 10 minutes from the city, this farm café is a worthy lunch stop for those exploring the countryside or returning from a trip to the Te Apiti Wind Farm. Not surprisingly, the fare is local, organic, and includes healthy infusions of fresh herbs—homemade tofu herb fritters being a prime example. It serves a wholesome selection of Kiwi breakfast standards, including free-range bacon and eggs; tasty sandwiches and salads dominate the lunch menu. Walk off the meal and

calm the spirit by wandering through 2 acres of herb gardens (NZ$3.50 self-guided, map provided); the herbs are used in healing products that are made and sold here. $ *Average main: NZ$18* ⌧ *88 Grove Rd.* ☎ *06/326–8633* ⊕ *herbfarm.co.nz* ⊘ *No dinner.*

$$$$
MODERN NEW
ZEALAND
Fodor's Choice
★

✕ **Nero Restaurant.** In a charming old Victorian-style villa on a quiet inner-city street, Nero consistently wins regional restaurant awards and has received New Zealand's prestigious Beef and Lamb Excellence Award. Head chef and owner Scott Kennedy describes the cuisine as "contemporary New Zealand, along with a touch of fusion to celebrate our cultural diversity." Thus the menu features garlic pizza bread and flat Turkish bread starters as well as Asian-flavored lunch dishes, such as crispy duck leg curry and Thai beef salad. Options like locally farmed beef fillet with smoked mushrooms and potato-leek rösti or phyllo-wrapped chicken breast with pumpkin risotto entice diners at dinner. $ *Average main: NZ$37* ⌧ *36 Amesbury St.* ☎ *06/354–0312* ⊕ *www.cafenero.co.nz* ⊘ *Closed Sun. No lunch Sat.*

WHERE TO STAY

$$
HOTEL

⌂ **Distinction Hotel Palmerston North.** Just minutes by foot from shops, theaters, and cafés, the city's largest, Qualmark-rated four-star hotel occupies a 1927 heritage building (check out the cage-style elevator, one of the country's oldest). **Pros:** in the city; good facilities; off-street parking; elevator access. **Cons:** though comfortable, guest rooms lack character; traffic noise. $ *Rooms from: NZ$160* ⌧ *175 Cuba St.* ☎ *06/355–5895, 0800/554-490* ⊕ *www.travelodge.co.nz* ⊷ *85 rooms* ⦵ *No meals.*

$$$$
B&B/INN

⌂ **Hiwinui Country Estate.** For a luxurious farm stay and spa day, make the 18-km (11-mile) drive from Palmerston North to this 1,600-acre sheep-and-dairy farm, where you'll be hosted by a family that has worked the land for five generations; photos and artifacts relate their history. **Pros:** luxury on a working farm; interesting artwork; spa. **Cons:** not handy to town; no kids allowed. $ *Rooms from: NZ$440* ⌧ *465 Ashhurst–Bunnythorpe Rd.* ☎ *06/329–2838* ⊕ *www.hiwinui.co.nz* ⊷ *2 rooms* ⦵ *Breakfast.*

$$
B&B/INN

⌂ **Riverhills.** Friendly hosts Ken and Marie Baird, who have worked in hospitality in Britain and France, built their home with views in mind—and you can enjoy them from the cozy lounge overlooking the river or from one of the warm, comfortable rooms in the separate guest wing, all of which have private decks. **Pros:** thoughtful, knowledgeable hosts; river and mountains views; riverside walkway by the front door. **Cons:** so popular it's often booked up; five-minute drive from town center. $ *Rooms from: NZ$130* ⌧ *41 Dittmer Dr.* ☎ *06/357–8140* ⊕ *www.riverhills.biz* ⊘ *Closed July and Aug.* ⊷ *3 rooms* ⦵ *Breakfast.*

NIGHTLIFE AND PERFORMING ARTS
NIGHTLIFE

The Fish Cocktail Bar. Along with other cafés, bars, and pubs in this trendy little brick lane beside the city's grand Regent Theatre, The Fish is a popular late-night haunt. Open Wednesday to Saturday, its interior is a mix of tapa cloth and warm woods. ⌧ *Regent Arcade* ☎ *06/357–9845.*

PERFORMING ARTS

Several theaters in the city center host local and visiting productions.

Centrepoint. The only professional theater company outside New Zealand's main cities has a regular schedule of changing performances. ⊠ *Pitt and Church Sts.* ☎ *06/354–5740* ⊕ *www.centrepoint.co.nz.*

Regent on Broadway. Ballet troupes, traveling musical productions, opera companies, and rock groups take the stage at this opulent theater, which was built in 1930. ⊠ *63 Broadway* ☎ *06/350–2100* ⊕ *www. regent.co.nz.*

SHOPPING

Palmerston North's shopping is concentrated around the Square; Broadway Avenue and the Plaza shopping centers are within easy walking distance. George Street, which is also just off the Square, has a number of specialty shops, galleries, and cafés.

Bruce McKenzie Books. This is considered among New Zealand's leading independent bookstores (and they are becoming a rare breed). ⊠ *51 George St.* ☎ *06/356–9922.*

Taylor Jensen Fine Arts. This gallery sells contemporary and traditional New Zealand and international art, sculpture, jewelry, crafts, and furniture. ⊠ *33 George St.* ☎ *06/355–4278.*

7

WELLINGTON AND
THE WAIRARAPA

WELCOME TO
WELLINGTON AND THE WAIRARAPA

TOP REASONS TO GO

★ **Arts and Culture:**
The national symphony, ballet, and opera are based here. And the biennial New Zealand International Arts Festival offers a wide program of drama, music, dance, plus other arts events.

★ **A Wealth of Wineries:**
Spend a day or two wine tasting your way through the Wairarapa, home to more than 30 vineyards.

★ **Eclectic Cuisine:**
The great variety of Wellington's restaurants allows you to sample foods from dozens of cuisines, while also enjoying plenty of down-to-earth Kiwi fare.

★ **Ferry Tales:** Wellington is the North Island terminal for the ferry crossing to the South Island. In good weather, this is undoubtedly one of the world's finest boating experiences.

★ **The Waterfront:**
Meandering along Wellington's waterfront is a great way to spend a day. You can visit both the Museum of New Zealand Te Papa Tongarewa and the Wellington Museum for free.

1 Wellington. People are never far from the water here; surfers can be happy on beaches that are virtually in the city, and families can take a meal overlooking the harbor. Wellington has also gained a reputation for fostering the arts, and it's easily explored on foot.

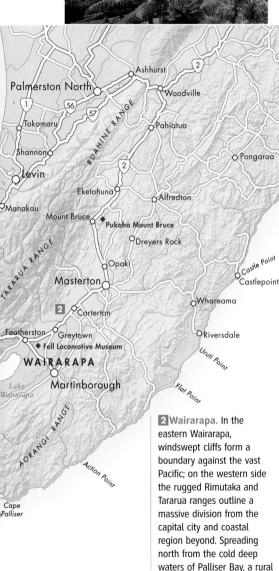

GETTING ORIENTED

All main roads from Wellington and the adjacent Wairarapa head north, as these regions are at the North Island's southern point where the sometimes-stormy waters of Cook Strait divide the country's two major islands. Separated by mountain ranges that virtually tumble into the Strait, road travel between the two regions is via the Hutt Valley and the winding Rimutaka Hill road. Expect peaceful river scenery, a green and pleasant outlook, and spectacular views.

7

2 **Wairarapa.** In the eastern Wairarapa, windswept cliffs form a boundary against the vast Pacific; on the western side the rugged Rimutaka and Tararua ranges outline a massive division from the capital city and coastal region beyond. Spreading north from the cold deep waters of Palliser Bay, a rural panorama of fields and quiet vineyards stretches north as far as the eye can see.

Updated by
Bob Marriott

Wellington has developed the lively, friendly, and infectious spirit of a city coming into its own. From the windswept green heights overlooking New Zealand's capital, a crystal-clear winter morning reveals stunning views over the deceptively quiet waters of Cook Strait stretching to the snowcapped mountains of the South Island; and it's sheer heaven on a mild summer night when a silver medallion of moon tops mysterious misty hillsides. People are making their way to Wellington, and not merely because it's the sailing point for ferries heading south.

You might find yourself content to laze around the harbor, perhaps sipping a chilled glass of Chardonnay from a nearby vineyard. The burgeoning film industry—thanks to the *Lord of the Rings (LOTR)* and *The Hobbit* extravaganzas—has injected life into the local arts scene. Ardent film fans can still visit the many *LOTR* sites around the region, but everyone benefits from the lively cafés and the rapidly expanding restaurant culture. On the waterfront the first-class Museum of New Zealand Te Papa Tongarewa has many hands-on exhibits equally fascinating for children and adults, while the Wellington Museum is dedicated to the city's history.

Wellington and the adjacent Hutt Valley are the southern gateway to the Wairarapa, a region whose name has become synonymous with wine. Journey over the hills and meander along quiet byways from vineyard to vineyard for a day—or two, or three—of wine tasting. If wine isn't your thing, the Wairarapa is still worth an excursion for its gardens, walking trails, and fishing opportunities. Head for the coast, too, where waves crash against craggy beaches, and the dramatic sunsets intoxicate you with their beauty.

PLANNING

In Wellington make time to enjoy a relaxing day on the waterfront; it's a stone's throw from the city center. This area is mainly flat, easy walking with interesting shopping and numerous cafés and restaurants. You don't need a car in the city, but to explore the Wairarapa and its vineyard-rich countryside, it's best to make a day trip of it and drive. You also need to drive to go north to the long sweeping beaches of the Kapiti Coast.

WHEN TO GO

November to mid-April is the best time weather-wise in the Wellington area. Most establishments are open (apart from Christmas Day, New Year's Day, and Good Friday). In Wairarapa book well ahead if you're traveling during summer school holidays from mid-December to the end of January. From February to April, you can expect fewer crowds and many brilliant, warm days. Winters bring more rain, but they're rarely bitterly cold. Be prepared for unpredictable weather, though; rain and southerly gales are possible even during the summer.

FESTIVALS

Matariki. One of the key Māori occasions in Wellington is Matariki, the North Island Māori New Year in late May–early June, which begins with the first new moon after the appearance of Matariki (Pleiades). The Museum of New Zealand Te Papa Tongarewa hosts nearly a month of musical, storytelling, and dance performances; events kick off with a ceremony at dawn. Brochures, available at the museum, have details. For a unique gift or souvenir, Te Papa Press also publishes a superbly illustrated Matariki calendar; it runs from June until May and is based on traditional lore of the seasons. ⊠ *Museum of New Zealand Te Papa Tongarewa, 55 Cable St., Wellington* ⊕ *www.tepapa.govt.nz/WhatsOn/ Matariki.*

New Zealand International Arts Festival. The country's major arts event is held February through March on even-numbered years at venues across the city. A huge array of international talent in music, drama, dance, the visual arts, and media descends upon Wellington. Events fill up quickly; check online for program information, and book a month in ahead if you can. ⊠ *Wellington* ☎ *04/473–0149* ⊕ *www.festival.co.nz.*

Summer City. One of the largest summer fests spans six weeks and hosts more than 70 events throughout the city. ⊠ *Wellington* ⊕ *wellington. govt.nz/events/annual-events/summer-city.*

GETTING HERE AND AROUND

AIR TRAVEL

Wellington International Airport (WLG) lies about 8 km (5 miles) from the city. Domestic carriers serving Wellington include **Air New Zealand, Qantas, Jetstar,** and **Sounds Air.** You can rent a car on-site or catch a shuttle into town; a taxi from the airport to central Wellington costs about NZ$35.

Airport Wellington Airport. ⊠ *Stewart Duff Dr., Rongotai* ☎ *04/385–5100* ⊕ *www.wellingtonairport.co.nz.*

Airline Contacts Air New Zealand. ☎ *0800/737–000* ⊕ *www.airnewzealand. co.nz.* **Jetstar.** ☎ *0800/800–995* ⊕ *www.jetstar.com.* **Qantas.** ☎ *0800 /808–767* ⊕ *www.qantas.com.* **Sounds Air.** ☎ *0800/505–005* ⊕ *www.soundsair.com.*

Airport Transfers Airport Flyer. ⊠ *Wellington* ☎ *0800/801–7000* ⊕ *www.airportflyer.co.nz.* **Co-operative Shuttle.** ⊠ *Wellington* ☎ *04/387–8787.*

BOAT AND FERRY TRAVEL

The **Interislander** runs a ferry service between Wellington and Picton; the boats take three hours. Fares vary by time of year, ranging from NZ$55 to NZ$75 one-way per person; for a car and driver, fares are NZ$174 to NZ$250. You can book up to six months in advance. A free bus leaves Platform 9 at the Wellington Railway Station for the ferry terminal 50 minutes before sailings. **Bluebridge Cook Strait Ferry** vessels, *The Strait Feronia* and *The Straitsman,* sail up to four times per day between Wellington and Picton. Fares are NZ$53 to NZ$73 one-way per person, and NZ$173 to NZ$199 for a driver with car up to 20 feet long. Most car-rental agencies offer North Island–South Island transfer programs.

Boat and Ferry Contacts Bluebridge Cook Strait Ferry. ⊠ *Wellington* ☎ *0800/844–844* ⊕ *www.bluebridge.co.nz.* **Interislander.** ⊠ *Wellington* ☎ *0800/802–802* ⊕ *www.interislander.co.nz.*

BUS TRAVEL

InterCity and the **Nakedbus** both operate daily long-distance bus services, connecting Wellington to most other cities and major towns in New Zealand.

Bus Depot Wellington Bus Depot. ⊠ *Wellington Railway Station, Bunny St. and Waterloo Quay, Wellington.*

Bus Contacts InterCity. ☎ *09/913–6100* ⊕ *www.intercity.co.nz.* **Nakedbus.** ☎ *09/979—1616* ⊕ *nakedbus.com.*

CAR TRAVEL

The main access to the city is via the Wellington Urban Motorway, which starts just after Highways 1 and 2 merge, a few miles north of the city center. The motorway links the city center with all towns and cities to the north.

TRAIN TRAVEL

Metlink operates trains connecting the Wellington Railway Station with the Hutt Valley and Masterton. If you're a fan of scenic train trips, try the *Northern Explorer*; linking Wellington and Auckland, it stops in Paraparaumu, Palmerston North, Ohakune, National Park, Otorohanga (near Waitomo), Hamilton, and Papakura. The train travels southbound on Monday, Thursday, and Saturday and northbound on Tuesday, Friday, and Sunday.

Train Station Wellington Railway Station. ⊠ *Bunny St. and Waterloo Quay, Wellington.*

Train Contacts Metlink. ⊠ *Wellington* ☎ *0800/801–700* ⊕ *www.metlink.org.nz.* **Northern Explorer.** ☎ *0800/872–467* ⊕ *www.kiwirailscenic.co.nz.*

RESTAURANTS

In Wellington, restaurants, cafés, and sports bars spring up overnight like mushrooms. Although you'll never be without the classic meal of steak, fries, and ale, city eateries have also embraced more adventurous fare. Chinese, Thai, Japanese, Malaysian, Mexican, and Italian cuisines are increasingly common. Indigenous food, too, is appearing in restaurants around the city—native plants might be paired with traditional seafood or made into sauces to accompany meat or sweet-potato dishes.

In rural areas outside Wellington, the wine industry has revolutionized local tables, with excellent dining and wine-tasting spots. In the Wairarapa, restaurants are winning a reputation for creative cuisine.

Generally, lunch runs from noon until 2, and most restaurants close for a few hours before opening for dinner around 6. On Monday, many restaurants are shuttered. Dress codes are still really relaxed; jeans would be frowned on only in the top restaurants.

HOTELS

Accommodations in Wellington range from no-frills backpacker hostels and motel units to sleek central hotels and classic bed-and-breakfasts in colonial-era villas.

As more people move into the city, apartments moonlighting as "serviced-apartment" hotels are also gaining steam. Rates are significantly more expensive than those of the average motel, but they're a good option if you're planning to stay a while. Most of these apartment-hotel hybrids have weekend or long-term specials.

Lodgings generally do not have air-conditioning, but the temperate weather in Wellington rarely warrants it.

Hotel reviews have been shortened. For full information, visit Fodors. com. Use the coordinate (⊕ B2) at the end of each listing to locate a site on the corresponding map.

WHAT IT COSTS IN NEW ZEALAND DOLLARS				
	$	$$	$$$	$$$$
Restaurants	under NZ$15	NZ$15–NZ$20	NZ$21–NZ$30	over NZ$30
Hotels	under NZ$125	NZ$125–NZ$200	NZ$201–NZ$300	over NZ$300

Restaurant prices are the average cost of a main course at dinner or, if dinner is not served, at lunch. Hotel prices are the lowest cost of a standard double room in high season.

VISITOR INFORMATION

There is a comprehensive information service for the city and surrounding districts—Positively Wellington Tourism—which covers everything you need to know. The Wellington i-SITE Visitor Information Centre, in Civic Square, can provide you with brochures, tour bookings, theater tickets, and more. It also has a number of computers available for Internet access, plus a souvenir shop.

Contacts Positively Wellington Tourism. ✉ *Wellington* ☎ *04/916–1205* ⊕ *www.WellingtonNZ.com.* **Wellington i-SITE Visitor Information Centre.** ✉ *Civic Administration Bldg., Victoria and Wakefield Sts., Wellington* ☎ *04/802–4860* ⊕ *www.wellingtonNZ.com.*

WELLINGTON

Wellington, the seat of government since 1865, is between the sea and towering hillsides that form a natural arena with the harbor as the stage. Ferries carve patterns on the green water while preening seabirds survey the scene. Houses cascade down the steep hills, creating a vibrant collage of colorful rooftops against a spectacular green backdrop. An old brick monastery peers down on the marina—a jigsaw of masts and sails bobbing alongside the impressive Museum of New Zealand Te Papa Tongarewa. Modern high-rises gaze over Port Nicholson, one of the finest natural anchorages in the world. Known to local Māori as the Great Harbor of Tara, its two massive arms form the "jaws of the fish of Maui" (Maui being the name of a god from Māori legend).

Civic Square represents the heart of the city and forms a busy shopping area with Willis and Cuba streets. The entertainment district is centered on Courtenay Place, south of Civic Square. Thorndon, the oldest part of the city, is notable for its many historic wooden houses just north of the Parliamentary district, which includes the distinctive (some might say bizarre) "Beehive" government building.

At the northern end of the waterfront, the Westpac Trust Stadium, home to rugby matches, soccer games, and rock concerts, dominates the skyline, and Lambton Quay is part of a seafront constructed on reclaimed land. At the southern end of the harbor, Norfolk pines line the broad sweep of Oriental Bay, a suburb with a small beach and a wide promenade, backed by art deco buildings and Wellington's most expensive real estate.

GETTING HERE AND AROUND

Wellington is a great **walking** city. The compact area around Lambton Quay and on Cuba Street is flat. A stroll along the waterfront around Oriental Bay provides outstanding sea views. If you head for the hills, take the cable car, and see the sights before walking down.

For **cyclists,** designated bike lanes in and around Wellington are marked with a continuous white line and a white bike image on the pavement. More details about urban cycling are on the city's website, ⊕ *www.wcc.govt.nz.*

Buses are a great way to navigate the city, though service outside the city center is sporadic. In Wellington, buses are operated by several companies; for information on all routes and fares contact Metlink (☏ *0800/801–700* ⊕ *www.metlink.org.nz*). The main terminals are at the Wellington Railway Station (Bunny Street and Waterloo Quay) and at Courtenay Place. For all inner-city trips, pay when you board the bus. Bus stops are marked with red-and-white signs. A Bus-about ticket costs NZ$9.50 but is not available for the Airport Flyer.

You don't need a **car** to get around central Wellington—and you probably don't want one as its many one-way streets can frustrate drivers. Having one, however, is essential if you hope to fully explore the outlying regions.

Taxi ride rates are NZ$3.50 on entry, then NZ$3.10 per 1 km (½ mile). Taxis idle outside the railway station, on Dixon Street, and along Courtenay Place and Lambton Quay.

TOURS

BOAT TOURS

Fodor's Choice
★

Dominion Post Ferry. East by West Ferries runs the *Dominion Post*, a commuter service between the city and Days Bay, on the east side of Port Nicholson; it's one of the best value tours around. En route you can stop at Matiu/Somes Island; this former quarantine station makes a unique picnic spot on a warm afternoon. Days Bay itself has seaside village character, a lovely swimming beach, local craft shops, and great views of Wellington. Weekdays the catamaran departs from Queens Wharf every 25 minutes between 6:25 am and 8:45 am, then at 10, noon, and 2:15, and every half hour from 4:30 until 7 pm. The return boats leave Days Bay roughly 30 minutes later. The sailing schedule is cut back on weekends and holidays but additional Harbour Explorer Tours visit Petone Wharf and Seatoun Wharf. You can pick up tickets at the ferry terminal between 8 and 5; otherwise, tickets can be bought on board. All sailings may be canceled in stormy weather. ⊠ *Queens Wharf* ☎ *04/499–1282, 04/494–3339* ⊕ *www.eastbywest.co.nz* ⊠ *NZ$11 one-way fare; NZ$22 round-trip with Matiu/Somes Island stop.*

BUS TOURS

Wellington Rover. This outfit's options range from a half-day city tour to a full-day *Lord of the Rings* sites tour, which includes a picnic lunch. A seal colony tour is also available. All leave from the i-SITE Visitor Information Centre. Reservations are essential. ⊠ *Wellington* ☎ *0800/426–211* ⊕ *www.wellingtonrover.co.nz* ⊠ *From NZ$95.*

PRIVATE GUIDES

Hammonds Wellington Tours. For wine tastings and a gourmet vineyard lunch, take the Martinborough wine tour by coach or train. Other choices include the Kapiti Coast Kiwi Experience and the Wellington City Sights and Coastline Tour. Run by an award-winning team, all are good value. ⊠ *Wellington* ☎ *04/472–0869* ⊕ *www. wellingtonsightseeingtours.com* ⊠ *From NZ$55.*

VISITOR INFORMATION

Contacts Wellington i-SITE Visitor Information Centre. ⊠ *Civic Administration Bldg., Victoria and Wakefield Sts.* ☎ *04/802–4860* ⊕ *www.wellingtonnz.com.*

EXPLORING

TOP ATTRACTIONS

Kelburn Cable Car. The Swiss-built funicular railway makes a short-but-sharp climb to Kelburn Terminal, from which you get great views across parks and city buildings to Port Nicholson. Sit on the left side during the six-minute journey for the best scenery. At the top, a small Cable Car Museum in the old winding house has a free display of restored cable cars. ⊠ *280 Lambton Quay, at Grey St. and Upland Rd.* ☎ *04/472–2199* ⊕ *www.wellingtonnz.com/cablecar* ⊠ *NZ$4 one-way fare; NZ$7 round-trip* ☉ *Departures about every 10 mins, weekdays 7 am–10 pm, weekends 9 am–10 pm.*

Lady Norwood Rose Garden. On a fine summer day you couldn't find a better place to enjoy the fragrance of magnificent flowers. This rose garden is the most popular part of the **Wellington Botanic Garden.** Situated on a plateau, the formal circular layout consists of 106 beds, each planted with a single variety of modern and traditional shrubs. Climbing roses cover a brick-and-timber colonnade on the perimeter. Adjacent to the rose beds, the Begonia House conservatory is filled with delicate plants. ⊠ *North end of Wellington Botanic Garden* ☎ *04/499–1400* ✉ *Free* ⊙ *Main gardens daily sunrise–sunset.*

NEED A BREAK?

Picnic Botanic Garden Café. In a sun-drenched corner of the Botanic Gardens, this delightful café is in a large conservatory attached to the Begonia House. You can't go wrong with the menu, which includes goodies such as potato-and-feta hash cakes and eggs Benedict. There's also a selection of delicious muffins and cakes. Sit outside, sip a latte, and smell the roses. ⊠ *Tinakori Rd.* ☎ *04/472–6002* ⊕ *www.picniccafe.co.nz* ⊙ *Daily 8:30–4.*

FAMILY

Fodor's Choice

★

Museum of New Zealand Te Papa Tongarewa. Te Papa Tongarewa (the Māori translation is "container of treasures") provides an essential introduction to the country's people, cultures, landforms, flora, and fauna; bringing together the latest technology, interactive exhibits, and storytelling, it shares New Zealand's past and present. Whether you want to enter a carved *marae* (Māori meetinghouse), walk through living native bush, be shaken in the Earthquake House, or see a colossal squid, there's inspiration for everyone. Don't miss *Gallipoli: The Scale of Our War.* Working closely with Weta Workshop, the museum has created a wrenching exhibit that uses giant sculptures, 3-D maps, models, and more to detail New Zealand's involvement in the World War I landings at Anzac Cove. ⊠ *55 Cable St.* ☎ *04/381–7000* ⊕ *www.tepapa.govt.nz* ✉ *Free; guided tours from NZ$12; some exhibitions from NZ$15* ⊙ *Daily 10–6.*

Otari-Wilton's Bush. Devoted to gathering and preserving indigenous plants, Otari's collection is the largest of its kind. With clearly marked bushwalks and landscape demonstration gardens, it aims to educate the public and ensure the survival of New Zealand's unique plant life. While in the garden, you'll learn to identify forest plants, from the various *blechnum* ferns underfoot to the tallest trees overhead. An aerial walkway crosses high above the bush, giving an unusual vantage point over the gardens. Look and listen for the native birds that flock to this haven: the bellbird (*korimako*), New Zealand wood pigeon (*kereru*), and parson bird (*tūī*) among others. Take the No. 14 Wilton bus from downtown (20 minutes) and ask the driver to let you off at the gardens. ⊠ *Wilton Rd., Wilton* ☎ *04/475–3245* ✉ *Free* ⊙ *Daily dawn–dusk.*

Wellington Botanic Garden. In the hills overlooking downtown is a concentration of splendidly varied terrain. Woodland gardens under native and exotic trees fill the valleys, water-loving plants line a pond and mountain streams, and lawns spread over flatter sections with beds of bright seasonal bulbs and annuals. The lovely **Lady Norwood Rose Garden** is in the northeast part of the garden. If you don't want to walk the hill up, the **Kelburn Cable Car** can take you. Or catch the No. 12 bus (direction: Karori) from Lambton Quay to the main (Glenmore Street)

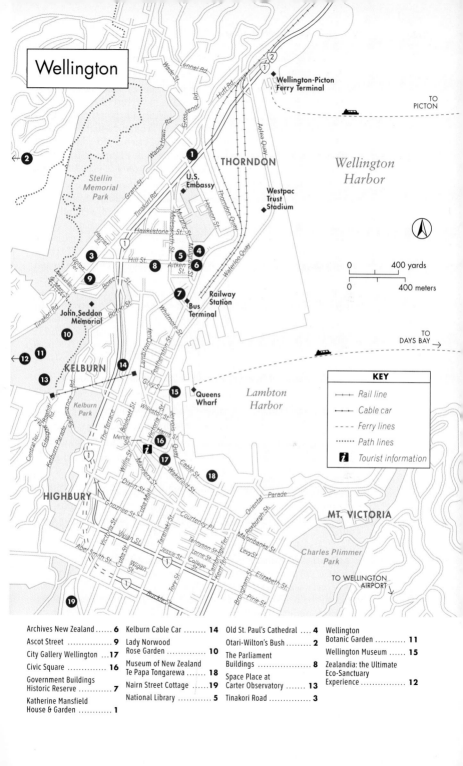

Wellington

THORNDON

Wellington-Picton
Ferry Terminal

TO
PICTON

*Wellington
Harbor*

Stellin
Memorial
Park

U.S.
Embassy

Westpac
Trust
Stadium

John Seddon
Memorial

Railway
Station

Bus
Terminal

KELBURN

Kelburn
Park

Queens
Wharf

*Lambton
Harbor*

TO
DAYS BAY →

KEY	
⊢——⊣	*Rail line*
•——•	*Cable car*
- - - -	*Ferry lines*
··········	*Path lines*
🛈	*Tourist information*

HIGHBURY

MT. VICTORIA

Charles Plimmer
Park

TO WELLINGTON
AIRPORT

0 ____ 400 yards
0 ____ 400 meters

entrance. ✉ *Upland Rd. and Glenmore St., parking lot on Tinakori Rd.* ☎ *04/499–1400 gardens* 🔗 *Free* ☽ *Main gardens daily sunrise–sunset.*

Wellington Museum. You can smell the burlap sacks, hear the gulls, and see the (mechanical) rats scuttling around in this refurbished 1892 bond store, now a museum that portrays the history of the original Māori tribes and the European settlers who arrived around 1840. Spread over four floors, the displays cover work, leisure, crime, and education in Wellington, telling stories of local life that will be of interest to visitors of all ages. ✉ *The Bond Store, Queens Wharf* ☎ *04/472–8904* ⊕ *www. museumswellington.org.nz* 🔗 *Free* ☽ *Daily 10–5.*

Zealandia: The Ultimate Eco-Sanctuary Experience. Just minutes from downtown Wellington, 623 acres of regenerating forest and wetland have been turned into a unique safe haven for some of New Zealand's most-endangered native animals. A specially designed fence creates a cage-free sanctuary for species that had disappeared from the mainland. Tuatara, New Zealand's unique "living fossil," are breeding, as are takahe and saddleback, which have both been brought back from the brink of extinction. Pick up a map and explore at your leisure, or take a free 45-minute guided walk. The flashlight-led night-time tour is also very popular; departing about 30 minutes before sunset, it provides a glimpse into the nocturnal world—you might even spy a little spotted kiwi (NZ$75; 2½ hours; no children under 12). ✉ *Waiapu Rd., end of Waiapu Rd., Karori* ☎ *04/920–9213* ⊕ *www.visitzealandia.com* 🔗 *NZ$17.50* ☽ *Daily 10–5.*

NEED A BREAK?

Smith the Grocer. Sip your coffee at this character-filled spot, where ornaments range from old radios and beer crates to an ancient set of golf clubs. The menu features Kiwi comfort food, like a bacon-beef burger with smoked cheese or savory mince on toast with two poached eggs. There is a selection of tempting cakes and scones as well. ✉ *The Old Bank Arcade, 233–237 Lambton Quay* ☎ *04/473–8591* ⊕ *www.smiththegrocer.co.nz.*

WORTH NOTING

Archives New Zealand. History buffs should make a beeline here, as the national archives are a gold mine of documents, photographs, and maps. Records of New Zealand ancestry from as far back as the early 1800s trace the country's development, making this a great place for New Zealanders to research their family history. One special highlight is *Te Tiriti o Waitangi,* the Treaty of Waitangi, which is now on display in a new purpose-built interactive visitor space around the corner in the Molesworth Street building. This controversial 1840 agreement between the British crown and more than 500 Māori chiefs is considered the founding document of modern New Zealand. The oldest document on display is the Declaration of Independence of the Northern Chiefs, signed by more than 30 northern Māori chiefs on October 28, 1835, a confederation agreement that led up to the Waitangi treaty. Also on view is the 1893 Women's Suffrage Petition, which led to New Zealand becoming the world's first nation to grant women the vote. ✉ *10 Mulgrave St., Thorndon* ☎ *04/499–5595* ⊕ *www.archives.govt. nz* 🔗 *Free* ☽ *Weekdays 9–5.*

DID YOU KNOW?

The silver fern, or ponga, has great significance. It is New Zealand's national symbol as well as that of the All Blacks. A furled one, known as a *koru* (Māori for "loop"), represents new life in Māori culture.

Performers welcome visitors to the marae at the Museum of New Zealand Te Papa Tongarewa.

Ascot Street. Built in the 1870s, the little doll-like cottages along Ascot remain the finest example of a 19th-century streetscape in Wellington. A bench at the top has been thoughtfully provided in the shady courtyard should you need to catch your breath. ⊠ *Off Glenmore St. and Tinakori Rd., northeast of Wellington Botanic Garden, Thorndon.*

City Gallery Wellington. This gallery offers world-class exhibitions of contemporary New Zealand and international art with specific programs dedicated to local artists, Māori and Pacific arts, and the City Art Collection. Visitors can view sometimes challenging but always captivating work. ⊠ *Civic Sq., Wakefield St.* ☎ *04/913–9037* ⊕ *www. citygallery.org.nz* ⊠ *Most exhibitions free; charges for special exhibits vary* ⊙ *Daily 10–5.*

Civic Square. Wellington's Civic Square is reminiscent of an Italian piazza; its outdoor cafés, benches, lawns, and harbor viewpoints make both a social hub and a delightful sanctuary from the traffic. The **City Gallery** (one of the nation's finest), the library, and the Town Hall concert venue are just steps apart. Architect Ian Athfield's steel sculptures of *nikau* palms are a marvel, and Māori artist Para Matchitt contributed the impressionistic sculptures flanking the wide wooden bridge that connects the square to the harbor. With its sweeping water views, this bridge is a popular place to enjoy a picnic or just sit down and dream. ⊠ *Wakefield, Victoria, and Harris Sts.*

Government Buildings Historic Reserve. The second-largest wooden structure in the world is now home to Victoria University's law faculty. After the earthquakes of 1848 and 1855, it was found that wooden buildings suffered less damage than brick. This one was constructed in 1876 and designed to look like stone, though it was actually fashioned entirely from kauri timber. Inside are historic exhibits about the building and an information center, but it's the exterior that most captivates. ⊠ *55 Lambton Quay* 🎫 *Free* ⊙ *Weekdays 9–4.*

Katherine Mansfield House & Garden. The writer, born in 1888, lived the first five years of her life here. Katherine Mansfield (née Kathleen Beauchamp) left to pursue her career in Europe when she was only 20, but many of her short stories take place in Wellington. A year before her death in 1923, she wrote, "New Zealand is in my very bones. What wouldn't I give to have a look at it!" The house, which has been restored as a typical Victorian family home, contains furnishings, photographs, and videos that elucidate Mansfield's life and times. ⊠ *25 Tinakori Rd., Thorndon* 🕾 *04/473–7268* ⊕ *www.katherinemansfield.com* 🎫 *NZ$8* ⊙ *Tues.–Sun. 10–4.*

Nairn Street Cottage. Built in 1858 as a family home by immigrant carpenter William Wallis, this cottage is Wellington's oldest remaining building. With its steep shingled roof and matchboard ceilings, kauri wood paneling, and somber Victorian wallpapers, the house has been kept almost completely in its original state. The spinning wheel, smoke-blackened cooking pot, hand-pegged rugs, and oil lamps re-create the feeling of those pioneer days. Outside, a garden of flowers and herbs blooms in a riot of color during the summer. ⊠ *68 Nairn St.* 🕾 *04/384–9122* ⊕ *www.museumswellington.org.nz* 🎫 *NZ$8* ⊙ *Jan.–Mar. daily; other months weekends. Tours at noon, 1, 2, and 3.*

National Library. Opposite the Parliament Buildings is the country's national library. The Alexander Turnbull Library, a "library within a library," specializes in archival materials about New Zealand and the Pacific. Its books, manuscripts, photographs, newspapers, maps, and oral history tapes are available for research. Exhibitions are regularly held in the National Library Gallery. It also has a lively public events program. ⊠ *Molesworth St. at Aitken St., Thorndon* 🕾 *04/474–3000* ⊕ *www.natlib.govt.nz* 🎫 *Free* ⊙ *Mon.–Sat. 10–5.*

Old St. Paul's Cathedral. Consecrated in 1866, the church is a splendid example of the English Gothic Revival style executed entirely in native timbers. Even the trusses supporting the roof transcend their mundane function with splendid craftsmanship. ⊠ *Mulgrave St., Thorndon* 🕾 *04/473–6722* ⊕ *www.oldstpauls.co.nz* 🎫 *Free* ⊙ *Daily 9:30–5.*

The Parliament Buildings. These buildings include **Parliament House** with its **Debating Chamber,** a copy of the one in the British House of Commons right down to the Speakers Mace. Here legislation is presented, debated, and voted on. There is fine Māori artwork in the Māori **Affairs Select Committee Room.** The adjoining building is the **Parliamentary Library.** The neighboring **Executive Wing** is known for architectural reasons as **The Beehive**; it's where the Prime Minister and Cabinet Ministers of the elected Government have their offices and hold Cabinet meetings. Across the road at the corner of Bowen Street and Lambton Quay, **Bowen House** is also part of the complex. Tours start in The Beehive, and a guide explains the Parliamentary process in detail. ⊠ *Molesworth St.* 🕾 *04/817–9503* ⊕ *www.parliament.nz* 🎫 *Free* ⊙ *Daily 10–4; tours depart on the hr.*

7

FAMILY **Space Place At Carter Observatory.** Here you can lie back and watch an almost limitless range of virtual space journeys in the planetarium; or, on a clear night, view the heavens through the observatory telescope. Such experiences—plus state-of-the-art displays and a remarkable collection of artifacts that includes the oldest working telescope of its kind in the country—make this a popular stop. The observatory is only a two-minute walk from the top of the Kelburn Cable Car, but you can also wander up from the botanical gardens. ⊠ *40 Salamanca Rd.* ☎ *04/910–3140* ⊕ *www.museumswellington.org.nz* ✉ *NZ$12.50* ☽ *Tues. and Thurs. 4–11, Sat. 10 am to 11 pm, Sun. 10–5:30; extended hrs during school holidays.*

Tinakori Road. The lack of suitable local stone, combined with the collapse of most of Wellington's brick buildings in the earthquake of 1848, ensured the almost-exclusive use of timber for building here in the second half of the 19th century. Most carpenters of the period had learned their skills as cabinetmakers and shipwrights in Europe, and the sturdy houses on this street are a tribute to their craftsmanship. Two notables are the tall and narrow **No. 306** and **Premier House.** ⊠ *Wellington.*

NEARBY WELLINGTON
TOP ATTRACTIONS

FAMILY **Southward Car Museum.** Housing the southern hemisphere's largest private car collection, this museum has more than 400 automobiles and
Fodor'sChoice
★ 140 motorcycles, plus aircraft, bicycles, vintage tools, and an old fire engine. Among the most popular are Marlene Dietrich's 1934 Cadillac Town Cabriolet, a 1915 Stutz Indianapolis race car, a gull-winged Mercedes-Benz, a 1950 Cadillac "Gangster Special" that had belonged to gangster Mickey Cohen, and an 1895 Benz Velo. ⊠ *Otaihanga Rd., Paraparaumu* ☎ *04/297–1221* ⊕ *www.southwardcarmuseum.co.nz* ✉ *NZ$17* ☽ *Daily 9–4:30.*

Fodor'sChoice **Weta Cave & Workshop.** In Weta Cave, you get a fascinating "behind
★ the scenes look" at a compact but comprehensive display detailing the characters and equipment used in special effects for *The Lord of the Rings, The Hobbit, The Chronicles of Narnia, King Kong,* and other Academy Award–winning films. A wonderfully furnished theater shows continuous clips from them; and memorabilia (think models, limited-edition sculptures, books, posters, and T-shirts) are sold at the on-site shop. Standing alongside the Cave, the Workshop has a larger display of props and costumes; you might even see Weta artists and technicians at work. Daily tours run half hourly from 9:30 to 5; an extended version, departing four times a day from Wellington's i-SITE Visitor Information Centre, takes in filming locations along the way. ⊠ *Corner of Weka St. and Camperdown Rd.* ☎ *04/909–4000* ⊕ *www.wetaNZ.com* ✉ *Cave free; workshop tour NZ$25; extended tour NZ$65* ☽ *Daily 9–5:30.*

WORTH NOTING
The Dowse Art Museum. Near Petone, this museum stages a changing array of exhibitions—including ones focused on extraordinary jewelry, fashion, photography, and ceramics—that showcase the creativity of New Zealand's artisans. ⊠ *45 Laings Rd., Lower Hutt* ☎ *04/570–6500* ⊕ *www.dowse.org.nz* ✉ *Free* ☽ *Daily 10–5.*

Dry Creek Quarry. Heading north from Petone on State Highway 2, you can enjoy views of the distant Tararua Ranges, which are snow covered in winter. If you're a *Lord of the Rings* fan, stop by the Dry Creel Quarry, where the scenes of Helms Deep and Minas Tirith were filmed; it's at the bottom of Haywards Hill Road—look for the traffic lights for the turnoff from the highway. ✉ *Haywards Hill Rd., Lower Hutt.*

Eastbourne. From Petone, a winding road leads south about 10 km (6 miles) to the suburb of Eastbourne. Have an alfresco bite in its tiny shopping area before driving on to where the road eventually transforms into a 4-km (2½-mile) walking trail, following the coast to Pencarrow Head and its lighthouse, with views across the strait. (There's a kiosk where you can rent a bike if you wish.) ✉ *Lower Hutt.*

Hutt River Trail. Starting at Hikoikoi Reserve on Petone Marine Parade, near the Hutt River mouth, this scenic trail follows the river for more than 32 km (20 miles) to Upper Hutt. Intended specifically for walkers and cyclists, it is now extended to link up with the Rimutaka Track to the Wairarapa. ✉ *Petone Marine Parade, Lower Hutt.*

Kaitoke Regional Park. From Upper Hutt, continuing north on State Highway 2 takes you to the Wairarapa region. But if you have time to spare, stop into Kaitoke Regional Park. Just beyond Upper Hutt, it's a great camping and picnic spot with pleasant walks by the river. *LOTR* lovers can check out the bridge, which stood in for Rivendell, the great homeland of the elves. Pause by the crystal-clear river, flanked by towering trees and native bush, and listen to the birdsong. ✉ *Waterworks Rd., off State Hwy. 2, Upper Hutt* ☎ *04/526–7322 for rangers.*

Petone. A 15-minute drive north of Wellington on State Highway 2—with magnificent harbor views all the way—leads you to the Hutt Valley and its namesake river. Start exploring it by paying a visit to pretty Petone. The Petone Esplanade, on the eastern side of the harbor, has good fishing from the wharf and is overlooked by houses clinging to steep bush-clad hills. While on the waterfront, visit the small but interesting Petone Settlers Museum; it's open Wednesday through Sunday from 10 to 4. Housed in the historic Wellington Provincial Centennial Memorial building, the free museum stands near the 1840 landing site of New Zealand's first organized European settlement. ✉ *Lower Hutt* ☎ *04/568–8373 museum* 🌐 *www.petonesettlers.org.nz* 🎟 *Free.*

WHERE TO EAT

$$$ NEW ZEALAND

🍴 **The Back Bencher Gastropub.** Right across the way from the Parliament buildings sits "the house that has no peers," a landmark watering hole where politicians grab a cold beer after a hot debate. The walls have become a gallery of political cartoons and puppets tweaking government characters and well-known sports figures. Don't labor over the prices; it'll be a national disaster if you miss this one. Try the pan-roasted ground beef and venison patty, followed by rich chocolate cake. [$] *Average main: NZ$28* ✉ *34 Molesworth St.* ☎ *04/472–3065* 🌐 *www.backbencher.co.nz* ✣ *B3.*

7

$$$$ ╳ **Boulcott Street Bistro.** A well-respected institution on the Wellington
ECLECTIC   dining scene, this old colonial-style house conveys tradition and class.
Fodor's Choice   Start with crumbed calamari or house-made mushroom ravioli; then
★   move on to main courses like the aged beef fillet with béarnaise sauce.
The crème brûlée with poached seasonal fruit is a classic dessert that
will satisfy the most discerning palate. $ *Average main: NZ$36* ✉ *99
Boulcott St.* ☎ *04/499–4199* ⊕ *www.boulcottstreetbistro.co.nz* ⊘ *No
lunch Sat.* ⊕ *B4.*

$$$ ╳ **The Crab Shack.** Set on the waterfront, the Crab Shack is an American-
SEAFOOD   style diner with a Kiwi twist. Crab-pots and ropes hang from the ceiling.
FAMILY   The walls are bedecked in old-world maps and colorful recycled timber.
A wide-planked floor, glazed brick walls behind the bar, and bottle-
globe lighting complete the nautical theme. Try the Cajun catch of the
day, grilled in a charcoal barrel and served with red pepper-lime sauce,
potato hash, and chipotle slaw. Or how about the King? That's nearly
2 pounds of Red King crab with jalapeño crème fraîche and Bloody
Mary mayonnaise. Youngsters will love old-school dishes like fish-and-
chips or bangers-and-mash. $ *Average main: NZ$25* ✉ *Shed 5, Queens
Wharf* ☎ *04/916–4250* ⊕ *www.crabshack.co.nz* ⊕ *B4.*

$$ ╳ **Dixon Street Deli.** The owner's grandfather opened this establishment
CAFÉ   in 1920; the friendly staff and excellent pickings have kept it a local
FAMILY   favorite ever since. You could snag provisions for a picnic lunch or get
a table inside. In the morning, opt for the Dixon Big Breakfast (eggs on
toast, bacon, sausage, mushrooms, potatoes, and baked beans); later in
the day, try the chicken and bacon bagel-burgers. The cakes and confec-
tions here are also delicious. $ *Average main: NZ$17* ✉ *45–47 Dixon
St.* ☎ *04/384–2436* ⊕ *www.dixonstreetdeli.co.nz* ⊘ *No dinner* ⊕ *B5.*

$$$$ ╳ **Dockside Restaurant & Bar.** A wood-beam roof and oiled floorboards
NEW ZEALAND   enhance the nautical vibe at this former warehouse on the wharf.
You can get close to the water, too, on the large harbor-front deck.
Inside or out, it's a lively spot, particularly on Friday nights. The
menu includes crumbed lamb chops with roasted pumpkin, feta, and
radicchio. For dessert, the lemon cheesecake with passion fruit and
ginger sorbet is divine. The place draws crowds on weekends and can
be a bit noisy. $ *Average main: NZ$35* ✉ *Shed 3, Queens Wharf, Jervois Quay* ☎ *04/499–9900* ⊕ *www.docksidenz.com* ⌂ *Reservations
essential* ⊕ *B4.*

$$$ ╳ **Dragonfly.** Cylindrical orange shades hovering over polished wood
ASIAN   tables and brightly colored parasols hanging from a dark ceiling give
this modern Asian eatery a warm, intimate atmosphere. Have a drink
in the exotic garden bar before enjoying dishes like red duck curry, lem-
ongrass chicken, or "Salmon 2 Ways" (char-grilled salmon fillet with a
green-tea smoked salmon salad). Don't miss out on Dragonfly's mini-
tasting dessert, four tiny delights that are perfect for sharing. $ *Average
main: NZ$29* ✉ *70 Courtenay Pl.* ☎ *04/803-3995* ⊕ *www.dragon-fly.
co.nz* ⊘ *Closed Sun. No lunch* ⊕ *C5.*

$$$$ ╳ **The Green Parrot.** Talk about character: this stalwart steak-and-seafood
NEW ZEALAND   joint, which has been serving meals continuously since 1926, has a grill
made from melted-down gun barrels. Kosta Sakoufakis, the welcom-
ing chef and co-owner, makes people feel at home and can talk about

American Marines visiting the place during World War II. Politicians and celebrities like Peter Jackson gravitate here, and a mural depicts notable clients ranging from famous writers to two former prime ministers. You definitely won't walk out feeling hungry. [$] *Average main: NZ$32* ✉ *16 Taranaki St.* ☎ *04/384–6080* 🌐 *www.greenparrot.co.nz* 🕒 *No lunch* ✥ *B5.*

$$$$ CONTEMPORARY

🍴 **Juniper.** In this narrow space, red leather couch-style seating blends with plum-color walls under muted lighting. An upstairs dining area is more open. The aged Angus beef tenderloin comes wrapped in pancetta with potato gratin and Te Mata mushrooms on the side. For dessert you can't go wrong with the warm apple-and-plum crumble topped with vanilla ice cream. [$] *Average main: NZ$32* ✉ *Corner of Featherston and Johnston Sts., Wellington Central* ☎ *04/499–3668* 🌐 *www.juniperrestaurant.co.nz* 🕒 *Closed Sun.* ✥ *B3.*

$$$ ITALIAN

🍴 **La Bella Italia.** Within sight of Petone Wharf, this old warehouse has been transformed into a vibrant Italian restaurant and delicatessen; in-your-face murals, photographs, and posters with an Italian theme cover the walls. Savor the vibe while enjoying dishes from the ever-changing menu of authentic Italian cuisine. The ravioli and linguine with clams are both very popular. For lunch on Tuesday and Wednesday and dinner Thursday through Saturday, the wood-fired oven produces piping hot pizzas. [$] *Average main: NZ$26* ✉ *10 Nevis St., Petone* ☎ *04/566–9303* 🌐 *www.labellaitalia.co.nz* 🕒 *No dinner Mon.–Wed.* ✍ *Reservations essential* ✥ *D1.*

$$$$ NEW ZEALAND Fodor's Choice ★

🍴 **Logan Brown.** Occupying a 1920s bank building with Corinthian columns and a classical dome, Logan Brown is a winner. An aquarium tank is set into the bar top, so that fish swim by under your cocktail. The menu highlights New Zealand's produce and exemplary wines; the service is swift and unpretentious. Ensure a memorable meal by ordering line-caught *hāpuku* (groper) with *tuatua* (clam) fritters and pickled beets or, perhaps, venison with black-pudding sweetbreads, followed by a delicious lemon pudding with a dollop of citrus-oil ice cream. [$] *Average main: NZ$40* ✉ *Cuba St. at Vivian St.* ☎ *04/801–5114* 🌐 *www.loganbrown.co.nz* 🕒 *Closed Sun. and Mon.* ✥ *B5.*

$$$$ NEW ZEALAND

🍴 **Matterhorn.** A long passage from the street leads you to this hidden treasure where the bar stretches nearly as far. A large wood burner lends warmth to rather plain walls and basic furniture. For warm days there is a covered outside area with its own bar. Main courses here include market-fresh fish with squid-ink tagliatelle and grain-fed beef rump with potato fondant. Look for DJ music and live events on weekend nights. [$] *Average main: NZ$32* ✉ *106 Cuba St., Te Aro* ☎ *04/384–3359* 🌐 *www.matterhorn.co.nz* 🕒 *No lunch* ✥ *B5.*

$$$$ EUROPEAN

🍴 **Pravda.** Three king-size chandeliers dominate the high ceilings in this classic, old Wellington building. The café area has half-paneled walls and a matching bar that gives a touch of understated class. The *pesce spada* (a swordfish steak with capers and shaved radish) is one top pick. Leave room for the dark chocolate fondant with house-made ice cream. The menu changes to capture the best of the season's produce. [$] *Average main: NZ$35* ✉ *105 Custom House Quay, Wellington Central* ☎ *04/801–8858* 🌐 *www.pravdacafe.co.nz* 🕒 *Closed Sun.* ✥ *B4.*

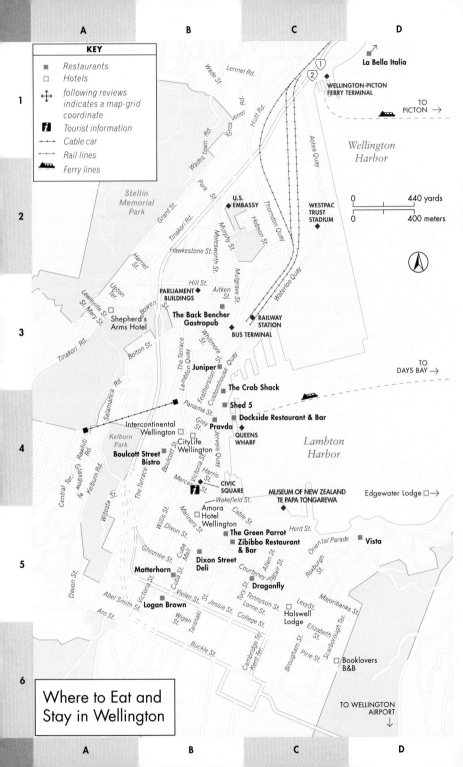

KEY

- ■ Restaurants
- □ Hotels
- ✛ *following reviews indicates a map-grid coordinate*
- ℹ️ *Tourist information*
- ┼┼┼ Cable car
- ┼┼┼ Rail lines
- ⛴ Ferry lines

Stellin Memorial Park

Wellington Harbor

La Bella Italia

WELLINGTON-PICTON FERRY TERMINAL

TO PICTON →

0 ___ 440 yards
0 ___ 400 meters

U.S. EMBASSY

WESTPAC TRUST STADIUM

Lennel Rd.

Wade St.

Grosvenor Rd.

Wadestown Rd.

Park St.

Grant St.

Tinakori Rd.

Hawkestone St.

Harriet St.

Upton Ter.

Lewisville St. / St. Mary St.

Shepherd's Arms Hotel

Tinakori Rd.

Bolton St.

Bowen St.

Hill St.

PARLIAMENT BUILDINGS

Aitken St.

The Back Bencher Gastropub

Murphy St.

Molesworth St.

Mulgrave St.

Hobson St.

Thorndon Quay

Waterloo Quay

Aotea Quay

Whitmore St.

RAILWAY STATION

BUS TERMINAL

The Terrace

Lambton Quay

Featherston St.

Customhouse Quay

Juniper

The Crab Shack

Shed 5

Dockside Restaurant & Bar

Pravda

Panama St.

Grey St.

Jervois Quay

QUEENS WHARF

TO DAYS BAY →

Lambton Harbor

Salamanca Rd.

Intercontinental Wellington

Kelburn Park

CityLife Wellington

Rawhiti Rd.

Kelburn Rd.

Glasgow St.

Central Ter.

Boulcott St. Bistro

Boulcott St.

Mercer St.

Victoria St.

Harris St.

CIVIC SQUARE

Wakefield St.

Cable St.

MUSEUM OF NEW ZEALAND TE PAPA TONGAREWA

Edgewater Lodge □ →

Wijeeta St.

The Terrace

Willis St.

Manners St.

Dixon St.

Amora Hotel Wellington

Herd St.

Devon St.

Ghuznee St.

Cuba Mall

Cuba St.

The Green Parrot

Zibibbo Restaurant & Bar

Oriental Parade

Roxburgh St.

Vista

Matterhorn

Dixon Street Deli

Courtenay Pl.

Blair St.

Allen St.

Dragonfly

Abel Smith St.

Victoria St.

Vivian St.

Jessie St.

Tory St.

Tennyson St.

Lorne St.

College St.

Logan Brown

Wigan St.

Taranaki St.

Buckle St.

Cambridge Ter.

Kent Ter.

Levy St.

Halswell Lodge

Majoribanks St.

Elizabeth St.

Scarborough Ter.

Brougham St.

Pirie St.

Booklovers B&B

TO WELLINGTON AIRPORT ↓

Aro St.

Where to Eat and Stay in Wellington

$$$$ ✕ **Shed 5.** Huge windows facing the harbor belie the fact that this historic
ECLECTIC building on the wharf was once a woolshed. Crisp white tablecloths and
sparkling tableware gleam under the dark-wood beams in the spacious
dining room. On the menu, seafood stands out; the daily fish selection
is sourced and filleted on-site by Shed 5's fishmonger. Seafood risotto
changes daily depending on what the tide brings in. Another popular
choice is wild venison and smoked-mushroom duxelle baked in butter-
crust pastry. Desserts include a lovely raspberry-pistachio gateaux with
ice-wine ganache. $ *Average main: NZ$33* ✉ *Shed 5, Queens Wharf,
Jervois Quay* ☎ *04/499–9069* ⊕ *www.shed5.co.nz* ✛ *B4.*

$$$ ✕ **Vista.** For a breezy meal and some morning sunshine, grab an outdoor
CAFÉ table at this busy café with views across Oriental Parade to the bustling
harbor. Breakfast is available until 4 pm; try the kedgeree (house-smoked
fish with jasmine rice, poached egg, and chutney). Small plates and light
fare, like the roasted-pumpkin-and-caramelized onion tart, are available
for lunch. Char-grilled meats and paella (the house specialty) are added
to the mix at dinner. $ *Average main: NZ$29* ✉ *106 Oriental Parade*
☎ *04/385–7724* ⊕ *www.vistacafe.co.nz* ⊗ *No dinner Sun.–Tues.* ✛ *D5.*

$$$$ ✕ **Zibibbo Restaurant & Bar.** Sit in the cozy downstairs bar with its imita-
ECLECTIC tion log fireplace or try the upstairs restaurant, which has dark leather
seating. The off-beat wall hangings and muted decor make for a sooth-
ing experience. Tapas are served in both areas. More sustaining main
courses range from Canterbury duck with Gorgonzola gnocchi to
roasted Wairarapa lamb with a minty crushed pea salad. The crème
brûlée with rum-and-raisin financier makes a sweet finish for either.
There is also a prix-fixe menu with wine pairings available. $ *Average
main: NZ$35* ✉ *25–29 Taranaki St.* ☎ *04/385–6650* ⊕ *www.zibibbo.
co.nz* ⊗ *No lunch Sat.–Thurs.* ✛ *B5.*

WHERE TO STAY

$$$ ⊡ **Amora Hotel Wellington.** Near the waterfront, this hotel is also close to
HOTEL the central business district and shopping, with the vibrant entertain-
ment area of Courtenay Place at the back door. **Pros:** right by the action;
extremely convenient parking; an excellent restaurant. **Cons:** can get
busy at times. $ *Rooms from: NZ$250* ✉ *170 Wakefield St.* ☎ *04/473–
3900, 0800/655–555* ⊕ *www.amorahotels.com* ⤳ *174 rooms, 18 suites*
⦿ *No meals* ✛ *B5.*

$$$ ⊡ **Booklovers B&B.** Residents of the Mount Victoria neighborhood claim
B&B/INN to live in the sunniest part of Wellington; local author Jane Tolerton has
set up house in a Victorian villa here and, true to her passion, has lined
the hallway with books. **Pros:** walk to virtually all the city attractions;
free off-street parking and Wi-Fi. **Cons:** due to Jane's writing commit-
ments personal service may not always be available. $ *Rooms from:
NZ$260* ✉ *123 Pirie St.* ☎ *04/384–2714* ⊕ *www.booklovers.co.nz* ⤳ *3
rooms* ⦿ *Breakfast* ✛ *C6.*

$$$ ⊡ **CityLife Wellington.** This apartment-style hotel is smack-dab in the
HOTEL middle of the city—and if you can snag a suite at a weekend or spe-
cial summer rate, it's one of the best-value lodgings in town. **Pros:** in
the heart of the city; just an elevator ride to Lambton Quay; good for
families or large groups. **Cons:** more suited to a longer stay. $ *Rooms*

Visitors dine alfresco in Courtenay Place, Wellington's entertainment center.

from: NZ$250 ✉ *300 Lambton Quay* ☎ *04/922–2800, 0800/368–888* 🌐 *www.heritagehotels.co.nz/citylife-wellington* 🛏 *61 suites, 9 studios* 🍴 *No meals* ✥ *B4.*

$$$ B&B/INN Fodor's Choice ★ **Edgewater Lodge.** Right by the water's edge, with stunning harbor views from every room, this place exudes class. **Pros:** superbly comfortable accommodation; you'll see more boats pass by than cars. **Cons:** 15-minute ride into the city; parking can be tight. [$] *Rooms from: NZ$270* ✉ *423 Karaka Bay Rd.* ☎ *04/388–4446, 021/613–357* 🌐 *www.edgewaterwellington.co.nz* 🛏 *3 suites* 🍴 *Breakfast* ✥ *D4.*

$ HOTEL **Halswell Lodge.** For restaurant, theater, and cinema going, you can't beat this hotel's location, right by the eastern end of Courtenay Place. **Pros:** reasonably priced; close to all the action. **Cons:** some traffic noise; budget rooms are extremely small; parking is first-come, first-served. [$] *Rooms from: NZ$100* ✉ *21 Kent Terr.* ☎ *04/385–0196* 🌐 *www.halswell.co.nz* 🛏 *25 rooms, 11 motel units* 🍴 *No meals* ✥ *C5.*

$$$$ HOTEL Fodor's Choice ★ **InterContinental Wellington.** In the heart of the business district, and a stone's throw from the waterfront, this landmark high-rise gets the details right. **Pros:** comfortable; on the doorstep of the city happenings. **Cons:** can get booked up with corporate functions. [$] *Rooms from: NZ$329* ✉ *Featherston and Grey Sts.* ☎ *04/472–2722* 🌐 *www.intercontinental.com* 🛏 *232 rooms, 12 suites* 🍴 *No meals* ✥ *B4.*

$ HOTEL **Shepherd's Arms Hotel.** New Zealand's oldest hotel is a place to soak up history and mingle with the locals. **Pros:** reasonably priced; fairly close to the city; a short walk to the Botanic Gardens. **Cons:** there can be some noise from the bar crowd; limited parking. [$] *Rooms from: NZ$99* ✉ *285 Tinakori Rd., Thorndon* ☎ *04/472–1320* 🌐 *www.shepherds.co.nz* 🛏 *14 rooms* 🍴 *Breakfast* ✥ *A3.*

NIGHTLIFE AND PERFORMING ARTS

For current event listings in Wellington, check the entertainment section of the *Dominion Post,* Wellington's daily newspaper. The website for Positively Wellington Tourism (⊕ *www.WellingtonNZ.com*) also has up-to-date entertainment listings, covering everything from movies to theater and music.

Ticketek. Buy tickets for local performances at this spot between the Michael Fowler Center and the Town Hall. ⊠ *111 Wakefield St.* ☎ *04/384–3840* ⊕ *www.ticketek.co.nz.*

NIGHTLIFE

Wellington's after-dark scene splits between several main areas. The "alternative" set spends its time at **Cuba Street**'s funky cafés, bars, and clubs, which stay open until around 1 am during the week and about 3 am or later on weekends; cocktails are innovative, and the music is not top-20 radio.

Courtenay Place is home to the traditional drinking action with a selection of pubs, sports bars, and a few upscale establishments. It's packed on Friday and Saturday nights, especially when a rugby game is on, and the streets fill with beery couples in their late teens and early twenties lining up to get plastered (New Zealand's legal drinking age is 18).

In the downtown business district—between Lambton Quay and Manners Street—a couple of brewpubs and a few taverns cater to the after-work mob. Down by the harbor, a flashy corporate crowd hangs out in several warehouse-style bars, sipping martinis on weeknights and filling the dance floor on weekends.

BARS

Arizona Bar. For a bit of Tex-Mex—New Zealand style—plus plenty of great beers, head downtown and make an early start at this bar and grill adjoining the Hotel InterContinental. ⊠ *Grey and Featherston Sts.* ☎ *04/495–7867* ⊕ *www.arizona.co.nz.*

Dockside. This restaurant and bar has a pleasant nautical theme with antique boats hanging from the ceiling. It's a popular watering hole with the locals. In good weather, everyone spills outside for the best close-up harbor views in Wellington. ⊠ *Shed 3, Queens Wharf, Jervois Quay* ☎ *04/499–9900* ⊕ *www.docksidenz.com.*

Good Luck. Although it's right on bustling Cuba Street, Good Luck is a little hard to find. Stairs take you below street level to a club done in the style of a Shanghai opium den, glowing with candles in Chinese teapots. ⊠ *126 Cuba St.* ☎ *04/801–9950* ⊕ *www.goodluckbar.co.nz.*

The Grand. This well-lived-in spot, once a brewery and then a distillery, has exposed brick walls, timber floors, and four levels with everything from a 400-person main bar to a garden bar, plus a couple of pool tables. ⊠ *69–71 Courtenay Pl.* ☎ *04/801–7800* ⊕ *www.thegrandwellington.co.nz.*

Green Man Pub. In the heart of Wellington's central business district, this pub is a little bit Kiwi and a little bit Irish. The atmosphere is warm and friendly, the service excellent. Expect it to be packed on

weekends. ⊠ *At Victoria and Willeston Sts.* ☎ *04/499–5440* ⊕ *www. thegreenmanpub.co.nz.*

Kitty O'Shea's. A good-size crowd gathers nightly on Kitty O'Shea's outside veranda; traditional live music is regularly played. ⊠ *28 Courtenay Pl.* ☎ *04/384–7392* ⊕ *www.kittyosheas.co.nz.*

Malthouse. Modern with polished wood and plate glass aplenty, Malthouse's long bar with illuminated lettering is an attractive place to drink a pint. ⊠ *48 Courtenay Pl.* ☎ *04/802–5484* ⊕ *www.themalthouse.co.nz.*

Matterhorn. The centrally located Matterhorn, which also has a good restaurant, draws a mix of urban hipsters and after-work corporate types with its indoor-and-outdoor fireplaces, laid-back DJ, and live music on Friday and Saturday nights. It has a list of inventive cocktails, too. ⊠ *106 Cuba St.* ☎ *04/384–3359* ⊕ *www.matterhorn.co.nz.*

Mishmosh. Look for the bright cluster of lights on the overhead awning of this gastropub. It's a popular venue with a lively atmosphere. ⊠ *36 Courtenay Pl.* ☎ *04/384-8015* ⊕ *www.mishmosh.co.nz.*

Motel. Wellington's hipsters gravitate toward Motel, with its dimly lighted booths. There's an array of cocktails and finger food, plus a DJ who plays funky, down-tempo hip-hop. Although it's not formal, you'll want to leave the jeans and sneakers behind. ⊠ *4D Forresters La.* ☎ *04/384–9084.*

LIVE MUSIC AND DANCE CLUBS

Bodega. Local music, couches at the front, and a dance floor by the stage help Bodega pull in a predominantly student crowd. On nights when cheap drink specials are offered, it fills up fast. ⊠ *101 Ghuznee St.* ☎ *04/384–8212* ⊕ *www.bodega.co.nz.*

TSB Bank Arena. Headlining tours head to this venue. ⊠ *Queen's Wharf, Jervois Quay* ☎ *04/801–4231* ⊕ *www.pwv.co.nz/our-venues/ tsb-bank-arena-convention-centre.*

Valhalla. One of the best places to catch live local rock, Valhalla is a classic hole-in-the-wall: small, dark, and a little seedy, with concrete floors. ⊠ *154 Vivian St.* ☎ *04/385–4361.*

PERFORMING ARTS

Bats Theatre. Wellington's long-standing source for experimental, sometimes off-the-wall theater hosts the Fringe Festival during the International Arts Festival as well as a range of performances throughout the year. ⊠ *1 Kent Terr., Te Aro* ☎ *04/802–4175* ⊕ *www.bats.co.nz.*

Circa Theatre. Catch contemporary New Zealand pieces along with established masterworks from Harold Pinter to Oscar Wilde. It's on the wharf next to the Museum of New Zealand Te Papa Tongarewa. ⊠ *1 Taranaki St.* ☎ *04/801–7992* ⊕ *www.circa.co.nz.*

Michael Fowler Centre. Named after a former long-standing mayor, this venue regularly hosts shows ranging from the New Zealand Ballet to orchestral and pop concerts. ⊠ *111 Wakefield St.* ☎ *04/801–4231* ⊕ *www.pwv.co.nz/our-venues.*

Opera House. The well-preserved Opera House, with its plush carpets and tiered seating, has a similar lineup to the St. James Theatre. Because both are under the same ownership, the NBR New Zealand Opera and the Royal New Zealand Ballet use either venue as schedules allow. ✉ *111–113 Manners St.* ☎ *04/384–3840.*

St. James Theatre. The ornate, turn-of-the-20th-century St. James Theatre hosts dance performances, musicals, and opera. ✉ *77–83 Courtenay Pl.* ☎ *04/802–4060* ⊕ *www.stjames.co.nz.*

SHOPPING

The main downtown shopping area, for department stores, clothes, shoes, books, outdoor gear, and souvenirs, is the so-called **Golden Mile—** from Lambton Quay, up Willis, Victoria, and Manners streets. For smaller, funkier boutiques, visit **Cuba Street.**

DEPARTMENT STORE AND MALLS

Old Bank Arcade. A couple of indoor malls are on upper Lambton Quay: **Harbour City** and **Capital on the Quay** have a decent range of jewelry, lingerie, housewares, and clothing shops. A better mall is **The Old Bank Arcade** in the old-fashioned former Bank of New Zealand building, which is becoming something of a fashion enclave. The Arcade contains a slew of well-known boutiques, including New Zealand designer Andrea Moore's. There is classic jewelery at The Gold Exchange and de Spa Chocolatier sells delicious handmade sweets. If you miss your favorite coffee there's even a Starbucks. ✉ *233–237 Lambton Quay, at Customhouse Quay and Willis St.* ☎ *04/922–0600* ⊕ *www.oldbank.co.nz.*

BOOKS AND MAPS

Arty Bee's Books. This friendly store sells secondhand books and sheet music. ✉ *The Oaks, Manners St.* ☎ *04/384–5339* ⊕ *www.artybees.co.nz.*

Unity Books. Find a generous supply of New Zealand and Māori literature here. ✉ *57 Willis St.* ☎ *04/499–4245* ⊕ *www.unitybooksonline.co.nz.*

CLOTHING AND ACCESSORIES

Area 51. Street-savvy clothing brands like Diesel fill the shelves, but the real reason to come in is to check out the popular, local Huffer label. ✉ *Cuba and Dixon Sts.* ☎ *04/385–6590* ⊕ *www.area51store.co.nz.*

Jane Daniels. A comprehensive range of Jane Daniels's New Zealand ladies fashions are offered here, all locally manufactured. ✉ *97c Customhouse Quay* ☎ *04/473–7400* ⊕ *www.janedaniels.co.nz.*

Karen Walker. The eponymous owner has made a name for herself overseas. This Wellington store carries her own designs and also stocks Escentric Molecules fragrances. ✉ *126 Wakefield St.* ☎ *04/499–3558* ⊕ *www.karenwalker.com.*

Zambesi. Well-established New Zealand designer Elisabeth Findlay of Zambesi whips up innovative but extremely wearable clothes. ✉ *103 Customhouse Quay* ☎ *04/472–3638* ⊕ *www.zambesi.co.nz.*

MARKETS

Harbourside Market. On Sunday, between 7:30 am and 1 pm, folks flock to this outdoor food market on the waterfront. Organic produce, cheese, and fresh fish and meats are the main draws. ✉ *At Cable and Barnett Sts., by side of Te Papa* ⊕ *www.harboursidemarket.co.nz.*

Outdoor Night Markets. Two outdoor markets—one Friday night at Left Bank, Cuba Mall, and the other Saturday night on lower Cuba Street—lure crowds with a variety of international foods and entertainment from local performers. They're open from 5 to 10. ⊠ *Cuba St.*

Porirua Market. For a look at the weekly market of a close-knit ethnic community, catch an early train or take a drive north of Wellington on State Highway 1 to Porirua and hit the Porirua Market. Stalls sell everything from eggplants and pineapples to colorful clothing, basketry, and beadwork. Entertainers and hoarse-voiced evangelists play to the crowd. If you get hungry, there are food stalls galore selling curry and roti, chop suey, banana pancakes, and nearly every other treat you can imagine. The stalls open Friday at midnight and close Saturday at noon. ⊠ *Cobham Ct., Porirua.*

OUTDOOR EQUIPMENT

Gordons. This spot sells camping and outdoor clothing as well as footwear. ⊠ *Cuba and Wakefield Sts.* ☎ *04/499–8894.*

Kathmandu. Wellington is a fine place to stock up on camping supplies before hitting the great outdoors. Kathmandu carries its house brand of clothing and equipment. ⊠ *15 Willis St.* ☎ *04/472–0113* ⊕ *www. kathmandu.co.nz.*

SOUVENIRS

Kura Aotearoa Art + Design. Part gallery, part gift store, this establishment has a strong Māori current running through the work. Some of the smaller, less-expensive items make unique souvenirs. ⊠ *19 Allen St.* ☎ *04/802–4934* ⊕ *www.kuragallery.co.nz.*

Simply New Zealand. As its name suggests, this store focuses on New Zealand-made handcrafts, including ceramics, wooden items, jewelery, knitwear, and accessories. ⊠ *195 Lambton Quay* ☎ *04/472–6817* ⊕ *www.simplynz.co.nz.*

SIDE TRIPS FROM WELLINGTON

AKATARAWA VALLEY

40 km (25 miles) northeast of Wellington.

Winding through the steep bush-clad hills north of Wellington, the narrow road to the Akatarawa Valley (in the Māori language, Akatarawa means "place of tangled vines") requires a degree of driving care, but it leads to a number of hidden gems. About 35 minutes north of Wellington on State Highway 2, turn left at the clearly marked Brown Owl turnoff north of Upper Hutt. About two minutes after the turnoff, look for **Harcourt Park,** where a number of scenes in the *Lord of the Rings* movies were filmed.

A kilometer (½1 mile) farther on, a bridge spanning the junction of the Hutt and Akatarawa rivers leads into the Akatarawa Valley proper. Drive over the bridge, go past the cemetery, and then on the left, look for the Blueberry Farm and nearby Bluebank Blueberry and Emu Farm. After picking to your heart's content, continue uphill on the very winding road. On the right is the Staglands Wildlife Reserve. It's around 7 km (4½ miles) to the summit, then the narrow road winds downhill. Look for the tiny wooden Church of St. Andrews nearby and turn right immediately for the Reikorangi Potteries. The road continues for about 3 km (2 miles) to join State Highway 1 at the Waikanae traffic lights, where you can head back to Wellington; from here, you're about 45 minutes north of the city.

VISITOR INFORMATION

Contacts Upper Hutt i-SITE Visitor Information Centre. ⊠ *836 Fergusson Dr., Upper Hutt* ☎ *04/527-2168* ⊕ *www.huttvalleynz.com.*

EXPLORING

Bluebank Blueberry and Emu Farm. This property produces delicious blueberries and raises the large flightless emus. ⊠ *1301 Akatarawa Rd., Upper Hutt* ☎ *04/526-9540* ⊕ *www.bluebank.co.nz* ☉ *Jan., daily 10-5; Dec., Feb., Mar., and Apr., Wed.-Sun. 10-5. Check website for up-to-date info during picking season.*

Blueberry Farm. Pick your own blueberries (January to March), or go for a swim in the river. ⊠ *1229 Akatarawa Rd., Upper Hutt* ☎ *04/526–6788* ⊕ *www.theblueberryfarm.co.nz* ☉ *Jan., daily 10-5; Feb., Mar., and Apr., Wed.-Sun. 10-5. Check website for up-to-date info during picking season.*

FAMILY **Reikorangi Potteries.** Wilf and Jan Wright display their own pottery here along with local handicrafts and paintings. After perusing the gallery, you can wander around the small animal park to view assorted critters (including alpaca, wallaby, sheep, deer, and a bevy of different birds), then cool off with a dip in the river. ⊠ *27 Ngatiawa Rd., Reikorangi* ☎ *04/293-5146* ⊕ *www.reikorangi.com* ☜ *NZ$8* ☉ *Wed.-Sun. 10-5.*

NEED A BREAK? **The Potters Kiln Café.** If you've worked up an appetite, the tiny café at Reikorangi Potteries is just the ticket. Pottery and paintings fill the walls, as do interesting curios. Chicken-and-apricot pie or ground-beef lasagna, both of which come with salad on the side, are great lunch choices; mouth-watering cakes and pies can be ordered as well. Dinner, served Friday and Saturday night only, must be booked a week ahead. ⊠ *27 Ngatiawa Rd., Reikorangi* ☎ *04/293-5146* ⊕ *www.reikorangi.com* ☉ *Closed Mon. and Tues. No dinner Sun.-Thurs.* ☜ *Reservations essential.*

FAMILY
Fodor'sChoice
★
Staglands Wildlife Reserve. Staglands offers visitors the opportunity to feed and freely interact with wildlife in a beautiful natural environment. As you wander around its 25 peaceful acres, you can walk through aviaries to ogle kea, kaka, and many more brilliantly colored birds. At the stables you'll meet the native *kune kune* pig and impressive Clydesdale horse. Watch rainbow and brown trout fighting over their dinner at the Trout and Eel Pool. Have fun exploring the nooks and crannies of the re-created Old Bush Settlement. Climb to the Deer Park lookout for stunning views; then enjoy a picnic on the banks of the beautiful Akatarawa River, or dig into the scrumptious food served at the log cabin café. ⊠ *2362 Akatarawa Rd., Upper Hutt* ☎ *04/526-7529* ⊕ *www.staglands. co.nz* ☜ *NZ$20* ☉ *Daily 9:30-5.*

KAPITI COAST

50 km (31 miles) north of Wellington.

A drive up the West Coast from Wellington is not to be missed. State Highway 1 leads you north, and about a half hour out of the city you hit the water at Paremata. From here you can take State Highway 1 straight up the Kapiti Coast, so called for the view of Kapiti Island. Alternatively, you can take the longer—but infinitely more scenic—drive around the Pauatahanui Inlet and Bird Sanctuary, following the road along the ridge of the rugged, winding, and windy Paekakariki Hill, where stunning views of the coastline and Kapiti Island await. Both routes lead to **Paekakariki** (pie-*kahk*-a-reeky), a small, artsy beach town.

VISITOR INFORMATION

Contacts Paraparaumu i-SITE Visitor Information Centre. ⊠ *134 Rimu Rd., Paraparaumu* ☎ *04/298–8195* ⊕ *www.kapiticoast.govt.nz.*

EXPLORING

Queen Elizabeth Park. Paekakariki's draw is the shore, but it's also the main entry point for Queen Elizabeth Park. Covering more than 1,600 acres, the park is edged by sand dunes and swimmable beaches. Walking, horseback riding, and cycling are popular activities here; there is also a playground for kids. ⊠ *State Hwy. 1, Paraparaumu* ☎ *04/292–8625* ⊘ *Daily 8 am–dusk.*

KAPITI ISLAND

50 km (31 miles) north of Wellington and 5 km (3 miles) off the coast of Paraparaumu.

Paraparaumu is the departure point for one of Wellington's best-kept secrets: Kapiti Island. A protected reserve since 1897, the island is a fantastic place to hike. All pests have been eliminated from it, and birdlife—including saddlebacks, stitchbirds, and colonies of little spotted and South Island brown kiwi—is abundant. Don't be surprised if a curious and fearless weka bird investigates your day pack or unties your shoelaces. Climb to the Tuteremoana lookout point, which is more than 1,700-feet high, for stellar views.

The island's most famous inhabitant was the Ngati Toa chief Te Rauparaha, who took the island by ruse in 1822. From this stronghold, he launched bloodthirsty raids before he was captured in 1846. He died in 1849, but his burial place is a mystery. Old tri-pots (used for melting down whale blubber) on the island bear testimony to the fact that Kapiti was also used as a whaling station in the late 19th century.

The reserve is 5 km (3 miles) from the mainland. Sign on with a tour operator for the boat trip out; all depart from the Kapiti Boating Club, Paraparaumu Beach. Crossings are weather dependent.

TOURS

Kapiti Explorer. This outfit offers scenic cruises to and guided walks around the island. The round-trip boat ride costs NZ$75; guided walks are an extra NZ$10. ⊠ *Paraparaumu* ☎ *04/905–6610, 04/297–2585* ⊕ *www.kapitiexplorer.nz.*

Kapiti Island Nature Tours. Sample genuine Māori hospitality with Kapiti Island Nature Tours. Options range from a day trip with an introductory talk, lunch, and a guided walk to an overnight stay with accommodations, three meals, and a kiwi-spotting night walk. Passage to the island and Department of Conservation park permits are included. Tours start at NZ$165; return transport only costs NZ$75. ⊠ *Paraparaumu* ☎ *0800/547–5263, 021/126–7525* ⊕ *www.kapitiislandnaturetours.co.nz.*

VISITOR INFORMATION

Contacts Paraparaumu i-SITE Visitor Information Centre. ⊠ *134 Rimu Rd., Paraparaumu* ☎ *04/298–8195* ⊕ *www.kapiticoast.govt.nz.*

THE WAIRARAPA

To cross the Rimutaka Ranges, which form a natural barrier between Wellington and the Wairarapa, you climb a twisting snake of a road known locally as "The Hill." Near a small plateau at the road's peak, at a height of about 1,800 feet, a footpath leads to even higher ground with spectacular views on all sides. Heading down from the summit, the road plunges through a series of hairpin turns to reach the plain that the Māori called "Land of Glistening Water."

For some years, the rather-daunting access road gave a sense of isolation to the Wairarapa, which was essentially a farming area. But the emergence of the wine industry has triggered a tourism boom in the region. Red grape varieties flourish in the local soil (the Pinot Noir is particularly notable), and Wairarapa wines, produced in small quantities, are sought after in New Zealand and overseas. These days, vineyards, wine tastings, olive farms, and the twice-yearly Martinborough Fair are firmly established attractions. Sea-and-freshwater fishing, walking, the "Golden Shears" shearing competition, and other outdoor activities have also brought visitors over "The Hill."

GETTING HERE AND AROUND

Public transportation options are very limited, so you'll need a car to properly explore the area. State Highway 2 runs north–south through the region between Napier and Wellington. From Wellington you drive through Upper Hutt (the River Road bypasses the town), over the hills into the gateway town of Featherston. Highway 53 takes you to Martinborough; turn southwest here on Lake Ferry Road for Lake Ferry and Cape Palliser. Masterton is farther north along State Highway 2, roughly a 30-minute drive from Martinborough. The journey from Wellington to Martinborough takes about 75 minutes; Masterton is another 15. From Napier, Masterton is about three hours.

MARTINBOROUGH

70 km (44 miles) north of Wellington.

The pleasant town of Martinborough embodies the changes that have taken place in the Wairarapa as a result of the burgeoning wine industry. The town gets its name from its founder, John Martin, who, in 1881, laid out the streets in a union jack pattern, radiating from the square that forms the hub. Most restaurants and shops are on or close to the square.

To tap into the Wairarapa wine world, Martinborough is the place to come. More than 20 vineyards are within a few miles of it—an easy walk or bike ride to some and a pleasant drive to most.

GETTING HERE AND AROUND

During weekdays the roads are mostly quiet, ideal for cycling and relaxed motoring; however, driving on rural roads can be deceptive. Keep a sharp eye out for livestock movement—large herds of cattle or sheep can be just around that bend.

Weekends at virtually any time of the year can bring a flood of visitors. The first Saturday in February and March, the two Martinborough Fair Days, can see traffic jams for miles. On a good, sunny winter weekend, Wellington people regularly pop "over the hill" to sample a vineyard meal and a glass of vino. Plan your visit if you want to avoid the crowds.

VISITOR INFORMATION

Contacts Martinborough i-SITE Visitor Information Centre. ⊠ *18 Kitchener St.* ☎ *06/306–5010* ⊕ *www.wairarapanz.com.*

EXPLORING

Martinborough Fair. The town's signature event, held in the Square on the first Saturday of February and March, draws thousands of people and packs the place with crafts stalls. ⊠ *Martinborough* ☎ *06/304–9933* ⊕ *www.martinboroughfair.org.nz.*

Olivo. For a taste-bud-tickling exercise that doesn't involve grapes, head to Helen and John Meehan's olive grove, 3 km (2 miles) north of Martinborough. You can visit the grove and its 5 acres of gardens to learn how oils are produced. Tastings (and sales) of their extra-virgin and infused olive oils are encouraged. ⊠ *Hinakura Rd.* ☎ *06/306–9074* ⊕ *www.olivo.co.nz* ☜ *Tours NZ$15 (bookings essential)* ♡ *Jan. and Feb. 6, daily 10:30–5; other months, weekends, and public holidays 10:30–5 or by appointment.*

Toast Martinborough Wine, Food & Music Festival. Devoted to the hedonist's holy trinity, this festival occurs on the third Sunday of November. Tickets cost NZ$70, and thousands of them are typically sold within hours—you can get yours online through Ticketek (*www.ticketek. co.nz*). ☎ *06/306–9183* ⊕ *www.toastmartinborough.co.nz.*

WINERIES

Ata Rangi Vineyard. This family-owned and family-managed winery makes exceptional Chardonnay, Sauvignon Blanc, Pinot Noir, and Célèbre (a Cabernet-Merlot-Shiraz blend) in small quantities. You can taste at least six wines for a NZ$5 fee. ⊠ *Puruatanga Rd.* ☎ *06/306–9570* ⊕ *www.atarangi.co.nz* ☜ *Tastings NZ$5 (refundable with purchase)* ♡ *Tastings weekdays 1–3, weekends noon–4.*

Coney Wines. Have lunch here for a view over vines that produce a terrific Pinot Noir and Pinot Gris plus a rosé you can get only on-site. ⊠ *107 Dry River Rd.* ☎ *06/306–8345* ⊕ *www.coneywines.co.nz* ☜ *Tastings NZ$5 (refundable with purchase)* ♡ *Tastings Dec.–Mar., Fri., Sat., and Sun. 11–4; Apr.–Nov., weekends 11–4.*

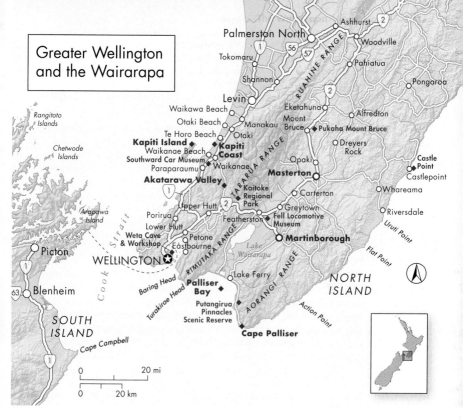

Greater Wellington and the Wairarapa

Palmerston North
Ashhurst 2
Woodville
Tokomaru 56
Pahiatua
57
Shannon
Pongaroa
Levin 2
Waikawa Beach
Eketahuna
Alfredton
Otaki Beach
Mount
Te Horo Beach Otaki Manakau Bruce Pukaha Mount Bruce
Kapiti Island
Waikanae Beach Kapiti
Dreyers
Southward Car Museum Coast
Rock
Paraparaumu Waikanae
Opaki
Castle
Akatarawa Valley Masterton
Point
Castlepoint
Kaitoke
Regional
Whareama
Upper Hutt 2 Park Carterton
Porirua
Greytown
Riversdale
Lower Hutt
Featherston Fell Locomotive
Uruti Point
Weta Cave
Museum
& Workshop Petone
Eastbourne
Martinborough
WELLINGTON
Lake
Wairarapa
Flat Point
Rangitoto
Islands

Chetwode
Islands

Arapawa
Island

Picton

Baring Head Lake Ferry
NORTH
Palliser ISLAND
Turakirae Head Bay
Putangirua
Pinnacles
Scenic Reserve
Action Point
Cape Palliser

Blenheim
Cook Strait

SOUTH
ISLAND

Cape Campbell

0   20 mi
0   20 km

Rangitoto
Islands

Martinborough Vineyard. This fine regional winery was the first to convince the world of the Wairarapa's Pinot Noir potential. The Chardonnay is also exceptional. ✉ *Princess St.* ☎ *06/306–9955* ⊕ *www.martinborough-vineyard.co.nz* 🗃 *Tastings NZ$5 (refundable with purchase)* ☾ *Tastings daily 11–4.*

Martinborough Wine Merchants. For an overview of area wines, take an oenophile's shortcut and hit Martinborough Wine Merchants. The shop stocks a thorough selection of local vintages for sipping and buying (arrangements can be made to have your purchases shipped home). It also carries books and wine accessories. ✉ *6 Kitchener St.* ☎ *06/306–9040* ⊕ *www.martinboroughwinemerchants.com.*

Murdoch James Vineyard. This premium producer of handcrafted wines is a scenic 10-minute drive from town. Try the smooth Blue Rock Pinot Noir or the very elegant Blue Rock Syrah. Both can be sampled in the on-site restaurant, Bloom, where the menu is designed with both the vineyard's wines and the changing seasons in mind. Daily tastings and wine tours (NZ$35, reservations required) are also available. ✉ *Dry River Rd.* ☎ *06/306–9165* ⊕ *www.murdochjames.co.nz* 🗃 *Tastings NZ$5 (refundable with purchase)* ☾ *Tastings daily 11–5. Restaurant Thurs.–Mon. 10:30–3.*

Palliser Estate. Don't miss the whites here—they're some of the best around. Of particular note is the Sauvignon Blanc, which is renowned for its intense ripe flavors, and the Pinot Noir, which is made in an elegant classic style. ✉ *Kitchener St.* ☎ *06/306–9019* 🌐 *www.palliser.co.nz* 🎟 *Tastings NZ$5 (refundable with purchase)* 🕓 *Tastings daily 10:30–4.*

WHERE TO EAT

$$$ NEW ZEALAND 🍴 **Martinborough Hotel Bar and Grill.** Polished floors, chandeliers, and glistening glassware are the hallmarks of this restaurant adjacent to the Martinborough Hotel. There are some interesting paintings on the walls, but the focus of attention is on the kitchen where diners can get a ringside view of the chefs at work. A good example of their handiwork would be the grilled salmon fillet with cumin-braised fennel, baby leeks, green beans, and orange brandy glaze. This could be topped off by a brownie with vanilla ice cream and berry coulis. As you'd expect, there's a great local wine list. If you prefer a more casual menu, try the adjoining bar. [$] *Average main: NZ$29* ✉ *The Square* ☎ *06/306–8350* 🌐 *www.mbbarandgrill.co.nz.*

$$$$ EUROPEAN 🍴 **Tirohana Estate and Cellars Restaurant.** The dark-tiled floor and white tablecloths put this classy dining area way above the usual winery restaurant. A wrought-iron door, black leather chairs, and polished-brass ceiling fan add to the aura. From the prix-fixe dinner menu, start with a glass of Sauvignon and a caramelized onion-and-feta tart, then choose the fish of the day *en papillotte* with baby potatoes and green beans, followed by pumpkin bread-and-butter pudding, and, to finish, petit fours. For a casual lunch, take a seat on the patio, where tasting platters, salads, pizzas, and such are complemented by vineyard views. It all comes with impeccable and friendly service. [$] *Average main: NZ$59* ✉ *42 Puruatanga Rd.* ☎ *06/306–9933* 🌐 *www.tirohanaestate.com* ✍ *Reservations essential.*

$$ NEW ZEALAND 🍴 **The Village Café.** At this barnlike café with a sunny outdoor courtyard, all the food is made from local ingredients. The cooks even smoke their own salmon and stuff their own sausages. One popular dish is the corned beef with poached egg and hollandaise sauce—it's hearty enough to keep you going all day. The rustic spot shares a building with Martinborough Wine Merchants. [$] *Average main: NZ$17* ✉ *6 Kitchener St.* ☎ *06/306–8814* 🕓 *No dinner.*

WHERE TO STAY

$$ HOTEL 🏨 **The Claremont.** In a quiet rural area just outside the village center, this motel complex has a variety of stylishly modern units to suit a range of budgets. **Pros:** quiet location out of the town center; good modern lodgings. **Cons:** no swimming pool or activities; you need to go into town for a restaurant. [$] *Rooms from: NZ$145* ✉ *38 Regent St.* ☎ *06/306–9162* 🌐 *www.theclaremont.co.nz* 🛏 *16 rooms, 7 apartments* 🍽 *No meals.*

$$$ HOTEL 🏨 **The Martinborough Hotel.** Sitting on a corner of the Martinborough Square, this vintage hotel was built in 1882 and has rooms that open onto either the veranda or the garden. **Pros:** fine accommodations in the town center; handy to everything. **Cons:** you'll need your best manners to match the design. [$] *Rooms from: NZ$280* ✉ *The Square* ☎ *06/306–9350* 🌐 *www.martinboroughhotel.co.nz* 🛏 *16 rooms.*

$$$ RESORT 🏨 **Peppers Parehua.** Located next to a vineyard, luxurious Peppers Parehua enjoys a park-like setting. **Pros:** modern luxury lodgings; outdoor pool; tennis court. **Cons:** a long way from the bright lights. [$] *Rooms from: NZ$299* ✉ *New York St. W.* ☎ *06/306–8405* 🌐 *www.peppers.co.nz* 🛏 *28 cottages* 🍴 *Breakfast.*

PALLISER BAY AND CAPE PALLISER

Southwest of Martinborough: 25 km (16 miles) to Lake Ferry, 40 km (25 miles) to Putangirua Pinnacles, 65 km (40 miles) to Cape Palliser.

This, the most southerly part of the North Island's coast, can be a wild and desolate area in winter. But the lighthouse and seal colony at Cape Palliser are well worth seeing, as are the eerie rock formations in Putangirua Pinnacles Scenic Reserve. Wedged between the bay and a lagoon, Lake Ferry is a great spot to enjoy rugged scenery on a good day.

EXPLORING

Cape Palliser. Named by Captain Cook, Cape Palliser marks the eastern end of Palliser Bay. You can't miss its lighthouse, a candy-striped classic erected in 1897. Climb the 250 (the sign says 258) wooden steps for terrific views up and down the wild coastline. Below the lighthouse, splashing in the surf and basking on the rocks, are members of the North Island's only resident **fur seal colony.** You'll be able to get pretty close for photos, but not too close—these animals are fiercely protective of their young. Don't get between seals and pups, or seals and the ocean.

To reach it from Martinborough, start at Memorial Square and turn left into Jellicoe Street, this becomes Lake Ferry Road. After 30 km (18½ miles) turn left at the Cape Palliser road sign; from there it's another 35 km (21½ miles) to the cape itself. You'll pass The Pinnacles on your left; after this the road deteriorates and is unpaved in places. It is a bleak and dramatic drive, though not particularly hard if you take care. The travel time from Martinborough is approximately 80 minutes. ✉ *Cape Palliser.*

Lake Ferry. The tiny settlement of Lake Ferry sits beside Palliser Bay, 40 km (25 miles) northwest of Cape Palliser. The lake in question, called Onoke, is actually a salt lagoon formed by the long sandbank here. Vacation homes, fishing spots, and remarkable sunsets bring in the weekend Wellingtonian crowd. If you're coming from Martinborough, expect a 25-km (16-mile) drive through rolling sheep country. ✉ *Lake Ferry.*

Putangirua Pinnacles Scenic Reserve. Just before Lake Ferry, turn left (coming from Martinborough) at the sign for Cape Palliser and drive another 15 km (9 miles) around Palliser Bay to Te Kopi, where the Putangirua Pinnacles Scenic Reserve is protected from the hordes by its relative isolation. The spectacular rocks have been formed over the last 120,000 years as rains have washed away an ancient gravel deposit, and pinnacles and towers now soar hundreds of feet into the air on both sides of a stony riverbank. An hour-long round-trip walk from the parking area takes you along the riverbank and close to the base of the pinnacles. If you're feeling adventurous, a three- to four-hour bushwalk involves some steep climbs and wonderful vistas of the coast—as far off as the South Island on a clear day. Stout footwear and warm clothing are essential. The Pinnacles are an hour's drive from Martinborough. ⊠ *Palliser Bay, Featherston.*

WHERE TO STAY

$$
B&B/INN
🛏 **Kawakawa Station.** On 5,000-acres of rolling hills with sheep, cattle, horses, and dogs is a cozy, self-contained hillside cottage that welcomes guests. **Pros:** a real Kiwi farm experience; not too far from the sea. **Cons:** not suitable for children; the silence might keep you awake at night. $ *Rooms from: NZ$135* ⊠ *2631 Cape Palliser Rd., Cape Palliser* 🕾 *06/307–8989* ⊕ *www.kawakawastationwalk.co.nz* ▭ *No credit cards* ↪ *1 cottage* ⍥ *Breakfast.*

$
HOTEL
🛏 **Lake Ferry Hotel.** This waterfront hotel is home to the North Island's southernmost pub, with breathtaking views across Cape Palliser to the South Island's Kaikoura Ranges. **Pros:** if you like the feeling of being at the end of the Earth, this is for you; you'll also love the food and friendly welcome. **Cons:** don't expect the Ritz; only one room is en suite. $ *Rooms from: NZ$75* ⊠ *2 Lake Ferry Rd., Lake Ferry* 🕾 *06/307–7831* ⊕ *www.lakeferryhotel.co.nz* ↪ *8 rooms, 2 bunkrooms* ⍥ *Breakfast.*

$$$$
HOTEL
Fodor's Choice
★
🛏 **Wharekauhau.** A working sheep station meets bygone-era elegance at this unique coastal getaway, 90 minutes from Wellington; the 5,000-acre estate comes complete with an Edwardian-style main lodge surrounded by 13 guest cottages, each with king-size bed, small patio, and open fireplace. **Pros:** local history and flavor; on-site working farm; unique range of activities; luxury and privacy; spa using local products and herbal remedies. **Cons:** steep price; you won't want to move far from the fireplaces in rough weather; don't expect the nightlife to set you alight. $ *Rooms from: NZ$2254* ⊠ *Western Lake Rd., Palliser Bay, Featherston* 🕾 *06/307–7581* ⊕ *www.wharekauhau.co.nz* ↪ *13 cottages* ⍥ *Some meals.*

MASTERTON AND ENVIRONS

Masterton is 40 km (25 miles) northeast of Martinborough.

Masterton is Wairarapa's major population center, and, like Martinborough to the south, it's in a developing wine region. There's not much to do in the town, but it's a handy gateway for hiking in the nearby parks and on the coast. Popular annual events include the Hot Air Balloon Festival in early April and the Golden Shears sheep-shearing competition, usually held the first weekend in March.

State Highway 2 strings together a handful of eye-catching small towns on its way north past the Rimutakas. Farther north on the arrow-straight highway is **Greytown,** where well-preserved Victorian buildings now filled with cafés and boutiques line the main street. After a few miles more you'll reach **Carterton,** another small town with a handful of tempting stores—especially Paua World.

Continued on page 349

SEARCHING FOR
MIDDLE-EARTH

By Debra A. Klein

✦

With the Oscar-winning *Lord of the Rings* trilogy Peter Jackson secured his place among great location directors like John Ford and Martin Scorsese. He also sealed New Zealand's reputation for otherworldly beauty, putting the country on the map by celebrating it on screen.

The sets have long been struck, but New Zealand's vistas will inspire your imagination to fill in the castles, coombs, and creatures. It seems as if half the country was involved in filming, so you can always ask a local to tell a tale of Middle-earth. Or take a tour—elf ears are optional!

The Lord of the Rings marked New Zealand scenery's star turn, but, like an aspiring actor, it has worked its way up, often as a stand-in for better-known, bigger names. Mountain peaks outside of Queenstown double for the Rockies in advertisements, and Mt. Taranaki on the North Island played Japan's Mt. Fuji alongside Tom Cruise in *The Last Samurai*.

Now, thanks to generous incentives and a favorable exchange rate, New Zealand has lured other large international productions such as *The Chronicles of Narnia*. And Jackson has given Tolkien fans three more reasons to celebrate with *The Hobbit* trilogy.

✦

Above: Scene from *The Lord of the Rings: The Two Towers*

MIDDLE-EARTH

TONGARIRO NATIONAL PARK
The peaks near Mt. Ruapehu, the country's largest ski slope and its largest and most active volcano, played **Emyn Muil**; its slopes starred as **Mount Doom.** Frodo and Sam tracked and caught Gollum on rocky cliffs here, and Gollum caught fish at Ohakune, a World Heritage Site.

MATAMATA, WAIKATO
Matamata stood in for **The Shire,** Bilbo Baggins's home and the starting point for Frodo's quest. The rolling hills are here, but those sod homes were struck; only the Hobbit holes are left. Tour with Hobbiton Tours for the backstory (⊕ www.hobbitontours.com).

Cape Reinga
Kerr Point
Bay of Islands
NORTHLAND
Whangarei
NORTH ISLAND
Great Barrier Island
Hauraki Gulf
Firth of Thames
Whangamata
Cape Runaway
Bay of Plenty
Tauranga
Hamilton
Matamata
WAIKATO
EASTLAND
Raglan
Rotorua
TE UREWERA NATIONAL PARK
Gisborne
Tasman Sea
Taupo
North Taranaki Bight
Lake Taupo
New Plymouth
Ohakune
TONGARIRO NATIONAL PARK
Hawke Bay
Mt. Taranaki
Mt. Ruapehu
Napier
Cape Egmont
TARANAKI
WANGANUI
HAWKE'S BAY
Wanganui
Palmerston North
MANAWATU
SOUTH PACIFIC OCEAN
WAIRARAPA
Upper Hutt
Lower Hutt
WELLINGTON
Putangirua Pinnacles
Cook Strait
SOUTH ISLAND

WELLINGTON
Wellington served as home base for the cast and crew, and digital work was done here. Scenes of **The Shire, the Tower of Saruman, Rivendell,** and **Dunharrow** were all shot in suburbs of Upper and Lower Hutt. Wairarapa's Putangirua Pinnacles were the movie's **Paths of the Dead.**

0   100 miles
0   100 km

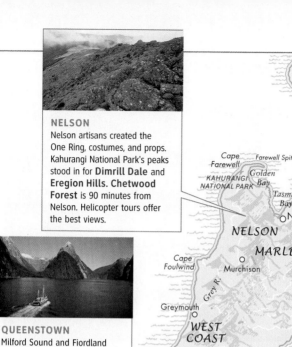

NELSON

Nelson artisans created the One Ring, costumes, and props. Kahurangi National Park's peaks stood in for **Dimrill Dale** and **Eregion Hills. Chetwood Forest** is 90 minutes from Nelson. Helicopter tours offer the best views.

QUEENSTOWN

Milford Sound and Fiordland National Park played **Amon Hen, Nen Hithoel,** and **Fangorn Forest.** Paradise became **Lothlorien,** where Frodo looks into the Mirror of Galadriel. Tour operators have a range of trips.

CANTERBURY

The Canterbury region became Gandalf's isolated fortress city of **Edoras** and the dramatic plains of **Rohan,** where Aragorn, Gimli, and Legolas track Merry and Pippin's captors in *The Two Towers.* And Twizel (a place, not a Hobbit) was the site of the winged-beast battle of **Pelennor Fields.**

Map labels

NORTH ISLAND

Cape Farewell
Farewell Spit
KAHURANGI NATIONAL PARK
Golden Bay
Tasman Bay
WELLINGTON
Nelson
Cook Strait
NELSON
Blenheim
MARLBOROUGH
Cape Foulwind
Murchison
Grey R.
Kaikoura
Greymouth
WEST COAST
Franz Josef
Christchurch
Fox Glacier
CANTERBURY
Akaroa
Lake Tekapo
Twizel
Lake Pukaki
Farlie
SOUTH ISLAND
Mt. Aspiring ▲
Lake Wanaka
Milford Sound
Paradise
Oamaru
FIORDLAND NATIONAL PARK
Queenstown
Doubtful Sound
Lake Te Anau
Lake Wakatipu
OTAGO
Lake Manapouri
Te Anau
Dunedin
SOUTHLAND
Invercargill
Foveaux Strait
Stewart Island
Muttonbird Islands

0   100 miles

0   100 km

TOURS OF THE *RINGS*

If you're familiar with the concept of "second breakfast," and know the difference between a smaug and a warg, you may want to break the bank for Glenorchy Air's **Three Ring Trilogy Tour,** an all-day adventure, including flying to and touching down at three filming locations on the South Island, or try their shorter **Two Ring** option for half a day. You can drive to some locations outside major cities on your own, but without a guide it may be difficult to "see" where the films were made (⊕ *www.trilogytrail.com*).

Hobbitontours (⊕ *www.hobbitontours. com*) offers guided tours of the Hobbiton Movie Set. Explore Hobbit Holes, the Green Dragon Inn, The Mill, and other structures from *The Hobbit* and *Lord of the Rings* sets that have been meticulously rebuilt. Based on a private farmland, The Hobbiton Movie Set is truly a journey into the Shire.

PRECIOUS MOMENTS

Many LOTR tours feature capes, swords, and flag replicas in the famous settings. Ogle the Weta Cave in Wellington, the museum of the movies' special-effects team (⊕ *www.wetanz.com*), or Minaret Lodge's Barliman's Room in Wanaka, featuring oversized furniture and a special Hobbit menu (⊕ *www.minaretlodge.co.nz*).

(top) The leisurely two-hour ride across the river flats at Glenorchy. (bottom) Mount Aspiring National Park

GETTING HERE AND AROUND

Approached on State Highway 2, Masterton is about a 90-minute drive from Wellington. Trains operated by Metlink come here from Wellington via the Hutt Valley, making the trip up to six times per day. Metlink buses also provide a very limited local bus service, but you need a car to explore the outlying areas.

Bus Depot Masterton Bus Depot. ✉ *Queen St., Masterton.*

Train Station Masterton Railway Station. ✉ *Perry St., Masterton.*

VISITOR INFORMATION

Contacts Featherston Visitor Centre. ✉ *The Old Courthouse, State Hwy. 2, Featherston* ☎ *06/308–8051.* **Masterton i-SITE Visitor Information Centre.** ✉ *At Dixon and Bruce Sts., Masterton* ☎ *06/370–0900* ⊕ *www.wairarapanz.com.*

EXPLORING

Castlepoint. An hour's drive east of Masterton along Te Ore-ore Road (which turns into the Masterton–Castlepoint Road), Castlepoint is perhaps the most spectacular site on the entire Wairarapa coast. Castle Rock rises a sheer 500 feet out of the sea; below, in **Deliverance Cove,** seals sometimes play. ✉ *Masterton.*

Fell Locomotive Museum. The tiny town of Featherston is worth a stop for the Fell Locomotive Museum. Along with photos, models, and memorabilia, it has the last remaining Fell locomotive in the world; built in 1875 and expertly restored, the engine is one of only six that clawed their way up the notorious Rimutaka Incline on the way to Wellington. ✉ *Lyon and Fitzherbert Sts., behind Information Center on State Hwy. 2, Featherston* ☎ *06/308–9379* ⊕ *www.fellmuseum.org.nz* ☞ *NZ$5* ☽ *Weekends 10–4, weekdays 10–2:30.*

Fodor's Choice ★ **Pukaha Mount Bruce.** Head 30 km (19 miles) north of Masterton for a fine introduction to the country's wildlife—particularly its endangered birds. An easy trail through the bush (one hour, round-trip) takes you past aviaries containing rare, endangered, or vulnerable birds, including the takahē, a flightless species thought to be extinct until it was rediscovered in 1948. The real highlight, though, is the nocturnal habitat containing foraging kiwis, endearing little bundles of energy that are the national symbol. Here you can also view the only white kiwi in captivity; she glows in the dark, so you won't have to wait for your eyes to adjust to the gloom to see her. Indigenous parrots are fed daily at 3, and the reserve's stream writhes when the long-finned eels are feed at 1:30. ✉ *State Hwy. 2, Masterton* ☎ *06/375–8004* ⊕ *www.pukaha.org. nz* ☞ *NZ$20* ☽ *Daily 9–4:30.*

Tararua Forest Park. For enjoyable bushwalks in gorgeous forests laced with streams, come to Tararua Forest Park. The Mt. Holdsworth area at the east end of the park is popular for tramping. If you're in the mood for an alfresco lunch, the park also has picnic facilities. To get here turn off State Highway 2 onto Norfolk Road, 2 km (1 miles) south of Masterton. ✉ *Masterton* ☎ *06/377–0700 DOC office.*

WHERE TO EAT

$$$$

MODERN NEW ZEALAND

✕ **The Farriers Bar & Eatery.** At The Farriers, you can watch the chefs in the open kitchen while waiting for your order to arrive. Much of the large menu is devoted to pub fare and wood-fired pizzas, all made from scratch; however, main courses like the Red Devon eye fillet with potato-spinach croquette tempt those with more ambitious appetites. Sustaining salads and a smattering of vegetarian dishes appeal to herbivores. In summer you can sit outside in the sunny courtyard. Ⓢ *Average main: NZ$34* ⊠ *4 Queen St. N, Masterton* ☎ *06/377–1102* ⊕ *www. thefarriers.co.nz.*

$$$

NEW ZEALAND

✕ **The White Swan Country Hotel.** A big open fireplace, light modern furniture, and glittering chandeliers create a warm, welcoming dining room where the service is impeccable. Try the grilled New Zealand rump steak with sautéed potatoes and herb mushrooms followed by a dark chocolate soufflé with orange mascarpone. For something more casual, choose from the excellent selection of light meals in the adjoining Veranda Bar. Ⓢ *Average main: NZ$24* ⊠ *109 Main St., Greytown* ☎ *06/304–8894* ⊕ *www.thewhiteswan.co.nz.*

WHERE TO STAY

$$

HOTEL

FAMILY

▢ **Copthorne Resort Solway Park Wairarapa.** With 24 acres of landscaped grounds and gardens, this spot on the southern outskirts of Masterton is a large resort for a small town. **Pros:** all single-story accommodations; indoor pool, squash court, and golf driving range; good off-road parking. **Cons:** weekdays popular for corporate conferences; can get crowded on weekends with special family rates. Ⓢ *Rooms from: NZ$160* ⊠ *High St. S, Masterton* ☎ *06/370–0500* ⊕ *www.solway.co.nz* ↩ *94 rooms, 8 apartments* ⏐◯⏐ *Breakfast.*

SHOPPING

Paua World. Just off the main highway in Carterton, Paua World is an interesting diversion. Akin to abalone, *paua* has been collected by the Māori since ancient times (they used it to represent eyes in their statues). The highly prized, rainbow-color shell interiors are polished, processed, then turned into jewelry and the like. ⊠ *54 Kent St., Carterton* ☎ *06/379–4247* ⊕ *www.pauaworld.com.*

UPPER SOUTH ISLAND AND THE WEST COAST

WELCOME TO UPPER SOUTH ISLAND AND THE WEST COAST

TOP REASONS TO GO

★ **Mountains, Glaciers, and Rain Forest:** Hiking, climbing, short rain forest and coastal walks, glacier walks and scenic flights, are all popular West Coast activities.

★ **Beaches:** Golden beaches and forest-fringed bays ring Upper South Island.

★ **Wildlife:** The Marlborough Sounds and Abel Tasman coast are home to several island sanctuaries where New Zealand seals and other rare native wildlife is protected. At Kaikoura, whales, dolphins, and ocean-traveling albatross come close to shore to feed.

★ **Wine:** In Marlborough and Nelson the sunny-day–cool-night climate means grapes come off the vines plump with flavor.

★ **Mining Legacy:** Marlborough, Murchison, Reefton, and the West Coast all have a strong legacy of mining, for gold and coal. This rich history comes alive in such places as the Denniston Mine near Westport.

1 Kaikoura. This is a rocky strip of Pacific coastline where whales breach just off shore, seals and dolphins play, and snowcapped mountains rise almost from the sea.

2 Marlborough. This region is all about vineyards, wide shingle riverbeds, and the sheltered, forest-lined waterways of the Marlborough Sounds.

3 Nelson and the Northwest. The northern coast encompasses the massive sand spit, Farewell Spit, the sheltered, golden-sand bays of the Abel Tasman National Park, and the wide expanse of Tasman Bay. A little inland, the economic heart of the region beats with farming, horticulture, viticulture, and forestry. To the south and west, from these productively

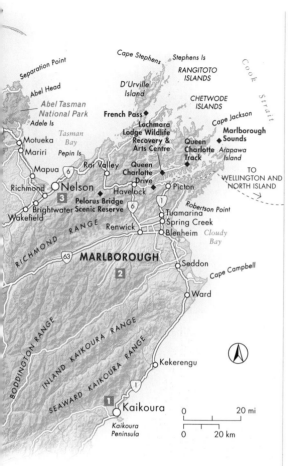

GETTING ORIENTED

In the northeast are the myriad waterways of the Marlborough Sounds. Heading south, you come to sunny Marlborough wine country. From Blenheim, the main town here, State Highway 1 travels south along the eastern coast, a narrow stretch between mountains and ocean to Kaikoura, then continues south through Canterbury farmland to Christchurch. Heading west, a series of forest-covered ranges separates Blenheim and Nelson. West of Nelson you'll pass through Motueka to Abel Tasman National Park and Golden Bay. Heading southwest on State Highway 6 brings you to big mountain country— Nelson Lakes and Kahurangi national parks—then through the Buller Gorge to the West Coast and south to the highest peaks of the Southern Alps. The highway follows the plains between the alps and Tasman Sea, passing settlements of Westport, Hokitika, and Greymouth before reaching glacier and world heritage country: Franz Josef and Fox glaciers in Westland/ Tai Poutini National Park.

8

intensive lowlands the landscape changes, to the mountains, beech forests, and glacial-formed lakes of Kahurangi and Nelson Lakes National Parks.

4 The West Coast. The Coast is a long narrow strip of land hemmed between the Tasman Sea and the Southern Alps. Landscapes encompass subtropical rain forests in the north and

icy glaciers in the south, where Westland/Tai Poutini National Park is a part of the massive Te Wahipounamu/ South West New Zealand World Heritage Area.

ABEL TASMAN NATIONAL PARK

Golden sand, sheltered bays, and granite headlands are washed by clear blue water and fast-moving tides; rocky inshore islands provide habitat for rare native birds, while migrant wading birds feed on the sand flats. It's a vibrant place of sun, sand, and sea.

Abel Tasman is New Zealand's smallest, and arguably most popular, national park. The terrain varies from forest-covered ranges to easy walking tracks that follow a forest-lined coastline with golden-sand beaches and sheltered bays. It's small enough that you can spend just a day here walking, kayaking, or simply cruising; or you can get serious and head off on a multiday trip combining all of the above. If you're new to outdoor experiences this is the perfect place to start. The park has a number of walking and water-based options, plus road access from the northeast and south. Shuttles and water taxis can take you to the trailheads and pick you up afterward.

BEST TIME TO GO

Anytime, but be wary during the peak summer holiday period, from Christmas to mid-January, when the locals flock here in great numbers. Most people prefer to visit in summer, November through April, but don't let winter put you off, especially if you prefer your solitude. Though colder, winter weather can be very settled and sunny.

BEST ACTIVITIES

Cruise or Water Taxi. In midsummer the coastline buzzes with little water taxis and bigger cruising catamarans delivering people to various parts of the track, picking up those who have walked or kayaked a section or two, and dropping off supplies and even kayaks. And if you just want to sit back and enjoy the scenery then join a cruise up the coast and back.

Kayak. Sea kayaking is popular, and several companies offer packages, often combining paddling and walking. These can be from half-day to multiday trips, freedom or fully guided and catered, with optional accommodations arranged. Water taxis can also be arranged to deliver your packs to your next stopover point. It's a pleasant, possibly invigorating trip, especially if the wind is going your way.

Sail. Almost without fail a healthy sea breeze comes up along the coast every summer afternoon. With this in mind catch a sailboat cruise out of Kaiteriteri in the morning. It's a slow gentle way to interact with the park. Then hang on as the skipper hooks the boat into that sea breeze on the way home behind a fully set spinnaker.

Walk. The entire 60 km (37 miles) Abel Tasman Coast Track, from Wainui Bay in the north to Marahau in the south, can be walked in three to five days, depending on your pace and how many swims you want along the way. This designated Great Walk is well formed and easy to follow. Alternatively you can walk short sections by arranging a drop-off and pickup by water taxi. Bark Bay to Torrent Bay and Awaroa to

Torrent Bay are ideal for this. There are a few tidal crossings along the track that can only be crossed at mid- to low tides. Each of these has a longer all-tide alternative, but plan ahead and remember to allow for this if you are meeting a water taxi. The park's inland tracks explore more rugged, forest-covered areas—best tackled by more experienced trampers.

WORD OF MOUTH

"Abel Tasman was gorgeous in a totally different way than the huge mountains and lakes we'd seen in other parts. It was forested with turquoise waters and reminded me a bit of Hawaii. We did a half-day kayak trip in the park and saw a little blue penguin, so that was a highlight. This was our last stop so we wanted to relax and also spent one day at the beach in Kaiteriteri."—nz2014

8

(above left) Abel Tasman Coastal Track; *(bottom)* Bark Bay; *(above)* Tonga Arches at Arch Point

KAHURANGI NATIONAL PARK

Kahurangi is a vast wilderness of marbled karst mountains, glaciated landforms, alpine tablelands, rivers, alpine tarns and beech, podocarp, and coastal rain forests. Underground are the country's longest, deepest, and oldest cave systems. Multiday hikes, short walks, caving, rafting, fly-fishing, and hunting are what people like to do here.

Kahurangi National Park spans 1.1 million acres, much of it untamed, yet crisscrossed by 570 km (353 miles) of hiking tracks of various levels. Most well known is the four- to five-day Heaphy Track, one of New Zealand's Great Walks. There are also several rafting and kayaking rivers and some serious caving challenges. Probably the most popular access from Nelson is the steep road to Flora Carpark on Mt. Arthur. More southern entry points include the Wangapeka River, near Tapawera, and Matiri Valley, near Murchison. The main West Coast access is through Karamea; this is also the southwestern entry to the Heaphy Track. Helicopters regularly transport fishing fans to secret river spots, though large areas of the park are designated wilderness, where no development or helicopter transport is permitted.

BEST TIME TO GO

Kahurangi can be visited any time of the year, although snow in winter will inhibit access to the higher areas like Mt. Arthur and the Mt. Owen massif. The Heaphy Track is generally passable year-round. It's particularly popular with walkers in summer, and mountain bikers are permitted on the track in winter (May to September).

BEST ACTIVITIES

Caving and Cave Diving. There is a spectacular network of caves beneath the park, in particular under "the mountains with plumbing," as Mt. Arthur and Mt. Owen are known. New passages are still being discovered and the cave systems at the northern end of Kahurangi join up with those under Abel Tasman. Local guides are essential if you want to explore these. The Pearce and Riwaka rivers, on the eastern side of Mt. Arthur, are both well-known cave-diving spots with well-defined resurgence caves. The Riwaka resurgence is popular with scuba enthusiasts. A local guide is essential.

Helicopter or Fixed Wing Plane. In some areas of the vast Kahurangi there's absolutely no development permitted, and the only way to get there is to walk. In other areas, however, helicopters can be chartered to ferry hikers and rafters to remote rivers and tracks, to get trout fishermen to favored spots, and for general sightseeing. A helicopter flight to *Lord of the Rings* film locations on spectacular Mt. Owen and Mt. Olympus has also become popular.

Tramp. The five-day Heaphy Track is one of the country's Great Walks, traversing tussock-covered tablelands and remote, wild West Coast beaches in the northwest corner of the park, between Collingwood and Karamea. Other challenging and less-walked walks are available; while shorter, easier and popular tracks leave from the Flora Carpark (accessed from Motueka and Nelson) and the Cobb Valley (south of Takaka).

White-Water Rafting and Kayaking. The Grade V Karamea River offers some of the country's most remote white-water rafting and kayaking. Access is generally by helicopter and rafting trips last up to a week, thus involving overnight camping. There is also great white water on the Buller River near Murchison, which runs along part of the park's southern boundary. Local knowledge is essential on these trips so use a local guiding company of good repute.

8

(top left) Eroded limestone formations; *(bottom)* A tramper relaxes at the top of Mt. Owen; *(top)* Trampers on the Heaphy Track

NELSON LAKES NATIONAL PARK

Snow-covered peaks and alpine passes sit between two deep brooding, forest-surrounded lakes. Dense native forest, swampy wetlands, and tumbling rivers line the valleys, and birdlife join in a resounding dawn chorus. It's an exhilarating environment.

Two stunningly scenic glacial-formed lakes, Rotoroa and Rotoiti, are the central focus of Nelson Lakes National Park. Also in the park are rocky peaks and tussock-covered tops, glacier-gouged river valleys, and bush-lined trails. Native beech forest pours down to the lakeshores. On cloudy days, mist swirls through the trees, wetting the draping mosses. On sunny days the intense greens shine through and the birds' chorus resounds.

Of the two lakes, Rotoroa is less developed, with just a few fishing cottages, a campsite, and a lodge gathered on its northern shore. The village of St. Arnaud, at the northern end of Lake Rotoiti, is the major gateway to the park, with a small service center, accommodations, and the Department of Conservation (DOC) Visitor Center and campsites. Rainbow Ski Area, a small club field, operates nearby in winter.

BEST TIME TO GO

Summer is the most popular time of year to visit as the weather is warm (for an alpine region), the lakes are swimmable (barely), and, for climbers, the high-alpine passes are usually free of snow and avalanche risk. Voracious sand flies, however, are a problem at any time. Bring your repellent.

BEST ACTIVITIES

Climb. Experienced alpinists enjoy the challenges of the high passes and summit ridgelines that lead to the highest peaks of the park. Experience is vital; some of this climbing is technical and subject to severe and changeable weather.

Kayak. Both Rotoroa and Rotoiti are excellent places to kayak. Although both lakes can attract high winds, summer conditions are usually favorable. Pick your day, pack a lunch, and leave from the jetty at the head of either lake. At St. Arnaud in summer, kayaks can be hired from the Rotoiti lakeshore. Pull up to a quiet stretch of pebble beach, where all you will hear are the birds and the breeze singing through the trees. Don't forget your sand-fly repellent.

Ski. In winter a small club ski field welcomes visitors. Rainbow Ski Area is an hour's drive from St. Arnaud. It has basic facilities (rope tows and a café) and access is via a steepish mountain road (open June to October). There is also ski hire at Rainbow.

Walk. The park is laced with walking tracks, which center on the two lakes and range from easy 30-minute wanders to serious multiday treks deep into the mountains. In summer the longer walks are usually passable, although a cold snap can bring snow at any time to the passes between valleys. Day walks include the climb up Mt. Robert on the

zigzagging Pinchgut Track, the climb to Parachute Rocks, and the lakeside walk around Rotoiti. Popular longer hikes are overnight to Lake Angelus Hut (often crowded in summer) and the three- to four-day Travers-Sabine circuit, which leads up the Travers, crosses an alpine pass, and returns down the Sabine. You camp or stay in park huts along the way.

Water Taxi. During summer water taxis work on both lakes. They save a half-day walk at the start of some longer trails, such as the Travers/Sabine circuit, and give nonwalkers quick access into the park. Remember to take everything you need with you as there are no shops, cafés, or amenities away from St. Arnaud.

8

(top left) View of the Parachute Rocks; *(bottom)* Looking into a basin at Robert Ridge; *(top)* A pier on Lake Rotoiti

Updated by
Kathy Ombler

The South Island has been carved by ice, water, and tectonic uplift, all processes still rapidly occurring. Here, the mellow farmland greens and jumbled forest-covered ranges of the North Island are replaced by snowcapped mountains, glaciers, rivers that sprawl across wide-shingle beds and, in the northeast, drowned river valleys.

Marlborough occupies the northeast corner of the South Island. The bays and inlets of the Marlborough Sounds (these are the drowned river valleys) wash around bush-covered peninsulas and sandy coves. Marlborough is also the largest wine-growing region in New Zealand, with more than 27,000 acres of vineyards. It's a relatively dry and sunny area, and on a hazy summer day the inland plains can resemble the American West, with mountains rising beyond the arid flats.

The northwest corner of the island is the sun-drenched Nelson region, which enjoys a relatively mild climate that allows a year-round array of outdoor activities. Nelson city is a lively place to visit, with fine restaurants and a vibrant network of artists and craftspeople. It's also the gateway to three national parks, an internationally recognized wetland, beaches, hiking tracks, and boating opportunities. Abel Tasman National Park, to the west of the city, is ringed with spectacularly blue-green waters studded with golden beaches and craggy rocks, and it's home to the popular Abel Tasman Coast Track. To the southwest is Kahurangi National Park, with unique karst marble mountains and the popular Heaphy Track. Farther to the south Nelson Lakes National Park, with its glacial lakes, bushwalks, longer hiking trails, alpine passes, and snowcapped peaks, is a popular holiday spot for both Kiwi folk and overseas visitors.

After the gentler climes of Marlborough and Nelson, the wild grandeur of the West Coast is a dramatic contrast. This is Mother Nature with her hair down, flaying the coastline with huge seas and drenching rains and littering its beaches with tons of bleached driftwood. When it rains, you feel like you're inside a fishbowl; then the sun bursts out, and you swear you're in paradise. (Always check local conditions before taking an excursion.) This region has a rich heritage of mining for gold and coal, and milling, a legacy that has created a special breed of rough-hewn and powerfully independent locals—known to the rest of the country as Coasters—who occupy a special place in New Zealand folklore.

PLANNING

Anything less than three or four days through Nelson and Marlborough and an additional three to four days on the West Coast will be too few. Don't be deceived by the maps; steep, winding roads slow down the drive times. Campervans proliferate these roads in summer, and tend to move slowly so be patient and wait for a clear place to pass.

WHEN TO GO

Nelson and Marlborough are delightful year-round, but beach activities are best from December to mid-March if you plan to be *in* the water. From Christmas through January some places can be busy with New Zealanders on their own vacations so book ahead. Snow generally covers the mountains from June through October. Don't let this stop you from driving through these regions; scenically they will look even more stunning. Sperm whales and dolphins live year-round off the coast of Kaikoura. Humpback whales visit in early winter. The pleasures of winter weather around the West Coast glaciers—clear skies and no snow at sea level—are a well-kept local secret. Look into local festival schedules; they occur year-round.

GETTING HERE AND AROUND

AIR TRAVEL

Several daily Air New Zealand flights operate between Auckland, Wellington, and Christchurch and Blenheim and Nelson. Sounds Air flies smaller planes daily between Wellington and Blenheim, Picton, and Nelson. Origin Air flies between Nelson and Palmerston North and Wellington. Kiwi Regional Airlines connects Nelson with Hamilton and Dunedin. Jetstar flies between Nelson and Wellington and Auckland. Hokitika is also serviced by Air New Zealand flights. Picton and Golden Bay are serviced by smaller commuter aircraft.

Contacts Kiwi Regional Air. ☎ 07/444–2020 ⊕ flykiwiair.co.nz. **Origin Air.** ☎ 0800/380–380 ⊕ originair.co.nz. **Sounds Air.** ☎ 0800/505–005 ⊕ www. soundsair.com.

CAR TRAVEL

Roads through this region's mountain ranges and deep river gorges can be narrow and winding, and a 160-km (100-mile) drive might take more than three hours. However, the roads are generally good, and there's always something to look at. There are a number of one-way bridges along the way. Check the road sign with two colorful arrows: if the arrow is red for your side of the road, that means you give way if traffic is coming the other way. Remember always to keep left. It can also be a long way between gas stations, so fill up when you can.

Nelson is about a two-hour drive from Picton. From Nelson, State Highway 6 runs southwest to the West Coast, north to Westport, back south down the coast to the glaciers, then inland, over the Haast Pass where roads lead to Wanaka, Queenstown, and Central Otago. For the West Coast, count on at least seven hours solid driving (and photo stops) for the 458-km (284-mile) journey from Nelson to Franz Josef. (But seriously, don't even think about doing this in one haul. Take a few days.) For Nelson to Christchurch, allow up to five hours, whether you go through the mountains of the Lewis Pass or take the coastal route via Blenheim and Kaikoura. Heading direct west from Nelson, Highway 60 splits from State Highway 6 about 13 km (8 miles) out of the city, near Richmond, and continues to Motueka, Abel Tasman National Park, and Golden Bay.

Westport, gateway to the northern end of the West Coast, is roughly a three-hour trip from Nelson on State Highway 6 or a five- to six-hour drive over Arthur's Pass on Highway 7 from Christchurch. State Highway 7 climbs from Arthur's Pass and across the backbone of the Southern Alps before winding steeply down through rain forest to the tiny town of Otira and on to the coastal river plains of the mid–West Coast.

AUTO TRANSFERS
Some car rental agencies have North Island–South Island transfer programs for their vehicles: you leave one car in Wellington, travel as a foot passenger, and pick another car up in Picton on the same contract. Others let you keep one car that you drive on and off the ferry. Check first.

FERRY TRAVEL

Visitors traveling from the North Island can take either the Interislander or Bluebridge ferry from Wellington to Picton, the northern entrance to the South Island. The trip is scenic, especially through sheltered Tory Channel in the Marlborough Sounds, though Cook Strait itself can be rough at times. The one-way adult fare ranges from NZ$53 to NZ$75. Ferries dock in Picton, right beside the township.

Contact Bluebridge. ☎ 0800/844–844 ⊕ www.bluebridge.co.nz. **Interislander.** ☎ 0800/802–802 NZ only ⊕ www.interislander.co.nz.

TRAIN TRAVEL

Two of New Zealand's three scenic rail journeys serve these regions. The West Coast is connected with Christchurch by the **TranzAlpine Express,** which ranks as one of the world's great rail journeys. The train crosses the Southern Alps between Christchurch and Greymouth, winding through southern beech forests and snow-covered mountains. The **Coastal Pacific** meets some Cook Strait ferry sailings and travels through Marlborough and along the scenic Kaikoura coast to Christchurch. Both trains are modern and comfortable, with panoramic windows and a no-frills dining and bar service.

Contact The Coastal Pacific Train. ☎ 0800/872–467 ⊕ www.kiwirailscenic.co.nz. **The TranzAlpine Train.** ☎ 0800/872–467 NZ only ⊕ www.kiwirailscenic.co.nz.

RESTAURANTS

In Marlborough visit a winery restaurant—there's no better way to ensure that your meal suits what you're drinking. Cloudy Bay clams are harvested here, salmon and Greenshell mussels are farmed in the Marlborough Sounds, and local crops—besides grapes—include cherries and garlic. In Kaikoura try crayfish. The region is named after this delicacy

(In Māori, *kai means "food" and koura* means "lobster"). Nelson is also famous for seafood, in particular scallops, and for fresh produce and, yes, for wine. On the West Coast, try the local delicacy whitebait fritters—a sort of omelet filled with the whitebait—tiny, young eel-like fish netted at river mouths as they migrate upstream in late spring.

Some restaurants in more remote tourist regions close in winter (June through August); others may curtail their hours. In summer, all doors are open and it's best to make reservations. If a restaurant is open on a major holiday, it may add a surcharge to your bill.

Year-round, the restaurants and cafés around the glaciers and other remote spots can be quick to close their doors at night. Arrive by 8:30 (it's sometimes even earlier in winter) or you might go hungry. Some of the smallest towns, including Punakaiki, settlements in the Marlborough Sounds, and parts of Golden Bay, have few cafés and no general stores, so bring your own supplies.

HOTELS

Bed-and-breakfasts, farm stays, and homestays, all a variation on the same theme, abound in the South Island in some spectacular coastal and mountain environments. Your hosts will generally feed you great breakfasts and advise on where to eat and what to do locally. Other choices include boutique luxury lodges and hotels, or less expensive but well-equipped motel rooms and backpacker lodges.

Hotel reviews have been shortened. For full information, visit Fodors.com.

WHAT IT COSTS IN NEW ZEALAND DOLLARS			
$	$$	$$$	$$$$
Restaurants	under NZ$15	NZ$15–NZ$20	NZ$21–NZ$30	over NZ$30
Hotels	under NZ$125	NZ$125–NZ$200	NZ$201–NZ$300	over NZ$300

Restaurant prices are the average cost of a main course at dinner or, if dinner is not served, at lunch. Hotel prices are the lowest cost of a standard double room in high season.

VISITOR INFORMATION

Every large, and most small, towns have an information center or i-SITE office; watch for the blue-and-white "i" sign showing their location.

Several regional tourism organizations maintain helpful websites: Destination Marlborough (⊕ *www.lovemarlborough.com*), Nelson Tasman Tourism (⊕ *www.nelsonnz.com*), Tourism West Coast (⊕ *www.westcoast.co.nz*), and Glacier Country Tourism Group (⊕ *www.glaciercountry.co.nz*). The Department of Conservation (⊕ *www.doc.govt.nz*) is the best source for national parks, forest parks, and scenic reserves.

KAIKOURA

129 km (81 miles) south of Blenheim, 182 km (114 miles) north of Christchurch.

The town of Kaikoura sits at the base of a peninsula that juts into the ocean from the east coast, and is backed by the steep Kaikoura mountain range. Take it all in from the 360-degree **lookout** by the water tower up on Scarborough Street. In addition to its spectacular scenery, Kaikoura is famous for the abundant marine life that gathers here because of offshore sea canyons and the meeting of subtropical and cold southern sea currents, which support a rich and complex underwater food chain. Sperm whales feed closer to shore at Kaikoura than anywhere else in the world. Humpbacks, pilot whales, and orca join them during seasonal migrations. You are most likely to see the whales between October and August, though the sperm whale lives here year-round. Joining the marine melee are dolphins and seals, and the birdlife is equally prolific. On a good day, Kaikoura is considered one of the world's best places for watching pelagic (oceangoing) birds, such as albatross (many species), while Hutton's Shearwaters, also oceanic travelers, nest only here, high in the craggy peaks of the Seaward Kaikoura Range. Ecotourism, whale-watching and bird-watching cruises, and swimming with dolphins and seals have become the backbone of Kaikoura's economy, attracting thousands of visitors each year.

Kaikoura's main street runs close to the coast, behind a high, stony bank, protected from stormy swells. On the southern shoreline of the peninsula, a few minutes' drive away, is South Bay, the boarding point for whale-watching and dolphin-swimming operators.

GETTING HERE AND AROUND

Kaikoura township sits on State Highway 1, between Picton and Christchurch and the coastal route between Nelson and Christchurch. It's an easy 2½-hour drive south from Kaikoura to Christchurch and 1½ hours north to Blenheim.

InterCity and **Atomic Shuttles** run daily buses between Christchurch, Kaikoura, Blenheim, Picton, and Nelson.

The Coastal Pacific train follows the coast from Christchurch to Picton, meeting with the Cook Strait ferries. It stops at Kaikoura both ways.

VISITOR INFORMATION

Contacts Kaikoura i-SITE Visitor Centre. ⊠ *West End* ☎ *03/319–5641* ⊕ *www.kaikoura.co.nz.*

EXPLORING

TOP ATTRACTIONS

Lavendyl Lavender Farm. Inland and just north of the town center, rows of lavender stretch out against the stunning backdrop of Mt. Fyffe and the Seaward Kaikoura Range. At this working 5-acre farm, visitors are welcome to walk through the heavenly scented gardens and from December to February, watch the blossom harvest. In the shop, bunches of lavender hang from the ceiling and lavender mustards, chutneys, soaps, oils, and salves line the shelves. There's a café, of sorts, serving tea and coffee, ice creams, and cold drinks and a few lavender-flavor treats. They also have two rustic self-contained B&B cottages in the garden. ⊠ *268 Postmans Rd.* ☎ *03/319–5473* ⊕ *www.lavenderfarm. co.nz* ✉ *NZ$5 (peak summer months), otherwise NZ$2; check website for up-to-date information* ⊙ *Daily 10–4 (winter), 9–7 (summer); check website for up-to-date information.*

WORTH NOTING

Fyffe House. Kaikoura's oldest building, erected soon after Robert Fyffe's whaling station was established in 1842, is now a small museum. Partly built on whale-bone piles on a grassy rise overlooking the sea, the house provides a look at what life was like when people aimed at whales with harpoons rather than cameras. You can stop here on the way to the Point Kean seal colony. ⊠ *62 Avoca St.* ☎ *03/319–5835* ⊕ *www.heritage.org.nz* ✉ *NZ$10* ⊙ *Oct.–Apr., daily 10–5; May–Sept., Thurs.–Mon. 10–4.*

EN ROUTE

Mainline Station Cafe. When traveling between Christchurch and Kaikoura, this café at Domett stands out among the slim eating options along the way. Built in the 100-year-old ex-Domett railway station, in the middle of rural North Canterbury, it's a sunny spot with a sheltered area of tables outdoors and a rustic atmosphere inside. There's a scrummy selection of cakes and a small blackboard menu of tasty homemade brunch and lunch dishes. Sunday in summer and spring is market day with local foods, arts, and crafts available. ⊠ *Corner State Hwy. 1 and Old Main Rd., 106 km (71 miles) north of Christchurch, 7 km (5 miles) south of Cheviot, Cheviot* ☎ *03/319–8776* ⊕ *mainline-station-cafe.tripledash.co.nz* ⊙ *Closed Tues. and July and Aug. No dinner.*

Seafest. On one Saturday every October Kaikoura celebrates the best of this coastal area's food, wine, and beer. Enjoy the food and drink while top New Zealand entertainers perform on an outdoor stage. Tickets are available online or from the town's i-SITE Visitor Center; they do sell out so be sure to book ahead. ☎ *0800/473–2337 NZ only, 03/319–5641* ⊕ *www.seafest.co.nz.*

8

WHERE TO EAT

For a small place Kaikoura has an excellent choice of restaurants. But for a taste of the local crayfish visit one of the roadside caravans; on the coast north of town Nin's Bin at Rakautara has a strong fan base. Crays come cooked or uncooked, or you may prefer to get your crayfish fix at a local café, though they are expensive even at a casual place. Also try the whitefish-like *groper* (grouper) and *terakihi,*or the shellfish, for example abalone, known here as *paua.*

$$
CAFÉ
✕ **Café Encounter.** Here's a bright eatery along the Esplanade, sharing space with the Dolphin and Albatross Encounter operations and a pleasant gallery/shop. The partially glassed-in courtyard is sheltered in most winds, and there's plenty of indoor seating. It's kid friendly, with a bright little Kiddies Corner playground. Food is available off the menu or from the cabinet; breakfasts and light lunches are appealing; and their range of cakes and slices is always tempting. As at any

outdoor café in Kaikoura, don't leave your food unattended because the birds will snatch it quicker than you can say "seagull!" $ *Average main: NZ$15* ⊠ *96 The Esplanade* ☎ *03/319–6777* ⊗ *No dinner.*

$$$
CAFÉ
Fodor's Choice
★

✕ **Hislops Café.** This wholesome foodie café is a local institution, a few minutes' walk north of town and worth the trip. In the morning you'll find tasty free-range eggs and bacon, plus freshly baked, genuinely stone-ground whole-grain bread served with marmalade or their own honey. The lunch and dinner menus use organic ingredients wherever possible, and there are wheat- and gluten-free options as well. The menu changes seasonally but choices may include a potato and feta rosti and seafood chowder. On sunny days, snag a table on the veranda. $ *Average main: NZ$26* ⊠ *33 Beach Rd.* ☎ *03/319–6971* ⊕ *www.hislops-wholefoods.co.nz* ⊗ *Closed Mon. and Tues. No dinner.*

$$$$
NEW ZEALAND

✕ **The Pier Hotel.** In a two-story Victorian waterfront hotel overlooking Ingles Bay, one of Kaikoura's most dependable eateries serves traditional New Zealand pub fare with a bit of a makeover. The dining room serves consistently good, fresh local dishes, particularly seafood, with a good selection presented on the Seafood Platter. Their chowder is thick and creamy and is served as a lunch dish or dinner main course; or try the lamb or aged steak. The bar serves cheaper lunches and pub snacks if you're just looking to graze. $ *Average main: NZ$34* ⊠ *1 Avoca St.* ☎ *03/319–5037* ⊕ *www.thepierhotel.co.nz* ⊜ *Reservations essential.*

WHERE TO STAY

Accommodations in Kaikoura are a mix of country lodge and motels, apartments, and holiday parks in town. Another option is camping out of town, beside the coast at one of the Kaikoura Coastal Campgrounds. There are various spots available from Paia Point, south of town, along to Oari. They are all administered from the Kaikoura Coastal Camp at **Goose Bay** (☎ *03/319–5348* ⊕ *www.kaikouracamping.co.nz*), and it's necessary to call before grabbing a site. Powered and tent sites are available. Department of Conservation campsites are at Okiwi Bay and Puhipuhi.

$$
HOTEL
FAMILY

⊞ **Alpine-Pacific Holiday Park.** Just outside town, this nicely laid-out site has spotless cabins, studios, and full motel units available; there are also powered campervan sites and campsites. **Pros:** incredibly clean, tidy outfit layered down a terraced slope; trampoline for the kids; bikes for rent. **Cons:** campsites a little cramped if full. $ *Rooms from: NZ$135* ⊠ *69 Beach Rd.* ☎ *03/319–6275, 0800/692–322 free in New Zealand* ⊕ *alpine-pacific.co.nz* ⇥ *8 cabins, 4 studio units, 8 en suite studio units, 2 2-bedroom units, 50 campsites* ⦿❘ *No meals.*

$$$$
HOTEL
Fodor's Choice
★

⊞ **Hapuku Lodge and Tree Houses.** Featuring imaginative use of timbers and finishings, the rooms in the main lodge building are quietly tasteful, but out in the trees things get way more interesting in the luxurious tree houses. **Pros:** unique luxury accommodations; surf out the back window and snow out the front; walking track down to the sea through the olive grove. **Cons:** stay in the main lodge if you can't manage stairs; no kids in the main lodge (but they're welcome in the tree houses). $ *Rooms from: NZ$660* ⊠ *State Hwy. 1 at 1 Station Rd., 12 km (8 miles) north* *of Kaikoura* ☎ *03/319–6559, 0800/524–56872* 🌐 *www.hapukulodge.com* 🛏 *2 lodge rooms, 2 lodge suites, 5 1- and 2-bedroom tree houses, 1 villa* 🍴 *Some meals.*

$$$ B&B/INN 🏨 **Surfwatch Getaway Cottages.** Perched high on the cliffs overlooking Mangamaunu Beach and just 10 minutes north of town, a private en suite room attached to the main house and a character-filled, self-contained garden cottage stand true to the name of this homey property. **Pros:** views from the B&B suite are exceptional; 5-acre property is a small farm; lots of handcrafted furniture and wood detail. **Cons:** really steep access road; opens off a fast stretch of twisting coastal highway so take care crossing the road. [$] *Rooms from: NZ$240* ✉ *1137 State Hwy. 1, Mangamaunu* ☎ *03/319–6611* 🌐 *surf-watch.co.nz* 🛏 *1 room, 1 cottage* 🍴 *Breakfast* ☞ *NZ$205 self-catering option available.*

$$$ HOTEL 🏨 **The White Morph Heritage Boutique Collection.** A waterfront view is hard to ignore—even more so on the rugged Kaikoura coast—and this rather fancy apartment-style lodge is just across the road from the beach and a few minutes' walk from the town center. **Pros:** eminently comfortable units in a great Esplanade location; breakfast available in the neighboring Encounter Café. **Cons:** not all units have a sea view; on a busy road. [$] *Rooms from: NZ$230* ✉ *92 The Esplanade* ☎ *03/319–5014* 🌐 *www.whitemorph.co.nz* 🛏 *31 units (12 with whirlpool baths), 16 studios, 3 self-catering family units* 🍴 *No meals* ☞ *Breakfast packages available.*

SPORTS AND THE OUTDOORS

December to March are the most popular months for whale-watching and swimming with dolphins or seals, so book well in advance.

BIRD-WATCHING

Fodor's Choice ★ **Albatross Encounter.** Birding experts say that when the conditions are right Kaikoura is one of the leading pelagic (oceangoing) bird-watching destinations in the world. It's also one of the most accessible, as the birds come close to shore to feed. Boat tours provide an intimate encounter with some of the planet's most spectacular birds, including several albatross species and the Hutton's shearwater, which disperses all around the world yet breeds only in the Seaward Kaikoura Range. Tours last 2½ hours. Longer, specialist tours are available by arrangement. Book on their website or at the Encounter Kaikoura headquarters, café, and gallery (great bird photographs, taken by company founder, Dennis Buurman, are available here), where you can also book to swim with dolphins. ✉ *96 The Esplanade* ☎ *03/319–6777, 0800/733–365* 🌐 *www.albatrossencounter.co.nz* 🎟 *NZ$115* ⏲ *Daily Apr–Oct.*

HIKING

Kaikoura Coast Track. This two-day walk provides uncrowded, unguided hiking and two nights in rustic yet comfortable accommodation along spectacular coastal farmland south of Kaikoura, for 10 people at a time maximum. Take binoculars to search out seals, seabirds, and dolphins. The first day's trail follows the remote coast, you'll pass towering cliffs, sandy beaches, and an ancient buried forest. Day 2 you'll be shown to a trail that explores forest-filled valleys, open tussock country, and farmland. You can expect about 13 km (8 miles) walking each day.

Bags are transferred to the next night's accommodations, so you only need to carry a day pack. Reservations are essential. The start point is a ¾-hour drive south of Kaikoura; public transport can drop you at the gate. ⊠ *356 Conway Flat Rd., Cheviot* ☎ *03/319–2715* ⊕ *www. kaikouratrack.co.nz* ✉ *NZ$190 per person, including bag transfers. Inquire about all-inclusive meal prices* ⊗ *Daily Oct.–Apr.*

FAMILY **Kaikoura Peninsula Walkway.** Public walking trails around the Kaikoura Peninsula show off spectacular coastal scenery and get you close to seal and seabird colonies. You can walk one long circuit from town, around the tip of the peninsula, then back across the top; or just walk out and back along the tip at either the northern or southern sides. There are also shorter walks to lookout points. Consult the Department of Conservation's website for maps and track information. The southern entry point, at South Bay, recognizes the importance of the area to local Māori, whose ancestors lived on this stretch of coast for many generations before Europeans arrived. The first part of the track from South Bay leading to Limestone Bay is wheelchair accessible. The northern access point, by the Point Kean car park, is where you are most likely to encounter seals. They might look like they're sleeping but keep a safe distance, and don't, as observers have done, get yourself between a seal and its escape route to the sea. ⊠ *Penisula Walkway* ⊕ *www.doc.govt.nz.*

Kaikoura Wilderness Walks. Hike private country that penetrates deep into the towering Kaikoura Mountains, and sleep in luxury. There's no roughing it on this expedition. The three-day guided walk includes overnight accommodations in the purpose-built **Shearwater Lodge,** high above the Puhi Puhi Valley in the Seaward Kaikoura Range. Up to 12 guests can be accommodated in six super-king or twin en suite rooms, each with its own balcony. The all-inclusive meals are served in the warm lounge and dining room, with its huge window overlooking the mountains. Door-to-door pickup can be arranged from Kaikoura, your luggage is transferred to the lodge, all meals are provided, and the walks are fully guided. You need to be moderately fit and agile and be able to hike five to seven (mild) hours a day. ⊠ *1695 Puhi Puhi Rd.* ☎ *03/319– 6966, 0800/945–337 NZ only* ⊕ *www.kaikourawilderness.co.nz* ✉ *NZ$1,895* ⊗ *Sept.–Mar., departs Tues.* ⚏ *Reservations essential.*

RAFTING

Clarence River Rafting. The Clarence is one of New Zealand's least known yet most interesting and scenically stunning wilderness rivers. It follows a fault line between the Inland and Seaward Kaikoura ranges, the highest peaks outside the Southern Alps, through some of the oldest and most geologically significant limestone in the country. Vegetation is a mix of tussock-covered hills, shrublands, scree slopes, and bare rock, and public access to the river's isolated upper reaches is limited. This locally based company can organize the entire expedition: transport, rafts, trusted and knowledgeable guides, all meals, and tent accommodation. The river is bouncy at best, and is ideal for a beginners' or family trip (minimum age five). By far a raft is the best option to visit this wild and wonderful country. Anything from half-day to fully catered overnight and multiday trips are offered, including either vehicle shuttle to your journey's starting point. Helicopter shuttles can be arranged at extra cost. Trips end at the river mouth, at Clarence township, one hour north of Kaikoura; transfers can be arranged from the Picton ferries, Marlborough and Picton airports, or Hanmer Springs township. ✉ *3802 State Hwy. 1* 🕾 *03/319–6993* ⊕ *www.clarenceriverrafting.co.nz* 🖃 *From NZ$120* ⊙ *Closed May–Sept.*

SWIMMING WITH DOLPHINS AND SEALS

The dolphin- and seal-spotting opportunities are fantastic here. Although operators have led visitors to view and swim with dolphins and seals off the Kaikoura coast for years, and the animals may be familiar with boats, they are not tame. New Zealand fur seals are also common along this coast and, if you get into the water around the rock pools, you might spot crayfish. Pods of Dusky dolphins stay in the area year-round; you may even see them doing aerial jumps and flips.

Options to engage with seals and dolphins vary and operators will explain these before you book. Some boat operators go quite a ways offshore, whereas others hug the coast. If you have any questions about the suitability of a trip, pipe up; these guys are happy to help. Guides can prime you with information on the local species and will be in the water with you. Wet suits and other gear are provided.

Dolphin Encounter. Swim with, or just watch, the Dusky dolphins that live around here. Tours operate three times a day through summer and twice a day in winter. Because boats operate in the open ocean, you need to be confident in the water, and it's an advantage to have some snorkeling experience. Trips can cancel due to bad weather so prepare to be flexible. Book online or visit the Encounter Kaikoura headquarters, café, and gallery, where you can also organize a bird-watching cruise. ✉ *96 The Esplanade* 🕾 *03/319–6777, 0800/733–365* ⊕ *www. dolphinencounter.co.nz* 🖃 *NZ$95, NZ$175 to swim with the dolphins.*

Point Kean Sea Colony. You don't have to join an organized tour to get close to seals. You can drive to this seal colony just outside of town on the northern side of the Kaikoura Peninsula. Watch the seals in their natural habitat, lying in the sun or playing in the kelp-filled shallows. These are wild animals so don't approach closer than 30 feet. With seabirds wheeling above and waves breaking along the shore, this is a powerful place just minutes from the main street. Follow Fyffe Quay to the colony at the end of the road. ✉ *Pt. Kean.*

Seal Swim Kaikoura. New Zealand's original seal-swimming experience has several boat- and shore-based tours running daily from October to May. The swims are in shallow waters, sheltered by the Kaikoura Peninsula, and you're virtually guaranteed to see New Zealand fur seals up close and personal. Book online or phone in. ✉ *58 West End* 🕾 *03/319–6182, 0800/732–579* ⊕ *www.sealswimkaikoura.co.nz* 🖃 *NZ$80–NZ$110.*

WHALE-WATCHING

Fodor's Choice
★ **Whale Watch Kaikoura.** Sperm whales browse closer to shore at Kaikoura than anywhere else in the world. Humpbacks, pilot whales, and orca pass by on annual migrations. See these marine giants as they dive and breach with comparative ease on specialist whale-watching

8

cruises operated by Ngai Tahu, the predominant South Island *iwi* (tribe). Having cruised these waters since 1987, Whale Watch skippers can recognize individual whales and adjust operations, such as the boat's proximity to the whale, accordingly. Allow 3½ hours for the whole experience, 2¼ hours on the water (you need to check in at the Whaleway Station at the end of Whaleway Road and you will be transported to your boat). Dolphins, seals, and other species of whales may also be seen on any day.

Book in advance: 7 to 10 days during the peak season, November–April, 3 to 4 days at other times. The whale-watching boats are sturdy catamarans and fully enclosed for sea travel, but once the whales are spotted you can go out on the deck for a closer view. Trips depend on the weather, and should your tour miss seeing a whale, which is rare, you will get an 80% refund. No children under three. ■ TIP→ Take motion-sickness pills if you suspect you'll need them: even in calm weather the sea around Kaikoura often has a sizable swell. Trips are subject to cancellation if the weather is bad. ⊠ *Whaleway Station Rd.* ☎ *03/319–6767, 0800/655–121* ⊕ *www.whalewatch.co.nz* ⊠ *NZ$145* ☉ *Nov.–Mar., daily at 7:15, 10, 12:45, and 3:30.*

Wings over Whales. To get above the action, take a half-hour whale-viewing flight. From a small, fixed-wing aircraft you get a bird's-eye view of the giant sperm whales, and others that pass by. The planes will drop to 450 feet to view the whales while the pilots give an informative commentary. The stunningly scenic coastal flight is a bonus, and, of course, you won't get seasick. Wings over Whales claims a 95% success rate in spotting whales, and the planes can often fly when it's too rough for the boats to go out. ⊠ *Kaikoura Airfield, State Hwy. 1* ☎ *03/319–6580, 0800/226–629* ⊕ *www.whales.co.nz* ⊠ *NZ$180; shuttle to airfield NZ$10.*

EN ROUTE

The Store at Kekerengu. This big, indoor/outdoor café/restaurant overlooking a rolling surf beach on State Highway 1 makes one of the best road stops in the area, well, in the country really. You'll find it halfway between Kaikoura and Blenheim. It's a beautiful, wild oceanside spot with the Kaikoura Mountains towering in the background. There's a large outdoor deck and huge log fire inside. You can choose lunch from a selection of prepared dishes or order from the menu; try The Store's classic seafood chowder or a Thai beef salad with a glass of local wine, or something sweet with a coffee. ⊠ *5748 State Hwy. 1, Kekerengu* ✛ *64 km (40 miles) south of Blenheim* ☎ *03/575–8600* ⊕ *www.thestore.kiwi* ☉ *No dinner* ⚏ *Reservations essential.*

MARLBOROUGH

The Marlborough Sounds were originally settled 700 to 900 years ago by the seafaring Māori people who named the area Te Tau Ihu O Te Waka a Māui ("the prow of Maui's canoe"). As legend has it, the legendary Maui fished up the North Island from his canoe with the jawbone of a whale. Consequently, the North Island is called Te Ika a Māui—"the fish of Maui."

Whale-watchers delight in spotting a whale in the waters near Kaikoura.

European settlers arrived in the early 1800s to hunt whales and seals. By the 1830s the whale and seal population had dropped drastically, so the settlers looked inland, to farm the fertile river plains of the Wairau Valley, where Blenheim now stands. While surveyors were pressured to open territory for farming, local Māori were reluctant to part with more of their land and responded by sabotaging the surveyors' work and equipment.

A police magistrate and Captain Arthur Wakefield, accompanied by a group of European settlers from Nelson, arrived to confront the two Māori chiefs leading the protests. A fracas flared up beside the Tuamarina River (now marked by a memorial on the roadside between Picton and Blenheim), resulting in several deaths, both Māori and European, including Captain Wakefield, and chief Te Rauparaha's daughter. Governor Fitzroy later upbraided the Europeans for their "impudent behavior" in what is now referred to as the "Wairau Affray." The land was later sold reluctantly by the Māori tribes, and by 1850 the new settlers began farming.

Thirty years later, the unwittingly prescient Charles Empson and David Herd began planting red muscatel grapes among local sheep and grain farms. Their modest viticultural torch was rekindled in the next century by the Freeth family, and by the 1940s Marlborough wineries were successfully producing port, sherry, and Madeira. In 1973 New Zealand's largest wine company, Montana, planted vines in Marlborough to increase the supply of New Zealand grapes. This was the beginning of the region's success with Sauvignon Blanc. Other vintners followed suit, and within a decade today's major players—such as Hunter's and

Cloudy Bay—had established the region's international reputation. Marlborough now glories in being New Zealand's single largest area under vine, and many local growers sell grapes to winemakers outside the area.

BLENHEIM

29 km (18 miles) south of Picton, 120 km (73 miles) southeast of Nelson, 129 km (80 miles) north of Kaikoura.

Many people come to Blenheim (pronounced *bleh*-num by the locals) for the wine. There are dozens of wineries in the area, some with stylish cellar doors and restaurants, and Blenheim township is developing fast, though it still has a small-town veneer.

In 1973 the Montana (pronounced Mon- *taa*-na here) company paid two Californian wine authorities to investigate local grape-growing potential on a commercial scale. Both were impressed with what they found. It was the locals who were skeptical—until they tasted the first wines produced. After that, Montana opened the first modern winery in Marlborough in 1977, although there had been fledgling efforts over the past 100 years by pioneering wine growers. The region now has more than 100 vineyards and wineries. The Marlborough Wine and Food Festival held in mid-February each year celebrates the region's success in suitable style.

Don't bury your nose in a tasting glass entirely, though; the landscape shouldn't be overlooked. The vineyards sprawl across the large alluvial plains of the Wairau River, lined by mountains. From many points you can see Mt. Tapuae-o-Uenuku, which, at 9,465 feet, is the highest South Island mountain outside the Southern Alps. Blenheim is a 30-minute drive from the Marlborough Sounds to the north, and 90 minutes from the Nelson Lakes National Park to the west. Walk off your winery excesses in the Wither Hills Farm Park on the southern side of town, where you can climb through open farmland for a wide view across the Wairau Plains.

GETTING HERE AND AROUND

Marlborough Airport (BHE), near Blenheim, is served by Air New Zealand, with several return flights daily from Wellington, Christchurch, and Auckland. Local airline Sounds Air flies daily to and from Wellington to Marlborough Airport and to Picton's small Koromiko Airport (PCN).

InterCity runs daily between Christchurch, Picton, Blenheim, and Nelson. The ride between Christchurch and Blenheim takes about 4 to 5 hours, from Christchurch to Picton 5 to 6 hours, and from Picton to Nelson, about 2½ hours. At Blenheim, buses stop at the train station; at Picton, they use the ferry terminal. An alternative bus service is **Atomic Shuttles.** Once in Marlborough, if you're looking to explore the wineries you'll find them easily, on roads laid out more or less in a grid that extends from close to Blenheim and across the Wairau Plains. Rapaura Road is the central artery route for vineyard visits; wineries cluster around Jeffries and Jacksons roads, Fairhall, the area around Renwick village, the lower Wairau Valley, and State Highway 1 south of Blenheim. To access the Marlborough Sounds, take either the road to Picton, or head west on the main road to Nelson and turn off at Havelock. The main road inland from Renwick, that heads toward the West Coast, accesses Nelson Lakes National Park. ■ TIP➔ **Pick up a map of the Marlborough wine region at the Marlborough i-SITE Visitor Centre.**

FESTIVALS AND EVENTS

Garden Marlborough. Marlborough's climate and soils encourage great gardens and this is one of the country's most popular garden festivals. For five days in November you can wander through inspiring and beautifully kept gardens, and partake in workshops and social events. Watch the website for bookings; tickets go on sale at least a couple of months ahead. ☎ *03/577–5500, 0800/627–527* ⊕ *www.gardenmarlborough.co.nz.*

TOURS

Bubbly Grape Wine Tours. With a choice of times, wineries, and lunch stops, these tours are about as flexible as you can get. There's no minimum number of people required, and if you're into chocolate, owner Kerry will take you to a boutique chocolatier as well. Options include the Sauvignon Blanc Blended Tour (half day), Special Reserve Tour (full day), and Gourmet Lunch Wine Tour (full day). Tour prices include wine tastings. Pickup from your accommodations can be arranged. ☎ *0800/228–2253 NZ only, 027/672–2195* ⊕ *www.bubblygrape.co.nz* ▸ *From NZ$55.*

Longpoint Experience. Base yourself on a coastal Marlborough farm, in a character-filled and comfortable historic cottage. Spend your days exploring private farm tracks and the spectacular coastline, including Long Point Reef. Or you can wrap up with a book by the fire in the cottage, take a 4WD trip over the farm, or explore further, to a Marlborough winery or other walks in the region. Hosts work with guests to do whatever suits their interests and level of fitness. ⊠ *301 Ward Beach Rd., Marlborough* ☎ *03/575–6876* ⊕ *www.longpoint.co.nz* ▸ *From NZ$50 a person a day.*

Molesworth Tour Company. Molesworth Station is the largest high-country farm in the country, covering almost 450,000 acres behind the Kaikoura Mountains, south of Blenheim, extending through remote and beautiful country. Tours are one to four days, traversing Molesworth and the neighboring Rainbow Station by comfortable 4WD vehicle. Meet the farming families and share a meal, with optional stays at Hanmer Springs or a high-country homestead. There's also a four-day cycle tour, if you're feeling active. Pickups from Marlborough lodgings can be arranged. ⊠ *50 State Hwy. 63, Renwick* ☎ *03/572–8025, 027/435–1955* ⊕ *www.molesworthtours.co.nz* ▸ *Prices NZ$220 (day tour), NZ$815 (2 days), NZ$1,859 (4 days).*

VISITOR INFORMATION

Contacts Blenheim i-SITE Visitor Centre. ⊠ *Blenheim Railway Station, 8 Sinclair St.* ✛ *Beside State Hwy. 1* ☎ *03/577–8080, 0800/777–181* ⊕ *marlboroughnz.com.*

8

EXPLORING

FAMILY

Fodor's Choice

★

Omaka Aviation Heritage Centre. World War I–era planes, and the stories of their pilots, are showcased in the Knights of the Sky exhibition. Highlights include the world's only Caproni Ca22, an Etrich Taube, and a Morane-Saulinier Type BB, all part of movie-director Sir Peter Jackson's collection. War stories are brought to life by the talents of New Zealand's Oscar-winning special-effects teams Weta Digital and Wingnut Films. Dangerous Skies focuses on aviation development during World War II. The center is backed by the Classic Fighters Charitable Trust, which runs an amazing, three-day international air show in odd-numbered years when vintage and classic aircraft are on display both on the ground and in the sky. At the Centre, there's an on-site café and shop as well. ⊠ *Omaka Aerodrome, 79 Aerodrome Rd., off New Renwick Rd.* ☎ *03/579–1305* ⊕ *www.omaka.org.nz and www.classicfighters.co.nz* ⊠ *NZ$30* ⊗ *Dec.–Mar., daily 9–5; Apr.–Nov., daily 10–4.*

The Vines Village. Artisan food and craft products are as classy as the local wines in these artisan shops that showcase wines alongside olive oils, fudge, homeware, quilts, ceramics, glassware, jewelry, and recipe books. Let the kids loose in the playground, or you can all just relax in the tranquil lakeside grounds. ⊠ *193 Rapaura Rd.* ☎ *03/579–5424* ⊕ *www.thevinesvillage.co.nz* ⊗ *Daily, each business here opens at different times, 10–5 will be safe for most.*

WINERIES

The wineries described here include some of the country's largest and most notable, as well as some small, family-owned outlets. Generally speaking, you won't go wrong at any of the vineyards around Marlborough. Tastings are free at some; others charge a fee and might have varying prices depending on the number or styles of wine on offer. Some will waive the tasting fee if you make a purchase.

Allan Scott Family Winemakers. Allan Scott has been working in Marlborough vineyards since 1973 and launched his own company in 1990. Now he makes well-respected Sauvignon Blanc, Chardonnay, Pinot Gris, Pinot Noir, *methode traditionelle* (try the Blanc de Blancs), Gewürztraminer, and Riesling (the last two are particularly good). The whole family is involved: Allan's son Joshua is the winemaker, his younger daughter Sara a viticulturist, and elder daughter Victoria looks after marketing. Josh also makes NZ's first *methode traditionelle* beer—a tasty, rather manly brew called Moa, at his brewery just across the road. The Allan Scott cellar door adjoins the indoor-outdoor Twelve Trees restaurant, which opens out to a delightful herb garden. Marlborough salmon fillet and seafood chowder are menu classics. ⊠ *Jackson's Rd.* ☎ *03/572–9054* ⊕ *www.allanscott.com* ⊗ *Nov.–Apr., daily 9–5; May–Oct., daily 9–4:30.*

Brancott Estate Heritage Centre. At this estate where the region's first Sauvignon Blanc wines were planted, striking views stretch across the heart of Marlborough's Wairau Valley vineyards, and tastings are available along with a meal in what is arguably one of Marlborough's finest winery restaurants, open for lunch (book ahead in summer). Sauvignon Blanc is the star here, but the Pinot Noir also has great merit. You can

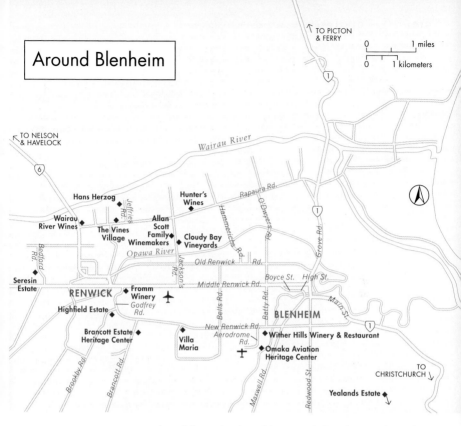

Around Blenheim

TO PICTON & FERRY

TO NELSON & HAVELOCK

Wairau River

Hans Herzog

Wairau River Wines

The Vines Village

Allan Scott Family Winemakers

Hunter's Wines

Cloudy Bay Vineyards

Opawa River

Old Renwick Rd.

Seresin Estate

RENWICK

Fromm Winery

Highfield Estate

Godfrey Rd.

Boyce St.   High St.

Middle Renwick Rd.

BLENHEIM

Brancott Estate Heritage Center

Villa Maria

New Renwick Rd.
Aerodrome

Wither Hills Winery & Restaurant

Omaka Aviation Heritage Center

TO CHRISTCHURCH

Yealands Estate

get some exercise while tasting by taking a guided cycle tour through the vineyard. Brancott is a major supporter of preservation efforts of the rare New Zealand falcon (which actually helps vineyards by keeping the mice at bay). The annual Marlborough Wine and Food Festival, one of New Zealand's original wine festivals, is held each summer at Brancott. ✉ *180 Brancott Rd., off New Renwick Rd.* ☎ *03/520–6975* ⊕ *www.brancottestate.com* ⊙ *Winery daily 10–4:30; restaurant daily 11:30–3:30; tours daily 11 and 2.*

Cloudy Bay Vineyards. From its first vintage in 1985, Cloudy Bay has produced first-class Sauvignon Blanc, along with a range that includes an equally impressive Pelorus sparkling, Chardonnay, Pinot Noir, Riesling, Pinot Gris, Gewürztraminer, and its unique barrel-aged Sauvignon Te Koko. The owner's Australian heritage can be seen in the eucalyptus plantings in the courtyard, where you can relax on couches in the summer. Various tasting options are available, as is light food year round. In summer Jack's Raw Bar offers clams and oysters, matched with in-house wines. ✉ *230 Jackson's Rd.* ☎ *03/520–9140* ⊕ *www.cloudybay. co.nz* ⊙ *Daily 10–4.*

Fromm Winery. Although Marlborough is best known for its Sauvignon Blancs, its reputation for Pinot Noir is climbing rapidly. Fromm pioneered the local use of Pinot Noir and is also known for Syrah, Malbec,

Continued on page 384

In recent decades New Zealand has emerged as a significant presence on the international wine stage. The country's cool, maritime climate has proven favorable for growing high-quality grapes, and winemakers now produce some of the world's best Sauvignon Blancs and Pinot Noirs, as well as excellent Chardonnays and Merlots.

Touring wineries in New Zealand is easy, as vineyards stretch virtually the entire length of the country, and most properties have tasting rooms with regular hours. Even if you just sample wines at a shop in Auckland, here's how to get the most out of your sipping experience.

(top) Pinot Noir grapes on a vine
(right) Rippon Vineyard, Lake Wanaka, Otago

Wines *of* New Zealand

By Sue Courtney

NEW ZEALAND WINES: THEN AND NOW

(top left) Nikola Nobilo was a New Zealand wine pioneer (right) Central Otago vineyard
(bottom left) Ripe Cabernet Sauvignon grapes

A BRIEF HISTORY

The first grapes were planted by missionaries on the North Island of New Zealand in 1819, and a British official (and hobbyist viticulturist) **James Busby** was the first to make wine almost 20 years later. For the next 150 years, the country's vineyards faced the significant challenges of powdery mildew and phylloxera, a root-killing louse.

New Zealand's modern-day wine production started in the 1970s, as European varietals were planted and started to show promise. Pioneers like Lebanese immigrant **Assid Corban** of Corbans Wines, and Croatian immigrants **Nikola Nobilo** of Nobilo and **Josip Babich** of Babich Wines settled in Henderson Valley, near Auckland, and helped shape the future of New Zealand wine production, innovating with cultured yeast, stainless steel tanks, and temperature-controlled fermentation, which have become widespread practices in many of the world's wine regions.

TODAY'S WINE SCENE

Ever since the country's Sauvignon Blancs captured the imagination of British wine critics at a major international tasting in 1985, wine drinkers worldwide have clamored for this crisp, fruity wine. New Zealand wines are now exported to 80 countries, with Australia biting a 20 percent chunk out of the export share, followed by the U.K. and the United States.

New Zealand is a long, narrow country of 1,000 miles between the north and south islands, with numerous microclimates and soil types, each suited to different varietals. Sauvignon Blanc is eminently well matched to the South Island, particularly Marlborough, while Chardonnay and Pinot Gris conveniently grow in most areas. Pinot Noir—NZ's most-planted red grape—and Riesling do best in Martinborough and on the South Island, with high-quality bottles coming from Marlborough, Nelson, Waipara, and Central

Grapevines at Fairmont Estate, a winery and vineyard in Gladstone, Wairarapa

WHY DID NZ SWITCH FROM CORK?

The New Zealand Screwcap Initiative was formed in 2001 by the country's top producers who were concerned that their wines were being compromised by cork taint and premature oxidation. Even though the public eschewed the screwcap 10 years previously, the winemakers regarded the closure as an evolution in quality packaging. Now, more than 90 percent of New Zealand wines sport screwcaps, and customers worldwide are becoming accustomed to this type of bottle closure.

Sauvignon Blanc grapes

Otago, the country's southernmost winegrowing area. Heavy-bodied red grapes like Cabernet Sauvignon, Merlot, Malbec, and Syrah excel in warmer Hawke's Bay and Auckland on the North Island.

As for the future, many winegrowers are playing around with new varieties, hoping to find the "next big thing." Gewürztraminer and Viognier are already well established, while varieties like Arneis and Grüner Veltliner are still rare. For red grapes, Sangiovese and Montepulciano show great promise, while Zinfandel and Tempranillo are making inroads.

NZ SAUVIGNON BLANC

New Zealand is best known for its celebrated Sauvignon Blanc wines, but the varietal wasn't planted in the country until the 1970s.

In recent years, Sauvignon Blancs from Marlborough have become the worldwide benchmark for the varietal, with concentrated grassy, herbal, and floral notes. Compared to the Sauvignon Blancs of France, New Zealand's wines are more intensely perfumed, with fruitier flavors.

Neudorf Vineyards, Nelson, produces several well-regarded wines

NEW ZEALAND'S WINE REGIONS

AUCKLAND One of the country's original wine regions, this warm area produces high-quality reds, especially from Waiheke Island and Matakana.

GISBORNE Distinctive Chardonnays with peach and melon flavors are the specialty here. The region is also known for its spicy Gewürztraminer wines.

NORTHLAND

AUCKLAND

○ Auckland ○

NORTH ISLAND

Tasman Sea

MARTINBOROUGH The area, which houses the Wairarapa subregion, is known for its rich Pinot Noirs and luscious Cabernet Sauvignons.

BAY OF PLENTY

GISBORNE

WAIKATO

HAWKE'S BAY

○ Napier

○ Hastings

Classic Wine Trail

PACIFIC OCEAN

CLASSIC WINE TRAIL

For the ultimate touring experience, take a weeklong excursion down the Classic Wine Trail. The well-marked, 240-mile touring route passes through towns and rural routes full of attractions, like farmer's markets and restaurants, artist's studios and museums, and outdoor activities, including hiking trails, horse riding, and fishing rivers. Download the trail guide at ⊕ www.classicwinetrail.co.nz.

MARTINBOROUGH

○ Wellington

○ Blenheim

SOUTH ISLAND

HAWKES BAY A geographically and climatically diverse wine region that produces many wines, such as Chardonnay, Merlot, and Cabernet Sauvignon.

IN FOCUS WINES OF NEW ZEALAND

8

NELSON A small wine region about two hours from Marlborough wineries. The region produces Chardonnay as its primary wine, followed by Riesling.

MARLBOROUGH The country's most important wine region, and the home of its world-class Sauvignon Blancs. Also common are Chardonnay and Riesling.

CANTERBURY This region is cool and dry, making it well-suited to Chardonnay and Pinot Noir. Riesling and Sauvignon Blanc are also produced here.

NELSON

Wellington
○

Tasman Mountains

Blenheim
○

MARLBOROUGH

Tasman Sea

Southern Alps

PACIFIC OCEAN

Christchurch
○

CANTERBURY

SOUTH
ISLAND

Queenstown
○

OTAGO

Dunedin
○

OTAGO This region is known for growing the world's southernmost grape vines. Its intensely concentrated Pinot Noirs have received great critical acclaim.

WINE-TASTING PRIMER

Ordering and tasting wine—whether at a winery, bar, or restaurant—is easy once you master a few simple steps.

LOOK AND NOTE

Hold your glass by the stem and look at the wine in the glass. Note its color, depth, and clarity.

For whites, is it greenish, yellow, or gold? For reds, is it purplish, ruby, or garnet? Is the wine's color pale or deep? Is the liquid clear or cloudy?

SWIRL AND SNIFF

Swirl the wine gently in the glass to intensify the scents, then sniff over the rim of the glass. What do you smell? Try to identify aromas like:

- **Fruits**—citrus, peaches, berries, figs, melon
- **Flowers**—orange blossoms, honey, perfume
- **Spices**—baking spices, pungent, herbal notes
- **Vegetables**—fresh or cooked, herbal notes
- **Minerals**—earth, steely notes, wet stones
- **Dairy**—butter, cream, cheese, yogurt
- **Oak**—toast, vanilla, coconut, tobacco
- **Animal**—leathery, meaty notes

Are there any unpleasant notes, like mildew or wet dog, that might indicate that the wine is "off"?

SIP AND SAVOR

Prime your palate with a sip, swishing the wine in your mouth. Then spit in a bucket or swallow.

Take another sip and think about the wine's attributes. Sweetness is detected on the tip of the tongue, acidity on the sides of the tongue, and tannins (a mouth-drying sensation) on the gums. Consider the body—does the wine feel light in the mouth, or is there a rich sensation? Are the flavors consistent with the aromas? If you like the wine, try to pinpoint what you like about it, and vice versa if you don't like it.

Take time to savor the wine as you're sipping it—the tasting experience may seem a bit scientific, but the end goal is your enjoyment.

WINE & FOOD PAIRING

Hospitality is a core value in Maori society, something you'll encounter in wineries and eateries

New Zealand cuisine is influenced by Pacific Rim, Asian, and European flavors and traditions. The diversity of the cuisine and its wide variety of ingredients—beef, lamb, venison, pork, poultry, and seafood—makes for a number of interesting food and wine pairings.

Sauvignon Blanc is delicious with shellfish and seafood, summer herbs, feta cheese, and salad greens.

Pinot Noir complements mushroom-based dishes. Lighter wines are best paired with tuna and salmon, while heavier wines suit lamb, duck, venison, and game.

Cabernet Sauvignon and **Merlot** work well with steaks and minted lamb.

Chardonnay goes well with rock lobster.

Pinot Gris matches beautifully with fresh salmon.

Riesling suits South Pacific-influenced dishes, such as seafood with coconut and lime.

Gewürztraminer is especially suited to lightly spiced Asian cuisine.

THE VISITING EXPERIENCE

Many wineries have tasting rooms where wines can be sampled for free or for a nominal fee. Facilities vary from grandiose buildings to rustic barns. Most larger wineries are open daily, all year round, while boutique vintners may close from Easter until Labour Weekend (end of October). If a winery is closed, you may still be able to make an appointment. Regional winegrower associations publish wine trail guides detailing opening hours and other attractions, such as tours, dining options, and vineyard accommodations. Pick up a guide at a visitors center or local wine shop.

(Left) A tour of Marlborough vineyards could last for three hours to three days, depending on your stamina

and Merlot reserves. All of their wines are produced from organically grown, handpicked grapes; the intense handcrafted vintages are made to cellar. Rieslings and Chardonnays are also Fromm strengths. As one of the region's smallest wineries, their tasting room is compact; visitors can look into the winery while tasting and watch the winemaker at work. Tastings are free. ⊠ *Godfrey Rd., Renwick* ☏ *03/572–9355* ⊕ *www.frommwinery.co.nz* ⊗ *Oct.–Apr., daily 11–5; May–Sept., Fri.–Sun. 11–4.*

Hans Herzog. Therese and Hans Herzog produce a superb range of wines on their organically managed estate vineyard. Standout wines are the Old World classics such as Montepulciano, and the wonderful Merlot-Cabernet, aptly named "The Spirit of Marlborough." Winery tours run daily, and bookings are essential. Cuisine is a hallmark of the Herzog estate; degustation menus with matching wines are offered from the Herzog Restaurant, widely considered one of Marlborough's best. For something slightly more casual but no less gourmet try the Bistro. Or join one of Winemaker's Table lunches and dine with the family's winemakers. ⊠ *81 Jeffries Rd., off Rapaura Rd.* ☏ *03/572–8770* ⊕ *www.herzog.co.nz* ⊗ *Weekdays 9–5, weekends 11–5. Closed weekends in July.*

Highfield Estate. This magnificent winery sits high on the Brookby Ridge, with spectacular views over the carpet of vineyards the lines the Wairau Plains and on a clear day all the way to the North Island. The winery building is signposted by an iconic Tuscan-inspired tower that visitors are welcome to climb. Highfield produces first-class Sauvignon Blanc, Pinot Noir, Chardonnay, and Riesling; their best, however, is a sparkling Elstree Cuvée Brut. You can relax and enjoy this magnificent setting in the Mediterranean-style winery restaurant, which opens for lunch daily. ⊠ *27 Brookby Rd., RD 2* ☏ *03/572–9244* ⊕ *www.highfield.co.nz* ⊗ *Daily 10–5.*

Hunter's Wines. Jane Hunter was described by the London *Sunday Times* as the "star of New Zealand wine," with a string of successes as long as a row of vines. Building on the success of her late husband and employing a top-notch winemakers, her wines have remained impressive; the Kaho Roa (oak-aged Sauvignon Blanc) and Pinot Noir are legendary. The Miru Miru (Māori for bubbles), a sparkling blend of Pinot Noir, Chardonnay, and Pinot Meunier grapes, is also a big seller. There's also garden café, an artist-in-residence, and a worthy walk through the 5-acre garden, which features endemic and threatened native plants from the Marlborough region. ⊠ *603 Rapaura Rd.* ☏ *03/572–8489, 0800/486–837 NZ only* ⊕ *www.hunters.co.nz* ⊗ *Daily 9:30–4:30.*

Seresin Estate. Named for owner Michael Seresin, a New Zealand filmmaker, this estate is known for its meticulous viticulture and subtle wine-making techniques, producing hand-grown, handpicked, and handmade wine. It's tricky to find—look out for the big stacked rocks on the edge of the river terrace. This vineyard is a pioneer in implementing high environmental standards, using both biodynamic and organic production methods. Seresin also produces a Tuscan-style, biodynamic olive oil and three citrus oils—lemon, lime, and orange. During vintage time guests can taste the handpicked grapes and fresh grape juice, and see the wine-making process firsthand. ⊠ *85 Bedford Rd.* ☎ *03/572–9408* ⊕ *seresin.co.nz* ⊗ *Daily 10–4:30.*

Villa Maria. Croatian-born George Fistonich was one of the pioneers of New Zealand wines. He established his first Villa Maria winery near Auckland in 1961. Now the company has several wineries around the country, including this one in Marlborough that's known for Sauvignon Blanc, as well as Pinot Noir, Chardonnay, Pinot Gris, and Riesling. Villa Maria wines from other regions, such as the heavier Hawke's Bay reds, are also available for tastings. ⊠ *Paynter Rd. at New Renwick Rd.* ☎ *03/520–8470* ⊕ *www.villamaria.co.nz* ⊗ *Oct.–May, daily 10–5; June–Sept., weekends noon–5.*

Wairau River Wines. Phil and Chris Rose were among the first contract grape growers in Marlborough. Now they produce award-winning Sauvignon Blanc and a notably good range of other varietals under their own label. The tasting room is made from mud bricks and has two log-fires in winter, while in summer you can relax on the sun-drenched lawns. The winery also operates a restaurant featuring local produce and is popular with the locals—reservations are recommended on weekends. ⊠ *Rapaura Rd. and State Hwy. 6* ☎ *03/572–9800* ⊕ *www.wairauriverwines.com* ⊗ *Daily 10–5.*

Wither Hills Winery & Restaurant. At this impressive complex of river rock, tile, concrete, and wood, fronted by dramatic plantings, the three-story tower gives a commanding view across the Wairau Valley and the Wither Hills. Tastings include award-winning Sauvignon Blancs and Rieslings. At the popular winery restaurant, guests can relax at alfresco tables, lounge on beanbags on the lawn, or opt for more formal seating inside. A "wine library" consists of vines of every wine grape grown in New Zealand—30 of them lined up across the front of the winery. ⊠ *211 New Renwick Rd.* ☎ *03/520–8284* ⊕ *www.witherhills.co.nz* ⊗ *Daily 10–4:30.*

Fodor's Choice
★

Yealands Estate. Peter Yealand has a vision as big as his vineyards. Sustainability is an absolute priority, and he has offset all greenhouse gas emissions from day one and is internationally recognized for his achievements. Sauvignon Blanc is the star but the winery also does great things with Pinot Gris, Riesling, Viognier, and Pinot Noir grapes. Yealands has free tastings of all their wines, including their noted Estate range, while audiovisual displays and interactive monitors will enhance your tasting experience. Visitors are also welcome to drive themselves around the vineyard on the "White Road" to see the natural mussel shell and grape waste compost and the baby doll sheep (non-fossil-fuel grass mowers). The drive also encompasses stunning views, from steep coastal cliffs to the snowcapped Kaikoura Mountains. ⊠ *Seaview Rd. and Reserve Rd., Seddon* ☎ *03/575–7618* ⊕ *www.yealands.co.nz* ⊗ *Daily 10–4:30.*

WHERE TO EAT

$$$$
MODERN NEW
ZEALAND

✕ **Arbour.** This friendly place suggests you stop in for a small taste and a drink before catching your flight at the airport down the road. If you do, take care not to miss your plane. Small dishes (artisan cheeses and Cloudy Bay clams), an ever-changing à la carte menu (groper cheeks, leg of lamb, and collar of pork), and degustation menus are available. A meal comes with views of the Richmond Ranges or into the kitchen to watch the well-reputed team at work. ⓢ *Average main: NZ$34* ✉ *36 Godfrey Rd., Renwick* ☏ *03/572–7898* ⊕ *www.arbour.co.nz* ⊟ *No credit cards.*

$
CAFÉ
✕ **Cafe Home.** Pop in for brunch, coffee, or lunch. The breakfast menu runs all day on the weekends, with options like hotcakes or toasted cranberry and orange muesli. There's fresh, simple lunch food, plenty of wheat- and gluten-free foods, and an impressive tea and coffee menu. Locals love this place, with its sharp, almost industrial decor. ⓢ *Average main: NZ$13* ✉ *1C Main St.* ☏ *03/579–5040* ☽ *No dinner.*

$$
NEW ZEALAND
Fodor's Choice
★
✕ **Dodson Street Beer Garden.** It's not all about wine in Marlborough. Craft beers are a fast-growing trend, and here you get to sample from arguably the largest selection of craft beers and ciders on the South Island. The adjacent Malthouse building has been a brewery since 1858 and is now the epicenter of a local craft beer Renaissance. In this cheery beer garden hearty ales are matched with traditional German cuisine (bratwurst and braised pork knuckles), Italian pizza, and a good range of classic Kiwi fare (seafood chowder and beer-battered fish-and-chips). There's also a good kids' menu, and yes, a range of Marlborough wines. Music is often on tap. ⓢ *Average main: NZ$20* ✉ *1 Dodson St.* ☏ *03/577–8348* ⊕ *www.dodsonstreet.co.nz.*

$$$$
NEW ZEALAND
Fodor's Choice
★
✕ **Herzog.** One of Marlborough's finest dining experiences is found at the Hans Herzog Estate, tucked away along a short side road leading down to the Wairau River. Superb three-, five-, or seven-course dinner menus pair Herzog wines with innovative dishes; the set and à la carte menus might include an appetizer of scampi and wild fennel, then a 70-day-aged Wakanui rib eye. Retire to the lounge after dinner for a coffee or a digestif. More casual lunches are available in the Herzog Cellar Door Bistro. ⓢ *Average main: NZ$46* ✉ *81 Jeffries Rd. off Rapaura Rd.* ☏ *03/572–8770* ⊕ *www.herzog.co.nz.*

$$$
NEW ZEALAND
✕ **Raupo.** An imposing structure of glass, wood, and river stone sits beautifully on a small bend in the Taylor River, and is named for the nearby bulrushes, or *raupo*, along the river. You can sit on the terrace in summer or cozy up to the fireplace in winter. Co-owner/chef Stephane is French and he works with the original owner Marcel Rood, of Dutch origin, and their meals are light, healthy, organic, and locally sourced when possible. Favorites include rib-eye beef, chicken breast, crispy pork belly, and locally caught fish of the day. Both à la carte and set menus for lunch and dinner are available, plus a five-course "surprise" degustation (by prior arrangement). Raupo is also a favored morning and afternoon coffee, tea, and cake stop and offers an indulgent selection of high-tea morsels and muffins. ⓢ *Average main: NZ$29* ✉ *6 Symons St.* ☏ *03/577–8822* ⊕ *www.raupocafe.co.nz.*

$$$
ECLECTIC
✕ **Scotch Wine Bar.** If you want a break from winery restaurants, this contemporary black-booth and brick-decor main street favorite should fit the bill—there's not a grapevine in sight. The dinner menu includes small plates, a few tasty main courses, and burgers, and though there may not be a vineyard attached, the wine list is one of the largest you'll find in any Marlborough eatery. Cocktails and craft beers are also in

Herzog offers outstanding food along with its own wines.

good supply. On summer nights the tables spill onto the public square outside—grab a beanbag for comfort. $ *Average main: NZ$21* ✉ *26 Maxwell Rd.* ☎ *03/579–1176* ⊕ *scotchbar.myshopify.com.*

$$$
MODERN NEW ZEALAND

✗ **The Vintners Room.** Toward the inland end of the Rapaura Road winery strip, this Sante Fe–style building that's part of the Marlborough Vintners Hotel is a good stop for afternoon or evening tapas (Nelson scallops) or a full meal. Local produce (from the restaurant garden and olive grove, when possible) appears in such choices as Dory fillet, pearl barley risotto, and lamb rum with polenta. The courtyard is shaded by cherry trees through summer. $ *Average main: NZ$28* ✉ *190 Rapaura Rd.* ☎ *03/572–5094* ⊕ *www.mvh.co.nz* ☾ *No lunch.*

WHERE TO STAY

$$$$
HOTEL

🏨 **Chateau Marlborough.** Overlooking the gardens of Seymour Square, spacious studios have luxurious furnishings and separate kitchenette areas, while the larger suites and apartments have full kitchens, dining areas, and laundry. **Pros:** comfy leather armchairs in the rooms; off-street parking. **Cons:** conferences can make it a busy spot. $ *Rooms from: NZ$340* ✉ *High St. at Henry St.* ☎ *03/578–0064* ⊕ *www.marlboroughnz.co.nz* ⇥ *45 rooms* ⦿ *No meals.*

$$$
HOTEL

🏨 **Hotel d'Urville.** Every room is unique in the well-preserved, art deco–style Old Public Trust Building, but all are stylish and enjoy a friendly, intimate atmosphere. **Pros:** fabulous old building right on the main street; the downstairs bar is a welcoming spot for an evening cocktail; affordable boutique stay. **Cons:** downstairs accommodation is very close to busy street; some rooms and bathrooms are quite small.

[$] *Rooms from: NZ$290* ✉ *52 Queen St.* ☎ *03/577–9945* 🌐 *www.durville.com* 🛏 *11 rooms* 🍴 *Breakfast.*

$$ HOTEL 🏨 **Marlborough Vintners Hotel.** Each of the 16 suites in contemporary-style Tuscan-style villas nestled on 6 acres of landscaped grounds enjoys views of vineyards and gardens and has a kitchenette, dining and lounge area, bedroom with king beds, and a spacious bath. **Pros:** delightful vineyard and Wither Hills views. **Cons:** country location out of town; weddings and small conferences can bring a crowd. [$] *Rooms from: NZ$185* ✉ *190 Raupara Rd.* ☎ *03/572–5094* 🌐 *www.mvh.co.nz* 🛏 *16 suites* 🍴 *No meals.*

$$$$ B&B/INN Fodor's Choice ★ 🏨 **Old St. Mary's Vineyard Estate.** Drive through the huge parklike grounds and lavender-lined driveway and you'll come to this striking turn-of-the-20th-century building, which was once a convent and is now a luxurious haven with beautifully decorated rooms, rambling lawns and gardens, and evening glasses of Marlborough wine (they produced their first vintage in 2009). **Pros:** in 60 acres of vineyard and rambling gardens; in the heart of Marlborough wine country; complimentary predinner drinks; a cold dinner platter can be arranged (charge). **Cons:** only downstairs rooms are easily accessible to guests with limited mobility. [$] *Rooms from: NZ$700* ✉ *776 Rapaura Rd., RD 3* ☎ *03/570–5700* 🌐 *www.convent.co.nz* 🕒 *Closed June–Aug.* 🛏 *5 rooms* 🍴 *Breakfast.*

$$$ HOTEL FAMILY 🏨 **St. Leonards Vineyard Cottages.** A rural retreat dotted around an expansive rambling garden and surrounded by vineyards offers accommodations in old farm buildings furnished in comfortable rural style with private outdoor spaces, barbecues, and verdant views. **Pros:** lots of sheep, deer, and chickens to amuse the kids; each accommodation is in a private setting. **Cons:** have to drive to get to area restaurants. [$] *Rooms from: NZ$220* ✉ *18 St. Leonards Rd., just off State Hwy. 6, 3 km (2 miles) from Blenheim* ☎ *03/577–8328* 🌐 *www.stleonards.co.nz* 🛏 *5 self-contained cottages* 🍴 *Breakfast.*

$$$$ HOTEL 🏨 **Straw Lodge.** Down a quiet lane near the Wairau River, these stylish rural accommodations on an organic vineyard are about as peaceful as it gets and occupy unique buildings of straw-bale construction, making them extra quiet, as well as warm in winter and cool in summer. **Pros:** beautiful vineyard setting; free use of bikes with lots of river trails nearby. **Cons:** a 15-minute drive from town. [$] *Rooms from: NZ$335* ✉ *17 Fareham La., off Wairau Valley Rd., Renwick* ☎ *03/572–9767* 🌐 *www.strawlodge.co.nz* 🛏 *2 suites* 🍴 *Breakfast.*

$$$$ B&B/INN Fodor's Choice ★ 🏨 **Timara Lodge.** Luxury, pure, simple luxury, is the hallmark of this1923 house, one of Marlborough's original homesteads, with a luxurious, finely crafted interior that evokes an elegant past and 25 acres of gardens. **Pros:** the huge garden is a highlight; the chef is one of the best in Marlborough; transfers available to/from Blenheim airport. **Cons:** strict cancellation policy applies; no children under 15. [$] *Rooms from: NZ$1600* ✉ *301 Dog Point Rd., RD 2* ☎ *03/572–8276* 🌐 *www.timara.co.nz* 🕒 *Closed July and Aug.* 🛏 *2 rooms, 2 suites* 🍴 *Some meals.*

$$$$ RESORT 🏨 **Vintners Retreat.** At the heart of Marlborough's wine district, these luxurious villas have patios that overlook six vineyards and the Richmond Ranges beyond. **Pros:** beautiful furnishings; easy access to world-class vineyards; prices are for up to four adults. **Cons:** on a busy main

road; out of town (though owner will organize a free shuttle to the local pub). $ *Rooms from: NZ$400* ✉ *55 Rapaura Rd.* ☎ *03/572–7420, 0800/484–686 NZ only* 🌐 *www.vintnersretreat.co.nz* 🛏 *14 villas* 🍴 *No meals.*

PICTON

29 km (18 miles) north of Blenheim, 110 km (69 miles) east of Nelson.

The maritime township of Picton (population 4,000) is a popular boating spot and has two sizable marinas, the smaller at Picton Harbour and the much larger at nearby Waikawa Bay. There's plenty to do in town, with crafts markets in summer, cafés and bars, historical sites, and museums (including one on a boat), and walking tracks through bushy scenic reserves to beaches and scenic lookouts over the Sounds. The Picton foreshore is a delightful parklike area looking up into Queen Charlotte Sound. It's a nice spot to wait for your ferry to the North Island, and to watch the comings and goings of smaller pleasure craft and water taxis.

GETTING HERE AND AROUND

Picton lies at the head of Queen Charlotte Sound and is the arrival point for ferries from the North Island, and summer-visiting international cruise ships. The town is the base for services and transport by water taxi to the Queen Charlotte Track, and to remote communities in the vast area of islands, inlets, and peninsulas of Queen Charlotte Sound.

Visitors from the North Island can take the Interislander or Bluebridge ferry from Wellington to Picton. Ferries dock in Picton wharf.

Car Rental Apex. ✉ *Ferry Terminal* ☎ *03/573–7009, 0800/422–744* 🌐 *www.apexrentals.co.nz.*

TOURS

Beachcomber Cruises. Scheduled daily scenic and eco-cruises run throughout Queen Charlotte Sound and include the Mail Boat cruise, which explores all the way to the outer reaches. Help deliver mail and supplies to families living in these wild, remote spots. They can also take you to and from points along the Queen Charlotte Walkway for one-day or longer unguided walks and bike rides. Boats depart from the Picton waterfront throughout the day (tours, times, and prices vary according to the time of year; check the website). ✉ *London Quay, The Waterfront* ☎ *03/573–6175, 0800/624–526* 🌐 *www.beachcombercruises.co.nz* 🎟 *From NZ$97.*

Cougar Line. Scheduled trips from Picton through the Queen Charlotte Sound operate three to four times daily, depending on the time of year, dropping passengers (sightseers included) at accommodations, private homes, or other points. Their scenic cruises range from a popular three-hour morning and afternoon cruises to shorter trips suitable for passengers waiting for the Cook Strait ferry. Cruises also include walking combos, an Earlybird Eco Cruise to Motuara Island bird sanctuary, and transport for walkers heading to the Queen Charlotte Track. A perfect end to the day is on board the "Blue Cod and Chips" twilight trip to watch the sunset, with fish-and-chips and a glass of Sauvignon Blanc in hand. (Bookings must be confirmed before 5 pm so the fish can be ordered.) Reservations for all trips are essential at peak times and recommended at others. Check the website for cruises times and prices. ⊠ *The Waterfront* ☎ *03/573–7925, 0800/504–090* ⊕ *www.cougarline. co.nz* ✇ *From NZ$85.*

Marlborough Sounds Adventure Company. Kayaking, walking, or biking, or all three, guided or independent, half-day or multiday trip—it's your choice with this company, one of the earliest to set up soft adventure tourism in the Sounds. Their three-day trip combines walking, biking, and kayaking in a fully guided experience with meals and lodging taken care of, and your luggage ferried ahead each day. Accommodation is in a quality lodge, and you need to be reasonably fit. The fee includes all water transfers, guide, accommodations, packed lunches, and equipment. The trip kicks off weekly from November through April. As well, four- and five-day guided walks on the Queen Charlotte Track include resort-style en suite accommodations, plus an ecotour of Motuara Island en route to the track. ⊠ *The Waterfront* ☎ *03/573–6078, 0800/283–283* ⊕ *www.marlboroughsounds.co.nz* ✇ *From NZ$995 for 3-day trip.*

Fodor's Choice   **Seafood Odyssea Cruise.** Cruise to a salmon farm on Queen Charlotte
★   Sound on board the Marlborough Tour Company's 65-foot catamaran MV *Odyssea.* Enjoy a taste of smoked salmon and locally farmed oysters, washed down with a top Sauvignon Blanc. Three-and-a-half-hour afternoon cruises depart daily at 1:30 (October to April) from Picton Marina. ⊠ *London Quay* ☎ *03/577–9997, 0800/990–800 NZ only* ⊕ *www.marlboroughtourcompany.co.nz* ✇ *NZ$145.*

Sounds Connection. Full-day and half-day tours are offered to Marlborough's most renowned wineries—and others less well known. The Gourmet Experience tour (November through April) combines a wine-and-food appreciation tour with behind-the-scenes glimpses and a four-course, wine-matched lunch. They also offer fishing trips. ⊠ *94 Wellington St.* ☎ *03/573–8843, 0800/742–866* ⊕ *www.soundsconnection. co.nz* ✇ *From NZ$69.*

Wilderness Guides. To see the glorious Marlborough Sounds in depth, try a four- or five-day fully catered and guided inn-to-inn walk on the Queen Charlotte Track with Wilderness Guides. The price includes land and water transport and three lodge nights along the track. Bookings are essential. Alternatively, they'll set you off to walk independently, organizing your accommodation, water taxi transport, a packed lunch, map, and directions; the price varies depending on the standard of accommodation you chose. Or you can just hire their guiding expertise for a day walk. These folk will also set you up on mountain biking and kayaking adventures. ⊠ *Picton Waterfront* ☎ *03/573–5432, 0800/266–266 toll-free in NZ* ⊕ *www.wildernessguidesnz.com* ✇ *From NZ$365 for guided day walk.*

VISITOR INFORMATION

Contacts Department of Conservation–Picton Field Base. ⊠ *Picton* ☎ *03/520–3002* ⊕ *www.doc.govt.nz.* **Picton i-SITE Visitor Centre.** ⊠ *Picton Foreshore* ☎ *03/520–3113* ⊕ *marlboroughnz.com.*

EXPLORING

TOP ATTRACTIONS

Lochmara Lodge Wildlife Recovery & Arts Centre. Take the short boat ride out to explore this delightful café, lodge, wildlife refuge, and art studio on the shore of Lochmara Bay. Follow the bushwalks to see native gecko and the *kakariki* (a native parrot) being nurtured here as part of the Lodge's wildlife recovery program. There's a pampering spa room and bathhouse above the beach, galleries of local art, and a sculpture trail. Artists-in-residence work here and art workshop, and events are held throughout the year. There are also chalets and units suitable for couples and families, if you plan to stay longer. ⊠ *Lochmara Bay, Queen Charlotte Sound* ☎ *03/573–4554* ⊕ *www.lochmara.co.nz.*

Marlborough Sounds. Locals will forgive you for thinking you've seen what the Marlborough Sounds are all about after crossing from the North Island to the South Island on the ferry—in reality, it's just a taste of better things to come. Picton is the base for cruising in this labyrinth of waterways that formed when the rising sea invaded a vast area of river valleys at the northern tip of the South Island. Backed by forested hills that rise gently from the water, the Sounds consist of sheltered bays and deep waterways, some little-changed since Captain Cook found refuge here in the 1770s. The Sounds are a wild, majestic place edged with tiny beaches and rocky coves and studded with islands where native wildlife is free from introduced animal predators. Māori legend tells how the Sounds were formed when a great warrior and navigator called Kupe fought with a giant octopus, *Te Wheke.* Its thrashings separated the surrounding mountains, and its tentacles became parts of the sunken valleys. You can hop on board the mail operator boats as they deliver the mail, groceries, and farming supplies to isolated residents and farms. From Havelock the *Pelorus Mail Boat* delivers mail and supplies to outlying settlements scattered around Pelorus Sound. To get on the ground in and around the Sounds, you can walk or cycle part or all of the scenic Queen Charlotte Track.

Fodor's Choice
★

Queen Charlotte Track. Starting northwest of Picton, the Queen Charlotte Track stretches 70 km (44 miles) south to north, playing hide-and-seek with the Marlborough Sounds along the way. Hike through lush native forests, stopping to swim or take photos along the way. Unlike other tracks, there are no Department of Conservation huts to stay in, just a few camping areas. One beauty of this walk, however, is the variety of other accommodations, including backpackers, lodges, resorts, and homestays. (Booking ahead is advised.) Boat companies Cougar Line or Beachcomber Cruises can drop you at various places for one- to four-day walks (guided or unguided). You can also mountain-bike on this track—it's the longest single track ride in New Zealand. (The outermost section, Ship Cove to Keneperu Sound, is closed to bikes during the busiest walking season from December 1 to February 28.) The boat companies can arrange for you and your bike to be dropped off and picked up at points along the track. For walkers and bikers they'll also carry your luggage between overnight stops. Some of the track passes through private land and users are required to purchase a pass for these sections; the funds contribute toward track maintenance.

■ TIP→ Though it's relatively easy to access, the track shouldn't be taken lightly. It has steep inclines and long drop-offs, and the weather can be unpredictable. The track is part of Te Araroa, the Long Pathway walking trail that runs the length of New Zealand. ⊕ *www.qctrack.co.nz.*

EN ROUTE

Kahikatea Flat DOC Campsite. This delightful campground, hidden in a beech forest clearing beside the Pelorus River, is part of a scenic reserve. The loudest noises are made by the songster bellbirds—or perhaps campers yelping when they jump into the not-always-so-warm river. Campsites come with or without power, plus access to very modern showers and a kitchen and dining area that opens to a riverside deck. There's also a café. Locals love this place so book ahead over midsummer, or plan your trip when it's not so hectic—the scenery is always the same. The river is the site of the famous "Barrel Scene" in the second *Hobbit* movie. ⊠ *Pelorus Bridge, State Hwy. 6, Rai Valley, Havelock* ☎ *03/571–6019* ⧖ *NZ$15 per person.*

EN ROUTE

Pelorus Bridge Scenic Reserve. Halfway between both Picton and Nelson, and Blenheim and Nelson, on State Highway 6 is this remnant of the native lowland forests that once covered this whole region. Easy walking trails explore the beech, *podocarp* (a species of evergreen), and broadleaf trees. In summer the river is warm enough (just) for swimming (watch for the sand flies). There's also a rare colony of endangered long-tailed native bats that come to play round the streetlight at the bridge at night. This is an utterly delightful place to take a pause, especially with a campground and café both in the vicinity. ⊠ *Pelorus Bridge, State Hwy. 6, Havelock* ⊕ *www.doc.govt.nz.*

WORTH NOTING

Edwin Fox Maritime Museum. The preserved hulk of the *Edwin Fox* demonstrates just how young New Zealand's European settlement is. The ship was used in the Crimean War, transported convicts to Australia, and brought settlers to New Zealand. Now dry-docked, it serves as a museum, bringing to life the conditions the early immigrants faced. Displays outline the ship's history and service. Walking through the ship, you can imagine how the settlers felt when shut belowdecks for months at a time, seasick, homesick, and unsure of what awaited them at landfall. ⊠ *Dunbar Wharf* ☎ *03/573–6868* ⊕ *www.edwinfoxsociety. com* ⧖ *NZ$15* ⊙ *Daily 9–5.*

Picton Heritage and Whaling Museum. Picton's seafaring history is captured with a wealth of memorabilia. The area was first a key Māori settlement called Waitohi, then an important whaling and sealing location for European immigrants in the early 19th century. Until 1860 there was no road access to Picton, so all trade and travel was done by sea. ⊠ *London Quay* ☎ *03/573–8283* ⊕ *www.pictonmuseum-newzealand. com* ⧖ *NZ$5* ⊙ *Daily 10–4.*

EN ROUTE

Queen Charlotte Drive. The main road out of Picton, State Highway 1, heads directly to Blenheim. If you're heading west toward Havelock and Nelson, and don't mind a slower, though much more scenic, route, Queen Charlotte Drive is for you. From Picton the drive climbs the hill to the west of the town, then winds in and out of bays along the edge of Queen Charlotte Sound. It then cuts across the base of the peninsula

A launch cuts a swathe through the calm waters of Queen Charlotte Sound.

that separates this waterway from Pelorus and Keneperu sounds, drops onto a small coastal plain, and follows the water's edge to Havelock township. (From here you join State Highway 6, which winds west through forested river valleys and hills to reach Tasman Bay and Nelson—allow two hours for this Picton-Nelson drive, despite how it might look on the map.) To find Queen Charlotte Drive from the Cook Strait ferry terminal in Picton, head out of the parking lot onto State Highway 1 and look for the sign indicating a right turn, which will take you on a road up the hill overlooking Picton.

Farther along, Governor's, Momorangi, and Ngakuta bays are gorgeous spots for a picnic or a stroll along the forested shore. Cullen Point, at the Havelock end of the drive, is a good vantage point to view the inland end of the Pelorus Sound and across the bay to Havelock. The short walk to the lookout is well worth the effort.

WHERE TO EAT

$$$ CAFÉ 🍴 **Cafe Cortado.** With a blend of South American and Mediterranean influences, tapas, seafood, and pizza are paired with top Marlborough wines and craft range beers at this prime waterfront spot. This is the second Cortado in the country, following the success of the original in Christchurch. The breakfasts—eggs any style or the breakfast burrito—will sufficiently fuel you up for a day out on the Sounds. [$] *Average main: NZ$27* ✉ *Corner of High St. and London Quay* ☎ *03/573–5630* 🌐 *cafecortado.co.nz.*

$$ IRISH 🍴 **The Irish Picton.** Even though the menu is all about pizza (good ones) this place definitely has the Irish bar vibe. Irish locals confirm they pour a good Guinness, for starters. Plus there's lots of live music, not

all Celtic, but it will get your toes tapping regardless. You'll find the bright red pub a short walk from the waterfront and it's open daily until the wee small hours so it's a great spot to wait for the late-night ferry. [$] *Average main: NZ$15* ✉ *25 Wellington St.* ☎ *03/573–8994* 🌐 *theirish.co.nz.*

$$$ CAFÉ 🍴 **Le Café.** Sitting outside Le Café on the waterfront you can look right down Queen Charlotte Sound and watch the local boats and the big Cook Strait ferries coming and going. Staff source organic, local, and free-range foods wherever possible—your fish was probably landed on the wharf at the end of the street and, if it's beef, they reckon they know the farmer. Casual meals, coffee, and baking are available all day before dinner kicks in; that's when the tempo at the bar picks up and live acts perform regularly. [$] *Average main: NZ$26* ✉ *London Quay* ☎ *03/573–5588* 🌐 *www.lecafepicton.co.nz.*

WHERE TO STAY

$$$$ RESORT Fodor's Choice ★ 🏨 **Bay of Many Coves.** Designed by the architect of the national museum Te Papa in Wellington, this contemporary waterfront lodge complements the surrounding native bush and seascape and offers wonderfully furnished units with private verandas. **Pros:** idyllic spot in a sheltered, iconic Marlborough Sounds location; great views from every unit. **Cons:** boat or foot access only; minimum stay requirement for two weeks over Christmas. [$] *Rooms from: NZ$710* ✉ *Bay of Many Coves, Queen Charlotte Sound* ☎ *03/579–9771, 0800/579–9771* 🌐 *www.bayofmanycoves.co.nz* 🛏 *11 1–3 bedroom apartments* 🍽 *No meals.*

$$$$ B&B/INN 🏨 **Escape To Picton.** Three sumptuously decorated suites each have their own character with large bathrooms, crisp linen, and big über-comfy beds; the bejeweled Formal Suite has honeymoon written all over it (well, not literally). **Pros:** a fruit platter with champagne on arrival; excellent restaurant on the property. **Cons:** some street noise. [$] *Rooms from: NZ$425* ✉ *33 Wellington St.* ☎ *03/573–5573, 0800/693–722* 🌐 *www.escapetopicton.com* 🛏 *3 rooms* 🍽 *Breakfast.*

$$ HOTEL 🏨 **Jasmine Court Travellers Inn.** Stylish, well-sized guest rooms done in soft pastels look down over the town to the main harbor. **Pros:** bike and luggage storage if you're off to walk the Queen Charlotte Track; handy for an early morning ferry sailing. **Cons:** often full in summer; kids by arrangement only. [$] *Rooms from: NZ$190* ✉ *78 Wellington St.* ☎ *03/573–7110, 0800/421–999* 🌐 *www.jasminecourt.co.nz* 🛏 *18 rooms, 1 apartment* 🍽 *No meals.*

$$ RESORT 🏨 **Punga Cove Resort.** Accommodations ranging from backpacker bunks to trimmed luxury suites sleeping up to five are tucked into the bush at this Queen Charlotte Track crossroads. **Pros:** chat with the locals at the boat shed bar on the jetty; a favorite stop on the Queen Charlotte Track. **Cons:** set over a steep site so check room access; you'll need to bring in supplies as there are no shops. [$] *Rooms from: NZ$200* ✉ *Punga Cove, Endeavour Inlet, Queen Charlotte Sound* ☎ *03/579–8561* 🌐 *www.pungacove.co.nz* 🛏 *3 suites, 14 chalets, 4 lodge rooms, 8 backpacker cabins.*

$$$ B&B/INN 🏨 **Sennen House.** Just a 1-km (½-mile) stroll from downtown Picton is this white, peak-roofed 1886 villa, with verandas overlooking 5 acres of lush landscaping and bush and suites and apartments equipped

with carved wooden bedsteads, stained glass, rich upholstery, and brass fixtures. **Pros:** two apartments have full kitchens and three have kitchenettes. **Cons:** ask for the downstairs rooms if you have limited mobility; short winter close-down that varies year to year. $ *Rooms from: NZ$290* ⊠ *9 Oxford St.* ✦ *Follow the western part of Oxford St. from Nelson Sq., crossing 2 roads, to reach the property* ☎ *03/573–5216* ⊕ *www.sennenhouse.co.nz* ⤴ *3 suites, 2 apartments* ⦿ *Breakfast.*

$
HOTEL
⛶ **The Villa Backpackers and Lodge.** There are flashier backpackers in town but the upbeat vibe and friendly atmosphere in this old character villa makes this place a great stay. **Pros:** doubles and en suite rooms have their own TVs; just half a kilometer (¼ mile) from the ferry terminal. **Cons:** the cheaper double rooms use shared facilities and are simply furnished. $ *Rooms from: NZ$70* ⊠ *34 Auckland St.* ☎ *03/573–6598* ⊕ *www.thevilla.co.nz* ⤴ *7 double rooms, 2 with en suite, 44 dorm beds.*

$$
B&B/INN
⛶ **Whatamonga Homestay.** From the seaview lounge and private balconies you can watch the ferries pass and hear fish splash. **Pros:** kitchenettes; magnificent Marlborough Sounds environment with great views. **Cons:** minimum two-night stay; particularly steep driveway with concealed exit. $ *Rooms from: NZ$170* ⊠ *425 Port Underwood Rd., Waikawa Bay* ☎ *03/573–7193* ⊕ *www.whsl.co.nz* ⤴ *2 apartments, 2 rooms* ⦿ *Breakfast.*

SPORTS AND THE OUTDOORS

DIVING

The Marlborough Sounds have an excellent dive site in the *Mikhail Lermontov*, recognized as one of the world's great wreck dives. In 1986, this Russian cruise ship came too close to shore and sank on her side in 100 feet of water in Port Gore, on the edge of Cook Strait. (One life was lost.) The 600-foot-long ship is now an exciting dive site for anyone with moderate diving skills. September and October generally have the best visibility but trips run all year.

E-Ko Tours. Swim with or watch dolphins from September through April. Rare Hector dolphins, plus bottlenose, Dusky, and common dolphins all frequent the sheltered Marlborough Sounds. Visits from orcas (killer whales) are another highlight. Or engage with the prolific birdlife on Motuara Island, an island wildlife reserve and home to rare and endangered species. Walk to the top of the island for a great view of the Sounds. Several tour options include Dolphin Swim and View, Motuara Island Bird Sanctuary and Dolphin Cruise, and Bird Watchers Expedition, including close-up encounters with King Shags. ⊠ *The Waterfront, Picton Foreshore* ☎ *03/573–8040, 0800/9453–5433* ⊕ *e-ko.nz* ⤴ *From NZ$99.*

Nine Dives Picton. Whether you're a qualified diver looking to explore a shipwreck, or a snorkeler keen to engage with seals, "Nine" is your man, PADI certified and a Department of Licensed company. He'll take you to top scuba diving sites, such as the Long Island Marine Reserve, teeming with fish, or the wreck site of the Russian cruise liner *Mikhail Lermontov*. He runs a small boat so it will be weather dependent, and he only takes qualified divers. But you don't need scuba qualifications to splash with the seals. Nine will take you to a sheltered bay with your snorkel and you can engage with Sammy, or with other fish if the seals go shy. Nine will also introduce you to other marine life and the birds above water. ⊠ *Picton* ☎ *03/573–7323, 0800/423–483 NZ only* ⊕ *www.ninedives.co.nz* ✉ *Seal swims NZ$150.*

FISHING

Sounds Connection. This long-standing Picton company runs a host of land- and water-based tours, including regular half-day fishing trips and full-day trips by request. All fishing trips leave from Picton, with pickup from accommodation in the Sounds for a small fee. They supply all the necessary gear—it's up to you to get the fish. Then they'll fillet it for you and prepare it for you to eat. They also run half- and full-day winery tours, scenic tours, and any kind of custom-designed tour you would like to organize, out of Picton and Blenheim. ⊠ *94 Wellington St., The Waterfront* ☎ *03/573–8843, 0800/742–866 NZ only* ⊕ *www. soundsconnection.co.nz* ✉ *NZ$495 for group of 6 for 3 hrs.*

KAYAKING

A great way to experience the Marlborough Sounds is by sea kayak—and the mostly sheltered waters of Queen Charlotte Sound are perfect for it.

Wilderness Guides. Offerings include one-day guided kayak trips with a tasty lunch, plus multiday trips of kayaking, walking, or mountain-biking along the Queen Charlotte Track. Accommodations for such excursions are in stylish, boutique lodges. Quality bike and kayak rentals are available if you want to do it on your own (minimum of two). A special combo day includes a guided kayak trip in the morning followed by an independent, afternoon hike or mountain bike ride along part of the Queen Charlotte Track. Reservations are recommended. ⊠ *Picton Waterfront* ☎ *03/573–5432, 0800/266–266 toll-free in NZ* ⊕ *www. wildernessguidesnz.com* ✉ *From NZ$99 for ½-day guided kayak tour of Queen Charlotte Sound.*

HAVELOCK

35 km (22 miles) west of Picton.

Known as the Greenshell mussel capital of the world (Greenshells are a variety of green-lipped mussel), Havelock is at the head of Pelorus and Keneperu sounds, and trips on the Pelorus Sound mail boat, *Pelorus Express,* depart from here. Pelorus Sound is larger than Queen Charlotte Sound but less accessible by commercial craft. Small, waterside Havelock (population 400) is a pretty place to stroll; check out the busy little marina, shop in the few arts and crafts shops, and enjoy those mussels.

TOURS

Greenshell Mussel Cruise. Leaving from Havelock marina, Marlborough Tour Company takes you into the largely untouched Kenepuru and Pelorus sounds, just some of the labyrinthine waterways that make up the Marlborough Sounds. The world's largest Greenshell mussel farms are in these waters. Your skipper will cruise to the rows of black buoys that mark the farms, then hook up ropes covered in great swathes of clinging mussels and harvest them for your gourmet delight. They'll prepare the mussels on board, steamed gently and washed down with a glass of Marlborough Sauvignon Blanc. You'll also hear about the pioneering history of the Sounds. Marlborough also runs a Seafood Odyssea cruise from Picton, plus Marlborough winery tours and a Marlborough Icons Tour—a full-day combo of wineries tour in the morning and mussel cruise in the afternoon. Transfers for both the mussel and combo tours are available from Blenheim and Picton. ☎ *03/577–9997, 0800/990–800 NZ only* 🌐 *www.marlboroughtourcompany.co.nz* 🎟 *NZ$125* 🕒 *Sept.–Mar.*

Pelorus Mail Boat. *Pelorus Express,* the Pelorus Sound Mail Boat, is a sturdy launch that makes a daylong trip around Pelorus Sound, delivering mail and supplies to residents, as it has since 1918. This is an excellent way to discover the waterway and meet the locals. The boat leaves from Havelock on Tuesday, Thursday, and Friday at 9:30 and returns in the late afternoon. Reservations are advised January through March. It leaves from the northern end of the Havelock Marina, next to the Slip Inn Restaurant. Bring your lunch; there is tea and coffee on board. ✉ *Havelock Marina 1* ☎ *03/574–1088* 🌐 *www.themailboat.co.nz* 🎟 *NZ$128, children under 16 free.*

EXPLORING

Shark Nett Gallery. A family-owned gallery located beside the Kaituna Estuary is touted as "the largest privately owned collection of Māori carving in the world," on the basis that other collections are held by museums and tribal groups. Nevertheless the carvings here, commissioned especially for the gallery, represent a striking blend of contemporary and traditional styles relating the stories of local tribal history, people, birds, and plants. The collection's main purpose is to carry on the stories of the Rangitane people of the Marlborough Sounds for future generations. Feather cloaks and contemporary jewelry also feature. This gallery is not a shop as such—it's all about learning the stories and understanding the art; thus guided tours are an essential element to a visit. You will receive the full treatment of *manaakitanga,* as in traditional Māori hospitality. ✉ *129 Queen Charlotte Dr.* ☎ *03/574–2877* 🌐 *www.sharknett.co.nz* 🎟 *NZ$12* 🕒 *Sept.–Apr., daily 10–4.*

8

WHERE TO EAT

$$$ SEAFOOD FAMILY 🍴 **The Mussel Pot.** Outside, giant, green fiberglass mussels play on the roof; inside, the real things are steamed for three minutes in the whole shell or grilled on the half shell. Choose a light sauce for both steaming and for topping: white wine, garlic, and fresh herbs or coconut, chili, and coriander. There are also smoked and marinated mussel salads, platters, and tasty mussel chowder. Marlborough Sauvignon Blanc perfectly pairs with almost any dish on the menu. There are also vegetarian, pasta, and meat choices for those who, shocking as it is, don't fancy the local treasures. On sunny days, head to the courtyard. [$] *Average main: NZ$25* ✉ *73 Main Rd.* ☎ *03/574–2824* 🌐 *www.themusselpot.co.nz.*

$ CAFÉ 🍴 **Pelorus Bridge Café.** One of the better on-the-road cafés in the area (actually one of the few) serves great breakfasts and wholesome, homemade lunches to both passersby and the happy campers in the adjacent

Kahikatea Flat DOC Campsite. The food is great (try the rabbit or venison pie) and so is the setting. The backdrop beside the rocky, tree-lined Pelorus River is lovely, especially in summer when you can eat under the trees. *Lord of the Rings* fans might recognize the river; it was here that the Hobbits performed their famous "Barrel Scene." This place can get busy in summer holiday time (January/February), though the staff seem to take it all in their stride and handle the crowds. $ *Average main: NZ$9* ✉ *State Hwy. 6, by Pelorus Bridge* ☎ *03/571–6019* ⊕ *pelorusnz.co.nz.*

$$$ ✕ **Slip Inn.** Down at the marina, and overlooking the main boat ramp
CAFÉ and working port area, this is a sunny spot to stop for a coffee, light lunch, or dinner. The café is smart and contemporary, with local art on the walls and a large deck overlooking the water. The menu is themed around local produce, and it's no surprise that mussels and salmon sourced from Havelock and the Marlborough sounds take up lots of tempting menu space. However, there's more on offer here: all-day breakfasts, antipasto, and a comprehensive dinner selection. Signature dishes include mussel chowder, beer-battered fish-and-chips, a seafood platter to share, and sirloin steak with grilled prawns. An extensive wine list features Marlborough wines. The coffee is also very good. $ *Average main: NZ$25* ✉ *Havelock Marina* ☎ *03/574–2345* ⊕ *www.slipinn.co.nz.*

WHERE TO STAY

$$$ 🏨 **Peppers Portage.** Views across Kenepuru Sound, a scenic location, and
HOTEL well-appointed accommodations add up to a memorable wilderness stay, well geared to hikers and mountain-bikers straight off the Queen Charlotte Track. **Pros:** stunning, relaxing location; friendly staff. **Cons:** off-the-beaten-track for sightseeing. $ *Rooms from: NZ$260* ✉ *2923 Kenepuru Rd., 19 km (12 miles) off Queen Charlotte Dr., Portage* ☎ *03/573–4309, 0800/762–742 toll-free in NZ* ⊕ *portage.co.nz* ⤶ *41 rooms, 8 dorm beds* ❍ *No meals.*

$$$$ 🏨 **Raetihi Lodge.** A grand old lodge that's been given a thorough over-
HOTEL haul to bring it into the modern world overlooks the forest-covered hills and the tree-lined waterfront. **Pros:** absolute peace and quiet and tranquillity; paddleboards, kayaks, mountain bikes, and more. **Cons:** remote, not easy to access in a hurry; hotel dining is your only option here. $ *Rooms from: NZ$305* ✉ *7124 Keneperu Rd., Keneperu Sound* ☎ *03/573–4300* ⊕ *raetihilodge.co.nz* ☾ *Closed Apr.–mid-Oct.* ⤶ *14 rooms.*

FRENCH PASS AND D'URVILLE ISLAND

They're not easy to get to, but if you have an adventurous spirit and don't mind a rough road, French Pass and D'Urville Island are two of the best-kept secrets in the whole top of the South Island.

The **road to French Pass** splits off State Highway 6 at Rai Valley, halfway between Havelock and Nelson. It's winding, rough, and steep in places, but quite passable in a regular vehicle if you're a confident driver (check that your rental car is allowed off the sealed road). The sign at the start says "French Pass 2 hrs," and although it's only 64 km (40 miles) to the

Greenshell mussels are Havelock's specialty.

pass, this estimate is basically true. The road first climbs over the Rongo Saddle and down to Okiwi Bay through native bush; not far from here, you'll have spectacular views of D'Urville Island in the distance. Then the road crosses to the Pelorus Sound catchment and climbs along the ridge separating the waters of that sound from Tasman Bay to the west. Small side roads drop precariously to hidden bays such as Te Towaka, Elaine Bay, and Deep Bay.

The last 12 km (7 miles) is a dramatic drop down to sea level, skirting Current Basin before arriving at French Pass, the narrow stretch of water separating Tasman Bay from Cook Strait, which moves at up to 9 knots during the tidal run. Both the waterway and the island were named for French explorer Dumont D'Urville, who navigated through the pass in the 1820s when it was uncharted by European cartographers. **D'Urville Island** is on the far side of this stretch of water, and it's a fabulous spot where you can get a sense of what isolated coastal New Zealand is all about. Plan to stay two nights as it's a long drive either way.

Between Okiwi Bay and French Pass there are no facilities—no gas stations, bathrooms, or cafés—so come prepared. Public facilities at French Pass are limited: a basic toilet and a small service station with petrol, diesel, and essential supplies, open only during limited hours.

WHERE TO STAY

$$ **D'Urville Island Wilderness Resort.** This secluded resort offers a truly
HOTEL remote experience in two-bedroom beachfront units, a Kiwi-style bach (holiday cottage), and a bunkhouse, all overlooking the sheltered waters of Catherine Cove. **Pros:** great wildlife; you can fish from

your own dinghy. **Cons:** incredibly remote. $ Rooms from: NZ$125
⊠ Catherine Cove, d'Urville Island, Rai Valley 🕾 03/576–5268 ⊕ www.
durvilleisland.co.nz ⇆ 4 2-bedroom units, 1 self-contained cottage, 1
bunkhouse ⓘⓞⓘ No meals.

NELSON AND THE NORTHWEST

On the broad curve of Tasman Bay with views of the Kahurangi Mountains to the west, Nelson is a top area for year-round adventure. To the west beckon the sandy bays and beaches of Abel Tasman National Park and Golden Bay. To the south, the long valleys, high peaks, and glacial lakes of Nelson Lakes National Park draw hikers, climbers, fishers, kayakers, and sightseers. There's a climatic allure here as well; Nelson usually has more hours of sunlight than any other city in the country. New Zealanders are well aware of these attractions, and in December and January the region is swamped with vacationers. Apart from this brief burst of activity, you can expect the roads and beaches to be relatively quiet.

Settled by Māori hundreds of years ago, the area, then called Whakatu, was chosen for its extremely sheltered harbor, good climate, and plentiful *kaimoana* (seafood). These enticements later caught the eye of the London-based New Zealand Company, and Nelson became the second town developed by that organization, with British immigrants arriving in the 1840s. These days Nelson is one of the country's chief fishing ports and a key forestry, orchard, hop-growing, and wine-producing area, and olive groves are developing into another significant industry. This setting has long attracted creatively minded people, and a significant community of artists, craftspeople, and writers is settled in the countryside around Nelson.

NELSON

116 km (73 miles) west of Blenheim.

Relaxed, hospitable, and easy to explore on foot, Nelson has a way of always making you feel as though you should stay longer. You can make your way around the mostly two-story town in a day, poking into craft galleries and stopping at cafés, but two days is a practical minimum. You can also use Nelson as a base for a variety of activities within an hour's drive of the town itself.

GETTING HERE AND AROUND

Nelson Airport (NSN) is a small regional airport 10 km (6 miles) south of the city center. **Air New Zealand** links Nelson with Christchurch, Auckland, and Wellington a number of times each day. **Sounds Air** flies to and from Wellington three times a day with a scenic, low-level flight over the Marlborough Sounds, weather permitting. **Origin Air** connects Nelson with Palmerston North and Wellington. **Kiwi Regional Airlines** flies between Nelson and Hamilton and Dunedin. **Jetstar** links Nelson with Wellington and Auckland.

Geographically Nelson is quite isolated, and you'll climb a range of hills to approach from any direction. It's a 2½-hour drive from Westport, 5½ hours from Christchurch via the Lewis Pass, and 2 hours from Blenheim. From Nelson, head west to Motueka and on to reach Abel Tasman Park, Golden Bay, and Kahurangi National Park. There is a big hill to climb to reach Golden Bay but the road is good, and it's well worth the trip.

InterCity buses run daily services between Christchurch, Blenheim, Nelson, and the West Coast.

Atomic Shuttles also operates between Christchurch, Blenheim, and Nelson, and has a ticket-sharing arrangement with InterCity for the West Coast. In the December and January holiday season, book at least a couple of days before you plan to travel; during the rest of the year a day's advance reservation should do the trick. Bus tickets can also be booked online with the bus companies or at i-SITE Visitor Centres.

Abel Tasman Coachlines runs from Nelson to Motuekaand to Kaiteriteri and Marahau, gateways to Abel Tasman National Park. **Golden Bay Coachlines** run from Nelson and Motueka to Golden Bay townships, and provide access to Abel Tasman National Park and Kahurangi National Park.

Many of the smaller routes cut their service frequency in winter, so double-check the schedules.

Airport Nelson Airport. ⊠ *Trent Dr.* ☎ *03/547–3199* ⊕ *www.nelsonairport.co.nz.*

Airport Transfers Super Shuttle. ☎ *03/547–5782, 0800/748–885.*

Bus Contacts Abel Tasman Coachlines. ☎ *03/548–0285* ⊕ *www.abeltasmantravel.co.nz.* **Golden Bay Coachlines.** ☎ *03/525–8352* ⊕ *www.goldenbaycoachlines.co.nz.*

Bus Depot Bus Depot Nelson. ⊠ *27 Bridge St.* ☎ *03/548–3290.*

TOURS

Bay Tours Nelson. Local, knowledgeable guides run daily half- and full-day tours of wine trails, craft breweries, arts-and-crafts tours, plus scenic adventure and custom-designed tours by arrangement. Wine tours can include tastings and platters or full lunches, depending on your preference. ☎ *03/540–3873, 0800/229–868* ⊕ *www.baytoursnelson. co.nz* ⊠ *From NZ$98, including wine tastings.*

Nelson Tours & Travel. Learn about the region's wines, winemakers, craft brewers, and artisan food producers with local guide (and fledgling winemaker himself) CJ. He offers one- and two-hour, half-day, and full-day tours and a full-day gourmet tour and he'll even take you over to Golden Bay to explore the best it has to offer. CJ is also happy to customize tours to suit any special interests they might have. ☎ *0800/222– 373 NZ only, 027/237–5007* ⊕ *www.nelsontoursandtravel.co.nz* ⊠ *From NZ$45.*

Wine Art and Wilderness. Engaging and enriching, these very premium, fully catered gourmet tours explore the Nelson region's "wine, art, and wilderness." Your host Noel is a great chap to have along—he's a true wine buff, knows several local artists, and will take you into their homes and studios. In a former life he worked for the Department of Conservation and is now licensed to guide in all three of the region's national parks. Tours range from half to full days, with heaps of options—check the website for your preference. ☎ *03/545–8485* ⊕ *www.wineartandwilderness.co.nz* ✉ *From NZ$1,200.*

VISITOR INFORMATION

Contacts Nelson i-SITE Visitor Centre. ⊠ *77 Trafalgar St. at Halifax St.* ☎ *03/548–2304* ⊕ *www.nelsonnz.com.*

EXPLORING

Once you arrive in Nelson get your bearings at the visitor center on the corner of Trafalgar and Halifax streets. The heart of town is farther up **Trafalgar Street,** between Bridge Street and the cathedral steps, also home to the region's museum. This area is lined with shops, and the block between Hardy Street and the cathedral steps is a sunny spot to enjoy a coffee. Lively Nelson Markets (produce and arts) are held at the Montgomery parking lot on Saturday and Sunday mornings (used goods and crafts) and on Wednesdays you'll find the Nelson Farmers Market selling fresh produce in Morrison Square. There are a few art stores and galleries on Nile Street, too. For a dose of greenery, the **Queens Gardens** are on Bridge Street between Collingwood and Tasman. You will find yourself, literally, in the center of New Zealand in this park. The Nelson Arts Guide, available at visitor centers and local shops, is a good resource for the area's crafts offerings.

A five-minute drive around the waterfront from town, Tahunanui Beach offers some of the safest swimming in the country. This long, open beach is perfect for watching the sky change during the sunset and is a favorite spot for paddleboarders and kite-boarders, with its rollicking summer sea breeze. There are also several bars and cafés, and one of the country's largest campgrounds.

TOP ATTRACTIONS

Seventy years ago the first potters were drawn by the abundant clays in the hills of the hinterlands. Over the decades not only potters, but painters, ceramicists, glass-artists, and mixed-media practitioners have continued to enjoy the climate, colors, and inspiring light of the region. Many artists continue to work in Nelson and Golden Bay and the locally published *Nelson Arts Guide* is at local visitor centers, bookshops, some hotels and cafés, and online. See ⊕ *www.nelsonartsguide. co.nz.*

Christ Church Nelson. On a hilltop surrounded by gardens is Nelson's historic and architectural highlight. The site is an integral part in Nelson's history, originally as a Māori *pā* or fortified village, then as the base for the initial city street survey. This hill also housed the immigration barracks when the city was first settled by Europeans. A tent church was erected in 1842, followed by more permanent ones in 1851 and 1887. Work on the current cathedral (the third on the site) began in 1925 and dragged on for 40 years. The grand Gothic vision was curtailed partway through construction with a modernist finish completed in the 1960s. The steps running down to Trafalgar Street have become a destination

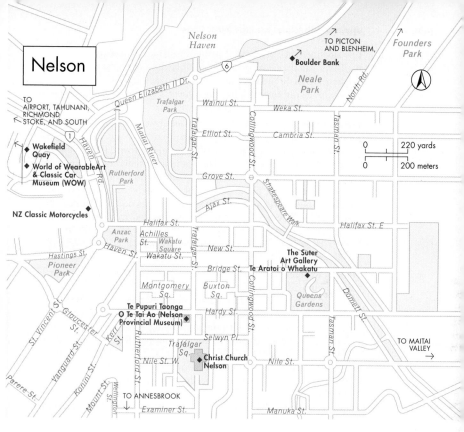

in their own right, a social hub in the city center. ✉ *Cathedral Sq.* ⊕ *nelsoncathedral.org* 🏷 *Free.*

NZ Classic Motorcycles. Even if you're not into motorbikes you might surprise yourself here. These classic and vintage machines evoke a wider sense of history, and they are beautiful to look at. When local businessman Tom Sturgess decided to share his private collection (more than 300 classic and vintage motorcycles and sidecars), he had this gallery built. He's included a glass-fronted workshop so you can watch the specialized mechanics restore machines. Then there's the art: Tom and his wife, Heather, show off their collection of more than 90 original works of vintage motorcycle themed art. ✉ *75 Haven Rd.* ☎ *03/546–7699* ⊕ *www.nzclassicmotorcycles.co.nz* 🏷 *NZ$20* ⊙ *Weekdays 9–4, weekends 10–3.*

The Suter Art Gallery Te Aratoi o Whakatu. These exhibits, reopening in late 2016 after a major museum renovation, show off both historical and contemporary art; this is a good place to see a cross section of work from an area that has long attracted painters, potters, woodworkers, and other artists. Many of them come for the scenery, the lifestyle, and the clay and, as a result, Nelson is considered the ceramics center of New Zealand. In recent years the gallery has increased its emphasis on painting and sculpture and there is a retail gallery with some of this quality work for sale. National touring exhibits come through regularly and they have a significant collection of nationally renowned artists such as John Gully and Toss Woollaston. A lunch café in the gallery looks out over neighboring Queen's Gardens. ⊠ *208 Bridge St.* ☎ *03/548–4699* ⊕ *www.thesuter.org.nz.*

Te Pupuri Taonga O Te Tai Ao (Nelson Provincial Museum). Nelson's regional museum occupies part of the original site of New Zealand's first museum. It explores the early settlement of the town, its development as an early port, the original Māori inhabitants, and other events that shaped the region. Exhibits include an outstanding collection of Māori musical instruments, plus a number of artifacts relating to the so-called Maungatapu murders, grisly goldfields killings committed near Nelson in 1866. There are heritage pieces donated from private collections, and regular visiting exhibitions. ⊠ *Hardy St. and Trafalgar St.* ☎ *03/548–9588* ⊕ *www.nelsonmuseum.co.nz* ⊠ *NZ$5* ⊙ *Weekdays 10–5, weekends 10–4:30.*

Fodor's Choice **World of WearableArt & Classic Car Museum (WOW).** Wacky and wonderful, ★ this museum displays garments from the World of WearableArt Awards Show, an event pioneered in Nelson but now presented in Wellington and exhibiting entries from designers worldwide. Art designed to be worn is best understood when facing moving mannequins in inventive ensembles. Imagine brightly colored, hand-painted silks draped into a giant winged headdress. Or papier-mâché fashioned into dramatic body suits, and glittering oceanic creations in the colors of *paua* shells. The elaborate sets, sound, and psychedelic lighting make this gallery a must-see. Exhibits change every six months. An adjoining gallery exhibits a superb collection of classic cars, New Zealand's largest, ranging from a pink Cadillac to E-type Jaguar to Aston Martin and more. They just don't make them like this anymore. Even if you're not a petrol head, not even a fan of cars, these sleek, shiny models will impress. An optional extra is the "Classic Collection"—an additional 70 classic cars parked out back because there simply isn't room for them all in the main gallery. At first the guys head for the cars, the women to the wearable art—then they'll surprise themselves by getting a huge kick out of both exhibitions. ⊠ *Cadillac Way off Quarantine Rd., Annesbrook* ☎ *03/547–4573* ⊕ *www.wowcars.co.nz* ⊠ *NZ$24* ⊙ *Daily 10–5.*

NEED A BREAK? **Penguino's Cafe.** A cool source for delicious gelato, like Rosemary & White Chocolate, Blueberry & Guava, Earl Grey, Manuka Honey, or a Mango-Lassie sensation. There are lots of dairy-free, low-fat, and low-sugar options and even a diabetic-friendly Lemon Sorbet. Oh, but there are waffles. And just try the enticing nine-flavor Tasting Platter for a real treat. Credit cards not accepted. ⊠ *85 Montgomery Sq.* ☎ *03/545–6450* ⊙ *Daily 10–5 (Fri.–Sun. 11–4 in winter).*

WORTH NOTING

Boulder Bank. One of the defining landscape features of Nelson is the 13-km (8-mile) natural stone bank, built up from eroding cliff faces farther north along the coast. In creating a sheltered harbor, the bank is essentially the reason Nelson was settled by early Māori in the first place. Haulashore Island, seen in the west, was originally part of the Boulder Bank, only becoming an island when The Cut was pushed through the bank as an entry for larger ships into the harbor. A lighthouse on the Boulder Bank served as a guiding light from the 1860s until the 1980s. For 27 years a lighthouse keeper and his wife lived at the lighthouse, raising 10 children on the isolated bank. The lighthouse can now be visited by a small harbor ferry. ⊠ *Boulder Bank Dr.* ✛ *Drive 9 km (5½ miles) north of town on State Hwy. 6, turn left onto Boulder Bank Dr., and go about 2 km (1 mile).*

Wakefield Quay. The waterfront area along the quay has been developing steadily for the past few years, and now has several cafés, along with a promenade that incorporates a historic stone seawall built by 19th-century prisoners. A statue commemorates the arrival of the early European pioneers, and Sunderland Quay houses a memorial to local fishermen lost at sea (Nelson is one of New Zealand's major fishing ports). It's also the site of the annual Blessing of the Fleet in July. ⊠ *Wakefield Quay, State Hwy. 6.*

WHERE TO EAT

$$$$
NEW ZEALAND

✕**Café Affair.** This busy city restaurant is a favorite with both locals and travelers looking for a quick-but-substantial meal. Morning options range from a quick muffin or big cooked breakfast, then switch to full lunch and dinner menus. The locals go for the stone-grill meals, especially the big chunky fillet steaks, the lamb kebabs, and seafood grills. There are a few outdoor tables and the indoor seating is split over two levels, with several big comfy couches upstairs above the dining room. Ⓢ *Average main: NZ$33* ⊠ *295 Trafalgar St.* ☎ *03/548–8295* ⊕ *www. caffeaffair.co.nz* ⊘ *No dinner Sun. in winter.*

$$$$
MODERN NEW ZEALAND

✕**Fords Restaurant & Bar.** Dining here is great throughout the day. Breakfast might be fish with tatties and house-made hollandaise or a carnivore's mixed grill delight. Lunch offerings include crispy duck salad and seafood chowder, while the dinner menu features signature Angus eye fillet with potato galette. There's also a really interesting tapas menu, and a quality local wine and craft beer list. Ⓢ *Average main: NZ$35* ⊠ *276 Trafalgar St.* ☎ *03/546–9402* ⊕ *fordsnelson.co.nz.*

$$$
ASIAN

✕**Harrys.** Asian cuisine is the focus at this local favorite, with an accent on Thai. Chilli-salt squid served with herb and sprout salad is a popular starter (also available as a main course); for other main courses try the "jungle" curry fish or pad Thai chicken. There's a wide selection of traditional and contemporary cocktails (try Harry's Houdini) and an ever-changing range of local craft beer on tap. On Friday night the bar fills with locals, often overflowing onto the sidewalk on warm evenings. The vibe here is upbeat and friendly. Ⓢ *Average main: NZ$28* ⊠ *296 Trafalgar St.* ☎ *03/539–0905* ⊕ *www.harrysnelson.co.nz* ⊘ *Closed Sun. and Mon.* ☙ *Reservations essential.*

$$$$
MODERN NEW ZEALAND
Fodor's Choice
★

✕**Hopgoods.** Nationally recognized chef Kevin Hopgood focuses on local produce and regularly wins national restaurant awards for his cooking. Try the Pure Angus beef fillet, always cooked to perfection, the fresh fish, the confit duck leg, or any of the ever-changing specials that come in from the farms and the sea, all simply cooked and fresh. This spot is likely to be busy, though the service remains attentive and

8

discreet. Reservations are recommended. [$] *Average main: NZ$36* ✉ *284 Trafalgar St.* ☎ *03/545–7191* 🌐 *www.hopgoods.co.nz* 🕑 *Closed Sun. No lunch.*

$$ ECLECTIC 🍴 **Morri Street.** With its pleasant outdoor terrace and open indoor spaces, this upbeat café is a favorite with the locals, and has great coffee. Along with a caffeine fix, come for the interesting breakfast menu (served all day) to enjoy Moroccan Spice Eggs; breakfast burrito with black beans, corn, spinach, and quinoa; or house muesli with natural yogurt. House-smoked Mt. Cook salmon and lots of interesting salads are on offer at lunch. The menu changes seasonally, as does the small wine list. [$] *Average main: NZ$17* ✉ *244 Hardy St.* ☎ *03/548–8110* 🌐 *www.morrisonstreetcafe.co.nz* 🕑 *No dinner.*

WHERE TO STAY

$$$$ B&B/INN 🏨 **Cambria House.** Built for a sea captain, this restored, 1880s Victorian villa pairs antiques with modern fabrics and conveniences, so each bedroom has an en suite bathroom with shower; the three luxury rooms also have a separate bathtub. **Pros:** elegant old house in leafy surroundings; close to the Maitai River and riverside walkway; easy walk to town and restaurants. **Cons:** tight off-street parking when at capacity (but plenty of street parking). [$] *Rooms from: NZ$325* ✉ *7 Cambria St.* ☎ *03/548–4681* 🌐 *www.cambria.co.nz* 🛏 *6 rooms* 🍽 *Breakfast.*

$$$ RENTAL 🏨 **Delorenzo's Studio Apartments.** These spacious and stylish studio apartments are a short walk from the city center and have plenty of conveniences, including washer-dryers and very comfy leather lounger chairs. **Pros:** walking distance to restaurants, the cinema, and the riverside walk; lots of flashy appliances. **Cons:** roadside units have some street noise. [$] *Rooms from: NZ$230* ✉ *43–55 Trafalgar St.* ☎ *03/548–9774, 0508/335–673* 🌐 *www.delorenzos.co.nz* 🛏 *25 suites* 🍽 *No meals.*

$$ HOTEL 🏨 **The Innbetween Lodge and Backpackers.** This grand old house in Trafalgar Square, just off the main street of Nelson, feels more like a small hotel than a typical hostel, with its rich brocade fabrics, strong colors, soundproofed rooms, and immaculate bathrooms with high-pressure showers. **Pros:** a terrific value; lovely old Victorian building with garden walks just across the road; outdoor bar area and small bistro out the back. **Cons:** lots of stairs inside. [$] *Rooms from: NZ$130* ✉ *335 Trafalgar Sq.* ☎ *03/548–8335* 🌐 *www.innbetween.co.nz* 🛏 *18 rooms, some en suites, 2 with bath, tent sites* 🍽 *No meals.*

$$ B&B/INN 🏨 **Joya.** This heavenly spot really encapsulates what Nelson is all about, with its focus on high eco-values in a B&B room and a studio unit in the main house and a delightful eco-friendly cottage in the garden, complete with its own water garden and turf roof. **Pros:** wide city views; fresh seasonal fruit in the rooms; Paulina speaks English, French, German, and Dutch. **Cons:** extremely steep driveway, so park on the street instead. [$] *Rooms from: NZ$150* ✉ *49 Brougham St.* ☎ *03/539–1350* 🌐 *www.joya.co.nz* 🛏 *1 B&B room, 1 studio, 1 cottage* 🍽 *Breakfast.*

$$$ B&B/INN 🏨 **Te Puna Wai Lodge.** The views from this 1857 three-story Victorian villa are stunning, and there are luxurious marble bathrooms in all rooms. **Pros:** walking distance to three excellent waterfront restaurants; complimentary spirits. **Cons:** short steep driveway with flat park at the top; steep staircase to the Fifeshire Suite makes it unsuitable for those

with limited mobility. $ *Rooms from: NZ$280* ✉ *24 Richardson St., Britannia Heights* ☎ *03/548–7621* ⊕ *www.tepunawai.co.nz* ⊋ *2 suites, 1 apartment* ⦿ *Breakfast.*

$$$$
B&B/INN
Fodor'sChoice
★

🖼 **Wakefield Quay House.** With just the road running between the front door and the sea, Woodi and John Moore's graceful 1905 villa has one of the best waterfront locations in town. **Pros:** 180-degree views of mountains, sea, and sunsets; easy walk to good waterfront restaurants. **Cons:** some road noise; limited off-street parking; bedrooms are both upstairs. $ *Rooms from: NZ$345* ✉ *385 Wakefield Quay* ☎ *03/546–7275, 027/265–7547* ⊕ *www.wakefieldquay.co.nz* ⊘ *Closed June–Aug.* ⊋ *2 rooms* ⦿ *Breakfast.*

NIGHTLIFE AND PERFORMING ARTS

If you like to party there are a few late-night clubs and music spots along Bridge Street. They change frequently as venues and acts come and go. Take a wander along the street after 11 pm to check out the options. To find out what's happening at night check ⊕ *www.itson.co.nz.*

FAMILY **The Free House.** Sorry, the ale isn't free here—the name means that this place isn't tied to any particular brewery, so you can try a whole range of the best crafted beer from this very crafty beer region. You can also order in light meals, pastas, and pizzas or bring takeout and eat with the locals out on the lawn—plates and blankets provided. There's live music some nights, in the adjoining Mongolian yurt, at other times maybe a poet or two. The Free House is family-friendly, even in the evening—and it's been voted one of New Zealand's best beer venues by a specialist beer magazine. Oh, and it's in a former church. ✉ *95 Collingwood St.* ☎ *03/548–9391* ⊕ *www.thefreehouse.co.nz.*

Nelson Arts Festival. A top music and performance event is the Nelson Arts Festival, usually held in October, likewise a magnet for top-notch Kiwi and international acts. ⊕ *www.nelsonartsfestival.co.nz.*

Nelson Jazz Fest. From January 1 to 5, Nelson hosts a terrific jazz festival. You'll find performances in local cafés, wineries, and at the Nelson School of Music. Check the website for who's playing where. ⊕ *www. nelsonjazzfest.co.nz.*

Sprig & Fern. Craft beer breweries are big in Nelson. This locale is one of seven Sprig & Fern outlets throughout Nelson, pouring 100% natural beers and ciders from the Nelson-based brewery. There is indoor and courtyard seating, a good bistro menu, and there's often live music on Saturday night. If you're looking for an even more casual tipple, the Sprig & Fern at nearby Milton Street has tasty, all-day bar food but also lets you order fish-and-chips or burgers from the takeaway shop next door—and they'll deliver. ✉ *280 Hardy St.* ☎ *03/548–1154.*

The Vic Mac's Brewbar. A historic building at the top of Trafalgar Street is the setting for live entertainment every weekend (check their website for gigs). A comprehensive lunch and dinner menu is noted for the tasty beer-battered blue cod and chips. ✉ *281 Trafalgar St.* ☎ *03/548–7631* ⊕ *vicbrewbar.co.nz.*

8

There's only one place to get an authentic replica of the One Ring; Jens Hansen Contemporary Gold & Silversmith in Nelson.

SHOPPING

Talented, creative artists live throughout the Nelson region, working full- or part-time in various media: ceramics, glassblowing, wood turning, fiber, sculpture, and painting. Not surprisingly there are many arts-and-crafts trails to follow, for which there is a brochure at the i-SITE Visitor Centre. There is also a colorful Montys Sunday Market in the central city, where you'll find both new and preloved crafts and goods.

Jens Hansen Contemporary Gold & Silversmith. Known now as "The Ring-maker," Jens Hansen craftspeople have long been known for skilled gold and silver jewelry creations. Contemporary pieces are handmade at the workshop/showroom, and many are set with precious stones or *pounamu* (jade) from the West Coast of the South Island. While they still do all this, the focus here has changed since Jens crafted the precious "One Ring" of *Lord of the Rings* film trilogy fame. You will find replicas of this ring all around the world, but here you can buy the officially authorized replica ring. The original prototype is on display, as is Frodo's chain. The studio opens by appointment outside regular hours. ⊠ *320 Trafalgar Sq.* ☎ *03/548–0640* ⊕ *www.jenshansen.com* ⊙ *Weekdays 9–5, Sat. 9–2, Sun. (summer only) 10–1.*

Nelson Markets. If you're in Nelson on a Saturday or Wednesday morning, check out the local markets. Saturday's Farmers Market, in Montgomery Square, has been established for more than 30 years and is one of the longest standing in the country. It gained its reputation from the wealth of local artists and craftspeople who sell their wares here, and now fresh produce, handmade breads, and artisan cheeses are also for sale. On Sunday morning Monty's Market in Montgomery Square sells vintage goods. On Wednesday morning the region's artisan growers come to Morrison Square, to the Wednesday Farmers Market. ⊠ *Montgomery Sq.* ⊕ *www.nelsonmarket.co.nz.*

South Street Gallery. A 19th-century, two-story cottage overflows with ceramic art, sculpture, and housewares. The gallery represents up to 25 Nelson artisans, most with a national, if not international, reputation. ⊠ *10 Nile St.* W ☎ *03/548–8117* ⊕ *www.nelsonpottery.co.nz.*

SPORTS AND THE OUTDOORS
BIKING

The Tasman Great Taste Trail, one of the Nga Herenga New Zealand Cycle Trail rides, offers riding on largely flat terrain, exploring the vineyards, orchards, cafés, and coastal areas from Nelson to Kaiteriteri and along the Motueka River valley. You can ride it independently or with a guide, in sections or in a multiday packages that include all accommodation, bike rental, and baggage-carrying service, with add-on options to walk or kayak in Abel Tasman National Park. Stops at cafés, wineries, craft beer breweries, beaches, orchards and art galleries you'll pass along the way are also optional, but you will be very welcome. In fact, many cycle companies incorporate tastings in their tours packages. You can even be met at the airport, your luggage swapped for a bike, and off you pedal. Check the Great Taste Trail on ⊕ *www.nzcycletrail.com.*

The Gentle Cycling Company. One of the first companies to set up in the region offers a range of guided rides, themed rides (Great Taste Beer, Great Taste Wine, for example), independent bike hire, and multiday packages including accommodation. They provide helmets, high-visibility vests, maps, and advice to make sure you get the most from your ride. They'll shuttle you and your bike to and from any start or finish point you prefer, pick you up from Nelson city if required, and also pick up any wine or craft purchases you might be tempted to make on your ride, so you don't have to carry it on your bike. ■TIP→ **They're based at Stoke, just around the corner from McCashins Brewery and Cafe, so plan your ride to finish there and slake your thirst.** ⊠ *411 Nayland Rd., Stoke* ☎ *03/929–5652, 0800/932–453 in NZ* ⊕ *www.gentlecycling.co.nz* ✉ *Bike rental NZ$30 ½-day, NZ$45 full-day.*

Trail Journeys Nelson. Bike rentals, day and multiday tour packages, and Mapua Ferry crossings (a vital link in the Great Taste Trail) are all provided by this highly experienced company. In addition to rides in the Mapua area, they also offer bike rentals from Nelson and Kaiteriteri Beach. ⊠ *Mapua Wharf, 10 Aranui Rd.* ☎ *03/540–3095,* ⊕ *trailjourneysnelson.co.nz* ✉ *Bike rental starts from NZ$35/3 hrs, e-bikes from NZ$30/1 hr, see website for more options and tour packages.*

Wheelie Fantastic. Bike hire, single-day and multiday rides, and luxury packages are all on offer from this experienced and knowledgeable outfit. They're based at Mapua but will deliver bikes and luggage wherever they're needed. ⊠ *8 Aranui Rd., Shed 6, Mapua Wharf* ☎ *03/543–2255, 0800/229–253 NZ only* ⊕ *wheeliefantastic.co.nz* ✉ *Bike hire from NZ$35/3 hrs, see website for longer rentals and tour options.*

8

NEARBY NELSON

Though Nelson's a bustling city, it retains a rural quality. Overlooking Tasman Bay and the foothills of the Bryant and Richmond ranges behind, open farmland, national parks, and vineyards are within easy reach. State Highway 6 winds southwest from the city through the outlying suburb of Stoke and through to Richmond, a good-size neighboring town. The commercial and civic center of the Tasman District, Richmond, has a good library and a modest shopping mall.

Just beyond Richmond, State Highway 60 branches northwest off State Highway 6, heading coastward to Mapua, Motueka, and Golden Bay. There's a wealth of vineyards along the strip toward Motueka, plus small farm and coastal communities with craft galleries and serious art studios tucked into valleys that run inland. If on a day drive, detour back along the inland route through historic **Upper Moutere,** with its blackcurrant and hop gardens. If you carry on south without turning to Motueka, look out for the birthplace of scientist Ernest Rutherford, on the right as you're leaving the small town of Brightwater. Five minutes south of Richmond the elaborate, atom-shape monument remembers this local boy's contribution to the world of nuclear science.

EXPLORING

TOP ATTRACTIONS

Hoglund Art Glass. One of New Zealand's best-known and longest-standing glass galleries is known internationally for its iconic collectible family of penguins as well as bold platters and vases. Their work creates a kaleidoscope of bright saturated colors and smooth curves. If the glassblowers are working during your visit you can watch them at their craft. They don't do this every day, so call ahead to confirm they are. ⊠ *52 Lansdowne Rd., Richmond* ☎ *03/544–6500* ⊕ *www.hoglundartglass.com* ⊡ *Free* ☉ *Daily 10–5.*

WORTH NOTING

Broadgreen. Cob houses, made from straw and horsehair bonded together with mud and clay, are common in Devon, the southern English home county of many of Nelson's pioneers. This 1855 house is typical of the style and is furnished as it might have been in the 1850s, with a fine collection of textiles and quilts, including one of the oldest-known quilts in New Zealand. Even the volunteer staff get dressed in the period style. The backdrop of tall trees and beautiful Samuel Rose Gardens completes the scene. ⊠ *276 Nayland Rd., Stoke* ☎ *03/547–0403* ⊡ *NZ$4* ☉ *Daily 10:30–4:30 (summer), 11–3 (winter).*

FAMILY **Grape Escape Complex.** Just a short drive from Richmond, this rustic complex is largely housed in a big old farm shed. A few galleries sell crafts, jewelry, and furniture, and wines and cheese are for sale as well. The very popular Grape Escape Cafe has been a long-standing success here, serving seriously and consistently good food. Kids can enjoy the playground while you shop or relax with a coffee, perhaps on the all-weather veranda. ⊠ *State Hwy. 60 and McShanes Rd., Nelson* ☎ *03/544–4341* ⊕ *www.thegrapeescapecafe.co.nz* ☉ *Daily 9–5.*

Isel House. This grand house, in the delightful tree-filled Isel Park in Stoke, was built for Thomas Marsden, one of the region's prosperous pioneers. It was Marsden who laid out the magnificent gardens surrounding the house, which include several towering California redwoods. The well-preserved stone house has had several rooms restored to their former glory, and contains stories of Isel and its surroundings, interpreted in part by local artists; also original anecdotal material, family items, and a herbarium. For some visitors, the sprawling woodland gardens are the highlight of a visit here. ✉ *16 Hilliard St., Isel Park, Stoke* ☎ *03/547–1347* ⊕ *www.iselhouse.co.nz* 🖂 *Donation* ⊗ *Oct.– May, Tues.–Sun. 11–4; May–Aug. by appointment.*

WINERIES

Grab a "Wine Nelson" brochure from the i-SITE Visitor Information Centre in Nelson before heading out. Or, visit ⊕ *www.wineart.co.nz* for all the information you need. Some of these wineries are a little tricky to find, even though they are signposted from the main roads.

Kahurangi Estate. This successful winery, in the idyllic little village of Upper Moutere, was one of the region's first, developed by Hermann Seifried in the 1970s. Greg and Amanda Day now produce a good range of Riesling, Pinot Gris, Pinot Noir, Montepulciano, Sauvignon Blanc, Chardonnay, and a fine Gewürztraminer. The cellar also has a selection of imported wines and cognacs. They also serve pizza on summer weekends, and they have a luxurious vineyard cottage accommodation on the property. ✉ *At Main and Sunrise Rds., Upper Moutere* ☎ *03/543–2980* ⊕ *www.kahurangiwine.com* ⊗ *Daily 10–4:30, to 8:30 Fri. and Sun. in summer.*

Fodor'sChoice **Mahana Estates.** This stunning winery and restaurant nestle unobtrusively on a hillside in Mahana. Views across the mountains and Tasman
★ Bay are superb, as are the estate's wines. In an area once known solely for apple production, the wines now being created from this district are maturing with style. Mahana produces Pinot Noir rose (from 100% Pinot Noir grapes), Sauvignon Blanc, Riesling, and Pinot Gris, and their Pinot Noir has received special accolades. Mahana Kitchen, the winery restaurant, champions local produce and complements Mahana wines. If you can take your eyes off the view, check out the artworks and sculptures around the estate, including some by internationally acclaimed Toss Woollaston, father of the original co-owner. Mahana Villa, a Pacific Mondernism-style luxury home with four suites, was built as the home of owner Glenn Schaeffer and is available to guests. ✉ *243 Old Coach Rd., Mahana* ☎ *03/543–2817* ⊕ *mahana.nz* ⊗ *Daily 11–4:30, extended summer hrs possible.*

Neudorf Vineyard. Despite its tiny size, Neudorf has established an international reputation for its Pinot Noir and Chardonnay. Riesling, Pinot Gris, and Sauvignon Blanc are also highly regarded. The top wines wear the Moutere designation on the label, as the winery is in the Moutere Valley surrounded by acres of vineyards and hop gardens. The Moutere Chardonnay is regarded as the vineyard's signature wine. Artisan cheeses are served in summer, and they also stock olives, cheese, and oat crackers in the small deli, to enjoy in the lovely grounds. ✉ *138*

8

Neudorf Rd., Upper Moutere ☎ *03/543–2643* 🌐 *www.neudorf.co.nz* 🕒 *Oct.–Apr., daily 11–5; May, June, and Sept., daily 11–5.*

Seifried Estate. One of Nelson's first wineries is a 20-minute drive from Nelson's main center, on the way to Motueka. Hermann Seifried was one of Nelson's pioneer winemakers and now the large family-run winery produces fresh, zippy Sauvignon Blanc, a creamy Chardonnay, a decidedly tasty Riesling, and a lush Pinot Noir. Petite Fleur, an independently run restaurant, serves lunch. You can dine inside or at a table in the garden. ✉ *184 Redwood Rd., Appleby* ☎ *03/544–1600* 🌐 *www.seifried.co.nz* 🕒 *Daily 10–5; Petite Fleur, Thurs.–Sun. 11–3.*

Waimea Estates. One of the largest and oldest Nelson wineries has been creating award-winning wines since 1997. The range includes Sauvignon Blanc, Chardonnay, Pinot Gris, Riesling, Viognier, Pinot Noir, and a delicious blended red called "Trev's Red," after the colorful owner. The well-crafted dessert wines and a funky "strawberries-and-cream" rosé are also worth trying. The Cellar Door Restaurant & Café is a bonus for visitors to the vineyard, specializing in local scallops, green-lipped mussels, and salmon, matched with the Waimea Estate wines. ✉ *59 Appleby Hwy., Appleby* ☎ *03/544–6385* 🌐 *www.waimeaestates.co.nz or www.thecellardoor.net.nz* 🕒 *Sun.–Wed. 10–5, Thurs.–Sat. 10–10.*

WHERE TO EAT

Richmond is a larger service town with some good cafés. While exploring craft galleries at Mapua, check out **Mapua Wharf** for its cafés and smokehouse, look for the craft brewery, and head into the café overlooking the estuary for some great fish-and-chips.

$$$$ MODERN NEW ZEALAND 🍴 **The Apple Shed Cafe.** The Mapua Wharf setting complements the food, and you can watch the boats go by while dining on quality produce, organic where possible, washed down with Nelson wines, ciders, and craft beers (including Mapua's own Golden Bear). You can dine inside or outside, just pick your day. All bread is baked in-house (try the banana bread with streaky bacon, maple syrup, and grilled banana for breakfast). Nelson's seafood is the choice for lunch and dinner: scallops, salmon, green-lipped mussels, and market fish. [$] *Average main: NZ$31* ✉ *Shed 3, Mapua Wharf* ☎ *03/540–3381* 🌐 *www.appleshed.co.nz.*

WHERE TO STAY

Throughout the Moutere, Mapua, Motueka region there are a number of delightful B&Bs and boutique lodges for accommodations.

$$$$ HOTEL 🏨 **Bronte Country Estate.** Sitting by the edge of the Waimea Estuary this estate in the true sense of the word encompasses both villas and suites and gets you right down to the water. **Pros:** excellent hosts with wide local knowledge; bird-watching opportunities on the sand flats; right in the heart of wine country. **Cons:** kids not encouraged. [$] *Rooms from: NZ$650* ✉ *133 Bronte Rd. E, off State Hwy. 60, Mapua* ☎ *03/540–2422* 🌐 *www.brontecountryestate.co.nz* 🕒 *Closed June–Sept.* 🛏 *2 villas, 2 suites, 1 luxury cottage* 🍽 *Breakfast.*

$$ B&B/INN FAMILY 🏨 **Matahua Cottages.** Two self-contained cottages on the shoreline of the Waimea Estuary began life as apple pickers' cottages and have been refurbished in a pleasing rustic style. **Pros:** intimate waterfront setting

Around Nelson

Tasman Bay

Cape Soucis

Whangamoa Head

Delaware Bay

PEPIN ISLAND

Cable Bay

TO FRENCH PASS & D'URVILLE ISLAND →

BRYANT RANGE

Rai Valley

TO PICTON & BLENHEIM →

Pelorus Bridge Reserve

6

Mount Richmond Forest Park

Pelorus River

0   5 mi
0   5 km

Happy Valley Adventures

6

The Glen

Atawhai

Boulder Bank

Nelson
see detail map

6

Stoke

Broadgreen
Isel House

Richmond

Green St.

Richmond

Hope

Abel Tasman N.P.
see detail map

Kahurangi
National Park

Marahau

Kaiteriteri

Riwaka

60

Motueka

Port Motueka

JACKETT ISLAND

Tasman

Harakeke

Mapua

RABBIT ISLAND

Ruby Bay

Seifried Estate

Hoglund Art Glass

Appleby

Grape Escape Complex

Waimea Estates

Moutere Hwy.

Redwood Rd.

Waimea Inlet

60

Motueka River

Motueka Valley

Neudorf Vineyard

Upper Moutere

Mahana Estates

Kahurangi Estate

ARTHUR RANGE

61

Brightwater

Wakefield

Waimea River

Wai-iti River

Nelson Lakes National Park

6

Kohatu Junction

Murchison

TO GOLDEN BAY & TAKAKA →

60

and views; fresh farm eggs and fruit when available. **Cons:** minimum two-night stay. [$] *Rooms from: NZ$165* ✉ *Apple Valley Rd. E, Mapua* ☎ *03/540–2214* 🌐 *www.matahuacottages.co.nz* 🛏 *1 1-bedroom cottage, 1 2- or 3-bedroom cottage.*

SHOPPING

Down at the Mapua wharf you'll find an aquarium, an ice-cream store, a gardening store, ceramics and craft stores, a few restaurant-bars, and a microbrewery.

Cool Store Gallery. Built in an old apple cool store (where apples were stored at cool temperatures after being picked), this gallery has well-priced 100% NZ-made art and craft work. Much of the work has a vibrant Pacific theme, produced by artists from the Nelson and West Coast regions; paintings, sculpture, textiles, *paua*-shell items, ceramics, glasswork, and jewelry line the walls. They have an arrangement with a local shipping company to get hard-to-travel-with purchases home for you in one piece. ✉ *7 Aranui Rd., Mapua* ☎ *03/540–3778* 🌐 *www.coolstoregallery.co.nz* 🕒 *Daily 11–4.*

SPORTS AND THE OUTDOORS

FAMILY **Happy Valley Adventures—4WD Motorbikes and SkyWire.** There's a ton of fun on this 1,600-acre farm just 10 minutes' drive from Nelson city, where the stock maybe play second fiddle to everything else going on: Quad bikes and reportedly the world's longest flying fox (zipline), for starters. Hop on a quad bike and climb a bush-lined track for 14 exciting km (8½ miles) before breaking out into the open to admire the ocean view across Delaware Bay. If the quad is not your thing, take the 4WD van tour. They also do a Tour of Discovery with a local guide explaining the culture and history of the land you cross. The Skywire—a mile-long zipline—takes you zooming across a forest-filled gully. If something more grounded is for you try a horse trek for some stunning views and steep trails. And if all that's not enough, they also offer paintball. Whatever you do you'll build up an appetite, so replenish in the Base Cafe. ✉ *194 Cable Bay Rd., 15-min drive north of Nelson, Nelson* ☎ *03/545–0304* 🌐 *www.happyvalleyadventures.co.nz.*

MOTUEKA

50 km (31 miles) west of Nelson.

Motueka (mo-too- *eh*-ka) is a horticultural center—hops, kiwifruit, and apples are among its staples. As a major gateway to two national parks, Kahurangi and Abel Tasman, Motueka also attracts kayakers, hikers, and holidaymakers. The town sits at the seaward end of the Motueka Valley, nestling close to the mountains of Kahurangi National Park. Like Golden Bay, Motueka is popular with the "alternative" communities around Nelson, and a few artisans and erstwhile hippies live alongside more traditional farming families. The hinterland is now also laced with vineyards, olive groves, and small, well-to-do farms often owned by absentee overseas owners. Many good cafés and places to stay are outside the town center, either in the sheltered inland valleys or out along the Abel Tasman coast and nearby bays, just north of town. South of town, the Motueka River is internationally known for its trout fishing, and the Great Taste Cycle Trail passes through the town.

GETTING HERE AND AROUND

Motueka is a 50-minute drive west of Nelson, on State Highway 60. You can also arrive from the south along the Motueka Valley Highway, which leaves State Highway 6 at Kohatu, 50 minutes north of Murchison. From Motueka it's a one-hour drive over the Takaka Hill to Golden Bay.

Abel Tasman Coachlines run from Nelson to Motueka, Kaiteriteri, and Marahau. Golden Bay Coachlines travel from Nelson to Motueka and on to Takaka, in Golden Bay.

VISITOR INFORMATION

Contacts Motueka i-SITE Visitor Centre. ⊠ *20 Wallace St.* ☎ *03/528–6543* ⊕ *www.motuekaisite.co.nz.*

WHERE TO EAT

$$ ✕ **Jester House Cafe.** This funky place is as much fun as the name sug-
CAFÉ gests, and is a great spot to bring the kids. The café is built in an
FAMILY eco-friendly style, echoing the owners' feelings about a sustainable environment. The food is all made on the premises and includes a raft of muffins, cakes, and biscuits to more hearty country fare like chowders, focaccia open sandwiches, and their famous twice-baked three-cheese soufflé. There's either cozy indoor seating or tables dotted through the garden and on a sunny veranda. For the kids there's a small playground, an enchanted forest, an outdoor chess set, and some extremely tame eels that can be hand-fed (September–May). ■ **TIP** ➜ **Down in the back garden, the Boot B&B has comfy accommodations for couples.** ⓢ *Average main: NZ$19* ⊠ *320 Aporo Rd.* ✛ *Follow the Ruby Bay Scenic Dr.* ☎ *03/526–6742* ⊕ *www.jesterhouse.co.nz.*

$$$ ✕ **Riverside Café.** You can chill in this rambling 150-year-old colonial
ECLECTIC cottage, along the Great Taste Trail cycle path and part of a community
FAMILY for Christian conscientious objectors established in 1941, the forerunner of many other communes later established around the country. It's decorated with hand-worked wood, copper, and fabric art, and enclosed with a grape-shaded veranda. The menu is built around organic veggies from the Riverside Community's gardens and focuses on nourishing, natural food, including milk from their own cows. Menu choices range from stylish restaurant fare to pizza and fries; desserts often include delights like chocolate-and-chili ice cream and spicy apple pie. If you're interested in the ethical side of this successful, long-running community, you're welcome to take a wander through after lunch. ⓢ *Average main: NZ$23* ⊠ *289 Main Rd., Inland Hwy., Lower Moutere* ✛ *South of Motueka toward Upper Moutere* ☎ *03/526–7447* ⊕ *www.riverside. org.nz/cafe* ⊗ *No dinner Sun.–Thurs.*

$$ ✕ **Toad Hall.** At this café, shop, and produce market in a former church,
CAFÉ enjoy breakfast (pancakes, salmon rosti, free-range eggs cooked heaps of ways), then stock up for your holiday travels, or just chill over a wholesome lunch (their slow-roast lamb burger is excellent). There's also an interesting kids menu, and you can indulge in the cakes and berry ice creams anytime. Weekend dinners in summer feature wood-fired

pizza oven and barbecue fare. [$] *Average main: NZ$19* ✉ *502 High St.* ☎ *03/528–6456* 🌐 *www.toadhallmotueka.co.nz* ⏲ *No dinner except in summer on Fri. and Sat.*

$$$ CAFÉ 🍴 **Up the Garden Path Cafe and Gallery.** You can mix art appreciation with fresh, wholesome culinary art at this delightful merging of café and art gallery on the main road into Motueka. You can dine in the main hall, among the art, on the wooden veranda, or in the peaceful garden, and any youngsters with you can happily exhaust themselves on the delightful playground. Breakfast? As well as the usual eggs, bacon, sausage suspects you could try an apple churro, or Mexican tortilla. The lunch menu is huge and offers soups, salads, burgers, pizzas, and sweet treats, too. [$] *Average main: NZ$21* ✉ *473 High St.* ☎ *03/528–9588* 🌐 *www.upthegardenpath.co.nz.*

WHERE TO STAY

$$ B&B/INN FAMILY 🏨 **Kairuru Farmstay Cottages.** Halfway up the Takaka Hill from Motueka, with distant views to the Abel Tasman coast, these homey cottages with timber interiors and wooden verandas have all you need for a comfy stay in the country. **Pros:** fantastic home base for area exploration; a real Kiwi sheep and cattle farm. **Cons:** a steep 15-minute drive up the Takaka Hill from Riwaka; long, narrow driveway onto the farm, though suitable for rental cars. [$] *Rooms from: NZ$150* ✉ *1014 State Hwy. 60, Takaka Hill* ☎ *03/528–8091, 0800/524–787 NZ only* 🌐 *www.kairurufarmstay.co.nz* 🛏 *2 cottages* 🍽 *No meals.*

$$$$ B&B/INN 🏨 **Motueka River Lodge.** Tranquillity, marvelous mountain views, and a superb standard of comfort are the hallmarks of this rustic lodge on 35 acres overlooking the Motueka River and accented with antiques from around the world. **Pros:** all meals can be arranged, and they are superb; fishing rivers all around. **Cons:** out in the countryside; 50-minute drive from Nelson airport. [$] *Rooms from: NZ$970* ✉ *Motueka Valley Hwy. (State Hwy. 61)* ☎ *03/526–8668* 🌐 *www.motuekalodge.com* 🛏 *5 rooms, 1 cottage* 🍽 *Some meals.*

$$$$ B&B/INN 🏨 **Stonefly Lodge.** Generous use of glass and balconies off each luxurious accommodation capture magnificent views over the Motueka River, with a peep of Kahurangi National Park's Mt. Arthur thrown in, all accented with lofty wooden spaces and river-stone pillars. **Pros:** a to-die-for setting; helipad out front; many area attractions can be explored. **Cons:** long drive in with a short, steep climb at the end. [$] *Rooms from: NZ$1300* ✉ *3256 Motueka Valley Hwy.* ☎ *03/522–4479* 🌐 *www.stoneflylodge.co.nz* 🛏 *4 rooms* 🍽 *Some meals.*

SPORTS AND THE OUTDOORS

FISHING

You won't lack for places to land some whopping brown trout in this region. Fishing season here runs from October to April. Fly-fishing excursions to local rivers and remote backcountry areas, for example Kahurangi National Park, involve hiking or helicopter trips and give plenty of excitement to visiting anglers. Daily guiding rates are generally around NZ$850 and include lunches, drinks, and 4WD transportation. (Helicopter access is additional.) Best areas to base yourself for trout fishing are: St. Arnaud, Motueka, Murchison, or at one of the dedicated though pricey fly-fishing lodges in country areas, close to these towns.

Strike Adventure Fishing. Zane Mirfin is a very experienced fly-fishing guide, with huge local knowledge. His company takes clients to the best spots throughout Nelson and Marlborough, as well as the West Coast and North Canterbury (He'll also take you sea fishing, if that's your preference.) ☏ *03/541–0020* ⊕ *www.strikeadventure.com.*

EN ROUTE

Motueka Valley. If you are headed for the West Coast from Motueka, turn south onto Highway 61 at the very obvious Motueka Clock Tower, following the sign to Murchison. The road snakes through the Motueka Valley alongside the Motueka River, with the green valley walls pressing close alongside. If this river could talk, it would probably scream, "Trout!" After the town of Tapawera, turn south on State Highway 6 at Kohatu and continue to the West Coast.

ABEL TASMAN NATIONAL PARK

77 km (48 miles) northwest of Motueka, 110 km (69 miles) northwest of Nelson.

Abel Tasman National Park is a stunning-yet-accessible swath of idyllic beaches and estuaries backed by a hinterland of native beech forests, granite gorges, and waterfalls. Unlike many of New Zealand's national parks, Abel Tasman has few serious challenges in its climate or terrain, making it a perfect place for an outdoor day trip.

GETTING HERE AND AROUND

From Motueka, the drive to the two southern entry points of Abel Tasman National Park is about 20 minutes. Tour boats leave from Kaiteriteri and Marahau—turn hard right off State Highway 60 just after the little townships of Riwaka to reach Kaiteriteri. Keep left at the same intersection to reach Marahau, but then take an immediate right for a road that leads over the Marahau Hill to Marahau. This is where the popular Abel Tasman Coast Track begins, although you can also get access to the track via water taxis at Kaiteriteri. Abel Tasman Coachlines service Abel Tasman National Park from Nelson and Motueka to Kaiteriteri and Marahau, the southern entry points. Golden Bay Coachlines travel to Totaranui, the Golden Bay entry point to the park. Many tour operators provide transfers as well.

Four companies provide boat transport to the coastal areas of the park, including day cruises, cruise/walk/kayak combos, and water taxi services for hikers and kayakers. These are Wilsons Abel Tasman, Abel Tasman Sea Shuttles, Marahau Water Taxis, and Abel Tasman Aqua Taxi.

Abel Tasman National Park information is available from the Motueka i-SITE Visitor Centre in Motueka.

Boat Transportation Abel Tasman Aqua Taxi. ⊠ *275 Sandy Bay Rd., Marahau, Motueka* ☏ *0800/278–282 NZ only* ⊕ *www.aquataxi.co.nz.* **Abel Tasman Sea Shuttles.** ⊠ *Kaiteriteri Beach* ☏ *03/527–8688, 0800/732–748 NZ only* ⊕ *www. abeltasmanseashuttles.co.nz.* **Marahau Water Taxis.** ⊠ *8 Franklin St., Marahau* ☏ *03/527–8176, 0800/808–018 NZ only* ⊕ *marahauwatertaxis.co.nz.* **Wilsons**

Abel Tasman. ⊠ *2 Inlet Rd., Kaiteriteri* ☎ *03/528–2027, 0800/223–582 NZ only* ⊕ *www.abeltasman.co.nz.*

VISITOR INFORMATION

Contacts Abel Tasman Centre. ⊠ *229 Sandy Bay–Marahau Beach Rd., Marahau* ☎ *03/527–8176* ⊕ *www.abeltasmancentre.co.nz.* **Department of Conservation Motueka.** ⊠ *At King Edward and High Sts., Motueka* ☎ *03/528–1810* ⊕ *www.doc.govt.nz.* **Motueka i-SITE Visitor Centre.** ⊠ *20 Wallace St., Motueka* ☎ *03/528–6543* ⊕ *www.motuekaisite.co.nz.*

EXPLORING

Fodor's Choice ★ **Abel Tasman National Park.** One of New Zealand's most easily accessible parks is also one of the most visited, with its golden sand beaches, sculptured granite headlands, and forest-lined tidal inlets and islands. Unlike other South Island parks, Abel Tasman has few extremes in weather and its coastal track, one of the Great Walks, is an ideal place to explore without the need of serious technical equipment or experience. Day- and multiday trips, walking, sea-kayaking, sailing, and scenic cruises, and combos of all of these, are popular ways to explore.

Keep in mind in the peak summer holiday season (Christmas to late January) this area is very busy and you will rarely be on that dream beach alone. Any time of the year, however, is perfectly suitable for an Abel Tasman trip, to wander the coastal track on golden beaches and through forest trails, or kayaking the sheltered bays and coves, perhaps in the company of seals.

The small settlements of **Kaiteriteri** and **Marahau** are the main gateways to the national park, both at the southern end 20- to 40-minutes' drive from Motueka. Stop first at the Nelson or Motueka i-SITE Visitor Centre for maps and information. If you're planning to stop overnight at a Department of Conservation campsite or hut, along the Abel Tasman Coast Track, you need to book ahead. You can do this online (⊕ *booking.doc.govt.nz*) or at the Nelson or Motueka i-SITE. It pays to book well ahead, especially in summer. Water taxis service the coastline, and they drop-off or pickup at many points along the way. At the northern end of the park, a road leads from Golden Bay through the park to Totaranui, where there is a large DOC campground and long, beautiful beach. This is a popular start/finish point for those walking the Abel Tasman Coast Track. ⊠ *Abel Tasman National Park* ⊕ *www.doc.govt.nz.*

BEACHES

Kaiteriteri Beach. The approach to Kaiteriteri Beach, through orchards then forest-lined coast, is lovely, and the beach is one of the area's prettiest, with its curve of golden sand, rocky islets offshore, and deep clear water. This place is packed in mid-summer, but once the four-week post-Christmas rush is over, the area returns to its usual less-frenzied pace. Many water-taxi and scenic cruises leave from here for Abel Tasman National Park. The Great Taste Trail cycle trail, which starts in Nelson, ends here. There is a popular campground and a few cafés in the village, although all prune their hours or close in winter. A number of private holiday homes are also located here. **Amenities:** accommodation; cruise- and water-taxi services; food and drink; parking (free); toilets; tour booking offices. **Best for:** swimming; walking. ⊠ *Kaiteriteri–Sandy Bay Rd., Motueka.*

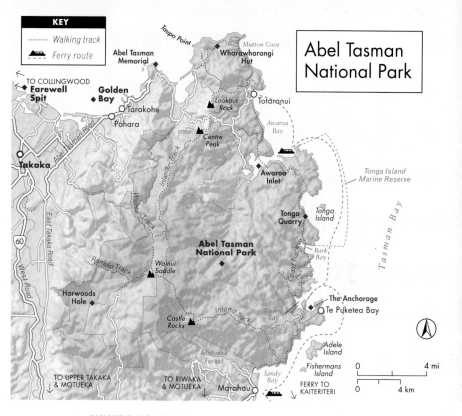

Abel Tasman National Park

WHERE TO STAY

$$$ 🏨 **Abel Tasman Marahau Lodge.** The location of these spacious chalets and
HOTEL studios, with native gardens between them, is hard to resist: Abel Tasman National Park is 200 yards in one direction and the Marahau beach is 200 yards in the other. **Pros:** close to everything in Marahau; travelers share tales in the communal kitchen; stylish, homey accommodations overlook the hills of Abel Tasman National Park. **Cons:** no breakfast in the room rate; studios don't have kitchen facilities. $ *Rooms from: NZ$220* ✉ *295 Sandy Bay–Marahau Rd., Marahau* ☎ *03/527–8250* ⊕ *www.abeltasmanmarahaulodge.co.nz* ⇆ *12 rooms* ⍟ *No meals.*

$$$ 🏨 **Kimi Ora Spa Resort.** The cozy wood walls and simple furnishings of
RESORT the guest quarters are part of the philosophy here: Kimi Ora means "seek health" in Māori, and this is meant to be an environmentally friendly, health-oriented resort. **Pros:** bordered by a mix of exotic forest and regenerating native bush; all the rooms have a distant sea view; some rooms have a whirlpool bath on the deck. **Cons:** 10-minute walk to Kaiteriteri Beach. $ *Rooms from: NZ$240* ✉ *Martins Farm Rd., Kaiteriteri* ☎ *03/527–8027, 0508/5464–672* ⊕ *www.kimiora.com* ⇆ *22 units* ⍟ *Breakfast.*

$$$$ 🏨 **The Resurgence.** Free-standing chalets and villas, and four lodge rooms
B&B/INN in the main house, are surrounded by native forest and stunning scenery and built of local timbers, plus they have every luxury. **Pros:** gorgeous

ABEL TASMAN: ONE-DAY ITINERARY

Try a walking/boat trip combo on the beautiful coastal track. Pack a picnic, your sunblock, and walking shoes and, if leaving from Nelson, hit the road by 8 am. Most operators will pick you up from accommodations; if you're driving, there's parking available at Kaiteriteri and Marahau beaches, the departure points for boat tours and water taxis. The drive across to the park takes around 80 minutes from Nelson, and around 30 minutes from Motueka.

Mid-morning, catch a big, modern catamaran or small, fast-water taxi along the coast to Bark Bay. On the way, if you've left from Kaiteriteri, you will pass Split Apple Rock, a giant granite marble in the sea that looks just like . . . a giant split apple. Farther up the coast you'll pass sandy beaches like Apple Tree Bay and Coquille Bay before cruising past birdlife sanctuary, Adele Island. Then, the boat hits open water for a short stretch before rounding Pitt Head and calling into Anchorage, a beautiful sheltered bay with a DOC hut and campsite that looks across to neighboring Torrent Bay, with its few private holiday homes. Your boat

will most likely drop off and pick up walkers, kayakers, and supplies here, then continue to Bark Bay, a little farther up the coast. Here is where you disembark. You'll walk off the boat ramp onto the beach and be shown where to join the Abel Tasman Coastal Track for your afternoon's walk back to Anchorage.

By now you'll be ready for lunch. There are few more idyllic spots than the forest-lined beach and estuary of Bark Bay for a picnic. From here it's an easy and scenic three-hour walk to Torrent Bay. The track climbs steeply at first, before ambling around several hillsides with pleasant outlooks through gaps in the trees. In summer you'll meet plenty of other walkers. Follow the track as it descends to Torrent Bay, then continue on to Anchorage, which you can now see across the bay. Depending on the tide you can either cross the estuary or walk around the all-tide track to Anchorage. Pass through the DOC campground and relax on the beach until your boat arrives to return you to Kaiteriteri or Marahau, all in good time for a well-earned sundowner.

scenery and terrific hosts; massage and therapeutic treatments available; walking tracks through the property. **Cons:** long, winding driveway is quite narrow and steep in places; villas and chalets are away from the main house, with gravel walks between; two-night minimum stay. $ *Rooms from: NZ$600* ✉ *574 Riwaka Valley Rd., Motueka* ☎ *03/528–4664* ⊕ *www.resurgence.co.nz* ☼ *Closed May–Sept.* ⤢ *4 lodge rooms, 3 chalets, 3 villas* ⦙◎⦙ *Breakfast.*

$$$
B&B/INN
⛺ **Split Apple Lodge B&B.** With breathtaking views across Tasman Bay and the jumbled, forested-covered ridges of Abel Tasman National Park, this lodge-style B&B seems miles from civilization, but it's not. **Pros:** convenience and beauty; sea-view rooms have private decks; comfortable beds. **Cons:** steep access drive. $ *Rooms from: NZ$210* ✉ *370 Kaiteriteri-Sandy Bay Rd., 5 km (3 miles) from Kaiteriteri, Nelson* ☎ *03/527–8502, 027/439–4009* ⊕ *www.splitapplelodge.co.nz* ⤢ *6 rooms* ⦙◎⦙ *Breakfast.*

OVERNIGHT IN ABEL TASMAN

Plan ahead if you want to stay in the park overnight, at either a Department of Conservation (DOC) campground or hut, like those at Anchorage, a four-hour, 12.4-km (7-mile) walk from the start of the track at Marahau. These huts and campsites are on the Abel Tasman Coast Track, which is a part of the national Great Walks system. Tickets (NZ$32 per night for huts and NZ$14 per night for campsites) must be bought beforehand, either at the Nelson or Motueka i-SITE Visitor Centres, DOC visitor centers throughout the country, or on the DOC website: ⊕ booking.doc.govt. nz. Huts are basic, with cooking, shower, and toilet facilities; filtered water; and sleeping bunks. There are

four huts and 18 campsites (some accessible by sea, for kayakers) plus Totaranui Campground. You will need to bring all your food (water taxis can be arranged to deliver fresh supplies, at a cost). You will also be expected to pack out all your rubbish. There are more salubrious park accommodations, lodges at Awaroa and Torrent bays, should comfort be your thing. Tip: From Torrent Bay, near Anchorage, there's a lovely short walk from the bridge over the Torrent River inland a short distance to Cleopatra's Pool. This rugged rock pool sits in between huge granite boulders and is surrounded by bush. But it's a frosty swim, even in summer.

SPORTS AND THE OUTDOORS
HIKING

Fodor's Choice ★ **Abel Tasman Coast Track.** One of the most popular multiday hikes in any New Zealand national park is the three- to five-day Abel Tasman Coast Track. From beach to golden beach, over gentle forest-covered hills and across tidal inlets, this is gourmet hiking. One of the premier-rated Great Walks, and traversed year-round, the track is popular because of its relatively easy terrain, short distances between huts and campsites, and the stunning landscapes. Water taxis can be booked to drop off and pick up hikers from several points along the track, allowing flexible options for walks of anything from one hour to five days. There are four huts and 19 campsites along the Coast Track, and spaces in both must be booked year-round. Bookings can be made online, through DOC visitor centers anywhere, and i-SITES in the Nelson region. ✉ *Abel Tasman Coast Track* ☎ *03/546–7393 Nelson i-SITE Visitor Centre, 03/546–8210 Department of Conservation Helpdesk* ⊕ *www.doc.govt.nz.*

MULTISPORT ADVENTURES AND TOURS

Wilsons Abel Tasman. One of the original operators of day excursions to this beautiful park, the Wilson family has expanded from their initial water taxi service to offering a whole gamut of scenic cruises, as well as single- and multiday walking and kayaking combos that include accommodation in their stylish family lodges at Torrent Bay and Awaroa. The flagship of their extensive fleet is the purpose-built, 24-meter catamaran, which cruises every day from Kaiteriteri—with several departures a day in summer, including an evening barbecue cruise. ✉ *265*

8

High St., Motueka ☎ *03/528–2027, 0800/223–582 NZ only* ⊕ *www. abeltasman.co.nz.*

SAILING AND KAYAKING

Abel Tasman Sailing Adventures. If you'd like a day in the park without breaking a sweat, call up the sailing gurus. Their large catamarans set sail daily from Kaiteriteri and glide into the heart of the park. Along the way you might call for a photo at Split Apple Rock, stop for a swim at a gorgeous beach such as Anchorage, or check out the seals on Adele Island. There's a delightful range of trips from which to chose; the most popular is a full day's sail that includes lunch. You can also arrange overnight trips, walking/sailing combos, and exclusive charters. ☎ *03/527–8375, 0800/467–245 NZ only* ⊕ *www.sailingadventures.co.nz* ▱ *Full-day sail NZ$185, with lunch.*

Kaiteriteri Kayaks. One of the long-standing local operators here offers the whole gamut of guided half-day, full-day, and multiday kayak trips, plus walk/kayak combos and kayak rental. They work with partner company Sea Shuttle Cruises to get you quickly into the best spots along this incredible coast—for example, to Tonga Island Marine Reserve, a trip that encompasses golden beaches, seals for company, a sheltered lagoon, and amazing rock formations. ✉ *Kaiteriteri-Sandy Bay Rd., Kaiteriteri* ☎ *03/527–8383, 0800/252–925 NZ only* ⊕ *www.seakayaks. co.nz* ▱ *NZ$199 for full-day catered sail.*

The Sea Kayak Company. Check out this little local company's guided kayaking trips, including stops on beaches and campsites that simply can't be reached by hikers. Popular options include the "Ab-Fab" Marine Reserve one-day paddle and walk, a two-day "More than Beaches" tour, and three- and five-day tours. All multiday tours are fully catered and all equipment is supplied. Reservations are recommended at least three weeks in advance. They'll also rent kayaks and gear for independent travel, and give you a heap of advice to help make your trip a happy and safe. ✉ *506 High St., Motueka* ☎ *03/528–7251, 0508/252–925 NZ only* ⊕ *www.seakayaknz.co.nz* ▱ *From NZ$85 (Split Apple Rock paddle).*

GOLDEN BAY AND TAKAKA

55 km (35 miles) northwest of Motueka, 110 km (70 miles) west of Nelson.

Fodor's Choice ★ The gorgeous stretch of coastline that begins at Separation Point, in Abel Tasman National Park, and runs westward past Takaka to Farewell Spit is known as **Golden Bay**, named for the gold discovered there in the 1850s. It's a 40-km (25-mile) crescent of beaches, farms, and orchards. Alternating sandy and rocky shores curve up to the sands of Farewell Spit, the arcing prong that encloses the bay. A 19th-century lighthouse station near its tip, here to warn shipping of the low-lying sandy spit, is the only man-made intrusion. Dutch navigator Abel Tasman anchored briefly in Golden Bay a few days before Christmas 1642. His visit ended abruptly when four of his crew were killed in an altercation with local Māori *iwi* (tribe), Ngāti Tūmatakōkiri. Tasman named the place Moordenaers Baij, or Murderers' Bay, and sailed away without ever setting foot on New Zealand soil. Today a relaxed crew of locals firmly believe they live in paradise, and a huge annual influx of summertime holidaymakers agree with them. The only road to Golden Bay climbs over the steep Takaka Hill from Motueka. You need to be determined to get here; it's not a place you pass on the way to somewhere else.

The Golden Bay lifestyle has for some years been considered "alternative"—a hideout for hippies, musicians, and artists. It's also the center of a rich dairy farming area, and its warm, sheltered climate nurtures crops such as citrus, avocados, and kiwifruit that struggle on the colder, Nelson side of "the hill." Overseas buyers have been snapping up Golden Bay properties to get their own little part-time spot of paradise, but local bylaws are changing to encourage full-time residents back to the bay.

GETTING HERE AND AROUND

Golden Bay Air flies scheduled flights from Wellington to Takaka, and to both ends of the Heaphy Track. They also run shuttles to the northern end of the Heaphy Track and the Abel Tasman Park.

The road into Golden Bay, over the Takaka Hill on State Highway 60, rises up 2,500 feet before plunging again to sea level to the tiny township of Takaka, a jumping-off point for Farewell Spit, Kahurangi National Park, and the Heaphy Track. This road is a 40-minute climb of twisting corners, steep drop-offs, and occasional passing bays. Don't be tempted to check the views while you're driving; wait until you reach Bob's Lookout, on the Nelson side of the hill, and Harwood Lookout, on the Takaka side, for safe viewings. The Ngarua Caves, on the Nelson side of the summit, are also worth a look, with their glittering caverns and stalactites and carbonated moa bones.

Airline Contacts Golden Bay Air. ☎ *03/525–8725, 0800/588–885 NZ only* ⊕ *www.goldenbayair.co.nz.*

Bus Contacts Golden Bay Coachlines. ☎ *03/525–8352* ⊕ *www.goldenbaycoachlines.co.nz.*

VISITOR INFORMATION

Contacts Department of Conservation Takaka Office. ⊠ *62 Commercial St., Takaka* ☎ *03/525–8026* ⊕ *www.doc.govt.nz.* **Golden Bay Visitor Centre.** ⊠ *Willow St., Takaka* ☎ *03/525–9136* ⊕ *www.goldenbaynz.co.nz.*

EXPLORING

Golden Bay begs to be explored, so if you take the trouble to cross the Takaka Hill into this spectacular area, plan to stay at least two nights or you'll spend your whole time driving and none enjoying the rewards of your travels. Golden Bay Coachlines runs daily services to Takaka, the Heaphy Track, and Totaranui (check times in winter).

Collingwood. After winding past several small farming districts and beach communities such as Paton's Rock, Onekaka, and Tukurua, State Highway 60 arrives at Collingwood, a small seaside village at the mouth of the giant Aorere River, 26 km (16 miles) west of Takaka. The earliest European settlers came here in the 1840s to build small ships from the timber lining the beaches and to farm the fertile river plains that spill out of the surrounding mountains. In the 1850s, gold was discovered nearby and Collingwood became a thriving port-of-entry town; at one time it was even under consideration to be the country's capital.

Collingwood is a bit out on a limb from main roads through the South Island. Nevertheless it's an interesting place with much to offer; for example, it's the northern access point for the Heaphy Track and the main base for trips to Farewell Spit and the wild, remote coastline of the northernmost West Coast. The old 1910 council office building houses the small Collingwood Museum, which has some interesting history displays; next door the Aorere Centre also has a good photographic record of the area's past. You can make a sweet stop by Rosy Glow Chocolates on Beach Road (not always open in winter) or buy a luscious gift at Living Light Candles on Tukurua Road, back toward Takaka a short way. For a really wacky experience, try a visit in August, when the town celebrates its annual "Gnome away from Home" Festival weekend. ⊠ *Collingwood.*

Waikoropupu Springs. Six kilometers (4 miles) west of Takaka are what the locals call Pupu Springs. This is the largest cold-water spring system in the southern hemisphere, and clear cold water bubbles into the Waikoropupu Valley after traveling underground from its source at the nearby Takaka Hill. The water in these springs is reportedly some of the clearest ever measured, anywhere. Swimming or touching the water is not allowed, to prevent the introduction of aquatic weeds and damage to the delicate flora within the springs; so leave your swimsuits and dive gear in the car. Instead, grab your shoes and take a leisurely stroll around the valley on the 40-minute, top-quality walk to the main spring, Dancing Sand Spring and Fish Creek Springs. Go quietly—the better to spot *tūī*, bellbirds, wood pigeons, and other birdlife. The turn-off from State Highway 60 to Pupu Springs Road is signposted, on the western side of the Takaka River bridge. ⊠ *Pupu Springs Rd., Takaka* ⊕ *www.doc.govt.nz.*

OFF THE BEATEN PATH

Totaranui. From Takaka the coast road heading northeast leads to the northern entry for Abel Tasman National Park, Totaranui. This scenic road passes through Pohara Beach, which has a few cafés and a holiday park, before winding around to Wainui Bay with its alternative Tūi community (a residential community that welcomes visitors) and cascading waterfall (a slightly rough 75-minute return walk from the road). From Wainui Bay, the road over the Totaranui Hill is a gravel surface. Take it slowly: it's a gorgeous drive through dense native bush to the coast. Totaranui Beach is a long golden-sand beach that is safe for swimming. This area can also be reached by boat from Kaiteriteri and Marahau, on the Motueka side of the Takaka Hill. It's a slice of pure beach bliss, and there's an unpowered campground with basic facilities. There's generally a wait-list to camp here for the first few weeks after Christmas, large though it is. Otherwise you should be fine—however, reservations are required no matter what time of year.

> ### ENCHANTED FOREST
>
> The Grove Scenic Reserve is a small patch of native forest at Rocklands, on the road from Takaka to Pohara, that escaped development when the area was cleared for farming. It's an enchanting collection of giant *rata*, elegant *nikau* palms, and trailing vines that grow between and over gnarly limestone outcrops and gulches. In early summer the *rata* wear a cloak of bright scarlet flowers. It's a 10-minute walk each way from the parking lot. Heading toward Pohara from Takaka, turn right off Abel Tasman Drive at Clifton. Follow the signs to the Grove; it's not far.

BEACHES

Golden Bay has miles of swimming beaches and small bays. Popular with families for its safe, shallow water is **Ligar Bay,** while **Tata Beach** is deeper—these are two of the best spots near Takaka.

Wharariki Beach. Out near Farewell Spit and too rough to be suitable for swimming, but with spectacular coastal landscapes, is Wharariki Beach. Among the massive sand dunes you're likely to come across sunbathing fur seals. If you get too close to them, they might charge or even bite, so keep a 30-foot distance, and never get between a seal and the sea. To get to this beach, drive past Collingwood to Pakawau and follow the signs. Go as far as the road will take you, and then walk over farmland on a well-defined track for 20 minutes. Allow at least an hour for the return circuit, along the beach and back via another well-marked track. This dramatic coast is quite remote, with few people (certainly no lifeguards) and tides change very quickly. Don't be one of those who get caught walking out to the offshore rocks to take photos and getting trapped by fast-rising water. **Amenities:** none. **Best For:** solitude; walking. ⊠ *Takaka ✢ Drive past Collingwood to Pakawau and follow signs.*

WHERE TO EAT

$$$

NEW ZEALAND

✕ **The Brigand.** This day/night bar and café is in a lovely old house on Takaka's main street and has a sunny courtyard, impressive handmade furniture, plenty of indoor seating, and roaring fires (indoor and out) for cozy nights. The menu consistently provides NZ faves like sticky pork spare ribs, 14-ounce sirloin steaks, and sea-run king salmon. Their daily specials and vegetarian selections provide plenty of other options, and there's a good range of light meals and snacks. The restaurant roasts and serves Takaka's very own fair-trade, organic Tuatara coffee. There's live music several nights a week, including an open-mike night every Thursday. [$] *Average main: NZ$29* ✉ *90 Commercial St., Takaka* ☎ *03/525–9636* 🌐 *www.virtualbay.co.nz/brigand.*

$$ NEW ZEALAND 🍴 **Courthouse Cafe.** In the lovely old former Collingwood Courthouse, on the main crossroads into town, this laid-back and popular café makes good use of local produce. Their breakfast "stacks" (rosti, bacon, egg, avocado) will set you up for a trip to the beach or Farewell Spit or Heaphy Track. Look also for the fresh muffins and quiches, the pies and pizzas, and daily blackboard special. The coffee is good, too. There are indoor and outdoor tables, but it gets packed in summer. [$] *Average main: NZ$15* ✉ *At Gibbs and Elizabeth St., Collingwood* ☎ *03/524–8194* 🕒 *No dinner Sun.–Fri.*

$$$ NEW ZEALAND FAMILY 🍴 **Mussel Inn.** Swing by for a quintessential slice of Golden Bay life, music, and craft beer. Locals come for the live music (usually several evenings a week and more in summer, starting around 8:30 pm), a bowl of mussel chowder, some fresh, steamed mussels, or local Anatoki salmon, washed down with some house-brewed beer. While new brews are always on the go, a perennial favorite is the famous Captain Cooker *manuka* beer—originally made from the native *manuka* tree by Captain Cook in the 1700s to combat scurvy on his ships. The plentiful options other than seafood are simple, tasty, and wholesome good. The design is wool-shed chic, self-described as "Kiwi woolshed meets Aussie farmhouse," which seems an apt description. Rough sawn timbers, handmade furniture, an outdoor fire pit, and leafy trees complete the rustic look. All the beers and ciders are made on-site. [$] *Average main: NZ$23* ✉ *State Hwy. 60, Onekaka* ☎ *03/525–9241* 🌐 *www.musselinn.co.nz* 🕒 *Closed mid-July–mid-Sept.* ✍ *Reservations not accepted.*

$$$ NEW ZEALAND 🍴 **The Naked Possum.** If you don't feel like you've quite hit the heart of backcountry Golden Bay then this place should do it. Here you can sit on the veranda and look across forest-clad hills, or down by the huge outdoor fire if there's a chill about. The well-presented food has a definite wild edge to it—wild game pies, open game meat sandwiches (Thar, anyone?), goat curries, wild pork pies, steak some nights, and a weekend Farmer's Brunch (venison sausage, cured bacon, and much more). Fresh garden salads and local beers and wines are also on the menu. Slow dining is encouraged, not because the service is slow, it isn't, but so you can soak up the country ambience. There's also a pleasant bushwalk (40-minute return to old gold workings along the start of the Kaituna Track, which continues for eight hours to Westhaven Inlet), plus an on-site tannery and possum products retail shop. [$] *Average main: NZ$22* ✉ *158 Carter Rd., Kaituna River* ☎ *03/524–8433* 🌐 *www.thenakedpossum.co.nz* 🕒 *No dinner Sun.–Thurs.*

$ CAFÉ 🍴 **Wholemeal Cafe.** Set in the old Takaka theater, this place is synonymous with the alternative, funky vibe that is Golden Bay. The decor and menu have evolved since the days of beanbags and bliss balls, but the essence remains. Best of all, the food is substantial and wholesome, and there's plenty of room to find a table, even at the height of summer. Eat indoors or out. There's a blackboard menu (try the pizza) and the coffee is notably good as well. $ *Average main: NZ$12* ⊠ *60 Commercial St., Takaka* ☎ *03/525–9426* ⊕ *www.wholemealcafe.co.nz* ⊗ *No dinner Sun.–Wed.*

WHERE TO STAY

$$$$
HOTEL
Fodor'sChoice
★

⛱ **Adrift In Golden Bay.** Pure romance here: a short walk across soft green grass from your own luxury cottage or studio unit gets you across your own quiet beach to the sea. **Pros:** calm, thoughtful atmosphere; Jacuzzi-style hot tubs; sundecks out front and private rear courtyards. **Cons:** a long driveway through farmland. $ *Rooms from: NZ$470* ⊠ *52 Tukurua Rd., 18 km (11 miles) north of Takaka, Takaka* ☎ *03/525–8353* ⊕ *www.new.adrift.co.nz* ⊗ *Closed July* ⇆ *5 1-bedroom cottages, 1 studio* ❍ *Breakfast.*

$$
HOTEL
FAMILY

⛱ **Anatoki Lodge Motel.** This might not be your paradise place at a Golden Bay beach but the studios and one- and two-bedroom units are spacious and comfortable and open out to a private patio and grass courtyard. **Pros:** barbecue cookouts in the garden; indoor solar-heated pool in summer; the two-bedroom family units are excellent value. **Cons:** the town backdrop is not typical of Golden Bay. $ *Rooms from: NZ$140* ⊠ *87 Commercial St., Takaka* ☎ *03/525–8047, 0800/262–333 NZ only* ⊕ *www.anatokimotels.co.nz* ⇆ *5 studios, 6 units* ❍ *No meals.*

$
HOTEL

⛱ **Pohara Top 10 Holiday Park.** Well-appointed cabins and motel units, with various bedding configurations and some with full kitchens, are set on five beachfront acres with plenty of trees for shelter. **Pros:** beachfront property. **Cons:** some units have shared bathroom facilities. $ *Rooms from: NZ$106* ⊠ *808 Abel Tasman Dr., Pohara* ☎ *03/525–9500, 0800/764–272 NZ only* ⊕ *www.poharabeach.com* ⇆ *24 units.*

$$
B&B/INN
FAMILY

⛱ **Sans Souci Inn.** A mellow spot just a two-minute walk from Pohara Beach has striking adobe and tile construction, wide verandas, and a turf roof, plus a touch of the Mediterranean about its decor. **Pros:** self-contained family unit sleeps up to four; you can cook in the restaurant kitchen for yourself; friendly, thoughtful hosts. **Cons:** restaurant is only open late October to Easter; shared bathroom. $ *Rooms from: NZ$140* ⊠ *11 Richmond Rd., Pohara* ☎ *03/525–8663* ⊕ *www.sanssouciinn.co.nz* ⊗ *Closed winter (exact dates flexible)* ⇆ *6 rooms without bath, 1 self-contained unit* ❍ *No meals.*

$$
B&B/INN

⛱ **Twin Waters Lodge.** Built on the edge of the Pakawau Estuary, this small but stunning lodge with curved timber ceilings and floor-to-ceiling windows overlooks the surrounding hills and wetlands, and is a two-minute walk from the sea on the other side of the peninsula.

ECO-STAYS

Twin Waters Lodge is a favored stopover for bird-watchers, who come to view the wading and migratory birdlife on the sand flats off Farewell Spit. The lodge features curved timber ceilings and uses a sound approach to ecological waste disposal, respecting its fragile coastal and estuarine setting. It is self-sufficient in water and uses solar heating for hot water throughout. It is an easy kickoff point for the western Kahurangi National Park, Farewell Spit Eco Tours, and the remote waters of Westhaven Inlet.

Pros: interesting tidal esturine. **Cons:** limited evening dining options in shoulder seasons. [$] *Rooms from: NZ$180* ✉ *30 Totara Ave., Pakawau, 9 km (5½ miles) past Collingwood on road to Farewell Spit, Collingwood* ☎ *03/524–8014* 🌐 *www.twinwaters.co.nz* 🕒 *Closed June–mid-Oct.* 🛏 *4 rooms* 🍴 *No meals.*

SPORTS AND THE OUTDOORS

FISHING

FAMILY **Anatoki Salmon.** Fishing at this salmon farm, on the edge of Kahurangi National Park next to the sparkling river of the same name, spares those prone to seasickness that particular unpleasantness. You can fish for salmon then have it cooked and prepared at the on-site café while you wait. Or put it through a hot smoker for freshly smoked salmon. Entry is free; just pay for what you catch. Fishing gear is provided, and no is experience necessary. Bring a picnic and the kids, and call it a day. ✉ *239 McCallum Rd., Anatoki Valley* ☎ *03/525–7251, 0800/262–865 NZ only* 🌐 *www.anatokisalmon.co.nz* 🎟 *Free* 🕒 *Daily 9–4:30.*

HORSE TREKKING

FAMILY **Cape Farewell Horse Treks.** Saddle up at Cape Farewell and ride off into the sunset, or to the beach. This outfit provides some of the best horse trekking in the country, on possibly the most spectacular beaches. For the best views, ride the combined Triangle and Old Man Range treks, or try the Puponga Beach ride for something more tranquil; it's also suitable for kids age five and up. If you're into wild beach gallops then join the Wharariki Beach Trek. ✉ *23 McGowan St., Puponga* ☎ *03/524–8031* 🌐 *www.horsetreksnz.co.nz* 🎟 *From NZ$80.*

FAREWELL SPIT

A 35-km (22-mile) sandspit that expands tenfold when the tide goes out, Farewell Spit is the home of tens of thousands of seabirds, many of them migrants from the northern hemisphere, and is an internationally recognized bird sanctuary. The landscape is wild.

GETTING HERE AND AROUND

The nearest town to Farewell Spit is Collingwood, 2½ hours from Nelson on SH60. The road continues 30 km (19 miles) from Collingwood to Puponga Farm Park, where the public road ends at the base of the Spit. Golden Bay Coachlines run a daily service from Nelson to Takaka, which includes a connection 23 km (14 miles) farther to Collingwood. Golden Bay Air flies from Wellington to Takaka. If you fly, rental vehicles can be hired in Takaka.

Access onto the Spit itself is only possible with the licensed tour operator Farewell Spit Eco Tours, based in Collingwood. Tours run daily, times depending on the tides.

TOURS

Fodor's Choice ★ **Farewell Spit Eco Tours.** This tidal spit stretches 30 km (19 miles) away from the northwestern tip of the South Island and is an internationally recognized bird sanctuary. More than 90 species of birds have been recorded here, including migrants flying around the globe to escape the northern hemisphere winter. Farewell Spit Eco Tours is one of the premier birding tours of New Zealand, traversing the vast windblown landscape. If you are in Golden Bay this trip is a spectacular must, even if you're not an avid birder. (Sliding down the massive sand dunes is a special treat.) The most popular trip is the 6½-hour Eco Tour, which travels along the sand in all-terrain vehicles to a lighthouse near the tip of the Spit. The Gannet Tour travels a little farther to a gannet colony that somehow survives on this sandy, windblown "edge" of the land. Bird enthusiasts should try the specialist, two-hour Wader Watch Tour. A shorter, 4½-hour Eco Tour onto the Spit is also offered. This company has been running tours for generations, and is the only one licensed by the New Zealnad DOC to travel on the Spit (which is closed to public access). Reservations are essential. Times vary with the tides. ✉ *6 Tasman St., Collingwood* ☎ *03/524–8257, 0800/808–257 NZ only* ⊕ *www.farewellspit.com* 🖾 *From NZ$120.*

KAHURANGI NATIONAL PARK

35 km (21 miles) west of Takaka.

New Zealand's second-largest national park, Kahurangi is 1.1 million acres of marbled mountains with fluted rock forms, arches, shafts, and sinkholes (featured in the *Lord of the Rings* films), remote river gorges, alpine tops, beech forests and coastal rain forests, and designated wilderness areas where no development or helicopter access is allowed. There are more than 350 miles of hiking tracks of various levels of difficulty, including the longest Great Walk, the Heaphy Track. Whitewater rafting and kayaking here is suitable for experienced paddlers and beneath the park are the deepest caving systems in the southern hemisphere. These are for serious cavers. Two of several entry points to the park are in Golden Bay, one into the Cobb Valley and the other 35 km (21 miles) west of Takaka, south of the town of Collingwood, which leads to the northern head of the Heaphy Track. The Department of Conservation Golden Bay Area Office (⊕ *www.doc.govt.nz*) provides local trail maps.

GETTING HERE AND AROUND

There are two main entry points to the park from Takaka. One is at the northern end of the Heaphy Track, south of Collingwood. However, most people walk the four- to five-day track one-way, and arrange a bus pickup or drop-off. The second entry point is up the Cobb Valley: turn left at East Takaka, at the base of the Takaka Hill on its western side. The Cobb Valley road ends approximately 22 km (15 miles) farther in. You'll find camping areas and short walks, plus the starting points to several park hiking trails in this valley. Golden Bay Coachlines also runs daily connections to the northern end of the Heaphy Track in summer.

SPORTS AND THE OUTDOORS

HIKING

Bush & Beyond Guided Walks. Walk with the locals: for guided walk and multiday hiking service throughout Kahurangi National Park, this company is a top choice. Trips are tailored to your level of fitness and interests, and their help on a multiday trail like the Heaphy Track can be invaluable. Trips can be self-catering (still guided) or fully guided, where your accommodation, food, and transfers are all taken care of. These guys operate year-round and know the Kahurangi area back to front, and beyond. They are also ardent conservationists, and founded the "Friends of Flora" conservation group, which aims to control predator pests and restore the wildlife of the beautiful Flora region of the park. ☎ *03/543–3742, 21/0270–8209* ⊕ *www.heaphytrackguidedwalks.co.nz.*

Heaphy Track. The most famous walk in Kahurangi National Park is the 78-km (49-mile), five-day Heaphy Track. The track is one of the Great Walks, regarded as the premier multiday walking trails of New Zealand. It traverses a grand landscape mix of beech forests, tussock-covered table lands, temperate rain forests, nikau palm forests, and coastal beaches as it crosses the national park from Golden Bay to Karamea, on the West Coast. The track can be approached from Karamea or Collingwood. Kiwi are often heard along the way. There are seven huts and nine campsites along the Heaphy Track, and spaces in both must be booked year-round. Bookings can be made online or through DOC offices or the Nelson or Motueka i-SITE Visitor Centres. Each end of this track is several hours' drive apart; shuttle transport (by coach or air) can be arranged. Mountain bikers are permitted on the track in winter (from May 1 to September 30). For help and advice contact the Great Walks Help Desk. ✉ *Kahurangi National Park* ☎ *03/546–8210 Great Walks Help Desk, Nelson DOC office* ⊕ *www.doc.govt.nz.*

Kahurangi Guided Walks. If you'd like some expert company on hikes around the national park, these specialists run half- and one-day treks on the best routes, as well as the full five-day Heaphy Track hike. More strenuous, multiday walks explore The Matiri Tops, Wangapeka Track, and remote, rarely visited spots such as Boulder Lake. Prices vary for each customized trip; these folk also run guided walks in Abel Tasman National Park and around Golden Bay. ☎ *03/391–4120* ⊕ *www.kahurangiwalks.co.nz.*

NELSON LAKES NATIONAL PARK

100 km (62 miles) south of Nelson.

Spread around mountains and two spectacular glacial lakes, Rotoroa and Rotoiti, the Nelson Lakes National Park also extends to high alpine passes and rocky peaks, clear-running rivers, and bush-lined trails. The native beech forests pour down to the lakeshore. On cloudy days, mist swirls through the trees, wetting the draping mosses. On sunny days the intense green shines through and the birdsong resounds. Lake Rotoiti is also the site of one of the Rotoiti Nature Recovery Project, through which long-term intensive pest control has helped the recovery of native birds and the reintroduction of some, including great spotted kiwi.

Of the two lakes, Rotoroa is less developed, with just a few fishing cottages, a campsite, and a lodge on its northern shore. The village of St. Arnaud, at the northern end of Lake Rotoiti, is the main gateway to the park. An accommodation lodge, a handful of B&Bs, a general store, a café, the DOC Nelson Lakes Visitor Centre, and a host of private holiday homes are located here. Each year in late February or early March the Antique and Classic Boat Show is held at Lake Rotoiti with close to 200 antique boats congregating for several days of boat racing and boat talk. The **DOC Visitor Centre** (☎ *03/521–1806* 🌐 *www.doc.govt.nz*) is particularly good, with information on the area's geology, ecology, and human history. Maps and details and advice on the hiking trails are available, and a mountain weather forecast is issued daily. DOC also administers two excellent campgrounds near the lake frontage. Bookings for these, at Kerr Bay and West Bay, can be made online or at the visitor center.

GETTING HERE AND AROUND

It's a 100-km (65-mile) drive south from Nelson to St. Arnaud, the hub of the park. Head south on State Highway 6; at Wai-iti, just south of Wakefield, veer left off the highway and follow the Golden Downs Road through to St. Arnaud. If coming up from the West Coast, pass through Murchison then after 35 km (21 miles), turn right at Kawatiri Junction. It's a further 30 minutes from here to St. Arnaud. From the East Coast, drive up the Wairau Valley from Blenheim, heading left (west) off State Highway 6 at Renwick.

Shuttle transport to the park is available through Nelson Lakes Shuttles; they will deliver to most track terminus points and the main stops as well. They can also link you between the various local national parks and track entry points.

Bus Contacts Nelson Lakes Shuttles. ☎ *03/547–6896* 🌐 *www.nelsonlakesshuttles.co.nz.*

VISITOR INFORMATION

Contacts DOC Nelson Lakes Visitor Centre. ✉ *View Rd., St. Arnaud* ☎ *03/521–1806* 🌐 *www.doc.govt.nz.*

WHERE TO STAY

$$ HOTEL **Alpine Lodge.** With the light wood paneling and dormer windows, the lodge feels somewhat European-alpine, but the view out the window is all Kiwi—wetlands, forest, and mountains. **Pros:** nice substitute for a backcountry lodge; the bushwalks are beautiful. **Cons:** bring repellent for the sand flies; book ahead in midsummer. $ *Rooms from: NZ$135* ✉ *Main Rd., St. Arnaud* ☎ *03/521–1869* 🌐 *www.alpinelodge.co.nz* 🛏 *28 rooms, 4 apartments, 1 dorm* 🍴 *No meals.*

$$$$ HOTEL **Lake Rotoroa Lodge.** This truly private haven sheltered beneath tall trees beside Lake Rotoroa lures anglers with a combination of old-fashioned personality and newfangled luxury, from the brass beds and hunting trophies to the expert fishing guides. **Pros:** lake views; some of the best brown trout fishing in the world; lovely walking tracks through native bush. **Cons:** a very scenic but 90-minute drive from Nelson; sand flies here are legendary. $ *Rooms from: NZ$340* ✉ *3 Gowan Valley Rd., Lake Rotoroa* ☎ *03/523–9121, 0800/574–634 NZ only* 🌐 *www.lakerotoroalodge.com* 🕓 *Closed May–Sept.* 🛏 *10 rooms* 🍴 *No meals.*

SPORTS AND THE OUTDOORS

Nelson Lakes has a number of half-, full-, and multiday trails that leave from the area around St. Aranud. The **Lake Rotoiti Circuit** gets you around the lake in an easy daylong walk. The rather steep **Mt. Robert**

There are numerous hiking tracks through the vast tracts of forest, deep river valleys, tussock tablelands, and mountain ridges of Kahurangi National Park.

Track zigzags up the face of Mt. Robert, giving you a superb view back across Lake Rotoiti toward St. Arnaud village. The return walk (fitness and good weather required) can be done in a loop by descending a marked track down Mt. Robert's eastern slopes to meet up with the Lake Rotoiti Circuit Track. Other tracks lead off these into the higher and more remote mountain areas and river valleys. Hut accommodations are available on a "first-in, first-served" basis. Backcountry experience (or traveling with someone who has this) and quality outdoor equipment are necessary on these longer tracks.

MURCHISON

125 km (78 miles) south of Nelson, 63 km (40 miles) west of Lake Rotoiti.

Surrounded by high mountains and roaring rivers, this small town is in some big country. With Nelson Lakes National Park to the east, Kahurangi National Park to the north, and the Matakitaki, Buller, Matiri, and Mangles rivers all converging on its doorstep, Murchison has gained the reputation as New Zealand's "white-water capital," and boasts the most-kayaked stretches of white water in the southern hemisphere. There are 13 rivers within 20 km (12½ miles) of town and white-water kayakers and rafters turn up every year to enjoy the sport these rivers offer. In particular, the first weekend in March brings more than 500 devotees to Murchison for Buller Fest, a churning gathering of white-water junkies. These local rivers are also teeming with trout and, as well as the white-water fans, fly-fishing enthusiasts worldwide converge to test their skills in what is one of the world's top fishing regions. Murchison residents still consider their landmark historic event "the earthquake," a major quake that hit in June 1929. The epicenter was nearby in the Buller Gorge, and the quake drastically altered the landscape. A second in 1968 (centered on nearby Inangahua) also rearranged the landscape considerably but was less destructive in human terms. Although most operators now accept credit cards, the only ATM in town accepts New Zealand cards only; so if yours is from elsewhere, make sure you have some cash on you.

GETTING HERE AND AROUND

Although it's 100 km (62 miles) from the nearest town, Murchison is easy to access by road, sitting right on State Highway 6. It's a 1¾-hour drive south of Nelson, 4¼ hours north of Christchurch, and 1½ hours east of Westport (without scenic stops). It is also one of only a couple of comfort and fuel stops on these long stretches so if (sadly) you are only passing through, take advantage of its conveniences.

InterCity buses pass through daily on its services between Nelson and Christchurch and Nelson and the West Coast.

VISITOR INFORMATION

Contacts Murchison Information Centre. ⊠ *47 Waller St.* ☏ *03/523-9350* ✉ *murchison@nelsonnz.com.*

EXPLORING

Murchison District Museum. For a small-town operation this local, community-run museum has a lot to look at. The rustic little building features an exhibit and memorial for the 1929 earthquake here, in which several locals died. There's also a good collection of farming and agricultural machinery from the town's colonial era, plus displays on the region's gold and coal mining history. The museum is run by a few volunteers, who make a brave attempt to open regularly. ⊠ *60 Fairfax St.* ☏ *03/523-9392* ⊘ *Daily, 11-3 or, as the door sign says, "maybe 10-4".*

The Natural Flames Experience. There are a handful of places in the world where you can find a natural gas flame, none in a natural ancient forest setting such as this one, near Murchison. It's been quietly glowing since the 1920s, when oil prospectors smelled natural gas seeping from the ground and put a match to it. This company has sole access rights, across a private deer farm then through Department of Conservation forest to the flame. The four-hour tour involves a short, scenic drive up the Mangles River valley, a talk about oil drilling history, farming, and the forest, then a one-hour backcountry walk (you might get wet feet) through farmland and forest to the flame, where you'll be treated to pancakes and tea, cooked up on the natural fire. You're likely to see farmed deer and lots of native birds. Tour groups are restricted to eight. Bookings are essential. ⊠ *47 Waller St.* ☏ *0800/687-244 NZ only* ⊕ *www.naturalflames.co.nz* ✉ *NZ$85* ⊘ *Tours leave from Murchison township daily at 9:30 am and 2 pm.*

WHERE TO EAT

Murchison has a great selection of casual cafés serving fresh, wholesome fare, just what you need after a day playing in white water.

$$ ✕**Beechwoods Cafe.** Lots of wholesome breakfast and lunch options, hot
CAFÉ snacks, and sweet treats are offered here. Some popular choices include
the snapper (fish) sandwich, Beechwood burgers, fish butties, and real
fruit ice cream. This is a great place to stoke up for your rafting or hik-
ing efforts. $ *Average main: NZ$15* ✉ *32 Waller St.* ☎ *03/523–9571.*

$$$ ✕**The Commercial Hotel.** In Murchison's historic hotel you'll find tasty café
NEW ZEALAND food during the day and, on the weekends, simple pub-style food (lamb
shanks, steak, salmon) for dinner. One table is set inside an actual bank
vault, this part of the building being a former bank. $ *Average main:*
NZ$26 ✉ *37 Waller St.* ☎ *03/523–9696* ⊕ *www.thecommercialhotel.*
co.nz ⊗ *No dinner Mon.–Thurs.*

$$ ✕**Red Barn Café.** About 10 km (6 miles) north of Murchison this rus-
CAFÉ tic, rural café also has a small farm park with sheep, goats, donkeys,
FAMILY and emus. As cafés go it's just your usual fare, however, this is a great
spot to let any youngsters with you have a break from the car. There's
a small fee to go into the actual animal park; however, there are also
little animal hutches on the expansive lawn. There's both indoor and
outdoor seating and they offer both a blackboard menu and premade
food. $ *Average main: NZ$15* ✉ *Mangarata, State Hwy. 6* ☎ *03/523–*
9400 ⊗ *No dinner.*

$$ ✕**Rivers Café.** Good food and good coffee is served every day in a wel-
CAFÉ coming, rustic setting. It's hard to find, tucked around a corner, so it's
mostly frequented by locals and those in the know. There's free Wi-Fi,
a bar, and an interesting little gift shop. Hours extend a touch in summer. $ *Average main: NZ$16* ✉ *51 Fairfax St.* ☎ *03/523–9009* ⊕ *www.*
riverscafemurchison.co.nz ⊗ *No dinner.*

WHERE TO STAY

$$ ☷**Kiwi Park Motels and Holiday Park.** These family motel units, luxury
HOTEL cottages, standard cabins, and campsites and powered sites are in a
delightfully peaceful rural setting close to the Matakitaki River, just a
10-minute walk from the shops, pubs, and cafés in Murchison. **Pros:**
barbecue area; playground; TV lounge; bikes and fishing rods for hire;
campsites are shady and cool in summer. **Cons:** busy in summer, so
book ahead over the Christmas rush. $ *Rooms from: NZ$150* ✉ *170*
Fairfax St. ☎ *03/523–9248, 0800/228–080 NZ only* ⊕ *www.kiwipark.*
co.nz ⇆ *2 cottages, 3 apartments, 5 motel units, 5 cabins* ⍟ *No meals.*

$$ ☷**Murchison Lodge.** Tucked in a tiny backstreet of Murchison, these
B&B/INN comfortably countrified guest rooms, with strong colors and lots of
wood, are within easy walking distance of the mighty Buller River.
Pros: private access to the Buller River through a grassy field; welcom-
ing hosts. **Cons:** a few stairs to climb. $ *Rooms from: NZ$180* ✉ *15*
Grey St. ☎ *03/523–9196* ⊕ *www.murchisonlodge.co.nz* ⊗ *Closed July/*
Aug. (dates vary) ⇆ *4 rooms, 1 with separate but private bathroom*
⍟ *Breakfast.*

$$$$ ☷**Owen River Lodge.** At one of the classiest of several top fly-fishing
HOTEL lodges in this region, six beautifully appointed cottages, each fronted by
Fodor's Choice sheltered verandas, overlook the Owen River valley. **Pros:** large garden;
★ fully equipped tackle room and fly-making table. **Cons:** the last mile
or two to the lodge is not paved but is easy enough to drive. $ *Rooms*
from: NZ$1490 ✉ *Owen Valley East Rd., 15 min north of Murchison*

8

☎ *03/523–9075* 🌐 *www.owenriverlodge.co.nz* ⏲ *Closed May–Sept.* 🛏 *6 cottage suites* 🍴 *Some meals.*

$$$$ B&B/INN Fodor's Choice ★ **River Haven Lodge.** This is essentially a fly-fishing lodge but if fishing isn't your thing, don't let that stop you from relaxing in these three stylish, comfortable, Colorado-style cabins on 5 acres of landscaped grounds set on the banks of the murmuring Mangles River, just outside of Murchison. **Pros:** home-cooked meals and warm hospitality; the river will lull you to sleep. **Cons:** beside the main road. [$] *Rooms from: NZ$750* ✉ *RD3, Longford* ☎ *03/523–9722* 🌐 *www.riverhaven.co.nz* 🛏 *3 cabins, 1 en suite bedroom* 🍴 *All meals.*

SPORTS AND THE OUTDOORS

Murchison's claim as a white-water destination is not to be ignored. They have some of the best white water anywhere.

RAFTING

Fodor's Choice ★ **New Zealand Kayak School.** Top professional instructors are based at this school, providing probably the best opportunity you'll get anywhere for learning the thrills of white-water paddling—all of it on great, scenic rivers. Enthusiasts love the area for the huge range of paddling available within 10 minutes' drive. The school offers tuition and training camps for groups and individuals, beginners to advanced, from a few hours to multiday trips on local rivers. Age is no barrier—the oldest (so far) couple they've taught to paddle were age 69 and 71. They also rent kayaks and supply guides for customised trips on the best local rivers. ✉ *111 Waller St.* ☎ *03/352–5786 year-round, for bookings* 🌐 *www.nzkayakschool.com* ⏲ *Closed May–Aug.*

FAMILY **Ultimate Descents New Zealand.** Highly experienced guides run rafting trips on the Maruia (Grade III), Clarence (Grade II), Buller (Grade III–IV), Mokihinui (Grade IV), and Karamea (Grade V) rivers. All half-day and day trips include a light snack, and the multiday trips are fully catered. They've been doing this for years and know the water well. ✉ *38 Waller St.* ☎ *03/523–9899, 0800/748–377 NZ only* 🌐 *www.rivers.co.nz* 🎟 *NZ$290 Buller Gorge full day, NZ$130 half-day; NZ$1,500 3-day Karamea River trip.*

Wild Rivers Rafting. Qualified guides introduce even first-time rafters to one of the premium white-water rafting experiences in the country, the legendary "Earthquake Rapids" on the Buller River in the rain forest. These are Grade III and IV rapids. The 25-foot cliff jump into the river is optional. River time is two hours; allow four hours total. Pickup is at the Iron Bridge on State Highway 6, 37 km (23 miles) from Murchison. ✉ *Iron Bridge, Upper Buller Gorge Rd., State Hwy. 6* ☎ *0508/467–238* 🌐 *www.wildriversrafting.co.nz* 🎟 *NZ$130 for 4-hr trip.*

EN ROUTE **Lewis Pass.** About 12 km (7½ miles) south of Murchison, State Highway 6 takes a sharp turn to the right over O'Sullivans Bridge toward the West Coast. If you've decided to skip the coast and head back to Christchurch from here, follow State Highway 65 straight through toward Lewis Pass. The first part of this road is known as "The Shenandoah," which follows the Maruia River valley as it climbs toward the main divide. This is prime farming country bounded by high mountains clothed in thick bush. Check the Maruia Falls, created by the 1929

Murchison Earthquake. Just 15 km (9 miles) before Springs Junction, Reids Store provides a welcome coffee and lunch stop, superior to the offerings farther on at Springs Junction. There's no fuel here, though, so you will have to get that at Springs Junction. From Springs Junction the road starts to climb to Lewis Pass, one of the lowest crossing points over the Southern Alps. Maruia Springs, just west of the pass, has traditional Japanese bathhouses and hot, outdoor rock pools, a restaurant, and accommodations (these are less salubrious and, accordingly, less-crowded than the waters at Hanmer Springs thermal resort town, farther east). Cross Lewis Pass and you're in Canterbury, where the countryside changes to high arid hills. Hanmer Springs is an hour southeast of the pass

THE WEST COAST

Heading southwest from the Nelson region brings you to the West Coast, a land unto itself and relatively remote from the rest of New Zealand. The mystical Pancake Rocks and blowholes around Punakaiki (poon-ah- *kye*-kee) set the scene for this big, rugged, sometimes forlorn landscape.

Māori, the first inhabitants, knew this area to be rich in *pounamu* (greenstone or jade). The Māori name for the South Island, Te Wai Pounamu, reflects this treasure. For hundreds of years the riverbeds, beaches, and mountain passes served as walking trails to access pounamu for intertribal trade, and you'll still hear references to "greenstone trails" throughout the area. Today, West Coast galleries sell traditional and contemporary greenstone carvings.

Early *Pākehā* (European) settlers carved out a hardscrabble life during the 1860s, digging for gold while constantly lashed by the West Coast rains. After the gold rushes, waves of settlers arrived to mine the vast coal reserves in the surrounding hills. Farmers and loggers followed; although the gold has mostly gone and magnificent native forests are now protected from milling, the coal mining and farming remain. The towns along this stretch of coastline are generally no-frills rural service centers, and make good bases for exploring the primeval landscape. These communities have also known mining tragedy: the most recent was at Pike River in late 2010, when 29 miners lost their lives in an underground explosion.

Near the southern glacier towns of Franz Josef and Fox, nature's spectacles are the high mountains, voluminous precipitation, and massive valleys of ice descending straight into rain forests (a combination also present on the southwest coast of South America). South of the glaciers, the road follows the coast, where majestic *kahikatea* rain forest grows closer to the ocean than anywhere else in New Zealand. On sunny days the Tasman Sea can take on an almost transcendent shade of blue.

In 2000, New Zealand's Labour-led government legislated to end commercial logging of the West Coast's native forests; since then the local communities have been in flux, as residents turn to tourism, farming, and a now struggling mining industry to sustain their livelihoods. But it's the environment that continues to determine the lifestyle here. Locals pride themselves on their ability to coexist with the wild landscape and weather. As a visitor, you may need a sense of adventure—be prepared for rain, swirling mist, and cold winter winds alternating with warm, clear days. "The Barber," Greymouth's infamous winter wind, blasts down the Grey River valley to the sea. The meteorological mix can mean that the glacier flight you planned at Franz Josef or Fox won't fly that day. So plan to stay an extra day, or more, as there are plenty of other things to do while you wait on the weather. Although the coast is well known for its rain, it also has clear, bright days when the mountains shine above the green coastal plains and the surf pounds onto sunny, sandy beaches; often the best, most settled weather is in winter.

EN ROUTE

If you're driving to the West Coast from Nelson or Motueka, State Highway 6 passes through Murchison before turning right at O'Sullivans Bridge 12 km (7 miles) farther south and heads down through the Buller Gorge toward the West Coast. This twisting, narrow road follows alongside the pristine **Buller River** as it carves a deep gorge below the jagged, earthquake-rocked mountain peaks. Not far from here are New Zealand's longest swaying footbridge, the **Buller Gorge Swing Bridge,** and the departure point for the **Buller Canyon Jet,** should you want to ride a few rapids. The upper gorge is tight and hilly but once past Inangahua the lower gorge is easier to negotiate. The Buller once carried a fabulous cargo of gold, but you'll have to use your imagination to reconstruct the days when places such as Lyell, 34 km (21 miles) west of Murchison, were bustling mining towns. There's now only a peaceful, Department of Conservation campsite at Lyell, and some good bushwalking. You'll pass high forest-clad mountains, narrow single-lane bridges, and the village of Inangahua along the way, sleepy now but not on the day a major earthquake centered here in 1968. **Hawk's Crag and Fern Arch,** where the highway passes beneath one-way rock overhangs with the river wheeling alongside, is another highlight, while a low-key café at Berlins offers a pit stop. At the end of the gorge, a left turn heads south along State Highway 6 toward Punakaiki. Continuing straight ahead leads to Westport and Karamea. Hopefully you will have allowed time to visit these northern West Coast regions before heading south. Although on a map the distances along the West Coast appear small, allow plenty of time to negotiate the hills and to explore the sights. When traveling in early to mid-summer, watch for the giant, spectacular crimson-flowering *rata* trees lighting the forest with their blooms. Watch also for campervans; they generally travel much slower.

Buller Gorge Swingbridge and Buller Canyon Jet Boat Ride. This adventure and heritage park is a delightful find, just when you think you're driving through the middle of nowhere. Be as active as you wish: jet-boat through the mighty Buller Gorge, swing over it on a zipline, cross it on New Zealand's longest swing bridge, explore a walking trail through dense native forest, try your luck panning for gold, or simply read about the massive earthquake that shook the land around here in 1968. Open daily 8–7 (summer), 9–5:30 (winter). Jet boats depart hourly through summer, 10 to 4 and by arrangement in winter. ⊠ *Upper Buller Gorge, State Hwy. 6, Murchison* ☎ *03/523–9809,*

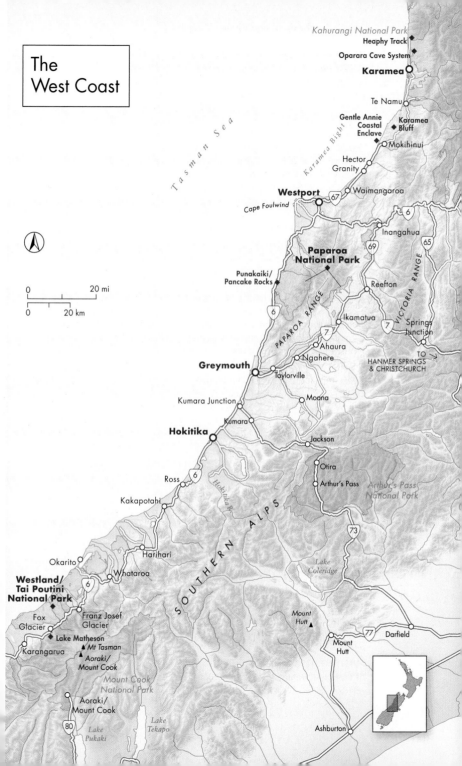

The West Coast

Kahurangi National Park

Heaphy Track

Oparara Cave System

Karamea

Te Namu

Gentle Annie
Coastal
Enclave

Karamea
Bluff

Mokihinui

Hector

Granity

Karamea Bight

Westport

67

Waimangaroa

Cape Foulwind

6

Inangahua

Tasman Sea

69

**Paparoa
National Park**

65

Reefton

VICTORIA RANGE

Punakaiki/
Pancake Rocks

PAPAROA RANGE

Ikamatua

7

7

Springs
Junction

Ahaura

TO
HANMER SPRINGS
& CHRISTCHURCH

6

Ngahere

Greymouth

Taylorville

Moana

Kumara Junction

Hokitika

Kumara

Jackson

Otira

Ross

6

Arthur's Pass

*Arthur's Pass
National Park*

Kakapotahi

Hokitika R.

SOUTHERN ALPS

73

Okarito

*Lake
Coleridge*

Harihari

Whataroa

**Westland/
Tai Poutini
National Park**

6

*Mount
Hutt*

Fox
Glacier

Franz Josef
Glacier

Lake Matheson

▲ *Mt Tasman*

Darfield

77

Karangarua

▲ *Aoraki/
Mount Cook*

Mount
Hutt

*Mount Cook
National Park*

Aoraki/
Mount Cook

80

*Lake
Pukaki*

*Lake
Tekapo*

Ashburton

0 — 20 mi
0 — 20 km

03/523–9883, 0800/285–537 NZ only ⊕ *www.bullergorge.co.nz*
⊠ *Jet boat NZ$105; zipline NZ$30; swing bridge NZ$10.*

KARAMEA

98 km (61 miles) north of Westport.

North of Westport, the coastline is squeezed between high mountain ranges and pounding surf. The highlight of the tiny settlements along this stretch is Karamea, known to most people as the southern entry to (or exit from) the renowned Heaphy Track, which crosses Kahurangi National Park from Golden Bay. Karamea is also a fine trout-fishing destination and the western entry point to the wilderness of Kahurangi National Park, with its wild rivers and network of hikes, and is home to the spectacular and easily visited Oparara cave system.

GETTING HERE AND AROUND

You can fly in direct from various places by either small plane or helicopter, although both are extremely weather dependent. **Karamea Helicopter Charters** specializes in scenic flights and operates helicopter transfers and day trips to and from Karamea. They provide a shuttle service to the Wangapeka and Heaphy Tracks, hunting and fishing, kayaking, and heli-rafting. **Adventure Flights Golden Bay** also offers transport for Heaphy Track hikers. **The Heaphy Bus** and **Karamea Connections** transport Heaphy Track hikers between the Brown Hut, in Golden Bay, and Kohaihai, near Karamea.

Karamea is a 100-km (62-mile) drive north of Westport on State Highway 67. Fill up with fuel before leaving Westport as there are no fuel stops until you reach Karamea. It's a 16-km (10-mile) drive north from Karamea to Kohaihai, the southern end and entrance to the Heaphy Track.

Hikers and (in winter) mountain bikers arrive at Karamea by the 78-km (48-mile), five-day hike over the Heaphy Track from Golden Bay.

It's a 45-minute drive from Karamea to the Oparara caves system. Follow the road north to Kohaihai for 10 km (6 miles) then turn right into McCallums Mill Road. Follow the signs along this gravel road. Note that the access road to the Oparara area is not suitable for large campervans. Walks range from 10 minutes to 10 hours (return); the spectacular and most popular Oparara Arch is a 25-minute walk each way from the parking lot. Contact the **Karamea Information & Resource Centre** for information on cave tours.

Contacts Adventure Flights Golden Bay. ☏ *03/525–6167*
⊕ *www.adventureflightsgoldenbay.co.nz.* **The Heaphy Bus.** ☏ *03/540–2042, 0800/128–735* ⊕ *www.theheaphybus.co.nz.* **Karamea Helicopter Charters.**
☏ *03/782–6111* ⊕ *www.karameahelicharter.co.nz.* **Karamea Connections.**
☏ *03/782–6767, 03/782–6838* ⊕ *www.karameaconnections.co.nz.*

VISITOR INFORMATION

Contacts Karamea Information & Resource Centre. ⊠ *106 Bridge St.*
☏ *03/782–6652* ⊕ *www.karameainfo.co.nz.*

EXPLORING

Oparara cave system. Magical rain forests and sculpted landforms here are encompassed in the Honeycomb Hill Caves Specially Protected Area, within Kahurangi National Park. Spectacular features at Oparara include a series of huge limestone arches (including the largest in the southern hemisphere, at 470 feet), passages, and caverns. Several short walks explore the caves, which are about a 45-minute drive northeast of Karamea. The Oparara Valley Project Trust, a community project, has enhanced visitor facilities, and offers guided tours that can include both walks and kayaking explorations. Also in this cave system is Honeycomb Hill, featuring underground passages of more than 13 km (8 miles) in length that contain the largest collection of subfossil bird bones found in New Zealand; many of them are extinct, including nine moa species and the giant NZ eagle. The caves are protected, and access is by guided tour only. ✉ *Karamea* ☎ 🌐 *www.oparara.co.nz* 🎫 *Guided tours NZ$95–NZ$240.*

EN ROUTE

Gentle Annie Coastal Enclave. On the drive up to Karamea from Westport you'll first pass through a series of sleepy coastal villages at Granity, Hector, and Ngakawau. If you want to stay over stop at the really laid-back Gentle Annie Coastal Enclave on the coastline north of the Mokihinui River. A local family oversees various accommodations, ranging from tasteful holiday homes to campsites and run a Cowshed Café in summer, all overlooking the coast or the bush. Kayaks and bikes are available, and a maze wends its way through native plantings, plus there's lots of interesting walks in the area. ✉ *de Malmanche Rd.* ✣ *Turn left directly after crossing Mokihinui River bridge (heading north)* ☎ *03/782–1826* 🌐 *www.gentleannie.co.nz.*

8

EN ROUTE

Karamea Bluff. The final hour of the drive from Westport crosses the incredibly scenic Karamea Bluff. In the gold-rush era of the 1800s and the farming days of the early 1900s this road didn't exist; road access to Karamea was by a more inland route up the Mokihinui Gorge and the Rough and Tumble Creek. But following the 1929 Murchison earthquake, which caused huge land upheaval over a vast area, the road was destroyed. The new road, which slowly pushed through over the bluff, is sealed. It climbs steeply from the Mokihinui River through virgin *podocarp* forest before breaking out on to a plateau of fertile farmland. It then drops away to Little Wanganui, some 15 km (9 miles) from Karamea before winding gently through coastal bush and farms for the last few kilometers. ✉ *Karamea.*

WHERE TO STAY

$$ HOTEL **The Last Resort.** Glowing hardwood beams salvaged from the forest floor, stylish local artwork, and unusual turf roof make this place (the last place to stay on the West Coast, heading north) look very much at one with its surroundings. **Pros:** down-to-earth, welcoming hosts; unique accommodations; decent restaurant. **Cons:** on the main street. [$] *Rooms from: NZ$130* ✉ *71 Waverley St.* ☎ *0800/505–042 NZ only* 🌐 *www.lastresortkaramea.co.nz* 🛏 *18 studios, 6 rooms with shared bath, 3 cottages, 3 dorm rooms* 🍴 *No meals.*

$$ HOTEL **Rough and Tumble Bush Lodge.** Just a few miles inland up the Mokihinui River from the highway, this wooden lodge occupies a stunning

spot on a bend in the river, surrounded by virgin forest and towering gorge walls. **Pros:** great spot for families; the nearby 10 km (6 miles) Charming Creek walkway is well worth doing; hosts are outdoor enthusiasts and play the fiddle; outdoor bath overlooking the river. **Cons:** the entry road is rough gravel, with a fjord crossing; watch those sand flies in summer. [$] *Rooms from: NZ$160* ✉ *Mokihinui Rd., Seddonville* ☎ *03/782–1337, 0800/333–746 NZ only* 🌐 *www.roughandtumble.co.nz* ⏲ *Closed May–Oct.* 🛏 *5 rooms* 🍴 *No meals.*

WESTPORT

230 km (144 miles) southeast of Nelson.

One of New Zealand's oldest ports sits at the mouth of the mighty Buller River. Once a boomtown for two separate gold rushes, it's now a quiet little hub (population 3,100) for the local farming and coal industries, plus the rapidly expanding adventure-tourism niche. It's an interesting place to stop before heading south toward Punakaiki and the glaciers or north to remote Karamea and the Heaphy Track; the best of Westport is out of town, either on the coast or up the rivers. The classic sights of the Westport region are breaking white-capped waves, blue sea, seals, rocky outcrops, and acres of flax and wetlands. In the town itself, several striking art deco buildings line the main street. Stop by the little **Coaltown Museum** at the i-SITE Visitor Centre on Palmerston Street to learn about the town's coal mining history. Or treat yourself to a tour for a real, hands-on underground coal mining experience in the original Banbury Mine, on the **Denniston Plateau,** 18 km (11 miles) northeast of town and high on a mountain plateau. It's a classic experience. A museum, information panels, and actual machinery detail life in this lonely outpost from the late 1800s through the early 1900s. Carving a living from the rich seams of coal in the surrounding tussock-covered hills, the miners and their families had to struggle with wild weather, isolation, and primitive conditions. Your best option here is to book the **Denniston Experience** *(see listing)* that guides you into the Banbury Mine, the region's oldest and longest-running, reopened (a bit) for visitors. A popular historical novel about these coal mining pioneers and their families, *The Denniston Rose,* by New Zealand writer Jenny Pattrick, details the area and the harsh colonial lifestyle.

The **Westport i-SITE Visitor Centre** can also provide information on Karamea township and Kahurangi National Park.

GETTING HERE AND AROUND

It's a 3-hour drive to Westport from Nelson to the north, or a 1½-hour drive south to Greymouth. Either way you'll pass along incredibly scenic coastlines or river gorges surrounded by thick native bush and high ranges. InterCity buses travel to Westport daily, en route between Nelson and the glaciers.

TOURS

Buller Adventure Tours. From the lower end of the Buller Gorge, before you reach Westport, jet-boat trips and horse treks explore the wild West Coast countryside. On the boat, you'll skim the rapids of the Lower Buller Gorge, coming pretty close to the rock walls. Horse treks take you into forest and along sandy river beaches. It's all a bit of quintessential New Zealand. ⊠ *State Hwy. 6, Lower Buller Gorge* ☎ *03/789–7286, 0508/486–877 NZ only* ⊕ *www.adventuretours.co.nz* ✈ *Horse trek NZ$89, jet-boat trip NZ$89.*

FAMILY

Fodor's Choice

★

The Denniston Experience. In 1879, one of the West Coast's largest coal mines started production on the Denniston Plateau. Coal was carried out on "The Incline," an incredibly steep railway dropping off the plateau. Some miners' families brought up this way never left this barren, windswept plateau—at least until a bridle track was constructed. Today you can drive a paved road to the top of the incline, where a wagon sits ready to descend. Better still, you get to ride a narrow gauge train around the bluff where coal-laden wagons once trundled out of the Banbury Mine, then you'll don your hard hat, be assigned your mining job, and head on into the mine. You'll walk in at least 1,000 feet (shafts head off in all directions) and get to play hands-on coal miner, maybe shoveling or sifting coal, pushing wagons, or setting off a charge. All the sounds of a working mine are around you, plus an intriguing hologram display tells of the harsh life of an old-time coal miner. You'll be glad you weren't one and you'll probably be glad to get back out in the open, looking down the sweeping vista to the coast. It's a fascinating, two-hour trip. You meet your guide up on the Denniston Plateau car park, about 40 minutes' drive from Westport. Reservations are essential. Minimum age is five years. ⊠ *Denniston Rd., Denniston Plateau* ☎ *0800/881–880 NZ only* ⊕ *www.denniston.co.nz* ✈ *Underground Union Experience NZ$99; Gorge Express (train ride only) NZ$45.*

OutWest Tours. Coal mining is a hot topic on the West Coast, where the history and the mines run deep. Past and recent tragedies in mines and current debates on open cast-mining and conservation versus employment are heatedly discussed. These tours into coal mining country make good use of off-road and 4WD vehicles. Micky will transport you in style up to the Denniston Plateau, site of historic and current mine sites, plus he's the exclusive operator for tours through the current Stockton Open cast site on the Stockton Plateau. He'll give you a local's views on coal mining, which plays a major role in the area's economy. ■ TIP→ Micky says to give him a call the day before your trip is planned to remind him. ☎ *027/641–8267, 0800/688–937 NZ only* ⊕ *www.outwest.co.nz* ✈ *NZ$65–NZ$130.*

8

FAMILY

Underworld Adventures. So many different adventures at once here. These popular soft adventure tours take you into the rain forest then under it, should you wish, off the main highway at Charleston. You can sign up for an open-sided bush-train ride through the dense temperate lowland forest, or take a cave walk into one of the giant limestone mountains up the Nile River valley (a glowworm grotto is a highlight). Their most popular trip is a slow drift in a raft through the glowworm caves before breaking out onto the river. For something more challenging, go for the daylong "Full On" caving adventure with a 154-foot abseil (rappel) down into the mountain, before crawling, swimming, and climbing your way back to the surface. The guides are great. Reservations are essential. ⊠ *Charleston Hotel, State Hwy. 6, Charleston* ☎ *03/788–8168* ⊕ *www.caverafting.com* 🚆 *Train ride NZ$25, cave walk NZ$120, boat trip NZ$185, rapel adventure NZ$350.*

VISITOR INFORMATION

Contacts Westport i-SITE Visitor Centre and Coaltown Museum. ⊠ *123 Palmerston St.* ☎ *03/789–6658* ⊕ *www.buller.co.nz.*

EXPLORING

Coaltown Museum. Westport is a town based around coal, and the stories, challenges, and hardships of mining on (and under) the high plateau behind the town are related in this modern, interactive museum. Hogging the limelight is the 8-ton coal wagon, perched on the 45-degree angle just as it would have been when descending the famous Incline, off the Denniston Plateau. Museum entry is through the Westport i-SITE Visitor Centre. ⊠ *123 Palmerston St.* ☎ *03/789–6658* 🏷 *NZ$10* ⊙ *Dec.–Mar., daily 9–7; Apr.–Nov., weekdays 9–4:30, weekends 10–4.*

WHERE TO EAT

There are several good daytime cafés in Westport. The Town House, down the port end of town, and Denniston Dog are local stalwarts for a wholesome down-home West Coast experience.

$$$
MODERN NEW ZEALAND
✕ **The Bay House.** Tucked among flax bushes beside the wild, foaming surf beach at Tauranga Bay, this busy little restaurant serves as fine a menu as you'll get anywhere in the South Island. The chef prepares top-quality local beef, lamb, and seafood dishes, and there are seasonal specialties like the whitebait (a local fish delicacy). Or try the West Coast beef fillet with chorizo and mustard-and-cream-cheese ravioli. There's lots of fish; the chowder is delicious, and the kitchen use local touches like *harakeke* seed, *paua*, and *kūmara* (native sweet potato). You'll find an extensive, mainly South Island wine list. It's worth the extra driving and, if you're heading south afterwards, you can follow the signposted shortcut toward Charleston to save going back into Westport. 💲 *Average main: NZ$30* ⊠ *Tauranga Bay, Cape Foulwind* ✛ *16 km (10 miles) west of Westport* ☎ *03/789–4151* ⊕ *www.bayhouse.co.nz.*

$$$
CAFÉ
FAMILY
✕ **Denniston Dog.** This old bank building, complete with a vault, is loaded with local character in its new guise as a cheerful pub and gathering spot. If the coal mining heritage of this town interests you, you will enjoy the memorabilia and photos on display. They serve good Kiwi tucker here, anything from breakfast and brunch to light meals to kids' meals to stone-grill steaks and seafood (where you get to cook the lovely presented food on your own, sizzling volcanic hot stone). The meals are hearty, and it's a very kid-friendly spot. There's a big covered courtyard for summer dining. 💲 *Average main: NZ$30* ⊠ *18 Wakefield St.* ☎ *03/789–5030* ⊕ *www.dennistondog.co.nz.*

$$$$
MODERN NEW ZEALAND
✕ **PortSide Bistro & Bar.** They're proud of their signature fish-and-chips on Friday. The fish is delivered straight off the boat, and there's also a huge range of other fare on the menu, be it for breakfast, lunch, or dinner. Breakfasts are served until 3 pm. Light lunch choices include salads, burgers, and lots of seafood, and the dinner menu showcases salmon, venison, and rib-eye beef. You'll be dining with the locals here, especially on the last Sunday every month when they come in for the

Great PortSide Roast (a special with all the trimmings and a drink). [$] *Average main: NZ$34* ✉ *13 Cobden St.* ☎ *03/789–7133* 🌐 *www.portsidebistro.co.nz* ⏲ *Closed Mon.* ✍ *Reservations essential.*

WHERE TO STAY

$$ B&B/INN 🏨 **Archer House.** Rooms are spacious, linens are fine, and the art collection is impressive at this villa that was built for a local trader in the late 1800s. **Pros:** sunny conservatory for coffee; short walk to Westport restaurants. **Cons:** children are welcome but are charged adult rates. [$] *Rooms from: NZ$190* ✉ *75 Queen St.* ☎ *03/789–8778, 0800/789–877 NZ only* 🌐 *www.archerhouse.co.nz* 🛏 *3 rooms* 🍴 *Breakfast.*

$$$$ B&B/INN Fodor's Choice ★ 🏨 **Birds Ferry Lodge.** Named for the old river ferry that crossed the nearby Totara River during the gold rush, this lodge and self-contained cottage set on 50 acres bring the place to life once more. **Pros:** lots of good walks; a superb three-course dinner is available on request; very comfortable. **Cons:** hard to find in the dark (watch closely for signs off the highway); entry road is rough gravel. [$] *Rooms from: NZ$380* ✉ *Birds Ferry Rd., Charleston* ☎ *021/337–217, 0800/212–207* 🌐 *www.birdsferrylodge.co.nz* 🛏 *2 rooms, 1 cottage* 🍴 *Breakfast.*

$ B&B/INN 🏨 **The Steeples Cottage, Studio & B&B.** Perched on the cliff top overlooking The Steeples rocks offshore, this self-contained cottage (with sea view) and studio and the rooms in the main house are all great value. **Pros:** very pleasant surroundings; safe swimming at nearby beach. **Cons:** parking can be a bit tight; a bit of a detour off the main road. [$] *Rooms from: NZ$120* ✉ *48 Lighthouse Rd., Cape Foulwind* ☎ *03/789–7876* 🌐 *www.steeplescottage.co.nz* 🛏 *1 cottage, 1 studio, 2 rooms* 🍴 *Breakfast.*

8

PAPAROA NATIONAL PARK

269 km (168 miles) southwest of Nelson.

Paparoa National Park extends from the forest-covered Paparoa Range inland, to the coast. With steep bluffs, limestone basins, canyons, caves, and fluted rock, it's a formidable environment. The cliffs, flood-prone rivers, dense rain forest, extensive cave systems, and collapsed sea caverns and cliffs along this dramatic coastline draw hikers, cavers, and, of course, photographers. The major track entry points—Bullock Creek, Fox River, and Pororari River—open onto an otherworldly zone of jungle green, striking *nikau* palms, rain forest, and rushing streams. There are several day hikes, canoeing in the Pororari River, horse treks, and entry-level cave experiences. Call into the **Paparoa National Park i-SITE Visitors Centre** (✉ *4293 Coast Rd., State Hwy. 6*) for maps and information.

One of the stars of the West Coast is the walk to the **Pancake Rocks & Blowholes,** one of New Zealand's most popular short walks. The huge swells that batter this coast have eroded the limestone cliffs, carving them into fantastical shapes. A paved walkway leads you past the curious pancake-stacked rocks and through the windswept cover of tenacious New Zealand flax and *nikau* palms to the most dramatic viewpoints, including the broiling cauldron called the Surge Pool (once a sea cavern before the roof collapsed) and the pumping fissure of the

Chimney Pot. In the right conditions, at high tide three blowholes spout a thundering geyser of spray. New Zealand's highest mountain, Aoraki/Mt. Cook, is sometimes visible across the sea to the south. To reach the rocks from the highway, take the easy 20-minute walk across the road from the visitor center. Keep turning left along the path so you don't miss the best bits out around the Surge Pool. High tide on a southwest swell under a full moon at midnight is an outstanding time to visit, if you dare. Otherwise, try for high tide and a big westerly swell. Look for the white-fronted terns, who nest on the spray-soaked rock stacks here.

GETTING HERE AND AROUND

At first glance, Punakaiki looks like nothing more than a small cluster of beach houses and shops—a blip on the radar without even a gas station or ATM. It's worth stopping, though, for its famous Pancake Rocks—a maze of limestone stacked high above the sea, and an easy walk from the road. Punakaiki is also the main entry point to the Paparoa National Park tracks and river activities. Punakaiki is roughly halfway along the coast between Greymouth and Westport on State Highway 6; 40 minutes north of Greymouth; and one hour south of Westport. The road is winding and steep in places, with high drop-offs to the coast on the stretch north of Punakaiki. InterCity buses pass through daily. Accommodations range from a holiday park to holiday homes, B&Bs, and a resort-style hotel.

If you have a spare half hour, follow the Truman Track, 3 km (2 miles) north of the village down to the coast. It's a delightful walk through native bush to a dramatic coastal bay. There's also easy access to the coast from the beach in front of the Punakaiki Resort just south of the Pancake Rocks.

The Paparoa National Park i-SITE Visitors Centre, across the road from the track to the Pancake Rocks, is a handy place to learn more about the rock formations and the park.

VISITOR INFORMATION

Contacts Paparoa National Park i-SITE Visitors Centre. ✉ *4294 Main Rd., State Hwy. 6, Punakaiki* ☎ *03/731–1895* 🌐 *www.doc.govt.nz.*

WHERE TO EAT

Eating options are limited in tiny Punakaiki, with just a pub and couple of daytime cafés open to the public. The oceanfront restaurant at Punakaiki Resort is pricey and only open to casual diners if in-house guests haven't booked it out. If you decide to stay in a self-catering unit, you'll need to bring in all your food, as there are no general stores in town.

$$ CAFÉ 🍴 **Pancake Rocks Cafe.** Not surprisingly, a pancake stack (edible) is the signature menu item at this busy little café and shop, directly opposite the Pancake Rocks and Blowholes Walk. Try it with bacon and caramelized banana. The café opens daily and offers a full breakfast and lunch menu (the burgers will set you right for beach-walking). There's also a small gallery/shop here, selling quality New Zealand souvenirs, including jewelry. [$] *Average main: NZ$18* ✉ *Coast Rd., Punakaiki* ☎ *03/731–1122* 🌐 *www.pancakerockscafe.com* 🕒 *No dinner.*

Paparoa National Park's eroded coastline includes the amazing Pancake Rocks.

WHERE TO STAY

Although tiny, Punakaiki is a popular tourist spot and therefore has some good accommodations available, including a sizable hotel and self-catering cottages with friendly hosts.

$$$ B&B/INN **Hydrangea Cottages.** You'll be lulled by the constant roar of the ocean in three brightly colored apartments with recycled native timbers and contemporary furniture, a rustic studio cottage, and a large cottage with sea views and a bath on the deck. **Pros:** ocean views; some units are family-size. **Cons:** steep driveway. [$] *Rooms from: NZ$270* ✉ *Main Rd., Punakaiki* ☎ *03/731–1839* 🌐 *www.pancake-rocks.co.nz* 🛏 *3 apartments, 2 cottages* 🍴 *No meals.*

$$$ HOTEL **Punakaiki Resort.** The modern beach-house design blends well with the dynamic coastal site; the front steps reach almost onto the beach, and driftwood, flax, sand, and surf are all part of the deal. **Pros:** prime seafront location; spectacular outlook from rooms and oceanfront restaurant and bar. **Cons:** some traffic noise in some units. [$] *Rooms from: NZ$300* ✉ *State Hwy. 6, 1 km (½ mile) south of Pancake Rocks, Punakaiki* ☎ *03/731–1168, 0800/706–707 NZ only* 🌐 *www.punakaiki-resort.co.nz* 🛏 *27 rooms, 12 eco-rooms, 22 villas* 🍴 *No meals.*

SPORTS AND THE OUTDOORS

FAMILY **Punakaiki Canoes.** For many, the essence of this gorgeous region is best understood by a paddle up the Pororari River, just to the north of the village. Glide silently through the dark yet clear waters between huge limestone cliffs, studded with *nikau* and giant *rata* trees. Pretend you're in the movies—*The Hobbit* cliff scenes were filmed here. Or head down the estuary toward the coast, where the waterway opens out into a more playful area. These trips are suitable for all abilities and ages, and ever changing with the tides and the rainfall. They are dependent on the state of the weather and the river. ⊠ *State Hwy. 6, by bridge, Punakaiki* ☎ *03/731–1870* ⊕ *www.riverkayaking.co.nz* ⚓ *NZ$40 per person for up to 2 hrs, NZ$60 for all day; guided tours from NZ$70.*

Punakaiki Horse treks. One of the most scenic horse riding options anywhere includes riding on the beach, through the forest beside huge limestone bluffs, and a river crossing. Treks run twice daily during summer months, and you will need to have some riding ability. ⊠ *4224 Main Rd., Punakaiki* ☎ *03/731–1839* ⊕ *www.pancake-rocks.co.nz* ⚓ *From NZ$170.*

GREYMOUTH

44 km (28 miles) south of Punakaiki, 258 km (160 miles) west of Christchurch.

The town of Greymouth is aptly named—at first take, it's a rather dispirited strip of motels and industrial buildings stretched along a wild beach. It sits, as the name suggests, at the mouth of the Grey River and is thus exposed to a bone-chilling wind in winter. But in warmer weather, its good points come to the fore. Many travelers arrive here on the TranzAlpine train from Christchurch—instead of captivating coastal drives, they've enjoyed a breathtaking ride on viaducts high above riverbeds, beneath steep peaks, and through dripping rain forest. If you're arriving and returning by train, take a day or two for a trip up to Punakaiki or down to the glaciers, to grasp the scope of the landscape in these parts.

GETTING HERE AND AROUND

Drive from Nelson or Westport in the north, from the glaciers to the south, or from Christchurch in the east, over Arthur's Pass. Be on your guard around Greymouth and Hokitika as there are a number of one-way bridges and unalarmed rail crossings. InterCity buses arrive in Greymouth daily.

The TranzAlpine train departs Christchurch daily at 8:15 am and arrives in Greymouth at 12:45 pm; the return train departs Greymouth at 1:45 pm and arrives at Christchurch at 6:05 pm. One-way fare options range from NZ$99–NZ$199.

Bus Depot Greymouth InterCity. ⊠ *Railway Station, 164 Mackay St.* ⊕ *www. intercity.co.nz.*

Train Contacts TranzAlpine Express. ☎ *04/495–0775, 0800/872–467 NZ only* ⊕ *www.kiwirailscenic.co.nz.*

VISITOR INFORMATION

Contacts Greymouth i-SITE Visitor Centre. ⊠ *Old Railway Station, 164 Mackay St.* ☎ *03/768-7080* ⊕ *www.westcoasttravel.co.nz.*

EXPLORING

The land around Greymouth (like Hokitika to the south) is particularly rich in *pounamu*, the greenstone (NZ jade) highly prized by Māori. This is all Ngai Tahu *iwi* (tribe) area, and as part of the 1997 Ngai Tahu

Settlement between the tribe and the Crown, the government recognized Ngai Tahu as having sole rights to collect and sell the precious *pounamu* in its natural form. If you want the authentic product, when buying greenstone on the West Coast, make sure it is local greenstone and not imported jade. The price will probably indicate this, but check anyway. Local greenstone is labeled as such.

Carey Dillon Photographer. Kumara, a tiny village at the start of the road over Arthur's Pass, is the home of photographer Carey Dillon. His rustic little gallery/shop is devoted to iconic landscape photography, and his work is superb—fine art prints that bring the West Coast landscape to life, catching all its light, drama, and moods. ⊠ *Main Rd., State Hwy. 73, Kumara* ☎ *03/736–9741* ⊕ *www.careydillon.com.*

Left Bank Art Gallery. The Left Bank Art Gallery on the corner of Tainui Street and Mawhera Quay is a good place to see and purchase a range of artworks, including contemporary pounamu (greenstone or jade) carvings. Housed in the old Greymouth branch of the Bank of New Zealand, this progressive little gallery supports local artists and holds regularly changing exhibitions. Displays in the old vault in this building include a collection of older pounamu artworks. ⊠ *1 Tainui St.* ☎ *03/768–0038* ⊕ *www.leftbankarts.org.nz* ⊗ *Tues.–Fri, 12:30–4, Sat. 11–2.*

Shades of Jade. Owner/carver Jeremy Dalzell has been working with jade since 2000, and brings his personal designs to the quality greenstone sourced from West Coast rivers from Punakaiki to Haast. Pendants, sculptures, and a variety of jade types are on display in his studio/gallery, and often you can watch Jeremy and fellow carvers at work. ⊠ *16 Tainui St.* ☎ *03/768–0794* ⊕ *www.shadesofjade.co.nz* ⊗ *Weekdays 8:30–5, Sat. 9:30–2:30, Sun. 10:30–2:30 (slightly shorter weekend hrs in winter).*

FAMILY **Shantytown Heritage Park.** On the southern outskirts of Greymouth is this lively, in-your-face reenactment of an industrial town of the 1880s. This is how the settlers who stayed on after gold rush days would have lived—minus the electricity, running water, and paved entry road. It was all about steam in them thar days as you'll discover. (There's even an official '"Steam School" here, teaching how to drive steam-driven engines.) Except for the church and the town hall, most of the buildings are reproductions, including a jail, a blacksmith shop, a railway station, and Chinatown. Gold-digging displays include a giant water jet for blasting the gold-bearing rock and soil from the hillside, water races, and a stamper—battery-powered by a 30-foot waterwheel—for crushing the ore. You can pan for gold for a very good chance of striking "color." Travel along an old bush tramline on a bone fide steam train (four trips daily) and check out other heritage trains. Watch a 3-D holographic show in an old parlor/theater. See why a foundry was so important via an interactive display created with the help of the movie design gurus Weta. Take a break in the café, or share a picnic on the shady lawns then go back for more. ⊠ *310 Rutherglen Rd.* ☎ *03/762–6634, 0800/742–689 NZ only* ⊕ *www.shantytown.co.nz* ⊠ *NZ\$33, train included* ⊗ *Daily 8:30–5; first train leaves at 9:45, last train at 4.*

8

NEED A BREAK? The 139-km (86-mile) West Coast Wilderness Cycle Trail, which was officially opened in 2013, is one of 23 Nga Herenga New Zealand Cycle Trail rides. It explores the West Coast backcountry; glacial rivers, rain forest, lakes, and wetlands along old tram and rail tracks and some purpose-built sections. The trail is graded as "easy" and can be completed in sections. Everything from bike rentals, shuttle transport, and accommodation to guided, fully catered multiday packages are available from local companies based in Hokitika and Greymouth. Among the best is Trail Transport in Greymouth, 🌐 *trailtransport.co.nz*. For full and updated details check out 🌐 *www.westcoastwildernesstrail.co.nz.*

WHERE TO EAT

$$ CAFÉ 🍴 **DP1 Cafe.** Homey hospitality in this colorful, retro-style spot comes with house-cooked breakfasts (scrambled eggs are as good as you'll find anywhere), lunches, and baked goods. Plus, the outlook over the Grey River is great. [$] *Average main: NZ$18* ✉ *104–108 Mawhera Quay* ☎ *03/768–4005* 🕒 *No dinner* 💳 *No credit cards.*

$$ CAFÉ 🍴 **Freddy's.** For a bright and breezy café stop, try this downtown favorite. They serve good coffee and all-day breakfast—their free-range eggs and a West Coast specialty, "Blackball Sausages," are a hit. Lunch offerings include seafood chowder, salads, pastas, and more. This place is handy to the railway station if you're just off the TranzAlpine and looking for lunch. [$] *Average main: NZ$18* ✉ *115 Mackay St.* ☎ *03/768–7443* 🕒 *No dinner.*

$$$ NEW ZEALAND 🍴 **Speight's Ale House.** This restored heritage building, once known as "The Brick House," indeed has a stately brick facade. It's one of Greymouth's original buildings and used to house government offices. Now the ale flows in an interior that's been stylishly restored with shiny, bold copper vents that look good against the wood and brick as well as carry heat from the fire throughout the premises. The bistro-style menu includes the signature whitebait (seasonal in September) and blue cod, along with the usual steaks, lamb, salmon, and mussels. There are also bar snacks and a kids menu. It makes for a good lunch spot, and of course the taps flow with the various brews of the famous southern brand. [$] *Average main: NZ$30* ✉ *130 Mawhera Quay* ☎ *03/768–0667* 🌐 *www.speights.co.nz.*

$$$ ECLECTIC 🍴 **Stationhouse Café.** You can come to beautiful Lake Brunner on a day drive from Greymouth, as part of a round-the-lake trip, or stop off the TranzAlpine train for lunch while it hops out to the coast and back—about a three-hour stop. The café is in an old railway house, perched on a terrace above the railway station, with a superb view across Lake Brunner and the *kahikatea* forests and wetlands beyond. Lunch options include chowders, salads, homemade pies with mashed potatoes and peas (like the old days), blue cod, and chips. The dinner menu features salmon, lamb Wellington, rib-eye steak, and venison, all served with generous fresh vegetables or salad. [$] *Average main: NZ$28* ✉ *Koe St., Moana* ☎ *03/738–0158* 🌐 *www.lakebrunner.net* 🕒 *Sometimes closed for dinner in winter* ✍ *Reservations essential.*

WHERE TO STAY

$$$$
B&B/INN
Fodor's Choice
★

Breakers. At this welcoming B&B between Greymouth and Punakaiki, two rooms in the main house and two suites in the garden overlook spectacular coastline, with penguins on the beach, native bush surroundings, and welcoming hosts. **Pros:** dinner by arrangement to save a late drive into Greymouth; scenic coastal views. **Cons:** 15-minute drive from Greymouth. $ *Rooms from: NZ$310* ⊠ *1367 State Hwy. 6, 14 km (9 miles) north of Greymouth* ☎ *03/762–7743, 0800/350–590 NZ only* ⊕ *www.breakers.co.nz* ⤴ *2 rooms, 2 suites* ⦿ *Breakfast.*

$$$
HOTEL

Lake Brunner Lodge. On the southern shore of Lake Brunner, a 40-minute drive southeast of Greymouth, this vintage bed-and-breakfast lodge is an enticing retreat at a price that is not as high as most of New Zealand's elite lodges. **Pros:** great for fishing, kayaking, and restoring; very relaxing ambience. **Cons:** the road in is narrow, winding, and gravel for the last couple of miles; two-night minimum stay over Christmas–New Year's week. $ *Rooms from: NZ$300* ⊠ *Mitchells, via Kumara or Jacksons* ☎ *03/738–0163* ⊕ *www.lakebrunner.co.nz* ⤴ *11 rooms* ⦿ *Breakfast.*

$$
B&B/INN

New River Bluegums B&B. Looking a bit like the little house on the prairie, yet just 12 km (7 miles) from town, this river-rock-and-timber homestay with two king rooms is a delight, full of rustic appeal. **Pros:** cycle trail at the front door; lovely bucolic setting and feel. **Cons:** railway crossing to get from the road to into the driveway has no bells or lights. $ *Rooms from: NZ$185* ⊠ *985 Main Rd. S* ✛ *9 km (5½ miles) south of Greymouth* ☎ *03/762–6678* ⊕ *www.bluegumsnz.com* ⤴ *2 rooms* ⦿ *Breakfast.*

$$$
B&B/INN

Rosewood. Rhonda and Stephan Palten run this traditional-style B&B in a restored 1920s home, with original oak paneling, leadlight windows, and cozy seats in the bay windows. **Pros:** good off-street parking and disabled access; near the town center. **Cons:** busy main street position. $ *Rooms from: NZ$230* ⊠ *20 High St.* ☎ *03/768–4674* ⊕ *www. rosewoodnz.co.nz* ⤴ *4 rooms* ⦿ *Breakfast.*

SPORTS AND THE OUTDOORS

FAMILY

On Yer Bike! If it's raining, your outdoor options just got a lot more exciting. On Yer Bike! makes the most of rain and mud with some wild fun. The two-hour Bush 'N' Bog tour and the one-hour Enchanted Forest tour will take you through beautiful native forest, streams, mud, and puddles on easy-to-ride quad motorbikes. Other tours include off-road go-karts, Hagglund, and argo rides (8WDs or ATVs). This is great fun for kids, though they must be at least 12 to ride the quads. ⊠ *511 State Hwy. 6* ✛ *5 km (3 miles) north of Greymouth* ☎ *03/762–7438, 0800/669–372 NZ only* ⊕ *www.onyerbike.co.nz* ⤴ *From NZ$115 for 1-hr quad biking.*

HOKITIKA

41 km (26 miles) south of Greymouth.

Hokitika is one of the larger towns along the West Coast, with the pounding ocean before it and bush-covered hills behind. It's a place of simple pleasures: scouting the craft galleries, taking a bushwalk, enjoying the seafood, and looking for evocatively shaped driftwood on the often stormy beach. Hokitika is central enough to take a day trip to Punakaiki or Arthur's Pass. During the height of the gold rushes in the 1860s, Hokitika was New Zealand's busiest port, and had more than 100 hotels. Pick up a Hokitika Heritage Walk brochure (50 cents) from the i-SITE Visitor Centre and explore this rich heritage, along with more recent colonial history. Start with a walk along the Quayside Heritage Area at the southern end of Tancred and Revell streets, and walk along to Sunset Point Lookout. See the old Custom House and river mouth; on a clear day you'll see Mt. Cook across the sea. West Coast rivers are the source of pounamu (jade), which has long been a precious resource for the South Island Māori people, Ngai Tahu. Hokitika is recognized as the center for artists and carvers who create stunning jewelry, from pounamu and other mediums. The town is filled with studios and galleries where you can watch the artists at work, and perhaps take home something special. Wood carvings, pottery, textiles, and photography are also showcased in the galleries, mostly found along Tancred and Weld streets.

GETTING HERE AND AROUND

There are daily flights to Hokitika from Christchurch with Air New Zealand. Arrive by road from Christchurch or Greymouth to the north, or from the glaciers to the south (via State Highway 6). Either way you will enjoy a spectacular drive through mountainous country, national parks, and scenic reserves. InterCity buses arrive in Hokitika daily and stop in front of the National Kiwi Center on Tancred Street.

VISITOR INFORMATION

Contacts Hokitika i-SITE Visitor Centre. ⊠ *36 Weld St* ☎ *03/755–6166* ⊕ *www.hokitika.org.*

EXPLORING

Hokitika Craft Gallery Co-operative. Works from local artists, including greenstone carvings, pottery, woodwork, and textiles, are showcased and for sale. ⊠ *25 Tancred St.* ☎ *03/755–8802* ⊕ *www.hokitikacraftgallery. co.nz* ⊗ *Daily 8:30–5 in summer (to 8:30 at summer peak); June–Aug. 9:30–5.*

Mountain Jade. The largest outlet in New Zealand to showcase *pounamu* has greenstone cutting and carving areas, and an extensive shop. Two or more artists are usually at work, plus they offer two tours each day that relates the history of *pounamu*, its significance to the Māori people, and its uses. There's also a stone-painting artist at work here. ⊠ *41 Weld St.* ☎ *03/755–8007* ⊕ *www.mountainjade.co.nz* ⊗ *Daily 8–6.*

Ocean Paua. Jewelry and other artworks at this shop and workshop is made from a range of *paua* shell, greenstone, and bone. ⊠ *25 Weld St.* ☎ *03/755–6128* ⊗ *Daily 9–5.*

Traditional Jade. This small family business creates carvings and sculptures, and has a collection of raw jade for you to admire. Visit in the mornings for the best chance of seeing one of the family artists at work. ⊠ *2 Tancred St.* ☎ *03/755–5233* ⊗ *Daily 9–5.*

Waewae Pounamu. Ngati Waewae is the Iwi (tribe) of this area, a subtribe of the South Island Ngai Tahu. The Iwi own and carve all the *pounamu* (jade) at this center. The artists will reveal how every stone has a story. If you buy a piece, they will give you its unique code, which you can use to trace the story of your stone on the center's website. ✉ *39 Weld St.* ☎ *03/755–8304* 🌐 *www.waewaepounamu.co.nz* 🕒 *Summer, weekdays 8:30–6, weekends 9–6; winter, weekdays 8:30–5, weekends 10–5.*

West Coast Treetop Walk and Cafe. Imagine being like a bird, able to wander the treetops of the ancient trees in the West Coast rain forest. Now you can, on this 1,500-foot long, 66-foot-high walkway through the forest canopy. You can go even higher on the Hokitika Tower, 130 feet above the forest floor. Views extend over the rain forest to dark, glacial Lake Mahinapua and beyond to the Southern Alps. The walkway is fully wheelchair-accessible. An excellent café and gift shop are on-site. It's a 15-minute drive south of Hokitika, and just off the main road. ✉ *1128 Woodstock Rimu Rd.* ☎ *03/755–5052, 0508/873–38677 NZ only* 🌐 *www.treetopsnz.com* 🎟 *NZ$38* 🕒 *Late Sept.–Mar., daily 9–5; Apr.–late Sept., daily 9–3:15.*

Westland Greenstone. Westland Greenstone is a long-established gallery, in business since 1962. There is an interesting walk-through workshop where you can watch greenstone being cut, shaped, and polished. Unlike some places, Westland uses local greenstone (*pounamu*) rather than imported jade. Check when you're buying that it's the real thing and not an imported stone. ✉ *34 Tancred St.* ☎ *03/755–8713* 🕒 *Daily 8–6.*

Wilderness Trail Shuttle. Hokitika is at about the halfway point of the West Coast Wilderness Trail, a purpose-built cycle trail that explores the alpine scenery, rivers, rural countryside, and history of the region. Whether you ride this in sections from one base or as a three- to four-day adventure, this company will move you and your luggage to wherever you need to go. ✉ *216 Revell St.* ☎ *03/755–5042, 21/263–3299* 🌐 *wildernesstrailshuttle.co.nz.*

Wildfoods Festival. This annual event celebrates bush tucker (food from the bush) from the West Coast's natural food sources. Bite into such delectables as *huhu* grubs, grasshoppers, beetles, whitebait patties (far more mainstream), and wild pork (as in from pigs running wild in the bush, not farmed—or angry), and follow it all with gorse wine, elderflower champagne, or Monteith's bitter beer. It's usually held in the second weekend of March. Book well ahead, as there's a cap of 10,000 participants and usually sells out. 🌐 *www.wildfoods.co.nz.*

WHERE TO EAT

$$$$ NEW ZEALAND

🍴 **Stations Inn.** The place that many locals consider to be a special-occasion destination provides visitors with a chance to experience high-quality, classic New Zealand fare. It's been a consistent winner of awards for the beef and lamb it serves, and has a reputation for matching foods with the West Coast brew, Monteiths. Stations Inn sits on a river terrace a couple of miles out of Hokitika, alongside a small number of accommodation suites and studios. On summer evenings you can sit outside and enjoy the view across the countryside; inside you can peruse the historic gold-mining photos. This was the site of the Blue Spur Gold fields, where some 2,500 people lived in the 1860s. [$] *Average main: NZ$33*

✉ *Blue Spur Rd., RD 2* ☎ *03/755–5499* ⊕ *www.stationsinnhokitika. co.nz* ⊗ *Closed Sun. and Mon. No lunch* ⚄ *Reservations essential.*

$$$
CAFÉ

✕ **Stella Cafe and Cheesery.** A live bee display provides much of the honey used in menu dishes in this friendly spot where owner Rachel says, "a menu is just the start of a conversation." A breakfast menu (eggs Benedict, Smokey Mushrooms, Bacon Buttie), baked goods (try the cheese scones), and lunch dishes that change with the seasons are on offer. Coffee is from Christchurch roaster, Empire. On your way out, stock up from the deli. During the height of summer, they'll stay open for evening meals, still café-style. $ *Average main: NZ$24* ✉ *84 Revell St.* ☎ *03/755–5432* ⊗ *No dinner in winter.*

$$$
MODERN NEW ZEALAND
Fodor's Choice
★

✕ **Theatre Royal Hotel Kumara.** Even though it's a 20-minute drive from either Hokitika or Greymouth, on the main State Highway 73, this popular spot draws locals from both towns. Built in 1876 during the heady Kumara gold rush days, the hotel fell into disrepair as Kumara township dwindled severely. Owners Kerrie and Mark Fitzgibbon spent two years restoring the property, and now the place hums. Local cured bacon, venison patties, wild pork sliders, house-made pies, and salads all vie for choice on the brunch/lunch menu. Bar snacks and baked goods are on offer all day, and dinner steps up with a small but stylish selection of appetizers (a little fish pie, or local Blackball chorizo perhaps?), mains, and desserts. The menu changes with the season but you can guarantee top-quality beef, wild venison, salmon, and beer-battered fish-and-chips. There's also a great locals' bar scene with live music and community events. Be sure to wander around the village, reading the information panels telling of its rich history. $ *Average main: NZ$30* ✉ *81 Seddon St., Kumara* ☎ *03/736–9277* ⊕ *www.theatreroyalhotel.co.nz.*

WHERE TO STAY

$$$$
B&B/INN

▦ **Rimu Lodge.** Just 10 minutes into the country east of Hokitika, this two-story lodge with four luxury rooms sits high above the Hokitika River valley and is the only five-star B&B on the West Coast. **Pros:** a birdwatchers delight; good local walks (Lakes Mahinapua and Kaniere and Hokitika Gorge) and heritage walks nearby; great breakfasts. **Cons:** bit hard to find at night. $ *Rooms from: NZ$330* ✉ *33 Seddons Terrace Rd., Rimu* ☎ *03/755–5255* ⊕ *www.rimulodge.co.nz* ⤴ *4 rooms* ⦿ *Breakfast.*

$$
HOTEL
FAMILY

▦ **Shining Star.** These stylish oceanfront wooden cabins and luxurious chalets are about as close to the beach as you'll get; the surf rolls in just beyond the dunes, the air has a salty tang, and the sky is filled with wheeling seabirds. **Pros:** facing wild surf and beach; very peaceful. **Cons:** on the edge of town; long walk to restaurants. $ *Rooms from: NZ$150* ✉ *16 Richards Dr.* ☎ *03/755–8921, 0800/744–646 NZ only* ⊕ *www. accommodationwestcoast.co.nz* ⤴ *12 chalets, 8 cabins, 3 1-bedroom apartments* ⦿ *No meals.*

$$$
B&B/INN

▦ **Teichelmann's Bed & Breakfast.** At this friendly, traditional B&B in the center of town, accommodation is in five rooms in the house (upstairs and downstairs) and in a cute, stand-alone cottage set in a delightful "miner's garden" behind the house. **Pros:** one of the West Coast's most historic accommodations; gracious hosts. **Cons:** no ocean or mountain views. $ *Rooms from: NZ$250* ✉ *20 Hamilton St.* ☎ *03/755–8232* ⊕ *teichelmanns.nz* ⤴ *5 rooms, 1 cottage* ⦿ *Breakfast.*

WESTLAND/TAI POUTINI NATIONAL PARK

North end 146 km (91 miles) south of Hokitika.

Fodor's Choice
★

Westland/Tai Poutini is a place of extremes, from the highest mountains to most ancient rain forest, and certainly extreme precipitation.

Try to allow more than a day in the region to increase your chance of clear weather. Otherwise, put your rain gear on and get out in it: walking in the rain forest, or in those massive glacial valleys with waterfalls roaring down the sheer sides, is a special experience. Annual rainfall here ranges from more than 120 inches at the coast to an incredible 16 feet on the alpine summits. Huge volumes of snow are dumped each year, feeding the 140 glaciers. The snow is compressed into ice on the névé, or head, of the glaciers (New Zealanders say "glassy-urs"), then moves steadily downhill under its own weight. The best known and most visited glaciers are Franz Josef and Fox. If, however, you're driving through on a cloudy or wet day—quite likely—you will get no idea of the size of the mountain ranges looming beside you. The main stopping places are townships near these glaciers, named simply **Fox Glacier** and **Franz Josef,** the latter slightly larger. Both towns have solid tourist infrastructures. The summer tourist rush means you should make reservations in advance for lodgings and restaurants, and in winter some places close. Check ahead.

GETTING HERE AND AROUND

State Highway 6 passes through this region and is the only road access in and out. Drive in from Hokitika in the north or Wanaka and Haast to the south. There are only a few fuel stops between Hokitika and Haast so plan ahead. InterCity buses travel daily from the north and the south, stopping at both glacier villages.

Bus Depot Fox Glacier. ⊠ *Northbound: Fox Glacier Guiding, Main Rd.; Southbound: opposite Fox Glacier Guiding, Main Rd., Westland National Park.* **Franz Josef.** ⊠ *Franz Josef Bus Stop, Main Rd.; Franz Josef YHA, 2–4 Cron St., Westland National Park.*

VISITOR INFORMATION

Contacts Fox Glacier Visitor Centre. ⊠ *Main Rd., Fox Glacier* ☎ *03/751–0807* ⊕ *www.glaciercountry.co.nz.* **Westland/Tai Poutini National Park Visitor Centre.** ⊠ *69 Cron St., Franz Josef* ☎ *03/752–0796* ⊕ *www.glaciercountry.co.nz or www.doc.govt.nz.*

EXPLORING

Westland/Tai Poutini National Park. Some wonderful walks follow the glacial valleys, bringing you to viewpoints within 500 feet or so of the glaciers. Topping the list, a five-minute drive west of Fox Glacier township, is the walk around Lake Matheson that leads to one of the country's most famous views. A trail winds along the lakeshore to where the snowcapped peaks of Aoraki/Mt. Cook and Mt. Tasman are reflected in the water. It's an easy 2.6-km (1-mile) walk right around the lake. The best times are sunrise and sunset, when the mirrorlike reflections are less likely to be fractured by the wind. Be wary at the car parks of the mischievous *kea* (*kee*-ah)—mountain parrots—that may delight in destroying the rubber of your windscreen wipers. Don't encourage

8

OKARITO LAGOON

Don't miss a visit to beautiful, coastal Okarito Lagoon, just a 13-km (8-mile) detour off the highway, 15 km (9.3 miles) north of Franz Josef township. An immense forest-fringed coastal lagoon, nestled in scenic splendor beneath the Southern Alps, Okarito is arguably one of the largest, most pristine wetlands remaining in New Zealand. It is home to thousands of sea and wading birds and is backed by the Okarito Kiwi Sanctuary, 27,000 acres of lowland forest and home of the Rowi, a rare species of kiwi. Back in 1866 Okarito was a thriving town of more than 1,200 people, with three theaters and 25 hotels. People came for the gold and for many years there was a working port inside the bar at the entrance to the lagoon. Things have changed dramatically and Okarito is now known for its natural values. A tiny settlement remains, most people just visit to kayak or cruise on the lagoon, watch the birds, walk the short forest and coastal trails, or head out at night for a kiwi-spotting expedition.

Okarito Boat Tours. Relax as this open-air, shallow-draught boat glides quietly across the lagoon, nosing into narrow channels lined with ancient rain forest. Watch the feeding birds, possibly a white heron visiting from its nearby breeding colony, or a godwit, one of thousands that fly here each summer from Arctic Siberia. Look up to the majestic backdrop of Aoraki/Mt. Cook and Franz Josef Glacier. Your host Swade runs three daily tours. Trips leave from Okarito Wharf; bookings are recommended. ⊠ *Okarito Wharf, Okarito* ☎ *03/753–4223* ⊕ *okaritoboattours.co.nz* 🖃 *From NZ$150.*

Okarito Kiwi Tours. Ian Cooper holds the only concession here to take visitors to see kiwi in their natural habitat. He is absolutely passionate about the Okarito kiwi. He'll have you walking softly through the bush, listening for their scuffles and calls, before catching a glimpse of these elusive flightless birds. It's an incredibly rare experience and Mr. Cooper promises a 98% chance of seeing one on a night tour; all you need to bring is patience and some warm, quiet clothes (no nylon windbreakers). Tours last three to five hours, depending on how shy the kiwi are. ⊠ *53 The Strand, Okarito* ☎ *03/753–4330* ⊕ *www.okaritokiwitours.co.nz* 🖃 *NZ$75* ☽ *Evenings only.*

Okarito Nature Tours. Explore the lagoon, the largest and possibly least modified coastal wetland in New Zealand, in a rented kayak or on a guided kayak. The lagoon is renowned for its birdlife. Look for the plucky godwits and other migrants that fly here all the way from Siberia each spring (and back in autumn). It's also a great spot to see white herons, who pop over here to feed from their sole New Zealand nesting ground in the Waitangiroto River, close by. Enjoy the views—dense rain forest backed by the Southern Alps—then nose your way into a tiny inlet, where the vegetation on each bank almost touches across the water. ⊠ *1 The Strand, Okarito* ☎ *03/753-4014* ⊕ *www.okarito.co.nz or www.birdingwestcoast.co.nz* 🖃 *From NZ$50 unguided and NZ$90 guided (minimum of 2 people).*

them, or potentially harm them, by feeding them. Guided walks can be booked to explore further. This is a dynamic environment, and access is sometimes closed for a day or so because of rock falls and river surges. Alternatively, from Fox township, drive about 4 km (2½ miles) toward the coast on Cook Flat Road for a roadside view of Fox Glacier (weather permitting). ■ TIP➜ Be sure to heed DOC closure signs, some who have ignored them have died as a consequence.

You can also fly over the glaciers in helicopters or planes and land on the stable névé, or hike on them with guides. Remember that these great ice structures are always in motion; guides know the hazardous areas to avoid.

Flights are generally best early in the morning, when visibility tends to be clearest. Summer may be warmer, but there is more rain and fog that can scuttle flightseeing and hiking plans. In winter, skies are clearer, which means fewer canceled flights and glacier hikes, and more spectacular views. In fact, in winter this area is a lot warmer than the snow resort towns east of the Southern Alps

Traveling south of the national park, look for the forest-framed views of Lakes Paringa and Moeraki, then 2 km (1 mile) south of Moeraki the ocean view over the rock stacks at **Knights Point.** Farther south, between Moeraki and Haast, stop and explore the walkways, wetlands, and beach at **Ship Creek.** There are few places where ancient rain forest grows so close to the coast as it does here. And check the waves—Hector's dolphins are sometimes seen surfing close to shore. Sand flies here can be voracious, so bring insect repellent and hope for a windy day (there are fewer sand flies in winter). ⊠ *Fox Glacier Hwy., Westland National Park.*

West Coast Wildlife Centre. Whether you make it to Okarito to see the rarest kiwi, Rowi, in their natural habitat, the opportunity to see firsthand the Department of Conservation's successful breeding program of this species is quite special. The center is a public-private partnership helping to build up the threatened kiwi population. Kiwi eggs are taken from their nests and incubated and hatched, safe from predator animals such as stoats and rats, then the chicks are raised in protected nursery areas and released back into the wild once they are able to defend themselves. You can simply wander through the Nocturnal House to see a few Rowi on display (wait a few moments on entering to let your eyes adjust to the deep gloom—these guys are truly nocturnal). However, the best option is to join the Kiwi Backstage Tour to witness the incubation and rearing program—and if your timing is lucky, perhaps a hatching chick. Other not-to-be-missed displays here include the West Coast storytelling hut, where you can learn from the "old-timers," and a quite lifelike "glacial exploration." ⊠ *At Cron and Cowan Sts., Franz Josef* ☎ *03/752–0600* ⊕ *www.wildkiwi.co.nz* ☝ *NZ$35; NZ$55 for Backstage Pass Tour.*

8

OFF THE BEATEN PATH

Glacier Hot Pools. After your day on the glacier fall into these pools nestled in a bewitching area of rain forest right in Franz Josef village. The three public pools range from family-friendly to completely relaxing. There is also a massage room, providing a range of five different therapies (from NZ$85), and three private hot tubs with their own shower, change areas, and towels. This is a great stop if the weather just won't cooperate, but the compact complex may fill up on such days. ✉ *Cron St., Franz Josef* ☎ *03/752–0099, 0800/044–044 NZ only* 🌐 *www.glacierhotpools.co.nz* 🎟 *Public pools NZ$26; private pools NZ$90 for up to 2* ⏲ *Daily 1–9.*

WHERE TO EAT

There are several dining options in the glacier villages. Remember these places shut early in winter, so get in soon after the sun goes down.

$$$ NEW ZEALAND

🍴 **The Alice May.** One of those cozy, buzzing places so prevalent on the West Coast serves country fare that is good and plentiful, with a welcome range of light meals (fish-and-chips, curries, venison burgers) and more substantial main courses (slow roasted pork belly, beef cheeks, and good vegetarian options). The wine and beer lists are stacked with mainstream NZ favorites. The Alice can get very busy over summer. [$] *Average main: NZ$27* ✉ *Cowan and Cron Sts., Franz Josef* ☎ *03/752–0740* 🌐 *www.alicemay.co.nz.*

$$$ NEW ZEALAND

🍴 **Café Neve.** This standout along Fox Glacier's main street sparks up no-nonsense options with fresh local flavors, such as the pizza topped with locally made Blackball salami, field mushrooms, spinach, rosemary, and tomato. From breakfast through to lunch and dinner the menu is big and varied, taking you through eggs Benedict, BLT sandwiches, soups and chowders, burgers, chicken, pizzas, and fillet steak—just what you need after a day exploring or driving. Everything is prepared on-site (muffins recommended). The wine list is all New Zealand vintage, and the beers are boutique. [$] *Average main: NZ$28* ✉ *21 Main Rd., Fox Glacier* ☎ *03/751–0110* ✍ *Reservations not accepted.*

$$$$ CAFÉ

🍴 **Matheson Cafe.** The food at this all-day café is decent if predictable (a huge breakfast menu, burgers at lunch, beef rib eye, and lamb cutlets for dinner) but the scenery steals the show. If the weather plays ball you'll be able to enjoy a memorably stunning view: an amphitheater of mountains (Aoraki/Mt. Cook and Mt. Tasman) and, in the foreground, tall *kahikatea* forest. Take time also to browse the Reflectionz Gifts and Galley next door. [$] *Average main: NZ$32* ✉ *Lake Matheson Rd., Fox Glacier* ☎ *03/751–0878* ⏲ *No dinner Apr.–Oct.*

WHERE TO STAY

As major tourist destinations both Fox and Franz Josef townships, and nearby areas, are well serviced with campsite, backpacker motel, B&Bs, hotels, and lodge accommodations.

$$$ HOTEL

🏨 **58 On Cron Motel.** Cater for yourself if you wish at this modern motel-style accommodation that offers great value, with well-appointed studios and apartments, excellent facilities, and a sunny environment. **Pros:** parking is right outside your door; property is well-managed. **Cons:** the units are a bit crowded on a small site but well laid-out. [$] *Rooms from:*

NZ$220 ✉ 58 Cron St., Franz Josef ☎ 03/752–0627, 0800/662–766 NZ only 🌐 58oncron.co.nz ⇨ 14 studios, 6 apartments.

$$$ B&B/INN FAMILY 🏨 **Glenfern Villas.** A short drive north of Franz Josef village, these very smart one- and two-bedroom villas are in a quiet rural environment away from the tourist bustle and helicopters. **Pros:** home-away-from-home in size and feel. **Cons:** some road noise from the highway. [$] *Rooms from: NZ$270 ✉ State Hwy. 6, Franz Josef ✣ 3.5 km (2 miles) north of Franz Josef village ☎ 03/752–0054 🌐 www.glenfern.co.nz ⇨ 10 1-bedroom units, 8 2-bedroom units 🍴 No meals.*

$$$$ HOTEL 🏨 **Te Waonui Forest Retreat.** Here you'll feel enfolded not only in luxury but also the rain forest, as the hotel has been built to fit in and not intrude on the trees—from concrete jungle to real jungle, as their mantra states. **Pros:** quiet; rain-forest surrounds; walking distance to village and spa. **Cons:** subdued guest room lighting for ambience makes reading difficult; no room-only rate. [$] *Rooms from: NZ$699 ✉ 3 Wallace St., Franz Josef ☎ 03/752–0555 🌐 www.tewaonui.co.nz ⏲ Closed May–Aug. ⇨ 100 rooms 🍴 Some meals.*

$$$$ B&B/INN 🏨 **Westwood Lodge.** For unpretentious luxury near the glaciers, turn into this spacious, modern lodge-style B&B just a few minutes' drive from Franz Josef village. **Pros:** light dinner platter available; alpine gardens; some private decks with mountain views. **Cons:** a bit away from town and its restaurants. [$] *Rooms from: NZ$386 ✉ 2796 State Hwy. 6, Franz Josef ☎ 03/752–0112, 0800/200–209 NZ only 🌐 www.westwoodlodge.co.nz ⇨ 8 rooms, 1 suite 🍴 Breakfast.*

$$$$ HOTEL Fodor's Choice ★ 🏨 **Wilderness Lodge Lake Moeraki.** In World Heritage rain forest beside the Moeraki River a 20-minute bushwalk from the Tasman Sea—the superb surroundings and passionate eco-guides make this lodge an ideal place to relax in and learn about the natural environment here. **Pros:** a top eco-experience; generates own hydropower. **Cons:** remote. [$] *Rooms from: NZ$495 ✉ State Hwy. 6, Westland National Park ✣ 90 km (56 miles) south of Fox Glacier ☎ 03/750–0881 🌐 www.wildernesslodge.co.nz ⏲ Closed June and July ⇨ 24 rooms, 4 suites 🍴 All-inclusive ☞ Rates also include 2 short guided activities daily.*

SPORTS AND THE OUTDOORS

BIRD-WATCHING

FAMILY Fodor's Choice ★ **White Heron Sanctuary Tours.** White heron (known to Māori as *kotuku*) are rare in New Zealand, not helped by the fact they have only one nesting colony in the entire country, which came under attack by introduced stoats and rats. Enter the local Arnold family, who for more than 25 years have been controlling these predators. The only way into the remote colony, isolated in wetlands and rain forest near the estuary of the Waitangiroto River, is by boat. The Department of Conservation has given the Arnolds exclusive rights to take visitors to the colony, and what a trip it is! A tranquil cruise along the Waitangiroto River, lined by rain forest and wetlands and teeming with wetland birds, brings you to Waitangiroto Nature Reserve. From here a short but beautiful boardwalk through the forest leads to a hide, just feet from the colony. The big white birds and their nests somehow balance on trees overhanging the river, their numbers slowly increasing as predators are controlled. They're joined by Royal Spoonbills and Little Shags, all crammed in

a tiny area as if ready for the inevitable photo shoot. The trips last just 2½ hours and run four times daily. Bookings are strongly recommended, and tour times can change depending on conditions. A tour introduces you to quintessential New Zealand and a great conservation story. ⊠ *State Hwy. 6, Whataroa* ☎ *03/753–4120, 0800/523–456 NZ only* ⊕ *www.whiteherontours.co.nz* ✉ *NZ$120* ⏱ *Sept.–Mar., daily, trips leave at 9, 11, 1, and 3 (can change with weather conditions)* ⌕ *Reservations essential.*

GLACIER TOURS

The walks to the Fox Glacier viewpoint and Franz Josef Glacier viewpoint are the easiest and cheapest ways to see the ice of a glacier. Landing on a glacier by helicopter and perhaps joining a guided walk on the ice is unforgettable. All the helicopter companies listed here offer similar tours and prices, as well as similarly stunning spectacles.

Fox and Franz Heliservices. These guys have been operating since 1986 and run the only 100% locally owned venture licensed to land on the glaciers. If your time is limited, try a 20-minute spin with a landing on either Fox or Franz Josef glacier. Longer flights also including glacier landings, explore around Mt. Aoraki/Mt. Cook and Mt. Tasman, and, weather permitting, across the Main Divide. Departures are from both Franz Josef and Fox Glacier townships. The company also runs the Cook Saddle Cafe & Saloon, in Fox Glacier township. ⊠ *Alpine Adventure Centre, Main Rd., Fox Glacier* ☎ *03/752–0793, 0800/800–793 NZ only* ⊕ *www.scenic-flights.co.nz.*

FAMILY **Fox Glacier Guiding.** Glacier walks and climbs suit all fitness levels, budgets, and time frames, and some are suitable for kids. Options range from the terminal face walk (you won't walk on the glacier but you will learn all about it's power—from five years and up), to walks up onto the glacier of varying durations (four hours to eight or nine). Kids aged from seven are allowed on the four-hour trip. For longer trips 13 is the minimum age. There's also heli-ice climbing on the upper icefall, plus an overnight heli-trek adventure where you stay high above the glacier in a historic alpine hut. Reservations are recommended. ⊠ *Fox Glacier Guiding Bldg., 44 Main Rd., Fox Glacier* ☎ *03/751–0825, 0800/111–600 NZ only* ⊕ *www.foxguides.co.nz* ✉ *From NZ$59 (valley walk) and NZ$115 (heli-hikes).*

Franz Josef Glacier Guides. You'll be flown up onto the ice field and guided on a glacier exploration on two heli-hike options, four hours (three on the ice) and three hours (two on the ice with additional scenic flight). They also offer a guided glacier valley walk up the canyon-like floor where the glacier once ground its icy way before retreating. You won't get onto the ice on this trip but you'll learn about its awesome power. Bookings are essential. ⊠ *63 Cron St., Franz Josef* ☎ *03/752–0763, 0800/484–337 NZ only* ⊕ *www.franzjosefglacier.com* ✉ *From NZ$75 (valley walk) and NZ$339 (heli-hike).*

Glacier Country Scenic Flights. Flights leave from Whataroa Valley, just a 30-minute drive north of Franz Josef township. The advantage is you get to see more mountains en route to the glaciers, and the weather can be more settled in the open valley, away from the glaciers. Both

The Southern Alps are reflected in Lake Matheson's calm waters in Westland/Tai Poutini National Park.

scenic flights and heli-hikes are available. You can be picked up from Franz Josef or Fox townships. ⊠ *Main Rd., Whataroa* ☎ *03/753–4096, 0800/423–463 NZ only* ⊕ *glacieradventures.co.nz* ✉ *From NZ$195 (scenic flights) and NZ$435 (heli-hikes).*

Glacier Helicopters. Offer scenic flights, starting from 20 minutes (NZ$235) to either Franz Josef or Fox Glacier, and a four-hour heli-hike, flying to and landing on Fox Glacier and walking on the ice (NZ$399). Bases in both Franz Josef and Fox townships. ⊠ *Main Rd., Franz Josef* ☎ *0800/800–732* ⊕ *glacierhelicopters.co.nz.*

Helicopter Line. Several scenic flights include quick flight over the glaciers (20 minutes) and/or longer trips around Aoraki/Mt. Cook, from heliports at either Franz Josef Glacier or Fox Glacier. Three-hour heli-hikes on Franz Josef Glacier are another option, with two hours up on the ice. Reservations are recommended in summer and essential for the heli-hikes. ⊠ *Main Rd., Franz Josef* ☎ *03/752–0767, 0800/807–767 NZ only* ⊕ *www.helicopter.co.nz/glaciers* ✉ *From NZ$235 (quick flights) and NZ$425 (heli-hikes).*

Mountain Helicopters. Fly out of either Franz Josef or Fox Glacier on helicopter flights as short as 10 minutes. Smaller choppers mean that everyone gets a window seat, and the experience is more intimate than it can be with the bigger operators. They also have an office on the main street at Fox Glacier. ⊠ *Fern Grove Souvenir Bldg., Main St., Franz Josef* ☎ *03/751–0045, 0800/369–423 NZ only* ⊕ *www.mountainhelicopters. co.nz* ✉ *From NZ$99.*

KAYAKING AND RAFTING

Glacier Country Kayaks. Glacial Lake Mapourika is (usually) mirror-still, reflecting its rain forest and mountain surrounds. On these three-hour trips you'll nose your kayak into an estuary that backs onto protected forest where Okarito Rowi kiwi live—on an evening paddle you might hear them calling. Kayak only trips and kayak-and-walk combos are available. Quality kayaks and gear are provided; you can meet your guides at the lake or in town. Reservations are essential. ■ TIP→ The best views are likely to be in winter, when the weather is clearer and calmer. ⊠ *64 Cron St., Franz Josef* ☎ *03/752–0230, 0800/423–262 South Island only* ⊕ *www.glacierkayaks.com* ✉ *From NZ$115 for 3-hr paddle.*

SKYDIVING

Skydive Franz. If you're going to skydive anywhere in New Zealand, above the glaciers and highest mountains is a spectacular option. New Zealand's highest tandem skydive takes you to 18,000 feet. You'll have a 75-second freefall and plenty of time to take in the amazing views. They also do 12,000- and 15,000-feet dives. Allow two hours for the experience. They operate every day, dawn to dusk, weather permitting. DVDs, photos, GoPro handcams, and free Internet upload ⊠ *Main Rd., Fox Glacier* ☎ *03/752–0714, 0800/458–677 NZ only* ⊕ *www. skydivefranz.co.nz* ✉ *NZ$319–NZ$599 per jump.*

CHRISTCHURCH AND CANTERBURY

WELCOME TO CHRISTCHURCH AND CANTERBURY

TOP REASONS TO GO

★ **The Arts:** Christchurch's galleries, museums, and cultural activities have reinvented themselves; thought-provoking art projects are dotted around the city. Expect the unexpected.

★ **The Great Outdoors:** You don't have to go far to be among mountains, forests, rivers, and beaches. There are an abundance of places to hike, trek, cycle, mountain-bike, boat, and ski; and it's easy to hire any gear you need.

★ **Parks and Gardens:** The Botanic Gardens and Hagley Park are Christchurch's green living rooms. In spring and summer, numerous public and private gardens are open for viewing.

★ **Superb Skiing:** Christchurch has 12 ski areas all within a few hours' drive. The season usually runs from June until early October.

★ **Fantastic Festivals:** Festivals celebrate the arts, music, seasons, heritage, wine, and food.

1 Christchurch. From the Port Hills New Zealand's second-largest city spreads out below, radiating from the central greenery of Hagley Park. The central city is now a city of the future—a city of cranes and new buildings, undergoing colossal change. To the west Christchurch's leafy suburbs are reminders of a genteel history. And to the east large areas of housing have been cleared. Their trees and gardens still remain, a poignant reminder of what happened when a series of strong earthquakes hit in 2010 and 2011.

2 Arthur's Pass and Canterbury. Arthur's Pass and Hanmer Springs are alpine regions; Akaroa is a seaside village tucked under high hills; and the southern areas around Geraldine and Timaru are the center of large, fertile farming areas. The Waipara Valley, just to the north of the city, is known for its excellent Pinot Noir, Chardonnay, Sauvignon Blanc, and Rieslings.

Arthur's Pass

Arthur's Pass National Park

73

SOUTHERN ALPS

TWO THUMB RANGE

Hakatere

Methven

Mount Somers

77

Lake Tekapo

Ashburton

Arundel

Hinds

Lake Tekapo

8

Hakatere

Geraldine

79

Fairlie

Orari

Coldstream

Pleasant Point

Winchester

8

Temuka

1

Timaru

↑ TO NELSON

Hanmer Springs

Waiau

Rotherham

CANTERBURY

Culverden

Cheviot

TO KAIKOURA

Huruni

PUKETERAKI RANGE

Waipara

Amberley

Oxford

Cust

Rangiora

Sefton

Springfield

Southbrook

Woodend

Kaiapoi

Pegasus Bay

WAIPARA VALLEY

Darfield

Belfast

Templeton

1 Christchurch

Rolleston

Halswell

Lyttelton Harbour

Lyttelton

BANKS PENINSULA

Dunsandel

Taitapu

Doyleston

Little River

Rakaia

Leeston

Akaroa

Southbridge

Lake Ellesmere

Akaroa Head

Pendarves

Akaroa Harbour

Canterbury Bight

0   20 mi

0   20 km

South Pacific Ocean

GETTING ORIENTED

Canterbury is the South Island's largest geographical region, with a natural boundary formed by the Main Divide (the peaks of the Southern Alps) in the west and stretching from Kaikoura in the north down to the Waitaki River in the south. *This chapter focuses on the section of Canterbury near the main city of Christchurch, including Banks Peninsula, the Waipara wine country, the ski town of Methven, and the alpine resort town of Hanmer Springs, north and west of the city, plus the towns sprinkled on the plains to the south. The chapter also includes Arthur's Pass National Park, a few hours northwest of Christchurch by car or train and a great mountain day trip from the city.*

9

ARTHUR'S PASS NATIONAL PARK

The journey is the thing. This Homeric phrase rings so true for the drive along Highway 73 to Arthur's Pass. In the heart of the Southern Alps, this area offers richly diverse landscapes: the beech forests and tussock grasslands of the eastern slopes give way to snowcapped mountains and wildflower fields; dense rain forests dominate the west.

Named Arthur's Pass for surveyor Arthur Dudley Dobson, who discovered the route over the Southern Alps in 1864, the east-west pass was long known to Māori hunters. Today, you can experience the thrilling mountain peaks, deep river gorges, and rain forest by car, train, or on foot. You can also spot kea, a native parrot, in the park and at Arthur's Pass Village.

BEST TIME TO GO
November through March brings gorgeous wildflowers to the park. Ski at Temple Basin from late June to early October. Remember: with 6,562-foot peaks, the weather in the park can change for the worse *anytime* at this altitude.

BEST WAYS TO EXPLORE
By Car. Driving offers the flexibility to stop for hikes and sightseeing when you please. The road, extensively revamped in the 1990s, is a feat of engineering, particularly the Otira Viaduct. Five thousand cubic meters (176,573 cubic feet) of concrete were used to create the viaduct on a steep unstable foundation in an area prone to flash floods and earthquakes. As you navigate the turns, spare some thoughts for the men who spent backbreaking years creating it.

By Foot. Everything from 10-minute strolls to multiday hikes are available in the park. We recommend the Punchbowl Falls Track (one-hour return from Arthur's Pass Village) and Dobson Nature Walk (30-minute return), which follows a lovely loop at the summit of Arthur's Pass. Marvel at brilliantly colored alpine lichen splashed across boulders and cliff faces. Kea, wrybill (with bent beaks), and green bellbirds populate the park. Lucky visitors will spot the roroa—or great-spotted kiwi—that roam the steep terrain.

By Mountain Climbing. There are plenty of ways up the peaks of Arthur's Pass. Mountain climbing in the area is prone to changeable weather and many routes involve river crossings, so check in with the Department of Conservation before any endeavor and make sure you are well equipped and up to the challenge.

By Train. Take to the tracks and relax on board the TranzAlpine Scenic Journey. It takes you from Christchurch ("ChCh" to locals) to Greymouth in 4½ hours, through 16 tunnels and over 5 viaducts. The train has an open-air carriage, which provides breathtaking views of the plains, gorges, valleys, and beech forests.

ECO-STAYS

As a guest at the **Arthur's Pass Wilderness Lodge,** you're invited to "walk the walk" and help remove invasive plants on nature hikes, and you're also welcome to do your own thing and take advantage of the extensive trails throughout the property. The owners are passionate about the conservation of this alpine environment and eager to share their knowledge with you. The lodge itself is built of local stone and wood. There's no need to worry about your cuisine's "food miles"—the delectable slow-cooked lamb on your plate was raised on the farm out the window. A more wallet-friendly but equally environment-conscious accommodation is the **Mountain House Arthur's Pass YHA.** The operators practice "responsible tourism" down to the last detail, using compact fluorescent lighting, organically based cleansers, recycled paper products, and nonnative firewood. They also initiated and run the recycling effort for the entire town. *(For more information see Where to Stay in Arthur's Pass National Park section.)*

9

(top left) Sunset at Arthur's Pass National Park; *(bottom)* There are spectacular views along the TranzAlpine train; *(top)* Arthur's Pass Wilderness Lodge

Updated by
Anabel Darby
With its vast food basket, water, and natural resources, Canterbury could be its own country. The expansive coast, fertile plains, and snow-lined Alps not only define the region's beauty, they also sustain a thriving agricultural industry. The province is served by a major international airport, several ports, and an excellent road network. The dynamic city of Christchurch with its growing immigrant population, has become known as the southern gateway to Antarctica, and has a keen arts community and a vibrant culinary scene.

Captain Cook sailed right past the Canterbury coast in 1770 and thought Banks Peninsula was an island. The Māori knew better, they were already well established (by some 500 years) around Te Waihora and Waiwera—Lakes Ellesmere and Forsyth. In 1850 the English were back to colonize the land. John Robert Godley had been sent by the Canterbury Association to prepare for the arrival of settlers for a planned Church of England community. That year, four settler ships arrived bearing roughly 800 pioneers, and their new town was named for Godley's college at Oxford.

Built in a Gothic Revival style of dark gray stone, civic buildings such as the Arts Center (originally Canterbury University) and Canterbury Museum give the city an English quality. This style, plus elements such as punting and cricket, often pegs Christchurch as a little slice of England. Though the city may have a conservative exterior, it has been a nursery for social change. It was here that Kate Sheppard began organizing a campaign that led to New Zealand being the first country in the world to grant women the vote.

Beyond Christchurch the wide-open Canterbury Plains sweep to the north, west, and south of the city. This is some of New Zealand's finest pastureland, and the higher reaches are sheep stations where life and lore mingle in the South Island's cowboy country. This is where young Samuel Butler dreamed up the satirical *Erewhon*—the word is an anagram of *nowhere*. But the towns here are no longer considered the back of beyond; communities such as Hanmer Springs, Akaroa, Timaru, and Geraldine are now favorite day-trip destinations. Arthur's Pass is probably the best place for a one-day-wonder experience of the Southern Alps while the Waipara Valley is now an established vineyard area, highly regarded for its Pinot Noir, Chardonnay and aromatics.

PLANNING

WHEN TO GO

November's New Zealand Cup and Show Week is a wacky time, when locals kick their heels up at Riccarton Park and Addington Raceway for horse racing and the country's largest agricultural and pastoral show where "country comes to town." If you've organized your accommodation well in advance it can be good fun but very busy. Wine and beer festivals follow over summer and the Garden City Summer Times festival runs from New Year's until late February, while mid-January brings the World Buskers Festival; the Electric Avenue Music Festival is in February. In winter the Christchurch Arts Festival and IceFest, a celebration of all the city's links to Antarctica, are held biennially.

Summer days can be amazingly changeable, while winter's weather is more settled but considerably colder. For skiing and snowboarding, this is *the* time to come. From June through October you can be assured of snow at Mt. Hutt. Snow on the ground in Christchurch is a rarity.

PLANNING YOUR TIME

Take at least four days to explore the Canterbury region. A full day in the city only skims the surface. An overnight trip to Hanmer, Arthur's Pass, or to Akaroa gives you a taste of the hinterland. Waipara and Hanmer Springs can be visited when heading north to Kaikoura or Nelson. Arthur's Pass is on the main road to the West Coast, and Timaru, Geraldine, and Tekapo are on the main routes south to Dunedin and Queenstown.

GETTING HERE AND AROUND

AIR TRAVEL

Direct flights arrive into Christchurch from the major New Zealand cities, the larger Australian cities, Singapore, China, and the Pacific Islands. There are no direct flights from North America. **Air New Zealand** connects Christchurch to most New Zealand centers. Jetstar has flights to all New Zealand's main centers, and several regional centers. For access to the Chatham Islands there's Air Chathams. Air New Zealand, Qantas, Jetstar, Virgin Australia, and Emirates fly direct from Australia. Charter helicopters connect to high country and remote lodges.

Contacts Air Chathams. ☎ *03/305-0209* ⊕ *www.airchathams.co.nz.* **Air New Zealand.** ☎ *0800/737-000 NZ only* ⊕ *www.airnewzealand.co.nz.* **Jetstar.** ☎ *0800/80-0995* ⊕ *www.jetstar.com/nz/en/home.* **Virgin Australia.** ☎ *0800/67-0000* ⊕ *www.virginaustralia.com/nz/en.*

CHRISTCHURCH EARTHQUAKES

The first earthquake was early in the morning of September 4, 2010, magnitude 7.1, centered beneath farmland on the Canterbury Plains. It caused considerable damage in the city but no loss of life. Collectively, Cantabrians believed they had been spared. But not so. At lunchtime, on February 22, 2011, a magnitude 6.3 aftershock, centered almost directly beneath the city, caused massive damage, injured several thousand people, and resulted in the loss of 185 lives. Many of the city's heritage buildings crumbled, suburban streets were swamped with liquefaction (a black silty deposit from underground), and even modern, inner-city buildings rocked and rolled on their foundations as the earth heaved. The central business district was cordoned off for more than two years afterward and more than half of the buildings there had to be demolished. On Madras Street, the odd assortment of empty white chairs is a memorial to each person who died. Spend a moment or two here, take a bus tour, or go to Quake City, an exhibition in Cashel Street mall, for a good insight into what people here have been dealing with. A special Memorial Wall is being constructed on the banks of the Avon River as a permanent place of contemplation.

More than five years on from New Zealand's biggest natural disaster, there is a feeling of excitement and anticipation in the air. Christchurch is now a future-focused city, rebuilding for new generations while carefully restoring its heritage. It is achieving international acclaim for creative and clever urban design, evidenced by inspiring street art, new high-tech structures, and a "Cardboard" Cathedral awarded the world's top architecture prize. As a visitor to this city you will be welcomed with open arms.

Today the city center is in active rebuild mode, with new office, shopping, and hospitality precincts now underway. Replacing many of the city's transitional colorful shipping containers are new sustainably designed buildings made of earthquake-strengthened steel, glass, and concrete.

Christchurch has been presented with a unique opportunity to redesign the city from the center outward, allowing for a new, energy-efficient, low-rise environment, and, where rebuilding is not possible, large areas of inner-city parklands. This will be a fascinating place to visit for years to come.

BUS TRAVEL

InterCity bus service connects Christchurch with major towns and cities in the South Island. The **Coastal Pacific** train runs from Christchurch to Blenheim and Picton at the top of the South Island and connects with the **InterIslander Ferry** to the North Island. The **TranzAlpine** train is one of the Great Train Journeys of the World. Christchurch has a good metropolitan bus service.

Contacts **InterCity Coachlines.** ☎ *03/377-7781* ⊕ *www.intercity.co.nz.* **InterIslander.** ☎ *0800/802-802* ⊕ *www.interislander.co.nz.* **KiwiRail Scenic Journeys.** ☎ *04/495-0775, 0800/872-467* ⊕ *www.kiwirailscenic.co.nz.*

CAR TRAVEL

Outside the city the best way to explore the region is by car. Roads across the Canterbury Plains tend to be straight and flat with good signage and low traffic volume. State Highway 1 runs the length of the region's coast, linking all the major towns. State Highway 72 follows the contours of the hills, farther inland, beneath the Alps. State Highway 7 leaves the main road at Waipara and heads inland to Hanmer Springs before heading north to Nelson, and State Highway 73 heads west across the plains before leaping into the Southern Alps on its way to the West Coast.

RESTAURANTS

Christchurch has an exciting foodie scene, and many new restaurants, cafés, and bars have opened in recent years. Restaurants are usually open every day; if they do close, it's either Sunday or Monday. Outside Christchurch, restaurants are more likely to close on Monday and Tuesday and during the winter.

The Waipara Valley is seeing a surge in exotic food production. North Canterbury is now a key producer in the country's fledgling black truffle industry. Locally sourced saffron, hazelnuts, *manuka* (an indigenous kind of tea tree) honey, olive oil, and ostrich meat are making their way onto area menus.

HOTELS

There's an extraordinary array of lodging in Christchurch to suit all tastes and budgets—from backpackers lodges to gorgeous boutique B&Bs, from modern multilevel contemporary hotels within the city center to plenty of motels heading out west and toward the airport. The more substantial lodges tend to be out in the hinterland. Many accommodations do not include breakfast in their room rates. Reservations are most necessary in summer, on public holidays, during rugby tests, and at festival times.

Outside Christchurch, it can be hard to find a place to stay in summer, especially over the holidays. If you're planning on going to Akaroa, Hanmer Springs, or Waipara during peak season, be sure to reserve well in advance. Bookings can also be heavy in winter around the ski areas and during school holidays.

Hotel reviews have been shortened. For full information, visit Fodors. com. Use the coordinate (✚ B2) at the end of each listing to locate a site on the corresponding map.

WHAT IT COSTS IN NEW ZEALAND DOLLARS			
$	$$	$$$	$$$$
Restaurants under NZ$15	NZ$15–NZ$20	NZ$21–NZ$30	over NZ$30
Hotels under NZ$125	NZ$125–NZ$200	NZ$201–NZ$300	over NZ$300

Restaurant prices are the average cost of a main course at dinner or, if dinner is not served, at lunch. Hotel prices are the lowest cost of a standard double room in high season.

VISITOR INFORMATION

The **Christchurch i-SITE Visitor Information Center** is open daily from 8:30 to 5, and until later in summer, in a temporary facility at the entrance to the Botanic Gardens, next to Canterbury Museum. Check the ⊕ *www. christchurchnz.com* website for details of their new permanent location. It is a great resource where you can find out about everything from lodging to bike rentals. *Avenues,* a local magazine with events listings and reviews, is also worth a browse. For a list of events and festivals go to the Be There website.

Contacts Be There. ⊕ *www.bethere.co.nz.* **Christchurch i-SITE Visitor Information Centre.** ☏ *03/379–9629* ⊕ *www.christchurchnz.com.*

CHRISTCHURCH

Earthquakes aside, the face of Christchurch is changing, fueled by both New Zealand residents drawn from other centers as well as immigrants, attracted by rebuild opportunities. The Māori community, although still below the national average in size, is growing. Ngai Tahu, the main South Island Māori tribe, settled Treaty of Waitangi claims in 1997 and has invested in many high-profile property and tourism ventures. There is a growing Asian population, reflected in the number of restaurants and stores catering to their preferences. Christchurch's population is rising, the arts scene is flourishing, and the city continues to attract cutting-edge technology companies.

Christchurch is also the forward supply depot for the main U.S. Antarctic base at McMurdo Sound, and if you come in by plane in summer, you are likely to see the giant U.S. Air Force transport planes of Operation Deep Freeze parked on the tarmac at Christchurch International Airport.

GETTING HERE AND AROUND

The inner city is reasonably compact and easiest to explore on foot or by bicycle; the central sights can be reached during an afternoon's walk. The city center was always defined by four avenues (Bealey, Fitzgerald, Moorhouse, and Rolleston) but now a more compact core has now emerged. Beyond this core are a number of special-interest museums and activities, about 20 minutes away by car.

Outside the central city, the best way to get around is to use the network of buses. There is a new indoor Bus Exchange on the corner of Lichfield and Colombo streets, and Metro has a great website (⊕ *www.metroinfo. co.nz*) that helps plan your route. Or call them at ☏ *03/366–8855.* Once in Christchurch you can purchase a Metrocard from the exchange or a Metro Agent (their website provides a list); a Metrocard is a preloaded card that will give 25% cheaper fares. You can also top-up these cards once you've used the initial funds. A number of tourist attractions, like the Antarctic Centre, Orana Park, and the Gondola provide shuttle services from the city; some are included in the entry price. Just check when you book. Spark is a bike-share system linking key city sites, with stations at Victoria Street, Gloucester Street, Cashel Street, Tuam Street, and Worcester Boulevard, where you can log in after preregistering online and pick up a bike. There is a one-off registration fee of NZ$4 for first-time users and the first 30 minutes is free. A NZ$4 per hour fee applies for trips more than 30 minutes. Each Spark Bike docking station also includes a map of the surrounding area and local attractions, and directions to the free Spark Wi-Fi hot spots. Bikes comes with helmets (compulsory to use) and locks.

Airport Christchurch International Airport. ✉ *30 Durey Rd., Harewood* ☎ *03/358–5029* ⊕ *www.christchurchairport.co.nz.*

Air Carriers Air New Zealand. ☎ *0800/737–000 within NZ,* ⊕ *www.airnewzealand.co.nz.* **Jetstar.** ☎ *0800/800–995 NZ only, 64/9975–9426* ⊕ *www.jetstar.com/nz/en/home.*

Bus Depot Christchurch Bus Exchange. ✉ *71 Lichfield St.* ☎ *03/366–8855* ⊕ *www.metroinfo.co.nz.*

Rental Bikes Spark Bike Share. ✉ *28 Worcester Blvd.* ☎ *09/373–4590* ⊕ *www.nextbike.co.nz.*

Rental Cars Apex. ✉ *Dakota Business Park, 28 Ron Guthrey Rd., Christchurch Airport* ☎ *03/357–4536, 0800/400–121 NZ only* ⊕ *www.apexrentals.co.nz.* **Avis.** ✉ *Christchurch International Airport, Terminal Bldg., 60 Durey Rd.* ☎ *03/358– 9661, 0800/284–722 NZ only* ⊕ *www.avis.co.nz.* **Budget.** ✉ *Christchurch International Airport, Terminal Bldg., Durey Rd.* ☎ *03/357–0231, 0800/283–438 NZ only* ⊕ *www.budget.co.nz.* **Hertz.** ✉ *Terminal Bldg., Christchurch International Airport, Durey Rd.* ☎ *03/358–6730* ⊕ *www.hertz.co.nz.* **Maui Motorhomes.** ✉ *Christchurch International Airport, 10 De Havilland Way* ☎ *03/357–5610, 0800/651–080 NZ only* ⊕ *www.maui.co.nz.*

Train Information TranzAlpine and Coastal Pacific. ☎ *0800/872–467 NZ only, 03/341–2588* ⊕ *www.kiwirailscenic.co.nz.*

Train Station Christchurch Railway Station. ✉ *Troup Dr., Addington* ☎ *03/341–2588.*

TOURS
BICYCLE TOURS

Fodor's Choice ★ **Christchurch Bike and Walking Tours.** Choose between a two-hour history and bush-themed bicycle tour that ambles through Hagley Park to the historic Riccarton House and Dean's Bush, Mona Vale Gardens, and Antigua Boat Sheds, or a CBD rebuild bike tour, which takes you to the Transitional Cardboard Cathedral, New Regent Street, and Cashel Mall. Bikes are comfortable and modern with thick tires and a basket for your goodies, and helmets and safety sash are provided. Tours meet outside the Antigua Boat Sheds for a 10 am or 2 pm start. For those who would prefer to keep their feet on the ground there are guided walking tours, too, which can start from a central spot of your choice. There's also a farmers' market tour at 10 am Saturday, and gourmet tours on bike or foot. Group sizes are kept small so book ahead. ✉ *Antigua Boat Shed, 2 Cambridge Terr.* ☎ *0800/733–257 NZ only, 021/280–8022* ⊕ *www.chchbiketours.co.nz* ⌖ *From NZ$35 (walk) or NZ$50 (bike).*

9

FAMILY   **Christchurch Segway Tours.** Informative and fun Segway tours with a knowledgeable local guide are popular with visitors to Christchurch. You can book a two-hour guided tour with three different route options. Full training and helmets are provided. Tours meet in South Hagley Park off Hagley Avenue. ⊠ *Hagley Ave.* ☎ *027/542–1887* ⊕ *www. urbanwheels.co.nz* ✉ *From NZ$109.*

SIGHTSEEING TOURS

Canterbury Leisure Tours. Canterbury Leisure Tours runs day trips to Hanmer Springs, Arthur's Pass, Kaikoura, and Akaroa. In addition to its Christchurch tours, it also offers half-day, full-day, and overnight tours and activities, including wine trails, whale-watching tours, horse trekking, night tours, sheep-farm visits, dolphin swimming, and skiing. Bookings are essential. ☎ *03/384–0999, 0800/484–485 NZ only* ⊕ *www.leisuretours.co.nz* ✉ *From NZ$65.*

Canterbury Trails. Canterbury Trails runs full-day guided tours from the Christchurch area to Akaroa (where you can join a dolphin-swimming tour), Arthur's Pass, and Kaikoura. They also have an exciting nine-day Wilderness South expedition and run small group tours around the South Island. If you're heading to Queenstown but don't want to drive yourself or go by coach, consider the one- or two-day tour (overnight at Aoraki/Mt. Cook). Groups are up to eight people. Reservations are essential. ☎ *03/384–6148* ⊕ *www.canterburytrails.co.nz* ✉ *From NZ$250.*

Christchurch Rebuild Tours. The Red Bus Rebuild Tour takes 1½ hours and departs every day at 11:30 from outside the Canterbury Museum. Tickets can be purchased from the nearby i-SITE Visitor Center. The coaches are modern and fully air-conditioned. Expert guides give visitors an insight into the new Christchurch, exciting plans for the city, and the history of the earthquakes. ⊠ *Rolleston Ave.* ☎ *03/379–4260, 0800/500–929 NZ only* ⊕ *www.redbus.co.nz* ✉ *From NZ$29.*

Fodor'sChoice   **Discovery Travel.** Discovery Travel runs day tours for small groups to
★   the Waipara wine district, Akaroa, Hanmer, and Arthur's Pass. These include dolphin swimming, whale watching, and an exciting safari jet-boat tour along the Waimakariri River. They also run special day tours for cruise ship passengers, and can tailor-make itineraries for visitors to explore beyond Christchurch and the South Island. ☎ *03/357–8262* ⊕ *www.discoverytravel.co.nz* ✉ *From NZ$155.*

Fodor'sChoice   **Hassle-Free Tours.** Discover Christchurch tours depart from outside the
★   Canterbury Museum, aboard classic red London double-decker buses, with open tops in summer. One-hour tours of central city with an expert guide are offered, as well as a 3½-hour tour of the city, plus Sumner and the Port Hills. There are regular departures from 10 until 2 daily. They also run four-wheel-drive tours of the Canterbury high country, including guided *Lord of The Rings* Tours, Alpine Safari, and four-wheel-drive and jet-boat river tours with regular departures and hotel pickups in Christchurch. Private and specialized tours can also be arranged. ⊠ *Rolleston Ave.* ☎ *03/385–5775* ⊕ *www.hasslefreetours. co.nz* ✉ *From NZ$32.*

WALKING TOURS

Canterbury Horticultural Society - Garden Tours. The Canterbury Horticultural Society began with the colonization of Canterbury in the 1850s, and continues to provide inspiration to gardeners throughout the region today. The Society runs seasonal tours of gardens and are happy to have nonmembers join in. Check their website for details of upcoming dates, and for a list of gardens that are open to view. ⊠ *Canterbury Horticultural Society, South Hagley Park* ☎ *03/366–6937* ⊕ *www.chsgardens. co.nz* ✉ *From NZ$20.*

FAMILY **Caterpillar Gardens Tour.** Take the hard work out of walking round the 52-acre Botanic Gardens on this hop-on, hop-off tour. The vehicles are environmentally powered (electric and solar) and a ticket lasts two days. You can buy tickets ahead online or give them a call. The full circuit with commentary from an expert guide takes approximately one hour. ⊠ *9 Rolleston Ave.* ☎ *0800/88–2223 NZ only* ⊕ *welcomeaboard.co.nz/ garden-tours/* ✉ *From NZ$20.*

EXPLORING

CENTRAL CHRISTCHURCH
TOP ATTRACTIONS

FAMILY
Fodor's Choice
★

Canterbury Museum. When this museum was founded in 1867, its trading power with national and international museums was in moa bones. These Jurassic birds roamed the plains of Canterbury and are believed to have been hunted to extinction by early Māori. The museum still houses one of the largest collections of artifacts from the moa hunting period. You'll also find an interactive natural-history center, called Discovery, where kids can dig for fossils. The Hall of Antarctic Discovery charts the links between the city and Antarctica, from the days when Captain Cook's ship skirted the continent in a small wooden ship. Among the 20th-century explorers celebrated here are the Norwegian Roald Amundsen, who was first to visit the South Pole, and Captain Robert Falcon Scott, who died returning from the continent. *Fred & Myrtle's Paua Shell House* tells the story of an iconic Kiwi couple and recreates their *paua* (abalone) shell–covered living room. The café looks out over the Botanic Gardens. ⊠ *11 Rolleston Ave.* ☎ *03/366–5000* ⊕ *www.canterburymuseum.com* ✉ *Free admission, donations appreciated. Entry to Discovery is NZ$2* ⊙ *Oct.–Mar., daily 9–5:30; Apr.– Sept., daily 9–5.*

FAMILY **Christchurch Botanic Gardens.** One of the largest city parks in the world, these superb gardens are known for the magnificent trees planted here in the 19th century. Pick up the Historic Tree Walk brochure from the information center for a self-guided Who's Who tour of the tree world. Spend time in the conservatories and the new award-winning Visitor Centre and ilex Cafe to discover tropical plants, cacti, and ferns on days when you'd rather not be outside. Go to the New Zealand plants area at any time of the year. There's also an interesting playground and some paddling pools—perfect for little ones on a hot day. ⊠ *Rolleston Ave.* ☎ *03/366–1701* ✉ *Free* ⊙ *Daily 7 am–dusk; conservatories daily 10:15–4.*

9

ChristChurch Cathedral. Sadly, this dominating landmark at the heart of the city was severely damaged in the 2011 earthquakes. Building of the original Gothic-style church started in 1864, 14 years after the arrival of the Canterbury Pilgrims, and was completed in 1904. There has been much angst in Christchurch over its fate and whether restoration is a viable option. However, the Anglican Church has deconsecrated the site and the Government has stepped in to help negotiate plans to restore or rebuild the cathedral within a decade. Until then the **Transitional "Cardboard" Cathedral** is its replacement. ✉ *Cathedral Sq.* ⊕ *www. cardboardcathedral.org.nz.*

FAMILY **Christchurch Tram.** There's something nostalgic and reassuring about the
Fodor's Choice *ding-ding* of these heritage trams. After the 2010 earthquake they disap-
★ peared from the cityscape for almost three years. Now they are back on the original route from New Regent Street with the addition of a new extended loop of the city. All-day tickets allow you to hop on and off and explore the inner city. You'll pass the remains of the ChristChurch Cathedral and continue along to the Avon River where you can get off for some punting. The Tramway Restaurant departs daily at 7 pm. The Tramway ticket office is in Cathedral Junction but you can buy tickets at other places en route and on board. Tickets can also be bought in a combination pass including Punting, Gondola, and the Caterpillar Botanic Gardens Tour. ✉ *Cathedral Junction* ☎ *03/366–7830* ⊕ *www. welcomeaboard.co.nz* 🎫 *NZ$10* ⏰ *Oct.–Mar., daily 9–6; Apr.–Sept., daily 10–5.*

Fodor's Choice **Transitional "Cardboard" Cathedral.** Locals call it the Cardboard Cathedral
★ because it is built largely from 98 cardboard tubes, covered in plastic. The Anglican church's Transitional Cathedral opened in August 2013 to help fill a little of the enormous gap left by the loss of the ChristChurch Cathedral. It can seat 700 and is the largest "emergency structure" to be designed by award-winning Japanese architect Shigeru Ban, who gifted the design (right down to its unusual chairs) to Christchurch. The large triangular window at the front contains images from ChristChurch Cathedral's original rose window. Built to last at least 50 years, it has been named by *Architectural Digest* magazine as one of the world's 10 daring buildings, and it won Shigeru Ban the Pritzker Architecture Prize in 2014. This striking venue is also used for functions and community events outside of church hours. ✉ *234 Hereford St.* ⊕ *www. cardboardcathedral.org.nz.*

WORTH NOTING

FAMILY **Antigua Boat Sheds & Cafe.** Built for the Christchurch Boating Club in 1882, this green-and-white wooden structure is the last shed standing of a half dozen that once lined the Avon. On sunny days, punts, canoes, and paddleboats take to the river paddled by visitors and families alike. Join them by renting a boat and taking a champagne picnic into the Botanic Gardens or farther up into the woodlands of Hagley Park. After exploring the waterway you can hire a bike for more action or rest a while at the boat shed's licensed café (open for breakfast and lunch) with a deck overlooking the Avon. ✉ *2 Cambridge Terr.* ☎ *03/366–5885 boat shed, 03/366–6768 café* ⊕ *www.boatsheds.co.nz* 🚣 *Single canoe NZ$12 per hr, double canoe NZ$24 per hr, rowboat NZ$24 per ½ hr*

Christchurch

↑ TO MAIN NORTH ROAD

◆ Mona Vale

◆ Willowbank

Bealey Ave.

Peacock St.

Beveridge St.

Harper Ave.

Little Hagley Park

← TO AIRPORT

←◆ International Antarctic Centre

North Hagley Park

Victoria Lake

Park Terrace

Papanui Rd.

Montreal St.

Victoria St.

Durham St.

Colombo St.

Manchester St.

Otley St.

Metrose St.

Ety St.

Salisbury St.

Peterborough St.

Madras St.

◆ Casino

Cranmer Square

Kilmore St.

◆ Town Hall

TO NEW BRIGHTON

Conservatories ◆

Chester St.

Chester St.

15

Oxford Terr.

Chester St. E.

Armagh St.

1

12

3

4

11

Worcester Blvd.

2

5

10

14

13

Isaac Theatre Royal

New Regent Street

Cathedral Square

17

16

19

i

Gloucester St.

Barbadoes St.

Visitor Centre

TO FITZGERALD AVE. →

Information Centre

Cambridge Terr.

9

Hereford St.

Cashel St.

20

Rolleston Ave.

Riccarton Ave.

Public Hospital

6

7

River Avon

Oxford Terr.

Lichfield St.

◆ Ballentynes

8

1

South Hagley Park

Hagley Ave.

Antigua St.

Montreal St.

Durham St.

Tuam St.

St. Asaph St.

Colombo St.

High St.

Madras St.

Ferry Rd.

Selwyn Ter.

Walter Ter.

Stewart St.

21

Christchurch Gondola ◆

← Airforce Museum of New Zealand

1

Moorhouse Ave.

TO LYTTELTON → & SUMNER

| 0 | 300 yards |
| 0 | 300 meters |

KEY
i Tourist information
⋯ Tramway

DID YOU KNOW?

Hagley Park includes, among other things, the botanic gardens, a hospital, 11 rugby fields, 13 soccer fields, a world-class cricket oval, polo ground, tennis courts, croquet lawns, a golf course, and a small lake—and there's plenty of space for the city's many festivals.

(3–4 people), paddleboat NZ$25 per ½ hr (minimum 2 people). Bike hire: NZ$10 per hr, NZ$30 all day ☉ Dec.–Apr., daily 9–4:30; May–Nov., daily 9–4.

Arts Centre. After major restoration, a large section of the historic Arts Centre (which was a popular arts, studios, theaters, shopping, and dining complex before the earthquakes) has reopened. Further careful restoration and strengthening is still underway on this fine collection of Gothic Revival stone buildings that were originally built as Canterbury's University. It was here that NZ-born physicist Ernest, Lord Rutherford (1871–1937) completed his undergraduate degree. Rutherford became one of the most influential scientists of the 20th century, a pioneer in nuclear physics, famous for his work with splitting the atom. ⊠ *Worcester Blvd. between Montreal St. and Rolleston Ave.* ⊕ *www.artscentre.org.nz.*

Bridge of Remembrance and Triumphal Arch. Arching over Cashel Street, this Oamaru limestone memorial arch and Avon River bridge was built in memory of the soldiers who crossed the river here from King Edward Barracks on their way to the battlefields of Europe during World War I. ⊠ *76 Cashel St. at Avon River.*

Cathedral of the Blessed Sacrament. The city's basilica-style Roman Catholic Cathedral was badly damaged in the 2011 earthquake and is now undergoing long-term restoration work. Built in 1860, this dramatically proportioned building is one of New Zealand's finest neo-Renaissance churches. ⊠ *122 Barbadoes St.* ⊕ *www.chch.catholic.org.nz.*

FAMILY **Chalice.** An artwork created by internationally acclaimed Christchurch sculptor Neil Dawson, this giant steel vessel was installed in Cathedral Square in 2001 to celebrate the 150th anniversary of the founding of Christchurch and Canterbury. It survived the earthquakes and is now a major city landmark. ⊠ *Cathedral Sq.* ⊕ *www.findchch.com.*

Fodor'sChoice **Christchurch Art Gallery—Te Puna O Waiwhetu.** The city's stunning art gal-
★ lery wows visitors as much for its architecture as for its artwork. Its tall, wavy glass facade was inspired by Christchurch's Avon River and the shape of the native *koru* fern. The museum's Māori name refers to an artesian spring on-site and means "the wellspring of star-reflecting waters." Free guided tours, entertaining events, and family activities make the gallery a must-see. Shop for a great selection of gifts, or relax at the café. Check the website for updates on the gallery program. ⊠ *Worcester Blvd. and Montreal St.* ☏ *03/941-7300* ⊕ *www. christchurchartgallery.org.nz* ⊡ *Free* ☉ *Daily 10–5, Wed. 10–9.*

FAMILY **Christ's College.** Founded in 1850, Christ's College is New Zealand's most well-known private school for boys. It is housed in a magnificent precinct of buildings designed by the city's leading architects over a period of 165 years. Set around an open quadrangle neighboring Hagley Park and the Botanic Gardens, the school's many heritage buildings are undergoing extensive repair and strengthening following the earthquakes. Guided tours of the school are available during summer from mid-October to late April, at 10 am for 80 minutes on Monday, Wednesday, and Friday. ⊠ *Rolleston Ave.* ⊕ *www.christscollege.com* ⊡ *NZ$10.*

CoCA - Centre of Contemporary Art. After a major four-year renovation, Christchurch's leading contemporary art home is back with a modern and stylish gallery space. Formed in 1880 as the Canterbury Society of Arts, CoCA is a not-for-profit art gallery run by a trust whose members include several of New Zealand's leading contemporary artists. The gallery commissions, produces, and collaborates with top artists to present four seasonal exhibition programs per year. There's an excellent café downstairs, too. ⊠ *66 Gloucester St.* ☎ *03/366–7261* ⊕ *www. coca.org.nz.*

Firefighters Memorial. Local artist Graham Bennett used crooked girders from the collapsed World Trade Center in this memorial sculpture. The work is dedicated not only to the firefighters who died in New York on September 11, 2001, but also to other firefighters who have died in the course of duty. You can reach the memorial along the riverside path; sit a while in the small park beside the Avon, not far from the central fire station. ⊠ *Kilmore and Madras Sts.*

FAMILY **Hagley Park.** Hagley Park was developed by European settlers in the mid-1800s with imported plants given trial runs in what would become the Botanic Gardens. Now the 407-acre park, includes a golf course, sports fields, world-class cricket oval, netball and tennis courts, cycling paths, walking and jogging tracks, and a 17-station fitness circuit. In spring you'll be treated to a magnificent blossom display from the flowering cherry trees and a host of golden daffodils. You can access the park from most of its perimeter. The Botanic Gardens is near the middle, closest to the city center. ⊠ *8 Riccarton Ave.* ⊕ *www.ccc.govt.nz.*

Peacock Fountain. This colorful sight at the entrance to the Botanic Gardens is a fine and rare example of Edwardian ornamental cast ironwork, set in a large circular pool. It was made in Shropshire, England, funded by a bequest to the city from politician and philanthropist John Peacock in 1911. ⊠ *Rolleston Ave.*

Provincial Council Chambers. This impressive complex of Gothic Revival stone and wooden buildings beside the Avon River was once the seat of Canterbury's government, which ran from 1853 to 1876. The Provincial Council Chambers were significantly damaged in the 2010–11 earthquakes, and will undergo major restoration work. They are the only surviving purpose-built Provincial Council chambers in the country and were some of the earliest buildings to be protected by the New Zealand Historic Places Trust. A large Victorian clock intended for the tower proved too big and normally stands a few blocks away, at the intersection of Victoria, Salisbury, and Montreal streets. For several years it was stopped at 12:51 pm (the time of the February 2011 earthquake) but has now been fully restored to working order. ⊠ *Durham St. at Gloucester St.* ☎ *03/941–7680.*

St. Michael and All Angels Anglican Church. The bell in this church's belfry came out with the Canterbury Pilgrims on one of the first four ships and was rung hourly to indicate time for early settlers; it is still rung every day. The original building was the first church to be built in Christchurch. The current white-timber church was built in 1872, entirely of *matai,* a native black pine, and has 26 English-made stained-glass windows dating back as far as 1858. It's one of the largest timber Victorian Gothic churches in Australasia. The building stood up to the 2010–11 earthquakes, apart from its 1872 Bevington pipe organ, which was badly damaged but has been beautifully restored. ⊠ *At Oxford Terr. and Durham St.* ☎ *03/379–5236* ⊙ *Weekdays 9–4.*

FAMILY **Victoria Square.** This square was named for Queen Victoria in her jubilee year. On its north side sits the damaged Town Hall, which is undergoing a restoration project, to reopen in 2018. Community consultation in 2015 resulted in a plan to restore the square, keeping its character and heritage. A *poupou*, a tall, carved, wood column in the square, acknowledges the site's history as a significant trading point between Māori and the European settlers. It is home to Christchurch's oldest iron bridge, a floral clock, two fountains, and statues of Queen Victoria and Captain Cook. ⊠ *Armagh and Colombo Sts.*

Women's Suffrage Memorial. This bronze memorial wall, unveiled in 1993, commemorates 100 years of votes for women. New Zealand was the first country in the world to grant women the vote, and Christchurch resident Kate Sheppard played a key role in petitioning Parliament for this essential right. The vote for all women over 21, including Māori women, was granted on September 19, 1893; the work of Sheppard and other activists is celebrated each year on that date at the memorial. ⊠ *Oxford Terr. and Worcester Blvd.*

NEED A
BREAK?

C1 Espresso. Sam and Fleur Crofskey are among the pioneers of Christchurch's new, edgy dining scene. At C1 an enthusiastic staff roasts and serves superb coffee and overhead pneumatic tubes speed-deliver burgers and fries to your table. Try the corn-and-coriander fritters with bacon and guacamole. There are intriguing stories behind everything—from the grapevines and beehives on the roof garden (look up before you walk inside), to the unusual drinking fountains and LEGO bar (look carefully). Alternatively, sit outside and feast your eyes on a beautifully laid-out vegetable garden. And another special touch, their own-designed matchbox tea selection gives you one to infuse there, and one to take home as a souvenir. ⊠ *185 High St.* ☎ *03/379–1917* ⊜ *Reservations not accepted.*

SOUTH OF CHRISTCHURCH

FAMILY **Air Force Museum of New Zealand.** Starting in 1916, New Zealand pilots learned how to fly at Wigram airfield. The Air Force's old hangars plus a brand-new state-of-the-art aircraft hall now hold exhibits on aviation history, including the Royal New Zealand Air Force, flight simulators, and 30 classic aircraft. Take the behind-the-scenes guided tour to see aircraft restoration projects in action in other hangars. ⊠ *45 Harvard Ave., Wigram* ✛ *By bus, take No. 5, 81, or Metro Star and walk from Main South Rd., just south of Sockburn Overbridge* ☎ *03/343–9532* ⊕ *www.airforcemuseum.co.nz* ⊡ *Free* ⊙ *Daily 10–5.*

9

Youngsters press in close to see penguins at the International Antarctic Centre.

EAST OF CHRISTCHURCH
TOP ATTRACTIONS

FAMILY

Fodor'sChoice

★

Christchurch Gondola. For one of the best vantage points to view Christ-church, the Canterbury Plains, and Lyttelton Harbour head to Christ-church Gondola. At the top, you can journey through the **Time Tunnel** to experience the history and geological evolution of the Canterbury region. Afterward, sit with a glass of local wine at the Red Rock Café. Ride the gondola with your back to the Port Hills for the best views of the Southern Alps. The adventurous can walk or mountain-bike back down (your bike can be transported to the top); it's steep in parts so watch your footing. If you don't have a car, hop on a No. 28 bus from the city center or take a Gondola shuttle from the i-SITE next to the Canterbury Museum (summer only). ⊠ *10 Bridle Path Rd., Heathcote* ☎ *03/384–0310* ⊕ *www.gondola.co.nz* ⊠ *NZ$25* ⊙ *Daily 10–5.*

FAMILY

Ferrymead Heritage Park. Ferrymead is the site of the country's first rail-way (built in 1863) and is now home to a replica Edwardian township and museum area. While exploring the shops and cottages, you can taste homemade scones or an old-fashioned *lamington* (chocolate-covered sponge cake dipped in coconut). You can watch an old-time movie at the Arcadia, see some knees-up dancing, or check out displays of fire engines, farming tools, and printing equipment. The park is home to 19 societies, particularly train and tram enthusiasts, who maintain their collections here, so trams and trains run on week-ends and public holidays. A steam train operates on the first Sunday of each month and every Sunday in mid-summer. Tram and train rides are included in the admission price if they are running. ⊠ *50*

Ferrymead Park Dr., Harewood ☎ *03/384–1970* ⊕ *www.ferrymead. org.nz* ✉ *NZ$20; steam days NZ$30* ⊙ *Daily 10–4:30.*

WORTH NOTING

Fodor's Choice
★

Riccarton House and Bush. The Deans, a Scottish family, beat even the Canterbury Association settlers to this region. Riccarton Bush, their home, is now run by a trust. You can view the small wooden cottage (built 1843) that was their first house. The larger Victorian/Edwardian wooden house, built between 1856 and 1900, now houses a daytime bistro called Local. Guided heritage tours are available; check the website for details. You can also amble through the last remnant of the original native floodplain forest still standing in Christchurch, with its 600-year-old *kahikatea* trees. The **Christchurch Farmers' Market** is held in the grounds of Riccarton House each Saturday morning from 9 to 1. And the **Artisans' Market** is held there each Sunday from 11 to 3. ✉ *16 Kahu Rd., Riccarton* ☎ *03/341–1018* ⊕ *www.riccartonhouse. co.nz* ✉ *Free entry to gardens* ⊙ *Daily dawn–dusk.*

WEST OF CHRISTCHURCH

TOP ATTRACTIONS

FAMILY

International Antarctic Centre. Ever since Scott wintered his dogs at nearby Quail Island in preparation for his ill-fated South Pole expedition of 1912, Christchurch has maintained a close connection with the frozen continent. You can experience a small taste of the modern polar experience here. Bundle up in extra clothing (provided) and brave a simulated storm with temperatures of minus 25 degrees Fahrenheit for a few minutes. Or take a ride on the Hägglund vehicle used to get around the ice. The 4-D extreme theater show of life at New Zealand's Scott Base is superb, and the Penguin Encounter lets you get up close with some blue penguins, the smallest penguin species. ■ **TIP→ There's a free shuttle service that leaves on the hour from outside the Canterbury Museum.** ✉ *38 Orchard Rd., Harewood* ☎ *03/357–0519* ⊕ *www.iceberg.co.nz* ✉ *NZ$39 or NZ$59 all-day pass with Hägglund ride and 4-D theater* ⊙ *Daily 9–5:30; café daily 8–5.*

FAMILY
Fodor's Choice
★

Orana Wildlife Park. Orana Wildlife Park is New Zealand's only openrange zoo and now home to a new Great Ape Center for gorillas and orangutans, making it the place to come to glimpse these endangered animals. You will also see both native (kiwi and tuatara) and exotic (tigers, wild dogs, cheetah, and zebras) animals.

Check out the different animal feeding times; hand-feeding the giraffes is a real highlight and even small kids manage with a bit of help. For a seriously close-up view of the lions being fed join the Lion Encounter; and watch from inside a specially modified vehicle (an extra cost but a memorable experience). A zebra-striped Safari Shuttle with commentary loops around the park, or you can join a guided walk. It's about a 15-minute drive from Christchurch airport, or there's an Orana Wildlife Park door-to-door shuttle (details on the website). ✉ *Orana Park, McLeans Island Rd., Harewood* ☎ *03/359–7109* ⊕ *www. oranawildlifepark.co.nz* ✉ *NZ$34.50* ⊙ *Daily 10–5, last entry at 4.*

9

WORTH NOTING

Mona Vale Gardens & Homestead. Come to stroll through the grounds along the Avon River, wandering under the trees and through the well-tended perennial gardens. The earthquakes dealt a severe blow to Mona Vale, one of Christchurch's great historic homesteads, and it has been undergoing extensive repair work, with only its grounds kept open to the public. The historic gate house at the Fendalton Road entrance is also under repair. Built in 1899, the house and 13½-acre gardens were almost lost to the city in the 1960s when the estate was in danger of being subdivided. A public campaign saw the homestead "sold" to individual Christchurch residents for NZ$10 per square foot. Catch a No. 9 bus from the city. ⊠ *63 Fendalton Rd., Fendalton ⊕ 2 km (1 mile) from city center* ☎ *03/348–9660* ⊠ *Free* ☉ *Grounds: gates open 24 hrs to pedestrians; vehicle access daily 7 am to 1 hr after dusk* ☉ *Restaurant and house closed till further notice.*

FAMILY **Willowbank Wildlife Reserve.** In addition to familiar farm animals and other zoo regulars, Willowbank has a section devoted to New Zealand's unique wildlife, from the national symbol, the kiwi, to the *tuatara*—the world's only living dinosaur. There's the cheeky mountain parrot, *kea*; the bush parrot, *kaka*; and the very rare but majestic *takahe*. To have all five of these iconic creatures in one place is a rarity. Willowbank is also home to *Ko Tane*, a fun, interactive Māori cultural experience followed by a traditional meal with a *hangi* main course. You'll be greeted with a *powhiri*, a welcome ceremony, and you can try your hand at swinging the *poi*, flaxen balls on long strings used in traditional Māori dances (it's not as easy as it looks), or the famous *haka*. *Ko Tane* provides complimentary return transport from the i-SITE Visitor Centre and most city hotels; phone for times. ⊠ *60 Hussey Rd., Harewood* ☎ *03/359–6226* ⊕ *www.willowbank.co.nz* ⊠ *NZ$28; Ko Tane and dinner: NZ$135* ☉ *May–Sept., daily 9:30–5; Oct.–Apr., daily 9:30–7.*

BEACHES

New Brighton Beach. About 8 km (5 miles) from the city center, this beach is popular with surfers and fishers. The long pier that goes well out into the surf is a great place to stroll when the sea is calm, but even better when it's rough. Yellow Line buses go here. **Amenities:** none. **Best for:** surfing; walking. ⊠ *8 km (5 miles) east of the city center.*

Sumner Beach. Sumner Beach is pleasant for the long relaxing walk along the sand to Cave Rock, the signal station at the top used to warn vessels approaching the Sumner bar in the 19th century. Children used to play at this large rock while their parents watched with a drink at the nearby beachside café but it's currently fenced off and the signal station's undergoing repairs. There are still a couple of those beachside cafés and the excellent Cornershop Bistro, but at this writing, Sumner is not yet back to the tourist destination it used to be. You can catch a Purple Line bus if you don't have a car. **Amenities:** food and drink; lifeguards. **Best For:** swimming; walking. ⊠ *12 km (7 miles) southeast of city center.*

Taylor's Mistake. Experienced surfers prefer Taylor's Mistake to Sumner Beach because the waves are often higher. You can drive here over the Scarborough Hill but there is no public transport. If you're lucky, you'll see tiny, rare Hector's dolphins playing off Sumner Head on your way out. **Amenities:** none. **Best for:** surfing. ✉ *16 km (10 miles) southeast of city center.*

WHERE TO EAT

Cuisine hubs are now dotted throughout the central city, in New Regent Street, High Street, Oxford Terrace, and Worcester Boulevard. **St. Asaph Street** hosts an array of ethnic cuisines. You can kick on into the night here, too, with live music and dancing. **Victoria Street,** near the city center, is packed with easygoing bars, top restaurants, and cafés. **Papanui Road,** starting across Bealey Avenue from Victoria Street and going all the way up to Merivale Mall, has several popular bars, cafés, and restaurants, while **Addington** also has a lively café and restaurant scene, plus bars and live music along Lincoln Road.

CENTRAL CHRISTCHURCH

$$ CAFÉ Fodor's Choice ★

🍴 **Addington Coffee Co-op.** Kick-start your senses and your day with the best coffee around—fair trade and organic-roasted on-site along with plenty of wholesome, tasty food, and some sweet treats to choose from the cabinet. Classic breakfast options like French toast or eggs Benedict are solid. While you're waiting for your order, take a look around the fair trade store, which shows this co-op's commitment to giving back to its suppliers. And on a more practical note, while you enjoy the lovely atmosphere in this café, you can even do your washing at its coin-operated laundromat. Both are open until 4 pm daily. [$] *Average main: NZ$17* ✉ *297 Lincoln Rd., Addington* ☎ *03/943–1662* 🌐 *www.addingtoncoffee.org.nz* ✍ *Reservations not accepted* ⊕ *A5.*

$$$ ITALIAN FAMILY

🍴 **Cafe Valentino.** Savor an Italian wood-fired pizza from one of Christchurch's favorite family-run restaurants. Try the signature Penne Basilicata or classic Picante pizza accompanied with a craft beer or a New Zealand wine, or go for a meat dish—it's been the winner of the New Zealand Beef and Lamb Gold Plate Award of Excellence for the past 17 years. For dessert it's hard to beat the Valentino *al cioccolota* chocolate cake. Kids can choose from a colorful menu designed just for them. On sunny days enjoy a relaxing lunch alongside the geranium boxes, or warm up for dinner inside with an impressive view of the roaring, mosaic pizza oven. Open daily for lunch and dinner. [$] *Average main: NZ$30* ✉ *168 St. Asaph St.* ☎ *03/377–1886* 🌐 *www.cafevalentino.co.nz* ⊕ *C5.*

$$$$ NEW ZEALAND

🍴 **Cook'n' with Gas.** This well-established fine-dining bistro serves the best local beef, lamb, and seafood on the menu, accompanied by a strong South Island wine list, including some exceptional reserve vintages. The dining rooms are themed—try the 1950s room, perhaps as you tuck into carved rack of lamb or mussels steamed in spruce beer. For a less pricey, more casual drink and good, substantial food head to the Astro Lounge garden bar out the back, and listen to mellow live music while you enjoy local wines and craft beers. The sturdy old house is opposite the Arts Centre and was once the university chaplain's home. $ *Average main: NZ$40* ⊠ *23 Worcester Blvd.* ☎ *03/377–9166* ⊕ *www.cooknwithgas.co.nz* ⊘ *No lunch* ⊹ *B4.*

$$$$
SPANISH
✕ **Curator's House.** Here you can dine in a 1920s Tudor-style house, looking out on the Botanic Gardens and the Peacock Fountain, or take a garden table and be part of it. The menu has tapas selections and a good variety of seafood, and owner/chef Javier Garcia adds Spanish flair with a grand paella (serves two). Try the slow-roasted Merino spring lamb or something a bit lighter like the West Coast whitebait. The kitchen garden supplies herbs, berries, and vegetables to the restaurant, and they have a strong environmental policy to keep things green. $ *Average main: NZ$39* ⊠ *7 Rolleston Ave.* ☎ *03/379–2252* ⊕ *www.curatorshouse.co.nz* ⊹ *B4.*

$$$
MODERN NEW
ZEALAND
FAMILY
Fodor's Choice
★
✕ **Dux Dine.** This Edwardian stationmaster's villa, not far from Hagley Park, is many locals' dream home. Plush dining rooms and a wide covered veranda lead to a manicured garden that is also a year-round source of produce for this busy kitchen. Award-winning Christchurch hospitality veteran Richard Sinke and his team have brought their vegetarian and seafood specialties here—you won't miss meat after this. The pizzas are hard to go past, and the lime-and-coriander-crusted fish is a treat. Staff go out of their way to make you feel at home for brunch, lunch, dinner, or a drink anytime. The Dux also brews its own acclaimed beers. $ *Average main: NZ$25* ⊠ *28 Riccarton Rd., Riccarton* ☎ *03/348–1436* ⊕ *www.duxdine.co.nz* ⊹ *A4.*

$$$$
ECLECTIC
✕ **Harlequin Public House.** On the site of an 1860s pub, the Public House part of the name is meant to show that it's once again inviting to all patrons. It is well worth a visit, but it's certainly not like an old pub. There are different spaces in the beautifully renovated old building including a "Snug" (fabulous cocktail lounge), as well as the bright, airy main dining room with lots of windows and lovely indoor/outdoor flow to the patio. The focus is on regional, seasonal food and Christchurch's renowned owner-chef Jonny Schwass knows what he's doing with it. Dine here if you can or drop in for champagne and oysters from the classy oyster bar. Or choose to do what Prince Harry did, and take a private dining room with your own choice of menu. ■ **TIP→ Check out their Facebook site for special nights.** $ *Average main: NZ$35* ⊠ *32 Salisbury St.* ☎ *03/377–8669* ⊕ *www.hphchch.com* ⊹ *B3.*

$$
CAFÉ
✕ **Hello Sunday.** Named the city's favorite café in the Christchurch Hospitality Awards, this quaint former Sunday school in one of Christchurch's oldest wooden buildings is often packed every day of the week. The owners have a focus on well-being and locals love the nourishing brunches and homemade foods on offer—even the jam and peanut butter are made here. Must-trys include the Za'atar eggs, and the homemade baked beans served in a cast-iron skillet with eggs and brioche. $ *Average main: NZ$18* ⊠ *6 Elgin St.* ☎ *03/260–1566* ⊕ *www.hellosundaycafe.co.nz* ⊘ *Closed evenings* ⊹ *C6.*

$$
CAFÉ
Fodor's Choice
★
✕ **ilex Cafe.** One of the city's must-see new buildings also houses one its most popular cafés. Christchurch Botanic Gardens' rare plants and nurseries sit alongside a busy dining room, named after one of its prized tree specimens, in this modern take on a glass conservatory. With their

own vegetables and herbs just outside, the ilex chefs are no doubt inspired by the 52 acres surrounding them. Line up with the locals for well-priced and inventive seasonal soups, pies, and salads washed down with organic soda, or a glass of wine. The clever cakes and desserts-in-a jar taste as good as they look. On a fine day grab a picnic blanket from the friendly staff and spread out on the impressive lawn. Keep the kids amused with their own appetizing mini-lunchboxes. Open daily until 5 pm. [$] *Average main: NZ$15* ✉ *Christchurch Botanic Gardens, Armagh St.* ✣ *Entrance off Armagh St., walk across bridge from car-park* ☎ *03/941–5556* 🌐 *www.vbase.co.nz/venues/ilex-botanic-gardens* ✣ *A4.*

$$$$ MODERN ASIAN Fodor's Choice ★

🍴 **King of Snake.** Named after its owner's signature cocktail (served up with half a fresh chili and slice of ginger), this restaurant and bar delivers on all levels. It's hard to recommend particular dishes because it all tastes so good. Try the spinach leaf with roasted coconut, peanuts, garlic, chili, and lime for a stunning starter or the light, crunchy texture of *moong dal* and mixed seed salad with fresh lime and avocado. The sticky beef wontons are popular but save room for the equally delicious main courses to follow. There's a good selection of wine and, of course, fabulous cocktails, served in a striking, seductive setting. The restaurant is offset from the road, so keep your eyes peeled to find it. ■ **TIP→ If you can't get a table at this popular spot, head to the bar and check out the snack menu so you don't miss out altogether.** [$] *Average main: NZ$32* ✉ *145 Victoria St.* ☎ *03/365–7363* 🌐 *www.kingofsnake.co.nz* ⏲ *No lunch weekends* ✣ *B2.*

$$$ MEXICAN FAMILY

🍴 **Mexicano's.** Don't feel uneasy about trying the unmarked double red doors to get in, you will be well rewarded inside. Mexicano's has an edgy atmosphere from the artwork and imported lamp shades peppered with real bullet holes. The menu delights with reasonable prices and dishes designed to be shared. If you're on a budget, or just want a great snack try the taco with cumin battered market fish, salsa mojito, and coriander. They whip up some exotic "Cocteles" at the bar and make great frozen margaritas. The same delicious snack menu is also at The Dirty Land bar next door. Come early with kids; youngsters are catered to with a tasty, nutritious kids menu up to 6:30 pm. [$] *Average main: NZ$27* ✉ *131 Victoria St.* ☎ *03/365–5330* 🌐 *www.mexicanos.co.nz* ✣ *B2.*

$$$$ NEW ZEALAND

🍴 **Pescatore.** It may have started out as a specialist seafood restaurant but Pescatore is now renowned for its creative, conceptual New Zealand cuisine. From the moment you set foot into the white space-age foyer, taste buds are tantalized. Situated on the second floor of the George hotel, there are great views over Hagley Park, but artfully prepared dishes are what should command your full attention. Choose from the à la carte or degustation menu and enjoy some unusual pairings (think celery sorbet with chocolate). There's an extensive wine list to accompany interesting food that will be a talking point and you will never walk away thinking you could have cooked it at home. [$] *Average main: NZ$44* ✉ *The George, 50 Park Terr.* ☎ *03/371–0257* 🌐 *www.thegeorge.com* ⏲ *Closed Sun. and Mon. No lunch* ✍ *Reservations essential* ✣ *B3.*

9

$$$$ EUROPEAN Fodor's Choice ★ 🍴 **Saggio di vino.** Saggio's knowledgeable owners and sommelier take both the wine and food to a whole new level with expert pairings. The menu is a mixture of old-world sentimental and new-world innovation. There are 650 wine labels and 60 of them can be bought by the glass. A flute of champagne at the bar is a lovely way to start. Choose from degustation and à la carte menus, changing daily, and check their website for special events. The winter truffle degustation dinner is always a treat. Save room for a final glass of wine with perfectly ripened cheese from the cheese trolley—which (like the wine) is temperature controlled to be at optimum taste. Don't worry about trying to read the long wine list, just put yourself in their hands and enjoy a night to remember. [$] *Average main: NZ$43* ✉ *179 Victoria St.* ☎ *03/379–4006* 🌐 *www.saggiodivino.co.nz* ⏲ *No lunch weekends* ✥ *B2.*

$$ BURGER 🍴 **Smash Palace.** Look out for the fairy lights and the big bus, and find your way through the construction sites to this cheerful, family-run oasis of beer, wine, and burgers. Head past the vegetable gardens and the foosball table to the cozy bar in this restored brick smokehouse. Ask for their own Bodgie Beer, and sample tap wines, all top-notch local drops from the Waipara region, easy on the palate and the wallet. A simple menu of burgers—beef with bacon and blue cheese, falafel, homemade buns and pickles, perfect large-cut fries, and tangy coleslaw—is dished up with superfriendly service. Musicians sometimes rock up to play, and every Thursday is Bike Night, when the street buzzes with big motorbikes, noisy scooters, and local petrolheads telling stories. [$] *Average main: NZ$15* ✉ *172 High St.* ☎ *03/366–5369* 🌐 *www.thesmashpalace.co.nz* ✍ *Reservations not accepted* ✥ *D5.*

$$ CAFÉ 🍴 **Supreme Supreme.** More than just a great coffee fix, this hip café is styled with a utilitarian look based on a distinctive red-and-white grid pattern. Tucked away off Colombo Street, it is well worth seeking out this former Land Rover dealership, where the roller doors are still a feature. Careful attention to detail is evident on the food side, too, with simple homemade, organic, locally sourced breakfast and lunch dishes (try the jerk chicken, the scrambled eggs with smoked salmon, or one of their many counter top goodies) served with excellent coffee, sodas, milk shakes (chocolate fish anyone?), and smoothies. Sit at a communal bar or smart wooden tables. A nice touch is the glass of freshly made sparkling water delivered as soon as you sit down. [$] *Average main: NZ$15* ✉ *10 Welles St.* ☎ *03/365–0445* 🌐 *www.supremesupreme.co.nz* ⏲ *Closed after 4 pm daily* ✥ *C5.*

$$$$ LATIN AMERICAN 🍴 **Tequila Mockingbird.** Spicy Latin-fusion shared plates are the mainstay of Tequila Mockingbird, in the heart of Victoria Street's busy food scene. Try at least two dishes per person from the meat, seafood, and vegetable options that span the Caribbean and South America. Cocktails are blended with the top tequilas, of course, and they make a mean Pisco Sour. Sharing jugs are also popular, and there's also an excellent wine list. For weekend brunch don't miss the fresh churros served with chili chocolate sauce. Upstairs, Boo Radley's shares the same flavors and delicious grazing plates with a live music venue. [$] *Average main: NZ$37* ✉ *98 Victoria St.* ☎ *03/365–8565* 🌐 *tequilamockingbird.co.nz* ⏲ *Closed until 5 on weekdays* ✥ *B2.*

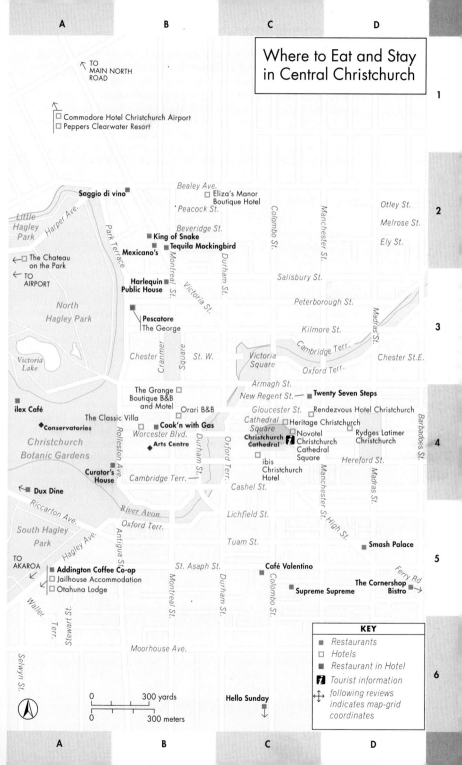

Where to Eat and Stay in Central Christchurch

A   B   C   D

1

↖ TO MAIN NORTH ROAD

↖
□ Commodore Hotel Christchurch Airport
□ Peppers Clearwater Resort

■ Saggio di vino

Bealey Ave.
□ Eliza's Manor Boutique Hotel
• Peacock St.

Otley St.

2

Little Hagley Park

Harper Ave.

Beveridge St.
■ King of Snake
■ Mexicano's   ■ Tequila Mockingbird

Melrose St.

Ely St.

Park Terrace

Colombo St.

Manchester St.

Salisbury St.

← □ The Chateau on the Park
← TO AIRPORT

■ Harlequin Public House

Montreal St.

Victoria St.

Durham St.

Peterborough St.

North Hagley Park

■ Pescatore
│ The George

Kilmore St.

Cambridge Terr.

Madras St.

3

Victoria Lake

Cranmer Square

Chester   St. W.

Victoria Square

Chester St.E.

Oxford Terr.

Armagh St.

The Grange □ Boutique B&B and Motel

New Regent St. ■ Twenty Seven Steps

■ ilex Café

The Classic Villa
♦ Conservatories

□ Orari B&B

Gloucester St.
Cathedral Square
■ Cook'n with Gas

■ Rendezvous Hotel Christchurch
□ Heritage Christchurch
□ Novotel Christchurch Cathedral Square

■ Rydges Latimer Christchurch

4

Christchurch Botanic Gardens

Rolleston Ave.

Worcester Blvd.
♦ Arts Centre

Durham St.

Oxford Terr.

Christchurch Cathedral 🛈

□ ibis Christchurch Hotel

Hereford St.

Madras St.

Barbadoes St.

Curator's House

Cambridge Terr.

Cashel St.

← ■ Dux Dine

Riccarton Ave.

River Avon

Oxford Terr.

Lichfield St.

Manchester St.

High St.

South Hagley Park

Hagley Ave.

Antigua St.

Tuam St.

5

TO AKAROA
↙

■ Addington Coffee Co-op
□ Jailhouse Accommodation
□ Otahuna Lodge

Montreal St.

St. Asaph St.

Durham St.

Colombo St.

■ Café Valentino

■ Smash Palace

Ferry Rd.
The Cornershop
Bistro →

Waller Terr.

Stewart St.

■ Supreme Supreme

6

Selwyn St.

Moorhouse Ave.

0 ——— 300 yards
0 ——— 300 meters

Hello Sunday
↓

KEY
■ Restaurants
□ Hotels
■ Restaurant in Hotel
🛈 Tourist information
⟷ following reviews indicates map-grid coordinates

A   B   C   D

$$$$
BISTRO
Fodor's Choice
★

✕ **Twenty Seven Steps.** This is one of the hottest locations in town. Climb exactly 27 steps to reveal a refined bistro spanning four shop fronts of New Regent Street's heritage row. Taking their cue from the blackboard menus, the intricate arched window frames stand out in black. A generous wine cellar, with an emphasis on Waipara locals, is tucked into the snug cocktail bar. Warmly welcoming staff deliver stand-out dishes. Try char-grilled Canterbury beef fillet with bone marrow crust, duck fat fondant potato and horseradish jus, or butter-roasted groper, chorizo spiced lentils, and silken mash, generously served with seasonal vegetables. $ *Average main: NZ$$35* ⊠ *16 New Regent St.* ☎ *03/366–2727* ⊕ *www.twentysevensteps.co.nz* ⊗ *Closed Sun. and Mon. No lunch* ✛ *C4.*

NORTH OF CENTRAL CHRISTCHURCH

$$$$
EUROPEAN/NEW
ZEALAND

✕ **The Cornershop Bistro.** Just a block back from Sumner Beach this urban-style establishment has drummed up an extremely loyal clientele. By day it's a busy café; at night it morphs in to something a little more serious. Brunch may include brioche French toast, eggs Benedict, or a breakfast grill. On the dinner menu contemplate dishes like aged-beef rib eye with sautéed spinach and walnut butter or coq au vin with creamed parsnip. This place is a favorite with locals and weekend drivers from the city so it can be busy. Book ahead if you're intent on eating here. Brunch is offered Friday–Sunday. $ *Average main: NZ$32* ⊠ *32 Nayland St., Sumner* ☎ *03/326–6720* ⊕ *www.cornershopbistro.co.nz* ⊗ *Closed Mon. and Tues.* ✛ *D5.*

WHERE TO STAY

Staying in the central city is a good choice, although there are strange road configurations and detours in place. Walking is probably still the easiest way to see the city sites and access its new restaurants and bars. Some good-quality hotels have come back on or near Cathedral Square (the Heritage, Novotel, or Rendezvous), and there's the brand-new Rydges Latimer Square. There are also some lovely little boutique B&Bs that offer more personal accommodation but you'll need to book early.

CENTRAL CHRISTCHURCH

$$$
HOTEL

🏨 **The Chateau on the Park.** Surrounded by 5 acres of landscaped gardens, this Kiwi take on a French château even has its own boutique vineyard. **Pros:** opposite Hagley Park and a pleasant walk to town; new outdoor swimming pool; free shuttle to Riccarton shops and restaurants. **Cons:** in a high-traffic area, so watch when arriving or leaving by car. $ *Rooms from: NZ$265* ⊠ *189 Deans Ave.* ☎ *03/348–8999, 0800/808–999* ⊕ *www.chateau-park.co.nz* ⇄ *186 rooms, 6 suites* ✛ *A2.*

$$$
B&B/INN

🏨 **The Classic Villa.** This bright-pink, Italian-style villa, directly opposite the Arts Centre, is one of Christchurch's cooler spots to stay. **Pros:** fabulous linen and duvets; a two-minute walk from Hagley Park, the Art Gallery, and museum and close to several top restaurants. **Cons:** tight off-street parking; accessed off one-way street system. $ *Rooms from: NZ$299* ⊠ *17 Worcester Blvd.* ☎ *03/377–7905* ⊕ *www.theclassicvilla. co.nz* ⇄ *11 rooms, 1 suite* ⦿ *Breakfast* ✛ *B4.*

$$$
B&B/INN
⊞ **Eliza's Manor Boutique Hotel.** Owner Ann warmly greats her guests no matter what unearthly time they arrive at this stately yet down-home bed-and-breakfast, with beautifully decorated rooms and unexpected little extras (home-baked biscuits in your room is just the start). **Pros:** warm, gracious host; sumptuous breakfasts. **Cons:** doesn't quite have that hideaway feel. Ⓢ *Rooms from: NZ$245* ⊠ *82 Bealey Ave.* ☎ *03/366–8584* ⊕ *www.elizas.co.nz* ↪ *8 rooms* ❤ *Breakfast* ✛ *B2.*

$$$$
HOTEL
Fodor'sChoice
★
⊞ **The George.** Overlooking the Avon River and Hagley Park, this small luxury hotel has spacious, modern guest rooms. **Pros:** consistently voted one of the country's best small hotels; has free parking and free Wi-Fi throughout the hotel. **Cons:** can get busy in the public areas with local functions and casual visitors. Ⓢ *Rooms from: NZ$465* ⊠ *50 Park Terr.* ☎ *03/379–4560* ⊕ *www.thegeorge.com* ↪ *41 rooms, 12 suites* ❤ *No meals* ✛ *B3.*

$$
B&B/INN
⊞ **The Grange Boutique Bed & Breakfast and Motel.** Lacking the immediate street appeal you might expect from a homestead built in 1874, this B&B in the center of the city slowly reveals its treasure as you walk through its dark wood-paneled entrance. **Pros:** delightful character accommodation; free Internet and Sky television ; close to plenty of live entertainment, good restaurants, bars, and the casino. **Cons:** on a busy corner. Ⓢ *Rooms from: NZ$145* ⊠ *56 Armagh St.* ☎ *03/366–2850* ⊕ *www.thegrange.co.nz* ↪ *14 rooms* ❤ *No meals* ✛ *B4.*

$$$
HOTEL
⊞ **Heritage Christchurch.** Inside the historic Old Government Building, with its sweeping central staircase and high ceilings, the Heritage has suites in an Italian Renaissance style complete with stained-glass windows and dark-wood paneling. **Pros:** centrally located; a decent spa and lap pool. **Cons:** short-term parking can be difficult. Ⓢ *Rooms from: NZ$275* ⊠ *28–30 Cathedral Sq.* ☎ *03/377–9722, 0800/368–888* ⊕ *www.heritagehotels.co.nz/christchurch* ↪ *42 suites* ❤ *No meals* ✛ *C4.*

$$
HOTEL
FAMILY
⊞ **ibis Christchurch Hotel.** Only a stone's throw from the new shopping and dining areas of Christchurch, this well-priced and cleverly designed hotel makes the most of every square inch, and many rooms interconnect if needed for family groups. **Pros:** restaurant/bar has a stylish outdoor patio area; good views; yoga next door. **Cons:** can be hard to find parking if the secure parking is full. Ⓢ *Rooms from: NZ$129* ⊠ *107 Hereford St.* ☎ *03/367–8666* ⊕ *www.accorhotels.com* ↪ *155 rooms* ❤ *No meals* ✛ *C4.*

$
HOTEL
Fodor'sChoice
★
⊞ **Jailhouse Accommodation.** Its email address is stay@jail.com, and certainly staying in an historic jail has a novelty factor, but this offers much more than that. **Pros:** free Wi-Fi throughout; free off-street parking; Netflix in the cinema and TV rooms. **Cons:** shared ablution facilities, which can be a bit cramped. Ⓢ *Rooms from: NZ$92* ⊠ *338 Lincoln Rd., Addington* ☎ *0800/524–546* ⊕ *www.jail.co.nz* ↪ *32 rooms, shared bath* ❤ *No meals* ✛ *A5.*

$$
HOTEL
⊞ **Novotel Christchurch Cathedral Square.** From the moment you walk in to the futuristic lobby you will receive a warm welcome from staff who know the city well and can help with directions and recommendations. **Pros:** right in the heart of the city, close to good dining and the Isaac Theatre Royal. **Cons:** the bathroom sink is set outside the bathroom door in

9

the living area. $ *Rooms from: NZ$198* ⊠ *52 Cathedral Sq.* ☎ *03/372–2111* ⊕ *www.accorhotels.com* ⤴ *154 rooms* ¶◯| *No meals* ⊹ *C4.*

$$
B&B/INN
Fodor's Choice
★

⛺ **Orari Bed & Breakfast.** Hidden behind an ivy-clad wall and pretty gardens, this lovely heritage villa boasts modern spacious rooms. **Pros:** no need for a car with so much nearby; the apartments are ideal for longer stays, and good for families who need adjoining rooms. **Cons:** two of the rooms have separate bathrooms, not en suites. $ *Rooms from: NZ$195* ⊠ *42 Gloucester St.* ☎ *03/365–6569, 0800/267–274 NZ only* ⊕ *www.orari.co.nz* ⤴ *10 rooms, 5 apartments* ¶◯| *Breakfast* ⊹ *B4.*

$$
HOTEL
FAMILY

⛺ **Rendezvous Hotel Christchurch.** Hard to miss, this city landmark is the tallest building in Christchurch with expansive central city, Port Hills, and mountain views. **Pros:** central city valet parking in a clever car-stacker inside the building. **Cons:** some rooms are on the small side and corridors are narrow; at busy times there can be a long wait for the elevators. $ *Rooms from: NZ$179* ⊠ *166 Gloucester St.* ☎ *03/943–3888* ⊕ *www.tfehotels.com* ⤴ *171 rooms* ¶◯| *No meals* ⊹ *C4.*

$$
HOTEL
FAMILY

⛺ **Rydges Latimer Christchurch.** Set on leafy Latimer Square, this newly built low-rise hotel is just a few minutes' walk from the central city, but far enough away to be quiet and relaxed. **Pros:** free Wi-Fi throughout the hotel; plenty of free parking on-site. **Cons:** this is Christchurch's biggest conference hotel and often busy with large groups. $ *Rooms from: NZ$199* ⊠ *30 Latimer Sq.* ☎ *0800/176–176 NZ only* ⊕ *www.rydges.com* ⤴ *138 rooms* ¶◯| *No meals* ⊹ *D4.*

WEST OF CENTRAL CHRISTCHURCH

$$$
HOTEL
FAMILY

⛺ **Commodore Hotel Christchurch Airport.** Just minutes from the airport and 10 minutes from central Christchurch, this family-owned, resort-style accommodation includes a heated indoor pool, sauna, spa, fitness center, and tennis court. **Pros:** free 24-hour shuttle service to and from the airport; free Wi-Fi throughout the hotel. **Cons:** there can be big functions here, keeping the lobby and the car park full. $ *Rooms from: NZ$240* ⊠ *449 Memorial Ave.* ☎ *03/358–8129* ⊕ *www.commodorehotel.co.nz* ⤴ *157 rooms* ¶◯| *No meals* ⊹ *A1.*

$$$
RESORT
FAMILY

⛺ **Peppers Clearwater Resort.** This contemporary resort, on the outer edge of Christchurch city, is wrapped around several small lakes and a large golf course. **Pros:** on the right side of the city for day trips to Hanmer Springs, Mt. Hutt, and Kaikoura; close to the airport; tennis, walks, golf, and a driving range on-site. **Cons:** you'll need a car to make the most of your stay; no ground-floor accommodation. $ *Rooms from: NZ$257* ⊠ *Clearwater Ave., Harewood* ☎ *03/360–1000* ⊕ *www.peppers.co.nz/clearwater* ⤴ *26 rooms, 44 suites, 5 apartments* ¶◯| *No meals* ⊹ *A1.*

SOUTH OF CENTRAL CHRISTCHURCH

$$$$
HOTEL

⛺ **Otahuna Lodge.** Just 20 minutes from Christchurch and almost hidden by glorious century-old gardens is one of New Zealand's most important historic homes, now an award-winning luxury retreat. **Pros:** memorable five-course degustation dinner included; lots of fresh homegrown fruits and vegetables and cooking classes are available. **Cons:** not for the budget-minded; TV only available by request. $ *Rooms from: NZ$2000* ⊠ *224 Rhodes Rd., 17 km (10 miles) from Christchurch, Tai Tapu* ☎ *03/329–6333* ⊕ *www.otahuna.co.nz* ⤴ *7 suites* ¶◯| *Some meals* ⊹ *A5.*

NIGHTLIFE AND PERFORMING ARTS

The *Press* (New Zealand's oldest surviving metropolitan daily) is a reliable source on the city's arts and entertainment scenes. Friday's *Go Guide* lists events and venues for theaters, galleries, music, and more. Also check out the website Be There (⊕ *www.bethere.co.nz*) for arts and entertainment listings.

Buses only run until about 12:30 am; after that you'll have to rely on a taxi.

Ticketek. Tickets for many performance venues and concerts are sold through Ticketek. You can find Ticketek outlets in shopping malls or online. ☎ *0800/842–538 NZ only* ⊕ *www.ticketek.co.nz.*

NIGHTLIFE
BARS AND PUBS

Baretta Bar & Restaurant. Step into another world at this most Italian of nightspots, but it's good Kiwi live music you'll hear in the evening or on a Sunday afternoon. With its fabulous turquoise walls and ornate, carved wooden bar, first impressions are of Milan. Second impressions are that these people know their Italian food. A great place to go for lunch and dinner or tasty pizza and then stay on as it starts to rock as a bar. There's a big piazza-style courtyard and another bar out the back, complete with heaters to warm the evening chill. Later on the live entertainment changes from acoustic duos to DJs and a separate dance floor. ✉ *174 St. Asaph St.* ☎ *03/260–2600* ⊕ *www.baretta.co.nz.*

Boo Radley's Food and Liquor. Hip music and top-notch craft beers go nicely together in this cozy Southern-style bar. Add great food and a heady cocktail list for a memorable night out. From the chefs at Tequila Mockingbird downstairs, enjoy substantial Cajun and creole Southern-style bar snacks. Favorites are the bourbon-and-coke-glazed ribs, and maple and moonshine salmon sliders with house-made pretzel buns. Don't expect to talk too much when the live music starts, it can get pretty loud in there. Open-mike comedy nights are fun, too. ✉ *Level 1, 98 Victoria St.* ☎ *03/366–9906* ⊕ *www.booradleys.co.nz.*

Engineers Bar. This rooftop bar in a revamped 1920s building really comes alive after dark when the DJ starts spinning. There's a great selection of cocktails and beers to go well with big sharing platters, making it a fun place to party. ✉ *178 St. Asaph St.* ☎ *03/365–7893* ⊕ *www.engineersbar.co.nz.*

The Last Word. Time for a wee dram anyone? Far from being a den for older male whisky drinkers, The Last Word is, just as its name suggests, the ultimate place to go if you are an up and-coming, discerning drinker looking for something different. And Christchurch's character-filled heritage row, New Regent Street, is the perfect location for this intimate whisky-and-cocktail lounge. There are close to 300 bottles to try from an extensive whisky library. There are some excellent local wines and beers on the menu, too. ✉ *Christchurch* ☎ *03/928–2381* ⊕ *www.lastword.co.nz.*

Mashina. The Russian contemporary "machine" theme is carried through this nightclub in its artwork and vodka selection (from 19 different countries). Don't worry, there are plenty of boutique beers to choose from, too. Live bands generally kick off the evening followed by a DJ; there's no excuse not to hit the large dance floor, but there are comfy leather couches that beckon. It's worth keeping an eye on their Facebook page and website for theme nights and there's usually no cover charge. It's a venue with a strict "no casual streetwear" dress code and you must be at least 20 years old. ■TIP→ Don't try to get to this nightclub through the casino. Its entrance is on Peterborough Street at the back of the casino. For some reason it doesn't have its own official address. ⊠ *30 Victoria St.* ☎ *03/365–9999* ⊕ *www.mashinalounge.co.nz* ⊗ *Closed Mon. and Tues.*

Revival Bar. Get yourself a bit of street cred and head out to Revival Bar. This is where it's cool to be seen, with funky DJs and quirky surrounds. From the street it's not immediately inviting, but follow the music and give it a chance. Built out of containers and using reclaimed material from the earthquake, there's plenty for the eye to feast on if the conversation's not doing it for you, with funky car-seat chairs and tables made from old blenders. A hydraulic roof ensures that good weather can quickly be brought in, and there's a custom-made fire table to keep the cold at bay—that's if you don't dance enough. ⊠ *92–96 Victoria St.* ☎ *03/379–9559* ⊕ *www.revivalbar.co.nz.*

Strange and Co. Join the throngs heading for the cocktails and live music in this architecturally stunning building set in a quirky laneway. Ask for one of their Strange Creations and you might receive a creative mix of flavors, with hints of chili, flowers, and fruits served in a jar. Soak it up with a honey-buttered toasted sandwich, poutine fries, or a tasty piece of BBQ salmon. Check their website or Facebook page for upcoming events. ⊠ *89 Lichfield St.* ☎ *03/365–7018* ⊕ *www.strangeand.co.*

CASINO

Christchurch Casino. When all else has closed, make your way to the Christchurch Casino for blackjack, American roulette, baccarat, and gaming machines. Open 24 hours over the weekend and until 3 am Monday to Thursday, there are four restaurant and bar areas. Places to dine and relax in the casino are The Grand Cafe, Chi Kitchen, Mashina, and the Monza Sports Bar. The latter has TV monitors at every vantage point plus one huge screen for watching live sports. The casino is strict on its dress code. If you're unsure check their website for details, and wear smart shoes. ■TIP→ Free shuttles go to and from some local hotels and motels daily from 6 pm to 2 am—book through the casino reception. ⊠ *30 Victoria St.* ☎ *03/365–9999* ⊕ *www.chchcasino.co.nz.*

PERFORMING ARTS

Christchurch has a strong arts scene, with orchestras, choirs, and theaters. A thriving Arts Precinct is key to the central city redevelopment, and part of this includes the new The Piano: Centre for the Music and Arts, home to the Christchurch Symphony Orchestra. Nearby, the Isaac Theatre Royal has been restored to its former glory, adding a grand venue for performances and film. Christchurch Town Hall is under way with a major restoration project and is set to reopen in 2018. Another mainstay of the arts scene is The Court Theatre, which has relocated to

Bernard Street in Addington. The professional theater company is well respected for productions that range from Shakespeare to musicals and comedies. Check the newspapers and websites for details.

Christchurch Arts Festival. In odd-numbered years (e.g., 2017) the city hosts a late-winter, monthlong Arts Festival, featuring everything from dance and theater to comedy, visual art, and cabaret. ⊕ *www. artsfestival.co.nz.*

SCAPE Public Art. SCAPE public art installs free-to-view contemporary art all year round in Christchurch city, with a focus on its biennial festivals on odd years (e.g., 2017) between September and November. The works are urban and alternative arts such as conceptual architecture, sculpture, and city murals. Check website for details. ⊕ *www. scapepublicart.org.nz.*

ART GALLERIES

Although the Christchurch Art Gallery Te Puna O Waiwhetu is the city's visual arts mother ship, there are many smaller galleries and plenty of street art to check out. For more information, check the Canterbury Art Trails website.

FILMS

Academy Gold Cinema. This luxury art house film center consists of a modern three-screen complex at The Colombo in Sydenham. Relax in their comfy seats and enjoy a glass of wine and delicious nibbles, including world-beating ginger crunch. There's easy parking. Check their website or call their information line for details. Rodney's Cheap Tuesdays are great value, and you can also reserve tickets for showings of NT Live Theatre and Met Opera. ⊠ *363 Colombo St., The Colombo* ☎ *03/377–9911* ⊕ *www.artfilms.co.nz* ▧ *NZ$16.*

Alice Cinematique. This boutique, luxury 38-seat art house cinema specializes in bringing rare, niche movies to the city center. Set in the restored High Street Post Office building it shares with the C1 Espresso, you can also hop next door for excellent drinks and snacks. ☎ *03/365–0615* ⊕ *cinematheque.aliceinvideoland.co.nz.*

MUSIC

Christchurch Town Hall. The Christchurch Town Hall is undergoing a NZ$127.5 million restoration after being damaged in the earthquakes and will reopen in 2018. The 2,500-seat auditorium is recognized as one of finest concert halls in the world. ⊠ *86 Kilmore St.*

Christchurch City Choir. This acclaimed choir of 100 singers regularly performs with the Christchurch Symphony Orchestra. The Christchurch Town Hall used to be where you'd hear them but since the earthquakes they perform at venues around the city, including the Transitional Cardboard Cathedral and the Air Force Museum. Check their website for upcoming performances. ⊕ *www.christchurchcitychoir.co.nz.*

Christchurch Symphony Orchestra. Christchurch Symphony Orchestra has been a Christchurch institution for more than 50 years. Left without a permanent base for five years, it is soon to move to a new home in the city's Piano: Centre for Music and the Arts. Check their website for upcoming concerts. If you're here in October, the Last Night of the Proms is a night to remember. ☎ *03/943–7797* ⊕ *www.cso.co.nz*.

SummerTimes Festival. If you're here in summer, be sure to check out the SummerTimes Festival, which includes several free concerts in Hagley Park. The festival kicks off with a New Year's Eve party and includes a spectacular orchestra concert punctuated with fireworks, usually held in late February or early March. ⊕ *www.summertimes.co.nz*.

THEATER

Court Theatre. Christchurch is proud of its strong and loyal theater following and the first thing to be rebuilt after the earthquakes was the Court Theatre. It's now in a temporary home in Addington, in an old granary with ample parking. The South Island's leading theater company perform everything from Shakespeare to contemporary plays by New Zealand playwrights. The Court Jesters run the ever-popular Scared Scriptless improv-comedy sessions on Friday and Saturday nights—now New Zealand's longest-running comedy show. Check their website to see what's on. ⊠ *Bernard St.* ☎ *03/963–0870* ⊕ *www. courttheatre.org.nz*.

Fodor's Choice **Isaac Theatre Royal.** The grand lady of Christchurch's theater scene, dat-
★ ing back to 1908, has returned with a magnificent face-lift. This opulent setting, complete with an intricate painted ceiling dome and marble staircase, hosts some of New Zealand's best touring shows including ballet and music. It is also home to a giant screen for the New Zealand International Film Festival, held every July. Get dressed up and enjoy the glamour of a bygone era, in the comfort of today's plushest seating. There are stylish bars on every level for a drink before the show or during the interval. ⊠ *145 Gloucester St.* ☎ *03/366–6326* ⊕ *www. isaactheatreroyal.co.nz*.

SHOPPING

The shopping scene in Christchurch is changing fast, and what you find will depend on how soon you get here. Re:START mall, the colorful container village of designer shops and eateries, caught everyone's imagination. In late 2016 it will be replaced by a set of glittering new retail spaces along Cashel Street including The Crossing, home to top New Zealand and international fashion and concept stores. Next door, Ballantynes has been a magnet for discerning shoppers since it was established in 1854 as New Zealand's first department store, and is still rated as its best. For a reliable mall that has most of what you'll need, the Westfield Riccarton mall is the South Island's biggest, but has little character. The Tannery boutique shopping emporium out at Woolston is a new Victorian-style shopping arcade and has some great places to eat. Victoria Street and Merivale are also good options for women's fashion and homewares. The city's large open-air craft market will reopen soon at the Arts Centre. For organic produce, flowers, coffee, and free music, Christchurch Farmers' Market at Riccarton House is one of New Zealand's most popular every Saturday morning, and there's a farmers' market at The Commons every Sunday morning, on the corner of Kilmore and Durham streets.

SHOPPING STREETS AND AREAS

Fodor's Choice
★

Ballantynes. Ballantynes is an institution in the South Island. Far from allowing its traditions to slow it down, it has morphed into a world-class shopping experience with some of the best New Zealand and international designer brand names all under one roof. Allow plenty of time to browse the racks and shelves, where you will find everything from the latest trends in designer concept stores to New Zealand gifts and wine, and the very best crystal and china. When you need a break there are three top cafés to choose from with tasty homemade fare, and a hair and beauty salon for pampering, too. They also have a store at Christchurch International Airport, where you can pick up your purchases and take advantage of tax-exempt shopping. ✉ *Cashel St.* ☎ *03/379–7400* ⊕ *www.ballantynes.co.nz.*

The Colombo. A new take on a neighborhood mall, this haven for food and fashion fans includes a stylish mix of designer clothes, eats, and gifts. Don't miss a sweet treat at J'aime les macarons. Their patisserie also includes divine eclairs, truffles, and tarts. Inside the main mall, The Colombo Emporium is a European concept store, featuring antiques, homewares, and another eatery. And other shops to spend time browsing include Bolt of Cloth for homewares, Annah Stretton for designer frocks, and the Beer Library, the largest craft beer retail outlet in the region. It's located just outside the central city, in Sydenham, and there's plenty of parking. ✉ *363 Colombo St.* ☎ *03/365–5091* ⊕ *www.thecolombo.co.nz.*

Merivale Mall. North of the city center, Merivale Mall has a range of classy boutiques and stores. Try Quinns for women's clothing and Bella Silver for jewelry; Copper and Pink for edgy homeware pieces, Rouche features big-name New Zealand designers, Robyn Pierre has beautiful shoes and handbags, and well-known fashion names Storm, Witchery, Kimberleys, and Max are all here, too. Outside on Papanui Road and surrounding streets the design stores and restaurants continue. You can also pick up a delicious takeaway meal and a bottle of wine from Traiteur (on the corner of Aikmans Road). You can also buy chopping boards here, an interesting souvenir of the city, crafted from wood from homes demolished in the earthquakes. ✉ *187 Papanui Rd.*

Re:START City Mall. It was only ever meant to be a temporary solution but this quirky shopping precinct with its colorful funky look has been kept in place for just a bit longer, because it's just so cute. It is set to close by January 2017 to make way for new shopping precincts now being built nearby. Made from shipping containers, there are more than 40 shops here, anchored by Ballantynes, one of the country's better-known department stores. There are trendy fashion boutiques and great cafés, and there's free Wi-Fi. ✉ *120 Cashel St., City Mall.*

The Tannery. It is one of those unlikely projects that would probably never have got off the ground in Christchurch before the earthquakes: turning an old former industrial tannery into a Victorian shopping mall. Not only that but the developer had each brick removed, cleaned, and put back, once the buildings were reinforced. The Tannery's now an interesting place to head, with quirky shops, fashion, and a fabulous

9

cake shop and deli. Try Mitchelli's Cafe Rinato for tasty food in a friendly atmosphere, Cassells &Sons Brewery for their boutique beers and superb wood-fired pizza. Gustav's Kitchen and Wine Bar has a great reputation, too. ⊠ *3 Garlands Rd.* ⊕ *www.thetannery.co.nz.*

Victoria Street. Victoria Street's new designer buildings are home to some of the city's best restaurants and cafés, and you will find a mix of clothing and small, eclectic designer shops here, too. Frogmore is a fabulous little store filled with jewelry, glass, fabrics, and lace; Redcurrent is a more contemporary take on the same selection, wonderful for gifts. Jane Daniels and Lynn Woods have contemporary urban fashion, and Zebrano's caters to larger sizes. Try Blax and Procope for great coffee, ⊠ *Victoria St., between Bealey Ave. and Kilmore St.*

SPECIALTY STORES

de Spa Chocolatier's. The delicious sweets at de Spa Chocolatier's pair Belgian chocolate with Kiwi ingredients and fruit fillings (among other delectable things). There's a small shop in Merivale Boutique, 121 Papanui Road. Their factory's on the way to Ferrymead Heritage Park and Sumner. Here you can watch the chocolatiers at work through a glass-walled kitchen, and they conduct factory tours. They also make a special line of sugar-free chocolate. ⊠ *121 Papanui Rd., Merivale Boutique, Merivale* ☎ *03/356–2203* ⊕ *www.despa.co.nz* ⊗ *Weekdays 9–4, Sat. 10–3. Closed Sun.*

Kathmandu. Kathmandu sells a colorful range of outdoor clothing, backpacks, accessories, and tents. This chain is found throughout New Zealand and has particularly good reductions at sale times. It has several stores throughout the city and a clearance outlet at 124 Riccarton Road. ⊠ *124 Riccarton Rd.* ☎ *03/343–4634* ⊕ *www.kathmandu.co.nz.*

Macpac. Macpac also sells good-quality outdoor (and merino) clothing, backpacks, accessories, sleeping bags, and tents. This store is now across New Zealand but it was founded in Christchurch in 1973. It also has good reductions at sale times, but if you're not here at the right time you can hunt for a bargain in its biggest clearance area—upstairs at Tower Junction off Mandeville Street, Riccarton. ⊠ *Tower Junction, Blenheim Rd.* ☎ *03/371–9342* ⊕ *www.macpac.co.nz.*

Scorpio Bookshop. This independent bookstore started in the early 1970s and has gathered a cult following over the years. The shop stocks a wide range of fiction, cooking, and history books as well as design studies, philosophy tomes, and travelogues. Scorpio has two stores, one in Cashel Street and a larger one on Riccarton Road. ⊠ *113 Riccarton Rd.* ☎ *03/379–2882, 0800/726–774* ⊕ *www.scorpiobooks.co.nz.*

Untouched World. All things hip and natural in New Zealand converge here. Although some outdoor labels appeal more to the backpacker end of the market, Untouched World has much more of a designer edge. Their stylish lifestyle clothing is easy on the Earth, too, with signature fabrics including Ecopossum (a mixture of possum fur and merino wool), organic cotton, and Mountainsilk—silky-fine machine-washable organic merino. The attached licensed café serves fresh food, organic where possible, in its native garden environment. Snowy Peak is its outlet store and it's just next door. ⊠ *155 Roydvale Ave., Burnside* ☎ *03/357–9399.*

SPORTS AND THE OUTDOORS

BALLOONING

Fodor's Choice
★

Ballooning Canterbury. Here's an activity worth getting up early for. Ballooning Canterbury picks you up from most central city places and takes you to Darfield, where you help set up the mighty balloon. Then you're away, floating above river gorges, the Canterbury Plains, and the foothills of the Southern Alps. You may see as far south as Aoraki/Mt. Cook, north up to the Kaikouras, and the ocean all the way down the coast to Timaru—much of the South Island in just an hour's flight. A glass of bubbly is the perfect finish. It's very weather dependent so don't leave it to the last minute to organize. Must be at least 4½ feet tall to ride. ⊠ *2136 Bealey Rd., Darfield* ☎ *03/318–0860* ⊕ *www. ballooningcanterbury.com* ⊠ *NZ$365 per person.*

BICYCLING

Christchurch's relative flatness makes for easy biking, and the city has cultivated good resources for cyclists. White lines, and sometimes red-color tarmac, denote cycling lanes on city streets, and holding bays are at the ready near intersections. A particularly nice paved pedestrian and cycling path is along the Avon running from the Bridge of Remembrance. Other popular cycle trails include the Rail Trail at Little River and the spectacular trails around the Port Hills.

You can pick up a route map from the city council or visit their transport website, which shows cycle lanes and mountain-bike routes and provides up-to-date information on roadworks. (⊕ *www. transportforchristchurch.govt.nz/cycling-2*).

City Cycle Hire. City Cycle Hire has mountain, touring, and tandem bikes. Rentals include helmets, locks, and cycle map; and they'll deliver your bike to your accommodation. ⊠ *132 Wrights Rd., Riccarton* ☎ *03/377–5952, 0800/424–534 NZ only* ⊕ *www.cyclehire-tours.co.nz* ⊠ *NZ$25 for a ½ day and NZ$35 for a full day.*

Cyclone Cycles. Cycles can be rented from Cyclone Cycles for a flat fee of NZ$45 per hire bike. Special rates are available for groups or longer periods. Book online. Closed Sunday. ⊠ *245 Colombo St.* ☎ *03/332–9588* ⊕ *www.cyclone.net.nz.*

Mountain Bike Adventure Company. The Mountain Bike Adventure Company offers a NZ$70 package including a ride up on the Christchurch Gondola to the summit station. Then there's the choice of either an off-road mountain-bike trail or a scenic-road route down to the beach and back to the Gondola base—cycle distance is approximately 16 km (10 miles). ☎ *03/377–5952, 0800/424–534 NZ only* ⊕ *www.cyclehire-tours.co.nz.*

BOATING

Punting on the Avon. Sit back and enjoy the changing face of the central city from water level, framed by weeping willows, tranquil parks, and ornate bridges. Replicating English punting at Oxford and Cambridge, the boat tours leave from the **Antigua Boat Sheds**, near the hospital, or the Worcester Street Bridge daily from 9 to 6 in summer and from 10 to 4 the rest of

9

the year. A 30-minute trip costs NZ$25. Call ahead to book a time. ✉ 2 *Cambridge Terr.* ☎ *03/366–0337* ⊕ *www.welcomeaboard.co.nz/punting.*

GOLF

Clearwater Golf Club. The 18-hole championship golf course at the Clearwater Golf Club was built on the old Waimakariri riverbed near Christchurch Airport. It's currently home to the ISPS Handa NZ Women's Open and is playable year-round and offers a choice of six tee positions. Rental equipment is on hand. The **Peppers Clearwater Resort** provides quality on-course accommodation. ✉ *Clearwater Ave., Harewood* ☎ *03/360–2146* ⊕ *www.clearwatergolf.co.nz* 🖅 *NZ$175; NZ$95 for resort guests.*

Terrace Downs. With extensive views of Mt. Hutt and Rakaia Gorge, the 18-hole championship course at Terrace Downs has to be one of the most scenic courses in the South Island. You can rent equipment, and you can even book a villa for the night. The luxurious suites and chalets overlook the golf course and the mighty Southern Alps. ✉ *Coleridge Rd.* ☎ *03/318–6943* ⊕ *www.terracedowns.co.nz* 🖅 *From NZ$110 per person.*

HIKING

Godley Head–Taylors Mistake Walkway. To reach this scenic track take the coast road through Sumner then take a left turn at the summit intersection. The road climbs and winds for several kilometers before breaking out above Lyttelton Harbour with startling views to the hills of Banks Peninsula. You'll see some of the World War II coastal defense battery built in 1939; rated one of the country's significant defense-heritage sites, but following the earthquakes, the gun emplacements are now fenced off. There's also a 1½-hour walking track from here back to Taylors Mistake near Sumner (although you'll need to arrange a pickup at the other end, or plan on a three-hour round-trip). The Godley Head lookout is particularly exciting in a strong southerly wind! ⊕ *www.doc. govt.nz/parks-and-recreation/tracks-and-walks.*

FAMILY **Port Hills Walks.** Christchurch's Port Hills are worth climbing for spectacular views of the city, the Southern Alps, and Banks Peninsula. This is the route the first settlers took when they arrived at the port of Lyttelton. Well-marked tracks include the Bridle Path, Rapaki Track, and the Bowenvale-Sugarloaf Circuit. ⊕ *www.christchurchnz.com/ walk-canterbury/christchurch/port-hills-walks.*

RUGBY

Canterbury fans are as rugby-mad as the rest of the country. In fact the first match ever played in New Zealand took place in 1862 in Cranmer Square, in central Christchurch. This is the home of the Crusaders, and the breeding ground for many famous All Blacks. Every Saturday in winter you can catch little All-Blacks-in-the-making playing games in Hagley Park and suburban parks.

AMI Stadium. Canterbury's professional rugby union team, the Crusaders, have won the most titles in the history of the Super Rugby competition, played between teams from South Africa, Australia, and NZ. So they're not a bad team to watch if you get the chance to cheer them

Continued on page 508

TAKING NEW ZEALAND HOME

By Debra A. Klein and Sue Courtney

You can't pack New Zealand's ocean breezes, pristine alpine pastures, rare birds, ubiquitous sheep, or quirky sense of humor, but you can take a bit of Kiwiana home in the form of colorful, practical, and often eco-friendly souvenirs.

"Kiwiana" refers to quirky items that celebrate New Zealand's identity: nature- and Māori-inspired prints on clothing; wood, shell, and stone products; and the cutest soft toys. The kiwibird appears on shirts and keychains and as plush toys. New Zealand's famous wool products are widely available, as are travel-friendly food items.

Major travel and tramping hubs like Christchurch, Auckland, Wellington, and Queenstown are retail havens with everything from boutiques to large souvenir shops. Outside the cities, look for roadside signs pointing to workshops and markets for local goods. Remem-ber that U.S. Customs and Border Patrol will confiscate plants, meats, fruits, and vegetables.

LAST-STOP SHOPPING

If you were too busy hiking to pick up souvenirs, never fear. Auckland International Airport's clothing, craft, and food shops (located both before and after security) are as good as those in town. Duty-free outlets have great selections of Kiwi-made lotions, soaps, and sweets all at prices that are comparable to those elsewhere in New Zealand.

Top: Paua, a native abalone with unique iridescent shell

NEW ZEALAND WOOL

New Zealand is the world's second-largest wool producer (after Australia). Fine pure-breed wool accounts for 5% of the market; high-country merino wool is the most sought after for fashion garments. Kiwi innovation has produced blended wool products that are usually practical, sometimes fashionable, and often eco-friendly.

Brush-tail possums, a non-native pest, threaten New Zealand's native flora and fauna. In 1991, the company Possumdown pioneered a method of weaving possum fur fibers with superfine merino wool. This resulted in a lighter, more durable yarn with a very soft, luxurious feel that provides more insulation and warmth. It also provided an economically advantageous method of pest control that has helped rejuvenate

Shearing at sheep show. Rotorua, North Island

the biological balance throughout the country. (Note that the WWF, Greenpeace New Zealand, and the New Zealand Forest and Bird organization support the culling of the possum and the sale of possum products.)

WOOL AND NATURAL PRODUCTS FOR . . .

...THE OUTDOORS PERSON

Swanndri (⊕ *www.swanndri.co.nz*) developed the now-iconic 100% wool, waterproof bush shirt in 1913, as well as the shearer's black, knee-length singlet made from coarse wool. Today Swanndri offers a range of clothing, footwear, and accessories. You'll still find the singlets, but they're more for fashion than function these days.

Hats, scarves, gloves, mittens, socks, and thermal underwear from natural wool and sheepskin products, as well as from merino-possum blends, are plentiful in sports shops throughout the country. The "baacode" that comes with **Icebreaker**'s (⊕ *www.icebreaker. com*) merino clothing allows customers to trace the wool in their outerwear back to the farm where it originated.

Hikers may be able to source their own wool too; just pick it off the fence lines in sheep farm country. Lanolin from natural wool soothes blistered toes and adds comfort while tramping.

Icebreaker wool wares

...THE FASHIONISTA

Some of the finest merino from the South Island high country becomes men's Italian designer suits. Wool and merino-possum blends can be found in boutiques and upmarket stores. Some jackets, sweaters, and cardigans even have luxurious possum fur trim. Away from the cities you'll find outlets where creative wool artists spin wool straight from the fleece for knitting, weaving, and making hand-felted products. Hand-knitted sweaters, cardigans, and beanies can provide an individual look, while a woven bag or a lacy merino shawl makes for an affordable fashion accessory. Beautiful gossamer-like scarves, made with felted merino wool and often embellished with silk, can be exquisite.

...THE COMFORT MAVEN

Wool and sheepskin products, such as sheepskin slippers, fleece-lined Ugg-style boots, 100% New Zealand wool leisure wear, wool underlays, and cozy wool blankets, sheepskin rugs, and fleece car seat covers have been comforting New Zealanders for generations.

Wool and sheep products are sold throughout New Zealand, particularly in tourist destinations, airports, and main city centers. The best stores will have a range of brands and will also

Newly shorn fleece

stock alpaca and other natural animal wool, fur, and skin products.

For babies you'll find hand-knitted lambswool hats, jackets, and booties. The well-known lightweight aircell baby blankets made from first-shear wool have an open weave that ensures circulation while retaining warmth and dissipating moisture. **Thermacell** is one of several brands; studies have shown that these types of blankets help the little ones get to sleep.

For extra-cuddly warmth on a chilly night, warm up with a possum fur hot water bottle cover. Lanolin creams extracted from merino wool will calm dry skin (⊕ *www. lanolin.co.nz*).

Merino Wool

TIPS FOR BUYING NEW ZEALAND WOOL PRODUCTS

Ensure that manufacturing was carried out in New Zealand. Look for labels that read "100% Pure New Zealand Merino," "Buy New Zealand," and "New Zealand Made."

You can spend as little as $NZ20 on lambswool gloves or socks, up to $500 for a lambskin trimmed jacket, or more than $1,000 for a full sheepskin jacket. Sheepskin rugs range from $NZ99 for a single fleece to $2,500 for a designer rug.

KIWIANA

Carry home a reminder of New Zealand's natural wonders, tastes, and culture with these great products.

FOR THE CRAFTY ONES

PUKEKO

The pukeko, or swamp hen, is a ubiquitous native bird, but it took artist Kevin Kilsby to turn the bright blue and red creature into an icon. His whimsical, decorative clay creations—with big red beaks, impossibly long, skinny legs, and gumboot-clad feet—come in several sizes and designs. The lovable design has inspired similar products from other artists, and there's even a plush version for the kids. Find the statuettes in souvenir shops all over, or go to the source: Kilsby has a shop in Auckland (⊕ www.kilsby.co.nz).

OTHER FEATHERED FRIENDS

During your travels you'll fall in love with other native birds such as the cheeky kea, the nectar-loving tui, the flitty piwakawaka (fantail), and the berry-loving kereru (wood pigeon). Bring home your favorite without causing an international incident at the airport by purchasing one of the soft toy versions sold at Department of Conservation and regional park information centers. If space is at a premium, look for Wild-Cards; when opened they play the distinctive song of the bird depicted on the card's front (⊕ www.wild-card.org).

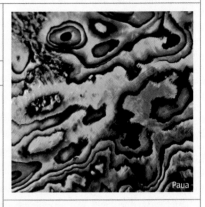
Paua

PAUA

Find the iridescent blue-gray paua (abalone) shell inlaid on wooden home wares or silver jewelry. You can even beachcomb to find slivers in the sand that wash ashore all over the country.

GREENSTONE

Local legend says that it's bad luck to buy jade (greenstone or *pounamu*) for yourself, so have a travel companion officially purchase greenstone for you. Māori tradition states you should wear jade for 24 hours before gifting it to infuse your spirit into the object. Take care to purchase authentic NZ pounamu, not the imported jade products.

CHILD'S PLAY

The brightly colored, wood-crafted **Buzzy Bee** toy has been delighting Kiwi toddlers since the 1940s. Check that you're buying an NZ-made one. Sports fans will delight in **All Blacks** uniforms, hats, and scarves from **Rebel Sport** stores throughout New Zealand. Buy online at the All Blacks Web site (⊕ www.allblackshop.com).

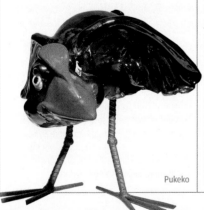
Pukeko

FOR SOME LOCAL FLAVOR

OLIVE OIL

More than 20 varieties of olive trees are available in New Zealand and olives are grown from Northland to Central Otago, but New Zealand's nascent olive oil industry varies widely in quality. The best olive oils have smooth, non-cloying texture and nutty, piquant, peppery flavors. Simunovich Olive Estate (south of Auckland), and Frog's End Estate (outside Nelson), have earned accolades for their extra, extra virgin presses.

CULINARY TREATS

Kinaki Wild Herbs (⊕ www.Maorifood.com) packages traditional Māori spices. Find *The Māori Cookbook*, written by Kinaki Wild Herbs founder and chef Charles Royal, at gourmet food stores and better supermarkets.

Seriously Good Chocolate Company (⊕ www.seriouslygoodchocolate.com) in Invercargill makes chocolates infused with New Zealand wine. At Mangawhai, on the North Island, you'll find **Bennetts of Mangawhai** (⊕ www.bennettsofmangawhai.com), which makes drool-inducing chocolate in traditional blocks.

You'll have to leave the great fruits behind, but consider taking home some feijoa or kiwi candy from **Remarkable Sweets** in Queenstown and Arrowtown (⊕ remarkablesweetshop.co.nz).

Chocolate making at Bennetts

HONEY

New Zealand honey is usually creamed, so it's thick, spreadable, and has a pearl-like sheen. You'll note subtle differences in taste but obvious differences in color of honey types. The lighter the color, the milder the taste. The rare, delicate Pohutukawa honey is sometimes white. Dark honeys, like manuka (prized for its medicinal qualities), are the most caramel-like.

Native flora honeys

FOR SOME PERSONAL PAMPERING

SKINCARE

Pacifica Skincare (⊕ www.pacificaskincare.co.nz) has a dazzling array of products made from native flowers, leaves, manuka honey, and flaxseed oil. Kowhai tree and pohutukawa essence products are popular. Wine fans will love the soaps made from the pulp of Chardonnay, Pinot Gris, or Pinot Noir. **Living Nature** (⊕ livingnature.com) in Kerikeri uses harakeke's (flax) natural gels in ointments, and Kumerahou plant in shampoos, soaps, and make-up remover.

on at their home turf. Their home turf is now a temporary stadium in Addington built in 100 days, after the original stadium was damaged beyond repair. The season goes from February through September. ⊠ *95 Jack Hinton Dr., Addington* ☎ *03/379–1765* ⊕ *crusaders.co.nz.*

EN ROUTE **Dunsandel Store.** If you've left Christchurch a bit late for breakfast, about 30 minutes south, stop at the Dunsandel Store. It's a fascinating mix of local store, deli, and café with excellent food. The cabinets are stuffed with tasty quiches, panini, and baked goods. They have a good range of breakfasts, and for an afternoon treat try the chocolate-and-almond cake with raspberries served with cream or yogurt. There are tables indoors and out, surrounded by a courtyard full of fruit trees and vegetables. ⊠ *3414 Main South Rd., Dunsandel* ☎ *03/325–4037* ⊕ *www. dunsandelstore.co.nz* ⊗ *Daily 7–5.*

ARTHUR'S PASS AND CANTERBURY

East of the city, you can explore the wonderful coastline of Banks Peninsula. The peninsula's two harbors, Lyttelton and Akaroa, were formed from the remnants of two ancient volcanoes; their steep grassy walls drop dramatically to the sea. Looking north, consider stopping in Waipara and its wineries if you're en route to or from Kaikoura or Hanmer Springs. Hanmer Springs' thermal baths are good for a relaxing soak, or you can ride the white water on the river, ski, or mountain bike. Head south or west of town into the Canterbury Plains countryside, and you can ski at Mt. Hutt (in winter) or drive the scenic inland highway to Geraldine and Timaru. Where once only sheep and cattle grazed, you're now just as likely to spot alpacas, deer, and ostriches. If you're heading to the West Coast by road or rail, then Arthur's Pass is worth investigating. You should set an entire day aside for any of these side trips, or, better still, stay overnight.

ARTHUR'S PASS NATIONAL PARK

153 km (96 miles) northwest of Christchurch.

Established in 1929, Arthur's Pass was the South Island's first national park. Follow in the footsteps of ancient Māori hunters, 1860s gold rushers, and 1990s road workers who constructed the 1,444-foot Otira Viaduct. Each of the many twists and turns reveals another photo op: waterfalls, fields of wildflowers, dizzying drops. And it's all easily accessible from Christchurch.

GETTING HERE AND AROUND

For any confident driver the road through Arthur's Pass is a glorious drive—sealed all the way, but with a few steep, gnarly sections in the middle. The train and bus tours are also good options, but you lose the flexibility to stop and do a walk or follow a waterfall track, or to just admire the breathtaking scenery if you're stuck on a tour.

To drive there from Christchurch head out on the West Coast Road—it is particularly well signposted from town. The turnoff is near the airport. There is only one road over the Alps within 100 km (62 miles)

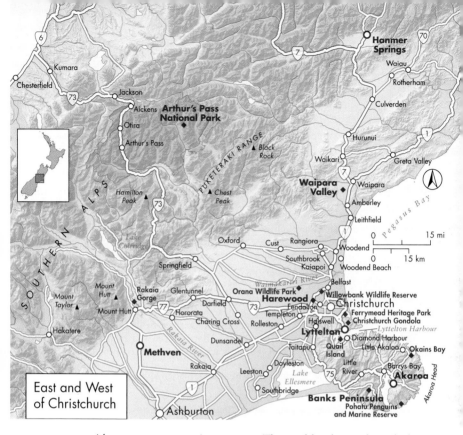

East and West of Christchurch

either way, so you can't go wrong. The road heads out through the small town of Springfield then heads up toward Porter's Pass and Cass before hitting the real stuff at Arthur's Pass.

Information on the park is available on the **Department of Conservation's** website and at the DOC-run **Arthur's Pass Visitor Center.** The **Arthur's Pass Mountaineering** site is another good source for information on local mountaineering conditions.

VISITOR INFORMATION

Contacts Arthur's Pass Mountaineering. ⊕ www.arthurspass.com. Department of Conservation Arthur's Pass Visitor Centre. ✉ State Hwy. 73, Arthur's Pass ☎ 03/318–9211 ⊕ www.doc.govt.nz.

EXPLORING

Arthur's Pass National Park. This spectacular alpine region is a favorite hiking destination. Initially hacked through as a direct route to the West Coast gold fields in 1865, the road over Arthur's Pass was a tortuous, dangerous track. It was frequently shut due to bad weather and slips. When the railway arrived, in 1923, the pass's skiing and hiking opportunities came to the fore, and the TranzAlpine train service now offers a supreme way to see this rugged area without getting your shoes dirty.

On the way to the pass, along State Highway 73 from Christchurch, you'll pass the **Castle Hill Conservation Area,** which is filled with interesting rock formations. The gray limestone rocks range in height from 3 to 164 feet and in spring and fall they're tackled by climbers keen to go bouldering. Nearby **Craigieburn Conservation Park** has wonderful beech and fern forests and some great mountain-biking trails—take the road leading to Broken River Ski Field. There's a campsite just half a mile up the road. Sheltered as they are by the Southern Alps, these parklands get far less precipitation than the western side of the mountains, which gets five times more rain than the eastern side. Still, the area is subject to some heavy snowfalls, so in winter carry chains and check the road conditions before you go. Above the tree line you'll find ski slopes and, between November and March, masses of wildflowers, including giant buttercups. Around the summit you'll also have a good chance of seeing *kea,* the South Island's particularly intelligent and curious mountain parrots.

Arthur's Pass Village, at 2,395 feet, is a true alpine village, so pack a jacket even in summer. A couple of restaurants and a store provide basic food supplies, and there are several places to stay, including an excellent wilderness lodge near Bealey. There's also a Department of Conservation visitor center to help with enjoying the vast selection of mountains and rivers in the area. Both the Devil's Punchbowl and Bridal Veil Falls are worth the short walk. The tracks are in good condition and, although they're a bit steep and rocky in places, no serious hiking experience is required. ☎ *0800/4–HIGHWAYS.*

WHERE TO EAT

$$$ NEW ZEALAND

🍴 **The Wobbly Kea Café and Bar.** This pleasant place is named for the cheeky mountain parrots that circle above it day after day. It's open from early in the morning until well into the evening—presuming people are around. The two most popular dishes are their bratwurst bangers and mash and the fresh beer-battered fish; both have people asking for more. They also have full breakfast and lunch menus and do pizza all day as well. [$] *Average main: NZ$24* ✉ *108 Main Rd., Arthur's Pass* ☎ *03/318–9101* 🌐 *www.wobblykea.co.nz.*

WHERE TO STAY

$$$$ B&B/INN Fodor's Choice ★

🏨 **Arthur's Pass Wilderness Lodge.** Surrounded by spectacular peaks, beech forests, and serene lakes, this sophisticated back-to-nature lodge shares 6,000 acres with its own high-country merino sheep station and nature reserve in a valley called Te Ko Awa a Aniwaniwa (Valley of the Mother of Rainbows). **Pros:** on alternate days, you can muster sheep with border collies and help blade-shear sheep the old-fashioned way. **Cons:** quite remote if you like shopping. [$] *Rooms from: NZ$749* ✉ *State Hwy. 73, Arthur's Pass* ☎ *03/318–9246* 🌐 *www.wildernesslodge.co.nz* 🕒 *Closed June and July* 🛏 *20 rooms, 4 suites* 🍽 *Some meals.*

$ B&B/INN

🏨 **Mountain House Arthur's Pass YHA.** This is the biggest spot in town with a main lodge that has private and shared rooms; two separate cottages, two motel units, and backpacker dorms in the old YHA lodge. **Pros:** a wing of newer facilities and private rooms is the pick for clean and tidy; YHA members get discounts and free Wi-Fi. **Cons:** the whole complex is spread over about a kilometer; no en suite bathrooms. $ *Rooms from: NZ$74* ⊠ *84 West Coast Rd., Arthur's Pass* ☎ *03/318–9258* ⊕ *www. trampers.co.nz* ↝ *12 double rooms, 2 cottages (4 bedrooms), 2 motel units, 11 share rooms* ⦿ *No meals.*

SPORTS AND THE OUTDOORS

HIKING AND WALKING

There are plenty of half- and full-day hikes and 10 backcountry trails with overnight huts for backpacking. A popular walk near Arthur's Pass Village is the short Punchbowl Falls Track, which passes through diverse subalpine forest to a 450-foott-high waterfall. It takes roughly one hour to do the track. For a full-day hike, trails leading to the summits of various mountains are all along State Highway 73. Be prepared for variable weather conditions. Two of the most popular and challenging overnight treks are the Cass/Lagoon Saddle trip and the Avalanche-Crow route over Avalanche Peak. For these, you'll need an experienced leader and full gear. The Department of Conservation Visitor Centre has up-to-date information on weather and trail conditions. Before you go into the outdoors, tell someone your plans and leave a date to raise the alarm if you haven't returned.

LYTTELTON

12 km (7½ miles) east of Christchurch.

Lyttelton, a sleepy port town, was the arrival point for many of the early Canterbury settlers. The Canterbury Pilgrims' landing place is marked by a rock near the road entrance to the port. A mix of renovated wooden villas and contemporary homes now rises halfway up what was once a volcanic crater. Today, though only 20 minutes' drive from Christchurch, Lyttelton has developed its own distinctive quality, attracting creative types who like the small-town character. Lyttelton was very badly hit by the earthquakes. The biggest loss, historically, was the Timeball Station where, in the days before GPS and atomic clocks, ships would make sure their chronometers were accurate by checking them when the large ball at the Timeball Station was lowered. There are some intriguing places to eat for all budgets; from Roots, which only offers a five- to eight-course degustation menu, to the superfriendly Port Hole Bar's burritos, to fish-and-chips. Saturday is a good day to come, with a farmers' market from 10 to 1, then sit and watch what's going on at this busy little shipping port. Governors Bay and farther round to Diamond Harbour makes a nice half-day drive from the city.

GETTING HERE AND AROUND

Lyttelton can be reached by driving down Ferry Road from Christchurch, heading toward Sumner, and then taking the road tunnel. Another scenic route is to follow the main street, Colombo, east out of the city, up the Port Hills, and over Dyers Pass to Governors Bay. Then turn left and head back along the harbor edge to Lyttelton. If you don't have a car, you can catch Bus 28 from Christchurch.

Lyttelton stretches along a terrace above the port. Norwich Quay runs along the waterfront, but the main street, London Street, runs parallel

Thematic Trails

Enterprising local tourist offices have sketched out thematically linked, self-guided sightseeing routes throughout the region. You can pick up maps at the Christchurch i-SITE Visitor Information Centre, or at visitor centers along the way. The following are the best of the bunch:

Alpine Pacific Triangle. This links three of the most popular getaways in Canterbury: Waipara, Hanmer Springs, and Kaikoura.

Selwyn Food and Wine Trail. Pick up a brochure from the i-SITE Visitor Center and follow the trail that starts 20 minutes west of the city to discover wineries, cheesemakers, farmers markets, and country stores.

Pioneer Trail. Connecting several historic sights between Timaru and Geraldine, this route includes the Richard Pearse Memorial, dedicated to a local aviation innovator.

Scenic Highway 72. Scenic Highway 72 runs from Amberley, north of Christchurch, along the foothills of the Southern Alps through two spectacular gorges, past Geraldine to Winchester. You can join up with it at various points along the way.

---

a block higher up the hill. London Street joins the road back over to Sumner, and in the other direction back past the tunnel entrance along Simeon Quay toward Governors Bay. Call the Lyttelton Harbor Information Center at 20 Oxford Street for maps and brochures.

VISITOR INFORMATION

Contacts Lyttelton Harbour Information Centre. ✉ *20 Oxford St.* ☎ *03/328– 9093* ⊕ *www.lytteltonharbour.info.*

EXPLORING

TOP ATTRACTIONS

Fodor's Choice   **Ohinetahi.** Sir Miles Warren is one of New Zealand's foremost architects
★   with a pedigree as large as his garden. Ohinetahi, which is also the Māori name for the area, features not only his large, stone, colonial villa, but also his immaculate garden—considered one of the best formal gardens in the country. Blending Sir Miles's eye for detail and design with a stunning situation this garden maximizes the use of "garden rooms"—the red room being particularly memorable—hedging, and color. ✉ *Governors Bay-Teddington Rd.* ☎ *03/329–9852* 💲 *NZ$15* ⊙ *Mid-Sept.–Mar. 30, weekdays 10–4; by appointment only on weekends.*

WORTH NOTING

Diamond Harbour. Diamond Harbour is the largest township on the far side of Lyttelton Harbour. You can drive to Diamond Harbour (around 40 minutes from Christchurch) or take a 10-minute journey on the Black Diamond ferry from Jetty B at Norwich Quay. Sailings are frequent. There's a small farmers' market once a fortnight over summer, some great walks, and the Charteris Bay Golf Club's beautiful. ✉ *"B" Jetty, 17 Norwich Quay* ☎ *03/328–9078, 0800/436–574* ⊕ *www.blackcat.co.nz* 💲 *NZ$12.40 return.*

Quail Island. Quail Island, in Lyttelton Harbour, was used by the early European settlers as a quarantine zone and leper colony and was named after the now-extinct native quail. It was once a significant area for collecting birds' eggs by local Māori. These days Quail Island, also known as Otamahua, is being restored as an ecological reserve, and is home to many native birds including kingfisher, fantail, *silvereye* (a small bird common in New Zealand), and various seabirds. The *Black Cat* ferry from Lyttelton can zip you out here for a hike or a picnic. ✉ *"B" Jetty, 17 Norwich Quay* ☎ *03/328–9078* 🌐 *www.blackcat.co.nz* 🎟 *NZ$30* 🕒 *Oct.–Apr., daily 10:20, return sailing at 3:30; Dec.–Feb., daily at 10:20 and 12:20, return at 12:30 or 3:30.*

Timeball Station. The New Zealand Historic Places Trust is committed to rebuilding the Timeball Station tower (but not a full rebuild of the station) in stages, over the next few years. This piece of maritime history was one of only five remaining timeball stations known to be in working order in the world, and it holds a special place in the hearts of Canterbury people. Built in the 1870s the ball would drop from its mast as a time signal for ships. The castle-like building was destroyed over the course of the 2010 earthquakes but much of the building was retrieved and stored so it's hoped the tower will be able to be rebuilt. ✉ *2 Reserve Terr.* 🌐 *www.historicplaces.org.nz.*

WHERE TO EAT

$$ TAPAS

🍴 **Civil and Naval.** This cozy haunt is packed with locals who come for tasty tapas-style food, produced in a tiny kitchen, and the excellent cocktails. Try the slow-cooked beef cheek, fried chicken, or cauliflower, and delectable hand-cut fries. There's an eclectic selection of international and New Zealand wines and craft beers. Or ask the owner to make you one of his own-recipe cocktails, like Pixy Stix, an anti-oxidant-laden fusion of black raspberry liqueur, blueberries, and cider vinegar. [$] *Average main: NZ$15* ✉ *16 London St.* ☎ *03/328–7206* 🌐 *www.civilandnaval.nz.*

$$$ NEW ZEALAND

🍴 **Governors Bay Hotel.** First granted a license in 1870, this historic old pub makes a great casual lunch or dinner stop if you're doing a round-trip from Christchurch through Lyttelton and back. Perched on a hill with fabulous views overlooking Lyttelton Harbour, it offers solid gastropub fare. There's a large sunny deck in summer and an open fire in winter. And you may stay the night in one of its recently renovated rooms; some have balconies overlooking the harbor, but none have en suite bathrooms. [$] *Average main: NZ$30* ✉ *52 Main Rd., Governors Bay* ☎ *03/329–9433* 🌐 *www.governorsbayhotel.co.nz.*

$$$$ MODERN NEW ZEALAND

Fodor's Choice ★

🍴 **Roots.** It's well worth making the journey to this award-winning haven for honest food, made from scratch by passionate people, using local organic and biodynamic ingredients. The philosophy here is all about bringing high-quality produce to the table, from the owners' garden, preserve cellar, and foraged nature. The degustation menu from the open kitchen includes seasonal specialities like blackfoot paua, Muscovy duck, wagyu beef, long-line caught fish, and guinea fowl. [$] *Average main: NZ$90* ✉ *8 London St.* ☎ *03/328–7658* 🌐 *www.rootsrestaurant.co.nz* 🖊 *Reservations essential.*

9

NIGHTLIFE

Wunderbar. Not your average bar, this Lyttelton institution prides itself on being different. Dolls' heads as lamp shades, a supersize Madonna, and 1950s newspapers on the bathroom walls give you an idea of the fun to be had here. There's live music just about every night. Pool and foosball tables will also keep you entertained. Great views out over Lyttelton port, too. ⊠ *19 London St.* ☎*03/328–8818* ⊕ *www.wunderbar.co.nz.*

SPORTS AND THE OUTDOORS

HIKING

Bridle Path. Quail Island is a good option, but if you'd rather stay on the mainland, you could instead follow in the trail of the early settlers by taking the Bridle Path. The steep zigzag track goes from Cunningham Street up to the crater rim. You can walk to the Gondola Summit Station, a few minutes' farther, to see the Canterbury Plains from the site of the memorial to the pioneer women, or walk down the rest of the trail to finish near the Christchurch Gondola base station. A No. 28 bus will take you to Lyttelton, and the same bus will pick you up on the other side. Allow 1½ hours for the walk—some of which is quite steep. ⊠ *Bridal Path at Cunningham Terr.*

AKAROA AND THE BANKS PENINSULA

82 km (50 miles) east of Christchurch.

Sheep graze almost to the water's edge in the many small bays indenting the coastline of Banks Peninsula, the nub that juts into the Pacific east of Christchurch. On the southern side of the peninsula, in a harbor created when the crater wall of an extinct volcano collapsed into the sea, nestles the fishing village of Akaroa (Māori for "long harbor"). The port is a favorite day trip for Christchurch residents on Sunday drives, and on weekends and over the summer holidays (December to February) it can be extremely busy. If you're planning to stay the night during the busy times (summer and weekends), book a room and dinner before you leave Christchurch.

Although Akaroa was chosen as the site for a French colony in 1838, the first French settlers arrived in 1840 only to find that the British had already established sovereignty over New Zealand by the Treaty of Waitangi. Less than 10 years later, the French abandoned their attempt at colonization, but the settlers remained and gradually intermarried with the local English community. Apart from the *rue* (street) names, a few family surnames, and architectural touches, there is little sign of a French connection anymore, but the village has splendid surroundings. A day trip from Christchurch will get you to and from Akaroa, including a drive along the Summit Road on the edge of the former volcanic dome, but take an overnight trip if you want to explore the peninsula bays as well as the town. It's an easy drive most of the way but the last hill over to Akaroa is narrow and winding with few passing areas. By the time you've taken a harbor cruise, driven around a few bays, and stopped for a meal, you'll be right in the mood to kick back overnight in this quiet spot.

9

GETTING HERE AND AROUND

The main route to Akaroa is State Highway 75, which leaves the southwest corner of Christchurch as Lincoln Road. The 82-km (50-mile) drive takes about 90 minutes. You can also head out through Lyttelton and Teddington, then over the hill to Little River for a really scenic but slightly longer trip.

If you'd rather not drive, the Akaroa Shuttle has a daily service between Christchurch and Akaroa from October to April for NZ$50 per person return, or NZ$35 one-way. Direct shuttles run from Rolleston Avenue in Christchurch and from outside the Akaroa Adventure Centre, and there is also a free pickup service from central city hotels.

Bus Companies Akaroa Shuttle. ☎ *0800/500–929 NZ only* ⊕ *www.akaroashuttle.co.nz.*

TOURS

One of the best ways to get to know Akaroa is to interact with the locals, and those quirky, innovative Kiwis have come up with a clever way to help you do that: delivering the mail. You'll get to see beautiful scenery, go off-the-beaten-path, and meet the folks who live and work in remote areas.

Eastern Bays Scenic Mail Run. To see nearly a dozen hideaway bays, sign up to ride with the mailman while he delivers the rural mail on the remote Eastern Bays Scenic Mail Run. This highly scenic trip covers the more remote areas and starts from Akaroa at 9 am, finishing its circuit around 2 pm. The van stops for a tasty, homemade morning tea by the beach. Reservations are essential, and it's not suitable for young children. Make reservations through the **Akaroa Adventure Centre** (tours leave from here, too). ⊠ *74a Rue Lavaud, Akaroa* ☎ *03/304–7784* ⊕ *www.akaroa.com* ☜ *NZ$70* ☽ *Weekdays.*

VISITOR INFORMATION

Contacts Akaroa Adventure Centre. ⊠ *74a Rue Lavaud, Akaroa* ☎ *03/304–7784* ⊕ *www.akaroa.com.*

EXPLORING

TOP ATTRACTIONS

Okains Bay. The contrast of the rim of the old volcanic cone and the coves below is striking—and when you drop into one of the coves, you'll probably feel like you've found your own little corner of the world. One of the easiest bays to access is Okains Bay. Take the Summit Road at Hilltop if approaching from Christchurch, or Ngaio Point Road behind Duvauchelle if approaching from Akaroa. It's about 24 km (15 miles) from Akaroa and takes about a half hour to drive. The small settlement lies at the bottom of Okains Bay Road, which ends at a beach sheltered by tall headlands. ⊠ *Okains Bay, Akaroa.*

WORTH NOTING

Akaroa Walks. Take the village walk, where you amble along the narrow streets past old-fashioned little cottages and historic buildings that reflect the area's multicultural background. If you are feeling more ambitious try the country walks on routes ranging from two hours to all day. For hikers, there are also 20 km (12.5 miles) of well-mapped tracks from summit to sea level. Start at the Akaroa Adventure Centre and choose from a range of free brochures and maps to enhance your experience. ⊠ *74a Rue Lavaud, Akaroa* ⊕ *www.akaroa.com/maps/ walking-tracks/peninsula.*

Akaroa Museum. The focus of historic interest is the Akaroa Museum, which has a display of Māori *pounamu* (greenstone) as well as alternating exhibits on the area's multicultural past. The peninsula supported a significant Māori population and the collections and displays tell some of the exciting stories of Kai Tahu, the people of the land. The building is being strengthened for earthquakes but the museum is still open. The Old Courthouse and Langlois-Eteveneaux House, the two-room cottage of an early French settler, are also part of the museum. ⊠ *Rue Lavaud at Rue Balguerie, Akaroa* ☎ *03/304–1013* ☞ *Free* ⊘ *Daily 10:30–4:30; closes at 4 in winter.*

Okains Bay Māori and Colonial Museum. This collection of buildings contains 20,000 Māori and 19th-century colonial artifacts, including *waka* (canoes) used in Waitangi Day celebrations and displays such as a smithy and print shop. There are also a *wharenui* (Māori meeting-house), colonial homes, including a *totara* slab cottage, and a saddlery and harness shop. If you happen to be in the area on Waitangi day (February 6), New Zealand's national day, the museum marks it in style. ⊠ *1146 Okains Bay Rd., Okains Bay* ☎ *03/304–8611* ⊕ *www. okainsbaymuseum.co.nz* ☞ *NZ$10* ⊘ *Daily 10–5.*

SCENIC TOUR

State Highway 75. State Highway 75 leads from Christchurch out onto the peninsula, curving along the southern portion past Lake Ellesmere. There are interesting stops on your way out to Akaroa. The small town of **Little River** used to be the end of the line for a now-defunct railway line from Christchurch; the route is now a walkway and bicycle trail. The old, wooden train station houses a crafts gallery and information office, and a café is next door in the grocery store. Look out for Silo Stay, where grain silos have been cleverly transformed into eco-accommodation units called Silococoons. When you reach **Hilltop,** pause for your first glimpse of Akaroa Harbour; on a sunny day it's magnificent. (At Hilltop the highway crosses the Summit Road, the other major route through the peninsula.) ⊠ *State Hwy. 75, Christchurch.*

Barry's Bay Cheese Factory. And if you're hungry after the drive over the hill, swing by Barry's Bay Cheese Factory and taste the local product, one of Akaroa's earliest exports; they've been making cheese since 1895. It's only made every second day and if you're there before about 2 in the cheese making season (October–May), you can watch the day's cheese

FRENCH FEST AKAROA

In recognition of how close this tiny town came to being the seat of a French government in New Zealand, a French Festival is held in early October every second year with a street party, fireworks, cabaret shows, local food, wine, and family entertainment—all themed "le Français."

being manufactured. They also sell local wines, preserves, honeys, and gifts. ✉ *5807 Christchurch Akaroa Rd., Akaroa* ☎ *03/304–5809* 🌐 *www.barrysbaycheese.co.nz* 🕒 *Daily 9–5.*

NEED A BREAK?

Little River Cafe & Store. What a buzz this place is—walk in and inhale deeply. It's a busy spot in mid-summer but otherwise is well worth the stop. The food is all handmade and delicious—pizzas, soup, samosa, chunky pies—and their coffee is excellent. There are also tasty treats to take away like the local honey, jams, aioli, or cakes. You can eat indoors or out, before wandering into the art gallery on one side or the general store and craft shop on the other. The date and citrus scones are delicious. ✉ *Main Rd., Little River* ☎ *03/325–1933* 🕒 *No dinner.*

WHERE TO EAT

$ CAFÉNEW ZEALAND

🍴 **Akaroa Fish and Chips.** Acclaimed around the country as having some of the best fish-and-chips available, this take-out–style eatery often has queues out the door. Buy deep-fried fish, served with a big side of perfectly cooked chips and a big chunk of lemon, and eat them out of the paper at one of the outdoor tables. You'll never want to eat fish-and-chips with a knife and fork again. But watch the seagulls, who also seem to like fish-and-chips—a lot. [$] *Average main: NZ$12* ✉ *59 Beach Rd., Akaroa* ☎ *03/304–7464.*

$$$$ NEW ZEALAND

🍴 **Bully Hayes Restaurant & Bar.** Named after a notorious American pirate, this modern restaurant occupies a great site. Dining is casual, either indoors or out, overlooking the yachts moored in the harbor. New Zealand cuisine is highlighted and there are light and full-size main courses. Options include seafood, lamb, venison, and a variety of beef cuts. Open for breakfast, lunch, and dinner, all year. [$] *Average main: NZ$35* ✉ *57 Beach Rd., Akaroa* ☎ *03/304–7533* 🌐 *www.bullyhayes.co.nz.*

$$$$ BISTRO

🍴 **The Little Bistro.** This is contemporary bistro style with a unique New Zealand twist set in a gorgeous seaside cottage. Be prepared for delicious seasonal produce and beautifully balanced dishes matched with a top wine list. Favorites include pumpkin and blue cheese risotto, braised short rib beef with truffle and bone marrow pudding in a red wine jus and, of course, the freshest catch of the day. If you can squeeze it in, desserts like the chocolate tart with beetroot meringue are very tempting. [$] *Average main: NZ$37* ✉ *33a Rue Lavaud, Christchurch* ☎ *03/304–7314* 🌐 *www.thelittlebistro.co.nz.*

$$$$ NEW ZEALAND

🍴 **The Trading Rooms Restaurant & Bar.** European spins on local produce, meat, and seafood, along with a seaside location, make for sought-after reservations here. Dark wooden floors, white tablecloths, and leather chairs lend a seaside chic quality and on a nice day you can sit outside. Seafood is the highlight, with Akaroa salmon and local grouper featuring, along with Banks Peninsula lamb and a duo of beef. Lunch is all about the sea with a salmon tasting plate, a seafood platter for two, and mussels marinière. Reservations essential for dinner. [$] *Average main: NZ$39* ✉ *71 Beach Rd., Akaroa* ☎ *03/304–7656* 🌐 *www.thetradingrooms.co.nz* 🕒 *Closed every June but may vary; check website.*

WHERE TO STAY

$$$$ B&B/INN **The Giant's House.** Named so because it looked like a giant's house to a visiting child, this grand old 1880 villa is full of art in unexpected places. **Pros:** fabulous, crazy mosaic artwork; pleasant garden and leafy outlook; contemporary art gallery. **Cons:** very steep driveway; garden tour visitors wander through in the afternoon. [$] *Rooms from: NZ$350* ✉ *68 Rue Balguerie, Akaroa* ☎ *03/304–7501* 🌐 *www.thegiantshouse.co.nz* 🛏 *3 rooms* 🍴 *Breakfast.*

$$$ B&B/INN **Oinako Bed and Breakfast.** Surrounded by a tranquil garden, just a two-minute walk from town and a few steps from Akaroa Harbour, this character Victorian manor house has its original, ornate plaster ceilings and marble fireplaces. **Pros:** old-fashioned leafy garden overlooking the harbor; tea and coffee and cookies, feather pillows, and duvets add a luxurious touch. **Cons:** Wi-Fi doesn't reach the rooms but it's free in the lounge and lobby areas. [$] *Rooms from: NZ$295* ✉ *99 Beach Rd., Akaroa* ☎ *03/304–8787* 🌐 *www.oinako.co.nz* 🕓 *Closed June–Aug.* 🛏 *6 rooms* 🍴 *Breakfast.*

SPORTS AND THE OUTDOORS

Akaroa Dolphins. With these nature cruises aboard a luxury vessel on Akaroa Harbour, a portion of your fare goes to the Department of Conservation for further research into the Hector's dolphin, which is threatened with extinction. Cruises depart three times daily in summer, and once a day in winter for two hours, from the main wharf. Informed guides give you an insight into the marine life found here, and a beverage and home-baked snacks are also included as part of the ticket price. ✉ *65 Beach Rd., Akaroa* ☎ *03/304–7866* 🌐 *www.akaroadolphins.co.nz* 🎟 *NZ$74.*

Akaroa Harbour Nature Cruises & Swimming With Dolphins. The *Black Cat* catamaran runs Akaroa Harbour Nature Cruises and Swimming with Dolphins (two different trips). On the Nature Cruise, you'll pull in beside huge volcanic cliffs and caves and bob around in the harbor entrance while tiny Hector's dolphins—an endangered and adorable species of dolphin with rounded dorsal fins that look like Mickey Mouse ears stuck on their backs—play in the wake of the boat. Trips leave daily and cost NZ$74. Or take your swimsuit and get in the water for the Swimming with Dolphins cruise, the only place in the world you can do so. Dolphin swim trips cost NZ$150 (NZ$79 to watch). Wet suits are provided and advance reservations are essential. ✉ *Main Wharf, Akaroa* ☎ *03/304–7641, 0800/436–574* 🌐 *www.blackcat.co.nz* 🕓 *Swimming with Dolphins not available in winter.*

FAMILY **Banks Peninsula Track.** The 35-km (22-mile) Banks Peninsula Track crosses lovely coastal terrain. From Akaroa hike over headlands and past several bays, waterfalls, and seal and penguin colonies, and you might even see Hector's dolphins at sea. Two-day and four-day self-guided hikes are available from October to April. The tracks follow the same route, so if you're a novice hiker or have plenty of time, take the four-day option. You will stay overnight in shared cabins with fully equipped kitchens. Rates include lodging, transport from Akaroa to the first hut, landowners' fees, and a booklet describing the features of the trail. No fear of overcrowding here—the track is limited to 16 people at a time. ⊠ *Banks Peninsula Track, Akaroa* ☎ *03/304–7612* ⊕ *www. bankstrack.co.nz* ⊠ *From NZ$185* ⊗ *Closed May–Sept.*

Pohatu Penguins, Nature & Sea Kayaking Safaris. Pohatu Marine Reserve is a key breeding area for the Little Penguin (*korora*), which are endemic to the Canterbury region. Best time for viewing is during the breeding season, September to January. You may also see the yellow-eyed penguin (*hoiho*), which also breed in the bay. Options range from day and evening penguin or nature tours (from NZ$65 per person) and sea-kayaking trips (from NZ$90). Price includes a scenic drive to Pohatu with photo stops along the way and there are several other tour options as well. An accommodation package is also available in a self-catering cottage inside the penguin colony—a rare opportunity—(from NZ$130 per person for 24-hour stay). All trips leave from Akaroa. ⊠ *Unit 2, 8 Rue Balguerie, Akaroa* ☎ *03/304–8542, 021/246–9556* ⊕ *www.pohatu. co.nz* ⊗ *Subject to penguin breeding season.*

WAIPARA VALLEY

65 km (40 miles) north of Christchurch.

Once known for its hot, dry summers and sheep farms, the Waipara Valley is now an established vineyard area. The local Riesling, Chardonnay, and Pinot Noir are particularly good. Sheltered from the cool easterly wind by the Teviotdale hills, the valley records hotter temperatures than the rest of Canterbury, and warm dry autumns ensure a longer time for the grapes to mature. Winemakers are also exploiting the area's limestone soil to grow Pinots—Pinot Noir, Pinot Gris, and *Pinotage*. There are 31 wineries in the valley, with nearly 3,700 acres planted out in vines.

GETTING HERE AND AROUND

To reach Waipara from Christchurch, take State Highway 1 north. Waipara's about 45 minutes away, north of Amberley, where State Highway 7 turns left off the main road. You can head from here to Hanmer Springs and Nelson on State Highway 7 and other northern towns along State Highway 1. The Hanmer Connection runs a daily service between Hanmer Springs and Christchurch, stopping in Waipara and elsewhere en route in the Waipara Valley. You can also join a wine tour from Christchurch.

Bus Company Hanmer Connection. ⊠ *Canterbury Museum, 11 Rolleston Ave., Christchurch* ☎ *0800/242–663, 03/382–2952* ⊕ *www.hanmerconnection.co.nz.*

WINERIES

Waipara's wines are celebrated each year at the Waipara Wine and Food Celebration (held in late March, it fills, ironically enough) the grounds of the local Glenmark Church. The oak-tree lined gardens are filled with music; local produce like olives, nuts, and breads; and, of course, plenty of wine from dozens of local vineyards.

Black Estate. With its distinctive black barn tasting room and restaurant on the warm, sunny slopes of the Omihi Hills, this family-run vineyard has become a local landmark. The award-winning architecture perfectly complements the acclaimed Pinot Noir, Chardonnay, and Riesling vintages hand-harvested and made on-site. Add to this a delicious lunch and tasting menu, focusing on the best local produce and superb service to match the wine. Enjoy a beautiful view while you dine and sip, overlooking the vineyards and west to the Main Divide. ⊠ *614 Omihi Rd., Waipara Valley, Amberley* ☎ *03/314–6085* ⊕ *www.blackestate.co.nz* ⊘ *Wed.–Sun. 10–5.*

Pegasus Bay. Family-run Pegasus Bay has one of the region's best reputations for wine and food in Canterbury, and the helicopters lined up on the lawn at lunchtime will confirm that. Taste the award-winning Rieslings, Chardonnay, and Pinot Noir while you look through a window at floor-to-ceiling stacks of oak aging casks. It has been ranked among the top five wine producers nationally by Robert Parker's buyer's guide and it's been named Best Winery Restaurant in NZ by *Cuisine* magazine six times. In good weather, dine outdoors in the garden or picnic in a natural amphitheater by a small man-made lake. It's best to book if visiting for a meal or large group tastings. There's a helipad if you're in a hurry. Reservations recommended. ⊠ *263 Stockgrove Rd., Waipara* ☎ *03/314–6869* ⊕ *www.pegasusbay.com* ⊘ *Tasting room daily 10–5; restaurant Thurs.–Mon., noon–4.*

Pukeko Junction Cafe & Deli. There is no specified wine trail or information center in the valley, but a good place to start your visit is the Pukeko Junction Cafe & Deli at Leithfield, on the main road 10 km (6 miles) south of Waipara. Rather than a cellar door, the center is a café, wineshop, information bureau, and gallery rolled into one. There's a solid range of local wines, often at particularly good prices, many from smaller wineries not open to the public. The café is a great place to stop for breakfast if you're heading out of Christchurch and later in the day it has an excellent range of light food, such as quiches, chowder, salads, and cakes. It's a busy spot at lunch time but they will hold a table if you call ahead. ⊠ *458 Ashworths Rd., (part of State Hwy. 1), Leithfield* ☎ *03/314–8834* ⊕ *www.pukekojunction.co.nz* ⊘ *Daily 9–4:30.*

Torlesse Wines. Kym and Ben Rayner are consummate winemakers, and Kym is one of the pioneers of Waipara winemaking. At Torlesse Wines they use grapes from several vineyards around Waipara and farther afield, and Riesling is their biggest seller. Sauvignon Blanc, Gewürztraminer, Chardonnay, Pinot Gris, Pinot Noir, and Rosé are also produced, as are the Omihi Road reserve wines and Old Reserve Port, made in the same barrels since 1992. While you're there you can also check out the local arts and crafts for sale. ⊠ *10 Loffhagen Dr., off State Hwy. 1, Waipara* ☎ *03/314–6929* ⊕ *www.torlesse.co.nz* ⊘ *Daily 11–5.*

Waipara Hills. The huge, cathedral-like European castle rock-and-timber building at Waipara Hills, although less than 20 years old, looks somewhat medieval. The Waipara Hills Riesling, Pinot Gris, and Pinot Noir are all worth trying. The label uses grapes from Marlborough, Otago, and Waipara so there's a lot happening in a bottle. The café in the Cloisters, the high ceiling–medieval style section of the building, is open for lunch and afternoon coffee. There's a cellar door across the entrance hall for tastings. ⊠ *780 Glasnevin Rd. (part of State Hwy. 1), Waipara* ☎ *03/314–6900* ⊕ *www.waiparahills.co.nz* ☉ *Daily 10–5.*

Waipara Springs Winery and Cafe. One of the valley's oldest wineries, Waipara Springs offers lunch or just a wine tasting (NZ$5). The café, in converted farm buildings, serves tasty dishes made with local foods such as olives, cheese, asparagus, and salmon. Try their antipasto platter for a sampling of each, with fresh homemade bread. These match well with their Southern Boundary Wines, top Pinot Noir, Riesling, Gewürztraminer, and Chardonnays. They also produce Sauvignon Blanc, Pinot Gris, and Rosé. ⊠ *State Hwy. 1, 409 Omihi Rd., Waipara* ☎ *03/314–6777* ⊕ *www.waiparasprings.co.nz* ☉ *Daily 11–5 in summer, 10–4 in winter.*

WHERE TO EAT

$ ✗ **Little Vintage Espresso.** Tucked away down a side street off the main
CAFÉ   road, this cute little café with a red door is packed with locals, and is fast becoming a popular visitor stop, too. Besides the great coffee, there's also an excellent selection of well-priced baked goods including delicious muffins, and a tasty brunch menu to suit all appetites. Try their amazing avocado-and-feta smash on sourdough with bacon, poached eggs, and homemade dukkah. $ *Average main: NZ$12* ⊠ *20 Markham St., Amberley* ☎ *03/314–9580* ☉ *Closed Sun.*

WHERE TO STAY

$$$ ⌂ **Old Glenmark Vicarage.** Once a real vicarage, Old Glenmark is now a
B&B/INN   funky rustic accommodation suitable for families, with lots of rough-sawn timber and colonial trimmings, providing a very comfortable base while touring the area. **Pros:** central to most Waipara wineries and restaurants; on-site boutique vineyard. **Cons:** close to busy State Highway 1. $ *Rooms from: NZ$210* ⊠ *161 Church Rd., Waipara* ☎ *03/314–6775* ⊕ *www.glenmarkvicarage.co.nz* ⌁ *2 rooms, 1 cottage* ⌾ *No meals.*

$ ⌂ **Waipara Sleepers.** Wake up to fresh-baked bread and newly laid eggs
B&B/INN   every morning at this basic-but-rather-quirky backpackers lodge housed in old railway carriages and huts. **Pros:** very rustic and rural; complete with all the sounds and smells of the country; a good stop for anyone cycle-touring. **Cons:** some of the accommodations and services are quite basic (where else in NZ advertises color TV!) but so is the price. $ *Rooms from: NZ$65* ⊠ *10–12 Glenmark Dr., Waipara* ☎ *03/314–6003* ⊕ *www.waiparasleepers.co.nz* ⌁ *4 rooms, 2 dorms* ⌾ *No meals.*

SPORTS AND THE OUTDOORS

Mt. Cass Walkway. Here's a moderately strenuous way to wear off some of those wine- and lunch-induced calories. This three-hour return climb up Mt. Cass produces a spectacular view over the surrounding countryside of the Waipara Valley. As it crosses through working farmland on the Tiromoana Station, be careful to leave gates and marker posts as you find them. Use the stiles provided for crossing fence lines and wear strong walking shoes. The track is closed each year in spring while the sheep are lambing. ⊠ *Mt. Cass Rd., Waipara* ⊕ *www.visithurunui.co.nz* ☉ *Closed approx. Aug.–Oct.*

EN
ROUTE

Hurunui Hotel. Built from limestone blocks, the Hurunui Hotel, New Zealand's oldest continually licensed hotel (since 1860), refreshed weary drovers bringing sheep down from Marlborough. There are seven quaint rooms in this stagecoach-style hotel. A bed for the night is relatively cheap (NZ$45 per person, including a cooked breakfast), and the restaurant with its old-fashioned pub serves à la carte dinners including a succulent fillet steak from NZ$21 and an all-day menu from NZ$10. Wednesday night is pizza night. You can dine in the pub, where there is a roaring fire in winter, or outside in the tree-lined beer garden. ⊠ *State Hwy. 7, about 20-min drive from Waipara turnoff, 1224 Karaka Rd., Hurunui* ☏ *03/314–4207* ⊕ *www.hurunuihotel.co.nz.*

HANMER SPRINGS

120 km (75 miles) northwest of Christchurch.

People used to come to Hanmer Springs to chill out with quiet soaks in the hot pools and to take gentle forest walks, but things have been changing fast. The number of boutique stores and restaurants has doubled, and an increasing number of off-road and backcountry activities are turning Hanmer Springs into Canterbury's adventure-sports hub. It is also a spa town in the true sense of the word, with relaxing and indulgent spa facilities available at the Hanmer Springs Thermal Pools and Spa and in the village. On holidays and weekends the springs can be busy. The Amuri Ski Field, a small ski area in the mountains behind town, attracts a dedicated following of local skiers in winter. Mountain biking is especially big, and Hanmer Springs is now the end point for several long-distance mountain-bike and endurance races through the backcountry. During the summer months Hanmer Springs is also the southern terminus of the drive along the Acheron road through the Molesworth Station, which runs through from the Awatere Valley in Marlborough. This backcountry trail is open for only a few months a year and is a solid six-hour drive on an unpaved road through some spectacular country. Go to the **Department of Conservation** website and search for Molesworth for more information. *(See Chapter 8, Blenheim, for tour operators. They leave from Blenheim.)*

GETTING HERE AND AROUND

The Hanmer Connection runs a daily service between Hanmer Springs and Christchurch. Service goes through Waipara on the way. By car, take State Highway 1 north out of Christchurch. About 45 minutes north, State Highway 7 turns left off the main highway toward Nelson. From here drive through the small town of Culverden and the foothills for another 45 minutes on State Highway 7, before turning onto Highway 7A toward Hanmer Springs (this is well signposted).

Navigation around Hanmer Springs is easy, as it's a really small place. The main road into town, Amuri Drive, is a wide tree-lined road, with the thermal resort and visitor center opening off it. Conical Hill Road carries on up the hill and has most of the stores and cafés along its lower portion. Jacks Pass Road to the left and Jollies Pass Road to the right lead to the great outdoors and many of the adventure activities.

9

Bus Company Hanmer Connection. ✉ *Hanmer Springs* ☎ *0800/242–663 NZ only, 03/382–2952* 🌐 *www.hanmerconnection.co.nz.*

Contacts Department of Conservation. 🌐 *www.doc.govt.nz.* **Hanmer Springs i-SITE Visitor Centre.** ✉ *42 Amuri Ave.* ☎ *03/315–0020, 0800/442–663 NZ only* 🌐 *www.visithanmersprings.co.nz.*

EXPLORING

FAMILY **Hanmer Springs Thermal Pools & Spa.** The Hanmer Springs Thermal Pools & Spa consists of 15 outdoor thermal pools of varying temperatures, a heated freshwater pool with lazy river, a family activity pool, and three waterslides. There are also six private mineral-rich thermal pools, as well as adults-only aquatherapy pools, private sauna, and steam rooms. Massage and beauty treatments are available at the on-site spa. The Greenhouse Cafe, a beautifully renovated 1904 building, has bar facilities, and there's a picnic area, too. The heated changing rooms are a real treat. ✉ *42 Amuri Ave.* ☎ *03/315–0000, 0800/442–663 NZ only* 🌐 *www.hanmersprings.co.nz* 🎟 *NZ$22 entry. NZ$30 private pool, steam, or sauna (includes outdoor pools); waterslide NZ$10* ⏲ *Daily 10–9.*

Jacks Pass. The scenic gravel drive along Jacks Pass, to the north of the village, crosses the lower slopes of Mt. Isobel before dropping into the upper Clarence River valley, an alpine area 15 minutes from Hanmer Springs. This is the beginning of some serious backcountry. The tiny stream trickling past the road at the end of the pass eventually reaches the coast north of Kaikoura at the rough and rumbling Clarence River—a favorite for rafters and kayakers. This is also the southern end of the Acheron Road through the Molesworth Station and the 4WD Rainbow Road through to St. Arnaud and the Nelson Lakes. There's restricted access at certain times of the year and the roads can be impassable during winter so before you go check with the Hanmer Springs i-SITE Visitor Centre.

WHERE TO EAT

$$$$ ASIAN 🍴 **Malabar Restaurant.** Looking out toward Conical Hill, this modern restaurant has a fine reputation for its Asian-fusion food presented with Kiwi flair. Dinner favorites are the lamb shank rogan josh, crispy duck, and ginger stir-fry, and a selection of traditionally cooked Indian curries. Their crème brûlée is a treat. [$] *Average main: NZ$32* ✉ *Alpine Pacific Centre, 5 Conical Hill Rd.* ☎ *03/315–7745* 🌐 *www.malabar.co.nz* ⏲ *No lunch Sun.–Fri.* ✍ *Reservations essential.*

$$$$ MODERN NEW ZEALAND 🍴 **No.31 Restaurant & Bar.** In a renovated villa on the main road into Hanmer, No. 31 serves exceptional food. Its well-established local chef specializes in modern NZ cuisine, using the best local produce, offered with a selection of wines from the Waipara/Hanmer area. Candle lighted, moody, and romantic inside, you can also dine alfresco in summer. Favorites include the seared venison fillet on creamed parsnip puree with pinot poached pear and for dessert the hot sticky licorice pudding with butterscotch sauce, but this place has a 2014 Beef and Lamb Excellence Award, too. It's recommended by locals as one of the best in town. Check their Facebook page for menus. [$] *Average*

main: NZ$38 ✉ *31 Amuri Ave.* ☎ *03/315–7031* ⏲ *Closed Mon. and 2 wks in winter (dates vary).*

$$ CAFÉECLECTIC 🍴 **Powerhouse Cafe and Restaurant.** Now a popular café for locals, the Powerhouse building used to contain a small hydroelectric generator that supplied power to the old Queen Mary Hospital and a few streetlights. It opens at 8 am with a great brunch menu to suit all tastes—from a hearty high-country breakfast to huevos rancheros to the Highland Fling (porridge with a "wee lick o'whisky liqueur, blow-torched to caramelized perfection"). There's home baking, and the food has a healthy, fresh feel about it with wonderful salads using local ingredients. [$] *Average main: NZ$18* ✉ *8 Jacks Pass Rd.* ☎ *03/315–5252* 🌐 *www.powerhousecafe.co.nz* ⏲ *No dinner Sun.–Fri.*

WHERE TO STAY

$$$$ HOTEL 🏨 **Braemar Lodge & Spa.** Part lodge, part boutique hotel, these new accommodations were built around all that remains of the original Braemar Lodge—an impressive two-story-high river stone fireplace. **Pros:** spa units have a hot tub on the deck; all units have a whirlpool bath in the bathroom; on-site day spa; packages available with outdoor activities included. **Cons:** a 10-minute drive from Hanmer; access is by several kilometers of gravel road, with a steep but sealed driveway. [$] *Rooms from: NZ$380* ✉ *283 Medway Rd.* ☎ *03/315–7555* 🌐 *www.selectbraemarlodge.com* 🛏 *24 suites* 🍽 *Breakfast.*

$$ HOTEL 🏨 **Heritage Hanmer Springs.** Set in beautifully landscaped gardens, this hotel is just a short walk from the thermal pools, and staying here in its carefully restored rooms will remind you of the grand, genteel era in which it was built. **Pros:** lovely old Spanish Mission–style building; in the middle of town within easy walk of most things. **Cons:** during NZ school holidays it can get busy. [$] *Rooms from: NZ$175* ✉ *1 Conical Hill Rd.* ☎ *03/315–0060* 🌐 *www.heritagehotels.co.nz* 🛏 *38 rooms, 11 villas, 16 garden rooms* 🍽 *No meals.*

$$ HOTEL 🏨 **Settlers Motel.** This property has peaceful apartments and studios set off Amuri Avenue, the main street into Hanmer. **Pros:** quiet, friendly motel-style establishment; short walk to town; flexible check-in and check-out times. **Cons:** units all open onto central courtyard and parking lot; reservations are essential over weekends and holiday periods. [$] *Rooms from: NZ$160* ✉ *6 Leamington St.* ☎ *03/315–7343, 0800/587–873* 🌐 *www.settlershanmer.co.nz* 🛏 *14 rooms* 🍽 *No meals.*

$$ B&B/INN FAMILY 🏨 **Tussock Peak Motor Lodge.** Adjacent to the thermal pools, this stylish 14-unit complex offers a choice of spacious one- and two-bedroom units, Most have sunny balconies with alpine views. **Pros:** Sky TV with 50-plus channels in each room; free Wi-Fi. **Cons:** can be busy with lots of families during NZ school holidays. [$] *Rooms from: NZ$145* ✉ *Corner Amuri Ave. and Leamington St.* ☎ *03/315–5191* 🌐 *www.tussockpeak.co.nz* 🛏 *14 units* 🍽 *No meals.*

9

NIGHTLIFE

Black Beech Wine Bar. This sophisticated meeting place in Oxford specializes in local boutique wine and craft beer served along with platters of nibbles sized to suit one or two, or large groups. Choices include everything from cheeseboards, to Ploughman's, seafood, Mexican-style, and their very popular dessert platters, plus the chef's daily specials board. It's an ideal place to stop for a drink and a snack on weekday evenings or weekends from 11 am. They also have a shop selling wine and beer to take away. ⊠ *Unit 1, 46 Main St.* ☎ *03/928–3124* ⊕ *www. blackbeechwinebar.kiwi.*

Saints Pizzeria and Bar. Saints Pizzeria and Bar is probably the closest thing to a nightclub in Hanmer Springs. It's open until 1 am Friday and Saturday, but closes around 11 other nights. It has a dance floor and pool table and features a DJ some Saturday nights. They do brunch and lunch, too, but not always during the week when it's quiet. Service can be a bit slow if they're really busy, but the wait is usually worth it. ⊠ *6 Jacks Pass Rd.* ☎ *03/315–5262* ⊕ *www.saintshanmer.co.nz.*

EN ROUTE
The northern section of State Highway 72, also known as the Inland Scenic Route, starts at Amberley, eventually joining the southern section near Sheffield on the West Coast Road through to Arthurs Pass. Cust is a tiny settlement 40 minutes from Christchurch, where Route 72 Cafe and Emporium is a great coffee, lunch, and gift shopping stop, with a gorgeous rural view. Oxford is a small town farther along this northern section, with several characterful shops and cafés including a bakery and pie shop. Don't miss Emma's in Oxford for books and gifts. There's a farmers' market every Sunday morning in Oxford, and one on the fourth Sunday of every month in Cust.

SPORTS AND THE OUTDOORS

ADVENTURE SPORTS

Hanmer Springs Adventure Centre. Hanmer Springs Adventure Centre runs quad-bike tours, clay-bird shooting, mountain biking, and archery in the backcountry behind Hanmer Springs. Quad-bike tours leave at 10, 1:30, and 4 each day, bouncing through some spectacular hill country, native bush, river crossings, hill climbs, and stunning scenery over their 24,000-acre Woodbank Station. ⊠ *20 Conical Hill Rd.* ☎ *03/315–7233, 0800/368–7386 NZ only* ⊕ *www.hanmeradventure.co.nz* ⊠ *From NZ$129.*

FAMILY **Thrillseekers Adventures.** Thrillseekers Adventures offer 115-foot bungy jumps off the 19th-century Ferry Bridge. You can also choose to raft or ride on a jet-boat through the scenic gorge or let the kids do a quad-bike safari. Try clay-bird shooting or paintball, or just peer off the 100-foot balcony and watch the bungy jumpers and jet-boats in the canyon below. ⊠ *839 Hanmer Springs Rd.* ☎ *03/315–7046, 0800/661–538 NZ only* ⊕ *www.thrillseekers.co.nz* ⊠ *From NZ$169.*

METHVEN

95 km (59 miles) southwest of Christchurch.

Methven's main claim to fame is as a ski town. It's a one-hour drive from Christchurch and the closest town to Mt. Hutt, which has New Zealand's longest ski season from June to October. You can't stay on the mountain, so Methven is après-ski central. It's also a great base to stay if you are skiing at the five boutique club fields within the region. The small boutique ski club fields are also open to the public—the accommodation is members-only during peak season but you can stay in Methven and go to these club fields for the day. They have basic facilities and are suited to more experienced skiers. Tow prices are cheaper if you are a member. An hour away is Canterbury's other major ski area, Porters. Some of New Zealand's best heli-skiing is available from Methven, too. In late September the famous Peak to Pub race challenges competitors to skiing, biking, and running across snow, dirt, and pavement from the top of the mountain to the famous Blue Pub. If you are here in summer, you will get a feel for the area's strong mountain bike culture. There's a range of established mountain bike trails and many more in the works, while uncrowded country roads provide great flat riding for road cyclists. You can also enjoy horse riding, hiking, salmon fishing, jet-boating, tandem skydiving, and hot-air ballooning.

GETTING HERE AND AROUND

The best way to get to Methven by car is the underused Scenic Highway 72, which you can join near Darfield, or via Hororata (but be wary of icy spots in the shade and hidden speed cameras on these straight roads). You could also travel down the busy State Highway 1 to Rakaia and take Thompson's Track (clearly signposted and paved) to Methven. Or join it from the north at Amberley, passing through Oxford and Sheffield. This stretch of highway, known as the **Inland Scenic Route,** makes a nice day drive from Christchurch, taking in the upper Rakaia and Rangitata River gorges, the small towns of Darfield, Methven, and Geraldine, scenic views of the Southern Alps, and the wide-open farmlands of the plains.

There are plenty of buses from Christchurch to Methven and Mt. Hutt in ski season, but the options drop off in summer. Mt. Hutt SNOWBUS runs daily in winter, and Methven Travel runs a daily bus in winter and four times a week in summer.

Bus Company InterCity Coachlines. ☎ *03/365–1113* ⊕ *www.intercity.co.nz.* **Methven Travel.** ☎ *03/302–8106, 0800/684–888* ⊕ *www.methventravel.co.nz.* **Snowman Shuttles.** ☎ *03/337–5750, 0800/766–928 NZ only* ⊕ *www.snowmanshuttles.co.nz.*

VISITOR INFORMATION

Contacts Methven i-SITE Visitor Centre. ✉ *160 Main St.* ☎ *03/302–8955* ⊕ *www.methveninfo.co.nz.*

9

The central Canterbury Plains area is the premier hot-air ballooning spot.

EXPLORING

Aoraki Balloon Safaris. Ballooning high above the Canterbury Plains looking out to the Southern Alps is a magical experience. This experienced team have been operating for more than 20 years from Methven and flights are all year round, weather dependent. Daybreak is the best time to fly when conditions are usually cool, calm, and tranquil. On a fine day you can expect to see for hundreds of miles, from Christchurch city to Timaru with full panoramas of Aoraki Mt. Cook and the Rakaia River. The NZ Army band fly with them every year before Christmas and play carols over selected country towns. ⊠ *121 Main St.* ☎ *03/66–7327* ⊕ *www.nzballooning.com* ✉ *NZ$385 including champagne-style buffet breakfast picnic.*

FAMILY **New Zealand Alpine and Agriculture Encounter.** This purpose-built new attraction brings to life the stories of the mountains, plains, and people who live there with multimedia and interactive displays. Get on board a huge combine harvester, operate a digger, explore a snow cave, view a ski film, and learn about Mid-Canterbury's dairying and seed growing. ⊠ *Methven Heritage Centre, 160 Main St.* ☎ *03/302–8954* ⊕ *www. methvenheritagecentre.co.nz* ✉ *NZ$12.50* ⊙ *Weekdays 9–5, winter weekends 9–5, summer weekends 10–3.*

WHERE TO STAY

Methven isn't a culinary hotbed, but it has several good casual places and is known for its two famous watering holes: the Blue Pub and the Brown Pub on opposite corners in the middle of town. Both have reasonably priced bistro-style meals and a courtyard where you can sit and have a beer. For a quintessential New Zealand café experience head to Cafe Primo set in a retro-vintage shop on MacMillan Street, where you'll find treasures along with their legendary bacon-and-egg sandwiches and excellent coffee. Grab a granola breakfast here and pack a muffin for later. Accommodations vary between larger resort- and hotel-style venues and backpacker lodges. Most accommodations are in Methven township, but there are some more remote country options as well as the large Terrace Downs resort. There is no accommodation at Mt. Hutt.

$
B&B/INN
FAMILY

Alpenhorn Chalet. This wonderfully pleasant backpacker lodge is in an old wooden villa built in the early 1900s, very typical of small-town Victorian architecture in New Zealand at the time. **Pros:** homey feel is far removed from the usual backpackers-hostel vibe; conservatory garden; free Internet; superb free espresso coffee. **Cons:** a short walk from the center of Methven; no credit cards. $ *Rooms from: NZ$65* ⊠ *44 Allen St.* ☎ *03/302–8779* ⊕ *www.alpenhorn.co.nz* ▭ *No credit cards* ⇩ *1 room with en suite, 2 dorm rooms and 2 double rooms share a double bathroom* ❏ *No meals.*

$$
RESORT
FAMILY

Brinkley Resort. These one- and two-bedroom apartment-style units are just two minutes' walk from the center of town, surrounded by landscaped gardens. **Pros:** tennis court, hot tub, children's playground and a putting green; plenty of off-street parking and a helipad. **Cons:** there is a convention center on-site, so sometimes it can be busy. $ *Rooms from: NZ$165* ⊠ *43 Barkers Rd.* ☎ *03/302–8855* ⊕ *www.brinkleyresort. co.nz* ⇩ *80 rooms* ❏ *No meals.*

$$$
RENTAL

Central Luxury Apartments. These modern apartments just off the main street of Methven offer all the amenities, and they're built to display the best of the Southern Alps' views. **Pros:** drying room downstairs for the skis and ski gear; good parking. **Cons:** style is neutral with minimal decoration. $ *Rooms from: NZ$270* ⊠ *7 Methven Chertsey Rd.* ☎ *03/302– 8829, 0800/128–829 NZ only* ⊕ *www.centralapartmentsmethven.co.nz* ⇩ *6 apartments* ❏ *No meals.*

$$
B&B/INN
FAMILY

Methven Motels and Apartments. This modern accommodation complex has both motels rooms and apartments for small or large groups. **Pros:** drying cupboard for ski clothing and short-term gear storage; electric blankets. **Cons:** road outside can be busy. $ *Rooms from: NZ$130* ⊠ *197 Main St., Methven* ☎ *03/302–9200* ⊕ *www.methvenmotels.co.nz* ⇩ *8 units* ❏ *No meals.*

$$
B&B/INN

Mt. Hutt Lodge. If you've come south for the views and outdoor activities then the Mt. Hutt Lodge delivers. **Pros:** close to great fishing spots, skiing, golf, and tramping. **Cons:** the building is very 1970s and a bit tired; it's a 15-minute drive from Methven, so you'll need a car to get here. $ *Rooms from: NZ$130* ⊠ *15 Zig Zag Rd.* ☎ *03/318–6898* ⊕ *www.mthuttlodge.co.nz* ⇩ *14 rooms* ❏ *No meals.*

$$$$
HOTEL

Terrace Downs. Considered a top golf resort in NZ, Terrace Downs is a good place to base yourself for a vacation away from the crowds. **Pros:** 18-hole championship golf course on-site; day spa and extended list of on- and off-site activities; kid's club and babysitting available. **Cons:** you'll need two nights if you want to really appreciate the surroundings and venue. $ *Rooms from: NZ$310* ⊠ *Coleridge Rd., Rakaia Gorge* ☎ *03/318–6943* ⊕ *www.terracedowns.co.nz* ⇩ *15 1- to 3-bedroom villas, 4 4- to 7-bedroom chalets* ❏ *Some meals.*

9

SPORTS AND THE OUTDOORS

BOATING

FAMILY **Discovery Jet.** Zoom along the glacier-fed Rakaia River with Discovery Jet as you journey through the deep canyon and braided courses of the river. The Rakaia's jewel-like aqua water contrasts wonderfully with the white limestone cliffs and views of Mt. Hutt ski field. Fishing and scenic tours are options or catch a ride up to the Rakaia Gorge Walkway. Tours vary from 15 to 45 minutes and are suitable for all ages. ☎ *0800/538–2628 NZ only, 021/538–386* ⊕ *www.discoveryjet.co.nz* ⬛ *From NZ$45 for 15 mins.*

HIKING

Mt. Somers Track. One of New Zealand's top 10 walkways, the Mt. Somers Track is a great way to get a taste of the subalpine New Zealand bush. Start at the Mt. Somers–Woolshed Creek end and hike downhill to the Staveley end and Sharplin Falls. The 16-km (10-mile) walk will take one to two days, and there are two huts to stay in along the way—or do it in reverse. Call the Staveley Village Store, which also has a great café, before you start your trip (☎ *03/303–0859*) for information on transport to the end of the trail; there are a number of small guiding companies. ⊕ *www.doc.govt.nz.*

Rakaia Gorge Walkway. Leaving from just below the Rakaia River gorge bridge, the Rakaia Gorge Walkway provides upstream access to the northern bank of the river and offers easy walking. You can also take a jet-boat upriver and walk back—just name your distance. ⊠ *State Hwy. 72* ⊕ *www.amazingspace.co.nz.*

MULTISPORT

Big Al's Snowsports. In summer Big Al's Snowsports turns into a cycling center for those keen to don Lycra and head to the trails. Al and his team have decades of experience and really know what they're talking about with trail maps, and the best riding tips for the region. You can rent full-suspension cross-country bikes and 29r xc hardtails from them, too. ⊠ *The Square* ☎ *03/302–8003* ⊕ *www.bigals.co.nz* ⬛ *Bike hire from NZ$45 per day or NZ$15 per hr.*

SKIING

Methven Heliski. Methven has access to some of New Zealand's best backcountry helicopter-accessed terrain and hundreds of square miles of pristine snow. You don't have to be an advanced skier to enjoy it—there is something for every range of ability here, including long runs in deep powder, gentle glaciers, plus a fabulous day out soaring over the Alps with a friendly team. They fly every fine day from July 1 until September 30. ⊠ *114 Main St.* ☎ *03/302–8108* ⊕ *www.methvenheli.co.nz* ⬛ *NZ$1,045 per person for full day, 5 runs.*

FAMILY **Mt. Hutt Ski Area.** The views across the Canterbury Plains are amazing from this high-country ski area. It has one of the longest vertical drops in the South Island and a complete terrain mix for all skiers and boarders. A great family ski spot, there is a beginner's area with a 140-meter-long enclosed Magic Carpet, and modern chairlifts. For advanced skiers

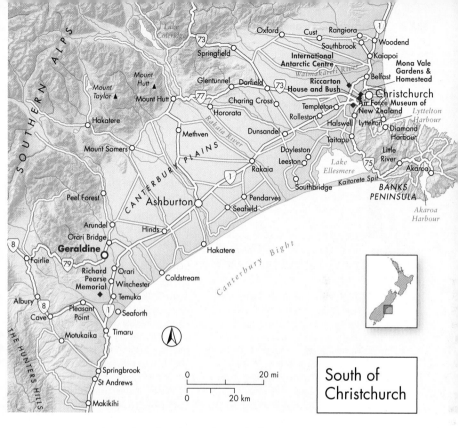

and snowboarders there's plenty of off-piste action, too. ✉ *Mt. Hutt Ski Area* ☎ *03/308–5074* ⊕ *www.nzski.com/mthutt* ☜ *Full day NZ\$98, ½ day NZ\$69. Free lift passes for children age 10 and under.*

FAMILY **Porters.** Take the drive from Methven along the Great Alpine Highway to the Porters ski area, with some spectacular views along the way. The access road is one of the shortest and least intimidating in the region, too. There are excellent learner facilities here, as well as a terrain park for boarders. A new Easyrider chairlift connects the base with the upper mountain. Two of New Zealand's legendary runs are here—Bluff Face and Big Mama. If you need a break, the café has great views over the Torlesse Range. ✉ *Porters Ski Area* ☎ *03/318–4002* ⊕ *www.skiporters. co.nz* ☜ *Full day NZ\$89, ½ day NZ\$59. Free lift pass for children under 12 with a full-day adult.*

GERALDINE

138 km (85½ miles) southwest of Christchurch.

For years, this lovely town has been a favorite stop on the road to Aoraki/Mt. Cook; these days, it's becoming a magnet in southern Canterbury for art mavens and foodies.

CLOSE UP

The Chatham Islands

Although officially part of New Zealand, the Chatham Islands, 800 km (500 miles) east of the South Island, are a land apart. Bearing the full force of the open Southern Ocean, the islands are wild and weather-beaten. The air has a salty taste to it, the colors of the landscapes are muted by salt spray, and the vegetation is stunted and gnarly. Many unusual plants and birds are about—including the extremely rare black robin—and the empty beaches invite fishing and diving (although the presence of sharks makes the latter unadvised).

Locals here refer to the mainland as New Zealand, as though it were an entirely separate country. Just 2 of the 10 islands are inhabited—the main island and tiny, neighboring Pitt Island which is well known for its extensive conservation programs. Most of the 600 residents are either farmers or fishermen, but tourism is increasing. The Chathams were first settled by the Moriori, a race of Polynesian descent, about 800–1,000 years ago, although there are now no full-blooded Moriori left. Māori and Europeans followed, and conflicts broke out between the separate populations throughout the 1800s. By the end of the 19th century, however, tensions had died down after the Native Land Court intervened in key disputes, and the new settlers established the strong maritime culture that still prevails on the islands.

When booking to fly to the Chathams, it's imperative that you make lodging reservations in advance. There is only one round-trip flight a week from Christchurch on Tuesday, but you can return earlier through Auckland or Wellington, and **Air Chathams** (☎ 03/305-0209 ⊕ www.airchathams. co.nz) is the only carrier. The islands are 45 minutes ahead of NZ time and, therefore, the first place on Earth to see the sun each day. Check out the Air Chathams website for more details on the islands, their natural history, accommodation, and activities. Allow at least three days to visit—you'll rarely get the chance to visit anywhere this remote. And don't forget to try the crayfish and blue cod.

GETTING HERE AND AROUND

State Highway 1 is the fastest route there from Christchurch; just after crossing the Rangitata River, turn inland for about 10 minutes on State Highway 79. State Highway 72—known as the Inland Scenic Route—gives you closer views of the mountains and river gorges but takes a bit longer. The rolling downs around Geraldine are especially breathtaking in the late afternoon, when the sun turns them golden.

Because Geraldine is between Christchurch and the popular draws of Aoraki/Mt. Cook and Queenstown, it's served by several bus companies, including InterCity and Atomic Shuttles.

Bus Companies Atomic Shuttles. ☎ 03/349-0697, 0508/108-359 NZ only ⊕ www.atomictravel.co.nz. **InterCity Coachlines.** ☎ 03/365-1113 ⊕ www. intercity.co.nz.

EXPLORING

You know you're in small-town New Zealand when the biggest store on the main street is the rural merchandiser. Luckily, along Geraldine's main drag, Talbot Street, you'll find other stores and galleries to browse as well. Or stop in at Talbot Forest Cheese for some delicious locally made cheeses, ice creams, fudge, and other tasty delights. Head farther to the Rangitata Valley and visit Peel Forest, the ancient podocarp remnant of the vast forest expanse that once covered much of Mid- and South Canterbury. The area is now a haven for birdlife and there are many trails for hikers and bikers.

Geraldine Vintage Car and Machinery Museum. At the Geraldine Vintage Car and Machinery Museum, there's some good rural stuff with more than 100 tractors (some dating back to 1912) and other farm machinery sharing space with vintage cars. ✉ *178 Talbot St.* ☎ *03/693–8756* 🎟 *NZ$10* 🕒 *Late Sept.–June, daily 9:30–4, Closed weekdays winter.*

WHERE TO STAY

$$$$ B&B/INN 🏨 **Peel Forest Lodge.** Tucked in among giant *kahikatea* trees and native forest, and overlooking Little Mt. Peel (which isn't so little), this comfortable oregon log lodge provides a haven of peace and quiet. **Pros:** café and bar just down the road at Peel Forest village; full kitchen for your use; big schist fireplace in the lounge; outdoor spa pool. **Cons:** a few trophy heads on the walls (if they're not your thing). [$] *Rooms from: NZ$380* ✉ *Brake Rd., off Dennistoun Rd., Peel Forest* ✥ *don't drive into Peel Forest Estate, take a right at their gate and continue another mile or so along the gravel road* ☎ *03/696–3703* 🌐 *www.peelforestlodge.co.nz* 🛏 *4 rooms* 🍴 *No meals.*

SHOPPING

Barker's. For foodie treats, stop by Barker's in the Four Peaks Plaza to try fruit chutneys, fruit syrups, sauces, spreads, and tasty jams. They do good gift boxes and they'll ship overseas for you, too. ✉ *76B Talbot St.* ☎ *0508/227–537 NZ only, 03/693–9727* 🌐 *www.barkers.co.nz.*

Louk NZ Clothing. Stop off at Louk NZ Clothing for a big range of designer merino wear and cool outdoor gear, for both males and females. They also have the biggest Swazi range (another hip outdoor label) in the South Island. They're in the old post office on the main street. ✉ *47 Talbot St.* ☎ *03/693–9070* 🌐 *www.louknzclothing.co.nz.*

The Tin Shed. Looking more like a shearing shed than a store, The Tin Shed is exactly that. Surrounded by farmland and animals, it is an authentic piece of rural New Zealand architecture being put to good use. Inside is a selection of lifestyle and handmade clothing. There's a good range of merino and possum fur knits and shawls, knitwear, and thermals, oilskins, sheepskin footwear, and locally produced skin-care items. This is a great spot to stock up with gifts before leaving the country, and they can arrange postage. Watch the turn-in off the main road as traffic moves fast here. ✉ *State Hwy. 79, just off State Hwy. 1 south of the Rangitata* ☎ *03/693–9416* 🌐 *www.thetinshed.co.nz* 🕒 *Weekdays 8:30–5, weekends 9–5.*

SPORTS AND THE OUTDOORS

Rangitata Rafts. Rangitata Rafts runs white-water rafting trips on the Grade V Rangitata River starting at 11:30 most days from October through May. The river grades build as you drop lower so if you can't face the Grade V section (the last part of the trip), you can walk around with the photographer then rejoin the raft. Rates include an early lunch, hot showers, spectacular scenery, a barbecue, and 2½ hours of rafting. Reservations are essential. They also do a more gentle Grade II trip that's suitable for anyone eight years or older; it's good fun and a nice introduction to white-water rafting. Nonrafters can relax at the lodge. ☎ *03/696–3534, 0800/251–251 NZ only* ⊕ *www.rafts.co.nz* ✉ *From NZ$210* ☾ *Closed June–Sept.*

THE SOUTHERN ALPS
AND FIORDLAND

WELCOME TO THE SOUTHERN ALPS AND FIORDLAND

TOP REASONS TO GO

★ **Action:** Jump, fly, splash, or swing; your inner daredevil will find its voice in Queenstown's multitude of adventurous activities.

★ **Clarity:** Everything is clearer here. Filmmakers comment on the quality of the light and you will see an extraordinary number of stars. This is where the world's largest International Dark Sky Reserve was declared in 2012.

★ **Fly-Fishing:** The crystal-clear lakes and rivers of the Southern Alps are some of the world's best fly-fishing spots.

★ **Hiking:** Tramping doesn't get any better than the Milford, the Kepler, the Routeburn, and the Hollyford tracks. Because trail traffic is carefully managed, you'll feel wonderfully alone in the wilderness.

★ **Scenery:** The landscape here is breathtaking: peaks, fjords, lakes, forest, and tussock lands lie in close proximity. A scenic flight to take it all in is money well spent.

1 The Southern Alps. In Mount Cook National Park, activities naturally revolve around the mountain—climbing, hiking, skiing, and scenic flights. But as you travel down into the foothills and valleys, the choices for adventure multiply. Stargaze at Lake Tekapo, or go gliding at Omarama, "the place of light." Enjoy the miles of hills and farmland as you travel through Lindis Pass; soon the uninhabited country will give way to Wanaka and the bustle of Queenstown.

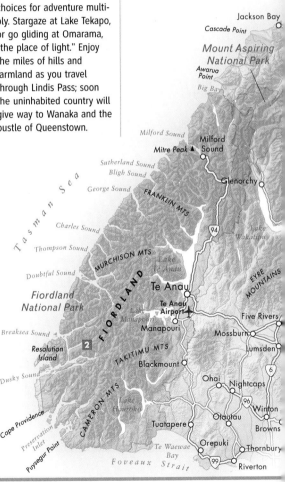

GETTING ORIENTED

The Southern Alps start in the northern end of the South Island around Kaikoura and stretch through the provinces of Canterbury, inland Otago, Westland, and Southland. These are serious mountains, with jagged 9,000-feet-plus peaks. The Mt. Cook area is the heart of Kiwi mountaineering. These majestic formations take center stage, and amazing landscapes unfurl at their feet—green rivers braided with white stone banks, acres of lupines, and lakes hued with indescribable blues. From Lake Tekapo, you finally come to "rest" at the adventure-friendly cities of Queenstown and Wanaka, historic Arrowtown, and the truly restful aura of the Otago vineyards. To the west, magnificent Milford Sound dominates Fiordland.

10

2 Fiordland. Te Anau is often referred to as a "jumping-off point" to explore Milford Sound. But the town, on the country's second-largest lake, is worth a stay to see the glowworms in Te Anau Caves. Doubtful Sound is actually closer to Te Anau than Milford but involves crossing Lake Manapouri and an alpine pass to get there.

FIORDLAND NATIONAL PARK

There is a reason Fiordland is considered a must-see destination. Prose, pixels, and paint all fail to describe Milford and its surrounding beauty. You simply have to experience the place yourself.

Encompassing more than 2 million acres of wilderness, Fiordland is the country's biggest national park. About half a million people visit each year to see playful dolphins and rain forest–coated mountains, but most converge on Milford and Doubtful sounds, the park's stars. Don't worry—the park is massive enough to easily absorb the crowds. The scenery actually quiets them, too: entire boatloads of visitors have been known to just *hush* out on the water. Sand flies and rain (along with your job, breaking news, and the rest of the world) will seem like tiny nuisances when you behold Milford Sound, with Mitre Peak rising along the coast and waterfalls tumbling into the sea. *I see the falls,* said one returning visitor, *and everything just falls away.*

BEST TIME TO GO

Spring and summer (October through April) are the best, but busiest, times to go. Still there are many opportunities to commune quietly with the park, such as kayaking, scuba diving, or hiking. If you only have time for a cruise, it is still well worth the trip; even the drive into Milford in itself is well worth the trip.

PARK HIGHLIGHTS

Milford's Waterfalls. Milford Sound mass-produces waterfalls. Silver threads of spontaneous waterfalls join Bowen Falls' 520-foot drop. Torrents of rain cause lush green walls to spring leaks. Occasionally, fierce winds stop the flow and appear to push water back *up* the cliff faces. That's Milford's drama: lovely on nice days, spectacular on nasty days. A scenic flight will take you over Sutherland Falls, the tallest in New Zealand at 1,904 feet; the only other way to see it is to walk the Milford Track.

Doubtful Sound. Doubtful Sound has all of the beauty of Milford, but it's less accessible and therefore less crowded and more serene. So if Milford's too hustle-bustle for you, arrange a trip to Doubtful, which will doubtless include a stop at its gateway, Lake Manapouri, and the enormous underground hydroelectric power station situated there.

Te Anau. This little town's restaurants, shops, and lodgings make it a perfect base for your Fiordland adventures. Situated on its picturesque namesake lake, it also has an excellent cinema/wine bar, which features the locally filmed *Ata Whenua: Shadowland*, well worth the ticket price. A short boat ride across the lake will take you to glowworm caves; it's a two-hour drive to Milford Sound and a 20-minute bus ride to Lake Manapouri.

BEST WAYS TO EXPLORE
Cruise the sound. Milford and Doubtful sound cruises run all day and include scenic, nature, and overnight trips. Most of Milford's day trips get you close to a waterfall. Kayak on Milford Sound (guided or not) for eye-level views of New Zealand fur seals, penguins, and dolphins. For high-seas adventure, charter a fishing trip in the Tasman Sea.

Walk the Finest Walk. New Zealand's most famous walk, the Milford Track, has been called the "Finest Walk in the World." Take the guided walk option if you want to stay warm and dry and have your meals cooked for you; otherwise it requires a bit of gumption and organization—and boat transport from either end—to complete the four-day track. The experience, which includes rain forest, glacial lakes, mountains, and several massive waterfalls, like Sutherland Falls (1,904 feet), is worth the effort. There are other wonderful walks, including the 60-km (37-mile) Kepler Track, which is accessible from Te Anau. Sights along this four-day walk include the Luxmore Cave, beech forests, mountains, and rivers.

Scuba. The thick layer of rainwater, pigmented by forest tannins, that sits atop the sounds' saltwater filters the sunlight and simulates deep-sea darkness. This means creatures of the deep in shallow waters. Scuba divers come here for uncommonly accessible glimpses of spiny sea dragons, sea pens, and black coral. If you don't want to suit up, visit the Milford Discovery Centre & Underwater Observatory.

(left above) Mitre Peak and Milford Sound; *(bottom)* Hiker and kea bird on Kepler Track; *(above)* Hollyford Track

10

Milford Sound and Mitre Peak

Drive Milford Road. Most visitors drive to the park themselves, traveling the scenic Milford Road. Places to stop and enjoy short walks include Mirror Lake, which lives up to its name on calm days, and the Avenue of the Disappearing Mountain. And don't drive past the Chasm walk in your haste to get to Milford Sound; it's worth the short walk (20-minute round-trip).

TOUR OPERATORS
By Air: Southern Lakes Helicopters has scenic flights that can take you right across Fiordland. **Fly Fiordland** has a range of scenic flights on its fixed-wing aircraft to Milford and Doubtful sounds. Combined packages include cruising. **Wings and Water Te Anau Ltd.** uses floatplanes to take travelers to inaccessible areas of Doubtful, Dusky, and Milford sounds.

By Land: Guided multiday treks with **Ultimate Hikes** require deep pockets but provide comfortable beds and a cook. Day hikes on either the Milford or Routeburn Track are available.

By Water: Real Journeys runs a range of combined bus and boat trips in and around Milford and Doubtful sounds, as well as overnight cruises. Southern Discoveries offers frequent daily cruises on its catamarans to Milford Sound that can be combined with kayaking and the Underwater Observatory. **Rosco's Milford Kayaks** specialize in kayaking. **Go Orange Kayaks** has kayaking day- and multiday trips on Milford and Doubtful sounds. Beginners are welcome.

Updated by
Mike Stearne

There are hundreds of glaciers locked in the Southern Alps, slowly grinding their way down to lower altitudes and melting into running rivers of uncanny blue-green hues. These conspire with the vast brown grasslands of the Mackenzie Basin and ancient green forests of Fiordland to humble you with their imposing presence, leaving you feeling very small and temporary. Nothing is permanent though—the freeze-thaw cycle constantly refreshes this mighty landscape making it feel absolutely *alive.*

Aoraki, or Mt. Cook, at 12,218 feet, is New Zealand's highest mountain, and 22 other peaks in this alpine chain are higher than 10,000 feet. Aoraki/Mount Cook National Park is a UNESCO World Heritage Area, and the alpine region around it contains the Tasman Glacier, at 27 km (17 miles), New Zealand's longest.

The Southern Alps region is great for hiking. Terrain varies from high alpine tundra to snow-covered peaks, heavily forested mountains, and wide, braided river valleys. A good network of trails and marked routes are throughout the mountains, but be well informed before venturing into them. Always make your intentions known: go to the Adventure Smart website for details (⊕ *www.adventuresmart. org.nz*); Aoraki/Mt. Cook is the only DOC office where you still sign your intentions in person.

There are many easier options for exploring the foothills and less arduous parts of the Southern Alps. On the southwest corner of the island, glaciers over millennia have cut the Alps into stone walls dropping into fjords, and walking trails take you into the heart of the wild Fiordland National Park. The Milford Track is the best known—it has been called the finest walk in the world since a headline to that effect appeared in the London *Spectator* in 1908. If you're not keen on walking to Milford Sound, hop on a boat and take in the sights from on deck. Most

10

river valleys with road access have well-marked walking trails leading to scenic waterfalls, gorges, and lookout points.

Floods of tourists have come to see the otherworldly landscape used in shooting *The Hobbit*, and *Lord of the Rings* film trilogies, and Hollywood directors have been drawn to the area for the magnificent backdrops that depicted Tolkien's Middle Earth. The vastness of the region keeps it from feeling crowded, even with all the new visitors. Queenstown, often billed as an adventure-sports hot spot, is perhaps the best-known destination in the Southern Lakes district. It and the nearby town of Wanaka are steeped in gold-rush history and surrounded by stunning mountain scenery.

PLANNING

Give yourself two to three days to explore the Aoraki/Mt. Cook area: two days is a good idea at Mt. Cook in case the namesake peak is hiding behind clouds, and you'll want to allow for an evening at the space observatory in Tekapo. Once you head south you can use Queenstown or Wanaka as a base from which you can visit Mount Aspiring National Park, wine country, and take on some exciting adrenaline-fueled activities around Queenstown—three days should be sufficient to pack it all in. Then head to Te Anau, which is a perfect base for seeing Fiordland National Park. An overnight on Milford or Doubtful Sound is recommended for unwinding and reflecting after the road-tripping, bungy-jumping excitement of the past week.

WHEN TO GO

Although the Southern Alps and Fiordland have four distinct seasons, it's not unusual for the mountains to get snow even in summer. If you're traveling in winter, check the weather forecasts and road conditions regularly. The road into Milford Sound can close for days at a time because of snow or avalanche risk and you must carry chains.

For winter sports, from July through September you can be assured of snow around Queenstown and Wanaka, where the ski scene is ushered in by the Queenstown Winter Festival. In the height of summer—from January to March—both resort towns have a lot of Kiwi holidaymakers. If you're planning on hiking one of the major trails, such as the Milford Track, summer or early autumn are the best times, but you'll need to book well ahead.

GETTING HERE AND AROUND
AIR TRAVEL

Air New Zealand flies from Auckland, Wellington, and Christchurch into Queenstown, the main hub. Jetstar flies in from Auckland and Wellington. Air NZ, Jetstar, Virgin Australia, and Qantas provide trans-Tasman flights (Brisbane, Sydney, and Melbourne). Tourist enterprises operate helicopters and fixed-wing planes, which buzz between Queenstown, Wanaka, Milford Sound, Franz Josef, and Mt. Cook. You can do fly-cruise-fly packages from Queenstown to Milford, although the flight from Wanaka to Milford is the most spectacular.

BUS TRAVEL

It may take a full day, but you can take buses to and from the major towns in the Southern Alps and Fiordland area. InterCity operates a daily bus service between Christchurch and Queenstown down the South Island's eastern flank via Dunedin or the longer, more scenic route via Mount Cook Village, with a one-hour stop at the Hermitage Hotel for lunch. Their coaches also make daily trips from the Franz Josef and Fox glaciers through Wanaka to Queenstown. InterCity also has a daily bus round-trip route from Queenstown and Te Anau to Milford Sound. Alpine ConneXions sends buses between Wanaka and Queenstown several times a day. They also run to Cardrona, Clyde, Cromwell, Dunedin, Ranfurly, Alexandra, and pickup and drop-off to various walking tracks and rail trails.

Contacts Alpine Connexions. ☎ *03/443–9120* ⊕ *www.alpineconnexions.co.nz.* **InterCity Coachlines.** ☎ *03/442–4922* ⊕ *www.intercity.co.nz.*

CAR TRAVEL

Exploring is best done by car on the state highways that weave through the vast mountain ranges, skirting several major lakes and rivers. Be prepared for rugged, quickly changing terrain, ice in winter, and frequent downpours, particularly around Milford Sound. Rental-car companies may discourage driving on some of the smaller, unpaved roads, so it is best to avoid them. That said, an ideal way to see the Alps is to "tiki-tour" (wander around) by car, as the main network of roads is paved and easy to negotiate.

RESTAURANTS

Queenstown, as the main regional resort, has the widest range of restaurants. Throughout the area, menus focus on local produce, seafood, lamb, and venison. Wine lists often highlight South Island wines, especially those from Central Otago and Gibbston Valley. Cafés and restaurants driven by the summer tourist trade shorten their hours in winter. Dress standards are generally relaxed, with jeans or khakis acceptable almost everywhere. At high-end places, particularly in Queenstown, you'll need to reserve a table at least a day in advance.

Outside of Queenstown and Wanaka dining options can be limited. In summer, meals of some sort are available almost everywhere, but outside the high season, there are fewer options in the smaller settlements and they don't tend to stay open late.

HOTELS

Lodgings in the Southern Alps and Fiordland milk the fantastic views for all they're worth. You can almost always find a room that looks out on a lake, river, or rugged mountain range. Queenstown and Wanaka are busy in summer (January through March) and winter (July through September), so you should reserve in advance. Luxury options are plentiful in Queenstown, and costs are correspondingly high. Other towns, such as Aoraki/Mount Cook Village, have extremely limited options, so you should plan ahead there, too. Air-conditioning is rare because it's rarely needed. Heating, though, is standard, and essential in winter.

10

*Hotel reviews have been shortened. For full information, visit Fodors.com.
Use the coordinate (✛ B2) at the end of each listing to locate a site on the
corresponding map.*

WHAT IT COSTS IN NEW ZEALAND DOLLARS			
$	**$$**	**$$$**	**$$$$**
Restaurants	under NZ$15	NZ$15–NZ$20	NZ$21–NZ$30	over NZ$30
Hotels	under NZ$125	NZ$125–NZ$200	NZ$201–NZ$300	over NZ$300

Restaurant prices are the average cost of a main course at dinner or, if dinner is
not served, at lunch. Hotel prices are the lowest cost of a standard double room in
high season.

VISITOR INFORMATION

The regional visitor bureaus are open daily year-round, with slightly
longer hours in summer. These local tourism organizations have helpful websites, including **Destination Fiordland, Destination Queenstown,** and
Aoraki/Mount Cook Mackenzie Region Tourism.

Contacts Aoraki/Mount Cook Mackenzie Region Tourism. ⊕ *www.mtcooknz.
com.* **Destination Fiordland.** ⊕ *www.fiordland.org.nz.* **Destination Queenstown.** ⊕ *www.queenstownnz.co.nz.*

THE SOUTHERN ALPS

The Canterbury Plains ring Christchurch and act as a brief transition
between the South Pacific and the soaring New Zealand Alps. The drive
south along the plain is mundane by New Zealand standards until you
leave State Highway 1 and head toward the Southern Alps.

The route south, along the eastern flank of the Alps, can leave you
breathless. Head through Lindis Pass by traveling inland to Fairlie
and Tekapo, then south to Omarama; you'll be entering the country's
adventure-sports playground, where Wanaka and Queenstown provide
at least a dozen ways to get your adrenaline pumping. A handful of
notable vineyards calm the nerves post-extreme-sport experience.

MACKENZIE COUNTRY AND LAKE TEKAPO

227 km (141 miles) west of Christchurch.

You will know you have reached the **Mackenzie Country** after you cross
Burkes Pass and the woodland is suddenly replaced by high-country
tussock grassland, which is full of lupines in the summer months. The
area is named for James ("Jock") McKenzie, one of the most intriguing
and enigmatic figures in New Zealand history. McKenzie was a Scot
who may or may not have stolen the thousand sheep found with him
in these secluded upland pastures in 1855. Arrested, tried, and con-
victed, he made several escapes from jail before he was granted a pardon
nine months after his trial—and disappeared from the pages of history.
Regardless of his innocence or guilt, McKenzie was a master bushman

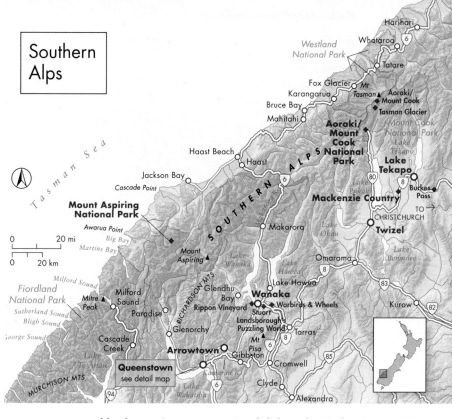

and herdsman. A commemorative obelisk marks Mackenzie Pass, 30 km (18 miles) off the main highway if you turn off at Burkes Pass.

GETTING HERE AND AROUND

From Christchurch take Highway 1 south. At the tiny town of Rangitata turn right onto Highway 79 to Lake Tekapo. Bus companies that serve Lake Tekapo include InterCity Coach, The Cook Connection (summer only), and several tour operators. Check ⊕ *www.mtcooknz. com* for a complete list.

VISITOR INFORMATION

Contacts Lake Tekapo Untouched. ⊕ *www.laketekapountouched.co.nz.* **Tekapo Springs Information Centre.** ✉ *State Hwy. 8, Village Center* ☎ *03/680–6579.*

EXPLORING

FAMILY **Earth and Sky.** If you're extremely lucky, you'll see the southern lights. Even if you don't, you're still at one of the best stargazing sites in the world. Earth and Sky operates from the Mt. John Observatory and studies the skies above Lake Tekapo. The Astro Café has ham-off-the-bone sandwiches, telescopes, and dizzying views. Stargazing trips leave from the town office in the evening, and reservations are essential. Earth and Sky also offers a shorter one-hour tour of the Cowan's Observatory, which is more suitable for those with younger children. You can do daytime tours of the facility, too, just book at the café. The coffee's good there, too. ✉ *Main St., State Hwy. 8, Lake Tekapo* ☎ *03/680–6960* 🌐 *www.earthandsky.co.nz* 🎟 *NZ$145.*

Lake Tekapo. The long, narrow expanse of Lake Tekapo anchors the area. Its extraordinary milky-turquoise color comes from rock flour, rock ground by glacial action and held in a soupy suspension. Tekapo, the country's highest large lake, has good fly-fishing in the lake and in the surrounding rivers and canals.

On the east side of the lakeside power station is the tiny **Church of the Good Shepherd.** The simple stone structure doesn't need stained glass; the view through the window is the lake's brilliant blue. A nearby memorial commemorates the sheepdogs of the area. As you drive into the small town, you'll notice a knot of restaurants with tour buses parked outside. It's a rather off-putting image, but it's relatively easy to keep the township at your back and your eyes on the lake and mountains. If you're not planning to stay at Mt. Cook, then Tekapo is the best place in the Mackenzie Basin to stop for the night. And once the buses have passed through for the day, it's a quiet spot—at least until the hordes of Cantabrians arrive for the summer break. A pleasant lakefront recreation area separates the town retail area from the lakeshore.

FAMILY **Tekapo Springs.** If you've taken advantage of the walks around Tekapo then you'll really appreciate this day spa and hot-pool complex with its beautiful views. There's a sauna and steam room and traditional plunge pool at lake temperature. In winter there's a skating rink and tube park. ✉ *6 Lakeside Dr., Lake Tekapo* ☎ *03/680–6550, 0800/2353–8283 free phone within New Zealand* 🌐 *www.tekaposprings.co.nz* 🎟 *From NZ$22* 🕘 *Daily 10 am–9 pm.*

OFF THE BEATEN PATH

Bullock Wagon Trail. This 268-km (167-mile) heritage highway, which stretches from Timaru to Twizel via Mt. Cook, recognizes the long, arduous journeys early settlers in the region made by bullock wagon. Leaving the Canterbury Plains at Geraldine or Pleasant Point (depending on whether you are coming directly from Christchurch or through from Timaru), the highways join at Fairlie and quickly climb toward the first of the alpine passes—Burkes Pass—along the Bullock Wagon Trail. The Burkes Pass monument marks the division between the high and low country, and from there the country immediately dries out and takes on the look of high-country tussock lands. To learn more about the trail and the history of the region, stop in at one of two information centers along the way.

WHERE TO EAT

$$$ JAPANESE FAMILY

🍴 **Kohan Japanese Restaurant.** For more than 20 years, Masato Itoh has run only Japanese restaurant in town, combining fresh local ingredients with imported spices and seasoning to produce a traditional Japanese menu. The barnlike space lacks personality, but has some of the best views over Lake Tekapo. The food is a refreshing change from the more traditional offerings in town and locals rate it highly. Any salmon dish is a winner, but the Bento Box is especially good value. [$] *Average main: NZ$25* ✉ *State Hwy. 8, Village Center* ☎ *03/680–6688* 🌐 *www.kohannz.com* 🕘 *No dinner Sun.*

$$$ NEW ZEALAND 🍴 **Reflections Cafe and Restaurant.** Great views of the lake are visible from almost every table at this rather rustically decorated restaurant. The menu is hearty, if not a little too meaty; a local favorite is the steak-and-bacon sandwich. The salmon from a nearby hatchery is also delicious. As many ingredients as possible are obtained locally to maintain freshness in the meals. You'll be dining with backpackers there for the Wi-Fi, and mature travelers looking to escape the coach tours. [$] *Average main: NZ$25* ✉ *State Hwy. 8, Lake Tekapo* ☎ *03/680–6234* 🌐 *www.reflectionsrestaurant.co.nz.*

WHERE TO STAY

$$$ RENTAL 🏨 **Aldourie Lodge at Parkbrae Estate.** With a fireplace, claw-foot bathtubs, lake views, and a library, Aldourie Lodge is an enchanting place to unwind. **Pros:** all properties are cozy and thoughtfully decorated; fantastic views. **Cons:** it books quickly, so reserve well in advance. [$] *Rooms from: NZ$285* ✉ *3 Sealy St., Lake Tekapo* ☎ *03/680–6607* 🌐 *www.parkbrae.co.nz* 🛏 *3 rooms, 6 cottages* 🍽 *No meals.*

$$ B&B/INN 🏨 **The Chalet.** The Chalet's seven fully self-contained apartments stretch beside the turquoise waters of Lake Tekapo. **Pros:** superb views; host is an experienced local guide. **Cons:** there's a NZ$30 surcharge if you only stay one night. [$] *Rooms from: NZ$190* ✉ *14 Pioneer Dr., Lake Tekapo* ☎ *03/680–6774* 🌐 *www.thechalet.co.nz* 🛏 *7 units* 🍽 *No meals.*

$$$$ B&B/INN Fodor's Choice ★ 🏨 **Lake Tekapo Lodge.** The large picture windows offer spectacular lake views, providing a blend of natural beauty and modern sophistication. **Pros:** the most luxurious stay in Lake Tekapo; dinner available by arrangement. **Cons:** hiding in a residential cul-de-sac; some buildings in the foreground of lake and mountain views; no children allowed. [$] *Rooms from: NZ$450* ✉ *25 Aorangi Cres, Lake Tekapo* ☎ *03/680–6566* 🌐 *laketekapolodge.co.nz* 🛏 *3 rooms* 🍽 *Breakfast* 💳 *No credit cards.*

$$ HOTEL 🏨 **Lake Tekapo Village Motel.** A nice mid-range alternative with good family-style facilities, this resort is in the center of town. **Pros:** good value; free Wi-Fi. **Cons:** busy during the holidays. [$] *Rooms from: NZ$170* ✉ *State Hwy. 8, Lake Tekapo* ☎ *03/680–6808, 0800/118–666* 🌐 *www.laketekapo.com* 🛏 *6 family units, 12 studios, 1 penthouse apartment.*

10

$$$ RENTAL 🏨 **Lakeview Tekapo.** Taking full advantage of the region's status as a dark sky reserve, each of Lakeview Tekapo's three suites have a stargazing window (with blind) directly over the bed. **Pros:** fully self-contained and superquiet. **Cons:** windows face directly on to street; no children allowed. [$] *Rooms from: NZ$259* ✉ *6 Lochinver Ave., Lake Tekapo* ☎ *03/680–6265* 🌐 *www.lakeviewtekapo.co.nz* 🛏 *3 suites* 🍽 *No meals.*

$$$ B&B/INN 🏨 **Three Rivers Lodge.** With few big accommodation providers in town, Three Rivers Lodge is a prime example of a local B&B filling the need, with a range of room options, including a self-contained two-bedroom apartment. **Pros:** all rooms have private entry; good base for Mount Cook. **Cons:** not all rooms have full lake view. [$] *Rooms from: NZ$240* ✉ *2 Lochinver Ave., Lake Tekapo* ☎ *03/680–6899* 🌐 *www.threeriverslodge.co.nz* 🕒 *Closed May and June* 🛏 *3 rooms, 1 2-bedroom apartment* 🍽 *Breakfast* 💳 *No credit cards.*

SPORTS AND THE OUTDOORS

If you're not up for tourist adventures on a particular day, a nice walk around Tekapo may suffice, which will lead you to spectacular views, and there's always the hot pools at Tekapo Springs to relax in afterward.

FISHING

Barry Clark Fly-Fishing & Small Game Hunting Guide. Barry's knowledge of the local spots is exhaustive. He'll take you fly-fishing or spinning, whatever your preference, to the most suitable lake or river spot of the day. All the gear's provided. ✉ *1 Esther-Hope St., Lake Tekapo, Lake Tekapo* ☎ *03/680–6513* ✆ *From NZ$300 a day.*

HIKING

Domain to Mt. John Lookout Track. At the **Tekapo Information Centre** you can pick up a walking-trail map and then take off to hike the Domain to Mt. John Lookout Track. In a couple of hours you can be well above the township, enjoying extensive views of the Mackenzie Basin, Southern Alps, and Lake Tekapo.

AORAKI/MOUNT COOK NATIONAL PARK

99 km (62 miles) from Lake Tekapo.

Endless rolling hills, bungy jumps off high bridges, the glittering Skytower of Auckland . . . so you think you've experienced the grandeur of New Zealand. Think again. Aoraki glowers severely at these puny sideshows as if to say *Try to bungy jump this, wee one!*

A few things about Aoraki/Mt. Cook: it's dually named with Māori and Anglo titles. Second, you may never see New Zealand's tallest mountain, as weather can shroud the peaks for days. Plan to stay in the park overnight in case your arrival coincides with curtains of clouds. Note that shopping in Aoraki/Mount Cook Village is very limited. If you don't intend to eat every meal in a restaurant, purchase food and necessary supplies in Twizel or Lake Tekapo. The ice cornices and granite faces are the realm of serious mountain climbers. Nonclimbers can still get a strong sense of the place with hikes, scenic flights, glacier ski trips, and a visit to the excellent Sir Edmund Hillary Alpine Centre at the Hermitage Hotel. And, finally, be prepared to be awed by these majestic peaks.

WHEN TO GO

For driving to and hiking in the park unhampered by bad weather, visit in the summer. Book accommodations and activities well in advance for November to March. If your trip revolves around skiing or snowboarding, then winter is a wonderland here, albeit a somewhat inaccessible one during snow storms.

GETTING HERE AND AROUND

The 330-km (205-mile) drive from Christchurch straight through to Aoraki/Mount Cook Village takes four hours. Take Highway 1 south out of Christchurch. At the tiny town of Rangitata turn right onto Highway 79 to Lake Tekapo. Pass through Lake Tekapo and look on the right for Highway 80 to Aoraki/Mount Cook Village. InterCity buses make daily stops at Mount Cook Village. The village itself is small and manageable on foot.

Bus Company InterCity Coachlines. ☎ *03/365–1113* ⊕ *www.intercity.co.nz.*

TOURS

Alpine Guides Ltd. Alpine Guides is NZ's longest-established mountain and ski guiding company. In summer they offer guided ascents and climbing instruction—trips are 6–10 days. In winter they have two heli-ski operations at Mount Cook and Methven, Ski the Tasman, and ski touring. ✉ *98 Bowen Dr., Aoraki Mount Cook* ☎ *03/435–1834* ⊕ *www. alpineguides.co.nz* 🏷 *From NZ$2,250.*

Glacier Explorers. Take a spectacular, almost surreal, boat trip on the terminal lake of New Zealand's largest and longest glacier, the Tasman Glacier. The lake formed in the mid-1980s, and every now and then icebergs calve and increase its size. It's the only place in the country where you can do a trip like this. The season starts once the lake has thawed, but generally runs from mid September to late May. It's a good idea to book ahead, and bring a warm jacket. ✉ *Aoraki Mount Cook* ☎ *03/435–1809, 0800/686–800* ⊕ *www.glacierexplorers.com* 🏷 *NZ$155.*

VISITOR INFORMATION

Contacts Aoraki/Mount Cook National Park Visitor Centre. ✉ *Aoraki/Mount Cook Village, 1 Larch Grove, Aoraki Mount Cook* ☎ *03/435–1186* ⊕ *www.doc. govt.nz.* **Weather Phone.** ☎ *03/435–1171.*

EXPLORING

Fodor's Choice
★ **Aoraki/Mount Cook National Park.** Aoraki Mt. Cook is New Zealand's highest peak at approximately 12,218 feet. There are 22 peaks over 10,000 feet in Aoraki/Mount Cook National Park. According to Māori legend, Aoraki was one of three sons of Rakinui, the sky father. Their canoe caught on a reef and froze, forming the South Island. South Island's oldest name to local Māori is Te Waka O Aoraki (Aoraki's canoe) and the highest peak is their ancestor Aoraki, frozen by the south wind, and turned to stone. The officially recognized names of this mountain and the national park were changed to their original Māori names of Aoraki (Aorangi to North Island Māori) as part of a 1998 settlement between the government and the major South Island Māori tribe, Ngai Tahu. The Māori and Anglo names are used interchangeably or together.

Aoraki was first scaled on Christmas Day 1894 by three New Zealanders—Tom Fyfe, George Graham, and Jack Clarke—just after it was announced that an English climber and an Italian mountain guide were about to attempt the summit. In the summer of 1991 a chunk of it broke away, but fortunately there were no climbers in the path of the massive avalanches. High Peak, the summit, is now about 66 feet lower, but its altered form makes for a much more difficult ascent.

The 273-square-mile national park surrounds tiny **Aoraki/Mount Cook Village**, which consists of a visitor center, an airfield, a pub, a little school, and a range of accommodation providers. Walking is always an option, and in winter there's heli-skiing. If the weather is clear, a

10

Safety in the High Country

The Fiordland region's remoteness and changeable weather make it necessary to take some sensible precautions. So, before you head out on that trek or boat trip, keep the following in mind:

Be sure to wear the right protective clothing: sturdy hiking boots, a waterproof jacket, and a warm layer such as a fleece or wool pullover. Weather in this region, especially at high altitude, can change dramatically in a short time.

Watch out for sunburn—take sunscreen and a hat with you. Also bring bug repellent for sand flies, which are impossible to avoid in this region unless you're traveling offshore by boat.

If you're heading off without a guide for more than an hour or two, let someone know where and when you're going and when you've returned. See the Adventure Smart website for advice (⊕ www.adventuresmart.org.nz). DOC visitor centers issue regular weather and trail updates.

Use extreme caution when crossing rivers. Especially after rain, mountain runoff can quickly turn a gentle stream into an angry torrent, and drowning is a major hazard. If you do get trapped on one side of a quickly rising river, wait for the water to recede rather than risk crossing.

For longer treks into serious country always carry a map and compass, first-aid gear, bottled water, high-energy foods, warm clothes and tent, and a mountain radio or EPIRB (locator beacon—these can be rented locally). Cell phones don't work in the mountains.

scenic flight can be the highlight of your stay in New Zealand. Contact the Aoraki/Mount Cook National Park Visitor Centre or the weather phone to check conditions before setting out on an unguided excursion. Hiking trails radiate from the visitor center, providing everything from easy walking paths to full-day challenges. Be sure to fill your car's gas tank and purchase essentials before leaving Twizel or Tekapo as services are very limited in the village.

10

For a unique hands-on educational experience take a half-hour hike to the fast-growing 2-km (1-mile) **Terminus Lake of the Tasman Glacier.** Fed by the retreating glacier and the Murchison River, the lake was formed only in the past couple of decades. From Terminus Lake you can examine up close the terminal face of the glacier, which is 3 km (2 miles) wide. A trip with Glacier Explorers takes you by boat to explore some of the large floating icebergs that have calved (fallen away) from the glacier. It's an eerie experience skimming across the milky-white water and closing in on icebergs.

From the airfield at Mount Cook Village, helicopters and fixed-wing aircraft make spectacular scenic flights across the Southern Alps. One of the most exciting is the one-hour trip aboard the ski planes that touch down on the **Tasman Glacier** after a gorgeous scenic flight. The 10-minute stop on the glacier doesn't allow time for much more than a snapshot, but the sensation is tremendous. The moving tongue of ice beneath your feet—one of the largest glaciers outside the Himalayas—is 27 km (17 miles) long and up to 2,000 feet thick in places. The intensity of light on the glacier can be dazzling, and sunglasses are a must. ✉ *Aoraki Mount Cook.*

WHERE TO EAT

$$$ CAFÉ 🍴 **The Old Mountaineers Cafe, Bar & Restaurant.** This cozy, very personable café/restaurant has big picture windows for grand views of the outside and all sorts of interesting mountaineering memorabilia and photos to peruse inside. There's a big roaring fire to keep you warm in winter. The meals are flavorful, hearty, and wholesome and they source a lot of organic produce, including organic wines and coffee (if you take it with milk, that's organic, too). A popular option is their Mountaineers' Breakfast—nitrate-free bacon, free-range eggs, sausages, tomato, mushrooms, hash browns, and ciabatta—served all day. Fresh burgers and pizza are a specialty here, too. They really push their underdog status, but after more than a decade in business it's probably time to let that go. They may close early if it's quiet at dinner, so be sure to get there by 7 pm. [$] *Average main: NZ$30* ✉ *Larch Grove Rd., Aoraki Mount Cook* ☎ *03/435–1890* 🌐 *www.mtcook.com.*

WHERE TO STAY

$$$ RENTAL 🏨 **Aoraki Court Motel.** Being fully self-catering is a huge plus with the lack of shopping in Mount Cook Village, and Aoraki Court Motel has 25 modern studio or two-bedroom units, all of which have kitchenettes. **Pros:** removed from the hordes of bus groups. **Cons:** free Wi-Fi is patchy, due to the remote location. [$] *Rooms from: NZ$265* ✉ *26 Bowen Dr., Aoraki Mount Cook* ☎ *03/435–1111* 🌐 *www.aorakicourt.co.nz* 🛏 *25 rooms* 🍽 *No meals.*

$$ B&B/INN 🏨 **Aoraki/Mt. Cook Alpine Lodge.** This lodge, run by a young local family, has twin, triple, and family rooms, all with private bathrooms and two have kitchenettes. **Pros:** great guest lounge with fireplace; caters to kids; bikes for hire. **Cons:** not many meal options, so be prepared to buy groceries and cook. [$] *Rooms from: NZ$169* ✉ *Bowen Dr., Aoraki Mount Cook* ☎ *03/435–1860* 🌐 *www.aorakialpinelodge.co.nz* 🛏 *16 rooms* 🍽 *No meals.*

$$$ HOTEL 🏨 **The Hermitage Hotel.** Famed for its stupendous mountain vistas, this rambling hotel has been substantially revamped over the past few years, and the improved layout now gives most of the rooms, as well as the lobby, views over Aoraki or Mt. Sefton. **Pros:** staff treat the property like home, and guests like family. **Cons:** summers can get very busy with tour groups; the best rooms get quite expensive. [$] *Rooms from: NZ$255* ✉ *Terrace Rd., Aoraki Mount Cook* ☎ *03/435–1809* 🌐 *www.hermitage.co.nz* 🛏 *163 rooms, 20 chalets* 🍽 *No meals.*

SPORTS AND THE OUTDOORS

You don't want to miss the chance to see Sir Edmund Hillary's playground or the backdrop of *Lord of the Rings*. Climbing the icy slopes yourself will provide a day full of exercise and an unforgettable experience.

CLIMBING AND MOUNTAINEERING

Adventure Consultants. Summer is the best climbing season in the Aoraki/Mount Cook National Park area. Adventure Consultants, a group specializing in the world's top peaks, guides ascents of Aoraki, Mt. Tasman, and throughout the Southern Alps. They also give private multiday mountaineering, alpine-climbing, and ice-climbing courses. The company is based in Wanaka and have a full range of equipment. ⊠ *20 Brownston St., Wanaka* ☎ *03/443–8711, 866/757–8722 toll-free in U.S* ⊕ *www.adventureconsultants.com* ✉ *From NZ$550 per day.*

FLIGHTSEEING

Flightseeing gives you an unparalleled view of the mountains, with the added thrill of landing on a glacier for a short walk. The light can be intensely bright in such dazzlingly white surroundings, so be sure to bring sunglasses. Generally, the best time for flights is early morning.

Air Safaris. Take a breathtaking 50-minute scenic flight over the two longest glaciers in New Zealand, the Tasman and the Murchison, as well as the Fox, and Franz Josef glaciers. You'll pass high-country sheep farms and see Aoraki/Mt. Cook and the rain forests on the west side of the Main Divide. There are helicopter charter options, too. ⊠ *253 Tekapo-Twizel Rd., Tekapo* ☎ *03/680–6880* ⊕ *www.airsafaris.co.nz* ✉ *Flights NZ$360 per person; helicopter from NZ$149 per person.*

Helicopter Line. The Helicopter Line runs flights from 20 to 50 minutes, all of which include a remote landing, from Glentanner Park, about 20 km (12 miles) toward Pukaki from the Hermitage. You can land on the glaciers or high ski slopes, depending on the weather. ⊠ *Glentanner Park, State Hwy. 80, Aoraki Mount Cook* ☎ *03/435–1801, 0800/650–651* ⊕ *www.helicopter.co.nz* ✉ *From NZ$235 per person.*

Mount Cook Ski Planes. Choose between a ski plane or helicopter; it's the way to go for a bird's-eye view of the stunning Mt. Cook. Flightseeing options include a 25-minute flight to the bottom of the Tasman Glacier or a 40-minute flight with a glacier landing. ⊠ *Mount Cook Airport, State Hwy. 80, Aoraki Mount Cook* ☎ *03/430–8034, 0800/800–702* ⊕ *www.mtcookskiplanes.com* ✉ *From NZ$245 per person.*

HIKING

The hiking trails spooling out from the visitor center range in difficulty and length, from the 10-minute Bowen Track to the 5½-hour climb to the 4,818-foot summit of Mt. Sebastopol. Several tracks can be done in running shoes and don't require hiking experience; the rest of the park's trails require some hiking experience, and the higher routes require serious mountaineering experience. The Mueller Hut route is a popular climb, taking three to four hours; a 28-bunk hut provides overnight accommodation (book and pay at the visitor center). The rewarding Hooker Valley walk, a four-hour round-trip, will take you across a couple of swingbridges to the Hooker Glacier terminus lake, and the Tasman Glacier Lake walk gives an intimate view of New Zealand's longest glacier.

10

TWIZEL

65 km (40 miles) from Lake Tekapo, 40 km (25 miles) from Aoraki/ Mt. Cook.

A service town to its core, Twizel was built in 1968 as a base for workers constructing a major hydroelectric power plant. When the hydroelectric scheme wrapped up, the residents fought to keep their town intact. Now it's a handy place for tourist overflow in the Aoraki/Mt. Cook area. There's good fishing to be done in its rivers and those hydro canals (a 45-pound brown trout was landed there in 2013). Birders should check with the visitor center about tours to the *kakī* aviary to see these striking endangered red-legged birds.

Twizel is close to five good-size boating and leisure lakes and has a couple of good places to eat. Having already passed Tekapo and Pukaki, you'll find Lake Ruataniwha a little tame. Lake Ohau is off the main road, but is another high-country fishing gem. A ski slope, Ohau Snow Fields, opens in July each winter, and a number of walks are in the nearby Ohau Forest Range.

GETTING HERE AND AROUND

Twizel is on State Highway 8. If you're driving south from Christchurch on Highway 1, turn onto Highway 8 at Fairlie. If you're coming north from Queenstown, follow Highway 6 to Cromwell, then turn onto Highway 8 and continue over the Lindis Pass to Twizel. InterCity Coachlines serve Twizel.

Bus Information InterCity Coachlines. ☎ *03/365–1113* ⊕ *www.intercity.co.nz.*

VISITOR INFORMATION

Contacts Twizel Information Centre. ⊠ *Market Pl.* ☎ *03/435–0066* ⊕ *www.twizel.info.*

WHERE TO EAT

$$$$ ✕**Poppies Cafe.** For years Poppies has been turning out good food in
CAFÉ Twizel. Meat, seafood, pizza, and pasta are complemented by organic
FAMILY produce from the garden, fresh-baked bread and pizza bases, and a good range of local wines. The selection of craft beer provides good company for the delicious wild venison pie. On hot days Poppies opens up into a garden with long tables: it's a great place to eat, drink, socialize, and bask in the sun. They'll put out cricket sets to keep the kids entertained, too. Poppies serves brunch and dinner daily. $ *Average main: NZ$32* ⊠ *1 Benmore Pl.* ☎ *03/435–0848* ⊕ *www.poppiescafe.com.*

WHERE TO STAY

$$ ▦**MacKenzie Country Hotel.** Its imposing stone-and-timber buildings
HOTEL make an impression in this otherwise nondescript town. **Pros:** reasonably priced. **Cons:** food isn't great—check out Poppies across the street; you still have to pay for Wi-Fi. $ *Rooms from: NZ$145* ⊠ *2 Wairepo Rd.* ☎ *03/435–0869, 0800/500–869* ⊕ *www.mackenzie.co.nz* ⤏ *28 deluxe, 80 superior rooms* ⦿❘ *No meals.*

$$$ ▦**Matuka Lodge.** Matuka Lodge is ideal for anyone wanting to enjoy
B&B/INN the hikes and activities of the Mt. Cook area, and is particularly nice for fly fishermen. **Pros:** endearing hosts; rooms have verandas

with mountain views. **Cons:** 50-minute drive to Mt. Cook. $ *Rooms from: NZ$285* ✉ *395 Glen Lyon Rd.* ☎ *03/435–0144* ⊕ *www.matukaluxurylodge.com* ⊘ *Closed June* ⇆ *2 suites with en suite, 2 suites with double spa bath* ⦅◯⦆ *Breakfast.*

MOUNT ASPIRING NATIONAL PARK

Roads only skirt the edge of this huge park, which compels you to hike, boat, and fly to see it. Only a winged, hoofed super-creature could possibly see the majority of Aspiring's wilderness. Daunting yet tantalizing: that's the magic draw of this unspoiled landscape.

At 877,224 acres, Mount Aspiring is the country's third-largest national park. The park's namesake mountain is only one of numerous geological wonders. The area has yielded much *pounamu* or greenstone, and the famous Otago schist featured in the architecture of the gateway communities. One unusual stretch of peaks is known as the Red Hills, where the toxic minerals in the soil rendered the landscape barren (and a deep rusty red). Most of the park is marked by beech forest and wildflower-filled valleys, with snow tussock grasslands and alpine herb fields above the snowline. The park is home to the famous Routeburn Track, a three-day Great Walk, and dozens of shorter hikes. Gateway communities include lively Wanaka, which offers a multitude of choices for lodging, dining, shopping, and those rewarding post-hike pints.

GETTING HERE AND AROUND

Gateway communities to the park are Wanaka, Makarora, Queenstown, Glenorchy, and Te Anau. These towns are all served by bus companies, and you can fly into Wanaka, Queenstown, and Te Anau. Major thoroughfares lead to them and driving to any of these locations is a treat—the scenery in this part of the country is dramatic and roadside attractions include gorgeous vineyards, fresh fruit stands, mountain passes, white-water rivers, and if you're en route to Wanaka from Queenstown you can stop and bungy jump.

For maps, information on local walks, and information on the three campgrounds and 20 backcountry huts in the park, contact the DOC. Many tours to the park leave from Wanaka. *See Tours in Wanaka for more details.*

VISITOR INFORMATION

Contacts Department of Conservation. ✉ *At Ardmore St. and Ballantyne Rd., Wanaka* ☎ *03/443–7660* ⊕ *www.doc.govt.nz.*

SPORTS AND THE OUTDOORS

Siberia Experience. Siberia Experience has one of the area's best adventure packages. The journey begins with a funky little yellow plane in a paddock-cum-airstrip. After a breathtaking 25-minute journey from Makarora, the pilot drops you off in the pristine wilderness of Mount Aspiring National Park's Siberia Valley, and points you to a trailhead. From there, embark on a magnificent three-hour hike on a well-marked, relatively easy trail. Finally, a jet-boat meets you at the Wilkin River and returns you to Makarora. There is a hut out

10

DID YOU KNOW?

New Zealand's Southern Alps are young by geological standards. In fact, they're still growing! Due to colliding tectonic plates, the mountains shoot up at a rate of about ¼ inch per year.

there if you'd like to arrange overnight stays. ⊠ *12 Lloyd Dunn Ave., Wanaka Airport, Luggate* ☎ *0800/345–666, 03/443–4385* ⊕ *www. siberiaexperience.co.nz* ✉ *NZ$355.*

WANAKA

70 km (44 miles) northeast of Queenstown, 140 km (87 miles) southwest of Twizel.

On the southern shore of Lake Wanaka, with some of New Zealand's most striking mountains behind it, Wanaka is the welcome mat for Mount Aspiring National Park. It has labeled itself the world's first "Lifestyle Reserve" and is a favorite of Kiwis on vacation, a smaller, quieter alternative to Queenstown. The region has two ski resorts, numerous trekking and river-sports opportunities, and if you arrive on a rainy day, you can hit a couple of unusual cultural attractions. These good points have not gone unnoticed, and Wanaka is one of the fastest-growing towns in New Zealand, with new housing popping up in record time.

GETTING HERE AND AROUND

If you're coming from Queenstown, you have two choices for getting to Wanaka: go over the Crown Range for stunning views (not recommended in snow) or take the winding road along the Kawarau River through wine and fruit country. From Christchurch, drive south through Geraldine and Twizel. Once in Wanaka it's easy to park and walk around town, and a taxi service can get you back to your accommodations if you take advantage of the nightlife. A short but pleasant drive to the western side of the lake brings you to Glendhu Bay. With nothing here but a campground and fabulous mountain and lake views, the real beauty in this drive lies in the unspoiled calm and surreal quiet (except in midsummer, when it is packed full of vacationing locals). This road also leads to the Aspiring region and the Treble Cone ski area. Several bus companies serve Wanaka.

Bus Companies Alpine Connexions. ⊕ *www.alpineconnexions.co.nz.*

TOURS

Deep Canyon. With the steep rugged waterways of the Matukituki and Wilkin valleys within easy reach, Wanaka is a key spot in the country for canyoning. Deep Canyon leads expeditions down the Niger Stream, Wai Rata Canyon, the Leaping Burn, and others. No experience is necessary but the minimum age is 12. ⊠ *100 Ardmore St.* ☎ *03/443–7922, 0800/327–853 NZ only* ⊕ *www.deepcanyon.co.nz* ✉ *From NZ$250.*

FAMILY **Eco Wanaka.** Visit the lake that's on top of an island that's on top of the
Fodor's Choice lake. Riddles aside, this is a journey to the Mou Waho Island Nature
★ Reserve in the middle of Lake Wanaka; a guided nature walk to the summit reveals the lake on top and hopefully you'll hear or catch a glimpse of rare native birds along the way. On every trip, guests plant a native tree. The guides are all locals, incredibly knowledgeable, and guide walks all over this World Heritage Area, including the Rob Roy Glacier. ⊠ *Lake Wanaka i-SITE, 103 Ardmore St.* ☎ *03/443–2869, 0800/926–326 NZ only* ⊕ *www.ecowanaka.co.nz* ✉ *From NZ$195.*

10

VISITOR INFORMATION

Contacts **Lake Wanaka i-SITE Visitor Information Centre.** ⊠ *103 Ardmore St.* ☎ *03/443–1233* ⊕ *www.lakewanaka.co.nz.*

EXPLORING

TOP ATTRACTIONS

FAMILY **Have a Shot.** Pretend you're Tiger Woods or Robin Hood at Have a Shot. At this excellent facility you can have a hand at clay bird or rifle shooting, archery, or get a basket of golf balls and chip away. It's fun for experts, and you get full instruction if you're a novice. There's an activity for everyone including the kids at the mini-golf course. A great option if the weather's misbehaving. ⊠ *87 Mt. Barker Rd., opposite Wanaka Airport* ☎ *03/443–6656* ⊕ *www.haveashot.co.nz* 🔗 *From NZ$9 to NZ$38.*

Rippon Vineyard. Lying spectacularly by the shores of Lake Wanaka, Rippon is one of the most photographed vineyards in the country. The vineyard's portfolio includes Riesling, Gewürztraminer, Chardonnay, Sauvignon Blanc, and fine Pinot Noir. Every other year, it's the venue for the Rippon Open Air Festival, one of the country's most popular music festivals. Head west from Wanaka along the lake on Mt. Aspiring Road for 4 km (2½ miles). ⊠ *246 Mt. Aspiring Rd.* ☎ *03/443–8084* ⊕ *www. rippon.co.nz* ⊗ *Dec.–Apr., daily 11–5; July–Nov., daily noon–5. Closed May–June.*

WORTH NOTING

FAMILY **Stuart Landsborough's Puzzling World.** The cartoonlike houses built at funny angles with the *Leaning Tower of Wanaka* is just the start. Turn off here for a number of puzzling life-size brainteasers, including the amazing Tumbling Towers, Hologram Halls, and Tilted House, which is on a 15-degree angle (is the water really running uphill?). There's a "3-D" Great Maze to get lost in and a new *Sculptillusion* gallery. For a break, head to the café, take on the puzzle of your choice, order a cup of coffee, and work yourself into a puzzled frenzy. ⊠ *Hwy. 84, 188 Wanaka Luggate Hwy.* ☎ *03/443–7489* ⊕ *www.puzzlingworld.co.nz* 🔗 *NZ$20* ⊗ *Nov.–Apr., daily 8:30–6; May–Oct., daily 8:30–5:30.*

Warbirds & Wheels. There are around 30 privately owned classic cars on display here. Their 1934 Duesenberg is the star of the show, with Packards, Lincolns, and Fords among the mix. You may have heard of the NZ Fighter Pilots Museum—it's long gone but you can still see some of the planes here, including a WWI SE5A, Hawker Hurricane, Vampire, Strikemaster, and impressive Skyhawk fighter jet. This is also home of New Zealand's largest contemporary touring art collection; at least half the collection stays here. ⊠ *11 Lloyd Dunn Ave., Wanaka Airport, Luggate* ☎ *03/443–7010* ⊕ *www.warbirdsandwheels.co.nz* 🔗 *NZ$20* ⊗ *Daily 9–5.*

WHERE TO EAT

$$$$

FRENCH

Fodor's Choice

★

✕ **Bistro Gentil.** Indulge with a modern fine French meal in a quiet setting with lake and mountain views on the outskirts of Wanaka. Each meal begins with a complimentary tasting of oils from the owner's olive grove in Provence, while the kitchen garden grows heirloom vegetables and herbs. The menu changes regularly, but the local Cardrona merino lamb is always there in one form or another. Help yourself to more oils and balsamic vinegars via the dispensing machines. You can opt to get your wine this way, too, allowing you to sample several wines by the taste, half, or full glass. If you want to make a real event of it, opt for the seven-course tasting menu (NZ$120). $ *Average main: NZ$38* ⊠ *76a Golf Course Rd.* ☎ *03/443–2299* ⊕ *www.bistrogentil.co.nz* ⚑ *Reservations essential* ▬ *No credit cards.*

$$ ✕ **Kai Whakapai.** This is a good place to sit shoulder to shoulder with
ECLECTIC the locals for breakfast on a crisp sunny morning with tables outside. It's just across the road from the lake, so the views range from pretty nice on a cloudy day to fantastic on a fine one. Meanwhile, the menu ranges from simple breakfast and lunch choices (coffee and croissants, salads, nachos, and kebabs), to beef ribs or rump roast for dinner. In addition to consistently good meals, "The Kai" has local beers on tap, fresh bread, and is a great place to wind down after a big day. $ *Average main: NZ$15* ⊠ *Helwick and Ardmore Sts.* ☎ *03/443–7795.*

$$$$ ✕ **Relishes Café.** You could hit this lakeside spot for every meal of the
NEW ZEALAND day, starting with the bacon or salmon eggs Benedict or check the counter food for something homemade and delicious, like their cinnamon sticky buns. At lunch and dinner, you'll find ever-changing blackboard specials, good service, and great coffee. Try the Southland lamb cutlets, crusted in *horopito* (pepper tree) and served with beetroot gnocci. The wine list is mainly local NZ, with a good selection sold by the glass. It gets busy here so it's advisable to book for dinner during the holidays. $ *Average main: NZ$32* ⊠ *99 Ardmore St.* ☎ *03/443–9018* ⊕ *www. relishescafe.co.nz.*

$$ ✕ **Sasanoki Japanese Kitchen.** It's cheating to say this is the best Japa-
JAPANESE nese place in Wanaka as it's the only one . . . but this take-out eatery really is a big hit among the locals. The most popular dish is the teriyaki chicken, and the Japanese chef serves dishes such as salmon sushi, crumbed fish, eel, and inari (tofu). If it's a chilly day you can get a miso soup for a two-dollar coin. $ *Average main: NZ$15* ⊠ *26 Ardmore St.* ☎ *03/443–6474.*

WHERE TO STAY

$$ ⛺ **Cardrona Hotel.** This classic old-country hotel and pub, 20 minutes
B&B/INN from Wanaka on the Crown Range Road, is the Cardrona après-ski spot for mulled wine in front of the outdoor fireplace. **Pros:** stay in a genuinely historic property. **Cons:** historic properties mean squeaky floorboards and hinges. $ *Rooms from: NZ$185* ⊠ *Cardrona Valley Rd.* ☎ *03/443–8153* ⊕ *www.cardronahotel.co.nz* ⮌ *16 rooms* ⦿*| Breakfast.*

$$$ ⛺ **Edgewater.** Directly by the water on the edge of town, the suites here
HOTEL have a full lounge and dining area and a well-equipped kitchenette, but it's the bathroom, complete with washer/dryer, that impresses most. **Pros:** free shuttle to town; good on-site café. **Cons:** it's a ½-hour stroll from the middle of town. $ *Rooms from: NZ$240* ⊠ *54 Sargood Dr.* ☎ *03/443– 0011* ⊕ *www.edgewater.co.nz* ⮌ *59 suites, 45 studio hotel rooms, 35 2-bedroom apartments (combined suite and room)* ⦿*| No meals.*

$$$ ⛺ **Lakeside Apartments.** These modern apartments provide nice family-
RENTAL size accommodation in a particularly central location. **Pros:** great loca-
FAMILY tion; lovely pool; use of a barbecue. **Cons:** can be hard to get into,

10

ECO-STAYS

Beautiful **Wanaka Homestead** (⊕ *www.wanakahomestead.co.nz*) combines luxury and sustainability. The lodge's hot water, which supplies the taps, hot tub, and cozy underfloor heating, is solar heated. This lodge has been highly commended with a New Zealand EnergyWise award, recognizing efforts that have reduced "brought-in" power needs by half. The lodge uses low-energy appliances and controllers, and it was designed and built with energy efficiency and environmental sensitivity in mind. Wanaka's **Minaret Lodge** (⊕ *www.minaretlodge.co.nz*) is another luxurious facility, which practices eco-sensitivity in its daily routines, using biodegradable cleansers, organic produce and fair-trade coffee, energy-efficient lightbulbs, and the great Kiwi answer to energy-efficient insulation: sheep's wool in the walls.

particularly over the NZ school holidays. $ *Rooms from: NZ$295* ⊠ *9 Lakeside Rd.* ☎ *03/443–0188, 0800/002–211 NZ only* ⊕ *www.lakesidewanaka.co.nz* ↝ *20 apartments* ⊘ *No meals.*

$$$$
B&B/INN

☰ **Minaret Lodge.** This five-star luxury retreat has eco-friendly accommodations, from the natural materials used in the chalets to organic coffee and cuisine. **Pros:** very quiet retreat in the Wanaka township; tennis and mountain bikes available; Lord of the Rings–themed rooms and menu are fun. **Cons:** a 15-minute walk from town; no direct lake views. $ *Rooms from: NZ$460* ⊠ *34 Eely Point Rd.* ☎ *03/443–1856* ⊕ *www.minaretlodge.co.nz* ↝ *5 rooms* ⊘ *Breakfast.*

$$$
B&B/INN
Fodor's Choice
★

☰ **Waiorau Homestead.** From the exceptionally good food to the warmth of the hospitality and finest linen on your bed, this is a memorable place to stay. **Pros:** lovely guest lounge; free bike use; outdoor hot tub; owner is a fantastic chef. **Cons:** 20-minute drive from Wanaka. $ *Rooms from: NZ$250* ⊠ *2127B Cardrona Valley Rd.* ☎ *03/443–2225* ⊕ *www.waiorauhomestead.co.nz* ↝ *3 rooms* ⊘ *Breakfast.*

$$$
B&B/INN

☰ **Wanaka Homestead Lodge and Cottages.** The owners used local schist and timber from the farm buildings that once stood here to build their fine solar-powered lakeshore lodge. **Pros:** outdoor fireplace; hot tub; free bike hire. **Cons:** occasional noise from the road disrupts tranquillity. $ *Rooms from: NZ$220* ⊠ *1 Homestead Close* ☎ *03/443–5022* ⊕ *www.wanakahomestead.co.nz* ↝ *5 rooms, 2 self-contained cottages* ⊘ *Breakfast.*

NIGHTLIFE

FAMILY

Cinema Paradiso. The local institution Cinema Paradiso is not your usual movie house—its seating includes couches, recliners, pillows, and even a yellow Morris Minor car. During intermission you can snack on homemade ice cream and warm cookies (straight out of the oven) or even have dinner with a glass of wine. Check the local paper or website for film details and make sure you book ahead. Opens half an hour before the first movie screens. ⊠ *72 Brownston St.* ☎ *03/443–1505* ⊕ *www.paradiso.net.nz* ▭ *NZ$15.*

The Cow. If you want a late bite and a good bottle of wine, pop into The Cow on Post Office Lane for good garlic bread and pizza. It's a very comfortable place, modeled in local stone and heavy timber, just like the original Cow in nearby Queenstown. In winter the open fireplace does an incredible job of warming the bones (and the wine). Feel free to add commentary to their restroom chalkboard walls. ⊠ *Post Office La., 33 Ardmore St.* ☎ *03/443–4269* ⊕ *www.thecowrestaurant.co.nz.*

Lake Bar. This bar's in an iconic spot at the top of Ardmore Street. Sit inside or out and soak up the amazing views of the lake and mountains; if you get hungry they turn out pub-style tapas and lunch, as well as dinner with a separate kids' menu. If you just want a pint in the sun, or after dark, the Lake Bar is a great place for visitors and locals alike. ⊠ *155 Ardmore St.* ☎ *03/443–2920* ⊕ *www.lakebar.co.nz.*

Water Bar. This is a very popular upmarket bar with an outdoor fire in winter and deck on the lakefront in summer. Head here for late-night entertainment. They have an attractive menu and all the meals are under NZ$25, with specials to be had at lunchtime and a ⊠ *145 Ardmore St.* ☎ *03/443–4345.*

SPORTS AND THE OUTDOORS

With the base of Mount Aspiring National Park on Wanaka's doorstep, renting a bicycle isn't such a bad idea. Soon mountains will surround you and then swingbridges will connect you to the trails, where you'll embark on foot.

BICYCLING

Rent a bicycle and explore along the shores of Lake Wanaka, and out along the Clutha River toward Albert Town. There are many places to rent bikes and get trail maps including Outside Sports (⊠ *17 Dunmore St.*) or Thunderbikes (⊠ *16 Helwick St.*). Both the Deans Bank Track near Albert Town, a scenic 11½ km (7 miles) intermediate-level loop track, and the Plantation or "Sticky Forest," as locals call it, have good networks of mountain bike trails for all abilities.

FISHING

Locals will tell you that fishing on Lake Wanaka and nearby Lake Hawea is better than at the more famed Taupo area. You won't want to enter that argument, but chances are good you'll catch fish if you have the right guide. Fishing is year-round.

If you're not keen on hiring a guide, you can rent fly-fishing gear and buy your fishing license at **Southern Wild** (⊠ *10 Helwick St.*) or **Lakeland Adventures** in the Log Cabin on Ardmore Street.

Hatch Fly Fishing Wanaka. If you've always loved the idea of fly-fishing but wouldn't know where to start, Craig Smith is a superb guide and a really nice guy who's happy to teach the basics. You can opt to get dropped in to your fishing spot by helicopter or jet-boat, and there are even overnight camp outs available. Rates include lunch and all equipment, as well as pickup and drop-off. ⊠ *9 Flora Dora Parade, Lake Hawea* ☎ *03/443–8446, 027/646–9419* ⊕ *www.hatchfishing.co.nz* 🛏 *From NZ$750 per day; NZ$790 with 2 anglers.*

10

Lake Hawea Fishing & Farmstay. Harry Urquhart has trolling excursions for rainbow trout, brown trout, and quinnat salmon on Lake Hawea. He's been doing it for 25 years and knows his stuff. He even offers a money-back guarantee: if you don't catch any fish you don't have to pay. He also has self-contained accommodation. ☎ *03/443–1535, 027/440–3070* ✉ *NZ$300 for a 2-hr trip or NZ$400 for 4 hrs (for up to 5 people).*

Telford Fishing and Hunting Services. Fishing and hunting guide Gerald Telford will tailor an experience just for you, whether you're fly-fishing, including night-fishing and multiday fishing expeditions, or hunting for trophy red stag. Hunting is free range, and you can choose rifle or bowhunting. Gerald has been doing this for more than 30 years and will show you the very best spots. ✉ *79 Riverbank Rd.* ☎ *027/535–6651* ⊕ *www.flyfishhunt.co.nz* ✉ *From NZ$700.*

Wanaka Fly Fishing. Wanaka Fly Fishing provides instruction, guided trips, and wilderness fishing safaris, including a heli-fishing option. Rates include gear, transport, lunch, flies, and photos. ☎ *03/443–7870* ⊕ *www.fly-fishing-guide-wanaka-new-zealand.co.nz* ✉ *NZ$470 ½ day for 2; NZ$780 full day.*

RAFTING

Pioneer Rafting. At Pioneer Rafting you can do some white-water rafting at a calmer pace. Lewis Verduyn is New Zealand's leading eco-rafting specialist. His highly informative eco-rafting adventure, suitable for most ages, retraces a historic pioneer log-raft route. Both full-day and half-day trips are available, and leave from the Visitor Information Centre in Wanaka. ✉ *Lake Wanaka i-SITE Visitor Centere, 103 Ardmore St.* ☎ *03/443–1246* ⊕ *www.ecoraft.co.nz* ✉ *From NZ$175.*

SCENIC FLIGHTS

The weather around Wanaka is clear much of the time, which has allowed it to become a scenic-flight base for fixed-wing planes and helicopters. Flights take in Mt. Cook and the West Coast glaciers, the Mt. Aspiring area, Queenstown, and Fiordland.

Aspiring Helicopters. It may be hard to believe the scenery can get any better but fasten your seat belt and prepare to be enthralled. Aspiring Helicopters does scenic and adventure trips ranging from a 20-minute local flight to a three-hour trip to Milford Sound. If you can, the longer flight to Milford goes via Mt. Aspiring and includes a landing at a high alpine lake and on a glacier. If you're after the serious wilderness spots to climb, ski, bike, fish, or even get married—they'll take you there, too. ✉ *2211 Wanaka-Mount Aspiring Rd.* ☎ *03/443–7152* ⊕ *www.aspiringhelicopters.co.nz* ✉ *From NZ$185 per person.*

Wanaka Flightseeing. Wanaka Flightseeing runs small Cessna aircraft to Mt. Cook, Mt. Aspiring, and Milford Sound. They also do private charters to create an itinerary of your choice. ✉ *Wanaka Airport, 10 Lloyd Dunn Ave.* ☎ *03/443–8787* ⊕ *www.flightseeing.co.nz* ✉ *From NZ$240.*

SKIING

With reliable snow and dry powder, Wanaka has some of the best skiing and snowboarding in New Zealand. Cardrona and Treble Cone are the two biggest winter-sports resorts, and Snow Farm specializes in cross-country ski. For more information about skiing and snowboarding in the area, check out ⊕ *www.lakewanaka.co.nz.*

Cardrona Alpine Resort. Cardrona, 34 km (21 miles) southwest of Wanaka, is great for families with its wide open trails, a kids' ski school and activity center, plus kid- and beginner-friendly lifts, and food outlets. A special "heavy metal" trail pours on the rails and jumps and there are two half pipes that are well used by international snowboarding teams (American snowboard star Shaun White landed his first back-to-back cork 10-80 in competition on one of them). The season is roughly mid-June–early October. A bonus at Cardrona is the 15 apartments up on the mountain, but you'll need to book early to get in. Daily shuttles are available from Wanaka, Queenstown, and Cromwell. ⊠ *Cardrona Valley Rd., Cardrona* ⊕ *www.cardrona.com* 📧 *1-day lift pass NZ$101.*

Treble Cone. Treble Cone, 19 km (11½ miles) west of Wanaka, is the South Island's largest ski area, with lots of advanced trails and off-piste skiing. You can purchase a single-day lift pass, or if you're planning to ski a few days you can buy a Flexi pass, which makes it a bit cheaper. You can call their Snow Phone to get up-to-date snow reports or check their website. If you're not a skier it's still worth getting a scenic chairlift ride on the home basin chairlift; the view is sensational. ⊠ *Wanaka-Mount Aspiring Rd.* ☎ *03/443–1406* ⊕ *www.treblecone.com* 📧 *Single-day lift pass NZ$106.*

WALKING AND TREKKING

The Mount Aspiring National Park provides serious hiking and mountaineering opportunities, including Wilkins Valley, Makarora River, and Mt. Aspiring tracks and trails.

Diamond Lake Track. The complete Diamond Lake Track takes three hours and starts 25 km (15½ miles) west of Wanaka, also on the Glendhu Bay–Mt. Aspiring road. The track rises to 2,518 feet at Rocky Peak, passing Diamond Lake along the way. If you've got time for only a short walk, take the one that heads to the lake; it takes only 20 minutes. The Diamond Lake area is also popular with mountain bikers and rock climbers. ⊠ *Matukituki Valley Rd.* ☎ *03/443–7660* ⊕ *www.doc.govt.nz.*

FAMILY **Lake Wanaka Outlet Track.** You get maximum views for minimal challenge on one of the prettiest local trails, which meanders along the Clutha River from the Lake Wanaka Outlet to Albert Town. This is a kid-friendly route, and also fly-fisherman-, bicyclist-, and picnicker-friendly. It takes about an hour one way. ⊠ *Outlet Track.*

Mt. Iron. If you have time for only one walk, Mt. Iron, rising 780 feet above the lake, is relatively short and rewarding. The access track begins 2 km (1 mile) from Wanaka, and the walk to the top takes 45 minutes. You can descend on the alternative route down the steep eastern face. ⊠ *124 Wanaka-Luggate Hwy.*

QUEENSTOWN

103 km (64 miles) southeast of Wanaka, 480 km (300 miles) southwest of Christchurch.

Fodor's Choice ★ Set on the edge of the glacial Lake Wakatipu, with stunning views of the sawtooth peaks of the Remarkables mountain range, Queenstown is the most popular tourist stop in the South Island. Once prized by the Māori as a source of greenstone, the town boomed when gold was discovered in the Shotover River during the 1860s; the Shotover quickly became famous as "the richest river in the world." By the 1950s Queenstown had become the center of a substantial farming area, and with ready access to mountains, lakes, and rivers, the town has since become the adventure capital of New Zealand. Today, New Zealanders' penchant for bizarre adventure sports culminates in Queenstown; it was here that the sport of leaping off a bridge with a giant rubber band wrapped around the ankles—bungy jumping—took root as a commercial enterprise. On a short walk along Shotover and Camp streets you can sign up for anything from white-water rafting and jet-boating to heli-skiing, parachuting, and paragliding. Queenstown unabashedly caters to adrenaline junkies, so height, G-force, and thrill factor are emphasized. Want to go on a nice rope swing? Queenstown has the world's biggest—120 meters (394 feet) long—in the Nevis Canyon; the ride is 120 kph (75 mph). In late June and early July, the 10-day Queenstown Winter Festival brings the winter-sport frenzy to a climax, with musical performers, ski-slope antics and races, and serious partying.

If you're not an extreme adventure enthusiast, you might recoil a bit and view the city with a cynical eye. Luckily there's a side to Queenstown that doesn't run on pure adrenaline: a large network of peaceful walks, several world-class golf courses, and you can always find a nice café, have wine by the lake, and sample the cuisine.

GETTING HERE AND AROUND

Highway 6 enters Queenstown from the West Coast; driving time for the 400-km (250-mile) journey from Franz Josef is eight hours. It takes approximately 1½ hours to drive between Queenstown and Wanaka; the drive between Queenstown and Te Anau generally lasts a little over two hours. Bus and airplane service are also available between Christchurch and Queenstown. The town is small and fun for seeing on foot. If you're out and about at night, there are several taxi services available.

Airport Queenstown Airport. ⊠ *Sir Henry Wigley Dr.* ☎ *03/450–9031* ⊕ *www.queenstownairport.co.nz.*

Airport Transfers Super Shuttle Queenstown. ☎ *09/522–5100, 0800/748–885 toll-free in NZ* ⊕ *www.supershuttle.co.nz.*

Bus Companies InterCity Coachlines. ☎ *03/442–4922 in Queenstown* ⊕ *www.intercity.co.nz.*

Bus Depot Frankton Bus Shelter. ⊠ *Kawarau Rd., Frankton.* **The Station - Queenstown.** ⊠ *At Camp and Shotover Sts.*

Rental Cars Apex. ⊠ *26 Shotover St.* ☎ *03/442–8040, 0800/531–111 NZ only* ⊕ *www.apexrentals.co.nz.* **Avis.** ⊠ *Terminal Bldg., Queenstown Airport* ☎ *03/442–3808* ⊕ *www.avis.co.nz.*

TOURS

COMBINATION TRIPS

FAMILY

Nomad Safaris. Nomad Safaris runs half-day 4WD trips to the old gold-rush settlements (or their remains), Skippers Canyon and Macetown. Try your hand at gold panning—they don't plant gold so any success or disappointment is genuine. Another off-roading trip takes you to see some of the areas filmed for the *Lord of the Rings* trilogy. ⊠ *37 Shotover St.* ☎ *03/442–6699, 0800/688–222* ⊕ *www.nomadsafaris.co.nz* ⌨ *From NZ$175.*

Queenstown Heritage Tours. Take a historical tour to Skippers Canyon in Queenstown Heritage's comfortable air-conditioned vehicles with delicious snacks. They also run separate wine-lovers tours in Gibbston Valley in the afternoon. If you book both as a combo it's cheaper, and includes lunch and tastings at three wineries. ⊠ *Unit 10, 174 Glenda Dr.* ☎ *03/409–0949* ⊕ *www.queenstown-heritage.co.nz* ⌨ *From NZ$160.*

Real Journeys. For a wide choice of fly-drive-cruise tour options to Milford and Doubtful sounds from Queenstown, Te Anau, and Milford, check out Real Journeys. ■ TIP➡ Do the overnight cruise if you really want to experience both sounds at their best; early in the morning and in the evening. The Doubtful Sound cruise is longer and more remote. The boat's engines are cut for a moment of silence, and what a moment it is—makes you realize how little true silence most of us have in our lives. The food's superb, too, and is all-inclusive. ⊠ *Steamer Wharf, Beach St.* ☎ *0800/656–501 within NZ, 03/442–7500* ⊕ *www. realjourneys.co.nz.*

VISITOR INFORMATION

Contacts **Queenstown i-SITE Visitor Information Centre.** ⊠ *Clocktower Bldg., 22 Shotover St., and Camp St.* ☎ *03/442–4100* ⊕ *www.qvc.co.nz.*

EXPLORING

TOP ATTRACTIONS

Fear Factory. A scary addition to the adventure scene in Queenstown, Fear Factory challenges you to walk through their haunted house in the center of town. Not for kids—thousands of people have chickened out (just yell chicken and you don't have to continue). It's best to do this half-hour activity with friends. Under 15 must be accompanied by an adult. ⊠ *54 Shotover St.* ⊕ *www.fearfactory.co.nz* ⌨ *NZ$35* ⊘ *Daily 11 am–10:30.*

Skippers Canyon. One of the enduring attractions in the area is the drive up Skippers Canyon. Harking back to the days when the hills were filled with gold diggers, the Skippers Road was hand carved out of rock, and it reaches into the deep recesses of the Shotover Valley. It's breathtakingly gorgeous but you could also be breathtakingly scared: there's a good reason that rental car companies don't insure you if you drive on this twisty, narrow, unsealed road fraught with slips and vertical drops. We suggest you take a tour instead. ⊠ *Skippers Rd.*

10

Skyline Gondola. Get the lay of the land by taking the Skyline Gondola up to the heights of Bob's Peak, 1,425 feet above the lake, for a smashing panoramic view of the town and the Remarkables. You can also get there by walking the One Mile Creek Trail. Once there, watch the paragliders jump off the summit for their slow cruise back down to lake level. There are restaurants at the summit (there's a great buffet) plus a *Kiwi Haka, or* Māori song-and-dance show, in the evening. For something a little faster, there's a luge ride, weather permitting. If even that isn't exciting enough, you can bungy jump from the summit terminal. ⊠ *Brecon St.* ☎ *03/441–0101* ⊕ *www.skyline.co.nz* ⊠ *Gondola from NZ$32* ⊗ *Daily 9 am–11:30 pm.*

T.S.S. *Earnslaw*. This lovely old ship is more than 100 years old, and one of the world's few coal-fired steamships still operating. It's in superb condition partly because it's only been on this lake and the water's so pure. T.S.S. (Twin Screw Steamer) *Earnslaw* runs across to Walter Peak and back on a 1½-hour cruise. You can do a stopover at **Walter Peak High Country Farm** and watch a sheep shearing and farm dog demonstration. But the best trip is to go to the Colonel's Homestead Restaurant for dinner (or lunch); it's an exceptional buffet—make sure you leave room for the sumptuous selection of desserts. The cruise back into Queenstown's particularly beautiful when the sun's going down. ⊠ *Steamer Wharf, Beach St.* ☎ *03/442–7500, 0800/656–501 NZ only* ⊕ *www.realjourneys.co.nz* ⊠ *Cruise only, NZ$57; cruise, dinner, and farm tour, NZ$125.*

WORTH NOTING

Queenstown Gardens. The public Queenstown Gardens on the waterfront peninsula are always worth a quiet stroll. It's one of the few places in Queenstown that hasn't changed. There's an easy path to wander along to wear off some of those calories you've consumed during your stay. Bring a disc and have a toss at the country's first Frisbee golf course. ⊠ *Park St.*

WINERIES

The vineyards across Central Otago and into the Queenstown and Wanaka areas constitute the world's southernmost wine region, and the country's highest and are particularly noted for producing outstanding Pinot Noir. Specifically, Bannockburn, Gibbston Valley, and Lowburn are home to big plantings. There are more than 90 wineries in the region with more than 4,774 acres planted in vines.

Amisfield Winery & Bistro. Step into this expansive winery and bistro and enjoy stunning lake and mountain views. Both the wines and the restaurant have earned accolades over the years, including Best Winery Restaurant from *Cuisine NZ* magazine in 2013. Go for a memorable lunch sharing locally sourced dishes that change with the season; sit in the sunny courtyard in summer, or by the fire in winter. The "Trust the Chef" menu is a good way to go. They're open for early dinner, closing around 8 pm. Wine tastings are available at the cellar door; the Pinot Noir, aromatic whites such as Riesling and Pinot Gris, and the Methode Traditionelle are all well worth sampling. ⊠ *10 Lake Hayes Rd.* ☎ *03/442–0556* ⊕ *www.amisfield.co.nz* ⊗ *Daily 11:30 am–8 pm.*

Carrick Wines. Spoil yourself and have lunch at Carrick Wines where the views of the mountains and Lake Dunstan are as satisfying as the cuisine. The Pinot Noir has been described as "archetypal Central Otago Pinot," which is a high compliment considering the caliber of the region's reds. ✉ *247 Cairnmuir Rd., Bannockburn* ☎ *03/445–3480* ⊕ *www.carrick. co.nz* ⊗ *Daily 11–5, lunch starts at noon. Closed June–mid-July.*

Chard Farm. The Chard Farm vineyard perches on a rare flat spot on the edge of the Kawarau Gorge, not far from Gibbston Valley and opposite AJ Hackett Bungy. Its location and the drive-in are beautiful and you'll find an excellent portfolio of wines to taste including Pinot Noir, Chardonnay, Gewürztraminer, Pinot Grigio, and Riesling. ✉ *Chard Rd., RD 1* ☎ *03/442–6110* ⊕ *www.chardfarm.co.nz* ⊗ *Weekdays 10–5, weekends 11–5.*

Gibbston Valley Wines. The wine-making industry in Central Otago began with the vines that were first planted here. The best-known vineyard in Central Otago, Gibbston Valley Wines is a beautiful spot for lunch and wine tasting. There are cheese platters and tasty sandwiches through to a full à la carte menu with wine recommendations. You can even taste wines in a cool, barrel-lined cave with cave tours on the hour. If you can't get out to the winery, Gibbston Valley also has a café in Arrowtown, where you'll get hint of what you've missed. ✉ *1820 State Hwy. 6, RD1, Gibbston* ⊹ *20-min drive east of Queenstown on State Hwy. 6* ☎ *03/442–6910* ⊕ *www.gibbstonvalleynz.com* ✉ *Wine-cave tour and tasting NZ$15* ⊗ *Tasting room 10–5, cave tours on the hr 10–4, restaurant noon–3.*

Mt. Difficulty. You could spend a lot of time in the tasting room with the large range of good wines on offer here, or you can keep it simple and grab one of their tasting trays, featuring a selection complete with notes. There are some sweet dessert wines that can only be bought at the cellar door to consider as well. Make sure you stay for lunch—the duck, slow-roasted in Pinot Noir with raspberry and cassis sauce, is a delight. Staff are friendly and know their stuff, and the view is pure Central Otago. ✉ *73 Felton Rd., Cromwell* ☎ *03/445–3445* ⊕ *www.mtdifficulty.co.nz* ⊗ *Cellar door 10:30–4:30, restaurant noon–4.*

The Winery. While the name is a bit misleading, the experience is very real. The Winery is a tasting room in the middle of Queenstown that provides an extensive winery tour with no driving. Purchase a wine card, peruse more than 90 bottles on tasting machines featuring New Zealand wines, insert the card into your chosen machine, and voilà, the machine debits your card and drops a taste (or more if you want) into your glass. You can buy any value card you like; NZ$10 buys 6–10 tastes. Recent upgrades mean you can now also taste whiskey, honey, and sparkling wine, and they do great cheeseboards to go with your tasting session. ✉ *14 Beach St.* ☎ *03/409–2226* ⊕ *www.thewinery.co.nz* ⊗ *Daily from 10:30.*

WHERE TO EAT

At first glance Queenstown's little side streets seem full of party bars and pizza joints, but that's because all the really great spots are hidden away or down at Steamer Wharf, which juts out into Lake Wakatipu.

Some places aren't easy to find, so ask if you can't find what you're looking for.

$$$

ECLECTIC

× **The Bathhouse.** In the early 1900s this space was a Victorian bathhouse, right on the beach, built to commemorate the coronation of Britain's King George V. Now a small kitchen turns out breakfast, lunch, fresh scones, tapas, and dinner. It's a beautiful spot and there are tables outside. The tapas menu starts at 3 pm, and there's beer and cider on tap; so grab your spot and watch the sun go down. $ *Average main: NZ$30* ⊠ *28 Marine Parade* ☎ *03/442–5625* ✧ *C2.*

$$

CAFÉ·ECLECTIC-NEW ZEALAND FAMILY

× **The Boat Shed Cafe & Bistro.** This charming historic wooden building in the Frankton Marina used to be the New Zealand Railways Shipping Office and is right beside the lake in a sunny spot looking out at the Remarkables Mountains. Take the Frankton Arm walk by the lake and head here for a great coffee and lovely breakfast or lunch. The menu's not extensive but is done well with focus on local, seasonal ingredients. There's also a small but good kids' menu. If the weather's bad, it's cozy and warm inside with a log burner and rustic wooden interior. $ *Average main: NZ$19* ⊠ *Sugar La., Frankton Marina* ☎ *03/441–4146* ⊕ *www.boatshedqueenstown.com* ✧ *D2.*

$$$$

ECLECTIC

× **The Bunker.** Log fires, leather armchairs, and a clubby vibe make the Bunker especially cozy. Whet your appetite with an aperitif at the bar before heading downstairs for some of the finest lamb, venison, duck, and quail you'll find in Queenstown. The wine list is equally impressive. The Bunker stays open really late and is often booked days in advance for dinner. It's a little hard to find, hidden behind an old wooden door down Cow Lane. If you can't do dinner, it's still a lovely place to pop in for a drink. $ *Average main: NZ$39* ⊠ *Cow La.* ☎ *03/441–8030* ⊕ *www.thebunker.co.nz* ⌂ *Reservations essential* ✧ *B2.*

$

BURGER

× **Fergburger.** A Queenstown institution, the famous Fergburger gets mentioned in media around the world. It began life as a burger bar serving from a hole in the wall and kept growing; now there's a permanent queue stretching outside. If you're not too hungry, but want to know what the fuss is about, just share one—they're big enough for two. And if the queue puts you off, there's always Fergbaker next door, selling freshly made gourmet pies as well as other French bakery–style delights. They're the place to go after a big night out. Both are open to 5 am. The most recent addition to the Ferg empire is Mrs. Ferg, selling a delicious range of gelati from the store next to Fergbaker. $ *Average main:* ⊠ *42 Shotover St.* ☎ *03/441–1232* ⊕ *www.fergburger.com* ✧ *B1.*

$$$$

NEW ZEALAND

× **Gantleys Restaurant.** Built in 1863 as an inn for gold miners, this beautifully renovated old stone building, set in 2 acres of garden, is a nostalgic and romantic place to dine. The food is superb, making the most of New Zealand's flavorful beef, lamb, and duck but with some unexpected combinations. They know their wine, too; there's a wine library and you'll find them on *Wine Spectator*'s award list. There's a six-course degustation menu with matching wine if you want to really settle in for the night. But the same dishes are on the à la carte menu if you'd rather pick and choose. ■ TIP→ **The restaurant will organize free pickup and drop-off for you from Queenstown—just ask when you** book your table. $ *Average main: NZ$42* ✉ *172 Arthurs Point Rd.* ☎ *03/442–8999* ⊕ *www.gantleys.co.nz* ⌕ *Reservations essential* ✢ *B1.*

$$$
ECLECTIC
✕ **Ivy & Lola's Kitchen & Bar.** Feast your eyes on a collection of relics from the 1940s to '60s, right down to the mismatched crockery and enjoy good food, great service, and a lovely atmosphere. The cuisine here is a delightfully eclectic mix, with flavors from NZ and around the world, though visitors to New Zealand are often looking for lamb. The Cecil Peak (just across the lake) lamb of the day comes served two ways and will satisfy any ovine cravings. Save room for dessert, or for a delightful finish to your evening ask for an espresso martini. $ *Average main: NZ$30* ✉ *Steamer Wharf, 88 Beech St.* ☎ *03/441–8572* ⊕ *www.ivyandlolas.com* ✢ *B2.*

$$$$
STEAKHOUSE
Fodor's Choice
★
✕ **Jervois Steak House.** Dine here and find out why New Zealand is so proud of its beef and lamb. This is how it should taste. You could take it to the next level with the Wagyu beef, but honestly it's hard to beat the standard Jervois fillet, with onion rings on the side and delicious sauces. Steak is the undisputed hero here, but like the great American steak houses on which Jervois models itself, there's fabulous seafood, too, and even a quality vegetarian menu. Warm, interesting decor, and welcoming, knowledgeable staff (they'll bring cuts of meat to your table to show what you're getting), ensure this place delivers a memorable night. If you can't do dinner, try lunch. $ *Average main: NZ$40* ✉ *Brecon St., Lower Steps* ☎ *03/442–6263* ⊕ *www.jervoissteakhouse.co.nz* ⌕ *Reservations essential* ✢ *B1.*

$$
CAFÉ
✕ **Joe's Garage.** There are now 10 outposts around New Zealand, but Queenstown is where the Joe's Garage concept began—good coffee in a laid-back, friendly spot, with a simple, reliable menu. You can have breakfast any time of the day. Try the *Tuska* (streaky bacon in a warm roll) with the delicious "rocket fuel" sauce on the side. There's counter seating with kitchen views. Seating outside can be a good choice as the music inside can seem a bit loud at times. $ *Average main: NZ$15* ✉ *Searle La.* ☎ *03/442–5282* ⊕ *www.joes.co.nz* ⊘ *No dinner* ✢ *C2.*

$$$$
NEW ZEALAND
✕ **Pier 19 Restaurant.** This bright and breezy eatery beside the lake on Steamer Wharf has picture-postcard views. In summer, if you don't mind being on display, sit outside for breakfast, lunch, or even dinner (and they'll make sure you're well looked after, with a hat and/or a blanket). Inside, it's cozy with a lovely atmosphere and friendly waitstaff. The regularly changing menu is fresh with regional tastes such as Pacific tuna nicoise salad, Stewart Island salmon, and Fiordland venison. If you're feeling adventurous, consider the Seafood Platter for two. $ *Average main: NZ$35* ✉ *Steamer Wharf* ☎ *03/442–4006* ⊕ *www.pier19.co.nz* ✢ *B2.*

$$$$
ITALIAN
✕ **Sasso.** Authentic Italian meets fresh New Zealand produce, topped off with fine local and Italian wines. If you have the time and appetite, go for the five-course Sapore di Sasso. Pair it with the recommended wines and the incredibly helpful staff and you'll have a great night; Sasso has done very well to build a culture of fine service and personality in a town not known for either. The beef carpaccio stays on the menu for good reason. $ *Average main: NZ$33* ✉ *14/16 Church St.* ☎ *03/409–0994* ⊕ *www.sasso.co.nz* ✢ *C2.*

10

$$

CAFÉ

✕ **Vudu Cafe.** This Queenstown institution is so popular it's opened a second venue, so if you can't get in to the main café try its "mini-me" version (Vudu Cafe & Larder) around the corner on Rees Street, just a short walk away. There's a solid breakfast and lunch menu with appealing homemade food at the counter to choose from, with plenty of gluten-free options, too. For breakfast try the poached eggs with grilled halloumi, or fill up with their blueberry and/or blackberry pancakes. Vudu has a pleasant cosmopolitan vibe but can get a bit noisy, so it's not the place to come for a quiet chat. $ *Average main: NZ$17* ⊠ *23 Beach St.* ☎ *03/442–5357* ⊕ *www.vudu.co.nz* ☾ *No dinner* ⚓ *Reservations not accepted* ✛ *B2.*

$$$

ECLECTICPIZZA

✕ **Winnie's.** A long-serving local favorite restaurant and bar with the winning combination of excellent pizza, pool tables, and a roof that opens to sunshine, snow, or stars. At night this place transforms into a happening spot, extremely popular with backpackers. Gluten-free pizzas are available for NZ$3 extra. Try and get a table on the balcony overlooking the mall. $ *Average main: NZ$25* ⊠ *7 The Mall, Mall St.* ☎ *03/442–8635* ⊕ *www.winnies.co.nz* ✛ *B2.*

WHERE TO STAY

$$$$

B&B/INN

⊡ **Blanket Bay.** Near the end of a long road, 40 minutes from Queenstown, this imposing schist lodge faces Lake Wakatipu and is surrounded by thousands of acres of sheep-station land. **Pros:** spectacular property; very private. **Cons:** 40-minute drive to Queenstown. $ *Rooms from: NZ$1590* ⊠ *Blanket Bay, 3 km (2 miles) south of Glenorchy* ☎ *03/441–0115* ⊕ *www.blanketbay.com* ↩ *5 rooms, 3 suites, 4 chalet suites* ❑ *Some meals* ✛ *A2.*

$$$$

HOTEL

⊡ **Eichardt's Private Hotel.** Once patronized by miners during the 1860s gold rush, Eichardt's now regularly receives awards as a boutique ski resort hotel. **Pros:** centrally located; great service. **Cons:** breakfast service can be slow. $ *Rooms from: NZ$1250* ⊠ *Marine Parade* ☎ *03/441–0450* ⊕ *www.eichardts.com* ↩ *5 hotel suites, 4 lakefront apartments (1–2 bedroom), 1 3-bedroom villa* ❑ *Breakfast* ✛ *B2.*

$$

HOTEL

⊡ **Heritage Queenstown.** Situated at the bottom of Fernhill, the Heritage is quieter than other local hotels and has panoramic views of the Remarkables and Lake Wakatipu. **Pros:** great service; pleasant rooms. **Cons:** 10-plus minute walk to downtown. $ *Rooms from: NZ$195* ⊠ *91 Fernhill Rd.* ☎ *03/450–1500* ⊕ *www.heritagehotels.co.nz* ↩ *136 rooms, 39 suites* ❑ *No meals* ✛ *A2.*

$$

RENTAL

⊡ **Queenstown Lakeview Holiday Park.** With everything from new two-bedroom motel units (that can sleep four to people) to spic-and-span, fully equipped apartments to studios, cabins, and campsites, this park is a varied budget pick. **Pros:** centrally located. **Cons:** can get a bit crowded. $ *Rooms from: NZ$135* ⊠ *45 Brecon St.* ☎ *03/442–7252, 0800/482–735 within New Zealand* ⊕ *www.holidaypark.net.nz* ↩ *16 rooms, 22 lodges, 8 cabins, 5 motel units* ❑ *No meals* ✛ *B1.*

$$$$

HOTEL

⊡ **Queenstown Park Boutique Hotel.** This plush hotel is located in the center of town and you can walk to the lake, shopping, dining, and tour departure points in just five minutes. **Pros:** leave your car at the hotel and walk; predinner drinks and canapes. **Cons:** street-view rooms can

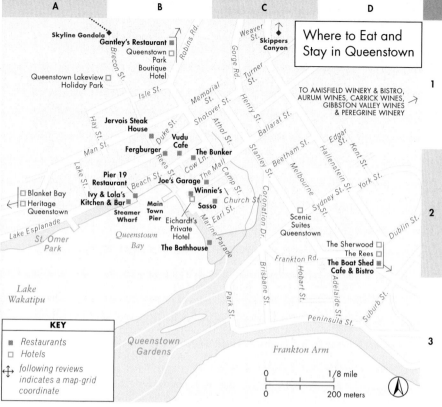

Where to Eat and Stay in Queenstown

TO AMISFIELD WINERY & BISTRO, AURUM WINES, CARRICK WINES, GIBBSTON VALLEY WINES & PEREGRINE WINERY

KEY

■ *Restaurants*
□ *Hotels*

following reviews indicates a map-grid coordinate

0   1/8 mile

0   200 meters

be noisy. $ *Rooms from: NZ$450* ⌧ *21 Robins Rd.* ☎ *03/441–8441* ⊕ *www.queenstownparkhotel.co.nz* ⛟ *19 rooms* ⊙ *No meals* ✛ *B1.*

$$$
HOTEL
Fodor's Choice
★

🛏 **The Rees.** Staff at The Rees are particularly attentive considering the large size of this place, named for Queenstown's first European settler, William Gilbert Rees, who oversaw the birth of the town during the 1860s gold rush. **Pros:** exceptional restaurant and wine selection; hourly shuttles to town. **Cons:** quite far from the town center. $ *Rooms from: NZ$255* ⌧ *377 Frankton Rd.* ☎ *03/450–1100* ⊕ *www.therees.co.nz* ⛟ *60 rooms, 90 apartments* ⊙ *No meals* ✛ *D2.*

$$$$
HOTEL

🛏 **Scenic Suites Queenstown.** Wide, floor-to-ceiling windows with views over the town, lake, and across to the mountains are the best part of these modern, spacious rooms. **Pros:** nice big rooms; well-equipped suites. **Cons:** steep (but short) walk to and from town. $ *Rooms from: NZ$322* ⌧ *27 Stanley St.* ☎ *03/442–4718* ⊕ *www.scenichotels.co.nz* ⛟ *42 rooms, 42 suites* ⊙ *No meals* ✛ *C2.*

$$
HOTEL

🛏 **The Sherwood.** Starting life in the 1980s as a mid-range motor inn, Sherwood has had a startling rebirth as one of the funkiest places to stay in Queenstown, with guest rooms furnished darkly in a retro industrial style. **Pros:** sociable bar and great restaurant; activities such as yoga and a BMX track on-site. **Cons:** looks quite ordinary from the street. $ *Rooms from: NZ$165* ⌧ *554 Frankton Rd.* ☎ *03/450–1090*

10

⊕ *www.sherwoodqueenstown.co.nz* ⮕ *78 rooms* ⦿ *No meals* ⊟ *No credit cards* ✛ *D2.*

NIGHTLIFE

After days spent testing limits, visitors cram Queenstown's clubs and bars, and often end up mingling with the friendly locals next to fireplaces, and catching up again as they walk between the popular venues, which are all close together. But in the very small hours, as with anywhere, be a little more careful; keep an eye out for those who've overindulged in the party spirit and don't be surprised to encounter a "hens' party" or "stag do." Kiwi guys are notoriously vile to their groom-to-be mates, so steer clear if you see a pack of rowdy bachelors as things can get messy in their midst. Grab a copy of the free weekly paper the *MountainScene* or check out the *Source* magazine, a monthly gig guide available in most cafés and bars or on Facebook.

Bardeaux. In winter Bardeaux has that upmarket mountain-après-ski atmosphere; even in summer there's a fair chance the fire will be roaring. There's a wide selection of whiskeys and reasonable (for Queenstown) prices. They know how to fix you up a cocktail at this pleasing bar that's good for a quiet, intimate evening. ⊠ *Eureka Arcade off The Mall* ☎ *03/442–8284.*

FAMILY **Minus 5° Ice Bar.** The ice-bar gimmick has been spreading over the past few years, but it's great fun if you've never tried one—if not for the beautiful ice sculptures alone. They deck you out in jackets and gloves prior to entering. In summer it's a good reminder of how close to Antarctica you are, and in winter it just adds to that alpine resort experience. Take the family during the day or to keep them amused while you have a predinner drink. The kids can have a "mocktail" in a "glass" made of ice. ⊠ *Steamer Wharf* ☎ *03/442–6050* ⊕ *www.minus5icebar. com* ⬜ *NZ$20.*

Searle Lane. With its roaring fire, good food, and quirky decor, Searle Lane is a popular Queenstown spot. There's plenty of beer on tap and a good selection of wine by the glass. They do a mean cocktail, too. The food is made for sharing with hearty choices; their specialty is rotisserie chicken, which is seriously good. ⊠ *15 Church St.* ☎ *03/441–3934* ⊕ *www.searlelane.co.nz.*

SPORTS AND THE OUTDOORS

You'll find many people raving about their bungy-jumping experience or their jet-boat tour from the day before. Any activity you choose around Queenstown will bring you deep into the scenery that you can only ogle from the wharf.

BUNGY JUMPING

AJ Hackett Bungy. This is where bungy began in New Zealand, at the original jump site: Kawarau Bridge, 20 minutes from Queenstown on State Highway 6. Even if you don't plan on taking the leap it's worth heading there to watch from the viewing decks. There's a zipride, too, that's way easier on the nerves but still gives something to write home about. Those who graduate from the 142-foot plunge might like to test themselves on the Nevis Bungy, suspended 440 feet above the Nevis

River, or try out what they claim is the world's biggest swing. If you're short on time, there's always the *Ledge* by the Skyline Gondola where you can also jump or swing. Be sure to check age, height, and weight requirements. ☒ *The Station, Camp and Shotover Sts.* ☎ *0800/286–4958 NZ only, 03/450–1300* ⊕ *www.bungy.co.nz* ☒ *From NZ$50 for zipride; NZ$195 for Kawarau or Ledge jump.*

Shotover Canyon Swing. For those who think bungy jumping doesn't keep the adrenaline pumping long enough, the Shotover Canyon Swing gives a terrifying jump with an added scenic boost. Choose your jump style—go forward, backward, or tied to a chair—and leave the edge of a cliff 358 feet above the Shotover Canyon. Price includes transfers to/from town and age, height, and weight requirements apply. ☒ *35 Shotover St.* ☎ *03/442–6990* ⊕ *www.canyonswing.co.nz* ☒ *NZ$219.*

HIKING

Several scenic walks branch out from town. For a history lesson with your ramble, head to the **Time Walk,** entering through an iron gateway on the Queenstown Hill trail. Narrative panels line the route; it takes about two hours, and you'll feel good when you see the view at the top. The **Ben Lomond Track** takes you to one of the highest peaks in the basin. Take the gondola to the Bob's Peak summit, then follow signs to the saddle and the steep climb to the peak (5,730 feet). You'll need to be reasonably fit and this can be a full-day walk, so make sure you bring all the necessary supplies.

Fodor's Choice ★ **Queenstown Trail.** For a wonderful journey around the Queenstown area, take a look at the trail map (see website) of this 120-km (74.5-mile) walking and cycling trail and start planning. The trail is well built and there are plenty of places to hire all the biking equipment you need (also on its website). The trail takes you over to Arrowtown and the wineries of Gibbston, past two lakes and three rivers, over some interesting bridges, and always through stunning scenery. You can do it all or just parts of it. The path's uphill from Queenstown so if you want to make it a little easier for yourself, start your trip in Arrowtown. ⊕ *www. queenstowntrail.co.nz.*

HORSE TREKKING

Dart Stables. There's no better way to absorb some of New Zealand's most spectacular scenery than on horseback. Dart Stables has been operating in Glenorchy since 1992 and has gained a well-earned reputation for providing great horse riding in a stunning part of New Zealand. With more than 50 horses of various breeds, knowledgeable and enthusiastic guides, and a wealth of experience, Dart Stables are able to provide riding for all levels. ☒ *58 Coll St., Glenorchy* ☎ *03/442–5688, 0800/474–3464* ⊕ *www.dartstables.com* ☒ *From NZ$85.*

Moonlight Stables. Moonlight Stables offers a 1½-hour ride with spectacular views of the mountains and rivers around the Wakatipu–Arrow Basin. Ride across an 800-acre deer farm in Australian stock saddles and western saddles. Both novice and experienced riders are welcome, and private rides can be arranged. Transportation from Queenstown is provided; allow 2½ hours return. ☒ *69 Morven Ferry Rd., Arrow Junction* ☎ *03/442–1229* ⊕ *www.moonlightstables.co.nz* ☒ *From NZ$120.*

10

JET-BOAT RIDES

Dart River Wilderness Jet. With Dart River you can get an unrivaled look at rugged Mount Aspiring National Park, one of the most spectacular parts of South Island. Their route includes jet-boating on the upper and lower Dart River, along with a bit of walking and a back-road tour of the "Paradise" area. The Funyak option takes you upstream by jet-boat, then you paddle gently downstream, exploring the Rockburn Chasm on the way. Start your adventure from their office in Glenorchy, or catch a shuttle bus, departing daily from Queenstown for the 45-minute ride to the boats. Rates include transfer. ⊠ *Corner of Camp and Shotover St.* ☎ *0800/327–853 NZ only, 03/442–9992* ⊕ *www.dartriver.co.nz* ⊠ *From NZ$219.*

Hydro Attack. Strap into the F-16–style cockpit of this shark-styled watercraft and fly across and under Lake Wakatipu. This is the world's first commercial operation using the Seabreacher X watercraft, and your expert pilot will tailor your personal trip to suit your comfort levels, from scenic cruise to wild ride. Riders are restricted by height and weight and you need to be somewhat flexible to board the craft. Not recommended if you are subject to seasickness. ⊠ *Lapsley Butson Wharf, Beach St.* ☎ *027/477–9074* ⊕ *www.hydroattack.co.nz* ⊠ *NZ$149.*

PARAGLIDING

KJet. With the sun sparkling off the lake, wind whistling past, and traveling way faster than you had imagined, this is good holiday fun. KJet takes you 42 km (27 miles) on Lake Wakatipu and down two rivers, the Kawarau and Shotover, with some 360 spins along the way. Boats leave from the Main Town Pier where there's also an interesting underwater observatory. Reservations recommended. ⊠ *Main Town Pier, Marine Parade* ☎ *03/442–6142* ⊕ *www.kjet.co.nz* ⊠ *From NZ$125.*

Shotover Jet. Shotover Jet's famous red boats lead high-speed, heart-stopping rides in the Shotover River canyons; it's got exclusive rights to operate in these waters. The boat pirouettes within inches of canyon walls. The boats are based at the Shotover Jet Beach beneath the historic Edith Cavell Bridge, a 10-minute drive from Queenstown. If you don't have transport, a free shuttle makes frequent daily runs. Reservations are essential. ⊠ *Gorge Rd., over the Edith Cavell Bridge at Arthur's Point* ☎ *03/442–8570, 0800/746-868 NZ only* ⊕ *www.shotoverjet.com* ⊠ *From NZ$135.*

MOTORSPORTS

Highlands Motorsport Park. Fulfill your dream of being a race car driver at Highlands. There's a range of activities including go-kart racing, self-drive hot laps, and ride-along hot laps. The Highlands Taxi is a Porsche Cayenne Turbo driven by a professional racer. The first lap is taken slowly and the driver talks about the facility, the second lap is full speed ahead. If you want to go faster, there is also a Lamborghini and a range of purpose-built race cars. Located in Cromwell, Highlands Motorsport Park is a 45-minute drive from Queenstown on State Highway 6, and you can call Highlands to arrange a free shuttle from Queenstown. The Highlands National Motorsport Museum is here, too. ⊠ *Corner State Hwy. 6 and Sandflat Rd., Cromwell* ☎ *03/445-4052* ⊕ *www.highlands.co.nz* ⊠ *Go karts NZ$35, Highlands Taxi NZ$95, self-drive from NZ$295.*

Jet-boats offer a thrillingly wet way to enjoy the Queenstown area's natural beauty.

RAFTING

Rafting is generally an adult thrill, with age restrictions for children. You'll need your swimsuit and a towel, but all other gear, including wet suit, life jacket, helmet, and wet-suit booties, are provided by the rafting companies. Instructors spend quite a bit of time on safety issues and paddling techniques before you launch.

Queenstown Rafting. Queenstown Rafting runs various half-, full-, and three-day white-water rafting trips in the Queenstown area year-round, with trips on the Shotover and Kawarau rivers. If you're not into the white water you can do the Flow (suitable for kids from four years), which is a scenic trip in a raft or inflatable kayak. Or go all out with the Nevis Quad Challenge, which includes a jet-boat ride, a helicopter trip, rafting on the Shotover, and a bungy jump, all in one day. ⊠ *35 Shotover St.* ☎ *03/442–9792, 0800/723–8464 NZ only* ⊕ *www. queenstownrafting.co.nz* ⊠ *From NZ$219; NZ$669 for Nevis Quad Challenge.*

Serious Fun River Surfing. This is serious—for the adventurous and those with surfing or water experience. You'll get kitted out in a full wet suit, helmet, life jacket, and fins. There's an introduction to river surfing on calm water first. Then grab your bodyboard and prepare to surf the waves of Queenstown's stunning Kawarau River. Where your guide ends up taking you will depend on the conditions but the Kawarau River has plenty of white water. They'll pick you up from town. ⊠ *39 Camp St.* ☎ *03/442–5262* ⊕ *www.riversurfing.co.nz* ⊠ *From NZ$215.*

SCENIC FLIGHTS

Over the Top Helicopters. Over the Top Helicopters runs a diverse selection of flights in their executive-style helicopters, including glacier and alpine ski slope landings, and scenic tours above Queenstown, the Remarkables, Fiordland, and Milford and Doubtful sounds. They'll also deliver you to fly-fishing spots absolutely miles from anywhere, or take you heli-skiing or on ecotours as far away as Stewart Island. ✉ *Blue Hangar, Tex Smith La.* ☎ *03/442–2233, 0800/123–359* ⊕ *www.flynz.co.nz* ✈ *From NZ$265 per person.*

SKIING

Coronet Peak. Queenstown's original ski resort, 20 minutes from town, rocks day and night to a ski and snowboard crowd that returns year after year. Not only is it accessible, but it also has a veritable army of ski guns to keep the snow topped up. It has a skiable area of 700 acres, a vertical drop of 1,360 feet, a high-speed six-seater, two express quads, and a T-bar, as well as four learner conveyor lifts in the learners area. The season usually runs June to October. Night skiing is available on Friday and Saturday night from early July to mid-September. Ski shuttles depart regularly from Queenstown Snow Centre. ✉ *Coronet Peak Station Rd.* ☎ *03/442–4620* ⊕ *www.nzski.com* ✈ *Day pass NZ$104.*

FAMILY   **The Remarkables.** Just across the valley, the Remarkables is a higher ski area that's a bit more of a drive but has something to suit all abilities from three terrain parks to wide sunny slopes to serious black runs. The vertical drop here is 1,160 feet and it has a fast-speed six-seater, and three quads. It's a great place to take kids with good vantage points to watch them on the learners slopes, and if skiing's not your thing you can take the family tubing—which is like sledding on a giant inner tube. It's a 45-minute drive from Queenstown and if you don't like heights or hairpin bends and unsealed roads you can catch the Ski Shuttle from the Queenstown Snow Centre in town. ✉ *Queenstown* ☎ *03/442–4615* ⊕ *www.nzski.com* ✈ *NZ$104.*

SKYDIVING

NZONE Skydive. Here's a different way of taking in the view of Queenstown—from a tandem skydive. At 15,000 feet the Earth is already taking on that round from-out-of-space look about it that says you're a long way up. You don't have to jump from that high: there are 12,000- and 9,000-feet options. Either way it's an unforgettable experience, helped by Jumpmasters who make you feel at ease (relatively speaking). And it's good to know this company has been operating successfully for more than 23 years. You have to be less than 220 pounds to do a tandem skydive. ✉ *Reservations and pickup, 35 Shotover St.* ☎ *03/442–5867* ⊕ *www.nzone.co.nz* ✈ *From NZ$299.*

ZIP-LINING

Ziptrek Ecotours. With Ziptrek you can zip every which way (upside down if you want) among the trees on the hills above Queenstown. It's a very scenic adventure and as each zipline stops at a tree platform, you learn about the ecology of the area. Most of all, it's good fun; but not for anyone who's scared of heights. Not suitable for children under six. ✉ *Gondola Hill* ☎ *03/441–2102, 0800/947–8735 NZ only* ⊕ *www.ziptrek.com* ✈ *From NZ$139.*

A former gold-rush town, Arrowtown now only sees gold in the autumn leaves.

ARROWTOWN

22 km (14 miles) northeast of Queenstown, 105 km (66 miles) south of Wanaka.

Arrowtown is tucked into a corner at the foot of the steep Crown Range. It's a quaint village that takes pride in the history of the area, with around 70 buildings from the original gold rush, a partially restored Chinese village from the 1880s, and a small but fantastic museum. Jack Tewa, or Māori Jack, as he was known, found gold along the Arrow River in 1861, and when William Fox, an American, was seen selling large quantities of the precious metal in nearby Clyde shortly afterward, the hunt was on. Eventually a large party of prospectors stumbled on Fox and his team of 40 miners. The secret was out, miners rushed to stake their claims, and Arrowtown was born. On the first gold escort in January 1863 a whopping 12,000 ounces of gold were carried out. At the height of the rush there were more than 30,000 hardy souls in this tiny settlement. After the gold rush ended in 1865, the place became another sleepy rural town until tourism created a second boom. Each April, Arrowtown celebrates the Autumn Festival when the trees are at their most spectacular, and includes the NZ Gold Panning championships. On a stroll along **Buckingham Street,** you can stop in the old post and telegraph office, still open for business. Take time to explore some of the lanes and arcades, filled with cafés and boutique shops, drop in to the Jade & Opal Factory shop to see hand carving done on-site and to Patagonia chocolates to see chocolate being made; as if that's not enough the ice-cream there's delicious, too (below Buckingham Street on Ramshaw Lane).

GETTING HERE AND AROUND

Arrowtown is a 20-minute drive from Queenstown, and you can take a bus there. Exploring the town is easily and enjoyably done on foot. If you'd like to venture out toward the old gold-mining settlement Macetown, you can walk or bike if you're a hearty sort (it's 16 km [10 miles] and entails 22 river crossings). A great way to explore the region is in a 4WD vehicle. Nomad Safaris provides a number of 4WD tour options. For a beautiful start to the day go up in a balloon and see Arrowtown and the Wakatipu Basin from the air.

Bus Companies Connectabus. ☎ *03/441–4471* 🌐 *www.connectabus.com.*

VISITOR INFORMATION

Contacts Arrowtown Visitor Information Centre. ✉ *Lakes District Museum, 49 Buckingham St.* ☎ *03/442–1824* 🌐 *www.arrowtown.com.*

EXPLORING

FAMILY **Chinese settlement.** In a less-visited part of the town is the former Chinese settlement. Chinese miners were common on the goldfields, brought in to raise a flagging local economy after the gold rush abated, but local prejudice from resident Europeans forced them to live in their own separate enclave. Some of their tiny 19th-century buildings, which have been restored, were built of sod, which endures well in the dry climate; others were built of layered schist stone, with roofs of corrugated iron or tussock thatch. Ah Lum's store (also now restored) was built in a style typical of the Canton delta region of China and operated until 1972. The settlement is a worthwhile part of any day-walk in the area. ✉ *Bush Creek, west end of town* 🎟 *Free.*

FAMILY Fodor's Choice ★ **Lakes District Museum.** Don't leave Arrowtown without dropping in to this small but very cleverly constructed museum. It gives a great insight into the history of the area, with artifacts of the gold-rush days, and even a whole streetscape underground, complete with Victorian schoolroom, bakery, and blacksmith. There's also an information center, small bookstore, and gallery. You can even rent a pan for NZ$3 and get gold-panning tips to try your luck in the nearby Arrow River. When your patience frays and your hands go icy, keep in mind that a hobby prospector found a 10 oz nugget in this very river in 2006. (He sold it on eBay for NZ$15,000.) ✉ *49 Buckingham St.* ☎ *03/442–1824* 🌐 *www.museumqueenstown.com* 🎟 *NZ$8* 🕒 *Daily 8:30–5.*

WHERE TO EAT

$$$ MEXICAN 🍴 **Agave.** Hidden down a small alleyway, Agave keeps the menu basic, with a focus on execution. The blue cod tacos nicely incorporate New Zealand seafood, and because former occupants Pesto's old pizza oven remains in the kitchen you can still order a pizza, albeit with a Mexican twist. After dinner, head next door to Blue Door bar. [$] *Average main: NZ$22* ✉ *18 Buckingham St.* ☎ *03/442–0885* 💳 *No credit cards.*

$$ CAFÉECLECTIC 🍴 **Cafe Mondo.** Tucked into a sheltered courtyard off the main street, this is the place for refreshing, eclectic cold drinks like the Mondo Combo, a blend of orange, carrot, and apple juices with a hint of ginger. They have

some great home baking and you could also dig into a substantial and interesting breakfast or lunch with Mexican, Thai, Italian, and Kiwi flavors. $ *Average main: NZ$17* ✉ *4/14 Buckingham St.* ☎ *03/442–0227* ⊕ *www.cafemondoarrowtown.com.*

$$$ ✕ **La Rumbla.** This is one of those rare places that's got all the elements
TAPAS right: food, service, and atmosphere. Put it down to the passion and interest of its owners who are either in the kitchen cooking or out front making sure this is the best experience it can be. Choose a few interesting dishes to share. It's a tapas restaurant but with generous servings—a mixture of Spanish and all sorts of interesting savory influences. There's a good wine list but they make wicked cocktails, too. Make a reservation if you want to be sure of a table; locals love this place. $ *Average main: NZ$30* ✉ *54 Buckingham St.* ☎ *03/442–0509.*

$$ ✕ **Provisions.** With a welcoming atmosphere and lovely garden Provi-
CAFÉ sions is a delightful place to have breakfast or lunch. The blackboard menu is enticing and there are homemade treats in the cabinet. People come from far and wide for their sticky buns, which go well with their great coffee. Set in a historic cottage, Provisions gets its name from the range of gourmet preserves they make. Try the roasted cherry chutney— it's Central Otago in a jar—along with homemade artisan breads to go with it. $ *Average main: NZ$16* ✉ *65 Buckingham St.* ☎ *03/442–0714* ⊕ *www.provisions.co.nz.*

WHERE TO STAY

$$$$ ☷ **Arrowtown House Boutique Hotel.** Arguably offering the best service
B&B/INN (and breakfast) in Arrowtown, Steve and Jeanette are famous for their
Fodor's Choice hospitality, winning numerous awards. **Pros:** the food is exceptional, as
★ is the service; located in the heart of Arrowtown. **Cons:** hard to get a booking in peak season. $ *Rooms from: NZ$530* ✉ *10 Caernarvon St.* ☎ *03/441–6008* ⊕ *www.arrowtownhouse.co.nz* ⤳ *5 rooms* ⦿ *Break-fast* ▬ *No credit cards.*

$$$$ ☷ **Millbrook Resort.** A 20-minute drive from Queenstown, this glamorous
RESORT resort has a special appeal for golfers: a 27-hole course first designed by New Zealand professional Sir Bob Charles and extended by another Kiwi golfing great, Greg Turner. **Pros:** terrific golf course; plenty of amenities. **Cons:** sprawling and somewhat impersonal. $ *Rooms from: NZ$350* ✉ *Malaghans Rd.* ☎ *0800/800–604, 03/441–7000* ⊕ *www.millbrook.co.nz* ⤳ *56 studios, 80 suites, 23 2- to 4-bedroom cottages* ⦿ *No meals.*

NIGHTLIFE

The Blue Door. What goes on behind the Blue Door? Whiskey, wine, and cocktails, served by knowledgeable and chatty (when it's quiet) staff. Sit in a dark corner near the fire, or at the bar, just not on the end nearest the door since you may get asked to move if their most regular patron comes in. Set in a beautiful old stone building with candles burning around the room, it's the perfect place for a nightcap before walking back to your accommodation. This venue is not child friendly. ✉ *18 Buckingham St.* ☎ *03/442–0131* ⊕ *www.saffronrestaurant.co.nz/bluedoor/index.html.*

10

Dorothy Brown's Boutique Cinema and Bar. It may not have a flashy marquee, but Dorothy Brown's Boutique Cinema and Bar is a truly memorable movie house. The theater doesn't seat many people, but the chairs are cushy and have plenty of legroom. Better yet, you can get a glass of wine at the fireplace bar and bring it with you, along with a cheeseboard to nibble from, and if you run out, all screenings have an intermission. The schedule mixes Hollywood releases with art and international films and they have 3-D screenings here, too. Book ahead—it's popular. ⊠ *Buckingham St.* ☎ *03/442–1964* ⊕ *www.dorothybrowns. com* ⊠ *NZ$18.50.*

The Fork and Tap. In this cozy historic building, there are 14 beers and ciders on tap, a great selection of local Central Otago wine, and a hearty pub-style menu for lunch and dinner. If you're looking for a lively spot to enjoy a beer and share stories after a big day of skiing or sightseeing, this is it. Don't sit too close to the fire if you can help it, it can get very hot. ⊠ *51 Buckingham St.* ☎ *03/442–1860* ⊕ *www. theforkandtap.co.nz.*

SPORTS AND THE OUTDOORS

There are several spectacular walks—**Tobin's Track, Sawpit Gully,** and the **Lake Hayes Walk**—to raise the fitness levels and give you a feeling for where you are. You can get details on all of them from the Lakes District Museum Information Centre. For easier ambles take the Arrow River Trail or the Bush Creek Trail. And if you want a real challenge tackle the hike out to the old gold settlement Macetown. Make sure you take your own picnic: although you might hear the Macetown Bakehouse mentioned, be aware the place is a ghost town now and there are only remnants of the settlement.

You can hire a bike from places like Arrowtown Bike Hire or Queenstown Bike Tours. Grab a map or check out ⊕ *www.queenstowntrail. co.nz* and head to Gibbston Valley for lunch or some wine tasting; the trail is well maintained and there are several interesting bridges to cross.

There are also three quite distinct golf courses within a 10-minute drive of Arrowtown that offer some of the most scenic golf holes you'll ever play; the most accessible is the Arrowtown Golf Course, but there's also Millbrook, and the Hills, which need booking well in advance.

FIORDLAND

Fiordland, on the southwest of the South Island, is a majestic wilderness of rocks, ice, and beech forest, where glaciers have carved mile-deep notches into the coast. Most of this terrain is officially designated **Fiordland National Park,** and in conjunction with South Westland National Park, is a designated UNESCO Te Wahipounamu World Heritage Area. Parts of the park are so remote that they have never been explored, and visitor activities are mostly confined to a few of the sounds and the walking trails. Te Anau serves as the base, with lodgings, a supermarket, cafés/restaurants, and sports outfitters. The most accessible scenic highlight of this area—and perhaps of the whole country—is Milford

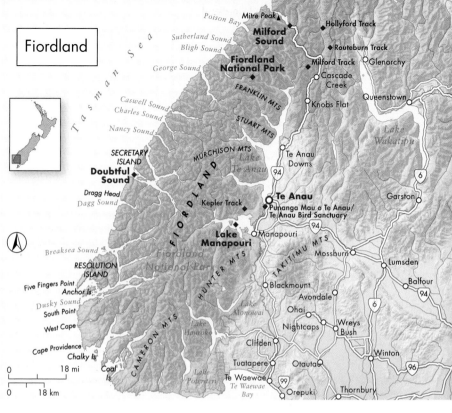

Sound, where trees cling to tremendous rock faces that plunge into the sea, and rare species of coral wait just below the water's surface.

The park is exceptional from a naturalist's point of view. More than 700 plants are found only here, and several rare birds as well. The flightless, blue-green *takahe*, for instance, was long thought to be extinct until one was discovered in Fiordland's Murchison Mountains in 1948. The last of the *kākāpo*, flightless nocturnal parrots, were also found in the park. The extreme landscape and soggy climate have prevented much development; neither the first Māori, the early European explorers, sealers, whalers, nor modern arrivals have made many inroads here. If you really want to take in the raw grandeur of Fiordland, hike one of the many trails in the area, among them the famous four-day Milford Track, long considered one of the finest walks in the world.

GETTING HERE AND AROUND

There are regular bus services to Te Anau and Milford Sound from Queenstown, Christchurch, and Invercargill. The town of Te Anau is small enough to explore on foot. If you want to see Doubtful Sound, it requires a bus and a boat so you will need to do an organized tour from Te Anau or Manapouri. The drive to Milford Sound is one of the most magnificent in the world. Once there, one of the best ways to experience the park is by boat. Te Anau has a small airport, but many people fly into the more regularly serviced Queenstown or Invercargill airports and then drive.

VISITOR INFORMATION

Fiordland National Park Visitor Centre. Fiordland National Park Visitor Centre hours vary a bit seasonally; summer hours are daily 8:30–6 and winter hours are 8:30–4:30. ⊠ *Lakefront Dr., Te Anau* ☎ *03/249–7924.*

TE ANAU

175 km (109 miles) southwest of Queenstown.

Lake Te Anau (tay- *ah*-no), which is 53 km (33 miles) long and up to 10 km (6 miles) wide, is the largest lake in New Zealand after Lake Taupo. The town of Te Anau, on the southern shores, serves as a base for Fiordland National Park. From Te Anau, you can set out on sightseeing trips by bus, boat, or plane to Milford and Doubtful sounds, or take off on one of the park's superb hiking trails. Of these, the most accessible to town is the Kepler Track. The town itself is very quiet and rural, but it does have its attractions and is very picturesque. It's busiest in summer; in winter, some cafés and shops close or reduce their hours.

GETTING HERE AND AROUND

Bus Companies InterCity Coachlines. ☎ *03/442–4922* ⊕ *www.intercity.co.nz.*

Bus Depot Te Anau. ⊠ *2 Miro St.*

EXPLORING

TOP ATTRACTIONS

Punanga Manu o Te Anau/Te Anau Bird Sanctuary. The lakeshore Te Anau Bird Sanctuary gives you the chance to preview some of the wildlife you're likely to encounter when hiking in Fiordland. The center houses one of New Zealand's rare flightless birds, the takahe, which was once thought to be extinct. The lakeside walk to the center makes for a pleasant one-hour stroll. The birds here have either been injured or involved in captive rearing programs. The injured birds are rehabilitated and sent back to the wild if they're strong enough. Entry's free, but if you have a NZ$1 or NZ$2 coin to donate it helps with the upkeep. ⊠ *Manapouri Rd., 1 km (½ mile) west of Te Anau* ☎ *03/249–7924* ⊠ *Donation requested* ☉ *Daily dawn–dusk.*

FAMILY **Te Anau Glowworm Caves.** Boats and walkways take you through a maze of caves containing underground whirlpools, waterfalls, and gushing streams. Then you'll reach the inner, quieter part and on the cave walls; glowworms shine like constellations in a clear night sky. It's a surreal experience. The caves can only be reached by water. This is a lovely family trip that takes around 2½ hours. Don't miss it if you're going through Te Anau; if you're short on time you can do it in the evening. ⊠ *Real Journeys, Lakefront Dr.* ☎ *03/249–6000, 0800/656–501* ⊕ *www.realjourneys.co.nz* ⊠ *NZ$75.*

WHERE TO EAT

$$$$ NEW ZEALAND Fodor's Choice ★ 🍴 **Redcliff Café & Bar.** If you want to try some of the good food that's produced in this area, Redcliff is the place to go. Even the atmosphere is true South at this cozy wooden cottage, with a roaring fire in winter. Cast and crew of the *Lord of the Rings* and *The Hobbit* trilogies were known to drop in for dinner or a drink during filming, including actor John Rhys-Davie, who famously snuck a Shakespearean soliloquy into a local poetry evening. Among the dishes served, the wild hare and venison are excellent. So, too, is the crème brûlée. There's a range of local and NZ wines and good beer and cider on tap. Reservations are advised as Redcliff is Te Anau's worst-kept secret. [$] *Average main: NZ$35* ✉ *12 Mokonui St.* ☎ *03/249–7431* 🌐 *www.theredcliff.co.nz* ⏲ *Closed July and Aug. No lunch in winter.*

SAND FLIES

Sand flies may be a useful cog in the great big eco-machine, but when you (inevitably) encounter them you'll just want them—and their irritating, itchy bites—to go away. They are drawn to warmth (your body heat) and dark colors (your navy or black clothing). Arm yourself with sand-fly repellent before hitting the park, and of course, always take a raincoat; and fill up with petrol before leaving Te Anau as there are no petrol stations farther south.

$ CAFÉ 🍴 **Sandfly Cafe.** The Sandfly Cafe just may have the best coffee in town, and a hearty breakfast from bacon and eggs to delicious corn-and-coriander fritters with smoked salmon to go with it. There's plenty of home baking to be found in the cabinet, too. In this part of the country you have to try a cheese roll—every café has its own recipe, and it's so much more than cheese and bread. Being popular with locals, it can get busy, but there's plenty to look at while you wait, with local photographer Barry Harcourt's stunning pictures of the area on the wall. [$] *Average main: NZ$14* ✉ *9 The Lane* ☎ *03/249–9529* ⏲ *No dinner.*

WHERE TO STAY

$$$ RENTAL 🏨 **Blue Thistle Cottages.** Five minutes' drive on from the town center on the Milford road, these four very cozy and comfortable cottages overlook the distant mountains and Lake Te Anau. **Pros:** quiet, rural setting; good base for exploring the area; cottage kitchens have fridges and microwaves. **Cons:** outside of walking distance to Te Anau. [$] *Rooms from: NZ$229* ✉ *168 Te Anau Milford Hwy.* ☎ *03/249–8338* 🌐 *www.bluethistlecottages.com* ⏲ *Closed June–Aug.* 🛏 *3 1-bedroom cottages, 1 2-bedrom cottage* 🍽 *No meals* 💳 *No credit cards.*

$$ B&B/INN 🏨 **Cats Whiskers B&B.** This basic but modern lakefront B&B is a 10-minute walk from the town center, opposite the National Park Visitor Centre. **Pros:** friendly hosts; cheerful place. **Cons:** fills up quickly, so try to book in advance. [$] *Rooms from: NZ$160* ✉ *2 Lakefront Dr.* ☎ *03/249–8112* 🌐 *www.catswhiskers.co.nz* 🛏 *4 rooms* 🍽 *Breakfast.*

$$$$ B&B/INN 🏨 **Fiordland Lodge.** A few kilometers out of Te Anau on the road to Milford Sound, glass, stone, and timber blend together to make a stylish place to spend a few days. **Pros:** room price includes dinner as well as breakfast. **Cons:** it's 5 km (3 miles) out of town. [$] *Rooms from: NZ$820*

✉ *State Hwy. 94, 472 Te Anau–Milford Hwy.* ☎ *03/249–7832* 🌐 *www.fiordlandlodge.co.nz* 🛏 *9 rooms, 2 cabins, 1 exec suite* 🍴 *Some meals.*

$$$ B&B/INN **Murrell's Grand View House.** Twenty minutes south of Te Anau, this B&B sits on one of New Zealand's prettiest and most pristine lakes—Lake Manapouri. **Pros:** leave your car here while on the overnight cruise in Doubtful Sound. **Cons:** it's a bit of a detour from the usual tourist circuit. [$] *Rooms from: NZ$260* ✉ *Murrell Ave., Manapouri* ☎ *03/249–6642* 🌐 *www.murrells.co.nz* 🕓 *Closed May–Oct.* 🛏 *4 rooms* 🍴 *Breakfast.*

$$$ RENTAL **Radfords on the Lake.** Fabulous lake views and the personal touches make this lakefront motel a great place to stay; it also has spacious, modern rooms and is a few minutes' walk from town. **Pros:** great location. **Cons:** popular over summer so need to book in early. [$] *Rooms from: NZ$285* ✉ *56 Lakefront Dr.* ☎ *03/249–9186* 🌐 *www.radfordsonthelake.co.nz* 🛏 *4 studios, 6 1-bedroom and 4 2-bedroom motel units.*

EN ROUTE

Milford Road. If there was nothing to see at the end of this road it would still be worth the journey. It's a spectacular route, on one of the highest highways in New Zealand, traveling through mossy beech forests, past waterfalls and grand sweeping valleys. The road is narrow and winding at times, so allow at least 2½ hours. Stop for some great photo ops at Mirror Lakes, Knobs Flat, and Lake Gunn before reaching the Divide, a watershed between rivers flowing both east and west and the starting point for the Routeburn Track. When you reach the **Homer Tunnel** think of the unemployed workers who began building it as a relief project in 1935 using picks and shovels. Before making the trip, check the transit website 🌐 *www.milfordroad.co.nz/* or phone ☎ *0800/444–449* for avalanche warnings (snow and trees) and between May and November come equipped with tire chains, which you can rent in any Te Anau service station. ⚠ **There have been a number of accidents on this stretch of road caused by overseas drivers unfamiliar with the conditions driving too fast or on the wrong side of the road.** Take care and drive to the conditions, and if you're just not comfortable, you can always take a bus from Te Anau or Queenstown

SPORTS AND THE OUTDOORS

Although Te Anau seems small, its lake serves as a larger and beautiful landmark. Trails around Fiordland reveal the natural blue color of the park's water with looming mountains in the distance.

HIKING

Fiordland National Park Visitor Centre. Information, transport options, and maps for the plethora of hikes near Te Anau, including the Kepler Track, can be obtained from the Fiordland National Park Visitor Centre. ✉ *Lakefront Dr.* ☎ *03/249–7924* 🌐 *www.doc.govt.nz.*

Kepler Track. The 60-km (37-mile) Kepler Track loops from the south end of Lake Te Anau and takes three to four days to complete. It goes through extensive beech forest, past limestone bluffs, and provides incredible views of the South Fiord and Te Anau Basin. It's a moderate walking trail but there are a number of hills to climb and a steep zigzag downhill section that takes a couple of hours and can be hard on the

STAY THE NIGHT AT FIORDLAND

Overnight cruises are a leisurely, thorough way to experience the sounds. If you choose Doubtful Sound, your tour company will provide a boat across Lake Manapouri and a bus ride to your cruise vessel. Drive to Lake Manapouri, or, for an extra fee, arrange for a coach transfer from Te Anau or Queenstown. Sleeping quarters aboard the vessel range from bunking with three others to a private cabin and bathroom. Dinner and breakfast are included, and you can arrange for a picnic lunch. The park's deepest sound, Doubtful, has three distinct arms and features the 619-meter (2,031-foot) Browne

Falls. If you are lucky, you will see Fiordland crested penguins on the rocks or bottle-nosed dolphins swimming at the bow. Cliffs rise from the sea to 900 meters (2,953 feet), often disappearing in a mist. You can explore the sound in kayaks once you anchor at the evening's mooring. Or you can sit on a viewing deck, sip a beverage from the bar, and take in the sights from your floating hotel. Milford overnight cruises generally leave around 4:30 pm and return around 9 the following morning; Doubtful cruises generally leave around noon and return around noon the next day.

knees. It also includes an alpine crossing and hikers should beware of high wind gusts while crossing the exposed saddle above the bush line. If you're on a tight schedule take a day hike to the Luxmore and Moturau huts. Huts cost NZ$54 in summer and you need to book; check online or call the Great Walks booking office for advice and conditions. ✉ *Te Anau* ☎ *03/249–8514 Great Walks booking* ⊕ *www.doc.govt.nz.*

KAYAKING

Go Orange Kayaks. If you're an intrepid adventurer at heart, love camping and the great outdoors, and you're pretty active, then you'll find Go Orange Kayaks' overnight Doubtful Sound trip an incredibly rewarding experience. It's not for the fainthearted; you can get wet and cold and the sand flies can be bad. But you'll be in a World Heritage area and you'll meet some wonderful like-minded people. If you're not keen on the overnight, go sea kayaking in Milford Sound for a day or half a day to gain the unique perspective on the fiord that being on the water gives you. Trips operate from September to May, with some differences according to location, so call ahead. ✉ *21 Town Centre* ☎ *03/249–8585, 0800/246–672 NZ only* ⊕ *www.goorangekayaks.co.nz* ✉ *From NZ$130 for ½-day; overnight trips from NZ$399.*

SCENIC FLIGHTS

Fly Fiordland. Fly Fiordland provides a range of scenic flights in its three Cessna fixed-wing aircraft; including to Milford and Doubtful sounds, and on the rare occasion that weather permits, an overfly of the most remote place in New Zealand, Dusky Sound. Prices don't include a cruise in Milford Sound, but you can add this as an option. ✉ *52 Town Centre* ☎ *03/249–4352, 0800/359–346 NZ only* ⊕ *www.flyfiordland.com.*

Fodor's Choice
★

Southern Lakes Helicopters. Once you've seen the movie *Ata Whenua* at Fiordland Cinema you'll want to take to the air and see some of this scenery for yourself (or do the flight first and see the movie after). Either way this helicopter company, privately owned by renowned helicopter pioneer Sir Richard "Hannibal" Hayes, has operated successfully here for more than 35 years. The Southern Lakes pilots have a wealth of knowledge and experience flying in this World Heritage area and offer a range of airborne services. ⊠ *Lakefront Dr.* ☎ *03/249–7167, 0508/249–7167* ⊕ *www.southernlakeshelicopters.co.nz* ⊠ *From NZ$230.*

Wings and Water Te Anau. Wings and Water Te Anau operates scenic flights with a floatplane that takes travelers to some of the region's most inaccessible areas, including a 10-minute trip over Lake Te Anau, Lake Manapouri, and the Kepler Track and longer flights over Doubtful, Dusky, and Milford sounds. ⊠ *Lakefront Dr.* ☎ *03/249–7405* ⊕ *www. wingsandwater.co.nz* ⊠ *From NZ$95.*

MILFORD SOUND

120 km (75 miles) northwest of Te Anau, 290 km (180 miles) west of Queenstown.

Fodor's Choice
★

Fiordland National Park's most accessible and busiest attraction is Milford Sound; in some ways it's also the most dramatic. Hemmed in by walls of rock that rise straight and sheer from the waterline up thousands of feet, the 13-km-long (18-mile-long) fiord was carved by a succession of glaciers as they gouged a track to the sea. Its dominant feature is the 5,560-foot pinnacle of Mitre Peak, which is capped with snow for all but the warmest months of the year. Opposite the peak, Bowen Falls tumbles 520 feet before exploding into the fiord. You'll often see seals on rocks soaking up the sun and dolphins sometimes flirt with the boats. Milford Sound is also spectacularly wet: The average annual rainfall is around 20 feet, and it rains an average of 200 days a year. In addition to a raincoat you'll need insect repellent—the sand flies can be voracious.

GETTING HERE AND AROUND
Highway 94 North out of Te Anau to Milford Sound is only 118 km (73 miles), but between the weather, the views, and the winding, hilly nature of the road, it's best to allow at least 2½ hours to get there safely. Most day tours in Milford Sound offer transport from Te Anau or Queenstown, and InterCity Coachlines run a daily service from Te Anau. If the weather is clear, there is an airport open to scenic fixed-wing and helicopter landings.

Bus Contact InterCity Coachlines. ☎ *03/442–4922* ⊕ *www.intercity.co.nz.*

EXPLORING
Milford Sound does not have a surrounding town. Here you'll fill your days with wondrous exploration. Because of excessive rain, make sure you come prepared with extra clothing and rain gear.

Milford Discovery Centre & Underwater Observatory. Even in heavy rain and storms Milford Sound is magical. Rainfall is so excessive that a coat of up to 20 feet of fresh water floats on the surface of the saltwater fjord.

Lightly stained with tannins from the plants and soil, it creates a unique underwater environment similar to that found at a much greater depth in the open ocean. Head downstairs at the Milford Underwater Observatory, and you can see rare black coral (that looks white) as well as anemones, starfish, octopus, and any number of fish swimming by. The Discovery Centre and Observatory is operated by Southern Discoveries and is only accessible by boat; you can add it on to most Milford Sound cruises. ✉ *Milford Sound* ☎ *03/441–1137, 0800/264–536 NZ only* 🌐 *www.milforddiscoverycentre.co.nz* 🎟 *NZ$36.*

WHERE TO EAT

Accommodations are scant at Milford Sound; pack your lunch in Te Anau before coming, or preorder the lunch box included on some boat tours. If you're staying overnight, be aware there is no shopping. You can buy dinner at Milford Sound Lodge, whether you are a guest or not.

$$ CAFÉ 🍴 **Discover Milford Information Centre.** Formerly the only pub in town, the Discover Milford Information Centre is the only place in Milford Sound to buy a coffee, snacks, and counter food. The view out the front window, across Milford Sound to Mitre Peak and the mountains beyond, is amazing. [$] *Average main: NZ$15* ✉ *Milford Sound* ☎ *03/249–7926* ⏲ *No dinner.*

WHERE TO STAY

$$$$ HOTEL Fodor's Choice ★ 🏨 **Milford Sound Lodge.** Just 1 km (½ mile) out of the Milford settlement, on the banks of the Cleddau River, this lodge provides Riverside Chalets with either one super-king or twin bed, kitchenette, and spectacular mountain and river views. **Pros:** beautiful chalets; good value; new lodge café serves breakfast, lunch, and early dinner. **Cons:** more like a hostel if you don't book a chalet. [$] *Rooms from: NZ$345* ✉ *Milford Sound* ☎ *03/249–8071, 0800/782–9645 NZ only* 🌐 *www.milfordlodge.com* 🛏 *6 riverside chalets, 8 mountainside chalets (en suite), 23 rooms with shared bath* 🍽 *No meals.*

SPORTS AND THE OUTDOORS

CRUISING

The gorgeous views from the water account for the popularity of cruising here. It's essential to book ahead between mid-December and March. All boats leave from the Milford wharf area. Avoid the midday sailings, as they link with tour buses and are the most crowded. Southern Discoveries and Real Journeys run more than a dozen cruises a day between them, with extra options in summer.

Real Journeys. By far the most satisfying way to experience Milford (or Doubtful) Sound is to do an overnight cruise; it gives you more time in the fjord when it's at its best—first thing in the morning and early evening. Kayaking off the boat gets you right up to that mossy bush and rock face. There are two overnight boats: the *Milford Mariner*'s the more luxurious cruise with roomier bunks (with en suites), but the *Milford Wanderer*'s not too far behind. Fewer passengers and shared facilities make it a very friendly boat. An overnight cruise includes a superb dinner and breakfast. But if you only want to do a day cruise, go for the Nature Cruise over the Scenic Cruise. It's more personal, a bit longer (2½ hours), and it's on a boat with more character and a nature

guide you can ask questions. Both trips cruise the full length of Milford Sound to the Tasman Sea and have the same extraordinary views of waterfalls, rain forest, mountains, and wildlife. ⌧ *Lakefront Dr., Te Anau* ☎ *03/249–6000, 0800/656–501* ⊕ *www.realjourneys.co.nz* ⌧ *From NZ$355 per person overnight; NZ$72 for day* ⊘ *Overnight cruises don't operate through winter (mid-May–Sept.).*

Fodor$Choice   **Southern Discoveries.** You can't miss Southern Discoveries' big red boats
★   in Milford Sound. If you're only here for the day the Cruise/Kayak option is great for getting close to the shore and seeing the edges of the fjord in all its lush detail—right down to its damp, green, earthy smell. It's an easy paddle on calm water so no experience is necessary. Kayaking starts at the Discovery Centre and Underwater Observatory, which is also included in the price and is well worth a visit. ⌧ *Milford Sound Wharf* ☎ *03/441–1137* ⊕ *www.southerndiscoveries.co.nz* ⌧ *From NZ$70.*

HIKING TRACKS AND GUIDES

Fiordland National Park Visitor Centre. To hike independently of a tour group for either the Milford, Kepler, or Routeburn Track, call the **Great Walks Booking Office** at the Fiordland National Park Visitor Centre or book online through the website. Reservations for the coming season can be made starting on the first of July every year. Book well in advance—especially if you plan to go in December or January. Independent walking, without a guide, requires that you bring your own food, utensils, bedding, and other equipment. You stay in clean, basic Department of Conservation huts. ⌧ *Lakefront Dr., Te Anau* ☎ *03/249–8514* ⊕ *www.doc.govt.nz.*

Hollyford Track. If you're itching to see some coastline during your hike, and have good fitness, consider the Hollyford Track. At 56 km (35 miles), it's usually a four-day endeavor, taking you from the Hollyford Road down to Martins Bay by roughly following the Hollyford River. You'll pass a couple of lakes and waterfalls on your way; at the coastline you'll likely spy seals and penguins. Be particularly careful of flooded creek crossings. Make sure you buy your hut tickets but you can't book in advance. It's a good idea to drop in to the Fiordland National Park Visitor Centre to check on conditions before you head off. ⌧ *Lakefront Dr., Te Anau* ☎ *03/249–7924* ⊕ *www.doc.govt.nz.*

Fodor$Choice   **Milford Track.** If you plan to walk the Milford Track—a rewarding four-
★   day bushwalk through Fiordland National Park—understand that it is one of New Zealand's most popular hikes. The 53½-km (33-mile) track is strictly one-way, and because park authorities control access, you can feel as though you have the wilderness more or less to yourself. The trail ends for the track are remote. Independent and guided groups stay in different overnight huts. Guided and unguided walks begin with a 1½-hour ferry ride to Glade Wharf on Lake Te Anau and end with a 20-minute ferry taking you from Sandfly Point over to the Milford Sound wharf. The track's well maintained during the restricted hiking season, which runs from late October to April (because of the risk of avalanche). ⌧ *Fiordland National Park.*

Great Walks Booking Office. For seasonal reservations on the Milford Track, Kepler Track, and the Routeburn Track contact the Great Walks

Booking Office or book online. Make sure you book well in advance. ☎ *03/249–8514, 0800/694–732 NZ only* ⊕ *www.greatwalks.co.nz.*

Real Journeys. If you don't have enough time for the whole Milford Track, you can still experience a good slice of what makes it New Zealand's most famous walk on a guided day-walk with Real Journeys. It includes a cruise across Lake Te Anau. You'll hike about 11 km (7 miles), lunch is included, and the good thing is there are no big hills. No children under 10. ✉ *Lakefront Dr., Te Anau* ☎ *03/249–6000, 0800/656–501* ⊕ *www.realjourneys.co.nz* ✉ *NZ$195.*

Routeburn Track. The 33-km (20.5-mile) Routeburn Track, like the Milford Track, is designated one of the country's Great Walks, so you need to book in season. The Routeburn goes between Lake Wakatipu, near Glenorchy, and the road between Milford and Te Anau; it takes about three days to hike. The alpine landscape is stunning, and once you're above the tree line, the sand flies back off. It's a linear track so make sure you organize your transport home. The track's well maintained but be prepared for rain and mud. Tramping out of season is not advised for most people as there's avalanche risk. ✉ *Milford Sound* ⊕ *www.doc.govt.nz.*

Ultimate Hikes. If you want to do the Milford Track but don't like the idea of hauling a heavy backpack for 34 miles with all your food and gear, then Ultimate Hikes is the rather wonderful alternative. All your meals are provided, you'll have a comfortable bed and hot showers, and you can wash and dry your gear if it rains. They'll organize your transport and provide backpacks. Their Milford Track journey includes a cruise on Milford Sound and transport to and from Queenstown; the Routeburn Track is a bit less expensive. If you're not up for a multiday trek, you can take a single-day "encounter" hike on either the Milford or Routeburn Track. ✉ *The Station Bldg., Duke St. entrance, Queenstown* ☎ *03/450–1940, 0800/659–255* ⊕ *www.ultimatehikes.co.nz* ✉ *From NZ$1,325 (in multishare accommodation).*

KAYAKING

Rosco's Milford Kayaks. If you like immersing yourself in nature then sea kayaking's a lovely way to see this extraordinary part of New Zealand and the creatures (seals, penguins, or dolphins if you're lucky) that live here. Rosco's Milford Kayaks leads a number of different guided kayaking options on Milford Sound that can even include a hike along part of the famous Milford Track. You can get picked up and dropped off from Te Anau. No children under 14. ✉ *Milford Sound* ☎ *03/249–8500, 0800/476–726 in New Zealand* ⊕ *www.roscosmilfordkayaks.com* ✉ *From NZ$99.*

SCENIC FLIGHTS

Glacier Southern Lakes Helicopters. You're in good hands flying with this company, which has highly sought-after helicopter pilots with a wealth of knowledge about the area. Helicopters are easily the best way to see this part of the country and even a short flight up the Remarkables or over the Skippers Canyon is an incredible experience. Flying to Milford Sound, the West Coast, and Mount Aspiring National Park, landing on a glacier on the way, could be life changing. There's a Middle

Earth flight to some of *The Lord of the Rings* and *The Hobbit* locations—about as authentic as you can get as one of this company's pilots, Alfie Speight, was the principal aerial pilot for the movies. ⊠ *35 Lucas Pl., Queenstown* ☎ *03/442–3016* ⊕ *www.glaciersouthernlakes.co.nz* ⊠ *From NZ$230 per person.*

LAKE MANAPOURI AND DOUBTFUL SOUND

Just 20 minutes south of Te Anau, Lake Manapouri has long had the reputation as one of New Zealand's prettiest lakes. The lake is hemmed by high mountains and studded by many bush-covered islands; it's 1,457 feet deep in parts. Cruises run several times a day to the head of the lake, where you can join a tour of the West Arm hydro-station, deep underground. West Arm is also the departure point for those traveling on to Doubtful Sound, a stunning stretch of water, largely untouched by visitors. A connecting bus crosses you over the 2,177-foot Wilmot Pass before dropping steeply down to sea level at Deep Arm, the head of Doubtful Sound.

GETTING HERE AND AROUND

To get to Lake Manapouri, head south of the Te Anau center onto Highway 95 to drive the 20 minutes to Manapouri township. Doubtful Sound is not accessible by car. Book a day trip or overnight tour and your tour will include a boat ride across Lake Manapouri and a bus ride across Wilmot Pass. You can park you car near the wharf at Pearl Harbour, which is the end of the road. Most tours will have the option to depart on a bus from Te Anau, allowing you to leave your car in town.

TOURS

Fiordland Expeditions. Fiordland Expeditions provides a very Kiwi overnight experience on their two boats, *Tutuko* and *Tutoko II*. With a maximum of 14 passengers, these are relaxed and personal trips and great if you want to do a bit of fishing, kayaking, or just soak up the splendid scenery. There are private or shared cabins, mostly with shared bathroom facilities. All meals (probably some crayfish for dinner), fishing gear, and transfers from Manapouri are included in the price. ⊠ *Deep Cove, Doubtful Sound* ☎ *03/249–9005* ⊕ *www.fiordlandexpeditions. co.nz* ⊠ *From NZ$450.*

Fodor's Choice ★ **Real Journeys.** Doubtful Sound is three times as long as Milford Sound and because there's no road access it receives far fewer visitors. The sides of the fiords aren't quite as in-your-face but they are just as beautiful, and there's a better chance of seeing dolphins and fur seals, too. Real Journeys runs a range of combined bus and boat trips. Most people take an eight-hour day trip from Lake Manapouri; there are bus connections from Te Anau and Queenstown. Some tours include a visit to the Lake Manapouri Power Station machine hall, an extraordinary engineering feat built deep beneath the mountain. Between October and May the ultimate experience is an overnight on the sound, aboard the *Fiordland Navigator.* Rates include meals and kayaking, and if you're brave enough, you can take a swim in the frigid waters. ⊠ *Lakefront Dr., Te Anau* ☎ *03/249–6000, 0800/656–501* ⊕ *www.realjourneys.co.nz* ⊠ *From NZ$250 day tour; NZ$435 (quad share overnight).*

OTAGO, INVERCARGILL, AND STEWART ISLAND

WELCOME TO OTAGO, INVERCARGILL, AND STEWART ISLAND

TOP REASONS TO GO

★ **Local Fare:** Partake in a fresh fillet of blue cod, salty muttonbird prepared the Māori way, succulent Bluff oysters, or a warm cheese roll.

★ **Bird-Watching:** See yellow-eyed penguin or an albatross on the peninsula or a kiwi on Stewart Island. Predator-free Ulva Island is the jewel in the crown of Rakiura National Park.

★ **Kiwi Sports:** Rugby puts New Zealand on the world stage, and for many Kiwis it's a passion. Provincial and international teams ruck and maul at Dunedin's Forsyth Barr Stadium.

★ **Pubs and Clubs:** Thanks to the presence of 25,000 university students, Dunedin is full of cafés, funky bars, late-night pubs, and rocking music venues.

★ **The Southern Sea:** The lower coast of the South Island is breathtakingly wild. Head south along the Catlins section of the Southern Scenic Route for ocean views, diving seabirds, and sandy beaches.

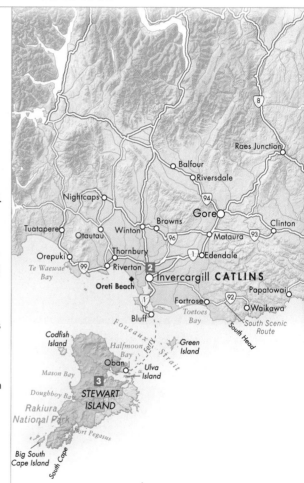

1 **Dunedin.** A university town, Dunedin has the austerity that old stone academic buildings lend a city. At the same time, it has the fresh, creative brio of young academics (aka partying 20-year-olds). The backdrop is a busy port, clanging and squealing with massive international freighters, while across the harbor, albatross chicks learn to fly, and penguins waddle anxiously past sea lions.

0 ⊢——⊣ 20 mi

0 ⊢——⊣ 20 km

GETTING ORIENTED

The region is bordered by the snowcapped Southern Alps to the west and a string of golden, albeit chilly, beaches to the east. The north is met by the wide Canterbury Plains and the south by the timeless Catlins region. The two major hubs of civilization in the "deep south" are both coastal cities: Dunedin to the east and Invercargill to the south. The Otago Peninsula stretches east from "Dunners" into the Pacific and is home to the Royal Albatross and yellow-eyed penguins. Take the winding coastal route south from Dunedin to explore the Catlins, where farms and forest meet the sea. Invercargill is flat and doesn't feel particularly coastal, as you can't see the sea from within the city. The southern port town of Bluff is the departure point for Stewart Island, across Foveaux Strait.

2 Invercargill. Cast your gaze upward! The architecture of Invercargill is a treat to behold. Due to its proximity to the sea, "Invers" has been called the "City of Water and Light." The wide flat roads of downtown and the enormous sweep of nearby Oreti Beach were perfect training grounds for homegrown hero Burt Munro (motorcycle land speed record holder).

3 Stewart Island. If your hand represents the island, your pinky fingernail would be the amount that is actually inhabited. Roads link the main township of Oban at Halfmoon Bay, to the other "neighborhoods"—a few homes nestled around adjoining bays. Beaches are pristine; the sea is crystal green and bountiful. Flowers spill from grounded dories. Beyond town is wilderness teeming with wonderful birds.

RAKIURA NATIONAL PARK

Between the rocky beach and a primitive forest at Lee Bay, a plaque at the park's entrance quotes a Stewart Islander: "I must go over to New Zealand some day." More than 200 km (124 miles) of trail unfurl at your feet into pure wilderness: the rest of the world is indeed far removed.

Even the most adventurous travelers to this 1,746 square-km (674 square-mile) island are liable to experience a growing feeling of utter isolation as they go about exploring the lush, bush-clad hills, sand dunes, unspoiled inlets, and beaches strewn with driftwood. Even the weather is inspiring, powering in from a vast ocean over which mollymawks and albatrosses soar. The show does not end with the daylight either, Rakiura in Māori means "glowing skies," referring to the exquisite sunsets and southern lights or *aurora australis* often visible from here.

Somewhere in the stands of ancient rimu trees and the thick tangle of supplejack vines and ferns are remnants of steam engines, try-pots, and wagon tracks— vestiges of human attempts over the centuries to live and work in these parts. Ancient Māori muttonbirders, Southern Ocean whalers, millers, and miners have all come and gone. A few commercial fishing boats still operate from Halfmoon Bay, the last of an industry that has dwindled over the years. While the rest of the planet succumbs to pavement and steel, Rakiura has become less developed, and the decision to make 85% of it a national park will preserve it so. As you adjust your pack, you may ponder what the island's industry is now. It's tourism (aka you).

BEST TIME TO GO

The summer (November through March) is the best time to visit. Weather is unpredictable this far south, and Christmas barbecues have been known to see a sudden hailstorm. But generally this is the best bet for lovely long days (and the local businesses are all open as opposed to the off-season).

BEST WAYS TO EXPLORE

Mud Walk. Eighty-five percent of the island is national park, and it's thrilling to think that much of that is impenetrable wilderness, never seen or trodden upon by people. Over 200 km (124 miles) of walking trails create some of New Zealand's greatest hikes, including the three-day Rakiura Track and the challenging 11-day Northern Circuit. A popular adventure is taking a water taxi to the trailhead at Freshwater on the east side of the island, and walking across to the West Coast's amazing Mason Bay beach, where you can arrange to have a plane pick you up. It takes close to three hours to walk to the end of the beach, along which is one of the best places to spot a few of the island's 20,000 kiwi birds. Unless you happen upon the island after a rare dry spell, you are sure to encounter copious quantities of mud on these trails so come prepared.

Sea-Sighting. Local companies offer a variety of boat tours: go fishing for Stewart Island blue cod, do a bird-viewing cruise, or view the gorgeous kelp gardens beneath the surface. Water taxi companies can drop you at bird sanctuary Ulva Island or at destinations along the Rakiura coast, or show you the aquaculture (mussel, salmon, and oyster farms) of Big Glory Bay. If the weather is right, nothing beats a kayak trip in Paterson Inlet, where you can visit Ulva, circumnavigate half a dozen tiny islands, and observe penguins (little blue and yellow-eyed).

Flightseeing. Seeing the island by helicopter is an unforgettable experience. If you don't have a week or more to properly tackle the trails, then heli-hiking makes a lot of sense—get dropped at Mason Bay and walk back, or spend a day visiting various far-flung bays and beaches and be back in Halfmoon Bay in time for dinner. Tours can show you the magnificent southern coast, and you will be privy to views of Stewart Island that many lifelong locals have never seen.

(top left) Beach on the Rakiura Track; *(bottom)* trampers on Stewart Island's Māori Beach; *(top)* the native Weka bird is a flightless rail, often referred to as a woodhen.

Updated
by Gerard
Hindmarsh

Otago Province takes up much of the southeast quadrant of the South Island and has two distinct regions, each a drawcard in its own right. Offering spectacular opportunities for wildlife and marine mammal watching, coastal Otago stretches across moist and verdant hills, its intricate coastline of headlands, inlets, and misty beaches strung with historic settlements. By comparison, inland Otago is stark yet jaw-droppingly beautiful, a drier landscape of spectacular schist outcrops and tussock grasslands, punctuated occasionally by small towns that still exude pioneering character. Draining much of Otago is the mighty Clutha River, the largest-volume waterway in the country.

In 1848 Dunedin was settled, and all the land from the top of the Otago Peninsula south to the Clutha River and sections farther inland were purchased from the Māori. By the mid-1860s Dunedin was the economic hub of the Otago gold rush. Dunedin's historical wealth and Scottish influence endures in monuments and institutions such as the University of Otago, the oldest in the country.

Invercargill, to the south, was born out of different economic imperatives. After wealthy graziers bought swaths of Southland for their sheep, they needed a local port to bring in more stock from Australia. The town of Bluff, already familiar to sealers, was selected as an ideal location. Invercargill became the administrative center to the port and then to the whole region. Until recent years, the town's economy focused on raising sheep and other livestock and crops; it is now becoming a more diverse metropolis.

Hanging off the bottom of the South Island and separated by 30-km-wide (19-mile-wide) Foveaux Strait, Stewart Island is a world all of its own. Commercial fishing and tourism accounts for most of the commercial activity in the island's only settlement, which soon gives way to bushland that the kiwi bird still haunts. At night, the nocturnal birds can be seen wandering remote beaches. Another late night show is the aurora australis, the southern hemisphere equivalent of the northern lights, which can light up the sky.

PLANNING

Most people spend a few days in Dunedin and migrate south via State Highway 1. Once you reach Balclutha, you can continue south either by staying on the State Highway heading straight for Invercargill or by going via the Catlins on the Southern Scenic Route. The Catlins route is more demanding, but much more scenic. Whichever route you take, by the time you reach Southland, all roads are wide, flat, and point to Invercargill.

WHEN TO GO

Dunedin gets more visitors in summer, but during the university vacations it's quieter. Inland Otago remains dry year-round, and you can expect crisp, sunny days in winter, but the coast gets more rain, and Dunedin can have day after day of clouds and showers. Southland in winter isn't any colder, but it is wetter.

It's often said of New Zealand that you may experience all four seasons in one day; on Stewart Island you may experience them all in an hour. In winter, there's a better chance of seeing the aurora australis, but some of the island's walking trails may be closed.

GETTING HERE AND AROUND

AIR TRAVEL

Most Air New Zealand flights to Dunedin and Invercargill go via Christchurch or come direct from Wellington, while Kiwi Regional Airlines connects Dunedin to Queenstown and Nelson (with onward flights to Hamilton). Fog occasionally causes delays, but Christchurch Airport has a slick, passenger-friendly terminal with shops and cafés as well as a family entertainment center where the little folks can wear themselves out. Stewart Island flights operate from Invercargill, or you can take a ferry to the island: one local described the choices as "either 60 minutes of fear or 20 minutes of terror," but that's true only on a bad day—both journeys afford breathtaking views.

BUS TRAVEL

InterCity's two daily runs between Christchurch and Dunedin take about five to six hours. Twice daily InterCity bus continues on from Dunedin to Invercargill; this takes another three hours. On both these routes the company makes an extra run on Friday and Sunday. Other bus companies operating in the region include Atomic Shuttles, Bottom Bus, Catch-A-Bus, Citibus, and Tracknet, as well as Nakedbus—clothing essential; the name refers to stripped-down costs such as no paper tickets.

CAR TRAVEL

The best way to explore the lower South Island is by car, particularly if you want to take your time seeing the Catlins. You cannot ferry your rental car to Stewart Island; there is secure parking in Invercargill and Bluff. Buses serve most places of interest, including daily routes between South Island cities. They go the direct route between Dunedin and Invercargill on State Highway 1. If you are driving and want to see the Catlins, leave State Highway 1 at Balclutha and take the well-marked Southern Scenic Route.

> **FUN FACT**
>
> Outside the terminal building at Dunedin Airport is Kiwi artist Sam Mahon's bronze sculpture of "The Southern Man." Stroking the horse's nose is said to bring good luck.

RESTAURANTS

Dunedin has the area's highest concentration of good restaurants. Seafood is a big player, in part because of Dunedin's coastal location but also because of its proximity to Bluff, the home of New Zealand's great delicacy, the Bluff oysters. Many of the least-expensive options are café-like Asian restaurants; these tend to close early, around 9 pm. Locals don't usually dress up or make reservations for anything other than the most exclusive establishments.

Invercargill has a more limited selection of mostly moderately priced restaurants. Stewart Island has a reasonable selection considering its location, but in winter some places limit their hours or close.

HOTELS

Dunedin has a full range of accommodations, from modest hostels to luxury hotels, while Invercargill has more motels than anything else. Local motels generally provide clean rooms with kitchens and TVs. Stewart Island lodging options include camping, hostels, rental houses, hotels, motels, and boutique B&Bs. Throughout the region air-conditioning is a rarity, but given the temperate climate, this isn't a problem. Heating, on the other hand, is standard in most places.

It's a good idea to make reservations, especially in summer. In Dunedin, rooms can be scarce around special events, such as graduation ceremonies and high-profile rugby games.

Hotel reviews have been shortened. For full information, visit Fodors. com. Use the coordinate (✛ B2) at the end of each listing to locate a site on the corresponding map.

WHAT IT COSTS IN NEW ZEALAND DOLLARS			
	$	$$	$$$	$$$$
Restaurants	under NZ$15	NZ$15–NZ$20	NZ$21–NZ$30	over NZ$30
Hotels	under NZ$125	NZ$125–NZ$200	NZ$201–NZ$300	over NZ$300

Restaurant prices are the average cost of a main course at dinner or, if dinner is not served, at lunch. Hotel prices are the lowest cost of a standard double room in high season.

Both Dunedin and Invercargill have centrally located i-SITE visitor centers: you can find Dunedin's in The Octagon in the city center and a kiosk branch at the wharf that only opens to greet cruise ships; the Invercargill i-SITE is in the Southland Museum. On Stewart Island check out the Department of Conservation office or the Stewart Island Experience office (in the red building at the ferry wharf).

DUNEDIN

280 km (175 miles) east of Queenstown, 362 km (226 miles) south of Christchurch.

Clinging to the walls of the natural amphitheater at the west end of Otago Harbour, the South Island's second-largest city is enriched with inspiring nearby seascapes and wildlife. Because Dunedin is a university town, floods of students give the city a vitality far greater than its population of 127,500 might suggest. The city's manageable size makes it easy to explore on foot—with the possible exception of Baldwin Street, the world's steepest residential street and home to the annual "gutbuster" race, in which people run up it, and the "Jaffa" race, in which people roll the namesake spherical chocolate candy down it.

INSIDE AND OUT

This region has plenty of indoor and outdoor options. If your temperament or the weather (which can be rather unpredictable in this neck of the country) are telling you to stay inside, stick around Dunedin for museums, galleries, cafés, and all the amenities that a city furnishes. But if you're game for exploring the natural world, venture onto the Otago Peninsula or farther into the Catlins; these can be a day trip from Dunedin. If you're truly feeling adventurous and ready to leave all urban comforts behind, take a few days and head down to Stewart Island.

Dunedin, the Gaelic name for Edinburgh, was founded in 1848 by settlers of the Free Church of Scotland, a breakaway group from the Presbyterian Church. The city's Scottish roots are still visible; you'll find New Zealand's first legal whisky distillery (now there are six), a statue of Scottish poet Robert Burns, and more kilts, sporrans, and gillies than you can shake a stick at. The Scottish settlers and local Māori came together in relative peace, but this wasn't true of the European whalers who were here three decades before, as places with names such as Murdering Beach illustrate.

Dunedin has always had a reputation for the eccentric. Wearing no shoes and a big beard here marks a man as bohemian rather than destitute, and the residents wouldn't have it any other way. The University of Otago was the country's first university and has been drawing writers ever since its founding in 1871, most notably Janet Frame and the poet James K. Baxter. Dunedin also has a musical heritage, which blossomed into the "Dunedin Sound" of the 1970s and '80s.

GETTING HERE AND AROUND

AIR TRAVEL

Dunedin Airport lies 20 km (13 miles) south of the city. Both Air New Zealand and Jetstar link Dunedin and Auckland daily; the flight takes just under two hours. Air New Zealand also flies daily from Dunedin to Christchurch and Wellington in around an hour, while Jetstar flies between Dunedin and Wellington three days a week. Kiwi Regional Airlines connects Dunedin direct to both Queenstown and Nelson most days of the week, and Virgin Australia flies between Dunedin and Brisbane four times a week.

Airport Contacts Dunedin International Airport. ✉ *25 Miller Rd., Momona* ☎ *03/486–2879* ⊕ *www.dunedinairport.co.nz.*

BUS TRAVEL

Local buses to the peninsula depart from Stand 5, outside City Centre New World on Cumberland Street.

Bus Contacts Dunedin Bus Station. ✉ *7 Halsey St.* ☎ *03/474–1699* ⊕ *www.orc.govt.nz.* **GoBus.** ✉ *1 Transport Pl., Princes St., Dunedin* ☎ *03/477–5577* ⊕ *www.gobus.co.nz.* **InterCity.** ✉ *7 Halsey St., Dunedin* ☎ *03/477–8860* ⊕ *www.intercity.co.nz.*

CAR TRAVEL

You can rent a car to explore the region at Dunedin airport on arrival, but confusing one-way roads and twisting hills in the suburbs make driving in Dunedin itself a challenge. Street parking is limited.

TOURS

City Walks Dunedin. Walks showcasing Dunedin's rich architectural heritage and colorful social history are offered daily except Sunday and depart from the Dunedin i-SITE Visitor Information Centre. The walk season is October through April, but tours may be offered at other times by arrangement. ✉ *Dunedin i-SITE Visitor Centre, 50 The Octagon* ☎ *027/356–9132, 0800/925–571 toll-free* ⊕ *www.citywalks.co.nz* 💰 *NZ$30.*

Elm Wildlife Tours. Passionate and enthusiastic guides lead walks through private conservation areas to penguin, fur seal, and sea lion colonies. A moderate degree of fitness is required to negotiate hilly terrain. ✉ *19 Irvine Rd., The Cove* ☎ *03/454–4121, 0800/356–563* ⊕ *www.elmwildlifetours.co.nz* 💰 *NZ$97–NZ$217.*

Mainland Air Scenic Flights. Scenic flights show off inland mountains and coastal sights as far south as Stewart Island. ✉ *Dunedin Airport, 3 Airport Dr.* ☎ *03/486–2200, 0800/284–284* ⊕ *www.mainlandair.com* 💰 *Flights from NZ$225 a person.*

VISITOR INFORMATION

Contacts Dunedin i-SITE Visitor Information Centre. ✉ *50 The Octagon* ☎ *03/474–3300* ⊕ *www.dunedin.govt.nz.* **Dunedin NZ Official Tourist Information.** ⊕ *www.dunedinnz.com.*

Luggage Storage Contacts Luggage Lockers. ✉ *Municipal La., Dunedin* ☎ *3/474–3300* ⊕ *www.dunedin.govt.nz.*

The extravagant Dunedin Railway Station is fronted by manicured grounds.

EXPLORING

As you explore Dunedin's city center, do look down. Beneath your feet are bronze plaques embedded in the sidewalks that highlight the city's Victorian history and heritage buildings. Around The Octagon, the thoughts of popular New Zealand writers are captured in bronze pavestones.

TOP ATTRACTIONS

FAMILY **Cadbury World.** Which came first, the Cadbury factory or the Cadbury Creme Egg? At Cadbury World you can watch chocolate candy in the making—and stand back as one ton of liquid chocolate gushes past you. Kiwis from as far away as Stewart Island have memories of school field trips here and ensuing tummy aches (the tour includes free samples of candy). Weekday tours include the factory; shorter weekend tours do not. This *is* a family-friendly place, but for safety reasons under-fives cannot be carried during tours unless you have a strap-on baby carrier and little kids may find all the steps—about 200 of them—challenging. The factory is usually closed for a week in June for maintenance. ⊠ *280 Cumberland St.* ☎ *03/467-7967, 0800/42462-8687* ⊕ *www.cadburyworld.co.nz* ✉ *NZ$20* ☺ *Closed 1 wk in June* ☞ *Reservations essential.*

Dunedin Railway Station. The 1906 Dunedin Railway Station, a cathedral to the power of steam, is a massive bluestone structure in Flemish Renaissance style, lavishly decorated with heraldic beasts, nymphs, scrolls, a mosaic floor, and even stained-glass windows of steaming locomotives. This extravagant building, considered one of the best examples

of railway architecture in the southern hemisphere, earned its architect, George Troup, a knighthood from the king—and the nickname Gingerbread George from the people of Dunedin because of the detailing on the outside of the building. It was once the busiest station in the country, with up to 100 trains a day coming and going. The station is also home to the Sports Hall of Fame, the country's finest sports museum with displays celebrating rugby, cricket, and other athletic pursuits. ⊠ *Anzac Ave. at Stuart St.* ☎ *03/477–4449 Station, 03/477–7775 Sports Hall of Fame* ⊕ *www.nzhalloffame.co.nz* ⊠ *Sports Hall of Fame $6* ⊙ *Station daily 8–6; Sports Hall of Fame daily 10–4.*

Speight's Brewery Heritage Centre. For a tasty indulgence, head to the Speight's Brewery Heritage Centre for a tour of the South's top brewery, which dates back to 1876. Here you can see the various stages of gravity-driven brewing, learn the trade's lingo such as *wort* and *grist,* and taste the results. Speight's makes several traditional beers, the most common being its Gold Medal Ale. The company claims that this is the drink of choice for every "Southern Man," which isn't far from the truth. Watch a video of various Speight's iconic television ads and learn to say the tough Southern way, *Good on ya, mate.* ⊠ *200 Rattray St.* ☎ *03/477–7697* ⊕ *www.speights.co.nz* ⊠ *NZ$28* ⊙ *Oct.–Apr., daily 10–7; May–Sept., daily noon–6* ☞ *Reservations essential.*

WORTH NOTING

FAMILY **Botanic Gardens.** Relax and enjoy the birdsong of bellbirds, woodpigeon, and *tūi* amid 70 acres of international and native flora at New Zealand's first ever public garden. Some 6,800 plant species thrive on flatlands and hillsides ranging up from Central Dunedin, providing amazing seasonal displays of foliage. Attractions include an aviary, a winter garden hothouse, a comprehensive native plant collection, and the spectacular Rhododendron Dell. Parking at the lower part of the gardens, off Cumberland Street, affords easier access than the Opoho end, which is steeper, but both parts are worth visiting. ⊠ *50 The Octagon* ☎ *03/477–4000* ⊕ *www.dunedinbotanicgarden.co.nz* ⊠ *Free* ⊙ *Gardens daily dawn–dusk, buildings daily 10–4.*

Dunedin Public Art Gallery. The shell of an original municipal building has been paired with a sweeping, modern, glass facade to house a collection that includes European masters Monet, Turner, and Gainsborough, as well as New Zealand and Otago artists. A special gallery highlights Dunedin native Frances Hodgkins, whose work won acclaim in the 1930s and '40s. Hodgkins's style changed throughout her career, but some of her most distinctive works are postimpressionist watercolors. ⊠ *30 The Octagon* ☎ *03/477–3240* ⊕ *www.dunedin.art.museum* ⊠ *Free* ⊙ *Daily 10–5.*

Milford Galleries. Milford Galleries, a major fine-art dealer, presents solo and group exhibitions of New Zealand paintings, drawings, sculpture, glasswork, ceramic art, and photography. Among the artists are Neil Frazer (who does large-scale abstract expressionist paintings) and Paul Dibble, one of New Zealand's most acclaimed sculptors. It's closed Sunday. ⊠ *18 Dowling St.* ☎ *03/477–7727* ⊕ *www.milfordgalleries.co.nz.*

OTAGO CENTRAL RAIL TRAIL

From Dunedin Railway Station, take the Taieri Gorge Train to Middlemarch (or Pukerangi, 19 km [12 miles] from Middlemarch), one end of the **Otago Central Rail Trail.** This 150-km (93-mile) pleasantly undulating bicycle path follows the old railway line and includes a dizzying wooden viaduct and a 500-foot-long tunnel, with places to eat, sleep, and drink along the way. The only traffic you'll encounter is the occasional herd of muddy-bottomed sheep. The ride takes about five days to complete, passing through sheep farms and lovely wee towns such as Ranfurly, an "oasis of art deco," and Alexander, one of the busier hubs in Central Otago on the banks of the paint-green Clutha River. The trail eventually ends in Thyme-scented Clyde. The route can be traversed in either direction; Clyde is approximately 80 km (50 miles) from Queenstown. The trail provides a great way to experience the sheep stations, with their puzzling gates and similarly puzzling locks, as well as mud, wind, rivers, pubs, and old gold fields. ⊕ *www. otagocentralrailtrail.co.nz.*

The Octagon. The city's hub is the eight-sided town center, lined with several imposing buildings, and a smattering of market stalls, cafés, and bars with tables spilling onto the pavement. In summer it's a meeting place, and it's also the site for the occasional student demonstration. Dunedin City Council provides free Wi-Fi in this grand arena. A **statue of Robert Burns** sits in front of **St. Paul's Cathedral,** a part-Victorian Gothic, part-modern building with an imposing marble staircase leading up to a towering facade of Oamaru stone. On Stuart Street at the corner of Dunbar, check out the late-Victorian **Law Courts.** Their figure of Justice stands with scales in hand but without her customary blindfold (she wears a low helmet instead).

FAMILY   **Otago Museum.** Galleries in an 1877 building are a throwback to Victorian times. The museum's first curator was a zoologist, and many of the original animals collected from 1868 are still on display in "Animal Attic," a restored, magnificent skylighted gallery. "Southern Land, Southern People" explores the cultural heritage of this region, and other galleries focus on Māori and Pacific Island artifacts, animal and insect specimens, and nautical items, including ship models and a whale skeleton. "The Tropical Forest" re-creates a jungle, complete with live butterflies and other tropical creatures. ⊠ *419 Great King St.* ☏ *03/474–7474* ⊕ *www.otagomuseum.nz* ✉ *Free; Discovery World NZ$10; guided tours NZ$12* ⊗ *Daily 10–5.*

FAMILY   **Taieri Gorge Railway.** A route along the now-closed Otago Central Railway runs from Dunedin to Pukerangi and Middlemarch, home of the annual Middlemarch Singles' Ball; each year this very train imports young city gals up to a dance with lonely Otago sheep shearers. The highlight of the trip is the run through the narrow and deep Taieri Gorge, with 10 tunnels and dozens of bridges and viaducts, all of which can be enjoyed from open-air viewing platforms. Also available is a seasonal *Seasider* route from Dunedin up the coast to Palmerston. The train runs every day; check the timetable for its destination. Reservations are essential. Cyclists can connect at Middlemarch to the wonderful Otago Central Rail Trail *(see box)*. ✉ *Dunedin Railway Station* ☎ *03/477–4449* 🌐 *www.taieri.co.nz* 🎟 *NZ $91–$113.*

Toitū Otago Settlers Museum. Documents, works of art, technological items, and forms of transport tell the stories of all Otago settlers, from Māori and early European and Chinese to later Pacific Islanders and Asians. The museum hosts changing exhibits and events, with a charge for some. ✉ *31 Queens Gardens* ☎ *03/477–5052* 🌐 *www.toituosm.com* 🎟 *Free* 🕓 *Daily 10–5.*

BEACHES

FAMILY **St. Clair Beach.** The sea at Dunedin can be a little wild; in summer an area between flags is patrolled by lifeguards. St. Clair has some good surfing; it hosts some prestigious competitions. Don't be too spooked by the shark bell on the Esplanade: a fatal attack hasn't occurred for 30 years, just the occasional nibble. Local residents show what they're made of at the annual "midwinter plunge" held on the beach at winter solstice. If the ocean is too cold for you try the Hot Salt Water Pool at the southern end of the beach (NZ$5.70 admission). South of town is the Tunnel Beach Walkway, a sandstone tunnel cut in 1870 by Edward Cargill so that his family could get down to the pretty beach below (this walk is closed from August through October for lambing). **Amenities:** food and drink; lifeguards; parking (free); showers; toilets. **Best for:** surfing; walking. ✉ *Beach St., St. Clair* ✥ *Drive south on State Hwy. 1 or hop on the Normanby–St. Clair bus from George St. or The Octagon.*

WHERE TO EAT

$$$ NEW ZEALAND 🍴 **The Ale House Bar & Restaurant.** A rugged interior with heavy wood furniture, old brewing equipment, and a huge schist fireplace makes the Speight's brewery restaurant welcoming. Its hub, naturally, is the bar. The menu includes a "drunken" steak (steak marinated in dark, malty porter) and beer-battered fish. You will get recommendations for the best Speight's ale to match your meal. Several special seasonal beers are released each year; in the past, these have included Harvest (an apricot beer), Chocolate, Samradh (a ginger-and-pimiento beer), and Spiced Amber Ale. You can order a "tasting try" to sample all the beer offerings. [$] *Average main: NZ$25* ✉ *200 Rattray St.* ☎ *03/471–9050* 🌐 *www.thealehouse.co.nz* ✥ *A2.*

$$ CAFÉ 🍴 **The Kitchen Table Cafe & Bake.** Paul is an artisan baker who crafts delicious wholesome food on-site as wife Louise fronts the counter to take your order. Porridge, pancakes, French toast, or good old eggs Benedict for breakfast, or how about a venison panini for lunch? Mindful of vegan taste buds and those with lactose and gluten intolerances, Paul has created a gooey brownie with blueberries, which you may want to try anyway, since it's so good. Large windows throw light into a warm and homey interior, while chunky wooden furniture with seating for 2 or 20 encourages conversation with a neighbor. [$] *Average main: NZ$15* ✉ *111 Moray Pl.* ☎ *03/477–0232* 🕓 *No dinner* ✥ *A1.*

$$ ✕ **Little India Dunedin.** Influenced by the flavors of northern India (and the
INDIAN kitchen of founder Sukhi's grandmother), this family business began in
Dunedin and has become a chain spanning the country. Spacious and
modern eateries meet traditional cooking methods, and warm hospital-
ity and generous portions of spicy vindaloos and Bengali fish prepara-
tions are among the hallmarks. A good selection of Indian beers and
excellent wines complement dishes. $ *Average main: NZ$20.50* ⊠ *308
Moray Pl.* ☎ *03/477–6559* ⊕ *www.littleindia.co.nz* ⊗ *No lunch week-
ends* ⌑ *Reservations essential* ✢ *B1.*

$$$$ ✕ **Plato Cafe.** A favorite among locals, this waterfront eatery provides
NEW ZEALAND great food and excellent service. Everything from the bread and house-
made duck liver–cognac pate, to the perfectly cooked seafood and
chicken dishes, is delicious. They do a mean coffee and great desserts,
too. Sunday brunch is popular. Licensed and BYO. $ *Average main:
NZ$34* ⊠ *2 Birch St.* ☎ *03/477–4235* ⊕ *www.platocafe.co.nz* ⊗ *No
lunch Mon. and Tues.* ✢ *C3.*

$$$ ✕ **Salt Bar Restaurant.** In an iconic art deco building, this is the place to
NEW ZEALAND dine in St. Clair's, a leafy seaside neighborhood that follows a spectacu-
lar beach. Sate yourself with beef Burgundy pie or venison; the less car-
nivorous may wish to try the roast pumpkin risotto. The bar's cool aura
of chrome finishing and art deco style is warmed by the dining area,
which has a brick fireplace. A huge brunch menu caters to all tastes,
and many dishes can be made gluten-free. The service is extremely
friendly. Brunch is available only on weekends from 9 am. $ *Average
main: NZ$26* ⊠ *240 Forbury Rd., St. Clair's* ☎ *03/455–1077* ⊕ *www.
saltbar.co.nz* ⌑ *Reservations essential* ✢ *A3.*

$ ✕ **Sampan Khmer Satay Noodle House.** This no-frills noodle bar is crowded
ASIAN with students and serves yummy, filling, and inexpensive soups. $ *Av-
FAMILY erage main: NZ$11* ⊠ *362 George St.* ☎ *03/477–3782* ▬ *No credit
cards* ✢ *B1.*

$$$ ✕ **Thai Hanoi.** Thai cuisine with some Vietnamese influences offers such
THAI choices as green or red Thai curries and a yellow or jungle (hot) Viet-
namese curry. The Rialto Cinema is across the way, making this a con-
venient pre- or post-movie dinner spot—but reserving a table is a good
idea. Licensed and BYO. $ *Average main: NZ$21* ⊠ *24 Moray Pl.*
☎ *03/471–9500* ⊗ *No lunch weekends* ✢ *B2.*

WHERE TO STAY

$$ ⊡ **Bluestone on George.** A short walk from restaurants and inner-city
RENTAL shopping, these contemporary-style studio apartments each has a patio
or balcony. **Pros:** centrally located; contemporary style. **Cons:** not terribly Dunediny, offering a bit of an impersonal business-trip vibe.
$ *Rooms from: NZ$195* ⊠ *571 George St.* ☎ *03/477–9201* ⊕ *www.
bluestonedunedin.co.nz* ⟿ *15 rooms* ⦿| *No meals* ✢ *B1.*

$$ ⊡ **Brothers Boutique Hotel.** This centrally located historic building that
HOTEL once housed members of the Christian Brothers Order now provides
plenty of charm, elegance, and character, and balconies off some rooms
and huge windows in the guest lounge take in views of the city and
harbor. **Pros:** clean rooms; quirky interior; friendly staff; great views

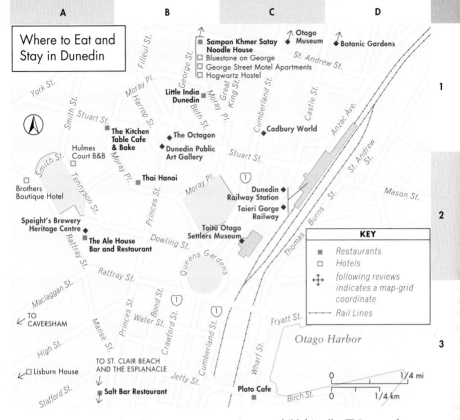

Where to Eat and Stay in Dunedin

A   B   C   D

York St.

Filleul St.

Moray Pl.

Harrop St.

George St.

Great King St.

Moray Pl.

Cumberland St.

Castle St.

Otago Museum

■ Sampan Khmer Satay Noodle House

□ Bluestone on George
□ George Street Motel Apartments
□ Hogwartz Hostel

◆ Botanic Gardens

St. Andrew St.

Little India Dunedin

Smith St.
Stuart St.

Beth St.

■ The Kitchen Table Cafe & Bake

◆ The Octagon

Hulmes Court B&B □

Smith St.

Moray Pl.

◆ Dunedin Public Art Gallery

◆ Cadbury World

Anzac Ave.

Stuart St.

St. Andrew St.

□ Brothers Boutique Hotel

Tennyson St.

■ Thai Hanoi

Princes St.

Moray Pl.

ⓘ

Dunedin ◆ Railway Station

Taieri Gorge ◆ Railway

Thomas Burns St.

Mason St.

Speight's Brewery Heritage Centre ◆

Rattray St.

■ The Ale House Bar and Restaurant

Dowling St.

Queens Gardens

Toitū Otago Settlers Museum

KEY

Maclaggan St.

TO CAVERSHAM

High St.

Manse St.

Princes St.

Water St.

Bond St.

Crawford St.

ⓘ

Cumberland St.

ⓘ

Fryatt St.

Wharf St.

■ Restaurants
□ Hotels
⊕ following reviews indicates a map-grid coordinate
⊢⊣ Rail Lines

Otago Harbor

□ Lisburn House

Stafford St.

TO ST. CLAIR BEACH AND THE ESPLANACLE

Jetty St.

■ Salt Bar Restaurant

Plato Cafe ■

Birch St.

0   1/4 mi
0   1/4 km

1

2

3

over city. **Cons:** some street noise; not child-friendly. $ *Rooms from: NZ$200* ⊠ *295 Rattray St.* ☎ *03/477–0043* ⊕ *www.brothershotel.co.nz* ⌕ *15 rooms* ⍩ *Breakfast* ⊕ *A2.*

$$
RENTAL   ⬚ **George Street Motel Apartments.** One block from Dunedin's main shopping and dining area, these clean and spacious apartments come with full kitchens in one-bedroom units and refrigerators and microwaves in the studios. **Pros:** large open kitchen/lounge rooms; central location; free Wi-Fi; helpful staff. **Cons:** some bathrooms are small and a little dated but upgrades are ongoing. $ *Rooms from: NZ$140* ⊠ *575 George St.* ☎ *03/477–9333, 0800/109–333* ⊕ *www.georgestreetmotel.co.nz* ⌕ *16 units* ⍩ *Breakfast* ⊕ *B1.*

$ ⬚ **Hogwartz Hostel.** Just opposite St. Joseph's Cathedral, this 1800s for-
RENTAL   mer bishop's residence is now a comfortable hostel with a few touches of Harry Potter (fans may want to look for Hedwig in Room 9 3/4) and plenty of nice spaces. **Pros:** central location; homey feel; helpful, friendly hosts; affordable rates. **Cons:** uphill access; most bathroom facilities are shared. $ *Rooms from: NZ$70* ⊠ *277 Rattray St.* ☎ *03/474–1487* ⊕ *www.hogwartz.co.nz* ⌕ *17 rooms, 4 with bath* ⍩ *No meals* ⊕ *B1.*

$ ⬚ **Hulmes Court Bed & Breakfast.** A character-filled home in a residential
B&B/INN   neighborhood just a three-minute walk to the center of town was built in 1860 for one of the founders of the Otago Medical School (it maintains scholarly ties by employing University of Otago students) and is

paired with a 1907 house. **Pros:** friendly staff; interesting decoration. **Cons:** not ideal for folks with cat allergies. $ *Rooms from: NZ$120* ✉ *52 Tennyson St.* ☎ *03/477–5319* ⊕ *www.hulmes.co.nz* ⤳ *11 rooms, 7 en suite, 4 without bath* ⦿ *Breakfast* ✛ *A2.*

$$
B&B/INN

⦿ **Lisburn House.** This Victorian-Gothic house is a romantic retreat set amid lovingly tended gardens and shows off such original details as decorative Irish brickwork, fishtail slate roof tiles, high, molded-plaster ceilings, and an impressive turn-of-the-20th-century stained-glass entrance. **Pros:** friendly hosts; antique-style rooms; fabulous dining in in-house restaurant; late breakfast and check-out. **Cons:** on the outskirts of city center; only one of the private baths is en suite. $ *Rooms from: NZ$185* ✉ *15 Lisburn Ave.* ☎ *03/455–8888* ⊕ *www.lisburnhouse.co.nz* ⤳ *3 rooms* ⦿ *Breakfast* ✛ *A3.*

NIGHTLIFE AND PERFORMING ARTS

You could spend all night bar-hopping and never leave The Octagon, with its many drinking establishments. Many venues are on or near George and Princes streets, often down dark alleys with no signs, so follow the crowd. Information about what's going on can be found on Radio One 91 FM (⊕ *www.r1.co.nz*) and in the student paper (⊕ *www.critic.co.nz*) the *Critic.*

NIGHTLIFE

Bacchus. Overlooking The Octagon, this high-ceilinged, upstairs wine bar and restaurant in 1880s surroundings is as elegant as the fine wines on offer. An accompanying menu showcases New Zealand beef and lamb. ✉ *12 The Octagon, 1st fl.* ☎ *03 /474–0824,* ⊕ *www. bacchuswinebarrestaurant.co.nz.*

The Craic. The Irish term for fun and banter certainly applies to this cozy tavern that plays host to live music and serves good pub grub and an excellent choice of beer, whisky, wine, and cocktails. ✉ *24 The Octagon* ⊕ *www.thecraic.co.nz.*

Ironic Cafe and Bar. A decor of steel and concrete with lots of natural light gives this modern space a semi-industrial look and a table comes with a view of the iconic Dunedin Railway Station building just across the road. You can enjoy market-fresh light fare by day and a lively cocktail scene come sunset. ✉ *9 Anzac Ave.* ☎ *03/477–9988* ⊕ *www. ironiccafebar.co.nz.*

Pequeno. Possibly the snuggest bar in Dunedin came to notoriety as the hangout of choice for Gwyneth Paltrow and Chris Martin, of the band Coldplay, during the Dunedin shoot of the film *Sylvia.* Leather chairs, an open fire, and a good selection of whisky and cigars add to the lounge atmosphere. The wine list is good as well, if pricey, and there's live music some nights. ✉ *Savoy Bldg., 50 Princes St., lower ground fl.* ☎ *03/477–7830* ⊕ *www.pequeno.co.nz.*

Refuel. A prime spot at the heart of the university campus ensures a predominantly student clientele, though everyone is welcome. Nights are split between local or national (or even international) live rock acts and DJ-driven nights of 1980s hits, hip-hop, house, and drum 'n' bass music. ✉ *640 Cumberland St.* ☎ *03/479–3875* ⊕ *www.dunedinmusic. com also www.refuel.co.nz.*

THEATER

Fortune Theatre. This local theater offers an international mix of plays, comedy, and musical theater presentations. If you can't decide what to see, go for a *"Lunchtime Bite"* at Dunedin's Public Library, where the cast performs a snippet of the Fortune's current show and offer a chance to win tickets and meet the cast. There's a late-night comedy improv show almost every second Friday, and this is a key venue for the annual Dunedin Fringe Festival. ✉ *231 Stuart St.* ☎ *03/477–8323* ⊕ *www.fortunetheatre.co.nz.*

Globe Theatre. Since 1961, the Globe has produced high-quality plays, some based on the work of local author and poet James K. Baxter. ✉ *104 London St.* ☎ *03/477–3274* ⊕ *www.globetheatre.org.nz* ✉ *NZ$25.*

Regent Theatre. A historic building hosts large-scale musicals as well as dance and theater performances and those of the Royal New Zealand Ballet. It is also the scene of the New Zealand Film Festival and the World Cinema Showcase each year. Stylish, 1930s-era The Bund is a café and tapas bar. ✉ *17 The Octagon* ☎ *03/477–8597 ticket reservations* ⊕ *www.regenttheatre.co.nz.*

SHOPPING

Nearly all the good shops are clustered around George Street and Moray Place.

Design Withdrawals. New Zealand artists and designers are well supported here. Unique jewelry, clothing, art, housewares, including David Trubridge furniture and lighting, are on offer. You'll find a gift for everyone in here, including yourself. ✉ *7 Moray Pl.* ☎ *03/477–9296* ⊕ *www.designwithdrawals.co.nz.*

Guilty by Confection. For sweets, drop by this shop for a hot chocolate or some homemade fudge. ✉ *44–46 Stuart St.* ☎ *03/474–0835.*

Koru NZ Art. A local artists' co-op gallery and interactive studio sells crafts made of *pounamu* (New Zealand greenstone), *paua* (abalone shell), and wood, as well as weaving and pottery. ✉ *2 Castle St.* ☎ *03/477–2138.*

Plume. Plume carries great New Zealand labels among a selection of major international designer clothes. New Zealand labels include Nom D, Zambesi, Rick Owens, Ksubi, Jimmy D, Palladium, Serge Thoraval, and Workshop. ✉ *310 George St.* ☎ *03/477–9358* ⊕ *www.plumestore.com.*

Slick Willy's. Girls: if you're looking for fun, funky sundresses, here's a great selection, along with women's denim, dresses, jackets, pants, skirts, shoes, shorts, skirts, and tops. ✉ *323 George St., upstairs* ☎ *03/477–1406* ⊕ *www.slickwillys.co.nz.*

University Bookshop. Bibliophiles will be in heaven amid this eclectic and diverse selection of books as well as a feast of quirky gifts, and bargain hunters will love the second floor, where there is a constant sale. ✉ *378 Great King St.* ☎ *03/477–6976* ⊕ *www.unibooks.co.nz.*

SPORTS AND THE OUTDOORS

Mix up your city adventure with some sightseeing on the outskirts of town. And when that's finished, pop over to one of the parks to watch kids in rugby practice after school.

HIKING AND WALKING

"Walking with Wheels" is a collection of well-groomed walks put together by Dunedin City Council detailing those suitable for wheelchair users and families with strollers (the three-wheeled rugged terrain kind). You can download a leaflet from the Dunedin i-SITE website *(see Visitor Information)*.

Signal Hill. This rise just northeast of the city center offers good views of the city below and the surrounding hills. It's a popular walking destination and an excellent mountain-biking venue. At the opposite end of town, Saddle Hill looks southward to Mosgiel and the Taieri Plain. The monument at the top was built in 1940 to mark 100 years of British sovereignty in New Zealand. ⊠ *Signal Hill Rd.*

RUGBY

Forsyth Barr Stadium. Is this real grass growing in a covered stadium? Originally developed for the space industry, a transparent polymer roof crowns this commanding 30,000 seater, which was completed in 2011. Take a tour of the stadium; scream yourself hoarse at a rugby match; soak up the atmosphere of a soccer game; choose a concert; or shop at the Stadium Market on a Sunday. Home games for super-rugby's Highlanders are played here, as are provincial rugby team Otago, and soccer's Southern United. Tickets sell out quick for international rugby fixtures; there's nothing like watching a pregame *haka* (Māori warrior dance) when national team, the All Blacks, are in town. Ticket prices start from NZ$25 but depend hugely on the type of match; internationals go well into hundreds of dollars. You can take a tour of the stadium (including up into the roof). ⊠ *130 Anzac Ave.* ☎ *03/479–2823, 0800/246–464* ⊕ *www.forsythbarrstadium.co.nz* ◷ *Tours NZ$20.*

THE NORTHERN OTAGO COAST

OAMARU

112 km (69 miles) north of Dunedin, 85 km (53 miles) south of Timaru.

In Oamaru's port district New Zealand's best-preserved collection of historical landmarks still gleam with ornate, limestone Victorian facades. During the second week of November the town hosts the Victorian Heritage Celebrations. Festivities include the New Zealand Penny Farthing Championships, a Heritage Golf Classic, a Heritage Ball, and a Victorian Garden Party. The town's visitor center has information about the festival and the buildings themselves.

Oamaru's other claim to fame is penguins. Each evening, enthusiastic blue penguins—the world's smallest penguin breed—emerge from the sea and waddle up the beach to their nests. The penguin colony is a five-minute drive from the town center in Oamaru. An even more significant population of yellow-eyed penguins, or *hoiho,* come ashore south of Oamaru. The best places to view them are Bushy Beach and Katiki Point, where hides (camouflaged viewing huts) have been constructed. The hide at Bushy Beach is wheelchair-accessible. These penguins are one of the world's rarest breeds, and they are considered an endangered species.

GETTING HERE AND AROUND

From Dunedin to Oamaru it's a 1½-hour drive north on State Highway 1. From Timaru to Oamaru it's a one-hour drive south on the same route. InterCity Coachlines connects Oamaru to Dunedin and Timaru three times daily. Exploring the mostly flat and ordered layout of Oamaru streets is easy and enjoyable on foot. South Hill Walkway follows the harbor to Lookout Reserve, which affords excellent views out over the town and port.

VISITOR INFORMATION

Oamaru i-SITE Info Centre. The town's visitor center has information about the locally popular Victorian Heritage Celebrations as well as the town's noteworthy buildings. ✉ *1 Thames St.* ☎ *03/434–1656* 🌐 *www.visitoamaru.co.nz* 🕒 *Daily 9—5.*

EXPLORING

FAMILY **Oamaru Blue Penguin Colony.** Penguins might be present any time of the year, and tours and viewing opportunities run day and evening. There's a small visitor center on-site with a shop and toilet facilities. The actual times penguins come ashore in the evening affects the nighttime open hours, but the center opens every morning at 10 am. ✉ *Waterfront Rd.* ☎ *03/433–1195* 🌐 *www.penguins.co.nz* 🎟 *Daytime NZ$10; NZ$16 for daytime tours; NZ$28 for evening/night viewing* 🕒 *Oct.–Mar., daily 10 am–11:30 pm; Apr.–Sept., daily 10 am–8:30 pm.*

WHERE TO EAT

$$$$ NEW ZEALAND FAMILY 🍴 **Riverstone Kitchen.** The mouthwatering menu focuses on organic, locally grown, seasonal produce, offering regional New Zealand cuisine with a few Asian accents (a Thai duck salad, for instance). While the atmosphere is casual, the food is serious. Chef Bevan Smith, who trained in Christchurch, has published two cookbooks. The "Little People" menu is just for kids. A prix-fixe menu let's you sample the best of the offerings for a fairly reasonable price. The restaurant is 12 km (7½ miles) north of the center of Oamaru. [$] *Average main: NZ$32* ✉ *1431 State Hwy. 1* ☎ *03/431–3505* 🌐 *www.riverstonekitchen.co.nz* 🕒 *Closed Tues. and Wed. No dinner Mon.*

MOERAKI

30 km (25 miles) south of Oamaru, 60 km (37 miles) north of Dunedin.

Between Oamaru and Dunedin, you can stop to see the striking Moeraki Boulders.

EXPLORING

Moeraki Boulders. These giant spherical rocks are concretions that were formed by a gradual buildup of minerals around a central core. Some boulders have sprung open, revealing—no, not alien life forms, but—interesting calcite crystals. The boulders stud the beach north of the town of Moeraki and south as well at Katiki Beach off Highway 1. Be warned that the boulders at Moeraki Beach have become a bit of a tourist attraction, and there are often whole busloads of people wandering the beach. Watch for little Hector's dolphins jumping in the surf just offshore; they're as interesting as the boulders. ⊠ *7 Moeraki Boulders Rd.*

WHERE TO EAT

$$$
SEAFOOD

✕ **Fleurs Place.** If you're feeling a bit hungry after the sea air, pop into this unpretentious place out on the old jetty in Moeraki. Here you can enjoy fish straight out of the sea, which is the highlight of the lunch and dinner menus, along with other delicacies such as *titi* (muttonbird). Sit upstairs and watch the fishing boats come in, gaze at the setting sun, or imagine the stories behind the eclectic mix of relics that adorn the walls. When a newspaper offered to send British restaurateur and chef Rick Stein anywhere in the world to write a travel article, he chose Fleurs Place as his subject. Praise indeed. $ *Average main: NZ$30* ⊠ *169 Haven St.* ☎ *03/439–4480* ⊕ *www.fleursplace.com* ۞ *Closed Mon. and Tues.*

OTAGO PENINSULA

The main items of interest along the claw-shape peninsula that extends northeast from Dunedin are an albatross colony and Larnach Castle. The road on the west side of the peninsula consists of 15 km (9½ miles) of tight curves along the harbor, so be careful while driving, or you could find yourself having an impromptu marine adventure. Along the road are a handful of settlements; these get progressively more rustic as you near the peninsula's tip. On the east side of the peninsula there's a string of rugged beaches; some are accessible via walking paths. On the journey back to Dunedin, the Highcliff Road, which turns inland at the village of Portobello, is a scenic alternative to the coastal Portobello Road and gives easiest access to Larnach Castle. Allow an hour to drive from the city.

GETTING HERE AND AROUND

Driving to the peninsula gives you freedom to stop when and where you choose, and the route is quite scenic, as much of the road hugs the water. The Dunedin city bus leaves throughout the day from Cumberland Street to the peninsula; check the GoBus website for the schedule. You can also see the peninsula sights via a harbor boat cruise.

Visitor information is available at the Dunedin i-SITE Visitor Information Centre, but for facts specific to the peninsula, check out the Visit Otago Peninsula website.

Contacts GoBus. ☎ *03/474-5577* ⊕ *www.gobus.co.nz.* **Otago Regional Council.** ⊠ *Dunedin Passenger Transport, 1 Transport Pl., Dunedin* ☎ *03/474–1669* ⊕ *www.orc.govt.nz.*

Otago Peninsula

Middlemarch

Sutton

87 Taieri Gorge Railway ◆

Clarks Junction

Evansdale ○ ○ Warrington

Orokonui Ecosanctuary ◆ ○ Waitati Aramoana

Port Chalmers ○ The Mole
Sawyers Bay ○

Outram ○ Larnach Castle ○ ○ Broad Bay

Lake Mahinerangi

Mosgiel ○ ○ Waverley

Allanton ○ ○ St Clair

Lawrence ○ Westwood Brighton

8

Kuri Bush

Milton ○

Balclutha
Invercargill
Kaitangata

Palmerston

85 1 ↑ TO CHRISTCHURCH

Waikouaiti
Cornish Head
Puketeraki

Royal Albatross Colony & Taiaroa Head
Yellow-Eyed Penguin Reserve
Otago Harbour
Portobello ○ "Disappearing Gun"

OTAGO PENINSULA

Dunedin see detail map

Toko Mouth

South Pacific Ocean

0 —————— 15 mi
0 —————— 15 km

TOURS

Monarch Wildlife Cruises. Experience the area's prolific wildlife on a guided, hour-long cruise from Dunedin to Taiaroa Head, including visits to the breeding sites of the northern royal albatross, New Zealand fur seals, and up to 20 species of coastal and pelagic birds. Very likely, an albatross will fly over your boat—the huge wingspan of these birds makes this a spectacular sight. Other trips include landing stops at the yellow-eyed penguin reserve or the Taiaroa visitor center. ⊠ *20 Fryatt St., Dunedin* ☎ *03/477–4276* ⊕ *www.wildlife.co.nz* ⊠ *From NZ$55.*

Natures Wonders Naturally. An all-terrain vehicle gets you to hard-to-reach parts of the Otago Peninsula. The one-hour Wildlife Tour includes visits to colonies of shags (cormorants), seals, and blue penguins, and you may even catch up with some yellow-eyed penguins coming ashore. The Sheep Shed Tour is exactly that and provides a look at life on a New Zealand sheep farm: watch talented shearers in action; feel the fleece; smell the lanolin (and the waft of a genuine sheep shed); walk alongside working dogs as they control the flow of sheep into holding pens. Make a day of it and combine both trips. ⊠ *Taiaroa Head, 1265 Harrington Point Rd., Dunedin* ☎ *03/478–1150, 0800/246–446* ⊕ *www.natureswonders.co.nz* ⊠ *From NZ$59.*

VISITOR INFORMATION

Contacts **Visit Otago Peninsula.** ⊕ *www.otago-peninsula.co.nz.*

EXPLORING

TOP ATTRACTIONS

Larnach Castle. High on a hilltop with commanding views from its battlements, the grand baronial fantasy of William Larnach, an Australian-born businessman and politician, was a vast extravagance even in the free-spending days of the gold rush in the 1870s. Larnach imported an English craftsman to carve the ceilings, which took 12 years to complete. The solid marble bath, marble fireplaces, tiles, glass, and even much of the wood came from Europe. The mosaic in the foyer depicts Larnach's family crest and the modest name he gave to his stately home: The Camp. Larnach rose to a prominent position in the New Zealand government of the late 1800s, but in 1898, beset by a series of financial disasters and possible marital problems, he committed suicide in Parliament House—when, according to one version of the story, his third wife, whom he married at an advanced age, ran off with his youngest son. The 35 acres of grounds around the castle include lodging, a rain-forest garden with kauri, rimu, and totara trees, statues of *Alice in Wonderland* characters (see if you can find the Cheshire Cat), a herbaceous walk, and a South Seas Walkway lined with palms and aloe plants. New Zealand's only castle is a 20-minute drive from Dunedin but can be tricky to find, so follow the directions on the website. ⊠ *145 Camp Rd., Otago, Dunedin* ☎ *03/476–1616* ⊕ *www.larnachcastle.co.nz* 🗟 *Castle and gardens NZ$30; gardens only NZ$15* ⊙ *Daily 9–5 including Christmas Day.*

Fodor's Choice ★ **Royal Albatross Colony & Taiaroa Head.** The wild and exposed eastern tip of the Otago Peninsula is the site of a breeding colony of royal albatrosses. Among the largest birds in the world, with a wingspan of up to 10 feet, they can take off only from steep slopes with the help of a strong breeze. With the exception of this colony and those in the Chatham Islands to the east, the birds are only on windswept islands deep in southern latitudes, far from human habitation. Under the auspices of the **Royal Albatross Centre,** the colony is open for viewing all year, except during a two-month break between mid-September and mid-November when the birds lay their eggs; the visitor center is open year-round. The greatest number of birds are present shortly after the young albatrosses hatch near the end of January. Between March and September parents leave the fledglings in their nests while they gather food for them. In September, the young birds fly away, returning about eight years later to start their own breeding cycle. Access to the colony is strictly controlled, and you must book in advance. From the visitor center you go in groups up a steep trail to the Albatross Observatory, from which you can see the birds through narrow windows.

Overlooking the albatross colony is the Armstrong "Disappearing" Gun at Fort Taiaroa, a 6-inch artillery piece installed during the Russian Scare of 1886, when Russia was making hostile maneuvers through the Pacific. The gun was shot in anger only once, during World War

A tramper gets close to a Royal Albatross.

II, when it was fired across the bow of a fishing boat that failed to observe correct procedures. Tours range from 30 to 90 minutes and can include albatross viewing, Fort Taiaroa, and an Albatross Insight presentation. ⊠ *1260 Harington Point Rd., Taiaroa Head* ☎ *03/478–0499, 0800/528–767* ⊕ *www.albatross.org.nz* ✉ *Albatross tour NZ$45; combined tour NZ$50* ⊗ *Mid-Nov.–mid-Sept., daily 11:30–dusk; tours from midday.*

FAMILY **Yellow-Eyed Penguin Reserve.** This conservation project is entirely funded by guided tours of the private reserve. If you'd like to observe the world's most endangered penguin in its natural habitat, visit Penguin Place, where a network of tunnels has been disguised so that you can get close. The penguins, also known as *hoiho* (meaning "noise shouter" in Māori), are characterized by their yellow irises and headbands. Tours are run throughout the afternoon but must be booked in advance. If you can't bring yourself to leave, Penguin Place Lodge offers basic and inexpensive farm-stay accommodation. ⊠ *45 Pakihau Rd., Harrington Point* ☎ *03/478–0286* ⊕ *www.penguinplace.co.nz* ✉ *NZ$52* ⊗ *Oct.– Mar., daily 10:15–dusk; Apr.–Sept., daily 3:15–dusk; call for specific tour times* ⚠ *Reservations essential.*

WORTH NOTING

The Mole. The Mole, which splits the picturesque white-sand beach at the end of the Aramoana Peninsula, is a 1-km-long (½-mile-long) artificial breakwater protecting the entrance to Otago Harbour. A walk atop the breakwater is especially exciting when there is a big running sea.

FAMILY **Orokonui Ecosanctuary.** A 30-minute drive northeast of Dunedin is a 759-acre forest where native plants and wildlife thrive in relative safety surrounded by an 8.7-km (5-mile) pest-proof fence. This is necessary because much of New Zealand wildlife is threatened by pests and predators introduced into the country before settlers knew any better, and Orokonui is unique because it's the only mainland ecosanctuary on the South Island. The park offers good walking tracks, informative displays, a café, and souvenir shop. Parents, grab a "Kiwi Ranger" booklet from the front desk, which lists lots of activities to keep the kids amused during the day; if they complete the tasks, they earn a "Kiwi Ranger" badge. ✉ *600 Blueskin Rd., Waitati* ☎ *03/482–1755* 🌐 *www.orokonui.org.nz* 🎟 *Self-guided NZ$16, guided NZ$30* 🕒 *Daily 9:30–4:30.*

WHERE TO EAT

$$$ CAFÉ 🍴 **Bay Café.** In the first settlement you reach on the peninsula, this well-known café has fine views across the harbor. Scallops, prawns, blue cod, and mussels are popular, as are the tasty pizzas with smoked salmon and prawns. The brunch menu is served between 11 and 3, and the dinner menu kicks in at 5. [$] *Average main: NZ$25* ✉ *494 Portobello Rd., Portobello* ☎ *03/476–0075* ✍ *Reservations essential.*

$$$$ ECLECTIC 🍴 **1908 Café & Bar.** There are good views of the harbor from this converted post office "where the high road meets the low road." The interior still feels Edwardian, and classic seafood dishes and steaks lead the menu. On a nice day sit outside in the courtyard or in winter beside the open fire. Reservation are recommended. [$] *Average main: NZ$31* ✉ *7 Harington Point Rd., Portobello* ☎ *03/478–0801* 🌐 *www.1908cafe.co.nz* 🕒 *No lunch Mon. and Tues. in Apr.–Sept.*

WHERE TO STAY

$$ B&B/INN 🏨 **Larnach Lodge.** It's hard to beat panoramic sea views, 35 acres of gardens, having Larnach Castle as a neighbor, and the choice of a luxury room or a more modest yet still character-filled accommodation. **Pros:** how often do you get to stay in the grounds of a castle?. **Cons:** cheaper rooms do not have private baths. [$] *Rooms from: NZ$160* ✉ *145 Camp Rd., Otago, 14 km (8.6 miles) northeast of Dunedin, Dunedin* ☎ *03/476–1616* 🌐 *www.larnachcastle.co.nz* 🛏 *23 rooms, 17 with private bath* 🍽 *Breakfast.*

SPORTS AND THE OUTDOORS

DIVING

Dive Otago. A dozen or so small ships were sunk between 1920 and 1950 to protect the breakwater from the relentless Southern Ocean. You can check these ships out, and the tall kelp forest that protects them, with Dive Otago, which run trips to the Mole and other dive sites when the weather allows. ✉ *2 Wharf St., Dunedin* ☎ *03/466–4370* 🌐 *www.diveotago.co.nz.*

The Southern Man

Speight's beer has gotten a lot of mileage from its Southern Man ad campaign, complete with a Southern Man theme song. ("Cuz here we just know/what makes a Southern boy tick/and it ain't margaritas/with some fruit on a stick.") But this stereotype is rooted in reality. There are plenty of good, hardy blokes in Otago and Southland who dress in shorts and Swannies (Swanndri woolen bush shirts), work on farms, and like to fix the ute (pickup truck), hit the bars for pool and beer, and drink Speight's beer. Before long some visitors may develop similar traits. If you find yourself saying things like "She's a hard road" and "She'll be right" when the going gets tough, then the process is well under way. To help the Southern Man find the right lady there is an annual Perfect Woman competition, with challenges such as digging in a fence post, backing a trailer loaded with hay, fitting snow chains, tipping a 242-pound ram, and opening a bottle of Speight's without a bottle opener. As the ad says, "It's a hard road to find the perfect woman."

—Joseph Gelfer and Sue Farley

EN ROUTE

The Southern Scenic Route, 440 km (273 miles) long, follows the coast south of Dunedin and the Otago Peninsula, picks up the highway to Balclutha, and swings around the Catlins coast before pushing through Invercargill to Milford Sound. The Catlins stretch (200 km, or 125 miles) is a treat, although some side roads are rough. Split your journey over at least two days. The *Southern Scenic Route* brochure, available at the Dunedin visitor center, describes the sights; attractions are sign-posted. Visit ⊕ *www.southernscenicroute.co.nz.*

When you leave the highway at Balclutha, you'll notice that the native bush is dense and relatively untouched. This, coupled with rich bird-song, gives the countryside a subtropical quality.

The first stop is **Nugget Point.** Its Māori name, Tokatā, means "rocks standing up out of water." Wildlife abounds, including yellow-eyed penguins, fur and elephant seals, and sea lions. The town at Nugget Point is **Kaka Point.** There are several places to stay the night, and you should spend time at the "hide" observing the yellow-eyed penguins coming in from the sea. If you want a coffee served with an excellent sea view, stop in the **Point Café & Bar** at Kaka Point. Inland is **Owaka,** the Catlins' only town. With a population of roughly 400, Owaka has a cluster of shops, a Department of Conservation Field Centre, a small museum, and basic services.

At the settlement of **Papatowai,** there's a convenient picnic spot behind a tidal inlet. Here you can enjoy rock pools with bush on one side and coastline on the other. Just south of here, stop at the **Florence Hill Lookout.** The view of Tautuku Bay is one of the best coastal views in New Zealand. There's a 30-minute loop walk onto the estuary at Tautuku Bay.

Farther on is **Curio Bay,** home to a petrified forest accessible at low tide. From Curio Bay a back road runs out to **Slope Point,** mainland New Zealand's southernmost point. Heavy rains or unusually high tides can make the road impassable. Slope Point is a bit of a disappointment—just some farmland sloping to the sea. However, it gets plenty of visitors. There is no access during the lambing season in September and October. If you skip Slope Point and continue on the main road, stop at the general store in Waikawa, where the art of the meat pie has been perfected. Worth checking out, too, is the Waikawa Museum and Information Centre, made from two old school buildings.

By now the rugged Catlins landscape smooths out into gentle green hills. From the township of Fortrose the roads are straight once more across the wide flats of Southland; before you know it, you've reached Invercargill. The road continues westward to Tuatapere, the self-proclaimed "sausage capital of New Zealand." Along the way check out the surfers at Colac Bay and make a detour to Cosy Nook, where a handful of fishing "cribs," or huts, have been likened to an old Cornwall fishing village.

INVERCARGILL

182 km (113 miles) south of Queenstown, 217 km (135 miles) southwest of Dunedin.

Originally settled by Scottish immigrants, Invercargill has retained much of its turn-of-the-20th-century character, with broad main avenues (Tay Street and Dee Street) and streetscapes with richly embellished buildings. You'll find facades with Italian and English Renaissance styles, Gothic stone tracery, and Romanesque designs on a number of its well-preserved buildings.

Invercargill was featured in the movie *The World's Fastest Indian* (2005) starring Sir Anthony Hopkins as Invercargill-bred Burt Munro, a local "petrolhead" who raced his Indian motorcycle on Oreti Beach in preparation for breaking a world land speed record. Mayor Tim Shadbolt had a cameo in the film, which is worth seeing. Invercargill has a reputation to this day for "boy racers," and you'll notice them roaring up and down the city streets in tricked-out cars. Indignant Invercargillites blame the epidemic on "Gorons," boy racers from neighboring city Gore. You might have a '50s flashback if you're waiting at a light and a lowrider next to you starts to rumble and rev its engine.

GETTING HERE AND AROUND

Invercargill's airport (IVC) is 3 km (2 miles) from the city center. From Invercargill, Air New Zealand runs direct flights to Christchurch and Wellington, and Stewart Island flights hops over to Stewart Island *(see Getting Here and Around in Stewart Island)*. Several rental car companies operate in the terminal. Taxis from Invercargill Airport into town cost NZ$12–NZ$15. A shuttle run by Executive Car Services (⊕ *www.executivecarservice.co.nz*) costs NZ$10–NZ$14 per person, and there's usually a shuttle waiting for each flight. Executive Car Service also rents secure car storage (NZ$10 per night). Invercargill is extremely walkable, and also particularly driver-friendly. Outside Reading Cinemas in Dee Street, BusSmart Central links the center of town with local districts; longer distance buses connect Invercargill to Christchurch, Dunedin, Te Anau, and Queenstown every day and leave from Queens Park adjacent to Southland Museum. Stewart Island Experience (⊕ *www.stewartislandexperience.co.nz*) operates the Bluff Bus, which stops at the museum and various accommodations (reservation essential).

Airport Contacts Invercargill Airport. ⊠ *106 Airport Ave.* ☎ *03/218–6366* ⊕ *www.invercargillairport.co.nz.*

Bus Contacts Atomic Travel. ☎ *03/349–0697* ⊕ *www.atomictravel.co.nz.* **Bottom Bus.** ☎ *0800/304–333, 03/477–9083* ⊕ *www.travelheadfirst.com.* **BusSmart.** ⊠ *Dee St.* ☎ *03/211–1777* ⊕ *www.icc.govt.nz.* **InterCity.** ☎ *03/471– 7143* ⊕ *www.intercity.co.nz.* **nakedbus.** ☎ *0900/62533* ⊕ *www.nakedbus.com.*

Bus Depot Invercargill Bus Terminal. ⊠ *Queens Park, 108 Gala St.*

TOURS

Catlins Wildlife Trackers Ecotours. To walk with Fergus and Mary Sutherland along a lonely beach has been described as the New Zealand equivalent of taking a tour through a Renaissance cathedral, and whatever wildlife you are into, they will track it down for you. The four-day/ three-night ecotour includes guided walks and conservation activities tailored to your ability as well as luxury cottage accommodation and meals. The two-day/three-night Catlins Traverse Walk requires reasonable fitness since you'll be walking for around seven hours a day carrying a daypack. ⊠ *5 Mirren St., Papatowai* ☎ *03/415–8613* ⊕ *www. catlins-ecotours.co.nz* ⊠ *From NZ$790.*

Lynette Jack Scenic Sights. Lynette Jack draws on an extensive knowledge of Invercargill and the surrounding area to illuminate local history during an exploration of gardens, beaches, historic houses, local hero Burt Munro, and even a smeltery. ⊠ *22 Willis St* ☎ *03/215–7741, 027/433– 8370* ✎ *scenic.sights@xtra.co.nz* ⊠ *From NZ$105.*

VISITOR INFORMATION

Contacts Invercargill Visitor Information Centre. ⊠ *Southland Museum, 108 Gala St.* ☎ *03/211–0895* ⊕ *www.invercargillnz.com.*

EXPLORING

TOP ATTRACTIONS

Bill Richardson Transport World. More than 300 trucks and VW Kombis (that's a VW bus, to Americans) are on display, alongside motoring memorabilia and petrol bowsers—or, again for Americans, gas pumps. Kids who get bored looking at old cars will enjoy a special Lego learning space geared to them. ⊠ *26 Dart St.* ☎ *03/217–1600* ⊕ *www. transportworld.co.nz* ☉ *Daily 10–6.*

E. Hayes and Sons. Invercargill's most famous sight is a 100-year-old hardware store that stocks every little thing you can think of. It's totally yin-yang (grandma-grandpa) with one half devoted to little glass lemon juicers and whisks and the other half filled with tools and wheelbarrows. The store also has a popular Motorworks Collection where you can view memorabilia of Invercargill's famous son Burt Munro, the "World's Fastest Indian." ⊠ *168 Dee St.* ☎ *03/218–2059.*

FAMILY **Queens Park.** These 200 acres in the center of town create a fine layout of public gardens. Included are two rose gardens with both modern and "antique" rose varieties; a Japanese garden complete with meditation area; and an impressive hothouse, which acts as a sanctuary on a wet day. The park has miles of gentle walking paths and waterways, an 18-hole golf course, a fitness trail, and a decent café. There's also a small zoo area and an aviary with a walk-through section that children love. The main entrance is through the stately Feldwick Gates next to the Southland Museum. ⊠ *Queens Dr. at Gala St.* ☎ *03/217–7368.*

FAMILY **Southland Museum and Art Gallery.** The Southland Museum and Art Gallery contains the largest public display of live *tuatara,* New Zealand's extremely rare and ancient lizards. The museum has also established a successful captive-breeding program for the creatures. It's usually easy to spot these minidinosaurs, but they do a successful job of hiding themselves if it gets too noisy. Southland also contains fine displays of Māori and settler artifacts, as well as a sub-Antarctic exhibit. The gallery has both older and modern New Zealand art on permanent display as well as temporary exhibits. It's in Queens Park, with an on-site café and information center. ⊠ *108 Gala St.* ☎ *03/219–9069* ⊕ *www.southlandmuseum.com* ✉ *Donation requested* ⊘ *Weekdays 9–5, weekends 10–5.*

WORTH NOTING

Water Tower. An exceptional example of Victorian architecture can be seen peaking above the city's gentle landscape. Built in 1889 to pressurize the water supply, the structure was recognized by New Zealand's Historic Places Trust as one of the country's most outstanding industrial monuments. This ornate landmark is still completely functional. On Sunday afternoons you can sometimes scale the internal staircase of the 139-foot-tall structure. ⊠ *Doon St.* ⊕ *www.icc.govt.nz.*

EN
ROUTE

Bluff. In the tiny township of Bluff (*The Bluff* to locals) you can taste the coveted namesake oysters. An annual festival, held in May, wallows in seafood delicacies; oyster-opening and oyster-eating competitions and cook-offs are part of the fun. (If you miss the festival, the most spectacular place for oysters, in season, is Lands End Restaurant overlooking the sea.) The Lands End Inn is the best place to stay the night. The bakery on Gore Street is open from 5:30 am and has nice pastries and meals. Don't miss the Maritime Museum on the Foreshore Road (the Oyster boat *Monica* sits beside it). Bluff is also home to the frequently photographed Stirling Point signpost, at the southern end of State Highway 1, which gives directions to places all over the world, including the South Pole. If it's a nice day follow the signs up to Bluff Lookout: the views encompass the Catlins and Stewart Island, and give you an excellent lay of the land. Good walking tracks are around Bluff; many begin at Stirling Point. The town is also the main jumping-off point for Stewart Island. It's about 30 km (19 miles) from Invercargill to Bluff, an easy half-hour drive south on State Highway 1. ⊕ *www.bluff.co.nz.*

BEACHES

Oreti Beach. The surf at this spot 11 km (7 miles) southeast of town is often too rough for swimming, but locals do swim in summer, and surfers and windsurfers take advantage of the wind and swells that whip the coast almost constantly. The annual Burt Munro Challenge in November sees motorcycles hurtle across the sand as riders pit their wits and machines against one another in honor of local hero and motorcycle land speed record holder from whom the race gets its name. **Amenities:** none. **Best for:** solitude; surfing; walking; windsurfing. ✉ *Dunns Rd.* 🌐 *www.burtmunrochallenge.com.*

COFFEE LOVERS

Invercargill is home to the world's southernmost Starbucks, so you might want to pop in for the mug that says as much. As for cafés, there are many other inviting options like the **Seriously Good Chocolate Company** (✉ *147 Spey St.*), the **Batch Café** (✉ *173 Spey St.*), and **Three Bean Cafe** (✉ *73 Dee St., corner of Don*).

WHERE TO EAT

$$$ NEW ZEALAND FAMILY 🍴 **Cabbage Tree.** A spacious room done in wood and brick offers a super-sized menu with more than 100 dishes. Popular choices are Stewart Island blue cod, lamb shanks, prawns, pan-seared venison, and Bluff oyster dishes. The wine list includes mostly New Zealand wines, with the occasional European bottle for the stubborn. The outdoor garden bar is a perfect place to enjoy the Southland sun with a glass of wine; forget driving and make use of a courtesy vehicle for pickup/drop-off within Otatara and Invercargill city. [$] *Average main: NZ$29* ✉ *379 Dunns Rd., Otatara* ☎ *03/213–1443* 🌐 *www.thecabbagetree.com.*

$$ INDIAN 🍴 **Little India Invercargill.** Influenced by the flavors of northern India (and the kitchen of founder Sukhi's grandmother) this family business began in Dunedin and now has restaurants spanning the country. Spacious and modern eateries offer traditional cookings methods; warm hospitality and generous portions keep diners coming back. The display of lamp shades covering one wall is an odd decorative choice given the lack of embellishment elsewhere, but an open fireplace adds a nice touch during winter. There's a good selection of Indian beers and an excellent choice of wines that complement the dishes. Reservations are a good idea but not an absolute requirement. [$] *Average main: NZ$18.50* ✉ *11 The Crescent* ☎ *03/214–1555* 🌐 *www.littleindia.co.nz* 🕒 *No lunch weekends.*

$$$ CONTEMPORARY 🍴 **The Rocks Restaurant Bar.** You could easily walk past this stylish place, tucked inside a shopping courtyard. Terra-cotta, brick, and river stone give off an urban-chic-meets-Tuscany vibe. The kitchen employs bounty from the nearby bush and sea paired with inventive sauces and sides. Share a "rummage board" (tapas-style plate loaded with seafood, chorizo, olives, cheese, and crusty bread) with friends while you ponder over the menu. [$] *Average main: NZ$30* ✉ *101 Dee St., at Courtville Arcade* ☎ *03/218–7597* 🌐 *www.shop5rocks.com* 🕒 *Closed Sun. and Mon.*

$$ ✕ **Ziff's Café and Bar.** This enormously popular restaurant on the way to Oreti Beach (past the airport) is a local favorite. Ziff's does steak, blue cod, chicken, and pasta, and customers love the home-smoked salmon and the venison hot pot. The establishment provides a taxi service for NZ$2 per person, so you can indulge in their excellent wines and cognacs, too. Breakfast is served until 2 for late sleepers. $ *Average main: NZ$18* ⊠ *143 Dunns Rd.* ☎ *03/213–0501* ⊕ *www.ziffs.co.nz.*

WHERE TO STAY

Many of Invercargill's motels are on Tay Street, handy if you're coming from Dunedin and North Road, convenient if you're arriving from Queenstown.

$$ 🏨 **Ascot Park Hotel.** The largest hotel in town, a five-minute drive from

HOTEL   the town center, is a rambling complex with spacious, modern rooms, all with small balconies and those in a motel-style building with kitchenettes. **Pros:** big rooms; some kitchenettes. **Cons:** restaurant pricey; tiny pool. $ *Rooms from: NZ$150* ⊠ *Tay St. at Racecourse Rd.* ☎ *03/219– 9076, 0800/272–687* ⊕ *www.ascotparkhotel.co.nz* ⇌ *82 rooms, 24 motel units* ⦿ *No meals.*

$ 🏨 **Invercargill Airport Hotel.** Don't let the name put you off, the "IAH"

RENTAL   is not at the end of the airport runway; rather, it's bang in the center of town, offering studio and one-, two-, or three-bedroom apartments, each with its own kitchenette. **Pros:** clean, comfortable units; central location; warm, superfriendly staff. **Cons:** some road noise at the front; bathrooms are small and basic; limited parking (reserve a space when booking). $ *Rooms from: NZ$99* ⊠ *15 Tay St.* ☎ *03/211–3800, 0508/454–845* ⊕ *www.iah.co.nz* ⇌ *65 units* ⦿ *No meals.*

$ 🏨 **Kelvin Hotel.** The big advantage of this modern but somewhat bland

HOTEL   full-service hotel is that it's really central, in just about the ideal location if you're not driving. **Pros:** couldn't be more centrally located. **Cons:** no gym on-site but pass to nearby facility included. $ *Rooms from: NZ$115* ⊠ *At Kelvin and Esk Sts.* ☎ *03/218–2829, 0800/802–829* ⊕ *www.kelvinhotel.co.nz* ⇌ *57 rooms, 3 suites, 1 3-bedroom apartment* ⦿ *No meals.*

$$ 🏨 **Mohua Park.** If you're traveling to Invercargill via the Southern Sce-

RENTAL   nic Route, these four lovely self-catering cottages make a perfect rest stop before you get to the city. **Pros:** beautiful outlooks on 35 acres of native forest. **Cons:** extra NZ$30 fee if you're only staying for one night; no TV or phone. $ *Rooms from: NZ$180* ⊠ *744 Catlins Valley Rd., Mohua* ☎ *03/415–8613* ⊕ *www.catlinsmohuapark.co.nz* ⇌ *4 cottages* ⦿ *No meals.*

SPORTS AND THE OUTDOORS

Take a picture of yourself on some of the world's southernmost beaches and send it home. But Invercargill doesn't exactly have perfect tanning weather. Even in summer, the south can still get a few chilly days. Some Stewart Island trips depart from here and include the ferry costs in their rate *(see Sports and the Outdoors in Stewart Island).*

11

HIKING

Estuary Walkway. Just 2½ km (1½ miles) south of Invercargill, this walking/cycling loop track where the Waihopai River meets the New River estuary traverses what was once a landfill site. The area has benefited from a community regeneration project and now provides a rich habitat for wildlife and people to enjoy. The walkway is accessible from the Stead Street Wharf car park. ⊠ *Stead St.*

Sandy Point. This good walking spot can be reached by taking a left after crossing the Oreti River on the way out to Oreti Beach. A 13-km (8-mile) network of easygoing trails covers the riverbanks, estuary, and the bush. A leaflet detailing the paths is available from the Invercargill Visitor Information Centre. ⊠ *Sandy Point Rd.*

Tuatapere Hump Ridge Track. On the western side of the Southern Scenic Route, this challenging, circular three-day, two-night walk combines beach, bush, and subalpine environments in its 53 km (33 miles). The track starts near Tuatapere, about two hours' drive west of Invercargill and right on the edge of the Fiordland National Park. It's no amble; you'll spend about nine hours walking each day, but two good huts along the route each sleep about 40 people. You'll need to buy hut tickets in advance. ⊠ *31 Orawia Rd., Tuatapere* ☎ *03/226–6739* ⊕ *www. humpridgetrack.co.nz.*

STEWART ISLAND

Stewart Island, home to New Zealand's newest national park, Rakiura, is the third largest and most southerly of New Zealand's main islands, separated from the South Island by the 30-km (19-mile) Foveaux Strait. Its original Māori name, Te Punga O Te Waka a Maui, means "the anchor stone of Maui's canoe." Māori mythology says the island's landmass held the god Maui's canoe secure while he and his crew raised the great fish—the North Island. Today the island is more commonly referred to by its other Māori name, Rakiura, which means "the land of the glowing skies." This refers to the spectacular sunrises and sunsets and to the southern lights, or aurora australis. The European name of Stewart Island dates back to 1809. It memorializes an officer William W. Stewart on an early sealing vessel, the *Pegasus,* who was the first to chart the island.

The island covers some 1,700 square km (650 square miles). It measures about 75 km (46 miles) from north to south and about the same distance across at its widest point. On the coastline, sharp cliffs rise from a succession of sheltered bays and beaches. In the interior, forested hills rise gradually toward the west side of the island. Seals and penguins frequent the coast, and the island's prolific birdlife includes a number of species rarely seen in any other part of the country. In fact, this is the surest place to see a kiwi. The Stewart Island brown kiwi, or *tokoeka,* is the largest species of this kind of bird. Unlike their mainland cousins, these kiwis can be seen during the day as well as at night. It's a rare and amusing experience to watch these pear-shape birds scampering on a remote beach as they feed on sand hoppers and grubs.

Māori have visited and lived on Stewart Island for centuries. Archaeologists' studies of 13th-century Māori middens (refuse heaps) indicate that the island was once a rich, seasonal resource for hunting, fishing, and gathering seafood. A commonly eaten delicacy at that time, the *titi*, also known as the muttonbird, is still traditionally harvested and occasionally appears on menus.

In the early 19th century, explorers, sealers, missionaries, and miners settled the island. They were followed by fishermen and sawmillers who established settlements around the edges of Paterson Inlet and Halfmoon and Horseshoe bays. In the 1920s Norwegians set up a whaling enterprise, and many descendants of these seafaring people remain. Fishing, aquaculture, and tourism are now the mainstays of the island's economy.

Even by New Zealand standards, Stewart Island is remote, raw, and untouched. The appeal is its seclusion, its relaxed way of life, and its untouched quality. Stewart Island is not for everyone: if you must have shopping malls, casinos, or umbrella drinks on the beach, don't come here. Visitors should be prepared for the fact that Stewart Island can be chilly, windy, and rainy, even in the middle of summer.

GETTING HERE AND AROUND

AIR TRAVEL

Stewart Island Flights has three scheduled flights daily between Invercargill and Halfmoon Bay. The 20-minute flight costs NZ$203 roundtrip; for the best views ask to sit up front with the pilot. The island's bare-bones-but-paved Ryan's Creek Airstrip is about 2 km (1 mile) from Oban (population 390). The shuttle that meets each flight is included in the airfare.

Contacts Stewart Island Flights. ☎ 03/218-9129 ⊕ www.stewartislandflights.com.

BOAT TRAVEL

Stewart Island Experience runs the ferry between the island and Bluff. There are three departures daily November to April, and one during the low season. The cost is NZ$75 each way. The company also offers an extensive list of organized tours, including trips aboard submersible craft with viewing windows that afford a close-up look at dozens of fish species and the mesmerizing kelp forests.

Contacts Rakiura Adventure Ulva Ferry. ☎ 03/219-1013. **Stewart Island Experience.** ✉ *Stewart Island Visitor Terminal, Main Wharf, Oban* ☎ *03/212-7660, 0800/000-511* ⊕ *www.stewartislandexperience.co.nz.* **Stewart Island Water Taxi & Eco Guiding.** ☎ *0800/469-283, 03/219-1394* ⊕ *www. stewartislandwatertaxi.co.nz.*

CAR, MOPED, AND BICYCLE TRAVEL

There are cars, mopeds, and bicycles for rent on the island, but there are only 20 km (13 miles) of paved road. Most of the traffic road signs you'll see are big yellow caution ones depicting silhouettes of kiwi and penguins.

FOOT TRAVEL

The best mode of transportation on the island is the "10-toe express." There are *some* sidewalks; when there isn't one, keep to the edge of the road and you'll endear yourself to locals by not strolling in the middle of traffic.

TAXI TRAVEL

Water taxis are an excellent option if you want to "mix it up" a bit when seeing the park. One-way fares start from NZ$45 depending on destination, and the Ulva Island return is NZ$25. Four taxis operate from Golden Bay Wharf, a scenic 15-minute walk from town. The visitor center can make a booking for you.

TOURS

Besides regular daily ferry services between Bluff and Halfmoon Bay (Stewart Island), Stewart Island Experience *(see above)* offers a range of island-based excursions. Get your bearings on the Village & Bays bus tour. There aren't many roads on Stewart Island but during the 90-minute tour you'll drive along most of them. Informative commentary, suitable for all ages, scheduled services at 11 am and 1 pm daily (more in summer). On the water: explore the coast near Halfmoon Bay and the underwater world on the Marine Nature Cruise. Sit beneath the waterline on a semisubmersible vessel and cruise past the kelp forests. From November through March, there are daily departures at noon (unsuitable for preschoolers). Or take a short cruise and guided walk on Ulva Island on the Paterson Inlet Cruise. From November through April there are daily departures at 12:45. Both cruises are 2 hours 30 minutes and are weather-dependent. Discounts are available for multibookings.

Island Explorer. If you're short of time, then hop on a scenic, 90-minute bus tour operated by Stewart Island Flights. There are no scheduled departure times (it's done on demand), so make sure to book ahead whenever possible. ✉ *Stewart Island Flights, Elgin Terr., Halfmoon Bay* ☎ *03/218–9129* ⊕ *www.stewartislandflights.com* ✉ *From NZ$35.*

VISITOR INFORMATION

The Department of Conservation Rakiura National Park Visitor Centre is open daily. The Environment Centre, located next to the Glowing Sky Merino Shop, has information about the habitat recovery projects on the island. The village library in the Community Centre has a complete collection of books about Stewart Island, as well as field guides of native flora and fauna. (The library is open only five hours per week, however.) For biased, vulgar, and amusing information about island goings-on ("the goss"), belly up to the bar at the pub and do some earwigging.

Contacts Department of Conservation Rakiura National Park Visitor Centre. ✉ *15 Main Rd., Oban* ☎ *03/219–0009* ⊕ *www.doc.govt.nz.* **Stewart Island Promotion Association.** ⊕ *www.stewartisland.co.nz.*

EXPLORING

Apart from the tiny township of Oban at Halfmoon Bay on Paterson Inlet, Stewart Island is practically uninhabited. Directly behind Oban's waterfront is a short main street with a small collection of

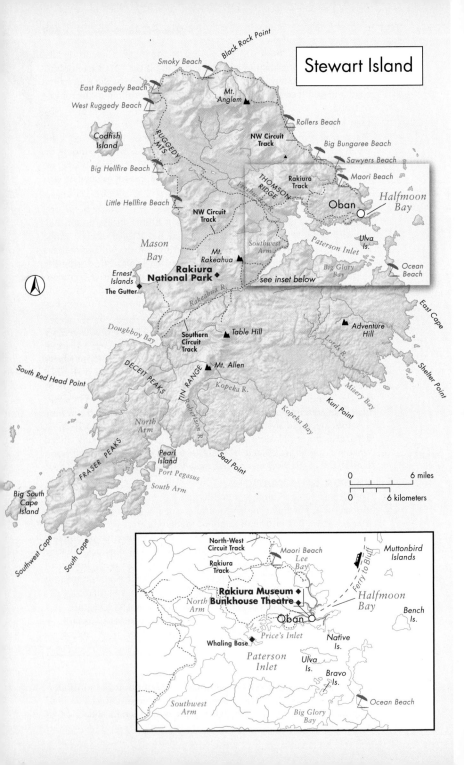

Stewart Island

Black Rock Point

Smoky Beach

East Ruggedy Beach

West Ruggedy Beach

Mt. Anglem

Rollers Beach

RUGGEDY MTS.

Codfish Island

NW Circuit Track

Big Bungaree Beach

Sawyers Beach

Big Hellfire Beach

THOMSON RIDGE

Rakiura Track

Maori Beach

Little Hellfire Beach

NW Circuit Track

Freshwater R.

Oban

Halfmoon Bay

Mason Bay

Mt. Rakeahua

Southwest Arm

Paterson Inlet

Ulva Is.

Ernest Islands

Rakiura National Park

Big Glory Bay

Ocean Beach

The Gutter

Rakeahua R.

see inset below

East Cape

Doughboy Bay

Southern Circuit Track

Table Hill

Adventure Hill

Lords R.

DECEIT PEAKS

Mt. Allen

Shelter Point

South Red Head Point

TIN RANGE

Kopeka R.

Robertson R.

Misery Bay

Kuri Point

Kopeka Bay

North Arm

Pearl Island

Seal Point

FRASER PEAKS

Port Pegasus

South Arm

Big South Cape Island

Southwest Cape

South Cape

| 0 | | | 6 miles |
| 0 | | | 6 kilometers |

North-West Circuit Track

Maori Beach

Lee Bay

Ferry to Bluff

Muttonbird Islands

Rakiura Track

Rakiura Museum

Bunkhouse Theatre

North Arm

Oban

Halfmoon Bay

Bench Is.

Price's Inlet

Native Is.

Whaling Base

Paterson Inlet

Ulva Is.

Bravo Is.

Southwest Arm

Big Glory Bay

Ocean Beach

establishments. A handful of roads head up the surrounding hills. The hills are mostly thick bush, with houses poking their heads out for a view of the bay.

TOP ATTRACTIONS

Rakiura Museum. A charmingly eclectic collection includes Māori arti-facts, ambergris, old schoolhouse memorabilia, tools from gold and tin-ning prospectors, and a china "moustache cup" (there's a story behind every item). The museum also forgivingly showcases an old-world globe that doesn't include Stewart Island. ⊠ *Ayr St., across from the Community Centre, Oban* ☎ *NZ$2* ⊗ *Mon.–Sat. 10–noon, Sun. noon–2.*

Rakiura National Park. Since spring 2002, about 85% of Stewart Island has been designated as Rakiura National Park. The park encompasses areas that were formerly nature reserves and the like. More than 200 walking trails thread through the park, and a dozen huts give shelter for overnight stays. The New Zealand Department of Conservation has more information on its website. ⊕ *www.doc.govt.nz/parks-and-recreation/national-parks/rakiura/* ☞ *For more information, see Rakiura National Park feature.*

WORTH NOTING

Bunkhouse Theatre. *A Local's Tail* is a quirky 40-minute movie about life on Stewart Island as told by Lola the dog. At three daily screenings (11 am, 2 pm, and 4 pm from October to April) in this neat 53-seater cinema, you'll be introduced to local characters and learn about island living. Write a review on the blackboard, pose for a photo with Lola herself, and perhaps add your name to the rogues gallery of moviegoers past. Additional screening times can be arranged for groups. On some weekend evenings classic old movies are shown. Be sure to grab a bucket of popcorn from the foyer. ⊠ *10 Main Rd., Oban* ☎ *027/867–9381* ☎ *NZ$10* ⊗ *Closed May–Sept.*

WHERE TO EAT

There are only a few places to eat on Stewart Island, and the only place open year-round for lunch and dinner is the South Sea Hotel Restaurant. The year-round center of island social life is the Pub, where at Happy Hour you'll encounter the "five o'clockers," retired fishermen who gather for a "few pints" and trade improbable yarns. After a life-time on the deck of storm-tossed boats, the sea stance remains—legs apart and knees slightly bent. There's almost an anti–dress code here: short-sleeved sweaters that are long in the back and often have burn holes from leaning against galley coal ranges and gum boots prevail. During oyster season, it's not uncommon to see customers in full wet suits squish-squashing around the bar. On Friday night a crowd gathers when the kitchen sends out platters of free greasy "nibbles"—heaps of fried mussels, cod, chips, and pies. The pool table is free. Be aware that folks play by "Island rules," which are posted on the wall. Locals take the "down-trow" seriously, and if you lose without sinking a ball and you are not willing to circle the table with your pants down, you ought to buy your opponent a drink. If you leave the jukebox idle, a certain resident will invariably play Three Dog Night and grab you for a whirl

Golden Pingao grows on sand dunes along the popular North West Circuit.

(whether you're a bloke or a lady) roaring "Jeremiah Was a Bullfrog." And that's on a quiet night! The Pub is a great place to enjoy a couple of "coldies," hear some local lore, and have a laugh. (Those sensitive to rough language might want to bring earplugs.) If you need a ride home, or help up the stairs, ask the bar staff for assistance.

$$ MODERN NEW ZEALAND

🍴 **Bird on a Pear.** Situated right in the thick of things on Halfmoon Bay Wharf, this popular café above the ferry terminal positively bustles from early morning into the afternoon with an eclectic mix of locals and visitors. An impressive menu includes breakfast treats, local seafood (try the divine Oyster soup), huge salads, and yummy cakes and muffins, all made on-site by owner/operator Jo Leask. Grab a window seat and watch the boats load and unload or spot little blue penguins darting beneath the clear waters below as you sip a tipple from the fully licensed bar. Evening meals are available weekends from December through March. [$] *Average main: NZ$16* ✉ *2 Elgin Terr., Main Wharf, Halfmoon Bay* ☎ *03/219–1019* 🕒 *Closed May–Sept.*

$$$$ SEAFOOD

🍴 **Church Hill Restaurant & Oyster Bar.** At the heart of the menu is food of the sea, or *kai moana*. Stewart Island blue cod, salmon, mussels, oysters, and *paua* (abalone) are all cooked to perfection and accompanied by fresh vegetables from the garden just yards away. This intimate little restaurant with a view out to sea is popular with both locals and visitors. There's also gourmet food to takeout in a picnic basket. The restaurant hosts popular themed nights in summer offering a special Asian or Italian menu. [$] *Average main: NZ$37* ✉ *36 Kamahi Rd., Oban* ☎ *03/219–1123* 🌐 *www.churchhill.co.nz* 🕒 *Closed Apr.–Aug. No lunch weekdays* ✍ *Reservations essential.*

CLOSE UP

Man of the Year

If you want to watch a bunch of young bucks get down and dirty on Halfmoon Bay beach right in front of the pub to compete against their fellow man in a test of strength, stamina, and guts—usually *paua* (abalone) guts—then be sure to come for the Stewart Island Man of the Year contest. It's challenging for the crowd to watch, too, as the guys shuck *paua*, eat the guts, and swig a bottle of beer to wash it down. Then they race on the beach dressed in snorkel and flippers; row in a boat race; chop wood; and tie ropes. It's all good family(ish) fun. The competition is usually held on Waitangi Weekend around February 6 and raises money for Rugrats (the local children's charity). The regular Sunday Quiz night at the South Seas Hotel is also a well-attended event.

$ NEW ZEALAND 🍴 **Kai Kart.** Come here for good old-fashioned fish-and-chips wrapped in a newspaper. There isn't an ounce of pretense in this cheerful little place between the museum and the "skateboard park" (a wooden ramp). The owner has a mussel farm in Paterson Inlet, and the cod comes from the Halfmoon Bay fishery. Try the bacon-wrapped mussels or chef Hilli's divine mussel chowder. [$] *Average main: NZ$10* ✉ *Ayr St., Oban* ☎ *03/219–1225* 🕒 *Closed May–Sept.*

$$$ FRENCH 🍴 **Kiwi French Cafe.** American owner Britt Moore makes coffee, a selection of sweet and savoury crepes, salads, and panfried fish of the day, making this a great place to stop and watch the world go by. Grab a take-out packed lunch or stay for coffee and cake. Dinner offers either an à la carte or set menu. Britt also owns New Zealand's southernmost spa, offering both massages or soaks in the hot tub, and treatments can be booked at the café. [$] *Average main: NZ$22* ✉ *6 Main Rd., Oban* ☎ *027/314–6192* 🌐 *www.stewartislandfood.co.nz* 🕒 *Closed June–Sept.* ✍ *Reservations essential.*

$$ NEW ZEALAND 🍴 **South Sea Hotel Restaurant.** You can have a relaxed meal in the seaside restaurant or an even more relaxed meal in the bar at this popular local spot. Food such as local seafood (including oysters), pizza, pasta, and steaks offer good value: seafood chowder is a popular choice, and if you give a 24-hour notice, you can try the crayfish. Reservations are strongly recommended in the busy summer season because there are so few places to eat in these parts. Renowned winter buffets draw the local crowd in on Tuesday night. [$] *Average main: NZ$19* ✉ *South Sea Hotel, 26 Elgin Terr., Oban* ☎ *03/219–1059* 🌐 *www.stewart-island.co.nz.*

WHERE TO STAY

In contrast with the lack of dining options there are scores of accommodations catering to every budget and fancy. All lodging is guaranteed to have a gorgeous view of bush, sea, or both. Look for accommodations on the Stewart Island website (🌐 *www.stewartisland.co.nz*). Around Christmastime and New Year's every available bed is often taken, including all the bunks in the DOC huts, so prebooking is a must.

$$ RENTAL **Bay Motel.** Clean, spacious, and comfortable apartment-like units and full apartments have decks with views that take in Halfmoon Bay, and from these "busybody" perches you can observe the comings and goings of the wharf and pub, as well as the antics of the *kakas* (parrots). **Pros:** central location; nice and clean; all rooms have cooking facilities. **Cons:** a slight walk uphill from town. [$] *Rooms from: NZ$172 ✉ 9 Dundee St., Oban ☎ 03/219–1119 🌐 www.baymotel.co.nz 🛏 12 rooms 🍴 No meals.*

$$$ B&B/INN **Glendaruel.** At this beautiful B&B a short walk from town, you can have private views over Golden Bay from two double rooms and a cozy wee single. **Pros:** lovely garden with birds; nice views. **Cons:** a bit of a walk uphill from town. [$] *Rooms from: NZ$240 ✉ 38 Golden Bay Rd., Oban ☎ 03/219–1092 🌐 www.glendaruel.co.nz 🛏 3 rooms 🍴 Breakfast.*

$$$$ B&B/INN **Greenvale Bed & Breakfast.** With a heritage woven from Māori, Portuguese, Irish, and English descent, owner Wendy' is legendary for her generous hospitality, and her en suite rooms with stunning views over Halfmoon Bay are comfortable. **Pros:** central location; clean, comfortable rooms; gracious host. **Cons:** uphill climb to get here. [$] *Rooms from: NZ$385 ✉ Elgin Terr., Oban ☎ 03/219–1357 🌐 www.greenvalestewartisland.co.nz 🛏 2 rooms 🍴 Breakfast.*

$$$$ B&B/INN **Port of Call.** From this modern B&B overlooking Halfmoon Bay and the Foveaux Strait you can wander the trails through 20 acres of native bush, bordering a lush wilderness teeming with birdlife. **Pros:** lovely, historic properties; courtesy transfers from flight or ferry. **Cons:** PoC and Bach are a 15-minute walk from town. [$] *Rooms from: NZ$385 ✉ Leask Bay Rd., Halfmoon Bay ☎ 03/219–1394 🌐 www.portofcall.co.nz 🛏 1 room 🍴 Breakfast.*

$ HOTEL **South Sea Hotel.** This handsome, historic building dominates the main road in Oban and offers comfortable rooms, some of which (in the front) have sea views. **Pros:** great value for a real island experience; in-house pub and restaurant. **Cons:** can be noisy some nights; shared bathrooms in some rooms. [$] *Rooms from: NZ$90 ✉ 26 Elgin Terr., Oban ☎ 03/219–1059 🌐 www.stewart-island.co.nz 🛏 9 studios, 8 rooms with shared bath 🍴 No meals.*

ECOSENSITIVE TOURISM ON STEWART ISLAND

Green comes naturally on Stewart Island. Reduce your carbon footprint by walking instead of driving; order the muttonbird, blue cod, groper, salmon, muscles, or oysters, and you'll be eating locally. Drinking water here is collected rainwater. Power costs four times as much on the island as it does on the mainland, so most accommodations are quite green: eco-friendly bulbs are used, and wet socks get dried by the fire. Property owners fill their gardens with native plants.

SPORTS AND THE OUTDOORS

You may explore the trails on Stewart Island, but the best way to have a true island experience is through the locals. Contact a native and not only will you get to see crayfish up close, but you might score a free dinner.

TRAIL RUNS

Are you the kind of traveler who packs running shoes? The park is paradise for **trail running**. Try trails leading to Fern Gully, Little River, and beyond.

BIRD-WATCHING

In New Zealand, you will encounter birds you've never seen before, and most of the country's exotic bird species reside on Stewart Island. If you brush up on your whistling, you might find yourself a feathered friend following you along a Rakiura trail.

BEST SPOTS

Halfmoon Bay. Birds are plentiful in Halfmoon Bay. If you walk up Argyle Street, which dead-ends into a drive and continue up (where it turns into a path), you'll be certain to see the noisy kaka (bush parrots) clowning in the trees around you. Ducks loiter at Mill Creek (locals have named many of them) and a little kingfisher often sits on the phone wire above them. Rare albino wood pigeons (*kereru*) reside in the *rimu* tree by the "*rimu* tree phone" on the road leading down into Horseshoe Bay. Little blue penguins are seen in Paterson Inlet, ditto yellow-eyed penguins and Stewart Island shags. Mollymawks soar past Acker's Point. *Tūī*, bellbirds, fantails, and robins can be seen throughout Halfmoon Bay gardens and on day walks. *Weka* have been reintroduced to the area and favor the gardens of Deep Bay Road (they cut through homes and steal shiny objects if residents leave the doors open). Oystercatchers live on every town beach, and pied oystercatchers like grazing the schoolyard. Kiwi are rarely seen around town but they are there; telltale tracks have been seen at Traill Park and their shrill unmistakable cry is heard some nights.

Ulva Island. One of the best places for bird-watching is Ulva Island, 620 acres of thick native bush. The rare birds that live here have no predators, so they have an excellent survival rate. Among the resident species are the weka, saddleback, kaka (a parrot), and kiwi. The forest, which has walking paths accessible to the public, is made up primarily of rimu, rata, and kamahi trees. To get here, take a boat or water taxi from Halfmoon or Golden Bay, or paddle a kayak from Thule Bay. You can also join a tour; the best guide is the aptly named Ulva Goodwillie. *For more information on Ulva Island, see Birding on Ulva Island.*

RECOMMENDED OUTFITTERS

Aurora Charters. Full- or half-day pelagic bird-watching tours are offered aboard the *Aurora, a* comfortable 58-foot catamaran on which to get your fix of seabirds. It's not uncommon to see five species of albatross during these trips, as well as penguins, petrels, terns, shearwaters, and more. The large open deck out back provides an excellent platform for spotting the birds (bring your binoculars but most of the birds get pretty close), and if the wind picks up the cabin can comfortably seat 20 to swig a hot drink. Advance booking is strongly recommended. The full-day trip usually goes to Port Pegasus, a rarely seen part of southern Stewart Island. These tours are not suitable for children. Fishing charters for large groups are available, too. ☎ *03/219–1126* ⊕ *www. auroracharters.co.nz* ✉ *From NZ$100.*

Bravo Adventure Cruises. Phillip Smith takes you on an evening cruise and guided bushwalk to spot kiwis as they forage on the beach. Phillip is extremely knowledgeable about island lore and local Māori history. The trip is limited to 15 people—you should have a reasonable level of fitness. Advance bookings are a must, but the trip may be canceled if the weather seems dodgy. ✉ *Stewart Island* ☎ *03/219–1144* ✎ *philldismith@xtra.co.nz* ⊕ *www.kiwispotting.co.nz/* ✉ *NZ$140.*

Ulva's Guided Walks. Let Ulva Goodwillie and her team of guides share their knowledge of flora, fauna, avian, and wildlife expertise with you on a three- to four-hour amble through this ancient podocarp forest. An open sanctuary since 1997, this predator-free refuge allows rare and endangered birds and plants to thrive. Ulva's guiding team all live and work on Stewart Island, and this becomes immediately apparent as they share their passion and enthusiasm for Ulva Island with you. Advanced booking is essential. Keen birders opt for the Birding Bonanza, a full-day wildlife trifecta of land birds, seabirds, and kiwi. ✉ *The Fernery, 20 Main Rd.* ☎ *03/219–1216* ⊕ *www.ulva.co.nz* ✉ *From NZ$125.*

FISHING

If you go fishing, your catch will likely be the succulent Stewart Island blue cod. Go with a guide and he or she will fillet and bag it for you. Some will cook it for your lunch. We recommend going out with one of the real salt dogs who have fished these waters all their lives. Aurora Charters can also arrange group fishing excursions *(see Bird-Watching).*

FAMILY   **Leask Bay Fishing Charters.** Join Andrew and Sharyn on the *Rawhiti,* a wooden launch built by Andrew's family in 1910. Half-day trips depart twice daily, weather permitting. Experience traditional hand-line fishing and catch blue cod, which is cooked on board for your lunch if you go on the morning trip. Advance bookings are strongly recommended; children are welcome, and ages under five go free. ✉ *19 RingaRinga Rd., Halfmoon Bay* ☎ *03/219–1530* ⊕ *www.leaskbaycharters.co.nz* ✉ *From NZ$80.*

Lo Loma Fishing Charters. Richard Squires (aka Squizzy) runs an old-school operation with a historic wooden boat and traditional hand-line fishing. You'll hear him belting out of *Lo Loma* as you near the wharf, and be regaled with some great stories once you're on board for a relaxed half-day fishing trip. Advance booking is recommended (half- or full-day charters are also possible). These trips are not suitable for preschoolers. ✉ *Oban* ☎ *03/219–1141* ⊕ *www.loloma.co.nz* ✉ *From NZ$80.*

FAMILY   **Rakiura Charters & Water Taxi.** Hop on board the *Rakiura Suzy,* a custom-built modern boat with heated cabin and covered fishing deck for a half-day of rod and reel fishing with Matt. Full-day tours, bird-watching for small groups, fish-and-hike combos, scenic cruises, and custom charters are also available. Whatever you choose, have a cuppa

Continued on page 642

BIRDING ON ULVA ISLAND

Ulva Island is not only a birdwatcher's paradise, but also a living time capsule. Visiting it gives you the chance to experience New Zealand in a time before human contact. Then, as now, birds seen nowhere else in the world find sanctuary and thrive here.　By Kathy Ombler

Isolated as it was for millions of years, New Zealand was the ideal environment for the evolution of unique birds and flora. Indeed, it was one of the last of the Earth's landmasses to be discovered, with only a 1,000-year history of settlement. Without native mammals, only those that could swim (sea lions, seals, and whales) made it to the islands, so flightless birds flourished absent of predators. It took just the last few hundred years of human contact to endanger many indigenous birds—some have become extinct.

In recent years, New Zealand conservationsts have developed ground-breaking techniques for creating predator-free sanctuaries on many islands, where native birds now flourish. Ulva Island's 250 hectares (618 acres) of forested land in a sheltered inlet of Stewart Island form one such sanctuary. Following the eradication of rats here in 1996 several previously endangered species are now flourishing.

The bird sightings begin on the 10-minute water-taxi ride from Golden Bay (Stewart Island), with glimpses of penguins, petrels, and, possibly, albatrosses. Beneath ancient rimu, totara, and miro trees, walk well-marked trails across rocky coasts and sandy beaches, while the forest resounds with bird chatter, song, and wing-flapping.

Above: Tui bird feeding on nectar of native Kakabeak flowers

ULVA ISLAND BIRDS

Early Maori settlers named New Zealand's distinctive birds, many according to the sounds of their calls. For example they gave the name "ruru" to the morepork, for its mournful nighttime cry and "whio" to the blue duck, echoing its high-pitched whistle. Many of these names (noted in parentheses below), some with tribal variations, remain in use along with more recently established English names.

Tui
(A) Possibly New Zealand's best-known native bird, the tui is abundant in both remote forests and private gardens, even in towns and cities. It's distinctive for the white tuft of feathers at its throat (some call it the parson bird) and loved for its melodious songs and mimicry.

Kiwi (Stewart Island tokoeka)
(B) One of New Zealand's five kiwi species, tokoeka live throughout Stewart Island where, unlike their strictly nocturnal mainland cousins, they feed during the day and night. The few that live on Ulva Island are rarely seen. However, Stewart Island guided tours—such as the Ocean Beach evening tour with Bravo Adventure Cruises—provide excellent chances to see kiwi. You might also get lucky while taking a solo evening stroll around Oban—kiwis are sometimes spotted in the town's parks and on trails.

Fantail (piwakawaka)
(C) Its eponymous fanlike tail makes this tiny bird easy to spot. The tail isn't just for show, though; the bird catches flies and other insects with it and uses it to navigate. Like robins, fantails are attracted to track walkers.

Northern Royal Albatross (torea)
(D) One of the world's largest albatrosses and the only one to breed on New Zealand's mainland (on Otago Peninsula, just one hour's drive from Dunedin city), the torea is also seen on the boat trip to Ulva. They're more likely seen, however, on a fishing or pelagic bird

watching cruise; ask at the visitor center for operator details. Alternatively, visit the Royal Albatross Centre on the Otago Peninsula, or take an Albatross Encounter cruise from Kaikoura.

Stewart Island Robin (toutouwai)
(E) The island's "friendliest" birds have a habit of following you on treks. They're not just trying to get into photographs (and they do); they nab the insects disturbed by your feet. Ulva's robin population has grown to more than 200 since 2000, when just 20 birds were transferred here following the rat eradication.

Parakeet (kakariki)
(F) Both red- and yellow-crowned parakeets live on Ulva. The bright green, red, and yellow colorings of these small parrots stand out against the darker forest greens. Their high-pitched "ka-ka-ka" chatter is also distinctive.

Saddleback (tieke)
(G) Ulva is the only place to see the South Island saddleback, named for the distinctive saddle-like reddish stripe across its back. The species has recovered from near extinction in the 1960s. The more prolific North Island saddleback lives on several island and mainland reserves.

Kaka
(H) These colorful, boisterous bush parrots screech their greetings, congregate in loud social groups, and commute over long distances between islands and forests. Look for bark torn by the kaka foraging for grubs and for the spectacle of their bright red underwings.

Yellowhead (mohua)
Island sanctuaries such as Ulva have become bastions for yellowhead as mainland populations dwindle. Their presence is signalled by persistent chatter, and they're found mostly in flocks high in the trees, especially in winter.

TIPS AND TOUR OPERATORS

Stewart Island robin on Ulva Island

KEEP ULVA PREDATOR FREE. Check your clothes and boots for seeds. Check and re-pack your belongings before getting off the boat. Rats have been known to stow away!

TAKE YOUR TIME. You will see more birds. Most guided tours take an unhurried three to four hours. If walking on your own, purchase the Ulva Island Charitable Trust self-guided brochure ($2) from the i-SITE Visitor Centre or Department of Conservation Visitor Centre.

ENJOY THE ISLAND'S FLORA. With no browsing from introduced animals the plants' abilities to fruit have increased and the forest has flourished. While giant totara, rimu, and miro dominate, there's also old, gnarled red-flowering rata; a tangled understorey of ferns; mosses; orchids; and rare, ancient plants now found in few other places.

COST. Guided Ulva Island trips cost around $100, water taxi included. For independent trips, water taxis cost $20 to $35 return (depending on passenger numbers). Several companies operate both scheduled and private charter trips daily.

BEST TIME TO GO. You can go to Ulva any time of the year. Winter will be colder but the weather is more predictable.

TOUR OPERATORS

The DOC has approved the following guided tours: **Ulva's Guided Walks** (⊕ *www.ulva.co.nz*); **Ruggedy Range™ Wilderness Experience** (⊕ *www.ruggedyrange.com*); **Stewart Island Water Taxi and Eco Guiding** (⊕ *www.portofcall.co.nz*); and **Sail Ashore** (⊕ *www.sailsashore.co.nz*)

USEFUL WEB SITES

Stewart Island i-SITE Visitors Centre (⊕ *www.stewartisland.co.nz*)

Department of Conservation and Ulva Island Charitable Trust (⊕ *www.doc.govt.nz*)

OTHER SOURCES

Where to Watch Birds in New Zealand, Kathy Ombler, New Holland, 2007. A guidebook to more than 30 of the country's best birding locations.

TOP BIRDING SPOTS IN NEW ZEALAND

Native weka seeking food from a visitor on Ulva Island

There are plenty of exceptional birding areas, and all are simply great places to visit even if birds aren't your main thing.

NORTH ISLAND

Cape Kidnappers Nature Reserve, Hawke's Bay. The world's largest mainland concentration of Australasian gannets congregates on dramatic sea cliffs. Visit November–April.

Kapiti Island Nature Reserve, Kapiti Island. Located 5 km off North Island's west coast, near Wellington, the bird population includes endangered little spotted kiwi and takahe. The Department of Conservation can book day trips; overnight stays are available at Kapiti Island Lodge. Visit anytime.

Kiwi Encounter/Rainbow Springs Nature Park, Rotorua. Visit this kiwi hatchery and nursery to learn about the ground-breaking work raising chicks for release into the wild. Daily tours are conducted all year; chicks hatch September to April.

Tiritiri Matangi Island Scientific Reserve, Hauraki Gulf (Auckland). This is one of the easiest places to see New Zealand's rarest birds, including takahe, kokako, saddleback, and stitchbird. Day trips depart from downtown Auckland. Walking treks range from one to five hours. Visit year-round.

Miranda Ramsar Site, Firth of Thames. From roadside viewings and hides, see some of the tens of thousands of Arctic migratory waders that live in the vast, tidal flats and shellbanks in the Firth of Thames. It's a one-hour drive south of Auckland. Visit September–March.

SOUTH ISLAND

Farewell Spit Nature Reserve, Golden Bay and Takaka. A massive sandspit and tidal flats at South Island's northeastern tip provide a summer home to thousands of Arctic waders and winter breeding grounds for other wetland birds. Guided 4WD tours are available. Visit year round; September–March for Arctic waders.

Kaikoura, between Christchurch and Picton. Feeding grounds, just a 10 minute boat trip from shore, attract some 16 albatross species, as well as prions, petrels, and more. Specialist pelagic tours and whale- and dolphin-watching cruises are available. Visit year round.

Otago Peninsula. A mainland colony of Northern Royal Albatross, several yellow-eyed penguin colonies, and a host of seabirds and shorebirds live on the peninsula's headlands, beaches, and tidal inlets, within one hour's drive of Dunedin city. Several guided tours operate from Dunedin. Visit year-round; summer is best for the Northern Royal Albatross.

on board and tuck into Alina's home baking. Advance booking is recommended, and children welcomed (and under five free). A water-taxi service is also available; price depends on destination. ✉ *10 Main Rd., Oban* 🕾 *0800/725–487, 03/219–1487* ⊕ *www.rakiuracharters.co.nz* ☞ *From NZ$115.*

Southern Isle Charters. Fast comfortable boats are available for charter and are suitable for large groups; fishing and scenic cruises are offered as well. Prices depend on the number of passengers and destination. ✉ *6 Petersons Hill Rd., Oban* 🕾 *03/219–1133.*

Southern Limits. Take a full- or half-day fishing charter with Brett on board the *Frances II*, a commercial fishing boat. All gear is supplied, and fish can be cooked on board. Minimum numbers apply; advance booking is a must. ✉ *46 Excelsior St., Oban* 🕾 *03/219–1234* ⊕ *www. southernlimits.co.nz* ☞ *From NZ$85.*

Tequila Charters. Want to crew for the day on the commercial fishing vessel *Tequila*? Learn how to prepare cod pots, process the catch, fillet fish, and use hand lines to catch your own blue cod to take home. "Chook," aka Anthony, has more than 28 years of experience in commercial fishing and will show you how things are done in the "roaring forties" (so called due to the unpredictable weather at 47 degrees south). Wet weather gear and equipment is provided; trips depart Halfmoon Bay wharf twice daily, weather permitting. Reservations are essential. 🕾 *03/219–1334, 027/251–7122* ⊕ *www.stewartislandfishing.com* ☞ *NZ$80.*

HIKING

Numerous day hikes on well-maintained trails are in and around the township. Free street maps are available at the Flight Centre–Post Office and Ferry Terminal; detailed maps and information are available at the Department of Conservation Office. Some walks, such as the Observation Rock and Fuchsia walks, are measured in minutes; others, such as the walks to Fern Gully, Ryan's Creek, and Horseshoe Point, are measured in hours.

For information on Rakiura National Park's walks, contact the Department of Conservation Rakiura National Park Visitor Centre in Oban.

BEST SPOTS

Acker's Point. If you only have a few hours, the walk from town out to the Acker's Point lighthouse is marvelous and encompasses town, boat sheds, a historic homestead, lush forest, and ocean views. This is nesting ground for *titi* (sooty shearwaters or muttonbirds), and little blue (fairy) penguins, which can often be seen from the lookout, along with albatross and fishing boats.

North West Circuit. This 9- to 11-day walk from Halfmoon Bay circles the north coast and then cuts through the interior. If that's not enough for you, five days can be tacked on by including the Southern Circuit. Stewart Island's climate is notoriously changeable, so be prepared for sun, wind, rain, and *lots* of mud. Take the usual safety precautions for these hikes: bring suitable boots, clothing, food, and a portable stove. Complete an Outdoors Intentions form at ⊕ *www.adventuresmart. org.nz* before setting out; and, ideally, bring along with you a locator beacon (available for hire from the Department of Conservation) or a guide who knows the trails. This hike may well reward you with a wild kiwi encounter.

Rakiura Track. One of New Zealand's great walks covers 32 km (19 miles) and takes three days. Day 1 goes from Halfmoon Bay to Port William Hut via Horseshoe and Lee bays. Day 2 heads inland through native bush and wood across the ridge, allowing for good views of Paterson Inlet and the Tin Range. Day 3 connects back to Halfmoon Bay via *rimu* and *kamahi* forest. Two huts on the route each accommodate up to 30 people on a first-come, first-served basis. They come with mattresses, a wood-burning stove, running water, and toilets. (If you're relatively fit and you leave early, you can do this track in one day, but you will be sore.)

RECOMMENDED OUTFITTERS

Stewart Island Flights *(see Getting Here and Around)* runs a flying, hiking, and boating adventure called Coast to Coast. For NZ$218 per person (with a three-person minimum) you can view the east and west coasts of the island, including Paterson Inlet and Mason Bay. The trip includes an easy four-hour hike on the North West Circuit and a water-taxi ride on the meandering Freshwater River. There's also an exciting plane landing on the beach and the chance to see kiwi birds. It's an interchangeable trip, so you can fly-hike-boat or boat-hike-fly.

Also consider Ulva's Guided Walks, with guided hikes focusing on the island's flora and fauna *(see Bird-Watching)*.

Kiwi Wilderness Walks. Get back to nature with a four- or five-day guided walk out in the Stewart Island bush. Highlights include Mason Bay with its staggering sand dune system; the possibility of seeing wild kiwi; historic Māori Beach, once the site of sawmills and a school in the early 1900s; and Port William's early sealing location. These tours depart from Invercargill. ☎ *021/359–592* ⊕ *www.nzwalk.com* ✉ *From NZ$1,295.*

Ruggedy Range Wilderness Experience & Aihe Eco Charters & Water Taxi. Offerings include guided walks, sea kayaking, boat cruises, water taxi, road tours, shuttle services, and an outdoor adventure gear shop. Bed-and-breakfast backpacking trips are available, and you can take a half-day guided walk of Ulva Island or do an entire wilderness escape. The company also offers guided kayaking and boat and land tours.

There's a range of outdoor gear available for sale or hire, so you can leave bulky camping equipment at home. The company does all of its own bookings. ✉ *14 Main Rd.* ☎ *03/219–1066* ⊕ *www.ruggedyrange. com* ✉ *From NZ$95.*

Sails Tours. With 80 years combined island experience, let Peter and Iris Tait escort you around Ulva Island for a four-hour tour. Your unhurried sojourn begins on the *Talisker,* a 55-foot yacht that will take you across to Ulva Island ready to explore. Group sizes are small; courtesy transfers to and from your accommodation are included in the tariff. Or you can take a leisurely road tour and learn what island life is like (at a discounted rate if you book and pay for both tours). Accommodation on

Stewart Island can also be arranged. ✉ *11 View St.* ☎ *0800/783–9278, 03/219–1151* ⊕ *www.sailsashore.co.nz* 🛳 *From NZ$175.*

KAYAKING

Share the water with penguins, seals, and occasionally dolphins in the mostly uninhabited Paterson Inlet; 100 square km (38 square miles) of bush-clad, sheltered waterways, it has 20 islands, four DOC huts, and two navigable rivers.

Phil's Sea Kayak. Suitable for beginners and experienced paddlers, this half-day guided trip in peaceful Paterson Inlet close to the shoreline is hard to beat. A full-day trip will get you into exposed coastal and intertidal waters, while a sunset/twilight tour rounds off the day as little blue penguins come ashore. Phil is very modest about his 30 years' experience on the water (which includes a circumnavigation of Stewart Island and crossing Foveaux Strait) and makes an amiable and patient guide. Small groups; tailored to experience; prices start from NZ$90 per person. ✉ *7 Leonard St., Oban* ☎ *027/444–2323* ✉ *philskayak@ observationrocklodge.co.nz.*

TRAVEL SMART
NEW ZEALAND

Visit Fodors.com for advice, updates, and bookings

GETTING HERE AND AROUND

▮ AIR TRAVEL

The least expensive airfares to New Zealand are priced for round-trip travel and must usually be purchased in advance. Airlines generally allow you to change your return date for a fee; most low-fare tickets, however, are nonrefundable. To expedite an airline fare search on the Web, check travel search engines with meta-search technology, such as ⊕ *www. mobissimo.com*. These search across a broad supplier base so you can compare rates offered by travel agents, consolidators, and airlines in one fell swoop.

Although air travel within New Zealand can be expensive compared with bus travel, the one-way fare system does make it easy to get around, especially if you don't want to spend all your time on the road. These days, booking your domestic flights in conjunction with your international flight won't necessarily save you any money, but it can help if connecting flights are running late—they will hold your next flight for you if possible. Luggage allowances are generally 1 x 23 kg (50 lb) bag when flying with Air New Zealand, and 1 x 30 kg (70 lb) bag when flying with Qantas, though these vary depending on online booking specials. Some airlines give great deals if you add stopovers to your flight itinerary. You'll need to stop in at a Pacific destination like Tahiti or Fiji for a limited time before heading to New Zealand. Check with the airline and see what they're offering; make sure that New Zealand is included in Pacific deals because sometimes it's the one exception. Qantas has a low-budget airline called Jetstar, which serves trans-Tasman and between major New Zealand hubs Auckland, Christchurch, Wellington, and Queenstown. When booking domestic flights with either Jetstar or Air New Zealand make sure you read the fine print regarding baggage allowance, as the cheaper fares have zero checked baggage allowance. If you hold an international student identification card, you'll save even more. But make sure you check in well before time! Jetstar is notorious for turning away passengers if they arrive even one second after cutoff time.

From New York to Auckland (via Los Angeles) flights take about 19 hours; from Chicago, about 17 hours; from Los Angeles to Auckland (nonstop), about 12 hours. From the United States and Canada, you will have to connect to a New Zealand–bound flight in Los Angeles, San Francisco, or Houston.

All international departure taxes are now factored into your airfare.

For domestic flights within New Zealand, check in at least a half hour before departure.

It is not required that you reconfirm outbound flights from or within New Zealand.

In line with all airlines, all New Zealand domestic and international bound flights are no-smoking.

Airline Security Issues Transportation Security Administration. ⊕ *www.tsa.gov.*

AIRPORTS

The major airport is Auckland International Airport (AKL). It is usually a bit cheaper to fly into and out of this airport, but the supplemental fees for flights to Wellington (WLG) or Christchurch (CHC) are reasonable. New Zealand's airports are relatively compact and easy to negotiate.

Auckland's international and domestic terminals are in separate buildings, a 10-minute walk apart. Free bus shuttles run constantly (however, after an incoming long-haul flight you may find that the walk and fresh air is great for the soul!). Christchurch International Airport is the main gateway to southern tourism destinations. After a major redevelopment, completed in 2013, it was awarded "New Zealand Major Airport of the Year" for its design and facilities.

New Zealand has a dense network of domestic air routes, so hopping from one area to another is fairly easy, if not inexpensive. Air New Zealand partners with other international airlines and serves smaller regional airports, so you can make these flight arrangements when booking your international flight. There are also several smaller regional and charter companies with planes carrying a dozen passengers or less. *For details on local services, see this guide's destination chapters.*

Airport Information Auckland International Airport. ☎ 09/275-0789 ⊕ www.aucklandairport.co.nz. **Christchurch International Airport.** ☎ 03/358-5029 ⊕ www.christchurchairport.co.nz. **Wellington International Airport.** ☎ 04/385-5100 ⊕ www.wellingtonairport.co.nz.

FLIGHTS

Air New Zealand flies two to three times a day from Los Angeles to Auckland and is the only carrier that extends a daily nonstop flight from San Francisco to Auckland. Qantas flies from Los Angeles to New Zealand daily, mostly through Sydney. United and Air Canada, affiliates of Air New Zealand, connect from points in North America to Los Angeles. Fiji Airways connects from Los Angeles through Nadi, Fiji, with Auckland, Wellington, and Christchurch.

Within New Zealand, Air New Zealand and Jetstar compete on intercity trunk routes, along with smaller airlines Sounds Air, Origin, and Air Chathams who fly several intercity routes. *For more information about regional travel, see the Getting Here and Around sections within regional chapters.*

Several airlines provide services to Australia: trans-Tasman flights are available from Auckland, Wellington, Christchurch, Dunedin, and Queenstown.

Airline Contacts Air Canada. ☎ 888/247-2262 in U.S. and Canada, 09/969-7470 in New Zealand, 0508/747-767 toll-free in New Zealand ⊕ www.aircanada.com. **Air Chathams.** ☎ 0800/580-127 toll-free in New Zealand ⊕ www.airchathams.co.nz. **Air New Zealand.** ☎ 800/262-1234 toll-free in U.S., 0800/737-000 toll-free in New Zealand ⊕ www.airnewzealand.co.nz. **British Airways.** ☎ 800/247-9297 in U.S., 09/966-9777 in New Zealand ⊕ www.britishairways.com. **Cathay Pacific.** ☎ 020/8834-8888 in U.K., 09/379-0833 in New Zealand, 800/233-2742 in U.S. ⊕ www.cathaypacific.com. **Fiji Airways.** ☎ 0800/800-178 ⊕ www.fijiairways. com. **Japan Airlines.** ☎ 800/525-3663 in U.S., 844/569-700 in U.K., 0800/885-880 toll-free in New Zealand ⊕ www.jal.com. **Jetstar.** ☎ 0800/800-995 toll-free in New Zealand, 866/397-8170 in U.S. ⊕ www.jetstar. co.nz. **Originair.** ☎ 0800/380-380 toll-free in New Zealand ⊕ www.originair.co.nz. **Qantas.** ☎ 800/227-4500 in U.S. and Canada, 0845/774-7767 in U.K., 0800/808-767 toll-free in New Zealand ⊕ www.qantas.com.au. **Singapore Airlines.** ☎ 800/742-3333 toll-free in U.S., 020/8961-6993 in U.K., 0800/808-909 toll-free in New Zealand ⊕ www.singaporeair. com. **Sounds Air.** ☎ 0800/505-505 ⊕ www. soundsair.com. **United Airlines.** ☎ 800/864-8331 for U.S. reservations, 800/538-2929 for international reservations, 0800/747-400 toll-free in New Zealand ⊕ www.united.com. **Virgin Australia.** ☎ 0800/670-000 toll-free in New Zealand, 07/3295-3000 in U.S. ⊕ www. virginaustralia.com.

▌ BOAT TRAVEL

To travel between the North Island and the South Island, take either the Interislander or Bluebridge ferry between Wellington and Picton. Both ferries carry cars. They also connect with KiwiRail trains. A free shuttle is available between the railway station and InterIslander ferry terminal in Wellington The Bluebridge terminal is right across the road from the station. The Picton railway station is a few minutes' walk from the ferry terminals. Both ferries travel four to five times a day. Standard one-way passenger fare can be as much as NZ$70, but there are off-peak deals to be had for as low as NZ$39. The fare for a medium-size sedan costs around NZ$200. Be sure to ask about specials, including ferry-train package deals through Kiwi-Rail, when you book. *For package ideas that include ferry travel, see Discounts and Deals.*

Schedules are available at i-SITE visitor-information centers around the country. Most will arrange Interislander and Blue-bridge ferry bookings. You can also check schedules and fares and book online via the Interislander and Bluebridge websites. Some fares allow you to make schedule changes up to the last minute and guarantee a full refund if you cancel prior to check-in. Discount fares can be booked once in New Zealand; these have some restrictions. No matter how you go about it, it's a good idea to reserve in advance, especially during holiday periods.

Information Bluebridge. ☎ 0800/844–844 *toll-free in New Zealand* ⊕ *www.bluebridge. co.nz.* **Interislander.** ☎ 644/498–3302 *in U.S., 0800/802–802 toll-free in New Zealand* ⊕ *www.interislander.co.nz.*

▌BUS TRAVEL

New Zealand is served by an extensive bus network. The InterCity Group operates the main bus line, InterCity and Newmans.

Some Newmans and InterCity bus routes overlap, but Newmans tends to have fewer stops and sticks to the key tourism routes, for example Christchurch to Queenstown and the West Coast. Inter-City buses, on the other hand, cover more remote areas.

There are also many regional bus services. For instance, Bottom Bus, operated by Travel Head First, runs from Dunedin through the Catlins to Southland, Queenstown, and Fiordland; while Atomic Travel covers much of the South Island.

See the Essentials sections in regional chapters for more details on local services.

Take a hop-on, hop-off bus if you prefer a more flexible itinerary, typically valid for 12 months. InterCity offers this, along with "backpacker-target" companies like Kiwi Experience and Stray Bus. Some passes cover all of New Zealand, whereas others are limited to specific regions. Most of the backpacker buses have affiliations with accommodation and activities and can offer priority bookings and special deals.

FARES AND PASSES

Fares vary greatly. A standard full fare between Auckland and Wellington is NZ$95 but can be obtained for as low as NZ$34. A certain number of seats are sold at a discounted rate, so book your tickets as early as possible, especially during the holidays. Individual company's websites are the best way to find out about special fares.

Look into the various flexible passes that allow coach travel over a set route in a given time frame, usually three or six months. You can travel whenever you like, without paying extra, as long as you stick to the stops covered by your pass. There is also the New Zealand Travelpass, which allows unlimited travel on buses and trains and on the Interislander ferries that link the North and South islands. *See Discounts and Deals, below.*

Flexipass. The Flexipass is sold in blocks of time during which you're eligible to travel on regular InterCity bus routes. This is such a good deal that locals even use this pass for their daily commute. Typically valid for a year, you can hop on and off, changing your plans without a penalty at least two hours prior to your departure. You must schedule in advance, as independent bus ticketing windows don't track your Flexipass hours. ⊕ *www. intercity.co.nz/bus-pass/flexipass.*

Kiwi Experience and Stray Bus also visit some pretty cool destinations with special accommodations not found on the mainstream traveler networks—remote farming settlements, small town pubs, and Māori *marae* (villages), for example.

Credit cards and traveler's checks are accepted by the major bus companies. Nakedbus, a true budget service, offers a backpacker bus pass where you choose how many trips you'd like to take in increments of five trips, or they offer an unlimited trip pass for just under NZ$600.

Bus Information Atomic Travel. ☎ 03/349–0697 in NZ ⊕ www.atomictravel.co.nz. **Bottom Bus.** ☎ 03/477–9083 ⊕ www.travelheadfirst. co.nz. **InterCity.** ☎ 09/583–5780 ⊕ www. intercity.co.nz. **Kiwi Experience.** ☎ 09/336–4286 ⊕ www.kiwiexperience.com. **naked-bus.** ☎ 0900–62533 $1.99 per-min cost per call ⊕ www.nakedbus.com. **Newmans.** ☎ 09/583–5780 ⊕ www.intercity.co.nz. **Stray Bus.** ☎ 09/526–2140 ⊕ www.straytravel. com. **Stray Travel.** ☎ 09/526–2140 ⊕ www. straytravel.co.nz.

▌ CAR TRAVEL

GETTING USED TO KIWI CARS

Nothing beats the freedom and mobility of a car for exploring. Even if you're nervous about driving on the "wrong" side of the road, driving here is relatively easy. Many rental cars will have a sticker right next to the steering wheel reading "stay to the left." Having said this, as tourism numbers increase so, too, have the number of driving accidents involving tourists. Tourism organizations have prepared a Voluntary Code to help rental vehicle companies advise their clients, and the Drive Safe website ⊕ *www.drivesafe.org. nz*, which gives some handy tips.

Remember this simple axiom: drive left, look right. That means keep to the left lane, and when turning right or left from a stop sign, the closest lane of traffic will be coming from the right, so look in that direction first. By the same token, pedestrians should look right before crossing the street. Americans and Canadians can blindly step into the path of an oncoming car by looking left as they do when crossing streets at home. You'll find yourself in a constant comedy of errors when you go to use directional signals and windshield wipers—in Kiwi cars it's the reverse of what you're used to.

RENTAL AGENCIES

Japanese brands dominate rental agencies in New Zealand. Most major agencies also offer higher end options, for example, convertibles and esteemed European models such as BMWs. Domestic agency Smart Cars specializes in luxury rentals such as Mercedes and Audi convertibles. Most Kiwi cars these days are automatic, though some stick shifts (manual) are included in hire fleets, so specify if you prefer an automatic.

Kiwi companies Maui New Zealand and Kea Campers are best known for wide selections of campers, motor homes, and 4X4 vehicles. Most major international car rental companies operate here; there are also reputable domestic agencies.

Rates in New Zealand begin at about NZ$35 a day and NZ$320 a week—although you can sometimes get even cheaper deals on economy cars with unlimited mileage. This does not include tax on car rentals, which is 12.5%. Reserve a vehicle well in advance if renting during holiday seasons, especially Christmas.

Most major international companies (and some local companies) have a convenient service if you are taking the ferry between the North and South islands and want to continue your rental contract. You simply drop off the car in Wellington and on the same contract pick up a car in Picton, or vice versa. It saves you from paying the fare for taking a car across on the ferry (though you will have to organize your luggage into carry-on). Your rental contract is terminated only at the far end of your trip, wherever you end up. In this system, there is no drop-off charge for one-way rentals, making an Auckland–Queenstown rental as easy as it could be.

Check for rates based on a south-to-north itinerary; it may be less expensive as it's against the normal flow. Special rates should be available whether you book from abroad or within New Zealand.

In New Zealand your own driver's license is acceptable. Still, an International Driver's Permit is a good idea; it's available from the American Automobile Association. These international permits are universally recognized, and having one in your wallet may save you problems with the local authorities.

For most major rental companies in New Zealand, 21 is the minimum age for renting a car. With some local rental companies, however, drivers under 21 years old can rent a car but may be liable for a higher deductible. Children's car seats are mandatory for kids under seven years old. Car-rental companies may ask drivers not to take their cars onto certain (rough) roads, so ask about such restrictions.

Local Rental Agencies Apex Rental Car. ☎ 800/7001–8001 toll-free in U.S, 0800/939–597 toll-free in New Zealand ⊕ www.apexrentals.co.nz. **Kea Campers.** ☎ 09/448–8800, 0800/520–052 toll-free in New Zealand ⊕ www.keacampers.com. **Maui New Zealand.** ☎ 1800/2008–0801 toll-free in U.S., 0800/651–080 toll-free in New Zealand ⊕ www.maui.co.nz. **Smart Car Rentals.** ☎ 09/307–3553, 0800/458–987 toll-free in New Zealand ⊕ www.smartcarrental.co.nz.

Major Rental Agencies Avis. ☎ 09/526–2847, 0800/655–111 toll-free in New Zealand ⊕ www.avis.com. **Budget.** ☎ 0800/283–438 toll-free in New Zealand, 800/472–3325 toll-free in U.S. for international reservations ⊕ www.budget.co.nz. **Hertz.** ☎ 0800/654–321 toll-free in New Zealand, 03/9698–2555 international ⊕ www.hertz.co.nz.

GASOLINE

On main routes you'll find stations at regular intervals. However, if you're traveling on back roads where the population is sparse, don't let your tank get low—it can be a long walk to the nearest farmer.

Credit cards are widely accepted.

Unleaded gas is widely available and often referred to as 91. High-octane unleaded gas is called 95. The 91 is usually a couple of cents cheaper than 95; most rental cars run on 91. Virtually all gas stations will have staff on hand to pump gas or assist motorists in other ways; however, they tend to have self-service facilities for anyone in a hurry. These are simply operated by pushing numbers on a console to coincide with the dollar value of the gas required. When you pump the gas, the pump will automatically switch off when you have reached the stated amount. Or push "fill" and the pump will stop when the tank is full. Mostly you can pay at the counter inside the station after you fill your tank, although a few stations—perhaps victims of previous dishonesty—now request payment first.

ROAD CONDITIONS

Roads are well maintained and generally not crowded (except for leaving major cities at peak holiday weekends). In rural areas, you may find some unpaved roads. On most highways, it's easier to use the signposted names of upcoming towns to navigate rather than route numbers.

Due to the less-than-flat terrain, many New Zealand roads are "wonky," or crooked. So when mapping out your itinerary, don't plan on averaging the speed limit of 100 kph (62 mph) too often. Expect two or three lanes; there are no special multi-occupant lanes on the major highways. In areas where there is only one lane for each direction, cars can pass, with care, while facing oncoming traffic, except where there is a double-yellow center line. Rural areas still have some one-lane roads. One-lane bridges are common. *See Rules of the Road.*

Dangerous overtaking, speeders, lack of indication, tailgating (following too close), and slow drivers in passing lanes are all afflictions suffered on New Zealand highways.

ROADSIDE EMERGENCIES

In the case of a serious accident, immediately pull over to the side of the road and phone ☎ 111. Except on city motorways, emergency phone boxes are not common; you may have to rely on a cellular phone. You will find New Zealanders quick to help if they are able to, particularly if you need to use a phone. Minor accidents are normally sorted out in a calm and collected manner at the side of the road. However, "road rage" is not unknown. If the driver of the other vehicle looks particularly angry or aggressive, you are within your rights to take note of the registration number and then report the accident at the local or nearest police station.

The New Zealand Automobile Association (NZAA) provides emergency road service and is associated with the American Automobile Association (AAA). If you are an AAA member, you will be covered by the service as long as you register in person with an NZAA office in New Zealand and present your membership card with an expiration date showing it is still valid. NZAA advises that you register before you begin your trip.

Should you find yourself at a panel beater (repair shop) after a prang (minor car accident), talking about your vehicle might end up sounding like more of an Abbott and Costello routine if you're not prepared with the appropriate vehicle vernacular. For instance, you might hear the panel beater say, "Geez mate! Doing the ton on loose metal when it was hosing down? You have a chip in the windscreen, the fender has to be reattached under the boot, and your axle is munted. Pop the bonnet and let's take a look." Translation: "Wow! Driving so fast on a gravel road in the rain? You chipped the windshield, the bumper needs to be reattached under the trunk, and the axle is broken. Pop the hood."

Emergency Services New Zealand Automobile Association. ⊠ *99 Albert St., Auckland* ☎ *09/966-8800* ⊕ *www.aa.co.nz.*

RULES OF THE ROAD

The speed limit is 100 kph (62 mph) on the open road, 50 kph (31 mph) in towns and cities, and 70 kph (44 mph) or 80 kph (50 mph) in some "in between" areas. Watch for the signs that show where these change. A circular sign with the letters LSZ (Limited Speed Zone) means speed should be governed by prevailing road conditions but still not exceed 100 kph. Speed cameras, particularly in city suburbs and on approaches to and exits from small towns, will snap your number plate if you're driving too fast. Fines start at about NZ$60 for speeds 10 kph (6 mph) over the speed limit. (If you're driving a rental, the company will track you down for payment.) It's easier and safer for everyone to obey the speed limit.

New Zealand law states that you must always wear a seat belt, whether you are driving or are a passenger. As the driver, you can be fined for any passenger not wearing a seat belt or approved child restraint if under the age of seven. If you are caught without a seat belt and you are clearly not a New Zealander, the result is likely to be a friendly but firm warning. Drunk drivers are not tolerated in New Zealand. The blood alcohol limit is 50 milligrams of alcohol per 100 milliliters of blood for adults), and it's safest to avoid driving altogether if you've had a drink. If you are caught driving over the limit you will most likely be taken to the nearest police station to dry out and be required to pay a high fine. Repeat offenses or instances of causing injury or death while under the influence of alcohol are likely to result in jail terms.

When driving in rural New Zealand, cross one-lane bridges with caution—there are plenty of them. A yellow sign with parallel black lines will usually warn you that you are approaching a one-lane bridge, and another sign will tell you whether you have the right-of-way. A rectangular blue sign with a bigger white arrow on the left side of a smaller red arrow means you have the right-of-way, and a circular sign with a red border and red arrow on the left side of a white arrow means you must pull over to the left and wait to cross until oncoming traffic has passed. Even when you have the right-of-way, slow down and take care. Roundabouts can be particularly confusing for newcomers. When entering a roundabout, yield to all vehicles coming from the right. A blue sign with a white arrow indicates that you should keep to the left of the traffic island as you come up to the roundabout. In a multilane roundabout, stay in the lane closest to the island until ready to exit the circle. You must indicate left just before you exit.

You can only pass on the left if there are two or more lanes on your side of the center line, if the vehicle you are passing has stopped, or if the vehicle ahead is signaling a right turn. At all other times, you must pass on the right, and only when you have enough clear road to do so.

When you encounter fog, try putting your headlights on low beam, this sometimes helps as high beams refract light and decrease visibility. It is illegal to drive with only your parking lights on.

In cities and towns, the usual fine for parking over the time limit on meters is NZ$10–NZ$15. In the last few years "pay-and-display" meters have been put up in cities. You'll need to drop a couple of dollars' worth of coins in the meter, take the dispensed ticket, and put it in view on the dashboard of your car. The fine for running over the time for these meters runs about NZ$12, but if you don't display your ticket at all, the fine will be at least NZ$40 and you may risk being towed. So carry a few coins at all times—any denomination will usually do (gold coins only in Auckland and Wellington). Credit cards also work in some machines. Make sure to observe all "no parking" signs. If you don't, your car is highly likely to be towed away. It will cost about NZ$100 to NZ$200 to have the car released, and most tow companies won't accept anything but cash.

For more road rules and safety tips, check the New Zealand Transport Agency website ⊕ *www.nzta.govt.nz.*

Contacts New Zealand Transport Agency. ☎ *0800/822-422 toll-free in NZ, 06/953-6200* ⊕ *www.nzta.govt.nz.*

TRAFFIC

The only cities with a serious congestion problem during rush hour are Auckland and Wellington, particularly on inner-city highways and on- and off-ramps. Avoid driving between 7:30 am and 9 am, and 5 pm and 6:30 pm. It is also worth taking this into account if you have important appointments or a plane to catch. Give yourself a spare 30 minutes to be on the safe side. Traffic around Christchurch also builds up at these times, and has been particularly problematic since the 2011 earthquake damaged many roads. Also, as the city is rebuilt, many roads become closed or changed to one-way. Even the locals get confused (and bemused).

■ CRUISE SHIP TRAVEL

Cruise companies are increasingly drawn to Auckland and Wellington's superb harbors, as well as to the gorgeous scenery in places such as the Bay of Islands, Tauranga, Napier, Marlborough Sounds, Akaroa, Dunedin, Fiordland, and Stewart Island. World-cruise itineraries with Crystal Cruises *and* Regent Seven Seas Cruises now include New Zealand. But some of the best cruising programs are those that concentrate entirely on the South Pacific and combine New Zealand with destinations such as Fiji, New Caledonia, Tonga, and Samoa. Generally, such cruises start and finish in Auckland and visit South Pacific islands in between.

P&O Cruises runs a couple of cruises out of Auckland to the South Pacific. Another choice is the Holland America Line vessel *Volendam* with its cruises around New Zealand, Australia, and the South Pacific.

Cruise Lines Crystal Cruises. ☎ *888/722–0021* ⊕ *www.crystalcruises.com.* **Holland America Line.** ☎ *877/932–4259* ⊕ *www.hollandamerica.com.* **P&O Cruises.** ☎ *0800/780–716 toll-free in New Zealand* ⊕ *www.pocruises.co.nz.* **Princess Cruises.** ☎ *0800/951–200 toll-free in New Zealand* ⊕ *www.princess.com.* **Regent Seven Seas Cruises.** ☎ *954/776–6123* ⊕ *www.rssc.com.*

▮ TRAIN TRAVEL

Don't rely on trains to get you around; train travel in New Zealand is limited to three routes operated by Kiwi Rail Scenic Journeys and commuter services in Wellington and Auckland. That said, the three long journeys are indeed scenic. They include the daily TranzAlpine Express, a spectacular ride over Arthur's Pass and the mountainous spine of the South Island between Greymouth, on the West Coast, and Christchurch on the east. The Coastal Pacific runs from Christchurch along the stunning Kaikoura coast (between mountains and sea), to Marlborough wine country and Picton. This runs daily between October and April and a few days a week through winter months (timetable varies). The Northern Explorer travels from Wellington to Auckland, departing Auckland on Monday, Thursday, and Saturday and Wellington Tuesday, Friday, and Sunday.

The trains do leave and arrive on time as a rule. They have one class, with standard comfortable seats and a basic food service selling light meals, snacks, beer, wine, and spirits. Special meals (diabetic, wheat free, or vegetarian) can be arranged, but you have to order at least 48 hours before you board the train. Most carriages have large windows from which to view the spectacular passing scenery, and you'll hear a commentary on passing points of interest. Most trains also have a viewing carriage at the rear.

Travelers can purchase a New Zealand Travelpass for unlimited travel by train, bus, and Interislander ferry for a variety of periods. *See Discounts and Deals.*

Senior citizens (over 60) get a 20% discount with proof of age.

You can obtain both schedules and tickets at i-SITE visitor information centers and at train stations. Major credit cards are accepted, as are cash and traveler's checks. Reservations are advised, particularly in the summer months. Book at least 48 hours in advance.

Information InterCity Travel Centres. ☎ *09/583–5780 in Auckland, 03/365–1113 in Christchurch, 04/385–0520 in Wellington.*

Train Information KiwiRail. ☎ *04/495–0775, 0800/801–070 toll-free in New Zealand for bookings* ⊕ *www.kiwirail.co.nz.*

▮ DISCOUNTS AND DEALS

Look into the New Zealand Travelpass to save money by combining bus, ferry, and train costs. The Travelpass has no fixed itineraries and gives you 3,000 different stops to choose from. You choose from a certain number of days of travel and kinds of transportation; there's also an option to tack on air travel. Most Travelpasses are valid for one year; the bus-only version is valid for unlimited travel on InterCity and Newmans coaches over a one-, two-, or three-month period, with an incremental-rate structure. You can purchase an open-ended pass from your travel agent prior to leaving and then call the Travelpass reservations center to make reservations.

KiwiRail Scenic Journeys also has a couple of deals worth checking out, including ThroughFares, which combine train trips with SoundsAir flights and the Interislander ferries.

▮ **TIP→ Ask the local tourist i-SITE visitor information center about hotel and local transportation packages that include tickets to major museum exhibits or other special events.**

Discount Resources New Zealand Travelpass. ☎ *0800/339–966 toll-free in New Zealand* ⊕ *www.travelpass.co.nz.*

ESSENTIALS

∎ ACCOMMODATIONS

Tourism New Zealand *(see Visitor Information)* publishes an online accommodation directory listing all properties that are accredited by Qualmark *(see below)*, the national tourism–quality assurance organization. While most reputable properties are Qualmark registered, some outstanding places to stay are not. You'll find a few of them in our listings. Another online directory, ⊕ *www.nztourism.net.nz*, also publishes a comprehensive accommodation directory.

BED-AND-BREAKFASTS

There are some helpful resources on the Web for researching and booking B&B choices. On websites such as those maintained by the Bed and Breakfast Association, you'll find hundreds of listings and advertisements for reputable B&Bs throughout the country. Heritage & Character Inns of New Zealand specializes in higher-end B&Bs.

Once in New Zealand you will find the *New Zealand Bed & Breakfast Book* in most major bookstores, or you can look at their listings online for free. It lists about 1,000 B&Bs, but be aware that property owners, not independent writers, provide the editorial copy.

Reservation Services Heritage & Character Inns of New Zealand. ⊕ *www.heritageinns.co.nz.* **The New Zealand Bed & Breakfast Book.** ⊕ *www.bnb.co.nz.* **Qualmark.** ⊕ *www.qualmark.co.nz.*

HOME AND FARM STAYS

If you think green acres is the place to be, New Zealand has plenty of them. Home and farm stays provide not only comfortable accommodations, but a chance to experience the countryside and the renowned Kiwi hospitality. Most operate on a B&B basis, though some also serve evening meals. Farm accommodations vary from modest shearers' cabins to elegant homesteads. Some hosts offer day trips, as well as horseback riding, hiking, and fishing. For two people, the average cost ranges from NZ$90 to NZ$400 per night, including meals. Check farmstay accommodation on Tourism New Zealand's ⊕ *www.newzealand.com* for options.

Farm Helpers in New Zealand (FHINZ) advertises dozens of positions throughout the country where you can stay for free in exchange for working on a farm. Tasks include fruit picking, gardening, and light carpentry.

Homestays, the urban equivalent of farm stays, are less expensive. Many New Zealanders seem to have vacation homes, called *baches* in the North Island, *cribs* in the South Island; these are frequently available for rent. New Zealand Vacation Homes lists houses and apartments for rent on both the North and South islands. Baches and Holiday Homes to Rent Ltd. publishes an annual directory of rental homes throughout the country, with color photos for each listing.

Contacts Baches and Holiday Homes to Rent Ltd. ☏ *09/585–2300* ⊕ *www.holidayhomes.co.nz.* **Farm Helpers in New Zealand.** ⊕ *www.fhinz.co.nz.* **New Zealand Vacation Homes Ltd.** ☏ *09/278–3839* ⊕ *www.nzvacationhomes.co.nz.* **Rural Holidays NZ Ltd.** ☏ *03/355–6218* ⊕ *www.ruralholidays.co.nz.*

HOME EXCHANGES

With a direct home exchange you stay in someone else's home while they stay in yours. Some outfits also deal with vacation homes.

Exchange Clubs Home Exchange.com. ☏ *800/877–8723 in U.S.* ⊕ *www.homeexchange.com.* **HomeLink International.** ☏ *09/959–077 in New Zealand* ⊕ *www.homelink.org.*

HOTELS
QUALMARK

When looking up hotel information, you'll often see a reference to Qualmark, New Zealand's official tourism quality-assurance agency. This nonprofit service grades hotels on a one- to five-star system and participation is voluntary. Each business applies and undergoes a strict assessment and licensing process to win Qualmark accreditation, shelling out some cash in the process. These ratings are generally fair gauges of each property's cleanliness and security. You can check a hotel's Qualmark rating on the website.

Information Qualmark. ⊕ *www.qualmark.co.nz.*

LUXURY LODGES

New Zealand does luxury lodges very, very well. At the high end of the price scale, luxury lodges put forth the best of country life, elegant dining, and superb accommodations. Some specialize in fishing, others in golf, but there is always a range of outdoor activities for nonanglers and nongolfers. Tariffs run about NZ$400–NZ$2,000 per day for two people; meals are generally included. For information, visit the New Zealand Lodge Association's website, where you can download an electronic catalog of New Zealand lodges. These properties are also listed in their very own Luxury Lodge category on the Qualmark website.

Information New Zealand Lodge Association. ⊕ *www.lodgesofnz.co.nz.*

MOTELS

Motels are popular accommodations, and most provide comfortable rooms with excellent self-service kitchen facilities for NZ$70–NZ$195 per night. Unlike in the United States, motels in New Zealand are not always below the standard of hotels. Many are set up like stylish apartments, with living and kitchen areas as well as bedrooms. Some motels are called "motor lodges." Accommodations with more basic facilities are called "serviced motels." The Motel Association of New Zealand (MANZ) is an independent

organization with nearly 1,000 members. Its website allows you to find properties by region or by motel name.

Information Motel Association of New Zealand. ⊕ *www.manz.co.nz.*

MOTOR CAMPS

The least expensive accommodations are the tourist cabins and flats in most of the country's 400 motor camps, or holiday parks as they are now described. Many of these also offer excellent motel and apartment units, as well as camping and powered sites. Tourist cabins provide basic accommodation and shared cooking, laundry, and bathroom facilities. Bedding and towels are usually provided. A notch higher up the comfort scale tourist flats provide fully equipped kitchens, and private bathrooms. Tent sites and powered caravan or motor home sites usually cost less than NZ$50 and overnight rates for cabins range anywhere from NZ$50 to NZ$100. More fully equipped tourist flats will cost NZ$80 to NZ$150.

Information New Zealand Holiday Parks Association. ⊕ *www.holidayparks.co.nz.*

▍ COMMUNICATIONS

INTERNET

Traveling with a laptop does not present any problems in New Zealand, where the electricity supply is reliable. However, you will need a converter and adapter as with other electronic equipment *(see Electricity)*. It pays to carry a spare battery and adapter, because they're expensive and can be hard to replace.

Most accommodations throughout the country, even in smaller, remote areas, provide Wi-Fi connections. Increasingly, connections are offered free for guests; however, there remains a lot of inconsistency with regard to the cost and speed. In many cases you will need to pay about NZ$2 or NZ$5 for 10 or 20 minutes, or NZ$10 to NZ$15 for 24-hour coverage. City hotels seem to offer either free or expensive connections, up to NZ$25 for 24 hours. The Cybercafes website lists more than 4,000 Internet cafés worldwide. Increasingly there are Free Spots in public areas around cities and holiday towns.

Contacts **Cybercafes.** ⊕ *www.cybercafes.com.*

PHONES

The country code for New Zealand is 64. When dialing from abroad, drop the initial "0" from the local area code. Main area codes within New Zealand include 09 (Auckland and the North), 04 (Wellington), and 03 (South Island). Dialing from New Zealand to back home, the country code is 1 for the United States and Canada, 61 for Australia, and 44 for the United Kingdom. The prefixes 0800, 0508, and 0867 are used for toll-free numbers in New Zealand.

Dial 018 for New Zealand directory assistance. For international numbers, dial 0172. To call the Telecom "calling assistance," dial 010; for international operator assistance, dial 0170. To find phone numbers within New Zealand go to the White Pages website ⊕ *www.whitepages.co.nz.*

CALLING OUTSIDE NEW ZEALAND

To make international calls directly, dial 00, then the international access code, area code, and number required. The country code for the United States is 1.

Access Codes **AT&T Direct.** ☏ *800/225–5288 in U.S.* **MCI WorldPhone.** ☏ *000–912.* **Sprint International Access.** ☏ *000–999.*

CALLING CARDS

With the increasing use of mobile phones there are fewer public pay phones to be found. Of those remaining, most phones accept PhoneCards or major credit cards rather than coins. PhoneCards, available in denominations of NZ$5, NZ$10, NZ$20, or NZ$50, are sold at post offices, dairies (convenience stores), tourist centers, and any other shops displaying the green PhoneCard symbol. To use a PhoneCard, lift the receiver, put the card in the slot in the front of the phone, and dial. The cost of the call is automatically deducted from your card; the display on the telephone tells you how much credit you have left at the end of the call. A local call from a public phone costs 70¢. Don't forget to take your PhoneCard with you when you finish your call or those minutes will be lost—or spent by a stranger.

Telecom has a reliable card called Easy Call, which covers calls to the United States for as low as 3¢ per minute. You can add minutes to the card by using your credit card; unlike a PhoneCard, you don't need to purchase a new one when you're running out of time. Other phone cards include KiaOra and Talk 'n' Save (both sold by Compass Phone Cards), which operate in the same way; you can call the United States for as low as 3.9¢ per minute. You can buy these phone cards at gas stations, dairies, and most hostels.

The Net2Phone Direct Calling Card provides an affordable solution by utilizing local access numbers to make calls utilizing the Internet. This is used in the same manner as a regular calling card, but depending on the area from which you are calling there is sometimes a slight voice delay. Of course, Internet connections such as Skype and Viber can make communications with those back home even easier. It is advisable to use a headset for the best clarity and, if using in a cybercafé or other public area, in consideration of others.

Calling Cards **Compass Phone Cards.** ☏ *0800/646–444 toll-free in New Zealand.* **Telecom Easy Call.** ☏ *0800/789–888 toll-free in New Zealand.*

MOBILE PHONES

Mobile-communications networks cover pretty much all of New Zealand, which operate on the GSM system. U.S.-based CDMA phones will work, as long as the phone has a dual-band switch so it can be switched to GSM. Contact your provider about specific requirements for your phone. Once in New Zealand you can purchase a SIM card (prices from NZ$25 to NZ$55). Keep in mind, however, that the phone must be unlocked.

Low-cost cell phones can also be purchased at Auckland, Queenstown, and Christchurch airports starting from NZ$29, or NZ$49 with credit, or a prepaid service plan. Look for a Vodafone stand in the arrival area of each airport.

Roaming fees can be steep: 99¢ a minute is considered reasonable. And overseas you normally pay the toll charges for incoming calls. It's almost always cheaper to send a text message than to make a call, since text messages have a really low set fee (often less than 5¢).

If you just want to make local calls, buying a SIM card or cheap phone means you'll then have a local number and can make local calls at local rates.

■**TIP→** **If you travel internationally frequently, save one of your old mobile phones or buy a cheap one on the Internet; ask your cell phone company to unlock it for you, and take it with you as a travel phone, buying a new SIM card with pay-as-you-go service in each destination.**

Contacts Cellular Abroad. ☎ 800/287–5072 ⊕ www.cellularabroad.com. **Mobal.** ☎ 888/888–9162 ⊕ www.mobal.com. **Planet Fone.** ☎ 888/988–4777 ⊕ www.planetfone.com. **Vodaphone.** ☎ 09/275–8154, ⊕ www.vodarent.co.nz.

It is illegal to drive and use a handheld mobile phone in New Zealand.

■ CUSTOMS AND DUTIES

New Zealand has stringent regulations governing the import of weapons, foodstuffs, and certain plant and animal material. Anti-drug laws are strict and penalties severe. In addition to personal effects, nonresidents over 17 years of age may bring in, duty-free, 200 cigarettes or 250 grams of tobacco or 50 cigars, 4.5 liters of wine, three bottles of spirits or liquor containing not more than 1,125 milliliters, and personal purchases and gifts up to the value of NZ$700.

Most stringent is the agricultural quarantine. New Zealand is highly dependent on its agriculture and horticulture industries and cannot risk unwanted introduction of pest plants or animals or disease. The authorities don't want any nonnative seeds (or popcorn kernels or honey) haplessly transported into the country. You must declare even a single piece of fruit, and all camping and hiking gear must be declared and inspected at customs. You'll be hit with an instant NZ$400 fine if you're caught bringing in fruit—those cute beagles at customs will bark if they smell even a whiff of a banana. And be truthful about your camping gear because they *will* want to take a look at it, unravel your tent and sleeping bag, and check for grass and muck. Do yourself a favor and make sure any camping gear and hiking boots are reasonably clean when entering the country. If you are unsure, simply declare it on the immigration card. An official will ask what you're declaring and if it's okay (like chocolate, for example), he'll send you straight through. Check the following websites for a more detailed description and explanations of no-nos. All bags coming into the country are X-rayed.

Information in New Zealand Biosecurity New Zealand. ⊕ www.biosecurity.govt.nz. **New Zealand Customs.** ⊕ www.customs.govt.nz.

U.S. Information U.S. Customs and Border Protection. ⊕ www.cbp.gov.

LOCAL DO'S AND TABOOS

CUSTOMS OF THE COUNTRY

In general, Kiwis are accommodating folk who are more likely to good-naturedly tease you about a cultural faux pas than to take offense, but there are a few etiquette points to keep in mind. First, the word "Kiwi" refers to either people (New Zealanders) or to the protected kiwi bird, but not the kiwifruit. (If you're asking for the fruit, ask for the whole thing: kiwifruit.) Also, don't lump New Zealanders in with Australians. A New Zealand accent does not sound just like an Australian one, or a British accent for that matter, and a Kiwi will be the first to point this out.

Be considerate of Māori traditions. For instance, *marae,* the area in front of a meetinghouse, should not be entered unless you are invited or unless it's in use as a cultural center. Only use the traditional *hongi* (touching foreheads and noses in greeting) when someone else initiates it.

If you're visiting someone's house, its not essential but it would be nice to take along a small gift. Among gestures, avoid the "V" symbol with the first two fingers with the palm facing in—an offensive vulgarity.

LANGUAGE

Kiwi English can be mystifying. The colloquialisms alone can make things puzzling, not to mention rural slang. Known as "cow cockie" talk, this is what you'll hear when "girls" refers to someone's cows, and "gummies" (galoshes) are the favored footwear.

The Māori language has added many commonly used words to the New Zealand lexicon. For instance, the Māori greeting is *kia ora,* which can also mean "thank you," "good-bye," "good health," or "good luck." You'll hear it from everyone, *Pākehā* (non-Māori) and Māori alike. Many place-names are Māori as well and can be so long as to seem unpronounceable. (A Māori word stands as the longest place-name in the world.) See the *Speak Like a Local* and *Māori Glossary* pages in the *Experience New Zealand* chapter for common phrases.

The biggest communication glitch between New Zealanders and visitors often involves the Kiwis' eloquent use of the understatement. This facet of Kiwi speech is both blessing and curse. Everything sounds relaxed and easygoing . . . but if you're trying to judge something like distance or difficulty you may run into trouble. No matter how far away something is, people often say it's "just down the road" or "just over the hill." Ask specific questions to avoid a misunderstanding.

SIGHTSEEING

If you are driving a road maggot (campervan), be considerate of the drivers behind you. Pull over when safe and possible to let them pass.

There is etiquette when visiting a marae, best illustrated in the book *Te Marae: A Guide to Māori Protocol,* available through Raupo Publishing (⊕ www.penguin.co.nz).

New Zealand is big on sheep, and you might lose smarty points if you ask dumb sheep questions. "When do you cut their fur?" or "When do their tails fall off?" will elicit laughter: sheep have wool, and their tails are cut off as young lambs, a month or so after they are born. And remember, there isn't a sheep joke here that hasn't been heard.

▌ EATING OUT

Some restaurants serve a fixed-price dinner, but the majority are à la carte. Remember that "entrée" in Kiwi English is the equivalent of an appetizer. Increasingly, restaurants are offering smaller, tapas-style plates for sharing. It's wise to make a reservation and inquire if the restaurant has a liquor license or is "BYOB" or "BYO" (Bring Your Own Bottle)—a few places have both. This only pertains to wine, not bottles of beer or liquor. Be prepared to pay a corkage fee, which can be up to NZ$10.

Many restaurants add a 15% surcharge on public holidays. Employers are required by law to pay staff a higher wage during holidays. This amount will be itemized separately on your bill.

New Zealand's *Cuisine* magazine has a special annual issue devoted to restaurants throughout the country; check their website if you'd like to get a copy before your trip. There are also a few helpful New Zealand dining websites worth a look. Through some, you can make online reservations. These include Dine Out and Zomato, two national databases with customer reviews.

For information on food-related health issues, see Health.

Information Cuisine Magazine. ⊕ www.cuisine.co.nz. **Dine Out.** ⊕ www.dineout.co.nz. **Zomato.** ⊕ www.zomato.com.

MEALS

BURGERS AND BACON

Burgers are a staple for a quick bite. However, you'll find there's a whole lot more than two all-beef patties and a bun—two of the most popular fillings are beetroot and a fried egg. Cheese on burgers (and sandwiches) is often grated bits sprinkled atop. Another Kiwi snack staple, meat pies, is sold just about everywhere. The classic steak-and-mince fillings are getting gussied up these days with cheese or mushrooms. And who could forget good ol' fish-and-chips in this former British colony? Appropriately called "greasies," this mainstay is often made of shark but called lemon fish or flake. You might notice bowls by the cash registers of take-out shops containing packets of tartar sauce or tomato sauce (catsup). These are usually not free for the taking; they cost about 50¢ each.

Be aware that "bacon" might consist of a thick blubbery slice of ham or a processed fatty, pink, spongy substance. If you love your bacon streaky and crisp, politely inquire what kind of bacon they serve before ordering a BLT.

LAMB

When in New Zealand, taste the lamb. No matter where you go in the country, it's sure to be on the menu along with locally farmed beef. Cervena, or farm-raised venison, is another local delicacy available all over New Zealand.

L&P

Lemon & Paeroa, otherwise known as L&P, is New Zealand's most famous soft drink. Keep in mind that if you order a lemonade you will be served a carbonated lemon-flavored drink. If you've a sweet tooth, nibble a chocolate fish, a chocolate-covered fish-shape marshmallow. This treat has become so popular in New Zealand that it's now synonymous with success. You'll often hear someone say, "you deserve a chocolate fish!" in place of "job well done!" And if you're traveling in the heat of the summer, don't leave town until you've tried a hokey pokey ice cream, another New Zealand mainstay. If you want to try a truly unique bit of New Zealand grub, and we do mean grub, taste the larvae of the huhu beetle. (Okay, this isn't readily available, probably only at the annual Hokitika Wildfoods Festival, on the South Island West Coast.)

MĀORI HĀNGI

Don't miss a Māori *hāngi*. This culinary experience is most likely to be available in conjunction with a cultural show, or marae visit. The traditional preparation involves steaming meat, seafood, and vegetables, for several hours, in a large underground pit. *See the "Dinner on the Rocks" Close-Up box in Chapter 5.* Also be sure to try the locally grown *kūmara*, or sweet potato. Some Kiwi folk view muttonbird (the cute name for young sooty shearwaters, harvested from their burrows on little islands around Stewart Island) as a special treat, but others balk at its peculiar smell and strong flavor. It is an acquired taste, but if you're an adventurous eater it's definitely one to try.

SEAFOOD

Of course, seafood is a specialty, and much of the fish is not exported so this is your chance to try it. The tastiest fish around is snapper in the North, and blue cod (not a true cod relative) in the South. Grouper (often listed by its Māori name of *hāpuku*), terakihi, and marine-farmed salmon are also menu toppers, as is whitebait, the juvenile of several fish species, in the whitebait-fishing season of spring. As for shellfish: try the Bluff oysters (in season March–August), Greenshell mussels (also known as green-lipped or New Zealand green mussels), scallops, crayfish (spiny lobster), and local clamlike shellfish, *pipi* and *tuatua*. *For more on native foods, see Tastes of New Zealand in Chapter 1.*

VEGETABLES

In New Zealand restaurants, many vegetables have two names, used interchangeably. Eggplants are often called aubergines, zucchini are also known as courgettes. The vegetable North Americans know as a bell pepper is a capsicum here. The tropical fruit papaya is known by its British name, pawpaw.

RESTAURANT HOURS

Hotel restaurants serve breakfast roughly between 7 and 10; cafés and restaurants often serve breakfast/brunch to 11 am, or even an "all-day breakfast." Lunch usually starts about noon and is over by 3. Dinners are usually served from 6 pm, but the most popular dining time is around 7 to 8. Restaurants in cities and resort areas will serve dinner well into the night, but some places in small towns or rural areas still shut their doors at around 8.

Unless otherwise noted, the restaurants listed *in this guide* are open daily for lunch and dinner.

PAYING

Credit cards are widely accepted in restaurants and cafés. There are a few exceptions to this rule, so check first. In some areas, American Express and Diners Club cards are accepted far less frequently than MasterCard and Visa. *For guidelines on tipping see Tipping below.*

RESERVATIONS AND DRESS

We only mention reservations specifically when they're essential or when they are not accepted. For popular restaurants, book as far ahead as you can (a week or more) and reconfirm as soon as you arrive. Large parties should always call ahead to check the reservations policy. We mention dress only when men are required to wear a jacket or a jacket and tie.

Attire countrywide is casual; unless you're planning to dine at the finest and more conservative of places, men won't need to bring a jacket and tie. At the same time, the most common dinner attire is usually a notch above jeans and T-shirts.

WINES, BEER, AND SPIRITS

New Zealand is well known for its white wines, particularly Sauvignon Blanc, Riesling, Pinot Gris, and Chardonnay. The country has also gained a reputation for red wines such as Cabernet Sauvignon, Pinot Noir, and Merlot. The main wine-producing areas are Hawke's Bay, Wairarapa, Marlborough, Nelson, Waipara (north Canterbury), and Central Otago. Restaurants almost without exception serve New Zealand products on their wine list. *For a rundown on New Zealand's wine industry, see Wines of New Zealand in Chapter 8.*

When ordering a beer, you'll get either a handle (mug), a one-liter jug (pitcher) with glasses, or a "stubby" (small bottle). If you've asked for one of these (a bottle), you might need to request a glass if you don't want to glug straight from the bottle (depending how casual the bar is). Two large mainstream breweries, DB and Lion, produce their own products along with smaller, well-known brands that initially started as independent breweries, such as Macs, Monteiths, and Speights. They also dispense international brands Steinlager, Stella Artois, Heinekin, and more. The big trend in recent years, however, has been to boutique microbreweries and craft beers. Innovation, international awards, and ever-changing brews are the features of brands where even the brewery names are interesting, for example, Tuatara, Garage Project, Epic and 8, Wired Brewing. Each brand has its own fan base and the good pubs will have at least a couple of ever-changing taps serving up these tasty brews. Most restaurants and liquor stores also sell beers from Australia, Europe, and other parts of the world. Some of the beer in New Zealand is stronger than the 4% alcohol per volume brew that is the norm in the United States. Many go up to 7% or 8% alcohol per volume, so check that number before downing your usual number of drinks.

Popular for its wacky marketing as well as the flavor is 42 Below vodka, which incorporates local flavors: feijoa, manuka honey, passion fruit, and kiwifruit. Most inner-city bars will have it on the menu if you want to try before you buy a bottle; and having won a slew of gold and silver medals at international wine and spirit competitions around the world, it makes a cool duty-free gift to bring to vodka connoisseurs back home. When it comes to gin, the Kiwi Lighthouse is an award winner and South is also tasty and comes in a gorgeous bottle.

Use your judgment about ordering "off the drinks menu." If you're in a small country pub, don't try to order an umbrella cocktail. By insisting on a margarita from an establishment that doesn't have the mix, the recipe, or the right glass, you're not gaining anything except a lousy

margarita and a reputation as an obnoxious customer.

Beer and wine can be purchased in supermarkets, specialized shops, and even little corner suburban shops—seven days a week. People under 18 are not permitted by law to purchase alcohol, and shops, bars, and restaurants strictly enforce this. If you look younger than you are, carry photo identification to prove your age.

▌ELECTRICITY

If you forget to pack a converter, you'll find a selection at duty-free shops in Auckland's airport and at electrical shops in towns and cities. The electrical current in New Zealand is 240 volts, 50 cycles alternating current (AC); wall outlets take slanted three-prong plugs (but not the U.K. three-prong) and plugs with two flat prongs set at a "V" angle.

Consider making a small investment in a universal adapter, which has several types of plugs in one lightweight, compact unit. Most laptops and mobile phone chargers are dual voltage (i.e., they operate equally well on 110 and 220 volts), requiring only an adapter. These days the same is true of small appliances such as hair dryers. Always check labels and manufacturer instructions to be sure. Don't use 110-volt outlets marked "for shavers only" for high-wattage appliances such as hair dryers.

Steve Kropla's Help for World Travelers has information on electrical and telephone plugs around the world. Walkabout

Travel Gear has a good coverage of electricity under "adapters."

Contacts Steve Kropla's Help for World Travelers. ⊕ *www.kropla.com.* **Walkabout Travel Gear.** ⊕ *www.walkabouttravelgear.com.*

▮ EMERGENCIES

For fire, police, or ambulance services, dial ☎ *111.*

In Auckland, the U.S. Consulate is open from 8:30 until around 5:30 on weekdays (closed last Wednesday of each month).

In Wellington, the U.S. Embassy is open weekdays 8:15 am to 5 pm.

United States U.S. Consulate. ⊠ *Level 3, Citigroup Bldg., 23 Customs St., Auckland* ☎ *09/303–2724* ⊕ *newzealand.usembassy.gov.* **U.S. Embassy.** ⊠ *29 Fitzherbert Terr., Thorndon* ☎ *04/462–6000* ⊕ *newzealand.usembassy.gov.*

▮ HEALTH

The most common types of illnesses are caused by contaminated food and water. In New Zealand that really shouldn't be an issue. New Zealand has high hygiene standards and strict health regulations when it comes to serving food and beverage from shops, restaurants, cafés, and bars. The tap water is fine to drink. Locals do it all the time.

Health Warnings National Centers for Disease Control and Prevention (*CDC*). ☎ *800/232–4636 international travelers' health line* ⊕ *www.cdc.gov.* **World Health Organization** (*WHO*). ⊕ *www.who.int.*

SPECIFIC ISSUES IN NEW ZEALAND

General health standards in New Zealand are high, and it would be hard to find a more pristine natural environment.

The major health hazard in New Zealand is sunburn or sunstroke. Even people who are not normally bothered by strong sun should cover up with a long-sleeve shirt, a hat, and pants or a beach wrap. At higher altitudes you will burn more easily, so

apply sunscreen liberally before you go out—even for a half hour—and wear a visor or sunglasses.

Dehydration is another serious danger that can be easily avoided, so be sure to carry water and drink often. Limit the amount of time you spend in the sun for the first few days until you are acclimatized, and avoid sunbathing in the middle of the day.

There are no venomous snakes, and the only native poisonous spider, the *katipo,* is a rarity. The whitetail spider, an unwelcome and accidental import from Australia, packs a nasty bite and can cause discomfort but is also rarely encountered.

One New Zealander you will come to loathe is the tiny black sand fly (some call it the state bird), common to the western half of the South Island, which inflicts a painful bite that can itch for several days. In other parts of the country, especially around rivers and lakes, you may be pestered by mosquitoes. Be sure to use insect repellent.

One of New Zealand's rare health hazards involves its pristine-looking bodies of water; as a precaution don't drink water from natural outdoor sources. Although the country's alpine lakes might look like backdrops for mineral-water ads, some in the South Island harbor a tiny organism that can cause "duck itch," a temporary but intense skin irritation. The organism is found only on the shallow lake margins, so the chances of infection are greatly reduced if you stick to deeper water. Streams can be infected by giardia, a waterborne protozoal parasite that can cause gastrointestinal disorders, including acute diarrhea. Giardia is most likely contracted when drinking from streams that pass through an area inhabited by mammals (such as cattle or possums). There is no risk of infection if you drink from streams above the tree line.

Less common, but a risk nevertheless, is the possibility of contracting amoebic meningitis from the water in geothermal pools. The illness is caused by an organism that can enter the body when the water is forced up the nose. The organism is quite rare, but you should avoid putting your head underwater in thermal pools or jumping in them. Also remember not to drink geothermic water.

OVER-THE-COUNTER REMEDIES
Popular headache, pain, and flu medicines are Nurofen (contains Ibuprofen), Panadol (contains Paracetamol), and Dispirin (contains Aspirin). Dispirin often comes as large tabs, which you must dissolve in water. Many Kiwi households and wheelhouses have a green tube of Berocca, the soluble vitamin supplement often taken the morning after a big night out.

■ HOURS OF OPERATION

Banks are open weekdays 9–4:30, but some cease trading in foreign currencies at 4.

Gas stations are usually open, at the least, from 7 to 9 daily. Large stations on main highways are commonly open 24 hours.

Museums around the country do not have standard hours, but many are open daily from 10 to 5. Larger museums and government-run collections are generally open daily, but the hours of small local museums vary, as many are run by volunteers. The New Zealand Museums website (⊕ *www.nzmuseums.co.nz*) is a helpful information source; you can search by collection, region, or museum name.

Pharmacies are generally open from 9 to 5, Monday through Saturday (and Sunday in cities). You will also find basic nonprescription drugstore items in supermarkets, many of which are open until 10 pm. During off-hours there will usually be emergency-hour pharmacies in the major cities. Phone the local hospital or i-SITE Visitor Centre for details.

Shops are generally open Monday through Saturday 9–5:30, although in small towns many shops close early on Saturday. In

cities shops are generally open on Sunday as well, while in smaller towns Sunday trading hours vary greatly from place to place. In many rural areas, stores are closed on Sunday. Liquor stores are often open daily. In major cities supermarkets and convenience stores, called "dairies," are usually open from 7 am to 10 pm; a few stay open 24 hours.

HOLIDAYS
On Christmas Day, Good Friday, Easter Sunday, and the morning of ANZAC Day, everything closes down in New Zealand except for a few gas stations, some shops selling essential food items, and emergency facilities. On other public holidays many museums and attractions stay open, as do transportation systems, though on a reduced schedule. Local anniversary days, which vary regionally, pop up as once-a-year three-day weekends in each particular area; some businesses close but hotels and restaurants stay open. Around Christmas and New Year's Kiwis go to the beach, so seaside resorts will be difficult to visit unless you have booked well in advance. You'll get plenty of sunshine and far fewer crowds if you visit from late January through to the colder period of late March. Cities such as Auckland and Wellington are pleasantly quiet over Christmas and New Year's. Fewer cars are on the road, and you'll get good prices from hotels making up for the lack of corporate guests, though some restaurants will be closed.

■ MAIL

Airmail should take around six or seven days to reach the United Kingdom or the United States and two or three days to reach Australia.

Most New Zealand Post shops are open weekdays 8:30–5, and in some areas on Saturday 9–12:30 or 10–1. The cost of mailing a letter within New Zealand is 80¢ standard post, NZ$1.40 fast post. Sending a standard-size letter by airmail costs NZ$2.40 to North America or

Europe and NZ$1.90 to Australia. Aerograms and postcards are NZ$1.90 to any overseas destination.

If you wish to receive correspondence, have mail sent to New Zealand, held for you for up to one month at the central post office in any town or city if it is addressed to you "c/o Poste Restante, CPO," followed by the name of the town. This service is free; you may need to show ID.

Postal Service New Zealand Post.
☎ *0800/501–501 toll-free in New Zealand* ⊕ *www.nzpost.co.nz.*

SHIPPING PACKAGES

Overnight services are available between New Zealand and Australia but to destinations farther afield "overnight" will in reality be closer to 48 hours. Even to Australia, truly overnight service is only available between major cities and can be subject to conditions, such as the time you call in. A number of major operators are represented in New Zealand and the services are reliable, particularly from cities.

You can use the major international overnight companies listed here or purchase packaging and prepaid mail services from the post office. Major duty-free stores and stores that deal frequently with travelers will be able to help with international shipping, but if you purchase from small shops, particularly in country areas, arrange shipping with a company in the nearest city.

Express Services DHL World Express.
⊕ *www.dhl.co.nz.* **Federal Express.**
⊕ *www.fedex.com/nz.* **TNT International Express.** ☎ *0800/275–868 toll-free in New Zealand* ⊕ *www.tnt.com.*

▮ MONEY

For most travelers, New Zealand is not an expensive destination. The cost of meals, accommodations, and travel prove comparable to larger cities within the United States and somewhat less than in Western Europe. Premium-grade gasoline costs more than it does in North America.

Prices here are given for adults. Substantially reduced fees are almost always available for children, students, and senior citizens.

▮TIP➜ **Banks never have every foreign currency on hand, and it may take as long as a week to order. If you're planning to exchange funds before leaving home, don't wait until the last minute.**

ATMS AND BANKS

Your own bank will probably charge a fee for using ATMs abroad; the foreign bank you use may also charge a fee. Nevertheless, you'll usually get a better rate of exchange at an ATM than you will at a currency-exchange office or even when changing money in a bank. And extracting funds as you need them is a safer option than carrying around a large amount of cash.

EFTPOS (Electronic Fund Transfer at Point of Sale) is widely used in New Zealand stores and gas stations. ATMs are easily found in city and town banks and in shopping malls. The number of ATMs in small rural communities continues to grow, but there are still areas where ATMs or banks are few and far between. All the major banks in New Zealand (Bank of New Zealand, Westpac, and Auckland Savings Bank) accept cards in the Cirrus and Plus networks. ▮TIP➜ **The norm for PINs in New Zealand is four digits. If the PIN for your account has a different number of digits, you must change your PIN number before you leave for New Zealand.**

CREDIT CARDS

MasterCard and Visa are the most widely accepted cards throughout New Zealand.

Reporting Lost Cards American Express.
☎ *800/528–4800 in U.S., 0800/656–660 in New Zealand* ⊕ *www.americanexpress. com.* **Diners Club.** ☎ *800/346–377 for New Zealand offices, 09/359–7796 from U.S* ⊕ *www.dinersclub.com.* **MasterCard.** ☎ *800/627–8372 in U.S., 0800/449–140 toll-free in New Zealand* ⊕ *www.mastercard.com.* **Visa.** ☎ *800/847–2911 in U.S., 09/522–3010*

for New Zealand offices, toll-free ⊕ *www.visa. com.*

CURRENCY AND EXCHANGE

New Zealand's unit of currency is the dollar, divided into 100 cents. Bills are in $100, $50, $10, and $5 denominations. Coins are $2, $1, 50¢, 20¢, and 10¢. At this writing the rate of exchange was NZ$1.45 to the U.S. dollar, NZ$1.15 to the Canadian dollar, NZ$2.12 to the pound sterling, NZ$1.64 to the euro, and NZ$1.12 to the Australian dollar. Exchange rates change on a daily basis.

Currency Conversion Oanda.com. ⊕ *www.oanda.com.* **XE.com.** ⊕ *www.xe.com.*

▌ PACKING

In New Zealand, be prepared for weather that can turn suddenly and temperatures that vary greatly from day to night, particularly at the change of seasons. Wear layers. You'll appreciate being able to remove or put on a jacket. Take along a light raincoat and umbrella, but remember that plastic raincoats and nonbreathing polyester are uncomfortable in the humid climates of Auckland and its northern vicinity. Many shops in New Zealand sell lightweight and mid-weight merino wool garments, which are expensive but breathe, keep you warm, and don't trap body odor, making them ideal attire for tramping. Don't wear lotions or perfume in southern places like Southland, either, because they attract mosquitoes and other bugs; carry insect repellent. Sand flies seem drawn to black and dark blue colors (so they say). Bring a hat with a brim to provide protection from the strong sunlight *(see Health)* and sunglasses for either summer or winter; the glare on snow and glaciers can be intense. There's a good chance you'll need warm clothing in New Zealand no matter what the season; a windbreaker is a good idea wherever you plan to be.

Dress is casual in most cities, though top resorts and restaurants may require a jacket. Some bouncers for big city bars will shine a flashlight on your shoes; if you like these kinds of places bring some spiffy spats. In autumn, a light wool sweater or a jacket will suffice for evenings in coastal cities, but winter demands a heavier coat—a raincoat with a zip-out wool lining is ideal. Comfortable walking shoes are a must. You should have a pair of what Kiwis call "tramping boots," or at least running shoes if you're planning to trek, and rubber-sole sandals or canvas shoes for the beaches.

Weather MetService. ⊕ *www.metservice.com.*

▌ RESTROOMS

Shopping malls in cities, major bus and train stations, gas stations, and many towns along main highways have public toilets. Look for a blue sign with white figures (ladies and gents) for directions to a public toilet. New Zealanders often use the word "loo," or, better yet, "superloo."

Most New Zealand public restroom facilities are clean and tidy and often have a separate room for mothers with young children.

Some gas stations, shops, and hotels have signs stating that only customers can use the restroom. Kiwis are generally fair-minded folk, so if you're genuinely caught short and explain the situation you will probably not be turned away.

Most gas stations in New Zealand have toilet facilities, but their standard is varied. As a rule of thumb, the newer and more impressive the gas station, the cleaner and better the toilet facilities.

▌ SAFETY

New Zealand is generally safe for travelers, but international visitors have been known to get into trouble when they take their safety for granted. Use common sense, particularly if walking around cities at night. Stay in populated areas, and avoid deserted alleys. Although New Zealand is an affluent society by world standards, it has its share of poor and homeless (some referred to as "street kids" if they are young), and violent gangs do exist. Avoid bus and train stations or city squares and parks late at night.

Hotels furnish safes for guests' valuables, and it pays to use them. Don't show off your wealth, and remember to lock doors of hotel rooms and cars. Sadly, opportunist criminals stake out parking lots at some popular tourist attractions. Put valuables out of sight under seats or lock them in your trunk *before* you arrive at the destination.

Most visitors have no trouble and find New Zealanders among the friendliest people in the world. Nine times out of 10, offers of help or other friendly gestures will be genuine.

Women will not attract more unwanted attention than in most other Western societies, nor will they be immune from the usual hassles. In cities at night, stick to well-lighted areas and avoid being totally alone. Hotel staff will be happy to give tips on any areas to avoid, and the times to avoid them. New Zealand is relatively safe for women, but don't be complacent. Female travelers have been victim to sexual assault in New Zealand; hitchhiking is not recommended, especially for solo females.

Some top Kiwi destinations have accommodations especially geared to women. Wellington, for instance, has a women-only guesthouse, and the Base Backpacker hostel chain (⊕ *stayatbase.com*), with locations in major New Zealand cities, created Sanctuary Floors, secure women-only zones with special amenities.

Contact Transportation Security Administration (TSA). ⊕ *www.tsa.gov.*

General Information and Warnings Australian Department of Foreign Affairs and Trade. ⊕ *www.smartraveller.gov.au.* **Consular Affairs Bureau of Canada.** ⊕ *www.voyage. gc.ca.* **U.K. Foreign & Commonwealth Office.** ⊕ *www.fco.gov.uk.* **U.S. Department of State.** ⊕ *www.travel.state.gov.*

▌ TAXES

Many restaurants add a 15% surcharge to your bill on public holidays, reflecting the need to pay staff a higher wage on holidays. This tax will be itemized separately on your bill when applicable.

A goods and services tax (GST) of 15% is levied throughout New Zealand. It's usually incorporated into the cost of an item, but in some hotels and some restaurants it is added to the bill.

▌ TIME

Trying to figure out just what time it is in New Zealand can get dizzying, especially because of cross-hemisphere daylight-saving times and multi-time-zone countries. Without daylight saving time, Auckland is 17 hours ahead of New York; 18 hours ahead of Chicago and Dallas; 20 hours ahead (or count back 4 hours and add a day) of Los Angeles; 12 hours ahead of London; and 2 hours ahead of Sydney.

Generally, from the States, call New Zealand after 5 pm EST.

Time Zones Timeanddate.com. ⊕ *www.timeanddate.com/worldclock.*

▌ TIPPING

Tipping is not as widely practiced in New Zealand as in the United States or Europe, but in city restaurants and hotels it's appreciated if you acknowledge good service with a 10% tip. Tour guides and drivers would also be used to receiving some gesture, even though it isn't mandatory.

Taxi drivers will appreciate rounding up the fare to the nearest NZ$5 amount, but don't feel you have to do this. Porters will be happy with a NZ$1 or NZ$2 coin. Most other people, like bartenders, theater attendants, gas-station attendants, or barbers, will probably wonder what you are doing if you try to give them a tip. The nice thing about this is good service in New Zealand is given because the person means it, not because they're aiming for a good tip.

▌ TOURS

Among companies that sell tours to New Zealand, the following are nationally known organizations with a proven reputation. The key difference between the categories listed here is usually in the accommodations, which run best to better-yet, and better to budget.

LUXURY

Abercrombie & Kent, otherwise known as A&K, is the benchmark for pairing deluxe accommodations with soft adventure. Its itineraries can be combined with a visit to Australia or focus solely on New Zealand. Sometimes better deals can be landed by booking a flight package with their affiliate airlines, Qantas.

The "Connoisseur Collection" tour series with Luxury Vacations New Zealand takes small groups of just eight people to both the North and South islands.

Luxury Tour Companies Abercrombie & Kent. ✉ *1520 Kensington Rd., Oak Brook* ☏ *800/554–7016* ⊕ *www.abercrombiekent. com.* **Antipodes Tours.** ✉ *5777 W. Century Blvd., Los Angeles* ☏ *800/354–7471* ⊕ *www. antipodestours.com.* **Luxury Vacations New Zealand.** ✉ *1/333 Remuera Rd., Remuera* ☏ *09/520–4963* ⊕ *www.luxuryvacationsnz.com.*

MODERATE

Scenic Pacific Tours promote North and South Island coach tours. These depart daily from Auckland, Wellington, Picton, Christchurch, and Queenstown. You can mix and match your tours and choose your level of accommodations to fit your budget. Travel2 and Australian Pacific Touring (APT) both specialize in South Pacific vacations and can arrange everything from self-drive to fully escorted tours.

Moderate Tour Companies Australian Pacific Touring (APT). ✉ *2 Augustus Terr., Parnell* ☏ *0800/278–687 toll-free in New Zealand, 800/290–8687 in U.S.* ⊕ *www. aptouring.co.nz.* **Scenic Pacific Tours.** ☏ *03/359–3999, 0800/500–388 toll-free in New Zealand* ⊕ *www.scenicpacific.co.nz.*

Travel2. ✉ *300 Continental Blvd., Suite 350, El Segundo* ☏ *888/282–4346* ⊕ *travel2-us.com.*

BUDGET

Thrifty Tours New Zealand packaged holidays are flexible, combining regular bus, train, and ferry services with prebooked accommodation. Flying Kiwi Adventure Tours helps tie up loose ends for those on a shoestring budget. It's geared to camping rather than hotels and sometimes the major means of transit are your two feet, but this tour company has been a long-time Kiwi favorite.

Budget Tour Companies Flying Kiwi Adventure Tours. ✉ *4B Forests Rd., Nelson* ☏ *03/547–0171, 0800/693–296 toll-free in New Zealand* ⊕ *www.flyingkiwi.com.* **Thrifty Tours New Zealand.** ✉ *5/18 Martins La., Grafton, Auckland* ☏ *09/359–8380* ⊕ *www. thriftytours.co.nz.*

SPECIAL-INTEREST TOURS

Several companies, for example, Grape Escape Food and Wine Tours, share astute insights on New Zealand's wine regions and top wines, the former with some time on top championship golf courses as well. The New Zealand Wine Tourism Network website is a useful directory for everything you want to know about wine regions, wines, and wine festivals. Birding New Zealand is a network of tours and accommodation that will bring you not only in touch with some of the world's rarest species, but also a diversity of great landscapes.

Lord of the Rings and *Hobbit* fans will find there are numerous companies giving tours of Middle Earth by helicopter, four-wheel drive, and bus. One of the most stunning trips is a horseback tour around Glenorchy—contact Dart Stables about the "Ride of the Rings."

Serious outdoor enthusiasts can take a walk on the wild side, or bike, kayak, or bungy jump with Active Adventures New Zealand. *For more New Zealand–based outfitters who organize multiday sports trips, see the Experience New Zealand chapter and individual chapters.*

Theme-Tour Companies Active Adventures New Zealand. ☎ *03/450–0414, 800/661–9073 in U.S.* ⊕ *www.activeadventures.com.* **Birding New Zealand.** ⊕ *www.birdingnz.co.nz.* **Dart Stables.** ✉ *Box 47, Glenorchy* ☎ *03/442–5688, 0800/474–3464 toll-free in New Zealand* ⊕ *www.dartstables.com.* **Grape Escape.** ☎ *0800/100–489 toll-free in New Zealand* ⊕ *www.grapeescapenz.co.nz.* **New Zealand Wine Tourism Network.** ⊕ *www.wtn.co.nz.*

▌ VISITOR INFORMATION

Tourism New Zealand is a government agency that markets New Zealand internationally. Their North American office is in Santa Monica. They have a website (⊕ *newzealand.com*) that lists all you'll want or need to know about your New Zealand holiday. There are also 30 locally funded Regional Tourism Organizations (RTOs) based throughout the country, some of these also market internationally, and they run most of the i-SITE visitor centers. Many of these have computerized booking systems in place, so rather than driving from lodge to B&B to hotel, making inquiries, the i-SITE can be a good place to let you know instantly which places are vacant. They also offer knowledgeable, independent advice about local attractions, activities, and transport. These centers are marked with blue signs and a lowercase white letter *i. Please see the individual chapter Planning sections for details on local visitor bureaus.*

Contact Tourism New Zealand. ✉ *501 Santa Monica Blvd., Los Angeles* ☎ *310/395–5453 in U.S.* ⊕ *newzealand.com.*

INDEX

PHOTO CREDITS

Front cover: Steve Taylor ARPS / Alamy Stock Photo [Description: Intricate wood carving at Te Po Maori cultural village, near Rotorua, New Zealand. Back cover, from left to right: Pichugin Dmitry / Shutterstock; irakite / Shutterstock; Pichugin Dmitry / Shutterstock. Spine: Cloudia Spinner / Shutterstock. 1, Kim Karpeles/age fotostock. 2, Gilbert van Reenen/Tourism New Zealand. 5, Destination Northland/Tourism New Zealand. Chapter 1: Experience New Zealand: 8-9, Fri Gilbert/Tourism New Zealand. 18 (left, top right and bottom right), Rob Suisted/www.naturespic.com. 18 (bottom center), Robert Cumming/Shutterstock. 19 (top left), Heliworks Queenstown Helicopters. 19 (bottom left), Rob Suisted/www.naturespic.com. 19 (bottom center), Chris McLennan /Tourism New Zealand. 19 (right), Rob Suisted/www.naturespic.com. 37, Rob Suisted/www.naturespic.com. 38, Paul Mercer/age fotostock. 39 (top left and bottom left), Jason Friend/www.jasonfriend.net. 39 (right) and 40 (left and right), Rob Suisted/www.naturespic.com. 41 (left), Cate Starmer. 41 (right) and 44, Rob Suisted/www.naturespic.com. Chapter 2: Auckland: 45, Evusha | Dreamstime.com. 48, ARCO/G Therin-Weise/age fotostock. 49 (Bottom), Linus Boman/iStockphoto. 49 (top), Shades0404/wikipedia.org. 50, Rob Suisted/www.naturespic.com, 51 (bottom), Simon Russell. 51 (top), Jocelyn Carlin/Tourism New Zealand. 52, Nigelspiers | Dreamstime.com. 62, Mark Carter. 67, Joe Gough/Shutterstock. 71, Chris Gin/Shutterstock. Chapter 3: Northland and the Bay of Islands: 101, Julia Thorne/age fotostock.103 (top), Ben Crawford/Tourism New Zealand. 103 (bottom), Rob Suisted/www.naturespic.com. 104 and 112-13, Rob Suisted/www.naturespic.com. 114, Kim Westerkov/Tourism New Zealand. 119, Marc von Hacht/Shutterstock. 124, GARDEL Bertrand/age fotostock. 126, Holger Leue/Tourism New Zealand. 127, Destination Northland/Tourism New Zealand. 128 (bottom left), jamie thorpe/Shutterstock. 128 (bottom center), Ruth Black/Shutterstock. 128 (bottom right), Gareth Eyres/Tourism New Zealand. 129 (top left), Small World Productions/Tourism New Zealand. 129 (bottom left), Scott Venning/Tourism New Zealand. 129 (right), Destination Rotorua. 130 (top), Becky Nunes/Tourism New Zealand. 130 (center), Rob Suisted/www.naturespic.com. 130 (bottom), Scott Venning/Tourism New Zealand. 131 (top left), Fay Looney/Tourism New Zealand. 131 (top right), Scott Venning/Tourism New Zealand. 131 (bottom), Adventure Films/Tourism New Zealand. Chapter 4: Coromandel Peninsula and the Bay of Plenty: 139, Colin Monteath/age fotostock. 141 (top), Rob Suisted/www.naturespic.com. 141 (bottom), Peter Morath/Tourism New Zealand. 142, 150-51, and 161, Rob Suisted/www.naturespic.com. 167, Rob Suisted/www.naturespic.com. 188, Greg Balfour Evans / Alamy. 191, Simon Russell. 192, Four Peaks Lodge/Tourism New Zealand. 193 (top left), Rob Suisted/www.naturespic.com. 193 (top right), Ben Crawford/Tourism New Zealand. 193 (bottom), 194 (left and right), and 195 (top and bottom), Rob Suisted/www.naturespic.com. 196, Four Peaks Lodge/Tourism New Zealand. Chapter 5: East Coast and the Volcanic Zone: 201, Jeremy Bright/age fotostock. 203, Bob McCree/Tourism New Zealand. 204, Pichugin Dmitry/Shutterstock. 205 (top), Destination Lake Taupo/Tourism New Zealand. 205 (bottom), Falk Kienas/Shutterstock. 206, Rob Suisted/www.naturespic.com. 207, Wai-o-tapu Thermal Wonderland/Tourism New Zealand. 222, Sircha/Wikipedia.org. 227, Rob Suisted/www.naturespic.com. 239, Rob Suisted/www.naturespic.com. 245, Chris McLennan/Tourism New Zealand. Chapter 6: North Island's West Coast: 253, Andy Belcher/age fotostock. 256, Colin Monteath/age fotostock. 257 (top), robinvanmourik/Flickr. 257 (bottom), Horizon/age fotostock. 258, Ben Crawford/Tourism New Zealand. 259 (top), Ian Trafford/Tourism New Zealand. 259 (bottom) and 260, Rob Suisted/www.naturespic.com. 267, Colin Monteath/age fotostock. 273, Tourism Holdings/Tourism New Zealand. 281, David Wall/age fotostock. 288-289, Rob Suisted/www.naturespic.com. 294, Don Fuchs/age fotostock. 299, Don Smith/age fotostock. Chapter 7: Wellington and the Wairarapa: 309, Hauke Dressler/age fotostock. 311 (top and bottom), Ian Trafford/Tourism New Zealand. 312 and 321, Rob Suisted/www.naturespic.com. 322, stefano brozzi/age fotostock. 330, Nick Servian/Tourism New Zealand. 332-33, Rob Suisted/www.naturespic.com. 345, New Line Cinema/Courtesy Everett Collection. 346 (top), David Wall/Tourism New Zealand. 346 (bottom) and 347 (top), Rob Suisted/www.naturespic.com. 347 (center), Holger Leue/Tourism New Zealand. 347 (bottom), Rob Suisted/www.naturespic.com. 348 (top), Miles Holden/Tourism New Zealand. 348 (bottom), Gilbert van Reenen/Tourism New Zealand. Chapter 8: Upper South Island and the West Coast: 351, Ian Trafford/age fotostock. 354, Ian Trafford/age fotostock. 355 (top), Rob Suisted/www.naturespic.com. 355 (bottom), Gunar Streu/age fotostock. 356, Colin Monteath/age fotostock. 357 (top), Gareth Eyres/Tourism New Zealand. 357 (bottom), Colin Monteath/age fotostock. 358, Ian Trafford / age fotostock. 359 (top), Carsten Lampe/iStockphoto. 359 (bottom), ©Rob Suisted/www.naturespic.com. 360, Gareth Eyres/Tourism New Zealand. 371, Whale Watch Kaikoura. 376, Rob Suisted/www.naturespic.com. 377, David Wall/Tourism New Zealand. 378 (top left), Cherryfarm22/wikipedia.org. 378 (bottom left), Rob Suisted/www.naturespic.com. 378 (right), David Wall/Tourism New Zealand. 379 (top left), Rob Suisted/www.naturespic.com. 379 (bottom), Ian Trafford/Tourism New Zealand. 379 (right), Filipe

NOTES

NOTES

NOTES

NOTES

NOTES

NOTES

NOTES

NOTES

ABOUT OUR WRITERS

Anabel Darby is a Christchurch-based writer and publicist. Early in her career she was editor of Air New Zealand's in-flight magazine, before moving abroad to edit magazines in Australia, Hong Kong, and Canada. She returned to New Zealand with her family in 2001 and is passionate about the Christchurch and Canterbury region, which she updated for this guide.

Gerard Hindmarsh trained as a cartographer before moving to Golden Bay in 1976, where he has lived ever since on his land at Tukurua on the edge of Kahurangi National Park. He began working as a journalist in 1991. He is the acclaimed author of *Kahawai: The People's Fish*, *Outsiders: Stories from the Fringe of New Zealand Society*, *Angelina: From Stromboli to D'Urville Island*, *Swamp Fever*, and *Kahurangi Calling*. He updated the Otago, Invercargill, and Stewart Island chapter.

Claire Kenny hopped on a plane right after college to explore New Zealand and has never regretted it. She immediately began to reap the benefits of travel and cultural immersion and constantly yearns for new adventures. She remains an avid singer, performer, and daydreamer. She updated Experience New Zealand this edition.

Bob Marriott was born in Nottingham, England, but has called the Hutt Valley near Wellington his home for many years. A freelance writer for 20 years, his travels have taken him to numerous countries and his work has been published extensively in New Zealand as well as Australia, Europe, Asia, and the United States. He has contributed to a number of Fodor's guides and for this edition updated the the East Coast and the Volcanic Zone and Wellington and Wairarapa chapters. He thanks Linda, his wife, for her help and understanding when the paper chase is on.

Kathy Ombler updated the Coromandel and the Bay of Plenty, North Island's West Coast, Upper South Island and the West Coast, and Travel Smart chapters this edition. She is a freelance writer focusing on tourism and conservation. Kathy has written several guidebooks, including *Where to Watch Birds in New Zealand* and *A Visitor's Guide to New Zealand National Parks*. Kathy grew up on a farm near Cambridge, has lived in many places throughout New Zealand, from cities to small rural settlements in national parks, and is now based in Wellington.

Richard Pamatatau was born in Auckland and grew up on the relaxed North Shore. As a child he spent some time mucking around in boats on the Waitemata Harbour, and spends as much time as he can sailing. Although he travels outside of the country, often he believes there is no place like home and he always discovers new things. For this edition he updated the Auckland and Northland and the Bay of Islands chapters.

Mike Stearne is a tour guide currently living and working in Wellington, New Zealand. He runs a small tour company, offering personalized private tours of New Zealand for individuals, couples, and small groups. Find out more at ⊕ *miketheguide.com*. He updated the Southern Alps and Fiordland chapter for this edition.